Campbell Biology
Concepts & Connections

Brief Contents

PEARSON ALWAYS LEARNING

Martha R. Taylor • Jean L. Dickey • Eric J. Simon
Kelly Hogan • Jane B. Reece

Campbell Biology
Concepts & Connections

Second Custom Edition for Inver Hills Community College

Taken from:
Campbell Biology: Concepts & Connections, Ninth Edition
by Martha R. Taylor, Jean L. Dickey, Eric J. Simon, Kelly Hogan, and Jane B. Reece

Cover Art: Courtesy of Photodisc/Getty Images.

Taken from:

Campbell Biology: Concepts & Connections, Ninth Edition
by Martha R. Taylor, Jean L. Dickey, Eric J. Simon, Kelly Hogan, and Jane B. Reece

This special edition published in cooperation with Pearson Education, Inc.

Pearson Education, Inc., 330 Hudson Street, New York, New York 10013
A Pearson Education Company
www.pearsoned.com

Printed in the United States of America

000200010272100420

IM

KV 10 29 2018 1202

ISBN 10: 1-323-74615-3
ISBN 13: 978-1-323-74615-8

About the Authors

Martha R. Taylor has been teaching biology for more than 35 years. She earned her B.A. in biology from Gettysburg College and her M.S. and Ph.D. in science education from Cornell University. At Cornell, Dr. Taylor has served as assistant director of the Office of Instructional Support and has taught introductory biology for both majors and nonmajors. Most recently, she was a lecturer in the Learning Strategies Center, teaching supplemental biology courses. Her experience working with students in classrooms, in laboratories, and with tutorials has increased her commitment to helping students create their own knowledge of and appreciation for biology. She was the author of the *Student Study Guide* for ten editions of *Campbell Biology*.

Eric J. Simon is a professor in the Department of Biology and Health Science at New England College in Henniker, New Hampshire. He teaches introductory biology to science majors and nonscience majors, as well as upper-level courses in tropical marine biology and careers in science. Dr. Simon received a B.A. in biology and computer science and an M.A. in biology from Wesleyan University, and a Ph.D. in biochemistry from Harvard University. His research focuses on innovative ways to use technology to improve teaching and learning in the science classroom. Dr. Simon also leads numerous international student field research trips and is a Scientific Advisor to the Elephant Conservation Center in Sayaboury, Laos. Dr. Simon is the lead author of the introductory nonmajors biology textbooks *Campbell Essential Biology*, Sixth Edition, and *Campbell Essential Biology with Physiology*, Fifth Edition, and the author of the introductory biology textbook *Biology: The Core*, Second Edition.

Jean L. Dickey is Professor Emerita of Biological Sciences at Clemson University (Clemson, South Carolina). After receiving her B.S. in biology from Kent State University, she went on to earn a Ph.D. in ecology and evolution from Purdue University. In 1984, Dr. Dickey joined the faculty at Clemson, where she devoted her career to teaching biology to nonscience majors in a variety of courses. In addition to creating content-based instructional materials, she developed many activities to engage lecture and laboratory students in discussion, critical thinking, and writing, and implemented an investigative laboratory curriculum in general biology. Dr. Dickey is author of *Laboratory Investigations for Biology*, Second Edition, and coauthor of *Campbell Essential Biology*, Sixth Edition, and *Campbell Essential Biology with Physiology*, Fifth Edition.

Kelly Hogan is a faculty member in the Department of Biology at the University of North Carolina at Chapel Hill, teaching introductory biology and genetics. Dr. Hogan teaches hundreds of students at a time, using active-learning methods that incorporate educational technologies both inside and outside of the classroom. She received her B.S. in biology at the College of New Jersey and her Ph.D. in pathology at the University of North Carolina, Chapel Hill. Her research interests focus on how large classes can be more inclusive through evidence-based teaching methods and technology. As the Director of Instructional Innovation at UNC, she encourages experienced faculty to take advantage of new professional development opportunities and inspires the next generation of innovative faculty. Dr. Hogan is the author of *Stem Cells and Cloning*, Second Edition, and co-author on *Campbell Essential Biology with Physiology*, Fifth Edition.

Jane B. Reece has worked in biology publishing since 1978, when she joined the editorial staff of Benjamin Cummings. Her education includes an A.B. in biology from Harvard University, an M.S. in microbiology from Rutgers University, and a Ph.D. in bacteriology from the University of California, Berkeley. At UC Berkeley, and later as a postdoctoral fellow in genetics at Stanford University, her research focused on genetic recombination in bacteria. Dr. Reece taught biology at Middlesex County College (New Jersey) and Queensborough Community College (New York). During her 12 years as an editor at Benjamin Cummings, she played a major role in a number of successful textbooks. She is coauthor of *Campbell Biology*, Eleventh Edition, *Campbell Biology in Focus*, Second Edition, *Campbell Essential Biology*, Sixth Edition, and *Campbell Essential Biology with Physiology*, Fifth Edition.

Neil A. Campbell (1946–2004) combined the inquiring nature of a research scientist with the soul of a caring teacher. Over his 30 years of teaching introductory biology to both science majors and nonscience majors, many thousands of students had the opportunity to learn from him and be stimulated by his enthusiasm for the study of life. While he is greatly missed by his many friends in the biology community, his coauthors remain inspired by his visionary dedication to education and are committed to searching for ever better ways to engage students in the wonders of biology.

See Connections

New Features of the ninth edition of ***Campbell Biology: Concepts & Connections*** provide students with a framework for understanding biological concepts and encourage students to see connections between concepts and the world outside of the classroom.

NEW! Unit Openers highlight the relevancy of the course to **careers** in a variety of fields.

Connection and **Evolution Connection Modules** present engaging examples and relate chapter content to evolution.

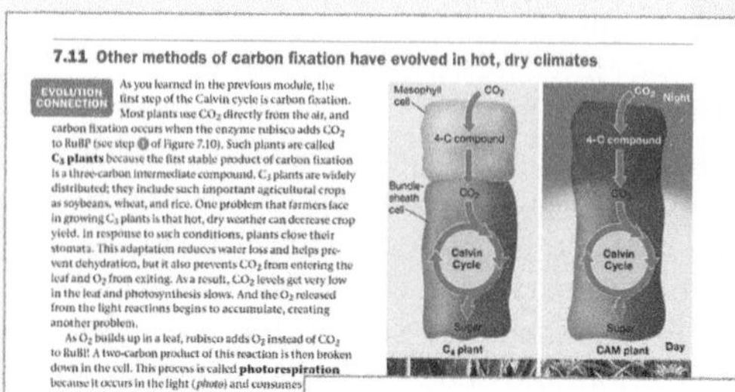

37.13 Invasive species can devastate communities

CONNECTION

▲ Figure 37.13A A Burmese python (*Python bivittatus*) captured in the Florida Everglades

▲ Figure 37.13B Kudzu (*Pueraria lobata*), a fast-growing vine

▲ Figure 37.13C A colony of zebra mussels (*Dreissena polymorpha*) attached to a native clam

Community Structure and Dynamics 753

NEW! A reframed focus on Major Themes in Biology provide students with a framework for understanding and organizing biological concepts. Icons throughout the text call students attention to examples of specific themes within each chapter.

Throughout the Ninth Edition, the five themes introduced in Chapter 1 are highlighted with specific references. Examples from Unit 1 include "Illustrating our theme of ENERGY AND MATTER, we see that matter has been rearranged, with an input of energy provided by sunlight" (Module 2.9); "The flow of genetic information that leads to gene expression, summarized as DNA → RNA → protein, illustrates the important biological theme of INFORMATION" (Module 3.15); "The interconnections among these pathways provide a clear example of the theme of INTERACTIONS in producing the emergent property of a balanced metabolism" (Module 6.15); and "The precise arrangements of these membranes and compartments are essential to the process of photosynthesis—a classic example of the theme of STRUCTURE AND FUNCTION" (Module 7.2). The theme of evolution is featured, as it is in every chapter, in an Evolution Connection module, such as Module 4.15, Mitochondria and chloroplasts evolved by endosymbiosis.

Build Science Literacy Skills

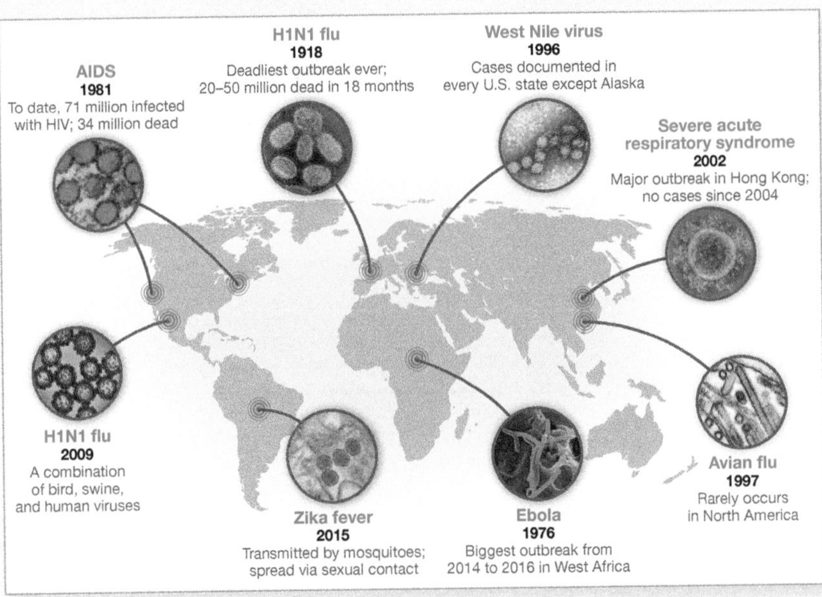

NEW! Visualizing the Data Figures are eye-catching infographics designed to provide students with a fresh approach to understanding concepts illustrated by quantitative information.

Scientific Thinking modules explore how scientists use the process of science and discovery. End-of-module questions prompt students to think critically.

24.11 Scientists measure antibody levels to look for waning immunity after HPV vaccination

SCIENTIFIC THINKING

Active adaptive immunity to a specific pathogen can be gained through a natural infection or through vaccination. With human papillomavirus (HPV), infections are common: Approximately 50% of all sexually active adults become infected by the virus. Usually there are no noticeable symptoms, and the immune system clears the HPV infection within two years. The individual now has active immunity to HPV—a second infection with the same viral strain would be cleared rapidly by the secondary immune response. Some individuals, however, have an HPV infection that escapes the immune system for many more years, interfering with the regulation of cell growth in the infected epithelial cells. Cells with a persistent infection can grow uncontrolled for years, increasing the likelihood that mutations will accumulate and result in cervical and anal cancers.

How long does the protection provided by HPV vaccination last?

Several vaccines have been developed to promote active immunity before individuals come into contact with cancer-causing strains of HPV. The first two vaccines approved in the United States were Gardasil and Cervarix. Both of these vaccines are made with HPV antigens. To determine the effectiveness of these vaccines, scientists have been conducting controlled studies. In these studies, participants are randomly assigned to one of two groups; those in the experimental group receive an injection of a vaccine, while those in the control group are injected with a placebo. Scientists then follow the participants to see if they develop precancerous lesions. For as many years as they have been studied, both vaccines have been 93–100% effective in preventing precancerous cervical lesions. These results are very good news, but scientists do not know how long this effectiveness lasts. The vaccines have not been in use long enough to provide the decades of data needed to determine the longevity of the immunity they confer.

Can scientists predict if or when an HPV vaccine's effectiveness will decrease? Not exactly, but they can analyze data about one component of the adaptive immune response: the level of antibodies being produced against HPV at various times after vaccination. If there is a significant decline of antibody levels, another dose of the antigen (vaccine) may be needed. An additional dose of a vaccine that is needed periodically is commonly known as a "booster shot."

Although you learned in Module 24.7 that the effector cells that produce antibodies are short-lived, the production of some antibodies continues for many years after vaccination. Scientists do not yet have a clear understanding of the process by which the immune system produces antibodies against certain antigens for long periods, but this enduring production of antibodies can be measured after some vaccinations.

To measure long-lasting antibody production against HPV, scientists designed and carried out two long-term studies. One study followed individuals for 5 years after vaccination with Gardasil and another followed individuals for 9.4 years after vaccination with Cervarix. Figure 24.11 provides data on the levels of two HPV-specific antibodies—anti-HPV-16 and anti-HPV-18—in the blood of individuals vaccinated with Gardasil (magenta bars) or Cervarix (blue bars). The two antibodies that were measured recognize two strains of HPV that cause cervical and anal cancer; both vaccines provide immunity against these two strains. On the *y* axis, you can see the percentage of individuals whose blood still contained measurable levels of HPV-specific antibodies. A person with no measurable antibodies might be susceptible to HPV infection.

Scientists hypothesize that higher levels of anti-HPV antibodies provide greater protection from HPV-related cancers than lower levels of antibodies, but they don't yet have strong evidence to support this hypothesis. Also unknown is whether there is a minimum antibody level necessary to prevent cancer. So far, the effectiveness of the vaccines remains high even in individuals where antibody levels have decreased, suggesting that long-term memory cells are marching into action when the virus is encountered. To know if booster shots will be necessary, vaccinated individuals will need to be followed for decades to see if there is a correlation between antibody levels and the onset of precancerous lesions. Such studies are ongoing. Stay tuned!

? **Based on the data in the graph, does it seem likely that either vaccine will require a booster in the future?**

Yes, Gardasil may require a booster: After 5 years, the antibody levels protecting against HPV-18 were undetectable in approximately 35% of individuals vaccinated.

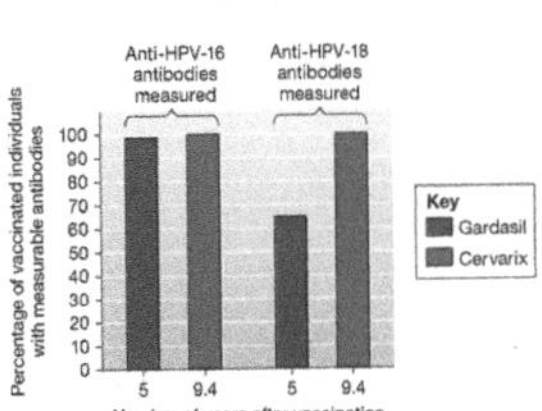

Data from S-E. Olsson et al., Induction of immune memory following administration of a prophylactic quadrivalent human papillomavirus (HPV) types 6/11/16/18 L1 virus-like particle (VLP) vaccine, *Vaccine* 25: 3931–4939 (2007); P. S. Naud et al., Sustained efficacy, immunogenicity, and safety of the HPV-16/18 AS04-adjuvanted vaccine: final analysis of a long-term follow-up study up to 9.4 years post-vaccination, *Human Vaccines Immunotherapeutics* 10: 2147–62 (2014).

▲ Figure 24.11 **The levels of anti-HPV-16 and anti-HPV-18 in blood after Cervarix and Gardasil vaccination**

500 CHAPTER 24 | The Immune System

Exploration and discovery: Observing, asking questions, reading literature

Formation and testing of hypotheses: Collecting and interpreting data

Societal benefits and outcomes: Solving problems, developing new technologies

Feedback from the scientific community: Peer-reviewed publications, replication of findings, consensus building

A new presentation of the process of science in chapter 1 demonstrates to students the iterative nature of scientific research.

Visualize Tough Topics

EXPANDED!
Visualizing the Concept Modules bring dynamic visuals and text together to walk students through tough concepts. The ninth edition features 28 of these immersive modules. Select modules are assignable in MasteringBiology as animated videos.

Embedded text **coaches students** through key points and **help address common misunderstandings.**

VISUALIZING THE CONCEPT **1.3 In life's hierarchy of organization, new properties emerge at each level**

Biologists study life across a very broad range of scales, from the molecules in a cell to the entire living planet. They divide this vast scope of biology into a series of structural

1. Biosphere:
All life on Earth and the places where life exists.
Florida
These places include most regions of land, bodies of water, and the lower atmosphere.

In this aerial view of a mangrove ecosystem, you see a forest of mangrove trees hugging the shoreline.
2. Ecosystem:
All the organisms in a particular area, as well as the physical components with which life interacts, such as soil, water, and light.
An emergent property of an ecosystem is the cycling of matter between organisms and the soil, water, and air.

3. Community:
All the organisms in an ecosystem.
In this community, we find mangrove trees and eel grass, crabs and barnacles, alligators and snakes, a huge diversity of insects, birds, and fish, and countless microorganisms.

4. Population:
All the individuals of a particular species living in a community.
Schoolmaster snappers swim together among the mangrove roots.

4 CHAPTER 1 | Biology: Exploring Life

and Develop Understanding

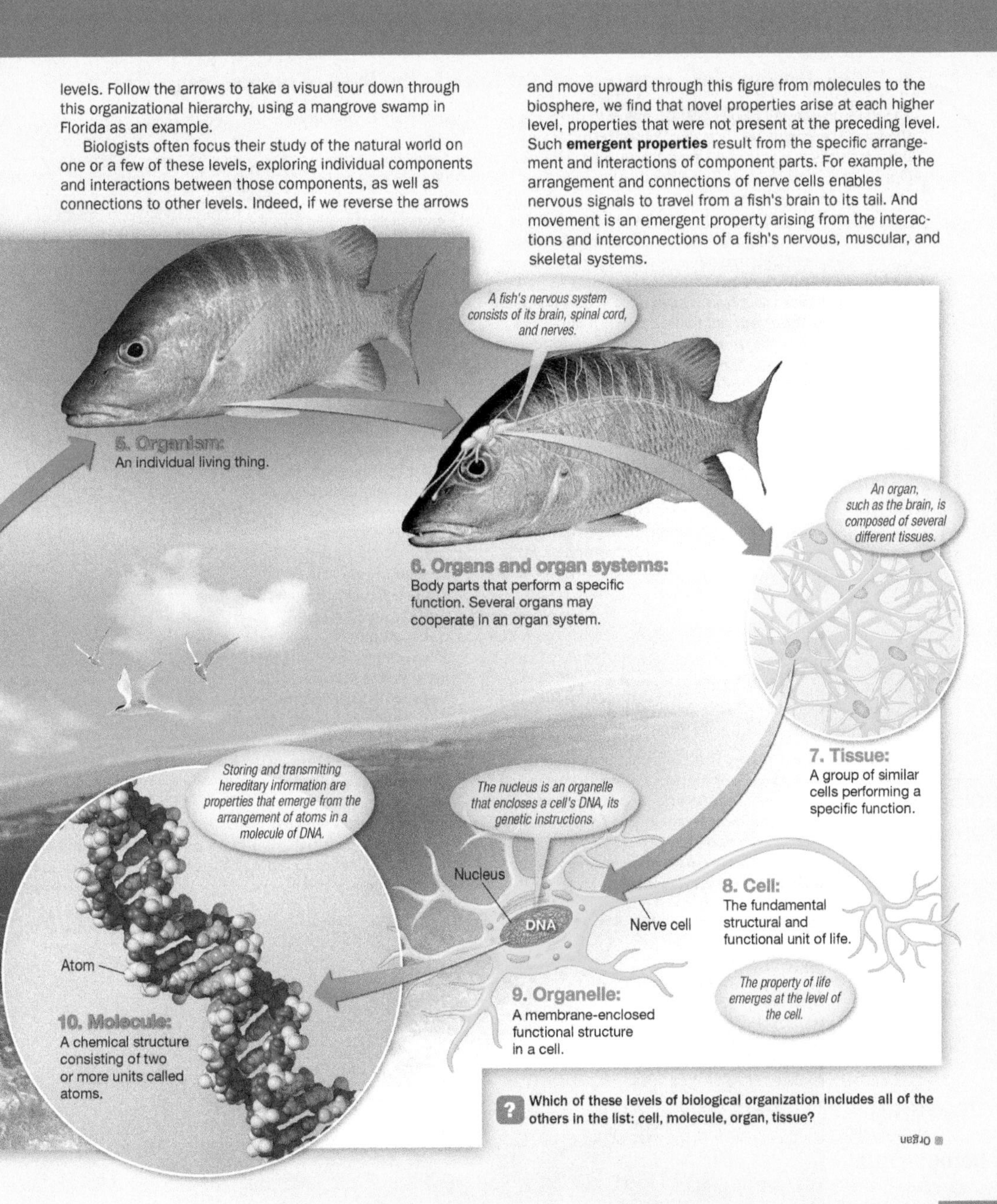

levels. Follow the arrows to take a visual tour down through this organizational hierarchy, using a mangrove swamp in Florida as an example.

Biologists often focus their study of the natural world on one or a few of these levels, exploring individual components and interactions between those components, as well as connections to other levels. Indeed, if we reverse the arrows and move upward through this figure from molecules to the biosphere, we find that novel properties arise at each higher level, properties that were not present at the preceding level. Such **emergent properties** result from the specific arrangement and interactions of component parts. For example, the arrangement and connections of nerve cells enables nervous signals to travel from a fish's brain to its tail. And movement is an emergent property arising from the interactions and interconnections of a fish's nervous, muscular, and skeletal systems.

A fish's nervous system consists of its brain, spinal cord, and nerves.
5. Organism:
An individual living thing.
6. Organs and organ systems:
Body parts that perform a specific function. Several organs may cooperate in an organ system.
An organ, such as the brain, is composed of several different tissues.
7. Tissue:
A group of similar cells performing a specific function.
Storing and transmitting hereditary information are properties that emerge from the arrangement of atoms in a molecule of DNA.
The nucleus is an organelle that encloses a cell's DNA, its genetic instructions.
Nucleus
DNA
Nerve cell
8. Cell:
The fundamental structural and functional unit of life.
Atom
9. Organelle:
A membrane-enclosed functional structure in a cell.
The property of life emerges at the level of the cell.
10. Molecule:
A chemical structure consisting of two or more units called atoms.

? Which of these levels of biological organization includes all of the others in the list: cell, molecule, organ, tissue?

Biology: The Scientific Study of Life 5

Streamlined text and illustrations **step students through the concept.**

NEW! Topics in the ninth edition include:

1.3: Hierarchy of Life
6.9: Oxidative Phosphorylation
8.17: Crossing Over
13.14: Natural Selection
25.4: Osmoregulation

Encourage Focus on

Main headings allow students to see the big picture.

A Central Concept at the start of each module helps students to focus on one concept at a time.

Cell Division and Reproduction

8.1 Cell division plays many important roles in the lives of organisms

The ability to transmit INFORMATION is one of the unifying themes that encompasses all levels of biological study. Such information flow is absolutely necessary for reproduction. Only people can make more people and only maple trees can make more maple trees because each species carries and transmits its own specific genetic information at the cellular level. When a cell undergoes reproduction, or **cell division**, the two "daughter" cells that result are genetically identical to each other and to the original "parent" cell. (Biologists traditionally use the word *daughter* in this context; it does not imply gender.) Before the parent cell splits into two, it duplicates its **chromosomes**, the structures that contain most of the cell's genetic information in the form of DNA. Then, during cell division, one set of chromosomes is distributed to each daughter cell. As a rule, the daughter cells receive identical sets of chromosomes from the lone, original parent cell. Each offspring cell will thus be genetically identical to the other and to the original parent cell.

Colorized TEM 5,000×

▲ Figure 8.1A A yeast cell producing a genetically identical daughter cell by asexual reproduction

Sometimes, cell division results in the reproduction of a whole organism. Many single-celled organisms, such as prokaryotes or the eukaryotic yeast cell in Figure 8.1A, reproduce by dividing in half, and the offspring are genetic replicas. This is an example of **asexual reproduction**, the creation of genetically identical offspring ...ent, without the participation of sperm and egg. ... that reproduces asexually gives rise to a **clone**, ...etically identical individuals. Many multicellu... can reproduce asexually to produce clones. For ...e sea star species and many house plants have the ability to grow new individuals from fragmented pieces (Figures 8.1B and 8.1C). In asexual reproduction, there is one simple principle of inheritance: The lone parent and each of its offspring have identical genes.

▲ Figure 8.1B A sea star reproducing asexually via fragmentation and regeneration of the body from the fragmented arm

Sexual reproduction is different; it requires the fusion of gametes, egg and sperm. The production of gametes involves a particular type of cell division that occurs only in reproductive organs (testes and ovaries in humans). A gamete has only half as many chromosomes as the parent cell that gave rise to it, and these chromosomes contain unique combinations of genes. In contrast to a clone, offspring produced by sexual reproduction are not identical to their parents or to each other (with the exception of identical twins), although they generally resemble their parents more closely than they resemble unrelated individuals of the same species. They are variations on a common theme of family resemblance, not exact replicas (Figure 8.1D). Each offspring inherits a unique combination of genes from its two parents,

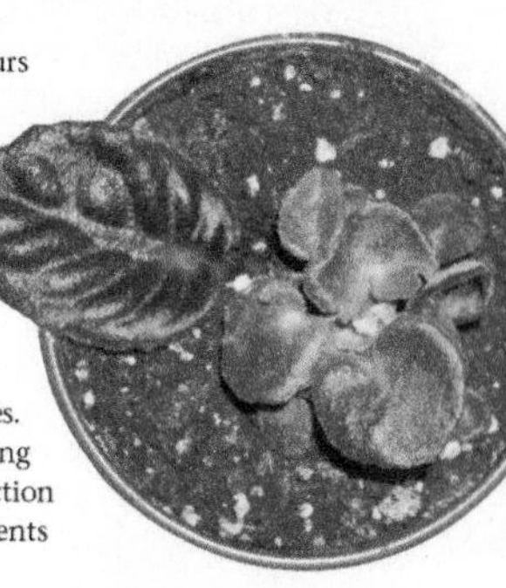

▲ Figure 8.1C An African violet reproducing asexually from a cutting (the large leaf on the left)

◀ Figure 8.1D Sexual reproduction produces offspring with unique combinations of genes

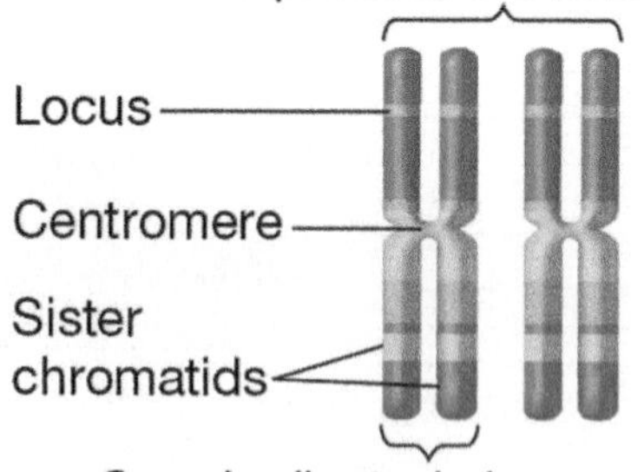

▲ Figure 8.11 A pair of homologous chromosomes

TRY THIS Cover this figure, and on a piece of paper, draw a pair of homologous chromosomes, and label the sister chromatids, the centromere, and one chromosome. Then, uncover this figure and compare it to your drawing.

Try This activities in every chapter encourage students to actively engage with the figures and develop positive study habits.

Key Concepts and Active Learning

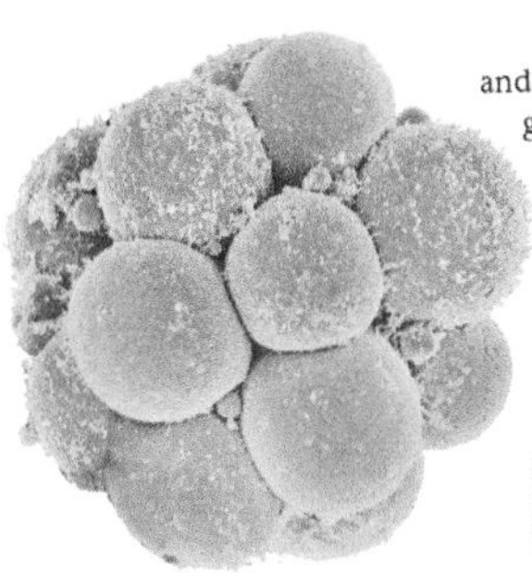

▲ Figure 8.1E Dividing cells in an early human embryo

and this one-and-only set of genes programs a unique combination of traits. As a result, sexual reproduction can produce great variation among offspring.

In addition to the production of gametes, cell division plays other important roles in multicellular organisms. Cell division enables sexually reproducing organisms to develop from a single cell—the fertilized egg, or zygote (Figure 8.1E)—into an adult organism. All of the trillions of cells in your body arose via repeated cell divisions that began in your mother's body with a single fertilized egg cell. After an organism is fully grown, cell division continues to function in renewal and repair, replacing cells that die from normal wear and tear or from accidents. Within your body, millions of cells must divide every second to replace damaged or lost cells (Figure 8.1F). For example, dividing cells within your epidermis continuously replace dead cells that slough off the surface of your skin.

The type of cell division responsible for the growth and maintenance of multicellular organisms and for asexual reproduction involves a process called mitosis. The production of egg and sperm cells involves a different type of cell division called meiosis. In the remainder of this chapter, you will learn the details of both mitosis and meiosis. To start, we'll look briefly at prokaryotic cell division.

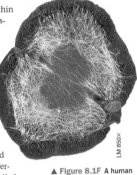

LM 850×

▲ Figure 8.1F A human kidney cell dividing

? What function does cell division play in an amoeba (a single-celled protist)? What functions does it play in your body?

■ Reproduction; development, growth, and repair

8.2 Prokaryotes reproduce by binary fission

Prokaryotes (single-celled bacteria and archaea) reproduce by a type of cell division called **binary fission**, a term that means "dividing in half." In typical prokaryotes, most genes are carried on one circular DNA molecule that, with associated proteins, constitutes the organism's single chromosome.

Although prokaryotic chromosomes are generally much shorter than those of eukaryotes, duplicating them in an orderly fashion and distributing the copies equally to two daughter cells are still formidable tasks. Consider, for example, that when stretched out, the chromosome of the bacterium *Escherichia coli* (*E. coli*) is about 500 times longer than the cell itself. It is no small feat to accurately replicate this molecule when it is coiled and packed inside the cell.

Figure 8.2A illustrates binary fission in a prokaryote. ① As the chromosome is duplicating, one copy moves toward the opposite end of the cell. ② Meanwhile, the cel... ③ When chromosome duplication is complet... has reached about twice its initial size, the plas... pinches inward and more cell wall is made, wh... divides the parent cell into two daughter cells...

Plasma membrane

Cell wall

Prokaryotic chromosome

① Duplication of the chromosome and separation of the copies

② Continued elongation of the cell and movement of the copies

③ Division into two daughter cells

▲ Figure 8.2A Binary fission of a prokaryotic cell

? Why is binary fission classified as asexual re...

...tically identical offspring inherit their DNA from a single

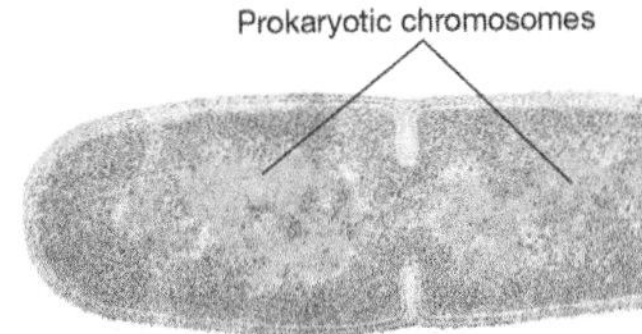

▲ Figure 8.2B An electron micrograph of a bacteriu... of dividing

Cell Division and Repro...

Checkpoint questions at the end of every module let students check their understanding right away.

Figures describing a process take students through a series of numbered steps keyed to explanations in the text.

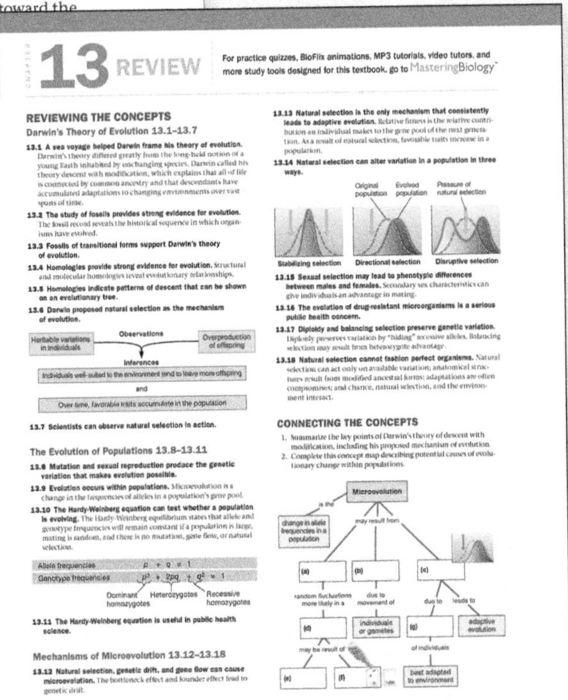

CHAPTER 13 REVIEW

For practice quizzes, BioFlix animations, MP3 tutorials, video tutors, and more study tools designed for this textbook, go to MasteringBiology™

REVIEWING THE CONCEPTS

Darwin's Theory of Evolution 13.1–13.7

13.1 A sea voyage helped Darwin frame his theory of evolution. Darwin's theory differed greatly from the long-held notion of a young Earth inhabited by unchanging species. Darwin called his theory descent with modification, which explains that all of life is connected by common ancestry and that descendants have accumulated adaptations to changing environments over vast spans of time.

13.2 The study of fossils provides strong evidence for evolution. The fossil record reveals the historical sequence in which organisms have evolved.

13.3 Fossils of transitional forms support Darwin's theory of evolution.

13.4 Homologies provide strong evidence for evolution. Structural and molecular homologies reveal evolutionary relationships.

13.5 Homologies indicate patterns of descent that can be shown on an evolutionary tree.

13.6 Darwin proposed natural selection as the mechanism of evolution.

13.7 Scientists can observe natural selection in action.

The Evolution of Populations 13.8–13.11

13.8 Mutation and sexual reproduction produce the genetic variation that makes evolution possible.

13.9 Evolution occurs within populations. Microevolution is a change in the frequencies of alleles in a population's gene pool.

13.10 The Hardy-Weinberg equation can test whether a population is evolving. The Hardy-Weinberg equilibrium states that allele and genotype frequencies will remain constant if a population is large, mating is random, and there is no mutation, gene flow, or natural selection.

13.11 The Hardy-Weinberg equation is useful in public health science.

Mechanisms of Microevolution 13.12–13.18

13.12 Natural selection, genetic drift, and gene flow can cause microevolution. The bottleneck effect and founder effect lead to genetic drift.

13.13 Natural selection is the only mechanism that consistently leads to adaptive evolution. Relative fitness is the relative contribution an individual makes to the gene pool of the next generation. As a result of natural selection, favorable traits increase in a population.

13.14 Natural selection can alter variation in a population in three ways.

13.15 Sexual selection may lead to phenotypic differences between males and females. Secondary sex characteristics can give individuals an advantage in mating.

13.16 The evolution of drug-resistant microorganisms is a serious public health concern.

13.17 Diploidy and balancing selection preserve genetic variation. Diploidy preserves variation by "hiding" recessive alleles. Balancing selection may result from heterozygote advantage.

13.18 Natural selection cannot fashion perfect organisms. Natural selection can act only on available variation; anatomical structures result from modified ancestral forms; adaptations are often compromises; and chance, natural selection, and the environment interact.

CONNECTING THE CONCEPTS

1. Summarize the key points of Darwin's theory of descent with modification, including his proposed mechanism of evolution.
2. Complete this concept map describing potential causes of evolutionary change within populations.

278 CHAPTER 13 How Populations Evolve

Chapter summaries include figures and text to help students review and check their understanding of the chapter concepts.

Continuous Learning
Before, During, and After Class

BEFORE CLASS
Interactive assignments introduce students to key concepts

NEW! Key Topic Overview videos introduce students to key concepts and vocabulary and are created by authors Eric Simon, Jean Dickey and Kelly Hogan. All 12 videos are delivered as a whiteboard style mini-lesson and are accompanied by assessment so that students can check their understanding.

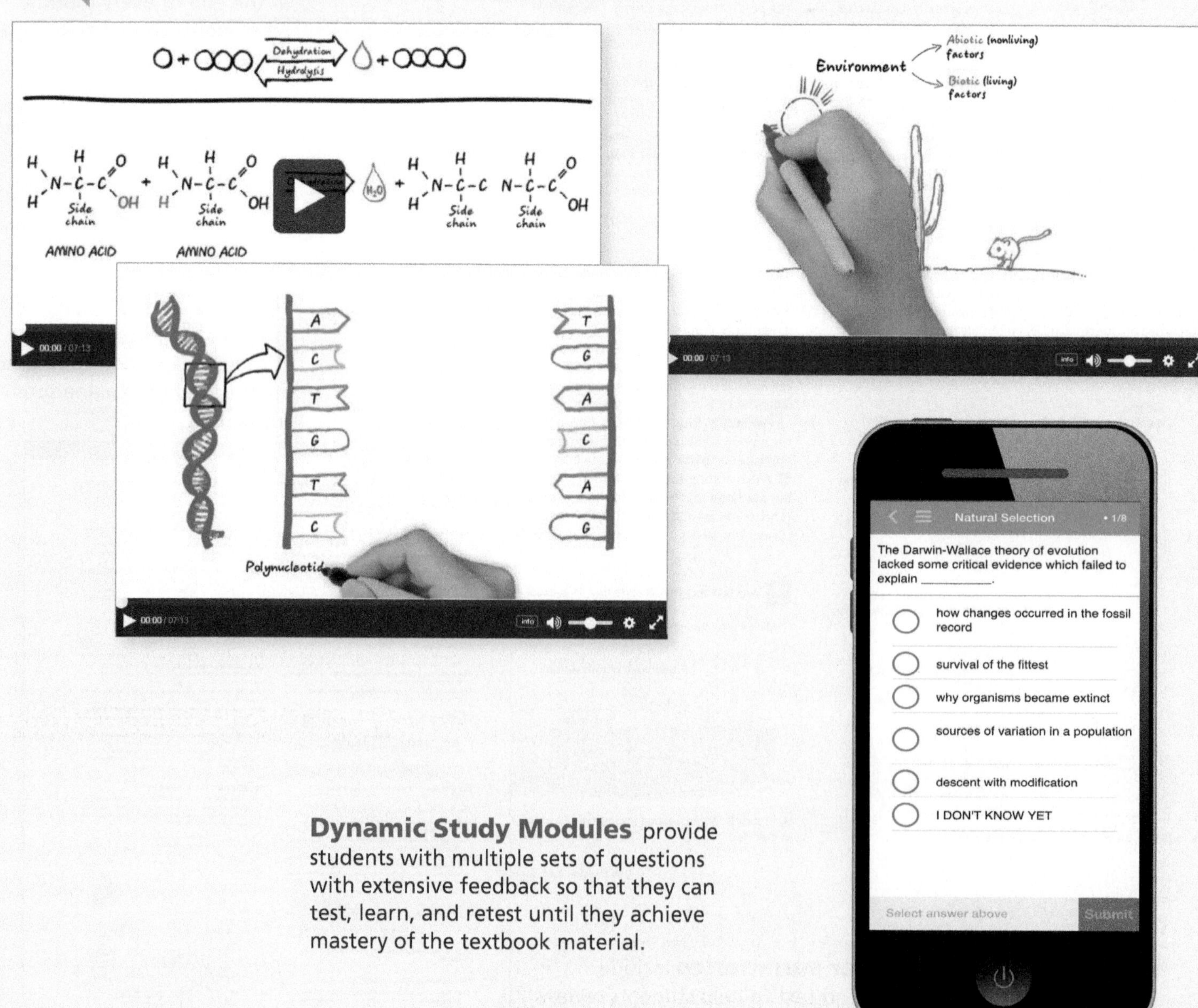

Dynamic Study Modules provide students with multiple sets of questions with extensive feedback so that they can test, learn, and retest until they achieve mastery of the textbook material.

with MasteringBiology

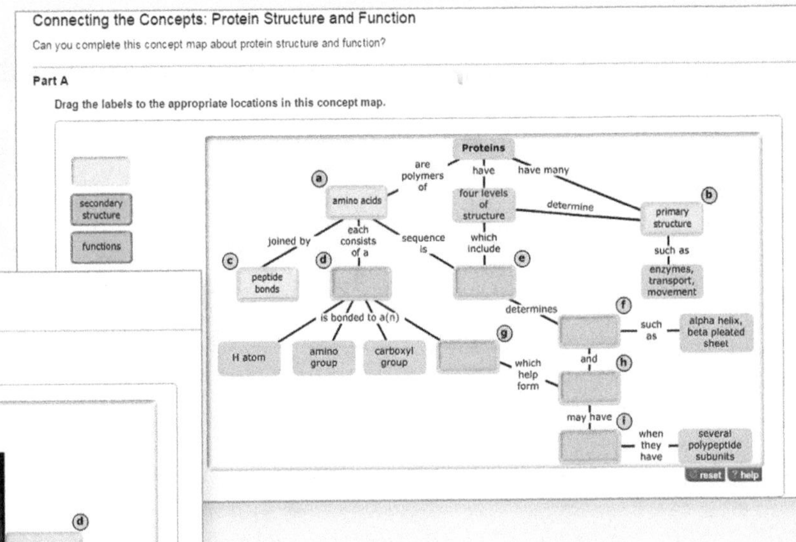

Create pre-lecture assignments with 170 **author created interactive coaching activities**.

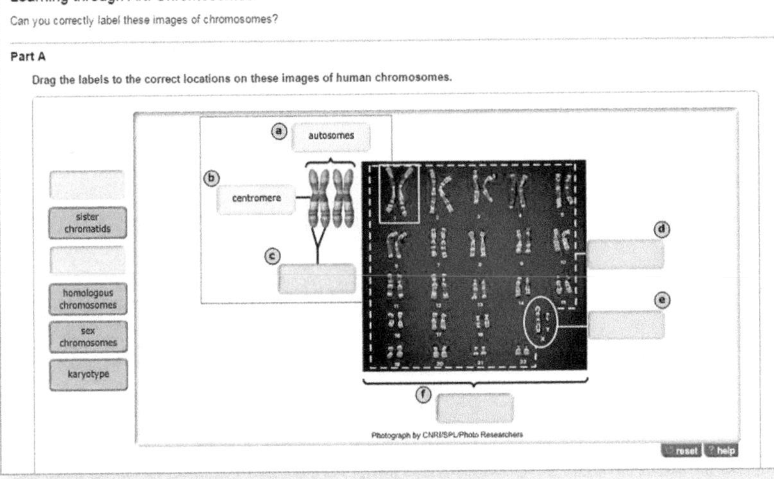

EXPANDED! Give students extra practice with **18 assignable Visualizing the Concept videos**, which pair with the select modules in the text.

Continuous Learning
Before, During, and After Class

DURING CLASS
Encourage engagement with dynamic videos and resources for in class activities

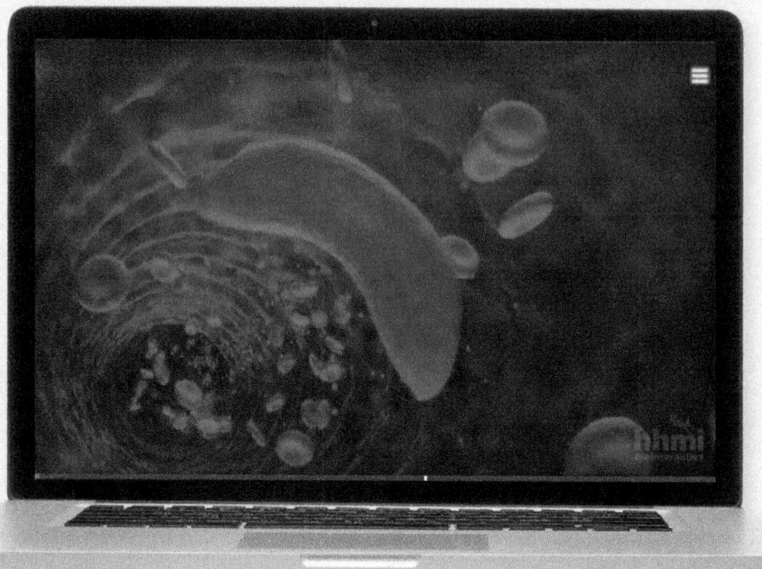

NEW! HHMI Short Films are documentary-quality movies from the Howard Hughes Medical Institute with explorations from the discovery of the double helix to evolution and include assignable questions.

Guided Reading Activities, in the MasteringBiology study area, accompany all chapters and are designed to help students stay on track and develop active reading skills.

Chapter 4: A Tour of the Cell

Big idea: The nucleus and ribosomes

Answer the following questions as you read modules 4.5–4.6:

1. DNA and its associated proteins are referred to as ____________.

2. Which of the following cells would be preparing to divide? Briefly explain your answer.

A

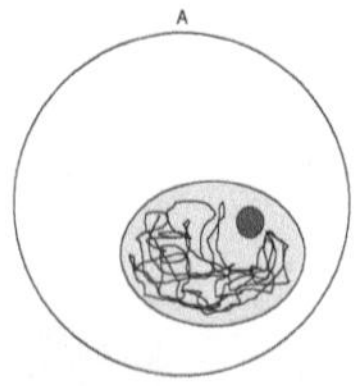

B

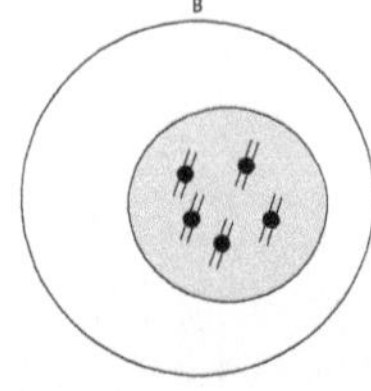

3. Complete the following table that compares rRNA to mRNA.

	rRNA	mRNA
Role in/part of . . .		
Made in . . .		
Travels to . . .		

4. Briefly describe the relationship between the nucleus and ribosomes. Your answer should include the following key terms: **mRNA, rRNA,** and **protein synthesis.**

Resources to help instructors plan dynamic lectures:

- **NEW! Ready-to-Go Teaching Modules** help instructors efficiently make use of the available teaching tools for the toughest topics.
- The **Instructor Exchange** provides active learning techniques from biology instructors around the nation. Co-author Kelly Hogan moderates the exchange.

with MasteringBiology

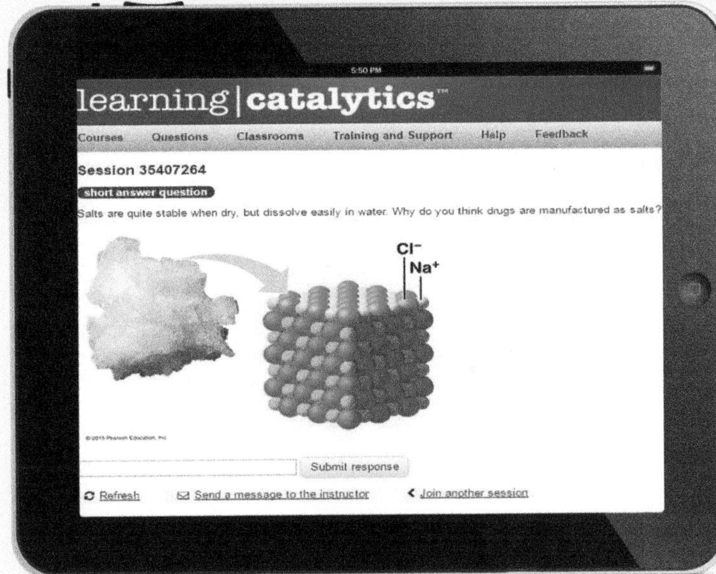

Learning Catalytics is a "bring your own device" (laptop, smartphone, or tablet) engagement, assessment, and classroom intelligence system that allows for active learning and discussion.

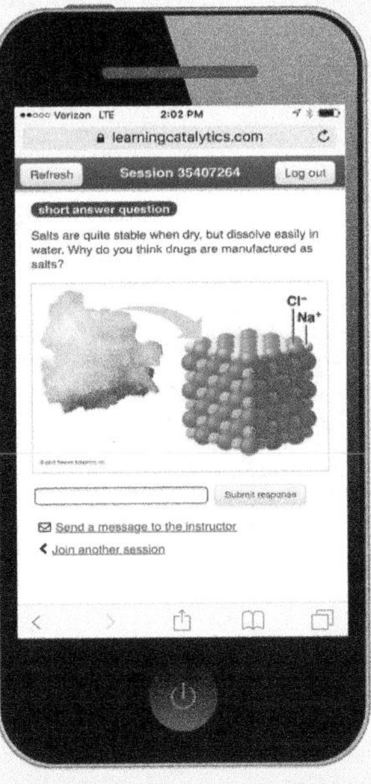

NEW! Try This questions in Learning Catalytics are easy to assign in-class active learning questions, based on the text "Try This" feature.

NEW! Everyday Biology Videos briefly explore interesting and relevant biology topics that relate to concepts that students are learning in class. These 20 videos, produced by the BBC, can be assigned in MasteringBiology.

Engage in Biology
anytime, anywhere

AFTER CLASS
Dynamic activities let students put skills into practice

Scientific Thinking Activities help students develop an understanding of how scientific research is conducted.

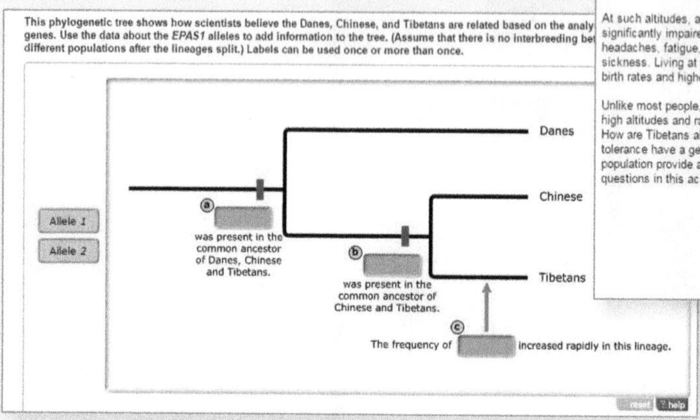

This phylogenetic tree shows how scientists believe the Danes, Chinese, and Tibetans are related based on the analy
genes. Use the data about the EPAS1 alleles to add information to the tree. (Assume that there is no interbreeding be
different populations after the lineages split.) Labels can be used once or more than once.
Allele 1
Allele 2
Danes
Chinese
Tibetans
a
was present in the common ancestor of Danes, Chinese and Tibetans.
b
was present in the common ancestor of Chinese and Tibetans.
c
The frequency of
increased rapidly in this lineage.
reset
help

Scientific Thinking: Is There a Genetic Basis for Adapting to Life at High Altitudes?
The Tibetan people have lived for many thousands of years in the Himalayan Plateau of Asia, a broad area nearly 15,000 feet above sea level (see map). That's higher than any point in the 48 states of the contiguous United States.
At such altitudes, a person's ability to extract oxygen from the air is significantly impaired. For most people, this quickly leads to headaches, fatigue, dizziness, and other symptoms of altitude sickness. Living at high altitudes long term can also lead to lower birth rates and higher infant mortality.
Unlike most people, the Tibetan people are well adapted to life at high altitudes and rarely display any symptoms of altitude sickness. How are Tibetans able to tolerate these conditions? Does this tolerance have a genetic basis? And what clues does this population provide about human evolution? You'll explore these questions in this activity.
RUSSIAN FEDERATION
KAZAKHSTAN
MONGOLIA
TAIWAN
© Dorling Kindersley

Examples of topics include:

- What Is the Role of Peer Review in the Process of Science?
- How Does "Citizen Science" Affect Scientific Data Collection?
- Do the Microorganisms in Our Digestive Tract Play a Role in Obesity?

The New York Times

Argentina Battles Major Outbreak of Dengue as Mosquito Population Swells

By JONATHAN GILBERT FEB. 17, 2016

A fumigation squad in Buenos Aires last month. Argentina reported nearly 4,900 cases of dengue in the first five weeks of 2016.
Natacha Pisarenko/Associated Press

BUENOS AIRES — Argentina is grappling with its worst outbreak of dengue in seven years as the population of

Current Events Activities cover a wide range of biological topics to demonstrate to students how science connects to everyday life.

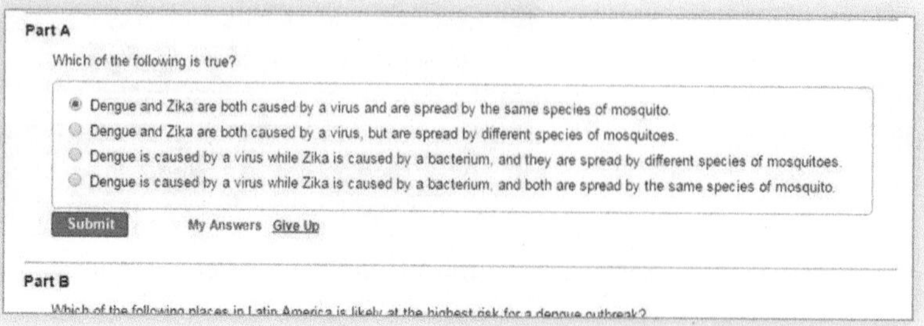

Part A
Which of the following is true?
Dengue and Zika are both caused by a virus and are spread by the same species of mosquito.
Dengue and Zika are both caused by a virus, but are spread by different species of mosquitoes.
Dengue is caused by a virus while Zika is caused by a bacterium, and they are spread by different species of mosquitoes.
Dengue is caused by a virus while Zika is caused by a bacterium, and both are spread by the same species of mosquito.
Submit
My Answers Give Up
Part B
Which of the following places in Latin America is likely at the highest risk for a dengue outbreak?

with MasteringBiology

NEW! Evaluating Science in the Media Activities teach students to recognize validity, bias, purpose, and authority in everyday sources of information.

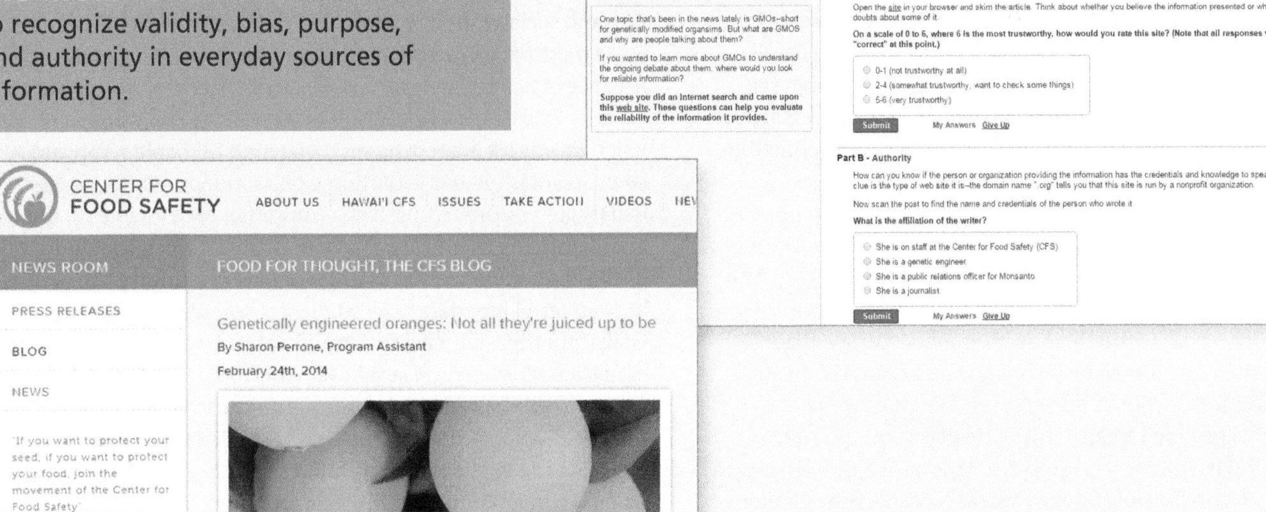

NEW! eText 2.0 is now available on smartphones, tablets and computers, featuring seamlessly integrated videos, and concept check questions. The eText 2.0 mobile app is available for most iOS and Android phones.

Powerful interactive and customization functions include integrated videos and concept check questions, accessible (screen-reader ready), note-taking, highlighting, bookmarking, search, and links to glossary terms.

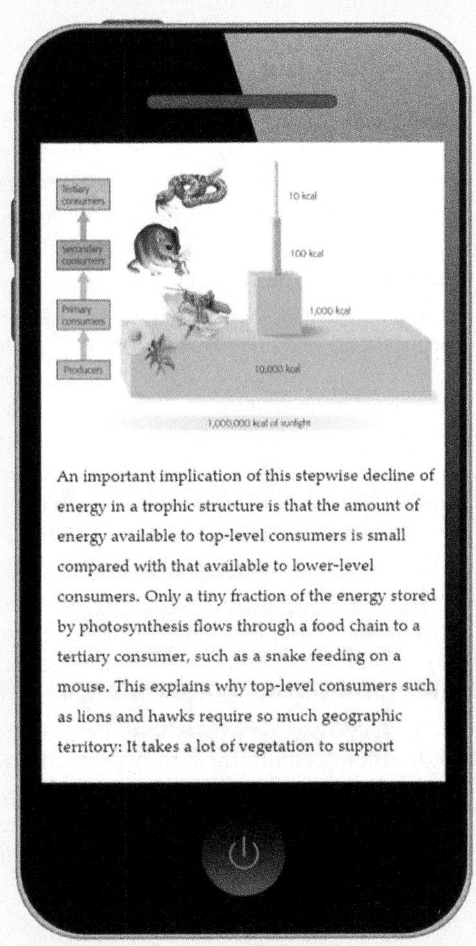

Tertiary consumers
Secondary consumers
Primary consumers
Producers
10 kcal
100 kcal
1,000 kcal
10,000 kcal
1,000,000 kcal of sunlight
An important implication of this stepwise decline of energy in a trophic structure is that the amount of energy available to top-level consumers is small compared with that available to lower-level consumers. Only a tiny fraction of the energy stored by photosynthesis flows through a food chain to a tertiary consumer, such as a snake feeding on a mouse. This explains why top-level consumers such as lions and hawks require so much geographic territory: It takes a lot of vegetation to support

Preface

Inspired by the thousands of students in our own classes over the years and by enthusiastic feedback from the many instructors who have used or reviewed our book, we are delighted to present this new, Ninth Edition. We authors have worked together closely to ensure that both the book and the supplementary material online reflect the changing needs of today's courses and students, as well as current progress in biology. Titled *Campbell Biology: Concepts & Connections* to honor Neil Campbell's founding role and his many contributions to biology education, this book continues to have a dual purpose: to engage students from a wide variety of majors in the wonders of the living world and to show them how biology relates to their own existence and the world they inhabit. Most of these students will not become biologists themselves, but their lives will be touched by biology every day. Understanding the concepts of biology and their connections to our lives is more important than ever. Whether we're concerned with our own health or the health of our planet, a familiarity with biology is essential. This basic knowledge and an appreciation for how science works have become elements of good citizenship in an era when informed evaluations of health issues, environmental problems, and applications of new technology are critical.

Concepts and Connections

Concepts Biology is a vast subject that gets bigger every year, but an introductory biology course is still only one or two semesters long. This book was the first introductory biology textbook to use concept modules to help students recognize and focus on the main ideas of each chapter. The heading of each module is a carefully crafted statement of a key concept. For example, "Helper T cells stimulate the humoral and cell-mediated immune responses" announces a key concept about the role of helper T cells in adaptive immunity (Module 24.12). Such a concept heading serves as a focal point, and the module's text and illustrations converge on that concept with explanation and, often, analogies. The module text walks the student through the illustrations, just as an instructor might do in class. And in teaching a sequential process, such as the one diagrammed in Figure 24.12A, we number the steps in the text to correspond to numbered steps in the figure. The synergy between a module's narrative and graphic components transforms the concept heading into an idea with meaning to the student. The checkpoint question at the end of each module encourages students to test their understanding as they proceed through a chapter. Finally, in the Chapter Review, all the key concept statements are listed and briefly summarized under the overarching section titles, explicitly reminding students of what they've learned.

Connections Students are more motivated to study biology when they can connect it to their own lives and interests—for example, when they are able to relate science to health issues, economic problems, environmental quality, ethical controversies, and social responsibility. In this edition, purple Connection icons mark the numerous application modules that go beyond the core biological concepts. For example, the new Connection Module 32.6 describes how humans tap into plant transport mechanisms for harvesting such materials as maple syrup and latex. In addition, our Evolution Connection modules, identified by green icons, connect the content of each chapter to the grand unifying theme of evolution, without which the study of life has no coherence. For example, a new Evolution Connection in Chapter 14 uses data from studies by Rosemary and Peter Grant and their students to demonstrate the continuing effects of natural selection on Darwin's finches. Explicit connections are also made between the chapter introduction and either the Evolution Connection module or the Scientific Thinking module in each chapter; high-interest questions introduce each chapter, drawing students into the topic and encouraging a curiosity to explore the question further when it appears again later in the chapter. And, connections are made in every chapter between key concepts and the core concepts of biology.

New to This Edition

New Focus on Five Underlying Themes of Biology

A major goal of this Ninth Edition is to provide students with an explicit framework for understanding and organizing the broad expanse of biological information presented in Concepts and Connections. This framework is based on the five major themes outlined in *Vision and Change in Undergraduate Biology Education: A Call to Action* published by the American Academy for the Advancement of Science. These major themes extend across all areas of biology: evolution, the flow of information, the correlation of structure and function, the exchange of energy and matter, and the interactions and interconnections of biological systems. Chapter 1 introduces each of these themes in a separate module. Specific examples of the themes are then called out in each chapter by green icons: INFORMATION, STRUCTURE AND FUNCTION, ENERGY AND MATTER, INTERACTIONS, and EVOLUTION CONNECTION (always in module form).

Expanded Coverage of the Process of Science

Chapter 1 also includes an enhanced focus on the nature of science and the process of scientific inquiry, setting the stage for both the content of the text and the process by which our biological knowledge has been built and continues to grow. We continue this emphasis on the process of scientific inquiry through our Scientific Thinking modules in every chapter, which are called out with an orange icon. New concept check questions for these modules focus on aspects of the process of science: the forming and testing of hypotheses; experimental design; variables and controls; the analysis of data; and the evaluation and communication of scientific results.

Additional Visualizing the Concept Modules These modules, which were new to the Eighth Edition, have raised our hallmark art–text integration to a new level. Visualizing the Concept modules take challenging concepts or processes and walk students through them in a highly visual manner, using engaging, attractive art; clear and concise labels; and instructor "hints" called out in light blue bubbles. These short hints emulate the one-on-one coaching an instructor might provide to a student during office hours and help students make key connections within the figure. Examples of the eight new Visualizing the Concept modules include Module 6.9, Most ATP production occurs by oxidative phosphorylation; Module 8.17, Crossing over further increases genetic variability; Module 13.14, Natural selection can alter variation in a population in three ways; Module 28.6, Neurons communicate at synapses, and Module 34.18, The global water cycle connects aquatic and terrestrial biomes.

New Visualizing the Data Figures Also new to this edition are figures that present data in an infographic form, marked by Visualizing the Data icons. These 19 eye-catching figures provide students with a fresh approach to understanding the concepts illustrated by graphs and numerical data. Figure 10.19 maps emergent virus outbreaks, showing that they originate throughout the world. Figure 12.17 summarizes a wealth of bioinformatics data on genome sizes versus the number of genes found in various species. Figure 13.16 illustrates the growing threat of antibiotic resistant bacteria. Figure 21.14 allows students to directly compare caloric intake (via food) with caloric expenditure (via exercise). Figure 30.5B shows changes in bone mass during the human life span. Figure 36.11 offers an illuminating visual comparison of the per capita and national ecological footprints of several countries with world average and "fair share" footprints. Figure 38.3 shows graphic evidence of global warming by tracking annual global temperatures since 1880.

New Unit Openers That Feature Careers Related to the Content of the Unit Expanding our emphasis on the connections of biology to students' lives, each unit opener page now includes photos of individuals whose professions relate to the content of the unit. For instance, Unit I features a brewery owner and a solar energy engineer. Unit IV portrays a hatchery manager and a paleoanthropologist. These examples are intended to help students see how their biology course relates to the world outside the classroom and to their own career paths.

New Design and Improved Art The fresh new design used throughout the chapters and the extensive reconceptualization of many figures make the book even more appealing and accessible to visual learners. Much of the art in Chapter 6, How Cells Harvest Chemical Energy, for example, has been revised to help students work through the complex reactions of cellular respiration. Other examples of improved art are found in Figures 5.15B, 10.11A, and 37.22B.

The Latest Science Biology is a dynamic field of study, and we take pride in our book's currency and scientific accuracy. For this edition, as in previous editions, we have integrated the results of the latest scientific research throughout the book. We have done this carefully and thoughtfully, recognizing that research advances can lead to new ways of looking at biological topics; such changes in perspective can necessitate organizational changes in our textbook to better reflect the current state of a field. For example, Chapter 12 uses both text and art to present the innovative CRISPR-Cas9 system for gene editing. You will find a unit-by-unit account of new content and organizational improvements in the "New Content" section on pages xix–xx following this Preface.

MasteringBiology® MasteringBiology, the most widely used online tutorial and assessment program for biology, continues to accompany *Campbell Biology: Concepts & Connections*. In addition to 170 author-created activities that help students learn vocabulary, extend the book's emphasis on visual learning, demonstrate the connections among key concepts (helping students grasp the big ideas), and coach students on how to interpret data, the Ninth Edition features new assignable videos. These videos bring this text's Visualizing the Concept modules to life, help students learn how to evaluate sources of scientific information for reliability, and include short news videos that engage students in the many ways course concepts connect to the world outside the classroom. MasteringBiology® for *Campbell Biology: Concepts & Connections*, Ninth Edition, will help students to see strong connections through their text, and the additional practice available online allows instructors to capture powerful data on student performance, thereby making the most of class time.

This Book's Flexibility

Although a biology textbook's table of contents is by design linear, biology itself is more like a web of related concepts without a single starting point or prescribed path. Courses can navigate this network by starting with molecules, with ecology, or somewhere in-between, and courses can omit topics. *Campbell Biology: Concepts & Connections* is uniquely suited to offer flexibility and thus serve a variety of courses. The seven units of the book are largely self-contained, and in a number of the units, chapters can be assigned in a different order without much loss of coherence. The use of numbered modules makes it easy to skip topics or reorder the presentation of material.

■ ■ ■

For many students, introductory biology is the only science course that they will take during their college years. Long after today's students have forgotten most of the specific content of their biology course, they will be left with general impressions and attitudes about science and scientists. We hope that this new edition of *Campbell Biology: Concepts & Connections* helps make those impressions positive and supports instructors' goals for sharing the fun of biology. In our continuing efforts to improve the book and its supporting materials, we benefit tremendously from instructor and student feedback, not only in formal reviews but also via informal communication. Please let us know how we are doing and how we can improve the next edition of the book.

Martha Taylor
(Chapter 1 and Unit I),
mrt2@cornell.edu

Eric Simon
(Units II and VI and Chapters 21 and 27),
SimonBiology@gmail.com

Jean Dickey
(Units III, IV, and VII and Chapters 22 and 30),
dickeyj@clemson.edu

Kelly Hogan
(Chapters 20, 23–26, 28, and 29),
leek@email.unc.edu

Jane Reece
janereece@cal.berkeley.edu

New Content

Below are some important highlights of new content and organizational improvements in *Campbell Biology: Concepts & Connections*, Ninth Edition.

Chapter 1, Biology: Exploring Life This chapter has been extensively reorganized and revised. Our expanded coverage of the nature of science and scientific inquiry has now moved to the forefront of Chapter 1. The first of the five modules in this section provides a general description of data, hypothesis formation and testing, the centrality of verifiable evidence to science, and an explanation of scientific theories. The module describing how hypotheses can be tested using controlled experiments now includes a subsection on hypothesis testing in humans. A new Scientific Thinking module entitled Hypotheses can be tested using observational data, describes how multiple lines of evidence, including DNA comparisons, have helped resolve the classification of the red panda. Another new module—The process of science is repetitive, nonlinear, and collaborative—presents a more accurate model of the process of science that includes four interacting circles: Exploration and Discovery; Forming and Testing Hypotheses: Analysis and Feedback from the Scientific Community; and Societal Benefits and Outcomes. The chapter concludes with the introduction of five core themes that underlie all of biology: evolution; information; structure and function; energy and matter; and interactions.

Unit I, The Life of the Cell This unit guides students from basic chemistry and the molecules of life through cellular structures to cellular respiration and photosynthesis. Throughout the Ninth Edition, the five themes introduced in Chapter 1 are highlighted with specific references. Examples from Unit 1 include "Illustrating our theme of ENERGY AND MATTER, we see that matter has been rearranged, with an input of energy provided by sunlight" (Module 2.9); "The flow of genetic instruction that leads to gene expression, summarized as DNA → RNA → protein, illustrates the important biological theme of INFORMATION" (Module 3.15); "The interconnections among these pathways provide a clear example of the theme of INTERACTIONS in producing the emergent property of a balanced metabolism" (Module 6.15); and "The precise arrangements of these membranes and compartments are essential to the process of photosynthesis—a classic example of the theme of STRUCTURE AND FUNCTION" (Module 7.2). The theme of evolution is featured, as it is in every chapter, in an Evolution Connection module, such as Module 4.15, Mitochondria and chloroplasts evolved by endosymbiosis. Two new Visualizing the Concept modules are Module 2.6, Covalent bonds join atoms into molecules through electron sharing, and Module 6.9, Most ATP production occurs by oxidative phosphorylation. Both use new and highly revised art to guide students through these challenging topics. The Connection Module 2.2, Trace elements are common additives to food and water, uses added information on water fluoridation to emphasize the process of science and societal interactions. Two new Connection modules are Module 3.6, Are we eating too much sugar? (which includes a Visualizing the Data figure on recommended and actual sugar consumption), and Module 7.14, Reducing both fossil fuel use and deforestation may moderate climate change (which includes information on the 2015 Paris climate accord). New orientation diagrams help students follow the various stages of cellular respiration and photosynthesis in Chapters 6 and 7.

Unit II, Cellular Reproduction and Genetics The purpose of this unit is to help students understand the relationship between DNA, chromosomes, and organisms and to help students see that genetics is not purely hypothetical but connects in many important and interesting ways to their lives, human society, and other life on Earth. The content has been reinforced with updated discussions of relevant topics, such as DCIS (also called stage 0 breast cancer), increased use of genetically modified organisms (GMOs), recent examples of DNA profiling, information about the 2015 California measles outbreak, a new infographic that charts emergent virus outbreaks, and new data on the health prospects of clones. This edition includes discussion of many recent advances in the field, such as an updated definition of the gene, and a largely new presentation of DNA technologies and bioinformatics, including extensive discussion in both text and art of the CRISPR-Cas9 system, GenBank, and BLAST searches. In some cases, sections within chapters have been reorganized to present a more logical flow of materials. Examples of new organization include an improved presentation of the genetics underlying cancer, a new Visualizing the Concept module on crossing over, a new circular genetic code chart that should improve student understanding, and a new Visualizing the Data that summarizes relevant information about different types of cancer and their survival rates. Material throughout the unit has been updated to reflect recent data, such as the latest statistics on cancer, cystic fibrosis, and Down syndrome, an improved model of ribosomes, new information about prions, expanded coverage of noncoding small RNAs, new human gene therapy trials, and recent information about Y chromosome inheritance.

Unit III, Concepts of Evolution This unit presents the basic principles of evolution and natural selection, the overwhelming evidence that supports these theories, and their relevance to all of biology—and to the lives of students. For example, a new Visualizing the Data figure (13.16) illustrates the growing threat of antibiotic resistance. Chapter 13 also includes a new Visualizing the Concept module (13.14) on the effects of natural selection that shows experimental data along with hypothetical examples. Chapter 14 contains a new

Evolution Connection module (14.9) featuring the work of Rosemary and Peter Grant on Darwin's finches. Modules 15.14 to 15.19 were revised to improve the flow and clarity of the material on phylogenetics and include updates from genomic studies and new art (for example, Figures 15.17 and 15.19A).

Unit IV, The Evolution of Biological Diversity The diversity unit surveys all life on Earth in less than a hundred pages! Consequently, descriptions and illustrations of the unifying characteristics of each major group of organisms, along with a small sample of its diversity, make up the bulk of the content. Two recurring elements are interwoven with these descriptions: evolutionary history and examples of relevance to our everyday lives and society at large. With the rapid accumulation of molecular evidence, taxonomic revisions are inevitable. These changes are reflected in Chapter 16, Microbial Life, with a new module and figure (16.13) on protist supergroups, and in Chapters 18 and 19, Evolution of Invertebrate Diversity and Evolution of Vertebrate Diversity, with three modules about animal phylogeny (18.10, 18.11, and 19.1). The importance of metagenomics to the study of microorganisms is highlighted in Modules 16.1 and 16.7 (prokaryotes) and 17.14 (fungi). New examples of relevance include valley fever, a fungal disease linked to climate change (Module 17.19), and a Visualizing the Data figure (19.16) on the evolution of human skin color.

Unit V, Animals: Form and Function This unit combines a comparative animal approach with an exploration of human anatomy and physiology. The introduction to Chapter 20, Unifying Concepts of Animal Structure and Function, begins with the question "Does evolution lead to the perfect animal form?" and the question is answered in the Evolution Connection, Module 20.1, in discussion of the lengthy laryngeal nerve in giraffes. By illustrating that a structure in an ancestral organism can become adapted to function in a descendant organism without being "perfected," this example helps to combat a common student misconception about evolution. The main portion of every chapter in this unit is devoted to detailed presentations of human body systems, frequently illuminated by discussion of the health consequences of disorders in those systems. The Chapter 22 opening essay and Scientific Thinking module (22.7) were revised to compare the conclusions from long term studies on the health hazards of cigarette smoking with the very recent research on the effects of e-cigarettes. In Chapter 23, Circulation, the Scientific Thinking module (23.6) discusses the consequences of treating coronary artery disease with medicine or both medicine and stents. Chapter 29, The Senses, incorporates new material on common eye conditions, glaucoma and cataracts. In many areas, content has been updated to reflect newer issues in biology. New modules include 24.9 on the importance of community vaccination, 28.18 on neuronal plasticity, and 29.12 about the contribution of genes in one's perception of the taste of cilantro. New Visualizing the Concept modules on osmoregulation (25.4) and neuronal synapses (28.6) help students better envision big concepts. New Visualizing the Data figures detail data on hypertension in the United States (23.9B), worldwide HIV infection and treatments (24.14B), and changes in bone mass during the human life span (30.5B). Chapter 21, Nutrition and Digestion, includes a new discussion of human microbiome and microbiota as well as presentation of the forthcoming changes to food nutritional labels. Module 22.9, Breathing is automatically controlled, was heavily revised. The equation showing the formation and dissociation of carbonic acid now accompanies the discussion of how the medulla regulates breathing, a process illustrated by new art. Improvements to this unit also include a significant revision to the presentation of the kidney as a water-conserving organ (25.7) and a clearer four-step process by which a sensory stimulus results in a perception (Module 29.1). Chapter 27, Reproduction and Embryonic Development, presents data on the decreased incidence of cervical cancer due to early detection, a new Visualizing the Data (Figure 27.8) that summarizes different methods of contraception, and new information on reproductive technologies.

Unit VI, Plants: Form and Function To help students gain an appreciation of the importance of plants, this unit presents the anatomy and physiology of angiosperms with frequent connections to the importance of plants to society. New Connections modules in this edition include an improved discussion of agriculture via artificial selection on plant parts and via plant cloning in Chapter 31; updated discussions of organic farming, human harvesting of plant transport products (such as maple syrup and rubber), and GMOs in Chapter 32; and a new discussion of caffeine as an evolutionary adaptation that can prevent herbivory in Chapter 33. Throughout the unit, the text has been revised with the goal of making the material more engaging and accessible to students. For example, the discussion of plant nutrients has been entirely reorganized into a large Visualizing the Data in Module 32.7, and the presentation of the potentially confusing topic of the effect of auxin on plant cell elongation benefits from a new visual presentation (Figure 33.3B). All of these changes are meant to make the point that human society is inexorably connected to the health of plants.

Unit VII, Ecology In this unit, students learn the fundamental principles of ecology and how these principles apply to environmental problems. The Ninth Edition features a new Visualizing the Concept module that explains the global water cycle (34.18) and Visualizing the Data figures that compare ecological footprints (36.11), track global temperatures since 1880 (38.3A), and illustrate the results of a study on optimal foraging theory (35.12). Module 35.16 has been updated with new examples of the effects of endocrine-disrupting chemicals on animal behavior and the EPA's progress in evaluating endocrine disruptors in pesticides as potential hazards to human health. Other content updates in this unit include human population data (36.9 and 36.10), species at risk for extinction (38.1), and the new federal law banning the use of microbeads in health and beauty products (38.2). Module 37.13 has been heavily revised to include more examples of invasive species. The unit-wide emphasis on climate change and sustainability continues in this edition. For example, the module on ecological footprints (36.11) has been updated and revised, and Module 37.23 includes a new emphasis on the role of wetlands in mitigating the effects of climate change. Figures 38.3B and 38.4A were updated with the most recent data available, and Module 38.3 was heavily revised.

Acknowledgments

This Ninth Edition of *Campbell Biology: Concepts & Connections* is a result of the combined efforts of many talented and hardworking people, and the authors wish to extend heartfelt thanks to all those who contributed to this and previous editions. Our work on this edition was shaped by input from the biologists acknowledged in the reviewer list on pages xxii–xxiv, who shared with us their experiences teaching introductory biology and provided specific suggestions for improving the book. Feedback from the authors of this edition's supplements and the unsolicited comments and suggestions we received from many biologists and biology students were also extremely helpful. In addition, this book has benefited in countless ways from the stimulating contacts we have had with the coauthors of *Campbell Biology*, Eleventh Edition.

We wish to offer special thanks to the students and faculty at our teaching institutions. Marty Taylor thanks her students at Cornell University for their valuable feedback on the book. Eric Simon thanks his colleagues and friends at New England College, especially within the collegium of Natural Sciences and Mathematics, for their continued support and assistance. Jean Dickey thanks her colleagues at Clemson University for their expertise and support. And Kelly Hogan thanks her students for their enthusiasm and colleagues at the University of North Carolina, Chapel Hill, for their continued support.

We thank Paul Corey, managing director of Higher Education Learning Services. In addition, the superb publishing team for this edition was headed up by courseware portfolio management specialist Alison Rodal, with the invaluable support of courseware portfolio management director Beth Wilbur. We cannot thank them enough for their unstinting efforts on behalf of the book and for their commitment to excellence in biology education. We are fortunate to have had once again the contributions of courseware director of content development Ginnie Simione Jutson. We are similarly grateful to the members of the editorial development team—Debbie Hardin, Evelyn Dahlgren, Julia Osborne, Susan Teahan, and Mary Catherine Hager—for their steadfast commitment to quality. We thank them for their thoroughness, hard work, and good humor; the book is far better than it would have been without their efforts. Thanks also to supplements project editor Melissa O'Conner on her oversight of the supplements program and to editorial coordinator Alison Cagle for the efficient and enthusiastic support she provided.

This book and all the other components of the teaching package are both attractive and pedagogically effective in large part because of the hard work and creativity of the production professionals on our team. We wish to thank managing producer Mike Early and content producers Mae Lum and Courtney Towson. We also acknowledge copy editor Jon Preimesberger, proofreaders Pete Shanks and Joanna Dinsmore, and indexer Tim Engman. We again thank photo researcher Kristin Piljay for her contributions, as well as text permissions manager K. Ganesh and photo permissions manager Eric Shrader. Integra was responsible for composition, headed by production project manager Alverne Ball, and the art house Lachina, headed by project manager Whitney Philipp, who was responsible for overseeing the rendering of new and revised illustrations. We also thank manufacturing overseer Stacey Weinberger.

We thank Elise Lansdon for creating a beautiful and functional interior design and a stunning cover, and we are again indebted to design manager Mark Ong for his oversight and design leadership.

The value of *Campbell Biology: Concepts & Connections* as a learning tool is greatly enhanced by the hard work and creativity of the authors of the supplements that accompany this book: Ed Zalisko (*Instructor's Guide* and *PowerPoint® Lecture Presentations*); Jean DeSaix, Kristen Miller, Justin Shaffer, and Suann Yang (*Test Bank*); Dana Kurpius (*Active Reading Guide*); Bob Iwan and Sukanya Subramanian (*Reading Quizzes*); Cheri LaRue (media correlator), and Brenda Hunzinger (*Clicker Questions* and *Quiz Shows*). In addition to supplements project editor Melissa O'Conner, the editorial and production staff for the supplements program included supplements production project manager Alverne Ball (Integra), Marsha Hall (PPS), and Jennifer Hastings (PPS). And the superlative MasteringBiology® program for this book would not exist without Lauren Fogel, Stacy Treco, Katie Foley, Sarah Jensen, Chloé Veylit, Jim Hufford, Charles Hall, Caroline Power, and David Kokorowski and his team. And a special thanks to Arl Nadel and Sarah Young-Dualan for their thoughtful work on the Visualizing the Concepts interactive videos.

For their important roles in marketing the book, we are very grateful to marketing manager Christa Pelaez and vice president of marketing Christy Lesko. The members of the Pearson Science sales team have continued to help us connect with biology instructors and their teaching needs, and we thank them.

Finally, we are deeply grateful to our families and friends for their support, encouragement, and patience throughout this project. Our special thanks to Paul, Dan, Maria, Armelle, and Sean (J.B.R.); Josie, Jason, Marnie, Alice, Jack, David, Paul, Ava, and Daniel (M.R.T.); Amanda, Reed, Forest, and dear friends Jamey, Nick, Jim, and Bethany (E.J.S.); Jessie and Katherine (J.L.D.); and Tracey, Vivian, Carolyn, Brian, Jake, and Lexi (K.H.)

Jane Reece, Martha Taylor, Eric Simon, Jean Dickey, and Kelly Hogan

Reviewers

Reviewers of the Ninth Edition

Ellen Baker, *Santa Monica College*
Deborah Cardenas, *Collin College*
Marc DalPonte, *Lake Land College*
Tammy Dennis, *Bishop State Community College*
Jean DeSaix, *University of North Carolina, Chapel Hill*
Cynthia Galloway, *Texas A&M University*
Jan Goerrissen, *Orange Coast College*
Christopher Haynes, *Shelton State*
Andrew Hinton, *San Diego City College*
Duane Hinton, *Washburn University*
Brenda Hunzinger, *Lake Land College*
Robert Iwan, *Inver Hills Community College*
Cheri LaRue, *University of Arkansas, Fayetteville*
Barbara Lax, *Community College of Allegheny County*
Brenda Leady, *University of Toledo*
Sheryl Love, *Temple University*
David Luther, *George Mason University*
Steven MacKie, *Pima County Community College*
Thaddeus McRae, *Broward Community College*
Kristen Miller, *University of Georgia*
Debbie Misencik, *Community College of Allegheny County*
Justin Shaffer, *University of California, Irvine*
Erica Sharar, *Santiago Canyon College*
Patricia Steinke, *San Jacinto College Central*
Jennifer Stueckle, *West Virginia University*
Sukanya Subramanian, *Collin County Community College*
Brad Williamson, *University of Kansas*
Suann Yang, *Presbyterian College*
Edward Zalisko, *Blackburn College*

Media Review Panel, Ninth Edition

Bob Iwan, *Inver Hills Community College*
Cheri LaRue, *University of Arkansas*
Linda Logdberg
Lindsay Rush, *Quinnipiac University*
Sukanya Subramanian, *Collin County Community*

Reviewers of Previous Editions

Michael Abbott, *Westminster College*
Tanveer Abidi, *Kean University*
Daryl Adams, *Mankato State University*
Dawn Adrian Adams, *Baylor University*
Olushola Adeyeye, *Duquesne University*
Shylaja Akkaraju, *Bronx Community College*
Felix Akojie, *Paducah Community College*
Dan Alex, *Chabot College*
John Aliff, *Georgia Perimeter College*
Sylvester Allred, *Northern Arizona University*
Jane Aloi-Horlings, *Saddleback College*
Loren Ammerman, *University of Texas at Arlington*
Dennis Anderson, *Oklahoma City Community College*
Marjay Anderson, *Howard University*
Steven Armstrong, *Tarrant County College*
Bert Atsma, *Union County College*
Yael Avissar, *Rhode Island College*
Gail Baker, *LaGuardia Community College*
Caroline Ballard, *Rock Valley College*
Andrei Barkovskii, *Georgia College and State University*
Mark Barnby, *Ohlone College*
Chris Barnhart, *University of San Diego*
Stephen Barnhart, *Santa Rosa Junior College*
William Barstow, *University of Georgia*
Kirk A. Bartholomew, *Central Connecticut State University*
Michael Battaglia, *Greenville Technical College*
Gail Baughman, *Mira Costa College*
Jane Beiswenger, *University of Wyoming*
Tania Beliz, *College of San Mateo*
Lisa Bellows, *North Central Texas College*
Ernest Benfield, *Virginia Polytechnic Institute*
Rudi Berkelhamer, *University of California, Irvine*
Harry Bernheim, *Tufts University*
Richard Bliss, *Yuba College*
Lawrence Blumer, *Morehouse College*
Dennis Bogyo, *Valdosta State University*
Lisa K. Bonneau, *Metropolitan Community College, Blue River*
Mehdi Borhan, *Johnson County Community College*
Kathleen Bossy, *Bryant College*
William Bowen, *University of Arkansas at Little Rock*
Robert Boyd, *Auburn University*
Bradford Boyer, *State University of New York, Suffolk County Community College*
Paul Boyer, *University of Wisconsin*
William Bradshaw, *Brigham Young University*
Agnello Braganza, *Chabot College*
James Bray, *Blackburn College*
Peggy Brickman, *University of Georgia*
Chris Brinegar, *San Jose State University*
Chad Brommer, *Emory University*
Charles Brown, *Santa Rosa Junior College*
Stephen T. Brown, *Los Angeles Mission College*
Carole Browne, *Wake Forest University*
Delia Brownson, *University of Texas at Austin and Austin Community College*
Becky Brown-Watson, *Santa Rosa Junior College*
Michael Bucher, *College of San Mateo*
Virginia Buckner, *Johnson County Community College*
Joseph C. Bundy, Jr., *University of North Carolina at Greensboro*
Ray Burton, *Germanna Community College*
Nancy Buschhaus, *University of Tennessee at Martin*
Warren Buss, *University of Northern Colorado*
Linda Butler, *University of Texas at Austin*
Jerry Button, *Portland Community College*
Carolee Caffrey, *University of California, Los Angeles*
George Cain, *University of Iowa*
Beth Campbell, *Itawamba Community College*
John Campbell, *Northern Oklahoma College*
John Capeheart, *University of Houston, Downtown*
James Cappuccino, *Rockland Community College*
M. Carabelli, *Broward Community College*
Jocelyn Cash, *Central Piedmont Community College*
Cathryn Cates, *Tyler Junior College*
Russell Centanni, *Boise State University*
David Chambers, *Northeastern University*
Ruth Chesnut, *Eastern Illinois University*
Vic Chow, *San Francisco City College*
Van Christman, *Ricks College*
Craig Clifford, *Northeastern State University, Tahlequah*
Richard Cobb, *South Maine Community College*
Glenn Cohen, *Troy University*
Mary Colavito, *Santa Monica College*
Jennifer Cooper, *Itawamba Community College*
Bob Cowling, *Ouachita Technical College*
Don Cox, *Miami University*
Robert Creek, *Western Kentucky University*
Hillary Cressey, *George Mason University*
Norma Criley, *Illinois Wesleyan University*
Jessica Crowe, *South Georgia College*
Mitch Cruzan, *Portland State University*
Judy Daniels, *Monroe Community College*
Michael Davis, *Central Connecticut State University*
Pat Davis, *East Central Community College*
Lewis Deaton, *University of Louisiana*
Lawrence DeFilippi, *Lurleen B. Wallace College*
James Dekloe, *Solano Community College*
Veronique Delesalle, *Gettysburg College*
Loren Denney, *Southwest Missouri State University*
Jean DeSaix, *University of North Carolina at Chapel Hill*
Mary Dettman, *Seminole Community College of Florida*
Kathleen Diamond, *College of San Mateo*
Alfred Diboll, *Macon College*
Jean Dickey, *Clemson University*
Stephen Dina, *St. Louis University*
Robert P. Donaldson, *George Washington University*
Gary Donnermeyer, *Iowa Central Community College*
Charles Duggins, *University of South Carolina*
Susan Dunford, *University of Cincinnati*
Lee Edwards, *Greenville Technical College*
Betty Eidemiller, *Lamar University*
Jamin Eisenbach, *Eastern Michigan University*
Norman Ellstrand, *University of California, Riverside*
Thomas Emmel, *University of Florida*
Cindy Erwin, *City College of San Francisco*
Gerald Esch, *Wake Forest University*
Nora Espinoza, *Clemson University*
David Essar, *Winona State University*
Cory Etchberger, *Longview Community College*
Nancy Eyster-Smith, *Bentley College*

William Ezell, *University of North Carolina at Pembroke*
Laurie Faber, *Grand Rapids Community College*
Terence Farrell, *Stetson University*
Shannon Kuchel Fehlberg, *Colorado Christian University*
Jerry Feldman, *University of California, Santa Cruz*
Eugene Fenster, *Longview Community College*
Dino Fiabane, *Community College of Philadelphia*
Kathleen Fisher, *San Diego State University*
Edward Fliss, *St. Louis Community College, Florissant Valley*
Linda Flora, *Montgomery County Community College*
Dennis Forsythe, *The Citadel Military College of South Carolina*
Karen E. Francl, *Radford University*
Robert Frankis, *College of Charleston*
James French, *Rutgers University*
Bernard Frye, *University of Texas at Arlington*
Anne Galbraith, *University of Wisconsin*
Robert Galbraith, *Crafton Hills College*
Rosa Gambier, *State University of New York, Suffolk County Community College*
George Garcia, *University of Texas at Austin*
Linda Gardner, *San Diego Mesa College*
Sandi Gardner, *Triton College*
Gail Gasparich, *Towson University*
Janet Gaston, *Troy University*
Shelley Gaudia, *Lane Community College*
Douglas Gayou, *University of Missouri at Columbia*
Robert Gendron, *Indiana University of Pennsylvania*
Bagie George, *Georgia Gwinnett College*
Rebecca German, *University of Cincinnati*
Grant Gerrish, *University of Hawaii*
Julie Gibbs, *College of DuPage*
Frank Gilliam, *Marshall University*
Patricia Glas, *The Citadel Military College of South Carolina*
David Glenn-Lewin, *Wichita State University*
Robert Grammer, *Belmont University*
Laura Grayson-Roselli, *Burlington County College*
Peggy Green, *Broward Community College*
Miriam L. Greenberg, *Wayne State University*
Jennifer Greenwood, *University of Tennessee at Martin*
Sylvia Greer, *City University of New York*
Eileen Gregory, *Rollins College*
Dana Griffin, *University of Florida*
Richard Groover, *J. Sargeant Reynolds Community College*
Peggy Guthrie, *University of Central Oklahoma*
Maggie Haag, *University of Alberta*
Richard Haas, *California State University, Fresno*
Joel Hagen, *Radford University*
Martin Hahn, *William Paterson College*
Leah Haimo, *University of California, Riverside*
James Hampton, *Salt Lake Community College*
Blanche Haning, *North Carolina State University*
Richard Hanke, *Rose State College*
Laszlo Hanzely, *Northern Illinois University*
David Harbster, *Paradise Valley Community College*
Sig Harden, *Troy University Montgomery*
Reba Harrell, *Hinds Community College*
Jim Harris, *Utah Valley Community College*
Mary Harris, *Louisiana State University*
Chris Haynes, *Shelton State Community College*
Janet Haynes, *Long Island University*
Jean Helgeson, *Collin County Community College*
Ira Herskowitz, *University of California, San Francisco*
Paul Hertz, *Barnard College*
Margaret Hicks, *David Lipscomb University*
Jean Higgins-Fonda, *Prince George's Community College*
Duane A. Hinton, *Washburn University*
Phyllis Hirsch, *East Los Angeles College*
William Hixon, *St. Ambrose University*
Carl Hoagstrom, *Ohio Northern University*
Kim Hodgson, *Longwood College*
Jon Hoekstra, *Gainesville State College*
Kelly Hogan, *University of North Carolina at Chapel Hill*
Amy Hollingsworth, *The University of Akron*
John Holt, *Michigan State University*
Laura Hoopes, *Occidental College*
Lauren Howard, *Norwich University*
Robert Howe, *Suffolk University*
Michael Hudecki, *State University of New York, Buffalo*
George Hudock, *Indiana University*
Kris Hueftle, *Pensacola Junior College*
Barbara Hunnicutt, *Seminole Community College*
Brenda Hunzinger, *Lake Land College*
Catherine Hurlbut, *Florida Community College*
Charles Ide, *Tulane University*
Mark Ikeda, *San Bernardino Valley College*
Georgia Ineichen, *Hinds Community College*
Robert Iwan, *Inver Hills Community College*
Mark E. Jackson, *Central Connecticut State University*
Charles Jacobs, *Henry Ford Community College*
Fred James, *Presbyterian College*
Ursula Jander, *Washburn University*
Alan Jaworski, *University of Georgia*
R. Jensen, *Saint Mary's College*
Robert Johnson, *Pierce College, Lakewood Campus*
Roishene Johnson, *Bossier Parish Community College*
Russell Johnson, *Ricks College*
John C. Jones, *Calhoun Community College*
Florence Juillerat, *Indiana University at Indianapolis*
Tracy Kahn, *University of California, Riverside*
Hinrich Kaiser, *Victor Valley College*
Klaus Kalthoff, *University of Texas at Austin*
Tom Kantz, *California State University, Sacramento*
Jennifer Katcher, *Pima Community College*
Judy Kaufman, *Monroe Community College*
Marlene Kayne, *The College of New Jersey*
Mahlon Kelly, *University of Virginia*
Kenneth Kerrick, *University of Pittsburgh at Johnstown*
Joyce Kille-Marino, *College of Charleston*
Joanne Kilpatrick, *Auburn University, Montgomery*
Stephen Kilpatrick, *University of Pittsburgh at Johnstown*
Erica Kipp, *Pace University*
Lee Kirkpatrick, *Glendale Community College*
Peter Kish, *Southwestern Oklahoma State University*
Cindy Klevickis, *James Madison University*
Robert Koch, *California State University, Fullerton*
Eliot Krause, *Seton Hall University*
Dubear Kroening, *University of Wisconsin, Fox Valley*
Kevin Krown, *San Diego State University*
Dana Kurpius, *Elgin Community College*
Margaret Maile Lam, *Kapiolani Community College*
MaryLynne LaMantia, *Golden West College*
Mary Rose Lamb, *University of Puget Sound*
Dale Lambert, *Tarrant County College, Northeast*
Thomas Lammers, *University of Wisconsin, Oshkosh*
Carmine Lanciani, *University of Florida*
Vic Landrum, *Washburn University*
Deborah Langsam, *University of North Carolina at Charlotte*
Geneen Lannom, *University of Central Oklahoma*
Brenda Latham, *Merced College*
Liz Lawrence, *Miles Community College*
Steven Lebsack, *Linn-Benton Community College*
Karen Lee, *University of Pittsburgh at Johnstown*
Tom Lehman, *Morgan Community College*
William Lemon, *Southwestern Oregon Community College*
Laurie M. Len, *El Camino College*
Peggy Lepley, *Cincinnati State University*
Richard Liebaert, *Linn-Benton Community College*
Kevin Lien, *Portland Community College*
Harvey Liftin, *Broward Community College*
Ivo Lindauer, *University of Northern Colorado*
William Lindsay, *Monterey Peninsula College*
Kirsten Lindstrom, *Santa Rosa Junior College*
Melanie Loo, *California State University, Sacramento*
David Loring, *Johnson County Community College*
Sheryl Love, *Temple University*
Eric Lovely, *Arkansas Tech University*
Paul Lurquin, *Washington State University*
James Mack, *Monmouth University*
David Magrane, *Morehead State University*
Joan Maloof, *Salisbury State University*
Joseph Marshall, *West Virginia University*
Presley Martin, *Drexel University*
William McComas, *University of Iowa*
Steven McCullagh, *Kennesaw State College*
Mitchell McGinnis, *North Seattle Community College*
James McGivern, *Gannon University*
Colleen McNamara, *Albuquerque TVI Community College*
Caroline McNutt, *Schoolcraft College*
Mark Meade, *Jacksonville State University*
Scott Meissner, *Cornell University*
Joseph Mendelson, *Utah State University*
John Mersfelder, *Sinclair Community College*
Timothy Metz, *Campbell University*
Iain Miller, *University of Cincinnati*
Robert Miller, *University of Dubuque*
V. Christine Minor, *Clemson University*
Andrew Miller, *Thomas University*
Brad Mogen, *University of Wisconsin, River Falls*
James Moné, *Millersville University*
Jamie Moon, *University of North Florida*
Juan Morata, *Miami Dade College*
Richard Mortensen, *Albion College*
Henry Mulcahy, *Suffolk University*
Christopher Murphy, *James Madison University*
Kathryn Nette, *Cuyamaca College*
James Newcomb, *New England College*
Zia Nisani, *Antelope Valley College*
James Nivison, *Mid Michigan Community College*
Peter Nordloh, *Southeastern Community College*

Stephen Novak, *Boise State University*
Bette Nybakken, *Hartnell College*
Michael O'Donnell, *Trinity College*
Camellia M. Okpodu, *Norfolk State University*
Steven Oliver, *Worcester State College*
Karen Olmstead, *University of South Dakota*
Steven O'Neal, *Southwestern Oklahoma State University*
Lowell Orr, *Kent State University*
William Outlaw, *Florida State University*
Phillip Pack, *Woodbury University*
Kevin Padian, *University of California, Berkeley*
Kay Pauling, *Foothill College*
Mark Paulissen, *Northeastern State University, Tahlequah*
Debra Pearce, *Northern Kentucky University*
David Pearson, *Bucknell University*
Patricia Pearson, *Western Kentucky University*
Kathleen Pelkki, *Saginaw Valley State University*
Andrew Penniman, *Georgia Perimeter College*
John Peters, *College of Charleston*
Gary Peterson, *South Dakota State University*
Margaret Peterson, *Concordia Lutheran College*
Russell L. Peterson, *Indiana University of Pennsylvania*
Paula Piehl, *Potomac State College*
Ben Pierce, *Baylor University*
Jack Plaggemeyer, *Little Big Horn College*
Barbara Pleasants, *Iowa State University*
Kathryn Podwall, *Nassau Community College*
Judith Pottmeyer, *Columbia Basin College*
Donald Potts, *University of California, Santa Cruz*
Nirmala Prabhu, *Edison Community College*
Elena Pravosudova, *University of Nevada, Reno*
James Pru, *Belleville Area College*
Rongsun Pu, *Kean University*
Charles Pumpuni, *Northern Virginia Community College*
Kimberly Puvalowski, *Old Bridge High School*
Rebecca Pyles, *East Tennessee State University*
Shanmugavel Rajendran, *Baltimore City Community College*
Bob Ratterman, *Jamestown Community College*
James Rayburn, *Jacksonville State University*
Jill Raymond, *Rock Valley College*
Michael Read, *Germanna Community College*
Brian Reeder, *Morehead State University*
Bruce Reid, *Kean College*
David Reid, *Blackburn College*
Stephen Reinbold, *Longview Community College*
Erin Rempala, *San Diego Mesa College*
Michael Renfroe, *James Madison University*
Tim Revell, *Mt. San Antonio College*
Douglas Reynolds, *Central Washington University*
Fred Rhoades, *Western Washington University*
Ashley Rhodes, *Kansas State University*
John Rinehart, *Eastern Oregon University*
Laura Ritt, *Burlington County College*
Lynn Rivers, *Henry Ford Community College*
Bruce Robart, *University of Pittsburgh at Johnstown*
Jennifer Roberts, *Lewis University*
Laurel Roberts, *University of Pittsburgh*
Lori B. Robinson, *Georgia College & State University*
Luis A. Rodriguez, *San Antonio Colleges*
Ursula Roese, *University of New England*
Duane Rohlfing, *University of South Carolina*
Jeanette Rollinger, *College of the Sequoias*
Steven Roof, *Fairmont State College*
Jim Rosowski, *University of Nebraska*
Stephen Rothstein, *University of California, Santa Barbara*
Donald Roush, *University of North Alabama*
Lynette Rushton, *South Puget Sound Community College*
Connie Rye, *East Mississippi Community College*
Linda Sabatino, *State University of New York, Suffolk County Community College*
Douglas Schamel, *University of Alaska, Fairbanks*
Douglas Schelhaas, *University of Mary*
Beverly Schieltz, *Wright State University*
Fred Schindler, *Indian Hills Community College*
Robert Schoch, *Boston University*
Brian Scholtens, *College of Charleston*
John Richard Schrock, *Emporia State University*
Doreen J. Schroeder, *University of St. Thomas*
Julie Schroer, *Bismarck State College*
Fayla Schwartz, *Everett Community College*
Justin Shaffer, *North Carolina A&T State University*
Judy Shea, *Kutztown University of Pennsylvania*
Daniela Shebitz, *Kean University*
Thomas Shellberg, *Henry Ford Community College*
Cara Shillington, *Eastern Michigan University*
Lisa Shimeld, *Crafton Hills College*
Brian Shmaefsky, *Kingwood College*
Marilyn Shopper, *Johnson County Community College*
Mark Shotwell, *Slippery Rock University*
Jane Shoup, *Purdue University*
Michele Shuster, *New Mexico State University*
Ayesha Siddiqui, *Schoolcraft College*
Linda Simpson, *University of North Carolina at Charlotte*
Gary Smith, *Tarrant County Junior College*
Marc Smith, *Sinclair Community College*
Michael Smith, *Western Kentucky University*
Phil Snider, *University of Houston*
Sam C. Sochet, *Thomas Edison Career and Technical Education High School*
Gary Sojka, *Bucknell University*
Ralph Sorensen, *Gettysburg College*
Ruth Sporer, *Rutgers University*
Ashley Spring, *Brevard Community College*
Thaxton Springfield, *St. Petersburg College*
Linda Brooke Stabler, *University of Central Oklahoma*
David Stanton, *Saginaw Valley State University*
Amanda Starnes, *Emory University*
Patrick Stokley, *East Central Community College*
John Stolz, *Duquesne University*
Ross Strayer, *Washtenaw Community College*
Donald Streuble, *Idaho State University*
Megan Stringer, *Jones County Junior College*
Mark Sugalski, *New England College*
Sukanya Subramanian, *Collin County Community College*
Gerald Summers, *University of Missouri*
Marshall Sundberg, *Louisiana State University*
Christopher Tabit, *University of West Georgia*
David Tauck, *Santa Clara University*
Hilda Taylor, *Acadia University*
Franklin Te, *Miami Dade College*
Gene Thomas, *Solano Community College*
Kenneth Thomas, *Northern Essex Community College*
Kathy Thompson, *Louisiana State University*
Laura Thurlow, *Jackson Community College*
Anne Tokazewski, *Burlington County College*
John Tolli, *Southwestern College*
Lori Tolley-Jordan, *Jacksonville State University*
Bruce Tomlinson, *State University of New York, Fredonia*
Nancy Tress, *University of Pittsburgh at Titusville*
Jimmy Triplett, *Jacksonville State University*
Donald Trisel, *Fairmont State College*
Kimberly Turk, *Mitchell Community College*
Virginia Turner, *Harper College*
Mike Tveten, *Pima College*
Michael Twaddle, *University of Toledo*
Rani Vajravelu, *University of Central Florida*
Leslie VanderMolen, *Humboldt State University*
Cinnamon VanPutte, *Southwestern Illinois College*
Sarah VanVickle-Chavez, *Washington University*
John Vaughan, *Georgetown College*
Martin Vaughan, *Indiana University*
Mark Venable, *Appalachian State University*
Ann Vernon, *St. Charles County Community College*
Rukmani Viswanath, *Laredo Community College*
Frederick W. Vogt, *Elgin Community College*
Mary Beth Voltura, *State University of New York, Cortland*
Jerry Waldvogel, *Clemson University*
Robert Wallace, *Ripon College*
Dennis Walsh, *MassBay Community College*
Patricia Walsh, *University of Delaware*
Lisa Weasel, *Portland State University*
James Wee, *Loyola University*
Harrington Wells, *University of Tulsa*
Jennifer Wiatrowski, *Pasco-Hernando Community College*
Larry Williams, *University of Houston*
Ray S. Williams, *Appalachian State University*
Lura Williamson, *University of New Orleans*
Sandra Winicur, *Indiana University, South Bend*
Robert R. Wise, *University of Wisconsin Oshkosh*
Mary E. Wisgirda, *San Jacinto College*
Mary Jo Witz, *Monroe Community College*
Neil Woffinden, *University of Pittsburgh at Johnstown*
Michael Womack, *Macon State University*
Patrick Woolley, *East Central College*
Maury Wrightson, *Germanna Community College*
Tumen Wuliji, *University of Nevada, Reno*
Mark Wygoda, *McNeese State University*
Tony Yates, *Seminole State College*
Jennifer J. Yeh, *San Francisco, California*
William Yurkiewicz, *Millersville University of Pennsylvania*
Gregory Zagursky, *Radford University*
Martin Zahn, *Thomas Nelson Community College*
Edward J. Zalisko, *Blackburn College*
David Zeigler, *University of North Carolina at Pembroke*
Uko Zylstra, *Calvin College*

Detailed Contents

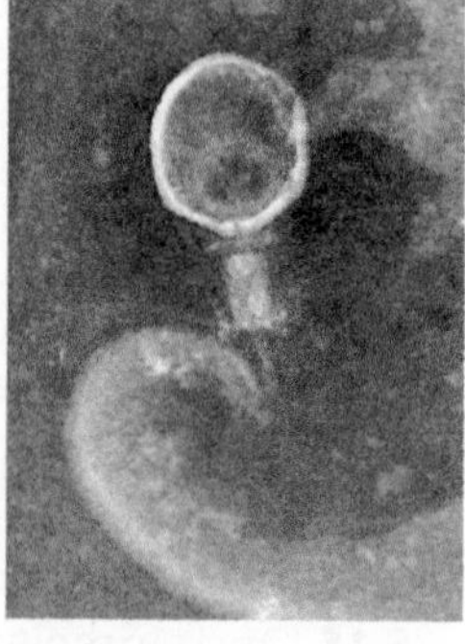

UNIT III

Concepts of Evolution

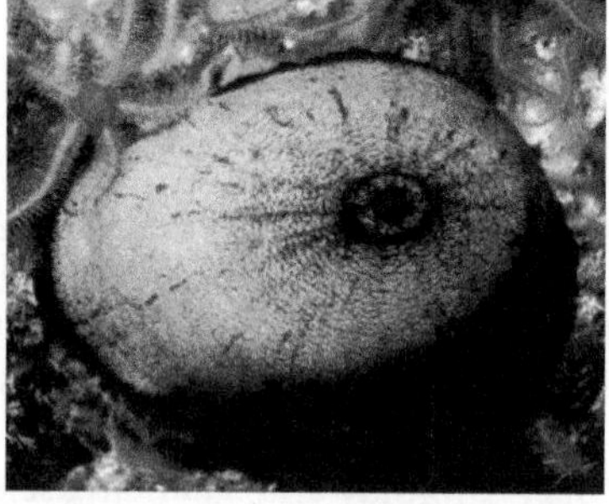

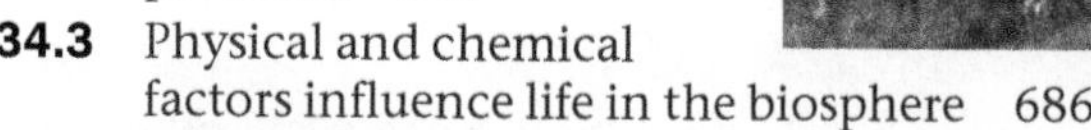

Biology: *Exploring Life*

CHAPTER 1

Red pandas (*Ailurus fulgens*), such as the one on the cover of this textbook and the one pictured to the right, have a characteristic kitten-like face and grow to be about the size of a large house cat. These captivating creatures are well adapted for life in the mountainous forests of Asia. Their cinnamon red and white coat camouflages them with the red mosses and white lichens of their environment, while their dark underbelly helps hide them from predators looking up from below. Their long bushy tail helps them balance in the trees and, when wrapped around their bodies, provides warmth during the winter. And a bony projection in their wrist helps them grasp one of their favorite foods, bamboo.

Who are a red panda's closest relatives?

You might think of the much larger, black and white pandas when you think about bamboo-eaters. Giant pandas live in similar regions in Asia. Are they closely related to red pandas? Scientists once thought so but have since reclassified red pandas into their own family. Later in the chapter we'll explore how scientists have traced the family tree of red pandas.

Despite their distinct lineages, the red panda and the giant panda do have something in common—they are both at risk of going extinct in the wild. Scientists don't have an accurate count of the red panda's numbers or know exactly where they live. The most recent counts estimate there are about 10,000 red pandas left in the world, a number that is likely to fall below 9,000 over the next 30 years. Finding and counting these shy, solitary animals in their remote habitats is difficult—just one example of the challenges and adventures encountered in biology, the scientific study of life.

We will begin this chapter by defining biology. Next we'll consider the nature and process of science. And we'll end the chapter with an exploration of five unifying themes that you will find woven throughout your study of biology.

BIG IDEAS

Biology: The Scientific Study of Life (1.1–1.3)

Life can be defined by a group of properties common to all living organisms and is characterized by both a huge diversity of organisms and a hierarchy of organization.

The Process of Science (1.4–1.8)

Science is based on verifiable evidence. In studying nature, scientists make observations, form hypotheses, and test predictions.

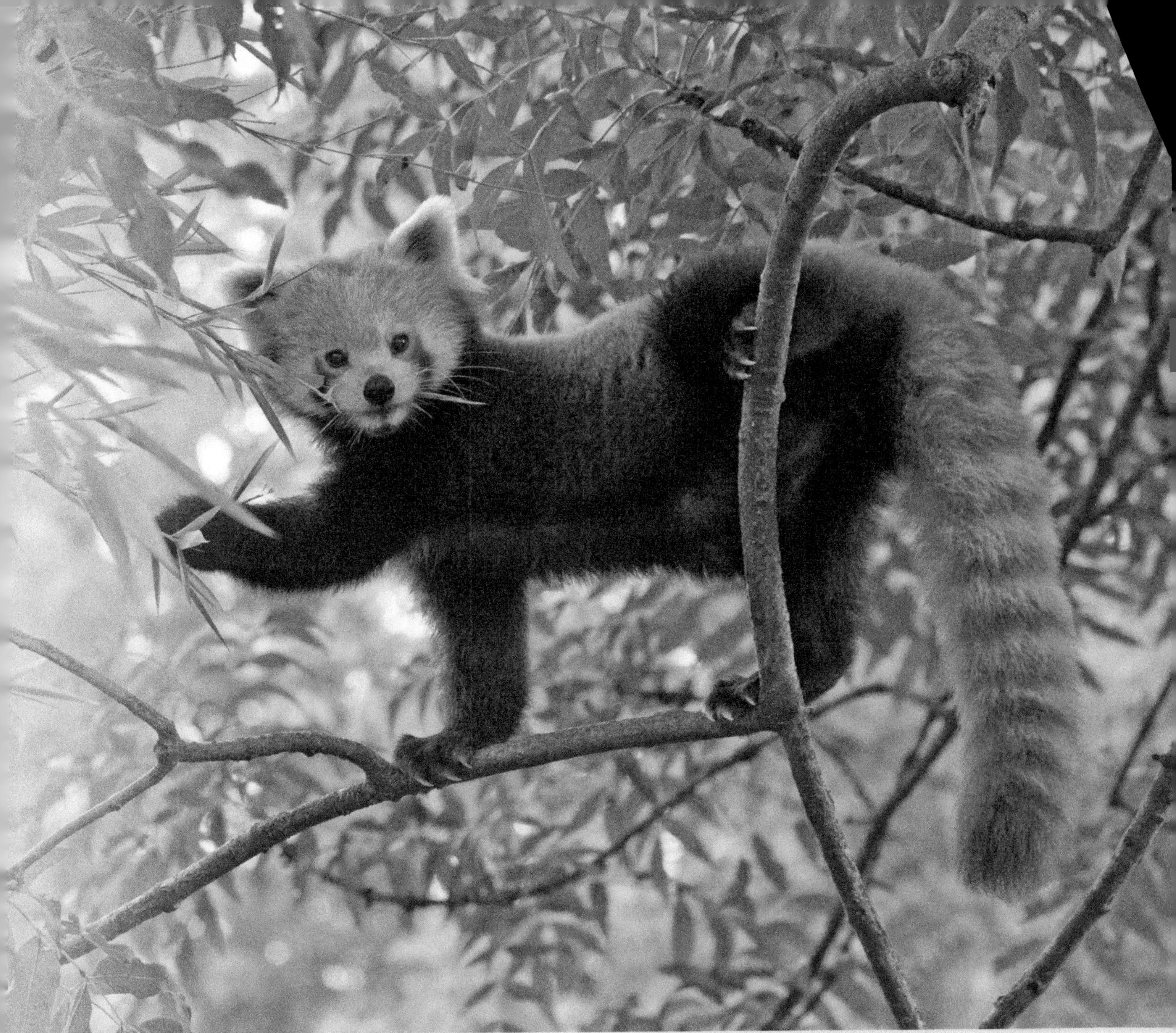

Five Unifying Themes in Biology (1.9–1.14)

Themes that run through all of biology are evolution, information, structure and function, energy and matter, and interactions.

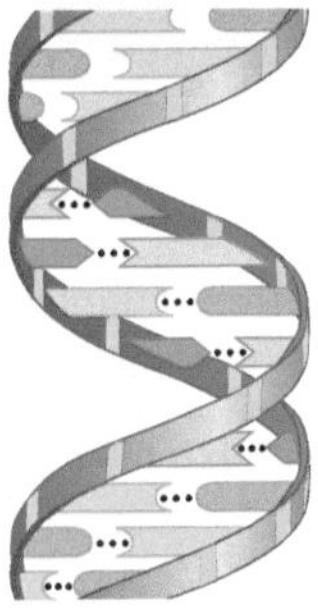

Biology: The Scientific Study of Life

1.1 What is life?

Defining **biology** as the scientific study of life raises the obvious question: What is *life*? Even a small child realizes that an ant or a plant is alive, whereas a rock or a car is not. But the phenomenon we call life defies a one-sentence definition. We recognize life mainly by what living things do. Figure 1.1 explores some of the properties and processes we associate with life.

All organisms, from ants to plants to people, are composed of **cells**—the structural and functional units of life. The phenomenon we call life emerges at the level of a cell: A cell can regulate its internal environment, take in and use energy, and respond to its environment. The ability of cells to give rise to new cells is the basis for all reproduction and for the growth and repair of multicellular organisms. A cell may be part of a complex plant or animal, or it may be an organism in its own right. Indeed, single-celled bacteria and other unicellular organisms far outnumber multicellular organisms on Earth.

Figure 1.1 also illustrates that the living world is wondrously varied. In the next module we see how biologists attempt to organize the remarkable diversity of life.

How would you define life?

Life can be characterized by its properties and processes, such as those depicted in Figure 1.1.

Order: Life is characterized by highly ordered structures.

Reproduction: Organisms reproduce their own kind.

Growth and development: Inherited information encoded in DNA controls the pattern of growth and development of all organisms.

Response to the environment: All organisms respond to environmental stimuli. This Venus flytrap rapidly closed its trap in response to a fly landing on it.

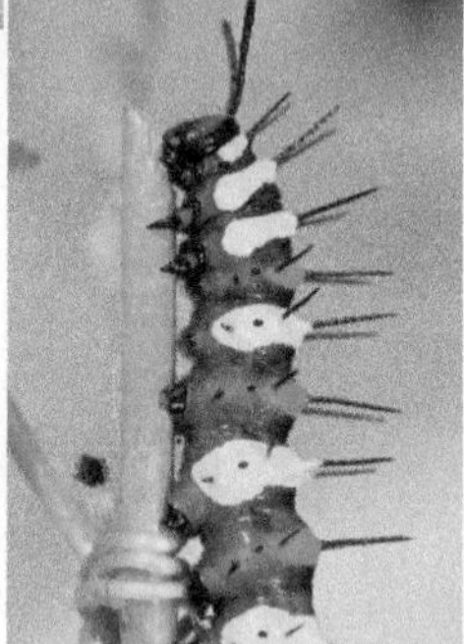

Energy processing: Organisms take in energy and use it to power all their activities.

Regulation: Organisms have regulatory mechanisms that maintain a beneficial internal environment. "Sunbathing" raises this lizard's body temperature on cold mornings.

Evolutionary adaptation: Adaptations, such as this red panda's warmth-providing tail, evolve over countless generations as individuals with heritable traits that are best suited to their environments have greater reproductive success.

▲ **Figure 1.1** Some properties of life

1.2 Biologists arrange the diversity of life into three domains

Diversity is a hallmark of life. One way in which biologists make sense of the vast array of organisms existing now and over the long history of life on Earth is to organize life's diversity into groups. Each unique form of life is called a species and is given a two-part, italicized, scientific name. The name identifies the genus and the particular species within that genus. For instance, the name for our species is *Homo sapiens*, meaning "wise man." Biologists have so far identified and named about 1.8 million species. Estimates of the total number of species range from 10 million to more than 100 million.

There seems to be a human tendency to group things, such as snakes or butterflies, although we recognize that each group includes many different species. And we often cluster groups into broader categories, such as reptiles (which include snakes) and insects (which include butterflies). Taxonomy, the branch of biology that names and classifies species, arranges species into a hierarchy of broader and broader groups, from genus, family, order, class, and phylum, to kingdom. A goal of this classification system is to reflect the evolutionary history and relationships of organisms.

Historically, biologists divided all of life into five kingdoms. But new methods for assessing evolutionary relationships, such as comparisons of DNA sequences, have led to an ongoing reevaluation of the number and boundaries of kingdoms. Although the debate continues on such divisions, there is consensus among biologists that life can be organized into three higher levels called **domains**. Figure 1.2 shows representatives of domains Bacteria, Archaea, and Eukarya.

Domains Bacteria and Archaea both consist of microscopic organisms with relatively simple cells. You are probably most familiar with bacteria, a very diverse and widespread group. Many members of domain Archaea live in Earth's extreme environments, such as salty lakes and boiling hot springs. Each rod-shaped or round structure in the photos of bacteria and archaea in Figure 1.2 is a single cell. These photos were made with an electron microscope, and the number along the side indicates the magnification of the image.

Domain Bacteria

Colorized SEM 7,500×

Bacteria

Domain Archaea

Colorized SEM 10,000×

Archaea

Domain Eukarya

LM 340×

Protists (multiple kingdoms)

Kingdom Plantae

Kingdom Fungi

Kingdom Animalia

▲ Figure 1.2 The three domains of life

All the organisms with more complex cells are called eukaryotes and are grouped in domain Eukarya. Protists are a diverse collection of mostly single-celled organisms. Figure 1.2 shows an assortment of protists in a drop of pond water. Biologists continue to assess how to group the protists to reflect their evolutionary relationships.

The three remaining groups within Eukarya are distinguished partly by their modes of nutrition. Kingdom Plantae consists of plants, which produce their own food by photosynthesis. The plant pictured in Figure 1.2 is a tropical bromeliad, a plant native to the Americas.

Kingdom Fungi, represented by the mushrooms in Figure 1.2, is a diverse group whose members mostly decompose organic wastes and absorb the nutrients into their cells.

Animals, which are grouped in Kingdom Animalia, obtain food by eating other organisms. The butterfly in Figure 1.2 is drinking nectar from a thistle flower.

Another way in which biologists make sense of the diversity and complexity of life is to organize it into a hierarchy of structural levels, extending from the microscopic level of cells to the global scale of the entire Earth. In the next module we take a visual journey through these levels.

? **To which of the three domains of life do we belong?**

■ Eukarya

VISUALIZING THE CONCEPT 1.3 In life's hierarchy of organization, new properties emerge at each level

Biologists study life across a very broad range of scales, from the molecules in a cell to the entire living planet. They divide this vast scope of biology into a series of structural

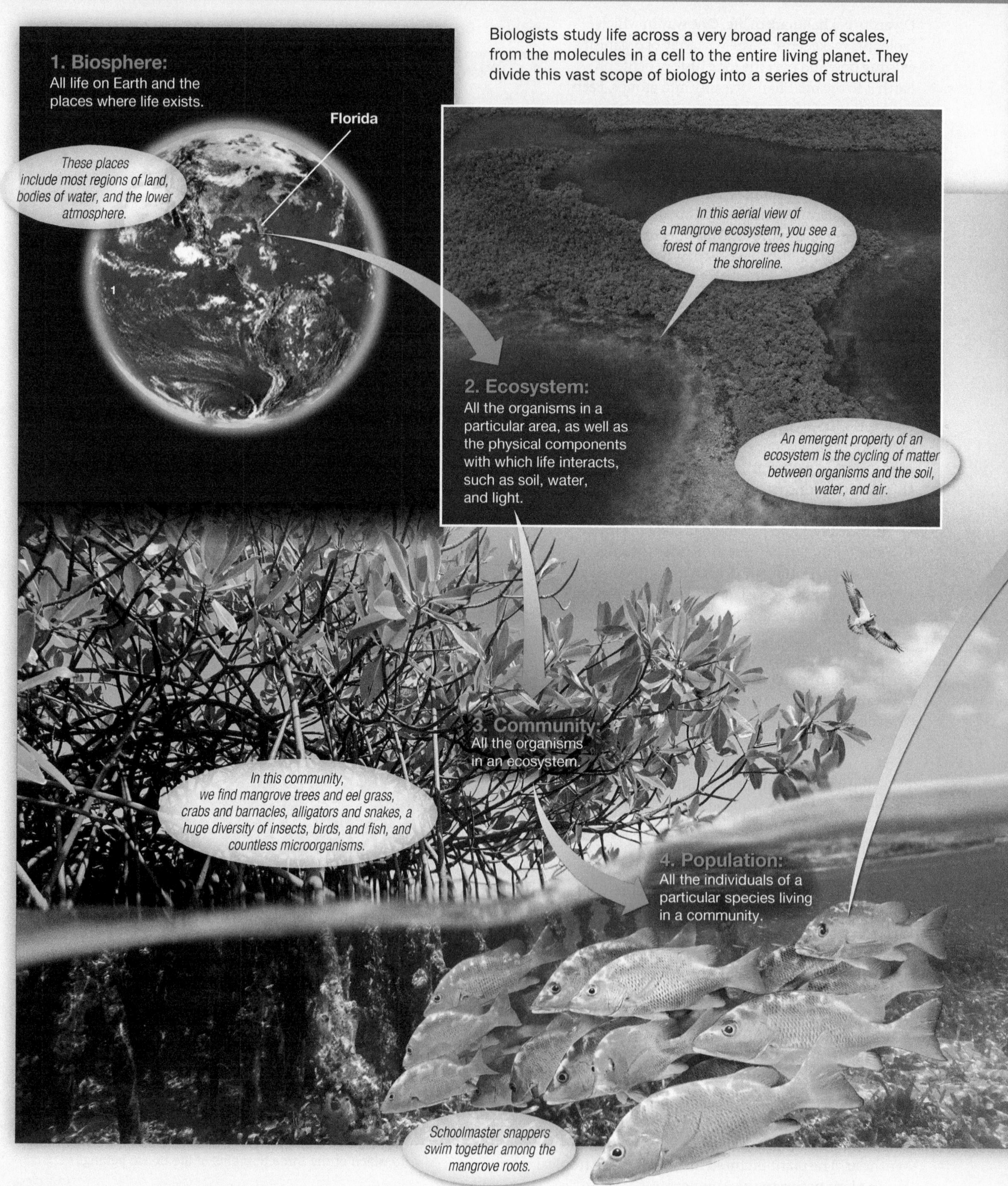
1. Biosphere:
All life on Earth and the places where life exists.
Florida
These places include most regions of land, bodies of water, and the lower atmosphere.
In this aerial view of a mangrove ecosystem, you see a forest of mangrove trees hugging the shoreline.
2. Ecosystem:
All the organisms in a particular area, as well as the physical components with which life interacts, such as soil, water, and light.
An emergent property of an ecosystem is the cycling of matter between organisms and the soil, water, and air.
3. Community:
All the organisms in an ecosystem.
In this community, we find mangrove trees and eel grass, crabs and barnacles, alligators and snakes, a huge diversity of insects, birds, and fish, and countless microorganisms.
4. Population:
All the individuals of a particular species living in a community.
Schoolmaster snappers swim together among the mangrove roots.

levels. Follow the arrows to take a visual tour down through this organizational hierarchy, using a mangrove swamp in Florida as an example.

Biologists often focus their study of the natural world on one or a few of these levels, exploring individual components and interactions between those components, as well as connections to other levels. Indeed, if we reverse the arrows and move upward through this figure from molecules to the biosphere, we find that novel properties arise at each higher level, properties that were not present at the preceding level. Such **emergent properties** result from the specific arrangement and interactions of component parts. For example, the arrangement and connections of nerve cells enables nervous signals to travel from a fish's brain to its tail. And movement is an emergent property arising from the interactions and interconnections of a fish's nervous, muscular, and skeletal systems.

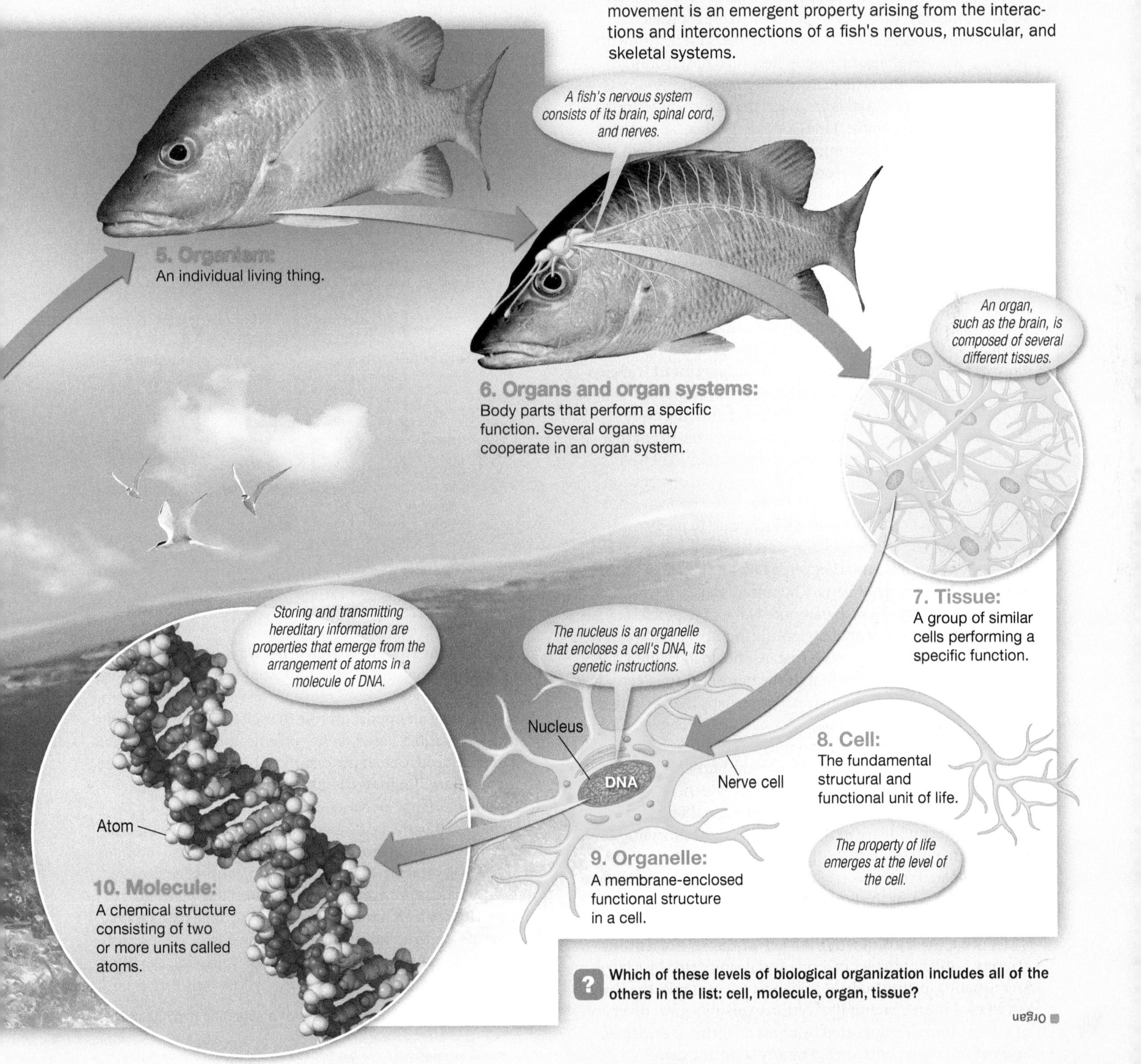

5. Organism:
An individual living thing.

A fish's nervous system consists of its brain, spinal cord, and nerves.

6. Organs and organ systems:
Body parts that perform a specific function. Several organs may cooperate in an organ system.

An organ, such as the brain, is composed of several different tissues.

7. Tissue:
A group of similar cells performing a specific function.

The nucleus is an organelle that encloses a cell's DNA, its genetic instructions.

Nucleus

DNA

Nerve cell

8. Cell:
The fundamental structural and functional unit of life.

The property of life emerges at the level of the cell.

9. Organelle:
A membrane-enclosed functional structure in a cell.

Storing and transmitting hereditary information are properties that emerge from the arrangement of atoms in a molecule of DNA.

Atom

10. Molecule:
A chemical structure consisting of two or more units called atoms.

? **Which of these levels of biological organization includes all of the others in the list: cell, molecule, organ, tissue?**

Organ

The Process of Science

1.4 What is science?

Science is a way of knowing—an approach to understanding the natural world. It stems from our curiosity about ourselves and the world around us. At the heart of science is inquiry, a search for information and explanations of natural phenomena.

Biology, like other sciences, begins with careful observation. In gathering information, biologists often use tools such as microscopes to extend their senses and precision instruments to facilitate careful measurement. Recorded observations are called **data**—the evidence on which scientific inquiry is based. Some data are *qualitative*, often in the form of recorded descriptions. For example, Jane Goodall spent decades recording her observations of chimpanzee behavior during field research in Tanzania (see Module 35.22). She also recorded volumes of *quantitative* data, such as the frequency and duration of specific behaviors. Quantitative data are generally numerical measurements, which may be organized into tables and graphs and analyzed with a type of mathematics called statistics.

Observations often prompt us to ask questions and then seek answers by forming and testing hypotheses. A **hypothesis** is a proposed explanation for a set of observations, and it leads to predictions that can be tested by making additional observations or by performing experiments. An **experiment** is a scientific test, often carried out under controlled conditions.

We all use hypotheses and predictions in solving everyday problems. Let's say you are preparing for a big storm that is approaching your area and find that your flashlight isn't working. That your flashlight isn't working is an observation, and the question is obvious: Why doesn't it work? **Figure 1.4** presents two hypotheses, each of which leads to predictions you can test. Predictions are the results we should expect if the hypothesis is correct, and they often take an "*if*. . . *then*" form. For example, *if* the dead-battery hypothesis is correct, *then* replacing the batteries with new ones will fix the problem.

An important point about scientific inquiry is that we can never *prove* that a hypothesis is true. As shown in Figure 1.4, the burned-out bulb hypothesis is the more likely explanation in our hypothetical scenario. But perhaps the old bulb was simply loose and the new bulb was inserted correctly. We could test this hypothesis by carefully reinstalling the original bulb. If the flashlight doesn't work, the burned-out bulb hypothesis is supported by another line of evidence. Testing a hypothesis in various ways provides additional support and increases our confidence in the hypothesis. Indeed, multiple rounds of hypothesis testing may lead to a scientific consensus—the shared conclusion of many scientists that a particular hypothesis explains the known data well and stands up to experimental testing.

How is a theory different from a hypothesis? A scientific **theory** is much broader in scope and is supported by a large and usually growing body of evidence. For example, the theory of evolution by natural selection explains a great diversity of observations, is supported by a vast quantity of evidence, and has not been contradicted by any scientific data.

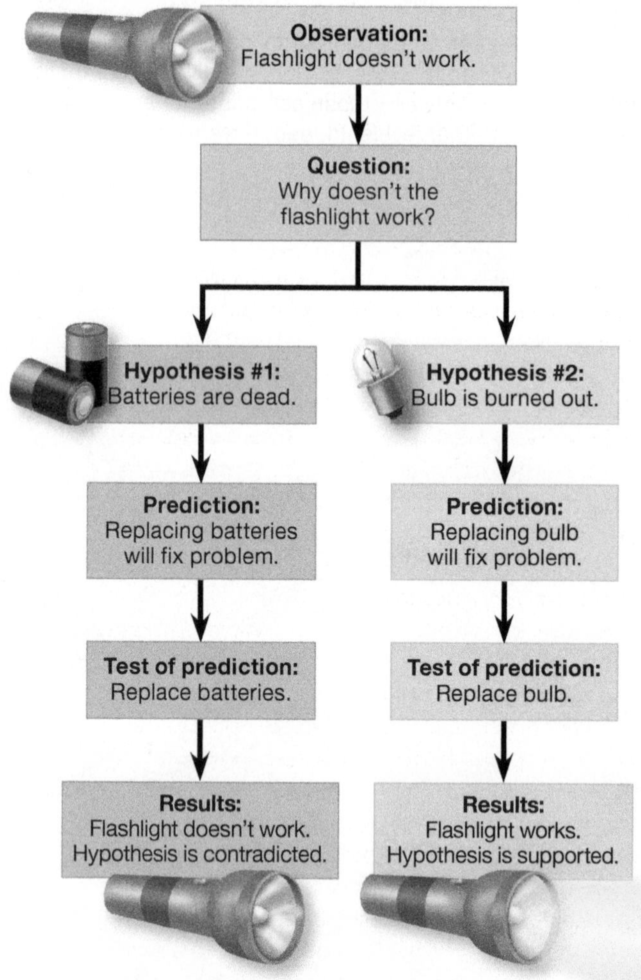

▲ **Figure 1.4** An everyday example of forming and testing hypotheses

How is science different from other ways of describing and explaining nature, such as philosophy or religion? Those endeavors also seek to make sense of the world around us, and they often play an important role in society. But the scientific view of the world is based on hypothesis testing and verifiable evidence. Indeed, one of the distinguishing characteristics of science is the willingness to follow the evidence—and to correct itself when new evidence is found.

To help you better understand what science is, we include a Scientific Thinking module in each chapter. These modules encompass several broad activities that scientists engage in: observing nature; forming hypotheses and testing them using various research methods; analyzing data; using tools and technologies to build scientific knowledge; communicating the results of scientific research; and evaluating the implications of such studies for society as a whole.

 **What is the main requirement for a scientific hypothesis?**

■ It must generate predictions that can be tested by experiments or gathering further observations.

1.5 Hypotheses can be tested using controlled experiments

Many animals match their environment: toads the color of dead leaves, green cabbage worms on green leaves, or white snowy owls in their arctic habitat. From these observations, one might hypothesize that such color patterns have evolved as adaptations that protect animals from predation. Can scientists test this hypothesis?

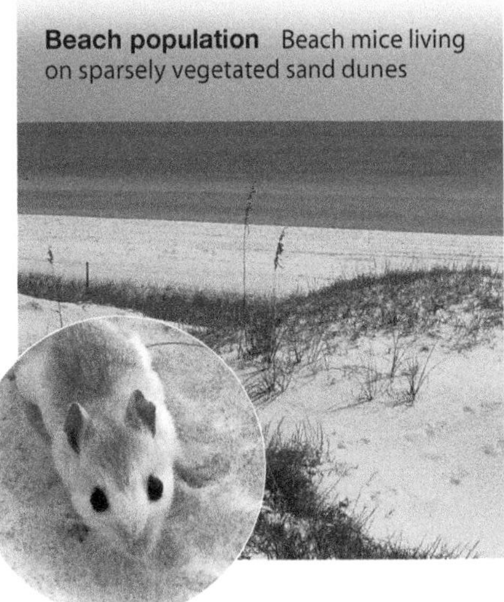

Beach population Beach mice living on sparsely vegetated sand dunes

Inland population Members of the same species living about 30 km inland

▲ **Figure 1.5** Beach mouse and inland mouse with their native habitat

Controlled Experiments In an experimental test of a hypothesis, a researcher often manipulates one component in a system and observes the effects of this change. Variables are factors that *vary* in an experiment. The factor that is manipulated by the researchers is called the **independent variable**. The measure used to judge the outcome of the experiment is called the **dependent variable**. This variable *depends* on, or is affected by, the manipulated variable. A **controlled experiment** is one in which an experimental group is compared with a control group. These groups ideally differ only in the one variable the experiment is designed to test.

Let's consider an example of a controlled experiment involving two populations of mice that belong to the same species (*Peromyscus polionotus*) but live in different environments. The beach mouse lives along the Florida seashore; the inland mouse lives on darker soil farther inland. As you can see in Figure 1.5, there is a striking match between mouse coloration and habitat. In 2010, biologist Hopi Hoekstra of Harvard University and a group of her students headed to Florida to test the camouflage hypothesis. They predicted that if camouflage coloration protects mice from predators, then mice that matched their environment would be preyed on less frequently than mice with coloration that did not match their habitat.

This experiment is an example of a field study, one not done in a laboratory but out in nature, using the natural habitat of the mice and their predators. The researchers built 250 plastic models of mice and painted them to resemble either beach or inland mice. Equal numbers of models were placed randomly in both habitats. The models resembling the native mice in each habitat were the control group. The mice with the non-native coloration were the experimental group. Signs of predation were recorded for three days.

As you can see by the results in Table 1.5, the noncamouflaged models had a much higher percentage of predation attacks in both habitats. The data thus support the camouflage hypothesis: Coloration that matches the environment protects animals from predation.

TABLE 1.5 Results from Camouflage Experiment

	Number of Attacks		
Habitat	**On Camouflaged Models**	**On Noncamouflaged Models**	**% Attacks on Noncamouflaged Models**
Beach (light habitat)	2	5	71%
Inland (dark habitat)	5	16	76%

Data from S. N. Vignieri et al., The selective advantage of crypsis in mice, *Evolution* 64: 2153–8 (2010).

TRY THIS Identify the independent and dependent variables in this experiment.

Testing Hypotheses in Humans Controlled experiments involving humans, such as tests of new medications, are called clinical trials or clinical studies. Subjects are usually randomly assigned to control and experimental groups. The control group participants are often given a placebo, a treatment (such as a sugar pill) that doesn't contain the substance being studied. In a double-blind trial, neither the researchers nor the subjects know who is in which group. Clinical trials must be cut short if preliminary results show that the treatment is either significantly harmful or significantly beneficial to the participants, because it would be unethical to knowingly harm participants or withhold effective treatment.

Observational studies are often used to test hypotheses in humans. In a retrospective study, researchers may interview people, use medical records, or examine death certificates in the attempt to identify factors that led to a specific outcome. In a prospective study, researchers enter the picture at the beginning, enrolling a group of participants, called a cohort, and then collecting data from them over a period of time. Observational studies have their limitations. A correlation between a factor and an outcome does not necessarily mean that the factor caused the outcome. Large cohort studies, however, have contributed a great deal to our understanding of the effects of many health-related factors, including diet, smoking, exercise, and environmental conditions.

? **In some studies, researchers try to match the sex, age, and general health of subjects in the control and experimental groups. What is this experimental design trying to do?**

■ Ensure that the two groups differ only in the one variable the experiment is designed to test.

1.6 Hypotheses can be tested using observational data

SCIENTIFIC THINKING

Controlled experiments are not the only way to test hypotheses. Scientists often use data from observations to form and test hypotheses. Let's consider an example of how scientists have answered the question of how to classify the red panda. As you will see, the red panda story provides an excellent example of observations leading to hypotheses and the willingness of scientists to revise hypotheses to incorporate new evidence.

Who are the red panda's closest relatives?

From its antics in YouTube videos, the red panda might remind you of a house cat. Indeed, its scientific name, *Ailurus fulgens*, means "shining cat." But it also looks like a raccoon, and it eats bamboo and has a false thumb like a giant panda. Common names such as lesser panda, red cat-bear, and firefox reflect the confusion over the red panda's relatives. How have scientists classified this animal?

To develop hypotheses about the evolutionary relationships among species, scientists use many kinds of evidence, including comparisons of both fossils and living organisms. Based on observations of physical similarities, scientists initially hypothesized that the red panda was most closely related to raccoons, and therefore classified the two species in the same biological family (**Figure 1.6**). Other scientists, observing that the diet and habitat of red pandas were similar to those of giant pandas, placed the two pandas together in their own family. As evidence accumulated that giant pandas are members of the bear family, it was proposed that the red panda also belonged in that family.

In recent years, scientists have increasingly used molecular evidence based on comparisons of DNA sequences to test hypotheses about evolutionary relationships. The underlying assumption is that the more closely the DNA sequences of two species match, the more closely they are related. A number of recently published molecular studies strongly support the hypothesis that red pandas are not part of either the bear or the raccoon family. As a result of this new evidence of differences in the DNA sequences of these groups, scientists now classify red pandas as the sole living species of their own family.

▼ Figure 1.6 **Two hypotheses for the group in which red pandas should be classified**

?
Should red pandas be grouped with raccoons or with giant pandas?
?

Explain why comparisons of DNA sequences are considered observational and not experimental data.

■ Scientists are not manipulating DNA sequences in any type of experiment but are simply recording and comparing the differences in sequences that they observe.

1.7 The process of science is repetitive, nonlinear, and collaborative

As discussed in Module 1.4, scientists use a process of inquiry that includes making observations, asking questions, forming hypotheses, and testing them. Very few scientific inquiries, however, adhere rigidly to the sequence of steps that are typically used to describe "the scientific method."

Figure 1.7, on the facing page, presents a more inclusive model of the scientific process. You can see that forming and testing hypotheses are at the center of science. This core set of activities is the reason that science does so well in explaining natural phenomena. These activities, however, are shaped by exploration and discovery (the upper circle in Figure 1.7) and influenced by interactions with other scientists and with society more generally (lower circles). The arrows pointing between the circles illustrate that the components of the scientific process interact and interconnect.

The process of science is typically repetitive and nonlinear. For example, scientists often work through several iterations of making observations and asking questions, with each round informing the next, before settling on hypotheses that they wish to test. In fine-tuning their questions, biologists rely heavily on scientific literature, the published contributions of fellow scientists—their peers. By reading about and understanding past studies, scientists can build on the foundation of existing knowledge.

Scientists rarely work alone in testing their ideas: they may learn methods from each other and share advice on experimental design and data analysis. An experimental design may need to be adjusted after initial data are collected. And results may lead to a revision of the original hypothesis or the formation of alternate ones, thus leading to further testing. In this way, scientists circle closer and closer to their best estimation of how nature works. As in all quests, science includes elements of challenge, adventure, and luck, along with careful planning, reasoning, creativity, patience, and persistence in overcoming setbacks. Such diverse elements of inquiry make science far less structured than most people realize.

Scientists share information with their community of peers through seminars, meetings, personal communication, and scientific publications. Before the results of hypothesis testing are published in a peer-reviewed journal, the research is evaluated by qualified, impartial, often anonymous experts who were not involved in the study. Reviewers often require authors to make revisions to their claims or perform additional experiments to provide more lines of evidence. It is not uncommon for a journal to "reject," or not publish, a paper if it doesn't meet the rigorous standards set by fellow scientists. When a study is published, scientists often check each other's claims by attempting to confirm observations or repeat experiments.

As indicated by the lower left circle in Figure 1.7, science is interwoven with the fabric of society. Much of scientific research is focused on particular problems that are of human concern, such as the push to cure cancer or to understand and slow the process of climate change. Societal needs often determine which research projects are funded and how extensively the results are discussed. To emphasize the connection between biology and society, each chapter of this text includes at least one Connection module. These modules also highlight the connections between biology and your own life.

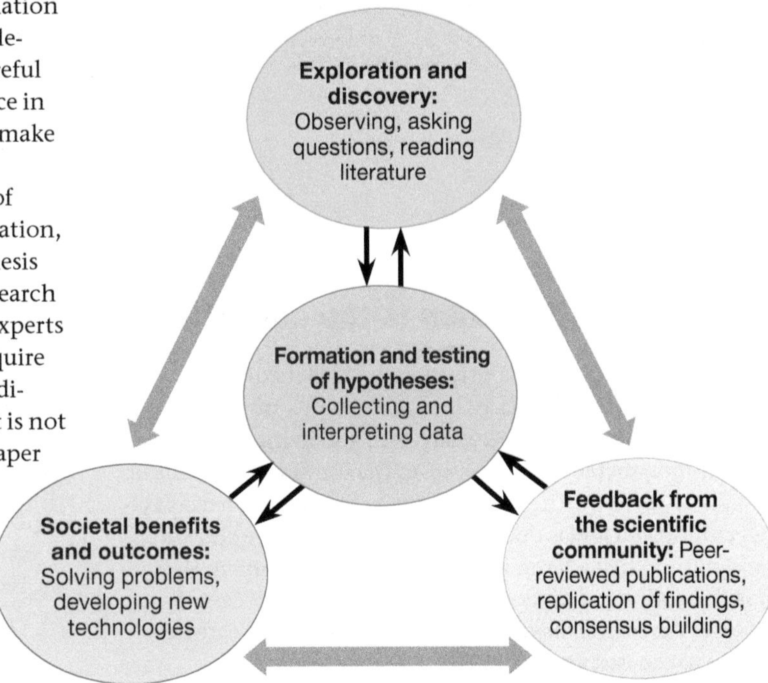

▲ **Figure 1.7** A more realistic model of the process of science. This illustration in based on a model (How Science Works) from the website Understanding Science (www.understandingscience.org).

? Why is hypothesis testing at the center of the process of science?

■ Hypothesis testing is central because a core component of science is testable explanations of nature.

1.8 Biology, technology, and society are connected in important ways

CONNECTION

Many of the current issues facing society are related to biology, and they often involve our expanding technology. What are the differences between science and technology? The goal of science is to understand natural phenomena. In contrast, the goal of **technology** is to apply scientific knowledge for some specific purpose. Scientists usually speak of "discoveries," whereas engineers more often speak of "inventions." These two fields, however, are interdependent. Scientists use new technology in their research, and scientific discoveries often lead to the development of new technologies.

The potent combination of science and technology can have dramatic effects on society. For example, the discovery of the structure of DNA by Watson and Crick more than 60 years ago was aided by the technology of X-ray crystallography. Subsequent advances in DNA science have led to the technologies of DNA manipulation that today are transforming applied fields such as medicine, agriculture, and forensics.

Technology has improved our standard of living in many ways, but not without consequences. Technology has helped Earth's population to grow tenfold in the past three centuries and to more than double in just the past 40 years. There are now more than 7.3 billion people on Earth. Climate change, toxic wastes, deforestation, and increasing rates of extinction are just some of the repercussions of more and more people wielding more and more technology. Science can help identify problems and provide insight into how to slow down or prevent further damage. But solutions to these problems have as much to do with politics, economics, and cultural values as with science and technology. Every citizen has a responsibility to develop a reasonable amount of scientific literacy to be able to participate in the debates regarding science, technology, and society.

The process of science we have just explored results in new biological discoveries every day. In the next section, we introduce broad themes that you will encounter throughout your study of life.

? How do science and technology interact?

■ New scientific discoveries may lead to new technologies; new technologies may increase the ability of scientists to discover new knowledge.

Five Unifying Themes in Biology

Biology is a subject of enormous scope. Within this ever-growing body of knowledge, however, we can identify some unifying themes. In the next few modules, we'll describe the themes of evolution, information, structure and function, energy and matter, and interactions. We'll also help you recognize them as they recur throughout your study of biology.

1.9 Theme: Evolution is the core theme of biology

Life is distinguished by both its unity and its diversity. Multiple lines of evidence point to life's unity, from the similarities seen among and between fossil and living organisms, to common metabolic processes, to the universal molecule of inheritance, DNA. The amazing diversity of life is on display all around you and is documented in zoos, nature shows, and natural history museums. The scientific explanation for this unity and diversity is **evolution**, the process of change that has transformed life on Earth from its earliest forms to the vast array of organisms living today.

Darwin's Theory of Evolution The history of life, as documented by fossils and other evidence, is the saga of a changing Earth billions of years old, inhabited by an evolving cast of living forms. This evolutionary view of life came into sharp focus in November 1859, when Charles Darwin published one of the most influential books ever written, entitled *On the Origin of Species by Means of Natural Selection*.

How does Darwin's work illustrate the process of science you just learned about? As a young man, Darwin made key observations that greatly influenced his thinking. During a five-year, around-the-world voyage, he collected and documented plants, animals, and fossils in widely varying locations—from the isolated Galápagos Islands to the heights of the Andes mountains to the rain forests of Brazil. He was particularly struck by the adaptations of these varied organisms that made them well suited to their diverse habitats. After returning to England, Darwin spent more than two decades continuing his observations, performing experiments, corresponding with other scientists, and refining his thinking before he finally published his work.

The first of two main points that Darwin presented in *The Origin of Species* was that species living today arose from a succession of ancestors that were different from them. Darwin called this process "descent with modification." This insightful phrase captures both the unity of life (descent from a common ancestor) and the diversity of life (modifications that evolved as species diverged from their ancestors). Figure 1.9A illustrates this unity and diversity among birds. The flamingo, penguin, and hummingbird all have a common "bird" body plan of wings, beak, feet, and feathers, but these structures are highly specialized for each bird's unique lifestyle.

Darwin's second point was to propose a mechanism for evolution, which he called **natural selection**. Darwin started with two observations, from which he drew two inferences.

OBSERVATION #1: Individual variation. Individuals in a population vary in their traits, many of which seem to be heritable (passed on from parents to offspring).

OBSERVATION #2: Overproduction of offspring. All species can produce far more offspring than the environment can support. Competition for resources is thus inevitable, and many of these offspring fail to survive and reproduce.

INFERENCE #1: Unequal reproductive success. Individuals with inherited traits best suited to the local environment are more likely to survive and reproduce than are less well-suited individuals.

INFERENCE #2: Accumulation of favorable traits over time. As a result of this unequal reproductive success over many generations, a higher and higher proportion of individuals in the population will have the advantageous traits.

▲ **Figure 1.9A** Unity and diversity among birds

TRY THIS For each bird, describe some adaptations that fit it to its environment and way of life.

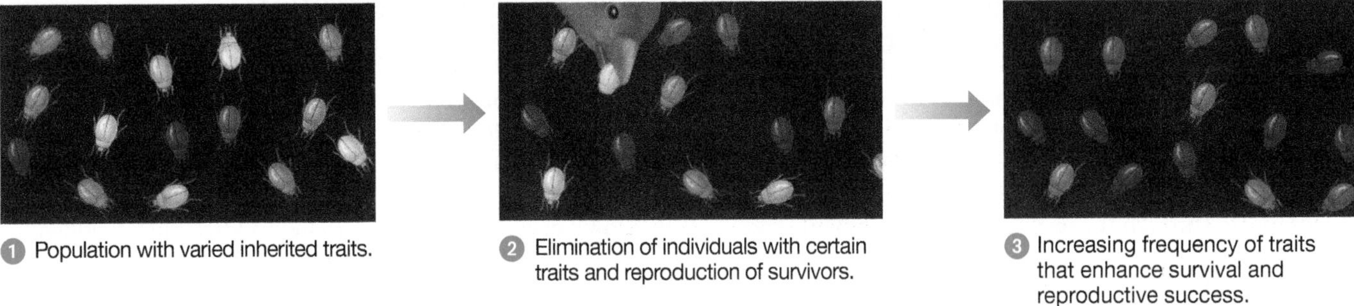

1 Population with varied inherited traits.
2 Elimination of individuals with certain traits and reproduction of survivors.
3 Increasing frequency of traits that enhance survival and reproductive success.

▲ **Figure 1.9B** An example of natural selection in action

TRY THIS Predict what might happen if some of these beetles colonized a sand dune habitat.

Figure 1.9B uses a simple example to show how natural selection works. ① An imaginary beetle population has colonized an area where the soil has been blackened by a recent brush fire. Initially, the population varies extensively in the inherited coloration of individuals, from very light gray to charcoal. ② A bird eats the beetles it sees most easily, the light-colored ones. This selective predation reduces the number of light-colored beetles and favors the survival and reproductive success of the darker beetles, which pass on the genes for dark coloration to their offspring. ③ After several generations, the population is quite different from the original one. As a result of natural selection, the frequency of the darker-colored beetles in the population has increased.

Darwin realized that numerous small changes in populations as a result of natural selection could eventually lead to major alterations of species. He proposed that new species could evolve as a result of the gradual accumulation of changes over long periods of time. This could occur, for example, if one population fragmented into subpopulations isolated in different environments. In these separate arenas of natural selection, one species could gradually divide into multiple species as isolated populations adapted over many generations to different sets of environmental factors.

The Tree of Life Just as you have a family tree, each species on Earth today has a family history. A species represents one twig on a branching tree of life that extends back in time through ancestral species more and more remote. For example, the fossil record indicates that red pandas, raccoons, and weasels share an ancestor that existed close to 30 million years ago. Tracing back farther in time, these groups and bears share a common ancestor that lived about 40 million years ago. All mammals have hair and milk-producing mammary glands, and such similarities are what we would expect if all mammals descended from a common ancestor. Evidence indicates that the ancestral mammal arose more than 200 million years ago.

Figure 1.9C traces some of the family tree of the red panda, based on the most recent molecular evidence (see Module 1.6). Diagrams of evolutionary relationships generally take the form of branching trees, usually turned sideways and read from left to right. You can see that giant pandas, red pandas, and racoons are placed in three separate families. Red pandas are now classified as the sole living species of the family Ailuridae.

The theory of evolution by natural selection is supported by multiple lines of evidence—the fossil record, experiments, observations of natural selection in action, and ever-increasing numbers of DNA comparisons. Evolution is the central theme that makes sense of everything we know and learn about biology. Throughout this text, we'll see many more examples of both the process and products of evolution. To emphasize evolution as the central theme of biology, we include an Evolution Connection module, called out with a green icon, in each chapter.

? **Explain the cause and effect of unequal reproductive success.**

Those individuals with heritable traits best suited to the local environment produce the greatest number of offspring. Over many generations, the proportion of these adaptive traits increases in the population.

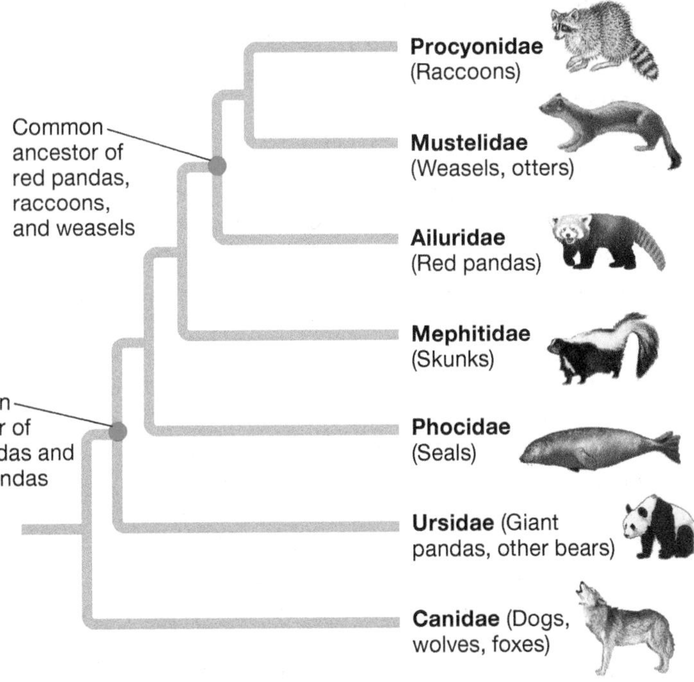

▲ **Figure 1.9C** An evolutionary tree of the red panda based on recent molecular data

1.10 Evolution is connected to our everyday lives

EVOLUTION CONNECTION

You just learned that natural selection is the primary mechanism of evolution, in which the environment "selects" for adaptive traits when organisms with such traits are better able to survive and reproduce. Through the selective breeding of plants and animals, humans also act as agents of evolution. As a result of **artificial selection**, our crops, livestock, and pets bear little resemblance to their wild ancestors. Humans have been modifying species for millennia by choosing which organisms reproduce, and recent advances in biotechnology have increased our capabilities. Plant biologists can now identify genes for beneficial traits in relatives of our crop plants or even in totally unrelated species, and then use genetic engineering to produce enhanced crops. For example, genes for such traits as drought tolerance, improved growth, and increased nutrition have been introduced into rice plants.

But humans also affect evolution unintentionally. The impact of habitat loss and climate change can be seen in the loss of species. Indeed, scientists estimate that the current rate of extinction is 100 to 1,000 times the typical rate seen in the fossil record. Our actions are also driving evolutionary changes in species. For example, our widespread use of antibiotics and pesticides has led to the evolution of antibiotic resistance in bacteria and pesticide resistance in insects.

How can evolutionary theory help address such worldwide problems? Understanding evolution can help us develop strategies for conservation efforts and prompt us to be more judicious in our use of antibiotics and pesticides. It can also help us create flu vaccines and HIV drugs by tracking the rapid evolution of these viruses. Identifying shared genes and studying their actions in closely related organisms may produce new knowledge about cancer or other diseases and lead to new medical treatments. Our understanding of evolution can yield many beneficial results.

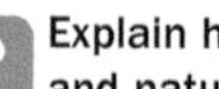

Explain how humans are agents of both artificial selection and natural selection.

We use artificial selection when choosing specific traits or genes in organisms that we breed. Our intentional and unintentional manipulations change the environment and thus affect natural selection.

1.11 Theme: Life depends on the flow of information

The processes of life, such as reproduction, growth and development, internal regulation, and response to the environment, all depend on the transmission and use of information. Genetic information encoded in DNA determines an organism's structures and functions. But such properties also depend on the stimuli, signals, and pathways that regulate where, when, and how an organism's genetic information is expressed. Indeed, the integrated flow of genetic and other types of information is essential for life.

Genetic Information DNA provides the master instructions for all of a cell's functions. It is also the heritable information that is passed from one generation to the next. How does the molecular structure of DNA account for its ability to encode and transmit information? Each DNA molecule is made up of two long chains, called strands, coiled together into a double helix. The strands are made up of four kinds of chemical building blocks called nucleotides. Figure 1.11A (left side) illustrates these four nucleotides with different colors and letter abbreviations of their names. The right side of the figure shows a short section of a DNA double helix.

Before a cell divides, its DNA is first replicated, or copied. The two strands "unzip," and new complementary strands assemble along the separated strands—so that the information in the two resulting sets of DNA remains the same. Thus, each new cell inherits a complete set of DNA that is identical to that of the parent cell. You began as a single cell stocked with DNA inherited from your two parents. Each round of cell division transmitted copies of that DNA to what eventually became the trillions of cells in your body.

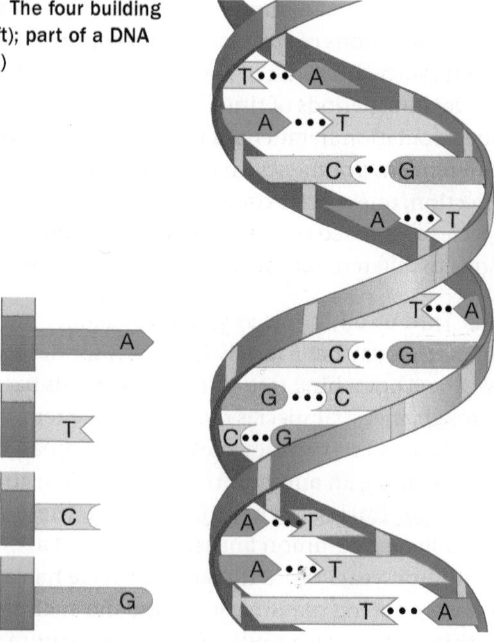

▶ **Figure 1.11A** The four building blocks of DNA (left); part of a DNA double helix (right)

The way DNA encodes a cell's information is analogous to the way we arrange letters of the alphabet into precise sequences with specific meanings. The word *rat*, for example, conjures up an image of a rodent; *tar* and *art*, which contain the same letters, mean very different things. We can think of the four nucleotides as the alphabet of inheritance. Specific sequences of these four chemical letters encode precise information in units of inheritance called **genes**, which are

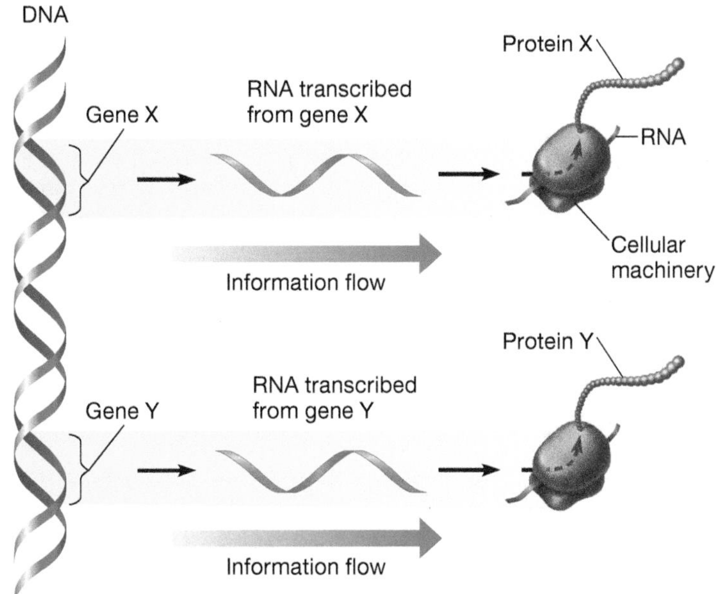

▲ **Figure 1.11B** The flow of information from DNA to RNA to protein

typically hundreds or thousands of "letters" long. For most genes, the sequence provides the blueprint for making a protein, and proteins are the major players in building and maintaining the cell and carrying out its activities.

Making a protein from the instructions contained in a gene involves a sequential flow of information, which is illustrated in **Figure 1.11B**. A gene's information is first transcribed from DNA to an intermediate molecule, RNA. An RNA molecule carries the information to the protein-manufacturing machinery in the cell. There, the sequence of nucleotides in the RNA is translated into a chain of protein building blocks. Once completed, the chain forms a specific protein with a unique shape and function. This process is called **gene expression**.

All forms of life use essentially the same chemical language to translate the information stored in DNA into proteins. Called the genetic code, this universal language is a strong piece of evidence that all living organisms are related. The universal genetic code also makes it possible to engineer cells to produce proteins normally found only in some other organism. Thus, bacteria can be used to produce insulin for the treatment of diabetes by inserting a gene for human insulin into bacterial cells.

Signaling Information What Figure 1.11B does not show is that the flow of genetic information from DNA to RNA to protein is usually linked with information from the external and internal environment. For example, the information your body receives includes external stimuli such as light, sound, or chemicals, and internal stimuli such as food in your stomach or an excess of sugar in your blood. The stimulus is usually received by some type of receptor and its information is relayed within your body in the form of nervous signals, hormones, or other types of signals. This flow of information ultimately reaches individual cells and influences their behavior, often by changing the activity of existing proteins or by regulating gene expression and the production of specific proteins.

Figure 1.11C illustrates the importance of the flow of information in controlling the level of sugar in your blood. All body cells have the same genetic information, but the gene for insulin is only expressed in certain cells in your pancreas. What signals tell those cells to produce and release insulin? (1) After a meal, the level of the sugar glucose in your blood rises. (2) This internal signal stimulates cells in your pancreas to secrete the hormone insulin, which travels throughout your body in your blood. (3) Insulin binds to receptors on body cells, causing them to take up glucose. (4) The now-lowered blood glucose level removes the signal, and insulin secretion decreases. Information flow through such regulatory systems enables organisms to maintain relatively stable and beneficial internal conditions.

Receiving and relaying information is evident at all levels of biological organization. The plaque that forms on your teeth is made up of bacteria, which exchange signals that influence their growth and community organization. Cells in a developing embryo exchange and respond to signals that affect their gene expression and ultimately lead to a highly organized body form. Organisms depend on information to maintain favorable internal conditions in response to environmental changes. The flow of information within and between organisms is central to the structure and functioning of all communities.

Throughout this text, you'll find many more examples of the flow of information. Some of these examples will be highlighted by this icon: INFORMATION.

? **How is signaling information involved in the expression of genetic information?**

■ Information from the internal and external environment affects gene expression—where and when particular genes are activated and proteins made.

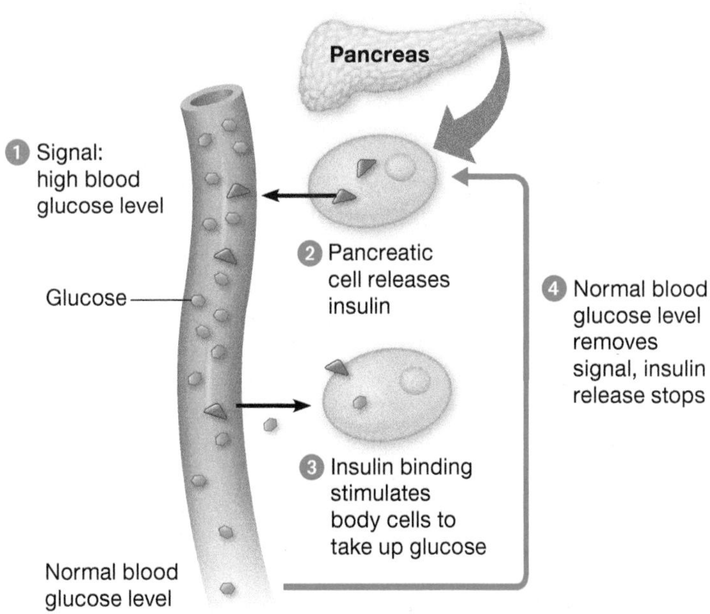

▲ **Figure 1.11C** The flow of information in the regulation of the level of glucose in the blood

TRY THIS Describe the action of insulin as a signaling molecule in this regulatory pathway.

1.12 Theme: Structure and function are related

A third theme that pervades all of biology is the correlation of structure and function. When considering useful objects around your home, you may note that form generally fits function. A screwdriver tightens or loosens screws, a hammer pounds nails. Because of their form, these tools can't do each other's jobs. You use a spoon to eat soup, but if you are spearing a piece of meat, you use a fork. Similarly, in biological systems, structure (the shape of something) and function (what it does) are almost always related, with each providing insight into the other.

The relationship between structure and function can be observed at every level of life. At the molecular level, the structure of a protein correlates with its function, whether it is part of the strong ligaments holding your bones together or the hemoglobin molecules transporting oxygen in your blood. On the cellular level, the long extensions of nerve cells enable them to transmit impulses from your spinal cord to your toes. The long, thin cells of fungi enable them to extend through their food source and absorb nutrients. The thick walls surrounding plant cells provide structural support to the plant leaf pictured in **Figure 1.12A**, just as the tough exoskeleton of the beetle supports its body.

Let's consider the red panda's hand as another example. In **Figure 1.12B**, you can see a red panda holding some bamboo. Scientists using an X-ray technique known as computed tomography (CT) produced a scan of the hand and wrist of a red panda (upper left part of the figure) to highlight the small bone protruding from the wrist, called the radial sesamoid. In red pandas, this bone is much larger than in related animals and is often referred to as a "false thumb." What might be its function? Just as your thumbs are useful in grasping objects, the red panda's wrist projection helps it grasp bamboo. By studying the fossil record, scientists propose that this projection originally evolved in the red panda's carnivorous ancestor as an adaptation that enabled it to move along branches in trees. Secondarily, this projection enabled the plant-eating red panda to hold on to bamboo. In the evolutionary history of life, we will encounter many examples of the remodeling of existing structures to new functions.

▲ **Figure 1.12A** Structural adaptations in the form of plant cell walls and insect exoskeletons that function in physical support

▲ **Figure 1.12B** A red panda grasping bamboo; a CT scan showing the "false thumb" of a red panda (inset)

Interestingly, the giant panda also has a "false thumb," yet much larger. As discussed in Module 1.6, this shared "panda thumb" and bamboo diet once led biologists to classify the red panda and the giant panda as close relatives. However, evidence from fossils and comparisons of DNA indicate that these similar structural adaptations evolved separately in the two distinct lineages.

The close match of form and function in the structures of life can be explained by natural selection. The organisms whose structures best performed their functions would have been most likely to have reproductive success, thereby passing those adaptations on to their offspring. Given that existing structures are often remodeled for new functions, however, we don't expect evolutionary adaptations to be perfect (see the introduction to Chapter 20).

Throughout the text we will see how the theme of structure and function applies to life at all levels of organization, from molecules and cells, to the internal organization of plants and animals, to whole ecosystems. To help you recognize this theme, specific examples will be highlighted with this icon: STRUCTURE AND FUNCTION.

? **Look at the structure of your hand and explain how its structure supports its function.**

■ The finger joints and opposable digits allow you to manipulate objects.

1.13 Theme: Life depends on the transfer and transformation of energy and matter

The activities of life—movement, growth, reproduction, regulation, and most cellular processes—require energy. The input of energy, primarily from the sun, and the conversion of energy from one form to another make life possible. **Figure 1.13** is a simplified diagram of the transfer and transformations of energy and matter taking place in a forest in Canada. Plants are the producers that provide the food for a typical terrestrial ecosystem. A tree, for example, absorbs water (H_2O) and minerals through its roots, and its leaves take in carbon dioxide (CO_2) from the air. In the process of photosynthesis, energy from sunlight is stored as chemical energy as the atoms in CO_2 and H_2O are rearranged into sugar molecules that are rich in chemical energy.

The consumers in an ecosystem eat plants and other animals. The moose in Figure 1.13 eats the grasses and tender shoots and leaves of trees in the forest ecosystem. To release the chemical energy in food, animals (as well as plants and most other organisms) use the process of cellular respiration, taking in O_2 from the air and releasing CO_2. Consumers use both the energy and the atoms (matter) obtained from food to build new molecules. For example, proteins in the moose's fur were assembled from atoms that were once in its food. An animal's wastes return matter to the environment.

Vital parts of this ecosystem are the small animals, fungi, and bacteria in the soil that decompose wastes and the remains of dead organisms. These decomposers act as recyclers, changing complex matter into simpler chemicals that return to the environment and are once again available to producers.

As illustrated in Figure 1.13, the dynamics of ecosystems can be summarized with two major processes—the flow of energy and the cycling of matter. An ecosystem gains and loses energy constantly. Energy flows into most ecosystems as sunlight (yellow arrow), and photosynthetic organisms convert it into the chemical energy in sugars and other energy-rich molecules. Chemical energy in food (orange arrow) is then passed through a series of consumers and, eventually, to decomposers, powering each organism in turn. In the process of these energy conversions between and within organisms, some energy is always converted to heat, which is then lost from the ecosystem (red arrow). Thus, energy flows through an ecosystem in one direction, entering as light and exiting as heat. By contrast, matter cycles within an ecosystem, from the air and soil to producers, to consumers and decomposers, and back to the air and soil (shown by the blue arrows in the figure).

This "chemical square dance" in which molecules swap chemical partners as they receive, convert, and release energy is never-ending in all forms of life. Throughout your study of biology, you will see many examples of this theme, from microscopic cellular processes to ecosystem-wide cycles of carbon and other nutrients. To help you recognize this theme, some examples will be highlighted with this icon: ENERGY AND MATTER.

? Describe how photosynthesis transforms energy and matter.

■ Using the energy of sunlight, CO_2 and H_2O (matter) are converted into sugar molecules with stored chemical energy.

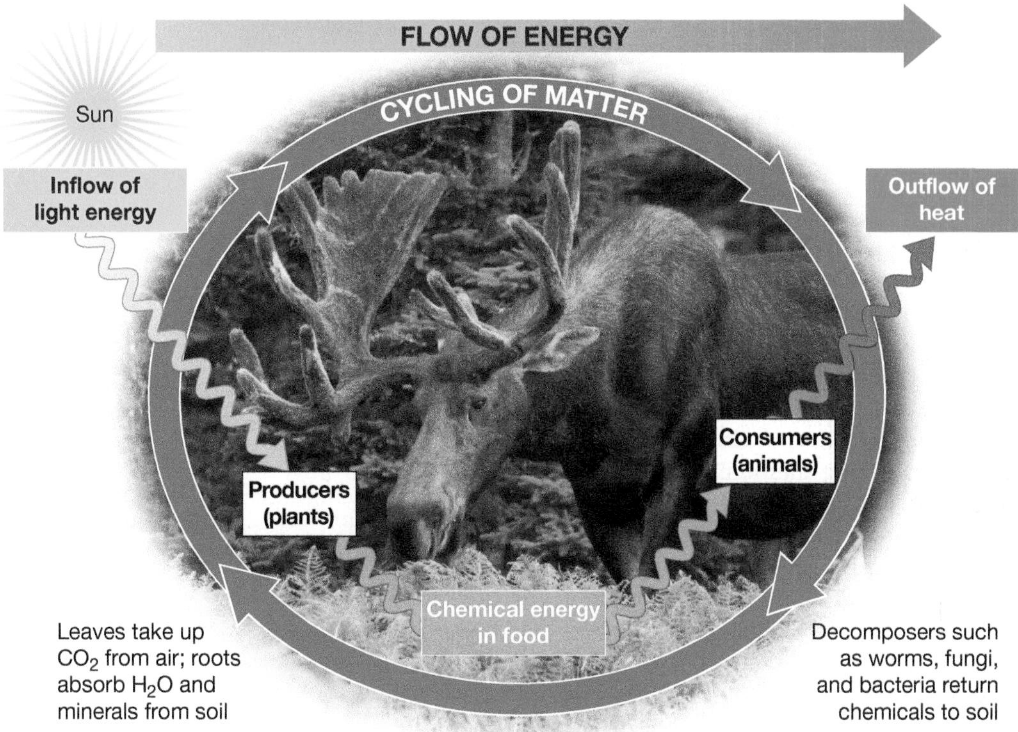

▲ **Figure 1.13** The flow of energy and cycling of matter in an ecosystem

1.14 Theme: Life depends on interactions within and between systems

As you saw in Module 1.3, the study of life extends from the microscopic scale of the molecules and cells that make up an organism to the global scale of the entire living planet. Working our way upward through this hierarchy, we noted that novel properties arise at each higher level. Such emergent properties represent an important concept in biology. The familiar saying that "the whole is greater than the sum of its parts" captures this idea. The emergent properties of each level result from the specific arrangement and interactions of its parts. Such a combination of components forms a more complex organization called a *system*. Biological systems can range from the molecular machinery of a cell to the functioning of an ecosystem or the entire biosphere.

Your body is a system, and it is the interactions between the parts (molecules, cells, tissues, organs) that allow you to maintain a relatively stable internal environment. Interactions and connections between your circulatory, digestive, and endocrine (hormonal) systems—your blood, pancreatic cells, molecules of insulin, and body cells—enable the regulation of blood glucose level (see Figure 1.11C). An alteration in one of the components of such a system disrupts its functioning and can lead to disease. For example, type 1 diabetes is the result of pancreatic cells no longer producing insulin; type 2 diabetes develops when body cells no longer respond to insulin.

Using an approach called **systems biology**, scientists attempt to model the behavior of biological systems by analyzing the interactions among their parts. For example, researchers have produced a complex systems map of the interactions among 2,346 proteins in a fruit fly cell, based on a huge database of known proteins and their actions. One goal of developing such models is to be able to predict how a change in one component will affect the other parts of the system. Thus the systems map of fruit fly proteins might show how an increase in the activity of a certain protein can ripple through a cell's molecular circuitry to affect other proteins and functions of the cell.

Recent technological advances have enabled scientists to pose new kinds of questions about system interactions at the molecular level. Faster and less expensive sequencing techniques have greatly increased the rate at which the nucleotide sequences in DNA can be determined. New computational tools are being used to store, organize, and analyze this huge volume of data. Scientists can now study and compare whole sets of genes and proteins in a species and across multiple species, asking questions about the functions of individual genes as well as the interactions among their protein products. These molecular techniques have also enabled the identification of organisms that were previously unknown, ranging from the communities of bacteria living in our bodies to the vast array of microorganisms that play essential roles in every ecosystem.

Systems biology often involves interdisciplinary research as well as mathematical or computer modeling of the dynamic behavior of an integrated network of components. Thus, scientists can study and predict the effects of climate change by modeling increases in atmospheric levels of CO_2 and global warming, monitoring weather patterns, and investigating impacts on individual populations as well as the diversity of biological communities.

▲ **Figure 1.14** Interactions among some of the components of an ecosystem

TRY THIS Identify the interconnections and interactions of the abiotic and biotic components illustrated in this photograph.

Life is characterized by interconnections and interactions. Consider the sloth in **Figure 1.14**. This denizen of South American rain forests is sporting a luxuriant growth of photosynthetic bacteria (the greenish tinge in its hair). The sloth depends on trees for food and shelter; the tree uses nutrients from the decomposition of the sloth's feces; the bacteria gain access to the sunlight necessary for photosynthesis by living on the sloth; and the sloth is camouflaged from predators by its greenish-brown coat. We can find these types of interactions among component parts at every level of biological organization. To help you recognize the theme of system interactions and interconnections in this text, some examples will be identified with this icon: INTERACTIONS.

As you embark on your study of biology, watch for the five themes: evolution, information, structure and function, energy and matter, and interactions. These unifying themes can provide a framework to help you organize your growing biological knowledge. And remember how this knowledge came to be in the first place: through the exciting and rewarding process of science.

? **A box of bicycle parts won't do anything, but if the parts are properly assembled, you can take a ride. What does this illustrate?**

Emergent properties of the interacting components of a system

CHAPTER **1** REVIEW

For practice quizzes, BioFlix animations, MP3 tutorials, video tutors, and more study tools designed for this textbook, go to MasteringBiology™

REVIEWING THE CONCEPTS

Biology: The Scientific Study of Life (1.1–1.3)

1.1 What is life? Biology is the scientific study of life. Properties of life include order, reproduction, growth and development, energy processing, regulation, response to the environment, and evolutionary adaptation. The cell is the structural and functional unit of life.

1.2 Biologists arrange the diversity of life into three domains. Taxonomists name species and classify them into broader groups. Domains Bacteria and Archaea contain organisms with simple cells. Domain Eukarya includes various protists and the kingdoms Fungi, Plantae, and Animalia.

1.3 In life's hierarchy of organization, new properties emerge at each level. Biological organization unfolds as follows: biosphere > ecosystem > community > population > organism > organ system > organ > tissue > cell > organelle > molecule. Emergent properties result from the interactions among component parts.

The Process of Science (1.4–1.8)

1.4 What is science? Science uses an evidence-based process of inquiry to investigate the natural world. The scientific approach involves observations, hypotheses, predictions, tests of hypotheses via experiments or additional observations, and analysis of data. A scientific theory is broad in scope and supported by a large body of evidence.

1.5 Hypotheses can be tested using controlled experiments. The use of control and experimental groups can demonstrate the effect of a single variable. Hypotheses can be tested in humans with clinical trials, as well as retrospective or prospective observational studies.

1.6 Hypotheses can be tested using observational data. Scientists tested hypotheses about the evolutionary relationships of red pandas. Recent studies comparing DNA sequences classify the red panda as the only living species in its family.

1.7 The process of science is repetitive, nonlinear, and collaborative. Forming and testing hypotheses is at the core of science. This endeavor is influenced by three spheres: exploration and discovery; analysis and feedback from the scientific community; and societal benefits and outcomes.

1.8 Biology, technology, and society are connected in important ways. Technological advances stem from scientific research, and research benefits from new technologies.

Five Unifying Themes in Biology (1.9–1.14)

1.9 Theme: Evolution is the core theme of biology. Darwin synthesized the theory of evolution by natural selection.

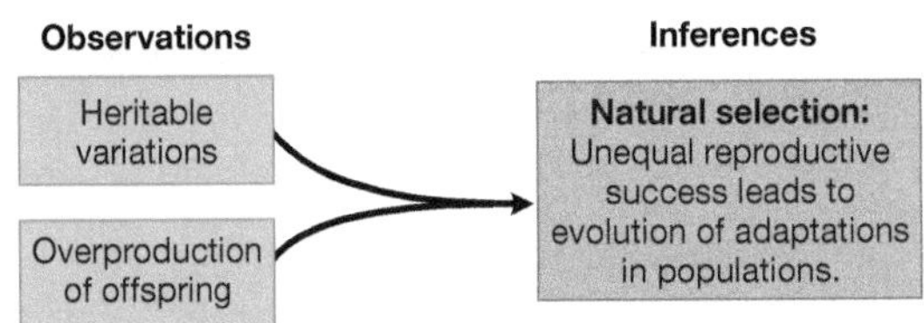

1.10 Evolution is connected to our everyday lives. Evolutionary theory is useful in medicine, agriculture, and conservation. Human-caused environmental changes are powerful selective forces that affect the evolution of many species.

1.11 Theme: Life depends on the flow of information. DNA is responsible for heredity and for programming the activities of a cell by providing the blueprint for proteins. Information from the external and internal environment includes the stimuli, signals, and pathways that regulate body processes and gene expression.

1.12 Theme: Structure and function are related. Structure is related to function at all levels of organization.

1.13 Theme: Life depends on the transfer and transformation of energy and matter. Energy flows through an ecosystem in one direction—entering as sunlight, converted to chemical energy by producers, passed on to consumers, and exiting as heat. Ecosystems are characterized by the cycling of matter from the atmosphere and soil through producers, consumers, decomposers, and back to the environment.

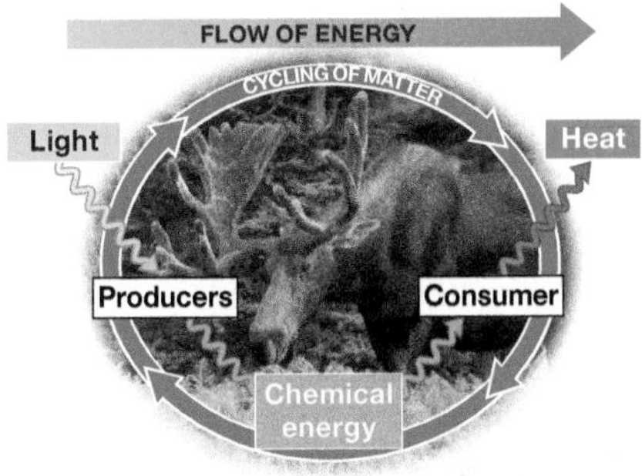

1.14 Theme: Life depends on interactions within and between systems. Emergent properties are the result of interactions between the components of a system. Systems biology models the complex behavior of biological systems.

CONNECTING THE CONCEPTS

1. Complete the following map organizing one of biology's major themes.

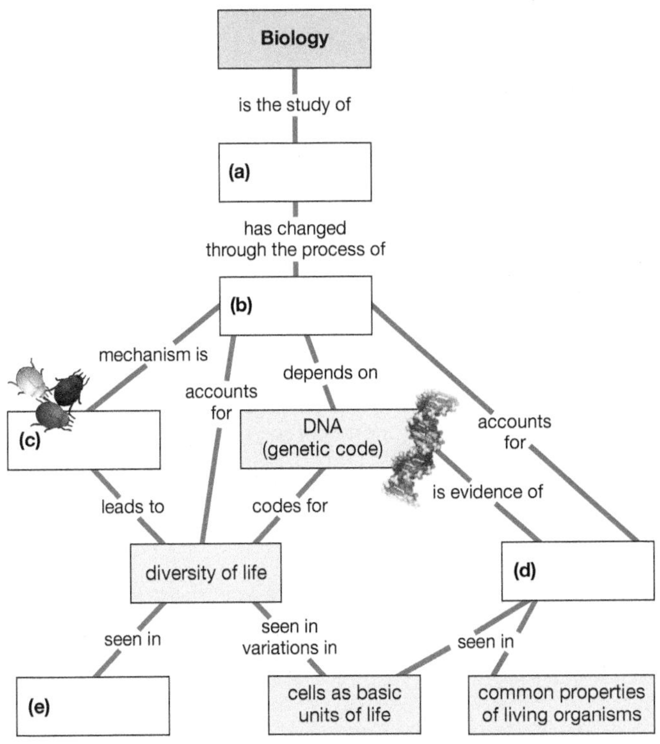

TESTING YOUR KNOWLEDGE

Level 1: Knowledge/Comprehension

2. All the organisms on your campus make up
   a. an ecosystem.
   b. a community.
   c. a population.
   d. the biosphere.
3. Which of these is *not* a property of all living organisms?
   a. capable of reproduction
   b. uses energy
   c. composed of multiple cells
   d. responds to the environment
4. Which of the following statements best distinguishes hypotheses from theories in science?
   a. Theories are hypotheses that have been proven.
   b. Hypotheses usually are narrow in scope; theories have broad explanatory power.
   c. Hypotheses are tentative guesses; theories are correct answers to questions about nature.
   d. Hypotheses and theories are different terms for essentially the same thing in science.
5. Which of the following best demonstrates the unity among all living organisms?
   a. structure correlated with function
   b. DNA and a common genetic code
   c. emergent properties
   d. natural selection
6. A controlled experiment is one that
   a. proceeds slowly enough that a scientist can make careful records of the results.
   b. keeps all variables constant.
   c. is repeated many times to make sure the results are accurate.
   d. tests experimental and control groups in parallel.
7. Which of the following is a *true* statement of observational data?
   a. It is always qualitative, not quantitative.
   b. It is used to form hypotheses, but not to test them.
   c. It can include comparisons of fossils as well as DNA sequences.
   d. It is the type of data used for the independent variable in a controlled experiment.

Level 2: Application/Analysis

8. A biologist studying interactions among the bacteria in an ecosystem could *not* be working at which level in life's hierarchy? (*Choose carefully and explain your answer.*)
   a. the population level
   b. the molecular level
   c. the organism level
   d. the organ level
9. Which of the following best describes the logic of scientific inquiry?
   a. If I generate a testable hypothesis, my experiments will support it.
   b. If my prediction is correct, it will lead to a testable hypothesis.
   c. If my observations are accurate, they will support my hypothesis.
   d. If my hypothesis is correct, I can expect certain test results.
10. In an ecosystem, how is the flow of energy similar to that of matter, and how is it different?
11. Explain the role of heritable variations in Darwin's theory of natural selection.
12. Describe the process of scientific inquiry and explain why it is not a rigid method.
13. Contrast technology with science. Give an example of each to illustrate the difference.

Level 3: Synthesis/Evaluation

14. Biology can be described as having both a vertical scale and a horizontal scale. Explain what that means.
15. Explain what is meant by this statement: Natural selection is an editing mechanism rather than a creative process.
16. The graph below shows the results of an experiment in which mice learned to run through a maze.

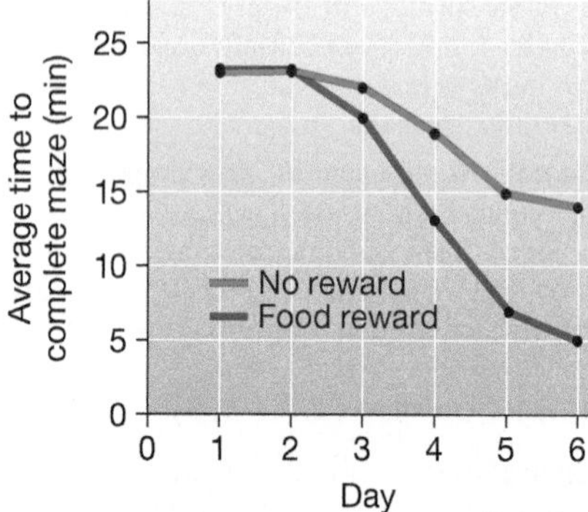

   a. State the hypothesis and prediction that you think this experiment tested.
   b. Which was the control group and which the experimental? Why was a control group needed?
   c. List some variables that must have been controlled so as not to affect the results.
   d. Do the data support the hypothesis? Explain.
17. SCIENTIFIC THINKING Suppose that in an experiment similar to the camouflage experiment described in Module 1.5, a researcher observed and recorded more total predator attacks on dark-model mice in the inland habitat than on dark models in the beach habitat. From comparing these two pieces of data, the researcher concluded that the camouflage hypothesis is false. Do you think this conclusion is justified? Why or why not?
18. The fruits of wild species of tomato are tiny compared with the giant beefsteak tomatoes available today. This difference in fruit size is almost entirely due to the larger number of cells in the domesticated fruits. Plant biologists have recently discovered genes that are responsible for controlling cell division in tomatoes. Why would such a discovery be important to producers of other kinds of fruits and vegetables? To the study of human development and disease? To our basic understanding of biology?
19. The news media and popular magazines frequently report stories that are connected to biology. In the next 24 hours, record the ones you hear or read about in three different sources and briefly describe the biological connections in each story.

Answers to all questions can be found in Appendix 4.

The Life of the Cell

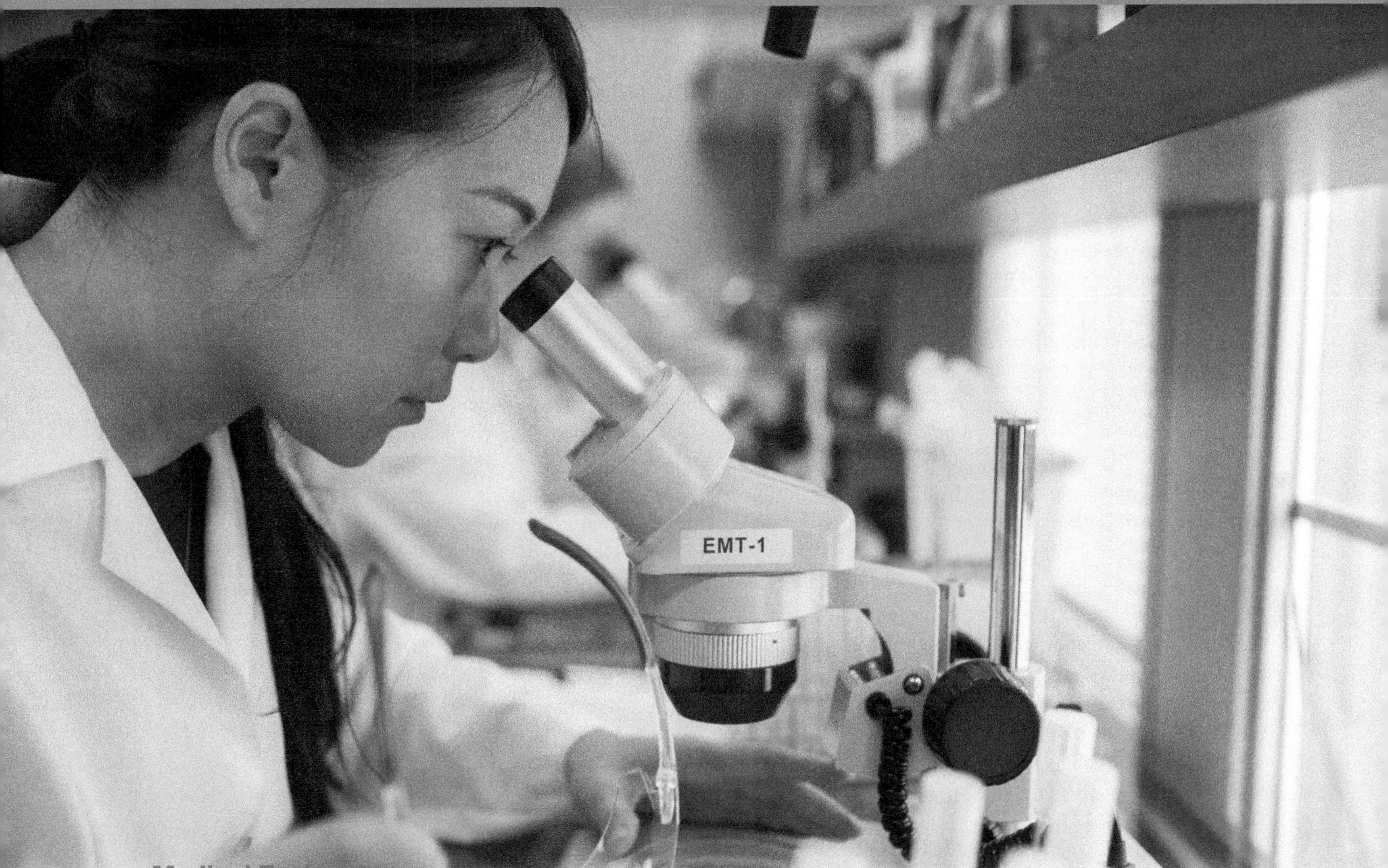

▲ **Medical Technician**

A laboratory technician studies a tissue sample using a light microscope (see Module 4.1).

▲ **Brewer**

Matt Licata removes a mash sample from a lauter tun, a vessel used to separate sweet wort from grain when brewing beer (see Module 6.12).

▲ **Solar Energy Engineer**

Crista Shopis helps install solar panels on the solar installation she has designed (see Module 7.14).

CHAPTER 2

The Chemical Basis of Life

Coral reefs are among the most diverse ecosystems on Earth. They are formed from the gradual buildup of the calcium carbonate skeletons of small coral animals. As you can see in the photo on the right, these structurally diverse habitats provide havens for a huge diversity of fish and other marine organisms. But in recent years, something in the air is threatening coral reefs. How might a chemical compound in the air harm such a vibrant ecosystem? The answer is chemistry. When carbon dioxide (CO_2) dissolves in water, it reacts with water to form an acid, which then makes the water more acidic. Later in the chapter we will see how scientists are exploring the effects of this ocean acidification on coral reefs.

Will rising atmospheric CO_2 harm coral reefs?

Why do we begin our study of biology with a chapter on chemistry? Well, chemistry is the basis of life—it explains how elements combine into the compounds that make up your body and the bodies of all other living organisms and how chemical reactions underlie the functions of all cells.

Life and its chemistry are tied to water. Life began in water and evolved there for 3 billion years before spreading onto land. And all life, even land-dwelling life, is still dependent on water. Your cells are about 70% water, and that is where the chemical reactions of your body take place. What properties of the simple water molecule make it so indispensable to life on Earth? You'll find out in this chapter.

Life is organized into a hierarchy of structural levels, with new properties emerging at each successive level (as you learned in Chapter 1). You will see that emergent properties are apparent even at the lowest levels of biological organization—the ordering of atoms into molecules and the interactions of those molecules. Thus we begin our study of biology with some basic concepts of chemistry that will apply throughout our study of life.

BIG IDEAS

Elements, Atoms, and Compounds (2.1–2.4)

Living organisms are made of atoms of certain elements, mostly combined into compounds.

Chemical Bonds (2.5–2.9)

The structure of an atom determines what types of bonds it can form with other atoms.

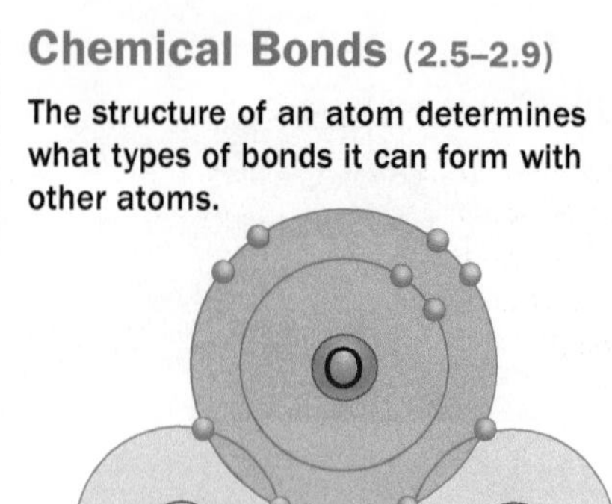

Water's Life-Supporting Properties (2.10–2.16)

The unique properties of water derive from the polarity and hydrogen bonding of water molecules.

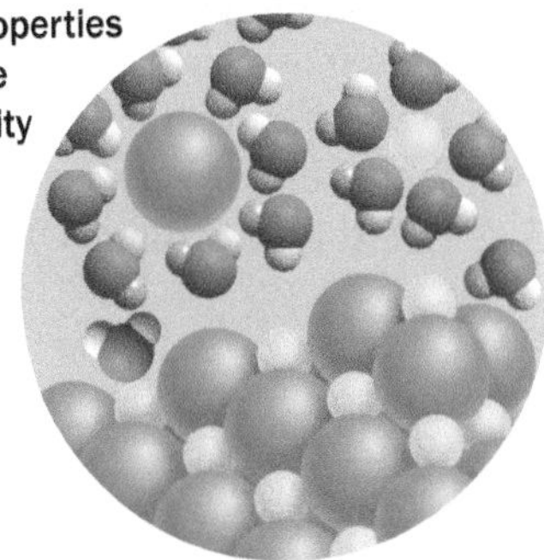

Elements, Atoms, and Compounds

2.1 Organisms are composed of elements, usually combined into compounds

You and all things around you are made of matter—the physical "stuff" of the universe. **Matter** is defined as anything that occupies space and has mass. (In everyday language, we think of mass as an object's weight.) Matter is found on Earth in three physical states: solid, liquid, and gas.

Types of matter as diverse as water, rocks, air, and biology students are all composed of chemical elements. An **element** is a substance that cannot be broken down to other substances by ordinary chemical means. Chemists recognize 92 elements that occur in nature; gold, copper, carbon, and oxygen are some examples. Chemists have also made a few dozen synthetic elements. Each element has a symbol made up of the first letter or two of its English, Latin, or German name. For example, the symbol O comes from the English word *oxygen*; the symbol for sodium, Na, is from the Latin word *natrium*.

A **compound** is a substance consisting of two or more different elements combined in a fixed ratio. For example, table salt (sodium chloride, NaCl) has equal parts of the elements sodium (Na) and chlorine (Cl). Pure sodium is a metal and pure chlorine is a poisonous gas. Chemically combined, however, they form an edible compound (Figure 2.1A). Hydrogen (H) and oxygen (O) are elements that typically exist as gases. Chemically combined in a ratio of 2:1, however, they form the most abundant compound on the surface of Earth—water (H_2O). Water and table salt are examples of organized matter having emergent properties: A compound has characteristics different from those of its elements.

Most of the compounds in living organisms contain at least three or four elements. Sugar, for example, is formed of carbon (C), hydrogen, and oxygen. Proteins, which make up about 20% of your body, are compounds containing carbon, hydrogen, oxygen, nitrogen (N), and a small amount of sulfur (S).

How many elements are essential for life? The requirements are similar among organisms, but there is some variation. For example, humans need 25 elements, but plants require only 17. As you can see in Figure 2.1B, six elements—oxygen, carbon, hydrogen, nitrogen, calcium, and phosphorus—make up about 99% of your body. The first four (O, C, H, and N) are the main ingredients of the biological molecules proteins, carbohydrates, and lipids. Calcium (Ca) and phosphorus (P) are the major components of your bones and teeth. Accounting for most of the remaining 1% of your body, potassium (K), sulfur, sodium, chlorine, and magnesium (Mg) are involved in functions such as nerve signaling and chemical reactions.

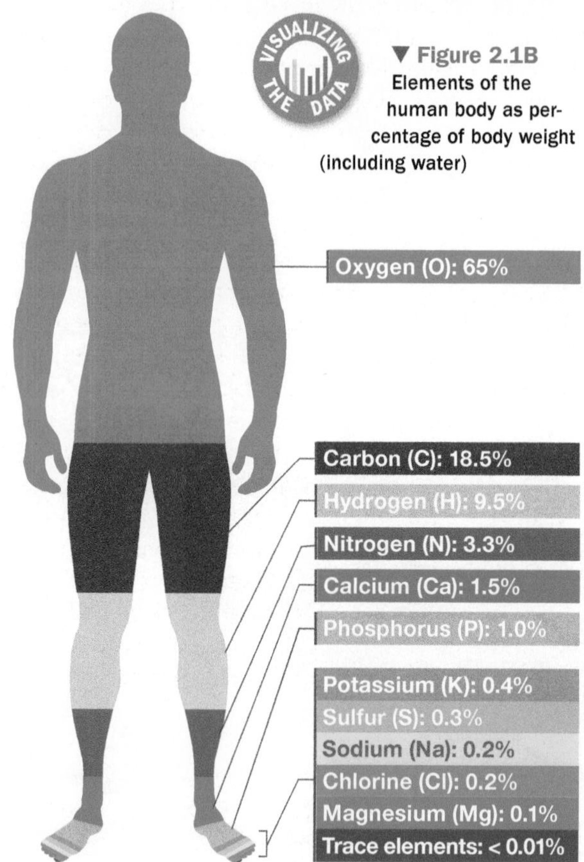

▼ **Figure 2.1B** Elements of the human body as percentage of body weight (including water)

What about that last tip of the toe in Figure 2.1B? The so-called **trace elements** are present in minute quantities, making up less than 0.01% of human body weight. They include boron, chromium, cobalt, copper, fluorine, iodine, iron, manganese, molybdenum, selenium, silicon, tin, vanadium, and zinc. Iron makes up only about 0.004% of your body weight but is vital for energy processing and for transporting oxygen in your blood. Iron (Fe) is a trace element needed by all forms of life. Others are required only by certain species. For example, iodine (I) is essential only for vertebrates—animals with backbones, which include you. We explore the importance of trace elements to your health next.

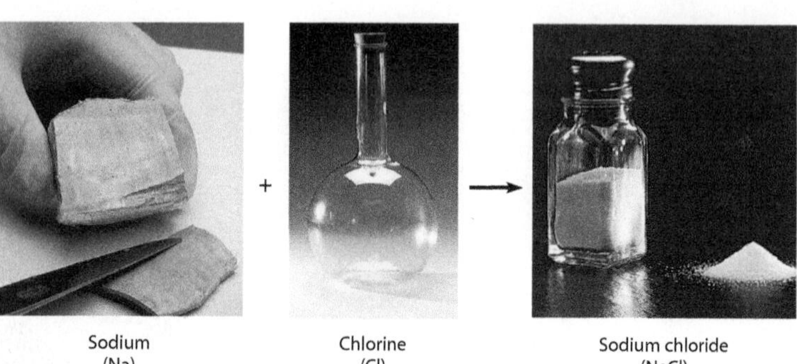

▲ **Figure 2.1A** The emergent properties of table salt

? Explain how table salt illustrates the concept of emergent properties.

■ The elements that make up the edible crystals of table salt, sodium and chlorine, are in pure form a metal and a poisonous gas.

2.2 Trace elements are common additives to food and water

CONNECTION Trace elements are required in very small quantities, but, in some cases, even those small requirements are difficult to fulfill.

Iodine is an essential component of a hormone produced by the thyroid gland. An iodine deficiency in the diet causes the thyroid gland to grow to abnormal size, a condition called goiter (**Figure 2.2A**). The most serious effects of iodine deficiency take place during fetal development and childhood, leading to miscarriages, poor growth, and mental impairment. Seafood, kelp, dairy products, and dark, leafy greens are good natural sources. Thus, deficiencies are often found in inland regions, especially in areas where the soil is lacking in iodine. A global strategy to eliminate iodine deficiency involves universal iodization of all salt used for human and animal consumption. Unfortunately, about 30% of global households still do not have access to iodized salt. Although most common in developing nations, iodine deficiencies may also result from excessive consumption of highly processed foods (which often use non-iodized salt).

▲ **Figure 2.2A** Goiter, a symptom of iodine deficiency, in a Burmese woman

A deficiency in another trace element—iron—is the world's most common nutritional disorder, with as many as 2 billion people affected, in particular children and women in developing countries. Strategies for addressing the challenge of iron deficiency include food fortification, iron supplements, and diet diversification and improvement. **Figure 2.2B** illustrates some iron-rich foods. In the United States, wheat flour has been fortified with iron since the 1940s, and iron is commonly added to processed foods, such as cereal.

But can an excess of trace elements also pose a problem? Recent studies indicate that older Americans are less likely to suffer from iron deficiency than from iron overload, which can damage organs and may increase the risk of certain diseases. And because of the risk of accidental fatal poisoning in children, warning labels are required on iron supplements.

Trace elements have also been added to water to improve public health. Fluoride is a form of fluorine (F), which is found in small amounts in all water sources. For more than 70 years, the American Dental Association has supported fluoridation of community drinking water. Indeed, the Centers for Disease Control and Prevention (CDC) listed water fluoridation as one of 10 great public health achievements of the 20th century. The history of water fluoridation illustrates both the process of science and societal benefits and interactions. In the early 1900s, a dentist began searching for the cause of brown-stained teeth (then called Colorado brown stain and now known as fluorosis). With the help of other researchers, he established the cause as a high concentration of fluoride in local water supplies. But he also noted that stained teeth were correlated with a greatly reduced incidence of cavities and tooth loss. By the 1940s, scientists at the U.S. National Institutes of Health published several studies showing that reduced tooth decay was associated with a fluoride concentration that was low enough not to cause fluorosis. A five-year controlled study of water fluoridation in Grand Rapids, Michigan, showed significant reductions in cavities, and by 1951, fluoridation became an official policy of the U.S. Public Health Service. Numerous research studies continue to show the effectiveness of water fluoridation on reducing cavities in both children and adults.

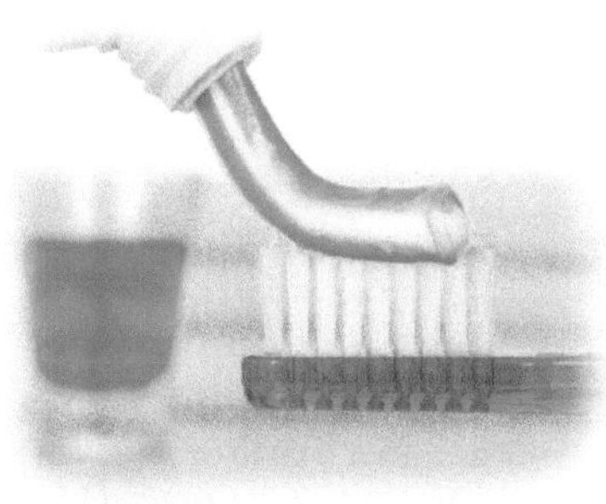

▲ **Figure 2.2C** Mouthwash and toothpaste with added fluoride

But this public health achievement is not without controversy. When first introduced in the 1950s, some groups asserted that fluoridated water, along with the polio vaccine, was part of a communist conspiracy. Fluoridation efforts in some U.S. communities have met with strong opposition, based sometimes on conflicting studies, a distrust of science, or a strong belief in individual rights. With the advent of fluoridated toothpaste and other fluoride treatments (**Figure 2.2C**), some opponents maintain that this public health practice should not be forced on everyone. Proponents assert that this intervention benefits those who may be least able to afford proper dental care. As is often the case, citizens need to educate themselves about all sides of such controversies and critically evaluate the types of scientific evidence on which decisions are based.

? A serving of cereal fortified to provide 100% of the recommended daily intake contains 18 mg of iron. The recommended tolerable upper intake level is 45 mg (before causing gastrointestinal upset). How many bowls of cereal before you exceed that level?

■ 2.5 servings

▲ **Figure 2.2B** Foods rich in iron

2.3 Atoms consist of protons, neutrons, and electrons

Each element has its own type of atom, which is different from the atoms of other elements. An **atom**, named from a Greek word meaning "indivisible," is the smallest unit of matter that still retains the properties of an element. Atoms are so small that it would take about a million of them to stretch across the period printed at the end of this sentence.

Subatomic Particles Physicists have split the atom into more than a hundred types of subatomic particles. However, only three kinds of particles are relevant here. A **proton** is a subatomic particle with a single positive electrical charge (+). An **electron** is a subatomic particle with a single negative charge (−). A **neutron**, as its name implies, is electrically neutral (has no charge).

Figure 2.3 shows two very simple models of an atom of the element helium (He), the "lighter-than-air" gas that makes balloons rise. Notice that two protons (+) and two neutrons (●) are tightly packed in the atom's central core, or **nucleus**. Two rapidly moving electrons (−) form a sort of cloud of negative charge around the nucleus. The attraction between the negatively charged electrons and the positively charged protons holds the electrons near the nucleus. The left-hand model shows the two electrons on a circle around the nucleus. The right-hand model, slightly more realistic, represents the electrons as a spherical cloud of negative charge. Neither model is drawn to scale. In real atoms, the electrons are very much smaller than the protons and neutrons, and the electron cloud is very much bigger compared with the nucleus. Imagine that this atom was the size of a baseball stadium: The nucleus would be the size of a pea in center field, and the electrons would be like two tiny gnats buzzing around inside the stadium.

Atomic Number and Mass Number So what makes the atoms of different elements different? All atoms of a particular element have the same unique number of protons. This number is the element's **atomic number**. Thus, an atom of helium, with 2 protons, has an atomic number of 2. Unless otherwise indicated, an atom has an equal number of protons and electrons, and thus its net electrical charge is 0 (zero).

What other numbers are associated with an atom? An atom's **mass number** is the sum of the number of protons and neutrons in its nucleus. For helium, the mass number is 4. The mass of a proton and the mass of a neutron are almost identical and are expressed in a unit of measurement called the dalton. Protons and neutrons each have masses close to 1 dalton. An electron has only about 1/2,000 the mass of a proton, so it contributes very little to an atom's mass. Thus, an atom's **atomic mass** (or weight) is approximately equal to its mass number—the sum of its protons and neutrons—in daltons.

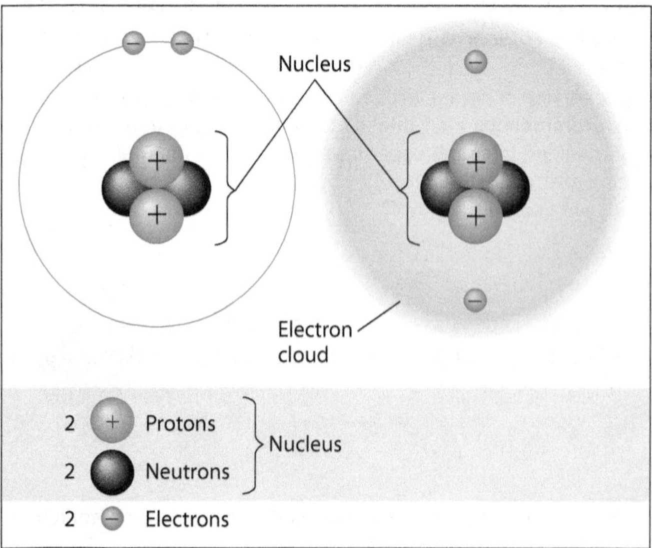

▲ Figure 2.3 Two models of a helium atom. (Note that these models are not to scale; they greatly overestimate the size of the nucleus in relation to the electron cloud.)

Isotopes All atoms of an element have the same atomic number, but some atoms of that element may differ in mass number. The different **isotopes** of an element have the same number of protons and behave identically in chemical reactions, but they have different numbers of neutrons. Table 2.3 shows the numbers of subatomic particles in the three isotopes of carbon. Note that carbon's atomic number is 6—all of its atoms have 6 protons. Carbon-12 (named for its mass number), with 6 neutrons, accounts for about 99% of naturally occurring carbon. Most of the remaining 1% consists of carbon-13, with a mass number of 13 and thus 7 neutrons. A third isotope, carbon-14, with 8 neutrons, occurs in minute quantities. Of course, all three isotopes have 6 protons—otherwise, they would not be carbon.

Both carbon-12 and carbon-13 are stable isotopes, meaning that their nuclei remain intact more or less forever. The isotope carbon-14, on the other hand, is unstable, or radioactive. A **radioactive isotope** is one in which the nucleus decays spontaneously, giving off particles and energy. Radiation from decaying isotopes can damage cellular molecules and thus can pose serious risks to living organisms. But radioactive isotopes can be helpful, as in their use in dating fossils (see Module 15.5). They are also used in biological research and medicine, as we see next.

TABLE 2.3 Isotopes of Carbon

	Carbon-12		Carbon-13		Carbon-14	
Protons	6	Mass number 12	6	Mass number 13	6	Mass number 14
Neutrons	6		7		8	
Electrons	6		6		6	

? **A nitrogen atom has 7 protons, and its most common isotope has 7 neutrons. A radioactive isotope of nitrogen has 9 neutrons. What is the atomic number and mass number of this radioactive nitrogen?**

■ Atomic number = 7; mass number = 16

2.4 Radioactive isotopes can help or harm us

CONNECTION Living cells cannot readily distinguish between isotopes of the same element. Consequently, organisms take up and use compounds containing radioactive isotopes in the usual way. Because radioactivity is easily detected and measured by instruments, radioactive isotopes are useful as tracers—biological spies, in effect—for monitoring the fate of atoms in living organisms.

Basic Research Biologists often use radioactive tracers to follow molecules as they undergo chemical changes in an organism. For example, researchers have used carbon dioxide (CO_2) containing the radioactive isotope carbon-14 to study photosynthesis. Using sunlight to power the conversion, plants take in CO_2 from the air and use it to make sugar molecules. Radioactively labeled CO_2 has enabled researchers to trace the sequence of molecules made by plants in the chemical route from CO_2 to sugar.

Medical Diagnosis and Treatment Radioactive isotopes may also be used to tag chemicals that accumulate in specific areas of the body, such as phosphorus in bones. After injection of such a tracer, a special camera produces an image of where the radiation collects. In most diagnostic uses, the patient receives only a tiny amount of an isotope.

Sometimes radioactive isotopes are used for treatment. As you learned in Module 2.2, the body uses iodine to make a thyroid hormone. Because radioactive iodine accumulates in the thyroid, it can be used to kill cancer cells there.

Substances that the body metabolizes, such as glucose or oxygen, may also be labeled with a radioactive isotope. Figure 2.4A shows a patient being examined by a PET (positron-emission tomography) scanner, which can produce images of areas of the body with high metabolic activity. PET is useful for diagnosing certain heart disorders and cancers and for basic research on the brain.

The early detection of Alzheimer's disease may be a new use for such techniques. This devastating illness gradually destroys a person's memory and ability to think. As the disease progresses, the brain becomes riddled with deposits (plaques) of a protein called beta-amyloid. Researchers have synthesized a radioactively labeled protein molecule called PIB that binds to beta-amyloid plaques and can be detected on a PET scan. Figure 2.4B shows PET images of the brains of a healthy person (left) and a person with Alzheimer's (right) injected with PIB. Notice that the brain of the Alzheimer's patient has high levels of PIB (red and yellow areas), whereas the unaffected person's brain has lower levels (blue). New therapies are focused on limiting the production of beta-amyloid or clearing it from the brain. A diagnostic test using PIB would allow researchers to monitor the effectiveness of new drugs in people living with the disease.

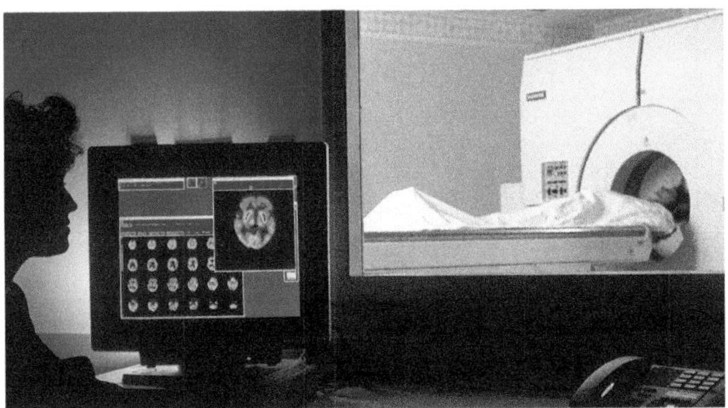

▲ **Figure 2.4A** Technician monitoring the output of a PET scanner

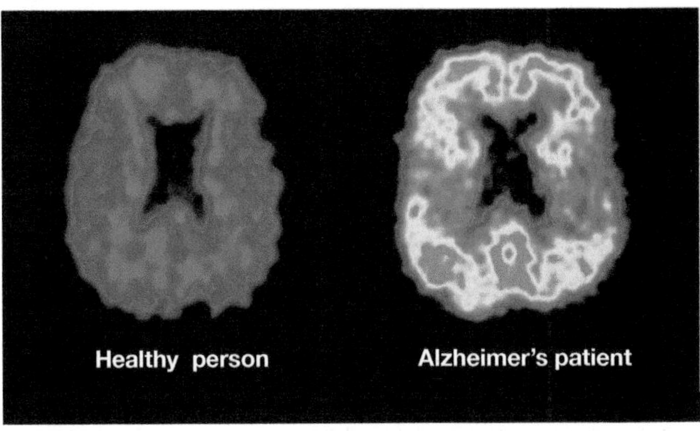

▲ **Figure 2.4B** PET images of brains of a healthy person (left) and a person with Alzheimer's disease (right). Red and yellow colors indicate high levels of PIB bound to beta-amyloid plaques.

Dangers Although radioactive isotopes have many beneficial uses, uncontrolled exposure to high levels of radiation can be lethal. The particles and energy thrown off by radioactive atoms can damage molecules, especially DNA. The explosion of a nuclear reactor in Chernobyl, Ukraine, in 1986 released large amounts of radioactive isotopes into the environment, which drifted over large areas of Russia, Belarus, and Europe. A few dozen people died from acute radiation poisoning within a few weeks of the accident, and more than 100,000 people were evacuated from the area. Increased rates of thyroid cancer in children exposed to the radiation have been reported. Likewise, scientists will carefully monitor the long-term health consequences of the 2011 post-tsunami Fukushima nuclear disaster in Japan, particularly for the 150 emergency workers at the plant.

Natural sources of radiation can also pose a threat. Radon, a radioactive gas, is the second-leading cause of lung cancer in the United States. Radon can contaminate buildings in regions where underlying rocks naturally contain uranium, a radioactive element. Homeowners can buy a radon detector or hire a company to test their home to ensure that radon levels are safe. If levels are found to be unsafe, technology exists to remove radon from homes.

? **Why are radioactive isotopes useful as tracers in research on the chemistry of life?**

■ Organisms incorporate radioactive isotopes into their molecules, and researchers can use special scanning devices to detect these isotopes in biological pathways or locations in the body.

Chemical Bonds

2.5 The distribution of electrons determines an atom's chemical properties

To understand how atoms interact with each other, we need to explore atomic structure further. Of the three subatomic particles—protons, neutrons, and electrons—only electrons are directly involved in the chemical activity of an atom.

If you glance back to the model of the helium atom in Figure 2.3, you see that its 2 electrons are shown together on a circle around the nucleus. But where should the electrons be shown in an atom with more than 2 electrons? Consider the model of carbon in **Figure 2.5A**. Two electrons are still located on an inner circle, but the remaining 4 are distributed on a larger outside circle. It turns out that electrons can be located in different **electron shells**, each with a characteristic distance from the nucleus. Depending on an element's atomic number, an atom may have one, two, or more electron shells.

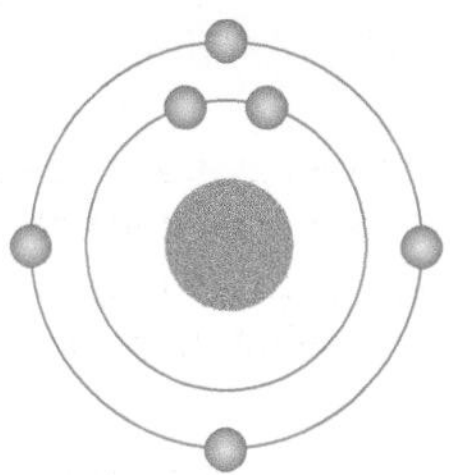

▲ **Figure 2.5A** An electron distribution model of carbon

Figure 2.5B is an abbreviated version of the periodic table of the elements (see Appendix 2 for the complete table). The figure shows the distribution of electrons for the first 18 elements, arranged in rows according to the number of electron shells (one, two, or three). Within each shell, electrons travel in different orbitals, which are discrete volumes of space in which electrons are most likely to be found. Each orbital can hold a maximum of 2 electrons. The first electron shell has one orbital and can hold only 2 electrons. Thus, hydrogen and helium are the only elements in the first row. For the second and third rows, the outer shell has four orbitals and can hold up to 8 electrons (four pairs).

It is the number of electrons present in the outermost shell, called the valence shell, that mostly determines the chemical properties of an atom. Atoms whose outer shells are not full tend to interact with other atoms in ways that enable them to complete or fill their valence shells.

Look at the electron shells of hydrogen, carbon, nitrogen, and oxygen—the four elements that are the main components of biological molecules (highlighted in green in Figure 2.5B). Because their outer shells are incomplete, these atoms react readily with other atoms. Atoms whose outer shells are full, such as helium, neon, and argon (in the right column of Figure 2.5B), will not interact readily with other atoms. These elements are said to be inert.

When two atoms with incomplete outer shells interact, they may give up, accept, or share electrons, so that both partners end up with completed outer shells. Such interactions usually result in atoms staying close together, held by attractions known as **chemical bonds**.

The actual transfer of an electron between atoms results in an attraction called an **ionic bond**. The sodium and chlorine atoms of salt (NaCl) are held together by ionic bonds. We will explore ionic bonds in Module 2.7.

In a **covalent bond**, atoms do not transfer electrons but actually share electrons between them. Sharing one or more pairs of electrons enables atoms to complete their outer shells. The number of covalent bonds an atom can form depends on the number of electrons needed to fill its valence shell. This number is called the valence, or bonding capacity, of an atom.

Let's look more closely at covalent bonds next.

? **Looking at the electron distribution diagrams for hydrogen, oxygen, nitrogen, and carbon, how many covalent bonds can each form?**

■ H = 1, O = 2, N = 3, C = 4

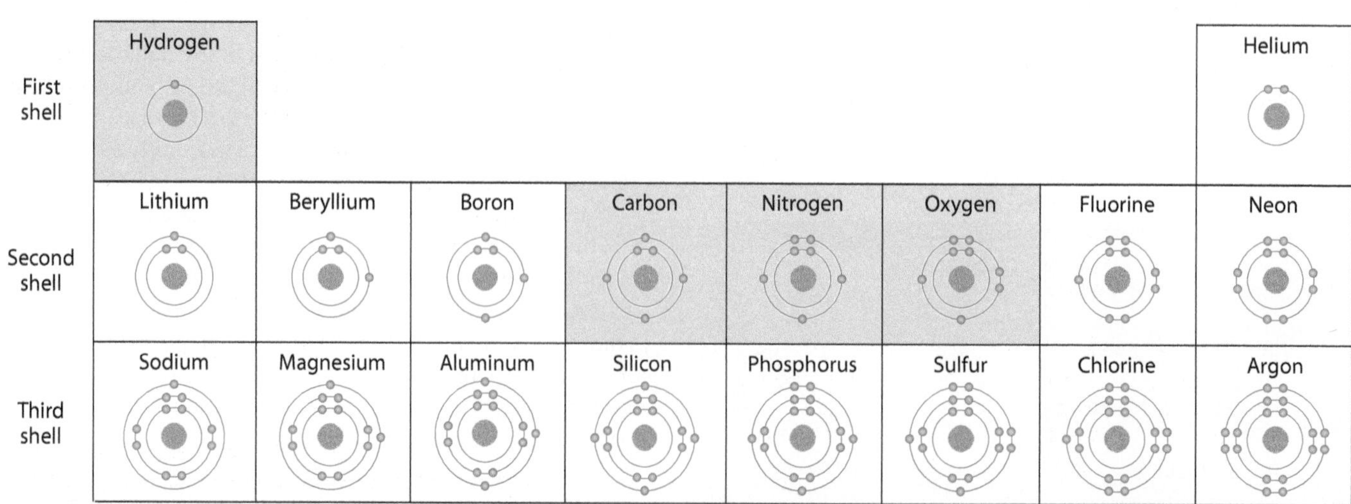

▲ **Figure 2.5B** The electron distribution diagrams of the first 18 elements in the periodic table

TRY THIS As you read from left to right across each row, describe how the number of electrons changes. Note that the electrons don't pair up until all orbitals have at least one electron.

VISUALIZING THE CONCEPT

2.6 Covalent bonds join atoms into molecules through electron sharing

A **molecule** consists of two or more atoms held together by covalent bonds. As shown below in the formation of a covalent bond, two hydrogen atoms, each with an unpaired electron, share a pair of electrons in a hydrogen molecule. The sharing of electrons in covalent bonds, however, is not always equal.

An atom's **electronegativity** is a measure of its attraction for shared electrons. In a covalent bond between two atoms of the same element, the electrons are shared equally because the two atoms have the same electronegativity. Such bonds are called **nonpolar covalent bonds**. Atoms of elements that are similar in electronegativity, such as carbon and hydrogen, also share electrons fairly equally between them.

When two atoms differ in electronegativity, they form a **polar covalent bond**. The negatively charged electrons are drawn more closely to the more electronegative element. As a result, that atom carries a partially negative charge and the other atom is partially positive. Oxygen is one of the most electronegative elements and is usually involved in polar covalent bonds.

To learn more about covalent bonds, study the four different ways to visually represent the four common molecules shown below.

Formation of a Covalent Bond

Proton

Electron cloud

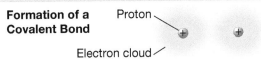

As two hydrogen atoms approach, the electron of each atom is also attracted to the proton in the other nucleus.

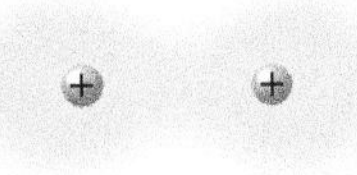

The two electrons become shared in a covalent bond, with each atom gaining a completed valence shell.

Four Common Molecules	Hydrogen	Oxygen	Methane	Water
Molecular Formula A molecular formula shows the number of atoms of each element in a molecule, using symbols and subscripts.	H_2	O_2	CH_4	H_2O
Electron Distribution Diagram An electron distribution diagram shows how each atom completes its outer shell by sharing one or more pairs of electrons.				
Structural Formula A structural formula shows a molecule's approximate shape and represents each covalent bond with a line.	H—H	O═O	H–C–H (with H above and below C)	O bonded to H and H
Space-Filling Model A space-filling model uses a color-coded ball for each atom and comes closest to representing a molecule's three-dimensional shape.				

Hydrogen has a single bond (a pair of shared electrons).

It takes 4 hydrogen atoms to satisfy carbon's valence of 4.

Oxygen has a double bond (indicated by a double line).

C and H are about equal in electronegativity and are joined by nonpolar covalent bonds.

(slightly –)

In a water molecule, shared electrons are pulled closer to the more electronegative oxygen atom, forming a polar covalent bond.

The oxygen atom has a slight negative charge as the negatively-charged electrons are pulled closer to it.

O

H

H

With its electron pulled closer to oxygen, the hydrogen atom has a slight positive charge.

(slightly +) (slightly +)

? Polarity refers to a separation of charges (think of the positive and negative poles of a battery). Explain why the bonds in a water molecule are polar covalent bonds?

The negatively charged electrons are pulled closer to oxygen, giving it a slight negative charge. With its electron pulled further away from its positively charged nucleus, the H is slightly positive.

2.7 Ionic bonds are attractions between ions of opposite charge

In some cases, two atoms are so unequal in their attraction for electrons that the more electronegative atom strips an electron completely away from its partner. Table salt (NaCl) is an example of how this transfer of electrons can bond atoms together. Notice in Figure 2.7A that sodium has only 1 electron in its outer shell, whereas chlorine has 7. When these atoms interact, the sodium atom's outer electron is transferred to chlorine. Sodium now has only two shells, the second shell having a full set of 8 electrons. And chlorine's outer shell is also now full with 8 electrons.

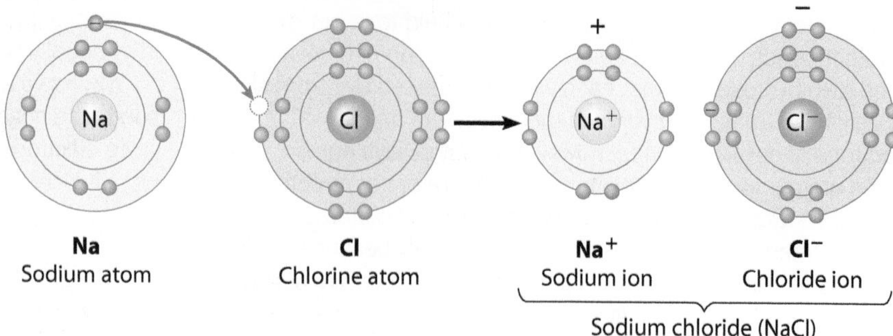

▲ Figure 2.7A Electron transfer and the formation of an ionic bond

TRY THIS Explain why the sodium ion has a positive charge and the chloride ion has a negative charge.

But how does this electron transfer result in an ionic bond between Na and Cl? Remember that electrons are negatively charged particles. The transfer of an electron moves one unit of negative charge from one atom to the other. Sodium, with 11 protons but now only 10 electrons, has a net electrical charge of 1+. Chlorine, having gained an extra electron, now has 18 electrons but only 17 protons, giving it a net electrical charge of 1−. In each case, an atom has become an **ion**—an atom or molecule with an electrical charge resulting from a gain or loss of one or more electrons. (Note that the names of negatively charged ions often end in *-ide*, such as *chloride.*) When the attraction between two ions with opposite charges holds them together, it is called an ionic bond. The resulting compound, in this case NaCl, is electrically neutral.

Sodium chloride is a familiar type of **salt**, a synonym for an ionic compound. Salts often exist as crystals in nature. Figure 2.7B shows the ions Na$^+$ and Cl$^-$ in a crystal of sodium chloride. An NaCl crystal can be of any size (there is no fixed number of ions), but sodium and chloride ions are always present in a 1:1 ratio. The ratio of ions can differ in the various kinds of salts.

The environment affects the strength of ionic bonds. In a dry salt crystal, the bonds are so strong that it takes a hammer and chisel to break enough of them to crack the crystal. If the same salt crystal is placed in water, however, the ionic bonds break when the ions interact with water molecules and the salt dissolves, as we'll discuss in Module 2.13. Most drugs are manufactured as salts because they are quite stable when dry but can dissolve easily in water.

▲ Figure 2.7B A crystal of sodium chloride

? Explain what holds together the ions in a crystal of table salt.

Opposite charges attract. The positively charged sodium ions (Na$^+$) and the negatively charged chloride ions (Cl$^-$) are held together by ionic bonds, attractions between oppositely charged ions.

2.8 Hydrogen bonds are weak bonds important in the chemistry of life

In living organisms, most of the strong chemical bonds are covalent, linking atoms to form a cell's molecules. But crucial to the functioning of a cell are weaker bonds within and between molecules, such as the ionic bonds we just discussed. One of the most important types of weak bonds is the **hydrogen bond**, which is best illustrated with water molecules.

As you saw in Module 2.6, the hydrogen atoms of a water molecule are attached to oxygen by polar covalent bonds. Because of these polar bonds and the wide V shape of the molecule, water is a **polar molecule**—that is, it has an unequal distribution of charges. It is slightly negative at the oxygen end of the molecule (the point of the V) and slightly positive at each of the two hydrogen ends. This partial positive charge allows each hydrogen to be attracted to—in a sense, to "flirt" with—a nearby atom (often an oxygen or nitrogen) that has a partial negative charge.

These "flirtations" are called hydrogen bonds because one atom in this type of attraction is always a hydrogen atom. Let's see how these weak bonds form between water molecules. Figure 2.8, on the facing page, shows how each hydrogen atom of a water molecule can form a hydrogen bond (depicted by dotted lines) with a nearby partially negative oxygen atom of another water molecule. The negative (oxygen) pole of a water

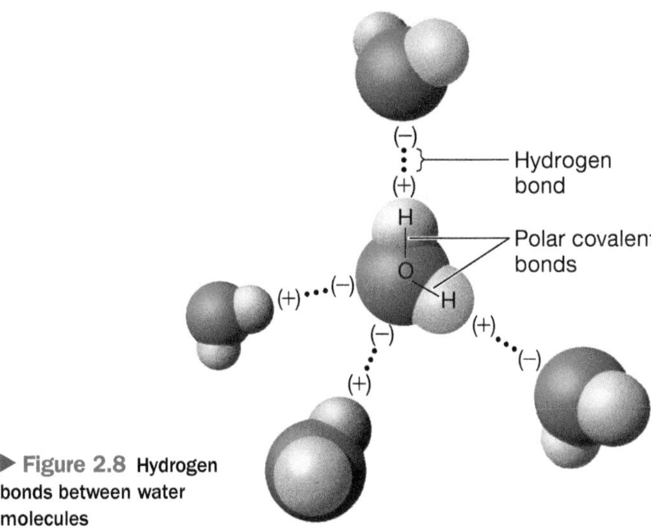

▶ **Figure 2.8** Hydrogen bonds between water molecules

TRY THIS Describe polar covalent bonds and hydrogen bonds and explain how they are related.

molecule can form hydrogen bonds to two hydrogen atoms. Thus, each water molecule can hydrogen-bond to as many as four partners.

You will learn later how hydrogen bonds help to create a protein's shape (and thus its function). The flow of INFORMATION, one of the core themes of biology, depends on hydrogen bonds. They hold the two strands of a DNA molecule together, and play key roles in translating hereditary information into proteins. Later in this chapter, we will explore how water's polarity and hydrogen bonds give it unique, life-supporting properties. But first we discuss how the making and breaking of bonds change the composition of matter.

? What enables neighboring water molecules to hydrogen-bond to one another?

■ The molecules are polar, with each positive end (hydrogen end) of one molecule attracted to the negative end (oxygen end) of another molecule.

2.9 Chemical reactions make and break chemical bonds

Your cells are constantly rearranging molecules in **chemical reactions**—breaking existing chemical bonds and forming new ones. A simple example of a chemical reaction is the reaction between hydrogen gas and oxygen gas that forms water (this is an explosive reaction, which, fortunately, does not occur in your cells):

$$2\,H_2 + O_2 \rightarrow 2\,H_2O$$

In this case, two molecules of hydrogen ($2\,H_2$) react with one molecule of oxygen (O_2) to produce two molecules of water ($2\,H_2O$). The arrow in the equation indicates the conversion of the starting materials, called the **reactants**, to the **product**, the material resulting from the chemical reaction. Notice that the same *numbers* of hydrogen and oxygen atoms appear on the left and right sides of the arrow, although they are grouped differently. Chemical reactions do not create or destroy matter; they only rearrange it in various ways. As shown in Figure 2.9, the covalent bonds (represented here as white "sticks" between atoms) holding hydrogen atoms together in H_2 and holding oxygen atoms together in O_2 are broken, and new bonds are formed to yield the H_2O product molecules.

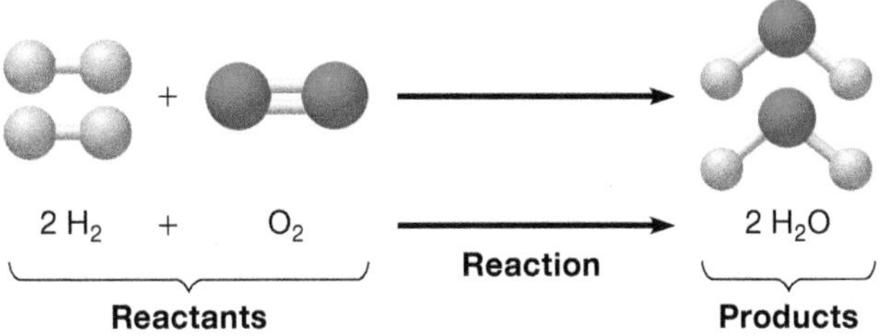

▲ **Figure 2.9** Breaking and making of bonds in a chemical reaction

Organisms cannot make water from H_2 and O_2, but they do carry out a great number of chemical reactions that rearrange matter in significant ways. Let's examine a chemical reaction that is essential to life on Earth: photosynthesis. The raw materials of photosynthesis are carbon dioxide (CO_2), which is taken from the air, and water (H_2O), which plants absorb from the soil. Within green plant cells, sunlight powers the conversion of these reactants to the sugar product glucose ($C_6H_{12}O_6$) and oxygen (O_2), a by-product that the plant releases into the air. The following chemical shorthand summarizes the process:

$$6\,CO_2 + 6\,H_2O \rightarrow C_6H_{12}O_6 + 6\,O_2$$

Although photosynthesis is actually a sequence of many chemical reactions, we still end up with the same number and kinds of atoms we started with. Illustrating our theme of ENERGY AND MATTER, we see that matter has been rearranged, with an input of energy provided by sunlight.

Your body routinely carries out thousands of chemical reactions. These reactions take place in the watery environment of your cells. We look at the life-supporting properties of water next.

? Fill in the blanks with the correct numbers in the following chemical process:

$$C_6H_{12}O_6 + \_\_O_2 \rightarrow \_\_CO_2 + \_\_H_2O$$

What process do you think this reaction represents? (*Hint:* Think about how your cells use these reactants to produce energy.)

■ $C_6H_{12}O_6 + 6\,O_2 \rightarrow 6\,CO_2 + 6\,H_2O$; the breakdown of sugar in the presence of oxygen to carbon dioxide and water, with the release of energy that the cell can use

Water's Life-Supporting Properties

2.10 Hydrogen bonds make liquid water cohesive

We can trace water's life-supporting properties to the structure and interactions of its molecules—their polarity and the resulting hydrogen bonding between molecules (review Figure 2.8).

Hydrogen bonds between molecules of liquid water last for only a few trillionths of a second, yet at any instant, many molecules are hydrogen-bonded to others. This tendency of molecules of the same kind to stick together, called **cohesion**, is much stronger for water than for most other liquids. The cohesion of water is important in the living world. Trees, for example, depend on cohesion to help transport water and nutrients from their roots to their leaves. The evaporation of water from a leaf exerts a pulling force on water within the veins of the leaf. Because of cohesion, the force is relayed all the way down to the roots. **Adhesion**, the clinging of one substance to another, also plays a role. As an example of the theme of STRUCTURE AND FUNCTION, the thinness of a plant's veins enhances the adhesion of water to its cell walls, helping to counter the downward pull of gravity.

▲ Figure 2.10 Surface tension allowing a water strider to walk on water

Related to cohesion is **surface tension**, a measure of how difficult it is to stretch or break the surface of a liquid. Hydrogen bonds give water unusually high surface tension, making it behave as though it were coated with an invisible film. You can observe the surface tension of water by slightly overfilling a glass; the water will stand above the rim. The water strider in Figure 2.10 takes advantage of the high surface tension of water to "stride" across ponds without breaking the surface.

? After a hard workout, you may notice "beads" of sweat on your face. Can you explain what holds the sweat in droplet form on your face?

■ The cohesion of water molecules and its high surface tension hold water in droplets. The adhesion of water to your skin helps hold the beads in place.

2.11 Water's hydrogen bonds moderate temperature

Thermal energy is the energy associated with the random movement of atoms and molecules. Thermal energy in transfer from a warmer to a cooler body of matter is defined as **heat**. **Temperature** measures the intensity of heat—that is, the *average* speed of molecules in a body of matter. If you have ever burned your finger on a metal pot while waiting for the water in it to boil, you know that water heats up much more slowly than metal. In fact, because of hydrogen bonding, water has a stronger resistance to temperature change than most other substances.

▲ Figure 2.11 Sweating as a mechanism of evaporative cooling

Heat must be absorbed to break hydrogen bonds, and heat is released when hydrogen bonds form. To raise the temperature of water, hydrogen bonds between water molecules must be broken before the molecules can move faster. Thus, water absorbs a large amount of heat (much of it used to disrupt hydrogen bonds) while warming up only a few degrees. Conversely, when water cools, water molecules slow down and more hydrogen bonds form, releasing a considerable amount of heat.

Earth's giant water supply moderates temperatures, helping to keep temperatures within limits that permit life. Oceans, lakes, and rivers store a huge amount of heat from the sun during warm periods. Heat given off from gradually cooling water warms the air. That's why coastal areas generally have milder climates than inland regions. Water's resistance to temperature change also stabilizes ocean temperatures, creating a favorable environment for marine life. Because water accounts for approximately 66% of your body weight, it also helps moderate your temperature.

When a substance evaporates (changes physical state from a liquid to a gas), the surface of the liquid that remains behind cools down. This **evaporative cooling** occurs because the molecules with the greatest energy (the "hottest" ones) leave. It's as if the 10 fastest runners on the track team left school, lowering the average speed of the remaining team. Evaporative cooling helps prevent some land-dwelling organisms from overheating. Evaporation from a plant's leaves keeps them from becoming too warm in the sun, just as sweating helps dissipate our excess body heat (Figure 2.11). On a much larger scale, the evaporation of surface waters cools tropical seas.

Explain the popular adage "It's not the heat, it's the humidity."

■ High humidity hampers cooling by slowing the evaporation of sweat.

2.12 Ice floats because it is less dense than liquid water

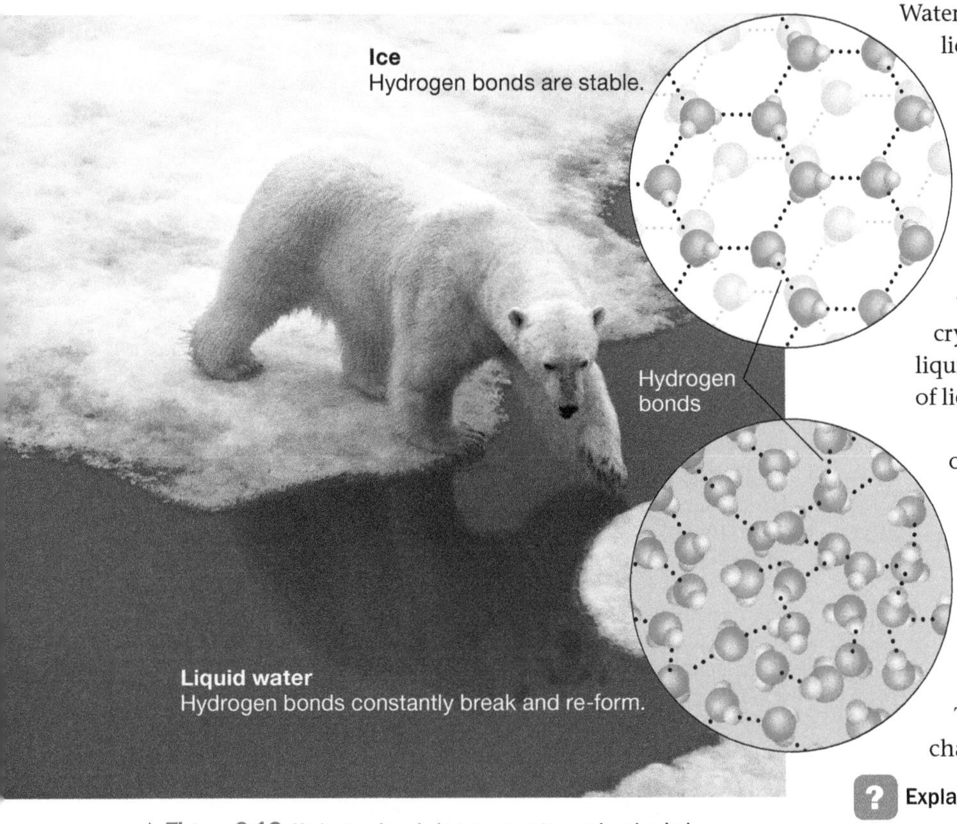

Ice
Hydrogen bonds are stable.

Hydrogen bonds

Liquid water
Hydrogen bonds constantly break and re-form.

▲ Figure 2.12 Hydrogen bonds between water molecules in ice and water

Water exists on Earth in three forms: gas (water vapor), liquid, and solid. Unlike most substances, water is less dense as a solid than as a liquid. As you might guess, this unusual property is due to hydrogen bonds.

As water freezes, each molecule forms stable hydrogen bonds with its neighbors, holding them at "arm's length" and creating a three-dimensional crystal. In Figure 2.12, compare the spaciously arranged molecules in the ice crystal with the more tightly packed molecules in the liquid water. The ice crystal has fewer molecules than an equal volume of liquid water. Therefore, ice is less dense and floats on top of liquid water.

If ice sank, then eventually ponds, lakes, and even oceans would freeze solid. Instead, when a body of water cools, the floating ice insulates the water from the colder air above it. This "blanket" of ice prevents the water from freezing and allows fish and other aquatic forms of life to survive under the frozen surface.

In the Arctic, this frozen surface serves as the winter hunting ground for polar bears (Figure 2.12). The shrinking of this ice cover as a result of climate change may doom these bears.

? **Explain how freezing water can crack boulders.**

Water in the crevices of a boulder expands as it freezes because the water molecules become spaced farther apart as ice crystals form.

2.13 Water is the solvent of life

If you add a teaspoon of salt to a glass of water, the salt will eventually dissolve, forming a solution. A **solution** is a liquid consisting of a uniform mixture of two or more substances. The dissolving agent (in our example, water) is the **solvent**, and a substance that is dissolved (in this case, salt) is a **solute**. An **aqueous solution** (from the Latin *aqua*, water) is one in which water is the solvent.

Water's versatility as a solvent results from the polarity of its molecules. Figure 2.13 shows how salt (NaCl) dissolves in water. The positively charged hydrogen ends of the water molecules are attracted to the negative chloride ions (Cl^-). And the oxygen ends of the water molecules, with their partial negative charge, cling to the positive sodium ions (Na^+). Working inward from the surface of each salt crystal, water molecules eventually surround and separate all the ions. Water dissolves other ionic compounds as well. Seawater, for instance, contains a great variety of dissolved ions, as do your cells.

A compound doesn't need to be ionic to dissolve in water. A spoonful of sugar will also dissolve in a glass of water. Polar molecules such as sugar dissolve as water molecules surround them and form hydrogen bonds with their polar regions. Even large molecules, such as proteins, can dissolve if they have ionic or polar regions on their surface.

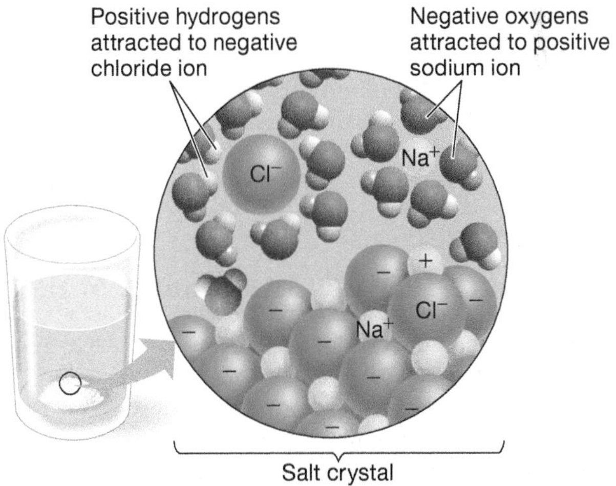

▲ Figure 2.13 A crystal of salt (NaCl) dissolving in water

As the solvent inside all cells, in blood, and in plant sap, water dissolves an enormous variety of solutes necessary for life.

? **Why are blood and most other biological fluids classified as aqueous solutions?**

The solvent in these fluids is water.

2.14 The chemistry of life is sensitive to acidic and basic conditions

In liquid water, a very small percentage of the water molecules dissociate or break apart into hydrogen ions (H^+) and hydroxide ions (OH^-). These ions are very reactive, and changes in their concentrations can drastically affect a cell's proteins and other complex molecules.

Some chemical compounds contribute additional H^+ to an aqueous solution, whereas others remove H^+ from it. A substance that donates hydrogen ions to solutions is called an **acid**. An example of a strong acid is hydrochloric acid (HCl), the acid in the gastric juice in your stomach. An acidic solution has a higher concentration of H^+ than OH^-.

A **base** is a substance that reduces the hydrogen ion concentration of a solution. Some bases, such as sodium hydroxide (NaOH), do this by donating OH^-; the OH^- combines with H^+ to form H_2O, thus reducing the H^+ concentration. Sodium hydroxide is a common ingredient in oven cleaners. Other bases accept H^+ ions from solution, resulting in a higher OH^- concentration.

We use the **pH scale** to describe how acidic or basic a solution is (pH stands for potential of hydrogen). As shown in Figure 2.14, the scale ranges from 0 (most acidic) to 14 (most basic). Each pH unit represents a 10-fold change in the concentration of H^+ in a solution. For example, lemon juice at pH 2 has 10 times more H^+ than an equal amount of a cola at pH 3 and 100 times more H^+ than tomato juice at pH 4.

Pure water and aqueous solutions that are neither acidic nor basic are said to be neutral; they have a pH of 7, and the concentrations of H^+ and OH^- are equal. The pH inside most cells is close to 7.

The pH of human blood is very close to 7.4. A person cannot survive for more than a few minutes if the blood pH drops to 7.0 or rises to 7.8. How can your body maintain a relatively constant pH in your cells and blood? Biological fluids contain **buffers**, substances that minimize changes in pH. They do so by accepting H^+ when it is in excess and donating H^+ when it is depleted.

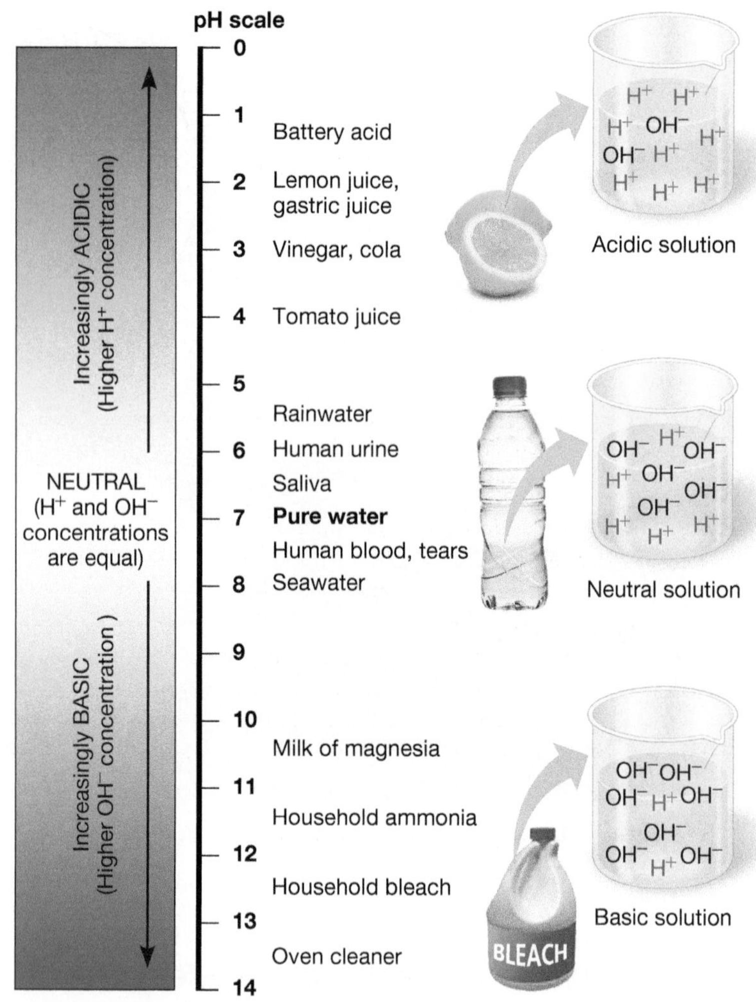

▲ Figure 2.14 The pH scale, which reflects the relative concentrations of H^+ and OH^-

? Compared to a basic solution at pH 9, the same volume of an acidic solution at pH 4 has ________ times more H^+.

■ 100,000

2.15 Scientists study the effects of rising atmospheric CO_2 on coral reef ecosystems

SCIENTIFIC THINKING

Will rising atmospheric CO_2 harm coral reefs?

Carbon dioxide is the main product of fossil fuel combustion, and its steadily increasing release into the atmosphere is linked to climate change (see Modules 7.14 and 38.4). About 25% of this CO_2 is absorbed by the oceans—and this naturally occurring remedy to excess CO_2 would seem to be a good thing. However, as CO_2 levels on the planet continue to rise, the increasing absorption of CO_2 is threatening to harm marine life and ecosystems.

In **ocean acidification**, CO_2 dissolving in seawater lowers the pH of the ocean. Recent studies estimate that the pH of the oceans is 0.1 pH unit lower now than at any time in the past 420,000 years and may rapidly drop another 0.3–0.5 pH unit from the current level of 8.1 by the end of this century. As an example of the importance of the theme of INTERACTIONS, scientists are studying the effects of such changes on marine organisms and ecosystems.

Several studies investigating the impact of a lower pH on coral reef ecosystems have looked at the process called calcification, in which coral animals combine calcium and carbonate ions to form their calcium carbonate skeletons. As seawater acidifies, the extra hydrogen ions (H^+) combine with carbonate ions (CO_3^{2-}) to form bicarbonate ions (HCO_3^-). This reaction reduces the carbonate ion concentration available to corals and other shell-building animals. Scientists predict that ocean acidification will cause the carbonate ion concentration to decrease by 40% by the year 2100.

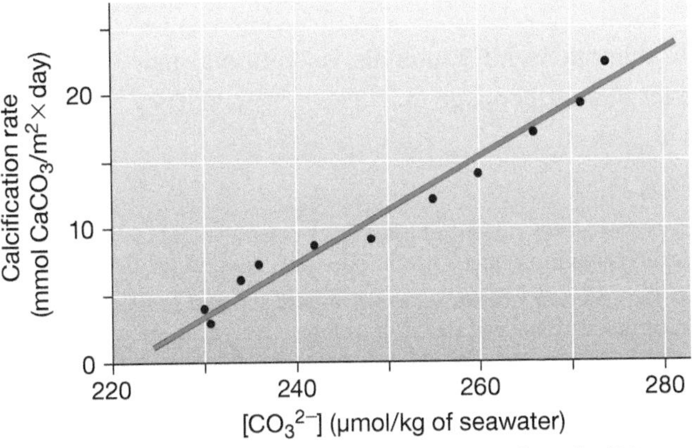

Source: Adaptation of figure 5 from "Effect of Calcium Carbonate Saturation State on the Calcification Rate of an Experimental Coral Reef" by C. Langdon, et al., from *Global Biogeochemical Cycles*, June 2000, Volume 14(2). American Geophysical Union.

▲ **Figure 2.15A The effect of carbonate ion concentration on calcification rate in an artificial coral reef system**

Scientists have looked at the effect of decreasing carbonate ion concentration on the rate of calcium deposition by reef organisms. The Biosphere 2 aquarium in Arizona contains a large coral reef system that behaves like a natural reef. Researchers measured how the calcification rate changed with differing amounts of dissolved carbonate ions. **Figure 2.15A** presents the results of one set of experiments, in which pH, temperature, and calcium ion concentration were held constant while the carbonate ion concentration of the seawater was varied. As you can see from the graph, the lower the concentration of carbonate ions, the lower the rate of calcification, and thus, the slower the growth of coral animals.

Controlled experiments such as this one have provided evidence that ocean acidification and the resulting reduction in carbonate ion concentration will negatively affect coral reefs. But scientists have also looked to natural habitats to study how ocean acidification affects coral reef ecosystems.

▲ **Figure 2.15B A "champagne" reef with bubbles of CO_2 rising from a volcanic seep**

A 2011 study looked at three volcanic seeps in Papua New Guinea. As you can see in **Figure 2.15B**, bubbles of CO_2 are released from underwater volcanoes around such "champagne reefs," lowering the pH of the water. Researchers surveyed three study sites in which the pH naturally varied from 8.1 to 7.8. They found reductions in coral diversity and the attachment of juvenile coral as the pH of the sites declined, both of which undermine the resiliency of a reef community. Researchers also found a shift to less structurally complex and slower-growing corals. The structural complexity of coral reef ecosystems makes them havens for a great diversity of organisms.

Scientists often synthesize their conclusions using multiple lines of evidence. The results from both controlled experimental studies and observational field studies of sites where pH naturally varies have dire implications for the health of coral reefs and the diversity of organisms they support.

? Identify the independent and dependent variables in the experiment depicted in Figure 2.15A.

■ The independent variable shown on the x axis is the concentration of carbonate ions, which the researchers manipulated. The dependent variable—the calcification rate, shown on the y axis—is what was measured in this experiment and was predicted to "depend on" or respond to the experimental treatment.

2.16 The search for extraterrestrial life centers on the search for water

EVOLUTION CONNECTION

When astrobiologists search for signs of life on distant planets, they look for evidence of water. Why? As we've seen in this chapter, the emergent properties of water support life on Earth in many ways. Is it possible that some form of life has evolved on other planets that have water in the environment? Scientists with the National Aeronautics and Space Administration (NASA) are exploring this question.

Like Earth, Mars has an ice cap at both poles, and scientists have found signs that water may exist elsewhere on the planet. In 2008, the robotic spacecraft Phoenix landed on Mars and sent back images showing ice present just under Mars's surface. The Curiosity rover, which landed on Mars in 2012, has measured a high percentage of water in its soil samples. And in 2013, the Opportunity rover, which has far outlasted its three-month mission begun in 2004, spotted types of clay in an ancient rock that suggest that neutral-pH water once flowed in the area.

Evidence of water has also come from the Mars Reconnaissance Orbiter. In 2011, high-resolution images sent to Earth revealed distinctive streaks along steep slopes during the Mars spring and summer, which then vanish during the winter, indicating that seasonal streams form when subsurface ice melts during the warm season. Then, in 2015, NASA announced that refined chemical readings taken from the orbiter identified waterlogged molecules in those streaks, providing evidence for liquid water on Mars' surface. These exciting finds have reinvigorated the search for signs of life, past or present, on Mars and other planets. If any life-forms or fossils are found, their study will shed light on the process of evolution from an entirely new perspective.

? Why is the presence of water important in the search for extraterrestrial life?

■ Water plays important roles in life as we know it, from moderating temperatures on the planet to functioning as the solvent for life.

CHAPTER 2 REVIEW

For practice quizzes, BioFlix animations, MP3 tutorials, video tutors, and more study tools designed for this textbook, go to MasteringBiology™

REVIEWING THE CONCEPTS

Elements, Atoms, and Compounds (2.1–2.4)

2.1 Organisms are composed of elements, usually combined into compounds. Oxygen, carbon, hydrogen, nitrogen, calcium, and phosphorus make up about 99% of living matter.

2.2 Trace elements are common additives to food and water.

2.3 Atoms consist of protons, neutrons, and electrons.

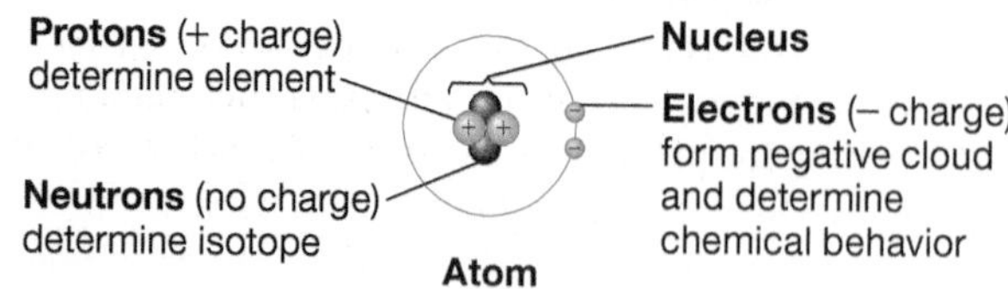

2.4 Radioactive isotopes can help or harm us. Radioactive isotopes are valuable in basic research and medicine.

Chemical Bonds (2.5–2.9)

2.5 The distribution of electrons determines an atom's chemical properties. An atom whose outer electron shell is not full tends to interact with other atoms and share, gain, or lose electrons, resulting in attractions called chemical bonds.

2.6 Covalent bonds join atoms into molecules through electron sharing. In a nonpolar covalent bond, electrons are shared equally. In polar covalent bonds, such as those found in water, electrons are pulled closer to the more electronegative atom.

2.7 Ionic bonds are attractions between ions of opposite charge. Electron gain and loss create charged atoms, called ions.

2.8 Hydrogen bonds are weak bonds important in the chemistry of life. The slightly positively charged H atoms in one polar molecule may be attracted to the partial negative charge of an oxygen or nitrogen atom in a neighboring molecule.

2.9 Chemical reactions make and break chemical bonds. The composition of matter is changed as bonds are broken and formed to convert reactants to products.

Water's Life-Supporting Properties (2.10–2.16)

2.10 Hydrogen bonds make liquid water cohesive. Cohesion creates surface tension and helps water to move from plant roots to leaves.

2.11 Water's hydrogen bonds moderate temperature. Heat is absorbed when hydrogen bonds break and released when hydrogen bonds form. This helps keep temperatures relatively steady. As the most energetic water molecules evaporate, the surface of a substance cools.

2.12 Ice floats because it is less dense than liquid water. Floating ice protects lakes and oceans from freezing solid, which in turn protects aquatic life.

Liquid water: Hydrogen bonds constantly break and re-form

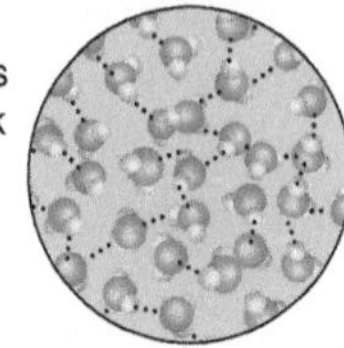

Ice: Stable hydrogen bonds hold molecules apart

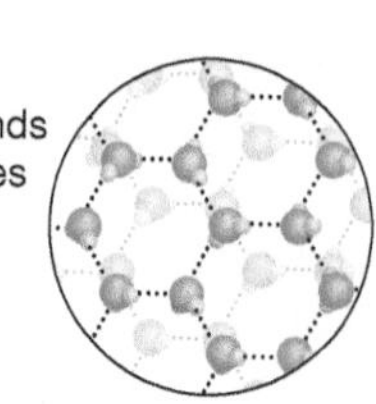

2.13 Water is the solvent of life. Polar or charged solutes dissolve when water molecules surround them, forming aqueous solutions.

2.14 The chemistry of life is sensitive to acidic and basic conditions. A compound that releases H^+ in solution is an acid, and one that accepts H^+ is a base. The pH scale ranges from 0 (most acidic) to 14 (most basic). The pH of most cells is close to 7 (neutral) and is kept that way by buffers.

2.15 Scientists study the effects of rising atmospheric CO_2 on coral reef ecosystems. The acidification of the ocean threatens coral reefs and other marine organisms.

2.16 The search for extraterrestrial life centers on the search for water. The emergent properties of water support life on Earth and may contribute to the potential for life to have evolved on other planets.

CONNECTING THE CONCEPTS

1. Fill in the blanks in this concept map to help you tie together the key concepts concerning elements, atoms, and molecules.

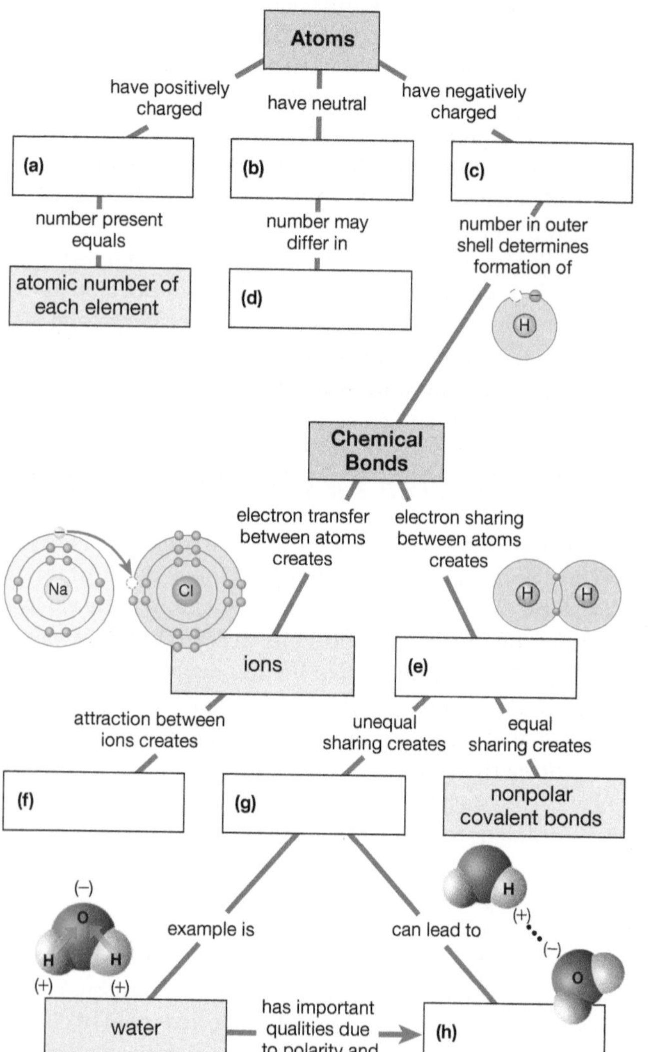

2. Create a concept map to organize your understanding of the life-supporting properties of water. A sample map is in the answer section, but the value of this exercise is in the thinking and integrating you must do to create your own map.

TESTING YOUR KNOWLEDGE

Level 1: Knowledge/Comprehension

3. Changing the ________ would change it into an atom of a different element.
   a. number of electrons surrounding the nucleus of an atom
   b. number of protons in the nucleus of an atom
   c. electrical charge of an atom
   d. number of neutrons in the nucleus of an atom
4. What is chemically nonsensical about this structure?

   H—C=C—H
5. A solution at pH 6 contains ________ H^+ than the same amount of a solution at pH 8.
   a. 20 times more
   b. 100 times more
   c. 2 times less
   d. 100 times less
6. Most of the unique properties of water result from the fact that water molecules
   a. are the most abundant molecules on Earth's surface.
   b. are held together by covalent bonds.
   c. are constantly in motion.
   d. are polar and form hydrogen bonds.
7. A can of cola consists mostly of sugar dissolved in water, with some carbon dioxide gas that makes it fizzy and makes the pH less than 7. In chemical terms, you could say that cola is an aqueous solution where water is the ________, sugar is a ________, and carbon dioxide makes the solution ________.
   a. solvent . . . solute . . . basic
   b. solute . . . solvent . . . basic
   c. solvent . . . solute . . . acidic
   d. solute . . . solvent . . . acidic

Level 2: Application/Analysis

8. The atomic number of sulfur (S) is 16. Sulfur combines with hydrogen by covalent bonding to form a compound, hydrogen sulfide. Based on the number of valence electrons in a sulfur atom, predict the molecular formula of the compound. (*Explain your answer.*)
   a. HS
   b. H_2S
   c. H_4S_2
   d. H_4S
9. In what way does the need for iodine or iron in your diet differ from your need for calcium or phosphorus?
10. Use carbon-12, the most common isotope of carbon, to define these terms: atomic number, mass number, valence. Which of these numbers is most related to the chemical behavior of an atom? Explain.
11. In terms of electron sharing between atoms, compare nonpolar covalent bonds, polar covalent bonds, and ions.
12. The diagram below shows the arrangement of electrons around the nucleus of a fluorine and a potassium atom. What kind of bond do you think would form between these two atoms?

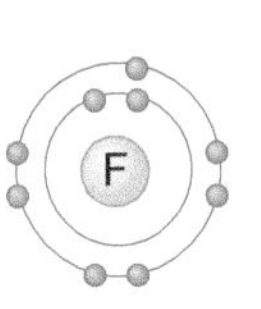

Fluorine atom

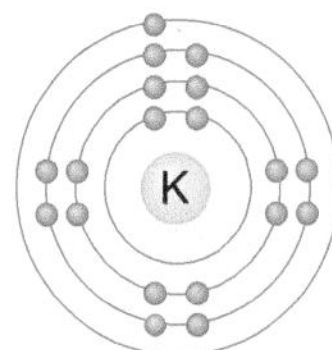

Potassium atom

Level 3: Synthesis/Evaluation

13. Look back at the abbreviated periodic table of the elements in Figure 2.5B. If two elements are in the same row, what do they have in common? If two elements are in the same column, what do they have in common? Would you predict that elements in the same row or the same column will have similar chemical properties? Explain.
14. What do you think the effect on the properties of water would be if oxygen and hydrogen had equal electronegativity?
15. **SCIENTIFIC THINKING** A recent experimental study looked at the combined effects of ocean acidification (see Module 2.15) and increased ocean temperatures, both aspects of climate change, on the growth of polyps, juvenile coral animals. Researchers reported the average polyp biomass (in μg/polyp) after 42 days of growth under four treatments: a control with pH and temperature maintained close to normal reef conditions, a pH lowered by 0.2 units, a temperature raised by 1°C, and a combined lower pH and higher temperature. The results showed that polyp biomass was reduced somewhat in both the low-pH and high-temperature treatments, but the combined treatment resulted in a reduction in growth by almost a third—a statistically significant result. Experiments often look at the effects of changing one variable at a time, while keeping all other variables constant. Explain why this experiment considered two variables—both a higher temperature and a lower pH—at the same time.
16. In agricultural areas, farmers pay close attention to the weather forecast. Right before a predicted overnight freeze, farmers spray water on crops to protect the plants. Use the properties of water to explain how this method works. Be sure to mention why hydrogen bonds are responsible for this phenomenon.
17. This chapter explains how the emergent properties of water contribute to the suitability of the environment for life. Until fairly recently, scientists assumed that other physical requirements for life included a moderate range of temperature, pH, and atmospheric pressure. That view has changed with the discovery of organisms known as extremophiles, which have been found flourishing in hot, acidic sulfur springs and around hydrothermal vents deep in the ocean. What does the existence of life in such environments say about the possibility of life on other planets?

Answers to all questions can be found in Appendix 4.

The Molecules of Cells

CHAPTER 3

Is a big glass of milk a way to a healthy diet—or an upset stomach? Quite often, the answer is the latter. Most of the world's adult populations cannot easily digest milk-based foods. Such people suffer from lactose intolerance, the inability to properly break down lactose, the main sugar found in milk. Almost all infants are able to drink breast milk or other dairy products, benefiting from the proteins, fats, and sugars in this nutritious food. But as they grow older, many people find that drinking milk comes with a heavy dose of digestive discomfort.

What does evolution have to do with drinking milk?

The young woman in the photograph on the right can enjoy drinking milk because her body continues to produce lactase—the enzyme that speeds the digestion of lactose into smaller sugars that her digestive system can absorb. In most human populations, the production of this enzyme begins to decline after the age of 2. In the United States, as many as 80% of African Americans and Native Americans and 90% of Asian Americans are lactase-deficient once they reach their teenage years. Americans of northern European descent make up one of the few groups in which lactase production continues into adulthood. Why are some people lactose tolerant while others are not? As you'll find out later in this chapter, the answer has to do with evolution and the inheritance of a genetic mutation that occurred in the ancestors of certain groups.

In people who easily digest milk, lactose (a sugar) is broken down by lactase (a protein), which is coded for by a gene made of DNA (a nucleic acid). Such molecular interactions, repeated in countless variations, drive all biological processes. In this chapter, we explore the structure and function of sugars, proteins, fats, and nucleic acids—the biological molecules that are essential to life. We begin with a look at carbon, the versatile atom at the center of life's molecules.

BIG IDEAS

Introduction to Organic Compounds (3.1–3.3)

Carbon-containing compounds are the chemical building blocks of life.

Carbohydrates (3.4–3.7)

Carbohydrates serve as a cell's fuel and building material.

Lipids (3.8–3.11)

Lipids are hydrophobic molecules with diverse functions.

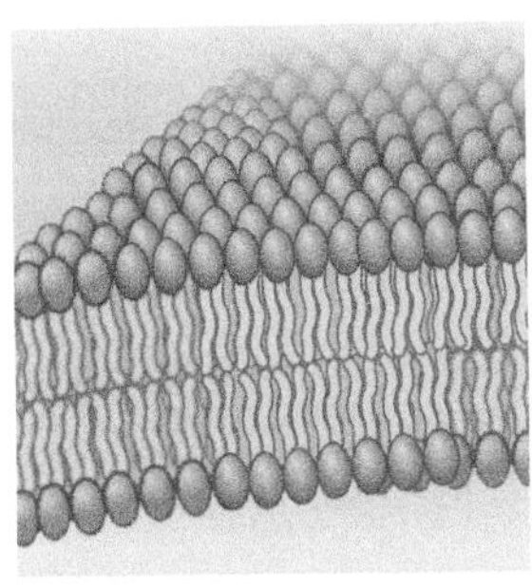

Proteins (3.12–3.14)

Proteins are essential to the structures and functions of life.

Nucleic Acids (3.15–3.16)

Nucleic acids store, transmit, and help express hereditary information.

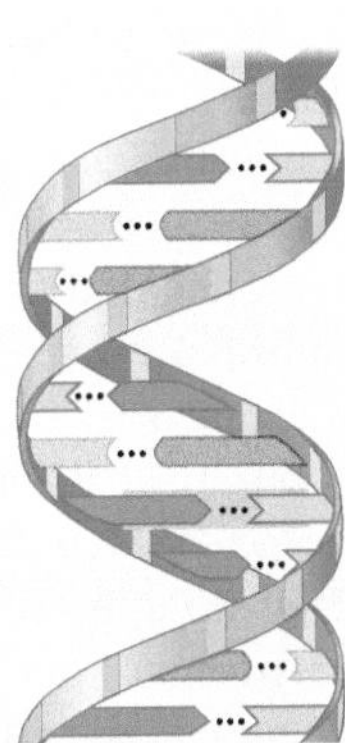

Introduction to Organic Compounds

3.1 Life's molecular diversity is based on the properties of carbon

When it comes to making molecules, carbon usually takes center stage. Almost all the molecules a cell makes are composed of carbon atoms bonded to one another and to atoms of other elements. Carbon is unparalleled in its ability to form large and complex molecules, which build the structures and carry out the functions required for life. Carbon-based molecules are called **organic compounds**, and they usually contain hydrogen atoms in addition to carbon.

Why are carbon atoms the lead players in the chemistry of life? Remember that the number of electrons in the outermost shell determines an atom's chemical properties. A carbon atom has 4 electrons in a valence shell that holds 8. Carbon completes its outer shell by sharing electrons with other atoms in four covalent bonds (see Module 2.6).

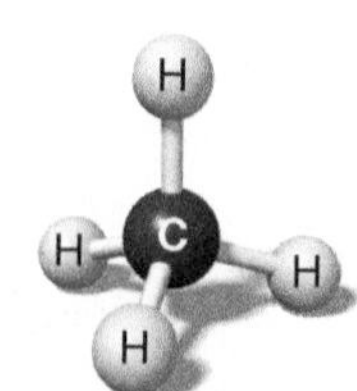

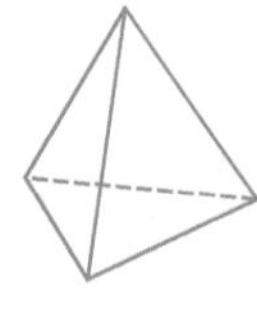

▲ **Figure 3.1A** A model of methane (CH_4) and the tetrahedral shape of a molecule (outlined in red) in which a carbon atom has four single bonds to other atoms

Figure 3.1A presents a ball-and-stick model of methane (CH_4), one of the simplest organic molecules and the main component of natural gas. It shows that carbon's four bonds (the white "sticks") angle out toward the corners of an imaginary tetrahedron (an object with four triangular sides, as sketched in red). This shape occurs wherever a carbon atom participates in four single bonds. In molecules with more than one carbon, each carbon atom is a connecting point from which a molecule can branch in up to four directions. In addition, different shapes occur when carbon atoms form double bonds. Thanks to the geometry of carbon's bonds, organic molecules can have very elaborate shapes. As you will see repeatedly, a molecule's shape usually determines its function.

Carbon chains form the backbone of most organic molecules. **Figure 3.1B** illustrates four ways in which such "carbon skeletons" (shaded in gray in the figure) can vary. They may differ in length and can be straight, branched, or arranged in rings. Carbon skeletons may also include double bonds, which can vary in number and location.

Notice that the two compounds on the bottom left of Figure 3.1B, butane and isobutane, have the same molecular formula, C_4H_{10}. They differ, however, in the arrangement of their carbon skeleton. The two molecules on the top right also have the same numbers of atoms (C_4H_8), but they have different three-dimensional shapes because of the location of the double bond. Compounds with the same formula but different structural arrangements are called **isomers**. The different shapes of isomers add greatly to the diversity of organic molecules and their properties.

Isomers can also result from the different spatial arrangements that can occur when four different partners are bonded to a carbon atom. This type of isomer is important in the pharmaceutical industry, because the two isomers of a drug may not be equally effective or may have different (and sometimes harmful) effects.

Methane (Figure 3.1A) and the compounds illustrated in Figure 3.1B are **hydrocarbons**, molecules consisting of only carbon and hydrogen. Hydrocarbons are the major components of petroleum and provide much of the world's energy. Hydrocarbons are rare in living organisms, but hydrocarbon chains are found in regions of some molecules. For instance, fats contain hydrocarbon chains that provide fuel to your body.

In the next module, we see how attaching atoms other than just hydrogen to carbon skeletons produces a huge diversity of biological molecules.

? **Methamphetamine occurs as two isomers: one is the addictive illegal drug known as "crank"; the other is a sinus medication. How can you explain these differing effects?**

■ Isomers have different structures, or shapes, and the shape of a molecule usually determines the way it functions in the body.

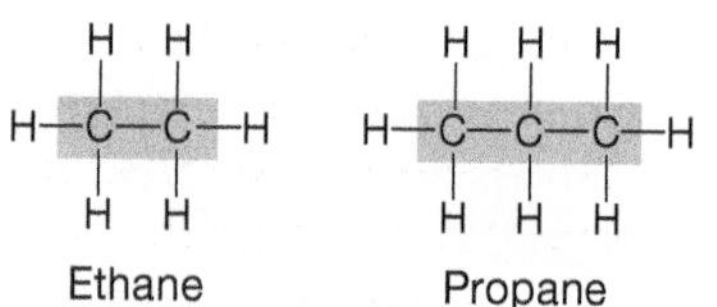

Length: Carbon skeletons vary in length.

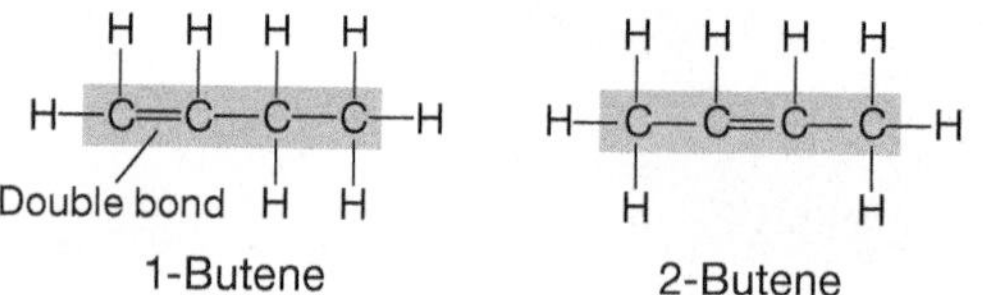

Double bonds: Carbon skeletons may have double bonds, which can vary in location.

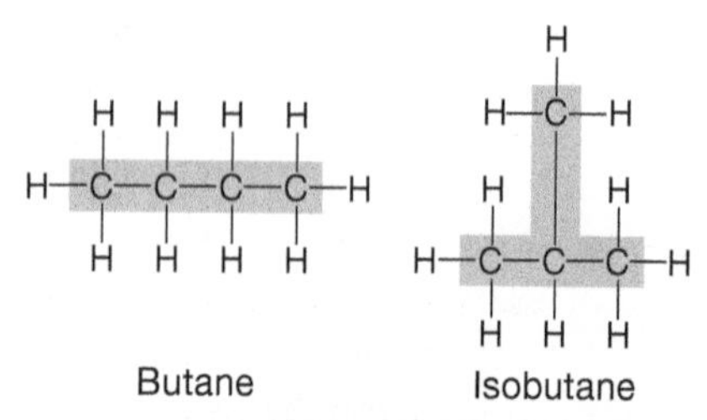

Branching: Carbon skeletons may be unbranched or branched.

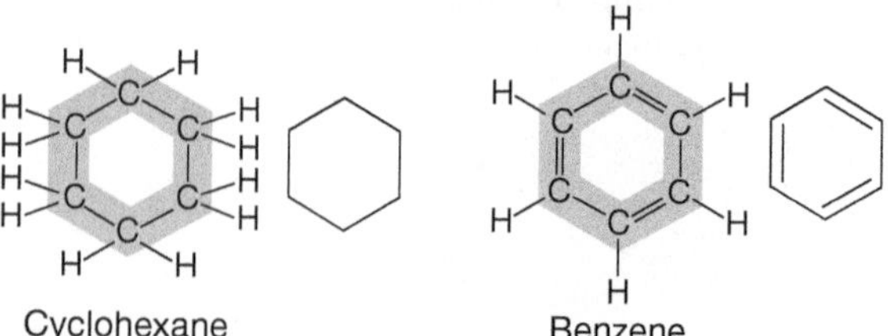

Rings: Carbon skeletons may be arranged in rings. (In the abbreviated ring structures, each corner represents a carbon and its attached hydrogens.)

▲ **Figure 3.1B** Four ways in which carbon skeletons can vary

TRY THIS Decide whether cyclohexane and benzene are isomers or not and then explain your decision.

3.2 A few chemical groups are key to the functioning of biological molecules

An organic compound's properties depend not only on the size and shape of its carbon backbone but also on the atoms attached to that skeleton.

Figure 3.2 shows what a difference chemical groups can make. The hormones testosterone and estradiol (a type of estrogen) differ only in the groups of atoms highlighted with colored boxes. These small differences affect how the molecules function, helping to produce male and female features in lions, humans, and other vertebrates.

Table 3.2 illustrates six important chemical groups. The first five are called **functional groups**. They affect a molecule's function by participating in chemical reactions. These groups are polar, which tends to make compounds containing them **hydrophilic** (water-loving) and therefore soluble in water—a necessary condition for their roles in water-based life. The sixth group, a methyl group, is nonpolar and not reactive, but it affects molecular shape and thus function.

A **hydroxyl group** consists of a hydrogen atom bonded to an oxygen atom. Ethanol, shown in the table, and other organic compounds containing hydroxyl groups are called alcohols.

In a **carbonyl group**, a carbon atom is linked by a double bond to an oxygen atom. The carbonyl group can be located within or at the end of a carbon skeleton. Simple sugars contain a carbonyl group and several hydroxyl groups.

A **carboxyl group** consists of a carbon double-bonded to an oxygen atom and also bonded to a hydroxyl group. As shown by the double arrows in the figure, the carboxyl group can act as an acid by contributing an H^+ to a solution (see Module 2.14) and thus becoming ionized. Compounds with carboxyl groups are called carboxylic acids.

TABLE 3.2 Important Chemical Groups Of Organic Compounds

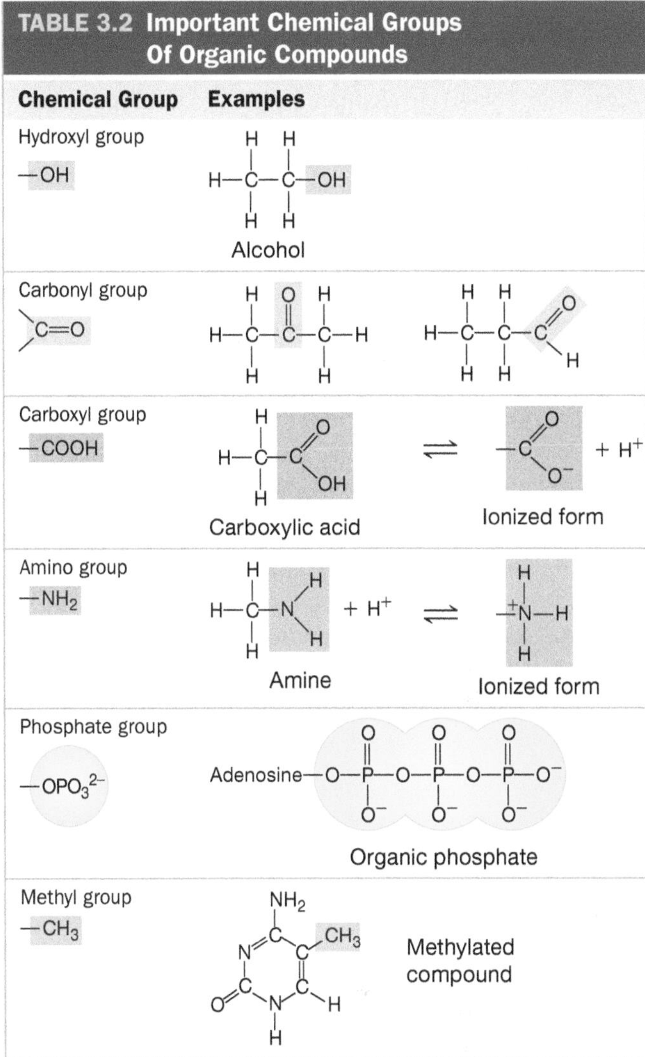

Chemical Group	Examples
Hydroxyl group $-OH$	Alcohol
Carbonyl group $>C=O$	
Carboxyl group $-COOH$	Carboxylic acid ⇌ Ionized form $+ H^+$
Amino group $-NH_2$	Amine $+ H^+$ ⇌ Ionized form
Phosphate group $-OPO_3^{2-}$	Adenosine—O—P—O—P—O—P—O⁻ Organic phosphate
Methyl group $-CH_3$	Methylated compound

▲ Figure 3.2 Differences in the chemical groups of sex hormones

An **amino group** has a nitrogen bonded to two hydrogens. It can act as a base by picking up an H^+ from a solution and becoming ionized. Organic compounds with an amino group are called amines. The building blocks of proteins—amino acids—contain an amino and a carboxyl group.

A **phosphate group** consists of a phosphorus atom bonded to four oxygen atoms. It too is usually ionized, as you can see by the negatively charged oxygens in the figure. Compounds with phosphate groups are called organic phosphates and are often involved in energy transfers, as is the energy-rich compound ATP (adenosine triphosphate), shown in the table.

A **methyl group** consists of a carbon bonded to three hydrogen atoms. The methylated compound in the table—a component of DNA—affects the expression of genes.

You will meet these chemical groups again as you learn about the four major classes of organic molecules. But first, let's see how your cells make large molecules out of smaller ones.

? **Identify the chemical groups that do *not* contain carbon.**

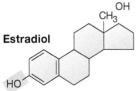

■ The hydroxyl, amino, and phosphate groups

3.3 Cells make large molecules from a limited set of small molecules

Given the rich complexity of life on Earth, we might expect there to be an enormous diversity of types of molecules. Remarkably, however, the important molecules of all living things—from bacteria to elephants—fall into just four main classes: carbohydrates, lipids, proteins, and nucleic acids. On a molecular scale, molecules of three of these classes—carbohydrates, proteins, and nucleic acids—can be gigantic; in fact, biologists call them **macromolecules**. For example, a protein may consist of thousands of atoms. How does a cell make such a huge molecule?

Cells make most of their macromolecules by joining smaller molecules into chains called **polymers** (from the Greek *polys*, many, and *meros*, part). A polymer is a long molecule consisting of many identical or similar building blocks strung together, much as a train consists of a chain of cars. The building blocks of polymers are called **monomers**.

Making Polymers Cells link monomers together to form polymers by a **dehydration reaction**, a reaction that removes a molecule of water as two molecules become bonded together. Each monomer contributes part of the water molecule that is released during the reaction. As you can see on the left side of Figure 3.3, one monomer (the one at the right end of the short polymer in this example) loses a hydroxyl group and the other monomer loses a hydrogen atom to form H_2O. As this occurs, a new covalent bond forms, linking the two monomers. Dehydration reactions are the same regardless of the specific monomers and the type of polymer the cell is producing.

Breaking Polymers Cells not only make macromolecules but also have to break them down. For example, most of the organic molecules in your food are in the form of polymers that are much too large to enter your cells. You must digest these polymers to make their monomers available to your cells. This digestion process is called **hydrolysis**. Essentially the reverse of a dehydration reaction, hydrolysis means to break (*lyse*) with water (*hydro-*). As the right side of Figure 3.3 shows, the bond between monomers is broken by the addition of a water molecule, with the hydroxyl group from the water attaching to one monomer and a hydrogen attaching to the adjacent monomer.

The lactose-intolerant individuals you learned about in the chapter introduction are unable to hydrolyze such a bond in the sugar lactose because they lack the enzyme lactase. Both dehydration reactions and hydrolysis require the help of enzymes to make and break bonds. **Enzymes** are specialized macromolecules that speed up chemical reactions in cells.

The Diversity of Polymers The diversity of macromolecules in the living world is vast. Surprisingly, a cell makes all its thousands of different macromolecules from a small list of ingredients—about 40 to 50 common components and a few others that are rare. Proteins, for example, are built from only 20 kinds of amino acids. Your DNA is built from just four kinds of monomers called nucleotides. The key to the great diversity of polymers is arrangement—variation in the sequence in which monomers are strung together.

The variety in polymers accounts for the uniqueness of each organism. The monomers themselves, however, are essentially universal. Your proteins and those of a tree or an ant are assembled from the same 20 amino acids. Life has a simple yet elegant molecular logic: Small molecules common to all organisms are ordered into large molecules, which vary from species to species and even from individual to individual in the same species.

In the remainder of the chapter, we explore each of the four classes of large biological molecules. Like water and simple organic molecules, large biological molecules have unique emergent properties arising from the orderly arrangement of their atoms. For these molecules of life, as for all things biological, STRUCTURE AND FUNCTION are related.

? Suppose you eat some cheese. What reactions must occur for the protein of the cheese to be broken down into its amino acid monomers and then for these monomers to be converted to proteins in your body?

■ In digestion, the proteins are broken down into amino acids by hydrolysis. New proteins are formed in your body cells from these monomers in dehydration reactions.

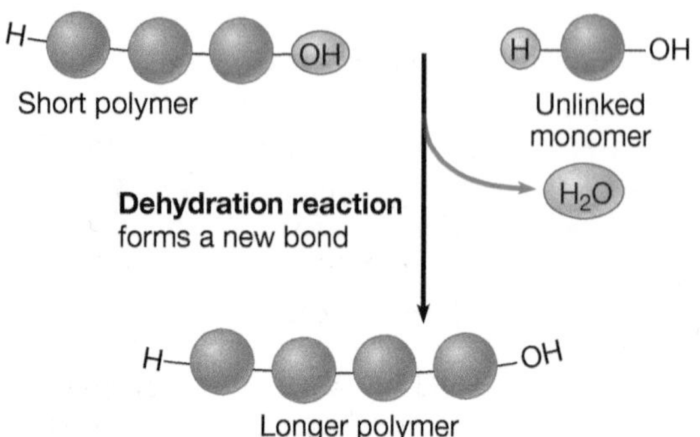

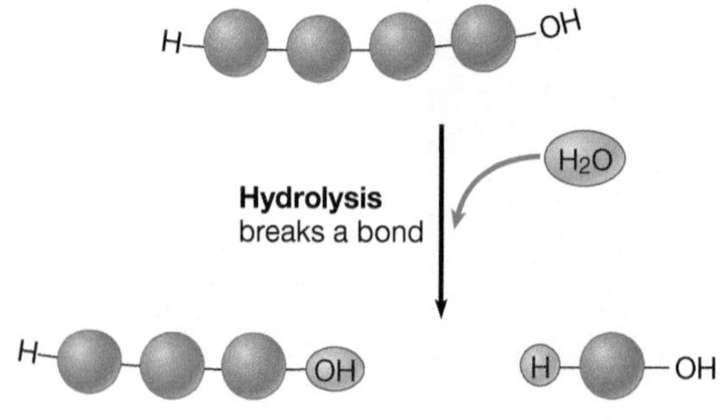

▲ **Figure 3.3** Dehydration reaction building a polymer (left); Hydrolysis breaking down a polymer (right)

Carbohydrates

3.4 Monosaccharides are the simplest carbohydrates

Let's start our survey of biological molecules with **carbohydrates**, the class of molecules that range from small sugar molecules, such as those dissolved in soft drinks, to large polysaccharides, such as the starch molecules we consume in pasta and potatoes.

Simple sugars, or **monosaccharides** (from the Greek *monos*, single, and *sacchar*, sugar), are the monomers of carbohydrates. The honey shown in Figure 3.4A consists mainly of monosaccharides called glucose and fructose. These and other single-unit sugars can be hooked together by dehydration reactions to form more complex sugars and polysaccharides.

Monosaccharides generally have molecular formulas that are some multiple of CH_2O. For example, the formula for **glucose**, a common monosaccharide of central importance in the chemistry of life, is $C_6H_{12}O_6$. Figure 3.4B illustrates the molecular structure of glucose, with its carbons numbered 1 to 6. This structure also shows the two trademarks of a sugar: a number of hydroxyl groups (—OH) and a carbonyl group ($>$C=O).

If you count the numbers of different atoms in the fructose molecule in Figure 3.4B, you will find that its molecular formula is $C_6H_{12}O_6$, identical to that of glucose. Thus, glucose and fructose are isomers; they differ only in the arrangement of their atoms (in this case, the positions of the carbonyl groups, highlighted in blue). Because the shape of molecules is so important, seemingly minor differences like this give isomers different properties, such as how they react with other molecules. These differences also make fructose taste considerably sweeter than glucose.

The carbon skeletons of both glucose and fructose are six carbon atoms long. Other monosaccharides may have three to seven carbons. Five-carbon sugars, called pentoses, and six-carbon sugars, called hexoses, are among the most common. (Note that most names for sugars end in *-ose*. Also, as you saw with the enzyme lactase, which digests the sugar lactose, the names for most enzymes end in *-ase*.)

It is convenient to draw sugars as if their carbon skeletons were linear, but in aqueous solutions, most five- and six-carbon sugars form rings, as shown for glucose in Figure 3.4C. To form the glucose ring, carbon 1 bonds to the oxygen attached to carbon 5, with carbon 6 extending above the ring. As shown in the middle representation, the ring diagram of glucose and other sugars may be abbreviated by not showing the carbon atoms at the corners of the ring. Also, the bonds in the ring are often drawn with varied thickness, indicating that the ring is a relatively flat structure with attached atoms extending above and below it. The simplified ring symbol on the right is often used in this text to represent glucose.

Monosaccharides, particularly glucose, are the main fuel molecules for cellular work. Because cells release energy from glucose when they break it down, an aqueous solution of glucose (often called dextrose) may be injected into the bloodstream of sick or injured patients; the glucose provides an immediate energy source to tissues in need of repair. Cells also use the carbon skeletons of monosaccharides as raw material for making other kinds of organic molecules, such as amino acids and fatty acids. The use of sugars as both energy resources and organic building blocks clearly illustrates the theme of the transformation of ENERGY AND MATTER.

? Write the formula for a monosaccharide that has three carbons.

■ $C_3H_6O_3$

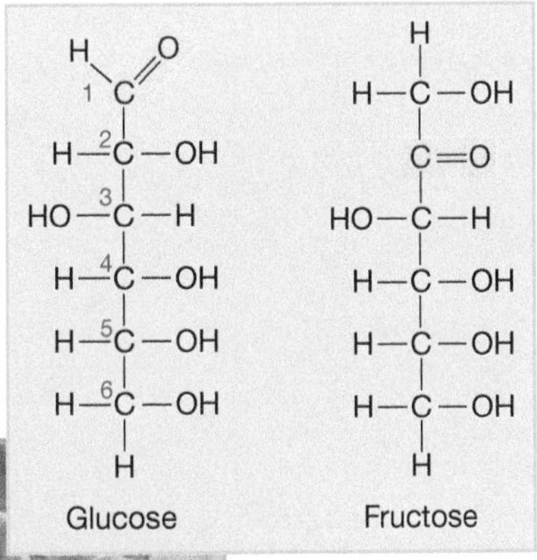

Glucose:
H—C(1)=O; H—C(2)—OH; HO—C(3)—H; H—C(4)—OH; H—C(5)—OH; H—C(6)—OH; H

Fructose:
H; H—C—OH; C=O; HO—C—H; H—C—OH; H—C—OH; H—C—OH; H

◀ **Figure 3.4B** Structures of glucose and fructose

TRY THIS In these structural formulas, identify the two functional groups that are characteristic of a monosaccharide.

▲ **Figure 3.4A** Bees with honey, a mixture of two monosaccharides

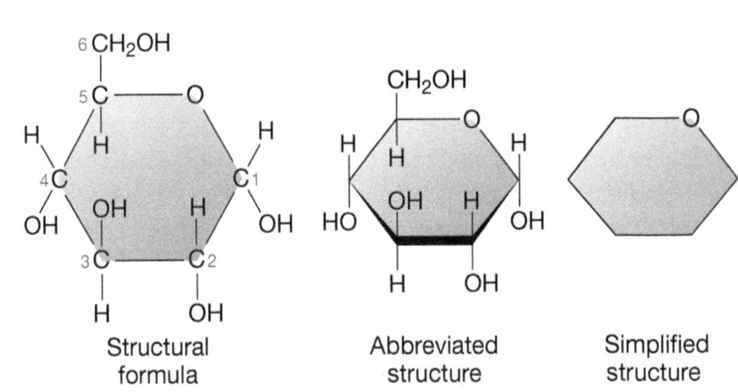

▲ **Figure 3.4C** Three representations of the ring form of glucose

3.5 Two monosaccharides are linked to form a disaccharide

Cells construct a **disaccharide** from two monosaccharide monomers by a dehydration reaction. Figure 3.5 shows how maltose, also called malt sugar, is formed from two glucose monomers. One monomer gives up a hydroxyl group and the other gives up a hydrogen atom. As H_2O is released, an oxygen atom is left, linking the two monomers. Malt sugar, which is common in germinating seeds, is used in making beer, malt whiskey, and malted milk candy.

Sucrose is the most common disaccharide. It is made of a glucose monomer linked to a fructose monomer. Transported in plant sap, sucrose provides a source of energy and raw materials to all the parts of the plant. We extract it from the stems of sugarcane or the roots of sugar beets to use as table sugar.

? **Lactose, as you read in the chapter introduction, is the disaccharide sugar in milk. It is formed from glucose and galactose. The formula for both these monosaccharides is $C_6H_{12}O_6$. What is the formula for lactose?**

■ $C_{12}H_{22}O_{11}$

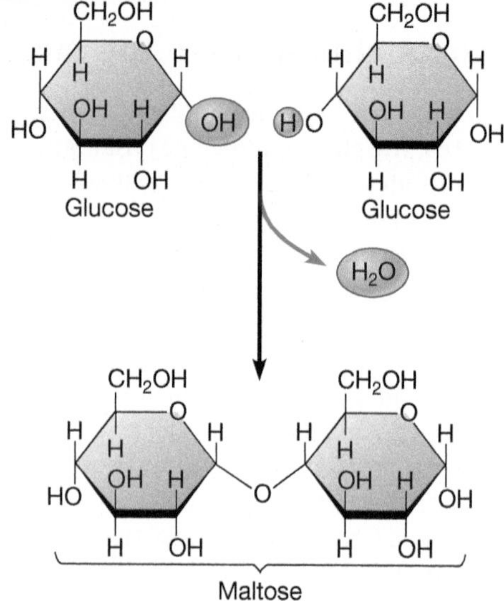

▲ **Figure 3.5** **Disaccharide formation by a dehydration reaction**

3.6 Are we eating too much sugar?

CONNECTION

If you are the typical American, you consume the equivalent of at least 22 teaspoons of sugar a day. The World Health Organization has recommended that only 5% of our daily calories should come from sugar—about 6 teaspoons a day. The U.S. Food and Drug Administration (FDA) recommends no more than 12 teaspoons of added sugar a day. If you drink one 16 ounce soda, you are already over your daily limit. And that doesn't count the sugar you use in your coffee or tea or that has been added to your yogurt, cereal, bread, snacks, and desserts. Every two weeks, the average American consumes more than a 5 pound bag of sugar, or 26 bags a year (Figure 3.6). So, is that a problem?

The main consequences previously associated with high sugar consumption have been dental cavities and obesity. The obesity rates in the United States have climbed to 36.5% of adults and 17% of children. The health risks of obesity are well established, from type 2 diabetes to high blood pressure to other chronic diseases.

Recent research, however, has documented a correlation between increased sugar consumption (independent of obesity) and health problems such as cardiovascular disease, high blood pressure, high cholesterol, and diabetes. For example, a 2014 study found that 71.4% of U.S. adults get more than the FDA-recommended 10% of their daily calories from added sugars in foods and drinks. The researchers used data from a large study updated every two years by the Centers for Disease Control and Prevention, called the National Health and Nutrition Examination Survey or NHANES, to track 11,733 participants over 15 years. The data analysis showed that those participants who consumed more than 25% of their daily calories from added sugars were almost three times as likely to die as a result of cardiovascular disease (a 275% greater risk) compared with those who consumed less than 10% of daily calories from sugar.

In response to studies such as this, the FDA has proposed changes to the nutrition facts on packaged food labels to include grams of added sugars. They are also considering adding the percentage of the recommended daily value of those added sugars. If this second change is instituted, the label on each can of your soda will now have to state that it contains 105% of the daily value for added sugars.

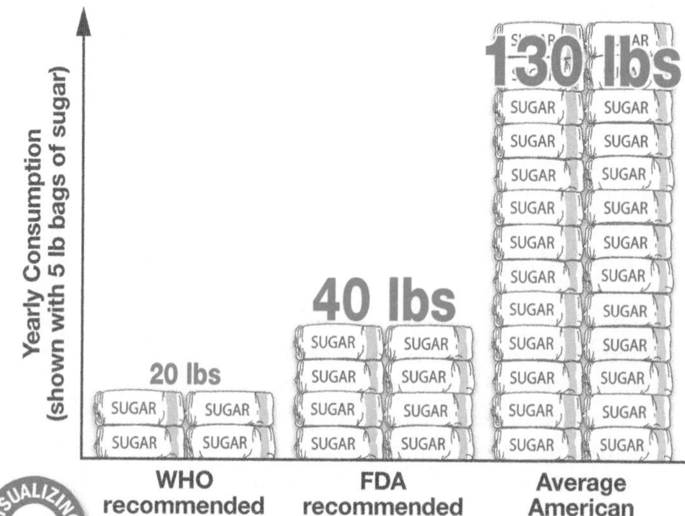

▲ **Figure 3.6** **The amount of sugar an average U.S. adult eats in a year compared to recommendations from the World Health Organization (WHO) and the Food and Drug Administration (FDA)**

? **Sugars are often described as "empty calories." What do you think that means from a nutrition standpoint?**

■ Added sugars provide energy but they do not provide other nutrients, such as protein, fats, vitamins, or minerals.

Data from Q. Yang et al., Added sugar intake and cardiovascular diseases mortality among U. S. adults, *JAMA Internal Medicine*, Volume 174, Number 4, 516–524 (April 2014).

3.7 Polysaccharides are long chains of sugar units

Polysaccharides are macromolecules, polymers of hundreds to thousands of monosaccharides linked together by dehydration reactions. Polysaccharides may function as storage molecules or as structural compounds. Figure 3.7 illustrates three common types: starch, glycogen, and cellulose.

Starch, a storage polysaccharide in plants, consists of long chains of glucose monomers. Starch molecules coil into a helical shape and may be unbranched (as shown in the figure) or branched. Starch granules serve as carbohydrate "banks" from which plant cells can withdraw glucose for energy or building materials. Humans and most other animals have enzymes that can hydrolyze plant starch to glucose. Potatoes and grains, such as wheat, corn, and rice, are the major sources of starch in the human diet.

Animals store glucose in a polysaccharide called **glycogen**. Glycogen is more highly branched than starch, as shown in the figure. Most of your glycogen is stored as granules in your liver and muscle cells, which hydrolyze the glycogen to release glucose when it is needed.

Cellulose, the most abundant organic compound on Earth, is a major component of the tough walls that enclose plant cells. Cellulose is also a polymer of glucose, but its monomers are linked together in a different orientation. (Carefully compare the oxygen "bridges" highlighted in yellow in the figure between glucose monomers in starch, glycogen, and cellulose.) Arranged parallel to each other, cellulose molecules are joined by hydrogen bonds, forming cable-like microfibrils. Layers of microfibrils combine with other polymers, producing strong support for trees and the structures we build with lumber.

Animals do not have enzymes that can hydrolyze the glucose linkages in cellulose. Therefore, cellulose is not a nutrient for humans, although it does contribute to digestive health. The cellulose that passes unchanged through your digestive tract is referred to as "insoluble fiber." Fresh fruits, vegetables, and whole grains are rich in fiber.

Some microorganisms do have enzymes that can hydrolyze cellulose. Cows and termites house such microorganisms in their digestive tracts and are thus able to derive energy from cellulose. Decomposing fungi also digest cellulose, helping to recycle its chemical elements within ecosystems.

Chitin is a structural polysaccharide used by insects and crustaceans to build their exoskeleton, the hard case enclosing the animal. Chitin is also found in the cell walls of fungi.

Almost all carbohydrates are hydrophilic owing to the many hydroxyl groups attached to their sugar monomers (see Figure 3.4B). Thus, cotton bath towels, which are mostly cellulose, are quite water absorbent due to the water-loving nature of cellulose. As you'll see next, not all biological molecules "love water."

? **Compare and contrast starch and cellulose, two plant polysaccharides.**

Both are polymers of glucose, but the bonds between glucose monomers have different shapes. Starch functions mainly for sugar storage. Cellulose is a structural polysaccharide that is the main material of plant cell walls.

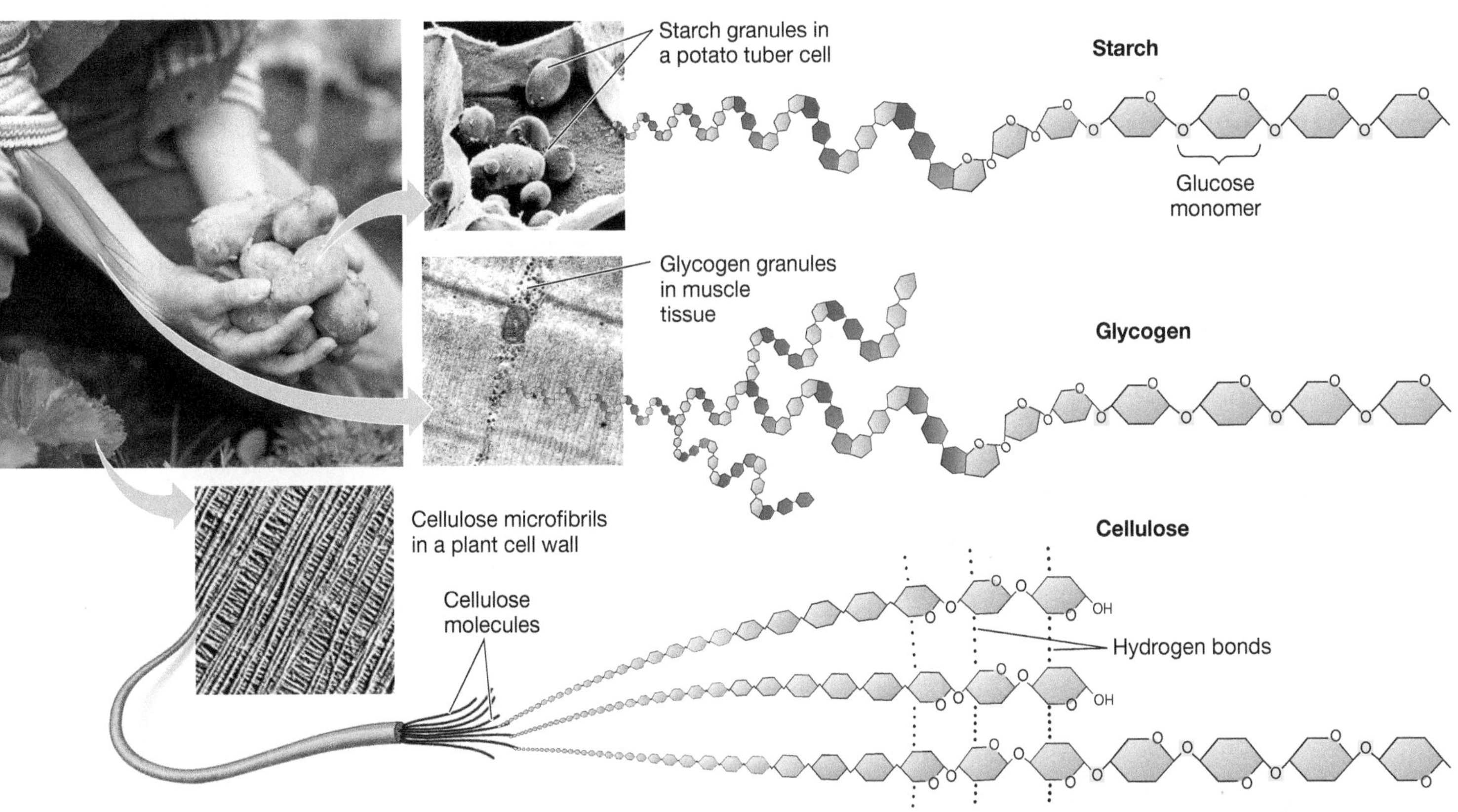

▲ Figure 3.7 Polysaccharides of plants and animals

Lipids

3.8 Fats are lipids that are mostly energy-storage molecules

Lipids are a diverse group of molecules that are classified together because they share one trait: They do not mix well with water. In contrast to carbohydrates and most other biological molecules, lipids are **hydrophobic** (water-fearing). You can see this chemical behavior in an unshaken bottle of salad dressing. The oil (a type of lipid) separates from the vinegar (which is mostly water).

Lipids also differ from carbohydrates, proteins, and nucleic acids in that they are neither huge macromolecules nor polymers built from similar monomers. In this and the next few modules, we consider the structures and functions of three important types of lipids: fats, phospholipids, and steroids.

A **fat** is a large lipid made from two kinds of smaller molecules: glycerol and fatty acids. Shown at the top in Figure 3.8A, glycerol consists of three carbons, each bearing a hydroxyl group (—OH). A fatty acid consists of a carboxyl group (the functional group that gives these molecules the name fatty *acid*, —COOH) and a hydrocarbon chain, usually 16 or 18 carbon atoms in length. The nonpolar C—H bonds in the hydrocarbon chains are the reason fats are hydrophobic.

Figure 3.8A shows how one fatty acid molecule can link to a glycerol molecule by a dehydration reaction. Linking three fatty acids to glycerol produces a fat, as illustrated in Figure 3.8B. A synonym for fat is *triglyceride*, a term you may see on food labels or on medical tests for fat in the blood.

A fatty acid whose hydrocarbon chain contains one or more double bonds is called an **unsaturated fatty acid**. Each carbon atom connected by a double bond has one fewer hydrogen atom attached to it. These double bonds usually cause kinks (or bends) in the carbon chain, as you can see in the third fatty acid in Figure 3.8B. A fatty acid that has no double bonds in its hydrocarbon chain has the maximum number of hydrogen atoms attached to each carbon atom (its carbons are "saturated" with hydrogen) and is called a **saturated fatty acid**.

Most animal fats are saturated: Their hydrocarbon chains—the "tails" of their fatty acids—lack double bonds and thus pack closely together, making them solid at room temperature (Figure 3.8C). In contrast, the fats of plants and fishes generally contain unsaturated fatty acids—the kinks in their tails prevent them from packing tightly together. Thus, unsaturated fats are usually liquid at room temperature and are referred to as oils.

When you see "partially hydrogenated oils" on a food label, it means that unsaturated fats have been converted to saturated fats by adding hydrogen. Unfortunately, the process of hydrogenation also creates **trans fats**, a form of fat that recent research associates with health risks. We will discuss some of that research in Module 3.9.

The main function of fats is energy storage. A gram of fat stores more than twice as much energy as a gram of polysaccharide. For immobile plants, the bulky energy storage form of starch is not a problem. (Vegetable oils are generally obtained from seeds, where more compact energy storage is a benefit.) Mobile animals, such as humans, can get around much more easily carrying their food reserves in the form of fat. Of course, the downside of this energy-packed storage form is that it takes more effort for a person to "burn off" excess fat.

It is important to remember that a reasonable amount of body fat is both normal and healthy. You stock these long-term fuel reserves in adipose cells, which swell and shrink as you deposit and withdraw fat from them. In addition to storing energy, fatty tissue cushions vital organs and insulates the body.

? Explain why fats are hydrophobic.

The three fatty acid tails of a fat molecule contain only nonpolar C—H bonds, which do not mix well with polar water molecules.

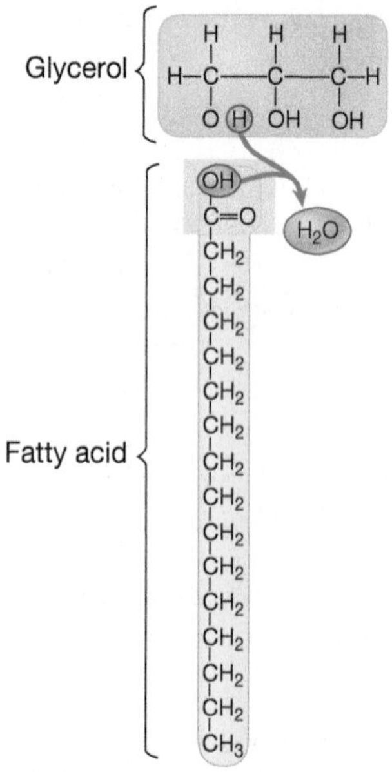

Glycerol

Fatty acid

▲ **Figure 3.8A** A dehydration reaction that will link a fatty acid to glycerol

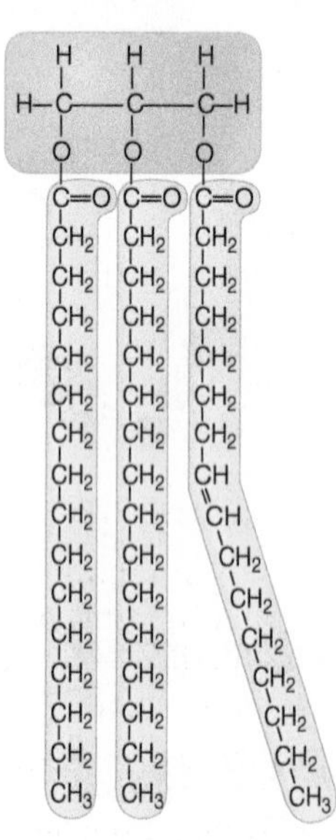

▲ **Figure 3.8B** A fat molecule (triglyceride) consisting of three fatty acids linked to glycerol

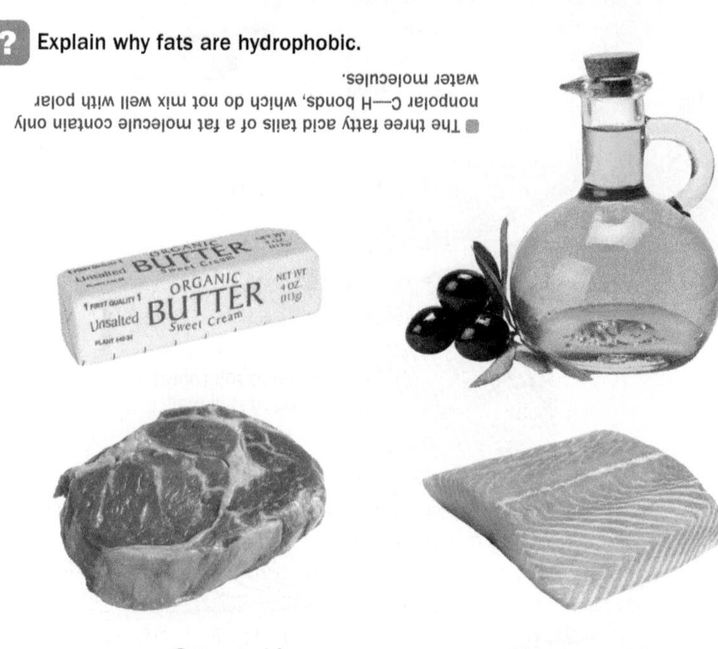

▲ **Figure 3.8C** Types of fats

3.9 Scientific studies document the health risks of trans fats

SCIENTIFIC THINKING

In the previous module, you learned about the difference between animal fats and vegetable oils and their saturated versus unsaturated fatty acids. In the 1890s, a process was invented that added hydrogen atoms to the double-bonded carbon atoms of unsaturated fats, producing partially hydrogenated vegetable oils. These new fats had several desirable traits: They didn't spoil as quickly as oils and could withstand repeated reheating for frying. In addition, in the 1950s and 1960s, scientific studies began to associate saturated fats with an increased risk of heart disease, leading to a public health campaign to reduce consumption of animal fats (such as butter) and replace them with unsaturated oils and the supposedly healthier partially hydrogenated oils (such as margarine).

Jump ahead to the 1990s, and partially hydrogenated oils were found in countless foods—cookies, crackers, snacks, baked goods, and fried foods. But new research began to show that the trans fats produced in the process of hydrogenation were an even greater health risk than were saturated fats. One study estimated that eliminating trans fats from the food supply could prevent up to one in five heart attacks! In 2006, the FDA required the listing of trans fat on food labels. Many cities and states passed laws to eliminate trans fats in the foods sold in restaurants and schools. And in 2015, the FDA made its final determination that partially hydrogenated oils are not "generally recognized as safe" and must be removed from foods within three years.

The scientific studies establishing the risks of trans fats were of two types: experimental and observational. In experimental controlled feeding trials, the diets of participants contained different proportions of saturated, unsaturated, and partially hydrogenated fats. The hypothesis of these studies was that trans fats adversely affect cardiovascular health; the prediction was that the more trans fats in the diet, the greater the risk. But how does one measure risk? Should the study proceed until participants start having heart attacks? For both ethical and practical reasons, controlled feeding trials are usually fairly short in duration, involve only limited dietary changes, generally use healthy individuals, and measure intermediary risk factors, such as changes in cholesterol levels, rather than actual disease outcomes.

Many scientific studies on dietary health effects are observational. The advantages of such studies are that they can extend over a longer time period, use a more representative population, and measure disease outcomes as well as risk factors. Observational studies may be retrospective (looking backward): Present health status is documented, and participants report their prior eating habits. Two difficulties with retrospective studies are that people may not accurately remember and report their dietary histories, and anyone who has already died, say, of a heart attack, is not included in the study. Prospective studies, on the other hand, look forward. Researchers conducting such studies enlist a study group, quantify participants' health attributes, and then collect data on the group over many years. Diet, lifestyle habits, risk factors, and disease outcomes can all be recorded and then analyzed.

A landmark example of a prospective study is the Nurses' Health Study, begun in 1976 with more than 120,000 female nurses. In a portion of the study that looked at dietary fat intake, 80,082 women were followed from 1980 to 1994. The researchers estimated the relative risk of coronary heart disease associated with the intake of different types of fats. In studies such as these, a relative risk of 1 indicates that there is no association between the factor under study and the disease. In the Nurses' Health Study, a relative risk of 1 indicated no difference in risk of coronary heart disease for a particular type of fat when compared to an equivalent energy intake from carbohydrates; a relative risk of less than 1 meant there was a decreased risk; a relative risk greater than 1 indicated a greater risk. As you can see in Figure 3.9, for each 5% increase in energy consumed in the form of monounsaturated or polyunsaturated fat, the relative risk of heart disease falls below 1. For each 5% increase in energy consumed as saturated fat, the relative risk rises to 1.17—indicating a 17% increase in the risk of heart disease. For each 2% increase in the amount of energy consumed in the form of trans fat, however, there is a 93% increase in risk. Trans fats are indeed a greater health risk than saturated fats.

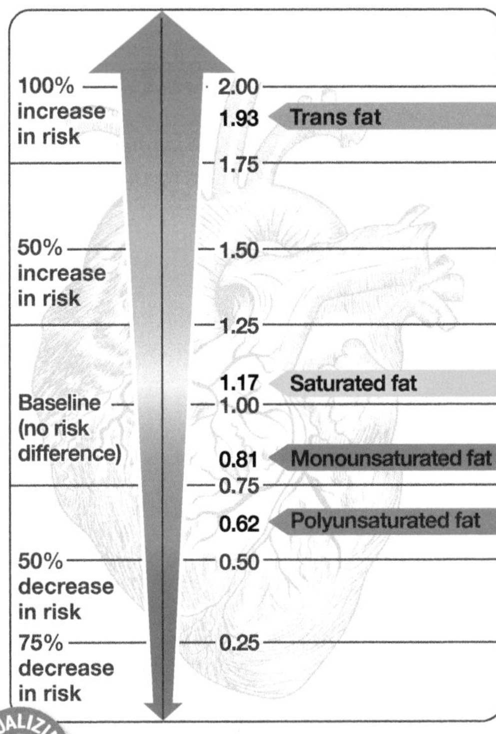

▲ **Figure 3.9** **Relative risk of heart disease associated with increased intake of specific types of fats**

Data from F. B. Hu et al., Dietary fat intake and the risk of coronary heart disease in women, *New England Journal of Medicine* 337: 1491–9 (1997).

Based on an accumulation of scientific evidence from many studies, U.S. governmental agencies have revised their policies—from promoting partially hydrogenated oils as a healthful alternative to saturated fats in the middle of the 20th century to banning them today. Such changes in policy reflect changes in our understanding based on current research. Scientific knowledge both expands and is revised as new questions are asked, new studies are done, and new evidence accumulates.

? **What is the difference between a retrospective and a prospective study?**

■ A retrospective study "looks backward" to assess risk factors or benefits that correlate with current health status. A prospective study follows a group forward, monitoring certain factors and recording health outcomes over a period of time.

3.10 Phospholipids and steroids are important lipids with a variety of functions

Cells could not exist without **phospholipids**, the major component of cell membranes. Phospholipids are structurally similar to fats, except that they contain only two fatty acids attached to glycerol instead of three. As shown in Figure 3.10A, a negatively charged phosphate group (shown as a yellow circle in the figure and linked to another small molecule) is attached to glycerol's third carbon.

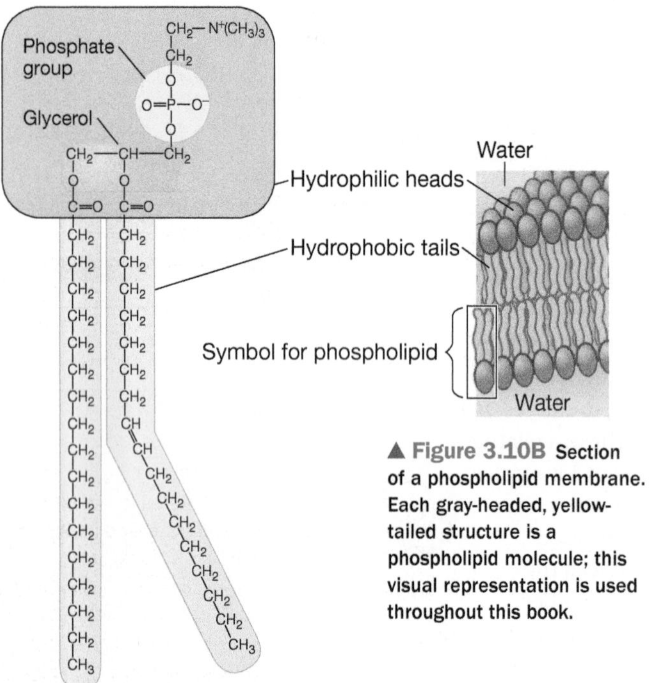

▲ **Figure 3.10A** Chemical structure of a phospholipid molecule

TRY THIS Explain why the gray region of this phospholipid is hydrophilic and why the yellow tails are hydrophobic.

▲ **Figure 3.10B** Section of a phospholipid membrane. Each gray-headed, yellow-tailed structure is a phospholipid molecule; this visual representation is used throughout this book.

The association between phospholipids and water in providing the structure of a membrane is an example of the theme of INTERACTIONS on a molecular level. The two ends of a phospholipid have different relationships with water. The interactions between phospholipid molecules within a watery environment result in their arrangement into a double-layered sheet (Figure 3.10B). The hydrophobic tails of the phospholipids cluster together in the center of the sheet, excluded from water, and the hydrophilic phosphate heads face the watery environment on either side of the resulting membrane. In cell membranes, various types of proteins are associated with such phospholipid membrane structures. (We will explore biological membranes in more detail in Chapter 5.)

Steroids are lipids in which the carbon skeleton contains four fused rings, as shown in the structural formula of cholesterol in Figure 3.10C. (The diagram omits the carbons and hydrogens making up the rings and the attached hydrocarbon chain.) **Cholesterol** is a common component in animal cell membranes and is also the precursor for making other steroids, including sex hormones. Different steroids vary in the chemical groups attached to the rings, as you saw in Figure 3.2. A high level of cholesterol in the blood may contribute to atherosclerosis.

? **Compare the structure of a phospholipid with that of a fat.**

■ A phospholipid has two fatty acids and a phosphate group attached to glycerol. Three fatty acids are attached to the glycerol of a fat molecule.

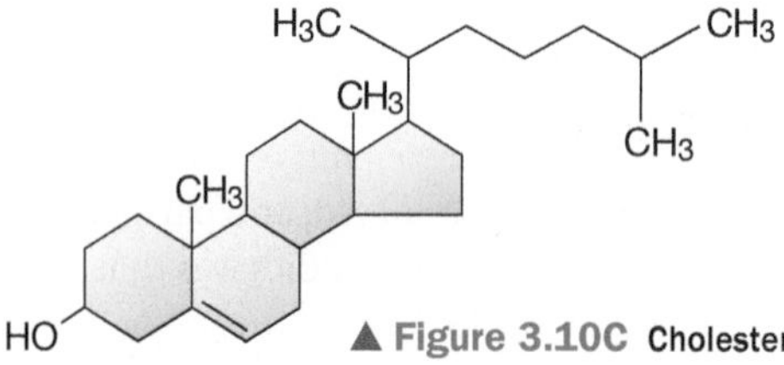

H_3C CH_3 CH_3 CH_3 CH_3 HO

▲ **Figure 3.10C** Cholesterol, a steroid

3.11 Anabolic steroids pose health risks

CONNECTION

Anabolic steroids are synthetic variants of the male hormone testosterone. Testosterone causes a general buildup of muscle and bone mass in males during puberty and maintains masculine traits throughout life. Because anabolic steroids structurally resemble testosterone, they also mimic some of its effects. (The word *anabolic* comes from *anabolism*, the building of substances by the body.)

Anabolic steroids are used to treat general anemia and diseases that destroy body muscle. Some athletes use these drugs to build up their muscles quickly and enhance their performance. But at what cost? Steroid abuse may cause violent mood swings ("roid rage"), depression, liver damage or cancer, and high cholesterol levels and blood pressure. Use of these drugs often makes the body reduce its output of natural male sex hormones, which can cause shrunken testicles, reduced sex drive, infertility, and breast enlargement in men. Use in women has been linked to menstrual cycle disruption and development of masculine characteristics. An effect in teens is that bones may stop growing.

Despite the risks, some athletes continue to abuse synthetic steroids, and unscrupulous chemists, trainers, and coaches try to find ways to avoid their detection. Meanwhile, the U.S. Congress, professional sports authorities, and school athletic programs ban the use of anabolic steroids, implement drug testing, and penalize violators in an effort to keep the competition fair and protect the health of athletes.

? **Explain why fats and steroids, which are structurally very different, are both classed as lipids.**

■ Fats and steroids are hydrophobic molecules, the key characteristic of lipids.

Proteins

3.12 Proteins have a wide range of functions and structures

Nearly every dynamic function in your body depends on proteins. A **protein** is a polymer of small building blocks called amino acids. Of all of life's molecules, proteins are structurally and functionally the most elaborate and varied.

You have tens of thousands of different proteins in your body. What do they all do? Probably their most important role is as enzymes, the chemical catalysts that speed and regulate virtually all chemical reactions in your cells. Lactase, which you read about in the chapter introduction, is just one example of an enzyme.

Other types of proteins include transport proteins that are embedded in cell membranes and move sugar molecules and other nutrients into your cells. Moving through your blood stream are defensive proteins, such as the antibodies of the immune system, and signal proteins, such as many of the hormones and other chemical messengers that help coordinate your body's activities. Receptor proteins built into cell membranes receive and transmit such signals into your cells.

Muscle cells are packed with contractile proteins, and structural proteins are found in the fibers that make up your tendons and ligaments. Indeed, the structural protein collagen, which forms the long, strong fibers of connective tissues, accounts for 40% of the protein in your body.

Some proteins are storage proteins, which supply amino acids to developing embryos. The proteins found in eggs and seeds are examples.

The functions of all of these different types of proteins depend on each protein's unique shape. Figure 3.12A shows a ribbon model of lysozyme, an enzyme found in your sweat, tears, and saliva. Lysozyme consists of one long polymer of amino acids, represented by the purple ribbon. Lysozyme's general shape is called globular. This overall shape is more apparent in Figure 3.12B, a space-filling model of lysozyme. In that model, the colors represent the different atoms of carbon, oxygen, nitrogen, and hydrogen. The barely visible yellow balls represent sulfur atoms that form the stabilizing bonds shown as yellow lines in the ribbon model. Most enzymes and many other proteins are globular. Structural proteins, such as those making up hair, tendons, and ligaments, are typically long and thin and are called fibrous proteins. Figure 3.12C shows a spider's web, made up of fibrous silk proteins. The structural arrangement within these proteins makes each silk fiber stronger than a steel strand of the same weight.

Descriptions such as *globular* and *fibrous* refer to a protein's general shape. Each protein also has a much more specific shape. The coils and twists of lysozyme's ribbon in Figure 3.12A may appear haphazard, but they represent the molecule's specific, three-dimensional shape. Nearly all proteins must recognize and bind to some other molecule to function. Lysozyme can destroy bacterial cells, but first it must bind to molecules on the bacterial cell surface. Lysozyme's specific shape enables it to recognize and attach to its molecular target, which fits into the groove you see on the right in the figures.

The dependence of protein function on a protein's shape becomes clear when a protein is altered. In a process called **denaturation**, a protein unravels, losing its specific shape and, as a result, its function. Excessive heat can denature many proteins. For example, visualize what happens when you fry an egg. Heat quickly denatures the clear proteins surrounding the yolk, making them solid, white, and opaque.

Given the proper cellular environment, a newly synthesized amino acid chain spontaneously folds into its functional shape. What happens if a protein doesn't fold correctly? Many diseases, such as Alzheimer's and Parkinson's, involve an accumulation of misfolded proteins. Prions are infectious misshapen proteins that are associated with serious degenerative brain diseases such as mad cow disease (see Module 10.21). Such diseases reinforce the important correlation between structure and function: A protein's unique three-dimensional shape determines its proper functioning. In the next two modules, we'll learn how a protein's structure takes shape.

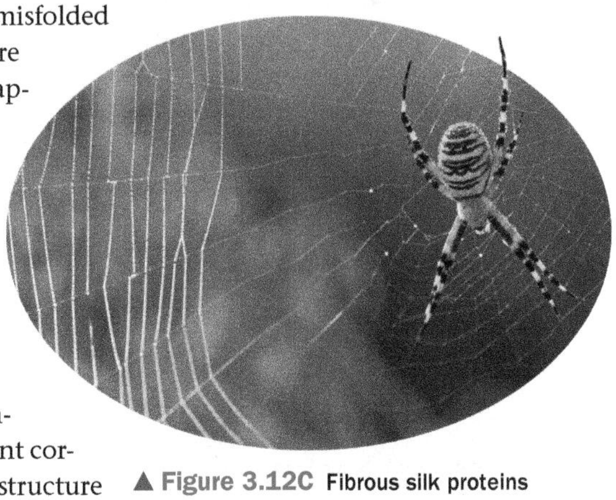

▲ Figure 3.12C Fibrous silk proteins of a spider's web

Why does a denatured protein no longer function normally?

The function of each protein is a consequence of its specific shape, which is lost when a protein denatures.

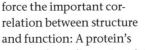

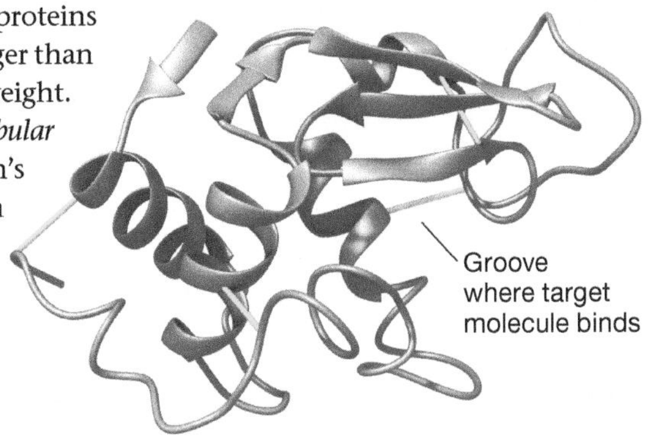

▲ Figure 3.12A Ribbon model of the protein lysozyme

▲ Figure 3.12B Space-filling model of the protein lysozyme

3.13 Proteins are made from amino acids linked by peptide bonds

Now let's see what the monomers of proteins look like. **Amino acids** all have an amino group and a carboxyl group (which makes it an acid, hence the name amino *acid*). As you can see in the general structure shown in Figure 3.13A, both of these functional groups are covalently bonded to a central carbon atom. The other two partners bonded to this carbon are a hydrogen atom and a variable chemical group symbolized by the letter R. In the simplest amino acid (glycine), the R group is just a hydrogen atom. In all others, the R group consists of one or more carbon atoms with various functional groups attached.

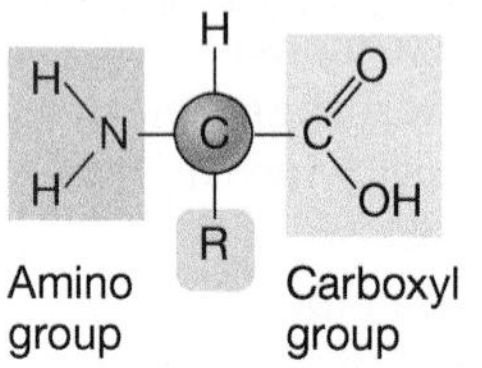

▲ **Figure 3.13A** General structure of an amino acid

All 20 amino acids are included in Appendix 3, grouped according to whether their R groups are hydrophobic or hydrophilic. Figure 3.13B shows representatives of these two main types. Hydrophobic amino acids have nonpolar R groups—note the nonpolar C—H bonds in the R group of leucine (abbreviated Leu) shown in the figure. The R groups of hydrophilic amino acids, on the other hand, may be polar or charged. R groups that contain acidic or basic groups are charged at the pH of a cell. Indeed, as you can see in Figure 3.13B, the amino and carboxyl groups attached to the central carbon are usually in their ionized form at cellular pH (see ionized forms in Table 3.2).

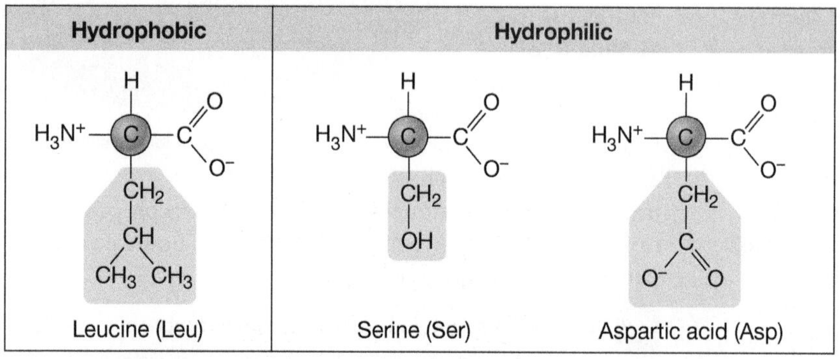

▲ **Figure 3.13B** Examples of amino acids with hydrophobic and hydrophilic R groups

TRY THIS Point out the bonds and functional groups that make the R groups of these three amino acids either hydrophobic or hydrophilic.

Now that we have examined amino acids, let's see how they are linked to form polymers. Can you guess? Cells join amino acids together in a dehydration reaction that links the carboxyl group of one amino acid to the amino group of the next amino acid as a water molecule is removed (Figure 3.13C). The resulting covalent linkage is called a **peptide bond**. The product of the reaction shown in the figure is called a *di*peptide, because it was made from *two* amino acids. Additional amino acids can be added by the same process to form a chain of amino acids, a **polypeptide**.

How is it possible to make thousands of different kinds of proteins from just 20 amino acids? The answer has to do with sequence. You know that thousands of English words can be made by varying the sequence of letters and word length. Although the protein "alphabet" is slightly smaller (just 20 "letters," rather than 26), the "words" are much longer. Most polypeptides are at least 100 amino acids in length; some are 1,000 or more. Each different polypeptide has a unique sequence of amino acids.

But a long polypeptide chain of specific sequence is not the same as a protein, any more than a long strand of yarn is the same as a sweater that can be knitted from that yarn. What are the stitches that coil and fold a polypeptide chain into its unique three-dimensional shape? This is where the R groups of the constituent amino acids play their role in influencing protein structure. Hydrophobic amino acids may cluster together in the center of a globular protein, while hydrophilic amino acids face the outside, helping proteins dissolve in the aqueous solution of a cell. Hydrogen bonds and ionic bonds between hydrophilic R groups also help determine a protein's shape, as do covalent bonds called disulfide bridges between sulfur atoms in some R groups. (Look back at the yellow lines in Figure 3.12A.) The unique sequence of the various types of amino acids in a polypeptide determines how a protein takes shape. Let's visualize this process in the next module.

? **By what process do you digest the proteins you eat into their individual amino acids?**

By hydrolysis, adding a molecule of water back to break each peptide bond

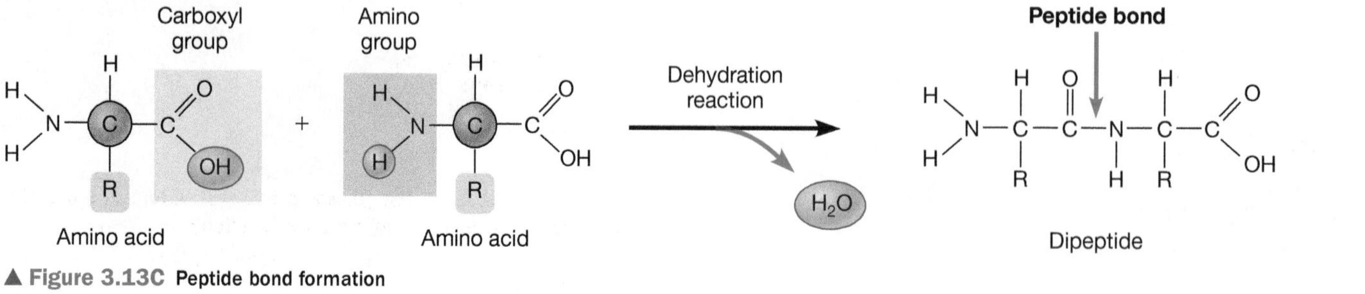

▲ **Figure 3.13C** Peptide bond formation

VISUALIZING THE CONCEPT 3.14 A protein's functional shape results from four levels of structure

The **primary structure** of a protein is the precise sequence of amino acids in the polypeptide chain. Segments of the chain then coil or fold into local patterns called **secondary structure**. The overall three-dimensional shape of a protein is called **tertiary structure**. Proteins with more than one polypeptide chain have **quaternary structure.**

To help you visualize how these structural levels are superimposed on each other to form a functional protein, let's look at transthyretin, an important transport protein found in your blood. Its specific shape enables it to transport vitamin A and one of the thyroid hormones throughout your body.

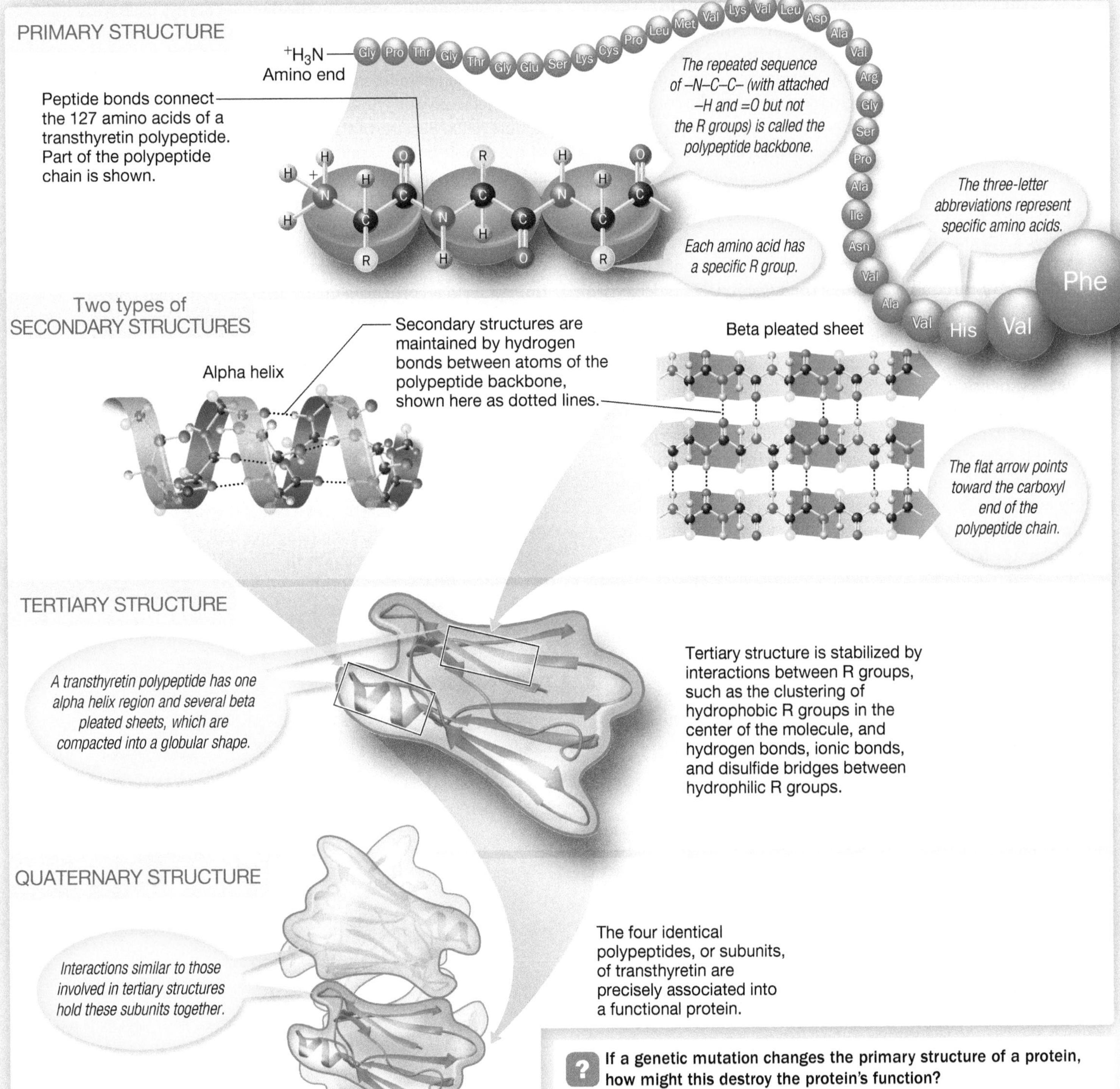

? If a genetic mutation changes the primary structure of a protein, how might this destroy the protein's function?

■ Primary structure determines the secondary and tertiary structure due to the chemical nature of the R groups of the amino acids in the chain. Even a slight change may affect a protein's shape and thus its function.

TRY THIS **Look back to the ribbon model of lysozyme in Figure 3.12A, and identify three regions of alpha helix and one of beta pleated sheet.**

Nucleic Acids

3.15 The nucleic acids DNA and RNA are information-rich polymers of nucleotides

As we just saw, the primary structure of a polypeptide determines the shape of a protein. But what determines this primary structure? The amino acid sequence of a polypeptide is programmed by a discrete unit of inheritance known as a **gene**. Genes consist of **DNA (deoxyribonucleic acid)**, one of the two types of polymers called **nucleic acids**. The name *nucleic* comes from DNA's location in the nuclei of cells. The other type of nucleic acid is **RNA (ribonucleic acid)**. Its role is in assembling the polypeptides according to the instructions of DNA. Let's begin by examining the composition and structure of nucleic acids. Then we will explore how they function in the storage, transfer, and expression of hereditary information.

Monomers of Nucleic Acids The monomers that make up nucleic acids are **nucleotides**. As indicated in Figure 3.15A, each nucleotide contains three parts. At the center of a nucleotide is a five-carbon sugar (blue); the sugar in DNA is deoxyribose, whereas RNA has a slightly different sugar called ribose. Linked to one side of the sugar in both types of nucleotides is a negatively charged phosphate group (yellow). Linked to the sugar's other side is a nitrogenous base (green), a molecular structure containing nitrogen and carbon. (The nitrogen atoms tend to take up H^+ in aqueous solutions, which explains why it is called a nitrogenous *base*.) Each DNA nucleotide has one of four different nitrogenous bases: adenine (A), thymine (T), cytosine (C), and guanine (G). Thus, all genetic information is written in a four-letter alphabet. RNA nucleotides also contain the bases A, C, and G; but the base uracil (U) is found instead of thymine.

Nucleotide Polymers Like polysaccharides and polypeptides, a nucleic acid polymer—a polynucleotide—is built from its monomers by dehydration reactions. In this process, the sugar of one nucleotide bonds to the phosphate group of the next monomer. The result is a repeating sugar-phosphate backbone in the polymer, as represented by the blue and yellow ribbon in Figure 3.15B. (Note that the nitrogenous bases are not part of the backbone.)

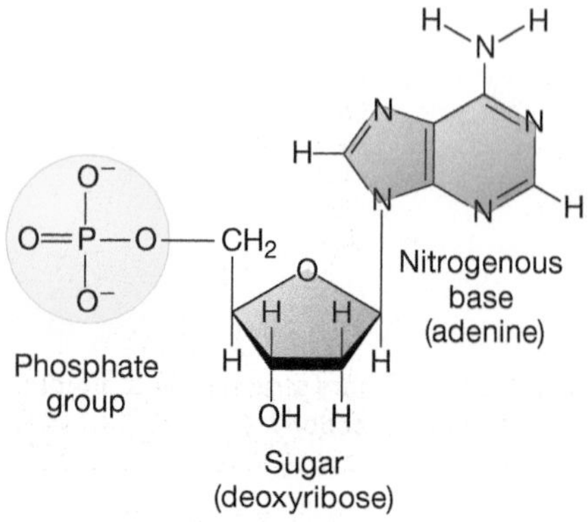

Phosphate group
Sugar (deoxyribose)
Nitrogenous base (adenine)

▲ **Figure 3.15A** A nucleotide

RNA usually consists of a single polynucleotide strand. DNA molecules contain two polynucleotides, which wind around each other forming a **double helix** (Figure 3.15C). The nitrogenous bases protrude from the two sugar-phosphate backbones and pair in the center of the helix. As shown by their diagrammatic shapes in the figure, A always pairs with T, and C always pairs with G. The two DNA chains are held together by hydrogen bonds (indicated by the dotted lines) between their paired bases. These bonds are individually weak, but collectively they hold the two strands together in a stable double helix. Because of the base-pairing rules, the two strands of the double helix are said to be *complementary*, each a predictable counterpart of the other. Thus, if a stretch of nucleotides on one strand has the base sequence -AGCACT-, then the same stretch on the other strand must be -TCGTGA-.

Functions of Nucleic Acids The genetic material that humans and all other organisms inherit from their parents consists of DNA. DNA resides in a cell as one or more very long structures called chromosomes, which each carry several hundred or more genes. Unique among molecules, DNA provides directions for its own replication. Every time a cell divides, it first makes two identical copies of each of its chromosomes. Why is the structure of DNA so important in this process? Complementary base pairing is the key—the double helix unzips and new complementary strands assemble along the separated strands. Thus, as a cell divides, its genetic instructions are passed to each daughter cell.

These instructions program all of a cell's activities by directing the synthesis of proteins. Figure 3.15D shows the roles of DNA and RNA in the production of proteins, a process called **gene expression**.

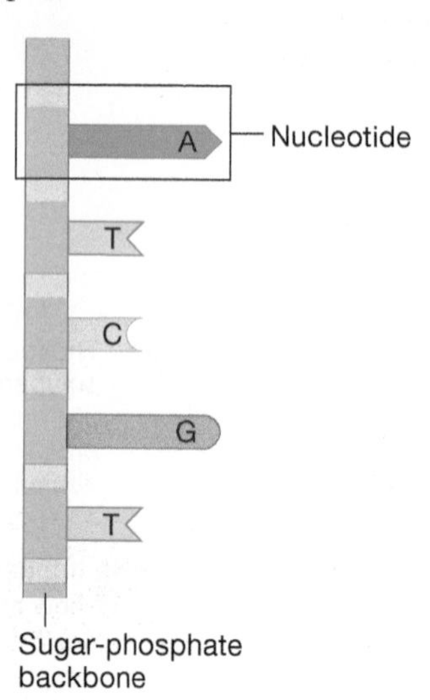

▲ **Figure 3.15B** A polynucleotide

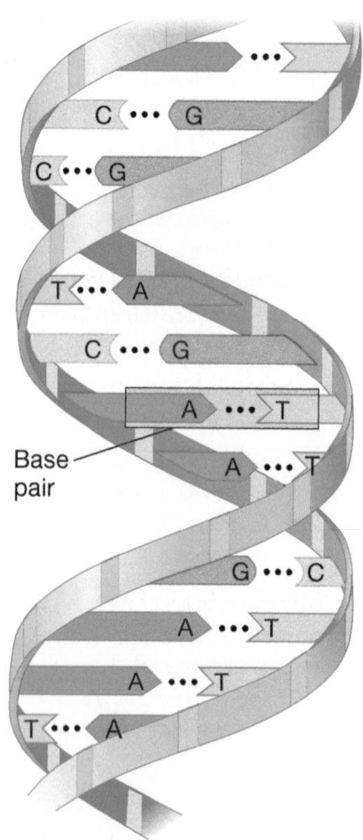

▲ **Figure 3.15C** DNA double helix

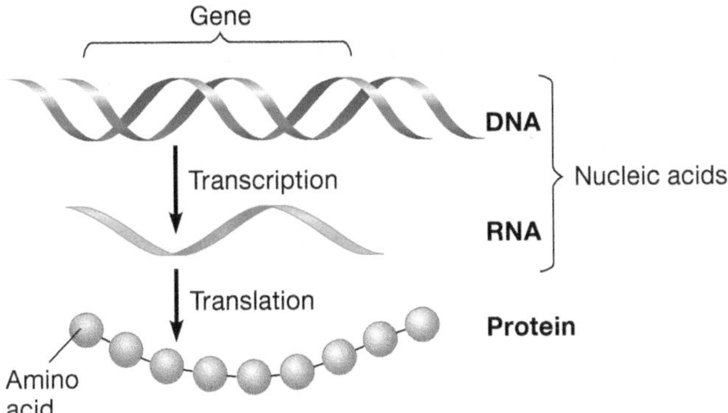

▲ **Figure 3.15D** **The flow of genetic information in the building of a protein**

A gene first directs the synthesis of an RNA molecule. We say that DNA is transcribed into RNA. The same base-pairing rules account for the precise transcription of information from DNA to RNA (with the exception that the U nucleotides of RNA pair with the A nucleotides of DNA). The RNA molecule then interacts with the protein-building machinery of the cell. There, the gene's instructions, written in "nucleic acid language," are translated into "protein language," the amino acid sequence of a polypeptide. The flow of genetic instruction that leads to gene expression, summarized as DNA → RNA → protein, illustrates the important biological theme of **INFORMATION**.

Complementary base pairing relays information from DNA to RNA. But base pairing can also occur between stretches of complementary nucleotides within RNA molecules, allowing these molecules to take on the particular three-dimensional shapes necessary for their various functions. Three types of RNA molecules are involved in the process of protein synthesis. Recent research has identified previously unknown types of RNA molecules that are involved in regulating gene expression. (The functions of DNA and RNA are explored in more detail in Unit 2.)

An organism's genes determine the proteins and thus the structures and functions of its body. Let's return to the subject of the chapter introduction—lactose intolerance—to see an example of how genes dictate function as we conclude our study of biological molecules. (In the next chapter, we move up in the biological hierarchy to the level of the cell.)

? **What roles do complementary base pairing play in the functioning of DNA?**

■ Complementary base pairing makes possible the precise replication of DNA, ensuring that genetic information is faithfully transmitted every time a cell divides. It also ensures that RNA molecules carry accurate instructions from DNA for the synthesis of proteins.

3.16 Lactose tolerance is a recent event in human evolution

EVOLUTION CONNECTION

As you'll recall from the chapter introduction, the majority of people stop producing the enzyme lactase in early childhood and thus do not easily digest the milk sugar lactose. Researchers were curious about the genetic and evolutionary basis for the regional distribution of lactose tolerance and intolerance. In 2002, a group of scientists completed a study of the genes of 196 lactose-intolerant adults of African, Asian, and European descent. They determined that lactose intolerance is actually the human norm. It is "lactose tolerance" that represents a relatively recent mutation in the human genome.

What does evolution have to do with drinking milk?

The ability to make lactase into adulthood is concentrated in people of northern European descent, and the researchers speculated that lactose tolerance became widespread among this group because it offered a survival advantage. Middle Eastern and North African populations domesticated cattle between 7,500 and 9,000 years ago, and these animals were later brought into Europe. In northern Europe's relatively cold climate, only one harvest a year is possible, and domesticated animals likely became an important source of food. With milk and other dairy products at hand year-round, natural selection would have favored anyone with a mutation that kept the lactase gene switched on into adulthood. The mutation that allows lactase production to persist appears to have spread rapidly in Europe within the past 5,000 years.

Researchers wondered whether the lactose tolerance mutation found in Europeans might be present in other cultures that kept dairy herds. Indeed, a study published in 2007 compared the genetic makeup and lactose tolerance of various ethnic groups in East Africa. The researchers identified three mutations, all different from each other and from the European mutation, that are associated with keeping the lactase gene permanently turned on.

Mutations that conferred a selective advantage, such as surviving cold winters or withstanding drought by drinking milk, spread rapidly in these early pastoral peoples. Mutations such as these are an example of convergent evolution—a similar adaptation evolving independently in different lineages (**Figure 3.16**). The evolutionary and cultural history of these groups is recorded in their genes and in their continuing ability to digest milk.

? **Explain how lactose tolerance involves three of the four major classes of biological macromolecules.**

■ Lactose, milk sugar, is a carbohydrate that is hydrolyzed by the enzyme lactase, a protein. The ability to make this enzyme and the regulation of when it is made are coded for in DNA, a nucleic acid.

▲ **Figure 3.16** **Lactose tolerance: two different cultures, two different mutations—same adaptation**

CHAPTER **3** REVIEW

For practice quizzes, BioFlix animations, MP3 tutorials, video tutors, and more study tools designed for this textbook, go to MasteringBiology™

REVIEWING THE CONCEPTS

Introduction to Organic Compounds (3.1–3.3)

3.1 Life's molecular diversity is based on the properties of carbon. Carbon's ability to bond with four other atoms is the basis for building large and diverse organic compounds. Hydrocarbons are composed of only carbon and hydrogen. Isomers have the same molecular formula but different structures.

3.2 A few chemical groups are key to the functioning of biological molecules. Hydrophilic functional groups give organic molecules specific chemical properties.

3.3 Cells make large molecules from a limited set of small molecules.

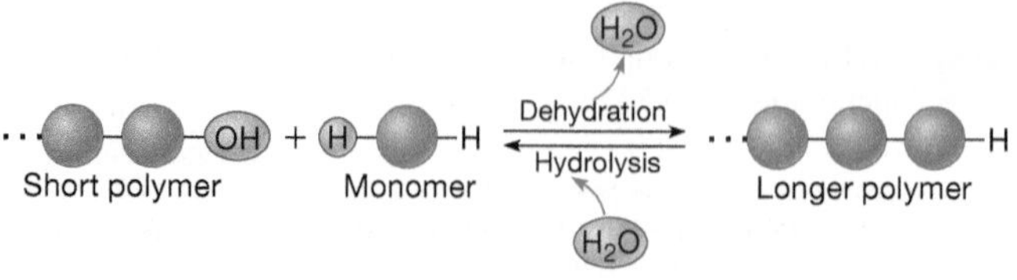

Carbohydrates (3.4–3.7)

3.4 Monosaccharides are the simplest carbohydrates. A monosaccharide has a formula that is a multiple of CH_2O and contains hydroxyl groups and a carbonyl group.

3.5 Two monosaccharides are linked to form a disaccharide.

3.6 Are we eating too much sugar? The FDA recommends that only 10% of daily calories come from added sugar. Research supports the correlation between high sugar intake and adverse health effects.

3.7 Polysaccharides are long chains of sugar units. Starch and glycogen are storage polysaccharides; cellulose is structural, found in plant cell walls. Chitin is a component of insect exoskeletons and fungal cell walls.

Lipids (3.8–3.11)

3.8 Fats are lipids that are mostly energy-storage molecules. Lipids are diverse, hydrophobic compounds composed largely of carbon and hydrogen. Fats (triglycerides) consist of glycerol linked to three fatty acids. Saturated fatty acids are found in animal fats; unsaturated fatty acids are typical of plant oils.

3.9 Scientific studies document the health risks of trans fats.

3.10 Phospholipids and steroids are important lipids with a variety of functions. Phospholipids are components of cell membranes. Steroids include cholesterol and some hormones.

3.11 Anabolic steroids pose health risks.

Proteins (3.12–3.14)

3.12 Proteins have a wide range of functions and structures. Proteins are involved in almost all of a cell's activities; as enzymes, they regulate chemical reactions.

3.13 Proteins are made from amino acids linked by peptide bonds. Protein diversity is based on different sequences of amino acids, monomers that contain an amino group, a carboxyl group, an H atom, and an R group, all attached to a central carbon. The R groups distinguish 20 amino acids, each with specific properties.

3.14 A protein's functional shape results from four levels of structure. A protein's primary structure is the sequence of amino acids in its polypeptide chain. Its secondary structure is the coiling or folding of the chain, stabilized by hydrogen bonds. The tertiary structure is the overall three-dimensional shape of a polypeptide, resulting from interactions among R groups. Proteins made of more than one polypeptide have quaternary structure.

Nucleic Acids (3.15–3.16)

3.15 The nucleic acids DNA and RNA are information-rich polymers of nucleotides. Nucleotides are composed of a sugar, a phosphate group, and a nitrogenous base. DNA is a double helix; RNA is a single polynucleotide chain. DNA and RNA serve as the blueprints for proteins and thus control the life of a cell. DNA is the molecule of inheritance.

3.16 Lactose tolerance is a recent event in human evolution. Different mutations in DNA have led to lactose tolerance in several human groups whose ancestors raised dairy cattle.

CONNECTING THE CONCEPTS

1. Complete the following table to help you review the structures and functions of the four classes of organic molecules.

Classes of Molecules and Their Components	Functions	Examples
Carbohydrates (CH_2OH, H, O, H, H, OH, H, HO, OH, H, OH)	Energy for cell, raw material	a. ______
	b. ______	Starch, glycogen
Monosaccharide	Plant cell support	c. ______
Lipids (don't form polymers)	Energy storage	d. ______
H H H / H–C–C–C–H / OH OH OH; OH, C=O, CH_2 ×7	e. ______	Phospholipids
Glycerol; Fatty acid; Components of a fat molecule	Hormones	f. ______
Proteins	j. ______	Lactase
g. ______ h. ______	k. ______	Hair, tendons
H, H, N, H, C, C, O, OH	l. ______	Muscle proteins
	Transport	m. ______
	Communication	Signal proteins
	n. ______	Antibodies
i. ______	Storage	Proteins in seeds
Amino acid	Receive signals	Receptor protein
Nucleic Acids	Heredity	r. ______
p. ______ o. ______	s. ______	DNA and RNA
Nucleotide q. ______		

TESTING YOUR KNOWLEDGE

Level 1: Knowledge/Comprehension

2. A glucose molecule is to starch as (*Explain your answer.*)
   a. a steroid is to a lipid.
   b. a protein is to an amino acid.
   c. a nucleic acid is to a polypeptide.
   d. a nucleotide is to a nucleic acid.
3. What makes a fatty acid an acid?
   a. It does not dissolve in water.
   b. It is capable of bonding with other molecules to form a fat.
   c. It has a carboxyl group that can donate an H^+ to a solution.
   d. It contains only two oxygen atoms.
4. Cows can derive nutrients from cellulose because
   a. they produce enzymes that recognize the shape of the glucose-glucose bonds and hydrolyze them.
   b. they re-chew their cud to break down cellulose fibers.
   c. their digestive tract contains microorganisms that can hydrolyze the bonds of cellulose.
   d. they convert cellulose to starch and can digest starch.
5. Of the following functional groups, which is/are polar, tending to make organic compounds hydrophilic?
   a. carbonyl
   b. amino
   c. hydroxyl
   d. all of the above
6. Unsaturated fats
   a. have double bonds in their fatty acid chains.
   b. have fewer fatty acid molecules per fat molecule.
   c. are associated with greater health risks than are saturated fats.
   d. are more common in animals than in plants.

Level 2: Application/Analysis

7. A shortage of phosphorus in the soil would make it especially difficult for a plant to manufacture
   a. DNA.
   b. proteins.
   c. cellulose.
   d. sucrose.
8. Which of the following substances is a major component of the cell membrane of a fungus?
   a. cellulose
   b. chitin
   c. cholesterol
   d. phospholipids
9. Which structural level of a protein would be *least* affected by a disruption in hydrogen bonding?
   a. primary structure
   b. secondary structure
   c. tertiary structure
   d. quaternary structure
10. Circle and name the functional groups in this organic molecule. What type of compound is this? For which class of macromolecules is it a monomer?

11. Most proteins are soluble in the aqueous environment of a cell. Knowing that, where in the overall three-dimensional shape of a protein would you expect to find amino acids with hydrophobic R groups?
12. Sucrose is broken down in your intestine to the monosaccharides glucose and fructose, which are then absorbed into your blood. What is the name of this type of reaction? Using this diagram of sucrose, show how this would occur.

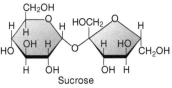

Sucrose

13. Explain the role of complementary base pairing in the functions of nucleic acids.
14. What are the two types of secondary structures found in polypeptides, and what maintains them? What stabilizes the tertiary structure of a polypeptide?

Level 3: Synthesis/Evaluation

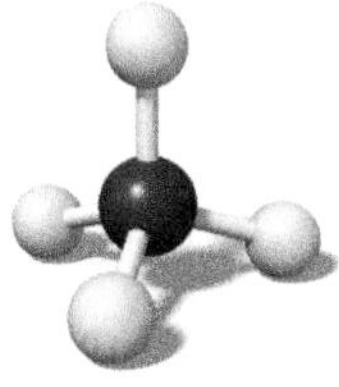

15. The diversity of life is staggering. Yet the molecular logic of life is simple and elegant: Small molecules common to all organisms are ordered into unique macromolecules. Explain why carbon is central to this diversity of organic molecules. How do carbon skeletons, chemical groups, monomers, and polymers relate to this molecular logic of life?
16. How can a cell make many different kinds of proteins out of only 20 amino acids? Of the myriad possibilities, how does the cell "know" which proteins to make?
17. Given that the function of egg yolk is to nourish and support the developing chick, explain why egg yolks are so high in fat, protein, and cholesterol.
18. Enzymes usually function best at an optimal pH and temperature. The following graph shows the effectiveness of two enzymes at various temperatures.

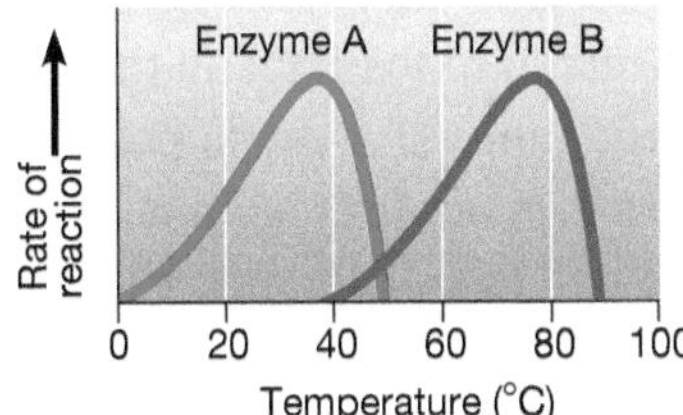

   a. At which temperature does enzyme A perform best? Enzyme B?
   b. One of these enzymes is found in humans and the other in thermophilic (heat-loving) bacteria. Which enzyme would you predict comes from which organism?
   c. From what you know about enzyme structure, explain why the rate of the reaction catalyzed by enzyme A slows down at temperatures above 40°C (140°F).
19. SCIENTIFIC THINKING Another aspect of the Nurses' Health Study introduced in Module 3.9 looked at the percentage of change in the risk of coronary heart disease associated with substituting one dietary component for another. These results estimated that replacement of 5% of energy from saturated fat in the diet with unsaturated fats would reduce the risk of heart disease by 42%, and that the replacement of 2% of energy from trans fat with unsaturated fats would reduce the risk by 53%. Explain what these numbers mean.

Answers to all questions can be found in Appendix 4.

A Tour of the Cell

CHAPTER 4

You can probably identify the blue blobs in this beautiful micrograph as the nuclei of the cells it depicts. But did you know that the brightly colored pink and green strands you also see form a cell's skeleton? These structures are part of a system of protein fibers called the cytoskeleton.

How has our knowledge of cells grown?

Much like the way your skeleton provides support and also enables you to move, the cytoskeleton provides structural support to a cell and allows some cells to crawl and others to swim. But even stationary cells have movement: Many of their internal parts bustle about, often traveling on cytoskeletal "roads." Later in the chapter you will learn more about the cytoskeleton and how our knowledge of its structures and functions has grown. As you will see, our understanding of nature often goes hand in hand with the invention and refinement of instruments that extend our senses. This certainly applies to how cells were first discovered.

In 1665, Robert Hooke used a crude microscope to examine a piece of bark from an oak tree. Hooke compared the structures he saw to "little rooms"—*cellulae* in Latin—and the term *cell* stuck. His contemporary, Antoni van Leeuwenhoek, working with more refined lenses, examined numerous subjects, from blood and sperm to pond water. He produced drawings and enthusiastic descriptions of his discoveries, such as the tiny "animalcules, very prettily a-moving" he found in the scrapings from his teeth.

Since the days of Hooke and Leeuwenhoek, improved microscopes and techniques have vastly expanded our view of the cell. For example, fluorescently colored stains reveal the cytoskeleton in the cells pictured to the right. In this chapter, you will see many micrographs using such techniques, and they will often be paired with drawings that help emphasize specific details.

Neither drawings nor micrographs, however, allow you to see the dynamic nature of living cells. For that, you need to look through a microscope or view videos. As you study the images in this chapter, keep in mind that the parts of a cell are moving and interacting. Indeed, the phenomenon we call life emerges from the interactions of the many components of a cell.

Introduction to the Cell

(4.1–4.4)

Microscopes reveal the structures of cells—the fundamental units of life.

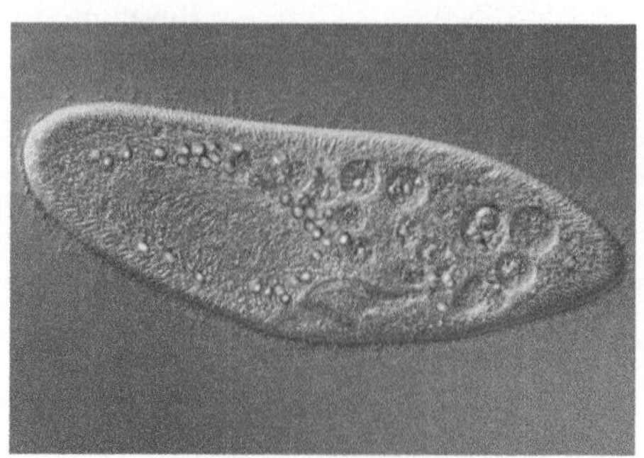

The Nucleus and Ribosomes

(4.5–4.6)

A cell's genetic instructions are housed in the nucleus and carried out by ribosomes.

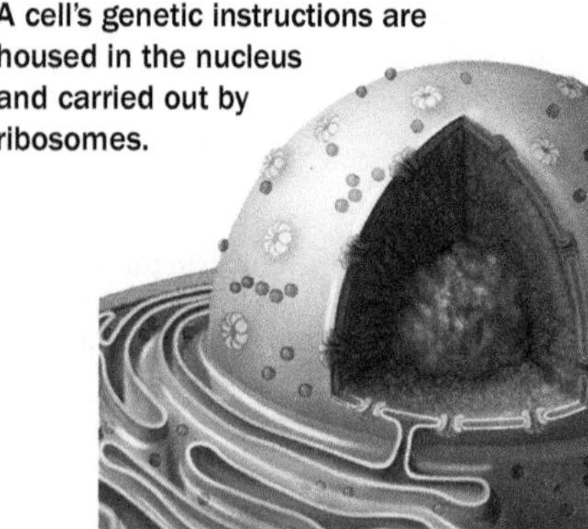

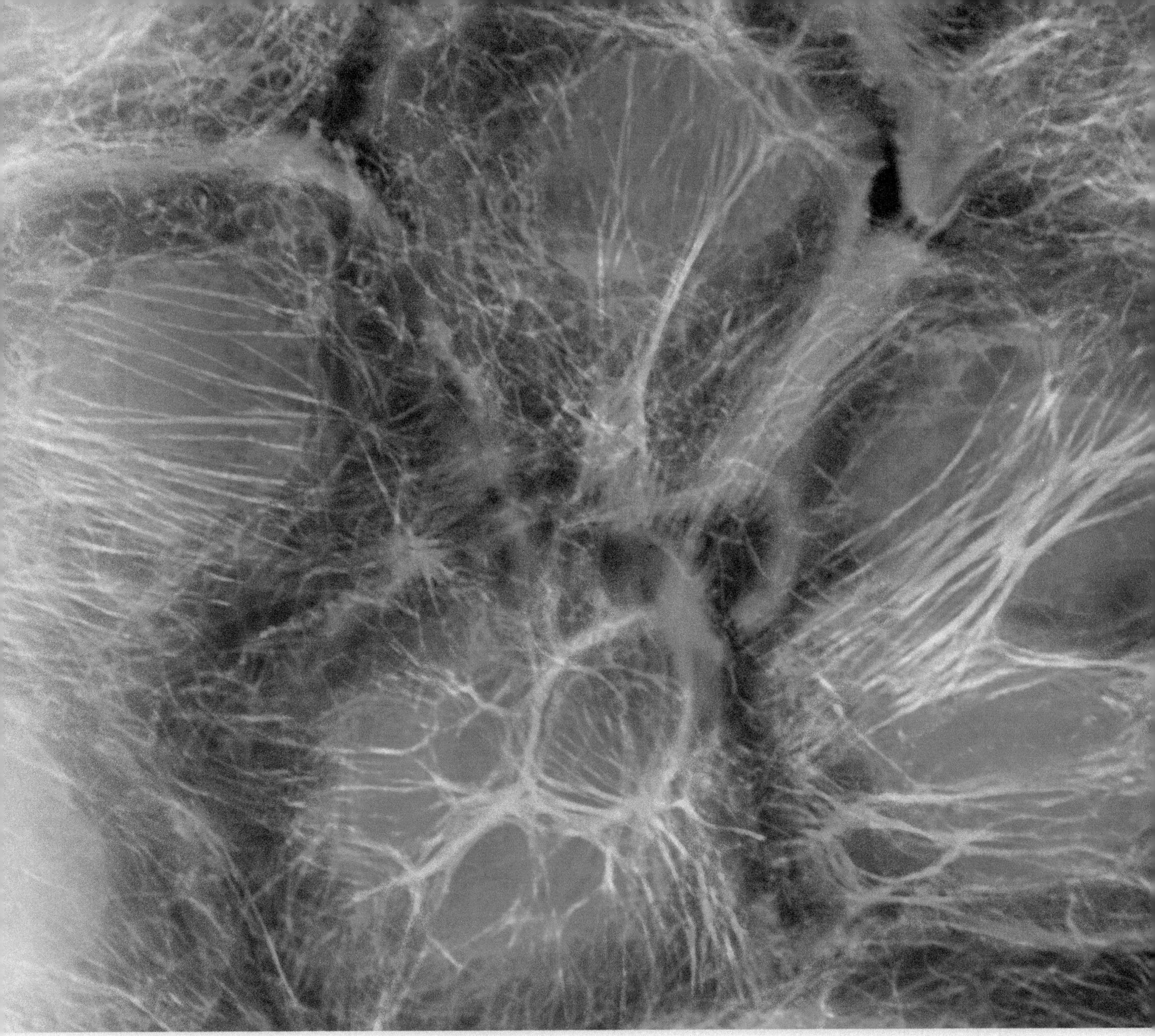

The Endomembrane System (4.7–4.12)

The endomembrane system participates in the manufacture, distribution, and breakdown of materials.

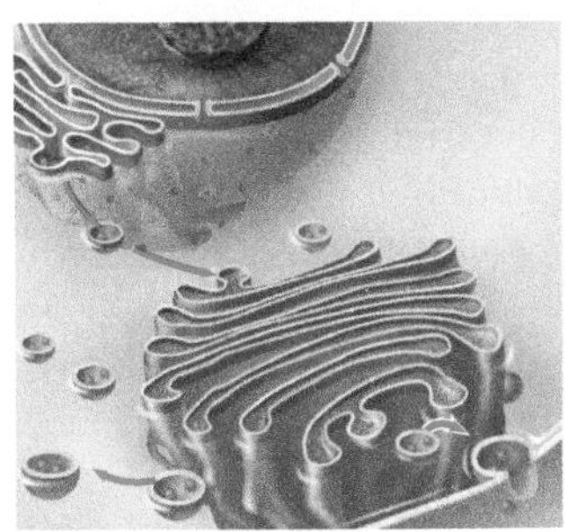

Energy-Converting Organelles (4.13–4.15)

Mitochondria in all eukaryotic cells and chloroplasts in plant cells function in energy processing.

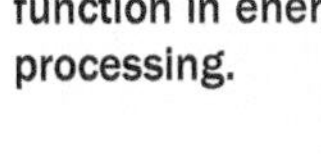

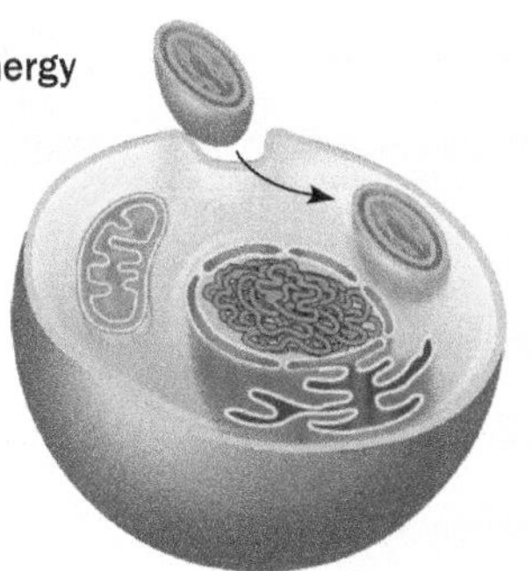

The Cytoskeleton and Cell Surfaces (4.16–4.22)

The cytoskeleton and extracellular components provide support, motility, and functional connections.

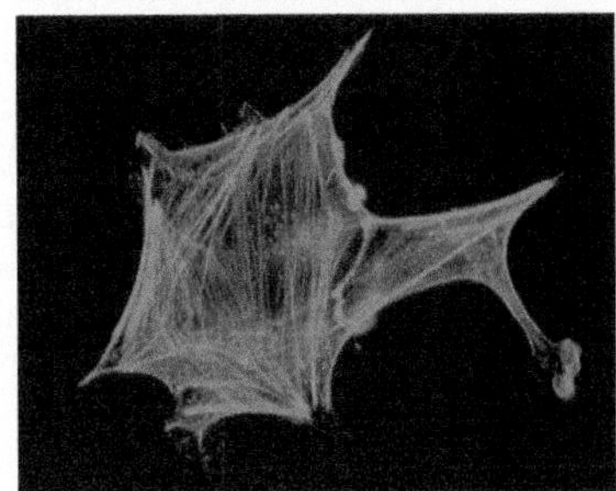

Introduction to the Cell

4.1 Microscopes reveal the world of the cell

Before microscopes were first used in the 1600s, no one knew that living organisms were composed of the tiny units we call cells. The first microscopes were light microscopes, like the ones you may use in a biology laboratory. In a **light microscope (LM)**, visible light is passed through a specimen, such as a microorganism or a thin slice of animal or plant tissue, and then through glass lenses. The lenses bend the light in such a way that the image of the specimen is magnified as it is projected into your eye or a camera.

Magnification is the increase in an object's image size compared with its actual size. Figure 4.1A shows a micrograph of a single-celled organism called *Paramecium*. The notation "LM 230×" printed along the right edge tells you that this photograph was taken through a light microscope and that the image is 230 times the actual size of the organism. This *Paramecium* is about 0.33 millimeter (mm) in length. Table 4.1 shows the most common units of length that biologists use.

An important factor in microscopy is resolution, a measure of the clarity of an image. Resolution is the ability to distinguish two nearby objects as separate. For example, what you see as a single star in the sky may be resolved as twin stars with a telescope. Each optical instrument—be it an eye, a telescope, or a microscope—has a limit to its resolution. The human eye can distinguish points as close together as 0.1 mm, about the size of a very fine grain of sand. A typical light microscope cannot resolve detail finer than about 0.2 micrometer (μm), about the size of the smallest bacterium. No matter how many times the image of such a small cell is magnified, the light microscope cannot resolve the details of its structure. Indeed, light microscopes can effectively magnify objects only about 1,000 times.

From the time that Hooke discovered cells in 1665 until the middle of the 1900s, biologists had only light microscopes for viewing cells. With these microscopes and various staining techniques to increase contrast between parts of cells, these early biologists discovered microorganisms, animal and plant cells, and even some structures within cells. By the mid-1800s, this accumulation of evidence led to the **cell theory**, which states that all living things are composed of cells and that all cells come from other cells.

Our knowledge of cell structure took a giant leap forward as biologists began using the electron microscope in the 1950s. Instead of using light, an **electron microscope (EM)** focuses a beam of electrons through a specimen or onto its surface. Electron microscopes can distinguish biological structures as small as about 2 nanometers (nm), a 100-fold improvement over the light microscope. This high resolution has enabled biologists to explore cell ultrastructure, the complex internal anatomy of a cell. Figures 4.1B and 4.1C show images produced by two kinds of electron microscopes.

TABLE 4.1 Metric Measurement Equivalents

1 meter (m) = 100 cm = 1,000 mm = 39.4 inches
1 centimeter (cm) = 10^{-2} m (0.01 or 1/100 m) = 0.4 inch
1 millimeter (mm) = 10^{-3} m (0.001 or 1/1,000 m)
1 micrometer (μm) = 10^{-6} m (0.000001 m) = 10^{-3} mm
1 nanometer (nm) = 10^{-9} m = 10^{-3} μm

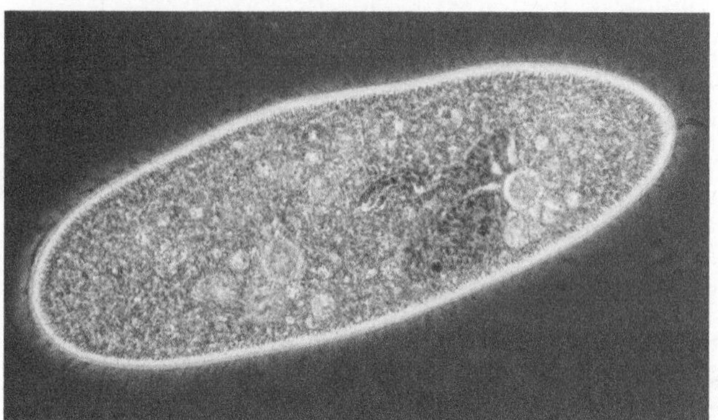

▲ Figure 4.1A Light micrograph of the unicellular organism *Paramecium*

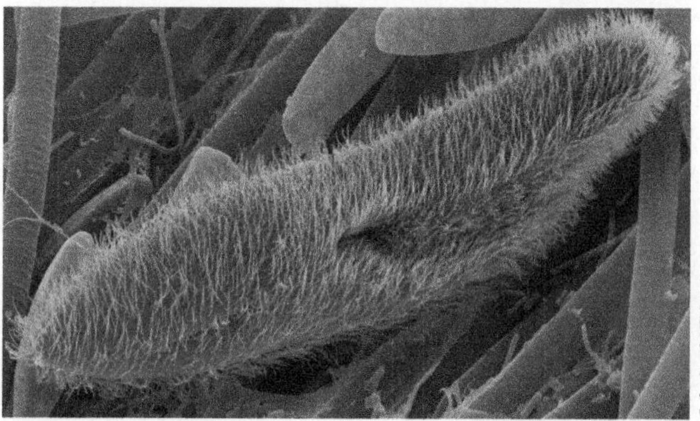

▲ Figure 4.1B Scanning electron micrograph of *Paramecium*

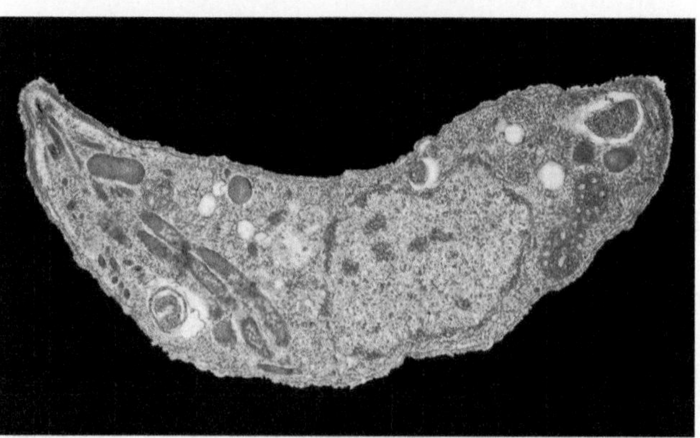

▲ Figure 4.1C Transmission electron micrograph of *Toxoplasma* (This parasite of cats can be transmitted to humans, causing the disease toxoplasmosis.)

TRY THIS Describe a major difference between the *Paramecium* in Figure 4.1B and the *Toxoplasma* in this figure. (Hint: Compare the notations along the right sides of the micrographs.)

Biologists use the **scanning electron microscope (SEM)** to study the detailed architecture of cell surfaces. The SEM uses an electron beam to scan the surface of a cell or other sample, which is usually coated with a thin film of gold. The beam excites electrons on the surface, and these electrons are then detected by a device that translates their pattern into an image projected onto a video screen. The scanning electron micrograph in Figure 4.1B highlights the numerous cilia on *Paramecium*, projections it uses for movement. Notice the indentation, called the oral groove, through which food enters the cell. As you can see, the SEM produces images that look three-dimensional.

The **transmission electron microscope (TEM)** is used to study the details of internal cell structure. The TEM aims an electron beam through a very thin section of a specimen, just as a light microscope aims a beam of light through a specimen. The section is stained with atoms of heavy metals, which attach to certain cellular structures more than others. Electrons are scattered by these more dense parts, and the image is created by the pattern of transmitted electrons. Instead of using glass lenses, both the SEM and TEM use electromagnets as lenses to bend the paths of the electrons, magnifying and focusing the image onto a monitor. The transmission electron micrograph in Figure 4.1C shows internal details of a single-celled organism called *Toxoplasma*. SEMs and TEMs are initially black and white but are often artificially colorized, as they are here, to highlight or clarify structural features.

Electron microscopes have truly revolutionized the study of cells and their structures. Nonetheless, they have not replaced the light microscope: Electron microscopes cannot be used to study living specimens because the methods used to prepare the specimen kill the cells. For a biologist studying a living process, such as the movement of *Paramecium*, a light microscope equipped with a video camera is more suitable than either an SEM or a TEM.

There are different types of light microscopy, and major technical advances in the past several decades have greatly expanded our ability to visualize cells. **Figure 4.1D** shows *Paramecium* as seen using differential interference contrast microscopy. This optical technique amplifies differences in density so that the structures in living cells appear almost three-dimensional. Other techniques use fluorescent stains that selectively bind to various cellular molecules (see the chapter introduction).

You will see many beautiful and illuminating examples of microscopy in this textbook. But even with the magnification shown beside each micrograph, it is often hard to imagine just how small cells are. **Figure 4.1E** shows the size range of cells compared with objects both larger and smaller and the optical instrument that allows us to view them. Notice that the scale along the left side of the figure is logarithmic to accommodate the range of sizes shown. Starting at the top with 10 meters (m), each reference measurement marks a tenfold decrease in length. Most cells are between 1 and 100 µm in diameter (yellow region of the figure) and are therefore visible only with a microscope. Certain bacteria are as small as 0.2 µm and can barely be seen with a light microscope, whereas chicken eggs are large enough to be seen with the unaided eye. A single nerve cell running from the base of your spinal cord to your big toe may be 1 m in length, although it is so thin you would still need a microscope to see it. In the next module, we explore why cells are so small.

? Which type of microscope would you use to study (a) the changes in shape of a living human white blood cell; (b) the finest details of surface texture of a human hair; (c) the detailed structure of an organelle in a liver cell?

(a) Light microscope; (b) scanning electron microscope; (c) transmission electron microscope

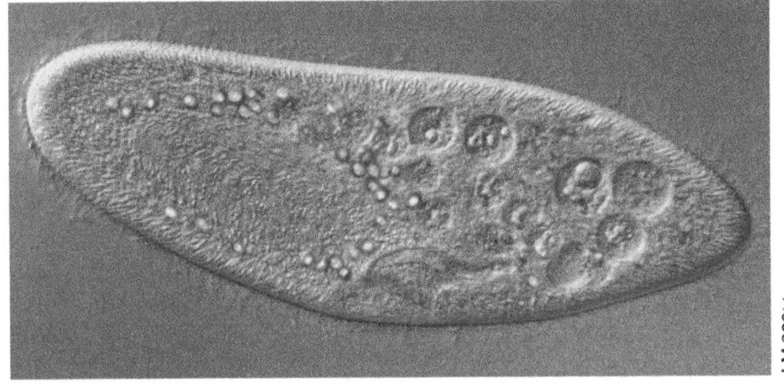

▲ **Figure 4.1D** Differential interference contrast micrograph of *Paramecium*

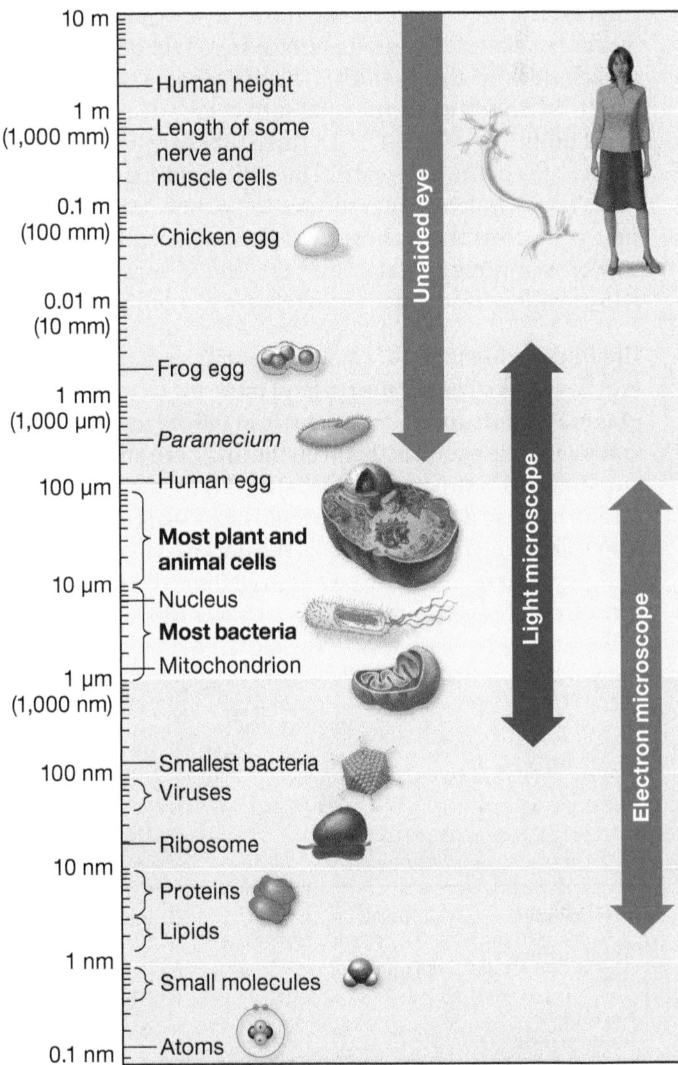

▲ **Figure 4.1E** The size range of cells and related objects

4.2 The small size of cells relates to the need to exchange materials across the plasma membrane

As you saw in Figure 4.1E, most cells are microscopic. Are there advantages to being so small? The logistics of carrying out a cell's functions appear to set both lower and upper limits on cell size. At minimum, a cell must be large enough to house enough DNA, protein molecules, and structures to survive and reproduce. But why aren't most cells as large as chicken eggs? The maximum size of a cell is influenced by geometry—the need to have a surface area large enough to service the volume of a cell. Active cells have a huge amount of traffic across their outer surface. A chicken egg cell isn't very active, but once a chick embryo starts to develop, the egg is divided into many microscopic cells, each bounded by a membrane that allows the essential flow of oxygen, nutrients, and wastes across its surface.

Surface-to-Volume Ratio Large cells have more surface area than small cells, but they have a much smaller surface area relative to their volume than small cells. Figure 4.2A illustrates this by comparing 1 large cube to 27 small ones. Using arbitrary units of measurement, the total volume is the same in both cases: 27 units^3 (height × width × length). The total surface areas, however, are quite different. A cube has six sides; thus, its surface area is six times the area of each side (height × width). The surface area of the large cube is 54 units^2, while the total surface area of all 27 cubes is 162 units^2 (27 × 6 × 1 × 1), three times greater than the surface area of the large cube. Thus, the combined smaller cubes have a much greater surface-to-volume ratio than the large cube. How about those neurons that extend from the base of your spine to your toes? Very thin, elongated shapes also provide a large surface area relative to a cell's volume.

The Plasma Membrane So what is a cell's surface like? And how does it control the traffic of molecules across it? The **plasma membrane**, also referred to as the cell membrane, forms a flexible boundary between the living cell and its surroundings. For a structure that separates life from nonlife, this membrane is amazingly thin. It would take a stack of more than 8,000 plasma membranes to equal the thickness of this page. And, as you have come to expect with all things biological, the structure of the plasma membrane correlates with its function.

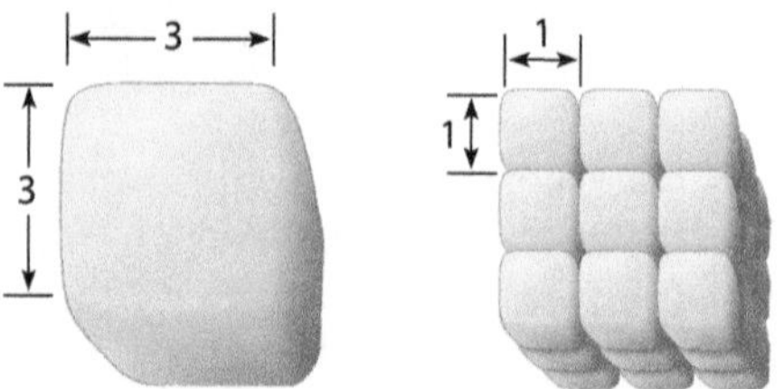

Total volume	27 units^3	27 units^3
Total surface area	54 units^2	162 units^2
Surface-to-volume ratio	2	6

▲ Figure 4.2A Effect of cell size on surface area and volume

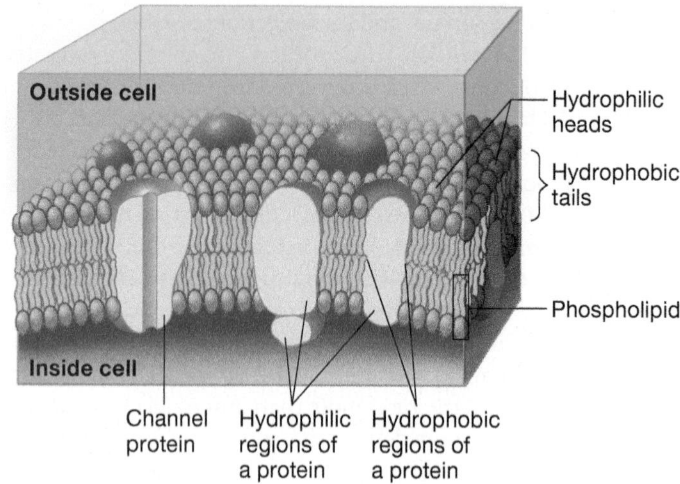

▲ Figure 4.2B The structure of a plasma membrane

Phospholipid molecules are well suited to their role as a major constituent of biological membranes. Each phospholipid is composed of two distinct regions—a head with a negatively charged phosphate group and two nonpolar fatty acid tails (see Module 3.10). Phospholipids group together to form a two-layer sheet called a phospholipid bilayer. As you can see in Figure 4.2B, the phospholipids' hydrophilic (water-loving) heads face outward, exposed to the aqueous solutions on both sides of a membrane. Their hydrophobic (water-fearing) tails point inward, mingling together and shielded from water. Embedded in this lipid bilayer are diverse proteins, floating like icebergs in a phospholipid sea. The regions of the proteins within the center of the membrane are hydrophobic; the exterior sections exposed to water are hydrophilic.

Illustrating our theme of STRUCTURE AND FUNCTION, the properties of the phospholipid bilayer and the proteins suspended in it relate to the plasma membrane's job as a traffic cop, regulating the flow of material into and out of the cell. Nonpolar molecules, such as O_2 and CO_2, can easily move across the membrane's hydrophobic interior. Some of the membrane's proteins form channels (tunnels) that shield ions and polar molecules as they pass through the hydrophobic center of the membrane. Still other proteins serve as pumps, using energy to actively transport molecules into or out of the cell.

We will return to the structure and function of biological membranes later (see Chapter 5). In the next module, we consider other features common to all cells and take a closer look at the prokaryotic cells found in two of the three major groups of organisms.

? **To convince yourself that a small cell has a greater surface area relative to volume than a large cell, compare the surface-to-volume ratios of the large cube and one of the small cubes in Figure 4.2A.**

■ Large cube: 54/27 = 2; small cube: 6/1 = 6 (surface area is 1 × 1 × 6 sides = 6 units^2; volume is 1 × 1 × 1 unit^3)

4.3 Prokaryotic cells are structurally simpler than eukaryotic cells

Cells are of two distinct types: prokaryotic and eukaryotic. **Prokaryotic cells** were the first to evolve and were Earth's sole inhabitants for more than 1.5 billion years. Evidence indicates that **eukaryotic cells** evolved from some of these ancestral cells about 1.8 billion years ago. Biologists recognize three domains or major groups of organisms. The microorganisms placed in domains Bacteria and Archaea consist of prokaryotic cells. These organisms are known as prokaryotes. All other forms of life are placed in domain Eukarya. They are composed of eukaryotic cells and are referred to as eukaryotes.

Eukaryotic cells are distinguished by having a membrane-enclosed nucleus, which houses most of their DNA, and many membrane-enclosed organelles that perform specific functions. Prokaryotic cells are smaller and simpler in structure.

Both types of cells, however, share certain basic features. In addition to being bounded by a plasma membrane, the interior of all cells is filled with a thick, jellylike fluid called **cytosol**, in which cellular components are suspended. All cells have one or more **chromosomes**, which carry genes made of DNA. They also contain **ribosomes**, tiny structures that make proteins according to instructions from the genes. The inside of both types of cells is called the **cytoplasm**. However, in eukaryotic cells, this term refers only to the region between the nucleus and the plasma membrane.

Figure 4.3 explores the structure of a generalized prokaryotic cell. Notice that the DNA is coiled into a region called the **nucleoid** ("nucleus-like"), but no membrane surrounds the DNA. The ribosomes of prokaryotes are smaller and differ somewhat from those of eukaryotes. These molecular differences are the basis for the action of some antibiotics, which specifically target prokaryotic ribosomes. Thus, protein synthesis can be blocked for the bacterium that's invaded you, but not for you, the eukaryote who is taking the drug.

Outside the plasma membrane of most prokaryotes is a fairly rigid, chemically complex cell wall. The wall protects the cell and helps maintain its shape. Some antibiotics, such as penicillin, prevent the formation of these protective walls. Again, because your cells don't have such walls, these antibiotics can kill invading bacteria without harming your cells. Certain prokaryotes have a sticky outer coat called a capsule around the cell wall, helping to glue the cells to surfaces or to other cells in a colony. In addition to capsules, some prokaryotes have surface projections. Short projections help attach prokaryotes to each other or their substrate. Longer projections called **flagella** (singular, *flagellum*) propel a cell through its liquid environment.

It takes an electron microscope to see the internal details of any cell, and this is especially true of prokaryotic cells. Notice that the TEM of the bacterium in Figure 4.3 has a magnification of 20,940×. Most prokaryotic cells are about one-tenth the size of a typical eukaryotic cell. (Prokaryotes will be described in more detail in Chapter 16.) Eukaryotic cells are the main focus of this chapter, so we turn to these next.

? List three features that are common to prokaryotic and eukaryotic cells. List three features that differ.

■ Both types of cells have plasma membranes, chromosomes containing DNA, and ribosomes. Prokaryotic cells are smaller, do not have a nucleus or other membrane-enclosed organelles, and have somewhat different ribosomes.

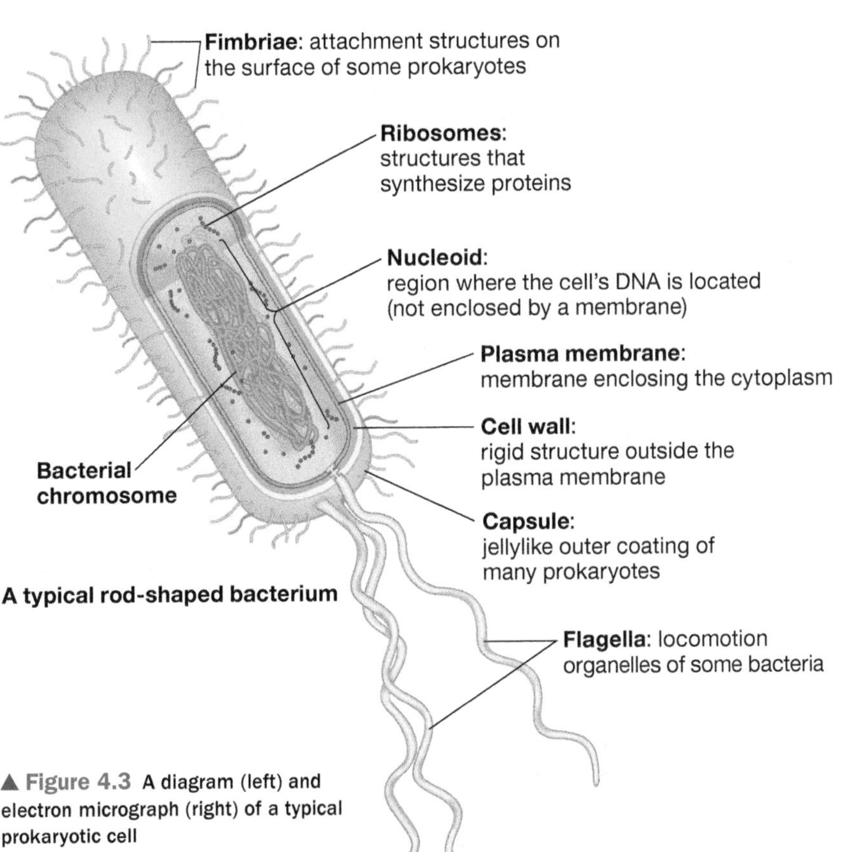

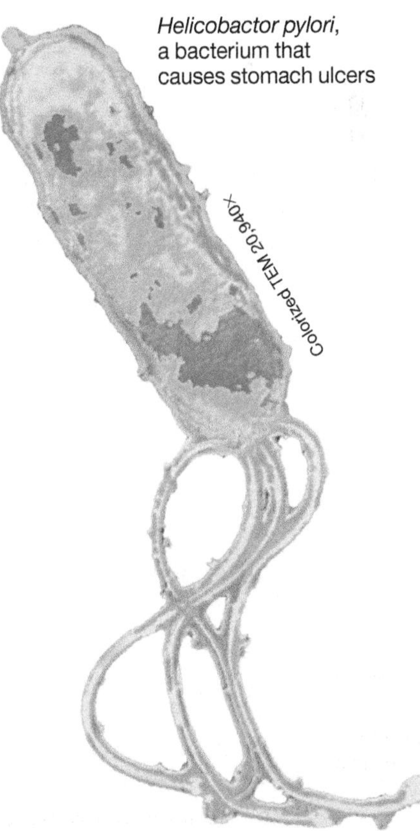

Helicobactor pylori, a bacterium that causes stomach ulcers
Colorized TEM 20,940×

▲ **Figure 4.3 A diagram (left) and electron micrograph (right) of a typical prokaryotic cell**

4.4 Eukaryotic cells are partitioned into functional compartments

All eukaryotic cells—whether from protists (a diverse group of mostly unicellular organisms), fungi, animals, or plants—are fundamentally similar to one another and profoundly different from prokaryotic cells. Let's look at an animal cell and a plant cell as representatives of the eukaryotes.

Figure 4.4A is a diagram of a generalized animal cell, and Figure 4.4B shows a generalized plant cell. We color-code the various structures in the diagrams for easier identification, and you will see miniature versions of these cells to orient you during our in-depth tour in the rest of the chapter. But no cells would look exactly like these. For one thing, cells have multiple copies of all of these structures (except for the nucleus). Your cells have hundreds of mitochondria and millions of ribosomes. A plant cell may have 30 chloroplasts packed inside. Cells also have different shapes and relative proportions of cell parts, depending on their specialized functions.

The most obvious hallmark of a eukaryotic cell is its nucleus. But it also contains various other **organelles** ("little organs"), which perform specific tasks. Just as the cell itself is wrapped in a membrane made of phospholipids and proteins that perform various functions, each organelle is bounded by a membrane with a lipid and protein composition that suits its function.

The organelles and other structures of eukaryotic cells can be organized into four basic functional groups: (1) The nucleus and ribosomes carry out the genetic control of the cell. (2) Organelles involved in the manufacture, distribution, and breakdown of molecules include the endoplasmic reticulum, Golgi apparatus, lysosomes, vacuoles, and peroxisomes. (3) Mitochondria in all cells and chloroplasts in plant cells function in energy processing. (4) Structural support, movement, and communication between cells are the functions of the cytoskeleton, plasma membrane, and plant cell wall. The cellular components identified in these two figures will be examined in detail in the modules that follow.

In essence, the internal membranes of a eukaryotic cell partition it into functional compartments in which many

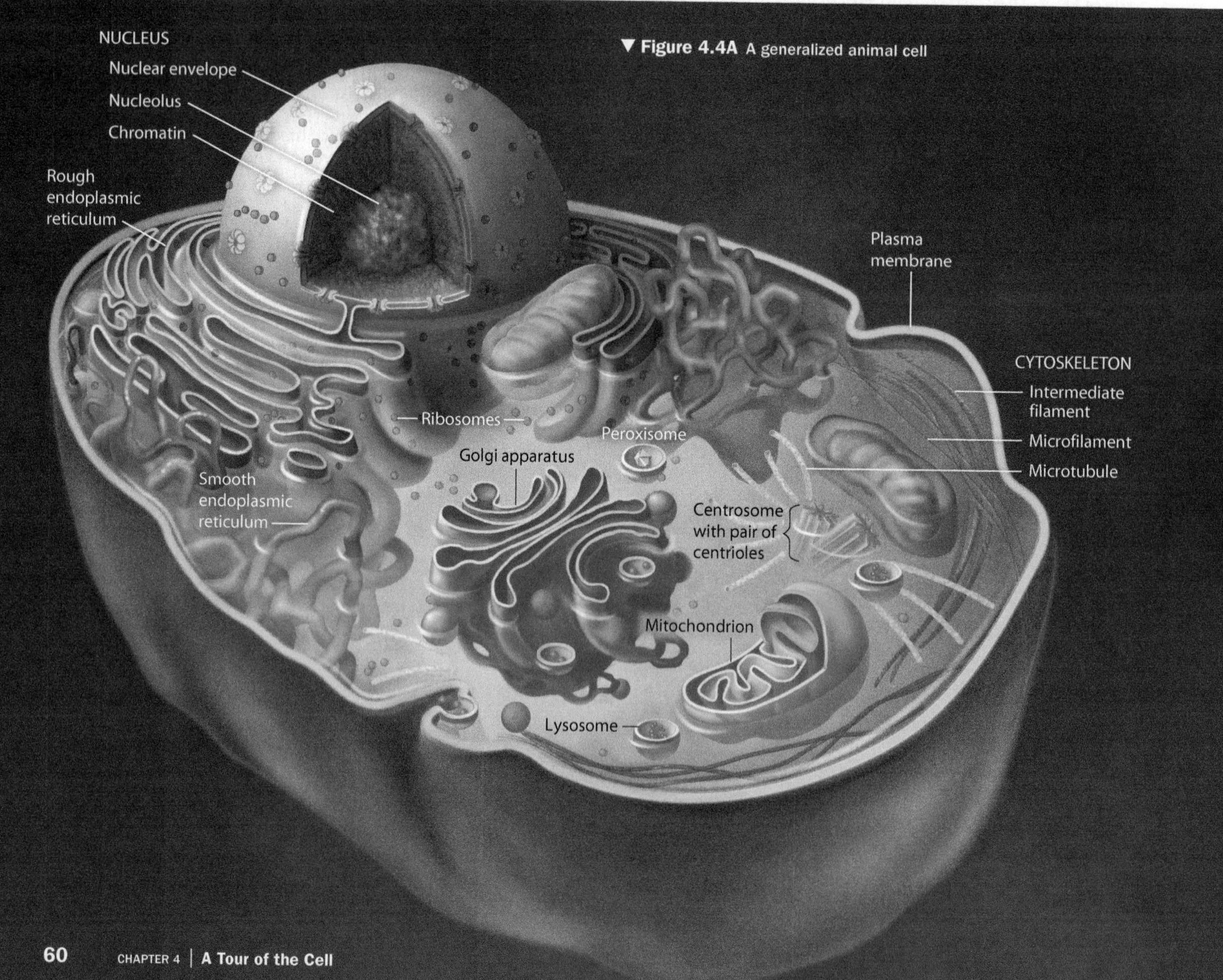

▼ **Figure 4.4A** A generalized animal cell

of its chemical activities—collectively called **cellular metabolism**—take place. In fact, various enzymes essential for metabolic processes are built into the membranes of organelles. The fluid-filled spaces within such compartments are locations where specific chemical conditions are maintained. These conditions vary among organelles and favor the metabolic processes occurring in each. For example, while a part of the endoplasmic reticulum is engaged in making hormones, neighboring peroxisomes may be detoxifying harmful compounds and making hydrogen peroxide (H_2O_2) as a poisonous by-product of their activities. But because the H_2O_2 is confined within the peroxisomes, where it is converted to H_2O by resident enzymes, the rest of the cell is protected.

Except for lysosomes and centrosomes, the organelles and other structures of animal cells are found in plant cells. Also, although some animal cells have flagella or cilia (not shown in Figure 4.4A), among plants, only the sperm cells of a few species have flagella.

A plant cell (Figure 4.4B) also has some structures that an animal cell lacks. For example, a plant cell has a rigid, rather thick cell wall. Chemically different from prokaryotic cell walls, plant cell walls contain the polysaccharide cellulose. Plasmodesmata (singular, plasmodesma) are cytoplasmic channels through cell walls that connect adjacent cells. An important organelle found in plant cells is the chloroplast, where photosynthesis occurs. Unique to plant cells is a large central vacuole, a compartment that stores water and a variety of chemicals.

Eukaryotic cells contain nonmembranous structures as well. The cytoskeleton, which you were introduced to in the chapter introduction, is composed of different types of protein fibers that extend throughout the cell. And ribosomes are found in the cytosol as well as attached to certain membranes.

After you preview these cell diagrams, let's move to the first stop on our detailed tour of the eukaryotic cell—the nucleus.

? **Identify the structures in the plant cell that are not present in the animal cell.**

Chloroplasts, central vacuole, cell wall, and plasmodesmata

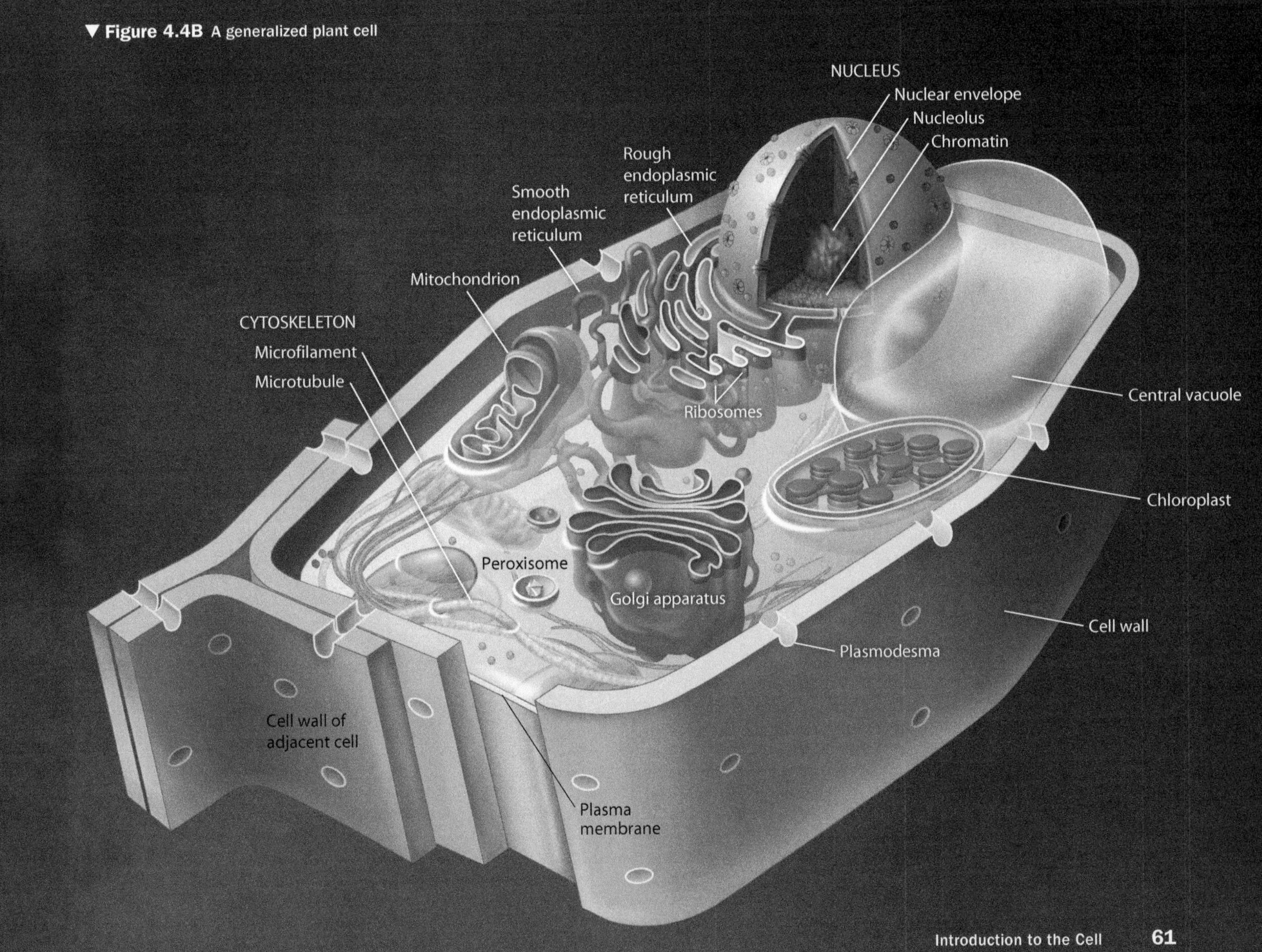

▼ **Figure 4.4B** A generalized plant cell

The Nucleus and Ribosomes

4.5 The nucleus contains the cell's genetic instructions

You just saw a preview of the many intricate structures that can be found in a eukaryotic cell. A cell must build and maintain these structures and also process energy to support its work of transport, movement, and communication. But who is in charge of this bustling factory? Who stores the master plans, gives the orders, changes course in response to environmental input, and, when called on, makes another factory just like itself? The cell's nucleus functions as this command center.

The **nucleus** contains the cell's genetic instructions encoded in DNA. These master plans control the cell's activities by directing protein synthesis. The DNA is associated with many proteins and organized into structures called chromosomes. The proteins help coil these long DNA molecules. Indeed, the DNA of the 46 chromosomes in one of your cells laid end to end would stretch to a length of more than 2 m, but it must coil up to fit into a nucleus only 5 μm in diameter. When a cell is not dividing, this complex of proteins and DNA, called **chromatin**, appears as a diffuse mass within the nucleus, as shown in the TEM (right half) and diagram (left half) of a nucleus in Figure 4.5.

As a cell prepares to divide, the DNA is copied so that each daughter cell can later receive an identical set of genetic instructions. Just prior to cell division, the thin chromatin fibers coil up further, becoming thick enough to be visible with a light microscope as the familiar separate structures you would probably recognize as chromosomes.

Enclosing the nucleus is a double membrane called the **nuclear envelope**. Each of the two membranes is a separate phospholipid bilayer with associated proteins. Similar in function to the plasma membrane, the nuclear envelope controls the flow of materials into and out of the nucleus. As you can see in the diagram of a nucleus in Figure 4.5, the nuclear envelope is perforated with protein-lined pores. These pores regulate the entry and exit of large molecules and also connect with the cell's network of membranes called the endoplasmic reticulum.

The **nucleolus**, a prominent structure in the nucleus, is the site where a special type of RNA called ribosomal RNA (rRNA) is synthesized according to instructions in the DNA. Proteins brought in from the cytoplasm are assembled with this rRNA to form the subunits of ribosomes. These subunits then exit to the cytoplasm, where they will join to form functional ribosomes.

Another type of RNA, messenger RNA (mRNA), directs protein synthesis. Essentially, mRNA is a transcription of protein-synthesizing instructions written in a gene's DNA (see Figure 10.7). The mRNA moves into the cytoplasm, where ribosomes translate it into the amino acid sequences of proteins. Let's look at ribosomes next.

? **Describe the processes that occur in the nucleus.**

■ DNA is copied and passed on to daughter cells in cell division; rRNA is made and ribosomal subunits assembled; protein-making instructions in DNA are transcribed into mRNA.

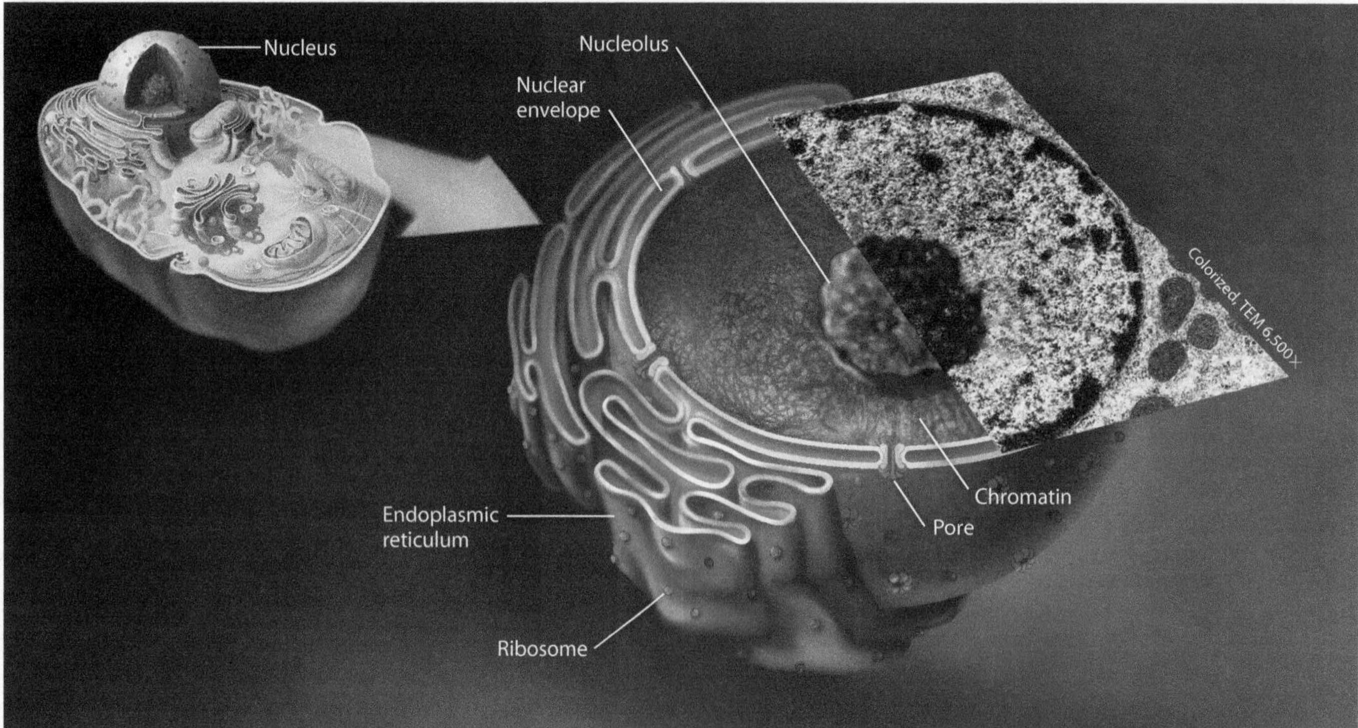

▲ Figure 4.5 A cross section of the nucleus with a superimposed TEM

4.6 Ribosomes make proteins for use in the cell and for export

If the nucleus is the cell's command center, then ribosomes are the machines that carry out those commands. Ribosomes are the cellular components that use instructions from the nucleus, written in mRNA, to build proteins. Cells that make a lot of proteins have a large number of ribosomes. For example, a cell in your pancreas that produces digestive enzymes may contain a few million ribosomes. What other structure is prominent in cells that are active in protein synthesis? Remember that the nucleolus in the nucleus is the site where the subunits of ribosomes are assembled.

As shown in Figure 4.6, ribosomes are found in two locations in the cell. Free ribosomes are suspended in the cytosol, while bound ribosomes are attached to the outside of the endoplasmic reticulum or nuclear envelope. Free and bound ribosomes are structurally identical, and they can function in either location, depending on the protein they are making.

Most of the proteins made on free ribosomes function within the cytosol; examples are enzymes that catalyze the first steps of sugar breakdown for cellular respiration. In Module 4.8, you will see how bound ribosomes make proteins that will be exported from the cell.

At the bottom right in Figure 4.6, you see how ribosomes interact with messenger RNA (carrying the instructions from a gene) to build a protein. The nucleotide sequence of an mRNA molecule is translated into the amino acid sequence of a polypeptide. The pathway from DNA to RNA to protein is a prime example of our theme of the flow of INFORMATION. (Protein synthesis is explored in more detail in Chapter 10.)

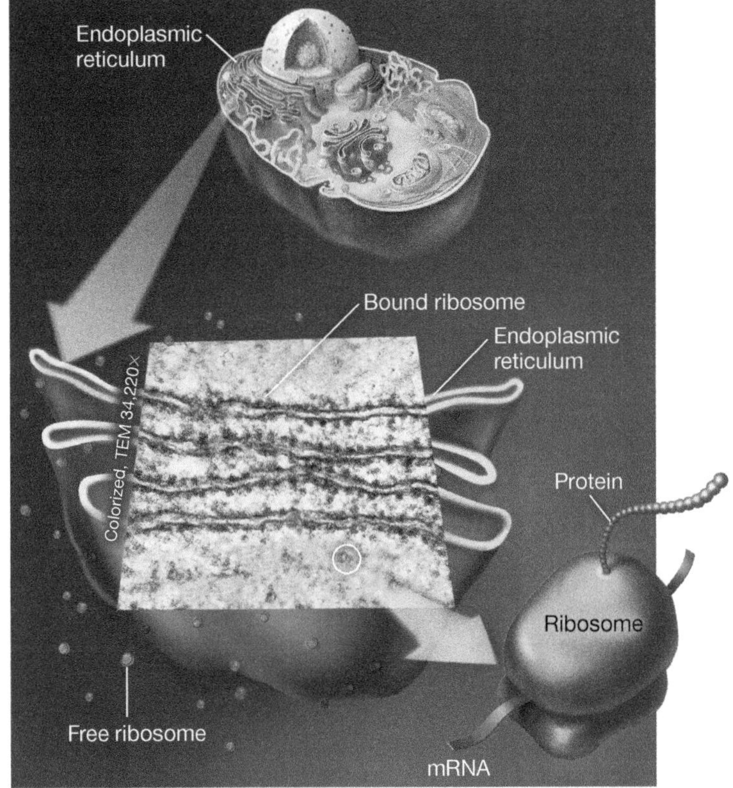

▲ **Figure 4.6 The locations and structure of ribosomes**

? What role do ribosomes play in carrying out the genetic instructions of a cell?

■ Ribosomes synthesize proteins according to the instructions of messenger RNA, which was transcribed from DNA in the nucleus.

The Endomembrane System

4.7 Many organelles are connected in the endomembrane system

Ribosomes may be a cell's protein-making machines, but running a factory as complex as a cell requires infrastructure and many different departments that perform separate but related functions. Internal membranes, a distinguishing feature of eukaryotic cells, are involved in most of a cell's functions. Many of the membranes of the eukaryotic cell are part of an **endomembrane system**. Some of these membranes are physically connected and others are linked when tiny **vesicles** (sacs made of membrane) transfer membrane segments between them.

The endomembrane system includes the nuclear envelope, endoplasmic reticulum, Golgi apparatus, lysosomes, various types of vesicles and vacuoles, and the plasma membrane. (The plasma membrane is not exactly an *endo* (inner) membrane in physical location, but it is related to the other membranes by the transfer of vesicles.) Many of these organelles interact in the synthesis, distribution, storage, and export of molecules.

The largest component of the endomembrane system is the **endoplasmic reticulum (ER)**, an extensive network of flattened sacs and tubules. (The word *endoplasmic* means "within the cytoplasm," and *reticulum* is Latin for "little net.") The ER is a prime example of the direct and indirect interrelatedness of parts of the endomembrane system. As shown in Figure 4.5 on the facing page, membranes of the ER are continuous with the nuclear envelope. And when vesicles bud from the ER, they travel to many other components of the endomembrane system.

The membranes of the ER enclose a space separate from the cytosol. Indeed, an important aspect of the components of the endomembrane system is dividing the cell into functional compartments, each of which may require different conditions.

? Which structure includes all others in the list: ER, vesicle, endomembrane system, nuclear envelope?

■ Endomembrane system

4.8 The endoplasmic reticulum is a biosynthetic workshop

One of the major manufacturing sites in a cell is the endoplasmic reticulum. The diagram in Figure 4.8A shows a cutaway view of the interconnecting membranes of the smooth and rough ER, which can be distinguished in the superimposed electron micrograph. **Smooth endoplasmic reticulum** is called *smooth* because its outer surface lacks attached ribosomes. **Rough endoplasmic reticulum** has bound ribosomes that stud the outer surface of the membrane; thus, it appears *rough* in the electron micrograph.

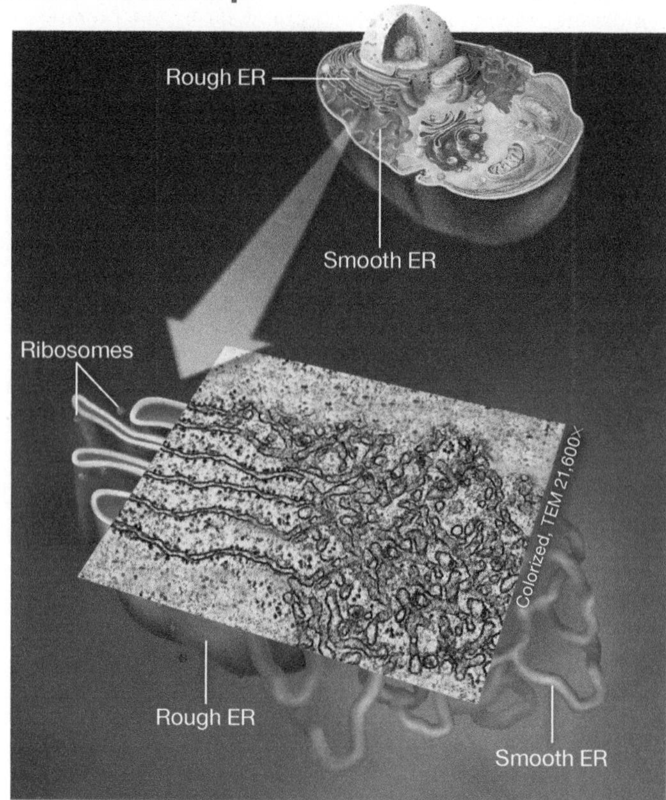

▲ Figure 4.8A **Smooth and rough endoplasmic reticulum**

Smooth ER The smooth ER of various cell types functions in a variety of metabolic processes. Enzymes of the smooth ER are important in the synthesis of lipids, including oils, phospholipids, and steroids. In vertebrates, for example, cells of the ovaries and testes synthesize the steroid sex hormones. These cells are rich in smooth ER, a structural feature that fits their function by providing ample machinery for steroid synthesis.

Our liver cells also have large amounts of smooth ER, with enzymes that help process drugs, alcohol, and other potentially harmful substances. The sedative phenobarbital and other barbiturates are examples of drugs detoxified by these enzymes. As liver cells are exposed to such chemicals, the amount of smooth ER and its detoxifying enzymes increases, thereby increasing the rate of detoxification and thus the body's tolerance to the drugs. The result is a need for higher doses of a drug to achieve a particular effect, such as sedation. Also, because detoxifying enzymes often cannot distinguish among related chemicals, the growth of smooth ER in response to one drug can increase the need for higher doses of other drugs. Barbiturate abuse, for example, can decrease the effectiveness of certain antibiotics and other useful drugs.

Smooth ER has yet another function, the storage of calcium ions. In muscle cells, for example, a specialized smooth ER membrane pumps calcium ions into the interior of the ER. When a nerve signal stimulates a muscle cell, calcium ions rush from the smooth ER into the cytosol and trigger contraction of the cell.

Rough ER Many types of cells secrete proteins produced by ribosomes attached to rough ER. An example of a secretory protein is insulin, a hormone produced and secreted by certain cells of the pancreas and transported in the bloodstream. Type 1 diabetes results when these cells are destroyed and a lack of insulin disrupts glucose metabolism in the body.

Figure 4.8B follows the synthesis, modification, and packaging of a secretory protein. As the polypeptide is synthesized by a bound ribosome following the instructions of an mRNA, ❶ it is threaded into the cavity of the rough ER. As it enters, the new protein folds into its three-dimensional shape. ❷ Short chains of sugars are often linked to the polypeptide, making the molecule a **glycoprotein** (*glyco* means "sugar"). ❸ When the molecule is ready for export from the ER, it is packaged in a **transport vesicle**, a vesicle that moves from one part of the cell to another. ❹ This vesicle buds off from the ER membrane.

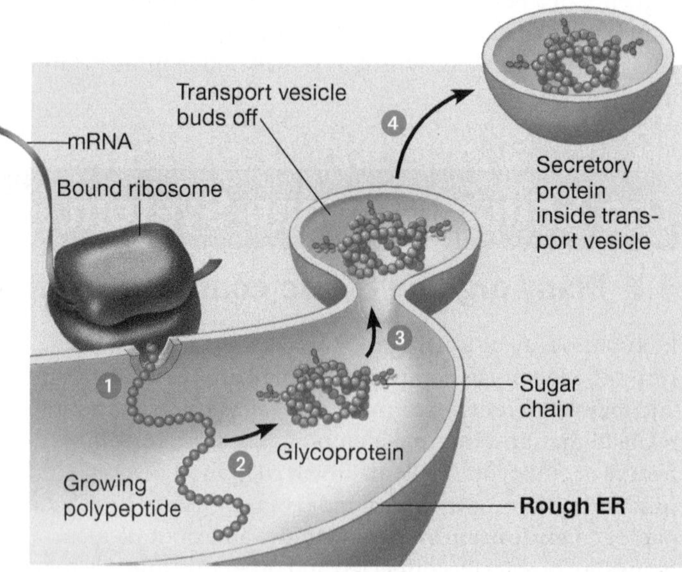

▲ Figure 4.8B **Synthesis and packaging of a secretory protein by the rough ER**

TRY THIS Explain where the protein-making instructions carried by the mRNA came from.

The vesicle now carries the protein to the Golgi apparatus for further processing. From there, a transport vesicle containing the finished molecule makes its way to the plasma membrane and releases its contents from the cell.

In addition to making secretory proteins, rough ER is a membrane-making machine for the cell. It grows in place by adding membrane proteins and phospholipids to its own membrane. As polypeptides destined to be membrane proteins grow from bound ribosomes, they are inserted into the ER membrane. Phospholipids are made by enzymes of the rough ER and also inserted into the membrane. Thus, the ER membrane grows, and portions of it are transferred to other components of the endomembrane system in the form of transport vesicles.

Now let's follow a transport vesicle carrying products of the rough ER to the Golgi apparatus.

? **Explain why we say that the endoplasmic reticulum is a biosynthetic workshop.**

■ The ER produces a huge variety of molecules, including phospholipids for cell membranes, steroid hormones, and proteins (synthesized by bound ribosomes) for membranes, other organelles, and secretion by the cell.

4.9 The Golgi apparatus modifies, sorts, and ships cell products

After leaving the ER, many transport vesicles travel to the **Golgi apparatus**. Using a light microscope and a staining technique he developed, Italian scientist Camillo Golgi discovered this membranous organelle in 1898. The electron microscope confirmed his discovery more than 50 years later, revealing a stack of flattened sacs, looking much like a pile of pita bread. A cell may contain many, even hundreds, of these stacks. The number of Golgi stacks correlates with how active the cell is in secreting proteins—a multistep process that, as you have just seen, is initiated in the rough ER.

The Golgi apparatus serves as a molecular warehouse and processing station for products manufactured by the ER. You can follow these activities in Figure 4.9. Note that, unlike the ER sacs, the flattened Golgi sacs are not connected. ① One side of a Golgi stack serves as a receiving dock for transport vesicles produced by the ER. ② A vesicle fuses with a Golgi sac, adding its membrane and contents to the "receiving" side. ③ Products of the ER are modified as they progress through the stack. ④ The "shipping" side of the Golgi functions as a depot, dispatching its products in vesicles that bud off and travel to other sites.

How might ER products be processed during their transit through the Golgi? Various Golgi enzymes modify the carbohydrate portions of the glycoproteins made in the ER, removing some sugars and substituting others. Molecular identification tags, such as phosphate groups, may be added that help the Golgi sort molecules into different batches for different destinations.

Finished secretory products, packaged in transport vesicles, move to the plasma membrane for export from the cell. Alternatively, finished products may become part of the plasma membrane itself or part of another organelle, such as a lysosome, which we discuss next.

? **What is the relationship of the Golgi apparatus to the ER in a protein-secreting cell?**

■ The Golgi receives transport vesicles budded from the ER that contain proteins synthesized by bound ribosomes. The Golgi finishes processing the proteins and dispatches transport vesicles to the plasma membrane, where the proteins are secreted.

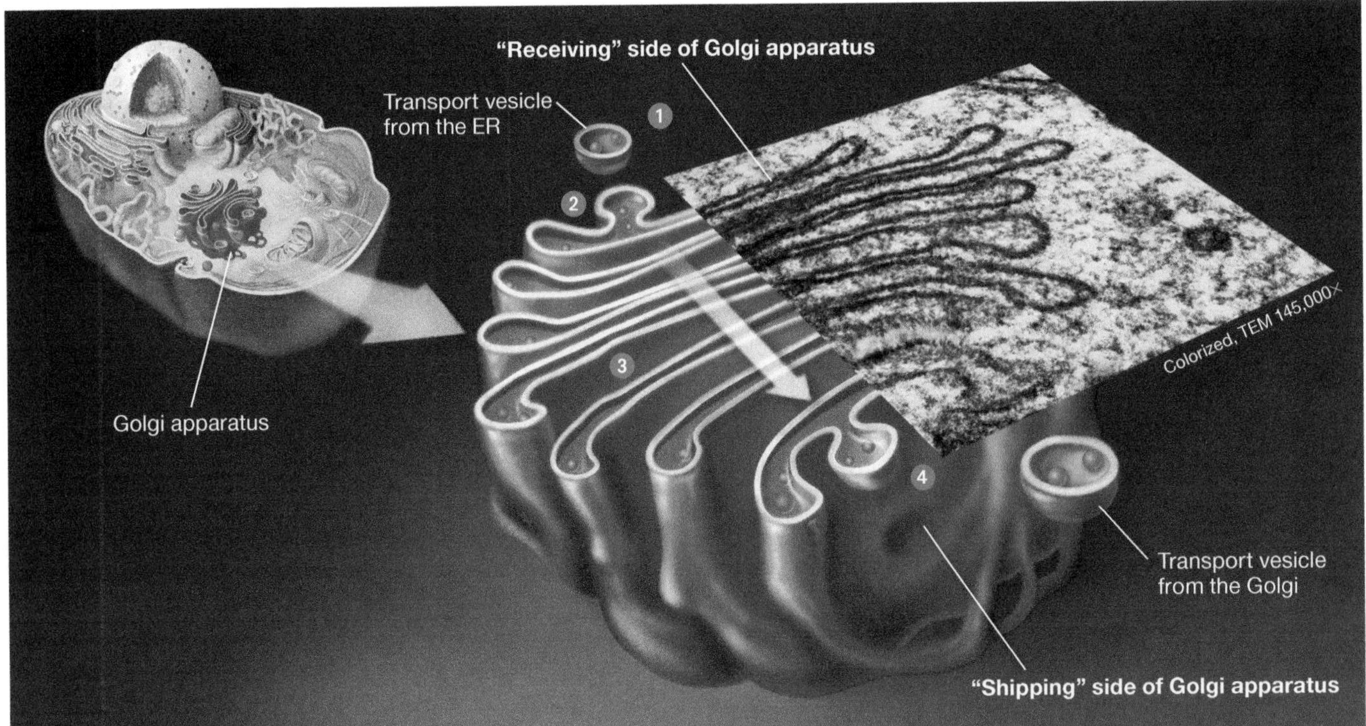

▲ Figure 4.9 The Golgi apparatus receiving, processing, and shipping products

4.10 Lysosomes are digestive compartments within a cell

A **lysosome** is a membrane-enclosed sac of digestive enzymes. The name *lysosome* is derived from two Greek words meaning "breakdown body." The enzymes and membranes of lysosomes are made by rough ER and processed in the Golgi apparatus. Illustrating a key characteristic of eukaryotic cells—compartmentalization—a lysosome provides an acidic environment for its enzymes, while safely isolating them from the rest of the cell.

Lysosomes have several types of digestive functions. Many protists engulf food particles into membranous sacs called food vacuoles. As Figure 4.10A shows, lysosomes fuse with food vacuoles and digest the food. The nutrients are then released into the cytosol. Our white blood cells engulf bacteria and then destroy them using lysosomes. Lysosomes also serve as recycling centers. Cells enclose damaged organelles or small amounts of cytosol in vesicles. A lysosome fuses with such a vesicle (Figure 4.10B) and dismantles its contents, making organic molecules available for reuse. With the help of lysosomes, a cell continually renews itself.

The cells of people with inherited lysosomal storage diseases lack one or more lysosomal enzymes. The lysosomes become engorged with undigested material, eventually interfering with cellular function. In Tay-Sachs disease, for example, a lipid-digesting enzyme is missing, and brain cells become impaired by an accumulation of lipids. Fortunately, lysosomal storage diseases are rare in the general population, as they are often fatal in early childhood.

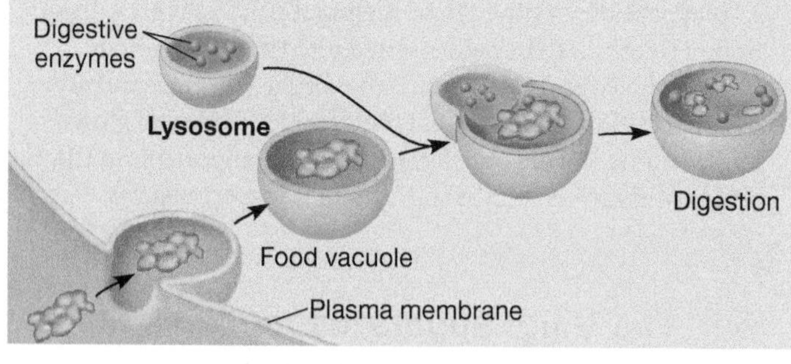

▲ Figure 4.10A Lysosome fusing with a food vacuole and digesting food, after which nutrients are released to the cytosol

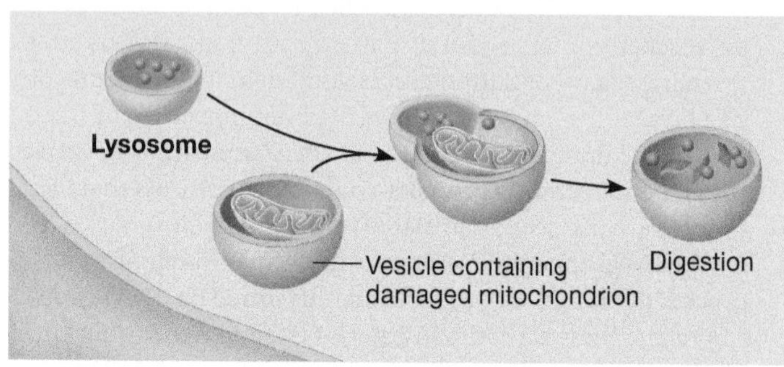

▲ Figure 4.10B Lysosome fusing with a vesicle containing a damaged organelle and then digesting and recycling its contents

 How is a lysosome like a recycling center?

■ It breaks down damaged organelles and recycles their molecules.

4.11 Vacuoles function in the general maintenance of the cell

Vacuoles are large vesicles that have a variety of functions. In Figure 4.10A, you saw how a food vacuole forms as a cell ingests food. Figure 4.11A shows two contractile vacuoles in the protist *Paramecium*, looking somewhat like wheel hubs with radiating spokes. The "spokes" collect water from the cell, and the hub expels it to the outside. Water constantly enters freshwater protists from their environment. Without a way to get rid of the excess water, the cell would swell and burst. In plants and fungi, certain vacuoles have a digestive function similar to that of lysosomes in animal cells. In the seeds of plants, small vacuoles in storage cells can hold reserves of proteins. Vacuoles in flower petals contain pigments that attract pollinating insects. Vacuoles may also help protect the plant against herbivores by storing compounds that are poisonous or unpalatable to animals. Examples include nicotine, caffeine, and various chemicals we use as pharmaceutical drugs.

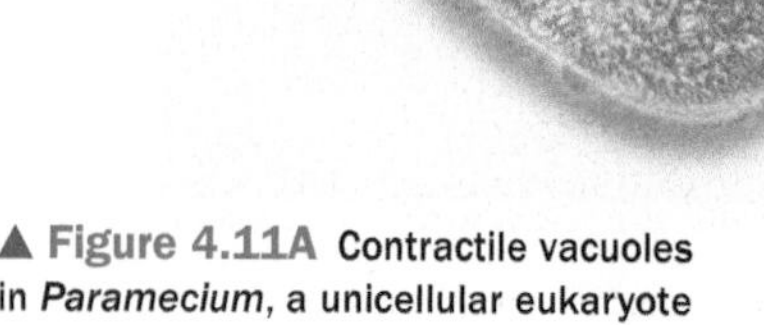

▲ Figure 4.11A Contractile vacuoles in *Paramecium*, a unicellular eukaryote

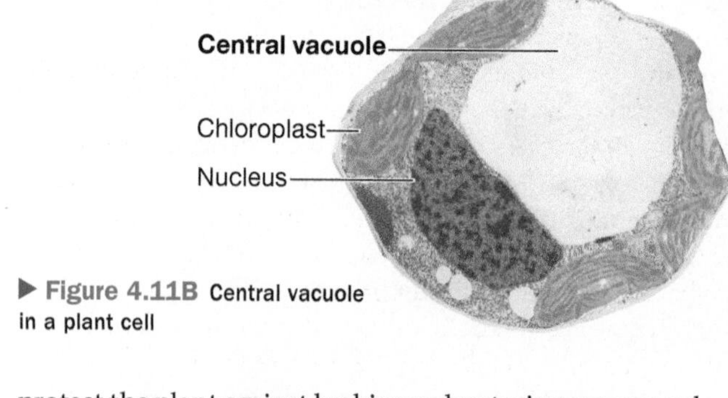

▶ Figure 4.11B Central vacuole in a plant cell

Figure 4.11B shows a plant cell's large **central vacuole**, which helps the cell grow in size by absorbing water and enlarging. It also stockpiles vital chemicals and may act as a trash can, safely storing toxic waste products.

? Is a food vacuole part of the endomembrane system? Explain.

■ Yes; it forms by pinching in from the plasma membrane, which is part of the endomembrane system.

4.12 A review of the structures involved in manufacturing and breakdown

Figure 4.12 summarizes the relationships within the endomembrane system. You can see the direct *structural* connections between the nuclear envelope, rough ER, and smooth ER. The red arrows show the *functional* connections, as membranes and proteins produced by the ER travel in transport vesicles to the Golgi and on to other destinations. Some vesicles develop into lysosomes or vacuoles. Others travel to and fuse with the plasma membrane, secreting their contents and adding their membrane to the plasma membrane.

Peroxisomes (see Figures 4.4A and 4.4B) are metabolic compartments that do not originate from the endomembrane system. In fact, how they are related to other organelles is still unknown. Some peroxisomes break down fatty acids to be used as cellular fuel. In your liver, peroxisomes detoxify harmful compounds. In these processes, enzymes transfer hydrogen from the compounds to oxygen, producing hydrogen peroxide (H_2O_2). Other enzymes in the peroxisome convert this toxic by-product to water—another example of the importance of a cell's compartmental structure.

A cell requires a continuous supply of energy to perform the work of life. Next we consider two organelles that act as cellular power stations—mitochondria and chloroplasts.

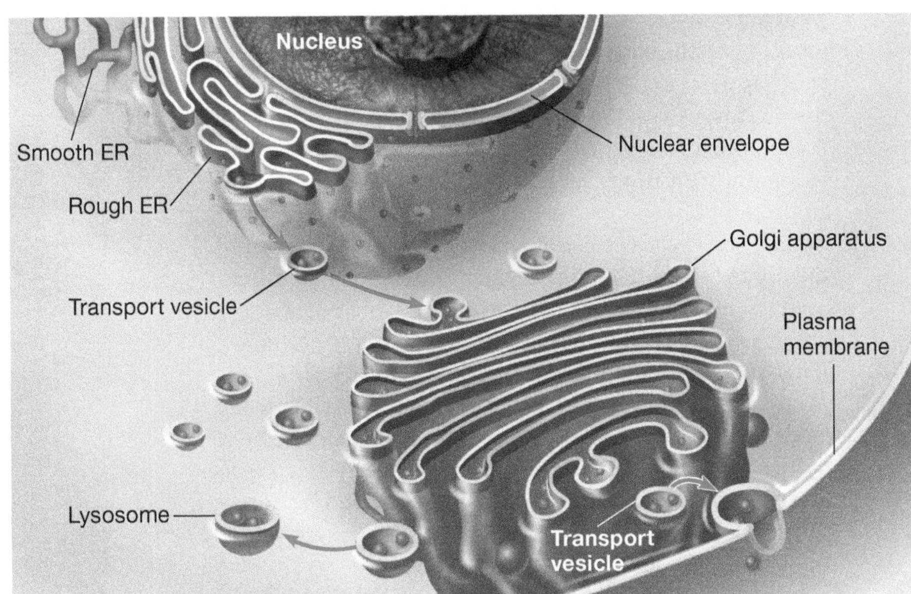

▲ Figure 4.12 Review of the endomembrane system

TRY THIS Explain how the endomembrane system enables a cell's compartmental organization.

? How do transport vesicles help tie together the endomembrane system?

■ Transport vesicles move membranes and the substances they enclose between components of the endomembrane system.

Energy-Converting Organelles

4.13 Mitochondria harvest chemical energy from food

Mitochondria (singular, *mitochondrion*) are organelles that carry out cellular respiration in nearly all eukaryotic cells. Illustrating the theme of ENERGY AND MATTER, mitochondria use O_2 and release CO_2 in transforming the chemical energy of foods to a form (ATP) that can be used for cellular work.

A mitochondrion is enclosed by two membranes, each a phospholipid bilayer with a unique collection of embedded proteins (Figure 4.13). The mitochondrion has two internal compartments. The first is the intermembrane space, the narrow region between the inner and outer membranes. The inner membrane encloses the second compartment, the **mitochondrial matrix**, which contains mitochondrial DNA and ribosomes, as well as enzymes that catalyze some of the reactions of cellular respiration. The inner membrane is highly folded and contains many embedded protein molecules that function in ATP synthesis. The folds, called cristae, increase the membrane's surface area, enhancing the mitochondrion's ability to produce ATP.

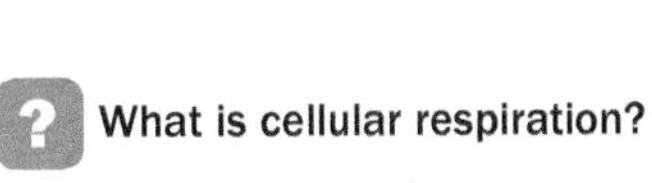

? What is cellular respiration?

■ A process that converts the chemical energy of food molecules to the chemical energy of ATP

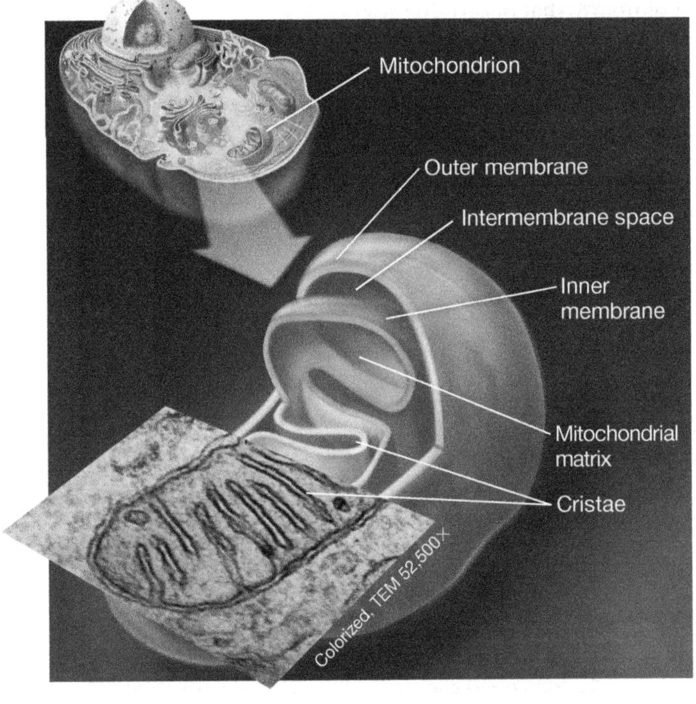

▲ Figure 4.13 The mitochondrion, site of cellular respiration

4.14 Chloroplasts convert solar energy to chemical energy

Most of the living world runs on the energy provided by photosynthesis, the conversion of light energy from the sun to the chemical energy of sugar molecules. **Chloroplasts** are the photosynthesizing organelles of plants and algae.

This organelle carries out complex, multistep processes, so it is not surprising that internal membranes partition the chloroplast into compartments (Figure 4.14). It is enclosed by an inner and outer membrane separated by a thin intermembrane space. The compartment inside the inner membrane holds a thick fluid called **stroma**, which contains chloroplast DNA and ribosomes as well as many enzymes. A network of interconnected sacs called **thylakoids** is suspended in the stroma. The sacs are often stacked like poker chips; each stack is called a **granum** (plural, *grana*). The compartment inside the thylakoids is called the thylakoid space.

The thylakoids are the chloroplast's solar power packs—the sites where the green chlorophyll molecules embedded in thylakoid membranes trap solar energy. In the next module, we explore the origin of mitochondria and chloroplasts.

? Which membrane in a chloroplast appears to be the most extensive? Why might this be so?

■ The thylakoids are the most extensive. The chlorophyll molecules that trap solar energy are embedded in them.

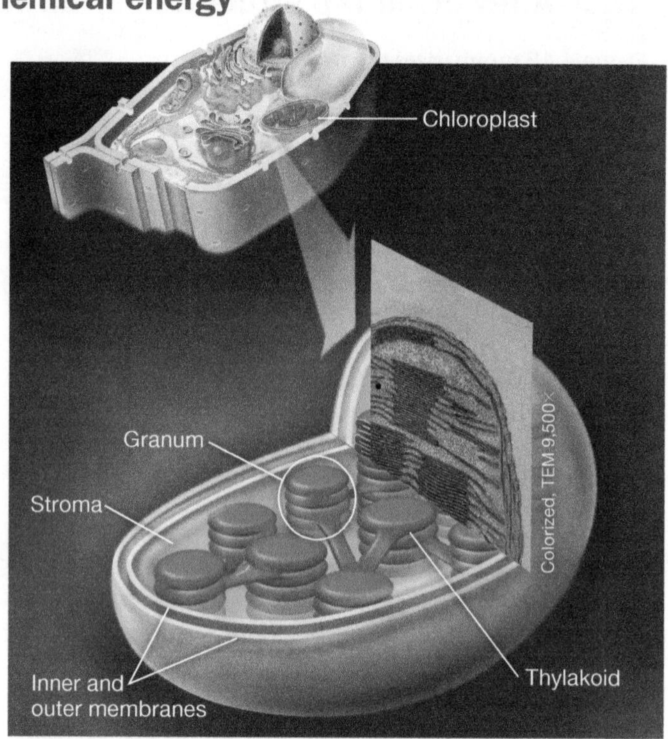

▲ **Figure 4.14 The chloroplast, site of photosynthesis**

4.15 Mitochondria and chloroplasts evolved by endosymbiosis

EVOLUTION CONNECTION

Mitochondria and chloroplasts contain a single circular DNA molecule, similar in structure to a prokaryotic chromosome, and ribosomes more similar to prokaryotic ribosomes than to eukaryotic ones. Interestingly, both organelles reproduce in a cell by a process resembling that of certain prokaryotes.

The **endosymbiont theory** states that mitochondria and chloroplasts were formerly small prokaryotes that began living within larger cells. These prokaryotes may have gained entry to the larger cell as undigested prey or parasites (Figure 4.15).

We can hypothesize how the symbiosis could have been beneficial. In a world that was becoming increasingly aerobic from the oxygen-generating photosynthesis of prokaryotes, a host would have benefited from an endosymbiont that was able to use oxygen to release large amounts of energy from organic molecules. Over the course of evolution, the host cell and its endosymbiont merged into a single organism—a eukaryotic cell with mitochondria. If one of these cells acquired a photosynthetic prokaryote, the prokaryote could provide the host cell with nourishment. An increasingly interdependent host and endosymbiont, over many generations, could become a eukaryotic cell containing chloroplasts.

? All eukaryotes have mitochondria, but not all have chloroplasts. What is the evolutionary explanation?

■ The first endosymbiosis would have given rise to eukaryotic cells containing mitochondria. A second endosymbiotic event gave rise to cells containing chloroplasts as well as mitochondria.

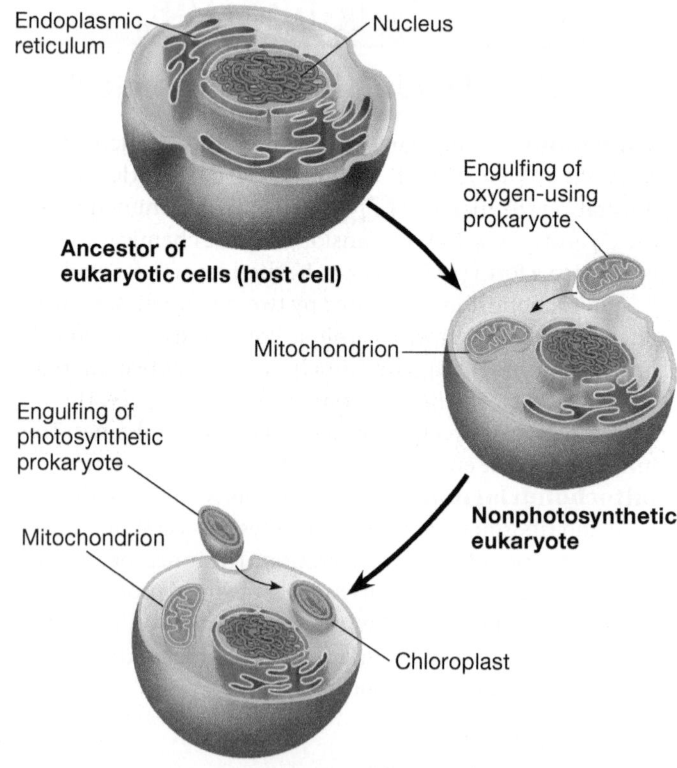

▲ **Figure 4.15 Endosymbiotic origin of mitochondria and chloroplasts**

The Cytoskeleton and Cell Surfaces

4.16 The cell's internal skeleton helps organize its structure and activities

As you saw in the chapter introduction, networks of protein fibers extend throughout a cell. Collectively called the **cytoskeleton**, these fibers act like a skeleton in providing for structural support as well as movement. Both the internal movement of cell parts and the swimming or crawling motility of some cells usually involve the interaction of the cytoskeleton with **motor proteins**.

Three main kinds of fibers make up the cytoskeleton: microtubules, the thickest fiber; microfilaments, the thinnest; and intermediate filaments, in between in thickness. Figure 4.16 shows three micrographs of cells of the same type, each stained with a different fluorescent dye that selectively highlights one of these types of fibers.

Microtubules are straight, hollow tubes composed of globular proteins called tubulins. As indicated in the bottom left of Figure 4.16, microtubules elongate by the addition of tubulin proteins, which consist of two subunits. Microtubules are readily disassembled, and their tubulin can be reused elsewhere in the cell. In animal cells, microtubules grow out from a region called the **centrosome**, which contains a pair of centrioles, each composed of a ring of microtubules (see Figure 4.4A). Plant cells lack centrosomes with centrioles and organize microtubules by other means.

Microtubules shape and support the cell and also act as tracks along which organelles equipped with motor proteins move. For example, a lysosome might use its motor protein "feet" to "walk" along a microtubule to reach a food vacuole. Microtubules also guide the movement of chromosomes when cells divide, and they are the main components of cilia and flagella. We will return to the structure of these locomotive appendages in Module 4.18.

Intermediate filaments are found in the cells of most animals. They are made of various fibrous proteins that supercoil into cables. Intermediate filaments reinforce cell shape and anchor some organelles. For example, the nucleus typically sits in a cage made of intermediate filaments. Whereas microtubules may be disassembled and reassembled elsewhere, intermediate filaments are often more permanent fixtures in the cell. The outer layer of your skin consists of dead skin cells packed full of intermediate filaments.

Microfilaments, also called actin filaments, are solid rods composed mainly of globular proteins called actin, arranged in a twisted double chain (bottom right of Figure 4.16). Microfilaments form a three-dimensional network just inside the plasma membrane that helps support the cell's shape. This is especially important for animal cells, which lack cell walls.

Microfilaments are also involved in cell movements. Actin filaments and thicker filaments made of a type of motor protein called myosin interact to cause contraction of muscle cells (see Figure 30.9B). Localized contractions brought about by actin and myosin are involved in the amoeboid (crawling) movement of the protist *Amoeba* and some of your white blood cells.

In the next module, we survey some of the techniques that led to the discovery of the cytoskeleton.

? **Which component of the cytoskeleton is most important in (a) holding the nucleus in place within an animal cell; (b) guiding transport vesicles from the Golgi to the plasma membrane; (c) contracting muscle cells?**

(a) Intermediate filaments; (b) microtubules; (c) microfilaments

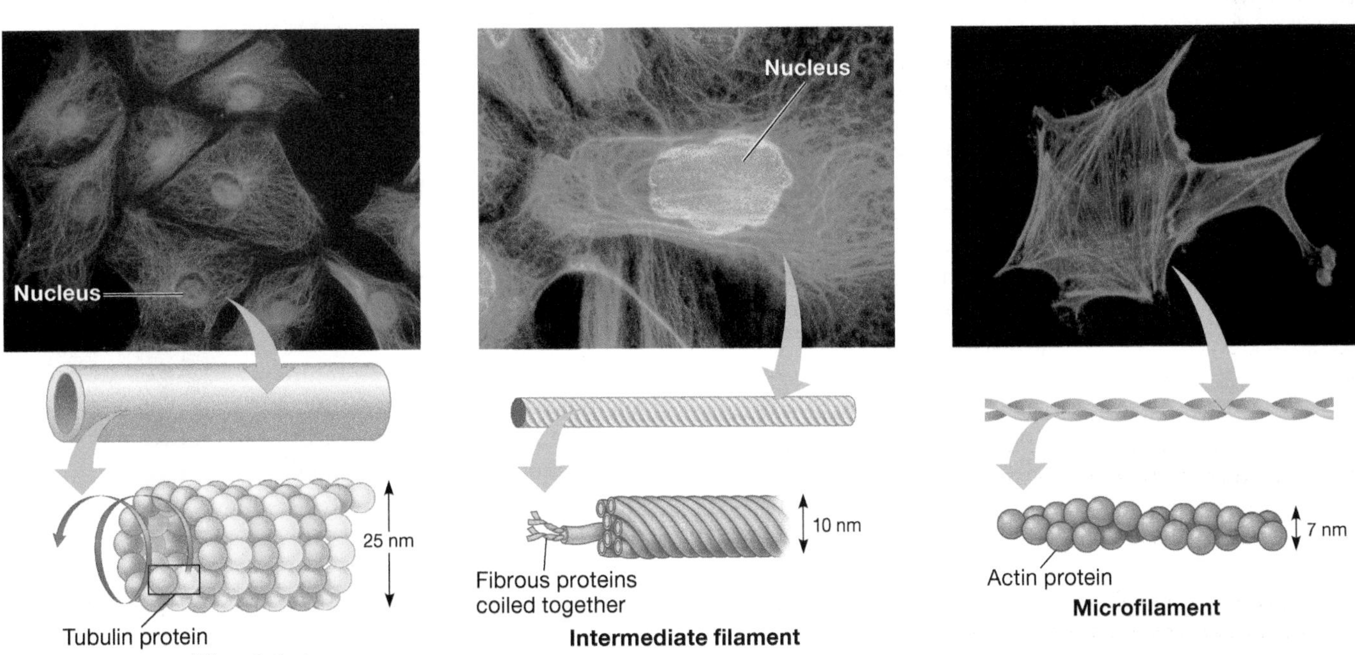

▲ **Figure 4.16** Three types of fibers of the cytoskeleton: microtubules labeled with green fluorescent molecules (left), intermediate filaments labeled yellow-green (center), and microfilaments labeled red (right)

4.17 Scientists discovered the cytoskeleton using the tools of biochemistry and microscopy

SCIENTIFIC THINKING

How has our knowledge of cells grown?

As you learned in Module 4.1, improvements in microscopes and staining techniques led to the discovery of organelles. But biologists originally thought that these structures floated freely in the cell. Let's trace the progressive sequence of new techniques that led to the discovery of microfilaments, the component of the cytoskeleton built from actin.

In the 1940s, biochemists first isolated and identified the proteins actin and myosin from muscle cells. In 1954, scientists, using newly developed techniques of microscopy, established how filaments of actin and myosin interact in muscle contraction. In the next decade, researchers developed a technique to stain and identify actin filaments with the electron microscope. Imagine their surprise when they found actin not just in the muscle cells they were studying but also in other cells present in their samples. Further study identified actin filaments in all types of cells.

Today we take for granted our ability to "see" the cytoskeleton (as you saw in the chapter introduction). But intact networks of microfilaments were not visualized in cells until 1974. Scientists developed antibody proteins that would bind to actin and attached fluorescent molecules to them. (When fluorescent molecules absorb light, they "glow" because they emit light of a specific wavelength or color.) These fluorescent antibodies revealed a remarkable and beautiful web of microfilaments. Figure 4.17 shows how different fluorescent tags can attach to various components of the cytoskeleton.

Researchers then tagged actin proteins themselves with fluorescent molecules and injected them into living cells. This technique enabled scientists to visualize the dynamic behavior of cytoskeletal proteins in living cells. By pairing video cameras with microscopes, scientists suddenly could "watch" what was happening in cells over time and follow the changing architecture of the cytoskeleton.

As scientists develop new techniques, our understanding of the cytoskeleton will continue to grow. Current research includes a molecular approach in which the genes for cytoskeleton proteins are sequenced and compared across diverse organisms. For example, the genes for actin are found to be highly conserved across evolutionary time—the actin proteins that facilitate the creeping movement of amoebas are remarkably similar to the actin proteins involved in the "amoeboid" movement of your white blood cells.

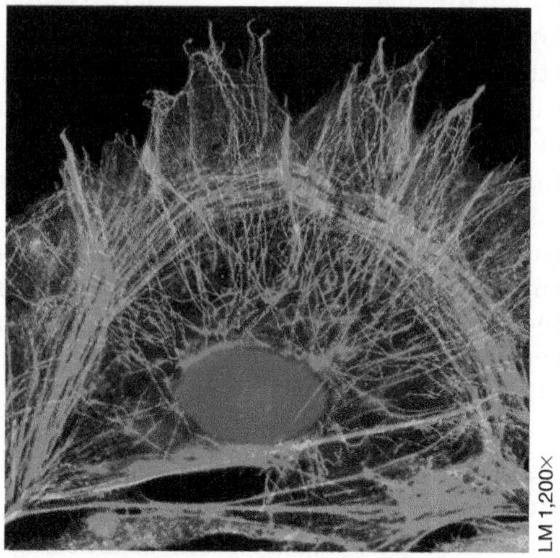

LM 1,200×

▲ **Figure 4.17** A fluorescence micrograph of the cytoskeleton (microtubules are green, microfilaments are reddish orange)

? **How does the discovery of the cytoskeleton illustrate the idea that advances in scientific knowledge often rely on advances in techniques and tools?**

■ Before electron microscopy and fluorescent dyes, biologists had no evidence that the cytoskeleton existed.

4.18 Cilia and flagella move when microtubules bend

The role of the cytoskeleton in movement is clearly seen in the motile appendages that protrude from certain cells. The short, numerous appendages that propel *Paramecium* (see Figure 4.1B) are called **cilia** (singular, *cilium*). Other protists may move using flagella, which are longer than cilia and usually limited to one or a few per cell.

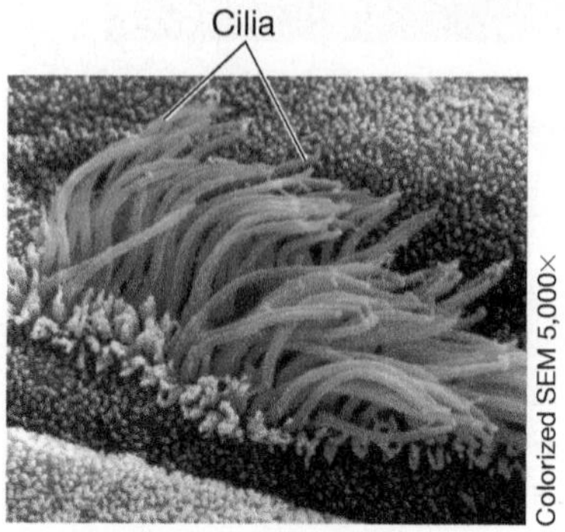

Some cells of multicellular organisms also have cilia or flagella. For example, Figure 4.18A shows cilia on cells lining the trachea (windpipe). These cilia sweep mucus containing trapped debris out of your lungs. (This cleaning function is impaired by cigarette smoke, which paralyzes the cilia.) Most animals and some plants have flagellated sperm. A flagellum, shown in Figure 4.18B, propels the cell by an undulating whiplike motion. In contrast, cilia work more like the coordinated oars of a rowing team.

Though different in length and beating pattern, cilia and flagella have a common structure and mechanism of movement (Figure 4.18C, on the facing page). Both are composed of microtubules wrapped in an extension of the plasma membrane. In nearly all eukaryotic cilia and flagella, a ring of nine microtubule doublets surrounds a central pair of microtubules. This arrangement is called the "9 + 2" pattern. The microtubule assembly is anchored in the cell by a basal

Cilia

Colorized SEM 5,000×

▲ **Figure 4.18A** Cilia on cells lining the respiratory tract

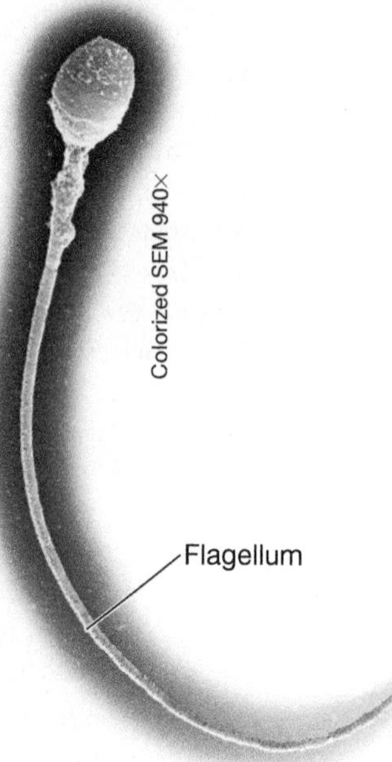

▲ **Figure 4.18B** Undulating flagellum on a human sperm cell

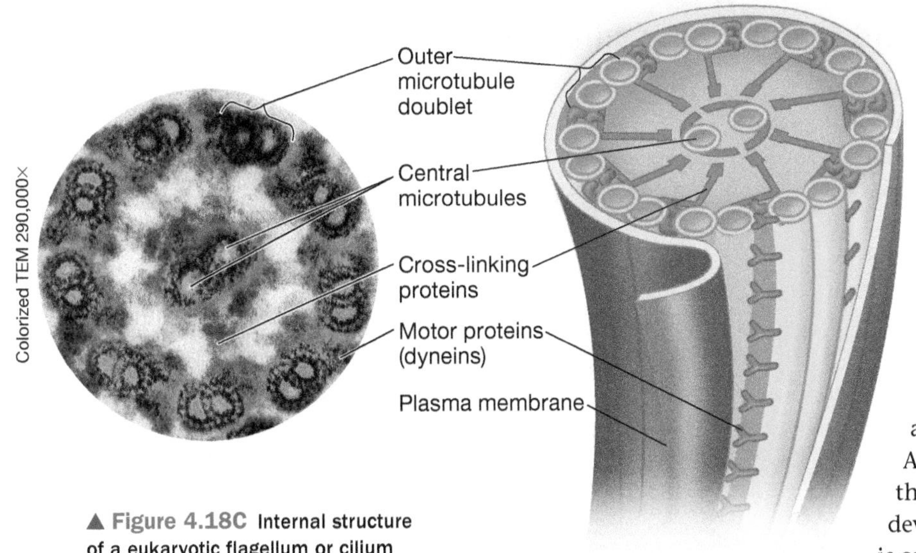

▲ **Figure 4.18C** **Internal structure of a eukaryotic flagellum or cilium**

body (not shown in the figure), which is structurally very similar to a centriole. In fact, in humans and many other animals, the basal body of the fertilizing sperm's flagellum enters the egg and becomes a centriole.

How does the microtubule assembly shown in Figure 4.18C produce the movement of cilia and flagella? Large motor proteins called dyneins (red in the figure) are attached along each outer microtubule doublet. A dynein protein has two "feet" that "walk" along an adjacent doublet. The walking movement is coordinated so that it happens on one side at a time. The microtubules are held together by flexible cross-linking proteins (purple in the diagram). If the doublets were not held in place, they would slide past each other. Instead, the "walking" of the dynein feet causes the microtubules—and consequently the cilium or flagellum—to bend.

A cilium may also serve as a signal-receiving "antenna" for the cell. Cilia with this function are generally nonmotile (they lack the central pair of microtubules), and there is only one per cell. In fact, in vertebrate animals, it appears that almost all cells have what is called a *primary cilium.* Although the primary cilium was discovered more than a century ago, its importance to embryonic development, sensory reception, and cell function is only now being recognized. Defective primary cilia have been linked to polycystic kidney disease and other human disorders.

? **Primary ciliary dyskinesia (PCD), also known as immotile cilia syndrome, is a fairly rare disease in which cilia and flagella are lacking motor proteins. PCD is characterized by recurrent respiratory tract infections and immotile sperm. How would you explain these seemingly unrelated symptoms?**

■ Without motor proteins, microtubules cannot bend. Thus cilia cannot cleanse the respiratory tract, and sperm cannot swim.

4.19 The extracellular matrix of animal cells functions in support and regulation

The plasma membrane is usually regarded as the boundary of the cell, but most cells synthesize and secrete materials that are external to the plasma membrane. Animal cells produce an **extracellular matrix (ECM)** (Figure 4.19). This elaborate layer helps hold cells together in tissues and protects and supports the plasma membrane.

The main components of the ECM are glycoproteins, proteins bonded with carbohydrates. The most abundant glycoprotein is collagen, which forms strong fibers outside the cell. In fact, collagen accounts for about 40% of the protein in your body. The collagen fibers are embedded in a network woven from large complexes that include hundreds of small glycoproteins connected to a long polysaccharide molecule (shown as green in the figure). The ECM may attach to the cell through other glycoproteins that then bind to membrane proteins called **integrins**. Integrins span the membrane, attaching on the other side to proteins connected to microfilaments of the cytoskeleton.

As their name implies, integrins have the function of integration: They transmit signals between the ECM and the cytoskeleton and can communicate changes occurring outside and inside the cell. Current research is revealing new and influential functions of the ECM. For example, it can regulate a cell's behavior by directing the path along which embryonic cells move. Researchers have also learned that a cell's ECM can even influence the activity of genes through the signals it relays.

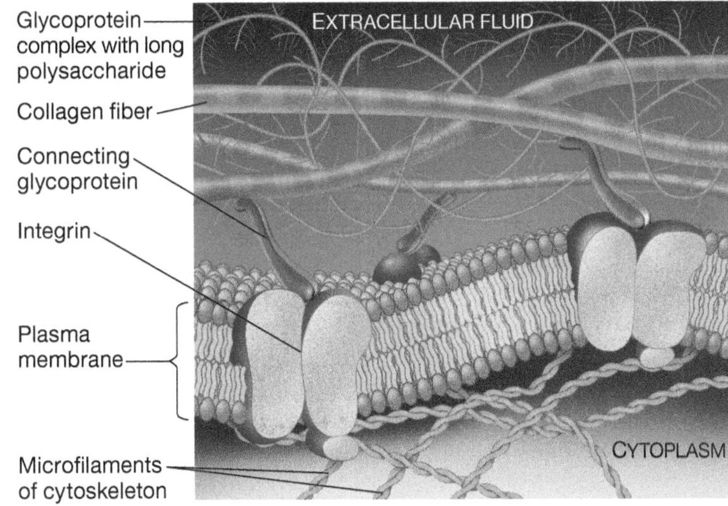

▲ **Figure 4.19** **The extracellular matrix (ECM) of an animal cell**

? **Referring to Figure 4.19, describe the structures that provide support to the plasma membrane.**

■ The membrane is attached through membrane proteins to microfilaments of the cytoskeleton and to connecting glycoproteins and collagen fibers of the ECM.

4.20 Three types of cell junctions are found in animal tissues

Neighboring cells in animal tissues often adhere, interact, and communicate through specialized junctions between them. **Figure 4.20** uses cells lining the digestive tract to illustrate three types of cell junctions. (The projections at the top of the cells increase the surface area for absorption of nutrients.)

At tight junctions, the plasma membranes of neighboring cells are knit tightly together by proteins. Tight junctions prevent leakage of fluid across a layer of cells. The dotted green arrows show how tight junctions prevent the contents of the digestive tract from leaking into surrounding tissues.

Anchoring junctions function like rivets, fastening cells together into strong sheets. Intermediate filaments made of sturdy proteins anchor these junctions in the cytoplasm. Anchoring junctions are common in tissues subject to stretching or mechanical stress, such as skin and muscle.

Gap junctions, also called communicating junctions, are channels that allow small molecules to flow through protein-lined pores between cells. The flow of ions through gap junctions in the cells of heart muscle coordinates their contraction. Gap junctions are common in embryos, where communication between cells is essential for development.

? **A muscle tear injury would probably involve the rupture of which type of cell junction?**

■ Anchoring junction

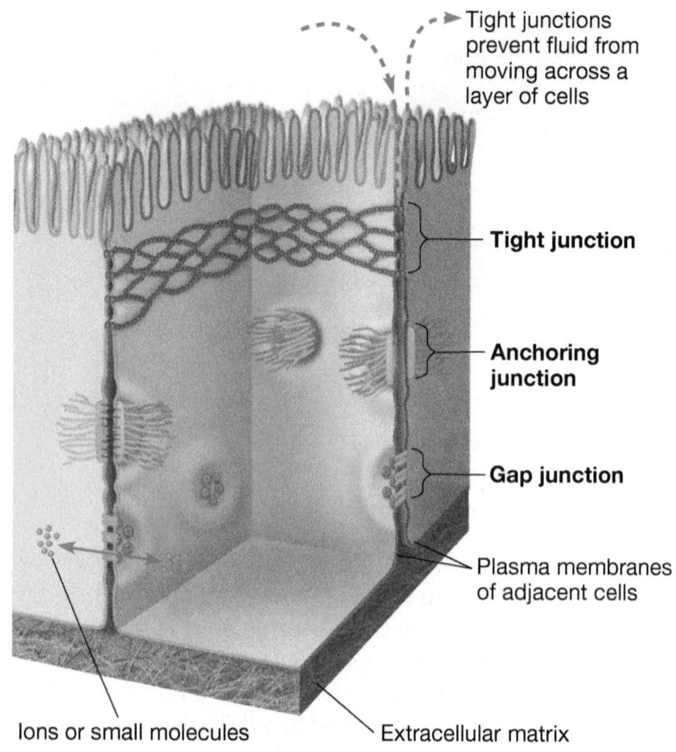

▲ **Figure 4.20** **Three types of cell junctions in animal tissues**

4.21 Cell walls enclose and support plant cells

The **cell wall** is one of the features that distinguishes plant cells from animal cells. This rigid extracellular structure not only protects the cells but also provides the skeletal support that keeps plants upright on land. Plant cell walls consist of fibers of cellulose (see Figure 3.7) embedded in a matrix of other polysaccharides and proteins. This fibers-in-a-matrix construction resembles that of steel-reinforced concrete, which is also noted for its strength.

Figure 4.21 shows the layered structure of plant cell walls. Cells initially lay down a relatively thin and flexible primary wall, which allows the growing cell to continue to enlarge. Between adjacent cells is a layer of sticky polysaccharides called pectins (shown here in dark brown), which glue the cells together. (Pectin is used to thicken jams and jellies.) When a cell stops growing, it strengthens its wall. Some cells add a secondary wall deposited in laminated layers next to the plasma membrane. Wood consists mainly of secondary walls, which are strengthened with rigid molecules called lignin.

Despite their thickness, plant cell walls do not totally isolate the cells from each other. Figure 4.21 shows the numerous channels that connect adjacent plant cells, called **plasmodesmata** (singular, *plasmodesma*). Cytosol passing through the plasmodesmata allows water and other small molecules to freely move from cell to cell. Through plasmodesmata, the cells of a plant tissue share water, nourishment, and chemical messages.

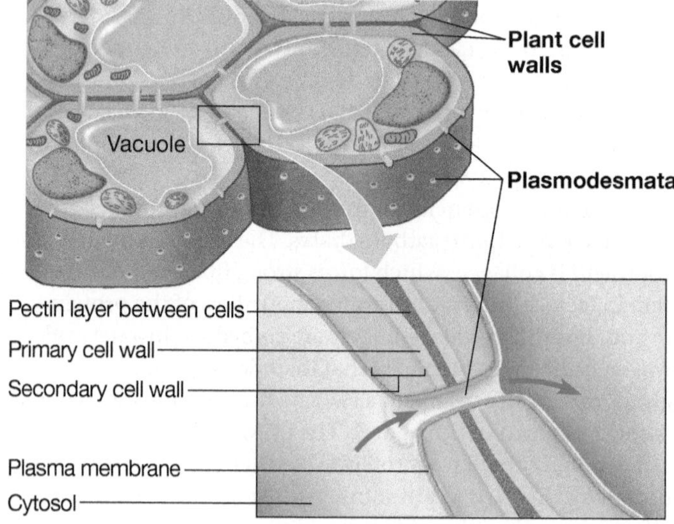

▲ **Figure 4.21** **Plant cell walls and plasmodesmata**

? **Which animal cell junction is analogous to a plasmodesma?**

■ A gap junction

4.22 Review: Eukaryotic cell structures can be grouped on the basis of four main functions

Congratulations: You have completed the grand tour of the cell. In the process, you have been introduced to many important cell structures. To provide a framework for this information and reinforce the theme that structure is correlated with function, we have grouped the eukaryotic cell structures into four categories by general function, as reviewed in Table 4.22.

The first category is genetic control. Here we include the nucleus that houses a cell's genetic instructions and the ribosomes that produce the proteins coded for in those instructions. The second category includes organelles of the endomembrane system that are involved in the manufacture, distribution, and breakdown of materials. The third category includes the two energy-processing organelles, mitochondria and chloroplasts. And the fourth category—structural support, movement, and intercellular communication—includes the cytoskeleton, extracellular structures, and connections between cells.

Within most of these categories, a structural similarity underlies the general function of each component. Manufacturing depends heavily on a network of structurally and functionally connected membranes. All the organelles involved in the breakdown or recycling of materials are membranous sacs, inside of which enzymatic digestion can safely occur. In the energy-processing category, expanses of metabolically active membranes and intermembrane compartments within the organelles enable chloroplasts and mitochondria to perform the complex energy conversions that power the cell. Even in the diverse fourth category, there is a common structural theme in the various protein fibers of most of these cellular systems.

We can summarize further by noting that the overall structure of a cell is closely related to its specific function. Thus, cells that produce proteins for export contain a large quantity of ribosomes and rough ER, while muscle cells are packed with microfilaments, myosin motor proteins, and mitochondria. And, finally, let us emphasize that these cellular structures form an integrated team—with the property of life emerging at the level of the cell from the coordinated functions of the team members. A cell beautifully illustrates our theme of INTERACTIONS: it is a living unit that is greater than the sum of its parts.

TABLE 4.22 Eukaryotic Cell Structures and Their Functions

Structure		Function
1. Genetic Control		
Nucleus	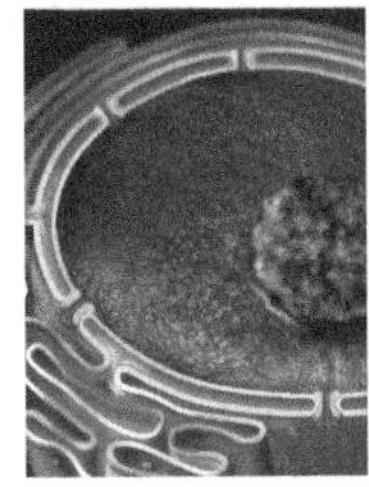	DNA replication, RNA synthesis; assembly of ribosomal subunits (in nucleolus)
Ribosomes		Polypeptide (protein) synthesis
2. Manufacturing, Distribution, and Breakdown		
Rough ER		Synthesis of membrane lipids and proteins, secretory proteins, and hydrolytic enzymes; formation of transport vesicles
Smooth ER		Lipid synthesis; detoxification in liver cells; calcium ion storage in muscle cells
Golgi apparatus	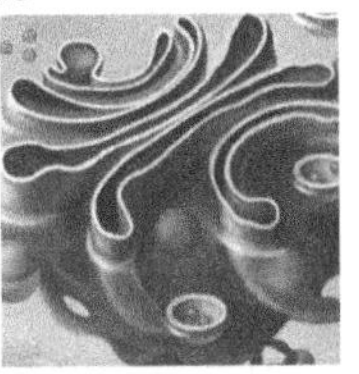	Modification and sorting of ER products; formation of lysosomes and transport vesicles
Lysosomes (in animal cells and some protists)		Digestion of ingested food or bacteria and recycling of a cell's damaged organelles and macromolecules
Vacuoles		Digestion (food vacuole); water balance (contractile vacuole); storage of chemicals and cell enlargement (central vacuole in plant cells)
Peroxisomes (not part of endomembrane system)		Diverse metabolic processes, with breakdown of toxic hydrogen peroxide by-product
3. Energy Processing		
Mitochondria		Cellular respiration: conversion of chemical energy in food to chemical energy of ATP
Chloroplasts (in plants and algae)		Photosynthesis: conversion of light energy to chemical energy of sugars
4. Structural Support, Movement, and Communication Between Cells		
Cytoskeleton (microfilaments, intermediate filaments, and microtubules)		Maintenance of cell shape; anchorage for organelles; movement of organelles within cells; cell movement (crawling, muscle contraction, bending of cilia and flagella)
Plasma membrane		Regulate traffic in and out of cell
Extracellular matrix (in animals)		Support; regulation of cellular activities
Cell junctions		Communication between cells; binding of cells in tissues
Cell walls (in plants)		Support and protection; binding of cells in tissues

? How do mitochondria, smooth ER, and the cytoskeleton all contribute to the contraction of a muscle cell?

■ Mitochondria supply energy in the form of ATP. The smooth ER helps regulate contraction by the uptake and release of calcium ions. Microfilaments function in the actual contractile apparatus.

CHAPTER

4 REVIEW

For practice quizzes, BioFlix animations, MP3 tutorials, video tutors, and more study tools designed for this textbook, go to MasteringBiology™

REVIEWING THE CONCEPTS

Introduction to the Cell (4.1–4.4)

4.1 Microscopes reveal the world of the cell. The light microscope can display living cells. The greater magnification and resolution of the scanning and transmission electron microscopes reveal the ultrastructure of cells.

4.2 The small size of cells relates to the need to exchange materials across the plasma membrane. The microscopic size of most cells provides a large surface-to-volume ratio. The plasma membrane is a phospholipid bilayer with embedded proteins.

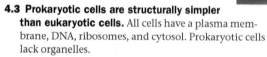

4.3 Prokaryotic cells are structurally simpler than eukaryotic cells. All cells have a plasma membrane, DNA, ribosomes, and cytosol. Prokaryotic cells lack organelles.

4.4 Eukaryotic cells are partitioned into functional compartments. Membrane-enclosed organelles compartmentalize a cell's activities.

The Nucleus and Ribosomes (4.5–4.6)

4.5 The nucleus contains the cell's genetic instructions. The nucleus houses the cell's DNA, which directs protein synthesis via messenger RNA. Subunits of ribosomes are assembled in the nucleolus.

4.6 Ribosomes make proteins for use in the cell and for export. Composed of ribosomal RNA and proteins, ribosomes synthesize proteins according to directions from DNA.

The Endomembrane System (4.7–4.12)

4.7 Many organelles are connected in the endomembrane system.

4.8 The endoplasmic reticulum is a biosynthetic workshop. The ER is a membranous network of tubes and sacs. Smooth ER synthesizes lipids and processes toxins. Rough ER produces membranes, and ribosomes on its surface make membrane and secretory proteins.

4.9 The Golgi apparatus modifies, sorts, and ships cell products. The Golgi apparatus consists of stacks of sacs in which products of the ER are processed and then sent to other organelles or to the cell surface.

4.10 Lysosomes are digestive compartments within a cell. Lysosomes house enzymes that break down ingested substances and damaged organelles.

4.11 Vacuoles function in the general maintenance of the cell. Some protists have contractile vacuoles. Plant cells contain a large central vacuole that stores molecules and wastes and facilitates growth.

4.12 A review of the structures involved in manufacturing and breakdown. The organelles of the endomembrane system are interconnected structurally and functionally.

Energy-Converting Organelles (4.13–4.15)

4.13 Mitochondria harvest chemical energy from food.

4.14 Chloroplasts convert solar energy to chemical energy.

4.15 Mitochondria and chloroplasts evolved by endosymbiosis. These organelles originated from prokaryotic cells that became residents in a host cell.

The Cytoskeleton and Cell Surfaces (4.16–4.22)

4.16 The cell's internal skeleton helps organize its structure and activities. The cytoskeleton includes microfilaments, intermediate filaments, and microtubules. Their functions include maintenance of cell shape, anchorage and movement of organelles, amoeboid movement, and muscle contraction.

4.17 Scientists discovered the cytoskeleton using the tools of biochemistry and microscopy.

4.18 Cilia and flagella move when microtubules bend. Eukaryotic cilia and flagella are locomotor appendages made of microtubules in a "9 + 2" arrangement.

4.19 The extracellular matrix of animal cells functions in support and regulation. The ECM consists mainly of glycoproteins, which bind tissue cells together, support the plasma membrane, and communicate with the cytoskeleton.

4.20 Three types of cell junctions are found in animal tissues. Tight junctions bind cells to form leakproof sheets. Anchoring junctions rivet cells into strong tissues. Gap junctions allow ions and small molecules to flow from cell to cell.

4.21 Cell walls enclose and support plant cells. Plant cell walls are made largely of cellulose. Plasmodesmata are connecting channels between cells.

4.22 Review: Eukaryotic cell structures can be grouped on the basis of four main functions. These functions are (1) genetic control; (2) manufacturing, distribution, and breakdown; (3) energy processing; and (4) structural support, movement, and communication between cells.

CONNECTING THE CONCEPTS

1. Label the structures in this diagram of an animal cell. Review the functions of each of these organelles.

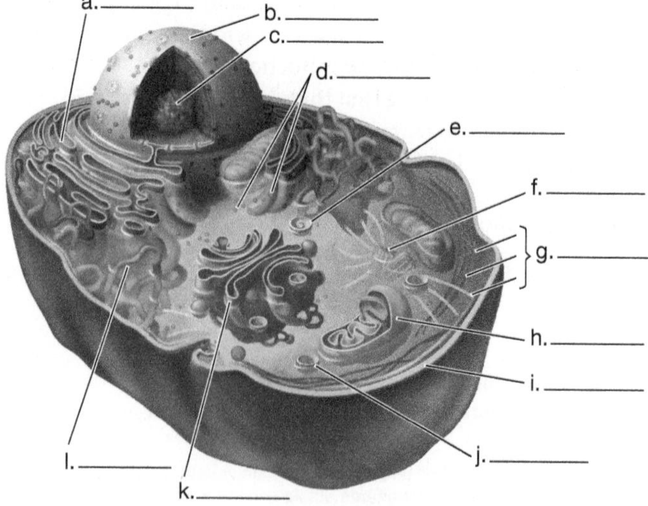

TESTING YOUR KNOWLEDGE

Level 1: Knowledge/Comprehension

2. The ultrastructure of a chloroplast is best studied using a
    a. light microscope.
    b. scanning electron microscope.
    c. transmission electron microscope.
    d. light microscope and fluorescent dyes.
3. The cells of an ant and an elephant are, on average, the same small size; an elephant just has more of them. What is the main advantage of small cell size? (*Explain your reasoning.*)
    a. A small cell has a larger plasma membrane surface area than does a large cell.
    b. Small cells can better take up sufficient nutrients and oxygen to service their cell volume.
    c. It takes less energy to make an organism out of small cells.
    d. Small cells require less oxygen than do large cells.
4. Which of the following clues would tell you whether a cell is prokaryotic or eukaryotic?
    a. the presence or absence of a rigid cell wall
    b. whether or not the cell is partitioned by internal membranes
    c. the presence or absence of ribosomes
    d. Both b and c are important clues.
5. Which of the following is one of the major components of the plasma membrane of a plant cell?
    a. phospholipids
    b. cellulose fibers
    c. collagen fibers
    d. pectins
6. What four cellular components are shared by prokaryotic and eukaryotic cells?
7. Describe two different ways in which cilia can function in organisms.

Level 2: Application/Analysis

Choose from the following cells for questions 8–11:

a. pancreatic cell that secretes digestive enzymes
b. ovarian cell that produces estrogen (a steroid hormone)
c. muscle cell in the thigh of a long-distance runner
d. white blood cell that engulfs bacteria

8. In which cell would you find the most lysosomes?
9. In which cell would you find the most smooth ER?
10. In which cell would you find the most rough ER?
11. In which cell would you find the most mitochondria?
12. In what ways do the internal membranes of a eukaryotic cell contribute to the functioning of the cell?
13. Is this statement true or false? "Animal cells have mitochondria; plant cells have chloroplasts." Explain your answer, and describe the functions of these organelles.
14. Describe the structure of the plasma membrane of an animal cell. What would be found directly inside and outside the membrane?
15. Imagine a spherical cell with a radius of 10 μm. What is the cell's surface area in μm^2? Its volume, in μm^3? (*Note:* For a sphere of radius *r*, surface area $= 4\pi r^2$ and volume $= 4/3\pi r^3$. Remember that the value of π is 3.14.) What is the ratio of surface area to volume for this cell? Now do the same calculations for a second cell, this one with a radius of 20 μm. Compare the surface-to-volume ratios of the two cells. How is this comparison significant to the functioning of cells?
16. Describe the pathway of the protein hormone insulin from its gene to its export from a cell of your pancreas.

Level 3: Synthesis/Evaluation

17. How might the phrase "ingested but not digested" be used in a description of the endosymbiotic theory?
18. Cilia are found on cells in almost every organ of the human body, and the malfunction of cilia is involved in several human disorders. During embryological development, for example, cilia generate a leftward flow of fluid that initiates the left-right organization of the body organs. Some individuals with primary ciliary dyskinesia (see Module 4.18 checkpoint question) exhibit a condition (*situs inversus*) in which internal organs such as the heart are on the wrong side of the body. Explain why this reversed arrangement may be a symptom of PCD.
19. **SCIENTIFIC THINKING** Microtubules often produce movement through their interaction with motor proteins. But in some cases, microtubules move cell components when the length of the microtubule changes. Through a series of experiments, researchers determined that microtubules grow and shorten as tubulin proteins are added or removed from their ends. Other experiments showed that microtubules make up the spindle apparatus that "pulls" chromosomes toward opposite ends (poles) of a dividing cell. The figures below describe a clever experiment done in 1987 to determine whether a spindle microtubule shortens (depolymerizes) at the end holding a chromosome or at the pole end of a dividing cell.

    Experimenters labeled the microtubules of a dividing cell from a pig kidney with a yellow fluorescent dye. As shown on the left half of the diagram below, they then marked a region halfway along the microtubules by using a laser to eliminate the fluorescence from that region. They did not mark the other side of the spindle (right side of the figure).

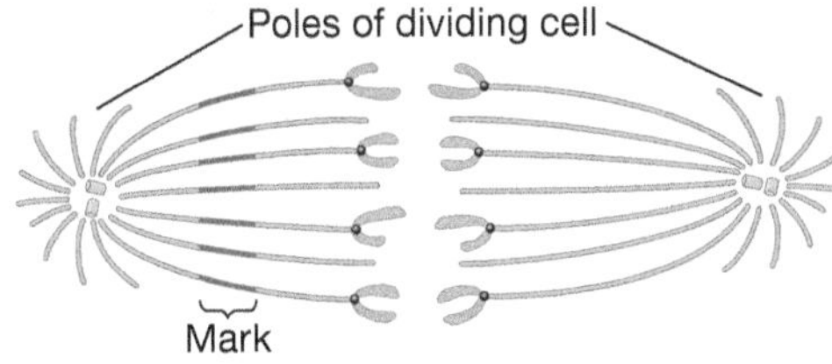

The figure below illustrates the results they observed as the chromosomes moved toward the opposite poles of the cell.

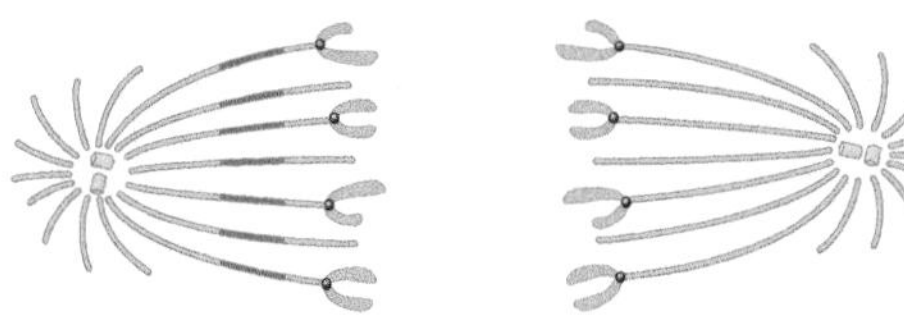

Describe these results. What would you conclude about where the microtubules depolymerize from comparing the length of the microtubules on either side of the mark? How could the experimenters determine whether this is the mechanism of chromosome movement in all cells?

Source: G. J. Gorbsky et al. Chromosomes move poleward in anaphase along stationary microtubules that coordinately disassemble from their kinetochore ends, *Journal of Cell Biology* 104:9–18 (1987).

Answers to all questions can be found in Appendix 4.

The Working Cell

CHAPTER 5

The illustration on the right is beautiful and intriguing—but what does it represent? This computer model shows a small section of a cell membrane. Notice the phospholipids that make up the lipid bilayer of this membrane: The yellow balls represent the phosphate heads and the green squiggles are the fatty acid tails of the phospholipids. You can see water molecules (depicted with red and gray balls) on both sides of the membrane. Notice also the single file of water molecules slipping along the blue ribbons embedded in the membrane. These ribbons represent regions of a membrane protein called aquaporin that function as water channels. Just one molecule of this protein enables billions of water molecules to stream through the membrane every second—many more than could wander through the lipid bilayer on their own.

How can water flow through a membrane?

Aquaporins are common in cells involved in water balance. For example, your kidneys filter and reabsorb many liters of water a day, and aquaporins are vital to their proper functioning. There are rare cases of people with defective aquaporins whose kidneys can't reabsorb water and who must drink 20 liters of water every day to prevent dehydration. On the other hand, if kidney cells have too many aquaporins, excess water is reabsorbed and body tissues may swell. A common complication of pregnancy is fluid retention, and it is likely caused by increased synthesis of aquaporin proteins. Later in the chapter you will learn about the serendipitous discovery of these water channels.

But aquaporins are only one example of how the plasma membrane and its proteins enable cells to survive and function. A cell expends energy to build membranes, and many functions of a membrane require energy. A cell's energy conversions involve enzymes, which control all of its chemical reactions. Indeed, everything that is depicted in this computer model of water molecules zipping through a membrane relates to how working cells use membranes, energy, and enzymes—which are the topics of this chapter.

Membrane Structure and Function (5.1–5.9)

A cell membrane's structure enables its many functions, such as regulating traffic across the membrane.

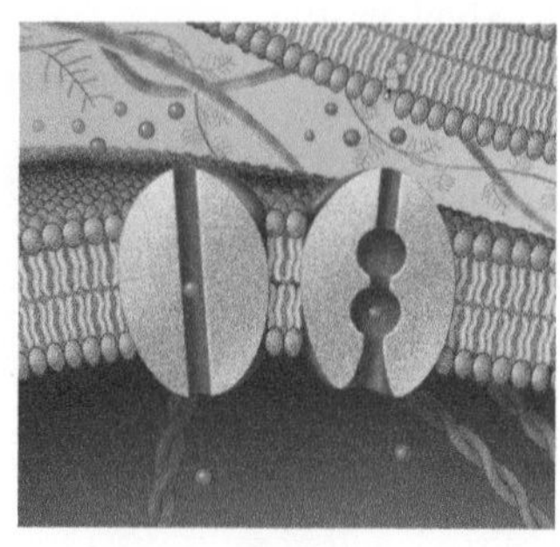

Energy and the Cell (5.10–5.12)

A cell's metabolic reactions transform energy, using ATP to drive cellular work.

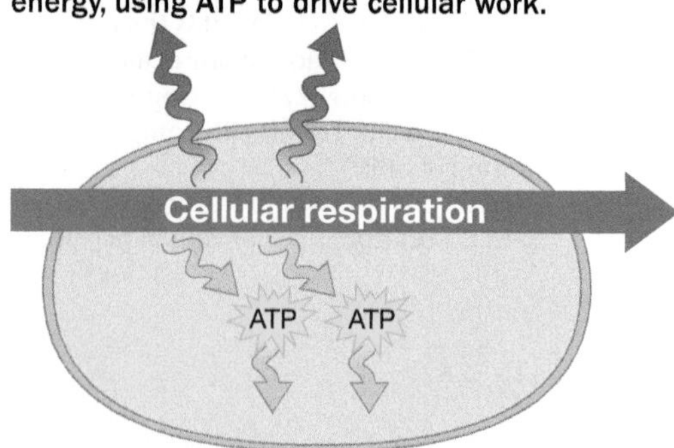

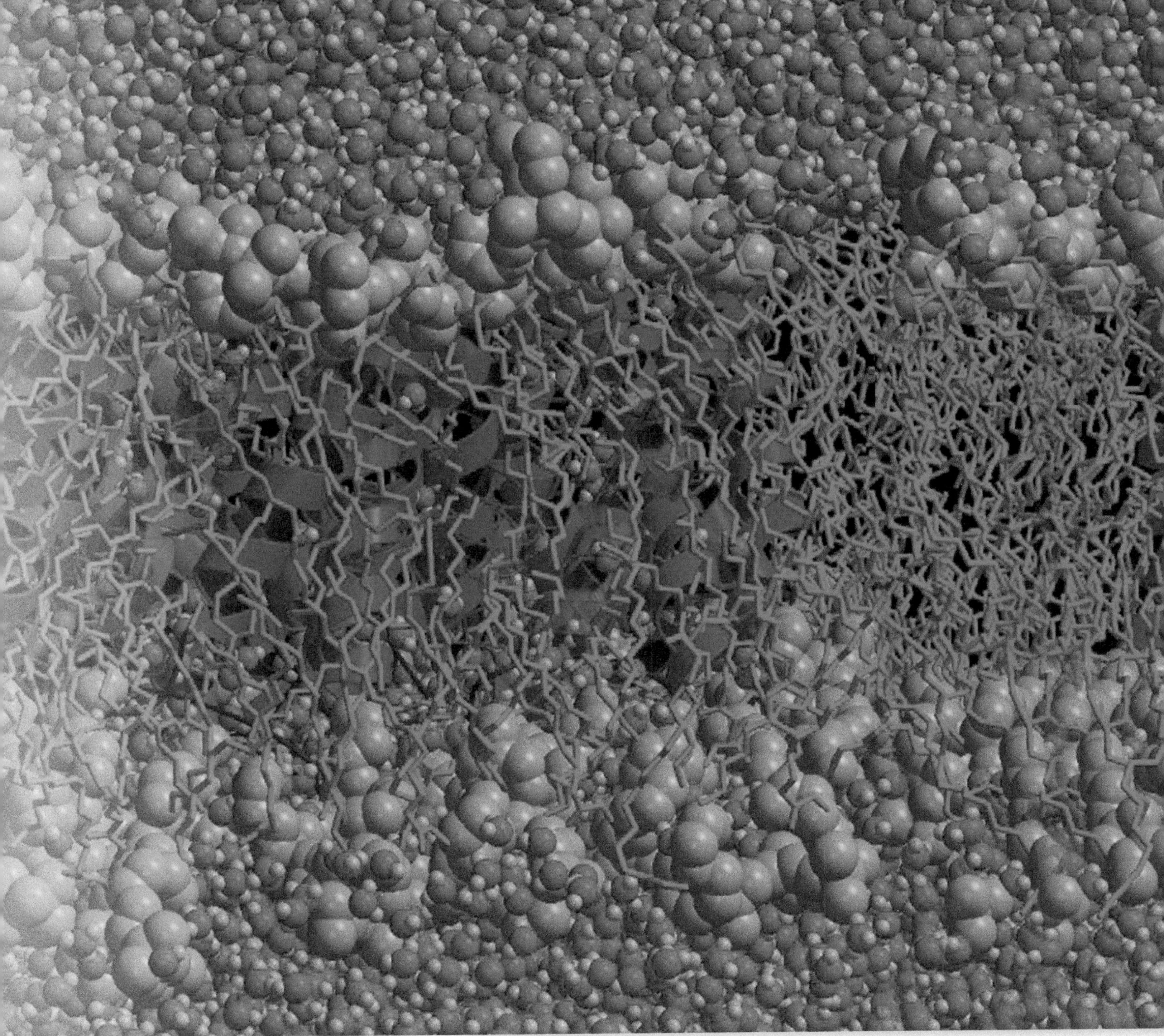

How Enzymes Function

(5.13–5.16)

Enzymes speed up a cell's chemical reactions and provide precise control of metabolism.

Membrane Structure and Function

VISUALIZING THE CONCEPT 5.1 Membranes are fluid mosaics of lipids and proteins with many functions

Biologists use the **fluid mosaic model** to describe a membrane's structure—diverse protein molecules suspended in a fluid phospholipid bilayer. This module illustrates the structure and function of a plasma membrane, the boundary that encloses a living cell. Like all cellular membranes, the plasma membrane exhibits **selective permeability**; that is, it allows some substances to cross more easily than others. But the plasma membrane does more than just regulate the exchange of materials. This figure will help you visualize all the activity taking place in and across the membranes of two adjacent cells.

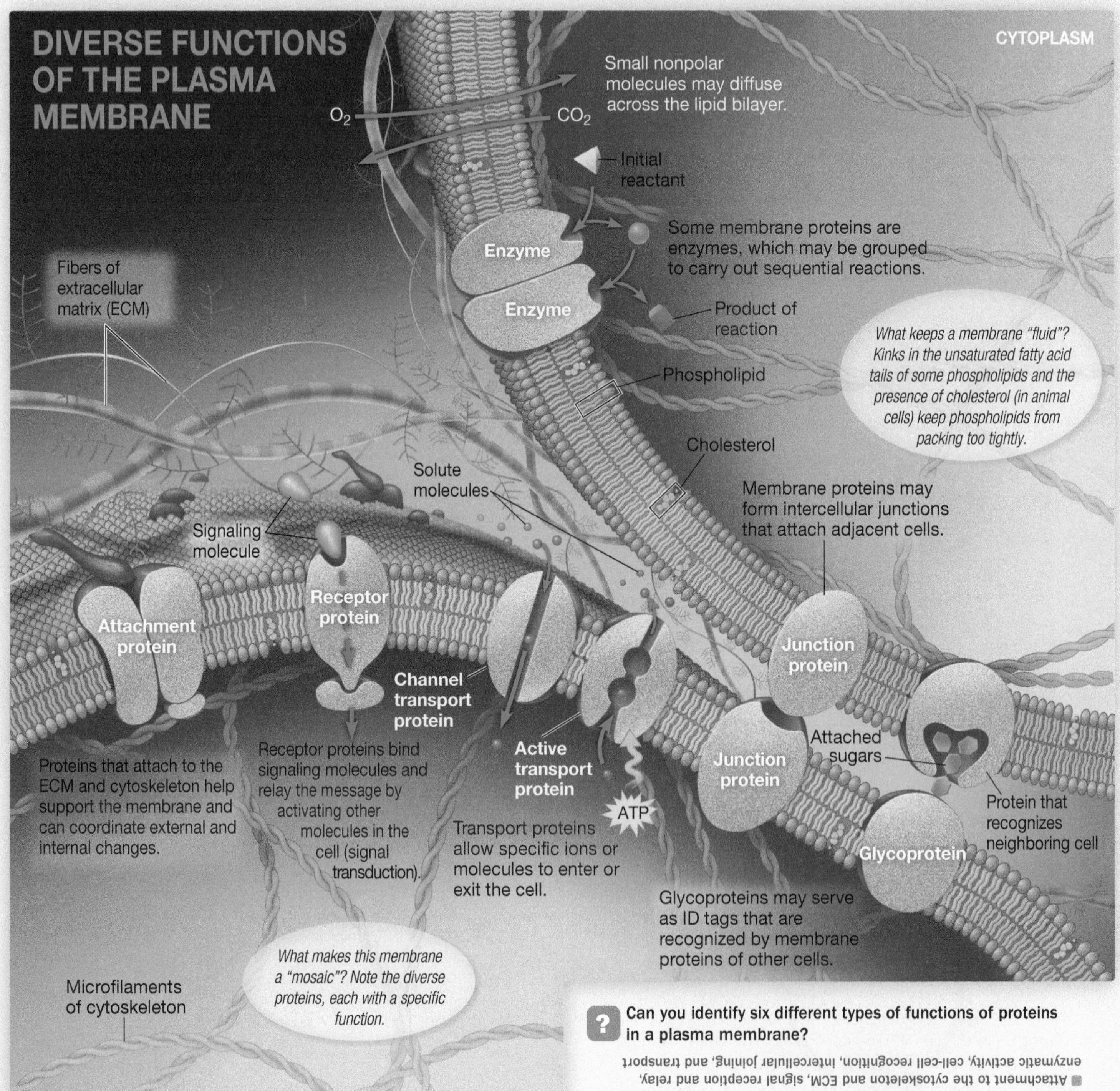

? **Can you identify six different types of functions of proteins in a plasma membrane?**

■ Attachment to the cytoskeleton and ECM, signal reception and relay, enzymatic activity, cell-cell recognition, intercellular joining, and transport

5.2 The spontaneous formation of membranes was a critical step in the origin of life

EVOLUTION CONNECTION

Phospholipids, the key ingredients of biological membranes, were probably among the first organic molecules that formed from chemical reactions on early Earth (see Module 15.2). These lipids could spontaneously self-assemble into simple membranes. Indeed, this property can be demonstrated by shaking a mixture of phospholipids and water—the phospholipids organize into bilayers surrounding water-filled bubbles (**Figure 5.2**).

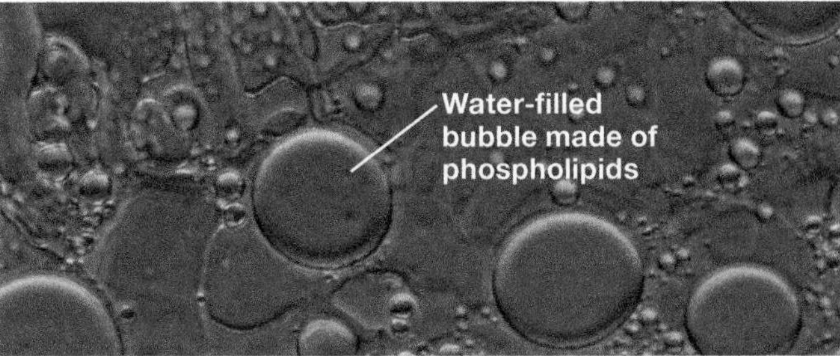

▲ **Figure 5.2** **Spontaneously formed membrane-bounded sacs**

The formation of membrane-enclosed collections of molecules would have been a critical step in the evolution of the first cells. A membrane can enclose a solution that is different in composition from its surroundings. If that solution included self-replicating molecules such as RNA and a beneficial assortment of other molecules, these combinations could be passed on to daughter cells as new membrane-enclosed vesicles budded off. A membrane that not only encloses a successful assembly of molecules but also regulates chemical exchanges with the environment is a basic requirement for life. Indeed, all cells are enclosed by a membrane similar in structure and function—illustrating the evolutionary unity of life.

? **In the origin of a cell, why would the formation of a simple lipid bilayer membrane not be sufficient? What else would have to be part of such a membrane?**

■ The membrane would need embedded proteins that could regulate the movement of substances into and out of the cell.

5.3 Passive transport is diffusion across a membrane with no energy investment

Molecules have a type of energy called thermal energy, due to their constant motion. One result of this motion is **diffusion**, the tendency for particles of any substance to spread out into the available space. Randomly moving molecules will diffuse through air and water—or into and out of a cell.

The figures to the right will help you visualize diffusion across a membrane. **Figure 5.3A** shows a solution of yellow dye separated from pure water by an artificial membrane. Assume that this membrane has microscopic pores through which dye molecules can move. Thus, we say the membrane is permeable to the dye. Although each molecule moves randomly, there will be a *net* movement from the side of the membrane where dye molecules are more concentrated to the side where they are less concentrated. Put another way, the dye diffuses down its **concentration gradient**. Eventually, the solutions on both sides will have equal concentrations of dye. At this dynamic equilibrium, molecules still move back and forth, but there is no *net* change in concentration on either side of the membrane.

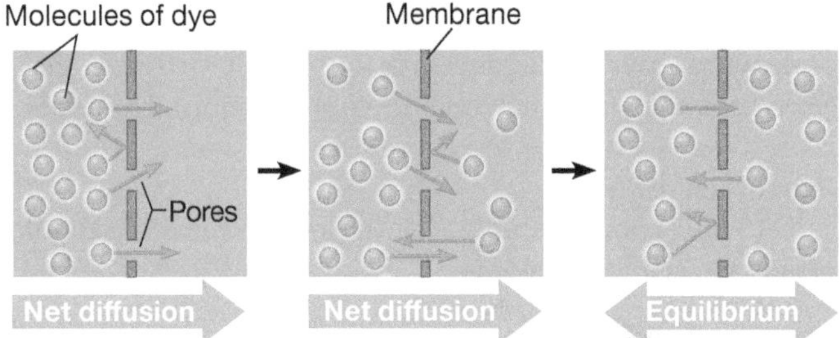

▲ **Figure 5.3A** **Diffusion of one type of molecule across a membrane**

Figure 5.3B illustrates the important point that two or more substances diffuse independently of each other; that is, each diffuses down its own concentration gradient.

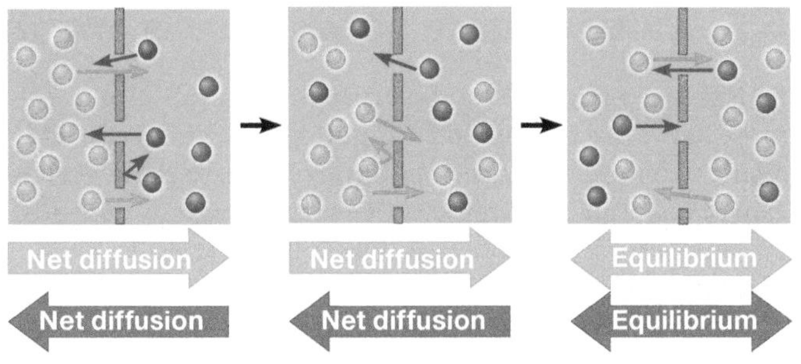

▲ **Figure 5.3B** **Diffusion of two types of molecules across a membrane**

TRY THIS **Explain why these two types of molecules initially move in opposite directions.**

Because a cell does not have to do work when molecules diffuse across its membrane, such movement is called **passive transport**. Much of the traffic across membranes occurs by diffusion. For example, diffusion down concentration gradients is the sole means by which oxygen (O_2), essential for the process of cellular respiration, enters your cells and carbon dioxide (CO_2), a metabolic waste, passes out of them.

Both O_2 and CO_2 are small, nonpolar molecules that diffuse easily across the phospholipid bilayer of a membrane. But can ions and polar molecules also diffuse across the hydrophobic interior of a membrane? They can if they are moving down their concentration gradients and if they have transport proteins to help them cross.

? **Why is diffusion across a membrane called passive transport?**

■ The cell does not expend energy to transport substances that are diffusing down their concentration gradients.

5.4 Osmosis is the diffusion of water across a membrane

One of the most important substances that crosses membranes by passive transport is water. In the next module, we consider the critical balance of water between a cell and its environment. But first let's explore a physical model of the diffusion of water across a selectively permeable membrane, a process called **osmosis**. Remember that a selectively permeable membrane allows some substances to cross more easily than others.

The top of Figure 5.4 shows what happens if a membrane permeable to water but not to a solute (such as glucose) separates two solutions that have different concentrations of solute. (A solute is a substance that dissolves in a liquid solvent. The resulting mixture is a solution.) The solution on the right side of the U-shaped tube initially has a higher concentration of solute than that on the left side. Water will cross the membrane until the solute concentrations are more nearly equal on both sides, as you can see in the U-tube on the right.

The close-up view at the bottom of Figure 5.4 will help you understand what is happening at the molecular level. Polar water molecules cluster around hydrophilic (water-loving) solute molecules. The effect is that on the right side of the U-tube, there are fewer water molecules that are *free* to cross the membrane. The less-concentrated solution on the left side has fewer solute molecules but more *free* water molecules available to move. There is a net movement of water down its concentration gradient, from the solution with more free water molecules (and lower solute concentration) to that with fewer free water molecules (and higher solute concentration). The result is the difference in water levels you see in the U-tube at the top right of Figure 5.4.

Let's now apply to living cells what we have learned about osmosis in artificial systems.

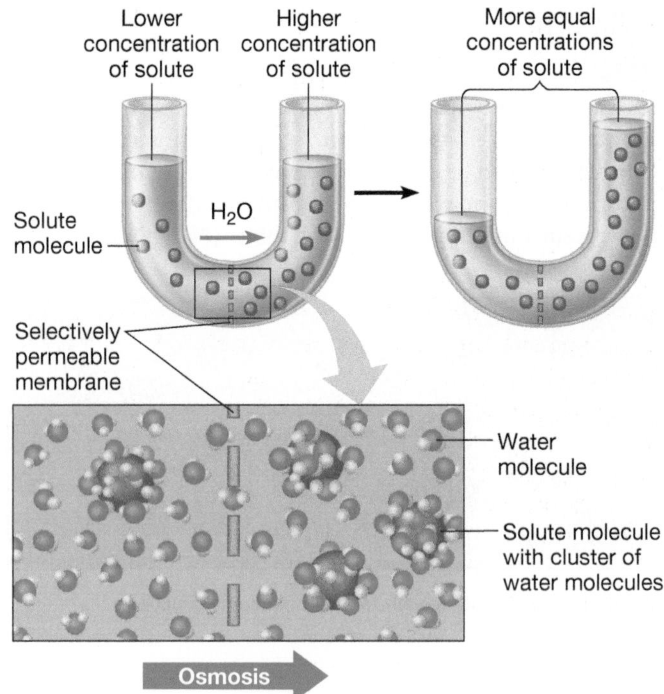

▲ Figure 5.4 **Osmosis, the diffusion of water across a membrane**

? Predict the net water movement between two solutions—a 0.5% sucrose solution and a 2% sucrose solution—separated by a membrane not permeable to sucrose.

Water will move from the 0.5% sucrose solution (lower solute concentration) to the 2% sucrose solution (higher solute concentration).

5.5 Water balance between cells and their surroundings is crucial to organisms

Biologists use a special vocabulary to describe how water will move between a cell and its surroundings. The term **tonicity** refers to the ability of a surrounding solution to cause a cell to gain or lose water. The tonicity of a solution mainly depends on its concentration of solutes relative to the concentration of solutes inside the cell.

Figure 5.5, on the facing page, illustrates the effects of placing animal and plant cells in solutions of different tonicities—solutions that have lower, equal, or higher concentrations of solutes compared to the cell.

When an animal cell, such as the red blood cell shown in the top center of the figure, is immersed in a solution that is **isotonic** to the cell (*iso*, same, and *tonos*, tension), the cell's volume remains constant. The solute concentration of a cell and its isotonic environment are essentially equal, and the cell gains water at the same rate that it loses it. In your body, red blood cells are transported in the isotonic plasma of the blood. Intravenous (IV) fluids administered in hospitals must also be isotonic to blood cells. The body cells of most animals are bathed in an extracellular fluid that is isotonic to the cells. And seawater is isotonic to the cells of many marine animals, such as sea stars and crabs.

What happens when an animal cell is placed in a **hypotonic** solution (*hypo*, below), a solution with a solute concentration lower than that of the cell? As shown in the upper left of the figure, the cell gains water, swells, and may burst (lyse) like an overfilled balloon. The upper right shows the opposite case—an animal cell placed in a **hypertonic** solution (*hyper*, above), a solution with a higher solute concentration. In which direction will water move? The cell shrivels and can die from water loss.

For an animal to survive in a hypotonic or hypertonic environment, it must have a way to prevent excessive uptake or loss of water and regulate the solute concentration of its body fluids. The control of water balance is called **osmoregulation**. For example, in a freshwater fish, which lives in a hypotonic environment, water enters its cells by osmosis and its kidneys must work constantly to remove excess water from the body. (We will discuss osmoregulation further in Module 25.4.)

Water balance issues are somewhat different for the cells of plants, prokaryotes, and fungi because of their cell walls. As shown in the bottom of Figure 5.5, in a hypotonic environment a plant cell is turgid (very firm), which is the healthy state for most plant cells. Although the plant cell swells as water enters by osmosis, the cell wall exerts a back pressure, called turgor pressure, which prevents the cell from taking in too much water and bursting. Plants that are not woody, such as most houseplants, depend on their turgid cells for mechanical support. In contrast, when a plant cell is surrounded by an isotonic solution, there is no net movement of water into the cell, and the cell is flaccid (limp). The plant itself may wilt.

In a hypertonic environment (bottom right), a plant cell is no better off than an animal cell. As a plant cell loses water, it shrivels, and its plasma membrane pulls away from the cell wall. This process, called plasmolysis, causes the plant to wilt and can be lethal to the cell and the plant. The walled cells of bacteria and fungi also plasmolyze in hypertonic environments. Thus, meats and other foods can be preserved with concentrated salt solutions because the cells of food-spoiling bacteria or fungi become plasmolyzed and eventually die.

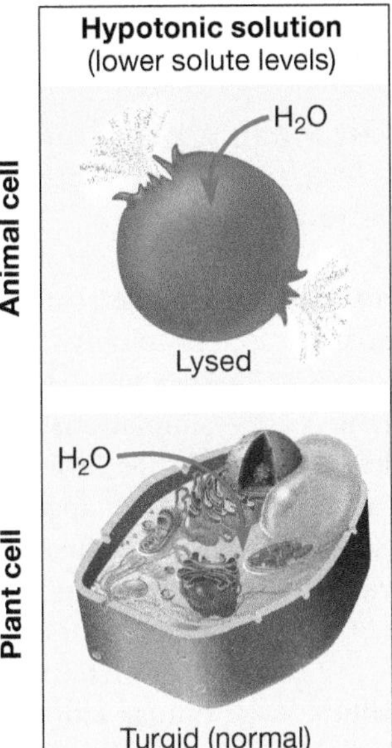

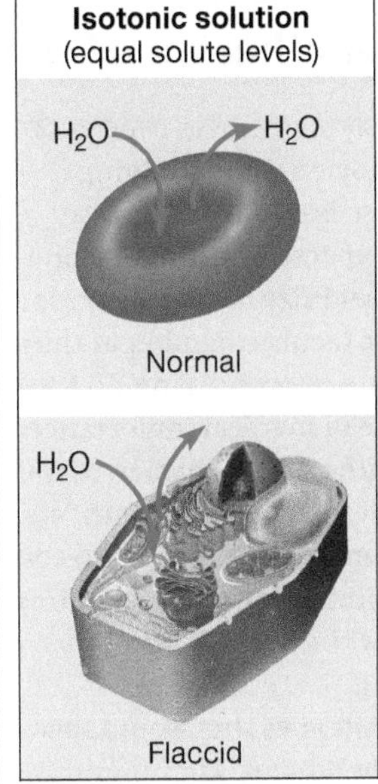

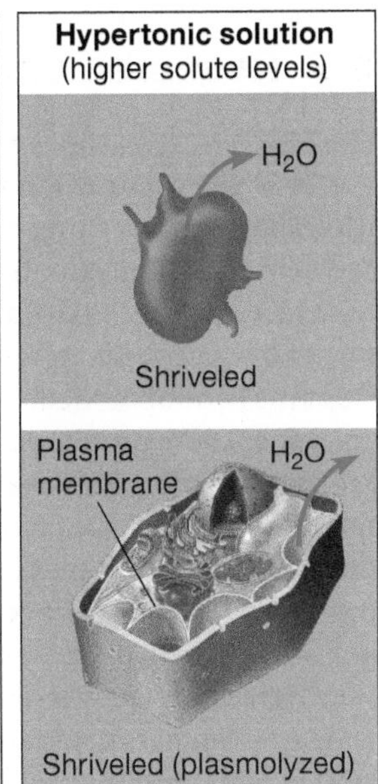

▲ **Figure 5.5** How animal and plant cells react to changes in tonicity (deeping shades of blue reflect increasing concentrations of solutes in the surrounding solutions)

TRY THIS Identify the panel above that depicts what would happen if an IV bag delivered pure water into a patient's vein. Explain.

? Explain the function of the contractile vacuoles in a freshwater *Paramecium* (shown in Figure 4.11A) in terms of what you have just learned about water balance in cells.

■ The pond water in which *Paramecium* lives is hypotonic to the cell. The contractile vacuoles expel the water that constantly enters the cell by osmosis.

5.6 Transport proteins can facilitate diffusion across membranes

Recall that nonpolar molecules, such as O_2 and CO_2, can dissolve in the lipid bilayer of a membrane and diffuse through it with ease. But how do polar or charged substances make it past the hydrophobic center of a membrane? Hydrophilic molecules and ions require the help of specific transport proteins to move across a membrane. This assisted transport, called **facilitated diffusion**, is a type of passive transport because it does not require energy. As in all passive transport, the driving force is the concentration gradient.

Figure 5.6 shows a common type of transport protein, which provides a channel that specific molecules or ions use as a passageway through a membrane. Another type of transport protein, called a carrier protein, binds its passenger, changes shape, and releases the transported molecule on the other side. In both cases, the transport protein helps a specific substance diffuse across the membrane down its concentration gradient and, thus, requires no input of energy.

Substances that use facilitated diffusion for crossing cell membranes include a number of sugars, amino acids, ions—and even water. The water molecule is very small, but because it is polar (see Module 2.6), its diffusion through a membrane's hydrophobic interior is relatively slow. For many cells, this slow diffusion of water is adequate. Cells such as plant cells,

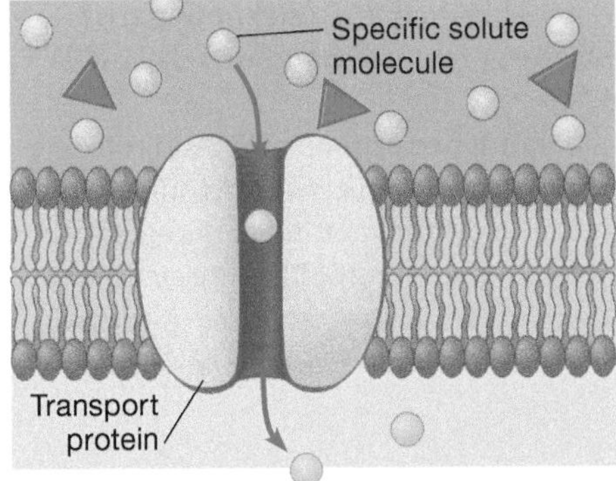

◀ **Figure 5.6** Transport protein providing a channel for the diffusion of a specific solute across a membrane

red blood cells, and the cells lining your kidney tubules, however, have greater water-permeability needs. As you saw in the chapter introduction, the very rapid diffusion of water into and out of such cells is made possible by a protein channel called an **aquaporin**. In the next module, we explore the discovery of these transport proteins.

? How do transport proteins contribute to a membrane's selective permeability?

■ Because they are specific for the solutes they transport, the numbers and kinds of transport proteins affect a membrane's permeability to various solutes.

5.7 Research on another membrane protein led to the discovery of aquaporins

SCIENTIFIC THINKING

How can water flow through a membrane?

Sometimes major advances in science occur when a scientist is studying something else but makes the wise decision to explore an unexpected finding. Peter Agre received the 2003 Nobel Prize in Chemistry for this sort of discovery. Dr. Agre, a faculty member at the Johns Hopkins School of Medicine, was studying Rh blood antigens. These proteins are of medical importance when Rh-negative mothers have Rh-positive babies. Membrane-spanning proteins are challenging to work with, and the samples that he and his team isolated seemed to consist of two proteins. They were certain that the smaller one was just a breakdown product of the larger Rh protein—and they were completely wrong.

The researchers made antibodies that would specifically bind to and label this smaller protein. They found two interesting results: The antibody did not bind to any part of the Rh protein, indicating that the smaller protein wasn't part of the Rh protein. And the antibody did bind in huge quantities to red blood cells, showing that this previously unknown protein is one of the most abundant proteins in blood cell membranes. Agre and his team also determined that an identical protein was even more abundant in certain kidney cells. But they didn't know what this protein did.

As is typical in science, Agre searched the scientific literature and consulted other researchers for ideas and advice. A colleague suggested that the protein might be the elusive water channel that physiologists had predicted would explain the rapid transport of water in some cells. To test this hypothesis, the researchers produced messenger RNA that coded for the mystery protein and injected the mRNA into frog eggs. (The plasma membranes of frog eggs are known to be quite water impermeable, a beneficial trait as they naturally develop in hypotonic pond water.) Biochemical tests showed that within 72 hours, the frog egg cells had translated the mRNA into the new protein.

The researchers then transferred a group of RNA-injected frog eggs and a control group of eggs injected with only a buffer solution to a hypotonic solution and monitored the eggs with videomicroscopy. The osmotic swelling of RNA-injected and control cells is plotted in Figure 5.7. As you can see by the red curve on the graph, the experimental egg cells exploded in 3 minutes. The control eggs showed minimal swelling, even for time periods exceeding an hour. The researchers concluded that the newly discovered protein enabled the rapid movement of water into the cells.

Since the results of that experiment were reported in 1992, much research has been done on aquaporins, determining their structure and dynamic functioning. The chapter introduction presented a model of aquaporin structure. Molecular biophysicists have produced computer simulations that show water molecules flipping their way single file through an aquaporin. Such simulations have revealed how aquaporins allow only water molecules to pass through them. Aquaporins have been found in bacteria, plants, and animals, and evolutionary biologists are tracing the relationships of these various aquaporins. Medical researchers study the function and occasional malfunction of aquaporins in the human kidney, lungs, brain, and lens of the eye. The serendipitous discovery of aquaporins has led to a broad range of scientific research and medical applications.

? **Why did the researchers use frog eggs to test the function of this unknown protein? Why did they also monitor the behavior of control eggs in the hypotonic solution?**

Frog eggs are quite impermeable to water. The control eggs confirmed this trait and provided a comparison to the bursting of the eggs that were making aquaporins.

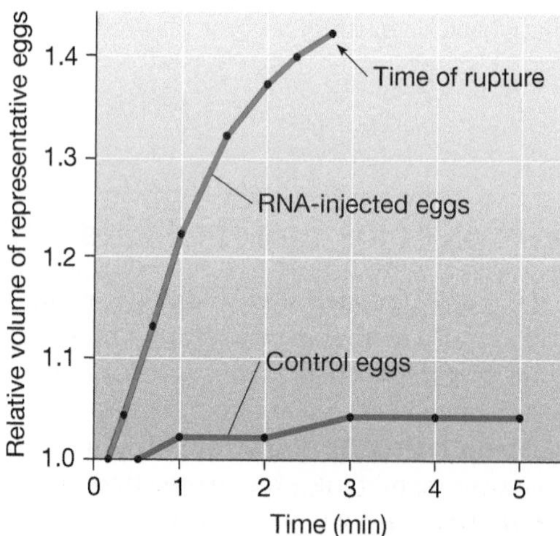

Source: Adaptation of Figure 2A from "Appearance of Water Channels in Xenopus Oocytes Expressing Red Cell CHIP28 Protein" by Gregory Preston et al., from Science, April 1992, Volume 256(5055) by AAAS.

▲ **Figure 5.7 Osmotic swelling of aquaporin RNA-injected and control-injected oocytes following transfer to a hypotonic solution**

5.8 Cells expend energy in the active transport of a solute

In **active transport**, a cell must expend energy to move a solute *against* its concentration gradient—that is, across a membrane toward the side where the solute is more concentrated. The energy molecule ATP (described in more detail in Module 5.12) supplies the energy for most active transport.

Active transport allows a cell to maintain internal concentrations of small molecules and ions that are different from concentrations in its surroundings. For example, the inside of an animal cell has a higher concentration of potassium ions (K^+) and a lower concentration of sodium ions (Na^+) than the solution outside the cell. The generation of nerve signals depends on these concentration differences, which a transport protein called the sodium-potassium pump maintains by actively moving Na^+ out of the cell and K^+ into the cell.

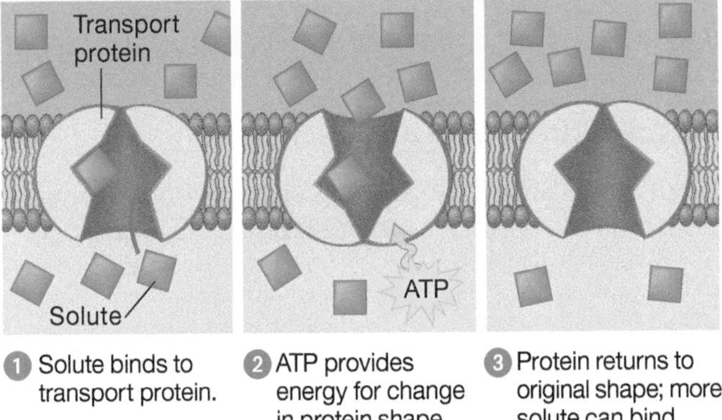

1 Solute binds to transport protein.
2 ATP provides energy for change in protein shape.
3 Protein returns to original shape; more solute can bind.

▲ **Figure 5.8** **Active transport of a solute across a membrane**

Figure 5.8 shows a simple model of an active transport system that pumps a solute out of the cell against its concentration gradient. 1 The process begins when solute molecules on the cytoplasmic side of the plasma membrane attach to specific binding sites on the transport protein. 2 With energy provided by ATP, the transport protein changes shape in such a way that the solute is released on the other side of the membrane. 3 The transport protein returns to its original shape, ready for its next passengers.

? **Cells actively transport Ca^{2+} out of the cell. Is calcium more concentrated inside or outside of the cell? Explain.**

■ Outside: Active transport moves calcium against its concentration gradient.

5.9 Exocytosis and endocytosis transport large molecules across membranes

So far, we've focused on how water and small solutes enter and leave cells. The story is different for large molecules.

A cell uses the process of **exocytosis** (from the Greek *exo*, outside, and *kytos*, cell) to export bulky materials such as proteins or polysaccharides. A transport vesicle buds from the Golgi apparatus and moves to the edge of the cell, where it fuses with the plasma membrane (see Figure 4.12). Its contents spill out of the cell as the vesicle membrane becomes part of the plasma membrane. For example, the cells in your pancreas that manufacture the hormone insulin secrete it into the extracellular fluid by exocytosis, where it is picked up by the bloodstream.

Endocytosis (*endo*, inside) is a transport process through which a cell takes in large molecules or droplets of fluid. Figure 5.9 shows two of the kinds of endocytosis. The top diagram illustrates **phagocytosis**, or "cellular eating." A cell engulfs a particle by wrapping extensions called pseudopodia around it and packaging it within a membrane-enclosed sac called a vacuole. The vacuole then fuses with a lysosome, whose hydrolytic enzymes digest the contents of the vacuole (see Figure 4.10A). Protists such as amoeba take in food particles this way, and some of your white blood cells engulf invading bacteria via phagocytosis.

The bottom diagram illustrates **receptor-mediated endocytosis**, which enables a cell to acquire specific solutes. Receptor proteins for specific molecules are embedded in regions of the membrane that are lined by a layer of coat proteins. The plasma membrane indents to form a coated pit, whose receptor proteins pick up particular molecules from the extracellular fluid. The coated pit pinches closed to form a vesicle, which then releases the molecules into the cytoplasm.

Your cells use receptor-mediated endocytosis to take in cholesterol from the blood for synthesis of membranes and as a precursor for other steroids. Cholesterol circulates in the blood in particles called low-density lipoproteins (LDLs). LDLs bind to receptor proteins and then enter cells by endocytosis. In humans with the inherited disease familial hypercholesterolemia, LDL receptor proteins are defective or missing.

Phagocytosis

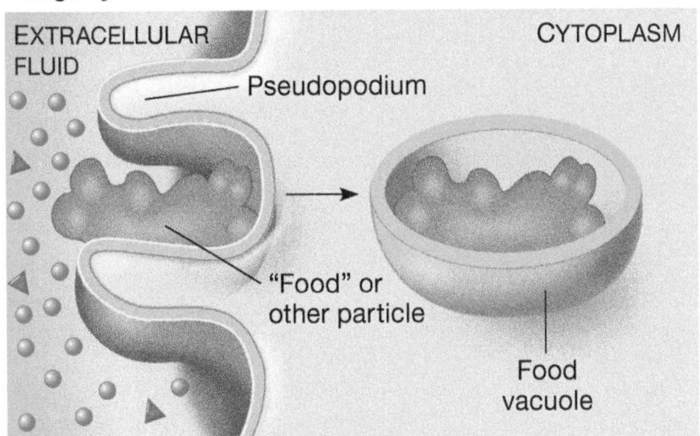

Receptor-mediated endocytosis

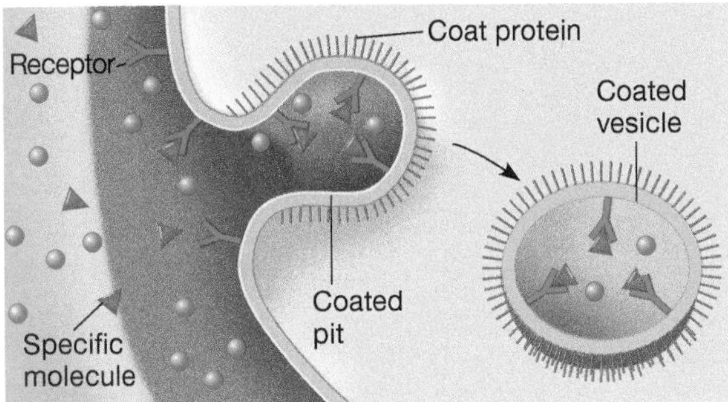

▲ **Figure 5.9** **Two kinds of endocytosis**

Cholesterol accumulates to high levels in the blood, leading to atherosclerosis, the buildup of fatty deposits in the walls of blood vessels (see Module 9.11).

Having explored the structure and function of the plasma membrane, let's now focus on how a cell transforms energy to perform its many types of work.

? **As a cell grows, its plasma membrane expands. Does this involve endocytosis or exocytosis? Explain.**

■ Exocytosis: When a transport vesicle fuses with the plasma membrane, its contents are released and the vesicle membrane adds to the plasma membrane.

Energy and the Cell

5.10 Cells transform energy and matter as they perform work

The title of this chapter is "The Working Cell." But just what type of work does a cell do? You just learned that a cell can actively transport substances across membranes. The cell also builds those membranes and the proteins embedded in them. A cell is a miniature chemical factory in which thousands of reactions occur within a microscopic space. All of these reactions involve the transformation of ENERGY AND MATTER, one of the core themes of biology. Before we begin our study of how the cell works, let's explore some basic concepts of energy.

Forms of Energy **Energy** is the capacity to cause change, especially to do work. There are two basic forms of energy: kinetic energy and potential energy. **Kinetic energy** is the energy of motion. Moving objects can perform work by transferring motion to other matter. For example, the movement of your legs can push bicycle pedals, turning the wheels and moving you and your bike up a hill. **Thermal energy** is a type of kinetic energy associated with the random movement of atoms or molecules. Thermal energy in transfer from one object to another is called **heat**. Light, which is also a type of kinetic energy, can be harnessed to power photosynthesis.

Potential energy, the second main form of energy, is energy that matter possesses as a result of its location or structure. Water behind a dam and you on your bicycle at the top of a hill possess potential energy. Molecules possess potential energy because of the arrangement of electrons in the bonds between their atoms. **Chemical energy** is the potential energy available for release in a chemical reaction. Chemical energy is the energy that can be transformed to power the work of the cell.

Energy Transformations The study of energy transformations that occur in a collection of matter is called **thermodynamics**. Scientists use the word *system* for the matter under study and refer to the rest of the universe—everything outside the system—as the *surroundings*. A system can be an electric power plant, a single cell, or the entire planet. An organism is an open system; that is, it exchanges both energy and matter with its surroundings.

The **first law of thermodynamics**, also known as the law of energy conservation, states that the energy in the universe is constant. Energy can be transferred and transformed, but it cannot be created or destroyed. A power plant does not create energy; it merely converts it from one form (such as the energy stored in coal) to the more convenient form of electricity. A plant cell converts light energy to chemical energy; the plant cell, too, is an energy transformer, not an energy producer.

If energy cannot be destroyed, then why can't organisms simply recycle their energy? It turns out that during every transfer or transformation, some energy becomes unavailable to do work—it is converted to thermal energy (random molecular motion) and released as heat. Scientists use a quantity called **entropy** as a measure of disorder, or randomness. The more randomly arranged a collection of matter is, the greater its entropy. According to the **second law of thermodynamics**, every energy conversion increases the entropy (disorder) of the universe.

Figure 5.10 uses a car and a cell to illustrate these two laws of thermodynamics, showing how energy can be transformed and how entropy increases as a result. Automobile engines and cells use the same basic process to make the chemical energy of their fuel available for work. The engine mixes oxygen with gasoline in an explosive chemical reaction that pushes the pistons, which eventually move the wheels. The waste products emitted from the exhaust pipe are mostly carbon dioxide and

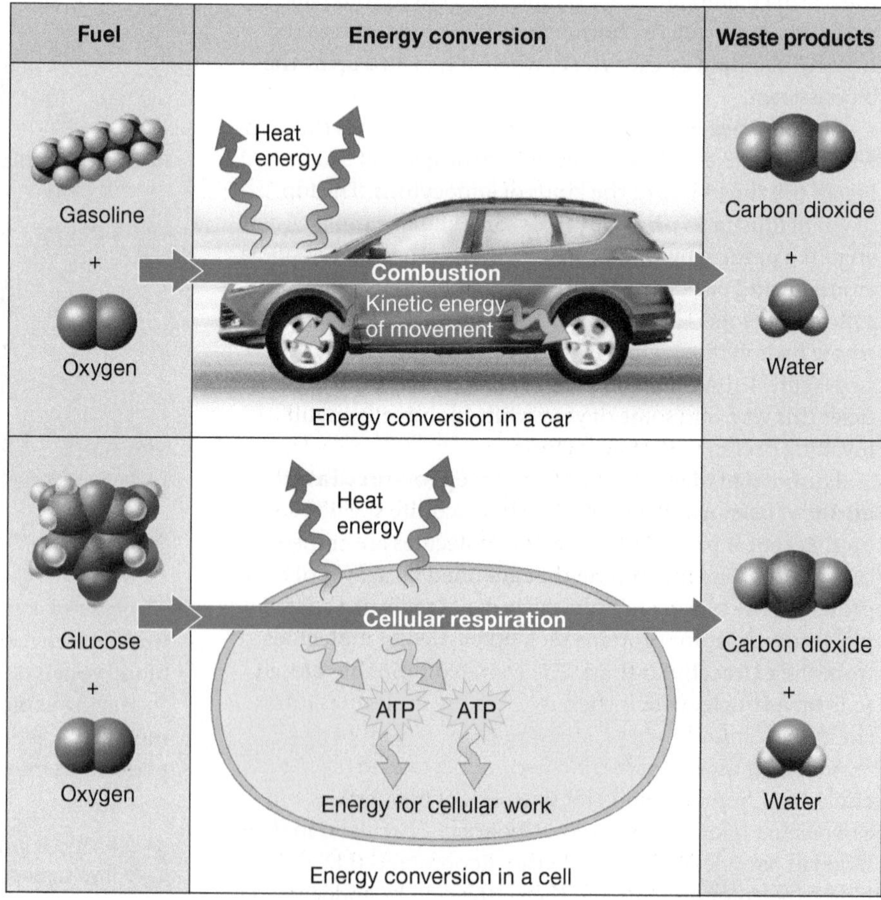

▲ **Figure 5.10** An illustration of the two laws of thermodynamics: transformation of energy and increase in entropy

water, energy-poor, simple molecules. Only about 25% of the energy stored in gasoline is converted to the kinetic energy of the car's movement; the rest is lost as heat.

Cells also use oxygen in reactions that release energy from fuel molecules. In the process called **cellular respiration**, the chemical energy stored in organic molecules is used to produce ATP, which the cell can use to perform work. Just like for the car, the waste products are carbon dioxide and water. Cells are more efficient than cars, however, converting about 34% of the chemical energy in their fuel to energy for cellular work. The other 66% generates heat, which explains why vigorous exercise makes you so warm.

According to the second law of thermodynamics, energy transformations result in the universe becoming more disordered. How, then, can we account for biological order? Although the intricate structures of a cell correspond to a decrease in entropy, their production is accomplished at the expense of ordered forms of matter and energy taken in from the surroundings. As shown in Figure 5.10, cells extract the chemical energy of glucose and return disordered heat and lower-energy carbon dioxide and water to the surroundings. In a thermodynamic sense, a cell is an island of low entropy in an increasingly random universe.

? How does the second law of thermodynamics explain the diffusion of a solute across a membrane?

■ Diffusion across a membrane results in equal concentrations of solute, which is a more disordered arrangement (higher entropy) than a high concentration on one side and a low concentration on the other.

5.11 Chemical reactions either release or store energy

Chemical reactions are of two types: exergonic or endergonic. An **exergonic reaction** releases energy (*exergonic* means "energy outward"). As Figure 5.11A shows, an exergonic reaction begins with reactants whose covalent bonds contain more potential energy than those in the products. The reaction releases to the surroundings an amount of energy equal to the difference in potential energy between the reactants and the products.

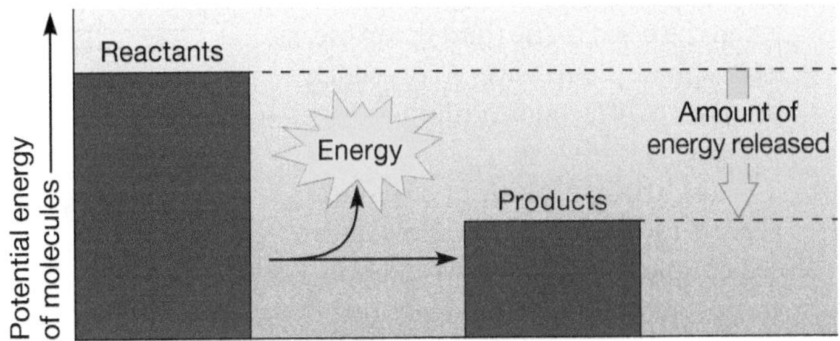

▲ **Figure 5.11A** Exergonic reaction, energy released

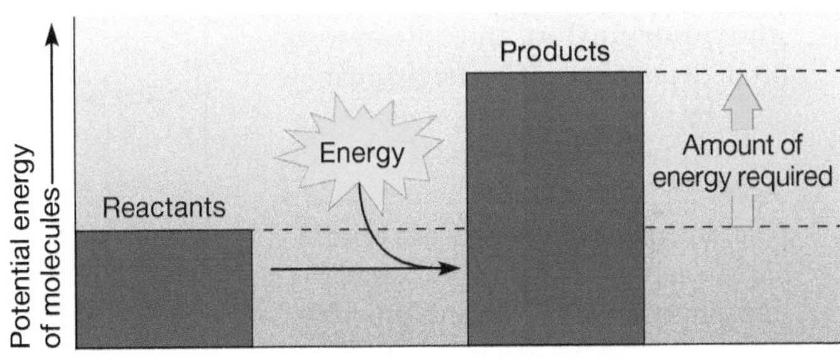

▲ **Figure 5.11B** Endergonic reaction, energy required

Consider what happens when wood burns. One of the major components of wood is cellulose, a large energy-rich carbohydrate composed of many glucose monomers. Burning wood releases the energy of glucose as heat and light. Carbon dioxide and water are the products of the reaction.

As you learned in Module 5.10, cells release energy from fuel molecules in cellular respiration. Burning and cellular respiration are alike in being exergonic. They differ in that burning is essentially a one-step process that releases all of a substance's energy at once. Cellular respiration, on the other hand, involves many steps, each a separate chemical reaction; you can think of it as a "slow burn." Much of the energy released by cellular respiration escapes as heat, but a substantial amount is stored in ATP, the immediate source of energy for a cell.

Endergonic reactions require a net input of energy and yield products that are rich in potential energy (*endergonic* means "energy inward"). As shown in Figure 5.11B, an endergonic reaction starts with reactants that contain relatively little potential energy. Energy is absorbed from the surroundings as the reaction occurs, so the products of an endergonic reaction contain more chemical energy than the reactants did.

Photosynthesis, the process by which plant cells make sugar, is an example of an endergonic process. Photosynthesis starts with energy-poor reactants (carbon dioxide and water molecules) and, using energy absorbed from sunlight, produces energy-rich sugar molecules.

Living cells carry out thousands of exergonic and endergonic reactions. The total of an organism's chemical reactions is called **metabolism**. We can picture a cell's metabolism as a road map of thousands of chemical reactions arranged as intersecting highways or metabolic pathways. A **metabolic pathway** is a series of chemical reactions that either builds a complex molecule or breaks down a complex molecule into simpler compounds. The "slow burn" of cellular respiration is an example of a metabolic pathway in which a sequence of reactions slowly releases the potential energy stored in sugar.

All of an organism's activities require energy, which is obtained from sugar and other molecules by the exergonic reactions of cellular respiration. Cells then use that energy in endergonic reactions to build molecules and do the work of the cell. **Energy coupling** is the use of energy released from exergonic reactions to drive endergonic reactions. As we see next, ATP molecules are the key to energy coupling.

? Remembering that energy must be conserved, what do you think becomes of the energy extracted from food during cellular respiration?

■ Some of it is stored in ATP molecules; the rest is released as heat.

5.12 ATP drives cellular work by coupling exergonic and endergonic reactions

ATP powers nearly all forms of cellular work. The abbreviation ATP stands for adenosine triphosphate, and as Figure 5.12A shows, ATP consists of an organic molecule called adenosine and a triphosphate tail of three phosphate groups (each symbolized by Ⓟ). All three phosphate groups are negatively charged (see Table 3.2). These like charges are crowded together, and their mutual repulsion makes the triphosphate tail of ATP the chemical equivalent of a compressed spring.

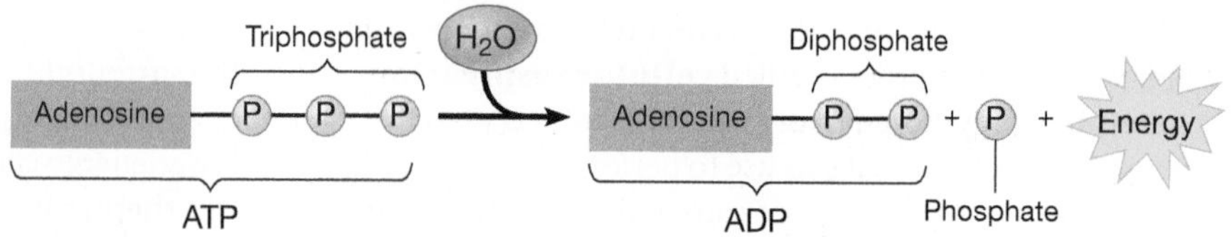

▲ Figure 5.12A The hydrolysis of ATP yielding ADP, a phosphate group, and energy.

As a result, the bonds connecting the phosphate groups are unstable and can readily be broken by hydrolysis, the addition of water. Notice in Figure 5.12A that when the bond to the third group breaks, a phosphate group leaves ATP—which becomes ADP (adenosine diphosphate)—and energy is released.

Thus, the hydrolysis of ATP is exergonic—it releases energy. How does a cell couple this reaction to an endergonic (energy-requiring) reaction? It often does so by transferring a phosphate group from ATP to another molecule. This phosphate transfer is called **phosphorylation**, and cellular work often depends on ATP energizing molecules by phosphorylating them.

What types of work does a cell do? As Figure 5.12B shows, the chemical, transport, and mechanical work of a cell are all driven by ATP. In chemical work, the phosphorylation of reactants provides energy to drive the endergonic synthesis of products. In transport work, ATP drives the active transport of solutes across a membrane against their concentration gradients by phosphorylating transport proteins. And in an example of mechanical work, the hydrolysis of ATP when attached to special motor proteins in muscle cells causes the proteins to change shape and pull on other protein filaments, in turn causing the cells to contract.

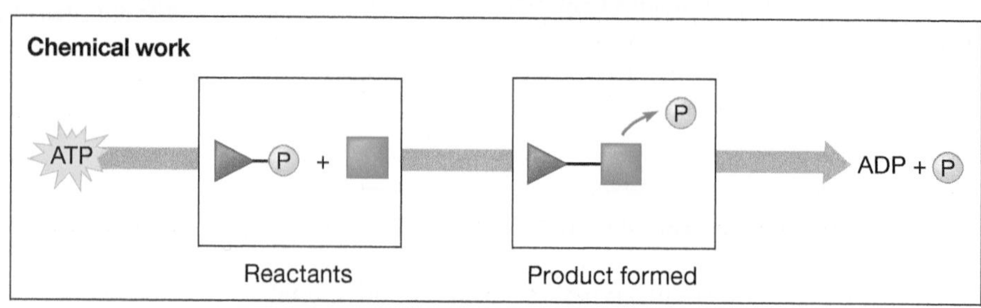

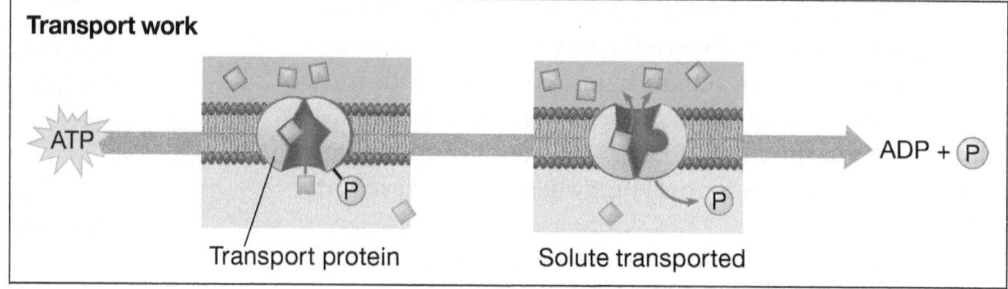

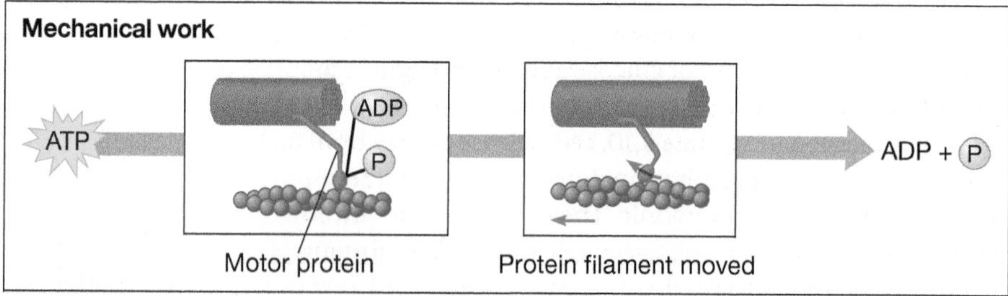

▲ Figure 5.12B How ATP powers cellular work

ATP is a renewable resource. A cell uses and regenerates ATP continuously. Figure 5.12C shows the ATP cycle. Each side of this cycle illustrates energy coupling. Energy released in exergonic reactions, such as the breakdown of glucose during cellular respiration, is used to generate ATP. In this endergonic process, a phosphate group is bonded to ADP, forming ATP. The hydrolysis of ATP releases energy that drives endergonic reactions. The ATP cycle runs at an astonishing pace. In fact, a working muscle cell may consume and regenerate 10 million ATP molecules each second.

Whether a cell's chemical reactions are exergonic or endergonic, they almost all require the assistance of enzymes, as we see next.

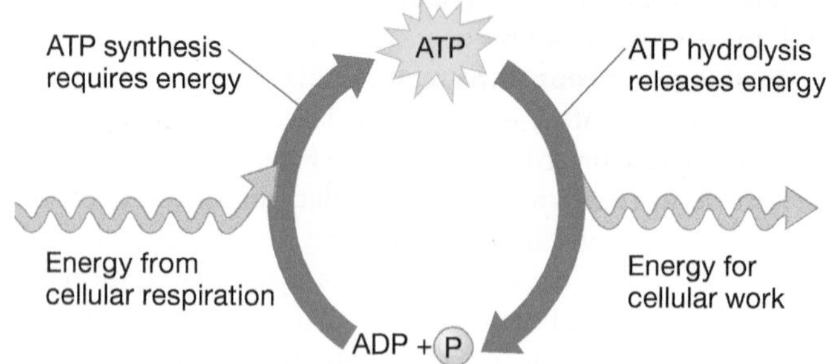

▲ Figure 5.12C The ATP cycle

TRY THIS Identify the exergonic and endergonic reactions shown by this cycle.

? Explain how ATP transfers energy from exergonic to endergonic processes in the cell.

■ Exergonic processes phosphorylate ADP to form ATP. ATP transfers energy to endergonic processes, often by phosphorylating other molecules.

How Enzymes Function

5.13 Enzymes speed up the cell's chemical reactions by lowering energy barriers

Your room gets messier; water flows downhill; sugar crystals dissolve in your coffee. Ordered structures tend toward disorder, and high-energy systems, which are inherently unstable, tend to change toward a more stable low energy state. Proteins, DNA, carbohydrates, lipids—these complex molecules of your cells are rich in potential energy. Why don't such high-energy, ordered molecules spontaneously break down into less-ordered, lower-energy components? They remain intact for the same reason that wood doesn't normally burst into flames or the gas in an automobile's gas tank doesn't spontaneously explode.

There is an energy barrier that must be overcome before a chemical reaction can begin. Energy must be absorbed to contort or weaken bonds in reactant molecules so that they can break and new bonds can form. We call this the **activation energy** (because it activates the reactants). We can think of activation energy as the amount of energy needed for reactant molecules to move "uphill" to a higher-energy, unstable state so that the "downhill" part of a reaction can begin.

The activation energy barrier protects the highly ordered molecules of your cells from spontaneously breaking down. But now we have a dilemma. Life depends on countless chemical reactions that constantly change a cell's molecular makeup. Most of the essential reactions of metabolism must occur quickly and precisely for a cell to survive. How can the specific reactions that a cell requires get over that energy barrier?

One way to speed reactions is to add heat. Heat speeds up molecules and agitates atoms so that bonds break more easily and reactions can proceed. Certainly, adding a match to kindling will start a fire, and the firing of a spark plug ignites gasoline in an engine. But heating a cell would speed up all chemical reactions, not just the necessary ones, and too much heat would kill the cell.

The answer to this dilemma lies in **enzymes**—molecules that function as biological catalysts, increasing the rate of a reaction without being consumed by the reaction. Almost all enzymes are proteins. (Some RNA molecules also function as enzymes.) An enzyme speeds up a reaction by lowering the activation energy needed for a reaction to begin. Figure 5.13 compares a reaction without an enzyme (left) and with an enzyme (right). In both cases, the reactant must absorb enough energy to reach the top of the activation energy barrier so that the reaction can proceed. Notice how much lower the activation energy barrier is when an enzyme is involved. This lowered barrier allows an enzyme-catalyzed reaction to proceed much more rapidly. In the next module, we explore how the structure of an enzyme enables it to lower the activation energy.

? **The graph below illustrates a reaction with and without an enzyme. Which curve represents the enzyme-catalyzed reaction? What do lines a, b, and c represent?**

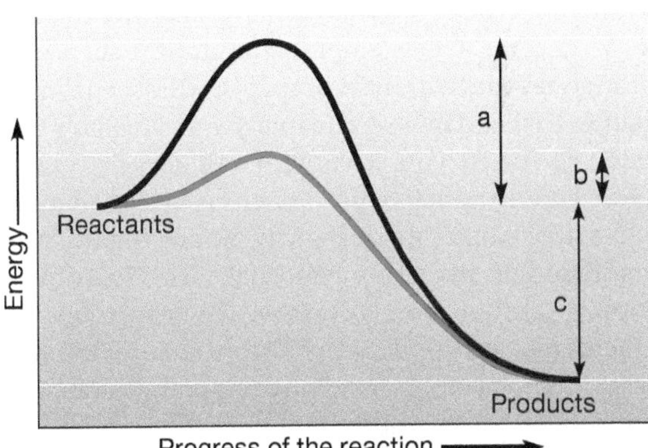

The red curve is the enzyme-catalyzed reaction. Line a is the activation energy without enzyme; b is the activation energy with enzyme; c is the change in energy between reactants and products, which is the same for both the catalyzed and uncatalyzed reactions.

Activation energy barrier
Reactant
Products
Energy
Reaction without enzyme

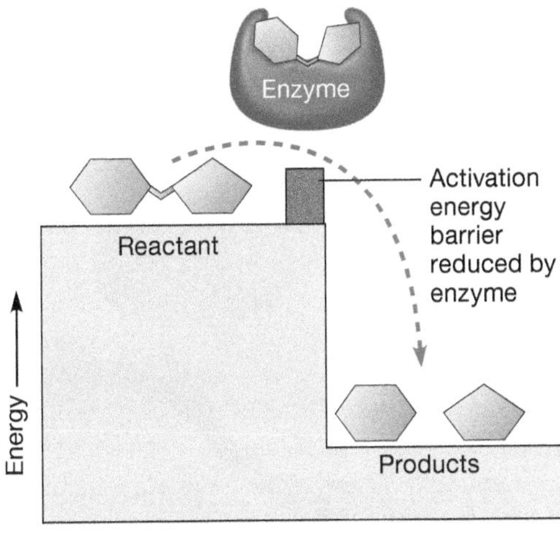

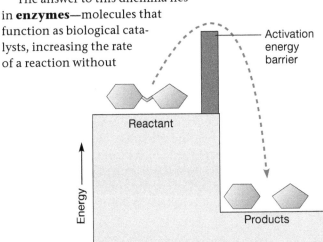

▲ **Figure 5.13 The effect of an enzyme in lowering the activation energy**

TRY THIS Relate these two figures to the graph shown in the checkpoint question.

5.14 A specific enzyme catalyzes each cellular reaction

You just learned that an enzyme catalyzes a reaction by lowering the activation energy barrier. How does it do that? With the aid of an enzyme, the bonds in a reactant are contorted into the higher-energy, unstable state from which the reaction can proceed. Without an enzyme, the activation energy barrier might never be breached. For example, a solution of sucrose (table sugar) can sit for years at room temperature with no appreciable hydrolysis into its components glucose and fructose. But if we add a small amount of the enzyme sucrase, all the sucrose will be hydrolyzed within seconds.

An enzyme is very selective in the reaction it catalyzes. Illustrating the core theme of STRUCTURE AND FUNCTION, an enzyme has a unique three-dimensional shape, and that shape determines the enzyme's specificity. The specific reactant that an enzyme acts on is called the enzyme's **substrate**. A substrate fits into a region of the enzyme called the **active site**—typically a pocket or groove on the surface of the enzyme. Enzymes are specific because only specific substrate molecules fit into their active sites.

The Catalytic Cycle Figure 5.14 illustrates the catalytic cycle of an enzyme. Our example is the enzyme sucrase, which catalyzes the hydrolysis of sucrose. (Most enzymes have names that end in *-ase*, and many are named for their substrate.) ① The enzyme starts with an empty active site. ② Sucrose enters the active site, attaching by weak bonds. The active site changes shape slightly, embracing the substrate more snugly, like a firm handshake. This **induced fit** may contort substrate bonds or place chemical groups of the amino acids making up the active site in position to catalyze the reaction. (In reactions involving two or more reactants, the active site holds the substrates in the proper orientation for a reaction to occur.)

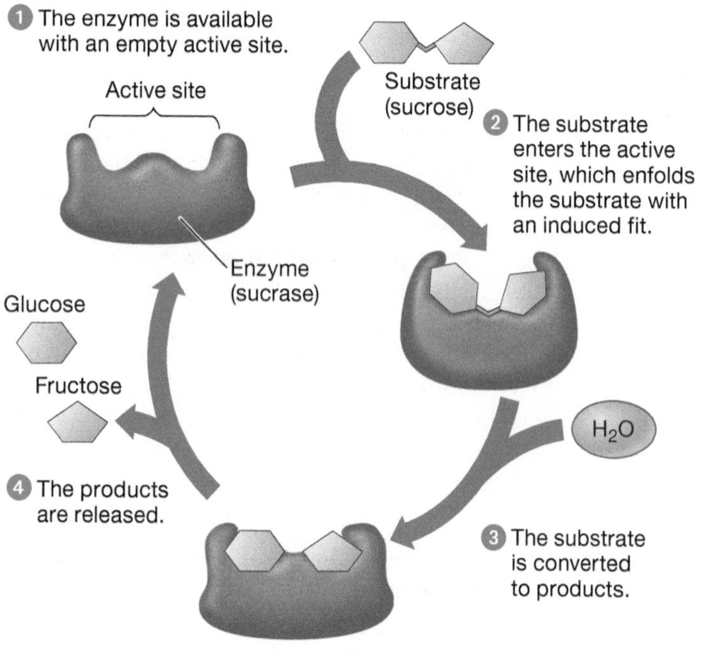

▲ Figure 5.14 The catalytic cycle of an enzyme

③ The strained bond of sucrose reacts with water, and the substrate is converted (hydrolyzed) to the products glucose and fructose. ④ The enzyme releases the products and emerges unchanged from the reaction. Its active site is now available for another substrate molecule, and another round of the cycle can begin. A single enzyme molecule may act on thousands or even millions of substrate molecules per second.

Optimal Conditions for Enzymes As with all proteins, an enzyme's shape is central to its function, and this three-dimensional shape is affected by the environment. For every enzyme, there are optimal conditions under which it is most effective. Temperature, for instance, affects molecular motion, and an enzyme's optimal temperature produces the highest rate of contact between reactant molecules and the enzyme's active site. Higher temperatures denature the enzyme, altering the protein's specific shape and thus destroying its function. Most human enzymes work best at 35–40°C (95–104°F), close to our normal body temperature of 37°C. Prokaryotes that live in hot springs, however, contain enzymes with optimal temperatures of 70°C (158°F) or higher. Scientists make use of the enzymes of these bacteria in a technique that rapidly replicates DNA sequences from small samples (see Module 12.12).

The optimal pH for most enzymes is near neutrality, in the range of 6–8. There are exceptions, of course. Pepsin, a digestive enzyme in your stomach, works best at pH 2. Such an environment would denature most proteins, but the structure of pepsin is most stable and active in this acidic environment.

Cofactors Many enzymes require nonprotein helpers called **cofactors**, which bind to the active site and function in catalysis. The cofactors of some enzymes are inorganic, such as the ions of zinc, iron, and copper. If the cofactor is an organic molecule, it is called a **coenzyme**. Most vitamins are important in nutrition because they function as coenzymes or raw materials from which coenzymes are made. For example, folic acid, a B vitamin, is a coenzyme for a number of enzymes involved in the synthesis of nucleic acids.

Chemical chaos would result if all of a cell's metabolic pathways were operating simultaneously. Illustrating the theme of INTERACTIONS between components in a system, a cell's carefully regulated metabolism depends on the connection and coordination of key molecular players. A cell must tightly control when and where its various enzymes are active. It does this either by switching on or off the genes that encode specific enzymes (as you will learn in Chapter 11) or by regulating the activity of enzymes once they are made. We explore this second mechanism in the next module.

? **Explain how an enzyme speeds up a specific reaction.**

■ An enzyme lowers the activation energy needed for a reaction when its specific substrate enters its active site. With an induced fit, the enzyme strains bonds that need to break or positions substrates in an orientation that aids the conversion of reactants to products.

5.15 Enzyme inhibition can regulate enzyme activity in a cell

A chemical that interferes with an enzyme's activity is called an inhibitor. Scientists have learned a great deal about enzyme function by studying the effects of such chemicals. Some inhibitors resemble the enzyme's normal substrate and compete for entry into the active site. As shown in the lower left of Figure 5.15A, such a **competitive inhibitor** reduces an enzyme's productivity by blocking substrate molecules from entering the active site. Competitive inhibition can be overcome by increasing the concentration of the substrate, making it more likely that a substrate molecule rather than an inhibitor will be nearby when an active site becomes vacant.

In contrast, a **noncompetitive inhibitor** does not enter the active site. Instead, it binds to a site elsewhere on the enzyme, and its binding changes the enzyme's shape so that the active site no longer fits the substrate (lower right of Figure 5.15A).

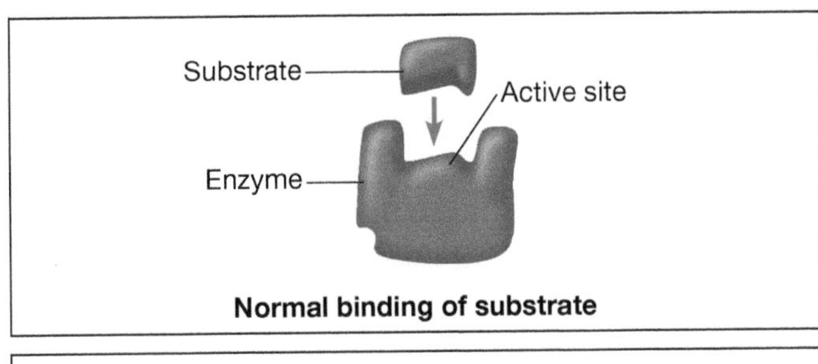

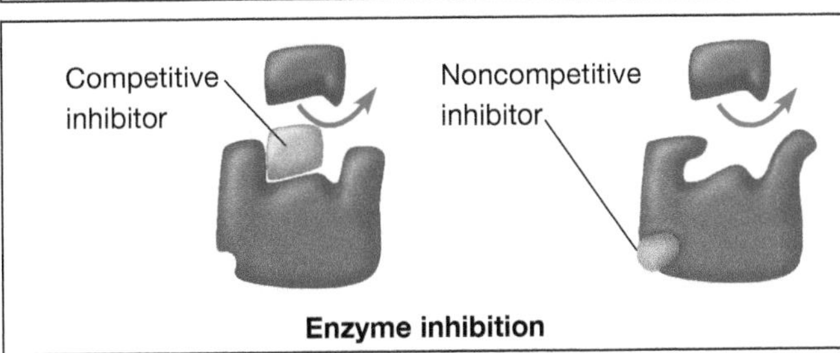

▲ Figure 5.15A How inhibitors interfere with substrate binding

Although enzyme inhibition sounds harmful, cells use inhibitors as important regulators of cellular metabolism. Many of a cell's chemical reactions are organized into metabolic pathways in which a molecule is altered in a series of steps, each catalyzed by a specific enzyme, to form a final product. If a cell is producing more of that product than it needs, the product may act as an inhibitor of one of the enzymes early in the pathway. Figure 5.15B illustrates this sort of inhibition, called **feedback inhibition**. Because only weak interactions bind inhibitor and enzyme, this inhibition is reversible. When the product is used up by the cell, the enzyme is no longer inhibited and the pathway functions again.

In the next module, we explore some ways that people make use of enzyme inhibitors.

? Explain an advantage of feedback inhibition to a cell.

It prevents the cell from wasting valuable resources by synthesizing more of a particular product than is needed.

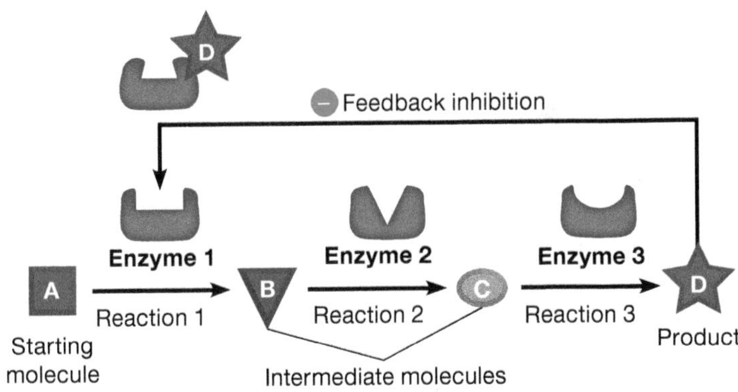

▲ Figure 5.15B Feedback inhibition of a metabolic pathway in which product D acts as an inhibitor of enzyme 1

5.16 Many drugs, pesticides, and poisons are enzyme inhibitors

CONNECTION

Many beneficial drugs act as enzyme inhibitors. Ibuprofen (Figure 5.16) is a common drug that inhibits an enzyme involved in the production of prostaglandins—messenger molecules that are released in response to injury. Prostaglandins increase our sensation of pain and cause inflammation, and inhibiting their production relieves these symptoms. Other drugs that function as enzyme inhibitors include some blood pressure medicines and antidepressants. Many antibiotics work by inhibiting enzymes of disease-causing bacteria. Penicillin, for example, blocks the active site of an enzyme that many bacteria use in making cell walls. Protease inhibitors are HIV drugs that target a key viral enzyme. And many cancer drugs are inhibitors of enzymes that promote cell division.

Humans have developed enzyme inhibitors as pesticides, and occasionally as deadly poisons for use in warfare. Such chemicals often attach to an enzyme by covalent bonds, making the inhibition irreversible. Poisons called nerve gases bind in the active site of an enzyme vital to the transmission of nerve impulses. The inhibition of this enzyme leads to rapid paralysis of vital functions and death. Pesticides such as malathion and parathion are toxic to insects (and dangerous to the people who apply them) because they also irreversibly inhibit this enzyme. Interestingly, some drugs reversibly inhibit this same enzyme and are used in anesthesia and treatment of certain diseases.

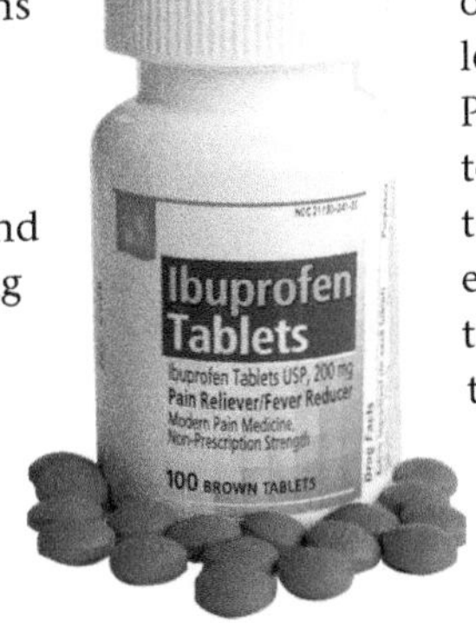

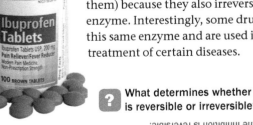

▲ Figure 5.16 Ibuprofen, an enzyme inhibitor

? What determines whether enzyme inhibition is reversible or irreversible?

If the inhibitor binds to the enzyme with covalent bonds, the inhibition is usually irreversible. When weak chemical interactions bind inhibitor and enzyme, the inhibition is reversible.

CHAPTER

5 REVIEW

For practice quizzes, BioFlix animations, MP3 tutorials, video tutors, and more study tools designed for this textbook, go to MasteringBiology™

REVIEWING THE CONCEPTS

Membrane Structure and Function (5.1–5.9)

5.1 Membranes are fluid mosaics of lipids and proteins with many functions. The proteins embedded in a membrane's phospholipid bilayer perform various functions.

5.2 The spontaneous formation of membranes was a critical step in the origin of life.

5.3 Passive transport is diffusion across a membrane with no energy investment. Solutes diffuse across membranes down their concentration gradients.

5.4 Osmosis is the diffusion of water across a membrane.

5.5 Water balance between cells and their surroundings is crucial to organisms. Cells shrink in a hypertonic solution and swell in a hypotonic solution. In isotonic solutions, animal cells are normal, but plant cells are flaccid.

5.6 Transport proteins can facilitate diffusion across membranes.

5.7 Research on another membrane protein led to the discovery of aquaporins.

5.8 Cells expend energy in the active transport of a solute.

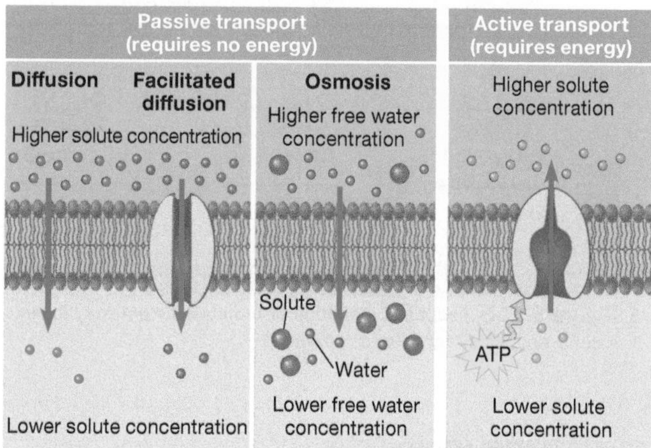

5.9 Exocytosis and endocytosis transport large molecules across membranes. A vesicle may fuse with the membrane and expel its contents (exocytosis), or the membrane may fold inward, enclosing material from outside the cell (endocytosis).

Energy and the Cell (5.10–5.12)

5.10 Cells transform energy and matter as they perform work. Kinetic energy is the energy of motion. Potential energy is energy stored in the location or structure of matter and includes chemical energy. According to the laws of thermodynamics, energy can change form but cannot be created or destroyed, and energy transfers or transformations increase disorder, or entropy, with some energy being lost as heat.

5.11 Chemical reactions either release or store energy. Exergonic reactions release energy. Endergonic reactions require energy and yield products rich in potential energy. Metabolism encompasses all of a cell's chemical reactions.

5.12 ATP drives cellular work by coupling exergonic and endergonic reactions. The hydrolysis of ATP and, often, the transfer of a phosphate group is involved in chemical, transport, and mechanical work.

How Enzymes Function (5.13–5.16)

5.13 Enzymes speed up the cell's chemical reactions by lowering energy barriers. Enzymes are catalysts (usually proteins) that decrease the activation energy needed to begin a reaction.

5.14 A specific enzyme catalyzes each cellular reaction. An enzyme's substrate fits specifically in its active site.

5.15 Enzyme inhibition can regulate enzyme activity in a cell. Inhibitors can be either competitive or noncompetitive. Feedback inhibition helps regulate metabolism.

5.16 Many drugs, pesticides, and poisons are enzyme inhibitors.

CONNECTING THE CONCEPTS

1. Fill in the following concept map to review the processes by which molecules move across membranes.

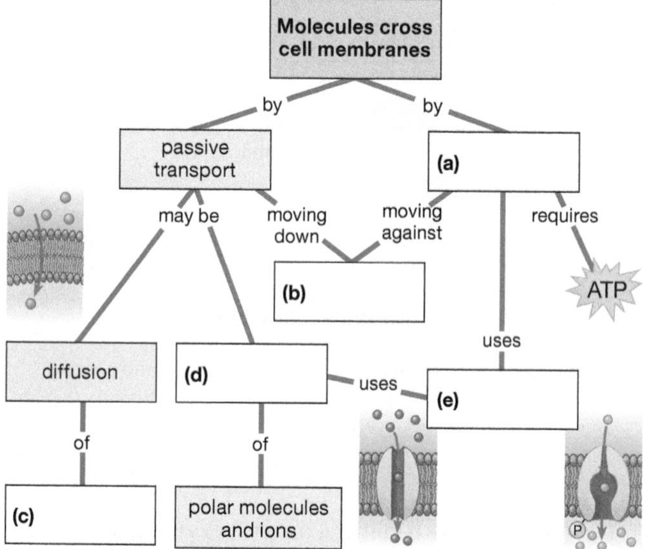

2. Label the parts of the following diagram illustrating the catalytic cycle of an enzyme.

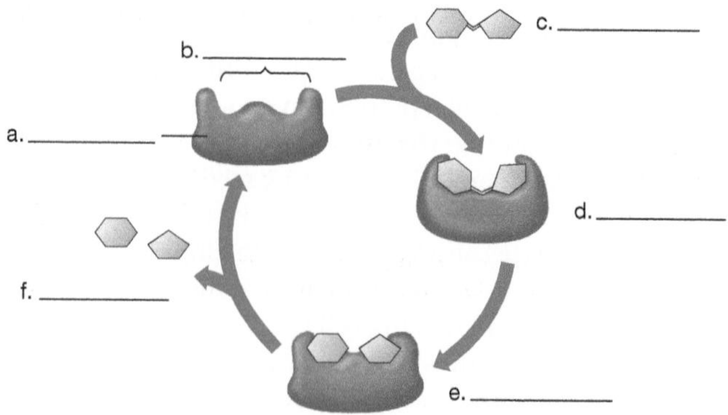

TESTING YOUR KNOWLEDGE

Level 1: Knowledge/Comprehension

3. Which best describes the structure of a cell membrane?
   a. proteins between two bilayers of phospholipids
   b. proteins embedded in a bilayer of phospholipids
   c. a bilayer of protein coating a layer of phospholipids
   d. cholesterol embedded in a bilayer of phospholipids
4. A plant cell placed in distilled water will ____________; an animal cell placed in distilled water will ____________.
   a. burst ... burst
   b. become flaccid . . . shrivel
   c. become turgid . . . be normal in shape
   d. become turgid . . . burst
5. The sodium concentration in a cell is 10 times less than the concentration in the surrounding fluid. How can the cell move sodium out of the cell? (*Explain your answer.*)
   a. passive transport
   b. receptor-mediated endocytosis
   c. active transport
   d. facilitated diffusion
6. The synthesis of ATP from ADP and (P)
   a. stores energy in a form that can drive cellular work.
   b. involves the hydrolysis of a phosphate bond.
   c. transfers a phosphate, priming a protein to do work.
   d. is an exergonic process.
7. Facilitated diffusion across a membrane requires ____________ and moves a solute ____________ its concentration gradient.
   a. transport proteins . . . up (against)
   b. transport proteins . . . down
   c. energy and transport proteins . . . up
   d. energy and transport proteins . . . down
8. What are the main types of cellular work? How does ATP provide the energy for this work?

Level 2: Application/Analysis

9. Why is the barrier of the activation energy beneficial for cells? Explain how enzymes lower activation energy.
10. Relate the laws of thermodynamics to living organisms.
11. How do the components and structure of cell membranes relate to the functions of membranes?
12. Sometimes inhibitors can be harmful to a cell; often they are beneficial. Explain.

Level 3: Synthesis/Evaluation

13. Cells lining kidney tubules function in the reabsorption of water from urine. In response to chemical signals, they reversibly insert additional aquaporins into their plasma membranes. In which of these situations would your tubule cells have the most aquaporins: after a long run on a hot day, right after a large meal, or after drinking a large bottle of water? Explain.
14. **SCIENTIFIC THINKING** Mercury is known to inhibit the permeability of water channels. To help establish that the protein isolated by Agre's group was a water channel (see Module 5.7), the researchers incubated groups of RNA-injected oocytes (which thus made aquaporin proteins) in four different solutions: plain buffer, low concentration and high concentration of a mercury chloride ($HgCl_2$) solution, and low concentration of a mercury solution followed by an agent (ME) known to reverse the effects of mercury. The water permeability of the cells was determined by the rate of their osmotic swelling. Interpret the results of this experiment, which are presented in the graph below.

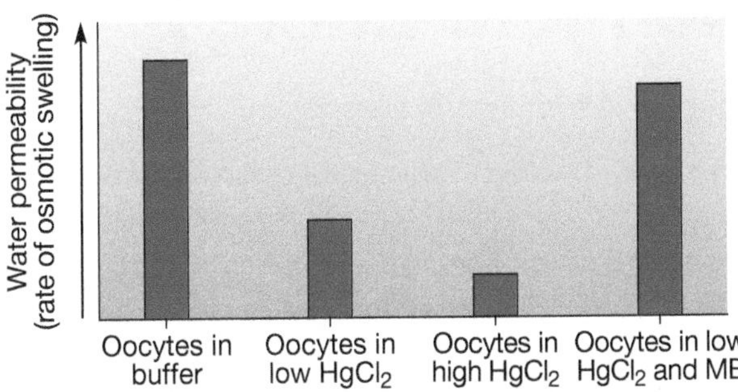

Data from G. M. Preston et al., Appearance of water channels in *Xenopus* oocytes expressing red cell CHIP28 protein, *Science* 256: 3385–7 (1992).

Control oocytes not injected with aquaporin RNA were also incubated with buffer and the two concentrations of mercury. Predict what the results of these treatments would be.

15. A biologist performed two series of experiments on lactase, the enzyme that hydrolyzes lactose to glucose and galactose. First, she made up 10% lactose solutions containing different concentrations of enzyme and measured the rate at which galactose was produced (grams of galactose per minute). Results of these experiments are shown in Table A below. In the second series of experiments (Table B), she prepared 2% enzyme solutions containing different concentrations of lactose and again measured the rate of galactose production.

TABLE A Reaction Rate and Enzyme Concentration

Lactose concentration	10%	10%	10%	10%	10%
Enzyme concentration	0%	1%	2%	4%	8%
Reaction rate	0	25	50	100	200

TABLE B Reaction Rate and Substrate Concentration

Lactose concentration	0%	5%	10%	20%	30%
Enzyme concentration	2%	2%	2%	2%	2%
Reaction rate	0	25	50	65	65

   a. Graph and explain the relationship between the reaction rate and the enzyme concentration.
   b. Graph and explain the relationship between the reaction rate and the substrate concentration. How and why did the results of the two experiments differ?

16. Organophosphates (organic compounds containing phosphate groups) are commonly used as insecticides to improve crop yield. Organophosphates typically interfere with nerve signal transmission by inhibiting the enzymes that degrade transmitter molecules. They affect humans and other vertebrates as well as insects. Thus, the use of organophosphate pesticides poses some health risks. On the other hand, these molecules break down rapidly upon exposure to air and sunlight. As a consumer, what level of risk are you willing to accept in exchange for an abundant and affordable food supply?

Answers to all questions can be found in Appendix 4.

How Cells Harvest Chemical Energy

CHAPTER 6

A baby's first cry! This welcome sound shows that the baby is breathing and taking in oxygen. But why is oxygen necessary for life? Oxygen is a reactant in cellular respiration—the process that breaks down sugar and other food molecules and generates ATP, the energy currency of cells. The process of cellular respiration also produces heat, which helps maintain a warm body temperature.

Cellular respiration occurred in this baby's cells before she was born, but the oxygen and sugar her cells required were delivered from her mother's blood. Now this baby takes in her own oxygen—although she still can't obtain her own food. And if this baby is exposed to the cold, she can't keep herself warm. If you get cold, you put on more clothes, move to a warmer place, or shiver—generating heat as your contracting muscles increase their production of ATP and heat. This baby can't do any of those things yet. Instead, along her back she has a layer of a special kind of "baby fat," called brown fat, that helps keep her warm. The cells of brown fat have a "short circuit" in their cellular respiration—they consume oxygen and burn fuel, but generate only heat, not ATP.

Can brown fat keep a newborn warm and help keep an adult thin?

Scientists have long known that brown fat is important for heat production in small mammals, hibernating bears, and newborn infants. Studies have also shown brown fat to be involved in weight regulation in mice. As you will learn later in the chapter, brown fat deposits have recently been discovered in adult humans. Scientists are now exploring whether this heat-generating, calorie-burning tissue could be tapped in the fight against obesity.

We begin this chapter with an overview of cellular respiration and then focus on its stages: glycolysis, pyruvate oxidation and the citric acid cycle, and oxidative phosphorylation. We also consider fermentation, an extension of glycolysis that has deep evolutionary roots. We complete the chapter with a comparison of the metabolic pathways that break down and build up the organic molecules of your body.

BIG IDEAS

Cellular Respiration: Aerobic Harvesting of Energy (6.1–6.5)

Cellular respiration oxidizes fuel molecules and generates ATP for cellular work.

Stages of Cellular Respiration (6.6–6.11)

The main stages of cellular respiration are glycolysis, pyruvate oxidation and the citric acid cycle, and oxidative phosphorylation.

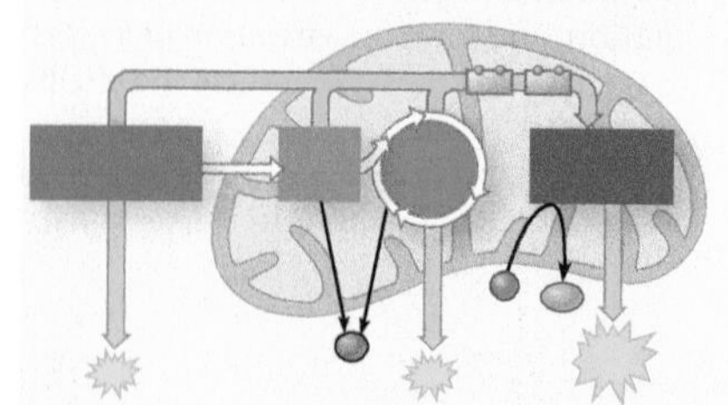

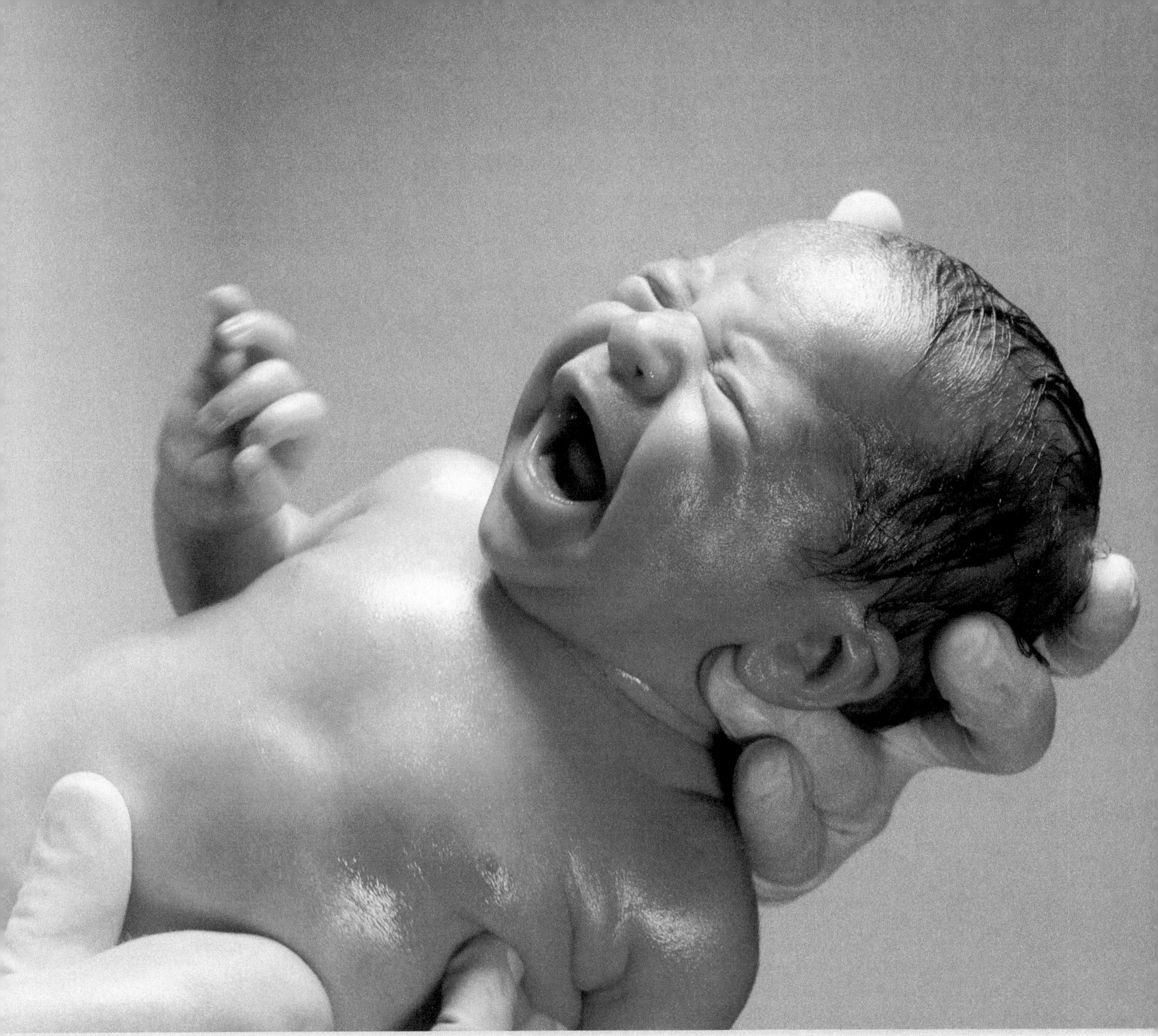

Fermentation: Anaerobic Harvesting of Energy (6.12–6.13)

Fermentation regenerates NAD^+, allowing glycolysis and ATP production to continue without oxygen.

Connections Between Metabolic Pathways (6.14–6.15)

The breakdown pathways of cellular respiration intersect with biosynthetic pathways.

Cellular Respiration: Aerobic Harvesting of Energy

6.1 Photosynthesis and cellular respiration provide energy for life

Life requires energy. **Figure 6.1** illustrates how photosynthesis and cellular respiration together provide energy for living organisms. In almost all ecosystems, that energy ultimately comes from the sun. In **photosynthesis**, the energy of sunlight is used to rearrange the atoms of carbon dioxide (CO_2) and water (H_2O), producing organic molecules and releasing oxygen (O_2). In **cellular respiration**, O_2 is consumed as organic molecules are broken down to CO_2 and H_2O, and the cell captures the energy released in ATP. Photosynthesis takes place in some prokaryotes and in the chloroplasts of plants and algae. Cellular respiration takes place in many prokaryotes and in the mitochondria of almost all eukaryotes—in the cells of plants, animals, fungi, and protists.

This figure also shows that, as in all energy conversions, some energy is lost as heat. Life on Earth is solar powered, and energy makes a one-way trip through an ecosystem. Matter, however, is recycled. The CO_2 and H_2O released by cellular respiration are converted through photosynthesis to sugar and O_2, which are then used in respiration. These processes are fundamental illustrations of the theme of ENERGY AND MATTER. (Photosynthesis will be explored in detail in Chapter 7.)

? What is misleading about the following statement? "Plant cells perform photosynthesis, and animal cells perform cellular respiration."

■ The statement implies that cellular respiration does not occur in plant cells. In fact, almost all eukaryotic cells use cellular respiration to obtain energy for their cellular work.

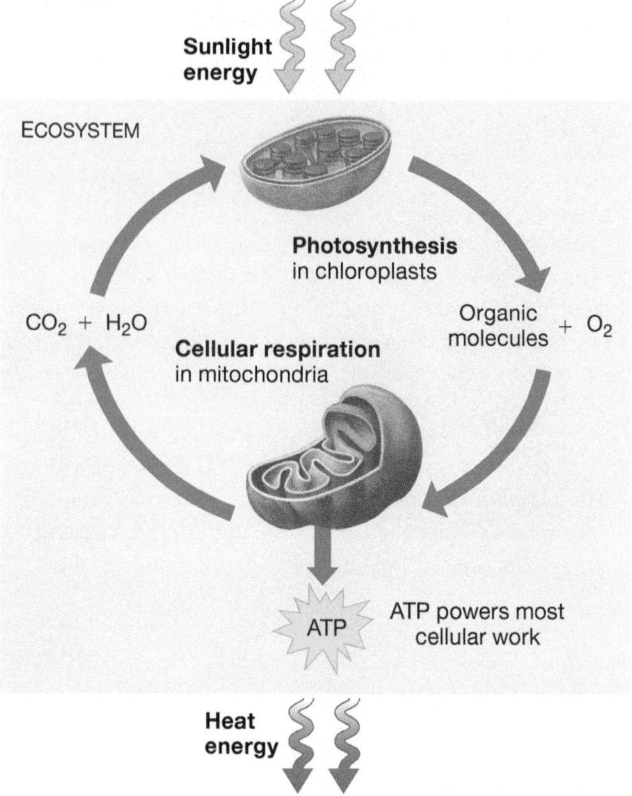

▲ **Figure 6.1** The connection between photosynthesis and cellular respiration

6.2 Breathing supplies O_2 for use in cellular respiration and removes CO_2

We often use the word *respiration* as a synonym for "breathing," the meaning of its Latin root. In that case, respiration refers to an exchange of gases: An organism obtains O_2 from its environment and releases CO_2 as a waste product. Biologists also define respiration as the aerobic (oxygen-requiring) harvesting of energy from food molecules by cells. This process is called cellular respiration to distinguish it from breathing.

Breathing and cellular respiration are closely related. As the runner in **Figure 6.2** breathes in air, her lungs take up O_2 and pass it to her blood. The bloodstream carries the O_2 to her muscle cells, where it is used in the process of cellular respiration to harvest energy from glucose and other organic molecules. Muscle cells use ATP generated by cellular respiration to power contractions. The runner's bloodstream and lungs also perform the vital function of disposing of CO_2, the waste produced in cellular respiration. Notice the positions of O_2 and CO_2 in the equation for cellular respiration at the bottom of the figure.

? How is your breathing related to your cellular respiration?

■ In breathing, CO_2 and O_2 are exchanged between your lungs and the air. In cellular respiration, cells use the O_2 obtained through breathing to break down fuel, releasing CO_2 as a waste product.

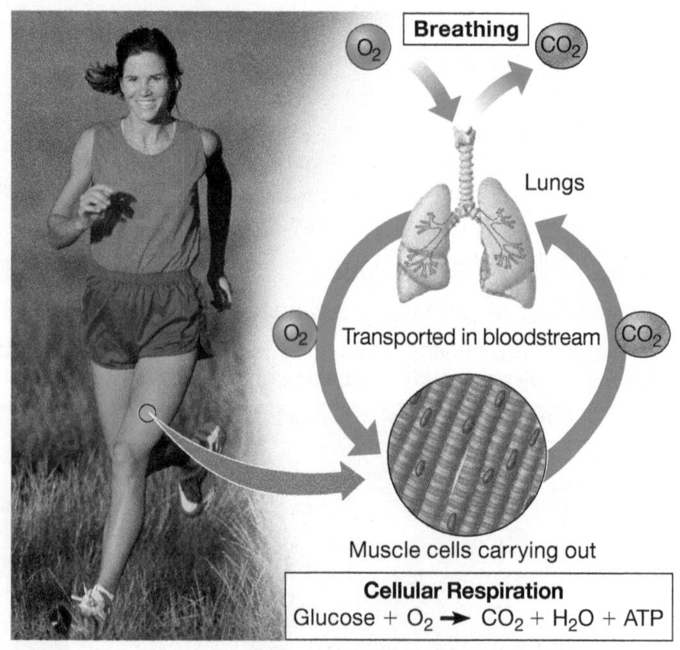

▲ **Figure 6.2** The connection between breathing and cellular respiration

6.3 Cellular respiration banks energy in ATP molecules

$$C_6H_{12}O_6 + 6\,O_2 \longrightarrow\longrightarrow\longrightarrow 6\,CO_2 + 6\,H_2O + \text{ATP} + \text{Heat}$$

Glucose   Oxygen   Carbon dioxide   Water

▲ **Figure 6.3** **Summary equation for cellular respiration**

You breathe air and eat food to supply your cells with the reactants needed for cellular respiration—the process that generates ATP for cellular work. The chemical equation in **Figure 6.3** summarizes cellular respiration. The simple sugar glucose ($C_6H_{12}O_6$) is the fuel that cells use most often, although other organic molecules can also be "burned" in cellular respiration. The equation tells us that the atoms of the reactant molecules $C_6H_{12}O_6$ and O_2 are rearranged to form the products CO_2 and H_2O. In this exergonic (energy-releasing) process, the chemical energy of the bonds in glucose is released, and some is stored (or "banked") in ATP (see Module 5.12) while the rest is released as heat. The series of arrows in Figure 6.3 indicates that cellular respiration consists of many steps.

Cellular respiration can produce up to 32 ATP molecules for each glucose molecule, a capture of about 34% of the energy originally stored in glucose. The rest of the energy is lost as heat (see Module 5.10). This may seem inefficient, but it compares very well with the efficiency of most energy-conversion systems. For instance, the average automobile engine is able to convert only about 25% of the energy in gasoline to the kinetic energy of movement. And, as you learned in the chapter introduction, heat released in cellular respiration helps maintain your warm body temperature.

How great are the energy needs of a cell? If ATP could not be regenerated through cellular respiration, you would use up nearly your body weight in ATP each day. Let's consider the energy requirements for various human activities next.

? **Why are sweating and other body-cooling mechanisms necessary during vigorous exercise?**

■ The demand for ATP is supported by an increased rate of cellular respiration, but about 66% of the energy released from food produces heat instead of ATP.

6.4 The human body uses energy from ATP for all its activities

CONNECTION

Your body requires a continuous supply of energy just to stay alive—to keep your heart pumping and to keep you breathing. Your brain especially requires a huge amount of energy; its cells burn about 120 grams (g)—a quarter of a pound!—of glucose a day, which accounts for about 20% of total energy consumption. Maintaining brain cells and other life-sustaining activities uses as much as 75% of the energy a person takes in as food during a typical day.

Above and beyond the energy you need for body maintenance, cellular respiration provides energy for voluntary activities. **Figure 6.4** shows the amount of energy it takes to perform some of these activities. The energy units are **kilocalories (kcal)**, a measure of the quantity of heat required to raise the temperature of 1 kilogram (kg) of water by 1°C. (The "Calories" listed on food packages are actually kilocalories, usually signified by a capital C.) The values shown do not include the energy the body needs for its basic life-sustaining activities, which may range from 1,300 to 1,800 kcal a day. This energy requirement is known as your basal metabolic rate (BMR).

The U.S. National Academy of Sciences estimates that the average adult needs to take in food that provides about 2,200 kcal of energy per day, although the number varies based on age, sex, and activity level. A balance of energy intake and expenditure is required to maintain a healthy weight. (We will explore nutritional needs further in Chapter 21.)

▲ **Figure 6.4** **Energy (kcal) consumed per hour by a 67.5-kg person doing various activities. Values do not include the kcal needed for body maintenance (BMR).**

Now we begin the study of how cells liberate the energy stored in fuel molecules to produce the ATP used to power the work of your cells and thus the activities of your body.

? **While walking at 3 mph, how far would you have to travel to "burn off" the equivalent of an extra slice of pizza, which has about 475 kcal? How long would that take?**

■ You would have to walk about 6 miles, which would take you about 2 hours. (Now you understand why the most effective exercise for losing weight is pushing away from the table!)

6.5 Cells capture energy from electrons "falling" from organic fuels to oxygen

How do your cells extract energy from fuel molecules? The answer involves the transfer of electrons.

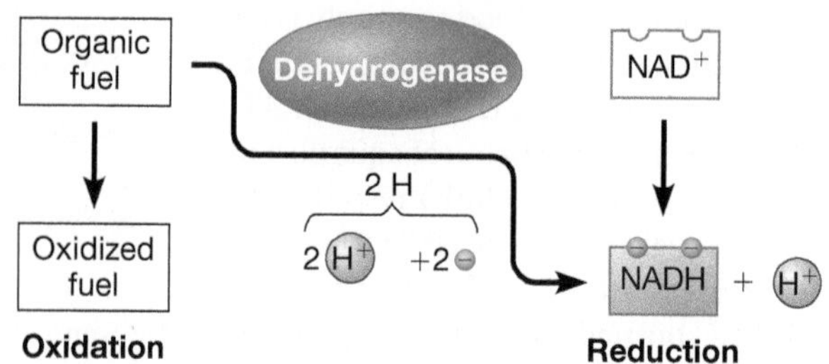

▲ **Figure 6.5B** Oxidation of an organic fuel with accompanying reduction of NAD^+ to NADH

TRY THIS Explain how the name *dehydrogenase* describes this enzyme's function in oxidation reactions.

Redox Reactions During cellular respiration, electrons are transferred from glucose or other organic fuels to oxygen, releasing energy. Oxygen attracts electrons very strongly, and an electron loses potential energy when it moves to oxygen. If you burn a cube of sugar, this electron "fall" happens very rapidly, releasing energy in the form of heat and light. Cellular respiration is a more controlled descent of electrons—more like stepping down an energy staircase, with energy released in small amounts that can be stored in the chemical bonds of ATP.

The transfer of electrons from one molecule to another is an oxidation-reduction reaction, or **redox reaction** for short. In a redox reaction, the loss of electrons from one substance is called **oxidation**, and the addition of electrons to another substance is called **reduction**. A molecule is said to become oxidized when it loses one or more electrons and reduced when it gains one or more electrons. Because an electron transfer requires both a donor and an acceptor, oxidation and reduction always go together.

In the cellular respiration equation in Figure 6.5A below, you cannot see any electron transfers. What you do see are changes in the location of hydrogen atoms. These hydrogen movements represent electron transfers because each hydrogen atom consists of an electron (⊖) and a proton (hydrogen ion, or H^+). Glucose ($C_6H_{12}O_6$) loses hydrogen atoms (with their electrons) as it becomes oxidized to CO_2; simultaneously, O_2 gains hydrogen atoms (and thus electrons) as it becomes reduced to H_2O. As they pass from glucose to oxygen, the electrons lose energy, some of which cells capture to make ATP.

NADH and Electron Transport Chains An important player in the process of oxidizing glucose is a coenzyme called **NAD^+**, which accepts electrons and becomes reduced to NADH. NAD^+, which stands for nicotinamide adenine dinucleotide, is an organic molecule that cells make from the vitamin niacin and use to shuttle electrons in redox reactions. Figure 6.5B depicts the oxidation of an organic fuel molecule and the accompanying reduction of NAD^+. An enzyme called dehydrogenase strips two hydrogen atoms from the organic fuel molecule and transfers two electrons and one proton to its coenzyme NAD^+, reducing it to NADH. The other proton is released into the surrounding solution. (NADH is represented throughout this chapter as a light brown box carrying two blue electrons.)

Using the energy staircase analogy for electrons passing from glucose to oxygen, the transfer of electrons from an organic molecule to NAD^+ is just the beginning. Figure 6.5C shows NADH delivering these electrons to the top of a chain of carrier molecules. Shown here as purple ovals, most of these carrier molecules are proteins. At the bottom of the staircase is an oxygen atom ($\frac{1}{2}\ O_2$), which accepts two electrons, picks up two H^+, and becomes reduced to water.

These carrier molecules form an **electron transport chain**. In a cell, a number of such molecules are built into the inner membrane of a mitochondrion. Through a series of redox reactions, electrons are passed from carrier to carrier, releasing energy that can be used to make ATP.

With an understanding of this basic mechanism of electron transfer and energy release, we can now explore cellular respiration in more detail.

? What chemical characteristic of the element oxygen accounts for its function in cellular respiration?

■ Oxygen is extremely electronegative (see Module 2.6), making it very powerful in pulling electrons down the electron transport chain.

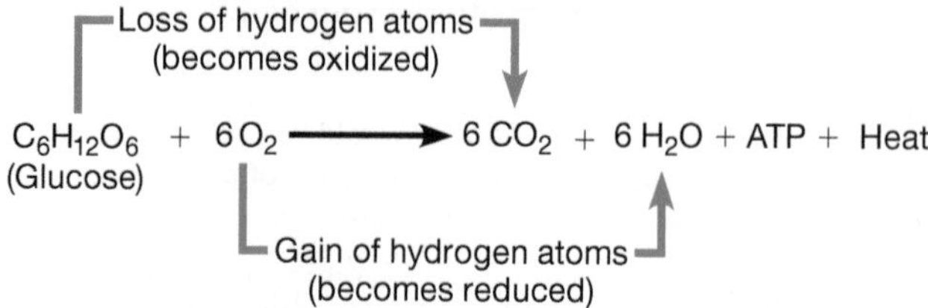

▲ **Figure 6.5A** Movement of hydrogen atoms (with their electrons) in the redox reactions of cellular respiration

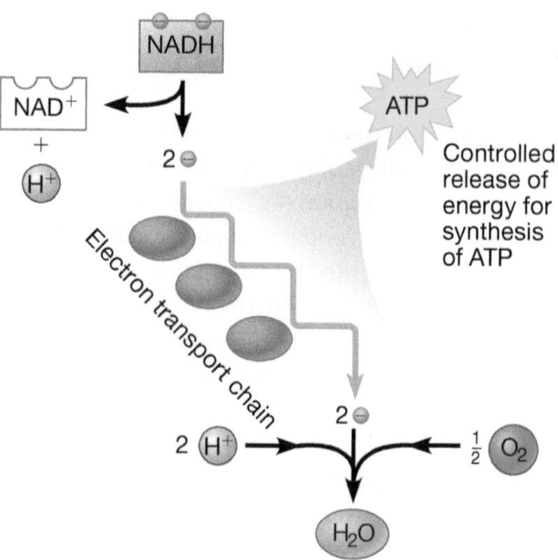

▲ **Figure 6.5C** Electrons releasing energy for ATP synthesis as they fall down an energy staircase from NADH through an electron transport chain to O_2

6.6 Overview: Cellular respiration occurs in three main stages

Cellular respiration consists of a sequence of many chemical reactions that we can divide into three main stages. Figure 6.6 gives an overview of these stages and shows where they occur in a eukaryotic cell. (In prokaryotic cells that use aerobic respiration, these steps occur in the cytosol, and the electron transport chain is built into the plasma membrane.)

Stage 1: Glycolysis (shown with a teal background throughout this chapter) occurs in the cytosol of the cell. Glycolysis begins cellular respiration by breaking glucose into two molecules of a three-carbon compound called pyruvate.

Stage 2: Pyruvate oxidation and the **citric acid cycle** (shown in shades of orange) take place within the mitochondria. Pyruvate is oxidized to a two-carbon compound. The citric acid cycle then completes the breakdown of glucose to carbon dioxide. Thus, the CO_2 that you exhale is formed in the mitochondria of your cells during this second stage of respiration.

As suggested by the smaller ATP symbols in the diagram, the cell makes a small amount of ATP during glycolysis and the citric acid cycle. The main function of these first two stages, however, is to supply the third stage of respiration with electrons (shown with gold arrows).

Stage 3: Oxidative phosphorylation (purple background) involves electron transport and a process known as chemiosmosis. NADH and a related electron carrier, $FADH_2$, shuttle electrons to electron transport chains embedded in the inner mitochondrial membrane. Most of the ATP produced by cellular respiration is generated by oxidative phosphorylation, which uses the energy released by redox reactions in the electron transport chain to make ATP. The electrons are finally passed to oxygen, which becomes reduced to H_2O.

What couples the electron transport chain to ATP synthesis? As electrons are passed down the energy staircase, the electron transport chain also pumps hydrogen ions (H^+) across the inner mitochondrial membrane into the narrow intermembrane space (colored darker salmon in the figure). The result is a concentration gradient of H^+ across the membrane. In **chemiosmosis**, the potential energy of this concentration gradient is used to make ATP. The details of this process are explored in Module 6.9.

In the next several modules, we look more closely at the stages of cellular respiration and the mechanisms by which ATP is synthesized.

? **Of the three main stages of cellular respiration, which one does not take place in the mitochondria?**

Stage 1, glycolysis, occurs in the cytosol.

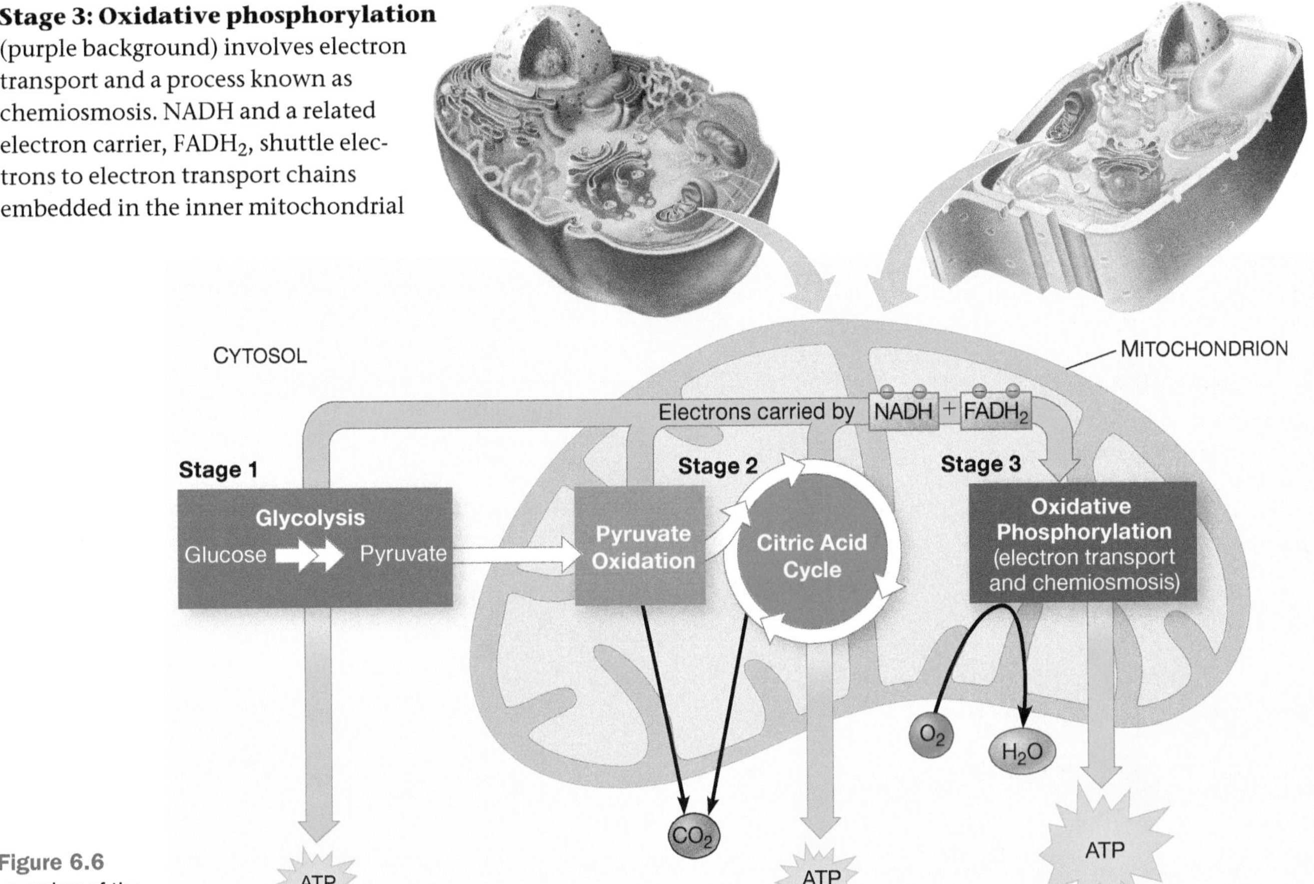

▶ **Figure 6.6**
An overview of the three stages of cellular respiration

6.7 Glycolysis harvests chemical energy by oxidizing glucose to pyruvate

Now that you have been introduced to the major players and processes, it's time to focus on the individual stages of cellular respiration. The term for the first stage, *glycolysis*, means "splitting of sugar" (*glyco*, sweet, and *lysis*, split), and that's exactly what happens during this phase.

Figure 6.7A below gives an overview of glycolysis, which begins with a single molecule of glucose and concludes with two molecules of pyruvate. (Pyruvate is the ionized form of pyruvic acid.) Each ● represents a carbon atom in the molecules; glucose has six carbons, and these same six carbons end up in the two molecules of pyruvate (three carbons in each). The straight arrow shown running from glucose to pyruvate actually represents nine chemical steps, each catalyzed by its own enzyme. As these reactions occur, two molecules of NAD^+ are reduced to two NADH, and a net gain of two molecules of ATP is produced.

Figure 6.7B illustrates how ATP is formed in glycolysis by **substrate-level phosphorylation**. In this process, an enzyme transfers a phosphate group (Ⓟ) from a substrate molecule to ADP, forming ATP. You will see that some ATP is also generated by substrate-level phosphorylation in the citric acid cycle.

The oxidation of glucose to pyruvate during glycolysis releases energy, which is stored in ATP and in NADH. The cell can use the energy in ATP immediately, but for it to use the energy in NADH, electrons from NADH must pass down an electron transport chain located in the inner mitochondrial membrane. And the pyruvate molecules still hold most of

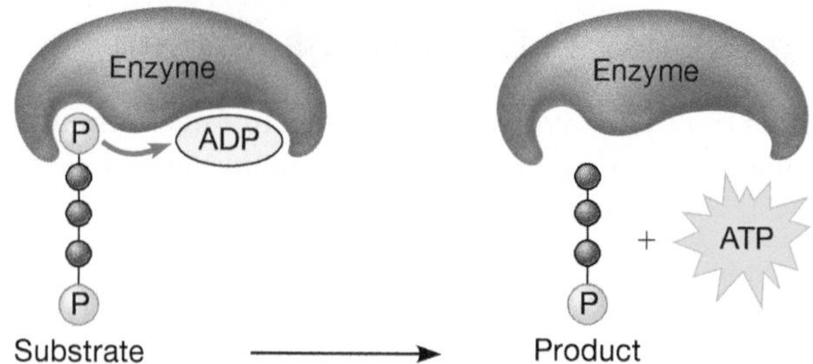

▲ **Figure 6.7B Substrate-level phosphorylation: transfer of a phosphate group from a substrate to ADP, producing ATP**

the energy of glucose; these molecules will be oxidized in the second stage of cellular respiration.

Let's take a closer look at glycolysis. Figure 6.7C, on the next page, shows simplified structures for all the organic compounds that form in the nine chemical reactions of glycolysis. Commentary on the left highlights the main features of these reactions.

The sequential steps of glycolysis illustrate how, in a metabolic pathway, each chemical step feeds into the next one. In other words, the product of one reaction serves as the reactant for the next. Compounds that form between an initial reactant and a final product are known as **intermediates**. A specific enzyme catalyzes each chemical step; however, the figure does not include the enzymes.

As indicated in Figure 6.7C, the steps of glycolysis can be grouped into two main phases. Steps ❶–❹, the energy investment phase, actually *consume* energy. In this phase, two molecules of ATP are used to energize a glucose molecule, which is then split into two small sugars.

Steps ❺–❾, the energy payoff phase, *yield* energy for the cell. This phase occurs after glucose has been split into two three-carbon molecules. Thus, the number 2 precedes all molecules in the diagram for these steps. As you can see, two NADH molecules are produced for each initial glucose molecule, and four total ATP are generated. Remember that the first phase used two molecules of ATP, so the net gain to the cell is two ATP molecules for each glucose that enters glycolysis.

These two ATP molecules from glycolysis account for only about 6% of the energy that a cell can harvest from a glucose molecule. Some organisms—yeasts and certain bacteria, for instance—can satisfy their energy needs with the ATP produced by glycolysis alone. And some cells, such as your muscle cells, may use this anaerobic production of ATP for short periods when they do not have sufficient O_2. Most cells and organisms, however, have far greater energy demands. The stages of cellular respiration that follow glycolysis release much more energy. In the next modules, we see what happens in most organisms after glucose is oxidized to pyruvate in glycolysis.

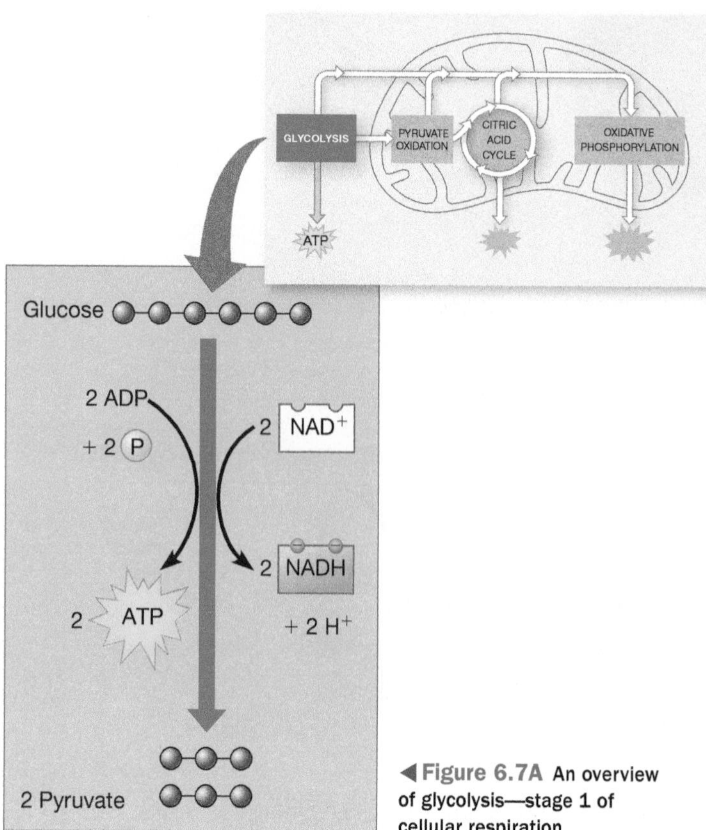

◀ **Figure 6.7A An overview of glycolysis—stage 1 of cellular respiration**

? **For each glucose molecule processed, what are the net molecular products of glycolysis?**

■ Two molecules of pyruvate, two molecules of ATP, and two molecules of NADH

Energy Investment Phase

Steps 1–3 Glucose is energized, using ATP. A sequence of three chemical reactions converts glucose to an energized intermediate. The curved arrows indicate the transfer of a phosphate group from ATP to another molecule. The cell invests 2 ATP, one at step 1 and one at step 3, to produce a more reactive molecule.

Step 4 A six-carbon intermediate splits into two three-carbon intermediates. An enzyme splits the highly reactive six-carbon molecule into two three-carbon molecules. Each of these molecules, called glyceraldehyde 3-phosphate (G3P), enters the next phase, so steps 5–9 occur twice per glucose molecule.

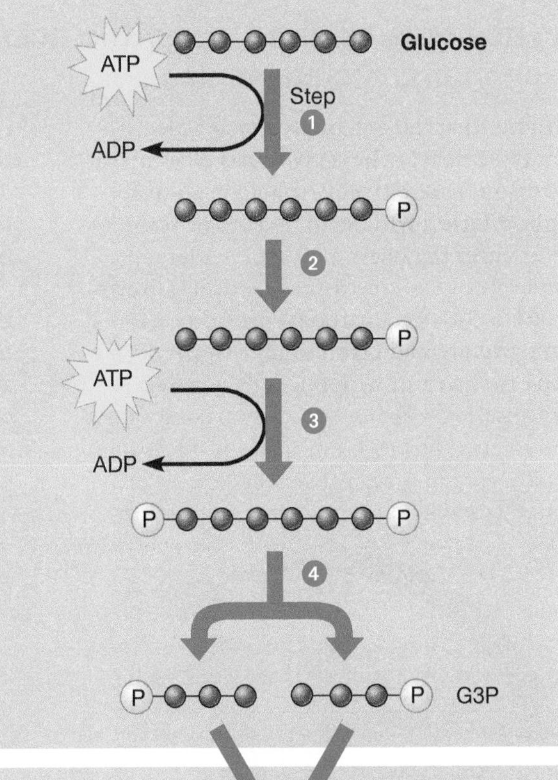

Energy Payoff Phase

Step 5 A redox reaction generates NADH. The curved arrow indicates the transfer of hydrogen atoms as each G3P is oxidized and NAD^+ is reduced to NADH. This reaction also attaches a phosphate group to the substrate.

Steps 6–9 ATP and pyruvate are produced. This series of four chemical reactions completes glycolysis, producing two molecules of pyruvate for each initial molecule of glucose. In steps 6 and 9, ATP is produced by substrate-level phosphorylation, yielding a total of 4 ATP produced in the energy payoff phase. (Water is produced at step 8 as a by-product.)

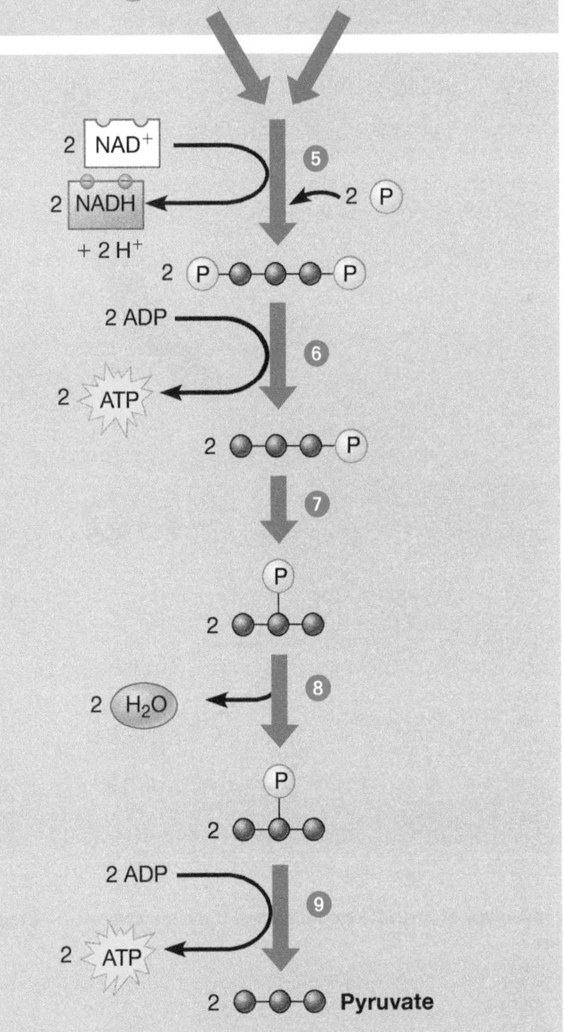

▲ **Figure 6.7C** Details of glycolysis

TRY THIS Identify the step of glycolysis that the substrate-level phosphorylation shown in Figure 6.7B represents.

6.8 After pyruvate is oxidized, the citric acid cycle completes the energy-yielding oxidation of organic molecules

As pyruvate is produced at the end of glycolysis, it is transported from the cytosol, where glycolysis takes place, into a mitochondrion, where the citric acid cycle and oxidative phosphorylation will occur. Pyruvate itself, however, does not enter the citric acid cycle. A large, multi-enzyme complex catalyzes three reactions (shown at the top of **Figure 6.8A**): ❶ A carboxyl group (—COO^-) is removed from pyruvate and given off as a molecule of CO_2 (this is the first step in which CO_2 is released during cellular respiration); ❷ the two-carbon compound remaining is oxidized while a molecule of NAD^+ is reduced to NADH; and finally, ❸ a compound called coenzyme A, derived from a B vitamin, joins with the two-carbon group to form a molecule called acetyl coenzyme A, abbreviated **acetyl CoA**.

For each molecule of glucose that enters glycolysis, two molecules of pyruvate are produced. These are oxidized, and then two molecules of acetyl CoA are ready to enter the citric acid cycle. This cycle is often called the Krebs cycle in honor of Hans Krebs, the German-British scientist who worked out much of this pathway in the 1930s.

The lower portion of Figure 6.8A summarizes the inputs and outputs of the citric acid cycle. Only the two-carbon part of the acetyl CoA molecule actually enters the citric acid cycle; coenzyme A splits off and is recycled. The outputs include two molecules of CO_2, one ATP molecule, three NADH molecules, and one molecule of the electron carrier, $FADH_2$. Remember that two acetyl CoA were derived from the two pyruvate molecules. Thus the cycle runs twice, and the outputs are doubled for each glucose molecule processed.

The citric acid cycle functions as a metabolic furnace that completes the oxidation of organic fuels. The inner workings of this cycle are shown and described in **Figure 6.8B** on the facing page. Each step is catalyzed by a specific enzyme located in the mitochondrial matrix or embedded in the inner mitochondrial membrane. As you can see, the two carbons entering the cycle from acetyl CoA are joined to a four-carbon molecule. As the resulting six-carbon molecule is processed through a series of redox reactions, two carbon atoms are removed as CO_2, and the four-carbon molecule is regenerated; this regeneration accounts for the word *cycle*. The six-carbon compound first formed in the cycle is citrate, the ionized form of citric acid; hence the name *citric acid cycle*. More detailed explanations of the steps of this cycle are provided at the bottom of Figure 6.8B.

Our main objective in this chapter is to learn how cells harvest the energy of glucose and other nutrients in food to make ATP. But the two stages of respiration we have dissected so far—glycolysis and pyruvate oxidation and the citric acid cycle—produce only 4 ATP molecules per glucose molecule, all by substrate-level phosphorylation: 2 net ATP from glycolysis and 2 ATP from the citric acid cycle. At this point, molecules of NADH (and $FADH_2$) account for most of the energy extracted from each glucose molecule. For the cell to be able to harvest the energy banked in NADH and $FADH_2$, these molecules must shuttle their high-energy electrons to an electron transport chain. There

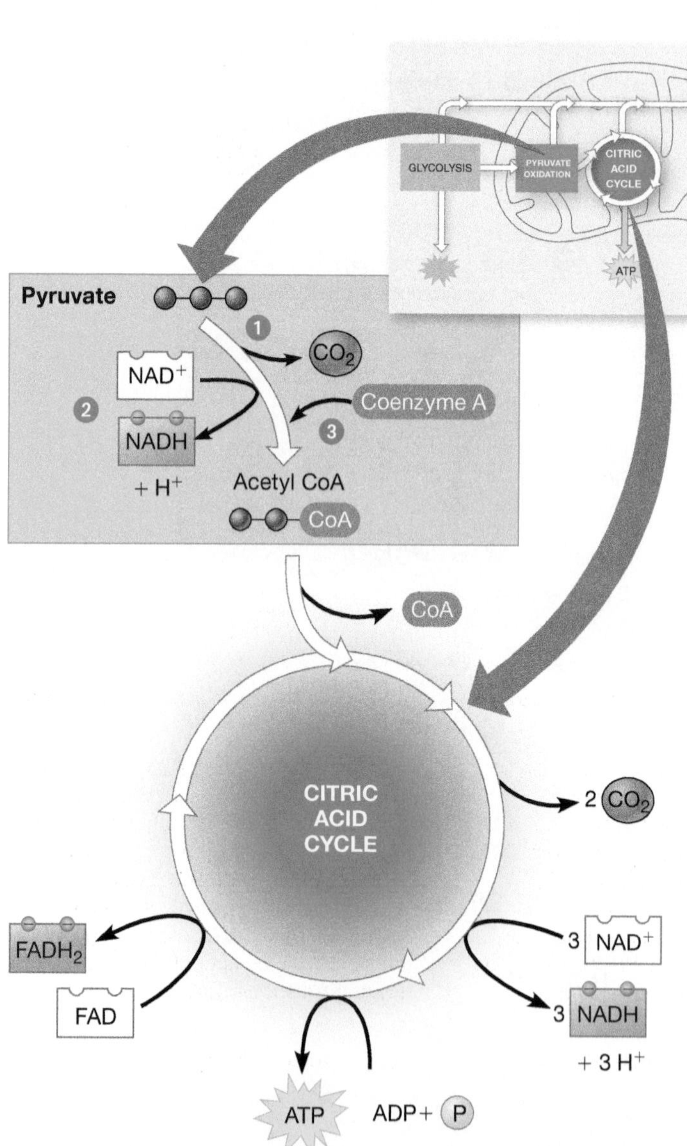

▲ **Figure 6.8A** An overview of pyruvate oxidation and the citric acid cycle—stage 2 of cellular respiration

TRY THIS Remember that 2 pyruvate are produced from each glucose. Use this figure to determine the per-glucose return of ATP, NADH, and $FADH_2$ from the second stage of cellular respiration.

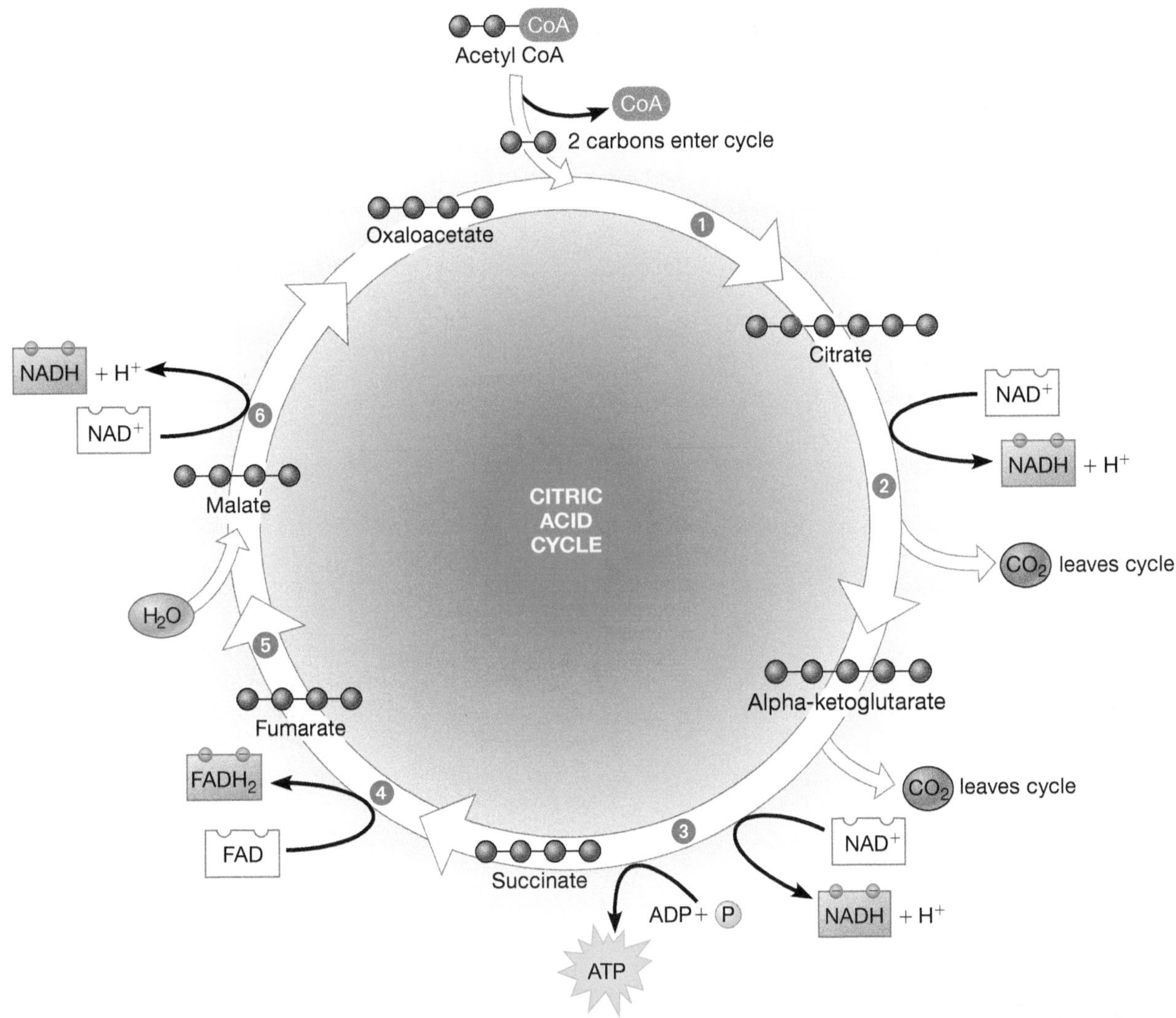

Step 1
Acetyl CoA stokes the furnace.

A turn of the citric acid cycle begins (top center) as enzymes strip the CoA portion from acetyl CoA and combine the remaining two-carbon group with the four-carbon molecule oxaloacetate (top left) already present in the mitochondrion. The product of this reaction is the six-carbon molecule citrate. All the acid compounds in this cycle exist in the cell in their ionized form, hence the suffix *-ate*.

Steps 2–3
NADH, ATP, and CO_2 are generated during redox reactions.

Successive redox reactions harvest energy by stripping hydrogen atoms from citrate and then alpha-ketoglutarate and producing energy-laden NADH molecules. In two places, an intermediate compound loses a CO_2 molecule. Energy is harvested by substrate-level phosphorylation of ADP to produce ATP. A four-carbon compound called succinate emerges at the end of step 3.

Steps 4–6
Further redox reactions generate $FADH_2$ and more NADH.

Succinate is oxidized as the electron carrier FAD is reduced to $FADH_2$. Fumarate is converted to malate, which is then oxidized as one last NAD^+ is reduced to NADH. One turn of the citric acid cycle is completed with the regeneration of oxaloacetate, which is then ready to start the next cycle by accepting an acetyl group from acetyl CoA.

▲ **Figure 6.8B** **A closer look at the citric acid cycle. (Remember that the cycle runs two times for each glucose molecule oxidized.)**

the energy that was captured from the *oxidation* of organic molecules is used to *phosphorylate* ADP to ATP—hence the name *oxidative phosphorylation*.

Almost 90% of the ATP generated in cellular respiration is made by oxidative phosphorylation, which involves electron transport and the process of chemiosmosis. We look at this final stage of cellular respiration next.

? What is the total number of NADH and $FADH_2$ molecules generated during the complete breakdown of one glucose molecule to six molecules of CO_2? (*Hint*: Combine the outputs discussed in Modules 6.7 and 6.8.)

■ 10 NADH: 2 from glycolysis, 2 from the oxidation of pyruvate, and 6 from the citric acid cycle; and 2 $FADH_2$ from the citric acid cycle. (Did you remember to double the output after the sugar-splitting step of glycolysis?)

VISUALIZING THE CONCEPT

6.9 Most ATP production occurs by oxidative phosphorylation

Oxidative phosphorylation clearly illustrates the theme of STRUCTURE AND FUNCTION. Electron transport chains embedded in the inner membrane of a mitochondrion pump hydrogen ions into the intermembrane space. (Recall that ions cannot move through a membrane on their own.) In the process called chemiosmosis, the resulting concentration gradient drives H^+ through the enzyme complex **ATP synthase**, whose molecular structure enables the synthesis of ATP.

Oxidative phosphorylation is illustrated below. Starting on the left, the gold arrows trace the transfer of electrons from the shuttle molecules NADH and $FADH_2$ through the electron transport chain to oxygen, the final electron acceptor. The electron carriers in the chain sequentially pass electrons down the "energy staircase." At three locations, the energy released from these electron transfers enables the active transport of H^+ into the intermembrane space. The flow of H^+ back through ATP synthase powers ATP synthesis.

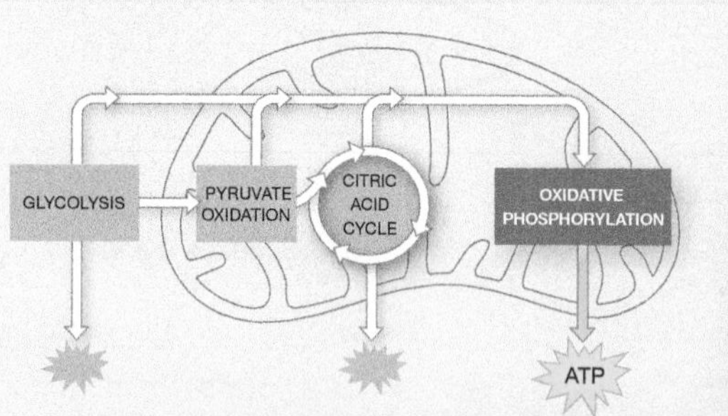

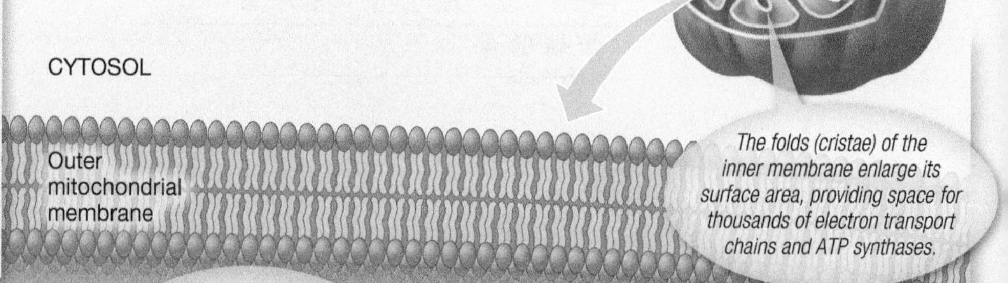

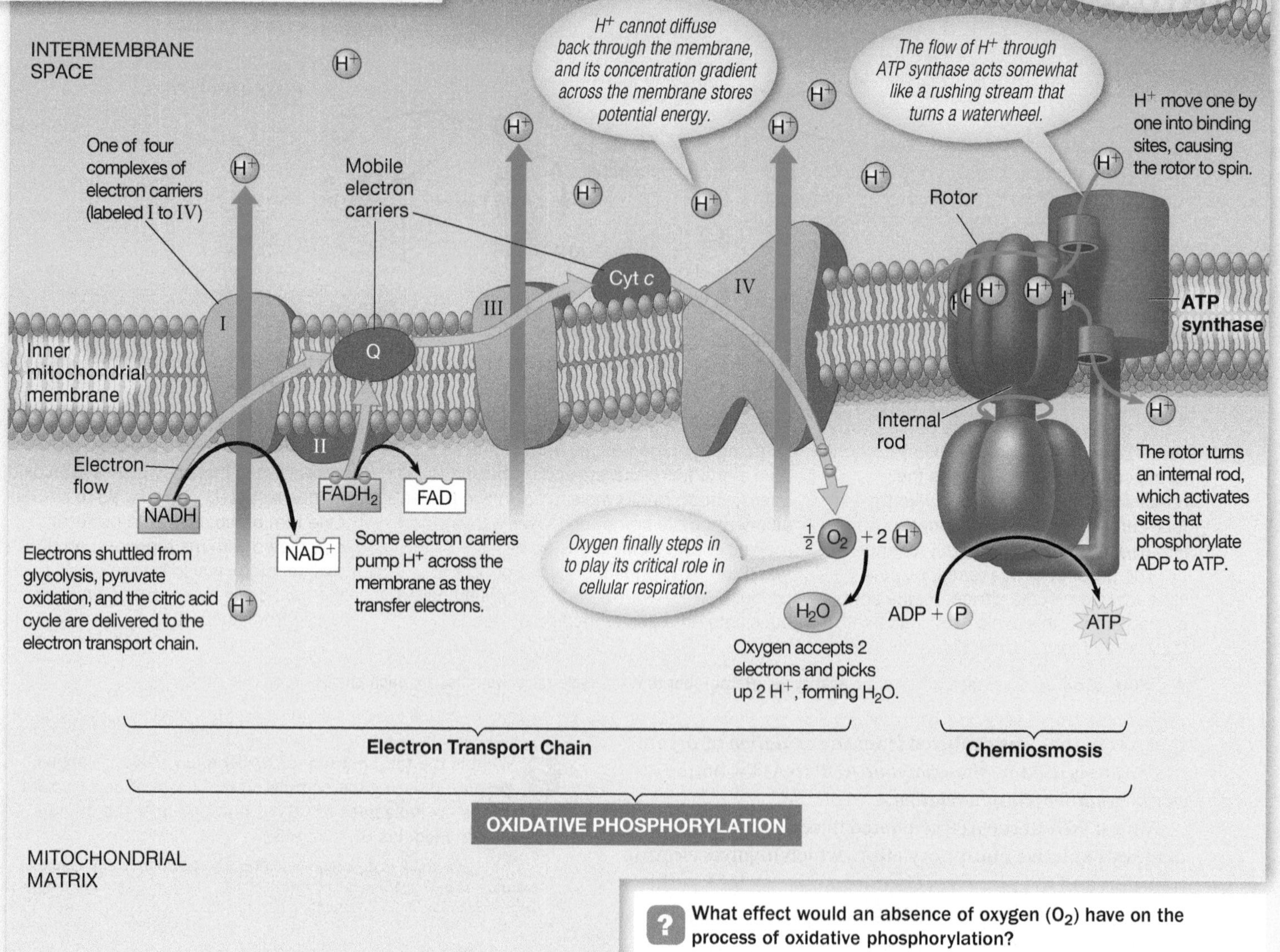

CYTOSOL

Outer mitochondrial membrane

The folds (cristae) of the inner membrane enlarge its surface area, providing space for thousands of electron transport chains and ATP synthases.

INTERMEMBRANE SPACE

H^+ cannot diffuse back through the membrane, and its concentration gradient across the membrane stores potential energy.

The flow of H^+ through ATP synthase acts somewhat like a rushing stream that turns a waterwheel.

H^+ move one by one into binding sites, causing the rotor to spin.

One of four complexes of electron carriers (labeled I to IV)

Mobile electron carriers

Rotor

I

Q

II

III

Cyt c

IV

ATP synthase

Inner mitochondrial membrane

Internal rod

Electron flow

NADH

NAD^+

$FADH_2$

FAD

Electrons shuttled from glycolysis, pyruvate oxidation, and the citric acid cycle are delivered to the electron transport chain.

Some electron carriers pump H^+ across the membrane as they transfer electrons.

Oxygen finally steps in to play its critical role in cellular respiration.

$\frac{1}{2} O_2 + 2 H^+$

H_2O

Oxygen accepts 2 electrons and picks up 2 H^+, forming H_2O.

ADP + P

ATP

The rotor turns an internal rod, which activates sites that phosphorylate ADP to ATP.

Electron Transport Chain

Chemiosmosis

OXIDATIVE PHOSPHORYLATION

MITOCHONDRIAL MATRIX

? What effect would an absence of oxygen (O_2) have on the process of oxidative phosphorylation?

Without oxygen to "pull" electrons down the electron transport chain, the energy stored in NADH and $FADH_2$ could not be harnessed for ATP synthesis.

6.10 Scientists have discovered heat-producing, calorie-burning brown fat in adults

SCIENTIFIC THINKING

You may recall from Module 6.3 that cellular respiration captures about 34% of the energy in glucose molecules as ATP, with the rest released as heat. But sometimes cellular respiration can be used primarily to generate heat, as happens in the mitochondria of brown fat cells.

Ordinary body fat, called white fat, has little metabolic activity. Each cell is filled with a single large droplet of fat. Brown fat, on the other hand, actively burns energy. You learned in the chapter introduction that brown fat helps keep infants warm. Brown fat is named for its color, which comes from the brownish mitochondria that pack its cells. These mitochondria are unique in that they can burn fuel and produce heat without making ATP. How can they do that? Look back at the figure in Module 6.9 and imagine ion channels spanning the inner mitochondrial membrane that allow H^+ to flow freely across the membrane. Such channels would dissipate the H^+ gradient that the electron transport chain had produced. Without that gradient, ATP synthase could not make ATP, and all the energy from the burning of fuel molecules would be released as heat. The mitochondria of brown fat cells have just such channels.

Can brown fat keep a newborn warm and help keep an adult thin?

Until recently, brown fat in humans was thought to disappear after infancy. The presence of unidentified tissue in the PET scans of cancer patients, however, caused researchers to question that conclusion. To test whether this tissue could be brown fat, researchers analyzed 3,640 PET-CT scans that had been performed on 1,972 patients for various diagnostic reasons. PET is a technique that identifies areas with high uptake of radioactively labeled glucose, and CT scans can detect adipose (fat) tissue. The combined PET-CT scans revealed small areas in the neck and chest of some patients that fit the criteria for brown fat—adipose tissue that was metabolically active (burning glucose). The researchers correlated the presence or absence of brown fat with each patient's sex, age, weight, and other parameters, including the outdoor temperature. The results showed that 7.5% of the women and 3% of the men examined had deposits of brown fat. The tissues were found to be more prevalent both in patients who were thinner and when the scans had been taken in cold weather.

As is typical in science, the results from one study led to new questions and new research. Is brown fat activated by cold temperatures and, thus, could a much higher percentage of adults have brown fat than shown in scans of patients who were presumably *not* cold? Is the prevalence of this fat-burning tissue in thinner individuals related to why some people are thin and others are obese?

A second study looked at the presence and activity of brown fat in 24 men exposed to cold temperatures. Combined PET-CT scans were taken of all research participants following a 2-hour exposure at 16°C (60.8°F). The scans of all but one participant (the one with the highest body mass index, or BMI) revealed activated brown fat tissues. One of the findings of this study is shown in Figure 6.10. The measured brown fat activity of the lean group was found to be significantly higher than that of the overweight/obese group.

Data from A. M. Cypess et al., Identification and importance of brown adipose tissue in adult humans, *New England Journal of Medicine* 360: 1509–17 (2009).

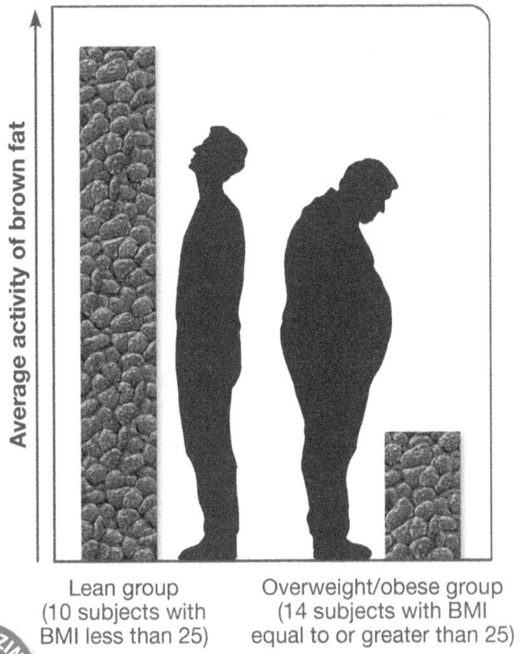

Average activity of brown fat

Lean group (10 subjects with BMI less than 25)

Overweight/obese group (14 subjects with BMI equal to or greater than 25)

VISUALIZING THE DATA

▲ **Figure 6.10** **Activity level of brown fat of lean and overweight/obese participants after cold exposure**

Data from W. D. van Marken Lichtenbelt et al., Cold-activated brown adipose tissue in healthy men, *New England Journal of Medicine* 360: 1500–8 (2009).

These results indicate that brown fat may be present in most people, and, when activated by cold, the brown fat of lean individuals is more active (burns more calories). Like before, this study raised interesting questions. Does the more active brown fat of thin individuals help keep them thin? Are there other ways to turn on brown fat besides exposure to cold? Could brown fat be a target for obesity-fighting drugs?

Research on this heat-producing, calorie-burning type of fat is continuing at a rapid pace. Many more experiments have confirmed that cold exposure stimulates brown fat activity. Illustrating the theme of INFORMATION, recent studies are focusing on the cell-signaling pathways and molecules involved in the changes in gene expression that activate such fat cells. Most of these studies have been done in mice, allowing for more control of variables such as calorie intake, temperature, and exercise, as well as precise manipulation of gene expression.

In a new discovery that involved distinguishing unique genetic markers on individual cells, scientists have identified a third type of fat. In response to stimulation by cold or other signals, some white fat cells appear to convert to so-called beige cells, which then function like brown fat. Increasing the amount and activity of brown or beige fat could burn off excess stored fat. Medical researchers are searching for ways to activate brown fat or convert white fat to beige fat as possible treatments for obesity and type 2 diabetes. Expect to see news on both basic science and medical applications of brown/beige fat research for years to come.

? **The initial study discussed identified brown fat in less than 10% of the patients whose scans were analyzed. The second study identified brown fat in 96% of participants. What accounts for this difference in research results?**

■ Brown fat was activated and thus identified in response to the cold temperature treatment of the second study.

6.11 Review: Each molecule of glucose yields many molecules of ATP

Let's review what you have learned about cellular respiration by following the oxidation of one molecule of glucose. Starting on the left in Figure 6.11, glycolysis, which occurs in the cytosol, oxidizes glucose to two molecules of pyruvate, produces 2 NADH, and produces a net of 2 ATP by substrate-level phosphorylation. Within the mitochondrion, the oxidation of 2 pyruvate yields 2 NADH and 2 acetyl CoA. The 2 acetyl CoA feed into the citric acid cycle, which yields 6 NADH and 2 $FADH_2$, as well as 2 ATP by substrate-level phosphorylation. Glucose has now been completely oxidized to CO_2. NADH and $FADH_2$ deliver electrons to the electron transport chain, where they are finally passed to O_2, forming H_2O. The electron transport chain pumps H^+ into the intermembrane space. The resulting H^+ gradient is tapped by ATP synthase to produce about 28 molecules of ATP by oxidative phosphorylation (according to current experimental data). Thus, the total yield of ATP molecules per glucose is about 32.

The number of ATP molecules cannot be stated exactly for several reasons. The NADH produced in glycolysis passes its electrons across the mitochondrial membrane to either NAD^+ or FAD. Because $FADH_2$ adds its electrons farther along the electron transport chain (see Module 6.9), it contributes less to the H^+ gradient and thus generates less ATP. In addition, some of the energy of the H^+ gradient may be used for work other than ATP production, such as the active transport of pyruvate into the mitochondrion.

Because most of the ATP generated by cellular respiration results from oxidative phosphorylation, the ATP yield depends on an adequate supply of oxygen to the cell. Without oxygen to function as the final electron acceptor, electron transport and ATP production stop. But as we see next, some cells can oxidize organic fuel and generate ATP *without* oxygen.

? Explain where O_2 is used and CO_2 is produced in cellular respiration.

■ O_2 accepts electrons at the end of the electron transport chain. CO_2 is released during the oxidation of intermediate compounds in pyruvate oxidation and the citric acid cycle.

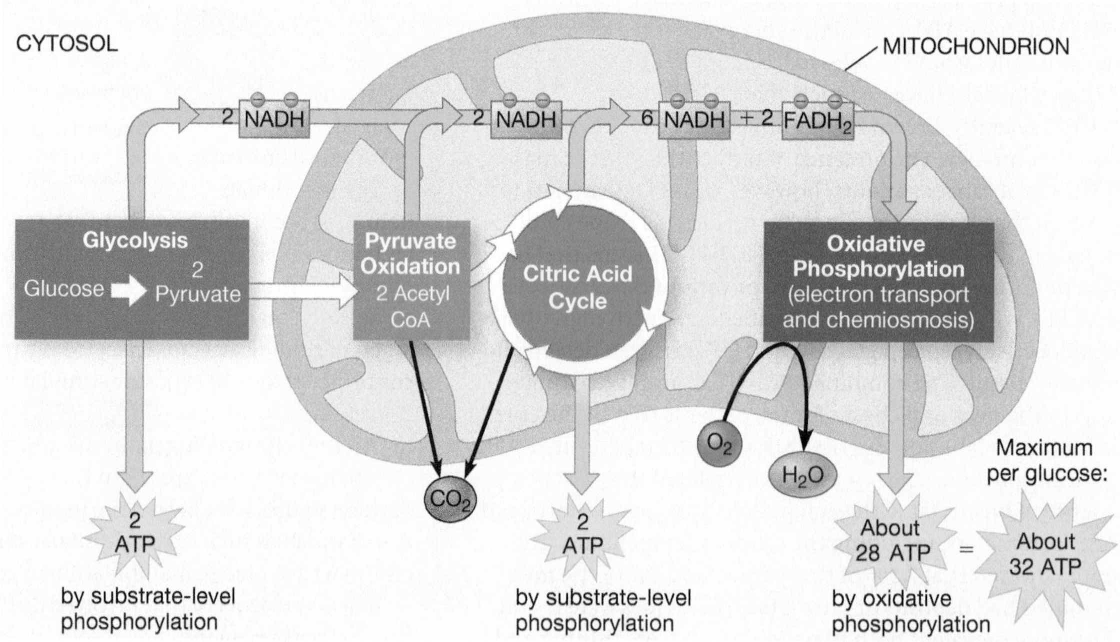

▶ **Figure 6.11**
An estimated tally of the ATP produced per molecule of glucose by substrate-level and oxidative phosphorylation in cellular respiration

Fermentation: Anaerobic Harvesting of Energy

6.12 Fermentation enables cells to produce ATP without oxygen

Fermentation is a way of harvesting energy that does not require oxygen. The pathway that generates ATP during fermentation is glycolysis, the same pathway that functions in the first stage of cellular respiration. Remember that glycolysis uses no oxygen; it simply generates a net gain of 2 ATP while oxidizing glucose to two molecules of pyruvate and reducing NAD^+ to NADH. The yield of 2 ATP is certainly a lot less than the possible 32 ATP per glucose generated during aerobic respiration, but it is enough to keep your muscles contracting for a short time when oxygen is scarce. And many microorganisms supply all their energy needs through glycolysis.

There is more to fermentation, however, than just glycolysis. To oxidize glucose in glycolysis, NAD^+ must be present as an electron acceptor. This is no problem under aerobic conditions, because the cell regenerates its pool of NAD^+ when NADH passes its electrons into the mitochondrion, to be transported to the electron transport chain.

Fermentation provides an anaerobic path for recycling NADH back to NAD^+.

Lactic Acid Fermentation One common type of fermentation is called **lactic acid fermentation**. Your muscle cells and certain bacteria can regenerate NAD^+ by this process, as illustrated in Figure 6.12A. You can see that NADH is oxidized back to NAD^+ as pyruvate is reduced to lactate (the ionized form of lactic acid). Muscle cells can switch to lactic acid fermentation when the need for ATP outpaces the delivery of O_2 via the bloodstream. The lactate that builds up in muscle cells was thought to cause the muscle soreness that occurs a day or so after intense exercise. Evidence shows, however, that within an hour, the lactate is carried by the blood to the liver, where it is converted back to pyruvate and oxidized. Muscle soreness is more likely caused by trauma to small muscle fibers, leading to inflammation and pain.

The dairy industry uses lactic acid fermentation by bacteria to make cheese and yogurt. Other types of fermentation turn soybeans into soy sauce and cabbage into sauerkraut.

Alcohol Fermentation For thousands of years, people have used **alcohol fermentation** in brewing, winemaking, and baking. Yeasts are single-celled fungi that normally use aerobic respiration to process their food. But they are also able to survive in anaerobic environments. Yeasts and certain bacteria recycle their NADH back to NAD^+ while converting pyruvate to CO_2 and ethanol (Figure 6.12B). The CO_2 provides the bubbles in beer and champagne. Bubbles of CO_2 generated by baker's yeast cause bread dough to rise. Ethanol (ethyl alcohol), the two-carbon end product, is toxic to the organisms that produce it. Yeasts release their alcohol wastes to their surroundings, where it usually diffuses away. When yeasts are confined in a wine vat, they die when the alcohol concentration reaches 14%.

Types of Anaerobes Unlike muscle cells and yeasts, many prokaryotes that live in stagnant ponds and deep in the soil are called *obligate anaerobes*, meaning they require anaerobic conditions and are poisoned by oxygen. Yeasts and many other bacteria are called *facultative anaerobes,* and they can make ATP either by fermentation or by oxidative phosphorylation, depending on whether O_2 is available. On the cellular level, our muscle cells behave as facultative anaerobes.

For a facultative anaerobe, pyruvate is a fork in the metabolic road. If oxygen is available, the organism will always use the more productive aerobic respiration. Thus, to make wine and beer, yeasts must be grown anaerobically so that they will ferment sugars and produce ethanol. For this reason, the wine barrels and beer fermentation vats in Figure 6.12C are designed to keep air out.

? A glucose-fed yeast cell is moved from an aerobic environment to an anaerobic one. For the cell to continue generating ATP at the same rate, how would its rate of glucose consumption need to change?

The cell would have to consume glucose at a rate about 16 times the consumption rate in the aerobic environment (2 ATP per glucose molecule is made by fermentation versus 32 ATP by cellular respiration).

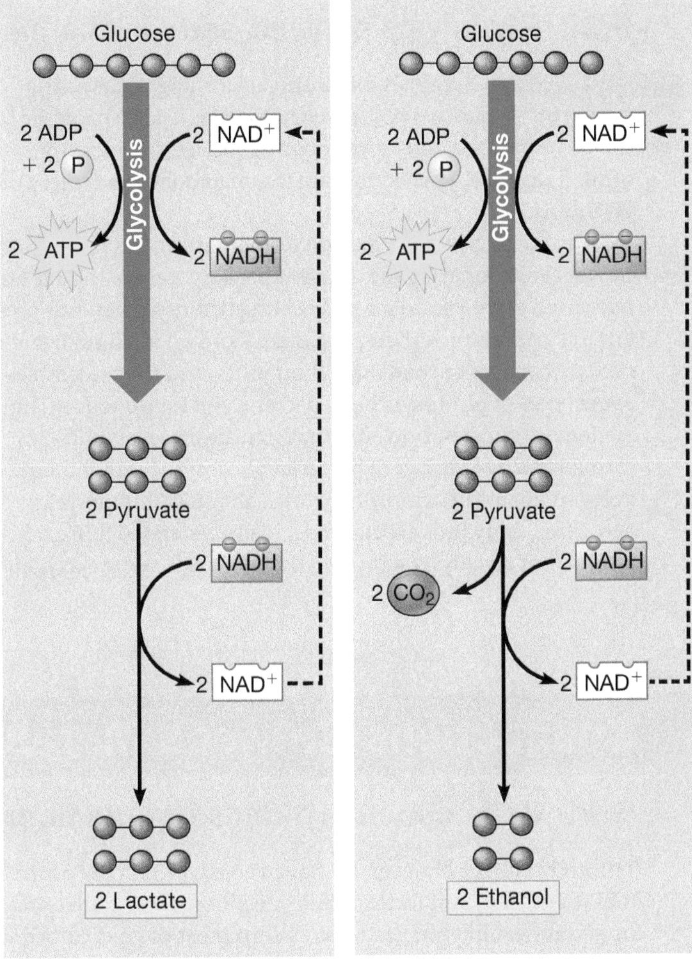

▲ **Figure 6.12A** Lactic acid fermentation. NAD^+ is regenerated as pyruvate is reduced to lactate.

▲ **Figure 6.12B** Alcohol fermentation. NAD^+ is regenerated as pyruvate is broken down to CO_2 and ethanol.

▲ **Figure 6.12C** Wine barrels and beer fermentation vats

6.13 Glycolysis evolved early in the history of life on Earth

EVOLUTION CONNECTION

Glycolysis is the universal energy-harvesting process of life. If you looked inside a bacterial cell, one of your body cells, or virtually any other living cell, you would find the metabolic machinery of glycolysis.

The role of glycolysis in both fermentation and respiration has an evolutionary basis. Ancient prokaryotes are thought to have used glycolysis to make ATP long before oxygen was present in Earth's atmosphere. The oldest-known fossils of bacteria date back more than 3.5 billion years, and they resemble some types of photosynthetic bacteria still found today. The evidence indicates, however, that significant levels of O_2, formed as a by-product of bacterial photosynthesis, did not accumulate in the atmosphere until about 2.7 billion years ago. Thus, early prokaryotes most likely generated ATP exclusively from glycolysis, a process that does not require oxygen.

The fact that glycolysis is the most widespread metabolic pathway found in Earth's organisms today suggests that it evolved very early in the history of life. The location of glycolysis within the cell also implies great antiquity; the pathway does not require any of the membrane-enclosed organelles of the eukaryotic cell, which evolved about a billion years after the first prokaryotic cell. Glycolysis is a metabolic heirloom from early cells that continues to function in fermentation and as the first stage in the breakdown of organic molecules by cellular respiration.

? **List some of the characteristics of glycolysis that indicate that it is an ancient metabolic pathway.**

■ Glycolysis occurs universally (functioning in both fermentation and respiration), does not require oxygen, and does not occur in a membrane-enclosed organelle.

Connections Between Metabolic Pathways

6.14 Cells use many kinds of organic molecules as fuel for cellular respiration

Throughout this chapter, we have spoken of glucose as the fuel for cellular respiration. But free glucose molecules are not common in your diet. You obtain most of your calories as carbohydrates (such as sucrose and other disaccharide sugars and starch, a polysaccharide), fats, and proteins. You consume all three of these classes of organic molecules when you eat a handful of peanuts, for instance.

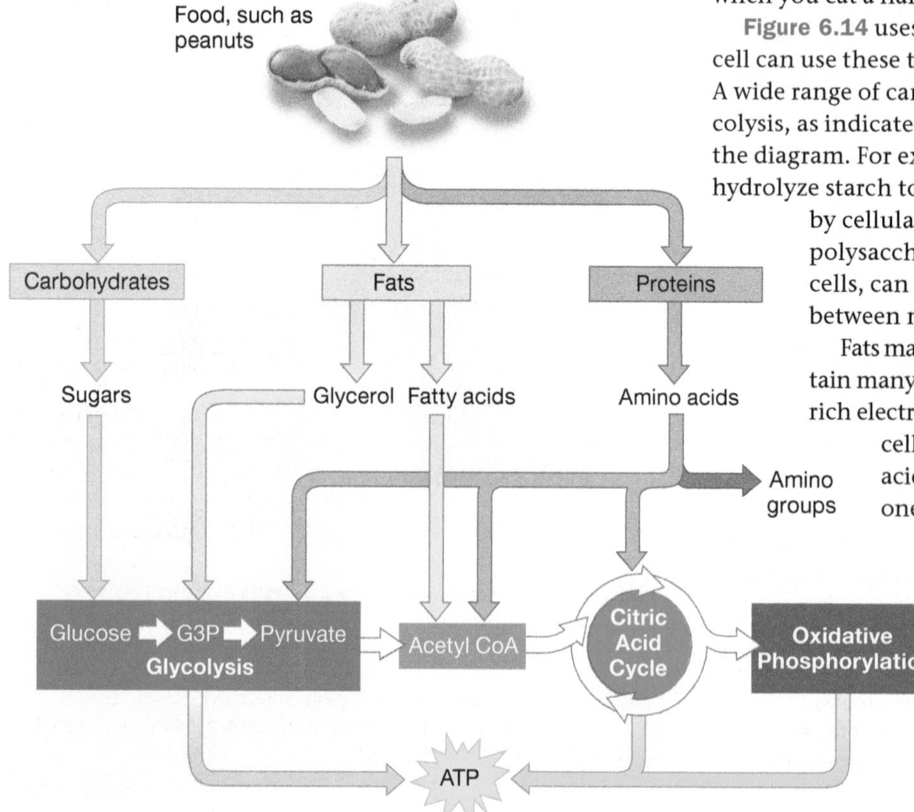

▲ **Figure 6.14** **Pathways that break down various food molecules**

Figure 6.14 uses color-coded arrows to illustrate how a cell can use these three types of molecules to make ATP. A wide range of carbohydrates can be funneled into glycolysis, as indicated by the blue arrows on the far left of the diagram. For example, enzymes in your digestive tract hydrolyze starch to glucose, which is then broken down by cellular respiration. Similarly, glycogen, the polysaccharide stored in your liver and muscle cells, can be hydrolyzed to glucose to serve as fuel between meals.

Fats make excellent cellular fuel because they contain many hydrogen atoms and thus many energy-rich electrons. As the diagram shows (tan arrows), a cell first hydrolyzes fats to glycerol and fatty acids. It then converts the glycerol to G3P, one of the intermediates in glycolysis. The fatty acids are broken into two-carbon fragments that enter the citric acid cycle as acetyl CoA. A gram of fat yields more than twice as much ATP as a gram of carbohydrate. Because so many calories are stockpiled in each gram of fat, you must expend a large amount of energy to burn fat stored in your body. This helps explain why it is so difficult for a dieter to lose excess fat.

Proteins (purple arrows in Figure 6.14) can also be used for fuel, although your body usually burns sugars and fats first. To be oxidized as fuel, proteins must first be digested to their constituent amino acids. Typically, a cell will use most of these amino acids to make its own proteins. Enzymes can convert excess amino acids to intermediates of glycolysis or the citric acid cycle, and their energy is then harvested by cellular respiration. During the conversion, the amino groups are stripped off and later disposed of in urine.

? Animals store most of their energy reserves as fats, not as polysaccharides. What is the advantage of this mode of storage for an animal?

■ Most animals are mobile and benefit from a compact and concentrated form of energy storage. Also, because fats are hydrophobic, they can be stored without extra water associated with them (see Module 3.8).

6.15 Organic molecules from food provide raw materials for biosynthesis

Not all food molecules are destined to be oxidized as fuel for making ATP. Food also provides the raw materials your cells use for biosynthesis—the production of organic molecules using energy-requiring metabolic pathways. A cell must be able to make its own molecules to build its structures and perform its functions. Some raw materials, such as amino acids, can be incorporated directly into your macromolecules. However, your cells also need to make molecules that are not present in your food. Indeed, glycolysis and the citric acid cycle function as metabolic interchanges that enable your cells to convert some kinds of molecules to others as you need them.

Figure 6.15 outlines the pathways by which your cells can make three classes of organic molecules using some of the intermediate molecules of glycolysis and the citric acid cycle. By comparing Figures 6.14 and 6.15, you can see clear connections between the energy-harvesting pathways of cellular respiration and the biosynthetic pathways used to construct the organic molecules of the cell.

The interconnections among these pathways provide a clear example of the theme of **INTERACTIONS** in producing the emergent property of a balanced metabolism. Basic principles of supply and demand regulate these pathways. If there is an excess of a certain amino acid, for example, the pathway that synthesizes it is switched off. The most common mechanism for this control is feedback inhibition: The end product inhibits an enzyme that catalyzes an early step in the pathway (see Module 5.15). Feedback inhibition also controls cellular respiration. If ATP accumulates in a cell, it inhibits an early enzyme in glycolysis, slowing down respiration and conserving resources. On the other hand, the same enzyme is activated by a buildup of ADP in the cell, signaling the need for more energy.

The cells of all living organisms—including those of the red panda shown in Figure 6.15 and the plants they eat—have the ability to harvest energy from the breakdown of organic molecules. In the process of cellular respiration, the atoms of the starting materials end up in carbon dioxide and water. In contrast, the ability to make organic molecules from carbon dioxide and water is not universal. Animal cells lack this ability, but plant cells can actually produce organic molecules from inorganic ones using the energy of sunlight in the process of photosynthesis. (We explore photosynthesis in Chapter 7.)

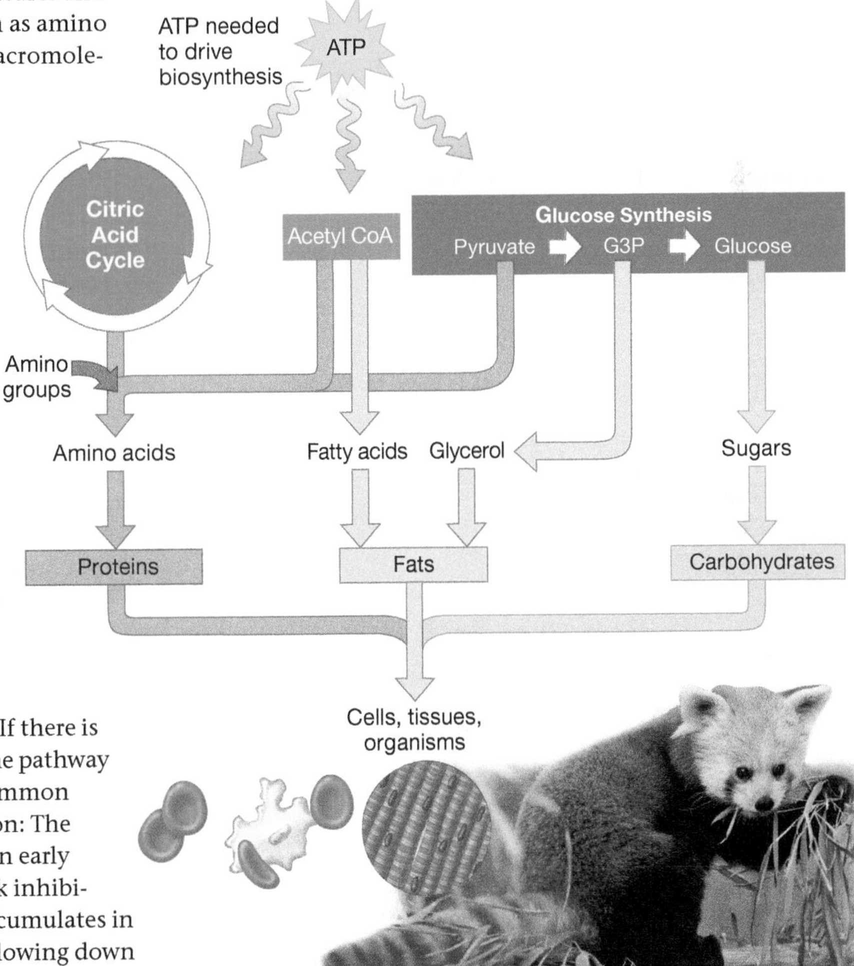

▲ **Figure 6.15** **Biosynthesis of organic molecules from intermediates of cellular respiration**

? Explain how someone can gain weight and store fat even when on a low-fat diet. (*Hint*: Look for G3P and acetyl CoA in Figures 6.14 and 6.15.)

■ If caloric intake is excessive, body cells use metabolic pathways to convert the excess to fat. The glycerol and fatty acids of fats are made from G3P and acetyl CoA, respectively, both produced from the oxidation of carbohydrates.

CHAPTER

6 REVIEW

For practice quizzes, BioFlix animations, MP3 tutorials, video tutors, and more study tools designed for this textbook, go to MasteringBiology™

REVIEWING THE CONCEPTS

Cellular Respiration: Aerobic Harvesting of Energy (6.1–6.5)

6.1 Photosynthesis and cellular respiration provide energy for life. Photosynthesis uses solar energy to produce organic molecules and O_2 from CO_2 and H_2O. In cellular respiration, O_2 is consumed during the breakdown of organic molecules to CO_2 and H_2O, and energy is released.

6.2 Breathing supplies O_2 for use in cellular respiration and removes CO_2.

6.3 Cellular respiration banks energy in ATP molecules.

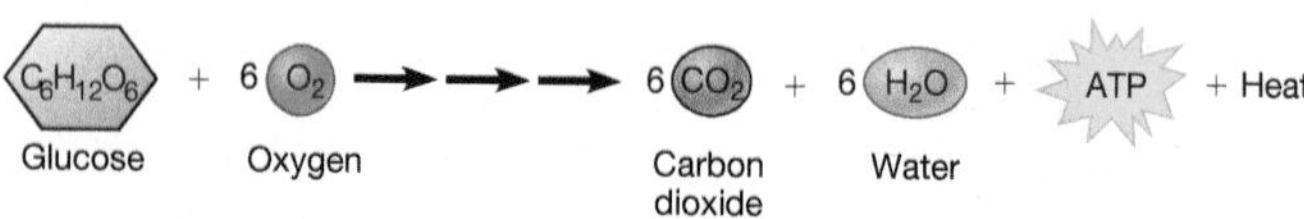

6.4 The human body uses energy from ATP for all its activities.

6.5 Cells capture energy from electrons "falling" from organic fuels to oxygen. Electrons removed from fuel molecules (oxidation) are transferred to NAD^+ (reduction). NADH passes electrons to an electron transport chain. As electrons "fall" from carrier to carrier and finally to O_2, energy is released.

Stages of Cellular Respiration (6.6–6.11)

6.6 Overview: Cellular respiration occurs in three main stages.

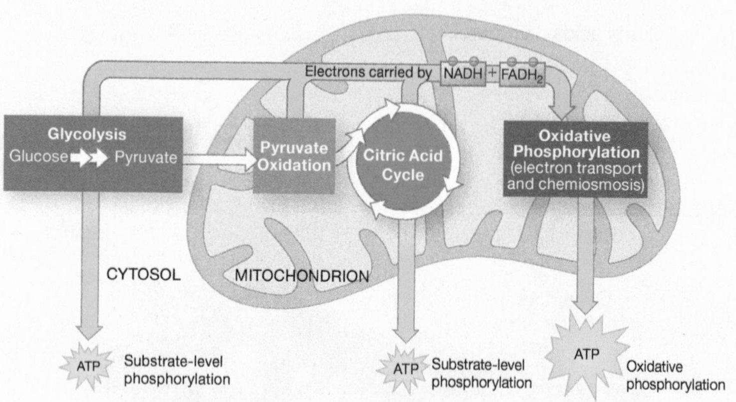

6.7 Glycolysis harvests chemical energy by oxidizing glucose to pyruvate. ATP is used to prime a glucose molecule, which is split in two. These three-carbon intermediates are oxidized to two molecules of pyruvate, yielding a net of 2 ATP and 2 NADH. ATP is formed by substrate-level phosphorylation, in which a phosphate group is transferred from an organic molecule to ADP.

6.8 After pyruvate is oxidized, the citric acid cycle completes the energy-yielding oxidation of organic molecules. The oxidation of pyruvate yields acetyl CoA, CO_2, and NADH. For each turn of the citric acid cycle, two carbons from acetyl CoA are added, 2 CO_2 are released, and 3 NADH and 1 $FADH_2$ are produced.

6.9 Most ATP production occurs by oxidative phosphorylation. In mitochondria, electrons from NADH and $FADH_2$ are passed down the electron transport chain to O_2, which picks up H^+ to form water. Energy released by these redox reactions is used to pump H^+ into the intermembrane space. In chemiosmosis, the H^+ gradient drives H^+ back through ATP synthase complexes in the inner membrane, synthesizing ATP.

6.10 Scientists have discovered heat-producing, calorie-burning brown fat in adults.

6.11 Review: Each molecule of glucose yields many molecules of ATP. Substrate-level phosphorylation and oxidative phosphorylation produce up to 32 ATP molecules for every glucose molecule oxidized in cellular respiration.

Fermentation: Anaerobic Harvesting of Energy (6.12–6.13)

6.12 Fermentation enables cells to produce ATP without oxygen. Under anaerobic conditions, muscle cells, yeasts, and certain bacteria produce ATP by glycolysis. NAD^+ is recycled from NADH as pyruvate is reduced to lactate (lactic acid fermentation) or alcohol and CO_2 (alcohol fermentation).

6.13 Glycolysis evolved early in the history of life on Earth. Glycolysis occurs in the cytosol of the cells of nearly all organisms and is thought to have evolved in ancient prokaryotes.

Connections Between Metabolic Pathways (6.14–6.15)

6.14 Cells use many kinds of organic molecules as fuel for cellular respiration.

6.15 Organic molecules from food provide raw materials for biosynthesis. Cells use intermediates from cellular respiration and ATP for biosynthesis of other organic molecules. Metabolic pathways are often regulated by feedback inhibition.

CONNECTING THE CONCEPTS

1. Fill in the blanks in this summary map to help you review the key concepts of cellular respiration.

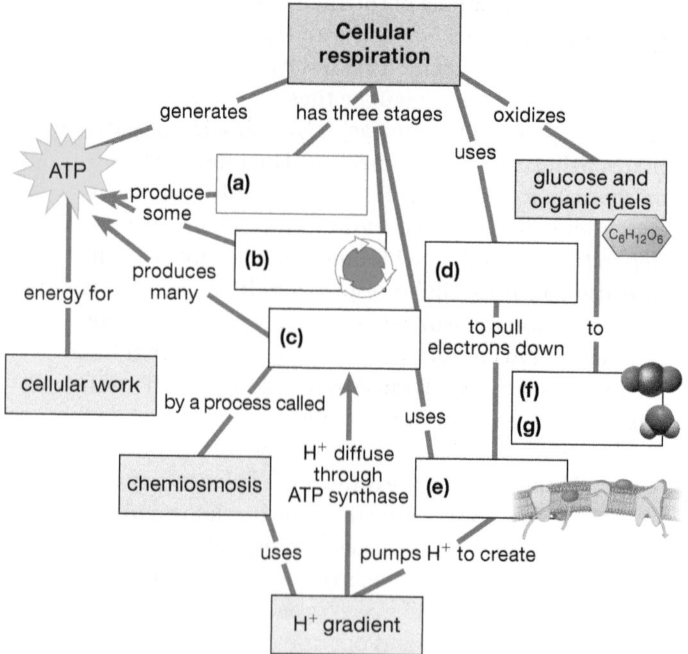

TESTING YOUR KNOWLEDGE

Level 1: Knowledge/Comprehension

2. A biochemist wanted to study how various substances were used in cellular respiration. In one experiment, she allowed a mouse to breathe air containing O_2 "labeled" by a particular isotope. In the mouse, the labeled oxygen first showed up in
   a. ATP.
   b. NADH.
   c. CO_2.
   d. H_2O.
3. In glycolysis, ________ is oxidized and ________ is reduced.
   a. NAD^+ ... glucose
   b. glucose ... oxygen
   c. ATP ... ADP
   d. glucose ... NAD^+
4. Most of the CO_2 from cellular respiration is released during
   a. glycolysis.
   b. pyruvate oxidation.
   c. the citric acid cycle.
   d. oxidative phosphorylation.
5. Which of the following is the most immediate source of energy for making most of the ATP in your cells?
   a. the transfer of (P) from intermediate substrates to ADP
   b. the movement of H^+ across a membrane down its concentration gradient
   c. the splitting of glucose into two molecules of pyruvate
   d. electrons moving through the electron transport chain
6. Which of the following is a true distinction between cellular respiration and fermentation?
   a. NADH is oxidized by passing electrons to the electron transport chain in respiration only.
   b. Only respiration oxidizes glucose.
   c. Substrate-level phosphorylation is unique to fermentation; cellular respiration uses oxidative phosphorylation.
   d. Fermentation is the metabolic pathway found in prokaryotes; cellular respiration is unique to eukaryotes.

Level 2: Application/Analysis

7. The poison cyanide binds to an electron carrier within the electron transport chain and blocks the movement of electrons. When this happens, glycolysis and the citric acid cycle soon grind to a halt as well. Why do you think these other two stages of cellular respiration stop? (*Explain your answer.*)
   a. They run out of ATP.
   b. Unused O_2 interferes with cellular respiration.
   c. They run out of NAD^+ and FAD.
   d. Electrons are no longer available.
8. In which of the following is the first molecule becoming reduced to the second molecule?
   a. pyruvate $\rightarrow$ acetyl CoA
   b. pyruvate $\rightarrow$ lactate
   c. glucose $\rightarrow$ pyruvate
   d. NADH + $H^+ \rightarrow NAD^+$ + 2H
9. Which of the three stages of cellular respiration is considered the most ancient? Explain your answer.
10. Compare and contrast fermentation as it occurs in your muscle cells and in yeast cells.
11. Explain how your body can convert excess carbohydrates in the diet to fats. Can excess carbohydrates be converted to protein? What else must be supplied?
12. An average adult human requires 2,200 kcal of energy per day. Suppose your diet provides an average of 2,300 kcal per day. How many hours per week would you have to walk to burn off the extra calories? Swim? Run? (See Figure 6.4.)
13. Your body makes NAD^+ and FAD from two B vitamins, niacin and riboflavin. The Recommended Dietary Allowance for niacin is 20 mg and for riboflavin, 1.7 mg. These amounts are thousands of times less than the amount of glucose your body needs each day to fuel its energy needs. Why is the daily requirement for these vitamins so small?

Level 3: Synthesis/Evaluation

14. Oxidative phosphorylation involves the flow of both electrons and hydrogen ions (H^+). Explain the roles of these movements in the synthesis of ATP.
15. In the citric acid cycle, an enzyme oxidizes malate to oxaloacetate, with the production of NADH and the release of H^+. You are studying this reaction using a suspension of bean cell mitochondria and a blue dye that loses its color as it takes up H^+. You set up reaction mixtures with mitochondria, dye, and three different concentrations of malate (0.1 mg/L, 0.2 mg/L, and 0.3 mg/L). Which of the following graphs represents the results you would expect, and why?

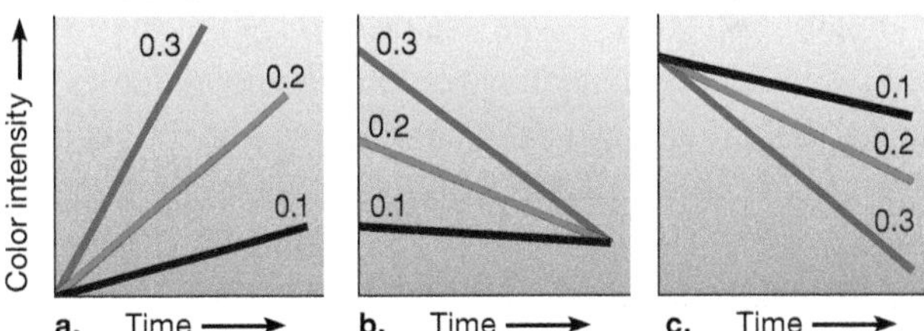

16. ATP synthase enzymes are found in the prokaryotic plasma membrane and in the inner membrane of a mitochondrion. What does this suggest about the evolutionary relationship of this eukaryotic organelle to prokaryotes?
17. **SCIENTIFIC THINKING** Several studies have found a correlation between the activity levels of brown fat tissue in research participants following exposure to cold and their percentage of body fat (see Module 6.10). Devise a graph that would present the results from such a study, labeling the axes and drawing a line to show whether the results show a positive or negative correlation between the variables. Propose two hypotheses that could explain these results.
18. For a short time in the 1930s, some physicians prescribed low doses of a compound called dinitrophenol (DNP) to help patients lose weight. This unsafe method was abandoned after some patients died. DNP uncouples the chemiosmotic machinery by making the inner mitochondrial membrane leaky to H^+. Explain how this drug could cause profuse sweating, weight loss, and possibly death.
19. Explain how the mechanism of brown fat metabolism is similar to the effect that the drug DNP described above has on mitochondria. Pharmaceutical companies may start targeting brown fat for weight loss drugs. How might such drugs help patients lose weight? What dangers might such drugs pose?

Answers to all questions can be found in Appendix 4.

Photosynthesis: *Using Light to Make Food*

CHAPTER 7

If you are among the 80% of people allergic to poison ivy, the thick patch of three-leaved plants pictured to the right may make you want to scrub with soap and water and rush to find calamine lotion. A close encounter with this noxious weed often leads to itchy and oozing blisters that can last for weeks. The allergic component of poison ivy sap, urushiol, binds to skin, clothing, and pet fur on contact, where it remains active until washed off. Even dead leaves or vines retain active urushiol for several years.

Will increasing atmospheric CO_2 make you itch?

Poison ivy is found throughout much of North America, often growing along the ground in both woods and open areas. It can also grow as a vine, climbing high up trees with its lateral branches that are sometimes mistaken for tree limbs. The rhymes "hairy vine, no friend of mine" and "raggy rope, don't be a dope" help alert hikers to the danger around them when the characteristic shiny leaves are hidden high in the tree foliage.

Like all plants, poison ivy produces energy for its growth by photosynthesis, the process that converts light energy to the chemical energy of sugar. Photosynthesis removes carbon dioxide (CO_2) from the atmosphere and stores it in plant matter. The burning of sugar in the cellular respiration of almost all organisms releases CO_2 back to the environment. Burning fossil fuels and deforestation also release CO_2, and these activities are contributing to the current rise in atmospheric CO_2 and the accompanying global warming and climate change. How might higher CO_2 levels affect plant growth? Unfortunately, many studies indicate that weeds grow faster under such conditions than do our crop plants or trees. Later in the chapter we will discuss one such study concerning the growth of poison ivy.

But first, let's learn how photosynthesis works. We begin with some basic concepts and then look more closely at the two stages of photosynthesis: the light reactions and the Calvin cycle. Finally, we explore ways in which photosynthesis affects our global environment.

BIG IDEAS

An Introduction to Photosynthesis (7.1–7.5)

Plants and other photoautotrophs use the energy of sunlight to convert CO_2 and H_2O to sugar and O_2.

The Light Reactions: Converting Solar Energy to Chemical Energy (7.6–7.9)

In the thylakoids of a chloroplast, the light reactions generate ATP and NADPH.

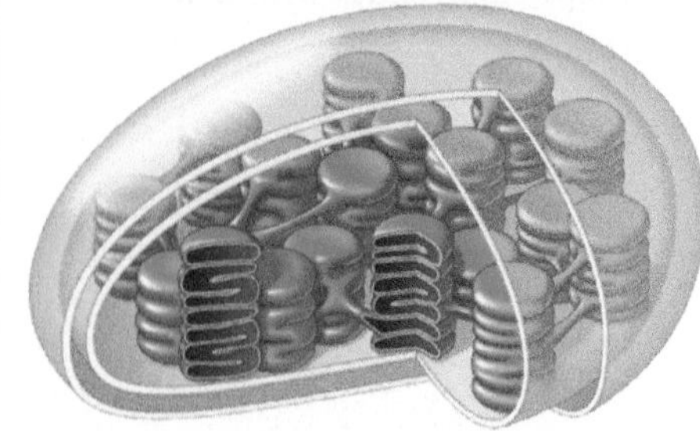

The Calvin Cycle: Reducing CO_2 to Sugar (7.10–7.11)

The Calvin cycle, which takes place in the stroma of the chloroplast, uses ATP and NADPH to reduce CO_2 to sugar.

The Global Significance of Photosynthesis (7.12–7.14)

Photosynthesis provides the energy and building material for ecosystems. It also affects atmospheric CO_2 levels and global climate.

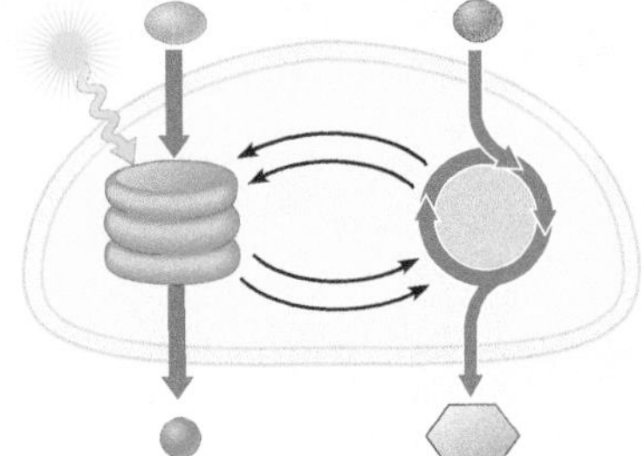

An Introduction to Photosynthesis

7.1 Photosynthesis fuels the biosphere

Life on Earth is solar powered. The chloroplasts in plant cells capture light energy that has traveled 150 million kilometers from the sun. Through the process of **photosynthesis**, plants use solar energy to convert carbon dioxide (CO_2) and water (H_2O) to sugars and other organic molecules, and they release oxygen gas (O_2) as a by-product. Plants are **autotrophs** (meaning "self-feeders" in Greek) in that they make their own food. Autotrophs not only feed themselves, but they are the ultimate source of organic molecules for almost all other organisms. Because they use the energy of light, plants and other photosynthesizers are specifically called **photoautotrophs**.

Photoautotrophs are often referred to as the producers of the biosphere because they produce its food supply. (In Chapter 16, you will learn about chemoautotrophs—prokaryotes that use inorganic chemicals as their energy source and are the producers in deep-sea vent communities.) Producers feed the consumers of the biosphere—the **heterotrophs** that cannot make their own food but must consume plants or animals or decompose organic material (*hetero* means "other"). You and almost all other heterotrophs are completely dependent on photoautotrophs for the raw materials and organic fuel necessary to maintain life and for the oxygen required to burn that fuel in cellular respiration.

Photoautotrophs not only feed us; they also clothe us (think cotton), house us (think wood), and provide energy for warmth, light, transport, and manufacturing. The fossil fuels we use as energy sources represent stores of the sun's energy captured by photoautotrophs in the far distant past.

The photographs shown on this page illustrate some of the diversity among today's photoautotrophs. On land, plants, such as those in the tropical forest in Figure 7.1A, are the producers. In aquatic environments, photoautotrophs include algae and some protists, as well as photosynthetic prokaryotes. Figure 7.1B shows kelp, a large alga that forms extensive underwater "forests" off the coast of California. Figure 7.1C is a micrograph of cyanobacteria, which are important producers in freshwater and marine ecosystems.

In this chapter, we focus on photosynthesis in plants, which takes place in chloroplasts. Illustrating the theme of INTERACTIONS, the remarkable ability of these organelles to harness light energy and use it to drive the synthesis of organic compounds emerges from the structural organization and interactions of their component parts. Photosynthetic pigments and enzymes are grouped together in membranes and compartments, facilitating the complex series of chemical reactions of photosynthesis. Photosynthetic bacteria have infolded regions of the plasma membrane containing such molecules. In fact, according to the widely accepted theory of endosymbiosis, chloroplasts originated from a photosynthetic prokaryote that took up residence inside a eukaryotic cell (see Module 4.15).

Let's begin our study of photosynthesis with an overview of the location and structure of plant chloroplasts.

? What do "self-feeding" photoautotrophs require from the environment to make their own food?

Light, CO_2, and H_2O. (Minerals are also required; you'll learn about the needs of plants in Chapter 32.)

▲ Figure 7.1A Tropical forest plants

▲ Figure 7.1B Kelp, a large alga

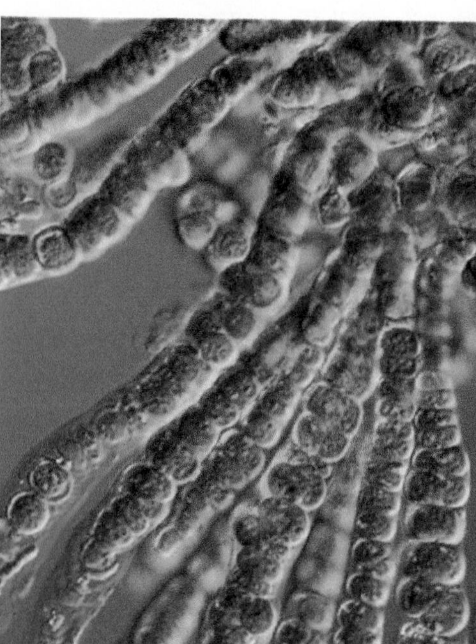

▲ Figure 7.1C Cyanobacteria (photosynthetic bacteria) LM 575X

7.2 Photosynthesis occurs in chloroplasts in plant cells

All green parts of a plant have chloroplasts in their cells, but leaves are the major sites of photosynthesis in most plants. Indeed, a section of leaf with a top surface area of 1 mm^2 has about a half million chloroplasts. A leaf's green color comes from **chlorophyll**, a light-absorbing pigment in the chloroplasts that plays a central role in converting solar energy to chemical energy.

Figure 7.2 zooms in to take you on a journey inside a leaf, then into a cell, and finally into a chloroplast—the actual site of photosynthesis. As you can see in the leaf cross section, chloroplasts are concentrated in the cells of the **mesophyll**, the green tissue in the interior of the leaf. CO_2 enters the leaf, and O_2 exits, by way of tiny pores called **stomata** (singular, *stoma*, meaning "mouth"). Water absorbed by the roots is delivered to the leaves in veins. Leaves also use veins to export manufactured sugar to roots and other parts of the plant.

As you will notice in the light micrograph of a single mesophyll cell, each cell has numerous chloroplasts. A typical mesophyll cell has about 30 to 40 chloroplasts. The bottom drawing and the electron micrograph show the structures in a single chloroplast. Membranes within the chloroplast form the framework for many of the reactions of photosynthesis, just as mitochondrial membranes provide the structure for much of the energy-harvesting machinery in cellular respiration (see Module 6.9).

In the chloroplast, an envelope of two membranes encloses an inner compartment, which is filled with a thick fluid called **stroma**. Suspended in the stroma is a system of interconnected membranous sacs, called **thylakoids**, which enclose another internal compartment, called the thylakoid space. In many places, thylakoids are concentrated in stacks called grana (singular, *granum*). Built into the thylakoid membranes are the chlorophyll molecules that capture light energy. The thylakoid membranes also house much of the machinery that converts light energy to chemical energy, which is then used in the stroma of the chloroplast to make sugar.

The precise arrangements of these membranes and compartments are essential to the process of photosynthesis—a classic example of the theme of STRUCTURE AND FUNCTION. Later in the chapter, we examine these structures and their functions in more detail. But first, let's look more closely at the general process of photosynthesis.

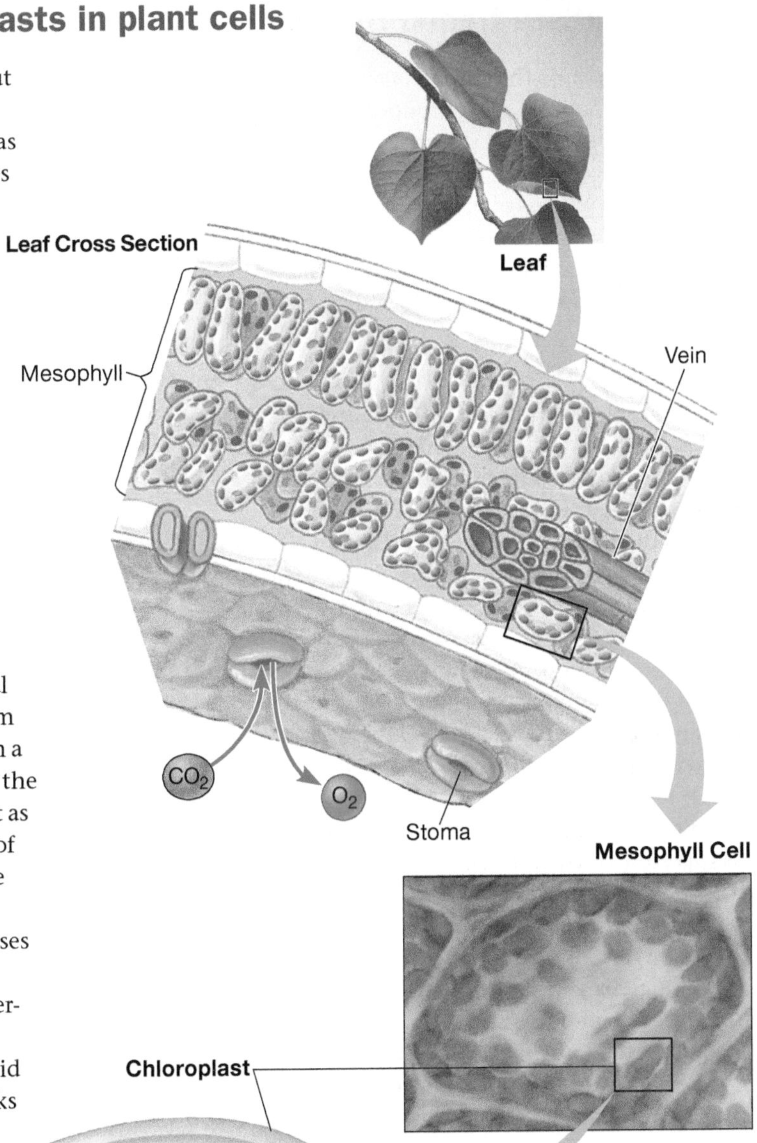

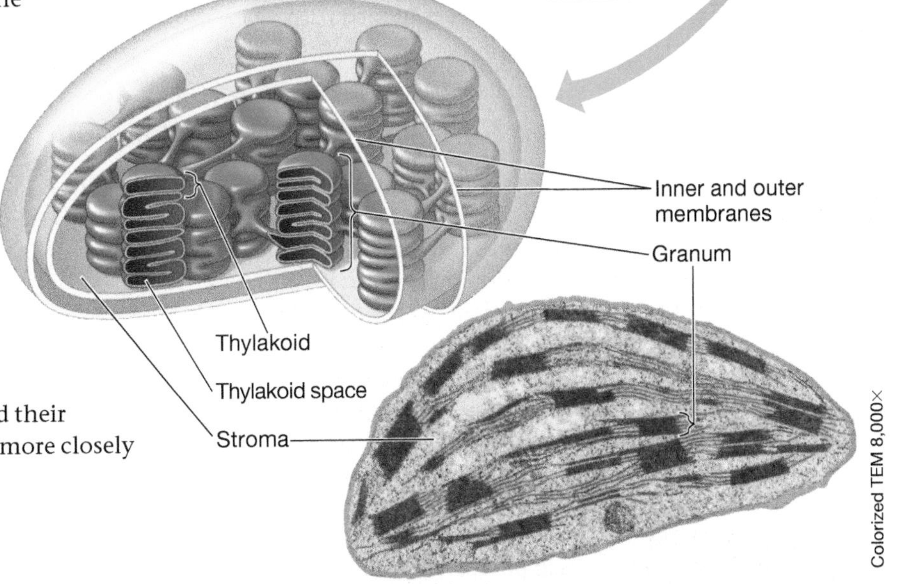

▲ **Figure 7.2** **Zooming in on the location and structure of chloroplasts**

TRY THIS Find the labels *Stoma* and *Stroma* in this figure. Describe the functions of these two similarly named structures.

? How do the reactant molecules of photosynthesis reach the chloroplasts in leaves?

■ CO_2 enters leaves through stomata, and H_2O enters the roots and is carried to leaves through veins.

7.3 Scientists traced the process of photosynthesis using isotopes

The leaves of plants that live in lakes and ponds are often covered with bubbles of O_2 produced during photosynthesis (Figure 7.3). How did scientists find out where this O_2 comes from?

The overall process of photosynthesis has been known since the 1800s: In the presence of light, green plants convert carbon dioxide and water into sugar and oxygen. Consider the basic summary equation for photosynthesis:

$$\text{Light energy} + 6\,CO_2 + 6\,H_2O \rightarrow C_6H_{12}O_6 + 6\,O_2$$

Looking at the equation, you can understand why scientists hypothesized that in photosynthesis, carbon dioxide is first split ($CO_2 \rightarrow C + O_2$) and O_2 released, and then water (H_2O) is added to the carbon to produce sugar. In the 1930s, this idea was challenged by C. B. van Niel, who was working with photosynthesizing bacteria that produce sugar from CO_2 but do not release O_2 in the process. These bacteria obviously did not split CO_2 in their photosynthesis. He hypothesized that in plant photosynthesis, it is H_2O that is split, with the hydrogen becoming incorporated into sugar and the O_2 released as gas.

It was almost 20 years before van Niel's hypothesis was confirmed. Using a heavy isotope of oxygen, O-18, scientists were able to follow the fate of oxygen atoms during photosynthesis. (See Module 2.3 to review isotopes.) O-18 has two more neutrons in the nucleus of its atom than the more common isotope O-16, and this slight difference in mass can be experimentally measured. To determine the source of the O_2 released by photosynthesis, researchers produced CO_2 and H_2O containing O-18, thus "labeling" the two reactant molecules. Experimental plants were provided with one or the other labeled reactant. The results were that plants produced O_2 containing O-18 only when supplied with labeled H_2O, never when provided with labeled CO_2. These experiments showed that the O_2 released during photosynthesis comes from water and not from CO_2.

The synthesis of sugar in photosynthesis involves numerous chemical reactions (as you will see in Module 7.10). Working out the details of these reactions also involved the use of isotopes, in this case, radioactive isotopes. In the mid-1940s, American biochemist Melvin Calvin and his colleagues began using radioactive C-14 to trace the sequence of the intermediate molecules formed in the cyclic pathway that produces sugar from CO_2. They worked for 10 years to elucidate this cycle, which is now called the Calvin cycle. Calvin received the Nobel Prize in 1961 for this work.

▲ **Figure 7.3** Oxygen bubbles on the leaves of an aquatic plant

? Photosynthesis produces billions of tons of carbohydrate a year. Where does most of the mass of this huge amount of organic matter come from?

■ Mostly from CO_2 in the air, which provides both the carbon and oxygen in carbohydrate. Water supplies only the hydrogen.

7.4 Photosynthesis is a redox process, as is cellular respiration

Let's compare the processes of photosynthesis and cellular respiration. Indeed, they appear to be opposite reactions: the reactants in one are the products of the other and vice versa. Both involve oxidation-reduction reactions (see Module 6.5), and both illustrate the theme of the transformation of ENERGY AND MATTER. Cellular respiration harvests energy stored in a glucose molecule by oxidizing the sugar to CO_2 and reducing O_2 to H_2O. This process involves a number of energy-releasing redox reactions, with electrons losing potential energy as they are passed down an electron transport chain to O_2. Along the way, the mitochondrion uses some of the energy to synthesize ATP.

Which way do electrons move in photosynthesis? Water is split, and its electrons are transferred along with hydrogen ions (H^+) to CO_2, reducing it to sugar. The potential energy of electrons increases as they move from H_2O to CO_2. The light energy captured by chlorophyll molecules in the chloroplast provides this energy boost. Figure 7.4 illustrates these energy-requiring redox reactions as CO_2 becomes reduced to sugar and water molecules are oxidized to O_2.

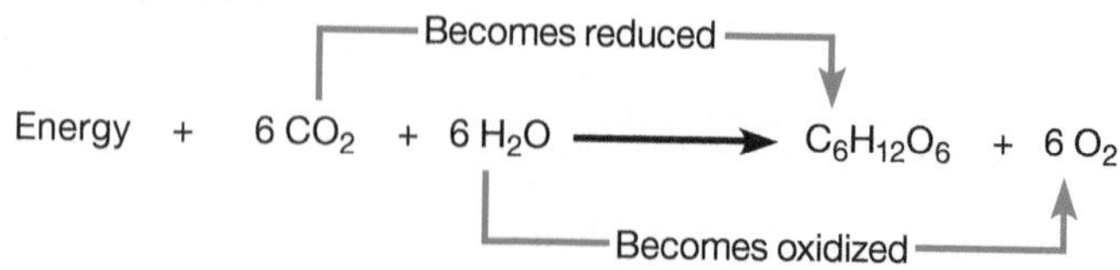

▲ **Figure 7.4** The redox reactions of photosynthesis

TRY THIS Write out the equation for cellular respiration, and indicate the molecules that are becoming reduced and oxidized.

? Which redox process, photosynthesis or cellular respiration, is exergonic? Is endergonic? (*Hint*: See Module 5.11.)

■ Cellular respiration; photosynthesis

7.5 Photosynthesis occurs in two stages, which are linked by ATP and NADPH

The summary equation for photosynthesis shown in Figure 7.5A is a rather simple synopsis of a very complex process. Actually, photosynthesis is not a single process, but two linked processes, each with multiple steps. Let's begin our study of photosynthesis with an overview of these two stages. Figure 7.5B presents a diagram of a chloroplast of a plant cell, showing the inputs and outputs of the light reactions and the Calvin cycle and how these two stages are related.

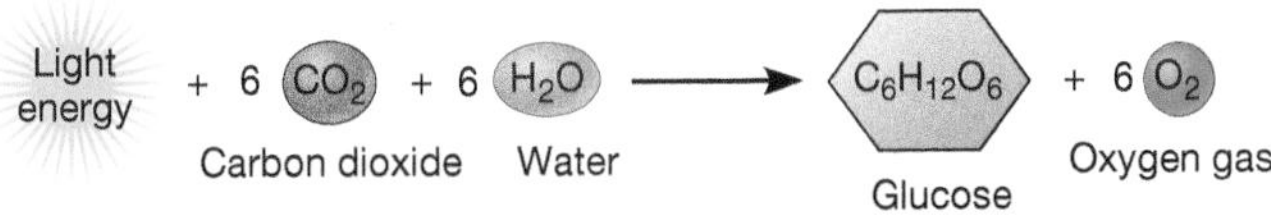

▲ Figure 7.5A The summary equation of photosynthesis

The **light reactions**, which occur in the thylakoids, include the steps that convert light energy to chemical energy and release O_2. Water is split, providing a source of electrons and giving off O_2 as a by-product. Light energy is absorbed by chlorophyll molecules built into the thylakoid membranes. This energy is used to drive the transfer of electrons (⊖) and H^+ from water to the electron acceptor **NADP$^+$**, reducing it to NADPH. NADPH is first cousin to NADH, which transports electrons in cellular respiration; the two differ only in the extra phosphate group in NADPH. NADPH temporarily stores electrons and provides "reducing power" to the Calvin cycle. The light reactions also generate ATP from ADP and a phosphate group.

In summary, the light reactions absorb solar energy and convert it to chemical energy stored in both ATP and NADPH. Notice that these reactions produce no sugar; sugar is not made until the Calvin cycle, which is the second stage of photosynthesis.

The **Calvin cycle** occurs in the stroma of the chloroplast. It is a cyclic series of reactions that assembles sugar molecules using CO_2 and the energy-rich products of the light reactions. The incorporation of carbon from CO_2 into organic compounds, shown in the figure as CO_2 entering the Calvin cycle, is called **carbon fixation**. After carbon fixation, the carbon compounds are reduced to sugars.

As the figure suggests, it is NADPH produced by the light reactions that provides the electrons for reducing carbon compounds in the Calvin cycle. And ATP from the light reactions provides chemical energy that powers several of the steps of the Calvin cycle. The Calvin cycle is sometimes referred to as the dark reactions, or light-independent reactions, because none of the steps requires light directly. However, in most plants, the Calvin cycle occurs during daylight, when the light reactions power the cycle's sugar assembly line by supplying it with NADPH and ATP.

The word *photosynthesis* encapsulates the two stages. *Photo*, from the Greek word for "light," refers to the light reactions; *synthesis*, meaning "putting together," refers to sugar construction by the Calvin cycle. In the next several modules, we look at these two stages in more detail. But first, let's consider some of the properties of light, the energy source that powers photosynthesis.

? For chloroplasts to produce sugar from carbon dioxide in the dark, they would need to be supplied with ________ and ________.

■ ATP . . . NADPH

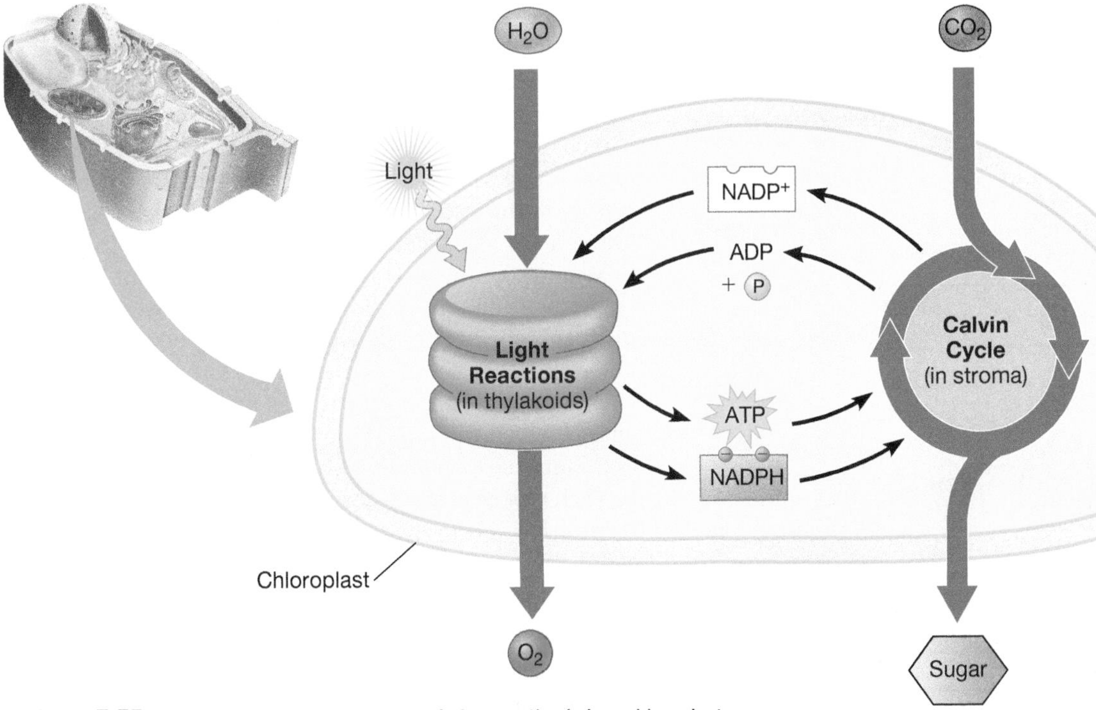

▲ Figure 7.5B An overview of the two stages of photosynthesis in a chloroplast

TRY THIS Relate the equation for photosynthesis shown in 7.5A to this overview diagram.

The Light Reactions: Converting Solar Energy to Chemical Energy

7.6 Visible radiation absorbed by pigments drives the light reactions

What do we mean when we say that photosynthesis is powered by light energy from the sun?

The Nature of Sunlight Sunlight is a type of energy called electromagnetic energy or radiation. Electromagnetic energy travels in space as rhythmic waves analogous to those made by a pebble dropped in a puddle of water. The distance between the crests of electromagnetic waves is called a **wavelength**. Figure 7.6A shows the **electromagnetic spectrum**, the full range of electromagnetic wavelengths from very short gamma rays to very long-wavelength radio waves. As you can see in the center of the figure, visible light is only a small fraction of the spectrum, consisting of wavelengths from about 380 nm to about 750 nm. A prism separates visible light into its component colors by bending different wavelengths at different angles. (Droplets of water in the atmosphere can act as prisms, forming a rainbow.)

The model of light as waves explains many of light's properties. However, light also behaves as discrete packets of energy called photons. A **photon** has a fixed quantity of energy, and the shorter the wavelength of light, the greater the energy of its photons. In fact, the photons of wavelengths that are shorter than those of visible light have enough energy to damage molecules such as proteins and nucleic acids. This is why ultraviolet (UV) radiation can cause sunburns and skin cancer.

Photosynthetic Pigments Figure 7.6B shows what happens to visible light in a chloroplast. Light-absorbing molecules called pigments, built into the thylakoid membranes, absorb some wavelengths of light and reflect or transmit other wavelengths. We do not see the absorbed wavelengths; their energy has been absorbed by pigment molecules. What we see when we look at a leaf are the green wavelengths that are not absorbed but are transmitted and reflected by the pigments.

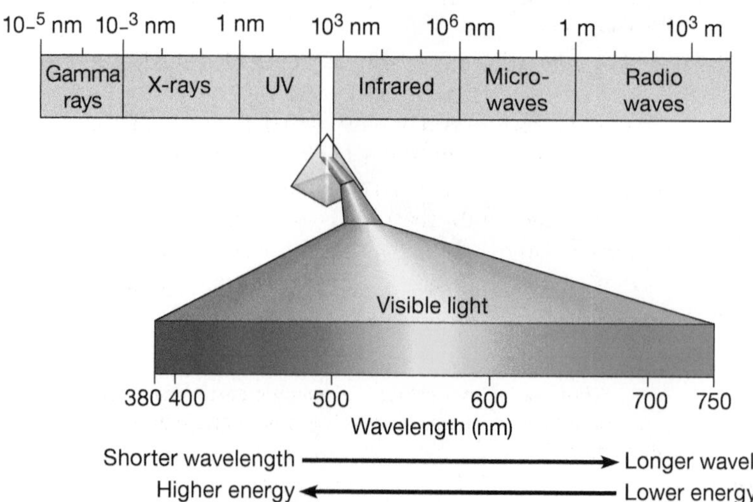

▲ **Figure 7.6A** The electromagnetic spectrum

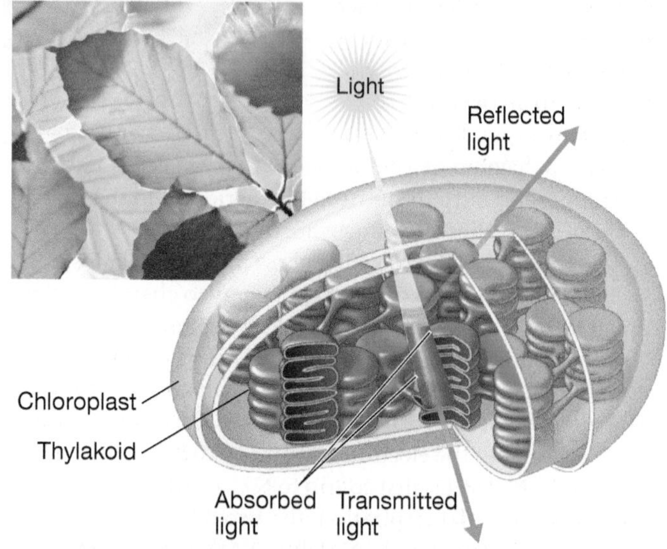

▲ **Figure 7.6B** The interaction of light with chlorophyll in a chloroplast

TRY THIS Use this diagram to explain why leaves are green.

Different pigments absorb light of different wavelengths, and chloroplasts contain more than one type of pigment. Chlorophyll *a*, which participates directly in the light reactions, absorbs mainly blue-violet and red light. A very similar molecule, chlorophyll *b*, absorbs mainly blue and orange light. Chlorophyll *b* broadens the range of light that a plant can use by conveying absorbed energy to chlorophyll *a*, which then puts the energy to work in the light reactions.

Chloroplasts also contain pigments called carotenoids, which are various shades of yellow and orange. The spectacular colors of fall foliage in certain parts of the world are due partly to the yellow-orange hues of longer-lasting carotenoids that show through once the green chlorophyll breaks down. Carotenoids may broaden the spectrum of colors that can drive photosynthesis. However, a more important function seems to be photoprotection: Some carotenoids absorb and dissipate excessive light energy that would otherwise damage chlorophyll or interact with oxygen to form reactive oxidative molecules that can damage cell molecules. Similar carotenoids, which we obtain from carrots and other vegetables and fruits, have a photoprotective role in our eyes.

Each type of pigment absorbs certain wavelengths of light because it is able to absorb the specific amounts of energy in those photons. Next we see what happens when a pigment molecule such as chlorophyll absorbs a photon of light.

? What color of light is least effective at driving photosynthesis? Explain.

Green, because it is mostly transmitted and reflected—not absorbed—by photosynthetic pigments.

7.7 Photosystems capture solar energy

Energy cannot be created or destroyed, but it can be transferred or transformed (see Module 5.10). Let's examine how light energy can be transformed to other types of energy. When a pigment molecule absorbs a photon of light, one of the pigment's electrons jumps to an energy level farther from the nucleus. In this location, the electron has more potential energy, and we say that the electron has been raised from a ground state to an excited state. The excited state, like all high-energy states, is unstable. Generally, when isolated pigment molecules absorb light, their excited electrons drop back down to the ground state in a billionth of a second, releasing their excess energy as heat. This conversion of light energy to heat is what makes a black car so hot on a sunny day (black pigments absorb all wavelengths of light).

Some isolated pigments, including chlorophyll, emit light as well as heat after absorbing photons. As shown on the left in Figure 7.7A, a brightly illuminated solution of chlorophyll isolated from chloroplasts produces a reddish afterglow called fluorescence. The right side of Figure 7.7A illustrates what happens in fluorescence: An absorbed photon boosts an electron of chlorophyll to an excited state, from which it immediately drops back to the ground state, emitting its energy as heat and light. The trick to harvesting the energy of light is to capture those excited electrons before they drop back down to the ground state. As you will see, that's what happens when chlorophyll molecules are embedded in intact chloroplasts.

In the thylakoid membrane, chlorophyll molecules are organized into clusters called photosystems (Figure 7.7B). A **photosystem** contains two kinds of complexes: a reaction-center complex surrounded by a number of light-harvesting complexes. A light-harvesting complex consists of various pigment molecules bound to proteins. The number and variety of pigment molecules can harvest light over a larger surface area and a larger portion of the spectrum than could any single pigment molecule alone. Together, the light-harvesting complexes function as a light-gathering antenna. When a pigment molecule absorbs a photon, the energy is transferred from molecule to molecule, somewhat like a human "wave" at a sporting event, until it is passed into the reaction-center complex. The reaction-center complex contains a pair of special chlorophyll *a* molecules and a molecule called the primary electron acceptor, which, as its name indicates, is capable of accepting electrons and becoming reduced. When an electron from a reaction-center chlorophyll *a* is boosted to a higher energy level, it is immediately captured by the primary electron acceptor. This is the first step in the transformation of light energy to chemical energy in the light reactions.

Two types of photosystems have been identified, and they cooperate in the light reactions. They are referred to as photosystem I and photosystem II, in order of their discovery, although photosystem II actually functions first in the sequence of steps that make up the light reactions. Each of the two types of photosystems has a characteristic reaction-center complex. Now let's see how the two photosystems work together in the light reactions to generate ATP and NADPH.

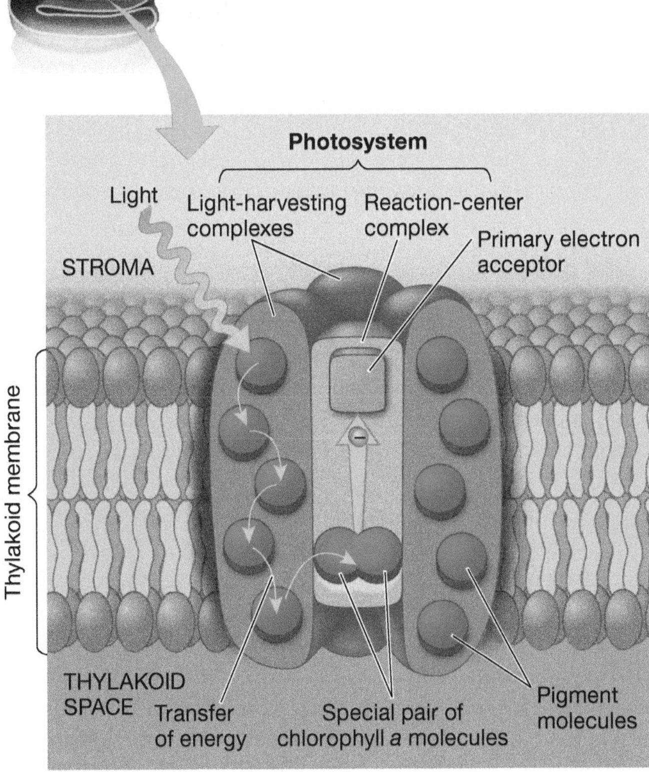

▲ **Figure 7.7B** A photosystem harvesting light energy and an excited electron being passed to the primary electron acceptor

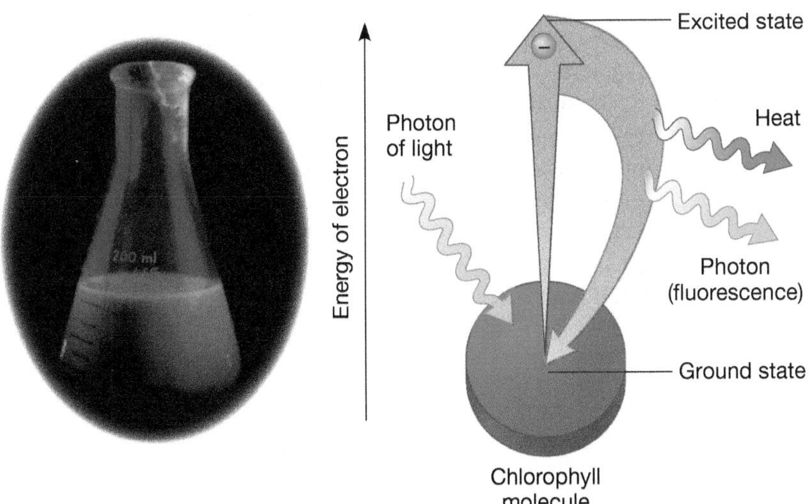

▲ **Figure 7.7A** A solution of chlorophyll glowing red when illuminated (left); an isolated chlorophyll molecule whose light-excited electron releases heat and light when it falls back to ground state (right)

? **Compared with a solution of isolated chlorophyll, why do intact chloroplasts not release heat and light when illuminated?**

In the chloroplasts, a light-excited electron from the reaction-center chlorophyll molecules is passed to a primary electron acceptor before it can fall back to the ground state.

7.8 Two photosystems connected by an electron transport chain convert light energy to the chemical energy of ATP and NADPH

You have just seen how light energy can boost an electron of chlorophyll *a* in the reaction center of a photosystem to an excited state, from which it is captured by a primary electron acceptor. But how do these captured electrons lead to the production of ATP and NADPH? Part of the explanation is found in the arrangement of photosystems II and I in the thylakoid membrane and their connection via an electron transport chain. Another part of the explanation involves the flow of electrons removed from H_2O through these components to NADPH. And the final part of the explanation, the synthesis of ATP, is linked (as it is in cellular respiration) to an electron transport chain pumping H^+ into a membrane compartment, from which the ions flow through an ATP synthase embedded in the membrane.

To unpack this rather complicated system, let's start with the simple mechanical analogy illustrated in **Figure 7.8**. Starting on the left, you see that the large yellow photon mallet provides the energy to boost an electron from photosystem II to a higher energy level, where it is caught by the primary electron acceptor standing on the platform. The electron is loaded onto an electron transport chain "ramp" leading to photosystem I. (Recall that photosystem II precedes photosystem I in the light reactions.) As electrons roll down the ramp, they release energy that is used for the production of ATP. When an electron reaches photosystem I, another photon mallet pumps it up to a higher energy level, where it is caught by a primary electron acceptor on the photosystem I platform. From there, the photoexcited electrons are thrown into a bucket to produce NADPH. This construction analogy shows how the coupling of two photosystems and an electron transport chain can transform the energy of light to the chemical energy of ATP and NADPH.

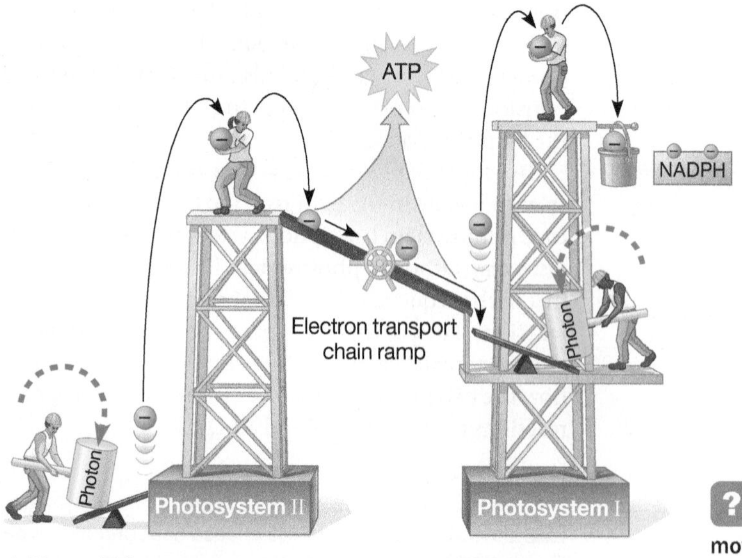

▲ **Figure 7.8** A mechanical analogy of the light reactions

TRY THIS Identify the two energy molecules that will be used in the Calvin cycle.

The simple analogy in Figure 7.8 does leave a few important unanswered questions: What is the source of the electrons that are moving through the photosystems to NADPH? Don't the light reactions produce O_2—where does that happen? And how does the flow of electrons down that ramp produce ATP?

The electrons that end up reducing $NADP^+$ to NADPH originally come from water. An enzyme in the thylakoid space splits H_2O into 2 electrons, 2 hydrogen ions (H^+), and 1 oxygen atom ($\frac{1}{2} O_2$). The oxygen atom immediately joins with another oxygen to form O_2. As you learned in Module 7.3, water is the source of the O_2 produced in photosynthesis, and these oxygen molecules diffuse out of the thylakoids, the chloroplast, and the plant cell, finally exiting the leaf through its stomata. The all-important electrons from water are passed, one by one, to the reaction center chlorophyll *a* molecules in photosystem II, replacing the photoexcited electron that was just captured by the primary electron acceptor. From photosystem II, the electrons pass through an electron transport chain to the reaction center chlorophyll *a* molecules in photosystem I, again replacing photoexcited electrons that had been captured by its primary electron acceptor. Although the illustration shows these electrons being dropped in a bucket, they actually are passed through a short electron transport chain to $NADP^+$, reducing it to NADPH.

Now that we have accounted for NADPH and O_2, all that is left is ATP. Making ATP in the light reactions involves an electron transport chain and chemiosmosis—the same players and process you met in the synthesis of ATP in cellular respiration. Recall that in chemiosmosis, the potential energy of a concentration gradient of H^+ across a membrane powers ATP synthesis. This gradient is created when an electron transport chain uses the energy released as it passes electrons down the chain to pump H^+ across a membrane. The energy of the concentration gradient drives H^+ back across the membrane through ATP synthase, spinning this rotary motor and phosphorylating ADP to produce ATP (see Module 6.9).

The next module, which presents a slightly more realistic model of the light reactions than this mechanical analogy, should help you visualize how photosystem II, the electron transport chain, photosystem I, and ATP synthase function together within the thylakoid membranes of a chloroplast to produce NADPH and ATP.

? **Looking at the model of the light reactions in Figure 7.8, explain why two photons of light are required in the movement of electrons from water to NADPH.**

■ One photon excites an electron from photosystem II, which is passed down an electron transfer chain to photosystem I. A second photon is then used in the reduction of $NADP^+$ to NADPH.

VISUALIZING THE CONCEPT

7.9 The light reactions take place within the thylakoid membranes

This diagram of the light reactions shows how the two photosystems and electron transport chain are embedded in a thylakoid membrane. All of the components shown here are present in numerous copies in each thylakoid. Moving from left to right, you can see how light energy absorbed by the two photosystems drives the flow of electrons from water to NADPH. Energy released as electrons pass down the electron transport chain powers the transport of H^+ into the thylakoid space. The concentration gradient of H^+ across the thylakoid membrane drives H^+ through ATP synthase, producing ATP. Because the initial energy input is light (*photo-*), this chemiosmotic production of ATP is called **photophosphorylation**.

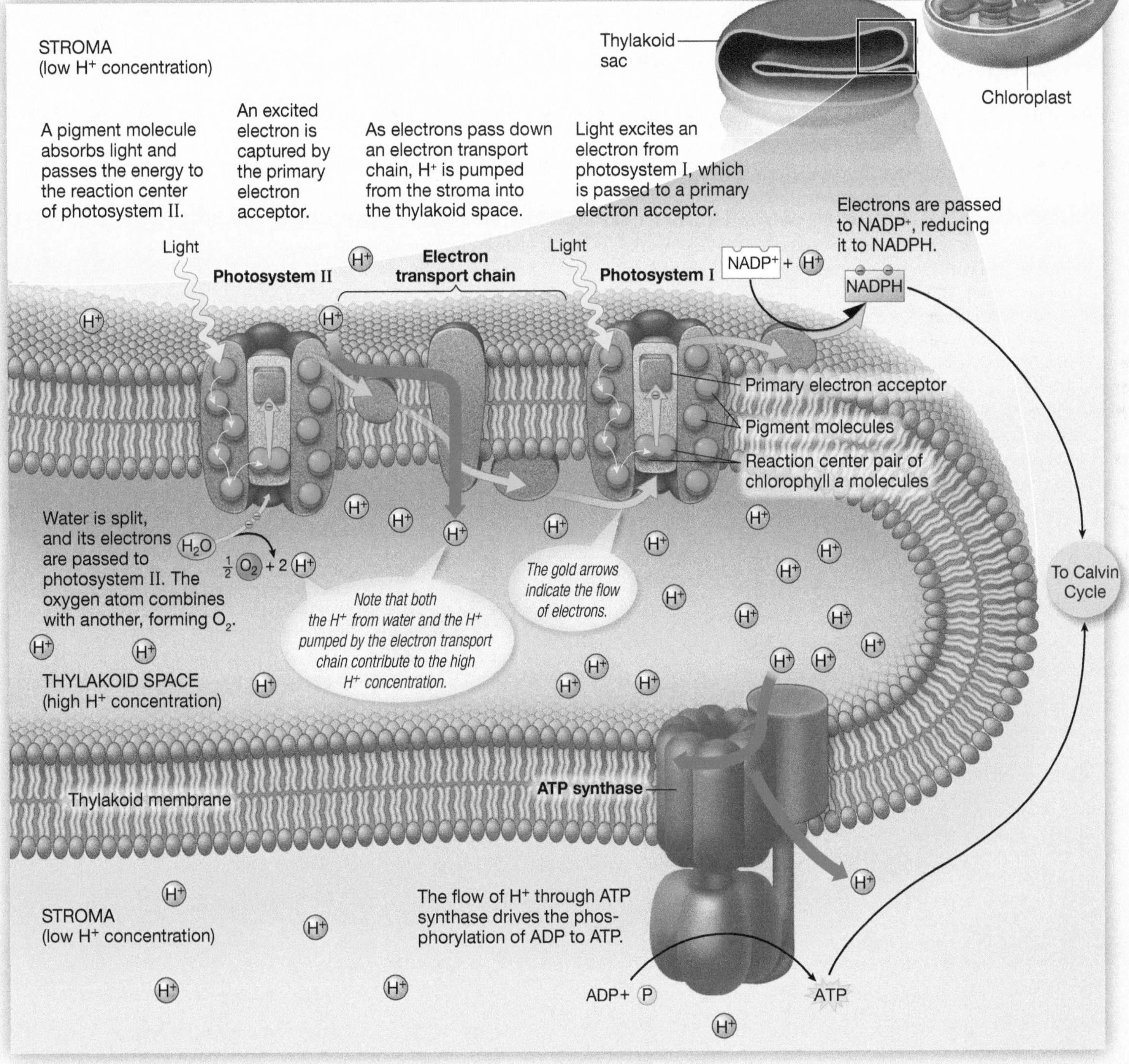

Thylakoid sac

Chloroplast

STROMA
(low H^+ concentration)

A pigment molecule absorbs light and passes the energy to the reaction center of photosystem II.

An excited electron is captured by the primary electron acceptor.

As electrons pass down an electron transport chain, H^+ is pumped from the stroma into the thylakoid space.

Light excites an electron from photosystem I, which is passed to a primary electron acceptor.

Electrons are passed to $NADP^+$, reducing it to NADPH.

Light

Photosystem II

Electron transport chain

Light

Photosystem I

$NADP^+$ + H^+

NADPH

Primary electron acceptor

Pigment molecules

Reaction center pair of chlorophyll *a* molecules

Water is split, and its electrons are passed to photosystem II. The oxygen atom combines with another, forming O_2.

H_2O → $\frac{1}{2}O_2 + 2H^+$

Note that both the H^+ from water and the H^+ pumped by the electron transport chain contribute to the high H^+ concentration.

The gold arrows indicate the flow of electrons.

To Calvin Cycle

THYLAKOID SPACE
(high H^+ concentration)

Thylakoid membrane

ATP synthase

STROMA
(low H^+ concentration)

The flow of H^+ through ATP synthase drives the phosphorylation of ADP to ATP.

ADP+ (P) → ATP

? Describe the two forces moving H^+ across the thylakoid membrane.

1) Energy released as electrons are passed down the electron transport chain pumps H^+ into the thylakoid space, and 2) the concentration gradient drives H^+ from the thylakoid space through ATP synthase.

The Calvin Cycle: Reducing CO_2 to Sugar

7.10 ATP and NADPH power sugar synthesis in the Calvin cycle

The Calvin cycle functions like a sugar factory within a chloroplast. The inputs to this all-important food-making process are CO_2 (from the air) and ATP and NADPH (both generated by the light reactions). ATP is used as an energy source and NADPH provides high-energy electrons for reducing CO_2 to sugar. The output of the Calvin cycle is an energy-rich, three-carbon sugar, glyceraldehyde 3-phosphate (G3P). A plant cell uses G3P to make glucose, the disaccharide sucrose, and other organic molecules as needed.

Figure 7.10 outlines the four main steps of the Calvin cycle. It is called a cycle because, like the citric acid cycle in cellular respiration, the starting material is regenerated after molecules enter and leave the cycle. In this case, the starting material is a five-carbon sugar named ribulose bisphosphate (RuBP). To make a molecule of G3P, the cycle must turn three times, incorporating three molecules of CO_2. We show the cycle starting with three CO_2 molecules so that we end up with a complete G3P molecule.

As you can see in step 1, carbon fixation, the enzyme rubisco attaches CO_2 to RuBP. (Recall that carbon fixation refers to the initial incorporation of CO_2 into organic compounds.) This unstable six-carbon molecule splits into two three-carbon molecules. In step 2, reduction, ATP and NADPH are used to reduce the three-carbon molecule to G3P.

For this to be a cycle, RuBP must be regenerated. In step 3, release of one molecule of G3P, you can see that for every three CO_2 molecules fixed, one G3P molecule leaves the cycle as product. In step 4, regeneration of RuBP, the remaining five G3P molecules are rearranged, using energy from ATP, to regenerate three molecules of RuBP.

For the synthesis of one G3P molecule, the Calvin cycle consumes nine ATP and six NADPH molecules, which were provided by the light reactions. Neither the light reactions nor the Calvin cycle alone can make sugar from CO_2. Photosynthesis is an emergent property of the structural organization of a chloroplast, which integrates the two stages of photosynthesis.

? **Explain why the large number of ATP and NADPH molecules used during the Calvin cycle is consistent with the value of glucose as an energy source.**

Glucose is a highly reduced molecule, storing lots of potential energy in its electrons. To reduce CO_2 to glucose, much energy and reducing power is required.

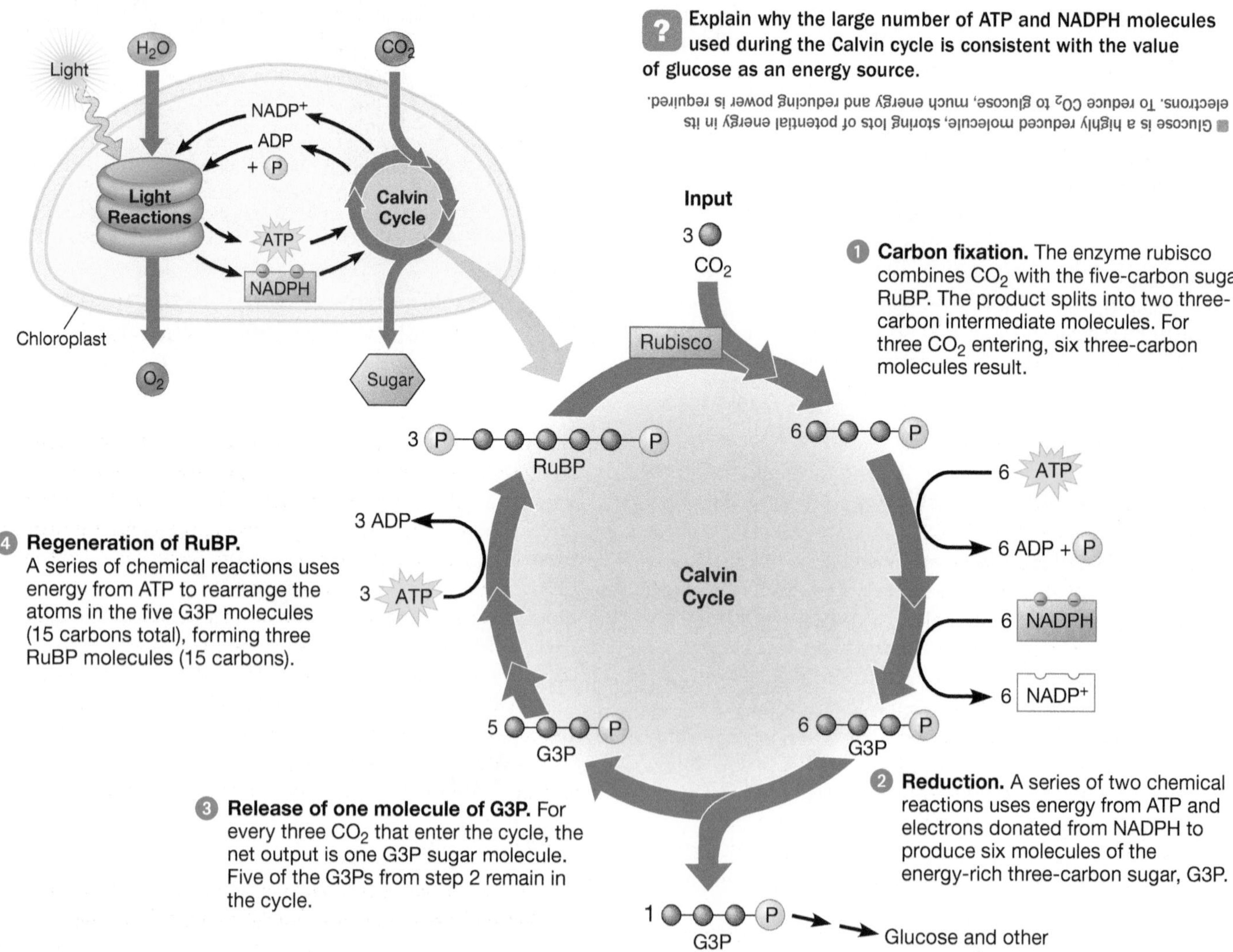

▲ **Figure 7.10** **Details of the Calvin cycle, which takes place in the stroma of a chloroplast**

7.11 Other methods of carbon fixation have evolved in hot, dry climates

EVOLUTION CONNECTION

As you learned in the previous module, the first step of the Calvin cycle is carbon fixation. Most plants use CO_2 directly from the air, and carbon fixation occurs when the enzyme rubisco adds CO_2 to RuBP (see step 1 of Figure 7.10). Such plants are called **C_3 plants** because the first stable product of carbon fixation is a three-carbon intermediate compound. C_3 plants are widely distributed; they include such important agricultural crops as soybeans, wheat, and rice. One problem that farmers face in growing C_3 plants is that hot, dry weather can decrease crop yield. In response to such conditions, plants close their stomata. This adaptation reduces water loss and helps prevent dehydration, but it also prevents CO_2 from entering the leaf and O_2 from exiting. As a result, CO_2 levels get very low in the leaf and photosynthesis slows. And the O_2 released from the light reactions begins to accumulate, creating another problem.

As O_2 builds up in a leaf, rubisco adds O_2 instead of CO_2 to RuBP. A two-carbon product of this reaction is then broken down in the cell. This process is called **photorespiration** because it occurs in the light (*photo*) and consumes O_2 and releases CO_2 (*respiration*). But unlike cellular respiration, it uses ATP instead of producing it; and unlike photosynthesis, it yields no sugar. Photorespiration can, in fact, drain away as much as 50% of the carbon fixed by the Calvin cycle.

According to one hypothesis, photorespiration is an evolutionary relic from when the atmosphere had less O_2 than it does today. In the ancient atmosphere that prevailed when rubisco first evolved, the ability of the enzyme's active site to bind O_2 as well as CO_2 would have made little difference. It is only after O_2 became so concentrated in the atmosphere that the "sloppiness" of rubisco presented a problem. There is also some evidence that photorespiration may play a protective role when the products of the light reactions build up in a cell (as occurs when the Calvin cycle slows due to a lack of CO_2).

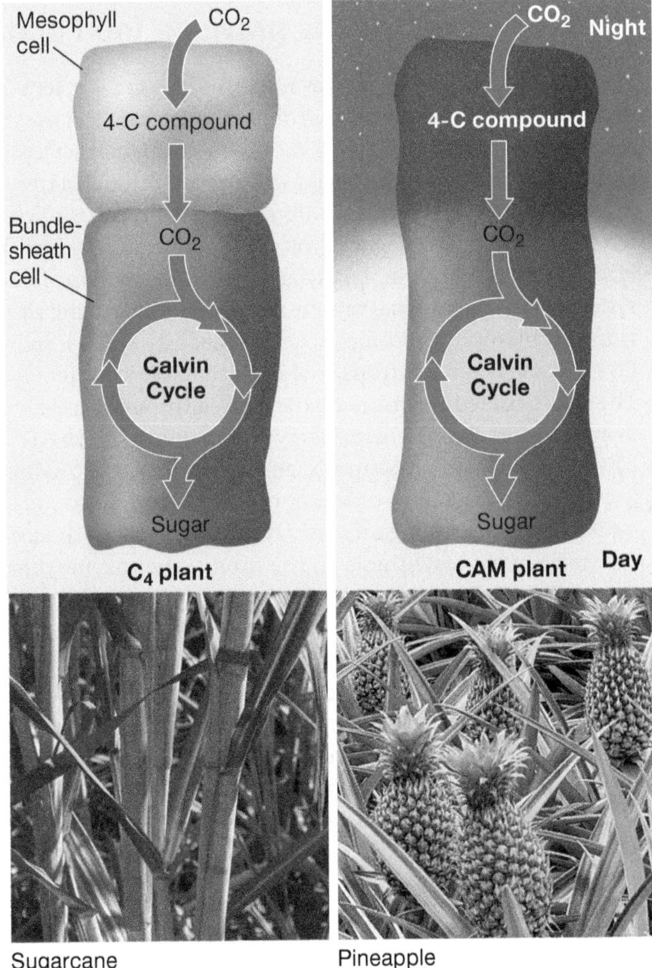

▲ **Figure 7.11** Adaptations for photosynthesis in hot, dry climates

TRY THIS Use these diagrams to explain the differences between C_4 and CAM photosynthesis.

C_4 Plants In some plant species found in hot, dry climates, alternate modes of carbon fixation have evolved that minimize photorespiration and optimize the Calvin cycle. **C_4 plants** are so named because they first fix CO_2 into a four-carbon compound. When the weather is hot and dry, a C_4 plant keeps its stomata mostly closed, thus conserving water. It continues making sugars by photosynthesis using the pathway and the two types of cells shown on the left side of Figure 7.11. An enzyme in the mesophyll cells has a high affinity for CO_2 and can fix carbon even when the CO_2 concentration in the leaf is low. The resulting four-carbon compound then acts as a CO_2 shuttle; it moves into bundle-sheath cells, which are packed around the veins of the leaf, and releases CO_2. Thus, the CO_2 concentration in these cells remains high enough for the Calvin cycle to make sugars and avoid photorespiration. Corn and sugarcane are examples of agriculturally important C_4 plants.

CAM Plants A second photosynthetic adaptation has evolved in pineapples, many cacti, and other succulent (water-storing) plants. Called **CAM plants**, these species are adapted to very dry climates. A CAM plant (right side of Figure 7.11) conserves water by opening its stomata and admitting CO_2 only at night. CO_2 is fixed into a four-carbon compound, which banks CO_2 at night and releases it during the day. Thus, the Calvin cycle can operate, even with the leaf's stomata closed during the day.

In C_4 plants, carbon fixation and the Calvin cycle occur in different types of cells. In CAM plants, these processes occur in the same cells, but at different times of the day. Keep in mind that CAM, C_4, and C_3 plants all eventually use the Calvin cycle to make sugar from CO_2. The C_4 and CAM pathways are two evolutionary adaptations that minimize photorespiration and maximize photosynthesis in hot, dry climates.

? Why would you expect photorespiration on a hot, dry day to occur less in C_4 and CAM plants than in C_3 plants?

■ Because of their initial fixing of carbon, both C_4 and CAM plants can supply rubisco with CO_2. When a C_3 plant closes its stomata, CO_2 levels drop and O_2 rises, making it more likely that rubisco will add O_2 to RuBP.

The Global Significance of Photosynthesis

7.12 Photosynthesis provides food and O_2 for almost all living organisms

Now that we have made our way from photons to food, let's step back and review the process of photosynthesis and then discuss its importance. Figure 7.12 shows the main reactants and products of photosynthesis as they move through a tree, a leaf, a leaf cell, and finally a chloroplast. Starting on the left of the chloroplast diagram, you see a summary of the light reactions, which occur in the thylakoid membranes. Two photosystems in the membranes capture solar energy, energizing electrons in chlorophyll molecules. Simultaneously, water is split, O_2 is released, and electrons are funneled to photosystem II. The photoexcited electrons are transferred through an electron transport chain, where energy is harvested to make ATP by the process of chemiosmosis, and finally to $NADP^+$, reducing it to the high-energy compound NADPH.

The chloroplast's sugar factory is the Calvin cycle, the second stage of photosynthesis. In the stroma, the enzyme rubisco combines CO_2 with RuBP. ATP and NADPH are used to reduce a three-carbon intermediate to G3P. Sugar molecules made from G3P serve as a plant's food supply.

About 50% of the carbohydrate made by photosynthesis is consumed as fuel for cellular respiration in the mitochondria of plant cells. Sugars also serve as starting material for making other organic molecules, such as a plant's proteins and lipids. Most plants make much more food each day than they need and store the excess as starch, a polymer of glucose. Glucose molecules are also linked together to make cellulose, the main component of cell walls. Cellulose is the most abundant organic molecule in a plant—and probably on the surface of the planet.

Plants (and other photosynthesizers) not only feed themselves but also are the ultimate source of food for virtually all other organisms. Humans and other animals make none of their own food and are totally dependent on the organic matter made by photosynthesizers. Even the energy we acquire when we eat meat was originally captured by photosynthesis. The energy in a steak, for instance, came from sunlight that was converted to a chemical form in the grasses eaten by cattle.

The products of photosynthesis provide us with more than just food. For most of human history, burning plant material has been a major source of heat, light, and cooking fuel. The use of fossil fuels is a relatively recent development, and these sources of energy come from the remains of organisms that had removed CO_2 from the atmosphere by photosynthesis over hundreds of millions of years. The burning of these ancient carbon stores is increasing the atmospheric level of CO_2, which has risen more than 45% since 1850, the start of the Industrial Revolution. In the next module, we explore how scientists study the effects of these rising CO_2 levels on plants.

? Explain this statement: No process is more important to the welfare of life on Earth than photosynthesis.

■ Photosynthesis is the ultimate source of the food for almost all organisms and the O_2 they need for cellular respiration.

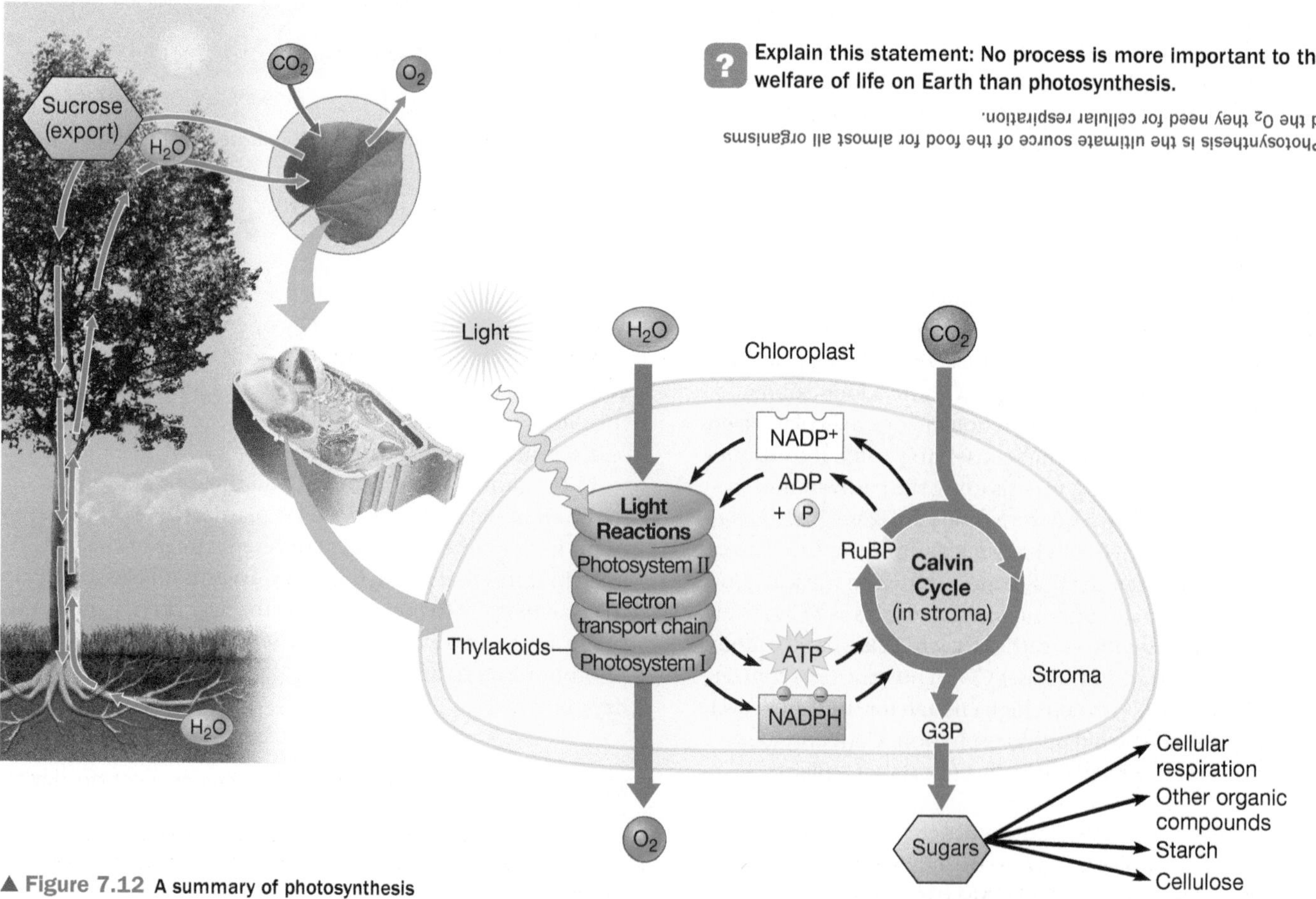

▲ **Figure 7.12** A summary of photosynthesis

7.13 Rising atmospheric levels of carbon dioxide may affect plants in various ways

SCIENTIFIC THINKING

How may increasing atmospheric levels of CO_2 affect plants? You might predict that, as a raw material for photosynthesis, increasing CO_2 levels would increase plant productivity. Indeed, research has documented such an increase, although results often indicate that the growth rates of weeds, such as the poison ivy described in the chapter introduction, increase more than those of crop plants and trees.

How do scientists study the effects of increasing CO_2 on plants? As is so often the case, scientists use different types of experiments to test their hypotheses. Many experiments are done in small growth chambers in which variables can be carefully controlled. But the availability of facilities and resources often limits such studies in scope and length. Some creative researchers have made use of study areas that naturally vary in CO_2 levels, such as comparing plant diversity and growth in experimental plots set in urban, suburban, and country locations.

Other scientists are turning to long-term field studies that include large-scale manipulations of CO_2 levels. In the Free-Air CO_2 Enrichment (FACE) experiment set up in Duke University's experimental forest, scientists monitored the effects of elevated CO_2 levels on an intact forest ecosystem over a period of 15 years. Six study sites were established, each 30 m in diameter and ringed by 16 towers (**Figure 7.13A**). In three of the plots, the towers released air containing CO_2 concentrations about 1½ times present-day levels. Monitoring instruments on a tall tower in the center of each plot adjusted the distribution of CO_2 to maintain a stable concentration. All other factors, such as temperature, precipitation, and wind patterns, varied normally for both experimental plots and adjacent control plots.

Figure 7.13B shows some results from a study that compared the growth of poison ivy in experimental and control plots. The poison ivy in the elevated CO_2 plots showed an average annual growth increase of 149% compared with control plots. This increase is much greater than the increase for woody plants that similar studies have documented. Indeed, over a 12-year monitoring period, the trees in the FACE experimental plots showed only about a 15% yearly increase in biomass compared with those in the control plots.

Will increasing atmospheric CO_2 make you itch?

There was one other significant finding of the poison ivy study. A chemical analysis showed that the high-CO_2 plants produced a more potent form of poison ivy's allergenic compound, urushiol. Thus, poison ivy is predicted to become both more abundant and more toxic ("itchy") as atmospheric CO_2 levels rise.

Next we explore the link between rising atmospheric CO_2 levels and changes in the global climate, and the role that photosynthesis may play in moderating those effects.

? **A key characteristic of science is the use of multiple lines of evidence in the testing of hypotheses. Describe three research methods that scientists use to test the hypothesis that increasing CO_2 levels will affect the growth of plants.**

■ Laboratory growth chambers, field studies in areas where CO_2 levels vary naturally, and large-scale field studies in which CO_2 levels are manipulated

▲ **Figure 7.13A Large-scale experiment in the Duke University Experimental Forest on the effects of elevated CO_2 concentration**

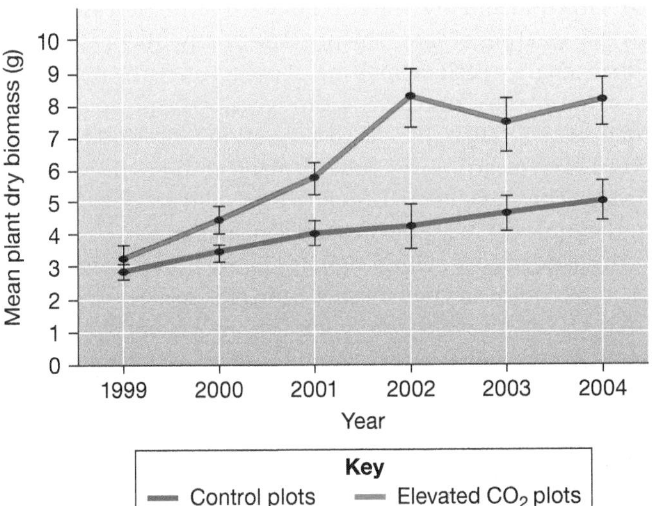

Source: Adaptation of Figure 1A from "Biomass and toxicity responses of poison ivy (*Toxicodendron radicans*) to elevated atmospheric CO_2," by Jacqueline E. Mohan, et al., from PNAS, June 2006, Volume 103(24). National Academy of Sciences.

▲ **Figure 7.13B The mean poison ivy biomass in control plots and elevated CO_2 plots (with error bars showing the variation around the mean)**

7.14 Reducing both fossil fuel use and deforestation may moderate climate change

CONNECTION How is the increase in atmospheric carbon dioxide affecting Earth's climate? First, let's consider the role of CO_2 as a so-called greenhouse gas. As you probably know, greenhouses are used to grow plants when the weather outside is too cold. Solar radiation can pass through their transparent walls, and much of the heat that accumulates inside is trapped.

An analogous process, called the **greenhouse effect**, operates on a global scale (Figure 7.14A). Solar radiation passes through the atmosphere and warms Earth's surface. Heat radiating from the warmed planet is absorbed by greenhouse gases, such as CO_2, water vapor, and methane, which then reflect some of the heat back to Earth. Without this natural heating effect, the average air temperature would be a frigid −18°C (−0.4°F), and most life as we know it could not exist. But this insulating blanket of greenhouse gases is starting to warm Earth *too* much. Scientists calculate that the CO_2 released by human activities has increased the average temperature of the planet by about 1°C (1.8°F) since 1900. Global models predict this temperature increase to continue at an ever-increasing rate unless actions are taken to reduce emissions of greenhouse gases.

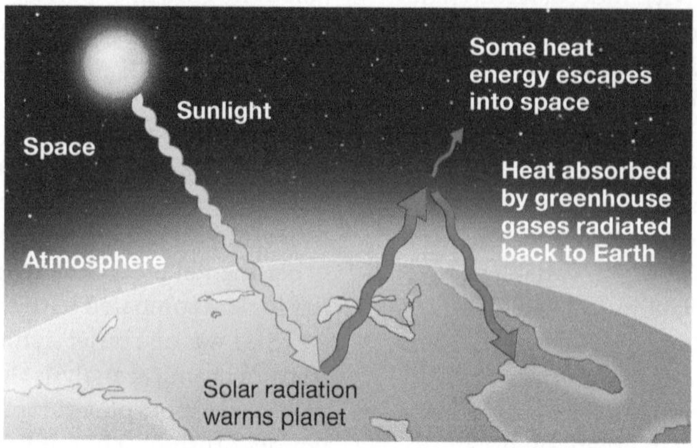

▲ Figure 7.14A The greenhouse effect

This ongoing global warming is a major aspect of **climate change**, a long-term directional change to the global climate that lasts for three decades or more (as opposed to short-term changes in the weather). But climate change also includes shifts in wind and precipitation patterns and increases in extreme weather events. The predicted consequences of climate change include melting of polar ice, rising sea levels, extreme weather patterns, droughts, widespread food and water shortages, increased extinction rates, and the spread of tropical diseases. Indeed, many of these effects are already being documented. (We'll discuss climate change and its consequences in greater detail in Chapter 38.)

The basic science behind climate change is well established, and scientists have been warning for decades that strong action is needed to limit greenhouse gas emissions. After more than 20 years of meetings and negotiations, the 2015 United Nations Climate Change Conference in Paris produced an agreement among 195 countries to limit global warming by the year 2100 to less than 2°C (3.6°F). Nearly every country committed to lowering emissions, using such approaches as increasing energy efficiency and reducing energy use, as well as shifting away from the use of coal, oil, and gas as primary energy sources toward zero-carbon sources such as wind, solar, and nuclear power.

But the Paris climate accord also emphasized the role of forests in the global response to climate change. Deforestation, particularly in the tropics, accounts for about 10% of greenhouse gas emissions—about as much as all the cars and trucks in the world combined. The Paris agreement includes a monetary commitment to help developing countries conserve their forests through both law enforcement and economic development to entice people away from illegal logging and land clearing.

Photosynthesis, the subject of this chapter, can be thought of as both a cause and a potential solution to climate change. The burning of the fossil products of photosynthesis and the destruction of vast swaths of forests pour enormous quantities of CO_2 into the atmosphere. Leaving some fossil fuels untapped and protecting and expanding forests, whose photosynthesis sucks CO_2 out of the atmosphere and stores it in biomass, can help to mitigate climate change. Reduced deforestation would not only slow the buildup of greenhouse gases in our atmosphere but also sustain native forests and preserve biodiversity. More than half of the world's animal and plant species live in tropical forests. Figure 7.14B illustrates one such rich forest ecosystem that is in a protected reserve in Costa Rica.

▲ Figure 7.14B Rich biodiversity of tropical forest protected from deforestation in Monteverde Cloud Forest Reserve, Costa Rica

With environmental problems as serious as global warming, the scientific research is often complicated and the solutions complex. The connections between science, technology, and society, a major theme of this text, are exemplified by scientists studying climate change, engineers and businesses searching for creative solutions, and citizens and their governments seeking international cooperation and commitment.

? Explain the greenhouse effect.

■ Sunlight warms Earth's surface, which radiates heat to the atmosphere. CO_2 and other greenhouse gases absorb and radiate some heat back to Earth.

CHAPTER 7 REVIEW

For practice quizzes, BioFlix animations, MP3 tutorials, video tutors, and more study tools designed for this textbook, go to MasteringBiology™

REVIEWING THE CONCEPTS

An Introduction to Photosynthesis (7.1–7.5)

7.1 Photosynthesis fuels the biosphere. Plants, algae, and some photosynthetic protists and bacteria are photoautotrophs, the producers of food consumed by virtually all heterotrophic organisms.

7.2 Photosynthesis occurs in chloroplasts in plant cells. Chloroplasts are surrounded by a double membrane and contain stacks of thylakoids and a thick fluid called stroma.

7.3 Scientists traced the process of photosynthesis using isotopes. Experiments using both heavy and radioactive isotopes helped determine the details of the process of photosynthesis.

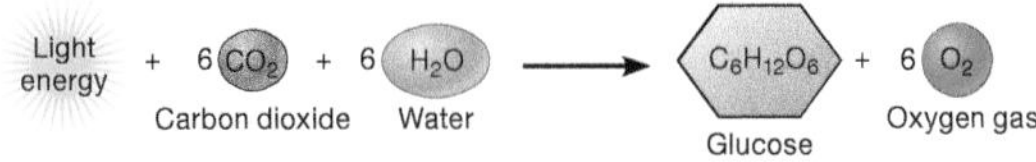

7.4 Photosynthesis is a redox process, as is cellular respiration. In photosynthesis, H_2O is oxidized and CO_2 is reduced.

7.5 Photosynthesis occurs in two stages, which are linked by ATP and NADPH. The light reactions occur in the thylakoids, producing ATP and NADPH for the Calvin cycle, which takes place in the stroma.

The Light Reactions: Converting Solar Energy to Chemical Energy (7.6–7.9)

7.6 Visible radiation absorbed by pigments drives the light reactions. Certain wavelengths of visible light are absorbed by chlorophyll and other pigments. Carotenoids also function in photoprotection from excessive light.

7.7 Photosystems capture solar energy. Thylakoid membranes contain photosystems, each consisting of light-harvesting complexes and a reaction-center complex. A primary electron acceptor receives photoexcited electrons from reaction-center chlorophyll *a*.

7.8 Two photosystems connected by an electron transport chain convert light energy to the chemical energy of ATP and NADPH. Electrons shuttle from photosystem II to photosystem I, providing energy to make ATP, and then reduce $NADP^+$ to NADPH. Photosystem II regains electrons as water is split and O_2 released.

7.9 The light reactions take place within the thylakoid membranes. In photophosphorylation, the electron transport chain pumps H^+ into the thylakoid space. The concentration gradient drives H^+ back through ATP synthase, powering the synthesis of ATP.

The Calvin Cycle: Reducing CO_2 to Sugar (7.10–7.11)

7.10 ATP and NADPH power sugar synthesis in the Calvin cycle. The steps of the Calvin cycle include carbon fixation, reduction, release of G3P, and regeneration of RuBP. Using carbon from CO_2, electrons from NADPH, and energy from ATP, the cycle constructs G3P, which is used to build glucose and other organic molecules.

7.11 Other methods of carbon fixation have evolved in hot, dry climates. In C_3 plants, a drop in CO_2 and rise in O_2 when stomata close divert the Calvin cycle to photorespiration. C_4 plants and CAM plants first fix CO_2 into four-carbon compounds that provide CO_2 to the Calvin cycle even when stomata close on hot, dry days.

The Global Significance of Photosynthesis (7.12–7.14)

7.12 Photosynthesis provides food and O_2 for almost all living organisms.

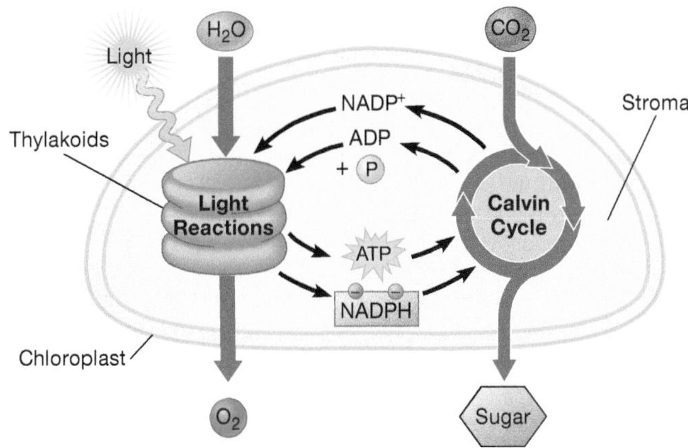

7.13 Rising atmospheric levels of carbon dioxide may affect plants in various ways. Scientists study the effects of rising CO_2 levels using laboratory growth chambers and field studies. Long-term field projects enable scientists to assess the effects of CO_2 levels on natural ecosystems.

7.14 Reducing both fossil fuel use and deforestation may moderate climate change. CO_2 and other gases in the atmosphere create the greenhouse effect. An international agreement reached at the Paris climate conference of 2015 seeks to reduce greenhouse gas emissions and limit global warming.

CONNECTING THE CONCEPTS

1. Complete this summary map of photosynthesis.

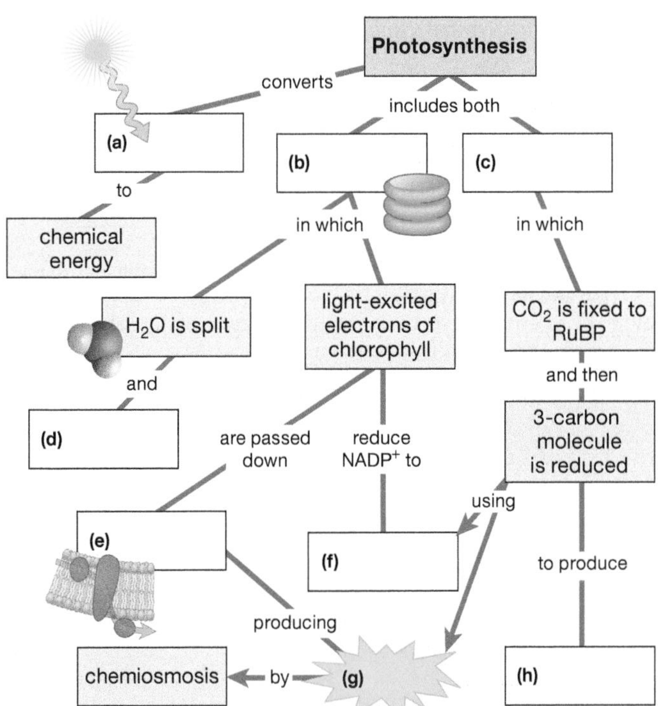

TESTING YOUR KNOWLEDGE

Level 1: Knowledge/Comprehension

2. In photosynthesis, ________ is oxidized and ________ is reduced.
   a. water . . . oxygen
   b. carbon dioxide . . . water
   c. water . . . carbon dioxide
   d. glucose . . . carbon dioxide
3. Which of the following are produced by reactions that take place in the thylakoids and consumed by reactions in the stroma?
   a. CO_2 and H_2O
   b. ATP and NADPH
   c. ATP, NADPH, and CO_2
   d. ATP, NADPH, and O_2
4. When light strikes chlorophyll molecules in the reaction-center complex, they lose electrons, which are ultimately replaced by
   a. splitting water.
   b. oxidizing NADPH.
   c. the primary electron acceptor.
   d. the electron transport chain.
5. The reactions of the Calvin cycle are not directly dependent on light, but they usually do not occur at night. Why? (*Explain your answer.*)
   a. It is often too cold at night for these reactions to take place.
   b. Carbon dioxide concentrations decrease at night.
   c. The Calvin cycle depends on products of the light reactions.
   d. Plants usually close their stomata at night.
6. Which of the following does *not* occur during the Calvin cycle?
   a. carbon fixation
   b. oxidation of NADPH
   c. consumption of ATP
   d. release of oxygen
7. Why is it difficult for C_3 plants to carry out photosynthesis in very hot, dry environments such as deserts?
   a. The light is too intense and destroys the pigment molecules.
   b. The closing of stomata keeps CO_2 from entering and O_2 from leaving the plant.
   c. They must rely on photorespiration to make ATP.
   d. CO_2 builds up in the leaves, blocking carbon fixation.

Level 2: Application/Analysis

8. How is photosynthesis similar in C_4 plants and CAM plants?
   a. In both cases, the light reactions and the Calvin cycle are separated in both time and location.
   b. Both types of plants make sugar without the Calvin cycle.
   c. In both cases, rubisco is not used to fix carbon initially.
   d. Both types of plants make most of their sugar in the dark.
9. To synthesize one glucose molecule, the Calvin cycle uses ________ molecules of CO_2, ________ molecules of ATP, and ________ molecules of NADPH.
10. Compare and describe the roles of CO_2 and H_2O in cellular respiration and photosynthesis.
11. Explain why a poison that inhibits an enzyme of the Calvin cycle will also inhibit the light reactions.
12. What do plants do with the sugar they produce in photosynthesis?

Level 3: Synthesis/Evaluation

13. Explain what is meant by saying the light reactions convert solar energy to chemical energy.
14. The following diagram compares the chemiosmotic synthesis of ATP in mitochondria and chloroplasts. Identify the components that are shared by both organelles and indicate which side of the membrane has the higher H^+ concentration. Then label on the right the locations within the chloroplast.

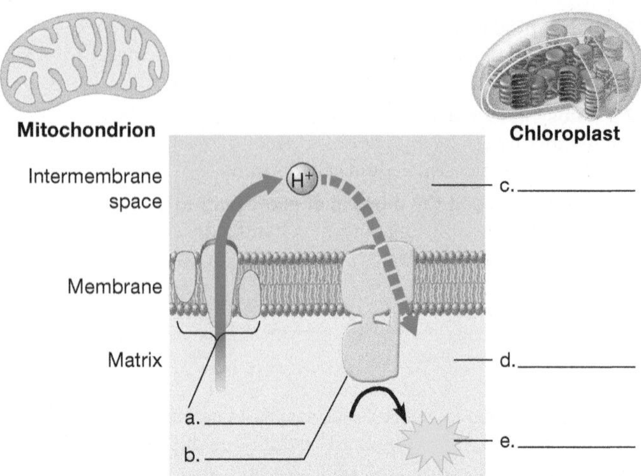

15. Continue your comparison of electron transport and chemiosmosis in mitochondria and chloroplasts. In each case,
    a. where do the electrons come from?
    b. how do the electrons get their high potential energy?
    c. what picks up the electrons at the end of the chain?
    d. how is the energy released as electrons are transferred down the electron transport chain used?
16. SCIENTIFIC THINKING Will increasing atmospheric levels of CO_2 make you sneeze as well as itch? Scientists studying the effects of rising CO_2 levels have looked at ragweed, whose pollen is the primary allergen for fall hay fever. They grew ragweed in three levels of CO_2: a pre-industrial concentration of 280 ppm, a year 2000 level of 370 ppm, and a projected level of 600 ppm. They found that pollen production increased by 131% and 320% in the plants exposed to the recent and projected CO_2 levels, respectively. What was the hypothesis of this experiment? Do the results support the hypothesis? Given what you know about climate change, what other variables would you like to test, and what other measurements would you like to take?
17. Most scientific experts agree that climate change is already occurring and has potentially catastrophic consequences for all of life on Earth. The Paris climate talks of 2015 have, for the first time, reached a global consensus on the need to reduce greenhouse gas emissions. Go online and research the main agreements reached in this historic global climate accord. What roles do you think scientists, politicians, and citizens will need to play to cut emissions and limit global warming?

Answers to all questions can be found in Appendix 4.

UNIT II Cellular Reproduction and Genetics

▲ Forensic Scientist

A forensic scientist collects tissue samples from a crime scene that will be analyzed via DNA profiling (see Module 12.11).

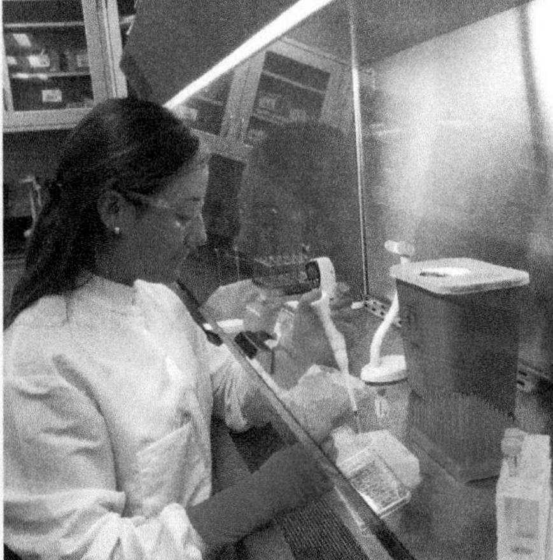

▲ **Microbiologist**

Samantha Dube, a microbiologist working at a pharmaceutical company, performs testing on a recombinant drug that helps patients living with hemophilia (see Module 12.1).

▲ **Medical Copywriter**

Ben Paramonte writes hospital brochures and content for pharmaceutical company websites (see Module 9.10).

CHAPTER 8

The Cellular Basis of Reproduction and Inheritance

Imagine a woman you care about received disturbing news: A routine mammogram (breast X-ray) revealed DCIS—ductal carcinoma in situ, also called stage 0 breast cancer. In DCIS, cancerous cells (such as those visible in the micrograph on the right) have not spread beyond the milk ducts of the breast. The cancer is therefore *in situ,* which means it remains "in the place" where it originated. She is now faced with a wide range of options, including a lumpectomy (surgical removal of part of a breast), single or double mastectomy (removal of most or all of one or both breasts), and radiation therapy.

Can cancer therapy be personalized?

Let's think about the underlying biology: What does it mean for cells to be cancerous? Cancer cells start as normal cells, but genetic mutations cause them to lose the ability to regulate their division. Like a car careening downhill with no brakes, unconstrained body cells will likely wreak havoc. Cancer cells divide and may spread, invading other tissues, disrupting organ function, and killing the host.

Mammograms uncover 60,000 cases of DCIS in the United States each year (almost all in women, but rarely in men). There is no consensus, however, about the best treatment after a diagnosis. Only patients with substantially higher risk should consider the most drastic measures, such as a mastectomy. How do patients decide which is the best treatment for them? Later in the chapter, we'll return to this question.

Although uncontrolled cell division is harmful, normal cell division is necessary in all forms of life. Some organisms, such as single-celled prokaryotes, reproduce themselves via cell division. In the bodies of all multicellular organisms, cell division allows for growth, replacement of damaged cells, and development of an embryo into an adult. In sexually reproducing organisms, eggs and sperm are produced by a particular type of cell division. In this chapter, we discuss the two main types of normal cell division—mitosis and meiosis—and explore how they function within organisms. Along the way, we'll consider the health consequences when those processes go awry.

BIG IDEAS

Cell Division and Reproduction (8.1–8.2)

Cell division is a key step in many of life's important processes.

The Eukaryotic Cell Cycle and Mitosis (8.3–8.10)

Cells produce genetic duplicates through an ordered, tightly controlled process.

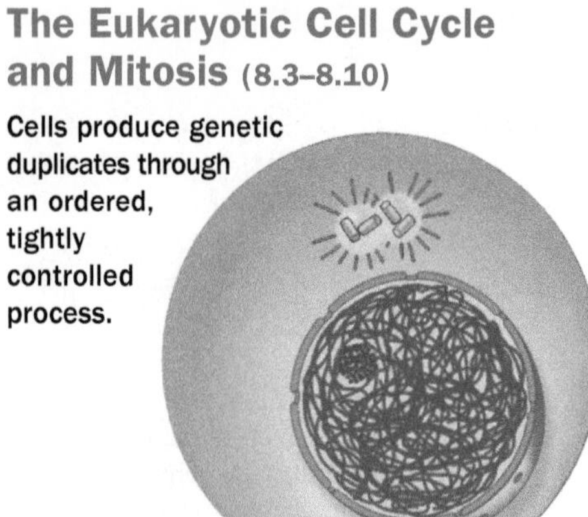

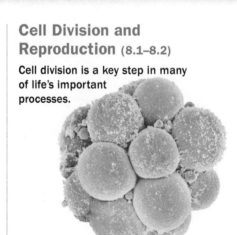

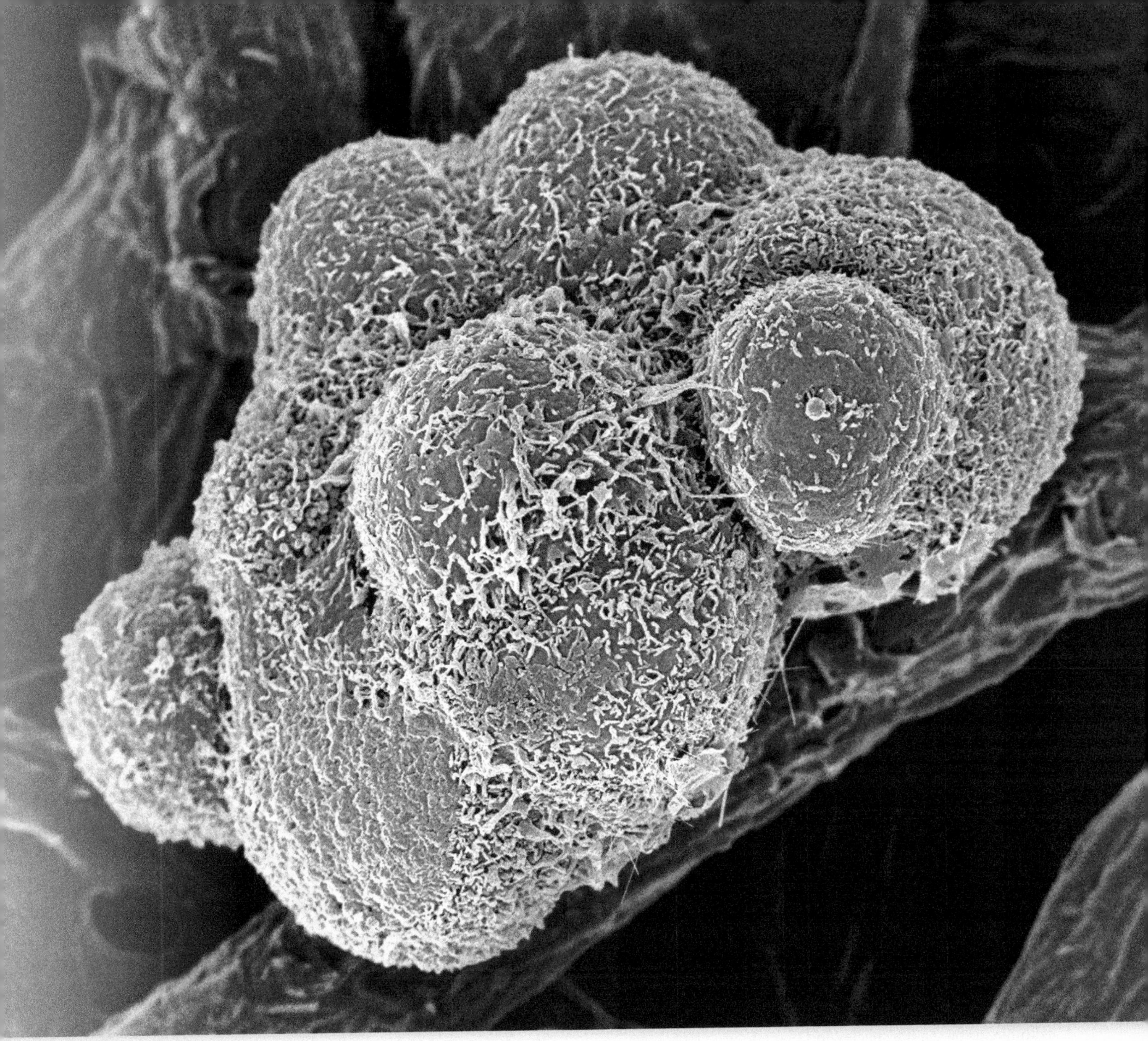

Meiosis and Crossing Over

(8.11–8.17)

The process of meiosis produces genetically varied haploid gametes from diploid cells.

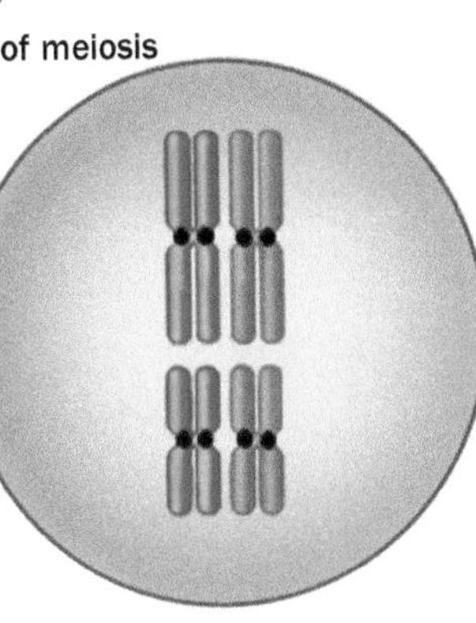

Alterations of Chromosome Number and Structure

(8.18–8.23)

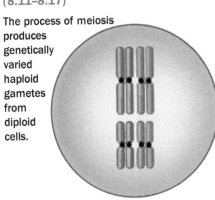

Errors in cell division can produce organisms with abnormal numbers of chromosomes.

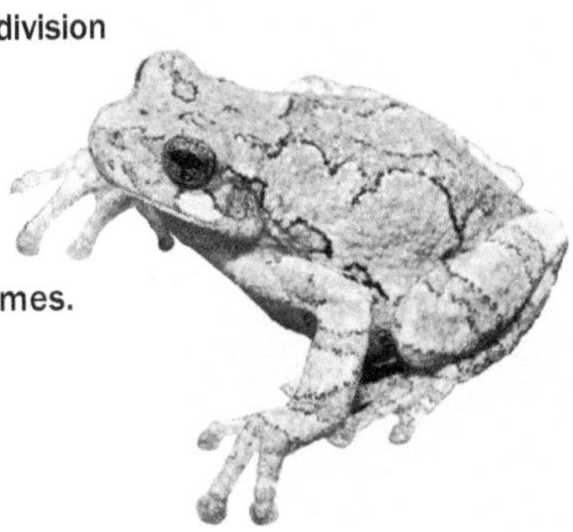

Cell Division and Reproduction

8.1 Cell division plays many important roles in the lives of organisms

The ability to transmit INFORMATION is one of the unifying themes that encompasses all levels of biological study. Such information flow is absolutely necessary for reproduction. Only people can make more people and only maple trees can make more maple trees because each species carries and transmits its own specific genetic information at the cellular level. When a cell undergoes reproduction, or **cell division**, the two "daughter" cells that result are genetically identical to each other and to the original "parent" cell. (Biologists traditionally use the word *daughter* in this context; it does not imply gender.) Before the parent cell splits into two, it duplicates its **chromosomes**, the structures that contain most of the cell's genetic information in the form of DNA. Then, during cell division, one set of chromosomes is distributed to each daughter cell. As a rule, the daughter cells receive identical sets of chromosomes from the lone, original parent cell. Each offspring cell will thus be genetically identical to the other and to the original parent cell.

Sometimes, cell division results in the reproduction of a whole organism. Many single-celled organisms, such as prokaryotes or the eukaryotic yeast cell in Figure 8.1A, reproduce by dividing in half, and the offspring are genetic replicas. This is an example of **asexual reproduction**, the creation of genetically identical offspring by a single parent, without the participation of sperm and egg. An individual that reproduces asexually gives rise to a **clone**, a group of genetically identical individuals. Many multicellular organisms can reproduce asexually to produce clones. For example, some sea star species and many house plants have the ability to grow new individuals from fragmented pieces (Figures 8.1B and 8.1C). In asexual reproduction, there is one simple principle of inheritance: The lone parent and each of its offspring have identical genes.

Colorized TEM 5,000×

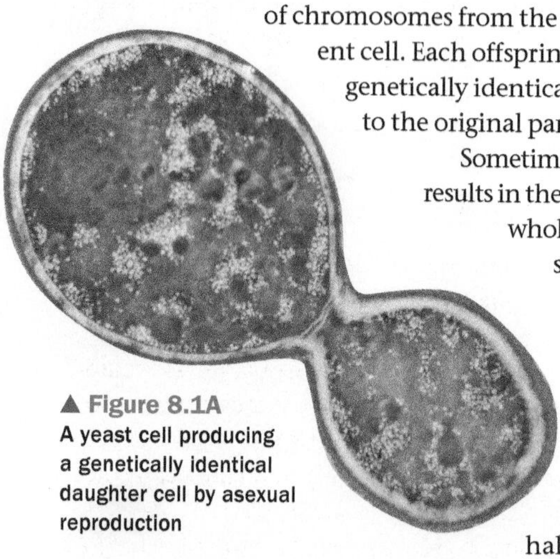

▲ **Figure 8.1A** A yeast cell producing a genetically identical daughter cell by asexual reproduction

▲ **Figure 8.1B** A sea star reproducing asexually via fragmentation and regeneration of the body from the fragmented arm

Sexual reproduction is different; it requires the fusion of gametes, egg and sperm. The production of gametes involves a particular type of cell division that occurs only in reproductive organs (testes and ovaries in humans). A gamete has only half as many chromosomes as the parent cell that gave rise to it, and these chromosomes contain unique combinations of genes. In contrast to a clone, offspring produced by sexual reproduction are not identical to their parents or to each other (with the exception of identical twins), although they generally resemble their parents more closely than they resemble unrelated individuals of the same species. They are variations on a common theme of family resemblance, not exact replicas (Figure 8.1D). Each offspring inherits a unique combination of genes from its two parents,

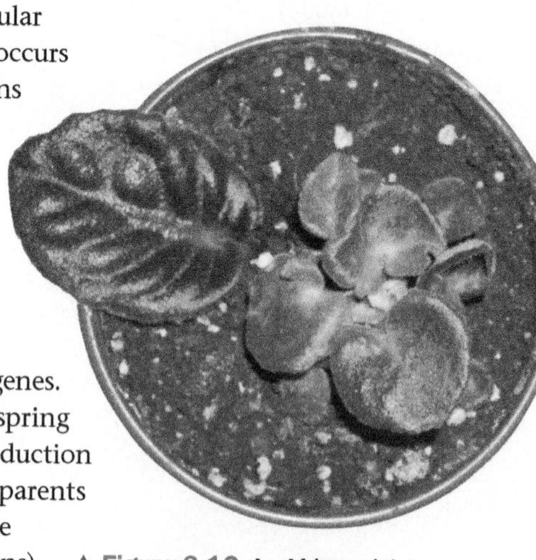

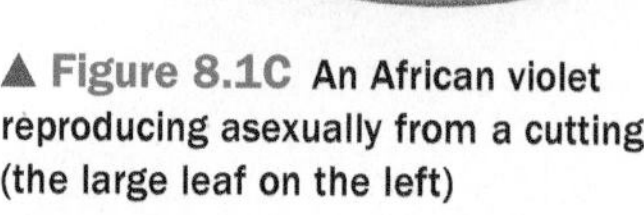

▲ **Figure 8.1C** An African violet reproducing asexually from a cutting (the large leaf on the left)

◀ **Figure 8.1D** Sexual reproduction produces offspring with unique combinations of genes

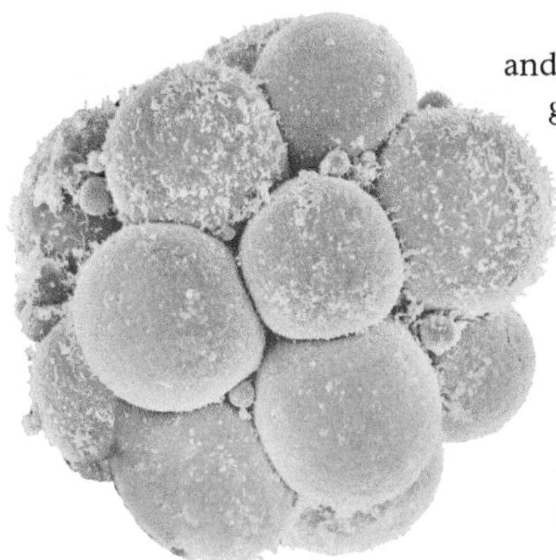

▲ **Figure 8.1E** Dividing cells in an early human embryo

and this one-and-only set of genes programs a unique combination of traits. As a result, sexual reproduction can produce great variation among offspring.

In addition to the production of gametes, cell division plays other important roles in multicellular organisms. Cell division enables sexually reproducing organisms to develop from a single cell—the fertilized egg, or zygote (Figure 8.1E)—into an adult organism. All of the trillions of cells in your body arose via repeated cell divisions that began in your mother's body with a single fertilized egg cell. After an organism is fully grown, cell division continues to function in renewal and repair, replacing cells that die from normal wear and tear or from accidents. Within your body, millions of cells must divide every second to replace damaged or lost cells (Figure 8.1F). For example, dividing cells within your epidermis continuously replace dead cells that slough off the surface of your skin.

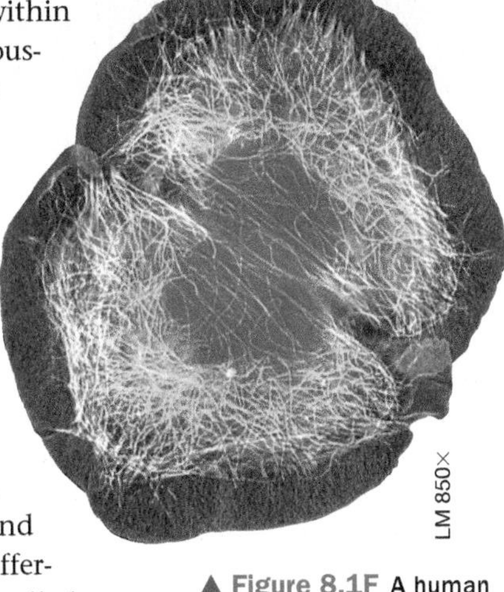

▲ **Figure 8.1F** A human kidney cell dividing

The type of cell division responsible for the growth and maintenance of multicellular organisms and for asexual reproduction involves a process called mitosis. The production of egg and sperm cells involves a different type of cell division called meiosis. In the remainder of this chapter, you will learn the details of both mitosis and meiosis. To start, we'll look briefly at prokaryotic cell division.

? **What function does cell division play in an amoeba (a single-celled protist)? What functions does it play in your body?**

■ Reproduction; development, growth, and repair

8.2 Prokaryotes reproduce by binary fission

Prokaryotes (single-celled bacteria and archaea) reproduce by a type of cell division called **binary fission**, a term that means "dividing in half." In typical prokaryotes, most genes are carried on one circular DNA molecule that, with associated proteins, constitutes the organism's single chromosome.

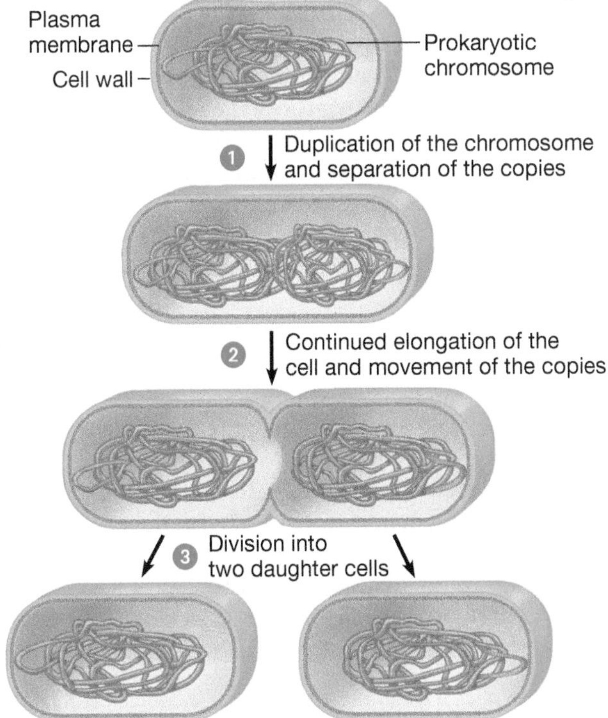

▲ **Figure 8.2A** Binary fission of a prokaryotic cell

Although prokaryotic chromosomes are generally much shorter than those of eukaryotes, duplicating them in an orderly fashion and distributing the copies equally to two daughter cells are still formidable tasks. Consider, for example, that when stretched out, the chromosome of the bacterium *Escherichia coli* (*E. coli*) is about 500 times longer than the cell itself. It is no small feat to accurately replicate this molecule when it is coiled and packed inside the cell.

Figure 8.2A illustrates binary fission in a prokaryote. ❶ As the chromosome is duplicating, one copy moves toward the opposite end of the cell. ❷ Meanwhile, the cell elongates. ❸ When chromosome duplication is complete and the cell has reached about twice its initial size, the plasma membrane pinches inward and more cell wall is made, which eventually divides the parent cell into two daughter cells (Figure 8.2B).

? **Why is binary fission classified as asexual reproduction?**

■ Because the genetically identical offspring inherit their DNA from a single parent

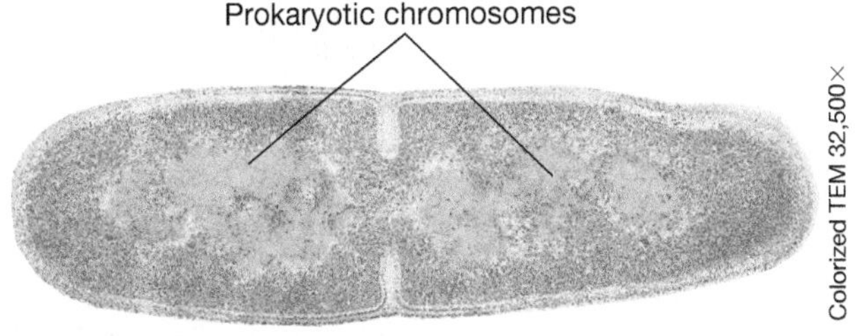

▲ **Figure 8.2B** An electron micrograph of a bacterium in a late stage of dividing

The Eukaryotic Cell Cycle and Mitosis

8.3 The large, complex chromosomes of eukaryotes duplicate with each cell division

Eukaryotic cells, in general, are more complex and much larger than prokaryotic cells. In addition, eukaryotic cells usually have many more genes, the units of information that specify an organism's inherited traits. Human cells, for example, carry just under 21,000 genes, versus about 3,000 for a typical bacterium. Almost all the genes in the cells of humans, and in all other eukaryotes, are found in the cell nucleus, grouped into multiple chromosomes. (The exceptions include genes on the small DNA molecules within mitochondria and, in plants, within chloroplasts.) Each eukaryotic species has a characteristic number of chromosomes in each cell nucleus. For example, human body cells have 46 chromosomes, while the body cells of a dog have 78 and those of a hedgehog have 90.

Each eukaryotic chromosome consists of one long DNA molecule—bearing hundreds or thousands of genes—and a number of protein molecules, which are attached to the DNA. The proteins help maintain the chromosome's structure and control the activity of its genes. Together, the entire complex—consisting of roughly equal amounts of DNA and protein—is called **chromatin**.

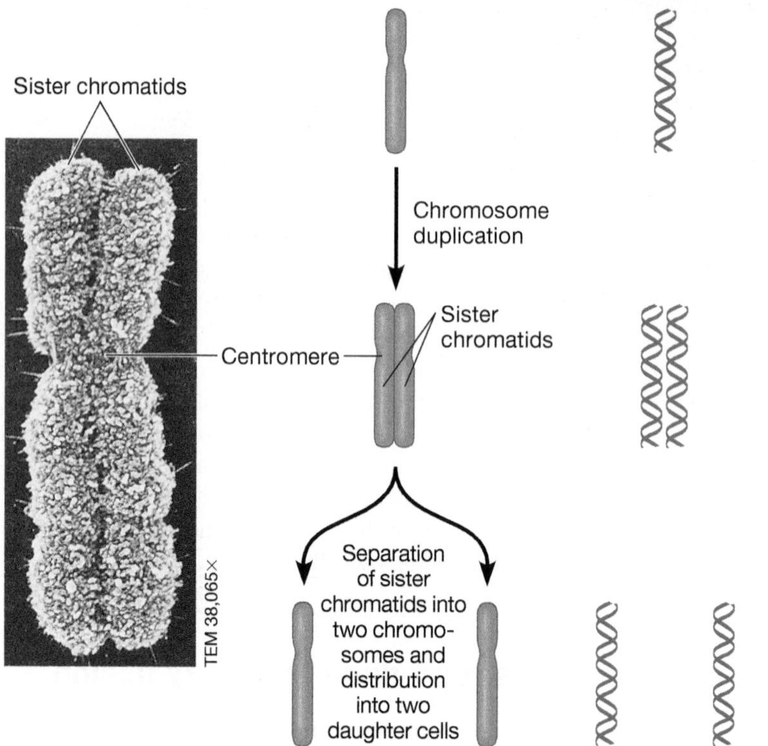

▲ **Figure 8.3B** **Chromosome duplication and distribution**

Most of the time, chromatin exists as a diffuse mass of long, thin fibers that, if stretched out, would be far too long to fit in a cell's nucleus. In fact, the total length of DNA in just one of your cells exceeds your height! Chromatin in this state is too thin to be seen using a light microscope.

As a cell prepares to divide, its chromatin coils up, forming tight, distinct chromosomes that are visible under a light microscope. Why is it necessary for a cell's chromosomes to be compacted in this way? Imagine that you have to move. Your belongings are spread throughout your home, but as you prepare to move, you gather them up and pack them into small containers to make them more easily sorted and transported. Similarly, before a cell can undergo division, it must compact all its DNA into manageable packages. Figure 8.3A shows a micrograph of a plant cell that is about to divide; each thick purple thread is actually an individual chromosome consisting of a single DNA molecule tightly wrapped around proteins.

▶ **Figure 8.3A** **A plant cell from an African blood lily (*Scadoxus multiflorus*) just before cell division**

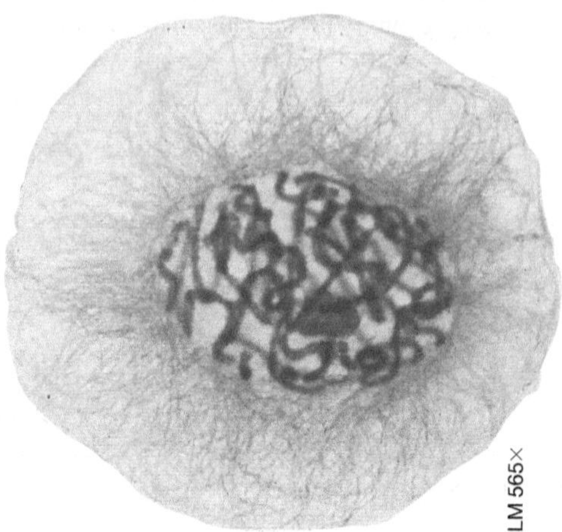

The chromosomes of a eukaryotic cell are duplicated before they condense and the cell divides. The DNA molecule of each chromosome is replicated (as you'll learn in Chapter 10), and new protein molecules attach as needed to maintain the chromosome's structure and regulate its genes. Each chromosome now consists of two copies called **sister chromatids**, joined copies of the original chromosome (Figure 8.3B). The two sister chromatids are attached together along their lengths by proteins, most closely at a region called the **centromere** (visible as a narrow "waist" near the center of each chromosome shown in the figure).

When the cell divides, the sister chromatids of a duplicated chromosome separate from each other. Once separated from its sister, each chromatid is considered an individual chromosome, and it is identical to the cell's original chromosome. During cell division, one of the newly separated chromosomes goes to one daughter cell and the other goes to the other daughter cell. In this way, each daughter cell receives a complete and identical set of chromosomes. In humans, for example, a typical dividing cell has 46 duplicated chromosomes (and thus 92 chromatids), and each of the two daughter cells that results from it has 46 single chromosomes.

? **When does a chromosome consist of two identical chromatids?**

■ When the cell is preparing to divide and has duplicated its chromosomes but before the duplicates actually separate

8.4 The cell cycle includes growth and division phases

How do chromosome duplication and cell division fit into the life of a cell and the life of an organism? As discussed in Module 8.1, all life depends on cell division: Cell division is the basis of reproduction for every organism; it enables a multicellular organism to grow to adult size; and it replaces worn-out or damaged cells. In your body, for example, millions of cells must divide every second to maintain the total number of about 200 trillion cells. Some cells divide once a day, others less often; and highly specialized cells, such as mature muscle and nerve cells, do not divide at all. The fact that some mature cells never divide explains why certain kinds of damage—such as the death of cardiac muscle during a heart attack or the death of brain cells during a stroke—can never be reversed.

The process of cell division is a key component of the **cell cycle**, an ordered sequence of events that run from the instant a cell is first formed from a dividing parent cell until its own division into two cells. The cell cycle consists of two main stages: a growing stage (called interphase), during which the cell approximately doubles everything in its cytoplasm and replicates its DNA, and the actual cell division (called the mitotic phase).

As Figure 8.4 indicates, most of the cell cycle is spent in **interphase**. During this time, the cell's metabolic activity is very high as it performs its normal functions. For example, a cell in your small intestine might release digestive enzymes and absorb nutrients. Your intestinal cell also grows in size during interphase, making more cytoplasm, increasing its supply of digestive proteins, and creating more cytoplasmic organelles such as mitochondria and ribosomes. In addition, the cell duplicates its chromosomes during this period. Typically, interphase lasts for at least 90% of the total time required for the cell cycle.

Interphase (illustrated in the beige portion of the figure) can be divided into three subphases: the G_1 phase ("first gap"), the S phase ("synthesis" of DNA—also known as DNA replication), and the G_2 phase ("second gap"). Calling the G phases "gaps" is a misnomer; cells are actually quite active and grow throughout all three subphases of interphase. The chromosomes are duplicated during the S phase, which typically lasts about half of interphase. At the beginning of the S phase, each chromosome is single. At the end of this subphase, after DNA replication, the chromosomes are doubled, each consisting of two sister chromatids joined along their lengths. During the G_2 phase, the cell completes preparations for cell division.

The **mitotic phase** (**M phase**; illustrated in the blue portion of the figure) is the interval of the cell cycle when the cell physically divides. Interphase accounts for only about 10% of the total time required for the cell cycle. The mitotic phase is divided into two overlapping stages, called mitosis and cytokinesis. In **mitosis**, the nucleus and its contents—most important, the duplicated chromosomes—divide and are distributed into two daughter nuclei. During **cytokinesis**, which usually begins before mitosis ends, the cytoplasm is

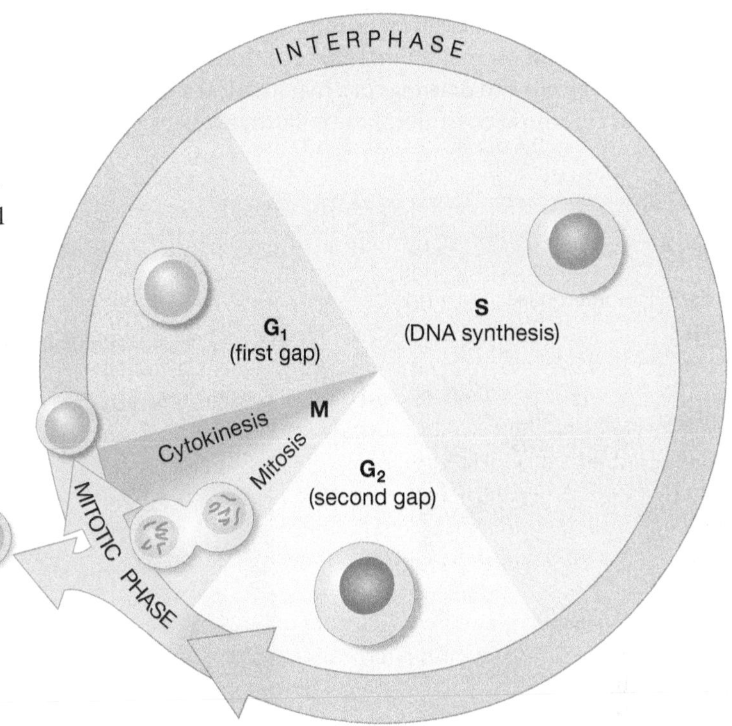

▲ Figure 8.4 The eukaryotic cell cycle. The relative size of each slice approximates the amount of time a typical human cell spends in that phase.

divided in two. The combination of mitosis and cytokinesis produces two genetically identical daughter cells, each with a single nucleus, surrounding cytoplasm stocked with organelles, and a plasma membrane. Each newly produced daughter cell may then proceed through G_1 and repeat the cycle.

Mitosis is unique to eukaryotes and is the evolutionary solution to the problem of allocating an identical copy of the whole set of chromosomes to two daughter cells. Mitosis is a remarkably accurate mechanism. Experiments with yeast, for example, indicate that an error in chromosome distribution occurs only once in about 100,000 cell divisions.

The extreme accuracy of mitosis is essential to the development of your own body. You began as a single cell. Mitotic cell division ensures that all your body cells receive copies of the 46 chromosomes that were found in this original cell. Thus, every one of the trillions of cells in your body today can trace its ancestry back through mitotic divisions to that first cell produced when your father's sperm and mother's egg fused about nine months before your birth.

During the mitotic phase, a living cell viewed through a light microscope undergoes dramatic changes in the appearance of the chromosomes and other structures. In the next module, we'll use these visible changes as a guide to the stages of mitosis.

? A researcher treats cells with a chemical that prevents DNA synthesis from starting. This treatment would trap the cells in which part of the cell cycle?

■ G_1 (printed upside down)

8.5 Cell division is a continuum of dynamic changes

Figure 8.5 illustrates the cell cycle using micrographs from a newt (with chromosomes stained blue and the mitotic spindle stained green) and drawings of a hypothetical animal cell with four chromosomes. Interphase is illustrated here, but the emphasis is on the dramatic changes that occur during cell division, the mitotic phase. Mitosis is a continuous process but biologists can distinguish five main stages: **prophase**, **prometaphase**, **metaphase**, **anaphase**, and **telophase**.

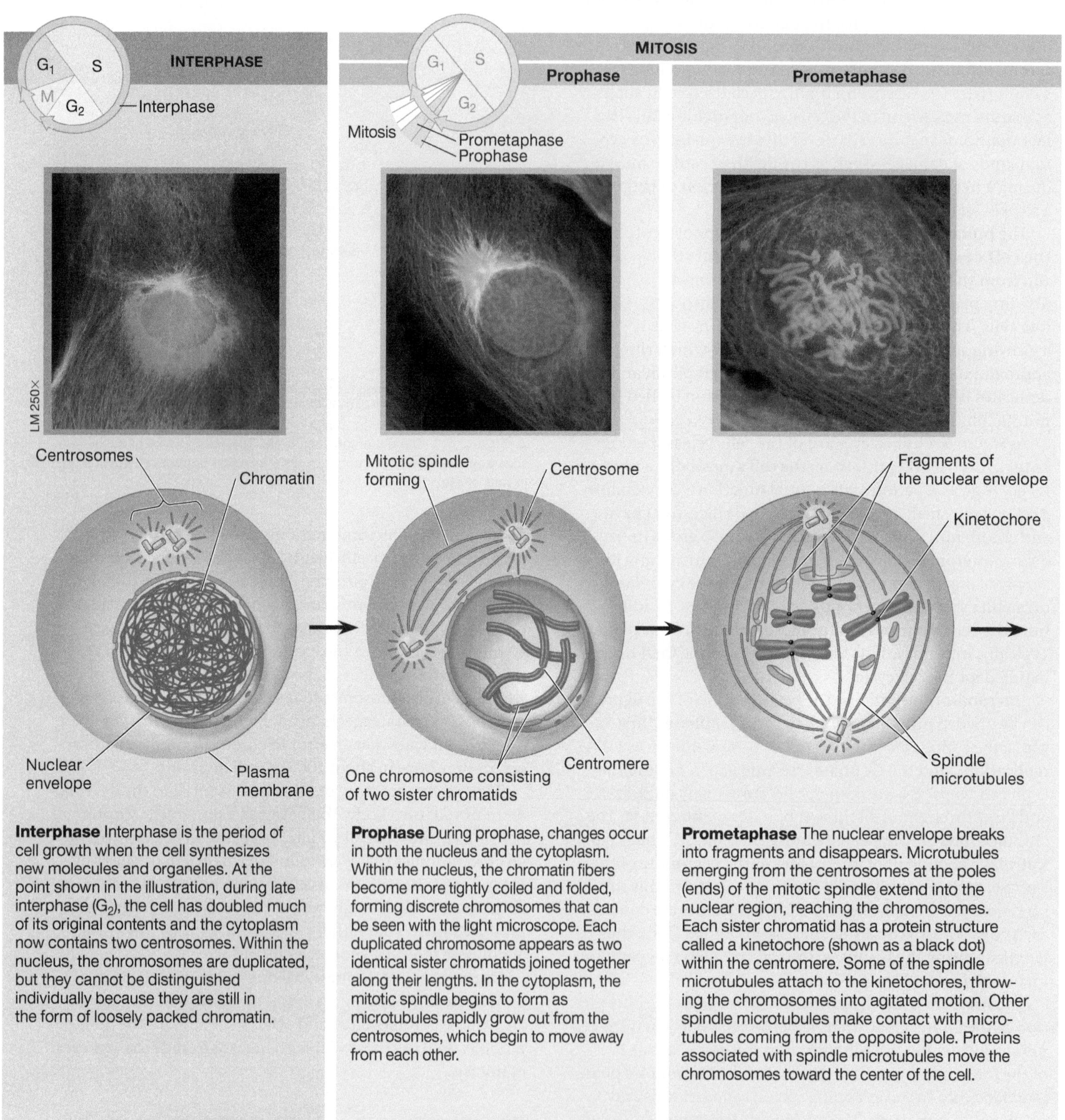

Interphase Interphase is the period of cell growth when the cell synthesizes new molecules and organelles. At the point shown in the illustration, during late interphase (G_2), the cell has doubled much of its original contents and the cytoplasm now contains two centrosomes. Within the nucleus, the chromosomes are duplicated, but they cannot be distinguished individually because they are still in the form of loosely packed chromatin.

Prophase During prophase, changes occur in both the nucleus and the cytoplasm. Within the nucleus, the chromatin fibers become more tightly coiled and folded, forming discrete chromosomes that can be seen with the light microscope. Each duplicated chromosome appears as two identical sister chromatids joined together along their lengths. In the cytoplasm, the mitotic spindle begins to form as microtubules rapidly grow out from the centrosomes, which begin to move away from each other.

Prometaphase The nuclear envelope breaks into fragments and disappears. Microtubules emerging from the centrosomes at the poles (ends) of the mitotic spindle extend into the nuclear region, reaching the chromosomes. Each sister chromatid has a protein structure called a kinetochore (shown as a black dot) within the centromere. Some of the spindle microtubules attach to the kinetochores, throwing the chromosomes into agitated motion. Other spindle microtubules make contact with microtubules coming from the opposite pole. Proteins associated with spindle microtubules move the chromosomes toward the center of the cell.

▲ **Figure 8.5** The stages of cell division by mitosis

TRY THIS Use simple drawings to illustrate the stages of mitosis for a cell that has six chromosomes.

The chromosomes are the stars of the mitotic dance. Their movements depend on the **mitotic spindle**, a football-shaped structure of microtubule fibers and associated proteins that guides the separation of the two sets of daughter chromosomes. The spindle microtubules emerge from two **centrosomes**, microtubule-organizing regions in the cytoplasm of eukaryotic cells.

? You view an animal cell through a microscope and observe dense, duplicated chromosomes scattered throughout the cell. Which state of mitosis are you witnessing?

Prophase (because the chromosomes are condensed but not yet aligned)

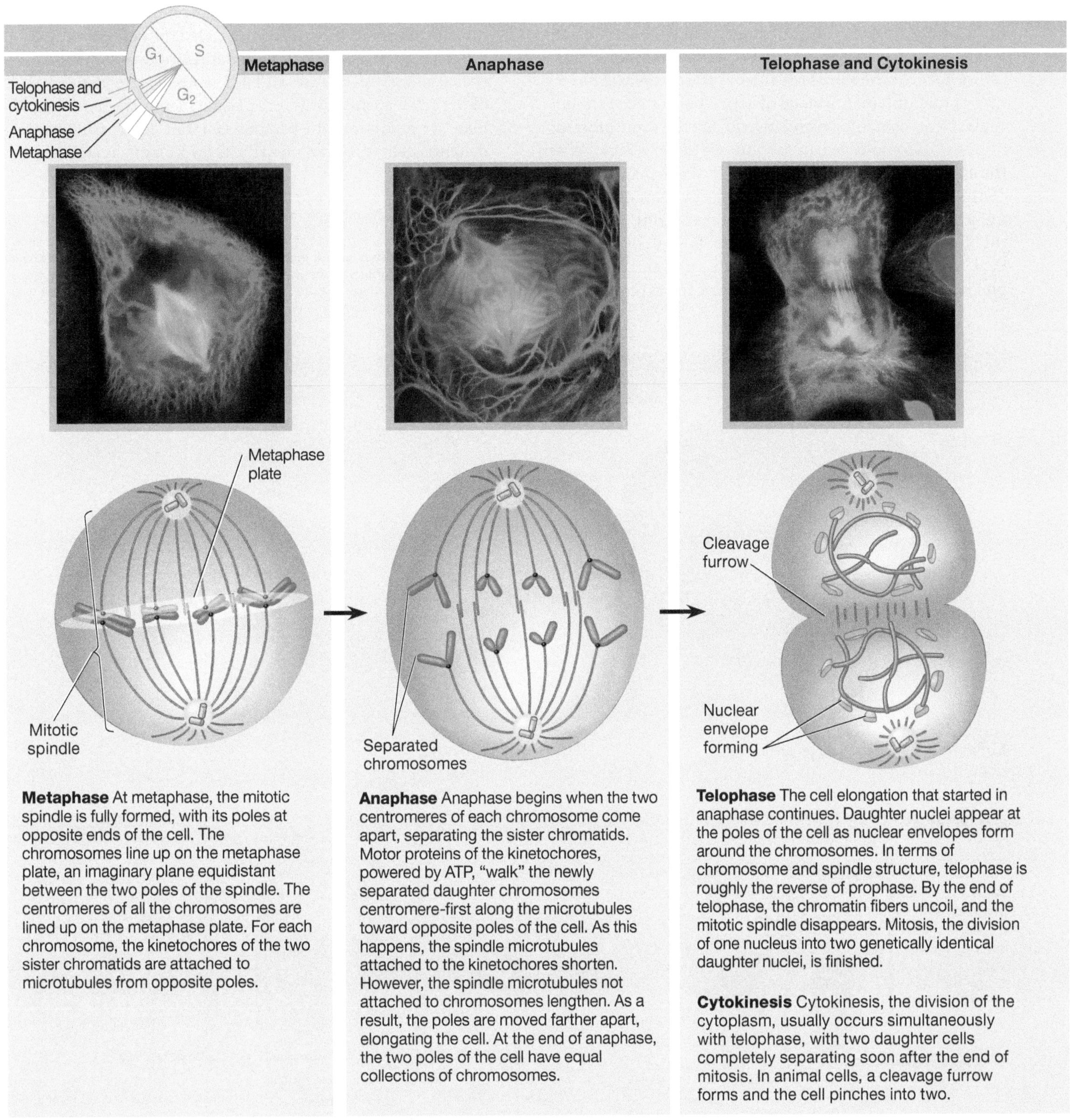

Metaphase At metaphase, the mitotic spindle is fully formed, with its poles at opposite ends of the cell. The chromosomes line up on the metaphase plate, an imaginary plane equidistant between the two poles of the spindle. The centromeres of all the chromosomes are lined up on the metaphase plate. For each chromosome, the kinetochores of the two sister chromatids are attached to microtubules from opposite poles.

Anaphase Anaphase begins when the two centromeres of each chromosome come apart, separating the sister chromatids. Motor proteins of the kinetochores, powered by ATP, "walk" the newly separated daughter chromosomes centromere-first along the microtubules toward opposite poles of the cell. As this happens, the spindle microtubules attached to the kinetochores shorten. However, the spindle microtubules not attached to chromosomes lengthen. As a result, the poles are moved farther apart, elongating the cell. At the end of anaphase, the two poles of the cell have equal collections of chromosomes.

Telophase The cell elongation that started in anaphase continues. Daughter nuclei appear at the poles of the cell as nuclear envelopes form around the chromosomes. In terms of chromosome and spindle structure, telophase is roughly the reverse of prophase. By the end of telophase, the chromatin fibers uncoil, and the mitotic spindle disappears. Mitosis, the division of one nucleus into two genetically identical daughter nuclei, is finished.

Cytokinesis Cytokinesis, the division of the cytoplasm, usually occurs simultaneously with telophase, with two daughter cells completely separating soon after the end of mitosis. In animal cells, a cleavage furrow forms and the cell pinches into two.

8.6 Cytokinesis differs for plant and animal cells

As discussed in the previous module, cytokinesis typically overlaps with telophase. Given the differences between plant and animal cells—particularly the stiff cell wall found in plant but not animal cells—it isn't surprising that cytokinesis proceeds differently for these two types of eukaryotic cells.

In animal cells, cytokinesis occurs by **cleavage**. As shown in Figure 8.6A, the first sign of cleavage in animal cells is the appearance of a **cleavage furrow**, a shallow groove in the cell surface. At the site of the furrow, the cytoplasm has a ring of microfilaments made of actin, associated with molecules of myosin. (Actin and myosin are the same proteins responsible for muscle contraction; see Module 30.8.) When the actin microfilaments interact with the myosin, the ring contracts. Contraction of the myosin ring is much like pulling a drawstring on a hoodie: As the drawstring is pulled, the ring of the hood contracts inward, eventually pinching shut. Similarly, the cleavage furrow deepens and eventually pinches the parent cell in two, resulting in two completely separate daughter cells, each with its own nucleus and share of cytoplasm.

Cytokinesis is markedly different in plant cells, which possess stiff cell walls that prevent contraction (Figure 8.6B). During telophase, membranous vesicles containing cell wall material collect at the middle of the parent cell. The vesicles fuse, forming a membranous disk called the **cell plate**. The cell plate grows outward, accumulating more cell wall materials as more vesicles fuse with it. Eventually, the membrane of the cell plate fuses with the plasma membrane, and the cell plate's contents join the parental cell wall. The result is two daughter cells, each bounded by its own plasma membrane and cell wall.

Contrast cytokinesis in animals with cytokinesis in plants.

In animals, cytokinesis involves a cleavage furrow in which contracting microfilaments pinch the cell in two. In plants, it involves formation of a cell plate, a fusion of vesicles that forms new plasma membranes and new cell walls between the cells.

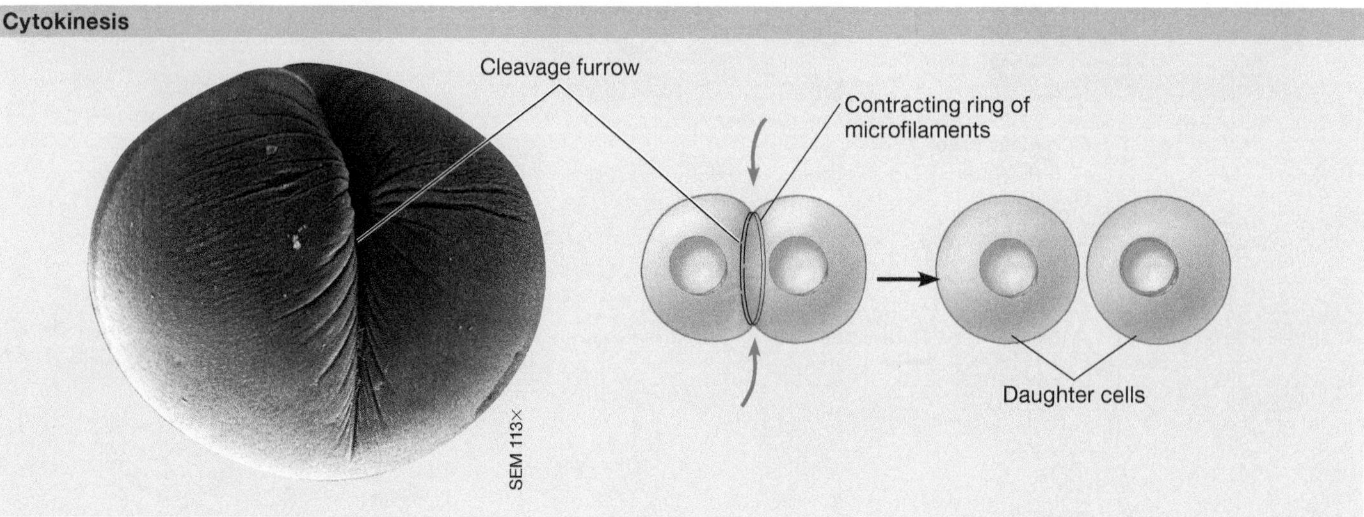

▲ **Figure 8.6A** Cleavage of an animal cell

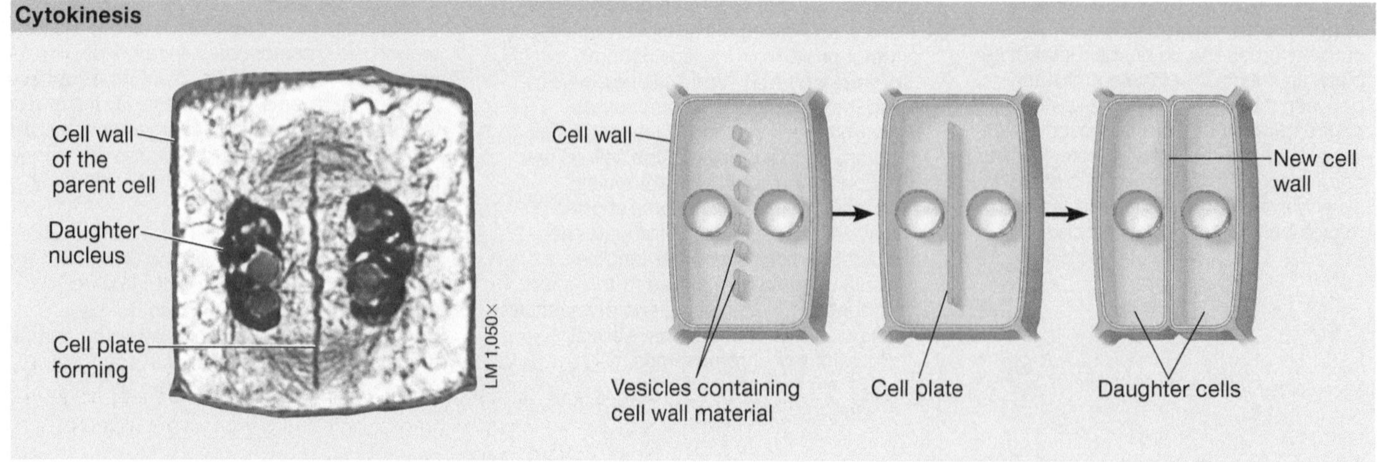

▲ **Figure 8.6B** Cell plate formation in a plant cell

8.7 The rate of cell division is affected by environmental factors

For a plant or an animal to grow, develop normally, and maintain its tissues once fully grown, the timing of cell division in different parts of its body must be carefully controlled. For example, your skin cells and the cells lining your digestive tract divide frequently, replacing cells that are constantly being abraded and sloughed off. In contrast, cells in your liver usually do not divide unless the liver is damaged. Other cells, such as your muscle cells, never divide.

By growing animal cells in culture—that is, in a laboratory growth medium, outside of the body—researchers have been able to identify many factors, both chemical and physical, that influence cell division. For example, most animal cells exhibit **anchorage dependence**; they must be in contact with a solid surface—such as the inside of a culture dish or the extracellular matrix of a tissue—to divide. Another physical factor that can regulate growth rate is **density-dependent inhibition**, a phenomenon in which crowded cells stop dividing (Figure 8.7A). Animal cells growing on the surface of a dish multiply to form a single layer and usually stop dividing when they touch one another. If some cells are removed, those bordering the open space begin dividing again and continue until the vacancy is filled. What actually causes the inhibition of growth? Studies of cultured cells suggest that physical contact of cell-surface proteins between adjacent cells is responsible for inhibiting cell division.

Chemical factors can also influence the rate of cell growth. For example, when grown in the laboratory, cells fail to divide if an essential nutrient is left out of the culture medium. Additionally, most types of mammalian cells will divide only if certain proteins, called **growth factors**, are present (Figure 8.7B). Dozens of different growth factors have been discovered, and different cell types respond only to certain growth factors or a certain combination of growth factors. For example, a protein called vascular endothelial growth factor (VEGF) stimulates the growth of new blood vessels during fetal development and after injury.

The importance of proper cell division to your own health becomes clear when you consider what happens if control is lost. Cancerous cells are different from normal body cells because they no longer exhibit the types of regulation discussed here. For example, cancer cells are not subject to anchorage dependence; they grow whether or not they are in contact with a suitable surface. Additionally, density-dependent inhibition fails in tumors; cancer cells continue to divide even at high densities, piling up on one another (bottom of Figure 8.7A). It is interesting to note that overproduction of VEGF is a hallmark of many dangerous cancers; several anticancer drug therapies work by inhibiting the action of VEGF. How do growth factors work? We will explore this question in the next module.

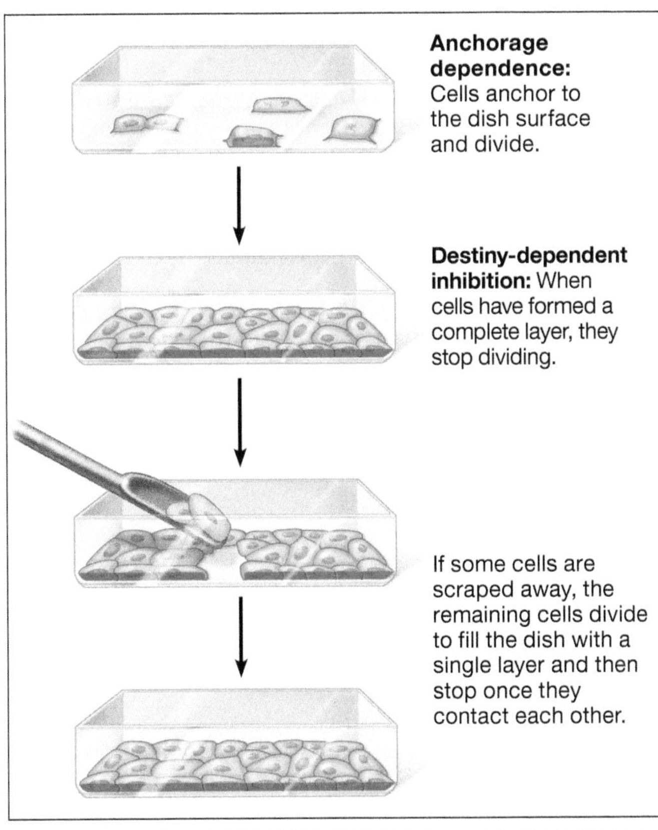

Anchorage dependence: Cells anchor to the dish surface and divide.
Destiny-dependent inhibition: When cells have formed a complete layer, they stop dividing.
If some cells are scraped away, the remaining cells divide to fill the dish with a single layer and then stop once they contact each other.

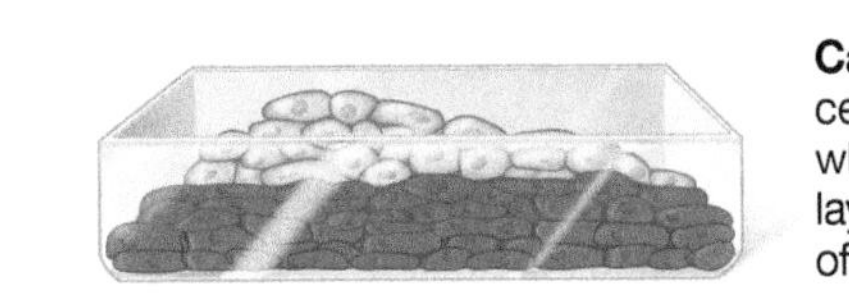

Cancer cells: Tumor cells keep dividing even when they have filled a layer, forming a clump of overlapping cells.

▲ **Figure 8.7A** An experiment demonstrating density-dependent inhibition, using animal cells grown in culture

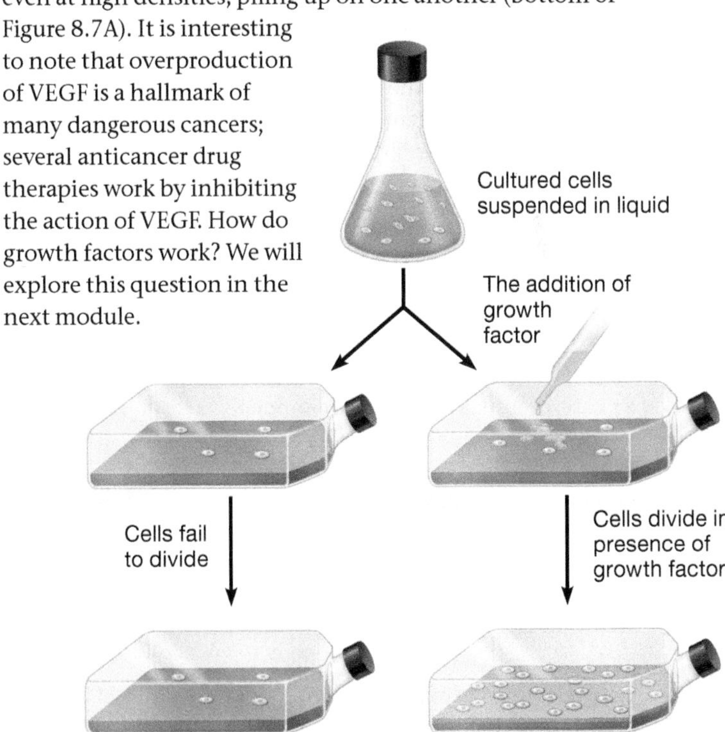

▲ **Figure 8.7B** An experiment demonstrating the effect of growth factors on the division of cultured animal cells

? **Compared with a control culture, the cells in an experimental culture are fewer but much larger in size when they cover the dish surface and stop growing. What is a reasonable hypothesis for this difference?**

■ The experimental culture is deficient in one or more growth factors.

8.8 Growth factors signal the cell cycle control system

The reproductive behavior of cells—whether to divide or not—results from INTERACTIONS among many different molecules. In a living animal, most cells are anchored in a fixed position and bathed in a solution of nutrients supplied by the blood, yet they usually do not divide unless they are signaled by other cells to do so. Growth factors are the main signals, and their role in promoting cell division leads us back to our earlier discussion of the cell cycle.

The sequential events of the cell cycle, shown in Figure 8.8A, are directed by a distinct cell cycle control system, represented by the gray circle in the center of the art. The thin gray bar extending from the circle represents the current position in the cell cycle. The **cell cycle control system** is a set of molecules that both triggers and coordinates key events in the cell cycle. The cell cycle is *not* like a row of falling dominoes, with each event causing the next one in line. During mitosis, for example, metaphase does not automatically lead to anaphase. Instead, proteins of the cell cycle control system must trigger anaphase to begin.

A checkpoint in the cell cycle is a critical control point where stop and go-ahead signals (represented by red/green traffic signals in the figure) can regulate the cycle. The default action in most animal cells is to halt the cell cycle at these checkpoints unless overridden by specific go-ahead signals in the form of growth factor proteins.

The red and white gates in Figure 8.8A represent major checkpoints in the cell cycle: during the G_1 and G_2 subphases of interphase and in the M phase. Intracellular signals detected by the control system tell the system whether key cellular processes up to each point have been completed and therefore whether the cell cycle should proceed past that point. The control system also receives messages from outside the cell, such as the general environmental conditions and the presence of growth factors. For many cells, the G_1 checkpoint is the most important one during cell division. If a cell receives a go-ahead signal at the G_1 checkpoint, it will usually enter the S phase, eventually going on to complete its cycle and divide. If such a signal never arrives, the cell will switch to a permanently nondividing state called the G_0 phase. Many cells in the human body, such as mature nerve cells and muscle cells, are in the G_0 phase.

Figure 8.8B shows a simplified model for how a growth factor might affect the cell cycle control system at the G_1 checkpoint. A cell that responds to a growth factor has molecules of a specific receptor protein in its plasma membrane. Binding of the growth factor (▽) to the receptor (⬠) triggers a signal transduction pathway in the cell. A signal transduction pathway is a series of protein molecules that conveys a message (see Modules 5.1 and 11.10). In this case, that message is a "go signal" that leads to cell division. The "signals" are changes that each protein molecule induces in the next molecule in the pathway. Via a series of relay proteins, a signal finally reaches the cell cycle control system and overrides the brakes that otherwise prevent progress of the cell cycle.

Research on the control of the cell cycle is one of the hottest areas in biology today. This research is leading to a better understanding of cancer, which we discuss next.

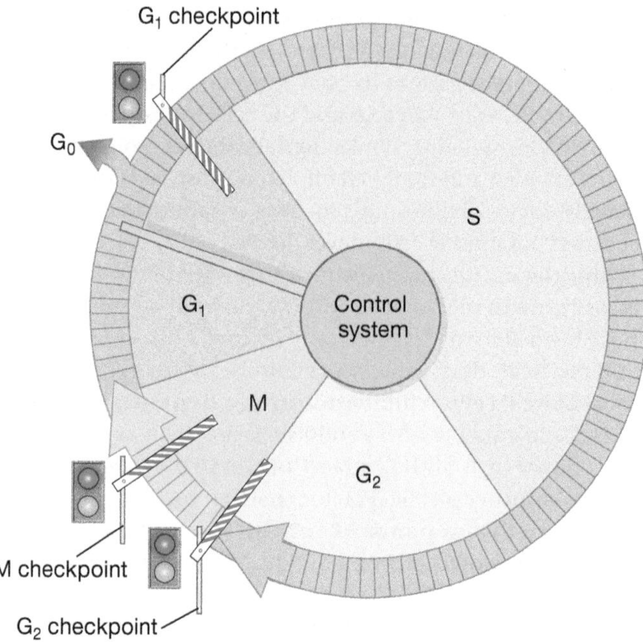

▲ **Figure 8.8A** A schematic model for the cell cycle control system

? At which of the three checkpoints described in this module do the chromosomes exist as duplicated sister chromatids?

■ G_2 and M checkpoints

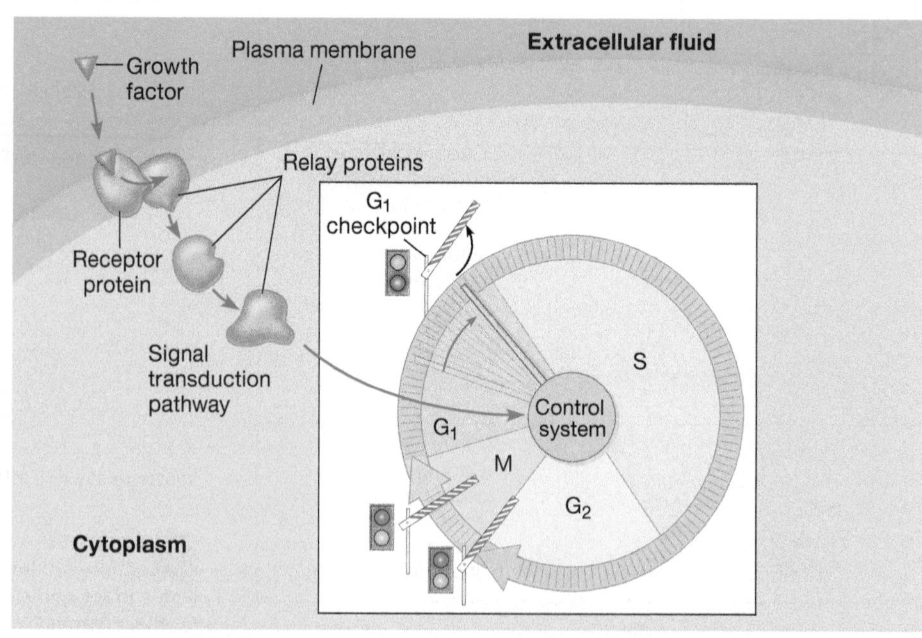

▲ **Figure 8.8B** How a growth factor signals the cell cycle control system

8.9 Growing out of control, cancer cells produce malignant tumors

CONNECTION

Cancer, which claims the lives of one out of every five people in the United States, is a disease of the cell cycle. Cancer cells do not heed the normal signals that regulate the cell cycle; they divide excessively and invade other tissues of the body. If unchecked, cancer cells may continue to grow and spread until they kill the organism.

Cancer begins when a single cell undergoes changes that convert a normal cell to a cancer cell. Such a cell often has altered proteins on its surface and the body's immune system normally recognizes the cell as an alien and destroys it. However, if the cell evades destruction, it may multiply to form a **tumor**, a mass of abnormally growing cells within otherwise normal tissue. If the abnormal cells remain at their original site, the lump is called a **benign tumor**. Benign tumors can cause problems if they grow in and disrupt certain organs, such as the brain, but often they can be completely removed by surgery or even (in cases in which they pose no imminent threat) left alone.

In contrast, a **malignant tumor** is a mass of abnormally reproducing cells that can spread into neighboring tissues and invade other parts of the body, with the potential to displace normal tissue and interrupt organ function as it grows (Figure 8.9). An individual with a malignant tumor is said to have **cancer**. Cancer cells may separate from the original tumor or secrete signal molecules that cause blood vessels to grow toward the tumor. A few tumor cells may then enter the blood and lymph vessels and thereby move to other parts of the body, where they may proliferate and form new tumors. The spread of cancer cells beyond their original site is called **metastasis**.

Cancers are named according to the organ or tissue in which they originate. Liver cancer, for example, starts in liver tissue and may or may not spread from there. Carcinomas are cancers that originate in the external or internal coverings of the body, such as the skin or the lining of the intestine. Leukemia is a broad term covering a number of diseases that originate in immature white blood cells within the blood or bone marrow.

From studying cancer cells in culture, researchers have learned that cancer cells do not heed the normal signals that regulate the cell cycle. For example, many cancer cells have defective cell cycle control systems that proceed past checkpoints even in the absence of growth factors. Other cancer cells synthesize growth factors themselves, causing the cells to divide continuously. If cancer cells do stop dividing, they seem to do so at random points in the cell cycle rather than at the normal cell cycle checkpoints. Moreover, in the laboratory, cancer cells are "immortal"; they can go on dividing indefinitely, as long as they have a supply of nutrients (whereas normal mammalian cells divide only about 20 to 50 times before they stop). A striking example of the immortality of cancer cells is a line that has been continuously multiplying in culture since 1951. Cells of this line are called HeLa cells, named for the original donor, Henrietta Lacks, who died of cervical cancer more than 65 years ago.

Luckily, many tumors can be successfully treated. A tumor that appears to be localized may be removed surgically. Alternatively, it can be treated with concentrated beams of high-energy radiation, which usually damages DNA in cancer cells more than it does in normal cells, perhaps because cancer cells have lost the ability to repair such damage. However, radiation also damages normal body cells, producing harmful side effects. For example, radiation damage to cells of the ovaries or testes can lead to sterility.

Chemotherapy is used to treat widespread or metastatic tumors. During periodic chemotherapy treatments, intravenous (IV) drugs are administered that disrupt specific steps in the cell cycle. For instance, the drug Taxol freezes the mitotic spindle after it forms, which stops actively dividing cells from proceeding past metaphase. Vinblastin, a chemotherapeutic drug first obtained from the periwinkle plant, prevents the mitotic spindle from forming in the first place.

The side effects of chemotherapy are due to the drugs' effects on cells that rapidly divide in parts of the body beyond those where the cancer resides. Nausea results from chemotherapy's effects on intestinal cells; hair loss comes from effects on hair follicle cells; and susceptibility to infection results from effects on immune cell production. (We will return to the topic of cancer—specifically, how mutations in genes that control cell division can lead to cancer—in Chapter 11.)

In the next module, you'll learn how understanding such mutations may aid in cancer treatment.

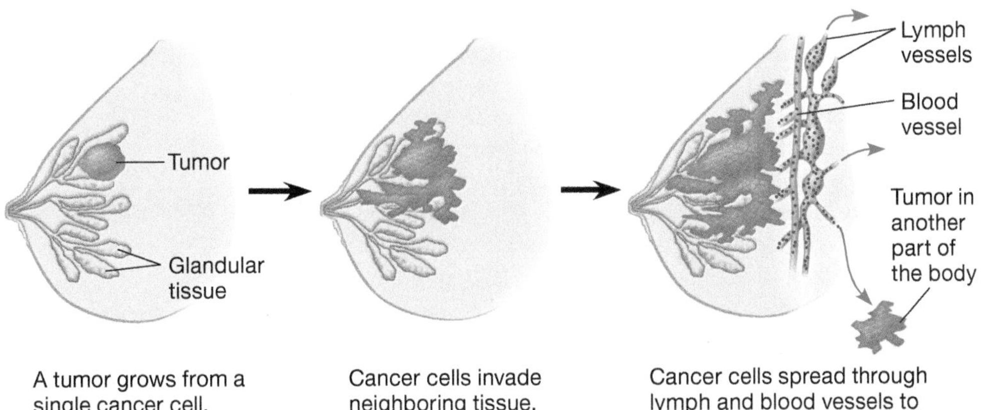
Tumor
Glandular tissue
Lymph vessels
Blood vessel
Tumor in another part of the body
A tumor grows from a single cancer cell.
Cancer cells invade neighboring tissue.
Cancer cells spread through lymph and blood vessels to other parts of the body.

▲ **Figure 8.9** Growth and metastasis of a malignant tumor of the breast

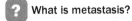

? **What is metastasis?**

Metastasis is the spread of cancer cells from their original site of formation to other sites in the body.

8.10 The best cancer treatment may vary by individual

SCIENTIFIC THINKING

Oncologists (doctors who treat cancer) have observed that different cancer patients respond in drastically different ways to the same treatment: Therapies that are effective for some patients may be unhelpful or even harmful for others. Treatment options for cancer are therefore changing from a "one-size-fits-all" model to a determination of the best therapies for each particular patient.

Can cancer therapy be personalized?

In 2015, researchers from Toronto published the most extensive analysis of data ever conducted on the treatment of DCIS (ductal carcinoma in situ, also called stage 0 breast cancer). Unlike more insidious forms of cancer, the progression of DCIS is uncertain: the abnormal cells might go away on their own, they might remain in place and never cause harm, or they might grow and spread, possibly leading to death. As discussed in the chapter-opening essay, treatment options for DCIS include lumpectomy, mastectomy, double mastectomy, and radiation therapy. How can cancer patients decide on their best course of treatment?

The 2015 study followed 108,000 American women for 20 years after diagnosis with DCIS. Death rates from breast cancer were examined and broken down by such factors as age at diagnosis, ethnicity, and socioeconomic status. This is an example of an observational study, one that draws inferences from a data set in the absence of controlled experiments. Such studies may be undertaken to help determine the possible benefit of a treatment on research participants with whom the use of controlled groups would be impractical.

Some important results of this research are summarized in Figure 8.10. Notice that a diagnosis of DCIS is far from a death sentence; the risk of dying from breast cancer is only 3.3% (1 in 30) in the 20 years after diagnosis. However, about 20% of DCIS patients, including women who are under 40 or are black, bear a substantially higher risk of death. The researchers concluded that, because of higher mortality, these women should consider the most aggressive treatment options.

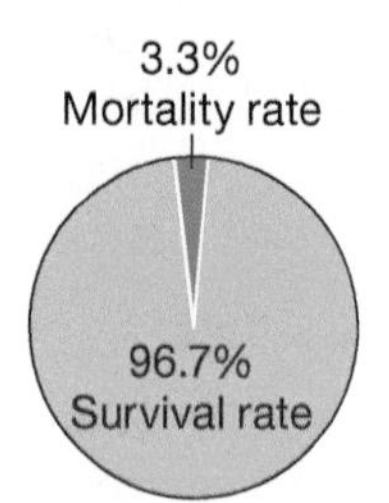

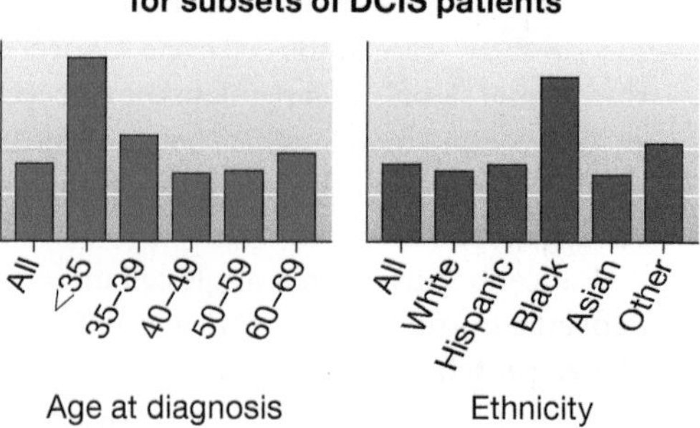

▲ **Figure 8.10** **Death rates due to breast cancer from a large observational study of DCIS**

Data from S. A. Narod et al., Breast cancer mortality after diagnosis of ductal carcinoma in situ, *JAMA Oncology* 1: 888–96 (2015).

Oncologists emphasize that additional research must be undertaken before any widespread changes can be made in DCIS treatment protocols. Additional studies could seek to determine which treatment options work best for which subsets of women. As more is learned about the underlying biology of cancer cells, cancer treatment will become even more personalized, with the most appropriate therapies chosen for each patient.

? Why must human cancer research often use an observational method when controlled studies could yield more definitive results?

■ It is clearly unethical to force cancer-causing behaviors on test subjects, so researchers can only observe what behaviors occurred during the study and how these behaviors correlated with outcomes.

Meiosis and Crossing Over

8.11 Chromosomes are matched in homologous pairs

In humans, a typical body cell, called a **somatic cell**, has 46 chromosomes. Chromosomes undergoing mitosis are condensed enough to be viewed with a microscope and arranged into matching pairs; Figure 8.11 illustrates one pair of condensed chromosomes, each consisting of two joined sister chromatids. A human somatic cell undergoing mitosis has 23 sets of duplicated chromosomes. Other species have different numbers of chromosomes, but these, too, usually occur in matched pairs. Moreover, when treated with special dyes, the chromosomes of a pair display matching staining patterns (represented by colored stripes in Figure 8.11).

Almost every chromosome has a twin that resembles it in length, centromere position, and staining pattern. The two chromosomes of such a matching pair are called **homologous chromosomes** (or a homologous pair) because each chromosome carries genes controlling the same inherited characters. For example, if a gene for freckles is located at a particular place, or **locus** (plural, *loci*), on one chromosome—say, within the narrow orange band in our drawing—then its homologous chromosome also has that same gene at that same locus. However, the two chromosomes of a homologous pair may have different versions

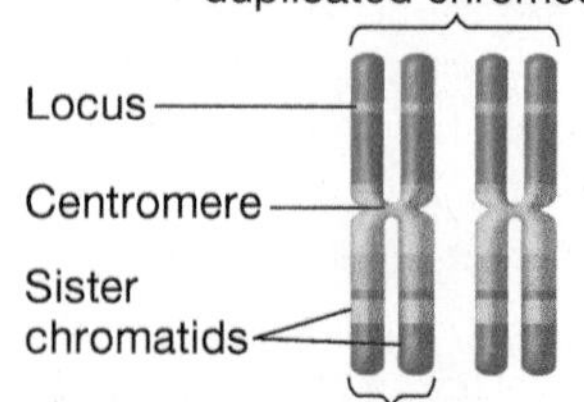

▲ **Figure 8.11** **A pair of homologous chromosomes**

TRY THIS Cover this figure, and on a piece of paper, draw a pair of homologous chromosomes, and label the sister chromatids, the centromere, and one chromosome. Then, uncover this figure and compare it to your drawing.

of the same gene. For example, one chromosome may have a gene encoding freckles, while the other chromosome has that same gene at the same place but in a version that encodes for the lack of freckles. The sequences of the two copies of the gene (whether identical or different) will ultimately affect the person's appearance.

The two distinct chromosomes referred to as X and Y are an important exception to the general pattern of homologous chromosomes. Human females have a homologous pair of X chromosomes (XX), but males have one X and one Y chromosome (XY). Only small parts of the X and Y are homologous. Most of the genes carried on the X chromosome do not appear on the tiny Y, and the Y chromosome has genes not present on the X. Because they determine an individual's sex, the X and Y chromosomes are called the **sex chromosomes**. Chromosomes other than sex chromosomes (44 of them in humans) are called **autosomes**.

? Are all of *your* chromosomes fully homologous?

If you were born female, yes. If you were born male, no.

8.12 Gametes have a single set of chromosomes

A **life cycle** is the sequence of generation-to-generation stages in the history of an organism, from fertilization to the production of its own offspring (Figure 8.12A). Having two sets of chromosomes, one inherited from each parent, is a key factor in the life cycle of all species that reproduce sexually.

Most animals and plants are said to be **diploid** organisms because all somatic cells contain pairs of homologous chromosomes. The total number of chromosomes is called the diploid number (abbreviated $2n$). For humans, the diploid number is 46; that is, $2n = 46$. The exceptions are the egg and sperm cells, collectively known as **gametes**. Each gamete has a single set of chromosomes: 22 autosomes plus a sex chromosome, either X or Y. A cell with a single chromosome set is called a **haploid** cell; it has only one member of each homologous pair. For humans, the haploid number (abbreviated n) is 23; that is, $n = 23$.

The human life cycle begins when a haploid sperm cell from the father fuses with a haploid egg cell from the mother in the process of **fertilization**. The resulting fertilized egg, called a **zygote**, has one set of homologous chromosomes from each parent, and so is diploid. As a human develops into an adult, mitosis of the zygote and its descendants generates all the somatic cells.

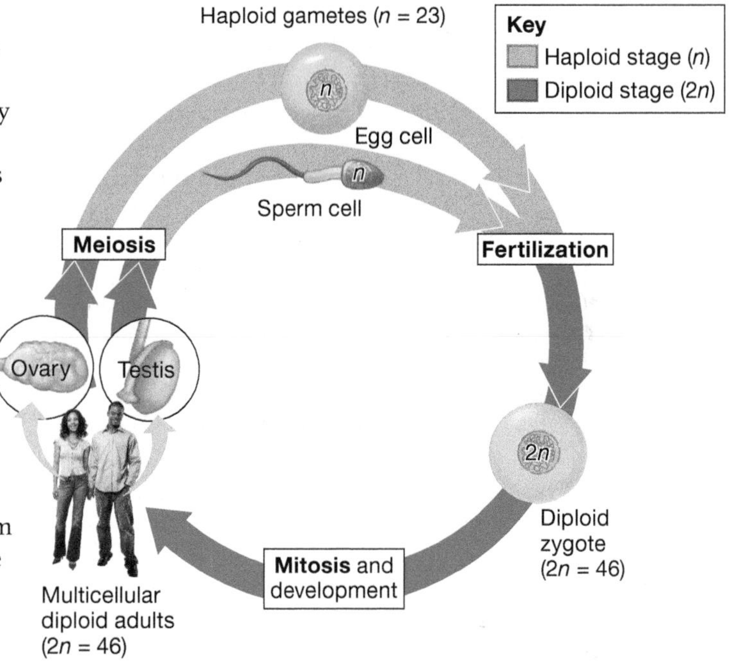

▲ Figure 8.12A Following chromosome number through the human life cycle

The only cells of the human body not produced by mitosis are the gametes. Gametes are made by a different form of cell division called meiosis, which occurs only in reproductive organs. Whereas mitosis produces daughter cells with the same number of chromosomes as the parent cell, meiosis reduces the chromosome number by half. Figure 8.12B tracks one pair of homologous chromosomes through the two divisions of meiosis. ❶ Each of the chromosomes is duplicated during interphase (before meiosis). ❷ The first division, meiosis I, segregates the two chromosomes of the homologous pair, packaging them in separate (haploid) daughter cells. But each chromosome is still doubled. ❸ Meiosis II separates the sister chromatids. Each of the four daughter cells is haploid and contains only a single chromosome from the homologous pair.

Next, we'll take a closer look at the process of meiosis.

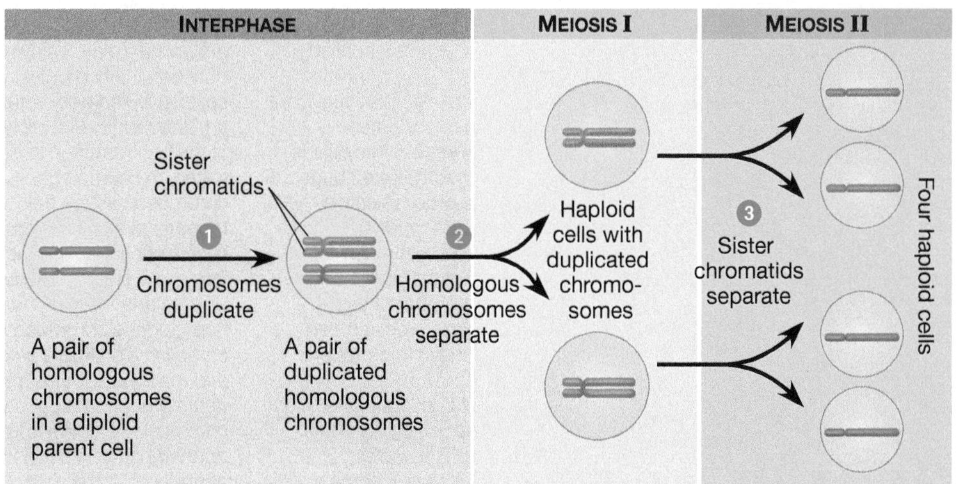

▲ Figure 8.12B How meiosis halves chromosome number through two sequential divisions

? How many autosomes are found in a human sperm cell? How many and which sex chromosomes?

22 autosomes plus either an X or Y sex chromosome

8.13 Meiosis reduces the chromosome number from diploid to haploid

Meiosis is a type of cell division that produces haploid gametes in diploid organisms. Two haploid gametes may then combine via fertilization to restore the diploid state in the zygote. Fertilization and meiosis alternate in sexual life cycles, which serves to maintain a constant number of chromosomes in each species from one generation to the next.

Many of the stages of meiosis closely resemble corresponding stages in mitosis. Meiosis, like mitosis, is preceded by the duplication of chromosomes. However, this single duplication is followed by not one but two consecutive cell divisions, called meiosis I and meiosis II. Because one duplication of the chromosomes is followed by two divisions, the result is four daughter cells, each with half as many chromosomes as the parent cell. The illustrations in Figure 8.13 show the two meiotic divisions for an animal cell with a diploid number of six. The members of a pair of homologous chromosomes in Figure 8.13 (and later figures) are colored red and blue to help distinguish them. (Imagine that the red chromosomes were inherited from the mother and the blue chromosomes from the father.)

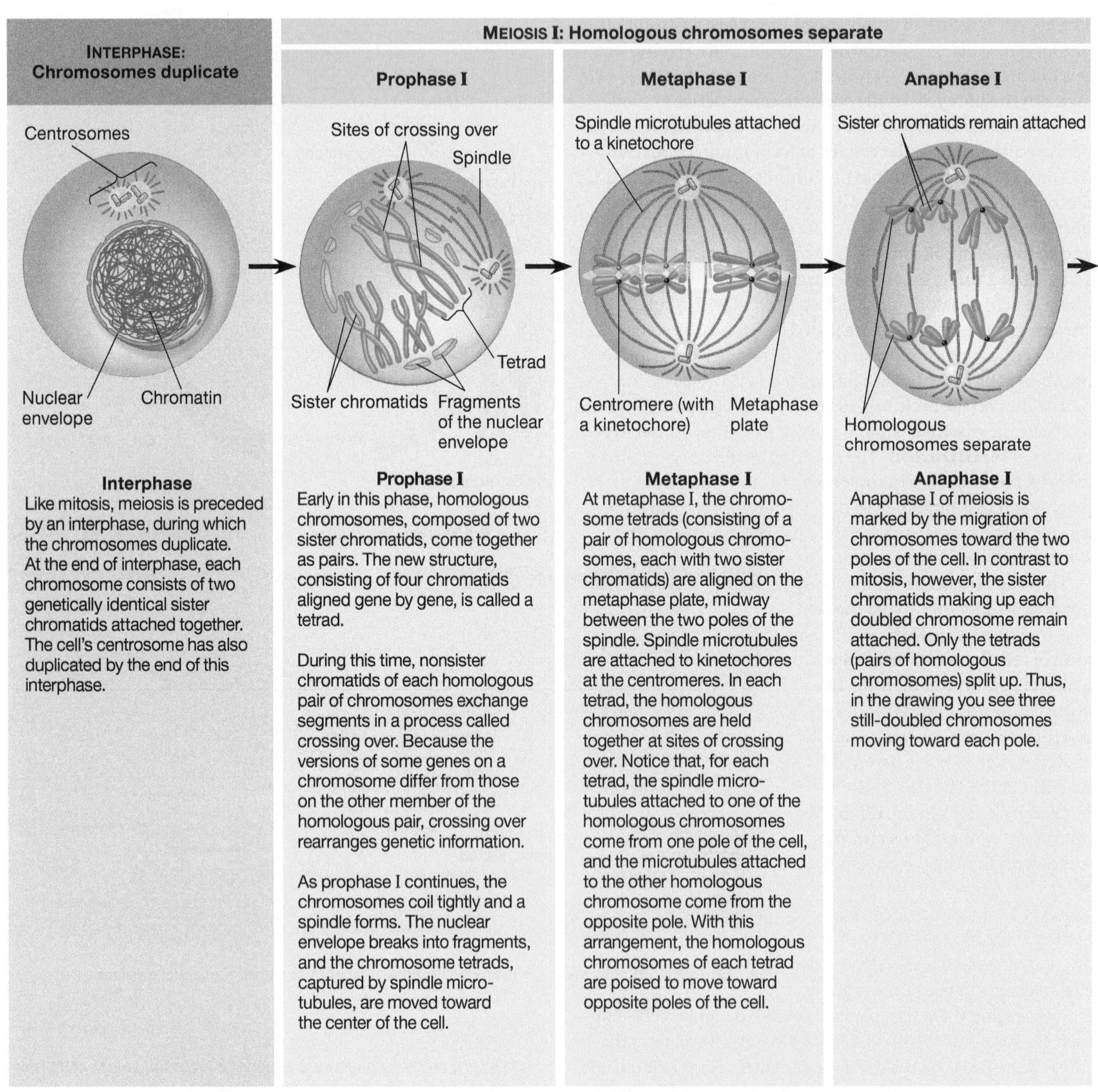

INTERPHASE: Chromosomes duplicate
MEIOSIS I: Homologous chromosomes separate
Prophase I
Metaphase I
Anaphase I
Centrosomes
Nuclear envelope
Chromatin
Sites of crossing over
Spindle
Tetrad
Sister chromatids
Fragments of the nuclear envelope
Spindle microtubules attached to a kinetochore
Centromere (with a kinetochore)
Metaphase plate
Sister chromatids remain attached
Homologous chromosomes separate
Interphase
Like mitosis, meiosis is preceded by an interphase, during which the chromosomes duplicate. At the end of interphase, each chromosome consists of two genetically identical sister chromatids attached together. The cell's centrosome has also duplicated by the end of this interphase.
Prophase I
Early in this phase, homologous chromosomes, composed of two sister chromatids, come together as pairs. The new structure, consisting of four chromatids aligned gene by gene, is called a tetrad.
During this time, nonsister chromatids of each homologous pair of chromosomes exchange segments in a process called crossing over. Because the versions of some genes on a chromosome differ from those on the other member of the homologous pair, crossing over rearranges genetic information.
As prophase I continues, the chromosomes coil tightly and a spindle forms. The nuclear envelope breaks into fragments, and the chromosome tetrads, captured by spindle microtubules, are moved toward the center of the cell.
Metaphase I
At metaphase I, the chromosome tetrads (consisting of a pair of homologous chromosomes, each with two sister chromatids) are aligned on the metaphase plate, midway between the two poles of the spindle. Spindle microtubules are attached to kinetochores at the centromeres. In each tetrad, the homologous chromosomes are held together at sites of crossing over. Notice that, for each tetrad, the spindle microtubules attached to one of the homologous chromosomes come from one pole of the cell, and the microtubules attached to the other homologous chromosome come from the opposite pole. With this arrangement, the homologous chromosomes of each tetrad are poised to move toward opposite poles of the cell.
Anaphase I
Anaphase I of meiosis is marked by the migration of chromosomes toward the two poles of the cell. In contrast to mitosis, however, the sister chromatids making up each doubled chromosome remain attached. Only the tetrads (pairs of homologous chromosomes) split up. Thus, in the drawing you see three still-doubled chromosomes moving toward each pole.

▲ Figure 8.13 The stages of meiosis

One of the most important events in meiosis occurs during prophase I. At this stage, the four chromatids (two sets of sister chromatids of each homologous pair) are aligned and physically touching each other. When in this configuration, nonsister chromatids may trade segments. As you will learn in Module 8.17, this exchange of chromosome segments—called crossing over—shuffles genes, making an important contribution to the genetic variability that results from sexual reproduction.

? A cell from a diploid organism has the haploid number of chromosomes, but each chromosome has two chromatids. The chromosomes are arranged singly at the center of the spindle. What is the meiotic stage?

Metaphase II (because the chromosomes line up two by two in metaphase I)

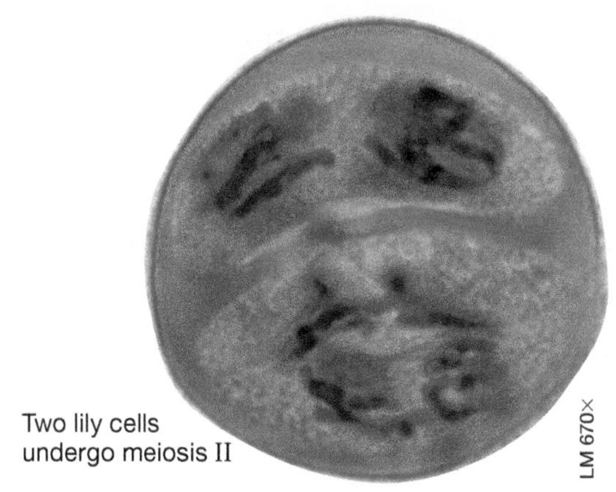

Two lily cells undergo meiosis II

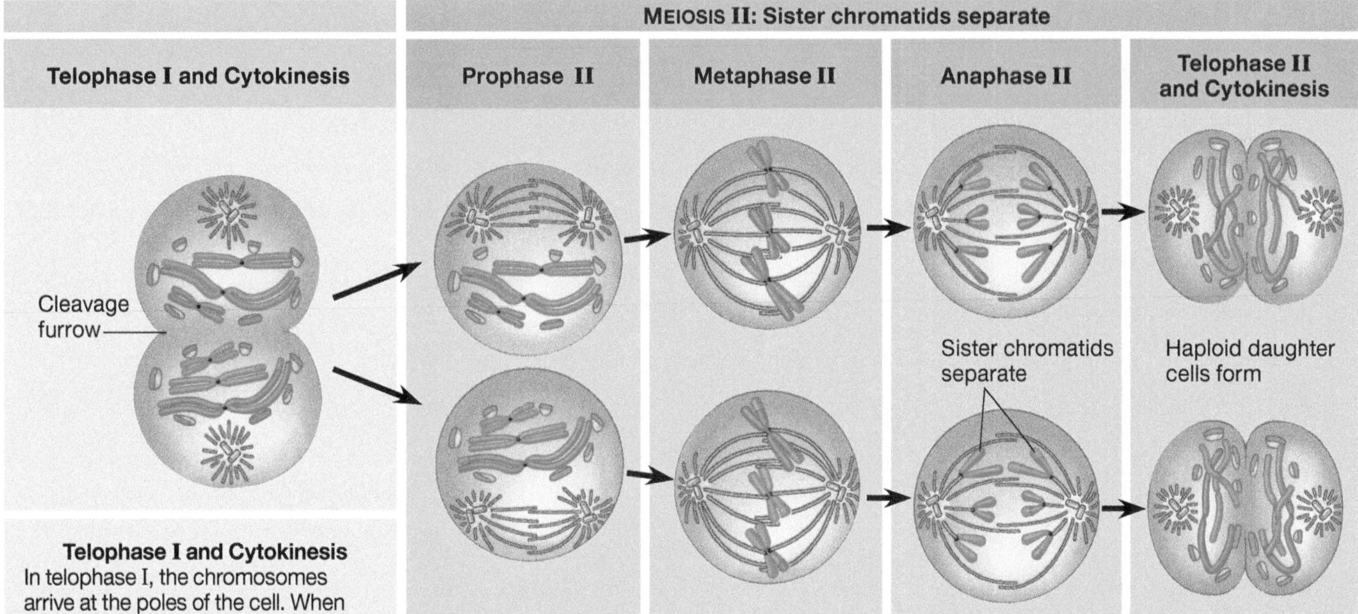

Telophase I and Cytokinesis

In telophase I, the chromosomes arrive at the poles of the cell. When the chromosomes finish their journey, each pole of the cell has a haploid chromosome set, although each chromosome is still in duplicate form (with two sister chromatids) at this point. Usually, cytokinesis (division of the cytoplasm) occurs simultaneously along with telophase I, and two haploid daughter cells are formed.

Following telophase I in some organisms, there is an interphase between telophase I and meiosis II. In other species, meiosis I immediately leads to meiosis II. In either case, no chromosome duplication occurs between telophase I and the onset of meiosis II.

Meiosis II

Meiosis II is essentially the same as mitosis. The important difference is that meiosis II starts with a haploid cell containing a single set of still-duplicated chromosomes.

During prophase II, a spindle forms and moves the chromosomes toward the middle of the cell. During metaphase II, the chromosomes are aligned on the metaphase plate as they are in mitosis, with the kinetochores of the sister chromatids of each chromosome pointing toward opposite poles. In anaphase II, the centromeres of sister chromatids separate, and the sister chromatids of each pair, now individual chromosomes, move toward opposite poles of the cell. In telophase II, nuclei form at the cell poles, and cytokinesis occurs at the same time. There are now four daughter cells, each with the haploid number of (single) chromosomes.

VISUALIZING THE CONCEPT

8.14 Mitosis and meiosis have important similarities and differences

Carefully review this figure, which compares mitosis and meiosis starting from a diploid parent cell with four chromosomes. Homologous chromosomes match in size (long versus short). Color (red versus blue) distinguishes the two chromosomes of each homologous pair. Note how the chromosomes differ in their movement in mitosis versus meiosis.

MITOSIS | **MEIOSIS I**

Parent cell
(before chromosome duplication)
$2n = 4$

Chromosome duplication
(Occurs once, during S phase of preceding interphase)

Prophase

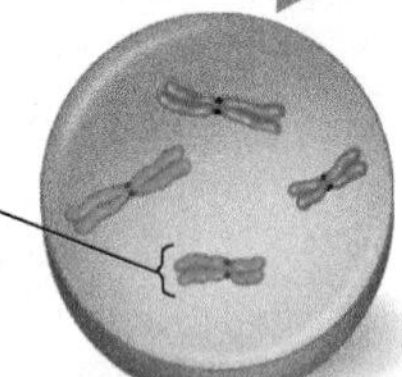

Duplicated chromosome (two sister chromatids)

In prophase of mitosis, each duplicated chromosome remains separate, while in prophase I of meiosis, chromosomes remain associated in homologous pairs.

Prophase I

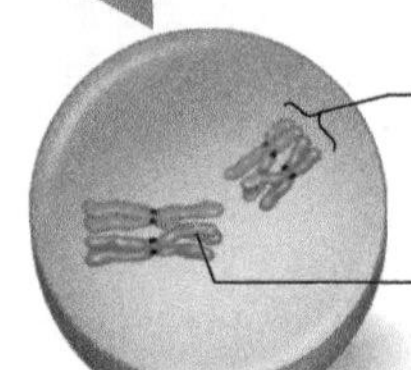

Homologous chromosomes come together in pairs

Site of crossing over between homologous (nonsister) chromatids

Metaphase

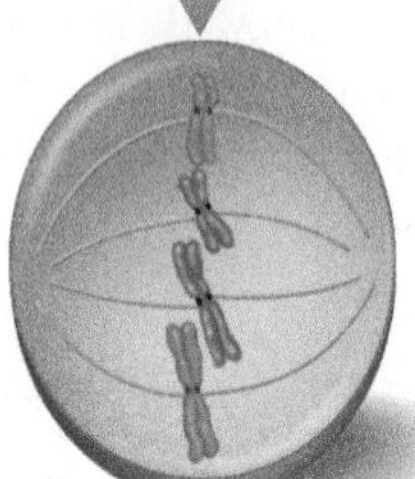

Individual chromosomes line up at the metaphase plate

In metaphase of mitosis, duplicated chromosomes line up singly, while in metaphase I of meiosis, duplicated homologous chromosomes line up in pairs.

Metaphase I

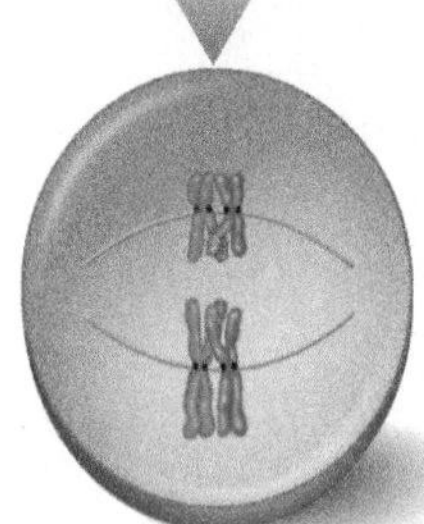

Tetrads (pairs of homologous chromosomes) line up at the metaphase plate

Anaphase Telophase

In anaphase of mitosis, sister chromatids separate, while in anaphase I of meiosis, pairs of homologous chromosomes separate.

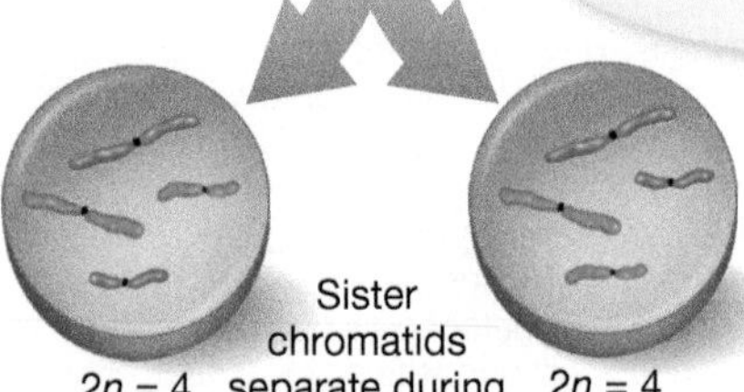

$2n = 4$ Sister chromatids separate during anaphase $2n = 4$

Anaphase I Telophase I

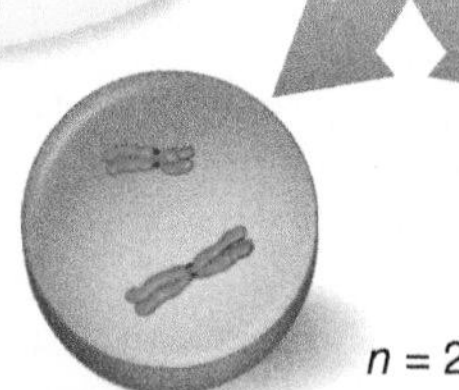

Homologous chromosomes separate during anaphase I; sister chromatids remain attached

$n = 2$

Mitosis involves one division of the nucleus and cytoplasm, while meiosis involves two divisions.

MEIOSIS II

Sister chromatids separate during anaphase II

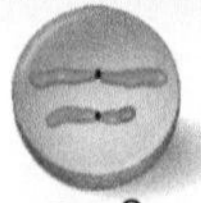

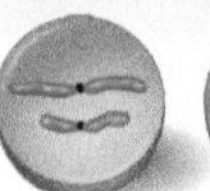

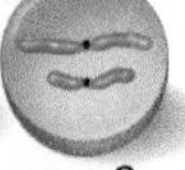

$n = 2$ $n = 2$ $n = 2$ $n = 2$

Result:	Two genetically identical diploid cells
Used for:	Growth, tissue repair, asexual reproduction

Result:	Four genetically unique haploid cells
Used for:	Sexual reproduction

? **Which stage of meiosis shown here most closely resembles mitosis?**

The movement of chromosomes during meiosis II very closely matches mitosis (except with half as many chromosomes).

8.15 Independent orientation of chromosomes in meiosis and random fertilization lead to varied offspring

Although they may share a family resemblance, offspring made via sexual reproduction are highly varied; they are genetically different from their parents and from one another. How can we account for this genetic variation?

Figure 8.15 illustrates one way: The arrangement of homologous chromosome pairs at metaphase I affects the resulting gametes. Our example is from a diploid organism with four chromosomes (two homologous pairs, with one set larger than the other to help make them distinct), and red represents chromosomes inherited from the mother, whereas blue represents chromosomes inherited from the father.

Recall that joined homologous chromosomes form tetrads, a set of four chromatids. At metaphase, the orientation of these tetrads—whether the maternal or paternal chromosome is closer to a given pole—is as random as the flip of a coin. Thus, there is a 50% chance that a given daughter cell will get the maternal chromosome of a certain homologous pair and a 50% chance that it will receive the paternal chromosome. In this example, there are two possible ways that the two tetrads can align during metaphase I. In possibility A, the tetrads are oriented with both red chromosomes on one side and both blue chromosomes on the other side (red/red and blue/blue). Therefore, the gametes produced in possibility A can each have either two red *or* two blue chromosomes (bottom row, combinations 1 and 2).

In possibility B, the tetrads are oriented differently (blue/red and red/blue). This arrangement produces gametes that each have one red and one blue chromosome. Furthermore, half the gametes have a big blue chromosome and a small red one (combination 3), and half have a big red chromosome and a small blue one (combination 4).

So we see that for this example, four chromosome combinations are possible in the gametes. In fact, the organism will produce gametes of all four types in equal quantities. For a species with more than two pairs of chromosomes, such as humans, *all* the chromosome pairs orient independently at metaphase I. (Chromosomes X and Y behave as a homologous pair in meiosis.)

For any species, the total number of combinations of chromosomes that meiosis can produce in gametes is 2^n, where n is the haploid number. For the organism in this figure, $n = 2$, so the number of chromosome combinations is 2^2, or 4. For a human ($n = 23$), there are 2^{23}, or about 8 million possible chromosome combinations! This means that each gamete you produce contains one of roughly 8 million possible combinations of chromosomes.

How many possibilities are there when a gamete from one individual unites with a gamete from another individual in fertilization? In humans, the random fusion of a single sperm with a single egg during fertilization will produce a zygote with any of about 64 trillion (8 million $\times$ 8 million) combinations of chromosomes! Although the random nature of fertilization adds a huge amount of potential variability to the offspring of sexual reproduction, there is in fact even more variety created during meiosis, as we will see in the next two modules.

? **A particular species of worm has a diploid number of 10. How many chromosomal combinations are possible for gametes formed by meiosis?**

32; $2n = 10$, so $n = 5$ and $2^n = 32$

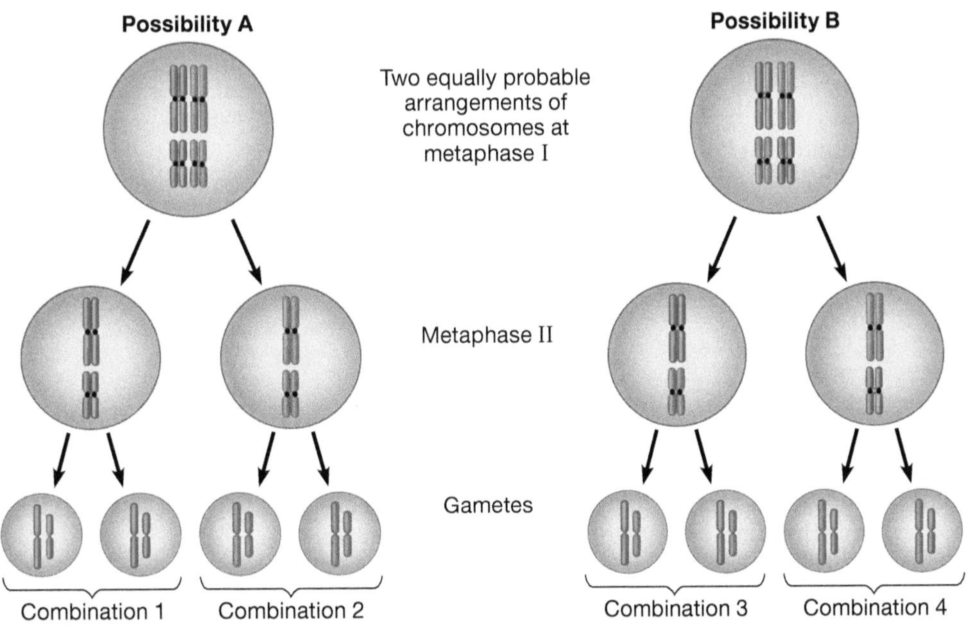

▲ **Figure 8.15** **Results of the independent orientation of chromosomes at metaphase I**

8.16 Homologous chromosomes may carry different versions of genes

So far, we have discussed two sources of genetic variability in the gametes and zygotes of sexually reproducing organisms: independent assortment and random fertilization. Both of these sources of variation operate at the whole chromosome level; that is, they are ways that entire chromosomes can be reshuffled. We have yet to discuss the actual genetic information—the genes—contained in the chromosomes. During meiosis, individual genes within chromosomes can also be shuffled, providing yet another source of increased genetic variation during sexual reproduction.

Recall that a tetrad is a pair of homologous chromosomes, where each chromosome contains a pair of sister chromatids, making four copies of each gene in total. **Figure 8.16A** shows one tetrad. The letters on the homologous chromosomes represent genes. Homologous chromosomes have genes for the same characteristic at corresponding loci. Our example involves hypothetical genes controlling the appearance of mice. *C* and *c* indicate different versions of a gene for one characteristic, coat color; *E* and *e* are different versions of a gene for another characteristic, eye color. (As you'll learn in later chapters, different versions of a gene contain slightly different nucleotide sequences in the chromosomal DNA.)

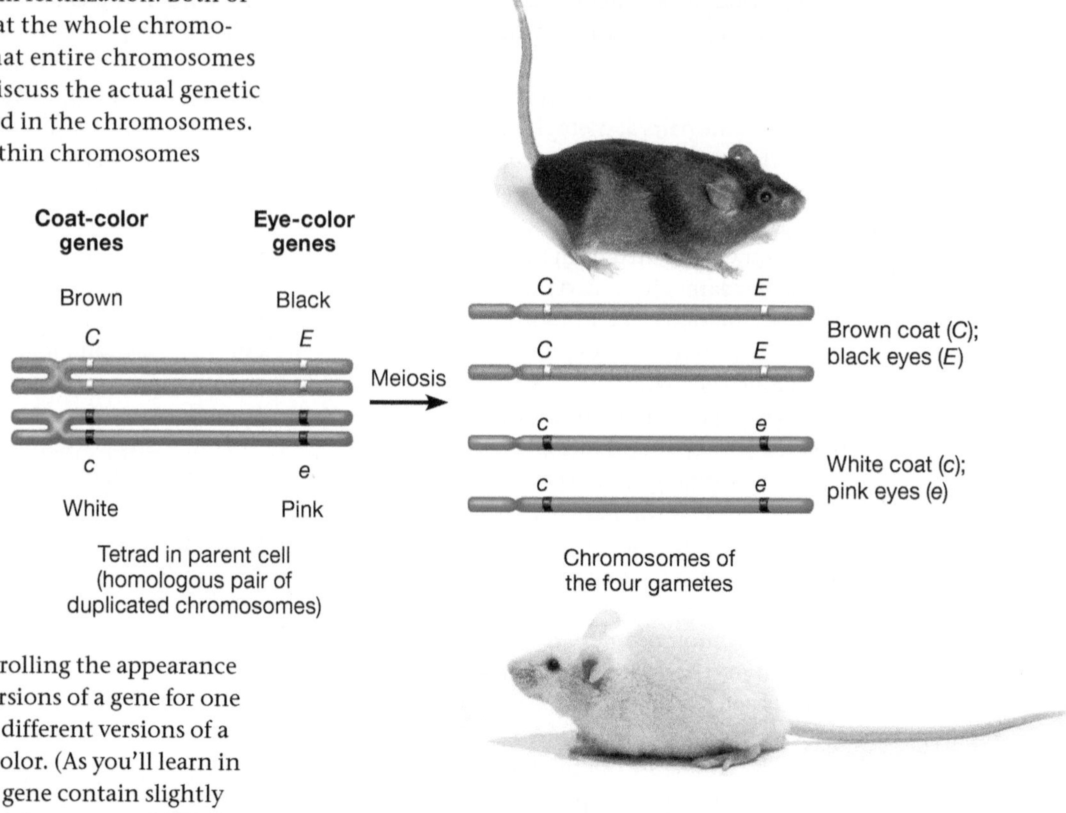

▼ **Figure 8.16A** Differing genetic information (coat color and eye color) on homologous chromosomes

Coat-color genes
Eye-color genes
Brown
Black
C
E
c
e
White
Pink
Tetrad in parent cell (homologous pair of duplicated chromosomes)
Meiosis
C E
C E
Brown coat (C); black eyes (E)
c e
c e
White coat (c); pink eyes (e)
Chromosomes of the four gametes

Let's say that *C* represents the gene for a brown coat and that *c* represents the gene for a white coat. Similarly, *E* is a version of a gene that produces a protein that results in black eyes, while *e* produces a protein that results in pink eyes. In the chromosome diagram, notice that *C* (brown coat) is at the same locus on the red chromosome as *c* (white coat) is on the blue one. Likewise, gene *E* (for black eyes) is at the same locus as *e* (pink eyes).

The fact that homologous chromosomes can bear two different kinds of genetic information for the same characteristic (for instance, coat color) is what really makes gametes—and therefore offspring—different from one another. In our example, a gamete carrying a red chromosome would have genes specifying brown coat color (*C*) and black eye color (*E*), whereas a gamete with the homologous blue chromosome would have genes for white coat (*c*) and pink eyes (*e*). Thus, we see that a tetrad can yield two genetically different kinds of gametes—in this case, half the gametes contain *C*/*E* while half the gametes contain *c*/*e*.

Now we come to the step that can actually shuffle genes. **Crossing over** is an exchange of corresponding segments between nonsister chromatids of homologous chromosomes. Crossing over occurs during the early stage of prophase I of meiosis. During this time, homologous chromosomes are closely paired all along their lengths, with a precise gene-by-gene alignment. The micrograph and drawing in **Figure 8.16B** show the results of crossing over between two homologous chromosomes. The sites of crossing over appear as X-shaped regions; each of these sites is called a **chiasma** (plural, *chiasmata*). A chiasma is a place where two homologous (nonsister) chromatids are attached to each other.

? **In the tetrad of Figure 8.16, use labels to distinguish the pair of homologous chromosomes from sister chromatids.**

Pair of homologous chromosomes
Sister chromatids
Sister chromatids

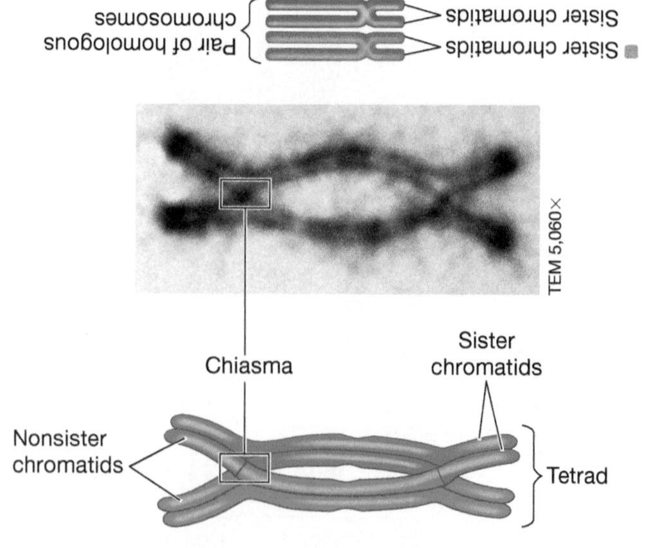

▲ **Figure 8.16B** Chiasmata, the sites of crossing over

VISUALIZING THE CONCEPT 8.17 Crossing over further increases genetic variability

In the figure below, we follow a single pair of homologous chromosomes as they cross over during meiosis and produce new combinations of genes. Such crossing over results in **recombinant chromosomes**, ones that carry DNA from two different parents. Recombinant chromosomes often have gene combinations different from those carried by the parent chromosomes.

MEIOSIS I

Very early in prophase I of meiosis, homologous chromosomes are paired all along their lengths, with a precise gene-by-gene alignment (only one pair is shown here).

Paternal chromosome (blue)

Centromere

Metaphase plate

Maternal chromosome (red)

Two sister chromatids are drawn in blue and two in red. Notice that a blue chromatid is lying directly atop a red nonsister chromatid.

The DNA molecules of two nonsister chromatids break at the same place, forming chiasma (plural *chiasmata*). The two homologous segments then trade places, or cross over, producing hybrid chromosomes.

Chiasma

During meiosis I in humans, an average of one to three crossover events occur per chromosome pair.

When the homologous chromosomes separate in anaphase I, half contain a new segment originating from the other member of the homologous pair.

Recombinant chromosomes resemble a cut-and-paste patchwork of two chromosomes (one from the mother and one from the father).

A recombinant chromosome contains a new combination of maternal and paternal genes.

MEIOSIS II

Finally, during meiosis II, the sister chromatids separate, each going to a different gamete.

The final result is two parental chromosomes that exactly match the originals, and two recombinant chromosomes that contain new combinations of genes not seen in the parents.

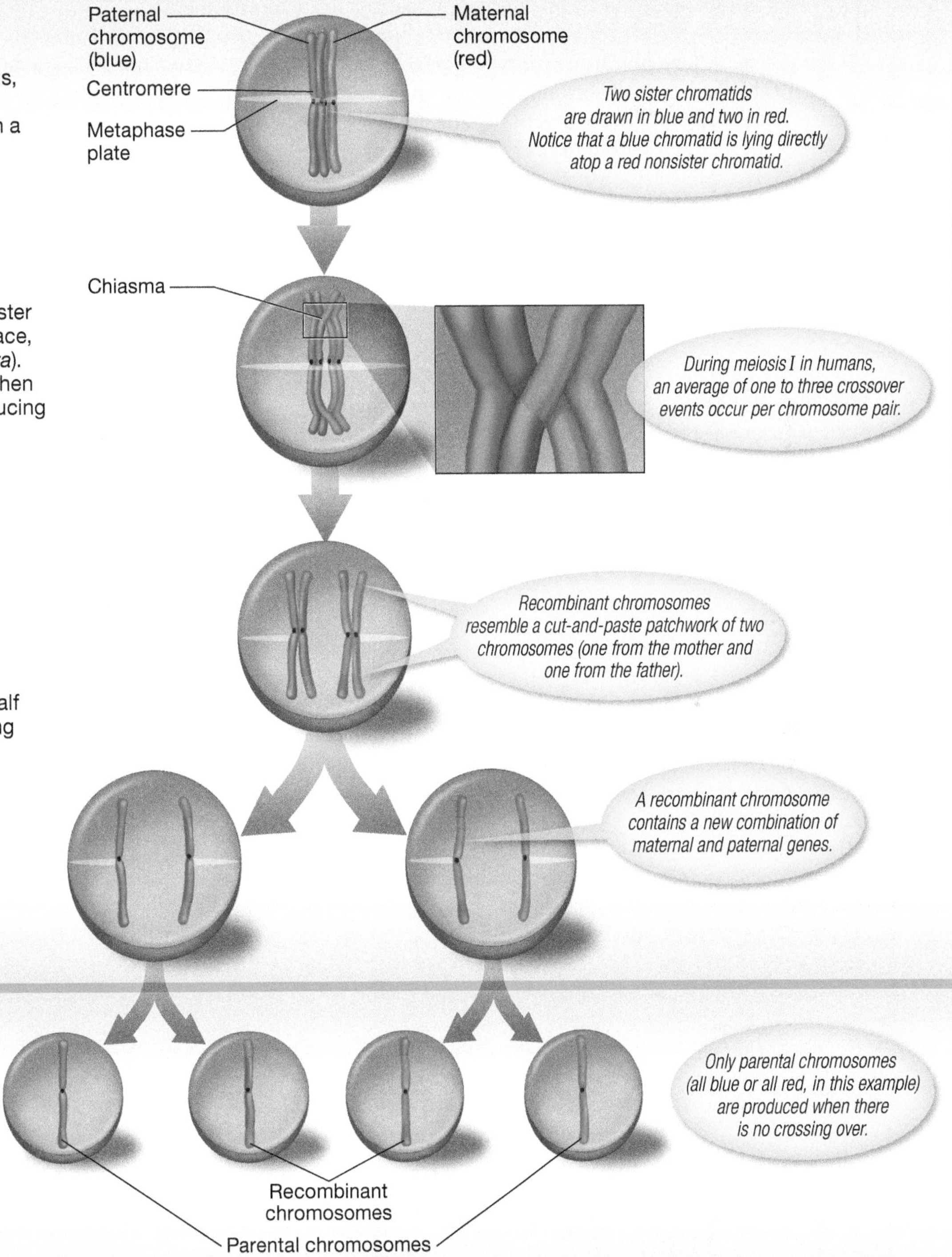

Recombinant chromosomes

Parental chromosomes

Only parental chromosomes (all blue or all red, in this example) are produced when there is no crossing over.

? If you were to examine a chromosome from one of your gametes, is it likely to look exactly like that same chromosome from one of your skin cells?

No, each chromosome probably looks like a cut-and-paste hybrid of segments derived from a pair of homologous chromosomes

Alterations of Chromosome Number and Structure

8.18 Accidents during meiosis can alter chromosome number

Within the human body, meiosis occurs repeatedly as the testes or ovaries produce gametes. In the vast majority of cases, the process distributes chromosomes to daughter cells without error. But there is an occasional mishap, called a **nondisjunction**, in which the members of a chromosome pair fail to separate. After a nondisjunction, one gamete receives two of the same type of chromosome and another gamete receives no copy of that chromosome. The other chromosomes (those not involved in the nondisjunction) are distributed normally.

Imagine a hypothetical organism whose diploid chromosome number is 4. In such an organism, the somatic cells are diploid ($2n = 4$), with two pairs of homologous chromosomes. Sometimes, a pair of homologous chromosomes does not separate during meiosis I (see left side of Figure 8.18). In this case, even though the rest of meiosis occurs normally, all the resulting gametes end up with abnormal numbers of chromosomes. Two of the gametes have three chromosomes; the other two gametes have only one chromosome each.

Alternatively, sometimes meiosis I proceeds normally, but one pair of sister chromatids fails to separate during meiosis II (see right side of Figure 8.18). In this case, two of the resulting gametes are abnormal—one with an extra chromosome and one that is missing a chromosome; the other two gametes are normal.

If an abnormal gamete produced by nondisjunction unites with a normal gamete during fertilization, the result is a zygote with an abnormal number of chromosomes. Mitosis will then transmit the mistake to all embryonic cells. If the organism survived, it would most likely display a syndrome of disorders caused by the abnormal number of genes. Nondisjunction is estimated to be involved in 10–30% of human conceptions and is the main reason for pregnancy loss. Biologists can detect such syndromes by taking an inventory of the chromosomes in a person's cells, as we'll see next.

? Explain how nondisjunction could result in a diploid gamete.

■ A diploid gamete would result if the nondisjunction affected all the chromosomes during one of the meiotic divisions.

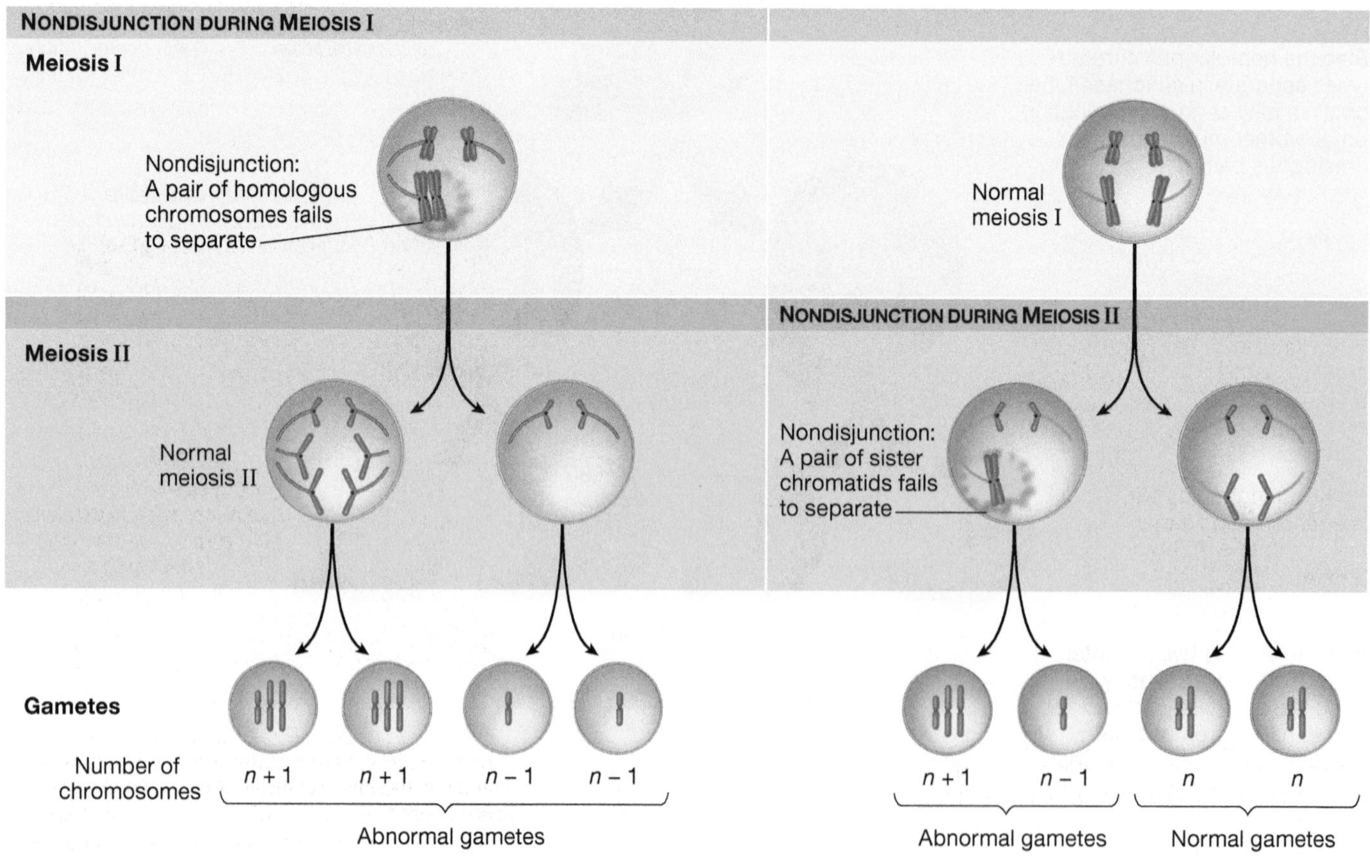

▲ **Figure 8.18** Nondisjunction in meiosis I and meiosis II

8.19 A karyotype is a photographic inventory of an individual's chromosomes

Chromosomal abnormalities can be readily detected in a **karyotype**, an ordered display of magnified images of an individual's chromosomes arranged in pairs. A karyotype shows the chromosomes condensed and doubled, as they appear in metaphase of mitosis.

To prepare a karyotype, scientists often use lymphocytes, a type of white blood cell. A blood sample is treated with a chemical that stimulates mitosis. After growing in culture for several days, the cells are treated with another chemical to arrest mitosis at metaphase, when the chromosomes, each consisting of two joined sister chromatids, are most highly condensed. Figure 8.19 outlines the steps of one method for the preparation of a karyotype from a blood sample.

The photograph on the right shows the karyotype of a normal human male. Images of the 46 chromosomes from a single diploid cell are arranged in 23 homologous pairs: autosomes numbered from 1 to 22 (starting with the largest) and one pair of sex chromosomes (X and Y in this case). The chromosomes have been stained to reveal band patterns, which are helpful in differentiating the chromosomes and in detecting structural abnormalities. Among the alterations that can be detected by karyotyping is trisomy 21, the basis of Down syndrome, which we discuss next.

? **How would the karyotype of a human female differ from the male karyotype in Figure 8.19?**

■ Instead of an XY combination for the sex chromosomes, there would be a homologous pair of X chromosomes (XX).

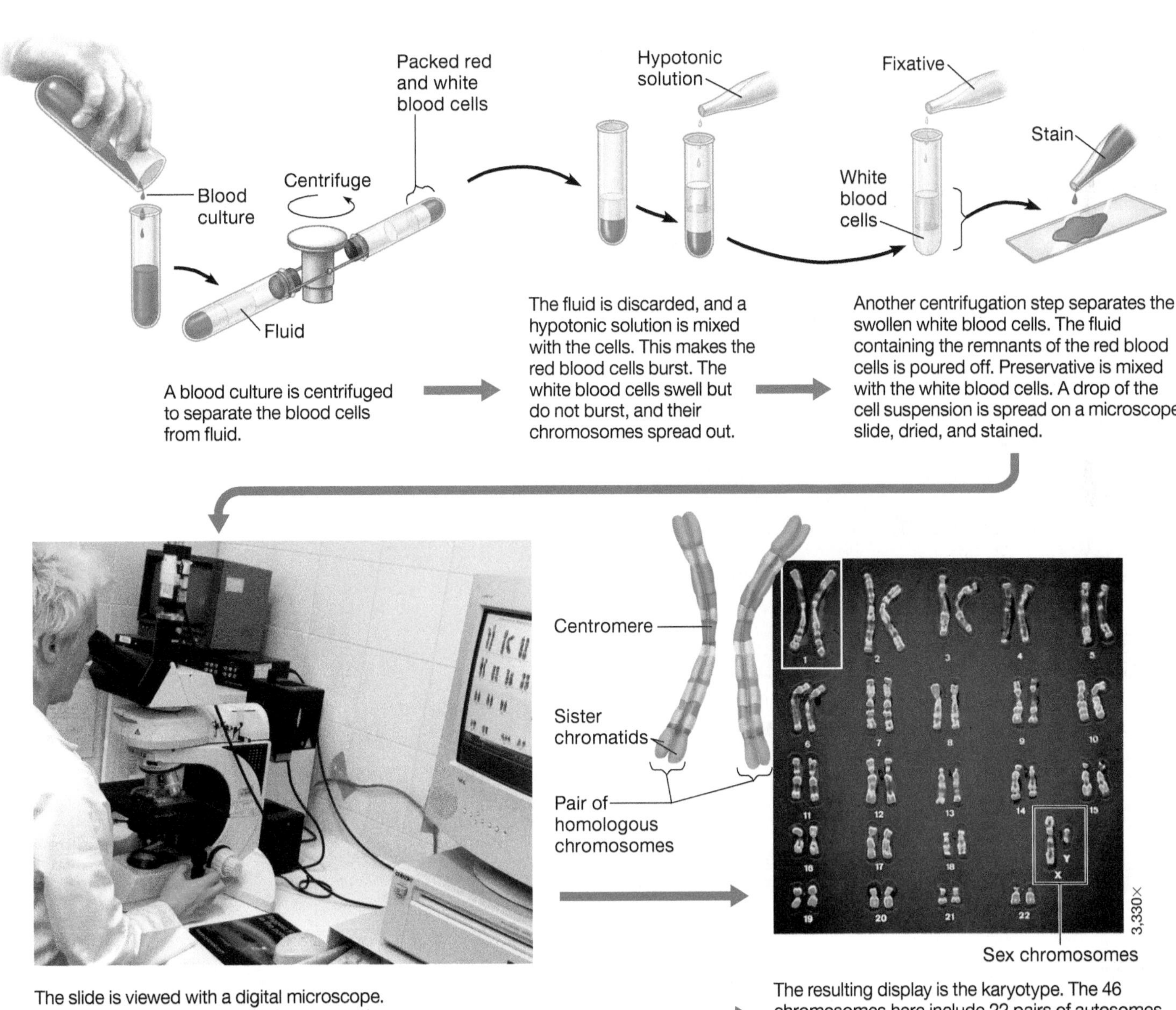

Packed red and white blood cells
Hypotonic solution
Fixative
Stain
Blood culture
Centrifuge
White blood cells
Fluid
A blood culture is centrifuged to separate the blood cells from fluid.
The fluid is discarded, and a hypotonic solution is mixed with the cells. This makes the red blood cells burst. The white blood cells swell but do not burst, and their chromosomes spread out.
Another centrifugation step separates the swollen white blood cells. The fluid containing the remnants of the red blood cells is poured off. Preservative is mixed with the white blood cells. A drop of the cell suspension is spread on a microscope slide, dried, and stained.
Centromere
Sister chromatids
Pair of homologous chromosomes
3,330×
Sex chromosomes
The slide is viewed with a digital microscope. Software is used to electronically arrange the photographed chromosomes by size and shape.
The resulting display is the karyotype. The 46 chromosomes here include 22 pairs of autosomes and two sex chromosomes, X and Y. Each of the chromosomes consists of two sister chromatids joined along their lengths (as shown in the diagram).

▲ **Figure 8.19** **Preparation of a karyotype from a blood sample**

8.20 An extra copy of chromosome 21 causes Down syndrome

CONNECTION The karyotype in Figure 8.19 shows the normal human complement of 23 pairs of chromosomes. Compare this figure with the karyotype shown in **Figure 8.20A**; besides having two X chromosomes (because it's from a female), notice that there are three number 21 chromosomes, making 47 chromosomes in total. This condition is called **trisomy 21**.

In most cases, an abnormal number of chromosomes is so harmful to development that an affected embryo is spontaneously aborted (miscarried) long before birth. But some aberrations in chromosome number, including trisomy 21, appear to upset the genetic balance less drastically, and individuals carrying such chromosomal abnormalities can survive into adulthood. Individuals with chromosomal abnormalities have a characteristic set of symptoms, collectively called a syndrome. A person with trisomy 21, for instance, has a condition called **Down syndrome**, named after John Langdon Down, a doctor who described the syndrome in 1866.

Trisomy 21 is the most common chromosome number abnormality. Affecting about one out of every 850 children, it is also the most common serious birth defect in the United States. Down syndrome includes characteristic facial features—frequently a round face, a skin fold at the inner corner of the eye, a flattened nose bridge, and small, irregular teeth—as well as short stature, heart defects, and susceptibility to respiratory infections, leukemia, and Alzheimer's disease.

People with Down syndrome usually have a life span shorter than normal. They also exhibit varying degrees of developmental delays. However, with proper care, many individuals with the syndrome live to middle age or beyond, and many are socially adept, live independently, and hold jobs. Almost all males and about half of females with Down syndrome are sexually underdeveloped and sterile. Half the eggs produced by a woman with Down syndrome will have the extra chromosome 21, so there is a 50% chance that she will transmit the syndrome to her child.

As indicated in **Figure 8.20B**, the incidence of Down syndrome in the offspring of normal parents increases markedly with the age of the mother. Down syndrome affects less than 0.05% of children (fewer than one in 2,000) born to women under age 30. The risk climbs to 1% (10 in 1,000) for mothers at age 40 and is even higher for older mothers. Prenatal screening for chromosomal defects in the embryo is now offered to all pregnant women.

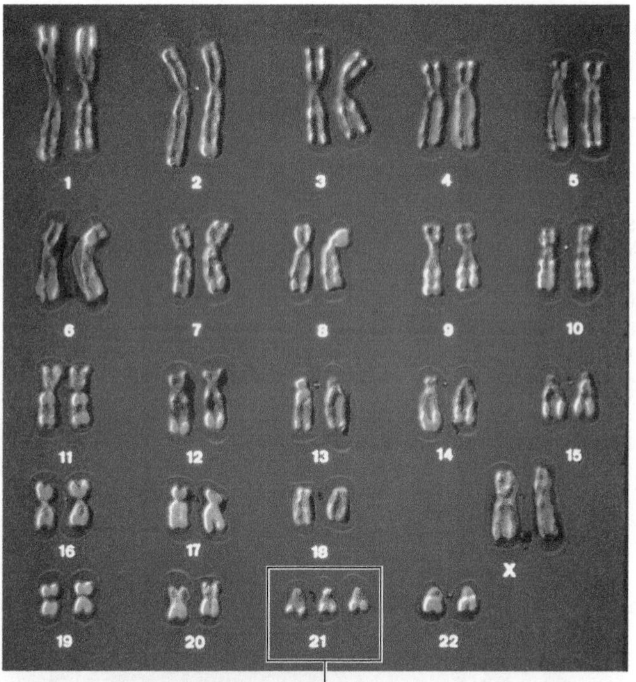

▲ **Figure 8.20A** A karyotype showing trisomy 21 and an individual with Down syndrome

? For mothers of age 47, the risk of having a baby with Down syndrome is about ______ per thousand births, or ______ %.

■ 40 . . . 4

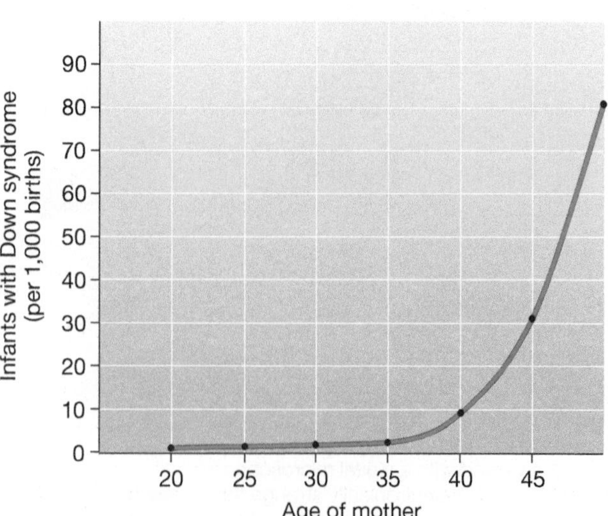

Source: Adapted from C. A. Huether et al., Maternal age specific risk rate estimates for Down syndrome among live births in whites and other races from Ohio and Metropolitan Atlanta, 1970–1989, *Journal of Medical Genetics* 35: 482–90 (1998).

▲ **Figure 8.20B** Maternal age and incidence of Down syndrome

8.21 Abnormal numbers of sex chromosomes do not usually affect survival

CONNECTION

Nondisjunction can result in abnormal numbers of sex chromosomes, X and Y. Unusual numbers of sex chromosomes seem to upset the genetic balance less than unusual numbers of autosomes. This may be because the Y chromosome is very small and carries relatively few genes. Furthermore, mammalian cells usually operate with only one functioning X chromosome because other copies of the chromosome become inactivated in each cell (as you'll learn in Module 11.2).

Table 8.21 lists the most common human sex chromosome abnormalities. An extra X chromosome in a male, making him XXY, causes Klinefelter syndrome. Such men have abnormally small testes, are usually sterile, may have subnormal intelligence, and may have female body characteristics such as enlarged breasts. Klinefelter syndrome is also found in individuals with more than three sex chromosomes, such as XXYY, XXXY, or XXXXY. These abnormal numbers of sex chromosomes result from multiple nondisjunctions; such men are more likely to have developmental disabilities than XY or XXY individuals.

Human males with an extra Y chromosome (such as XYY) do not have any well-defined syndrome, although they tend to be taller than average. Females with an extra X chromosome (XXX) are usually fertile and cannot be distinguished from XX females except by karyotype. Such women do tend to be slightly taller than average and have a higher risk of learning disabilities.

Females who lack an X chromosome are designated XO; the O indicates the absence of a second sex chromosome. These women have Turner syndrome. They have a characteristic appearance, including short stature and often a web of skin extending between the neck and the shoulders. Women with Turner syndrome are sterile because their sex organs do not mature at adolescence. If left untreated, girls with Turner syndrome have poor development of breasts and other secondary sexual characteristics. Artificial estrogen therapy can alleviate these symptoms, allowing such women to develop secondary sexual characteristics. Most women with Turner syndrome have normal intelligence. The XO condition is the sole known case where having only 45 chromosomes is not fatal in humans.

? **What is the total number of autosomes you would expect to find in the karyotype of a female with Turner syndrome?**

■ 44 (plus one sex chromosome)

TABLE 8.21 Abnormalities of Sex Chromosome Number in Humans

Sex Chromosomes	Syndrome	Origin of Nondisjunction	Symptoms
XXY	Klinefelter syndrome (male)	Meiosis in egg or sperm formation	Sterile; underdeveloped testes; secondary female characteristics
XYY	None (normal male)	Meiosis in sperm formation	None
XXX	None (normal female)	Meiosis in egg or sperm formation	Slightly taller than average
XO	Turner syndrome (female)	Meiosis in egg or sperm formation	Sterile; immature sex organs

8.22 New species can arise from errors in cell division

EVOLUTION CONNECTION

Errors in cell division do not always lead to problems. In fact, biologists hypothesize that such errors have been instrumental in the evolution of many species. Such new species are polyploid, meaning that they have more than two sets of homologous chromosomes in each somatic cell. At least half of all species of flowering plants are polyploid, including such crops as wheat, potatoes, and cotton.

Let's consider one scenario by which a diploid ($2n$) plant species might generate a tetraploid ($4n$) plant. Imagine that, like many plants, our diploid plant produces both sperm and egg cells and can self-fertilize. If meiosis fails to occur in the plant's reproductive organs and gametes are instead produced by mitosis, the gametes will be diploid. The union of a diploid ($2n$) sperm with a diploid ($2n$) egg during self-fertilization will produce a tetraploid ($4n$) zygote, which may develop into a mature tetraploid plant that can itself reproduce by self-fertilization. The tetraploid plants will constitute a new species, one that has evolved in just one generation. Although polyploid animal species are less common than polyploid plants, they are known to occur among the fishes and amphibians (Figure 8.22). Moreover, researchers in Chile have identified the first candidate for polyploidy among the mammals—the Viscacha rat (*Tympanoctomys barrerae*), a rodent whose cells seem to be tetraploid with 102 chromosomes. Tetraploid organisms are sometimes strikingly different from their recent diploid ancestors. Scientists don't yet understand exactly how polyploidy brings about such differences.

▲ **Figure 8.22 The gray tree frog (*Hyla versicolor*), a tetraploid organism**

? **What is a polyploid organism?**

■ An organism with more than two sets of homologous chromosomes in its body cells

8.23 Alterations of chromosome structure can cause birth defects and cancer

CONNECTION Errors in meiosis or damaging agents such as radiation can cause a chromosome to break, which can lead to four types of changes in chromosome structure (Figure 8.23A). A **deletion** occurs when a chromosomal fragment (along with its genes) becomes detached. The "deleted" fragment may disappear from the cell, or it may become attached as an extra segment to its sister chromatid or a homologous chromosome, producing a **duplication**. A chromosomal fragment may also reattach to the original chromosome but in the reverse orientation, producing an **inversion**. A fourth possible result of chromosomal breakage is for the fragment to join a nonhomologous chromosome, a rearrangement called a **translocation**. As shown in the figure, a translocation may be reciprocal; that is, two nonhomologous chromosomes may exchange segments.

Inversions are less likely than deletions or duplications to produce harmful effects, because in inversions all genes are still present in their normal number. Many deletions in human chromosomes, however, cause serious physical and mental problems. One example is a specific deletion in chromosome 5 that causes *cri du chat* ("cry of the cat") syndrome. Depending on the size of the deletion, the symptoms—developmental disabilities, a small head with unusual facial features, and a cry that sounds like the mewing of a distressed cat—can range from relatively mild to severe.

Like inversions, translocations may or may not be harmful. Some people with Down syndrome have only part of a third chromosome 21; as the result of a translocation, this partial chromosome is attached to another (nonhomologous) chromosome. Other chromosomal translocations have been implicated in certain cancers, including chronic myelogenous leukemia (CML). CML develops after a reciprocal translocation during mitosis of cells that will become white blood cells. In these cells, the exchange of a large portion of chromosome 22 with a small fragment from a tip of chromosome 9 produces a much shortened, easily recognized chromosome 22 (Figure 8.23B). Such an exchange causes cancer by creating a new "fused" gene that leads to an uncontrolled cell cycle.

Because the chromosomal changes in cancer are usually confined to somatic cells, cancer is not usually inherited. (We'll return to cancer in Chapter 11.) We continue our study of genetic principles (in Chapter 9), looking first at the historical development of the science of genetics and then at the rules governing the way traits are passed from parents to offspring.

? **How is reciprocal translocation different from crossing over?**

■ Reciprocal translocation swaps chromosome segments between nonhomologous chromosomes. Crossing over exchanges corresponding segments between homologous chromosomes.

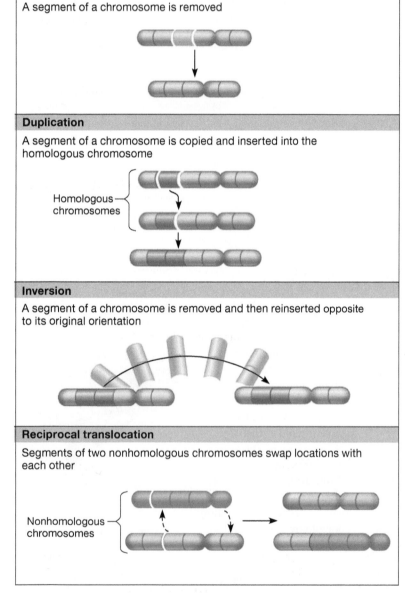

Deletion

A segment of a chromosome is removed

Duplication

A segment of a chromosome is copied and inserted into the homologous chromosome

Homologous chromosomes

Inversion

A segment of a chromosome is removed and then reinserted opposite to its original orientation

Reciprocal translocation

Segments of two nonhomologous chromosomes swap locations with each other

Nonhomologous chromosomes

▲ Figure 8.23A Alterations of chromosome structure

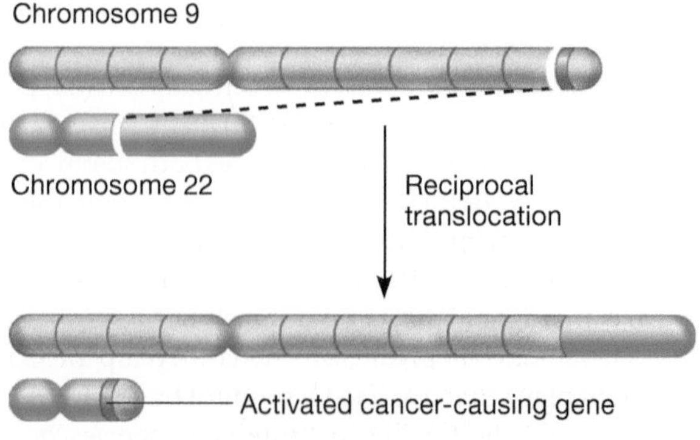

▲ Figure 8.23B The translocation associated with chronic myelogenous leukemia

CHAPTER 8 REVIEW

For practice quizzes, BioFlix animations, MP3 tutorials, video tutors, and more study tools designed for this textbook, go to MasteringBiology™

REVIEWING THE CONCEPTS

Cell Division and Reproduction (8.1–8.2)

8.1 Cell division plays many important roles in the lives of organisms. Cell division is at the heart of the reproduction of cells and organisms because cells originate only from preexisting cells. Some organisms reproduce through asexual reproduction, and in such instances their offspring are all genetic copies of the parent and identical to each other (clones). Other organisms reproduce through sexual reproduction, creating a variety of offspring.

8.2 Prokaryotes reproduce by binary fission. Prokaryotic cells reproduce asexually by cell division. As the cell replicates its single chromosome, the copies move apart; the growing membrane then divides the cell.

The Eukaryotic Cell Cycle and Mitosis (8.3–8.10)

8.3 The large, complex chromosomes of eukaryotes duplicate with each cell division. A eukaryotic cell has many more genes than a prokaryotic cell, and they are grouped into multiple chromosomes in the nucleus. Each chromosome contains one long DNA molecule. Individual chromosomes are visible under a light microscope only when the cell is in the process of dividing; otherwise, chromosomes are thin, loosely packed chromatin fibers too small to be seen. Before a cell starts dividing, the chromosomes duplicate, producing sister chromatids (containing identical DNA) that are joined together along their lengths. Cell division involves the separation of sister chromatids and results in two daughter cells, each containing a complete and identical set of chromosomes.

8.4 The cell cycle includes growth and division phases.

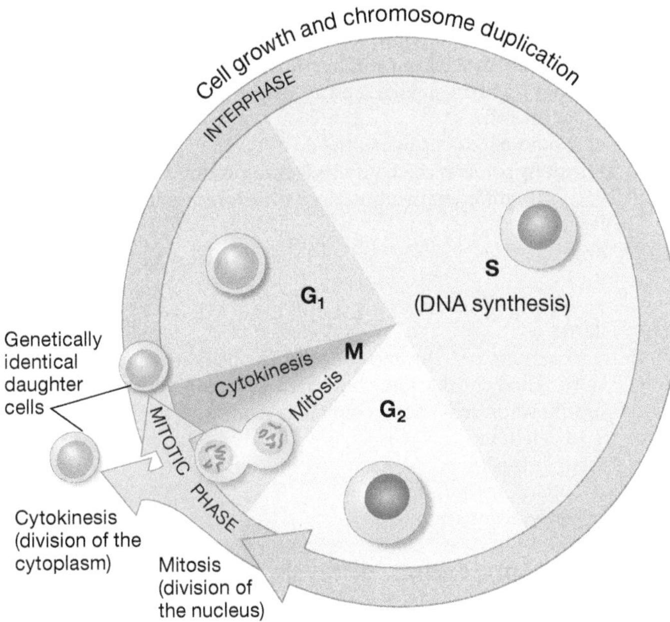

8.5 Cell division is a continuum of dynamic changes Mitosis distributes duplicated chromosomes into two daughter nuclei. After the chromosomes are coiled up, a mitotic spindle made of microtubules moves the chromosomes to the middle of the cell. The sister chromatids then separate and move to opposite poles of the cell, at which point two new nuclei form.

8.6 Cytokinesis differs for plant and animal cells. Cytokinesis, in which the cell divides in two, overlaps the end of mitosis. In animals, cytokinesis occurs when a cell constricts, forming a cleavage furrow. In plants, a membranous cell plate forms and then splits the cell in two.

8.7 The rate of cell division is affected by environmental factors. In laboratory cultures, most normal cells divide only when attached to a surface. The cultured cells continue dividing until they touch one another. Most animal cells divide only when stimulated by growth factors, and some do not divide at all. Growth factors stimulate cells to divide.

8.8 Growth factors signal the cell cycle control system. A set of proteins within the cell controls the cell cycle. Signals affecting critical checkpoints in the cell cycle determine whether a cell will go through the complete cycle and divide. The binding of growth factors to specific receptors on the plasma membrane is usually necessary for cell division.

8.9 Growing out of control, cancer cells produce malignant tumors. Cancer cells divide excessively to form masses called tumors. Malignant tumors can invade other tissues. Radiation and chemotherapy are effective as cancer treatments because they interfere with cell division.

8.10 The best cancer treatment may vary by individual. Mortality rates from cancer vary by age of diagnosis, race, and other factors. Taking such data into account may improve outcomes of cancer treatment.

Meiosis and Crossing Over (8.11–8.17)

8.11 Chromosomes are matched in homologous pairs. The somatic (body) cells of each species contain a specific number of chromosomes; for example, human cells have 46, consisting of 23 pairs of homologous chromosomes. The chromosomes of a homologous pair of autosomes carry genes for the same characteristics at the same place, or locus.

8.12 Gametes have a single set of chromosomes. Cells with two sets of homologous chromosomes are diploid. Gametes—eggs and sperm—are haploid cells with a single set of chromosomes. Sexual life cycles involve the alternation of haploid and diploid stages.

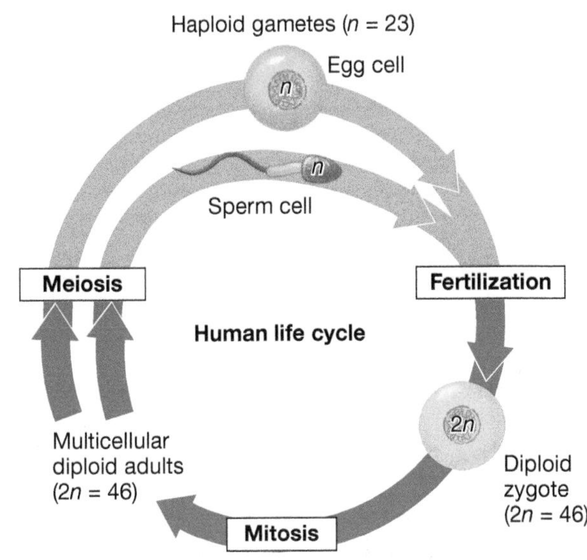

8.13 Meiosis reduces the chromosome number from diploid to haploid. Meiosis, like mitosis, is preceded by chromosome duplication, but in meiosis, the cell divides twice to form four daughter cells. The first division, meiosis I, starts with the pairing of homologous chromosomes. In crossing over, homologous chromosomes exchange corresponding segments. Meiosis I separates the members of each homologous pair and produces two daughter cells, each with one set of chromosomes. Meiosis II is essentially the same as mitosis: In each of the cells, the sister chromatids of each chromosome separate. The result is a total of four haploid cells.

8.14 Mitosis and meiosis have important similarities and differences. Both mitosis and meiosis begin with diploid parent cells that have chromosomes duplicated during the previous interphase. Mitosis produces two genetically identical diploid somatic daughter cells, whereas meiosis produces four genetically unique haploid gametes.

8.15 Independent orientation of chromosomes in meiosis and random fertilization lead to varied offspring. Each chromosome of a homologous pair differs at many points from the other member of the pair. Random arrangements of chromosome pairs at metaphase I of meiosis lead to many different combinations of chromosomes in eggs and sperm. Random fertilization of eggs by sperm greatly increases this variation.

8.16 Homologous chromosomes may carry different versions of genes. The differences between homologous chromosomes come from the fact that they can bear different versions of genes at corresponding loci.

8.17 Crossing over further increases genetic variability. Genetic recombination, which results from crossing over during prophase I of meiosis, increases variation still further.

Alterations of Chromosome Number and Structure (8.18–8.23)

8.18 Accidents during meiosis can alter chromosome number. An abnormal chromosome count is the result of nondisjunction, which can result from the failure of a pair of homologous chromosomes to separate during meiosis I or from the failure of sister chromatids to separate during meiosis II.

8.19 A karyotype is a photographic inventory of an individual's chromosomes. To prepare a karyotype, white blood cells are isolated, stimulated to grow, arrested at metaphase, and photographed under a microscope. The chromosomes are arranged into ordered pairs so that any chromosomal abnormalities can be detected.

8.20 An extra copy of chromosome 21 causes Down syndrome. Trisomy 21, the most common chromosome number abnormality, results in a condition called Down syndrome.

8.21 Abnormal numbers of sex chromosomes do not usually affect survival. Nondisjunction of the sex chromosomes during meiosis can result in individuals with a missing or extra X or Y chromosome. In some cases (such as XXY), this leads to syndromes that can affect the health of the individual; in other cases (such as XXX), the body is normal.

8.22 New species can arise from errors in cell division. Nondisjunction can produce polyploid organisms, organisms with extra sets of chromosomes. Such errors in cell division can be important in the evolution of new species.

8.23 Alterations of chromosome structure can cause birth defects and cancer. Chromosome breakage can lead to rearrangements—deletions, duplications, inversions, and translocations—that can produce genetic disorders or, if the changes occur in somatic cells, cancer.

CONNECTING THE CONCEPTS

1. Complete the following table to compare mitosis and meiosis.

	Mitosis	Meiosis
Number of chromosomal duplications		
Number of cell divisions		
Number of daughter cells produced		
Number of chromosomes in the daughter cells		
How the chromosomes line up during metaphase		
Genetic relationship of the daughter cells to the parent cell		
Functions performed in the human body		

TESTING YOUR KNOWLEDGE

Level 1: Knowledge/Comprehension

2. If an intestinal cell in a grasshopper contains 24 chromosomes, then a grasshopper sperm cell contains ________ chromosomes.
   a. 6
   b. 12
   c. 24
   d. 48
3. Which of the following is *not* a function of mitosis in humans?
   a. repair of wounds
   b. growth
   c. production of gametes from diploid cells
   d. replacement of lost or damaged cells
4. It is difficult to observe individual chromosomes during interphase because
   a. the DNA has not been replicated yet.
   b. they are in the form of long, thin strands.
   c. they leave the nucleus and are dispersed to other parts of the cell.
   d. homologous chromosomes do not pair up until division starts.
5. A fruit fly somatic cell contains 8 chromosomes. This means that ________ different combinations of chromosomes are possible in its gametes.
   a. 8
   b. 16
   c. 32
   d. 64
6. If a fragment of a chromosome breaks off and then reattaches to the original chromosome but in the reverse direction, the resulting chromosomal abnormality is called
   a. a deletion.
   b. an inversion.
   c. a translocation.
   d. a nondisjunction.

Level 2: Application/Analysis

7. Which of the following phases of mitosis is essentially the opposite of prophase in terms of changes within the nucleus?
   a. telophase
   b. metaphase
   c. interphase
   d. anaphase

8. A biochemist measured the amount of DNA in cells growing in the laboratory and found that the quantity of DNA in a cell doubled
   a. between prophase and anaphase of mitosis.
   b. between the G_1 and G_2 phases of the cell cycle.
   c. during the M phase of the cell cycle.
   d. between prophase I and prophase II of meiosis.
9. A micrograph of a dividing cell from a mouse showed 19 chromosomes, each consisting of two sister chromatids. During which of the following stages of cell division could such a picture have been taken? (*Explain your answer.*)
   a. prophase of mitosis
   b. telophase II of meiosis
   c. prophase I of meiosis
   d. prophase II of meiosis
10. Cytochalasin B is a chemical that disrupts microfilament formation. This chemical would interfere with
    a. DNA replication.
    b. formation of the mitotic spindle.
    c. cleavage.
    d. formation of the cell plate.
11. Why are individuals with an extra chromosome 21, which causes Down syndrome, more numerous than individuals with an extra chromosome 3 or chromosome 16?
    a. There are probably more genes on chromosome 21 than on the others.
    b. Chromosome 21 is a sex chromosome and chromosomes 3 and 16 are not.
    c. Down syndrome is not more common, just more serious.
    d. Extra copies of the other chromosomes are probably fatal.
12. In the light micrograph below of dividing cells near the tip of an onion root, identify a cell in interphase, prophase, metaphase, anaphase, and telophase. Describe the major events occurring at each stage.

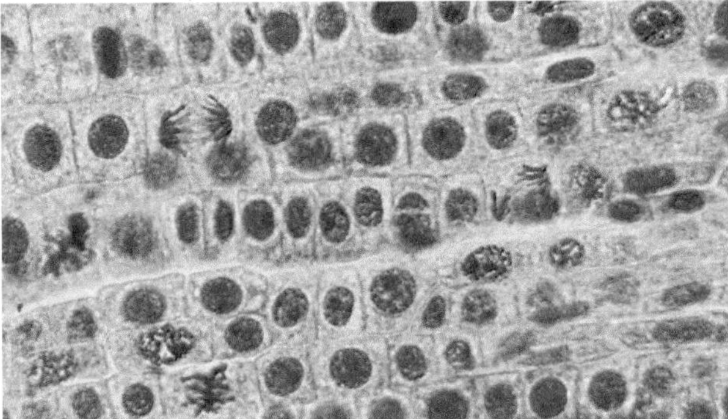

Level 3: Synthesis/Evaluation

13. An organism called a plasmodial slime mold is one large cytoplasmic mass with many nuclei. Explain how such a "megacell" could form.
14. Briefly describe how three different processes that occur during a sexual life cycle increase the genetic diversity of offspring.
15. Discuss the factors that control the division of eukaryotic cells grown in the laboratory. Cancer cells are easier to grow in the lab than other cells. Why do you suppose this is?
16. Compare cytokinesis in plant and animal cells. In what ways are the two processes similar? In what ways are they different?
17. Sketch a cell with three pairs of chromosomes undergoing meiosis, and show how nondisjunction can result in the production of gametes with extra or missing chromosomes.
18. Suppose you read in the newspaper that a genetic engineering laboratory has developed a procedure for fusing two gametes from the same person (two eggs or two sperm) to form a zygote. The article mentions that an early step in the procedure prevents crossing over from occurring during the formation of the gametes in the donor's body. The researchers are in the process of determining the genetic makeup of one of their new zygotes. Which of the following predictions do you think they would make? Justify your choice, and explain why you rejected each of the other choices.
    a. The zygote would have 46 chromosomes, all of which came from the gamete donor (its one parent), so the zygote would be genetically identical to the gamete donor.
    b. The zygote *could* be genetically identical to the gamete donor, but it is much more likely that it would have an unpredictable mixture of chromosomes from the gamete donor's parents.
    c. The zygote would not be genetically identical to the gamete donor, but it would be genetically identical to one of the donor's parents.
    d. The zygote would not be genetically identical to the gamete donor, but it would be genetically identical to one of the donor's grandparents.
19. Bacteria are able to divide on a faster schedule than eukaryotic cells. Some bacteria can divide every 20 minutes, while the minimum time required by eukaryotic cells in a rapidly developing embryo is about once per hour, and most cells divide much less often than that. State at least two testable hypotheses explaining why bacteria can divide at a faster rate than eukaryotic cells.
20. Red blood cells, which carry oxygen to body tissues, live for only about 120 days. Replacement cells are produced by cell division in bone marrow. How many cell divisions must occur each second in your bone marrow just to replace red blood cells? Here is some information to use in calculating your answer: There are about 5 million red blood cells per cubic millimeter (mm^3) of blood. An average adult has about 5 L (5,000 cm^3) of blood. (*Hint*: What is the total number of red blood cells in the body? What fraction of them must be replaced each day if all are replaced in 120 days?)
21. A mule is the offspring of a horse and a donkey. A donkey sperm contains 31 chromosomes and a horse egg cell contains 32 chromosomes, so the zygote contains a total of 63 chromosomes. The zygote develops normally. The combined set of chromosomes is not a problem in mitosis, and the mule combines some of the best characteristics of horses and donkeys. However, a mule is sterile; meiosis cannot occur normally in its testes (or ovaries). Explain why mitosis is normal in cells containing both horse and donkey chromosomes but the mixed set of chromosomes interferes with meiosis.
22. What you think of as "a banana" is a Cavendish, one variety of the species *Musa acuminate*. It is a triploid organism ($3n$) with three sets of chromosomes in every somatic cell. The Cavendish cannot be naturally bred; it can only be reproduced by cloning. Explain how its triploid state accounts for its inability to form normal gametes. Discuss how the lack of sexual reproduction might make the species particularly vulnerable to a new pest.
23. **SCIENTIFIC THINKING** The study described in Module 8.10 was purely observational; there were no controlled groups. Imagine that you are an oncologist. Design a hypothesis-driven study to determine whether mastectomy improves breast cancer survival over lumpectomy. What are your control groups? Would such a study be ethical to undertake? Why or why not?

Answers to all questions can be found in Appendix 4.

CHAPTER 9

Patterns of Inheritance

Are humans evolving?

The Inuit people (in the past, sometimes called Eskimos) are indigenous to the arctic regions of Greenland, Canada, and Alaska. With few plants available and no farming, the traditional Inuit diet consists of food obtained by hunting large land mammals (such as caribou and polar bears) and marine animals (whales, seals, and fish). This diet is one of the most extreme in the Western world: largely carnivorous, high in protein, and *very* high in fat. In fact, fat accounts for about 75% of the calories in the traditional Inuit diet. In contrast, U.S. dietary guidelines suggest we consume no more than 35% of our calories from fat. Yet the Inuit suffer heart attacks *less* often than people living in the United States.

What makes the Inuit people so able to tolerate high levels of dietary fat? The answer lies, at least in part, in their genes: Over tens of thousands of years, the Inuit population has accumulated genetic mutations that change the way the body metabolizes fats. For example, virtually every Inuit examined in a 2015 study carried a mutation in a gene for a fat-digesting enzyme, but only 25% of Chinese and 2% of Europeans had the mutation. Inheriting a copy of the mutated gene from each parent changes the regulation of different fats within the body in a way that reduces health risks associated with a high-fat diet.

In this chapter, we'll examine the rules that govern how inherited traits, such as the ability of many Inuit to metabolize high levels of fat, are passed from parents to offspring. We'll look at several different patterns of inheritance and investigate how we can predict the ratios of offspring with particular traits. Most importantly, we'll uncover a basic biological concept: how the behavior of chromosomes during gamete formation and fertilization (discussed in Chapter 8) accounts for the patterns of inheritance we observe. Along the way, we'll consider many examples of how genetic principles can help us understand the biology of humans, plants, and many other familiar creatures.

BIG IDEAS

Mendel's Laws (9.1–9.10)

A few simple rules explain many aspects of heredity.

Variations on Mendel's Laws (9.11–9.15)

Some inheritance patterns are more complex than the ones described by Mendel.

The Chromosomal Basis of Inheritance (9.16–9.19)

Hereditary rules can be understood by following the behavior of chromosomes.

Sex Chromosomes and Sex-Linked Genes (9.20–9.23)

Genes found on sex chromosomes display unique patterns of inheritance.

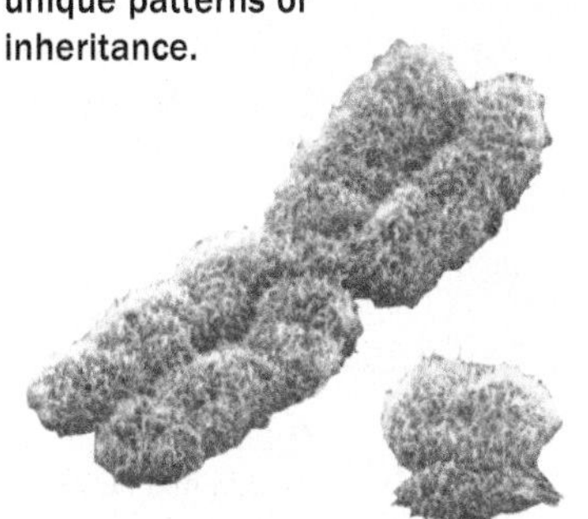

Mendel's Laws

9.1 The study of genetics has ancient roots

Attempts to explain inheritance date back at least to the ancient Greek physician Hippocrates (Figure 9.1). He suggested that particles called "pangenes" travel from each part of an organism's body to the eggs or sperm and then are passed to the next generation. Moreover, Hippocrates thought, changes that occur in the body during an organism's life are passed on in this way.

▲ Figure 9.1 Hippocrates (approximately 460–370 BCE)

Hippocrates's model is incorrect in several respects. The reproductive cells are not composed of particles from somatic (body) cells, and changes in somatic cells do not influence eggs and sperm. For instance, no matter how many years you endure braces on your teeth, cells in your mouth do not transmit genetic information to your gametes, and there is no higher likelihood that your offspring will have straight teeth just because you wore braces. This may seem like common sense today, but the idea that traits acquired during an individual's lifetime are passed on to offspring prevailed until the 19th century.

By observing inheritance patterns in ornamental plants, biologists of the early 19th century established that offspring inherit traits from both parents. The favored explanation of inheritance then became the "blending" hypothesis, the idea that the hereditary materials contributed by the male and female parents mix in forming the offspring similar to the way that blue and yellow paints blend to make green. According to this hypothesis, after the genetic information for the colors of black and chocolate brown Labrador retrievers is blended, the colors should be as inseparable as paint pigments. But this is not what happens: Instead, the offspring of a purebred black Lab and a purebred brown Lab will all be black, but some of the dogs in the next generation will be brown (you'll learn why in Module 9.5). The blending hypothesis was finally rejected because it does not explain how traits that disappear in one generation can reappear in later ones.

? Imagine you have two different birds of the same species, a female with a yellow beak and a male with a blue beak. Design a simple experiment to test the blending hypothesis.

■ Cross the two birds and observe the resulting beak color in the offspring. The blending hypothesis predicts the appearance of all green beaks.

9.2 The science of genetics began in an abbey garden

Heredity is the transmission of traits from one generation to the next. The field of **genetics**, the scientific study of heredity, began in the 1860s, when an Augustinian monk named Gregor Mendel (Figure 9.2A) deduced the fundamental principles of genetics by breeding garden peas. Mendel lived and worked in an abbey in Brunn, Austria (now Brno, in the Czech Republic). His research was strongly influenced by his study of physics, mathematics, and chemistry at the University of Vienna. His education helped Mendel design studies that were experimentally and mathematically rigorous, qualities that were largely responsible for his success.

▲ Figure 9.2A Gregor Mendel (1822–1884)

In 1866, Mendel published one of the most influential papers in the history of biology. In it, he correctly argued that parents pass discrete "heritable factors" on to their offspring. (Mendel's landmark publication appeared seven years after the publication of Darwin's *The Origin of Species*, making the 1860s a banner decade in the history of modern biology.) Mendel stressed that the heritable factors, today called genes, retain their individuality generation after generation. That is, genes are like playing cards: A deck may be shuffled, but the cards always retain their original identities, and no card is ever blended with another. Similarly, genes may be sorted, but each gene retains its identity.

Mendel probably chose to study garden peas because they had short generation times, produced large numbers of offspring from each mating, and came in many readily distinguishable varieties. For example, one variety has purple flowers, and another variety has white flowers. A heritable feature that varies among individuals, such as flower color, is called a **character**. Each variant for a character, such as purple or white flowers, is called a **trait**. Perhaps the most important advantage of pea plants as an experimental model is that matings can be strictly controlled. As Figure 9.2B shows, the petals of the pea flower almost completely enclose the reproductive organs: the stamens and carpel.

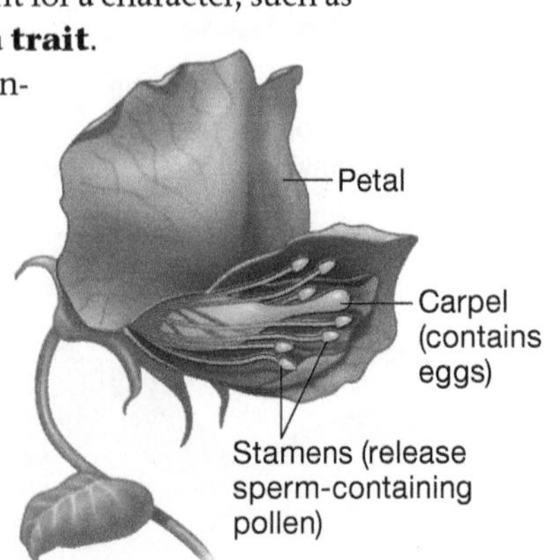

▶ Figure 9.2B The anatomy of a garden pea flower (with one petal removed to improve visibility)

Consequently, pea plants usually are able to self-fertilize in nature: Sperm-carrying pollen grains released from the stamens land on the egg-containing carpel of the same flower. Mendel could ensure self-fertilization by covering a flower with a small bag so that no pollen from another plant could reach the carpel. When he wanted cross-fertilization (fertilization of one plant by pollen from a different plant), he used the method shown in Figure 9.2C. ① He prevented self-fertilization by cutting off the immature stamens of a plant before they produced pollen. ② To cross-fertilize the stamenless flower, he dusted its carpel with pollen from another plant. After pollination, ③ the carpel developed into a pod, containing seeds (peas) that ④ he later planted. ⑤ The seeds grew into offspring plants (F_1). Through these methods, Mendel could always be sure of the parentage of new plants.

As noted earlier, Mendel's success was due in part to his experimental approach and choice of organism and to his selection of characters to study. He chose to observe seven characters, each of which occurred as two distinct traits (Figure 9.2D). Mendel chose **true-breeding** varieties—that is, varieties for which self-fertilization produced offspring all identical to the parent. For instance, he identified a purple-flowered variety that, when self-fertilized, produced offspring plants that all had purple flowers.

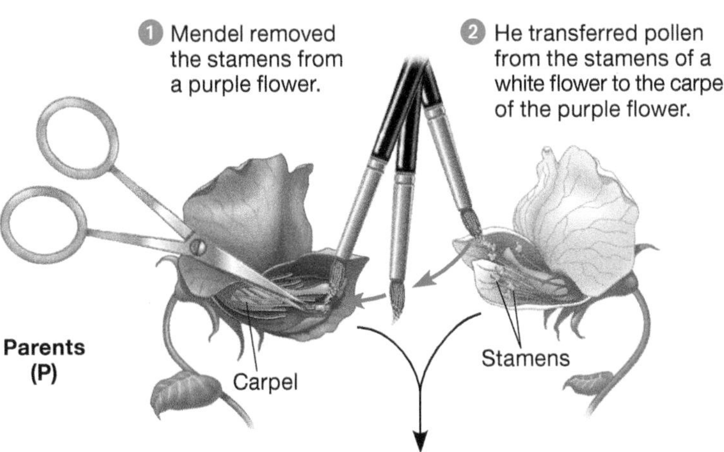

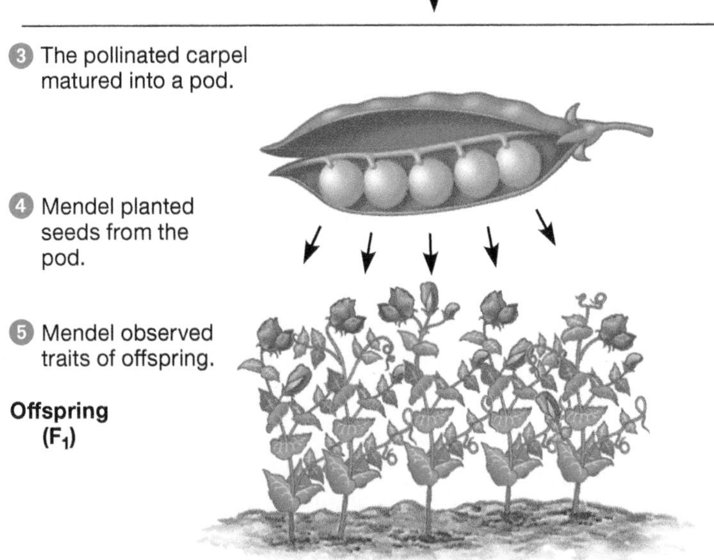

③ The pollinated carpel matured into a pod.
④ Mendel planted seeds from the pod.
⑤ Mendel observed traits of offspring.
Offspring (F_1)

▲ **Figure 9.2C** **Mendel's technique for cross-fertilization of pea plants**

Mendel was then ready to ask what would happen when he crossed his different true-breeding varieties with each other. For example, what offspring would result if plants with purple flowers and plants with white flowers were cross-fertilized? The offspring of two different varieties are called **hybrids**, and the cross-fertilization itself is referred to as a hybridization, or simply a genetic **cross**. The true-breeding parents are called the **P generation** (P for parental), and their hybrid offspring are called the **F_1 generation** (F for *filial*, from the Latin word for "son"). When F_1 plants self-fertilize or fertilize each other, their offspring are the **F_2 generation**.

Mendel's quantitative analysis of the F_2 plants from thousands of genetic crosses allowed him to deduce the fundamental principles of heredity. We turn to Mendel's results next.

? **Describe three generations of your own family using the terminology of a genetic cross (P, F_1, F_2).**

■ The P generation is your grandparents, the F_1 your parents, and the F_2 is you (and any siblings).

Character	Traits	
	Dominant	Recessive
Flower color	Purple	White
Flower position	Axial	Terminal
Seed color	Yellow	Green
Seed shape	Round	Wrinkled
Pod shape	Inflated	Constricted
Pod color	Green	Yellow
Stem length	Tall	Dwarf

▲ **Figure 9.2D** **The seven pea characters studied by Mendel**

9.3 Mendel's law of segregation describes the inheritance of a single character

Mendel performed many experiments in which he tracked the inheritance of characters that occur in two forms, such as flower color. The results led him to formulate several hypotheses about inheritance. Let's look at some of his experiments and follow the reasoning that led to his hypotheses.

Figure 9.3A starts with a cross between a true-breeding pea plant with purple flowers and a true-breeding pea plant with white flowers. Mendel observed that all resulting F_1 plants had purple flowers. Was the white-flowered plant's genetic contribution to the hybrids lost? By mating the F_1 plants with each other, Mendel found the answer to be no. Out of 929 F_2 plants, 705 (about $\frac{3}{4}$) had purple flowers and 224 (about $\frac{1}{4}$) had white flowers. That is, there are about three plants with purple flowers for every one with white flowers, or a 3:1 ratio of purple to white. Mendel reasoned that the heritable factor for white flowers did not disappear in the F_1 plants but was masked when the purple-flower factor was present. He also deduced that the F_1 plants must have carried two factors for the flower-color character, one for purple and one for white. From these results and others, Mendel developed four hypotheses, described here using modern terminology, such as "gene" instead of "heritable factor."

1. *There are alternative versions of genes that account for variations in inherited characters.* For example, the gene for flower color in pea plants exists in two versions: one for purple and the other for white. Alternative versions of a gene are called **alleles**.
2. *For each character, an organism inherits two alleles of a gene, one from each parent.* These alleles may be identical or they may differ. An organism that has two identical alleles for a gene is said to be **homozygous** for that gene (and is a "homozygote" for that trait). An organism that has two different alleles for a gene is said to be **heterozygous** for that gene (and is a "heterozygote").
3. *If the two alleles of an inherited pair differ, then one determines the organism's appearance and is called the* **dominant allele** and *the other has no noticeable effect on the organism's appearance and is called the* **recessive allele.** Geneticists use uppercase italic letters to represent dominant alleles and lowercase italic letters to represent recessive alleles.
4. *A sperm or egg carries only one allele for each inherited character because allele pairs separate (segregate) from each other during the production of gametes.* This statement is called the **law of segregation**. When sperm and egg unite at fertilization, each contributes its allele, restoring the paired condition in the offspring.

Do Mendel's hypotheses account for the 3:1 ratio he observed in the F_2 generation? Figure 9.3B illustrates

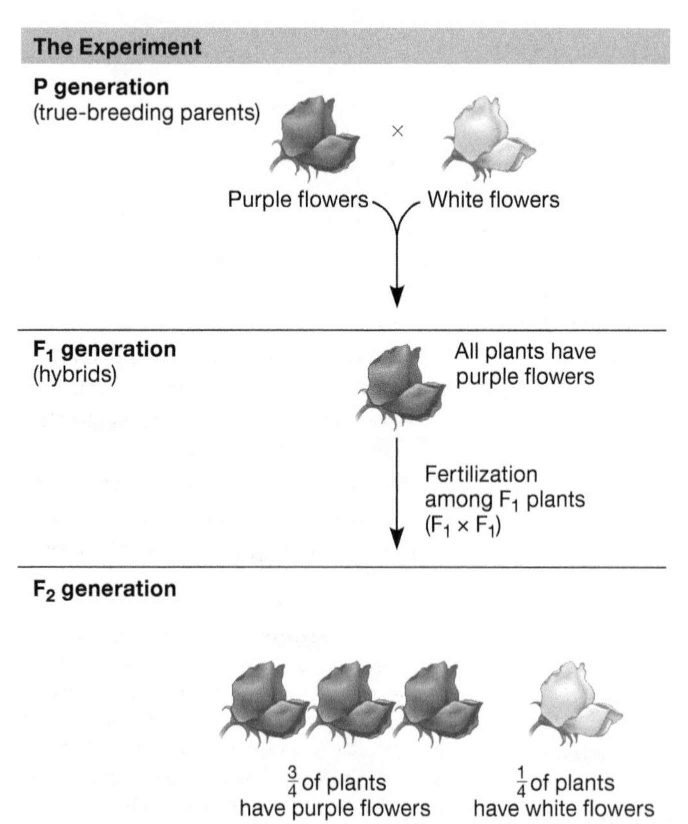

▲ Figure 9.3A A cross that tracks one character (flower color)

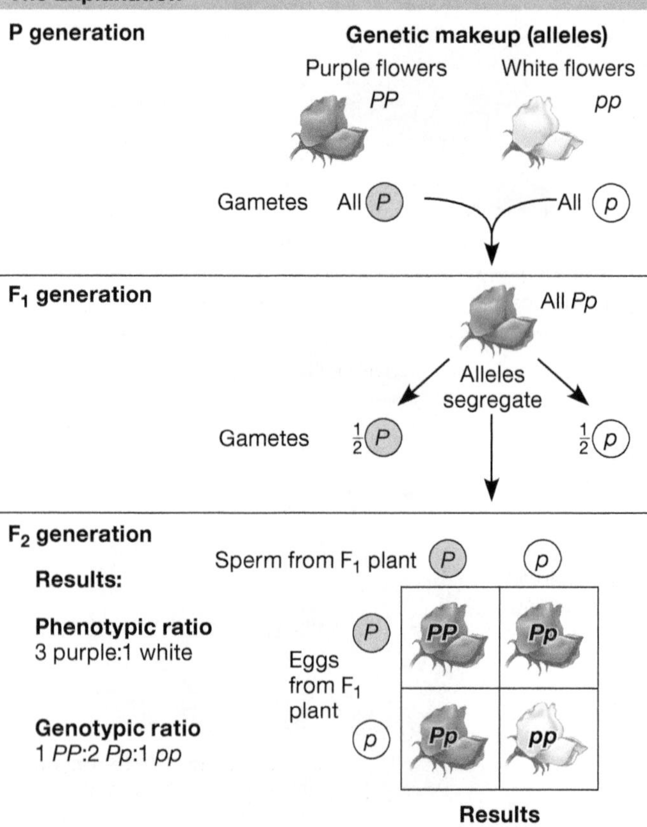

▲ Figure 9.3B An explanation of the crosses in Figure 9.3A

Mendel's law of segregation, which explains the inheritance pattern shown in Figure 9.3A. Mendel's hypotheses predict that when alleles segregate during gamete formation in the F_1 plants, half the gametes will receive a purple-flower allele (*P*) and the other half a white-flower allele (*p*). During pollination among the F_1 plants, the gametes unite randomly. An egg with a purple-flower allele has an equal chance of being fertilized by a sperm with a purple-flower allele or one with a white-flower allele (that is, a *P* egg may fuse with a *P* sperm or a *p* sperm). Because the same is true for an egg with a white-flower allele (a *p* egg with a *P* sperm or *p* sperm), there are a total of four equally likely combinations of sperm and egg in the F_2 generation.

The diagram at the bottom right of Figure 9.3B, called a **Punnett square**, repeats the cross shown in Figure 9.3A in a way that visually highlights the four possible combinations of gametes and the resulting four possible offspring in the F_2 generation. Each square represents an equally probable product of fertilization. For example, the box in the upper right corner of the Punnett square shows the genetic combination resulting from a *p* sperm fertilizing a *P* egg.

According to the Punnett square, what will be the physical appearance of these F_2 offspring? One-fourth of the plants have two alleles specifying purple flowers (*PP*); clearly, these plants will have purple flowers. One-half (two-fourths) of the F_2 offspring have inherited one allele for purple flowers and one allele for white flowers (*Pp*); like the F_1 plants, these plants will also have purple flowers, the dominant trait. (Note that *Pp* and *pP* are equivalent and usually written as *Pp*.) Finally, one-fourth of the F_2 plants have inherited two alleles specifying white flowers (*pp*) and will express this recessive trait. Thus, Mendel's model accounts for the 3:1 ratio that he observed in the F_2 generation.

Because an organism's appearance does not always reveal its genetic composition, geneticists distinguish between an organism's observable traits, called its **phenotype** (such as purple or white flowers), and its genetic makeup, its **genotype** (in this example, *PP*, *Pp*, or *pp*). So now we see that Figure 9.3A shows just phenotypes, whereas Figure 9.3B shows both phenotypes and genotypes in our sample crosses. For the F_2 plants, the ratio of plants with purple flowers to those with white flowers (3:1) is called the phenotypic ratio. The genotypic ratio, as shown by the Punnett square, is 1 *PP*:2 *Pp*:1 *pp*.

Mendel found that each of the seven characters he studied exhibited the same inheritance pattern: One parental trait disappeared in the F_1 generation, only to reappear in the F_2 offspring. The mechanism underlying this inheritance pattern is stated by Mendel's law of segregation: *Pairs of alleles segregate (separate) during gamete formation; the fusion of gametes at fertilization creates allele pairs once again.* Research since Mendel's time has established that the law of segregation applies to all sexually reproducing organisms, including humans.

Later in this chapter, we'll return to Mendel and his experiments with pea plants (in Module 9.5). But first, we'll investigate how cell division (the topic of Chapter 8) fits with what we've learned about genetics so far.

? How can two plants with different genotypes for a particular inherited character be identical in phenotype?

■ One could be homozygous for the dominant allele and the other heterozygous.

9.4 Homologous chromosomes bear the alleles for each character

Every diploid cell, whether from a pea plant or a person, has pairs of homologous chromosomes (one pair is shown in Figure 9.4). The chromosomes in a homologous pair carry alleles of the same genes at the same locations. One member of each pair comes from the organism's female parent and the other member of each pair comes from the male parent. The transmission of genetic traits from one generation to the next is an example of the theme of INFORMATION.

Each labeled band on the chromosomes in Figure 9.4 represents a gene **locus** (plural, *loci*), a specific location of a gene along the chromosome. You can see the connection between Mendel's law of segregation and homologous chromosomes: Alleles (alternative versions) of a gene reside at the same locus on homologous chromosomes. However, the two chromosomes may bear either identical alleles at a locus (as in the *P*/*P* and *a*/*a* loci) or different alleles (as in the *B*/*b* locus)—the organisms may be homozygous or heterozygous for the gene at any particular locus. We will return to the chromosomal basis of Mendel's law later in the chapter.

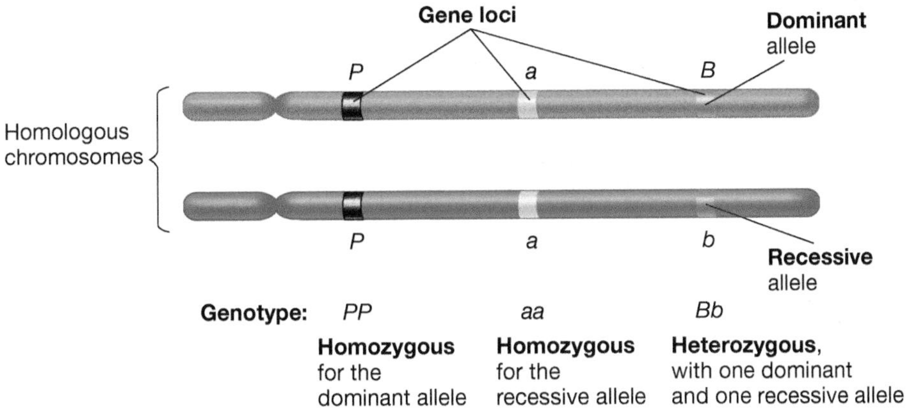

Gene loci
Dominant allele
P a B
Homologous chromosomes
P a b
Recessive allele
Genotype: PP aa Bb
Homozygous for the dominant allele
Homozygous for the recessive allele
Heterozygous, with one dominant and one recessive allele

▲ **Figure 9.4** Three gene loci on homologous chromosomes

? An individual is heterozygous, *Bb*, for a gene. According to the law of segregation, each gamete formed by this individual will have *either* the *B* allele *or* the *b* allele. Which step in the process of meiosis is the physical basis for this segregation of alleles? (*Hint:* See Figure 8.13.)

■ The *B* and *b* alleles are located at the same gene locus on homologous chromosomes, which separate during meiosis I and are packaged in separate gametes during meiosis II.

9.5 The law of independent assortment is revealed by tracking two characters at once

Recall from Module 9.3 that Mendel deduced his law of segregation by following one character through two generations. A cross between two individuals that are heterozygous for one character ($Pp \times Pp$ in this case) is called a **monohybrid cross**. By observing monohybrid crosses, Mendel knew that the allele for round seed shape (designated *R*) was dominant to the allele for wrinkled seed shape (*r*) and that the allele for yellow seed color (*Y*) was dominant to the allele for green seed color (*y*). Mendel wondered: What would happen if he crossed plants that differ in *both* seed shape and seed color?

To find out, Mendel crossed homozygous plants having round yellow seeds (genotype *RRYY*) with plants having wrinkled green seeds (*rryy*). Mendel knew that an *RRYY* plant would produce only gametes with *RY* alleles; an *rryy* plant would produce only gametes with *ry* alleles. Therefore, Mendel knew there was only one possible outcome for the F_1 generation: The union of *RY* and *ry* gametes would yield hybrids heterozygous for both characters (*RrYy*)—that is, dihybrids. All of these *RrYy* offspring would have round yellow seeds, the double dominant phenotype.

The F_2 generation is trickier to predict. To find out if genes for seed color and shape would be transmitted as a package, Mendel crossed the *RrYy* F_1 plants with each other. This is a **dihybrid cross**, a cross between two organisms that are each heterozygous for two characters being followed. Mendel hypothesized two outcomes from this experiment: Either the dihybrid cross would exhibit *dependent* assortment, with the alleles for seed color and seed shape inherited together as they came from the P generation, or it would exhibit *independent* assortment, with the genes inherited independently.

The hypothesis of dependent assortment leads to the prediction that each F_2 plant would inherit one of two possible sperm (*RY* or *ry*) and one of two possible eggs (*RY* or *ry*), for a total of four combinations (Figure 9.5A). The Punnett square shows that there could be only two F_2 phenotypes—round yellow or wrinkled green—in a 3:1 ratio. However, when Mendel actually performed this cross, he did not obtain these results, thus refuting the hypothesis of dependent assortment.

The alternative hypothesis—that the genes would exhibit independent assortment—leads to the prediction that the F_1 plants would produce four different gametes: *RY*, *rY*, *Ry*, and *ry* (Figure 9.5A, right). Each F_2 plant would receive one of four possible sperm and one of four possible eggs, for a total of 16 possible combinations. Fertilization among these gametes would lead to four different seed phenotypes—round yellow, round green, wrinkled yellow, or wrinkled green—in a 9:3:3:1 ratio. In fact, Mendel observed such a ratio in the F_2 plants, indicating that each pair of alleles segregates independently of the other.

From the 9:3:3:1 ratio, we can see that there are 12 plants with round seeds to 4 with wrinkled seeds, and 12 yellow-seeded plants to 4 green-seeded ones. These 12:4 ratios each reduce to 3:1, which is the F_2 ratio for a monohybrid cross. In other words, an independent monohybrid cross is occurring for each of the two characters. Mendel tried his seven pea characters in various dihybrid combinations and always obtained data close to the predicted 9:3:3:1 ratio. These results supported the hypothesis that each pair of alleles segregates independently of other pairs of alleles during gamete formation. Put another way, the inheritance of one character has no effect on the inheritance of another. This is referred to as Mendel's **law of independent assortment**.

Figure 9.5B shows how this law applies to the inheritance of two characters controlled by separate genes in Labrador retrievers: black versus chocolate coat color and normal vision versus progressive retinal atrophy (PRA), an eye disorder that leads to blindness. Black Labs have at least one copy of an allele (*B*) that gives their hairs densely packed granules of a dark pigment. The *B* allele is dominant to the *b* allele, which leads to a less tightly packed distribution of pigment. As a result, the coats of dogs with genotype *bb* are chocolate in color. The allele that causes PRA, *n*, is recessive to allele *N*, which is necessary for normal vision. Thus, only dogs of genotype *nn* become blind from PRA. In the top of this

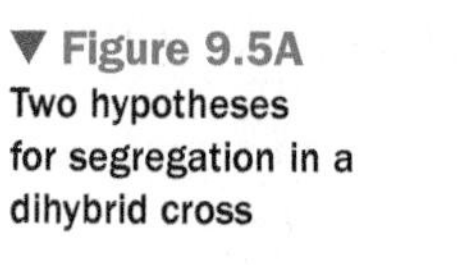

▼ Figure 9.5A Two hypotheses for segregation in a dihybrid cross

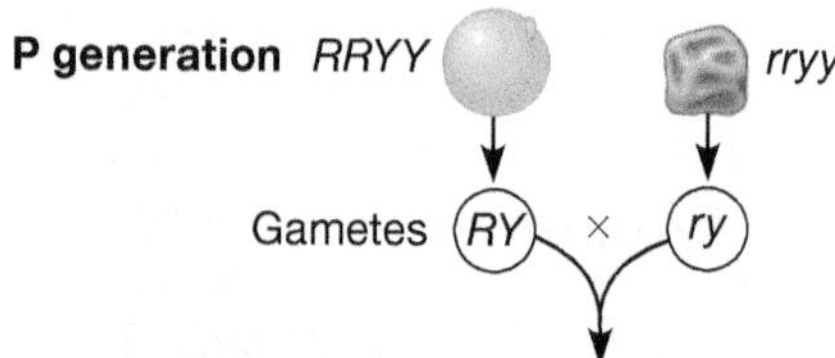

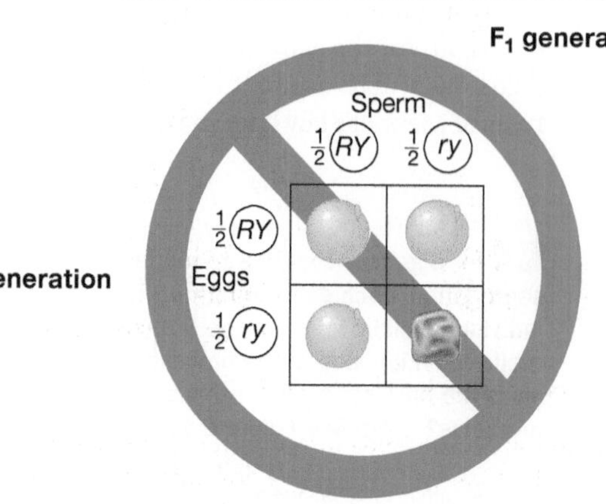

The hypothesis of dependent assortment

Not actually seen; hypothesis refuted

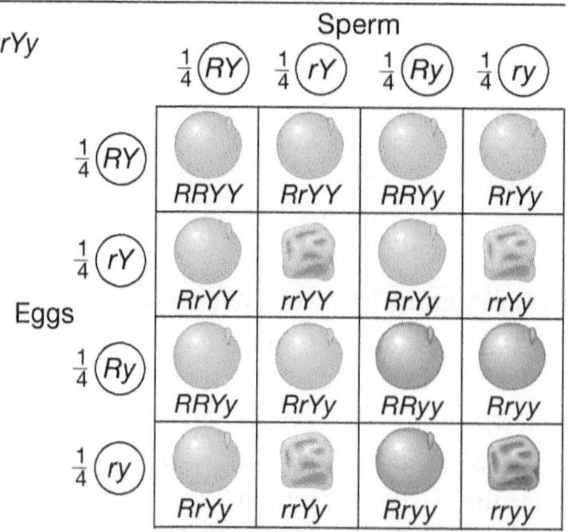

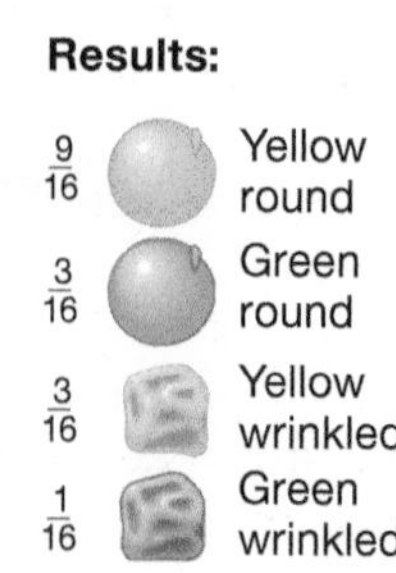

The hypothesis of independent assortment

Actual results; hypothesis supported

Four possible phenotypes and genotypes for coat color and vision in Labrador retrievers

Phenotypes	Black coat, normal vision	Black coat, blind (PRA)	Chocolate coat, normal vision	Chocolate coat, blind (PRA)
Genotypes	*B_N_*	*B_nn*	*bbN_*	*bbnn*

Mating of double heterozygotes (black coat, normal vision):

BbNn × *BbNn*

Phenotypic ratio of the offspring	9 Black coat, normal vision	3 Black coat, blind (PRA)	3 Chocolate coat, normal vision	1 Chocolate coat, blind (PRA)

▲ **Figure 9.5B** **Independent assortment of two genes in Labrador retrievers**

TRY THIS Rewrite the cross shown in this figure using a Punnett square, like the one used in the previous figure. You should get the same results!

figure, blanks in the genotypes are used where a particular phenotype may result from multiple genotypes. For example, a black Lab may have either genotype *BB* or *Bb*, which we abbreviate as *B_*.)

The lower part of Figure 9.5B shows what happens when we mate two heterozygous Labs, both of genotype *BbNn*. The F_2 phenotypic ratio will be nine black dogs with normal eyes to three black with PRA to three chocolate with normal eyes to one chocolate with PRA. These 9:3:3:1 results are analogous to the results in Figure 9.5A and demonstrate that the alleles for the *B* and *N* genes are inherited independently.

? Predict the phenotypes of offspring obtained by mating a black Lab homozygous for both coat color and normal eyes with a chocolate Lab that is blind from PRA.

■ All offspring would be black with normal eyes (*BBNN* × *bbnn* → *BbNn*).

9.6 Geneticists can use a testcross to determine unknown genotypes

Suppose you have a chocolate Lab. Referring to Figure 9.5B, you can tell that its genotype must be *bb*. But what if you had a black Lab? It could have one of two possible genotypes—*BB* or *Bb*—and there is no way to tell simply by looking at the dog. To determine your dog's genotype, you could perform a **testcross**, a mating between an individual of unknown genotype (your black Lab) and a homozygous recessive (*bb*) individual—in this case, a chocolate Lab.

Figure 9.6 shows the offspring that could result from such a mating. If, as shown on the bottom left, the black-coated parent's genotype is *BB*, all the offspring would be black because a cross between genotypes *BB* and *bb* can produce only *Bb* offspring. On the other hand, if the black parent is *Bb*, as shown on the bottom right, we would expect both black (*Bb*) and chocolate (*bb*) offspring. Thus, the appearance of the offspring reveals the original black dog's genotype.

To understand the results of any genetic cross, you need to understand the rules of probability. These rules are the topic of the next module.

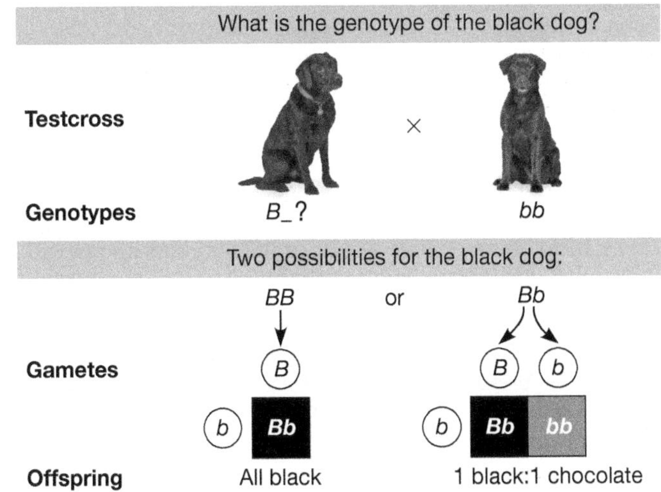

▲ **Figure 9.6** **Using a testcross to determine genotype**

? You use a testcross to determine the genotype of a Lab with normal eyes. Half of the offspring are normal and half develop PRA. What is the genotype of the normal parent?

■ Heterozygous (*Nn*)

9.7 Mendel's laws reflect the rules of probability

Mendel's strong background in mathematics served him well in his studies of inheritance. He understood, for instance, that the segregation of allele pairs during gamete formation and the re-forming of pairs at fertilization obey the rules of probability—the same rules that apply to the tossing of coins, the rolling of dice, and the drawing of cards. Mendel also appreciated the statistical nature of inheritance. He knew that he needed to obtain large samples—to count many offspring from his crosses—before he could begin to interpret inheritance patterns.

Let's see how the rules of probability apply to inheritance. The probability scale ranges from 0 to 1. An event that is certain to occur has a probability of 1, whereas an event that is certain *not* to occur has a probability of 0. For example, a tossed coin has a $\frac{1}{2}$ chance of landing heads and a $\frac{1}{2}$ chance of landing tails. These two possibilities add up to 1; the probabilities of all possible outcomes for an event to occur must always add up to 1. In another example, in a standard deck of 52 playing cards, the chance of drawing a jack of diamonds is $\frac{1}{52}$ and the chance of drawing any card other than the jack of diamonds is $\frac{51}{52}$, which together add up to 1.

An important lesson we can learn from coin tossing is that for each and every toss of the coin, the probability of heads is $\frac{1}{2}$. Even if heads has landed five times in a row, the probability of the next toss coming up heads is still $\frac{1}{2}$. In other words, the outcome of any particular toss is an independent event, unaffected by what has happened on previous attempts. If two coins are tossed simultaneously, the outcome for each coin is unaffected by the other coin.

What is the chance that both coins will land heads up when tossed together? The probability of such a dual event is the product of the separate probabilities of the independent events; for the coins, $\frac{1}{2} \times \frac{1}{2} = \frac{1}{4}$. This statistical principle is called the **rule of multiplication**, and it holds true for independent events in genetics as well as coin tosses.

Figure 9.7 offers a visual analogy of a cross between F_1 Labrador retrievers that have the *Bb* genotype for coat color. The genetic cross is portrayed by the tossing of two coins that stand in for the two gametes (a dime for the egg and a penny for the sperm); the heads side of each coin stands for the dominant *B* allele and the tails side of each coin the recessive *b* allele. What is the probability that a particular F_2 dog will have the *bb* genotype? To produce a *bb* offspring, both egg and sperm must carry the *b* allele. The probability that an egg will have the *b* allele is $\frac{1}{2}$, and the probability that a sperm will have the *b* allele is also $\frac{1}{2}$. By the rule of multiplication, the probability that the two *b* alleles will come together at fertilization is $\frac{1}{4}$. This is exactly the answer given by the Punnett square in Figure 9.7. If we know the genotypes of the parents, we can predict the probability for any genotype among the offspring.

Now consider the probability that an F_2 Lab will be heterozygous for the coat-color gene. As Figure 9.7 shows, there are two ways in which F_1 gametes can combine to produce a heterozygous offspring. The dominant (*B*) allele can come from the egg and the recessive (*b*) allele from the sperm, or vice versa. The probability that an event can occur in two or more alternative ways can be determined from the sum of the separate probabilities of the alternatives; this is known as the **rule of addition**. Using this rule, we can calculate the probability of an F_2 heterozygote as $\frac{1}{4} + \frac{1}{4} = \frac{1}{2}$. This is like asking the odds of turning over a playing card that is a heart or a club: the odds of drawing a heart ($\frac{1}{4}$) are added to the odds of drawing a club ($\frac{1}{4}$): $\frac{1}{4} + \frac{1}{4} = \frac{1}{2}$.

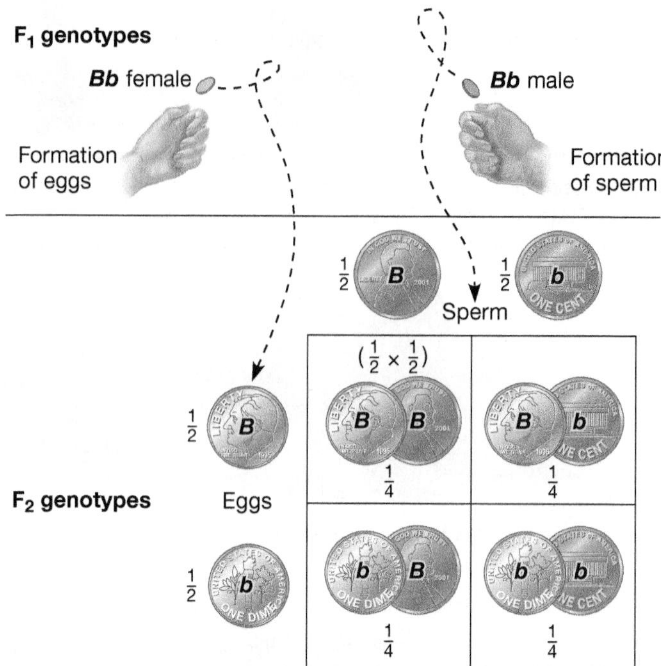

▲ **Figure 9.7** Segregation and fertilization as chance events

By applying the rules of probability to segregation and independent assortment, we can solve some rather complex genetics problems. For instance, we can predict the results of trihybrid crosses, in which three different characters are involved. Consider a cross between two organisms that both have the genotype *AaBbCc*. What is the probability that an offspring from this cross will be a recessive homozygote for all three genes (*aabbcc*)? Because each allele pair assorts independently, we can treat this trihybrid cross as three separate monohybrid crosses:

$$Aa \times Aa\text{: Probability of } aa \text{ offspring} = \tfrac{1}{4}$$
$$Bb \times Bb\text{: Probability of } bb \text{ offspring} = \tfrac{1}{4}$$
$$Cc \times Cc\text{: Probability of } cc \text{ offspring} = \tfrac{1}{4}$$

Because the segregation of each allele pair is an independent event, we use the rule of multiplication to calculate the probability that the offspring will be *aabbcc*:

$$\tfrac{1}{4}aa \times \tfrac{1}{4}bb \times \tfrac{1}{4}cc = \tfrac{1}{64}$$

We could reach the same conclusion by constructing a 64-section Punnett square, but that would take a lot of space!

? **A plant of genotype *AABbCC* is crossed with an *AaBbCc* plant. What is the probability of an offspring having the genotype *AABBCC*? (Hint: Treat this as 3 separate monohybrid crosses.)**

■ $\frac{1}{16}$ (that is, $\frac{1}{2} \times \frac{1}{4} \times \frac{1}{2}$.)

VISUALIZING THE CONCEPT

9.8 Genetic traits in humans can be tracked through family pedigrees

Although Mendel developed his laws of inheritance while working with peas, these principles apply to the inheritance of many human traits just as well. How are human traits studied? We obviously cannot perform controlled genetic crosses on people, so geneticists must analyze the results of matings that have already occurred. First, a geneticist collects information about a family's history for a trait. This information is assembled into a family tree, called a **pedigree**, that describes the traits of parents and children across generations. Here, you can see a pedigree that traces the incidence of a straight hairline versus a "widow's peak" (pointed) hairline through three generations of a hypothetical family. Notice that Mendel's laws and simple logic enable us to deduce the genotypes for nearly every person in the pedigree.

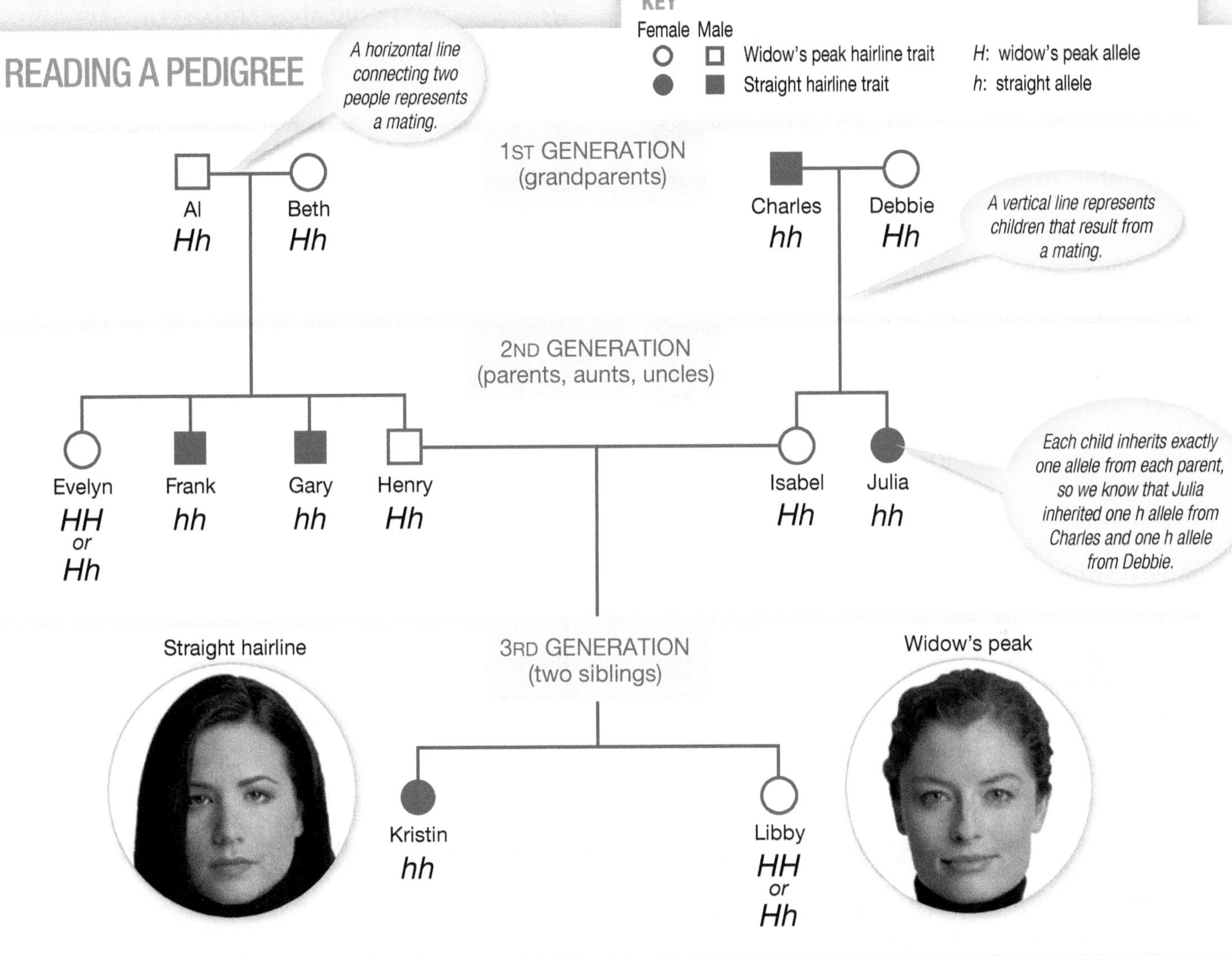

- Kristin has a straight hairline but neither of her parents (Henry and Isabel) do. This is only possible if the trait is recessive. We therefore know that Kristin and every other individual with a straight hairline must be homozygous recessive *hh*.
- Henry and Isabel must each have a copy of the *h* allele, because they each passed one on to daughter Kristin. And because they both have widow's peaks, they must each be heterozygous (*Hh*).
- Grandparents Al and Beth must both be *Hh* because they both had widow's peaks, but two of their sons (Frank and Gary) had straight hairlines and must therefore be *hh*.
- We cannot deduce the genotype of every member of the pedigree. Libby must have at least one *H* allele (since she has a widow's peak), but she could be either *HH* or *Hh*. We cannot distinguish between these two possibilities using the available data.

? If Libby had a child, which phenotype would allow her to deduce her own genotype for certain?

If her child had a straight hairline (*hh*), then Libby would know that she herself must be *Hh*.

9.9 Many inherited traits in humans are controlled by a single gene

CONNECTION

In the previous module, you studied an example of a human character (widow's peak) controlled by simple dominant-recessive inheritance of one gene. Figure 9.9A shows two more examples. (The genetic bases of many other human characters, such as eye and hair color, are more complex and poorly understood.) A trait being dominant does not mean that it is "normal" or more common than a recessive trait. Rather, dominance means that a heterozygote (*Aa*) displays the dominant phenotype. By contrast, the phenotype of a recessive allele is seen only in a homozygote (*aa*). Recessive traits may in fact be more common in the population than dominant ones. For example, the absence of freckles (a dominant trait) is more common than their presence. The term *mutant trait* refers to a trait that is less common in nature.

The genetic disorders listed in Table 9.9 are known to be inherited as dominant or recessive traits controlled by a single gene. These human disorders show simple inheritance patterns like the traits Mendel studied in pea plants. The genes discussed in this module are all located on autosomes, chromosomes other than the sex chromosomes X and Y (see Module 8.11).

▲ **Figure 9.9A** Examples of single-gene inherited traits in humans

Recessive Disorders Thousands of human genetic disorders—ranging in severity from relatively mild, such as albinism, to invariably fatal, such as Tay-Sachs—are inherited as recessive traits. Remember that the dominant phenotype results from either the homozygous genotype *AA* or the heterozygous genotype *Aa*. Recessive phenotypes result only from the homozygous genotype *aa*. Most people who have recessive disorders are born to normal parents who are both heterozygotes—that is, those parents who are **carriers** of the recessive allele for the disorder but are phenotypically normal.

Using Mendel's laws, we can predict the fraction of affected offspring likely to result from a mating between two carriers (Figure 9.9B). Suppose two people who are heterozygous carriers for albinism (*Aa*) had a child. What is the probability that this child would display albinism? Each child of two carriers has a $\frac{1}{4}$ chance of inheriting two recessive alleles, or about one-fourth of the children from such a mating are predicted to display albinism. We can also say that a child with normal pigmentation has a $\frac{2}{3}$ chance of being an *Aa* carrier; that is, on average, two out of three offspring with the pigmented phenotype will be carriers for albinism.

The most common lethal genetic disease in the United States is cystic fibrosis (CF), with 30,000 known cases in the United States and 70,000 worldwide. The recessive CF allele is carried by about one in 31 Americans—that means over 10 million Americans are silent carriers. A person with two copies of this allele has cystic fibrosis, which is characterized by an excessive secretion of very thick mucus from

TABLE 9.9 Some Autosomal Disorders in Humans

Disorder	Major Symptoms
Recessive Disorders	
Albinism	Lack of pigment in the skin, hair, and eyes
Cystic fibrosis	Excess mucus in the lungs, digestive tract, liver; increased susceptibility to infections; death in early childhood unless treated
Phenylketonuria (PKU)	Accumulation of phenylalanine in blood; lack of normal skin pigment; developmental disabilities
Sickle-cell disease	Sickled red blood cells; damage to many tissues
Tay-Sachs disease	Lipid accumulation in brain cells; mental deficiency; blindness; death in childhood
Dominant Disorders	
Achondroplasia	Dwarfism
Huntington's disease	Uncontrollable movements; cognitive impairments; strikes in middle age
Hypercholesterolemia	Excess cholesterol in the blood; heart disease

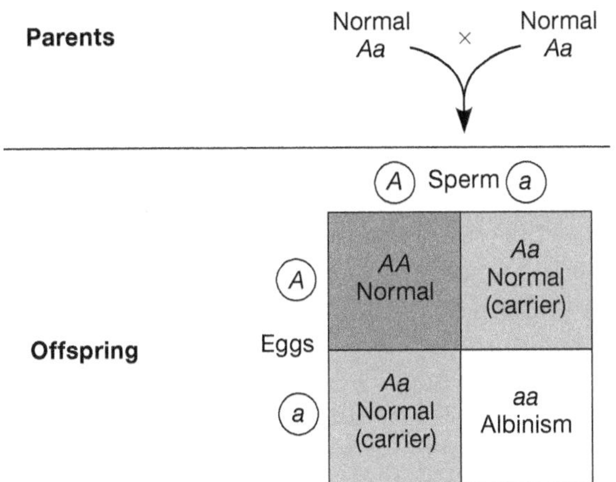

▲ **Figure 9.9B** Offspring produced by parents who are both carriers for albinism, a recessive disorder

the lungs and other organs. This mucus can interfere with breathing, digestion, and liver function and makes the person vulnerable to recurrent bacterial infections. Although there is no cure for CF, strict adherence to a daily health regimen—including gentle pounding on the chest and back to clear the airway, inhaled antibiotics, and a special diet—can have a profound impact on the health of the affected person. CF was once invariably fatal in childhood, but tremendous advances in treatment have raised the median survival age of Americans with CF to nearly 40.

Cystic fibrosis is most common in Caucasians. In fact, most genetic disorders are not evenly distributed across all ethnic groups. Such uneven distribution is the result of prolonged geographic isolation of certain populations. Isolation (as with settlers of a new island, for example) can lead to matings between close blood relatives. People with recent common ancestors are more likely to carry the same recessive alleles than are unrelated people. Therefore, matings between close relatives may cause the frequency of a rare allele (and the disease it causes) to increase within that community. Geneticists have observed increased incidence of harmful recessive traits among many types of inbred animals. For example, the detrimental effects of inbreeding are seen in some endangered species that recovered from small populations (see Module 13.11). With the increased mobility in most human populations today, it is relatively unlikely that two people who carry a rare, harmful allele will meet and mate.

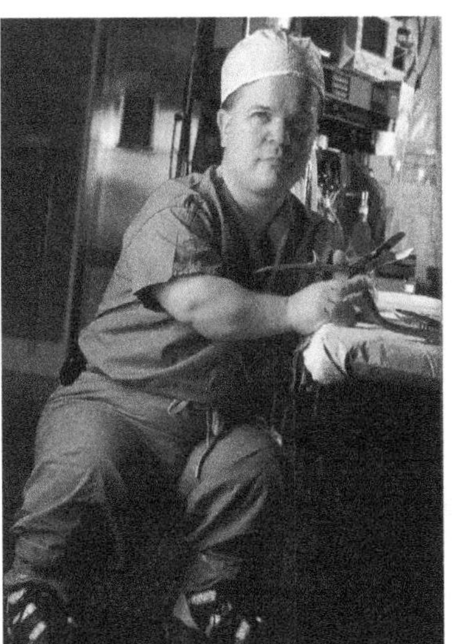

▲ **Figure 9.9C** Dr. Michael C. Ain, a specialist in the repair of bone defects caused by achondroplasia and related disorders

Dominant Disorders Although most harmful alleles are recessive, a number of human disorders are caused by dominant alleles. Some are harmless conditions, such as extra fingers and toes (called polydactyly) or webbed fingers and toes.

A more serious dominant disorder is achondroplasia, a form of dwarfism in which the head and torso of the body develop normally but the arms and legs are unusually short (**Figure 9.9C**). The homozygous dominant genotype (*AA*) causes death of the embryo; therefore, only heterozygotes (*Aa*) have this disorder. (This also means that a person with achondroplasia has a 50% chance of passing the condition on to any children.) Therefore, all those who do not have achondroplasia, more than 99.99% of the population, are homozygous for the recessive allele (*aa*). This example makes it clear that a dominant allele is not necessarily more common in a population than a corresponding recessive allele.

Dominant alleles that cause lethal diseases are much less common than recessive alleles that cause lethal diseases. One reason is that the dominant lethal allele cannot be carried by heterozygotes without affecting them. Many lethal dominant alleles result from mutations in a sperm or egg that subsequently kill the embryo. And if the afflicted individual is born but does not survive long enough to reproduce, he or she will not pass on the lethal allele to future generations. This is in contrast to lethal recessive mutations, which are perpetuated from generation to generation by healthy heterozygous carriers.

A lethal dominant allele can escape elimination, however, if it does not cause death until a relatively advanced age. One such example is the allele that causes **Huntington's disease**, a degenerative disorder of the nervous system that usually does not appear until a person is 35 to 45 years old. Once the deterioration of the nervous system begins, it is irreversible and fatal. Because the allele for Huntington's disease is dominant, any child born to a parent with the allele has a 50% chance of inheriting the allele and the disorder. This example makes it clear that a dominant allele is not necessarily "better" than a corresponding recessive allele.

Until relatively recently, the onset of symptoms was the only way to know if a person had inherited the Huntington's allele. This is no longer the case. A genetic test is now available that can detect the presence of the Huntington's allele in an individual's genome. This is one of several genetic tests currently available. We'll explore the topic of personal genetic screening in the next module.

? **Peter is a 30-year-old man whose father died of Huntington's disease. Neither Peter's mother nor a much older sister shows any signs of Huntington's. What is the probability that Peter has inherited Huntington's disease?**

■ Since his father had the disease, there is a $\frac{1}{2}$ chance that Peter received the gene. (The genotype of his sister is irrelevant.)

9.10 New technologies can provide insight into one's genetic legacy

CONNECTION

Some prospective parents are aware that they have an increased risk of having a baby with a genetic disorder. For example, many pregnant women over age 35 know that they have a heightened risk of bearing children with Down syndrome (see Module 8.20), and some couples are aware that certain genetic diseases run in their families. These prospective parents may want to learn more about their own and their baby's genetic makeup. Modern technologies offer ways to obtain such information.

Genetic Testing Because most children with recessive disorders are born to healthy parents, the genetic risk for many diseases is determined by whether the prospective parents are carriers of the recessive allele. For an increasing number of genetic disorders, including Tay-Sachs disease, sickle-cell disease, and one form of cystic fibrosis, tests are available that can distinguish between individuals who have no disease-causing alleles and those who are heterozygous carriers. Other parents may know that a dominant but late-appearing disease, such as Huntington's disease, runs in their family. Such people may benefit from genetic tests for dominant alleles. Information from genetic testing (also called genetic screening) can inform decisions about family planning.

Fetal Testing Several technologies are available for detecting genetic conditions in a fetus. Genetic testing before birth requires the collection of fetal cells. In **amniocentesis**, usually performed between weeks 14 and 16 of pregnancy, a physician carefully inserts a needle through the abdomen and into the mother's uterus while watching an ultrasound imager to guide the needle away from the fetus (Figure 9.10A, left). The physician extracts about 20 milliliters (4 teaspoons) of the amniotic fluid that bathes the developing fetus. Cells floating within this fluid are isolated and grown in the laboratory for several weeks. By then, enough dividing cells can be harvested to allow karyotyping (see Module 8.19) that will detect chromosomal abnormalities such as Down syndrome. Biochemical tests can also be performed on the cultured cells, revealing conditions such as Tay-Sachs disease.

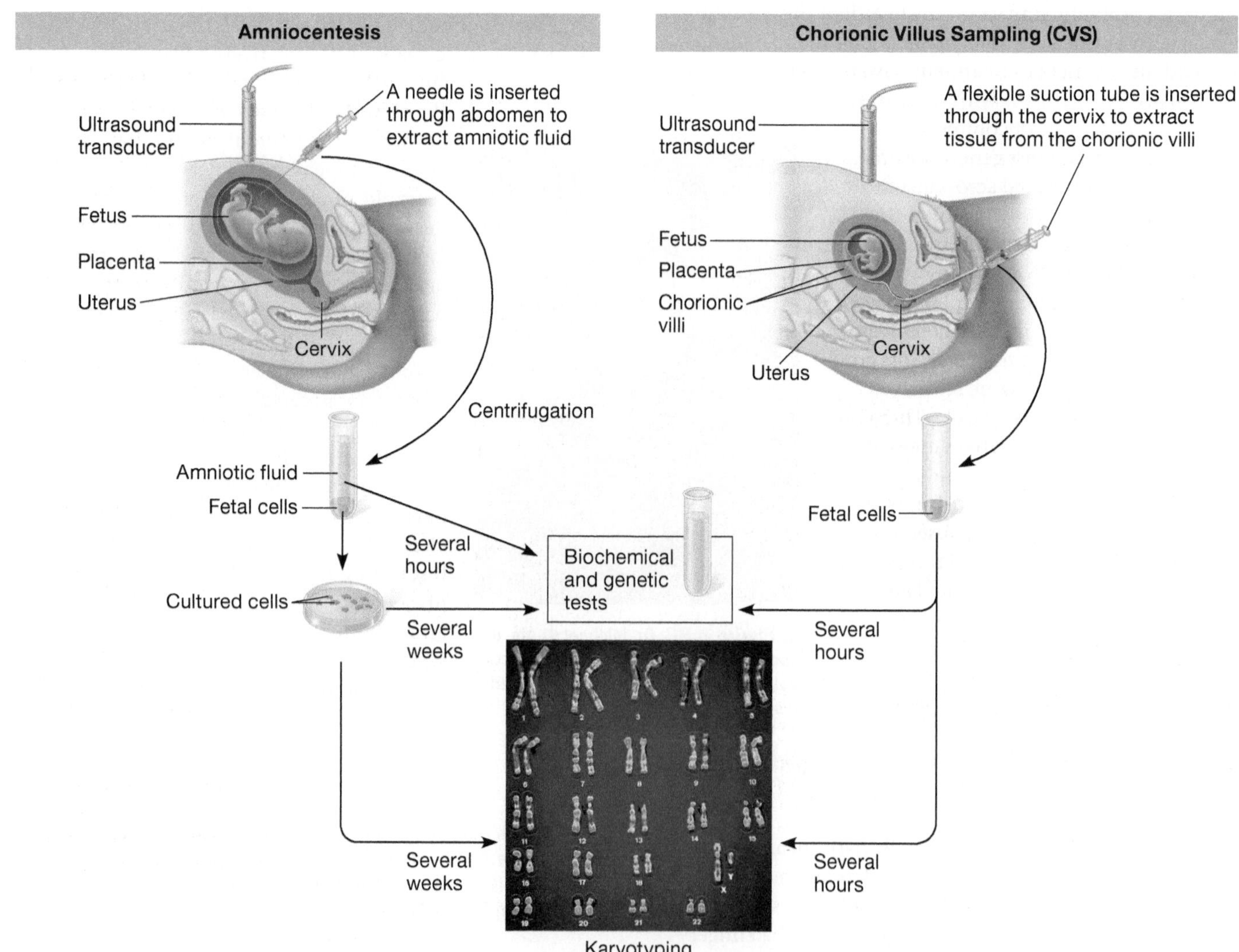

▲ Figure 9.10A Testing a fetus for genetic disorders

In another procedure, **chorionic villus sampling (CVS)**, a physician extracts a tiny sample of chorionic villus tissue from the placenta, the organ that carries nourishment and wastes between the fetus and the mother. The tissue can be obtained using a narrow, flexible tube inserted through the mother's vagina and cervix into the uterus (Figure 9.10A, right). Results of karyotyping and some biochemical tests can be available within 24 hours. The speed of CVS is an advantage over amniocentesis. Another advantage is that CVS can be performed early, usually from the 10th to the 12th (and as early as the 8th) week of pregnancy.

Unfortunately, both amniocentesis and CVS pose some risk of complications, such as maternal bleeding, miscarriage, or premature birth. Complication rates for both amniocentesis and CVS are about 1%. Because of the risks, these procedures are usually reserved for situations in which the possibility of a genetic disease is significantly higher than average. Newer genetic screening procedures involve isolating tiny amounts of fetal cells or DNA released into the mother's bloodstream. Although few reliable tests are yet available using this method, this promising and complication-free technology may soon replace more invasive procedures.

In addition, blood tests on the mother at 15 to 20 weeks of pregnancy can help identify fetuses at risk for certain birth defects—and thus candidates for further testing that may require more invasive procedures (such as amniocentesis). The most widely used blood test measures the mother's blood level of alpha-fetoprotein (AFP), a protein produced by the fetus. High levels of AFP may indicate a nervous systems defect in the fetus. Low levels of AFP may indicate Down syndrome. For a more complete risk profile, a woman's doctor may order a "triple screen test," which measures AFP as well as two other hormones produced by the placenta. Abnormal levels of these substances in the maternal blood may also point to a risk of Down syndrome.

Fetal Imaging Other techniques enable a physician to examine a fetus directly for anatomical deformities. The most common procedure is **ultrasound imaging**, which uses sound waves to produce a picture of the fetus. Figure 9.10B shows an ultrasound scanner, which emits high-frequency sounds, beyond the range of hearing. When the sound waves bounce off the fetus, the echoes produce an image on the monitor. The inset image in Figure 9.10B shows a fetus at about 20 weeks. Traditional ultrasound imaging is noninvasive—no foreign objects are inserted into the mother's body—and has no known risk. Transvaginal ultrasound imaging—during which a probe is placed in the woman's vagina—can be used to provide clear images in early pregnancy.

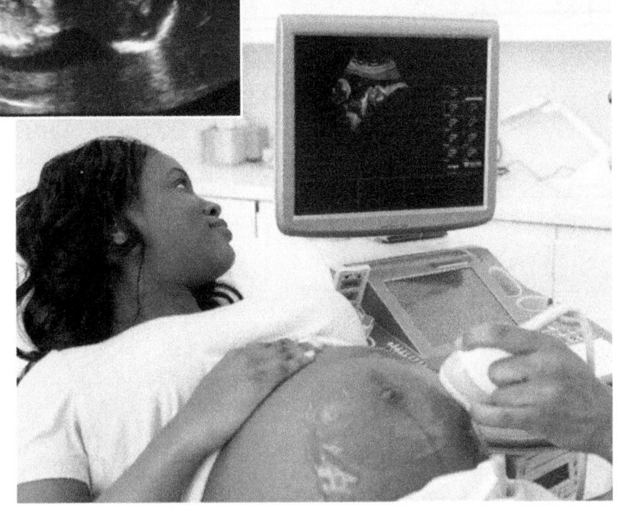

▲ Figure 9.10B Traditional ultrasound scanning of a fetus

In another imaging method, fetoscopy, a needle-thin tube containing a fiber-optic viewing scope is inserted into the uterus. Fetoscopy can provide highly detailed images of the fetus but, unlike ultrasound, carries risk of complications.

Newborn Screening Some genetic disorders can be detected at birth by simple tests that are now routinely performed in most hospitals in the United States. One common screening program is for phenylketonuria (PKU), a recessively inherited disorder that occurs in about one out of every 10,000 births in the United States. Children with this disease cannot properly break down the naturally occurring amino acid phenylalanine, and an accumulation of phenylalanine may lead to developmental disabilities. However, if the deficiency is detected in the newborn, a special diet low in phenylalanine can usually prevent symptoms. Unfortunately, few other genetic disorders are currently treatable.

Ethical Considerations As new technologies such as fetal imaging and testing become more widespread, geneticists are working to ensure that they do not cause more problems than they solve. Consider the tests for identifying carriers of recessive diseases. Such information may enable people with family histories of genetic disorders to make informed decisions about having children. But these new methods for genetic screening pose problems, too. If confidentiality is breached, will carriers be stigmatized? For example, will they be denied health or life insurance, even though they themselves are healthy? Geneticists stress that patients seeking genetic testing should receive counseling both before and after to clarify their family history, to explain the test, and to help them cope with the results. But with a wealth of genetic information increasingly available, a full discussion of the meaning of the results might be time-consuming and costly, raising the question of who should pay for such counseling.

Couples at risk for conceiving children with genetic disorders may now learn a great deal about their unborn children. What is to be done with such information? If fetal tests reveal a serious disorder, the parents must choose between terminating the pregnancy and preparing themselves for a baby with severe problems. Identifying a genetic disease early can give families time to prepare—emotionally, medically, and financially. The dilemmas posed by human genetics are a clear example of the immense social implications of biology.

? What is the primary benefit of genetic screening by CVS? What is the primary risk?

■ CVS allows genetic screening to be performed very early in pregnancy and provides quick results, but it carries a risk of miscarriage.

Variations on Mendel's Laws

9.11 Incomplete dominance results in intermediate phenotypes

Mendel's two laws explain inheritance in terms of discrete factors—genes—that are passed along from generation to generation according to simple rules of probability. These laws are valid for all sexually reproducing organisms, including garden peas, Labradors, and human beings. But just as the basic rules of musical harmony cannot account for all the rich sounds of a symphony, Mendel's laws stop short of explaining some patterns of genetic inheritance. In fact, for most sexually reproducing organisms, it is relatively rare for Mendel's laws alone to fully explain genetic traits. More often, the observed inheritance patterns are more complex, as we will see in this and the next four modules.

The F_1 offspring of Mendel's pea crosses always looked exactly like one of the two parental varieties. In this situation—called **complete dominance**—the dominant allele has the same phenotypic effect whether present in one or two copies. But for some characters, the appearance of F_1 hybrids falls between the phenotypes of the two parental varieties, an effect called **incomplete dominance**. For instance, when red snapdragons are crossed with white snapdragons, all the F_1 hybrids have pink flowers (Figure 9.11A). This third phenotype results from flowers of the heterozygote having less red pigment than the red homozygotes.

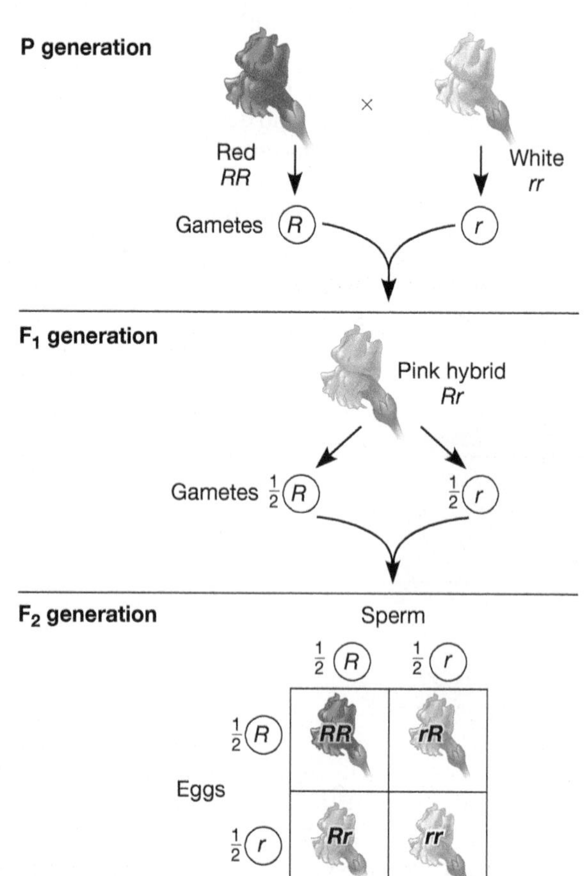

▲ Figure 9.11A Incomplete dominance in snapdragon flower color

As the Punnett square at the bottom of Figure 9.11A shows, the F_2 offspring appear in a phenotypic ratio of one red to two pink to one white, as the red and white alleles segregate during gamete formation in the pink F_1 hybrids. In incomplete dominance, the phenotypes of heterozygotes differ from the two homozygous varieties, and the genotypic ratio and the phenotypic ratio are both 1:2:1 in the F_2 generation.

We also see examples of incomplete dominance in humans. One case involves a recessive allele (*h*) that can cause hypercholesterolemia, dangerously high levels of cholesterol in the blood. Normal individuals are homozygous dominant (*HH*). Heterozygotes (*Hh*; about one in 500 people) have blood cholesterol levels about twice normal. They are unusually prone to atherosclerosis, the blockage of arteries by cholesterol buildup in artery walls, and they may have heart attacks from blocked heart arteries by their mid-30s. This form of the disease can often be controlled through changes in diet and by taking medications that lower blood cholesterol. Hypercholesterolemia is even more serious in homozygous recessive individuals (*hh*; about one in a million people). Homozygotes have about five times the normal amount of blood cholesterol and may have heart attacks as early as age 2. Homozygous hypercholesterolemia is harder to treat; options include high doses of cholesterol-lowering drugs, organ surgeries or transplants, or filtering lipids from the blood.

Figure 9.11B illustrates the molecular basis for hypercholesterolemia. The dominant allele (*H*), which normal individuals carry in duplicate (*HH*), specifies a cell-surface receptor protein called an LDL receptor. Low-density lipoprotein (LDL, known as "bad cholesterol") is transported in the blood. In certain cells, the LDL receptors mop up excess LDL particles from the blood and promote their breakdown. This process helps prevent the accumulation of cholesterol in arteries. Heterozygotes (*Hh*) have only half the normal number of LDL

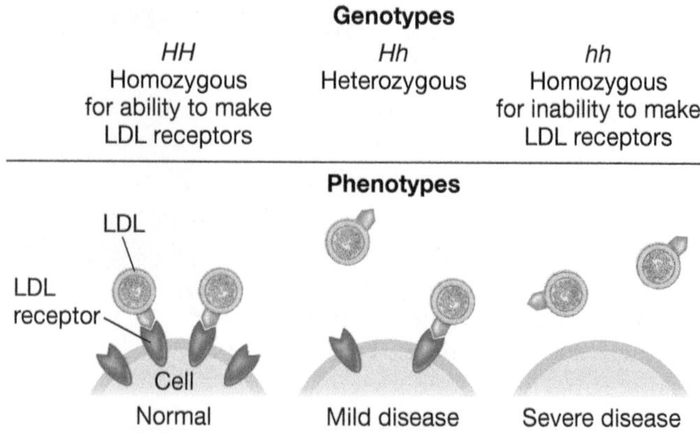

▲ Figure 9.11B Incomplete dominance in human hypercholesterolemia

receptors, and homozygous recessives (*hh*) have none. A lack of receptors prevents the cells from removing much of the excess cholesterol from the blood. The resulting buildup of LDL in the blood can be lethal.

? **Why doesn't the cross shown in Figure 9.11A support the blending hypothesis (see Module 9.1)?**

■ Although two of the F_2 offspring show a "blended" phenotype (pink flowers), the other two do not, and the white and red alleles are not lost to future generations.

9.12 Many genes have more than two alleles that may be codominant

So far, we have discussed inheritance patterns involving only two alleles per gene (*H* versus *h*, for example). But most genes can be found in populations in more than two versions, known as multiple alleles. Although each individual carries, at most, two different alleles for a particular gene, in cases of multiple alleles, more than two alleles exist in the population.

For instance, the **ABO blood group** phenotype in humans involves three alleles of a single gene. Various combinations of three alleles—called I^A, I^B, and *i*—produce four phenotypes: A person's blood type may be A, B, AB, or O (**Figure 9.12**). These letters refer to two carbohydrates, called A and B, that may be found on the surface of red blood cells. A person's red blood cells may be coated with carbohydrate A (in which case they are said to have type A blood), carbohydrate B (type B), both carbohydrates (type AB), or neither carbohydrate (type O). (In case you are wondering, the "positive" and "negative" notations on blood types—referred to as the Rh blood group system—are due to inheritance of a separate, unrelated gene.)

Matching compatible blood types is critical for safe blood transfusions. If a donor's blood cells have a carbohydrate that is foreign to the recipient, then the recipient's immune system produces proteins called antibodies (see Module 24.10) that bind specifically to the foreign carbohydrates and cause the donor blood cells to clump together, potentially killing the recipient. The clumping reaction is also the basis of a blood-typing test performed in the laboratory. In Figure 9.12, notice that AB individuals can receive blood from anyone without fear of clumping, making them "universal recipients," while donated type O blood never causes clumping, making those with type O blood "universal donors."

The four blood groups result from various combinations of the three different alleles: I^A (for an enzyme referred to as *I*, which adds carbohydrate A to red blood cells), I^B (which adds carbohydrate B), and *i* (which adds neither A nor B carbohydrate). Each person inherits one of these alleles from each parent. Because there are three alleles, there are six possible genotypes, as illustrated in the figure. Both the I^A and I^B alleles are dominant to the *i* allele. Thus, I^AI^A and I^Ai people have type A blood, and I^BI^B and I^Bi people have type B. Recessive homozygotes, *ii*, have type O blood, with neither carbohydrate. The I^A and I^B alleles are **codominant**: Both alleles are expressed in heterozygous individuals (I^AI^B), who have type AB blood. Be careful to distinguish codominance (the expression of two alleles in separate, distinguishable ways) from incomplete dominance (the expression of one intermediate trait).

? **Maria has type O blood, and her sister has type AB blood. The girls know that both of their maternal grandparents are type A. What are the genotypes of the girls' parents?**

■ Their mother is I^Ai; their father is I^Bi.

Blood Group (Phenotype)	Genotypes	Carbohydrates Present on Red Blood Cells	Antibodies Present in Blood	Reaction When Blood from Groups Below Is Mixed with Antibodies from Groups at Left: O	A	B	AB
A	I^AI^A or I^Ai	Carbohydrate A	Anti-B				
B	I^BI^B or I^Bi	Carbohydrate B	Anti-A				
AB	I^AI^B	Carbohydrate A and Carbohydrate B	None				
O	ii	Neither	Anti-A Anti-B				

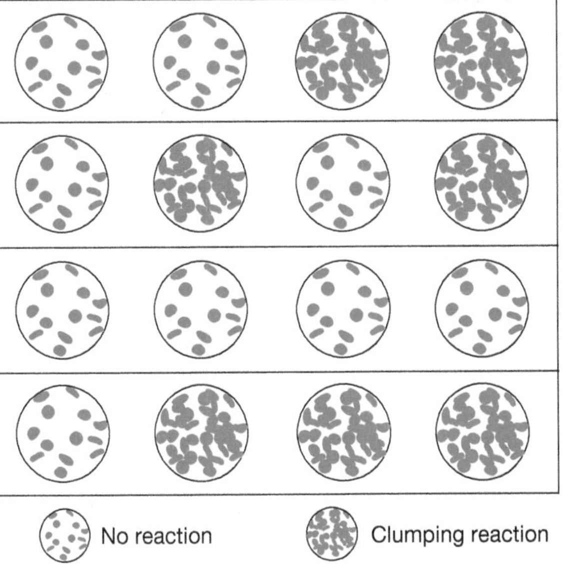

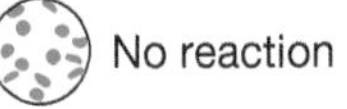 No reaction  Clumping reaction

▲ **Figure 9.12** Multiple alleles for the ABO blood groups

9.13 A single gene may affect many phenotypic characters

All of our genetic examples to this point have been cases in which each gene specifies only one hereditary character. In many cases, however, one gene influences multiple characters, a property called **pleiotropy**.

An example of pleiotropy in humans is **sickle-cell disease** (sometimes called sickle-cell anemia). The direct effect of the sickle-cell allele is to make red blood cells produce abnormal hemoglobin proteins. These molecules tend to link together and crystallize, especially when the oxygen content of the blood is lower than usual because of high altitude, overexertion, or respiratory ailments. As the hemoglobin crystallizes, the normally disk-shaped red blood cells deform to a sickle shape with jagged edges (Figure 9.13A). Sickled cells are destroyed rapidly by the body, and their destruction may seriously lower the individual's red cell count, causing anemia and weakness. Also, because of their angular shape, sickled cells do not flow smoothly in the blood and tend to accumulate and clog tiny blood vessels. Blood flow to body parts is reduced, resulting in periodic fever, severe pain, and damage to various organs, including the heart, brain, and kidneys. The overall result is the cascade of symptoms shown in Figure 9.13B. Blood transfusions and drug treatment may relieve some of the symptoms, but there is no cure; sickle-cell disease kills about 100,000 people each year.

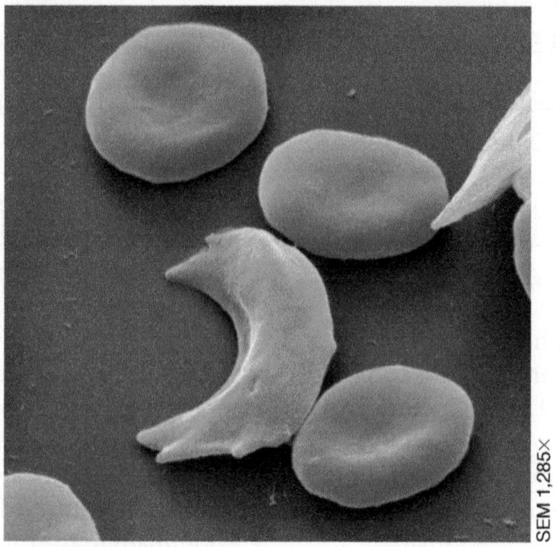

▲ **Figure 9.13A** Several jagged sickled cells in the midst of normal red blood cells.

In most cases, only people who are homozygous for the sickle-cell allele have sickle-cell disease. Heterozygotes, who have one sickle-cell allele and one normal allele, are usually healthy—hence, the disease is considered recessive. However, in rare cases, heterozygotes may experience some effects of the disease when oxygen in the blood is severely reduced, such as at very high altitudes. Thus, at the organismal level, a heterozygote displays incomplete dominance for the sickle-cell trait, with a phenotype between the homozygous dominant and homozygous recessive phenotypes. At the molecular level, however, the two alleles are actually codominant; the blood cells of heterozygotes contain both normal and abnormal (sickle-cell) hemoglobins. A simple blood test can distinguish homozygotes from heterozygotes.

Sickle-cell disease is the most common inherited disorder among people of African descent, striking one in 500 African Americans. About one in 12 African Americans is a heterozygous carrier. Among Americans of other ancestry, the sickle-cell allele is extremely rare.

One in 12 is an unusually high frequency of carriers for an allele with such harmful effects in homozygotes. We might expect that the frequency of the sickle-cell allele in the population would be much lower because many homozygotes die before passing their genes to the next generation. The high frequency appears to be a vestige of the ancestral history of African Americans. Sickle-cell disease is most common in tropical Africa, where the deadly disease malaria is also prevalent. The parasite that causes malaria spends part of its life cycle inside red blood cells. When it enters those of a person with the sickle-cell allele, it triggers sickling. The body destroys most of the sickled cells, killing the parasite with them. Consequently, sickle-cell carriers have increased resistance to malaria, and in many parts of Africa, they live longer and have more offspring than noncarriers who are exposed to malaria. In this way, malaria has kept the frequency of the sickle-cell allele relatively high in much of the African continent. To put it in evolutionary terms, as long as the environment harbors malaria, individuals with one sickle-cell allele will have a selective advantage.

? **Why is the sickle-cell trait considered codominant at the molecular level?**

■ Codominance means that both traits are expressed; a carrier for the sickle-cell allele produces both normal and abnormal hemoglobin.

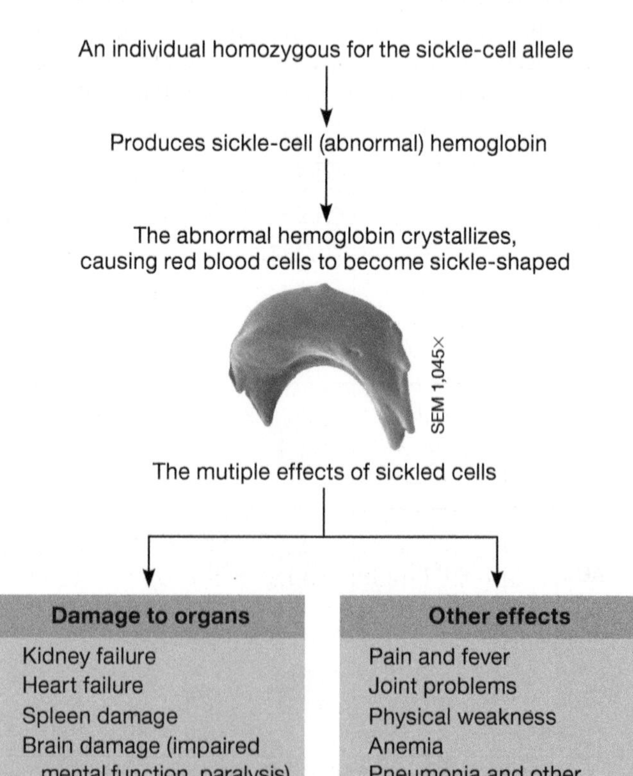

▲ **Figure 9.13B** Sickle-cell disease, an example of pleiotropy

9.14 A single character may be influenced by many genes

Mendel studied genetic characters that could be classified on an either-or basis, such as purple or white flower color. However, many characters, such as human skin color and height, vary in a population along a continuum. Many such features result from **polygenic inheritance**, the additive effects of two or more genes on a single phenotypic character. (This is the opposite of pleiotropy, in which one gene affects several characters.) For example, genomic studies have identified nearly 200 alleles that affect height. Many diseases—including diabetes, heart disease, and cancer—are also known to display polygenic inheritance. This concept is an example of the general theme of INTERACTIONS —that a novel property (in this case, a polygenic trait) can result from the interactions of many smaller parts (genes).

Let's consider a hypothetical example. Assume that the continuous variation in human skin color is controlled by three genes that are inherited separately, like Mendel's pea genes. (Actually, the character for skin color is probably affected by a great many genes, but we'll simplify it for now.) The "dark-skin" allele for each gene (*A*, *B*, or *C*) contributes one "unit" of darkness to the phenotype and is incompletely dominant to the other allele (*a*, *b*, or *c*). An *AABBCC* person would be very dark, whereas an *aabbcc* individual would be very light. An *AaBbCc* person would have skin of an intermediate shade. Because the alleles have an additive effect, the genotype *AaBbCc* would produce the same skin color as any other genotype with just three dark-skin alleles, such as *AABbcc*, because both of these individuals have three "units" of darkness.

The Punnett square in the middle of Figure 9.14 shows all possible genotypes from a mating of two triple heterozygotes (*AaBbCc*). The row of squares below the Punnett square shows the seven skin pigmentation phenotypes that would theoretically result from this mating. The seven bars in the graph at the bottom of the figure depict the relative numbers of each of the phenotypes in the F_2 generation. This hypothetical example shows how inheritance of three genes could lead to a wide variety of pigmentation phenotypes. As we will see in the next module, in actual human populations, skin color has even more variations than shown in the figure.

Up to this point in the chapter, we have presented four types of inheritance patterns that are extensions of Mendel's laws of inheritance: incomplete dominance, codominance, pleiotropy, and polygenic inheritance. It is important to realize that these patterns are extensions of Mendel's model, rather than exceptions to it. From Mendel's pea garden experiments came data supporting the idea that genes are transmitted according to the same rules of chance that govern the tossing of coins. This basic idea of genes as discrete units of inheritance holds true for all inheritance patterns, even the patterns that are more complex than the ones originally considered by Mendel. In the next module, we consider another important source of deviation from Mendel's standard model: the effect of the environment.

? An *AaBbcc* individual would be indistinguishable in phenotype from which of the following individuals: *AAbbcc*, *aaBBcc*, *AabbCc*, *Aabbcc*, or *aaBbCc*?

All except AabbCc

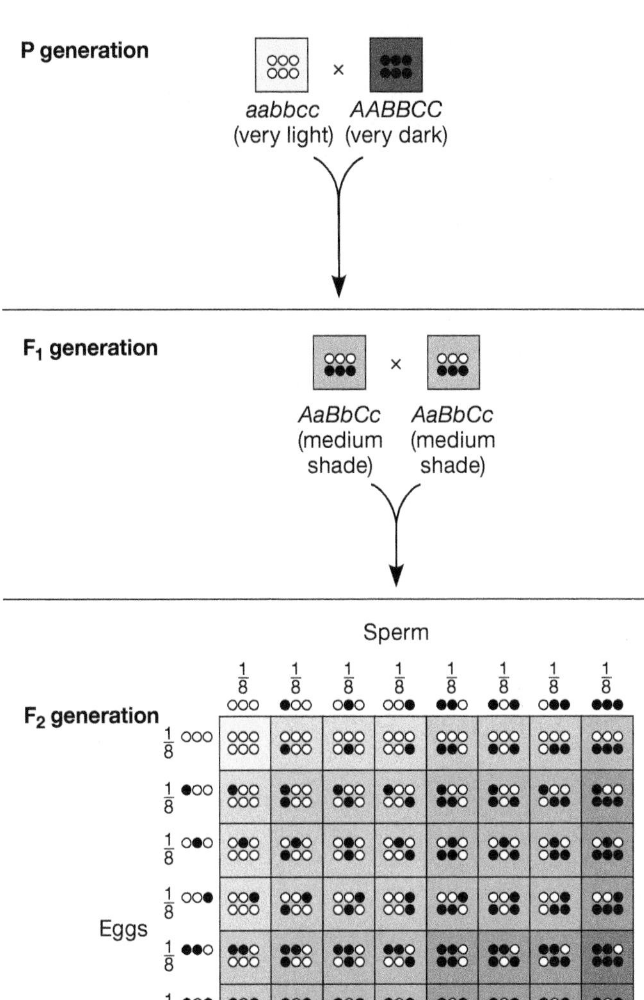

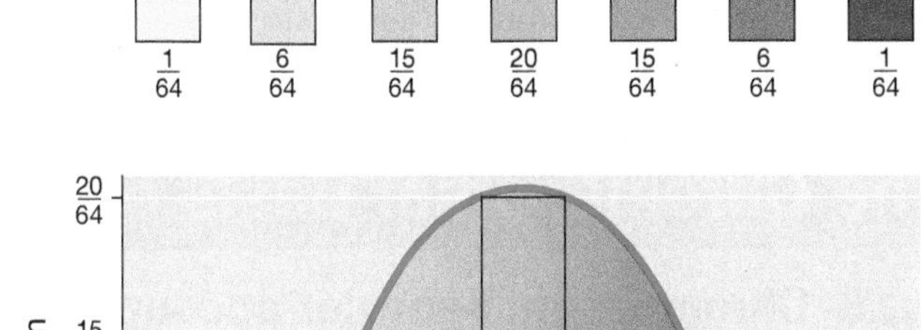

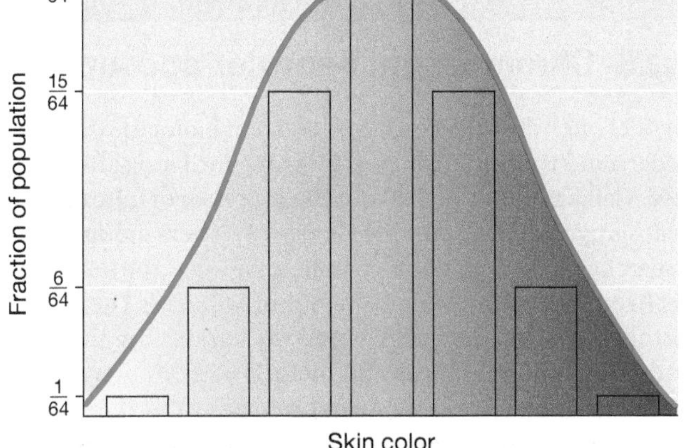

▲ **Figure 9.14** A model for polygenic inheritance of skin color

9.15 The environment affects many characters

In the previous module, we saw how a set of three hypothetical human skin-color genes could produce seven different phenotypes for skin color. But, of course, if we examine a real human population for skin color, we would see more shades than just seven. The true range might be similar to the entire spectrum of color under the bell-shaped curve in Figure 9.14. In fact, no matter how carefully we characterize the genes for skin color, a purely genetic description will always be incomplete. This is because skin color is also influenced by environmental factors, such as exposure to the sun (**Figure 9.15A**).

Many characters result from a combination of heredity and environment. For humans, nutrition influences height; exercise alters build; sun-tanning darkens the skin; experience improves performance on intelligence tests; and social and cultural forces greatly affect appearance. As geneticists learn more and more about our genes, it is becoming clear that many human characters—such as risk of heart disease and cancer and susceptibility to alcoholism and schizophrenia—are influenced by both genes and environment.

Whether human characters are more influenced by genes or by the environment—nature or nurture—is a very hotly contested debate. For some characters, such as the ABO blood group, a given genotype mandates a very specific phenotype, and the environment plays no role whatsoever. In contrast, how many red blood cells are circulating in your body is significantly influenced by environmental factors such as your overall health and the altitude at which you live.

It is important to realize that the individual features of any organism arise from a combination of genetic and environmental factors. Simply spending time with identical twins will convince anyone that environment, and not just genes, affects a person's traits (**Figure 9.15B**). Next, we turn to a discussion of the cellular basis of heredity: the behavior of chromosomes.

? If most characters result from a combination of environment and heredity, why was Mendel able to ignore environmental influences in his pea plants?

■ The characters he chose for study were all entirely genetically determined and all his test subjects were raised in a similar environment.

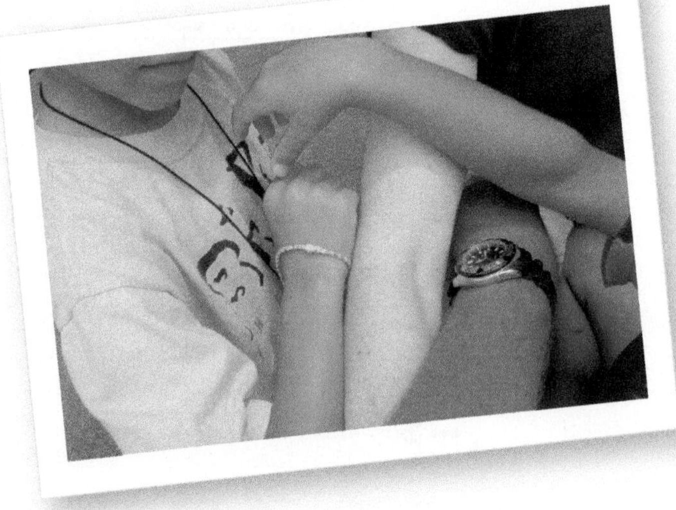

▲ **Figure 9.15A** The effect of genes and sun exposure on the skin of one of this book's authors and his family

▲ **Figure 9.15B** Varying phenotypes due to environmental factors in genetically identical twins, as displayed by the daughters of one of this book's authors

The Chromosomal Basis of Inheritance

9.16 Chromosome behavior accounts for Mendel's laws

Mendel published his results in 1866, but biologists did not understand the significance of his work until long after he died. Cell biologists worked out the processes of mitosis and meiosis by the late 1800s (see Chapter 8). Then, around 1902, researchers began to notice parallels between the behavior of chromosomes and the behavior of Mendel's "heritable factors" (what we now call genes). By combining this new understanding of mitosis and meiosis with an increasing understanding of genes, one of biology's most important concepts was formulated: The **chromosome theory of inheritance** holds that genes occupy specific loci (positions) on chromosomes, and it is the chromosomes that undergo segregation and independent assortment during meiosis. Thus, it is the behavior of chromosomes during meiosis and fertilization that accounts for inheritance patterns.

We can see the chromosomal basis of Mendel's laws by following the fates of two genes during meiosis and fertilization in pea plants. In **Figure 9.16**, the genes for seed shape (alleles *R* and *r*) and seed color (*Y* and *y*) are shown as black bars on different chromosomes. Notice that the Punnett square is repeated from Figure 9.5A; we will now follow the chromosomes to see how they account for the results of

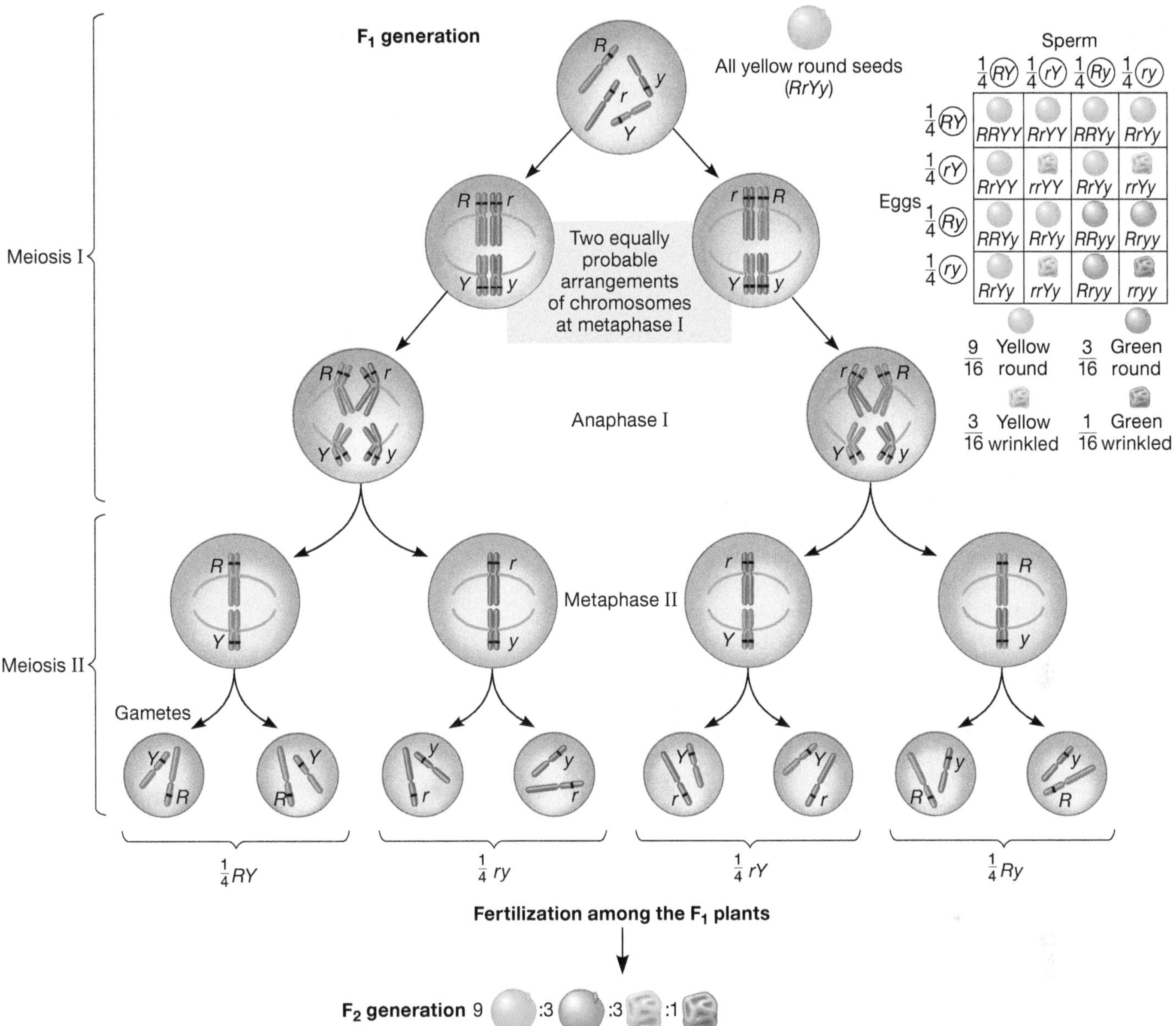

▲ **Figure 9.16** **The chromosomal basis of Mendel's laws**

the dihybrid cross shown in the Punnett square. We start with the F_1 generation, in which all plants have the *RrYy* genotype. To simplify the diagram, we show only two of the seven pairs of pea chromosomes and three of the stages of meiosis.

To see the chromosomal basis of the law of segregation (which states that pairs of alleles separate from each other during gamete formation via meiosis; see Module 9.3), let's follow just the homologous pair of long chromosomes, the ones carrying *R* and *r*, taking either the left or the right branch from the F_1 cell. Whichever arrangement the chromosomes assume at metaphase I, the two alleles segregate as the homologous chromosomes separate in anaphase I. At the end of meiosis II, a single long chromosome ends up in each of the gametes. Fertilization then randomly recombines the two alleles, resulting in F_2 offspring that are $\frac{1}{4}$ *RR*, $\frac{1}{2}$ *Rr*, and $\frac{1}{4}$ *rr*. The ratio of round to wrinkled phenotypes is thus 3:1 (12 round to 4 wrinkled), the ratio Mendel observed, as shown in the Punnett square in the figure.

To see the chromosomal basis of the law of independent assortment (which states that each pair of alleles sorts independently of other pairs of alleles during gamete formation; see Module 9.5), follow both the long and short (nonhomologous) chromosomes through the figure. Two alternative arrangements of tetrads can occur at metaphase I. The nonhomologous chromosomes (and their genes) assort independently, leading to four gamete genotypes. Random fertilization leads to the 9:3:3:1 phenotypic ratio in the F_2 generation.

? **Which of Mendel's laws have their physical basis in the following phases of meiosis: (a) the orientation of homologous chromosome pairs in metaphase I; (b) the separation of homologous chromosomes in anaphase I?**

(a) The law of independent assortment; (b) the law of segregation

9.17 Genes on the same chromosome tend to be inherited together

SCIENTIFIC THINKING

In 1908, British biologists William Bateson and Reginald Punnett (originator of the Punnett square) observed an inheritance pattern that seemed inconsistent with Mendelian laws. Bateson and Punnett were working with two characters in sweet peas: flower color and pollen shape. They crossed doubly heterozygous plants (*PpLl*) that exhibited the dominant traits: purple flowers (expression of the *P* allele) and long pollen grains (expression of the *L* allele). The corresponding recessive traits are red flowers (in *pp* plants) and round pollen (in *ll* plants).

The top part of **Figure 9.17** illustrates Bateson and Punnett's experiment. When they looked at just one of the two characters (that is, either cross *Pp* × *Pp* or cross *Ll* × *Ll*), they recorded a phenotypic ratio of approximately 3:1 for the offspring, in agreement with Mendel's law of segregation. However, when the biologists combined their data for the two characters, they did not see the 9:3:3:1 ratio predicted by Mendel's law of independent assortment (see Figure 9.16). Instead, as shown in the table, they found a disproportionately large number of plants with just two of the predicted phenotypes: purple long (almost 75% of the total) and red round (about 14%). The other two phenotypes (purple round and red long) were found in far fewer numbers than expected. It is often the case in science that a new discovery begins with a "failure," an experiment with results contrary to those expected. When scientists explore such unexpected results, the investigation may lead to deeper insight than was originally anticipated.

The number of genes in a cell is far greater than the number of chromosomes; in fact, each chromosome (except the Y) has hundreds or thousands of genes. Genes located close together on the same chromosome tend to be inherited together and are called **linked genes**. Linked genes may not follow Mendel's law of independent assortment.

Sweet-pea genes for flower color and pollen shape are located on the same chromosome. Thus, meiosis in the heterozygous (*PpLl*) sweet-pea plant yields mostly two genotypes of gametes (*PL* and *pl*) rather than equal numbers of the four types of gametes that would result if the flower-color and pollen-shape genes were not linked. The large numbers of plants with purple long and red round traits in the Bateson-Punnett experiment resulted from fertilization among the *PL* and *pl* gametes. But what about the smaller numbers of plants with purple round and red long traits? As you will see in the next module, crossing over accounts for these offspring.

The Experiment

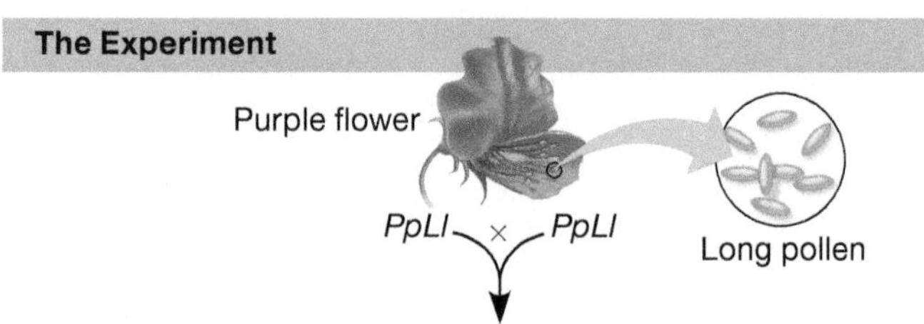

Phenotypes	Observed offspring	Prediction (9:3:3:1)
Purple long	284	215
Purple round	21	71
Red long	21	71
Red round	55	24

The Explanation: Linked Genes

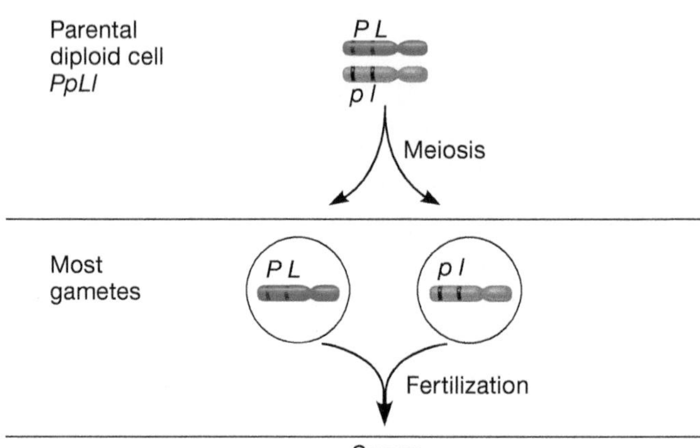

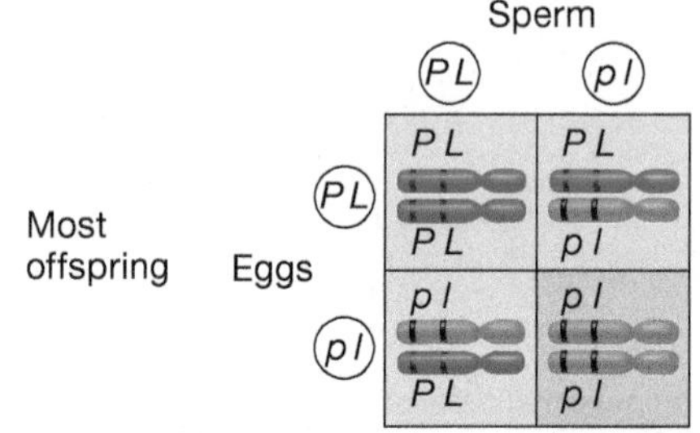

3 purple long:1 red round
Not accounted for: purple round and red long

▲ **Figure 9.17** The experiment revealing linked genes in the sweet pea

? In what way was Bateson and Punnett's success dependent upon failing at first?

■ The "failure" to obtain the expected results provided the insight that led to the discovery of linked genes.

9.18 Crossing over produces new combinations of alleles

During meiosis, crossing over between homologous chromosomes produces new combinations of alleles in gametes (as we saw in Module 8.17). Using the experiment shown in Figure 9.17 as an example, **Figure 9.18A** reviews this process, showing that two linked genes can give rise to four different gamete genotypes. Gametes with genotypes *PL* and *pl* carry parental-type chromosomes that have not been altered by crossing over. In contrast, gametes with genotypes *Pl* and *pL* are recombinant gametes. The exchange of chromosome segments during crossing over has produced new combinations of alleles. We can now understand the results of the Bateson-Punnett experiment presented in the previous module: The small fraction of offspring with recombinant phenotypes (purple round and red long) must have resulted from fertilization involving recombinant gametes.

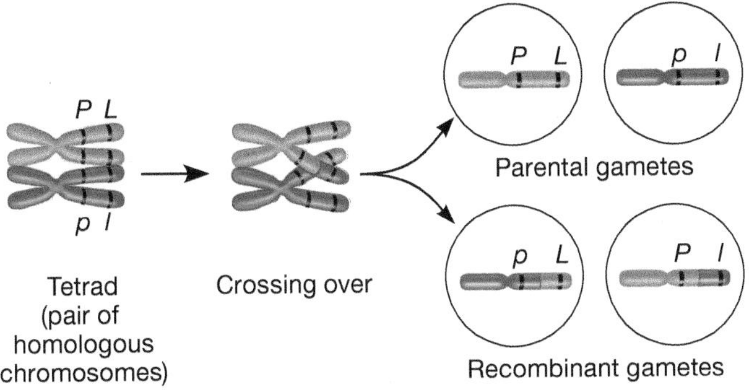

▲ **Figure 9.18A** Review: the production of recombinant gametes

The discovery of how crossing over creates gamete diversity confirmed the relationship between chromosome behavior and heredity. Some of the most important early studies of crossing over were performed in the laboratory of American embryologist Thomas Hunt Morgan in the early 1900s. Morgan and his colleagues used the fruit fly *Drosophila melanogaster* in many of their experiments (**Figure 9.18B**). *Drosophila* is a good research animal for genetic studies because it can be bred easily and inexpensively, producing each new generation in two weeks.

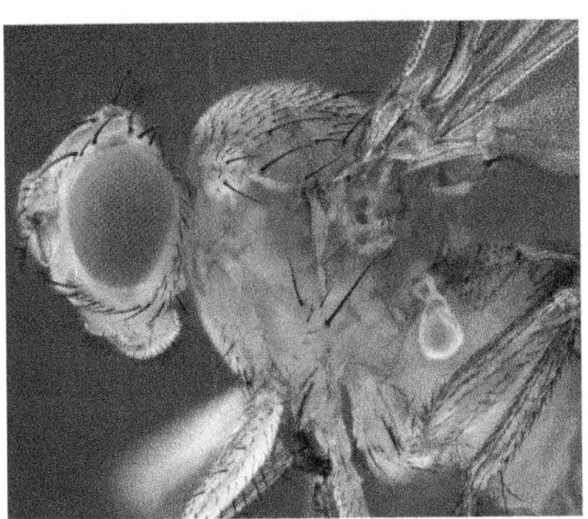

▲ **Figure 9.18B** *Drosophila melanogaster*

Figure 9.18C shows one of Morgan's experiments. The term **wild-type** refers to the traits most common in nature, while **mutant** refers to traits that are less common. (Note that wild-type has nothing to do with dominance; a mutant trait can be dominant.) This cross involves a wild-type fruit fly with a gray body and long wings and a mutant fly with a black body and vestigial wings. (Used here, the term *vestigial* describes the undeveloped, shrunken appearance of the wings and should not be confused with the evolutionary use of the word *vestigial*.) Morgan knew the genotypes of these flies from previous studies.

In mating a heterozygous gray fly with long wings (genotype *GgLl*) with a black fly with vestigial wings (genotype *ggll*), Morgan performed a testcross (see Module 9.6). If the genes were not linked, then independent assortment would produce offspring in a phenotypic ratio of 1:1:1:1 ($\frac{1}{4}$ gray body, long wings; $\frac{1}{4}$ black body, vestigial wings; $\frac{1}{4}$ gray body, vestigial wings; and $\frac{1}{4}$ black body, long wings). But because these genes are linked, Morgan obtained the results shown in the top part of Figure 9.18C: Most of the offspring had parental phenotypes, but 17% of the offspring flies were recombinants. The percentage of recombinant offspring among the total is called the **recombination frequency**.

The lower part of Figure 9.18C explains Morgan's results in terms of crossing over. A crossover between chromatids of homologous chromosomes in parent *GgLl* broke linkages between the *G* and *L* alleles and between the *g* and *l* alleles, forming the recombinant chromosomes *Gl* and *gL*. Later steps in meiosis distributed the recombinant chromosomes to gametes, and random fertilization produced the four kinds of offspring Morgan observed.

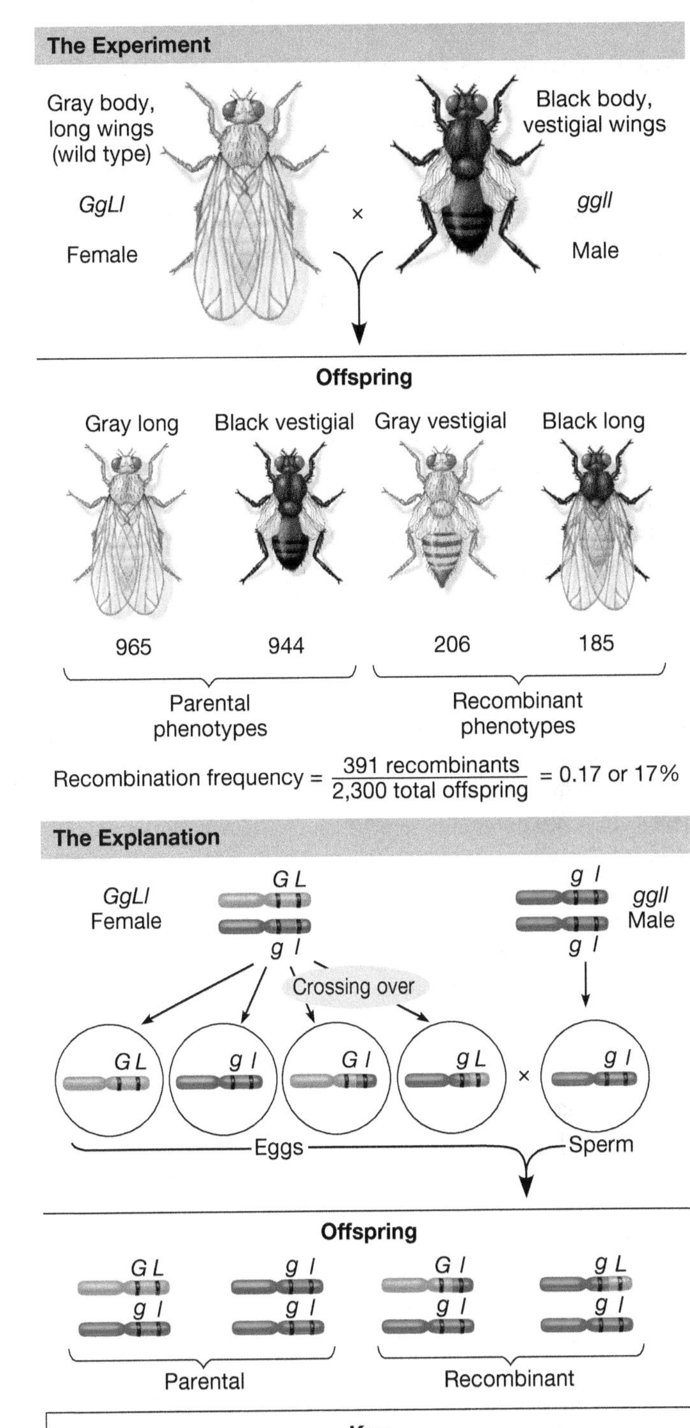

▲ **Figure 9.18C** A fruit fly experiment demonstrating the role of crossing over in inheritance

From T. H. Morgan and C. J. Lynch, The linkage of two factors in *Drosophila* that are not sex-linked, *Biological Bulletin* 23: 174–82 (1912).

? **Return to the data in Figure 9.17. What is the recombination frequency between the flower-color and pollen-length genes?**

■ 11% (42/381)

9.19 Geneticists use crossover data to map genes

While working with *Drosophila*, Alfred H. Sturtevant, one of Morgan's students, developed a way to use crossover data to create a **genetic map**, an ordered list of the genetic loci along a chromosome. This technique is based on the assumption that the chance of crossing over is approximately equal at all points along a chromosome. Sturtevant hypothesized that the farther apart two genes are on a chromosome, the more points there are between them where crossing over can occur. (This assumption is not entirely accurate, but it is good enough to provide useful data.) With this principle in mind, Sturtevant began using recombination data from fruit fly crosses to assign relative positions of the genes on the chromosomes—that is, to map genes.

Figure 9.19A represents a part of the chromosome that carries the linked genes for black body (*g*) and vestigial wings (*l*) that we described in Module 9.18. This same chromosome also carries a gene that has a recessive allele (we'll call it *c*) determining cinnabar eye color, a brighter red than the wild-type color. Figure 9.19A shows the actual crossover (recombination) frequencies between these alleles, taken two at a time: 17% between the *g* and *l* alleles, 9% between *g* and *c*, and 9.5% between *c* and *l*. Sturtevant reasoned that these values represent the relative distances between the genes. Because the crossover frequencies between *g* and *c* and between *l* and *c* are approximately half that between *g* and *l*, gene *c* must lie roughly midway between *g* and *l*. Thus, the sequence of these genes on one of the fruit fly chromosomes must be *g-c-l*. Such a genetic map based on recombinant frequencies is called a **linkage map**.

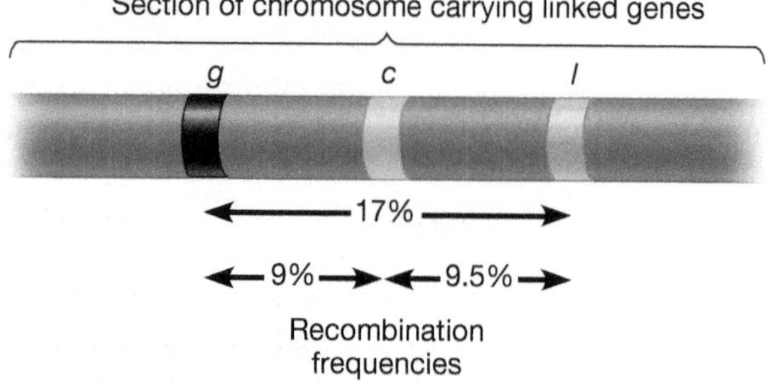

▲ Figure 9.19A Mapping genes from crossover data

Sturtevant's method of mapping genes helped establish the relative positions of many fruit fly genes. Eventually, enough data were accumulated to reveal that *Drosophila* has four groups of genes, corresponding to its four pairs of homologous chromosomes. Figure 9.19B is a genetic map showing just five of the gene loci on part of one chromosome.

The linkage-mapping method has proved valuable in establishing the relative positions of many genes in many organisms. The real beauty of the technique is that a wealth of information about genes can be learned simply by breeding and observing the organisms; no fancy equipment is required.

? **You design *Drosophila* crosses to provide recombination data for a gene not included in Figure 9.19A. The gene has recombination frequencies of 3% with the vestigial-wing (*l*) locus and 7% with the cinnabar-eye (*c*) locus. Where is it located on the chromosome?**

■ The gene is located between the vestigial and cinnabar loci, a bit closer to the vestigial-wing locus (because the vestigial-wing locus has a lower recombination frequency).

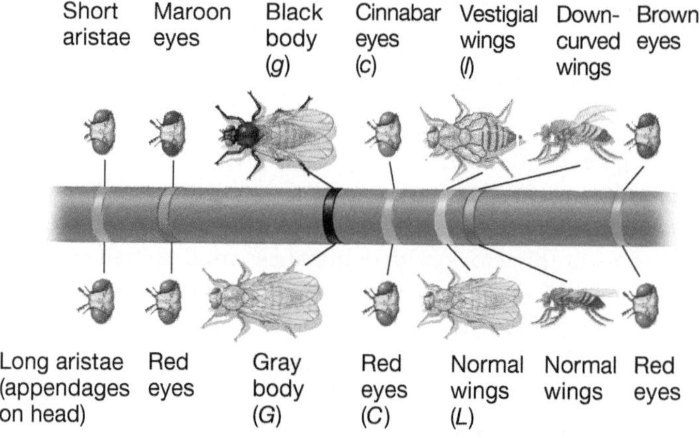

▲ Figure 9.19B A partial genetic map of one fruit fly chromosome

Sex Chromosomes and Sex-Linked Genes

9.20 Chromosomes determine sex in many species

Many animals, including fruit flies and all mammals, have a pair of **sex chromosomes**, designated X and Y, that determine an individual's sex (Figure 9.20A). Among humans, individuals with one X chromosome and one Y chromosome are males; XX individuals are females. In addition, human males and females both have 44 autosomes (nonsex chromosomes). After meiosis, each gamete contains one sex chromosome and a haploid set of autosomes (22 in humans). All eggs contain a single X chromosome. Of the sperm cells, half contain an X chromosome and half contain a Y chromosome. An offspring's sex depends on whether the sperm cell that fertilizes the egg bears an X chromosome or a Y chromosome (Figure 9.20B).

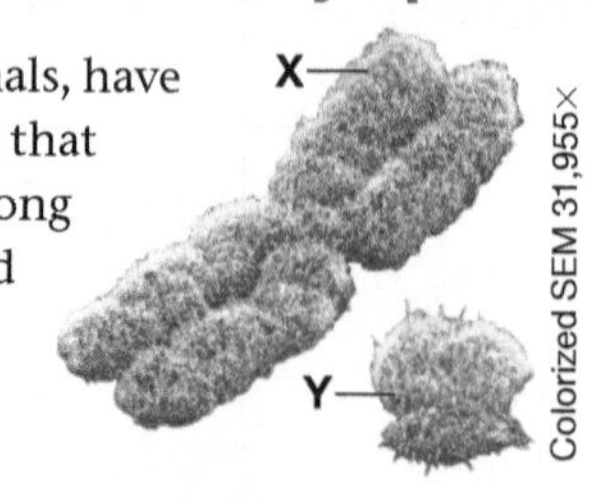

▲ Figure 9.20A The human sex chromosomes

Researchers have sequenced the human Y chromosome and identified 78 genes, about half of which are expressed only in the testis. One of

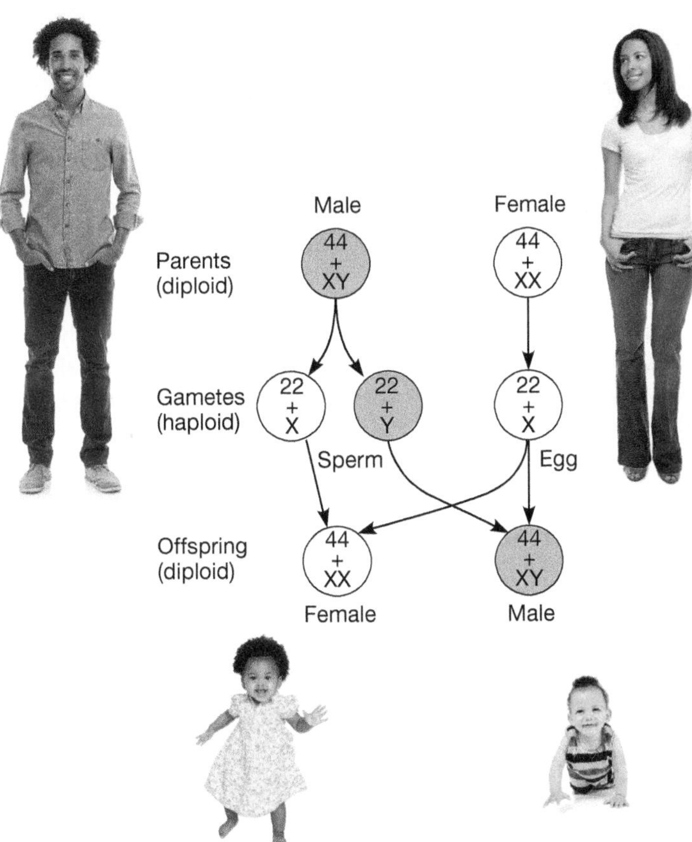

▲ **Figure 9.20B** **The X-Y system**

these genes is known to play a crucial role in sex determination. This gene is called *SRY* (for sex-determining region of Y) and triggers testis development. In the absence of *SRY*, ovaries develop rather than testes. *SRY* codes for proteins that regulate other genes on the Y chromosome. These genes in turn produce proteins necessary for normal testis development.

The X-Y system is only one of several sex-determining systems (**Table 9.20** summarizes three other systems). For example, grasshoppers, roaches, and some other insects have an X-O system, in which O stands for the absence of a sex chromosome. Females have two X chromosomes (XX); males have only one sex chromosome (XO). Males produce two classes of sperm: Half bear an X and half lack a sex chromosome. In this case, as in humans, sperm cells determine the sex of the offspring at fertilization.

In contrast to the X-Y and X-O systems, eggs determine sex in certain fishes, butterflies, and birds. The sex chromosomes in these animals are designated Z and W. Males have the genotype ZZ; females are ZW. In this system, sex is determined by whether the egg carries a Z or a W.

Some organisms lack sex chromosomes altogether. In most ants and bees, sex is determined by chromosome number rather than by sex chromosomes. Females develop from fertilized eggs and thus are diploid. Males develop from unfertilized eggs—they are fatherless—and are haploid.

Most animals have two separate sexes; that is, individuals are either male or female. Many plant species have sperm-bearing and egg-bearing flowers found on different individuals. Some plant species, such as date palms, have the X-Y system of sex determination; others, such as the wild strawberry, have the Z-W system. However, most plant species and some animal species have individuals that produce both sperm and eggs. In such species, all individuals have the same complement of chromosomes.

In Module 9.15, we discussed the role that environment plays in determining many characters. Among some animals, environment can even determine sex. For some species of reptiles, the temperature at which eggs are incubated during a specific period of embryonic development determines whether that embryo will develop into a male or female. For example, if green sea turtle hatchlings incubate above 30°C (86°F), nearly all the resulting turtles will be males. This leads some people to worry that global climate change might affect the makeup of turtle populations. Such temperature-dependent sex determination is an extreme example of the environment affecting the phenotype of an individual.

TABLE 9.20 Three Systems of Sex Determination

		Genetic Makeup	
System	**Example Organism**	**Males**	**Females**
X-O		22 + X	22 + XX
Z-W		76 + ZZ	76 + ZW
Chromosome number		16	32

? King Henry VIII of England was quick to blame his wives for bearing him only daughters. Explain how, from a genetic point of view, his thinking was wrong.

■ The male sperm bears either an X or Y, thereby determining the sex of the offspring; his wives' eggs always carried an X.

9.21 Sex-linked genes exhibit a unique pattern of inheritance

Besides bearing genes that determine sex, the sex chromosomes also contain genes for characters unrelated to femaleness or maleness. A gene located on either sex chromosome is called a **sex-linked gene**. Be careful not to confuse the term *sex-linked gene*, which refers to a single gene on a sex chromosome, with the term *linked genes*, which refers to genes on the same chromosome that tend to be inherited together. Because the human X chromosome contains many more genes than the Y (about 1,110 versus 78), the vast majority of sex-linked genes are **X-linked genes**.

The figures in this module illustrate inheritance patterns for white eye color in the fruit fly, an X-linked recessive trait. Wild-type fruit flies have red eyes; white eyes are very rare (Figure 9.21A). We use the uppercase letter *R* for the dominant, wild-type, red-eye allele and *r* for the recessive white-eye allele. Because these alleles are carried on the X chromosome, we show them as superscripts to the letter X. Thus, red-eyed male fruit flies have the genotype X^RY; white-eyed males are X^rY. The Y chromosome does not have a gene locus for eye color; therefore, the male's phenotype results entirely from his single X-linked gene. In the female, X^RX^R and X^RX^r flies have red eyes, and X^rX^r flies have white eyes.

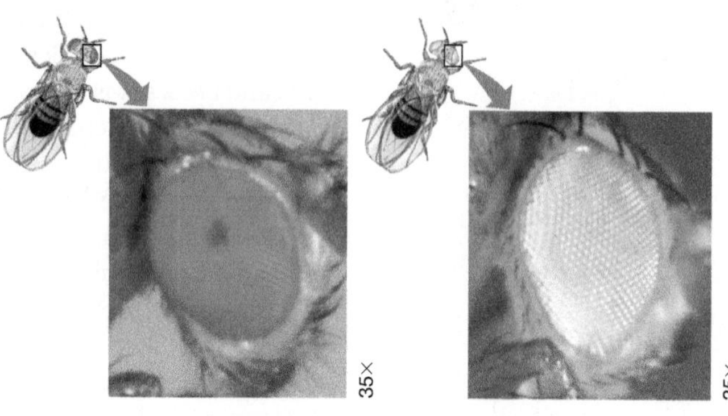

▲ **Figure 9.21A** **Fruit fly eye color determined by sex-linked gene**

A white-eyed male (X^rY) will transmit his X^r to all of his female offspring but to none of his male offspring. This is because his female offspring, in order to be female, must inherit his X chromosome, but his male offspring must inherit his Y chromosome.

As shown in Figure 9.21B, when the female parent is a dominant homozygote (X^RX^R) and the male parent is X^rY, all the offspring have red eyes, but the female offspring are all carriers of the allele for white eyes (X^RX^r). When those offspring are bred to each other, the classic 3:1 phenotypic ratio of red eyes to white eyes appears among the offspring (Figure 9.21C). However, there is a twist: The white-eyed trait shows up only in males. All the females have red eyes, whereas half the males have red eyes and half have white eyes. All females inherit at least one dominant allele (from their male parent); half of them are homozygous dominant, whereas the other half are heterozygous carriers, like their female parent. Among the males, half of them inherit the recessive allele their mother was carrying, producing the white-eye phenotype.

Because the white-eye allele is recessive, a female will have white eyes only if she receives that allele on both X chromosomes. For example, if a heterozygous female mates with a white-eyed male, there is a 50% chance that each offspring will have white eyes (resulting from genotype X^rX^r or X^rY), regardless of sex (Figure 9.21D). Female offspring with red eyes are heterozygotes, whereas red-eyed male offspring completely lack the recessive allele.

? **A white-eyed female *Drosophila* is mated with a red-eyed (wild-type) male. What result do you predict for the numerous offspring?**

■ All female offspring will be red-eyed but heterozygous (X^RX^r); all male offspring will be white-eyed (X^rY).

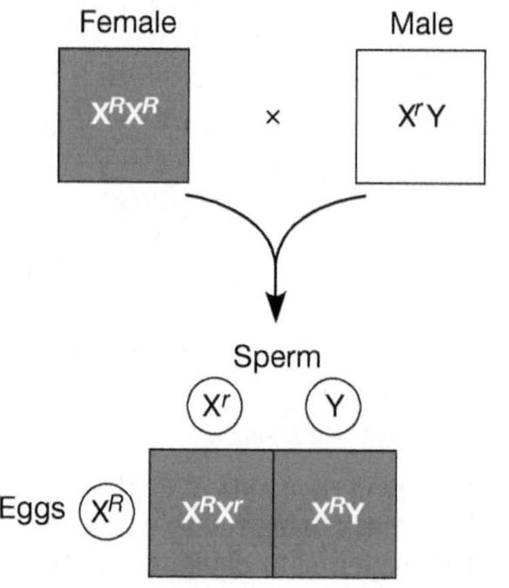

R = red-eye allele
r = white-eye allele

▲ **Figure 9.21B** **A homozygous, red-eyed female crossed with a white-eyed male**

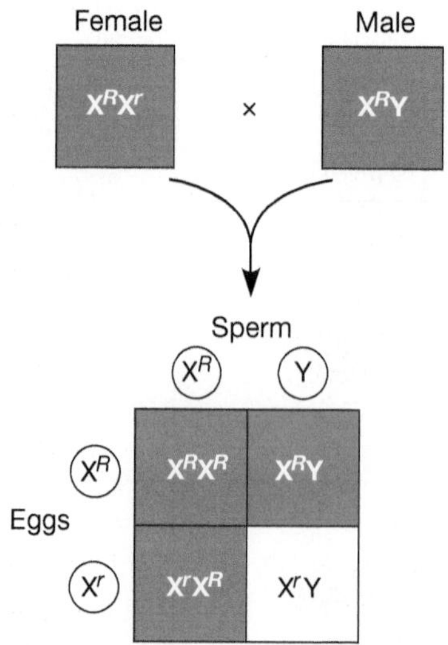

▲ **Figure 9.21C** **A heterozygous female crossed with a red-eyed male**

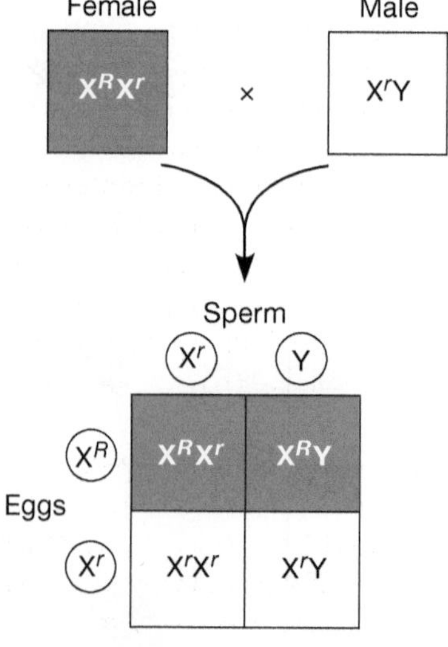

▲ **Figure 9.21D** **A heterozygous female crossed with a white-eyed male**

9.22 Human sex-linked disorders affect mostly males

CONNECTION

A number of human conditions are recessive X-linked traits. If a man inherits only one X-linked recessive allele—from his mother—the allele will be expressed. In contrast, a woman has to inherit two such alleles—one from each parent—to exhibit the trait. Thus, recessive X-linked traits are expressed much more frequently in men than in women.

Hemophilia is an X-linked recessive trait with a well-documented history. Hemophiliacs bleed excessively when injured because they lack one or more of the proteins required for blood clotting. A high incidence of hemophilia plagued the royal families of Europe. Queen Victoria (1819–1901) of England was a carrier of the hemophilia allele. She passed it on to one of her sons and two of her daughters. Through marriage, her daughters then introduced the disease into the families of Prussia, Russia, and Spain. The pedigree in Figure 9.22 traces the disease through one branch of the royal family. As you can see, Alexandra, like her mother and grandmother, was a carrier, and Alexis had the disease.

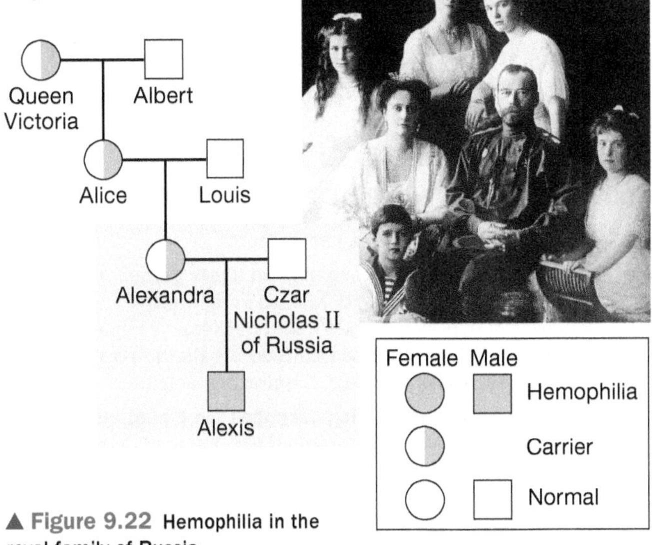

▲ **Figure 9.22** Hemophilia in the royal family of Russia

TRY THIS Alexis must have had an X^h chromosome (because he had hemophilia). Use your finger to trace back this mutant chromosome through three generations of his ancestors.

Another human X-linked recessive disorder is Duchenne muscular dystrophy, a condition characterized by a progressive weakening of the muscles and loss of coordination. The first symptoms appear in early childhood, when the child begins to have difficulty standing up. Eventually, muscle tissue becomes severely wasted, the individual becomes wheelchair-bound, and normal breathing becomes difficult. Affected individuals rarely live past their early 20s. Researchers have traced the disorder to a recessive mutation in a gene on the X chromosome that codes for a muscle protein.

? Neither Tom nor Sue has hemophilia, but their first son does. If the couple has a second child, what is the probability that he or she will also have the disease?

■ $\frac{1}{4}$ ($\frac{1}{2}$ chance of a male child × $\frac{1}{2}$ chance that he will inherit the mutant X)

9.23 The Y chromosome provides clues about human male evolution

EVOLUTION CONNECTION

As you learned in the chapter-opening essay about the Inuit, our genes often bear evidence of human evolution and can inform our understanding of history and culture. The Y chromosome can be particularly useful for tracing our past because, except for rare mutations, the human Y chromosome passes intact from father to son. Therefore, researchers can learn about the ancestry of human males by studying Y chromosome DNA.

In 2003, geneticists discovered that about 8% of males currently living in central Asia have Y chromosomes of striking genetic similarity. Additional analysis traced their common genetic heritage to a single man living about 1,000 years ago. In combination with historical records, the data led to the speculation that the Mongolian ruler Genghis Khan (Figure 9.23) is responsible for the spread of the telltale chromosome to nearly 16 million male descendants.

▲ **Figure 9.23** Genghis Khan (1162–1227)

Other analyses revealed several other highly successful lineages. Nearly 10% of Irish men are descendants of Niall of the Nine Hostages, a warlord who lived during the 5th century. The 16th-century Chinese ruler Giocangga has 1.5 million living male descendants. A 2015 study examining the Y chromosomes of 5,000 Asian men found nine additional widespread male lineages that have not yet been assigned to any individual.

Are humans evolving?

The discovery of the sex chromosomes and their pattern of inheritance was one of many breakthroughs in understanding how genes are passed from one generation to the next. During the first half of the 20th century, geneticists rediscovered Mendel's work, reinterpreted his laws in light of chromosomal behavior during meiosis, and firmly established the chromosome theory of inheritance. This work set the stage for discoveries in molecular genetics (an area we explore in the next three chapters).

? Why is the Y chromosome particularly useful in tracing recent human heritage?

■ Because it is passed directly from father to son, forming an unbroken chain of male lineage

CHAPTER 9 REVIEW

For practice quizzes, BioFlix animations, MP3 tutorials, video tutors and more study tools designed for this textbook, go to MasteringBiology™

REVIEWING THE CONCEPTS

Mendel's Laws (9.1–9.10)

9.1 The study of genetics has ancient roots.

9.2 The science of genetics began in an abbey garden. The science of genetics began with Gregor Mendel's quantitative experiments. Mendel crossed pea plants and traced traits from generation to generation. He hypothesized that there are alternative versions of genes (alleles), the units that determine heritable traits.

9.3 Mendel's law of segregation describes the inheritance of a single character. Mendel's law of segregation predicts that each set of alleles will separate as gametes are formed.

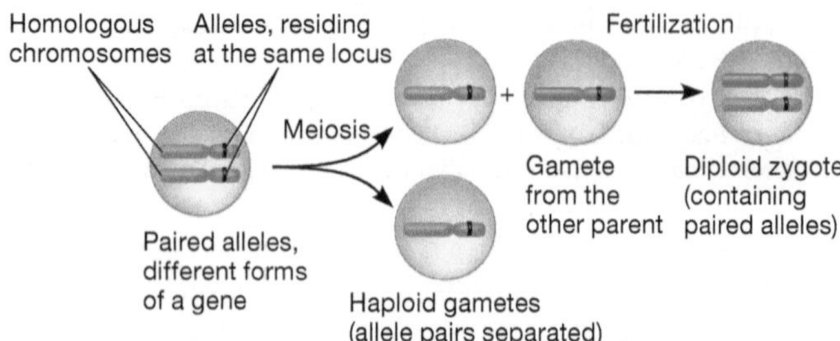

9.4 Homologous chromosomes bear the alleles for each character. When the two alleles of a gene in a diploid individual are different, the dominant allele determines the inherited trait, whereas the recessive allele has no effect.

9.5 The law of independent assortment is revealed by tracking two characters at once. Mendel's law of independent assortment states that the alleles of a pair segregate independently of other allele pairs during gamete formation.

9.6 Geneticists can use a testcross to determine unknown genotypes. The offspring of a testcross, a mating between an individual of unknown genotype and a homozygous recessive individual, can reveal the unknown genotype.

9.7 Mendel's laws reflect the rules of probability. The rule of multiplication calculates the probability of two independent events both occurring. The rule of addition calculates the probability of an event that can occur in alternative ways.

9.8 Genetic traits in humans can be tracked through family pedigrees. The inheritance of many human traits follows Mendel's laws. Family pedigrees can help determine individual genotypes.

9.9 Many inherited traits in humans are controlled by a single gene.

9.10 New technologies can provide insight into one's genetic legacy. Carrier screening, fetal testing, fetal imaging, and newborn screening can provide information for reproductive decisions but may create ethical dilemmas.

Variations on Mendel's Laws (9.11–9.15)

9.11 Incomplete dominance results in intermediate phenotypes. Mendel's laws are valid for all sexually reproducing species, but genotype often does not dictate phenotype in the simple way Mendel's laws describe.

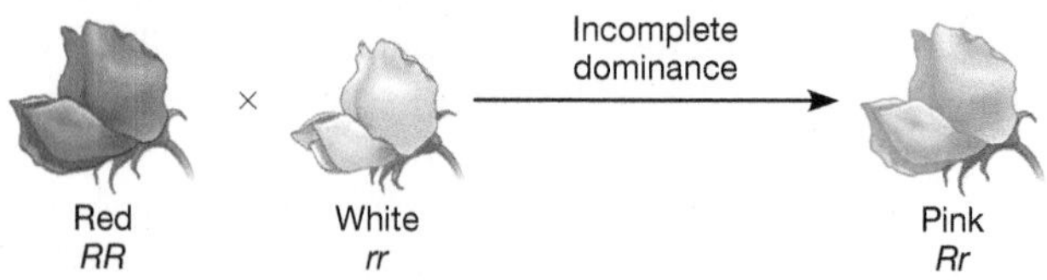

9.12 Many genes have more than two alleles that may be codominant. For example, the ABO blood group phenotype in humans is controlled by three alleles that produce a total of four phenotypes.

9.13 A single gene may affect many phenotypic characters.

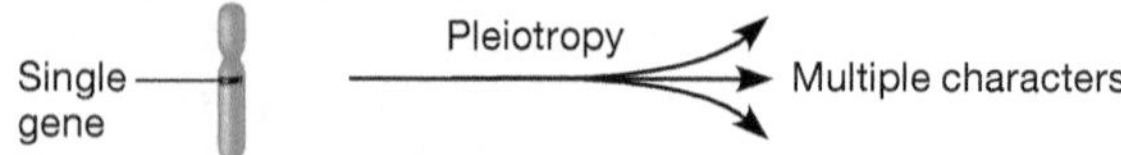

9.14 A single character may be influenced by many genes.

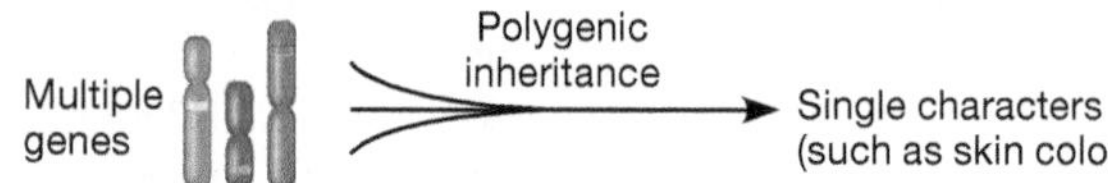

9.15 The environment affects many characters. Many traits are affected, in varying degrees, by both genetic and environmental factors.

The Chromosomal Basis of Inheritance (9.16–9.19)

9.16 Chromosome behavior accounts for Mendel's laws. Genes are located on chromosomes, whose behavior during meiosis and fertilization accounts for inheritance patterns.

9.17 Genes on the same chromosome tend to be inherited together. Such genes are said to be linked; they display non-Mendelian inheritance patterns.

9.18 Crossing over produces new combinations of alleles. Crossing over can separate linked alleles, producing gametes with recombinant chromosomes.

9.19 Geneticists use crossover data to map genes. Recombination frequencies can be used to map the relative positions of genes on chromosomes.

Sex Chromosomes and Sex-Linked Genes (9.20–9.23)

9.20 Chromosomes determine sex in many species. In mammals, a male has XY sex chromosomes, and a female has XX. The Y chromosome has genes for the development of testes, whereas an absence of the Y allows ovaries to develop. Other systems of sex determination exist in other animals and plants.

9.21 Sex-linked genes exhibit a unique pattern of inheritance. The X chromosome carries many X-linked genes that control traits unrelated to sex.

9.22 Human sex-linked disorders affect mostly males. Most X-linked human disorders are due to recessive alleles and therefore are seen mostly in males. A male receiving a single X-linked recessive allele from his mother will have the disorder; a female must receive the allele from both parents to be affected.

9.23 The Y chromosome provides clues about human male evolution. Because they are passed on intact from father to son, Y chromosomes can provide data about recent human evolutionary history.

CONNECTING THE CONCEPTS

1. Complete this concept map to help you review some key concepts of genetics.

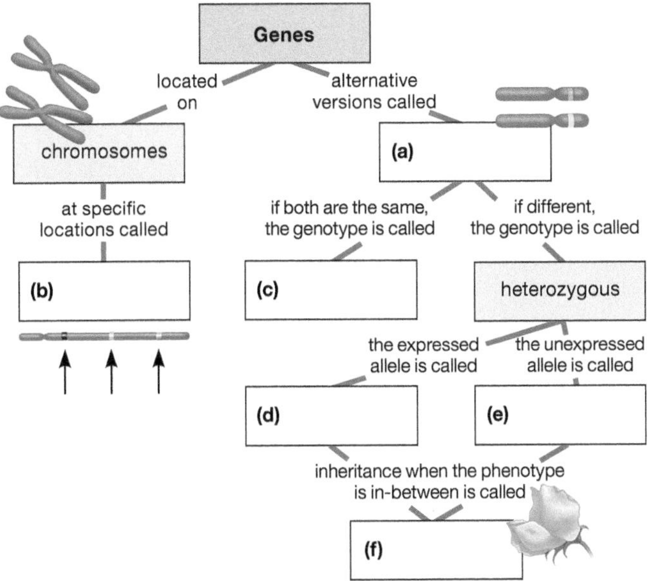

TESTING YOUR KNOWLEDGE

Level 1: Knowledge/Comprehension

2. Whether an allele is dominant or recessive depends on
   a. how common the allele is, relative to other alleles.
   b. whether it is inherited from the mother or the father.
   c. whether it or another allele determines the phenotype when both are present.
   d. whether or not it is linked to other genes.
3. Edward was found to be heterozygous (*Ss*) for sickle-cell trait. The alleles represented by the letters *S* and *s* are
   a. linked.
   b. on homologous chromosomes.
   c. both present in each of Edward's sperm cells.
   d. on the same chromosome but far apart.

Level 2: Application/Analysis

4. Two fruit flies with eyes of the usual red color are crossed, and their offspring are as follows: 77 red-eyed males, 71 ruby-eyed males, 152 red-eyed females. The allele for ruby eyes is
   a. autosomal (carried on an autosome) and dominant.
   b. autosomal and recessive.
   c. sex-linked and dominant.
   d. sex-linked and recessive.
5. A man with type B blood and a woman who has type A blood could have children of which of the following phenotypes?
   a. A or B only
   b. AB only
   c. AB or O
   d. A, B, AB, or O
6. Tim and Jan both have freckles (see Module 9.9), but their son Mike does not. Show with a Punnett square how this is possible. If Tim and Jan have two more children, what is the probability that both will have freckles?
7. Both Tim and Jan (problem 6) have a widow's peak (see Module 9.8), but Mike has a straight hairline. What are their genotypes? What is the probability that Tim and Jan's next child will have freckles and a straight hairline?
8. In rabbits, black hair depends on a dominant allele, *B*, and brown hair on a recessive allele, *b*. Short hair is due to a dominant allele, *S*, and long hair to a recessive allele, *s*. If a true-breeding black short-haired male is mated with a brown long-haired female, describe their offspring. What will be the genotypes of the offspring? If two of these F_1 rabbits are mated, what phenotypes would you expect among their offspring? In what proportions?
9. A fruit fly with a gray body and red eyes (genotype *BbPp*) is mated with a fly having a black body and purple eyes (genotype *bbpp*). What ratio of offspring would you expect if the body-color and eye-color genes are on different chromosomes (unlinked)? When this mating is actually carried out, most of the offspring look like the parents, but 3% have a gray body and purple eyes, and 3% have a black body and red eyes. Are these genes linked or unlinked? What is the recombination frequency?
10. A series of matings shows that the recombination frequency between the black-body gene (problem 9) and the gene for dumpy (shortened) wings is 36%. The recombination frequency between purple eyes and dumpy wings is 41%. What is the sequence of these three genes on the chromosome?
11. A couple are both phenotypically normal, but their son suffers from hemophilia, a sex-linked recessive disorder. What fraction of their children are likely to suffer from hemophilia? What fraction are likely to be carriers?

Level 3: Synthesis/Evaluation

12. Why do more men than women have colorblindness?
13. In fruit flies, the genes for wing shape and body stripes are linked. In a fly whose genotype is *WwSs*, *W* is linked to *S*, and *w* is linked to *s*. Show how this fly can produce gametes containing four different combinations of alleles. Which are parental-type gametes? Which are recombinant gametes? How are the recombinants produced?
14. Adult height in humans is at least partially hereditary; tall parents tend to have tall children. But humans come in a range of sizes, not just tall and short. Which extension of Mendel's model accounts for the hereditary variation in human height?
15. Heather was surprised to discover she suffered from red-green colorblindness. She told her biology professor, who said, "Your father is colorblind, too, right?" How did her professor know this? Why did her professor not say the same thing to the colorblind males in the class?
16. In 1981, a stray black cat with unusual rounded, curled-back ears was adopted by a family in Lakewood, California. Suppose you owned the first curl cat and wanted to breed it to develop a true-breeding variety. Describe tests that would determine whether the curl gene is dominant or recessive and whether it is autosomal or sex-linked. Explain why you think your tests would be conclusive. Describe a test to determine that a cat is true-breeding.
17. **SCIENTIFIC THINKING** The breakthrough that led Bateson and Punnett to recognize the existence of linked genes (Module 9.17) was the appearance of unexpected results after they crossed double heterozygous pea plants (*PpLl*) with each other. Imagine that you have a group of Labrador retrievers that are all heterozygous for both coat color and blindness (*BbNn*). If you used this group of dogs to produce 160 puppies, how many puppies of each phenotype do you expect to get if the genes are not linked? How would the results differ if the genes are in fact linked?

Answers to all questions can be found in Appendix 4.

Molecular Biology of the Gene

CHAPTER 10

Of all the visitors to California's Disneyland resort in 2014, one stood out. This unknown visitor (or perhaps a Disneyland employee) was sick with measles. Within a few months, at least 40 people who visited or worked at Disneyland had come into contact with this unknown person and become ill themselves. By the end of the outbreak in April 2015, 147 people in seven states had been infected. This outbreak is remarkable because scientists believed measles had been all but eradicated in the United States.

Where do deadly viruses come from?

Measles is caused by a highly contagious virus (pictured on the facing page) and is easily recognizable by the appearance of a red rash on the face. But the rash does not appear immediately. Infected people who cough or sneeze can therefore unknowingly spread the virus for several days before the telltale signs appear.

Just a few decades ago, measles killed more than a million people each year worldwide, many of them children. By 2007, widespread vaccination had reduced the number of cases to below 50 per year in the United States. But as the Disneyland outbreak demonstrates, measles has begun to make a comeback within communities that have low vaccination rates.

The measles virus, like all viruses, consists of a relatively simple structure of protein and nucleic acid (RNA in this case). Viruses share some of the characteristics of living organisms but are generally not considered alive because they are not cellular and cannot reproduce on their own. Because drugs are generally ineffective against viral infections, immunization is the only medical option that can prevent the disease.

Combating any virus thus requires a detailed understanding of nucleic acid—DNA and RNA—and how it serves as the molecule of heredity. Conversely, the study of viruses is responsible for our first understanding of the functions of DNA. In this chapter, we'll first explore the structure of DNA, how it replicates, and how it controls the cell by directing RNA and protein synthesis. We'll conclude by discussing the genetics of viruses and bacteria.

BIG IDEAS

The Structure of the Genetic Material (10.1–10.3)

A series of experiments established DNA as the molecule of heredity.

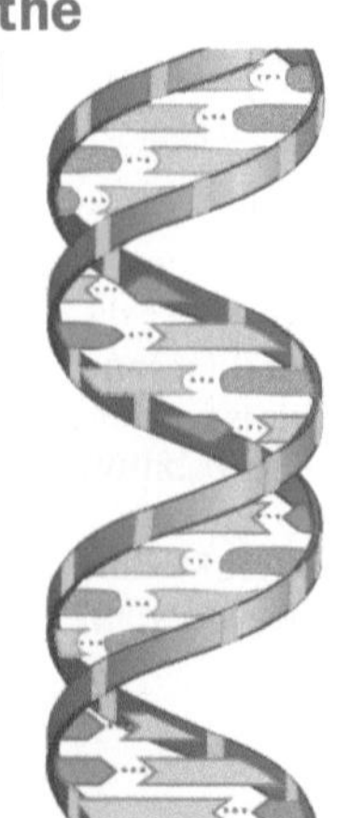

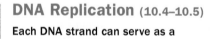

DNA Replication (10.4–10.5)

Each DNA strand can serve as a template for another.

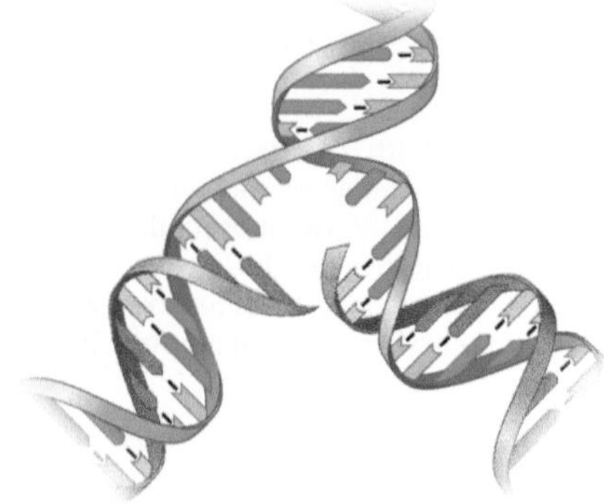

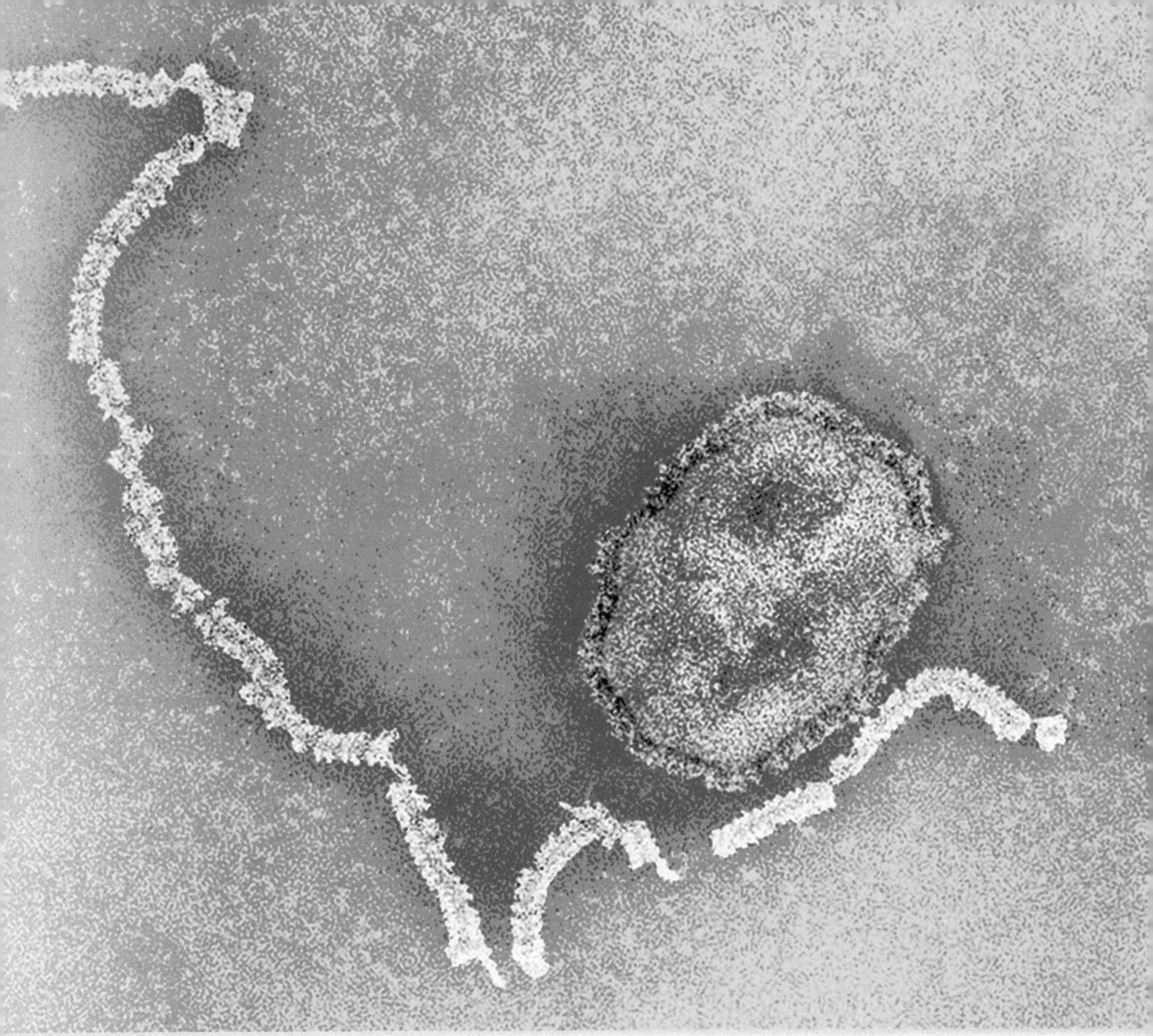

The Flow of Genetic Information from DNA to RNA to Protein (10.6–10.16)

Genotype controls phenotype through the production of proteins.

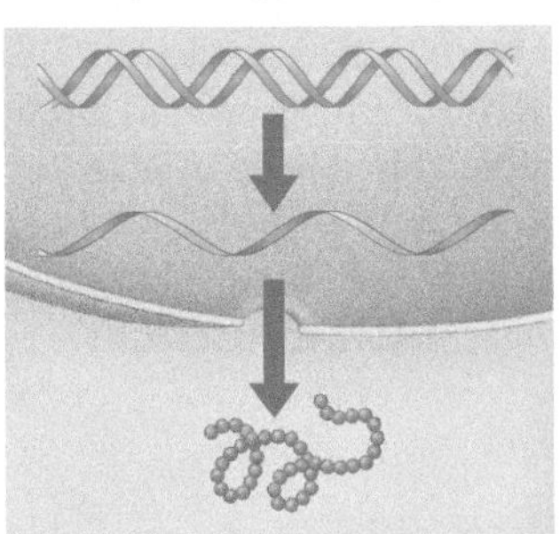

The Genetics of Viruses and Bacteria (10.17–10.23)

Viruses and bacteria are useful model systems for the study of nucleic acids.

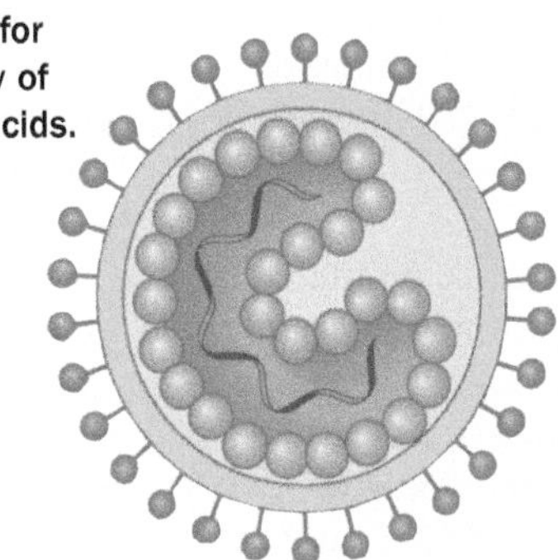

The Structure of the Genetic Material

10.1 Experiments showed that DNA is the genetic material

SCIENTIFIC THINKING

Today, scientists routinely manipulate DNA in the laboratory and use it to change the heritable traits of cells. Early in the 20th century, however, the molecular basis for inheritance was a mystery. Biologists did know that genes were located on chromosomes. The two chemical components of chromosomes—DNA and protein—were therefore the leading candidates to be the genetic material. Until the 1940s, the case for proteins seemed stronger than that for DNA because proteins appeared to be more structurally complex: Proteins were known to be made from 20 different amino acid building blocks, whereas DNA was known to be made from just four kinds of nucleotides. It seemed logical that the more complex molecule would serve as the hereditary material. Biologists finally established the role of DNA in heredity through experiments with bacteria and the viruses that infect them.

We can trace the discovery of the genetic role of DNA to 1928. British medical officer Frederick Griffith was trying to develop a vaccine against pneumonia by studying two strains (varieties) of a bacterium: a harmless strain and a pathogenic (disease-causing) strain that causes the disease in mammals. Griffith was surprised to find that when he killed the pathogenic bacteria and then mixed the bacterial remains with living harmless bacteria, some living bacterial cells became pathogenic. Furthermore, all of the descendants of the transformed bacteria inherited the newly acquired ability to cause disease. Clearly, some chemical component of the dead bacteria caused a heritable change in live bacteria.

Griffith's work set the stage for a race to discover the identity of the chemical basis of heredity. In 1952, American biologists Alfred Hershey and Martha Chase performed a very convincing set of experiments that showed DNA to be the genetic material of T2, a virus that infects the bacterium *Escherichia coli* (*E. coli*), a microbe normally found in the intestines of mammals (including humans). Viruses that exclusively infect bacteria are called **bacteriophages** ("bacteria-eaters"), or **phages** for short.

Hershey and Chase knew that T2 could reprogram its host cell to produce new phages, but they did not know what component of the virus conferred this capability. At the time, it was known that the structure of phage T2 consists solely of two types of molecules (Figure 10.1A): DNA (blue in the figure) and protein (gold). The researchers took advantage of this fact to devise an elegantly simple experiment that determined which of these molecules the phage transferred to *E. coli* during infection.

The Hershey and Chase experiment illustrates a point that arises repeatedly in the history of science: the importance of carefully designing an experiment and choosing the correct model organism to study. Like Mendel's garden peas (Module 9.2) and Morgan's fruit flies (Module 9.18), bacteriophage T2 had just the right properties (in this case, a simple structure consisting of just two contrasting elements) to allow for the design of a simple but conclusive experiment.

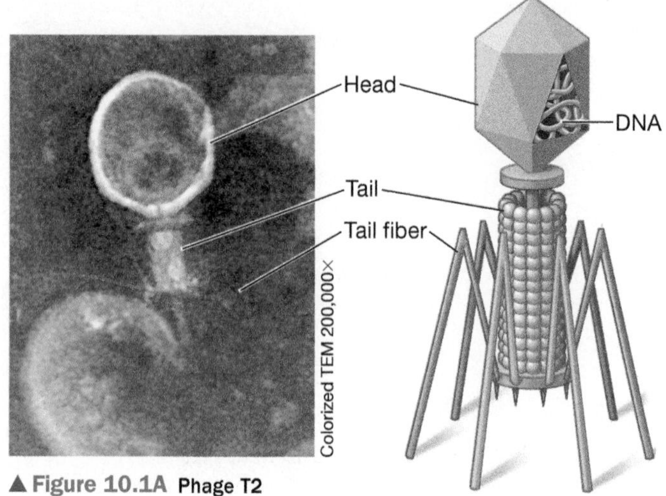

▲ **Figure 10.1A** Phage T2

To begin, Hershey and Chase grew T2 with *E. coli* in a solution containing radioactive sulfur (depicted in batch 1 beaker in yellow in Figure 10.1B on the facing page). Protein contains sulfur but DNA does not, so as new phages were made, the radioactive sulfur atoms were incorporated only into the proteins of the bacteriophage. The researchers grew a second batch of phages in a solution containing radioactive phosphorus (batch 2 beaker in green). Because nearly all the phage's phosphorus is in DNA, this labeled only the phage DNA.

Armed with the two batches of labeled T2, Hershey and Chase were ready to perform the experiment illustrated in Figure 10.1B. They allowed the two batches of T2 to infect separate samples of nonradioactive bacteria. Shortly after the onset of infection, they agitated the cultures in an ordinary kitchen blender to shake loose any parts of the phages that remained outside the bacterial cells. Then they collected the mixtures in tubes and spun the tubes in a centrifuge. The cells were deposited as a solid pellet at the bottom of the centrifuge tubes, but phages and parts of phages—because they were lighter—remained suspended in the liquid. The researchers then measured the radioactivity in the pellet and in the liquid.

Hershey and Chase found that when the bacteria had been infected with T2 phages containing labeled protein (batch 1), the radioactivity ended up mainly in the solution within the centrifuge tube, which contained phages but not bacteria. This result suggested that the phage protein did not enter the cells. But when the bacteria had been infected with phages whose DNA was tagged (batch 2), most of the radioactivity was in the pellet of bacterial cells at the bottom of the centrifuge tube. Furthermore, when these bacteria were returned to a liquid growth medium, they soon lysed, or broke open, releasing new phages that contained some radioactive phosphorus in their DNA.

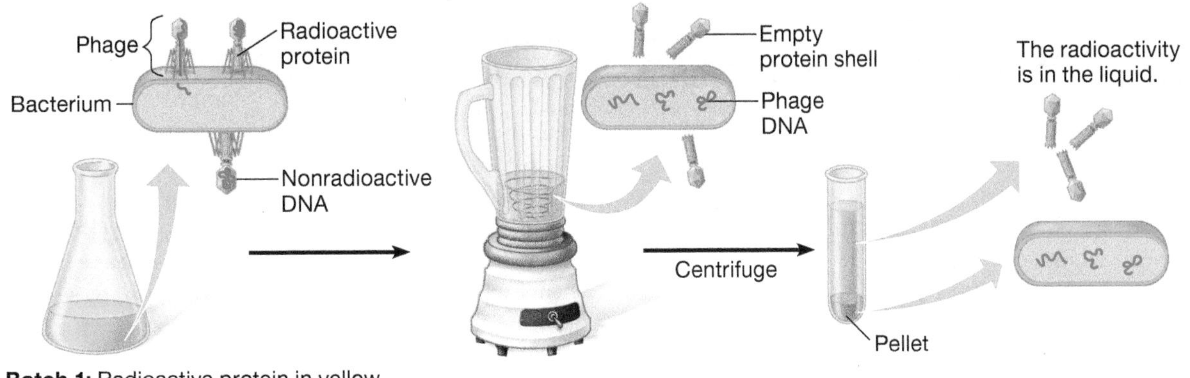

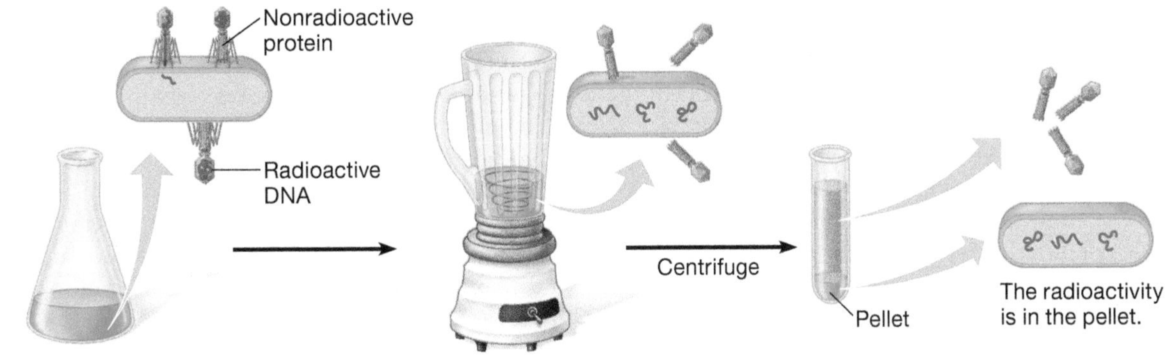

Hershey and Chase mixed radioactively labeled phages with bacteria. The phages infected the bacterial cells.

They agitated the cultures in a blender to separate the phages outside of the bacteria from the cells and their contents.

They centrifuged the mixture so that the bacteria formed a pellet at the bottom of the test tube.

Finally, they measured the radioactivity in the pellet and in the liquid.

▲ **Figure 10.1B** The Hershey-Chase experiment

Figure 10.1C outlines our current understanding of the replication cycle of phage T2. After the virus ❶ attaches to the host bacterial cell, it ❷ injects its DNA into the host. Notice that virtually all of the viral protein (yellow) is left outside of the bacterium (which is why the radioactive protein did not show up in the host cells during the experiment shown at the top of Figure 10.1B). Once injected into the bacteria, the viral DNA causes the bacterial cells to ❸ produce new phage proteins and DNA molecules—indeed, complete new phages—which soon ❹ cause the cell to lyse, releasing the newly produced phages. These phages may then attach to other host bacterial cells. As Hershey and Chase discovered, it is the viral DNA that contains the instructions for making phages.

Once DNA was shown to be the molecule of heredity, understanding its structure became the most important quest in biology. In the next two modules, we'll review the structure of DNA and discuss how it was discovered.

? **What structural feature of viruses like phage T2 made them ideally suited for the Hershey-Chase experiment?**

■ Phage T2 has a very simple structure consisting of just two "ingredients"—DNA and protein—making it easier to identify which component served as the genetic material.

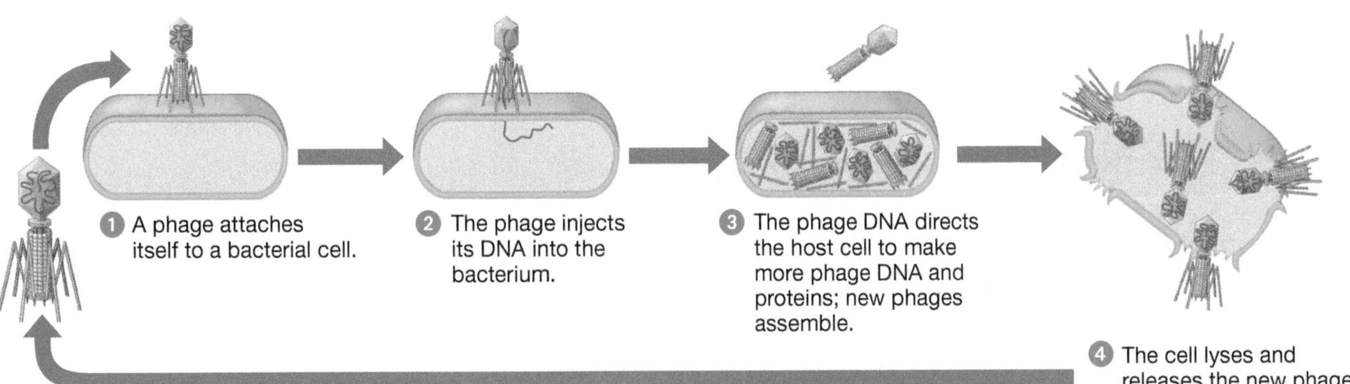

❶ A phage attaches itself to a bacterial cell.
❷ The phage injects its DNA into the bacterium.
❸ The phage DNA directs the host cell to make more phage DNA and proteins; new phages assemble.
❹ The cell lyses and releases the new phages.

▲ **Figure 10.1C** A phage replication cycle

10.2 DNA and RNA are polymers of nucleotides

Once biologists had confirmed that DNA was the molecule of heredity, they began to study its structure. DNA and its close chemical cousin RNA are nucleic acids, consisting of long chains (polymers) of chemical units (monomers) called **nucleotides** (see Module 3.15). **Figure 10.2A** shows four representations of various parts of the same molecule. At top left is a view of a DNA double helix. One of the strands is opened up (center) to show two different views of an individual DNA **polynucleotide**, a nucleotide polymer (chain). The view on the far right zooms in to a single nucleotide from the chain. Each type of DNA nucleotide has a different nitrogen-containing base: adenine (A), cytosine (C), guanine (G), or thymine (T). Because nucleotides can occur in a polynucleotide in any sequence and because polynucleotides can be very long, the number of possible polynucleotides is enormous. The chain shown in this figure has the sequence ACTGG, only one of many possible arrangements of the four types of nucleotides that make up DNA.

Looking more closely at the polynucleotide, we see in the center of Figure 10.2A that each nucleotide consists of three components: a nitrogenous base (in DNA: A, C, T, or G), a sugar (shown in blue), and a phosphate group (yellow). The nucleotides are joined to one another by covalent bonds between the sugar of one nucleotide and the phosphate of the next, forming a **sugar-phosphate backbone** with a repeating pattern of sugar-phosphate-sugar-phosphate. The nitrogenous bases are arranged like ribs that project from the backbone.

Examining a single nucleotide in even more detail (on the right in Figure 10.2A), you can see the chemical structure of its three components. The phosphate group has a phosphorus atom (P) at the center with four surrounding oxygen atoms. The sugar has five carbon atoms, called out in red in the figure for emphasis—four in its ring and one extending above the ring. The ring also includes an oxygen atom. The sugar is called deoxyribose because, compared with the sugar ribose (see Figure 10.2C), it is missing an oxygen atom. Notice that the C atom in the lower right corner of the ring is bonded to an H atom instead of to an —OH group, as it is in ribose. Hence, DNA is "deoxy"—which means "without an oxygen"—compared to RNA. The full name for **DNA** is **deoxyribonucleic acid**: *deoxyribo* refers to its form of the sugar, *nucleic* because DNA is located in the nuclei of eukaryotic cells, and *acid* because the phosphate

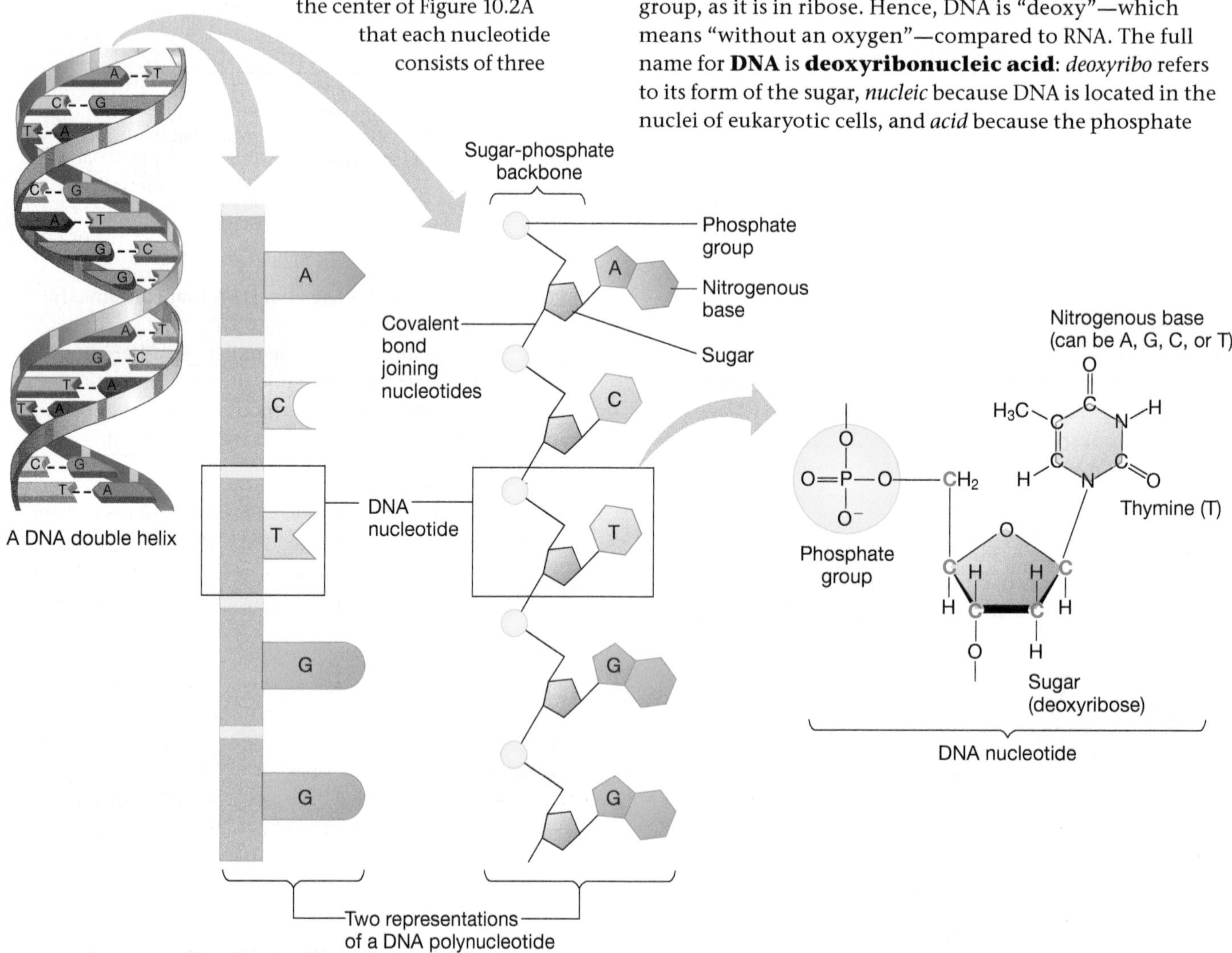

▲ **Figure 10.2A** **Breaking down the structure of DNA**

TRY THIS Use your finger to trace each part of the nucleotide—sugar, phosphate, and base—in all four parts of this figure.

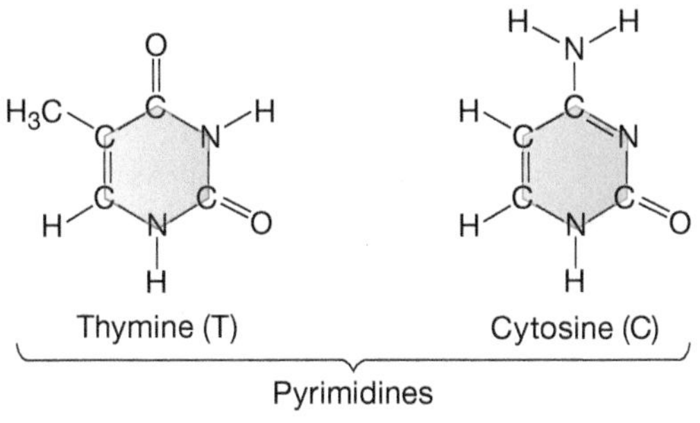

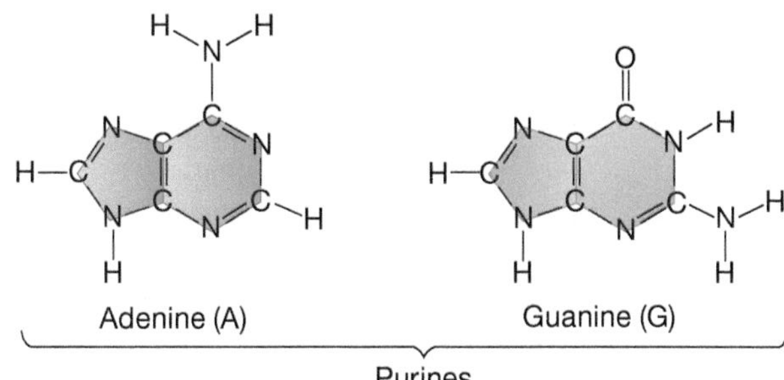

▲ **Figure 10.2B** The nitrogenous bases of DNA

group is in the ionized (negatively charged) form after donating a hydrogen atom.

Every nucleotide contains a nitrogenous base (thymine, in our example at the right in Figure 10.2A). In contrast to the acidic phosphate group, nitrogenous bases are basic—hence their name. Each base has a single or double ring consisting of nitrogen and carbon atoms with various functional groups attached (**Figure 10.2B**). Recall that a functional group is a chemical group that affects a molecule's function by participating in specific chemical reactions (see Module 3.2). In the case of DNA, the main role of the functional groups is to determine which other kind of bases each base can form hydrogen bonds with. For example, the NH_2 group hanging off cytosine is capable of forming a hydrogen bond to the C=O group hanging off guanine but not with the NH_2 group protruding from adenine. The chemical groups of the bases are therefore responsible for the specific base pairing found in DNA.

The four nucleotides found in DNA differ only in the structure of their nitrogenous bases. At this point, the structural details are not as important as is the fact that the bases are of two types. **Thymine (T)** and **cytosine (C)** are single-ring structures called pyrimidines. **Adenine (A)** and **guanine (G)** are larger, double-ring structures called purines. The one-letter abbreviations can be used either for the bases alone or for the nucleotides containing them.

What about RNA? As its name—ribonucleic acid—implies, its sugar is ribose rather than deoxyribose (**Figure 10.2C**).

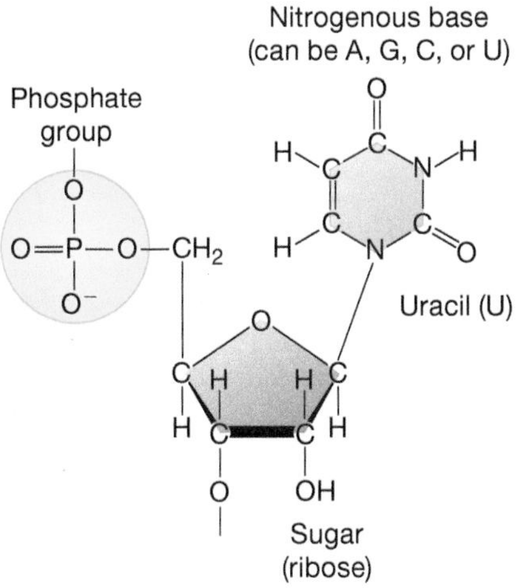

▲ **Figure 10.2C** An RNA nucleotide

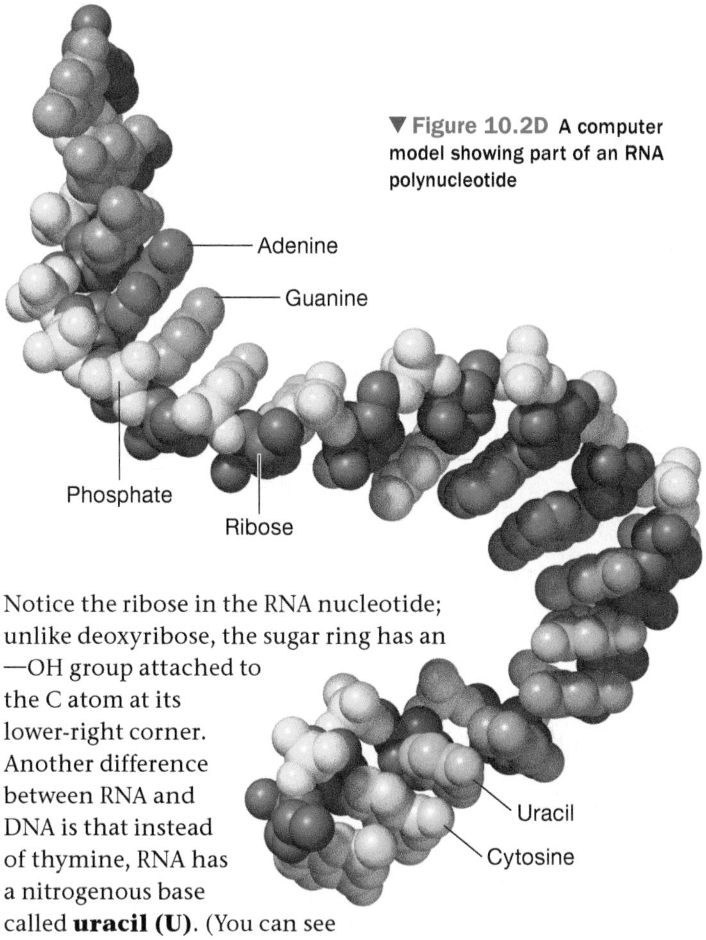

▼ **Figure 10.2D** A computer model showing part of an RNA polynucleotide

Notice the ribose in the RNA nucleotide; unlike deoxyribose, the sugar ring has an —OH group attached to the C atom at its lower-right corner. Another difference between RNA and DNA is that instead of thymine, RNA has a nitrogenous base called **uracil (U)**. (You can see the structure of uracil in Figure 10.2C; it is very similar to thymine.) Except for the presence of ribose and uracil, an RNA polynucleotide chain is identical to a DNA polynucleotide chain. **Figure 10.2D** is a computer graphic of a piece of RNA polynucleotide about 20 nucleotides long. In this three-dimensional view, each sphere represents an atom; notice that the color scheme is the same as in the other figures in this module. The yellow phosphate groups and blue ribose sugars make it easy to spot the sugar-phosphate backbone. In the next module, we'll see how two DNA polynucleotides join together in a molecule of DNA.

? **Compare and contrast DNA and RNA polynucleotides.**

■ Both are polymers of nucleotides consisting of a sugar, a nitrogenous base, and a phosphate. In RNA, the sugar is ribose; in DNA, it is deoxyribose. Both RNA and DNA have the bases A, G, and C, but DNA has a T and RNA has a U.

10.3 DNA is a double-stranded helix

After the 1952 Hershey-Chase experiment convinced most biologists that DNA was the material that stored genetic information, a race was on to determine how the structure of this molecule could account for its role in heredity. At the time, the arrangement of covalent bonds in a nucleic acid polymer was well established, and therefore, researchers focused on discovering the three-dimensional shape of DNA. First to the finish line were two scientists who were relatively unknown at the time—American James D. Watson and Englishman Francis Crick.

The partnership that solved the puzzle of DNA structure began soon after Watson, a 23-year-old newly minted Ph.D., journeyed to Cambridge University in England, where the more senior Crick was studying protein structure with a technique called X-ray crystallography. While visiting the laboratory of Maurice Wilkins at King's College in London, Watson saw an X-ray image of DNA produced by Wilkins's colleague, Rosalind Franklin (Figure 10.3A). A careful study of the image enabled Watson to deduce the basic shape of DNA to be a helix (spiral) with a uniform diameter and the nitrogenous bases located above one another like a stack of dinner plates. The thickness of the helix suggested that it was made up of two polynucleotide strands, forming a **double helix**. But how were the nucleotides arranged in the double helix?

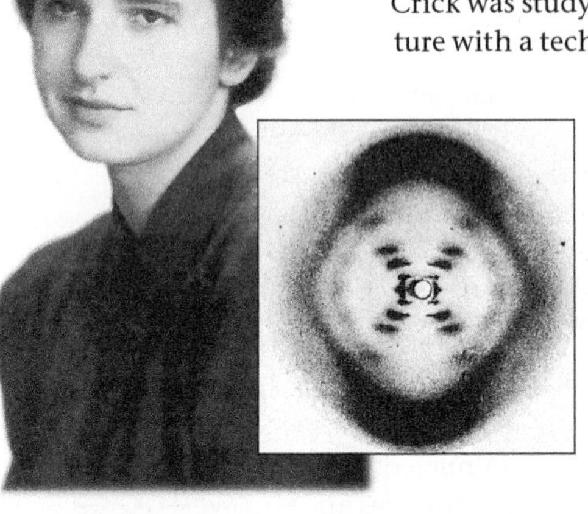

▲ Figure 10.3A Rosalind Franklin and her X-ray image of DNA

Watson and Crick began trying to construct a wire model of a double helix that would conform both to Franklin's data and to what was then known about the chemistry of DNA (Figure 10.3B). They knew that Franklin had concluded that the sugar-phosphate backbones must be on the outside of the double helix, forcing the nitrogenous bases to swivel to the interior of the molecule. But how were the bases arranged in the interior of the double helix?

At first, Watson and Crick imagined that the bases paired like with like—for example, A with A and C with C. But that kind of pairing did not fit the X-ray data, which suggested that the DNA molecule has a uniform diameter. An A-A pair, with two double-ring bases, would be almost twice as wide as a C-C pair, made of two single-ring bases. It soon became apparent that a double-ringed base (purine) on one strand must always be paired with a single-ringed base (pyrimidine) on the opposite strand to produce a molecule of uniform thickness. After considerable trial and error, Watson and Crick realized that the chemical structures of the bases dictated the pairings even more specifically. As discussed in the previous module, each base has protruding functional groups that can best form hydrogen bonds with just one appropriate partner (to review the hydrogen bond, see Module 2.8). Adenine can best form hydrogen bonds with thymine and only thymine, and guanine with cytosine and only cytosine. In the biologist's shorthand, A pairs with T, and G pairs with C. A is also said to be "complementary" to T and G to C.

Watson and Crick's pairing scheme both fit what was known about the physical attributes and chemical bonding of DNA and explained some data obtained several years earlier by American biochemist Erwin Chargaff. Chargaff had discovered that the amount of adenine in the DNA of any one species was equal to the amount of thymine and that the amount of guanine was equal to that of cytosine. Chargaff's rules, as they are called, are explained by the fact that A on one of DNA's polynucleotide chains always pairs with T on the other polynucleotide chain, and G on one chain pairs only with C on the other chain.

You can picture the model of the DNA double helix proposed by Watson and Crick as a rope ladder with wooden rungs, with the ladder twisting into a spiral (Figure 10.3C on the facing page). The side ropes represent the sugar-phosphate backbones, and the rungs represent pairs of nitrogenous bases joined by hydrogen bonds.

Figure 10.3D shows three representations of the double helix. The shapes of the base symbols in the ribbonlike diagram on the left indicate the bases' complementarity; notice that the shape of any kind of base matches only one other kind of base. In the center of the diagram is an atomic-level version showing four base pairs, with the helix untwisted and the hydrogen bonds specified by dotted lines. Notice that a

▲ Figure 10.3B Watson and Crick in 1953 with their model of the DNA double helix

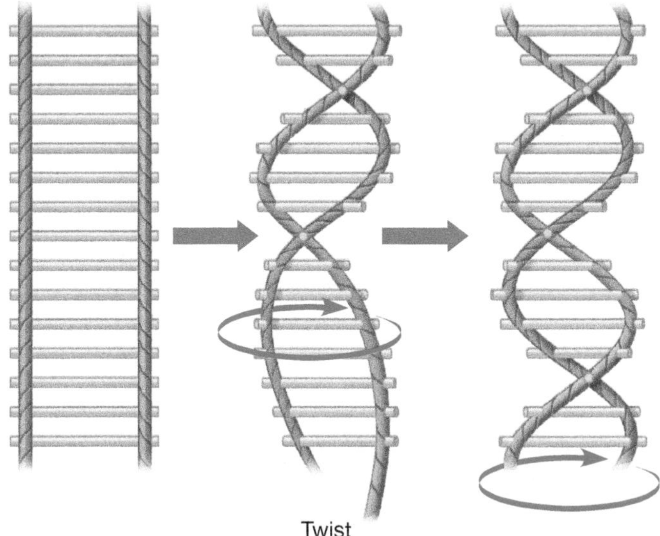

▲ **Figure 10.3C** **A rope ladder analogy for the double helix**

C-G base pair has functional groups that form three hydrogen bonds, whereas an A-T base pair has functional groups that form two hydrogen bonds. You can see that the two sugar-phosphate backbones of the double helix are oriented in opposite directions. (Notice that the sugars on the two strands are upside down with respect to each other.) On the right is a computer graphic showing most of the atoms of part of a double helix. (The atoms that compose the deoxyribose sugars are shown as blue, phosphate groups as yellow, and nitrogenous bases as shades of green and orange; you'll see this coloring convention throughout this text.)

Although the Watson-Crick base-pairing rules dictate the allowable combinations of nitrogenous bases that can form the rungs of the double helix, they place no restrictions on the sequence of nucleotides along the length of a DNA strand. In fact, the sequence of bases can vary in countless ways, and each gene has a unique order of nucleotides, or base sequence.

In April 1953, Watson and Crick rocked the scientific world with a succinct paper in the British scientific journal *Nature* that explained their molecular model for DNA. In 1962, Watson, Crick, and Wilkins received the Nobel Prize for their work. (Sadly, Rosalind Franklin died of multiple cancers in 1958 at the age of 38 and was thus ineligible for the prize; some suspect that her work with X-ray radiation may have caused her illness.) Few milestones in the history of biology have had as broad an impact as the discovery of the double helix, with its A-T and C-G base pairing.

The Watson-Crick model gave new meaning to the words *genes* and *chromosomes*—and to the chromosome theory of inheritance (see Module 9.16). With a complete picture of DNA, we can see that the genetic information in a chromosome must be encoded in the nucleotide sequence of the molecule. One powerful aspect of the Watson-Crick model is that the structure of DNA suggests a molecular explanation for genetic inheritance, as we will see in the next module.

? **Along one strand of a double helix is the nucleotide sequence GGCATAGGT. What is the complementary sequence for the other DNA strand?**

■ CCGTATCCA

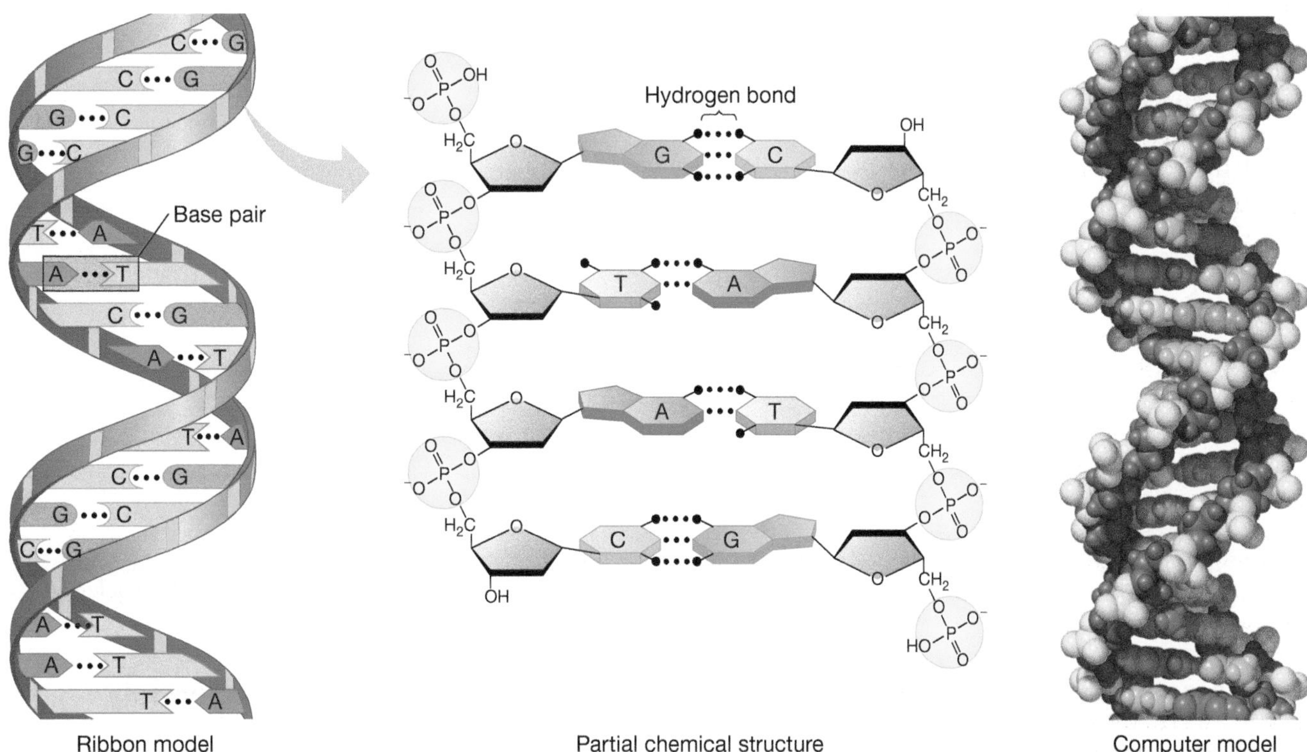

▲ **Figure 10.3D** **Three representations of DNA**

DNA Replication

10.4 DNA replication depends on specific base pairing

The primary function of DNA is to encode and store genetic information, thereby acting as the molecular basis of heredity. Genes are passed along from one cell to the next during cell division and from one generation to the next during reproduction (see Module 8.3). DNA's unique structure allows it to serve this information storage purpose. Thus, one of biology's overarching themes—the relationship of STRUCTURE AND FUNCTION—is evident in the double helix.

Watson and Crick proposed that the specific pairing of complementary bases accounts for the ability of DNA to be copied. You can see this by covering one of the strands in the parental DNA molecule in **Figure 10.4A**. You can determine the sequence of bases in the covered strand by applying the base-pairing rules to the unmasked strand: A pairs with T (and T with A), and G pairs with C (and C with G).

Watson and Crick predicted that a cell applies the same rules when copying its genes during each turn of the cell cycle. As shown in Figure 10.4A, the two strands of parental DNA (blue) separate. Each strand becomes a template for the assembly of a complementary strand from a supply of free nucleotides (gray) available within the nucleus. The nucleotides line up one at a time along the template strand in accordance with the base-pairing rules. Enzymes link the nucleotides to form the new DNA strands. The completed new molecules, identical to the parental molecule, are known as daughter DNA (although no gender should be inferred).

Watson and Crick's model predicts that when a double helix replicates, each of the two daughter molecules will have one old strand from the parental molecule and one newly created strand. This model for DNA replication is known as the **semiconservative model** because half of the parental molecule is maintained (conserved) in each daughter molecule.

Although the general mechanism of DNA replication is conceptually simple, the actual process is complex, requiring the coordination of more than a dozen enzymes and other proteins. Some of the complexity arises from the need for the helical DNA molecule to untwist as it replicates and for the two new strands to be made roughly simultaneously (**Figure 10.4B**). Another challenge is the speed of the process. *E. coli*, with about 4.6 million DNA base pairs, can copy its entire genome in less than an hour. Human cells, with more than 6 billion base pairs in 46 chromosomes, require only a few hours. Despite this speed, the process is amazingly accurate; typically, only about one DNA nucleotide per several billion is incorrectly paired. In the next module, we take a closer look at the mechanisms of DNA replication.

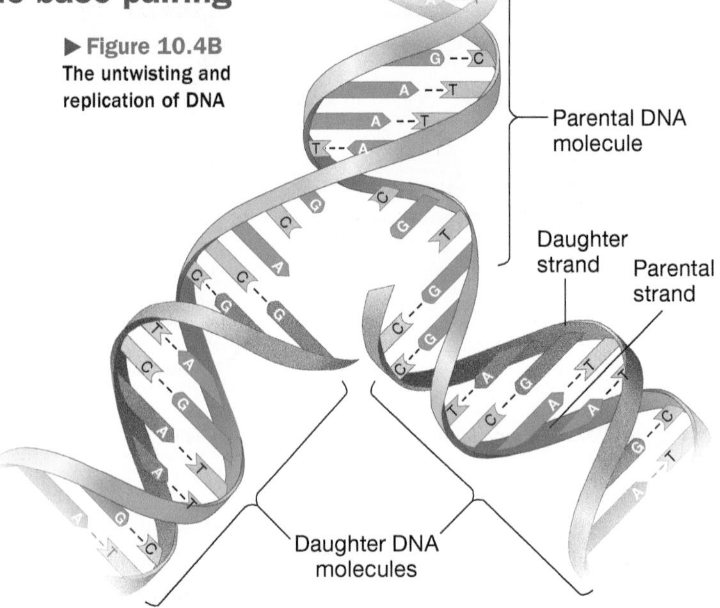

▶ **Figure 10.4B** The untwisting and replication of DNA

? How does complementary base pairing make possible the replication of DNA?

When the two strands of the double helix separate, free nucleotides can base-pair along each strand, leading to the synthesis of new complementary strands.

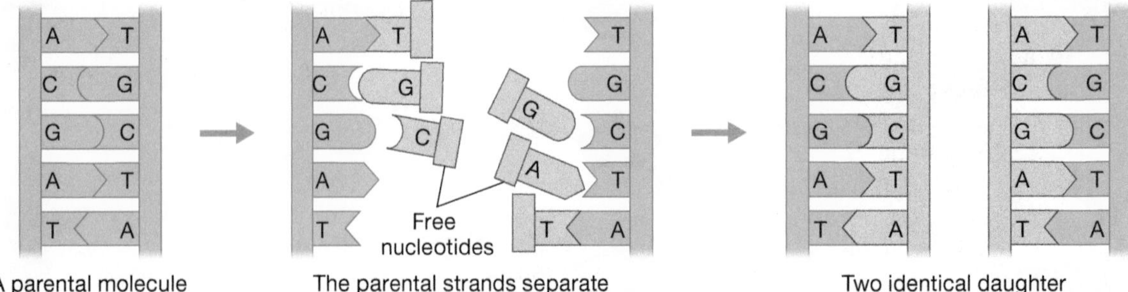

▶ **Figure 10.4A** A template model for DNA replication

10.5 DNA replication proceeds in two directions at many sites simultaneously

Replication of a chromosomal DNA molecule begins at particular sites called origins of replication, short stretches of DNA having a specific sequence of nucleotides. Proteins that initiate DNA replication attach to the DNA at an origin of replication, separating the two strands of the double helix (**Figure 10.5A** on the facing page). Replication then proceeds

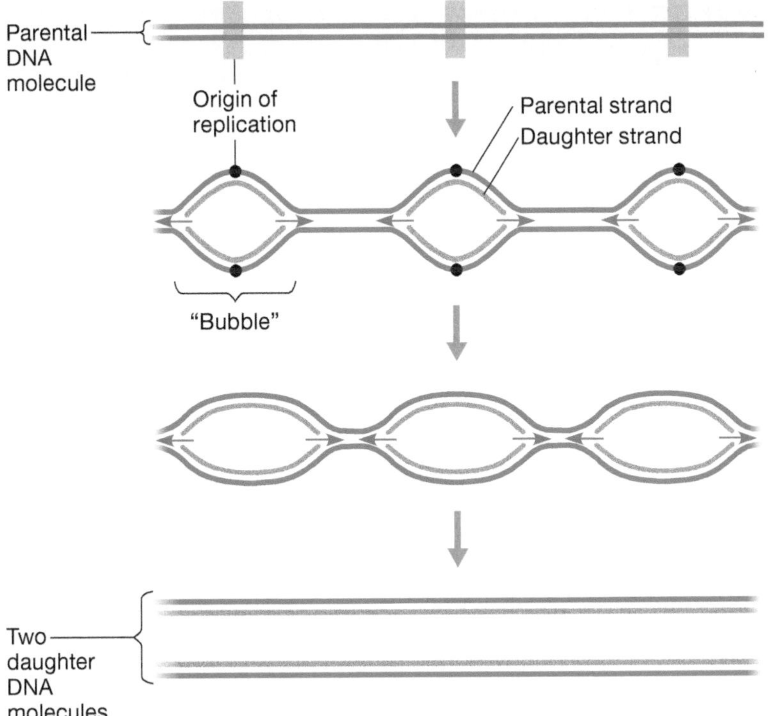

▲ **Figure 10.5A** Multiple replication bubbles in DNA

in both directions, creating replication "bubbles." The parental DNA strands (blue) open up as daughter strands (gray) elongate on both sides of each bubble. The DNA molecule of a eukaryotic chromosome has many origins where replication can start simultaneously, thereby shortening the total time needed for replication. Eventually, all the bubbles fuse, yielding two completed, double-stranded daughter DNA molecules (see the bottom of Figure 10.5A).

Figure 10.5B shows the molecular building blocks of a tiny segment of DNA. Notice that the sugar-phosphate backbones run in opposite directions. As a result, each strand has a 3′ ("three-prime") end and a 5′ ("five-prime") end. The primed numbers refer to the carbon atoms of the nucleotide sugars. At one end of each DNA strand, the sugar's 3′ carbon atom is attached to an —OH group; at the other end, the sugar's 5′ carbon is attached to a phosphate group.

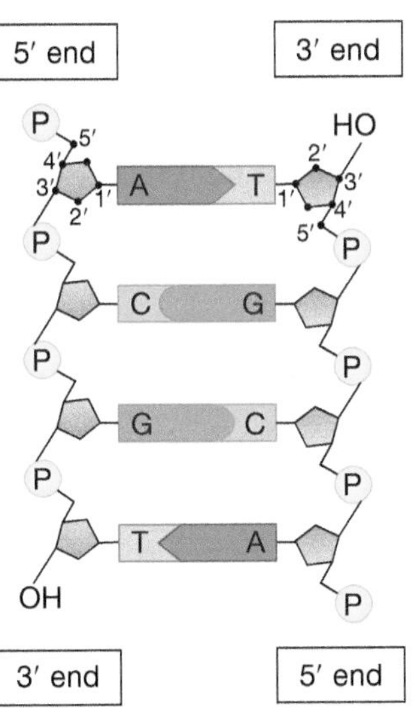

▲ **Figure 10.5B** The opposite orientations of DNA strands

TRY THIS On each polynucleotide strand, identify one complete nucleotide by drawing a circle around it. Notice that in one strand, the phosphate is on top, and in the other strand, it's on the bottom.

The opposite orientation of the strands is important in DNA replication. The enzymes that link DNA nucleotides to a growing daughter strand are called **DNA polymerases**. These enzymes add nucleotides only to the 3′ end of the strand, never to the 5′ end. Thus, a daughter DNA strand can only grow in the 5′ → 3′ direction. You see the consequences of this enzyme specificity in Figure 10.5C, where the forked structure represents one side of a replication bubble. One of the daughter strands (shown in gray) can be synthesized in one continuous piece by a DNA polymerase working toward the forking point of the parental DNA. However, to make the other daughter strand, polymerase molecules must work outward from the forking point. The only way this can be accomplished is if the new strand is synthesized in short pieces as the fork opens up. These pieces are called Okazaki fragments, after the Japanese husband and wife team of molecular biologists who discovered them. Another enzyme, called **DNA ligase**, then links, or ligates, the pieces together into a single DNA strand.

In addition to their roles in adding nucleotides to a DNA chain, DNA polymerases carry out a proofreading step that quickly removes nucleotides that have base-paired incorrectly during replication. DNA polymerases and DNA ligase are also involved in repairing DNA damaged by harmful radiation, such as ultraviolet light and X-rays, or toxic chemicals in the environment, such as those found in tobacco smoke.

DNA replication ensures that all the body cells in a multicellular organism carry the same genetic information. It is also the means by which genetic instructions are copied for the next generation of the organism. In the next module, we begin to pursue the connection between DNA instructions and an organism's phenotypic traits.

? **What is the function of DNA polymerase in DNA replication?**

■ As free nucleotides base-pair to a parental DNA strand, the enzyme DNA polymerase covalently bonds them to the 3′ end of a growing daughter strand.

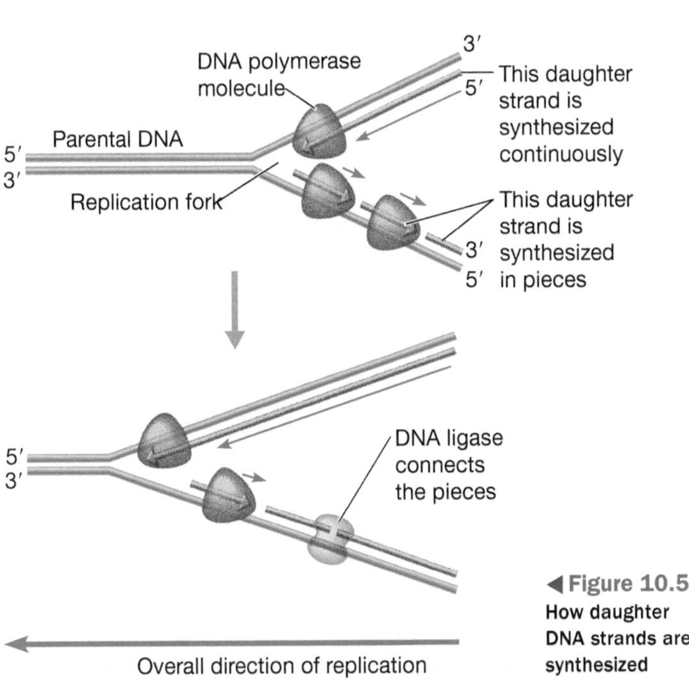

◀ **Figure 10.5C** How daughter DNA strands are synthesized

The Flow of Genetic Information from DNA to RNA to Protein

10.6 Genes control phenotypic traits through the expression of proteins

We can now define genotype and phenotype in terms of the structure and function of DNA. An organism's genotype, its genetic makeup, is the heritable information contained in the sequence of nucleotide bases in DNA. The phenotype is the organism's physical traits. So what is the molecular connection between genotype and phenotype?

The answer is that the DNA inherited by an organism specifies traits by dictating the synthesis of proteins (or, in some cases, just RNAs). In other words, proteins are the links between genotype and phenotype. However, a gene does not build a protein directly. Rather, a gene dispatches instructions in the form of RNA, which in turn programs protein synthesis. This fundamental concept in biology is summarized in Figure 10.6A. The molecular "chain of command" is from DNA in the nucleus of the cell to RNA to protein synthesis in the cytoplasm. The two main stages are **transcription**, the synthesis of RNA under the direction of DNA, and **translation**, the synthesis of protein under the direction of RNA.

The relationship between genes and proteins was first proposed in 1902, when English physician Archibald Garrod suggested that genes dictate phenotypes through enzymes, proteins that catalyze specific chemical reactions. Garrod hypothesized that an inherited disease reflects a person's inability to make a particular enzyme. He gave as one example the hereditary condition called alkaptonuria, in which the urine is dark because it contains a chemical called alkapton. Garrod reasoned that people with alkaptonuria inherited an inability to make an enzyme that breaks down alkapton. Years later, biochemists accumulated evidence in favor of Garrod's proposal that cells make and break down biologically important molecules via metabolic pathways, as in the synthesis of an amino acid or the breakdown of a sugar. Each step in a metabolic pathway is catalyzed by a specific enzyme (see Module 5.15). Therefore, individuals lacking one of the enzymes for a pathway are unable to complete that pathway.

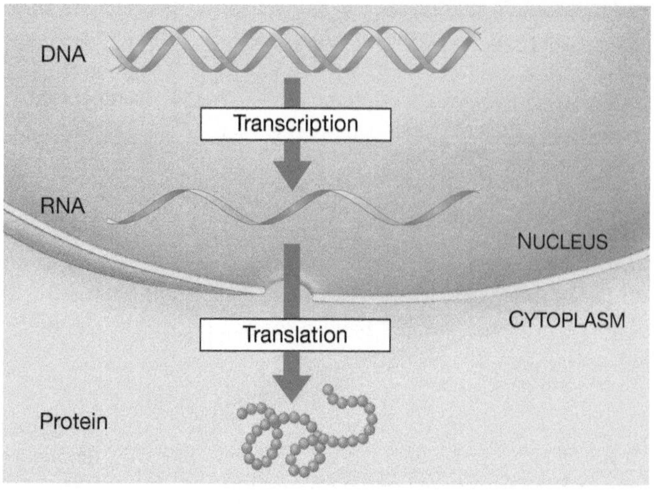

▲ Figure 10.6A The flow of genetic information in a eukaryotic cell

The major breakthrough in demonstrating the relationship between genes and enzymes came in the 1940s from American geneticists George Beadle and Edward Tatum and their work with the bread mold *Neurospora crassa* (Figure 10.6B). Beadle and Tatum studied strains of the mold that were unable to grow on a simple growth medium. Each of these so-called nutritional mutants turned out to lack an enzyme in a metabolic pathway that synthesized some molecule the mold needed, such as an amino acid. Beadle and Tatum also showed that each mutant was defective in a single gene. Accordingly, they hypothesized that the function of an individual gene is to dictate the production of a specific enzyme. This work won Beadle and Tatum the 1958 Nobel Prize in Chemistry.

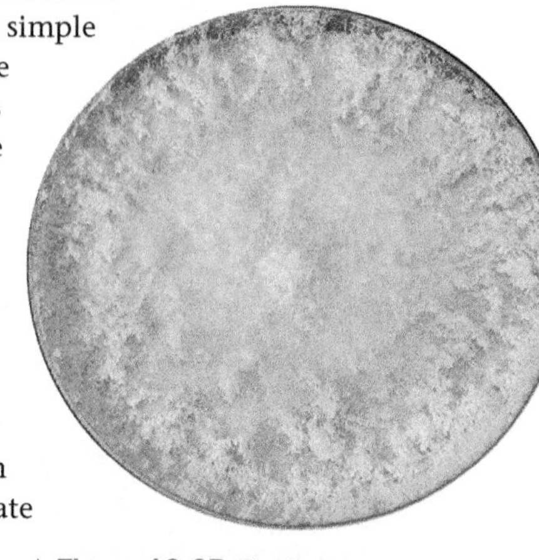

▲ Figure 10.6B The bread mold *Neurospora crassa* growing in a culture dish

The "one gene–one enzyme hypothesis" has since been modified. First, it was extended beyond enzymes to include *all* types of proteins. For example, keratin (the structural protein of hair) and the hormone insulin are two examples of proteins that are not enzymes. In addition, many proteins are made from two or more polypeptide chains, with each polypeptide specified by its own gene. For example, hemoglobin, the oxygen-transporting protein in your red blood cells, is built from two kinds of polypeptides, encoded by two different genes. In addition, many eukaryotic genes code for a set of polypeptides (rather than just one) by a process called alternative splicing (discussed in Module 11.4).

Even this description is incomplete because the RNA transcribed from some genes is not translated but nonetheless performs important functions itself (you'll learn about two such kinds of RNA in Modules 10.11 and 10.12). Putting all of this together brings us to the current definition of a gene: a region of DNA that can be expressed to produce a functional product that is either a polypeptide or an RNA molecule. The more biologists learn about the ways that genes act in cells, the more complicated the picture—and the more complicated the very concept of a gene—becomes. But for now, we'll focus on genes that do code for proteins. The nature of that code is our next topic.

? **What are the functions of transcription and translation?**

■ Transcription is the transfer of information from DNA to RNA. Translation is the use of the information in RNA to make a polypeptide.

10.7 Genetic information written in codons is translated into amino acid sequences

Genes provide the instructions for making specific proteins. But a gene does not build a protein itself. The bridge between DNA and protein synthesis is the nucleic acid RNA: DNA is transcribed into RNA, which is then translated into protein. Put another way, information within the cell flows as DNA → RNA → protein.

Transcription and translation are linguistic terms, and it is useful to think of nucleic acids and proteins as having languages. To understand how genetic information passes from genotype to phenotype, we need to see how the chemical language of DNA is translated into the different chemical language of proteins.

What exactly is the language of nucleic acids? Both DNA and RNA are polymers made of nucleotide monomers strung together in specific sequences that convey information, much as specific sequences of letters convey information in written language. In DNA, there are four types of nucleotides, which differ in their nitrogenous bases (A, T, C, and G). The same is true for RNA, although it has the base U instead of T.

Figure 10.7 focuses on a small region of one gene (gene 3, shown in light blue) on a DNA molecule. DNA's language is written as a linear sequence of nucleotide bases on a polynucleotide, a sequence such as the one you see on the enlarged DNA segment in the figure. Specific sequences of bases, each with a beginning and an end, make up the genes on a DNA strand. A typical gene consists of hundreds or thousands of nucleotides in a specific sequence.

The pink strand underneath the enlarged DNA segment represents the results of transcription: an RNA molecule. The process is called transcription because the nucleic acid language of DNA has been rewritten (transcribed) as a sequence of bases on RNA. Notice that the language is still that of nucleic acids, although the nucleotide bases on the RNA molecule are complementary to those on the DNA strand. As we will see in Module 10.9, this is because the RNA was synthesized using the DNA as a template.

The purple chain at the bottom of Figure 10.7 represents the results of translation, the conversion of the nucleic acid language to the polypeptide language. Like nucleic acids, polypeptides are polymers, but the monomers that compose them are the 20 different kinds of amino acids. Again, the language is written in a linear sequence, and the sequence of nucleotides of the RNA molecule dictates the sequence of amino acids of the polypeptide. The RNA acts as a messenger carrying genetic information from DNA.

During translation, there is a change in language from the nucleotide sequence of the RNA to the amino acid sequence of the polypeptide. How is this translation achieved? Recall that there are only four different kinds of nucleotides in DNA (A, G, C, T) and in RNA (A, G, C, U). In translation, these four nucleotides must somehow specify all 20 amino acids. Consider if each single nucleotide base were to specify one amino acid. In this case, only four of the 20 amino acids could be accounted for, one for each type of base. What if the language consisted of two-letter code words? If we read the bases of a gene two at a time—AG, for example, could specify one amino acid, whereas AT could designate a different amino acid—then only 16 arrangements would be possible (4^2), which is still not enough to specify all 20 amino acids. However, if the base code in DNA consists of a triplet, with each arrangement of three consecutive bases specifying an amino acid—AGT specifies one amino acid, for example, while AGA specifies a different one—then there can be 64 (that is, 4^3) possible code words, more than enough to specify the 20 amino acids. Thus, triplets of bases are the smallest "words" of uniform length that can specify all the amino acids (see the brackets below the strand of RNA in Figure 10.7). Indeed, the 64 triplets allow for more than one to represent an amino acid.

Experiments have verified that the flow of information from gene to protein is based on a **triplet code**: The genetic instructions for the amino acid sequence of a polypeptide chain are written in DNA and RNA as a series of nonoverlapping three-base "words" called **codons**. Notice in the figure that three-base codons in the DNA are transcribed into complementary three-base codons in the RNA, and then the RNA codons are translated into amino acids that form a polypeptide. We turn to the codons themselves in the next module.

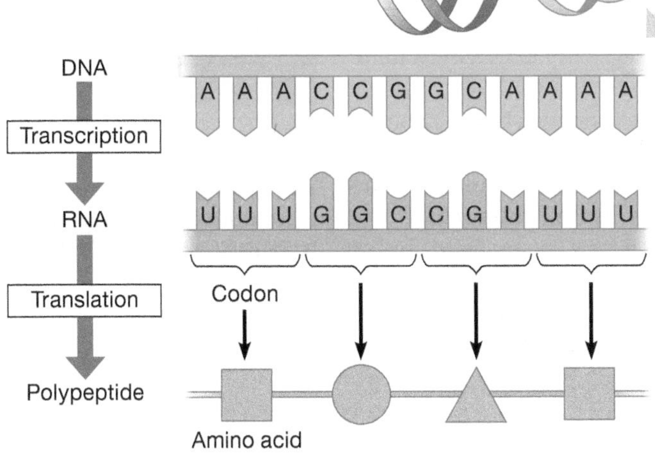

▲ Figure 10.7 Transcription and translation of codons

? What is the minimum number of nucleotides necessary to code for 100 amino acids?

300

10.8 The genetic code dictates how codons are translated into amino acids

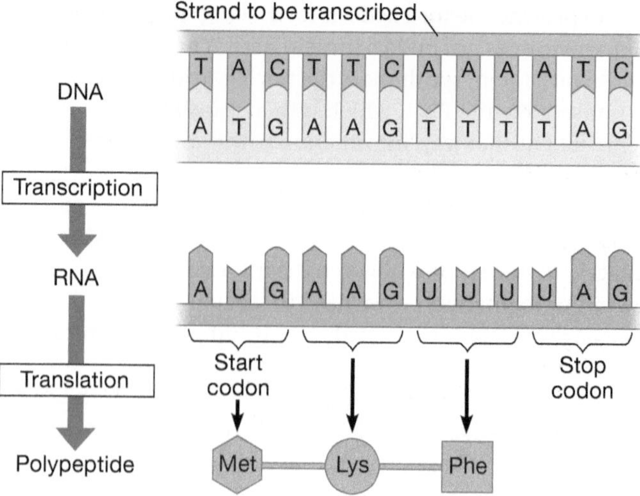

▲ **Figure 10.8B** **Deciphering the genetic information in DNA**

During the 1960s, molecular biologists used a series of elegant experiments to crack the **genetic code**, the amino acid translations of each of the nucleotide triplets. The first codon was deciphered by synthesizing an artificial RNA molecule using just uracil. No matter where this message started or stopped, it could contain only one type of triplet codon: UUU. When this "poly-U" was added to a test-tube mixture containing ribosomes and the other ingredients required for polypeptide synthesis, a polypeptide was translated that contained a single amino acid: phenylalanine (Phe). Thus, the RNA codon UUU must specify the amino acid phenylalanine. By variations on this method, the amino acids specified by all the codons were soon determined.

As shown in **Figure 10.8A**, 61 of the 64 triplets code for amino acids. The triplet AUG (green in the figure) has a dual function: It codes for the amino acid methionine (Met) and also can provide a signal for the start of a polypeptide chain. Three codons (UAA, UGA, and UAG) do not designate amino acids but serve as stop codons that mark the end of translation.

The codons in Figure 10.8A are the triplets found in RNA. They have a straightforward, complementary relationship to the codons in DNA, with UUU in the RNA matching AAA in the DNA, for example. The codons occur in a linear order along the DNA and RNA, with no gaps. Notice that there is redundancy in the code but no ambiguity. For example, although codons UUU and UUC both specify phenylalanine (redundancy), neither of them ever represents any other amino acid (no ambiguity).

As an exercise in translating the genetic code, consider the 12-nucleotide segment of DNA in **Figure 10.8B**. Let's read this as a series of triplets. Using the base-pairing rules (with U in RNA instead of T), we see that the RNA codon corresponding to the first transcribed DNA triplet, TAC, is AUG. As you can see in Figure 10.8A, AUG specifies, "Place Met as the first amino acid in the polypeptide." The second DNA triplet, TTC, dictates RNA codon AAG, which designates lysine (Lys) as the second amino acid. We continue until we reach a stop codon (UAG in this example).

The genetic code is nearly universal, shared by organisms from the simplest bacteria to the most complex plants and animals. Such universality is key to modern DNA technologies because it allows scientists to mix and match genes from various species (**Figure 10.8C**; see also Chapter 12). A language shared by all living things must have evolved early enough in the history of life to be present in the common ancestors of all modern organisms. A shared genetic vocabulary is a reminder of the evolutionary kinship that connects all life on Earth.

▲ **Figure 10.8C** **A cat (left) engineered to express a gene that produces a red fluorescent protein. Attaching a glowing reporter gene to a target gene allows researchers to track the expression of that target gene by observing the glow.**

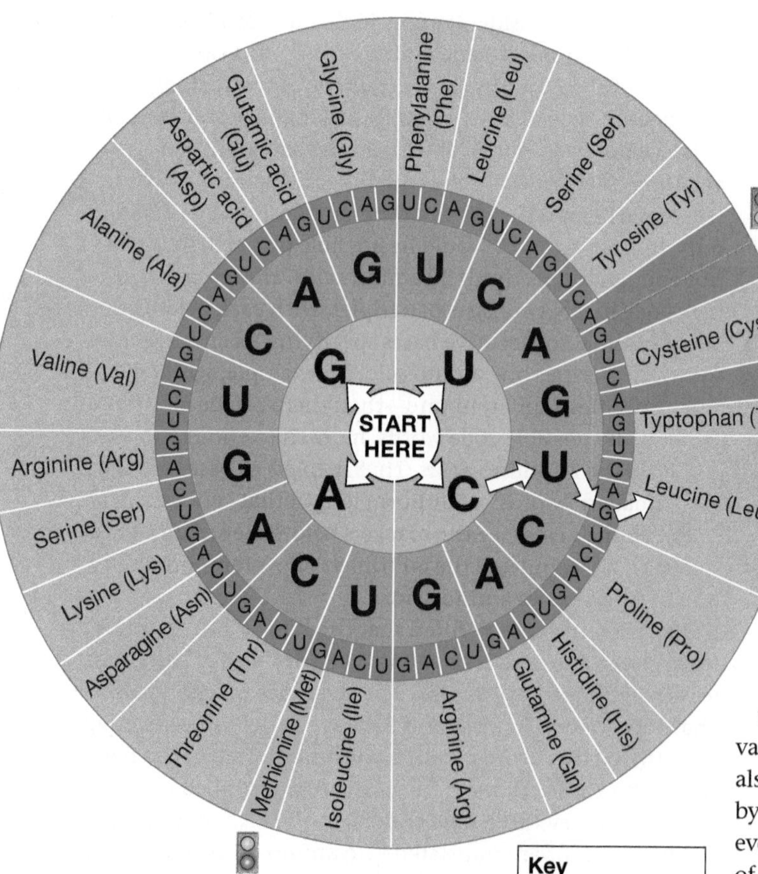

Key
- Start codon
- Stop codon

▲ **Figure 10.8A** **The genetic code used to translate RNA codons to amino acids. The white arrow shows that the RNA codon CUG corresponds to the amino acid leucine.**

TRY THIS Identify the DNA triplet that produces an RNA start codon, and identify the three DNA triplets that produce an RNA stop codon.

? **Translate the RNA sequence CCAUUUACG into the corresponding amino acid sequence.**

Pro-Phe-Thr

VISUALIZING THE CONCEPT

10.9 Transcription produces genetic messages in the form of RNA

Transcription is the transfer of genetic information from DNA to RNA. Here we focus on transcription in prokaryotic cells, which is a simpler process than in eukaryotic cells.

After separation of the two DNA strands, one strand serves as a template for a new RNA molecule; the other DNA strand is unused. The transcription enzyme **RNA polymerase** moves along the gene, forming a new RNA strand by following the base-pairing rules—but remember that in RNA, U replaces T. A specific nucleotide sequence called a **promoter** acts as a binding site for RNA polymerase and determines where transcription starts. RNA polymerase adds RNA nucleotides until it reaches a sequence of DNA bases called the **terminator**, which signals the end of the gene.

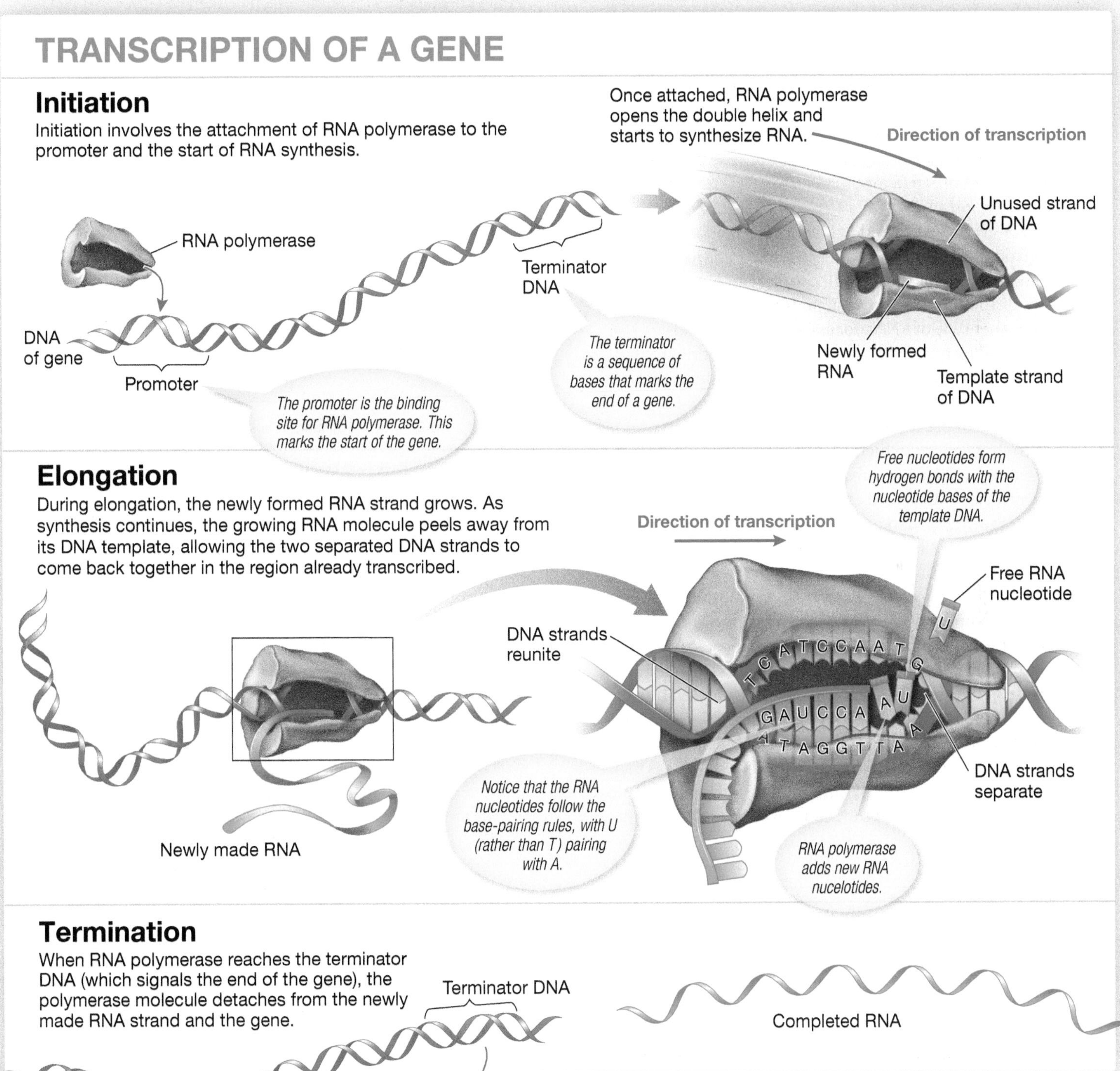

TRANSCRIPTION OF A GENE
Initiation
Initiation involves the attachment of RNA polymerase to the promoter and the start of RNA synthesis.
RNA polymerase
DNA of gene
Promoter
The promoter is the binding site for RNA polymerase. This marks the start of the gene.
Terminator DNA
The terminator is a sequence of bases that marks the end of a gene.
Once attached, RNA polymerase opens the double helix and starts to synthesize RNA.
Direction of transcription
Unused strand of DNA
Newly formed RNA
Template strand of DNA
Elongation
During elongation, the newly formed RNA strand grows. As synthesis continues, the growing RNA molecule peels away from its DNA template, allowing the two separated DNA strands to come back together in the region already transcribed.
Newly made RNA
Direction of transcription
Free nucleotides form hydrogen bonds with the nucleotide bases of the template DNA.
Free RNA nucleotide
DNA strands reunite
T C A T C C A A T G
G A U C C A A U
A T A G G T T A
U
DNA strands separate
Notice that the RNA nucleotides follow the base-pairing rules, with U (rather than T) pairing with A.
RNA polymerase adds new RNA nucelotides.
Termination
When RNA polymerase reaches the terminator DNA (which signals the end of the gene), the polymerase molecule detaches from the newly made RNA strand and the gene.
Terminator DNA
Completed RNA
RNA polymerase detaches

? How does RNA polymerase recognize the start and end of the gene?

■ Special DNA sequences mark the start (promoter) and end (terminator) of a gene.

10.10 Eukaryotic RNA is processed before leaving the nucleus as mRNA

The kind of RNA that encodes amino acid sequences is called **messenger RNA (mRNA)** because it conveys genetic messages from DNA to the translation machinery of the cell. Messenger RNA is transcribed from DNA, and the information in the mRNA is then translated into polypeptides. In prokaryotic cells, which lack nuclei, transcription and translation occur in the same place: the cytoplasm. In eukaryotic cells, however, mRNA molecules must exit the nucleus via the nuclear pores and enter the cytoplasm, where the machinery for polypeptide synthesis is located.

Before leaving the nucleus as mRNA, eukaryotic transcripts are modified, or processed, in several ways (**Figure 10.10**). One kind of RNA processing is the addition of extra nucleotides to the ends of the RNA transcript. These additions include a small cap (a modified form of a G nucleotide) at the 5′ end and a long tail (a chain of 50 to 250 A nucleotides) at the 3′ end. The cap and tail (yellow in the figure) facilitate the export of the mRNA from the nucleus, protect the mRNA from degradation, and help ribosomes bind to the mRNA. The cap and tail themselves are not translated into protein.

Another type of RNA processing is made necessary in eukaryotes by noncoding stretches of nucleotides that interrupt the nucleotides that actually code for amino acids. It is as if nonsense words were randomly interspersed in a story. Most genes of plants and animals include such internal noncoding regions, which are called **introns** ("intervening sequences"). The coding regions—the parts of a gene that are expressed—are called **exons**. As Figure 10.10 shows, both exons (shown in a darker color) and introns (in a lighter color) are transcribed from DNA into RNA. However, before the RNA leaves the nucleus, the introns are removed, and the exons are joined to produce an mRNA molecule with a continuous coding sequence. (The short noncoding regions just inside the cap and tail are considered parts of the first and last exons.) This cutting-and-pasting process is called **RNA splicing**. In most cases, RNA splicing is catalyzed by a complex of proteins and small RNA molecules. RNA splicing also provides a means to produce multiple polypeptides from a single gene (see Module 11.4). In fact, RNA splicing is believed to play a significant role in humans by allowing our approximately 21,000 genes to produce several times this number of polypeptides. This is accomplished by varying the exons that are included in the final mRNA.

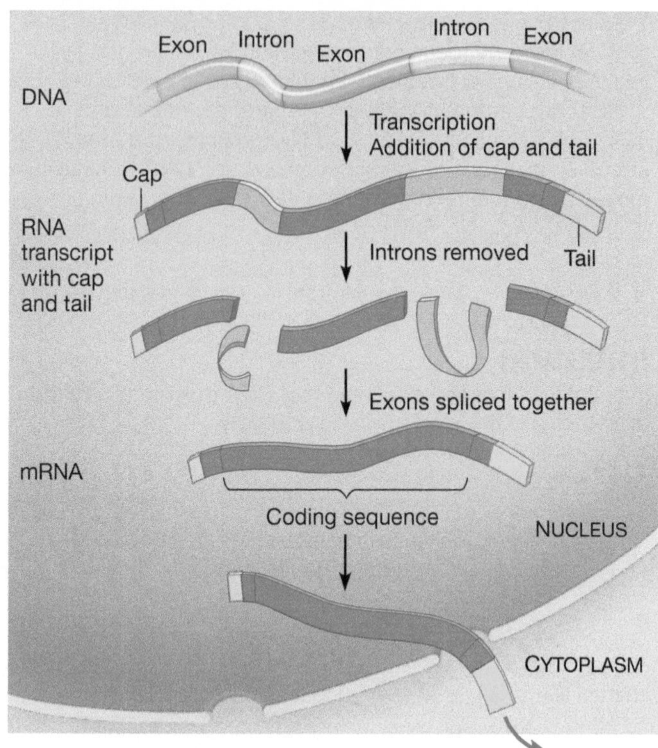

▲ **Figure 10.10** The production of eukaryotic mRNA

As we have discussed, translation is a conversion between different languages—from the nucleic acid language to the protein language—and it involves more elaborate machinery than transcription. The first important ingredient required for translation is the processed mRNA. Once it is present, the machinery used to translate mRNA requires enzymes and sources of chemical energy, such as ATP. In addition, translation requires two heavy-duty components: ribosomes and a kind of RNA called transfer RNA, the subject of the next module.

? **Explain why most eukaryotic genes are longer than the mRNA that leaves the nucleus.**

■ These genes have introns, noncoding sequences of nucleotides that are spliced out of the initial RNA transcript to produce mRNA.

10.11 Transfer RNA molecules serve as interpreters during translation

Translation of any language into another language requires an interpreter, someone or something that can recognize the words of one language and convert them to another. A cell that is producing proteins keeps its cytoplasm stocked with all 20 kinds of amino acids. But amino acids themselves cannot recognize the codons in the mRNA. Translation of a genetic message carried in mRNA into the amino acid language of proteins therefore requires an interpreter.

To convert the three-letter "words" of nucleic acids (codons) to the amino acid "words" of proteins, a cell uses a molecular interpreter, a special type of RNA called **transfer RNA (tRNA)**. The function of a tRNA is to transfer amino acids from the cytoplasmic pool to a growing polypeptide in a ribosome. To perform this task, tRNA molecules must carry out two functions: (1) picking up the appropriate amino acids and (2) recognizing the appropriate codons in the mRNA. The unique structure of tRNA molecules enables them to perform both tasks.

Figure 10.11A (on the facing page) shows three representations of a tRNA molecule. On the left is a flattened representation. It reveals that a tRNA molecule is made

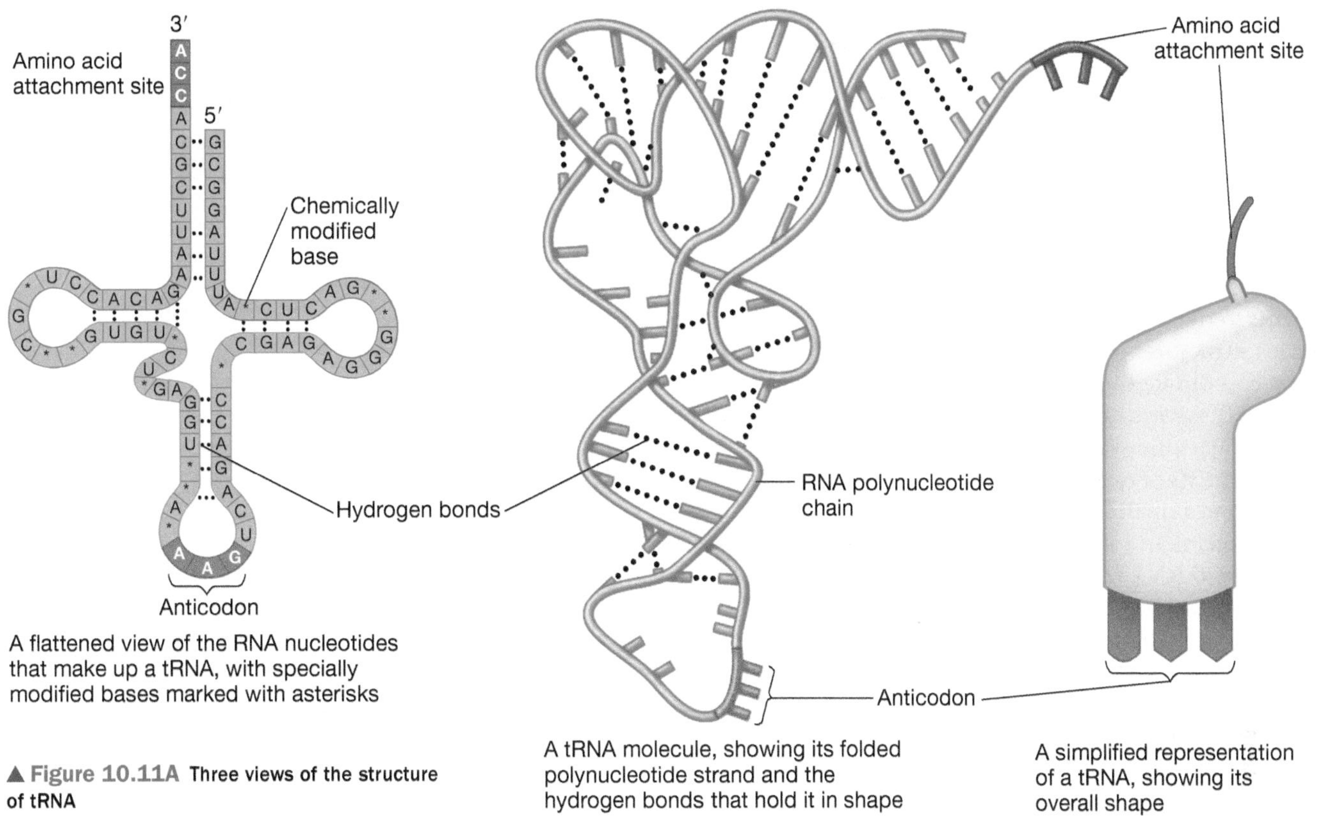

A flattened view of the RNA nucleotides that make up a tRNA, with specially modified bases marked with asterisks

A tRNA molecule, showing its folded polynucleotide strand and the hydrogen bonds that hold it in shape

A simplified representation of a tRNA, showing its overall shape

▲ **Figure 10.11A Three views of the structure of tRNA**

from a single strand of RNA—one polynucleotide chain—consisting of about 80 nucleotides. Overall, the molecule has a cloverleaf structure consisting of four arms. Each arm consists of nucleotides held together by hydrogen bonds (dotted lines). Most of the RNA sequence is common to all tRNAs, but the anticodon region (dark green at the bottom) varies from one type of tRNA to the next. As marked with asterisks, tRNAs contain special bases that have been chemically modified to be different than the standard versions. The modified bases are necessary for proper tRNA function, but no one yet knows why this is so.

The tRNA representation in the center of Figure 10.11A shows how the tRNA backbone twists and folds upon itself. A single-stranded loop at one end of the folded molecule (dark green at the bottom in this figure) contains a special triplet of bases called an **anticodon**. The anticodon is complementary to a codon triplet on mRNA. During translation, the anticodon on the tRNA recognizes a particular codon on the mRNA by using base-pairing rules. At the other end of the tRNA molecule is a site (at the top of the figure, colored purple) where one specific kind of amino acid attaches.

The structure on the right is a simplified schematic that emphasizes the most important parts of the tRNA structure. In the modules that follow, we represent tRNA as this simplified shape. This shape emphasizes the two parts of the molecule—the anticodon and the amino acid attachment site—that give tRNA its ability to match a particular nucleic acid "word" (a codon in mRNA) with its corresponding protein "word" (an amino acid). Although all tRNA molecules are similar, there is a slightly different variety of tRNA for each amino acid.

Each amino acid is joined to the correct tRNA by a specific enzyme (**Figure 10.11B**). There is a family of 20 versions of these enzymes, one enzyme for each amino acid. Each enzyme specifically binds one type of amino acid to all tRNA molecules that code for that amino acid, using a molecule of ATP as energy to drive the reaction. The resulting amino acid–tRNA complex can then contribute its amino acid to a growing polypeptide chain. This is accomplished within ribosomes, the cellular structures directly responsible for the synthesis of protein. We examine ribosomes in the next module.

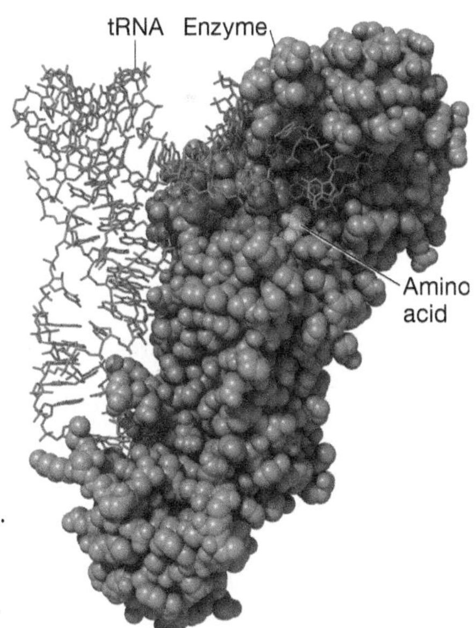

▲ **Figure 10.11B A computer graphic showing a molecule of tRNA (green sticks) with its amino acid (yellow) binding to an enzyme molecule (blue). Note the proportional sizes of these three molecules.**

? What is an anticodon, and what is its function?

■ It is the base triplet of a tRNA molecule that couples the tRNA to a complementary codon in the mRNA. This is a key step in translating mRNA to polypeptide.

10.12 Ribosomes build polypeptides

We have now looked at many of the components a cell needs to carry out translation: instructions in the form of mRNA molecules, tRNAs to interpret the instructions, a supply of amino acids and enzymes (for attaching amino acids to tRNA), and ATP for energy. The final components in translation are the **ribosomes**, structures in the cytoplasm that coordinate the functioning of mRNA and tRNA and catalyze the synthesis of polypeptides (**Figure 10.12**). A ribosome consists of two subunits—a large subunit and a small subunit—each made up of proteins and a kind of RNA called **ribosomal RNA (rRNA)**.

The ribosomes of bacteria and eukaryotes are very similar in function, but those of eukaryotes are slightly larger and different in structure. The differences are medically significant. Certain antibiotic drugs can inactivate bacterial ribosomes while leaving eukaryotic ribosomes unaffected. These drugs, such as tetracycline and streptomycin, are used to combat bacterial infections.

The simplified drawings on the right side of Figure 10.12 indicate how tRNA anticodons and mRNA codons fit together on ribosomes. A fully assembled ribosome has a binding site for mRNA on the small subunit and binding sites (referred to as the P site and the A site) for tRNA on the large subunit. The subunits of the ribosome act like a vise, holding the tRNA and mRNA molecules close together, allowing the amino acids carried by the tRNA molecules to be connected into a polypeptide chain. In the next two modules, we examine the steps of translation in detail.

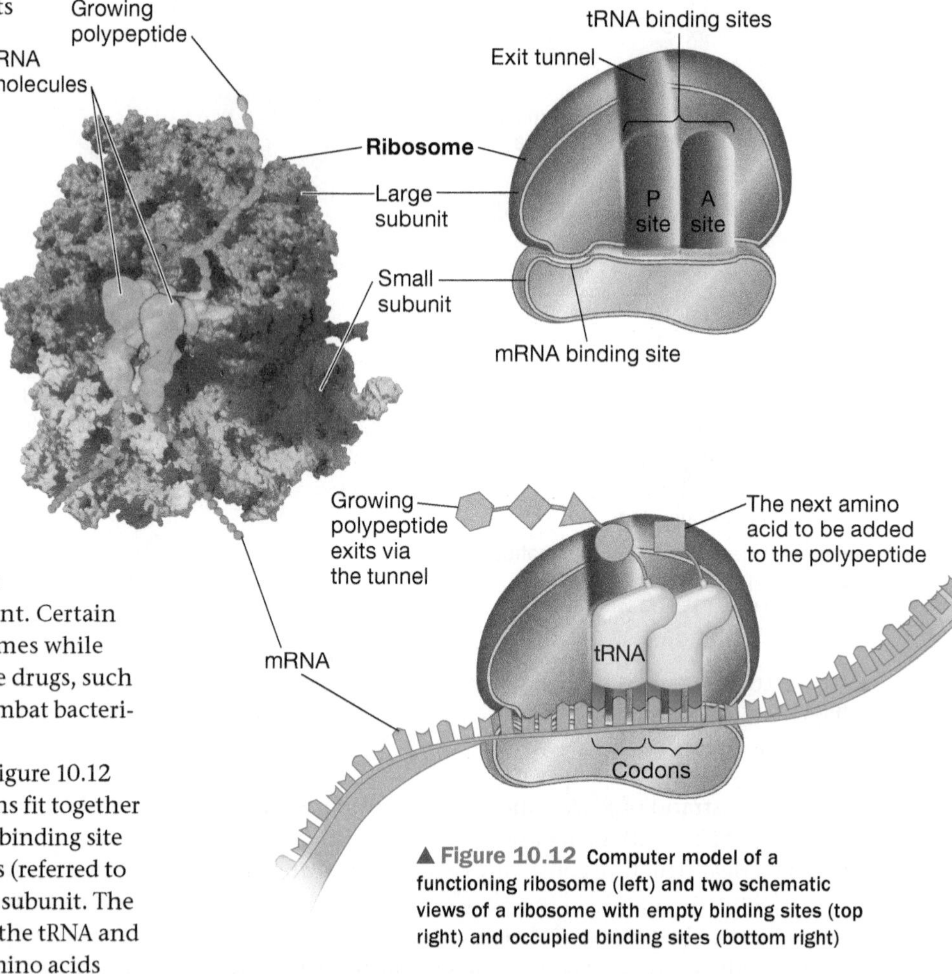

▲ **Figure 10.12** Computer model of a functioning ribosome (left) and two schematic views of a ribosome with empty binding sites (top right) and occupied binding sites (bottom right)

? **How does a ribosome facilitate protein synthesis?**

A ribosome holds mRNA and tRNAs together and connects amino acids from the tRNAs to the growing polypeptide chain.

10.13 An initiation codon marks the start of an mRNA message

Translation can be divided into the same three phases as transcription: initiation, elongation, and termination. We discuss initiation in this module; elongation and termination are discussed in the next module.

The process of initiation brings together the mRNA, a tRNA bearing the first amino acid, and the two subunits of a ribosome. An mRNA molecule is longer than the genetic message it carries (**Figure 10.13A**). The nucleotides at either end of the molecule (light pink in the figure) are not part of the message but help the mRNA to bind to the ribosome. The initiation process establishes exactly where translation will begin, ensuring that the mRNA codons are translated into the correct sequence of amino acids.

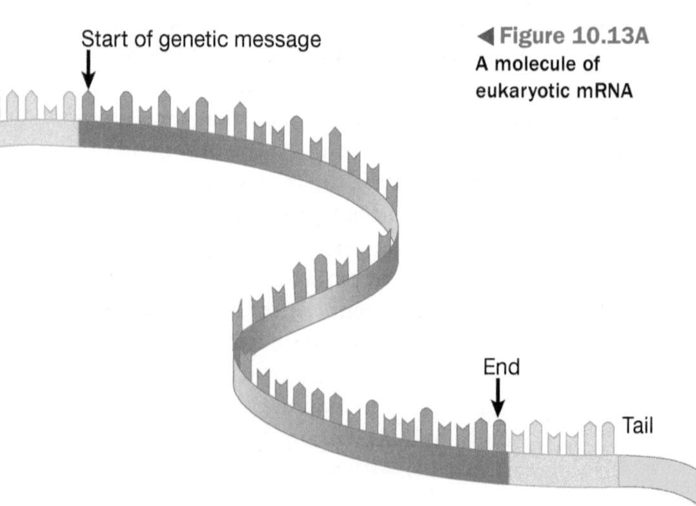

◀ **Figure 10.13A** A molecule of eukaryotic mRNA

Initiation occurs in two steps (**Figure 10.13B** on the facing page). ❶ An mRNA molecule binds to a small ribosomal subunit. A special initiator tRNA base-pairs with the specific

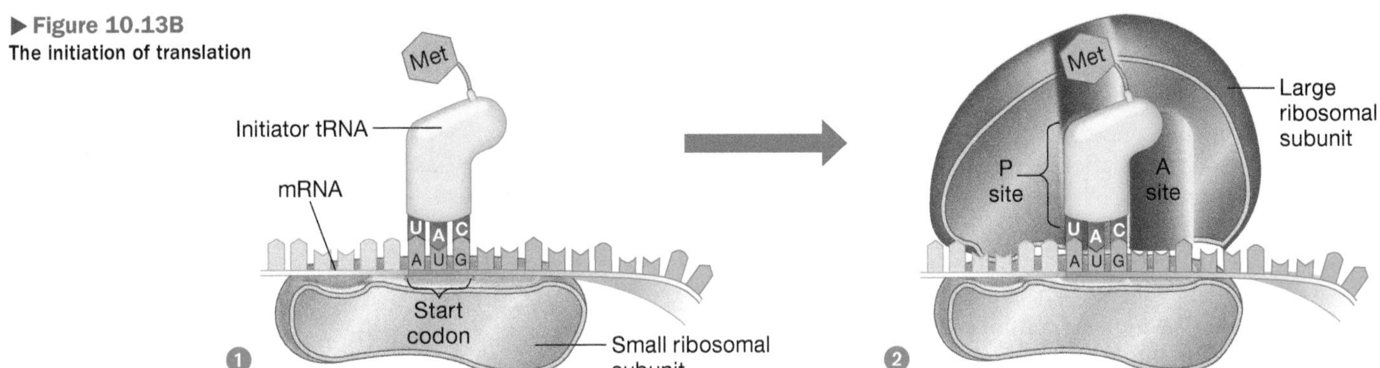

▶ **Figure 10.13B**
The initiation of translation

codon, called the **start codon**, where translation is to begin on the mRNA molecule. The initiator tRNA carries the amino acid methionine (Met); its anticodon, UAC, base-pairs with the start codon, AUG. ② Next, a large ribosomal subunit binds to the small subunit, creating a functional ribosome. The initiator tRNA fits into a tRNA binding site on the ribosome. This site, called the **P site**, will hold the growing polypeptide. The other tRNA binding site, called the **A site**, is shown vacant and ready for the next amino-acid-bearing tRNA.

? **What would happen if a genetic mutation in a gene changed a start codon to some other codon?**

■ The messenger RNA transcribed from the mutated gene would be nonfunctional because ribosomes could not initiate translation correctly.

10.14 Elongation adds amino acids to the polypeptide chain until a stop codon terminates translation

Once initiation is complete, amino acids are added one by one to the growing chain of amino acids. Each addition occurs in a three-step elongation process (**Figure 10.14**). ① The anticodon of an incoming tRNA molecule, carrying its amino acid, pairs with the mRNA codon in the A site of the ribosome. ② The polypeptide separates from the tRNA in the P site and attaches by a new peptide bond to the amino acid carried by the tRNA in the A site. The ribosome catalyzes the formation of the peptide bond, adding one more amino acid to the growing polypeptide chain, which snakes out of the ribosome via a tunnel through the molecule. ③ Then, the P site tRNA (which is now lacking an amino acid) leaves the ribosome, and the ribosome translocates (moves) the remaining tRNA (which holds the growing polypeptide) from the A site to the P site. The codon and anticodon remain hydrogen-bonded, and the mRNA and tRNA move as a unit. This movement brings into the A site the next mRNA codon to be translated, and the process can start again with step 1. These steps in the process of translation are powered by the breakdown of GTP, a molecule that is closely related to ATP.

Elongation continues until a **stop codon** reaches the ribosome's A site. As discussed earlier, stop codons—UAA, UAG, and UGA—do not code for amino acids but instead act as signals to stop translation. This is the termination stage of translation. The completed polypeptide is freed from the last tRNA, and the ribosome splits back into its separate subunits.

? **What would happen if a mutation caused a codon in the middle of an mRNA to change from UUA to UAA?**

■ Translation would stop prematurely, because a stop codon was introduced.

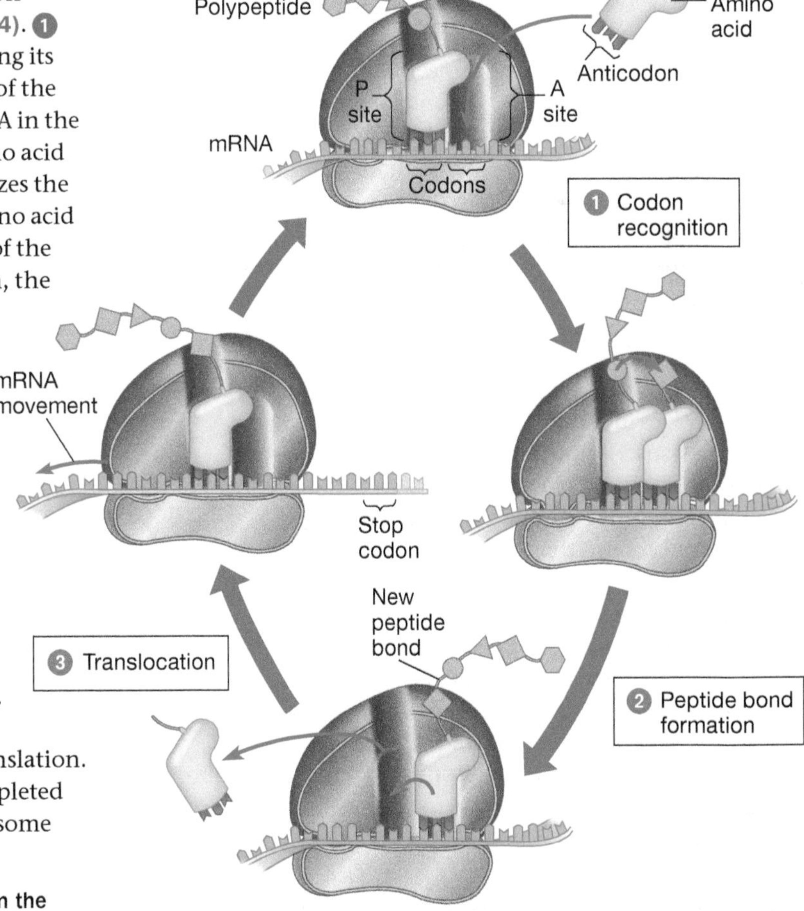

▲ **Figure 10.14** **Polypeptide elongation; the small green arrows indicate movement**

10.15 Review: The flow of genetic information in the cell is DNA → RNA → protein

The last six modules presented the processes of transcription and translation. Put it all together and you have an illustration of one of biology's most important themes: the flow of INFORMATION. In this instance, the instructions encoded in genes are used to create molecules of RNA, which are in turn used to create proteins. The proteins control an organism's structures and functions. This flow allows genetic information to influence an organism's traits.

Figure 10.15 summarizes the steps. ❶ In transcription (DNA → RNA), the mRNA is synthesized from a DNA template. In eukaryotic cells, transcription occurs in the nucleus, and the messenger RNA is processed before it travels to the cytoplasm (although the processing step is not shown here). In prokaryotes, transcription occurs in the cytoplasm.

❷–❺ Translation (RNA → protein) can be divided into four steps, all of which occur in the cytoplasm. When the polypeptide is complete at the end of step 5, the two ribosomal subunits come apart, and the tRNA and mRNA are released. Translation is rapid; a single ribosome can make an average-sized polypeptide in less than a minute. Typically, an mRNA molecule is translated simultaneously by a number of ribosomes. Once the start codon emerges from the first ribosome, a second ribosome can attach to it; thus, several ribosomes may trail along on the same mRNA molecule. As it is made, a polypeptide coils and folds, assuming a three-dimensional shape, its tertiary structure. Several polypeptides may come together, forming a protein with quaternary structure (see Module 3.14).

What is the overall significance of transcription and translation? These are the main processes whereby genes control the structures and activities of cells—or, more broadly, the way the genotype produces the phenotype. The chain of command originates with the information in a gene, a specific linear sequence of nucleotides in DNA. The gene serves as a template, dictating transcription of a complementary sequence of nucleotides in mRNA. In turn, mRNA dictates the linear sequence of amino acids in a polypeptide. Finally, the proteins that form from the polypeptides determine the appearance and the capabilities of the cell and organism.

Our discussion has focused on those regions of the genome that encode for proteins. It turns out, however, that a significant portion of the genome is transcribed into other types of RNA that do not code for proteins. (For example, other RNA molecules play critical roles in regulating gene expression—see Module 11.6.)

? Which of the types of nucleic acids you've learned about does not participate directly in translation?

DNA (answer printed upside down)

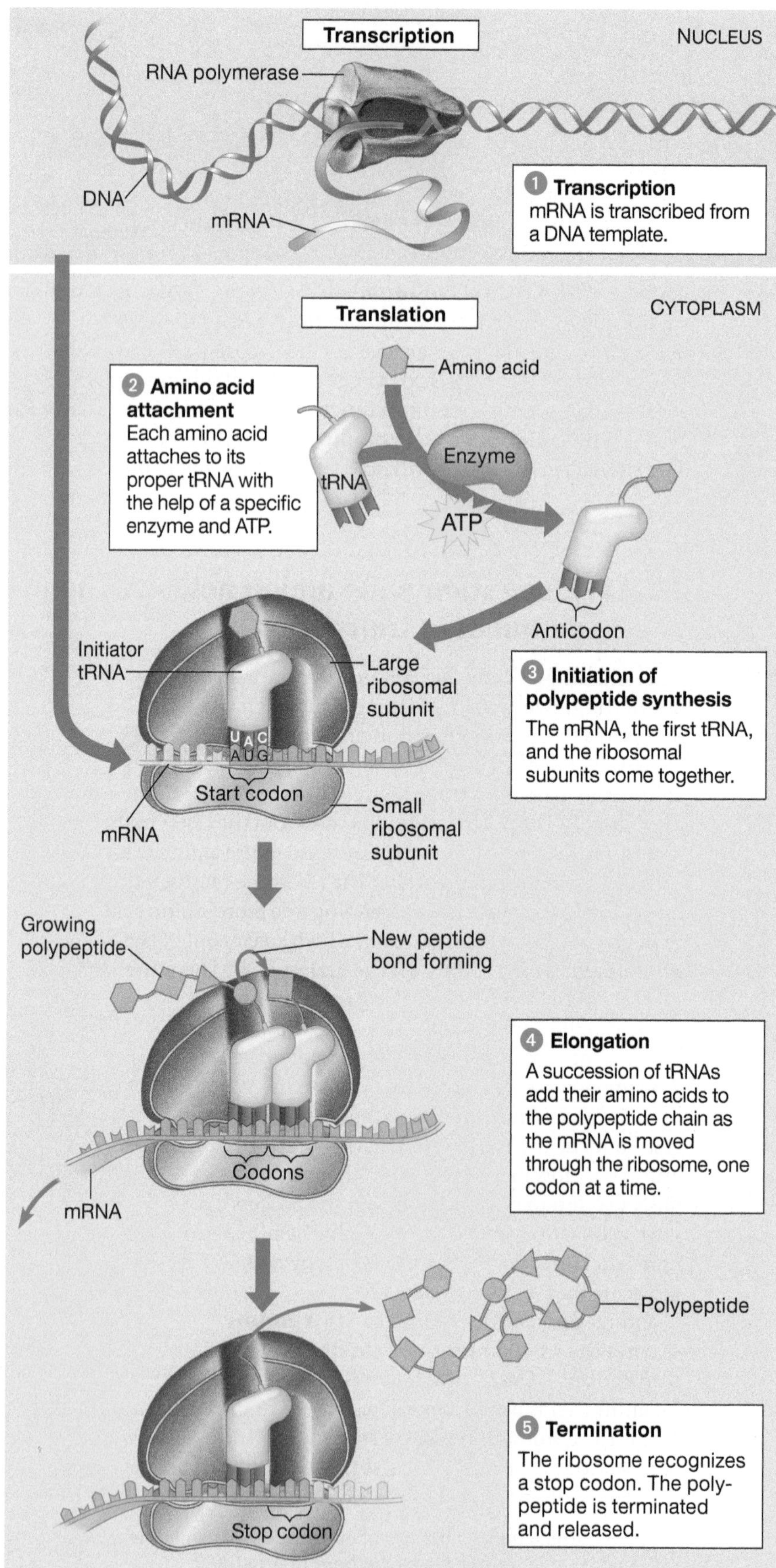

▲ Figure 10.15 A summary of transcription and translation

10.16 Mutations can affect genes

Many inherited traits can be understood in molecular terms. For instance, sickle-cell disease results from a change in a single amino acid in one of the polypeptides in the hemoglobin protein (see Module 9.13). This difference is caused by a single nucleotide difference in the DNA coding for that polypeptide (**Figure 10.16A**). In the double helix, one nucleotide pair is changed. Any change to the genetic information of a cell or virus is called a **mutation**. In this module, we'll explore several types of mutations.

A nucleotide substitution is the replacement of one nucleotide and its base-pairing partner with another pair of nucleotides. For example, in the second row in **Figure 10.16B**, A replaces G in the fourth codon of the mRNA. What effect can a substitution have? Some substitution mutations have no effect at all. For example, if a mutation causes an mRNA codon to change from GAA to GAG, no change in the protein product would result because GAA and GAG both code for the same amino acid (Glu; see Figure 10.8A). Such a change is called a **silent mutation**.

In contrast, a **missense mutation** changes one amino acid to another. For example, if an mRNA codon changes from GGC to AGC, as in the second row of Figure 10.16B, the resulting protein will have a serine (Ser) instead of a glycine (Gly) at this position. Some missense mutations have little or no effect on the resulting protein, but others, as in the case of sickle-cell disease, prevent the protein from performing its normal function. **Nonsense mutations** change an amino acid codon into a stop codon. For example, if an AGA (Arg) codon is changed to a UGA (stop) codon, the result will be a prematurely terminated protein, which probably will not function properly.

Because mRNA is read as a series of nucleotide codons (triplets) during translation, adding or subtracting nucleotides may alter the reading frame (triplet grouping) of the genetic message. Such a mutation, which is called a **frameshift mutation**, occurs whenever the number of nucleotides inserted or deleted is not a multiple of three. All the nucleotides after the insertion or deletion will be regrouped into different codons (Figure 10.16B, bottom two rows). Consider this example in the English language: The red cat ate the big rat. Deleting the second letter shifts the triplet frame and produces an entirely nonsensical message: Ter edc ata tet heb igr at. Frameshift mutations will most likely produce a nonfunctional polypeptide and often have disastrous effects.

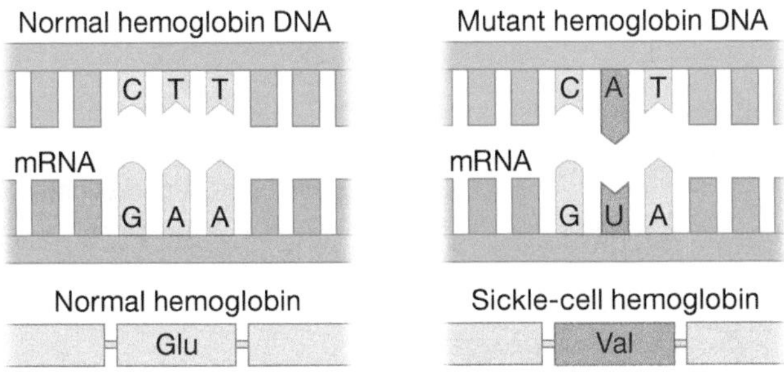

▲ **Figure 10.16A** The molecular basis of sickle-cell disease

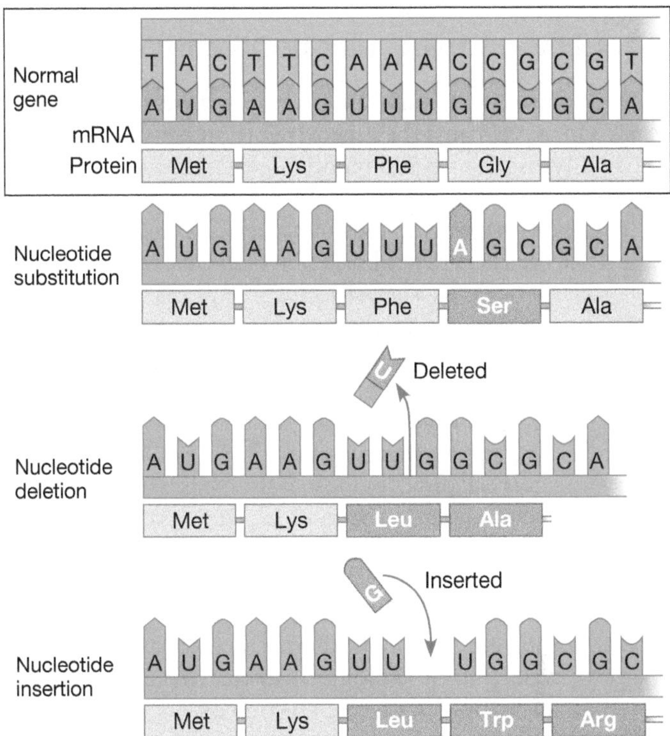

▲ **Figure 10.16B** Types of mutations and their effects. Note that mutations occur in the DNA; we show corresponding changes to the mRNA here.

Mutations can arise in a number of ways. Spontaneous mutations result from errors during DNA replication or recombination. Other mutations are caused by physical or chemical agents called **mutagens**. High-energy radiation, such as X-rays or ultraviolet light, is a physical mutagen. Some chemical mutagens are molecules that are similar to normal DNA bases but disrupt DNA replication. For example, the anti-AIDS drug AZT works because its structure is similar enough to thymine that viral polymerases incorporate it into newly synthesized DNA but different enough that the drug blocks further replication.

Occasionally, a mutation leads to a protein that enhances the success of the mutant organism and its descendants. Much more often, mutations are harmful to an organism. Mutations are, however, an important source of the rich diversity of genes in the living world, a diversity that makes evolution by natural selection possible.

? How could a single nucleotide substitution result in a shortened protein product?

■ A substitution that changed an amino acid codon into a stop codon would produce a prematurely terminated polypeptide.

The Genetics of Viruses and Bacteria

10.17 Viral DNA may become part of the host chromosome

As we discussed in Module 10.1, bacteria and viruses served as models in experiments that uncovered the molecular details of heredity. In the next four modules, we'll take a closer look at viruses.

In a sense, a **virus** is an infectious particle consisting of little more than "genes in a box": a bit of nucleic acid wrapped in a protein coat called a **capsid** and, in some cases, a membrane envelope. Unlike the genomes of all living cells, a viral genome may consist of DNA or RNA, and may be single- or double-stranded. Viral genomes usually consist of a single molecule of nucleic acid, which may be linear or circular.

Viruses are parasites that can reproduce only inside cells. In fact, the host cell provides most of the components used to produce new viruses. In Figure 10.1C, we described the replication cycle of phage T2. This sort of cycle is called a **lytic cycle** because it results in the lysis (breaking open) of the host cell and the release of the newly produced viruses. Some phages can also replicate by an alternative route called the lysogenic cycle. During a **lysogenic cycle**, viral DNA replication occurs without destroying the host cell.

Figure 10.17 illustrates the two kinds of cycles for a phage called lambda that infects *E. coli*. Both cycles begin when the phage DNA ❶ enters the bacterium and ❷ forms a loop. The DNA then follows one of two pathways. In the lytic cycle (left), ❸ lambda's DNA immediately turns the cell into a virus-producing factory, and ❹ the cell soon lyses and releases its viral products, which may then infect another cell.

In the lysogenic cycle, ❺ viral DNA is inserted into the bacterial chromosome. Once inserted, the phage DNA is referred to as a **prophage**, and most of its genes are inactive. ❻ Every time the *E. coli* cell prepares to divide, it replicates the phage DNA along with its own chromosome and passes the copies on to daughter cells. A single infected bacterium can thereby quickly give rise to a large population of bacterial cells that all carry the prophage. The lysogenic cycle enables viruses to spread without killing the host cells on which they depend. The prophages may remain in the bacterial cells indefinitely. Occasionally, however, an environmental signal—typically, one that indicates an unfavorable turn in the environment, such as an increase in radiation, drought, or certain toxic chemicals—triggers a switchover from the lysogenic cycle to the lytic cycle. This causes the viral DNA to be excised from the bacterial chromosome, eventually leading to death of the host cell.

Sometimes, the few prophage genes active in a lysogenic bacterium can cause medical problems. For example, the bacteria that cause diphtheria, botulism, and scarlet fever would be harmless to people if it were not for the prophage genes they carry. Certain of these genes direct the bacteria to produce the toxins responsible for making people ill. In the next module, we will explore viruses that infect animals and plants.

? Describe one way a virus can perpetuate its genes without destroying its host cell. What is this type of replication cycle called?

Some viruses can insert their DNA into a chromosome of the host cell, which replicates the viral genes when it replicates its own DNA prior to cell division. This is called the lysogenic cycle.

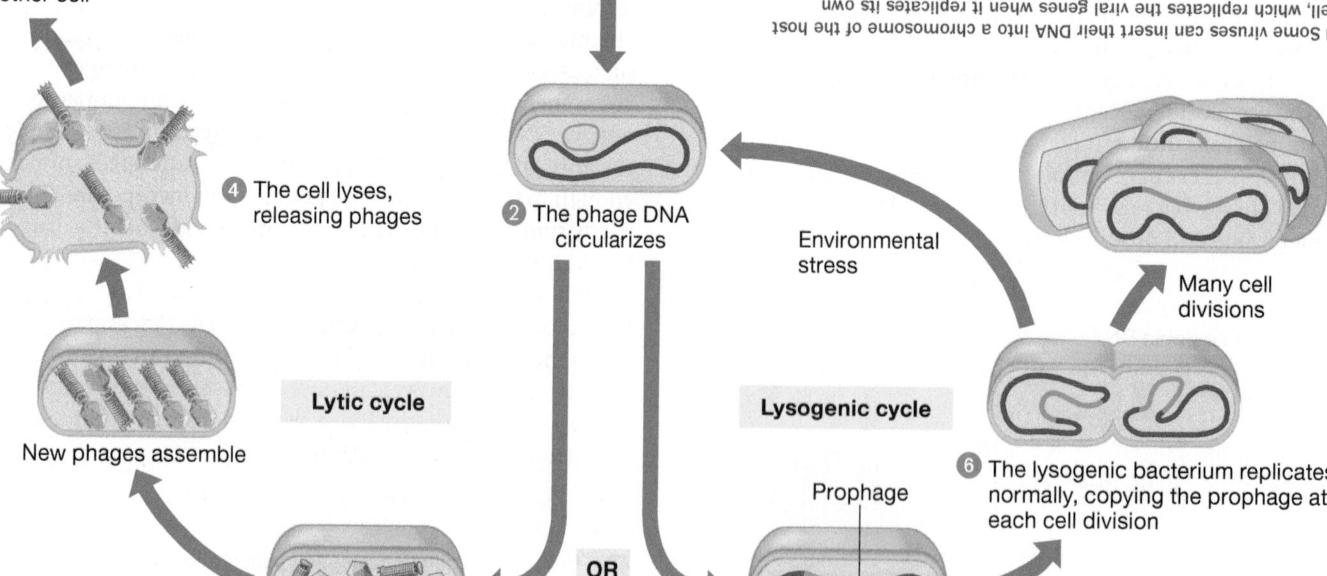

▲ **Figure 10.17** Two types of phage replication cycles

10.18 Many viruses cause disease in animals and plants

CONNECTION Viruses can cause disease in both animals and plants. A typical animal virus has a membranous outer envelope and projecting spikes of glycoprotein (protein molecules with attached sugars). The envelope helps the virus enter and leave the host cell. Many animal viruses have RNA rather than DNA as their genetic material. Examples of RNA viruses include those that cause the common cold, measles, mumps, polio, and AIDS. Examples of diseases caused by DNA viruses include hepatitis, chicken pox, and herpes infections.

Figure 10.18 shows the replication cycle of a typical enveloped RNA virus: the mumps virus. Once a common childhood disease characterized by fever and painful swelling of the salivary glands, mumps has become quite rare in industrialized nations thanks to widespread vaccination. When the mumps virus contacts a susceptible cell, the glycoprotein spikes attach to receptor proteins on the cell's plasma membrane. The viral envelope fuses with the cell's membrane, allowing the protein-coated RNA to ① enter the cytoplasm. ② Enzymes (not shown) then digest the protein coat. ③ An enzyme that entered the cell as part of the virus uses the virus's RNA genome as a template for making complementary strands of RNA (shown in pink). The new strands have two functions: ④ They serve as mRNA for the synthesis of new viral proteins and they serve as templates for synthesizing new viral genome RNA. ⑤ The new coat proteins assemble around the new viral RNA. ⑥ Finally, the viruses leave the cell by cloaking themselves in the host cell's plasma membrane. Thus, the virus obtains its envelope from the host cell, leaving the cell without necessarily lysing it.

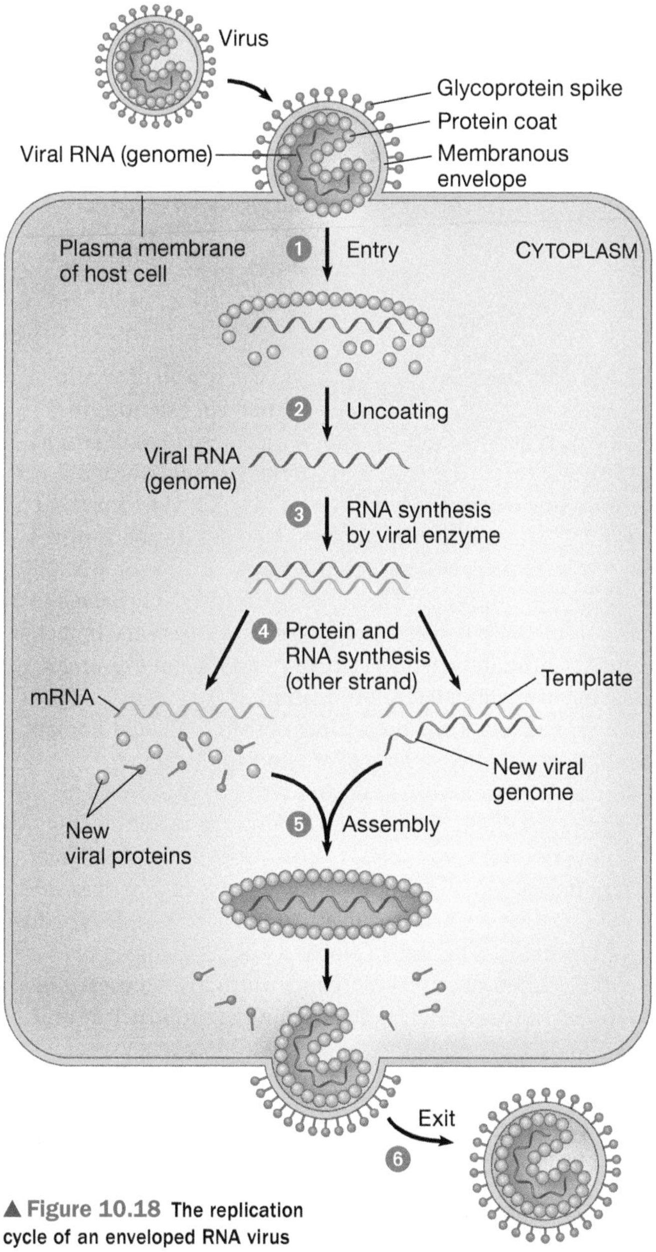

Not all animal viruses replicate in the cytoplasm. For example, herpesviruses—which cause chicken pox, shingles, cold sores, and genital herpes—are enveloped DNA viruses that replicate in the host cell's nucleus; they acquire their envelopes from the cell's nuclear membranes. While inside the nuclei of certain nerve cells, herpesvirus DNA may remain permanently dormant, without destroying these cells. From time to time, physical stress, such as a cold or sunburn, or emotional stress may stimulate the herpesvirus DNA to begin production of the virus, which then infects cells at the body's surface and causes symptoms.

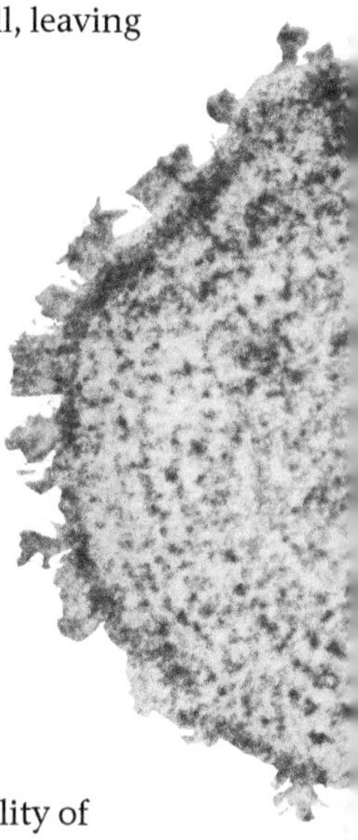

The amount of damage a virus causes our body depends partly on how quickly our immune system responds to fight the infection and partly on the ability of the infected tissue to repair itself. We usually recover completely from colds because our respiratory tract tissue can efficiently replace damaged cells by mitosis. In contrast, the poliovirus attacks nerve cells, which are not usually replaceable. The damage to the destroyed nerve cells is permanent. In such cases, we try to prevent the disease with vaccines (see Module 24.3).

Plants, like animals, are susceptible to viral infections. Viruses that infect plants can stunt plant growth and diminish crop yields. Most known plant viruses are RNA viruses. To infect a plant, a virus must first get past the plant's outer protective layer of cells (the epidermis). Once a virus enters a plant cell and begins replicating, it can spread throughout the entire plant through plasmodesmata, the cytoplasmic connections that penetrate the walls between adjacent plant cells (see Figure 4.21). Plant viruses may spread to other plants by insects, herbivores, humans, or farming tools. As with animal viruses, there are no cures for most viral diseases of plants. Agricultural scientists focus instead on preventing infections and on breeding resistant varieties of crop plants.

▲ **Figure 10.18 The replication cycle of an enveloped RNA virus**

? Explain how some viruses replicate without having DNA.

■ The genetic material of these viruses is RNA, which is replicated inside the host cell by special enzymes encoded by the virus. The viral genome (or its complement) serves as mRNA for the synthesis of viral proteins.

10.19 Emerging viruses threaten human health

EVOLUTION CONNECTION

Emerging viruses are ones that seem to burst on to the scene, becoming apparent to the medical community quite suddenly (**Figure 10.19**). One familiar example is **HIV** (human immunodeficiency virus, discussed in Module 10.20), the virus that causes **AIDS** (acquired immunodeficiency syndrome). HIV appeared in New York and California in the early 1980s, seemingly out of nowhere. Another example is the deadly Ebola virus, recognized initially in 1976 in central Africa; it is one of several emerging viruses that cause hemorrhagic fever, an often fatal syndrome characterized by fever, vomiting, massive bleeding, and circulatory system collapse. There have been several outbreaks of Ebola since it was first discovered; the largest started in 2014, eventually killing over 10,000 people on three continents.

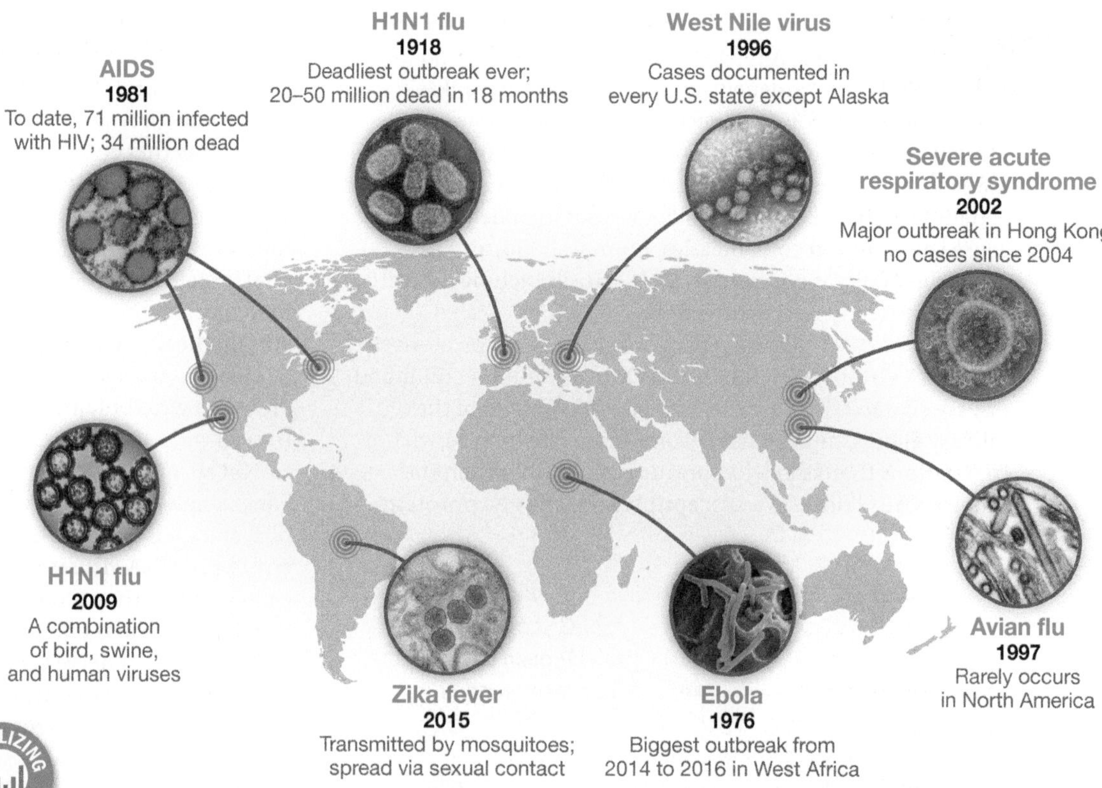

AIDS
1981
To date, 71 million infected with HIV; 34 million dead

H1N1 flu
1918
Deadliest outbreak ever; 20–50 million dead in 18 months

West Nile virus
1996
Cases documented in every U.S. state except Alaska

Severe acute respiratory syndrome
2002
Major outbreak in Hong Kong; no cases since 2004

H1N1 flu
2009
A combination of bird, swine, and human viruses

Zika fever
2015
Transmitted by mosquitoes; spread via sexual contact

Ebola
1976
Biggest outbreak from 2014 to 2016 in West Africa

Avian flu
1997
Rarely occurs in North America

VISUALIZING THE DATA

▲ **Figure 10.19** **A map of major emerging virus outbreaks of the past 100 years**

A number of other dangerous newly recognized viruses cause encephalitis, inflammation of the brain. One example is the West Nile virus, which appeared in North America in 1999 and has since spread to all 48 contiguous U.S. states. West Nile virus is spread primarily by mosquitoes, which carry the virus in blood sucked from one victim to the blood of another victim. West Nile virus cases surged in 2012, especially in Texas. Another recently recognized emerging pathogen is the Zika virus, which is spread by mosquitoes and causes Zika fever. This virus was recognized in the 1950s in equatorial Africa and Asia. Starting in 2013, the virus spread eastward across the Pacific Ocean. By 2015, Zika virus outbreak had reached pandemic levels in South America. As of 2016, there is no vaccine.

Where do deadly viruses come from?

How do such viruses emerge suddenly? Three processes contribute to the emergence of viral diseases: mutation, contact among species, and spread from isolated populations.

The mutation of existing viruses is a major source of new viral diseases. RNA viruses tend to have unusually high rates of mutation because errors in replicating their RNA genomes are not subject to the kind of proofreading and repair mechanisms that help reduce errors in DNA replication. Some mutations change existing viruses into new strains (genetic varieties) that can cause disease in individuals who have developed immunity to ancestral strains. That is why we need yearly flu vaccines: Mutations create new influenza virus strains to which previously vaccinated people have no immunity.

New viral diseases often arise from the spread of existing viruses from one host species to another. For example, in 2009, an epidemic of flu-like illness appeared in Mexico and the United States. The infectious agent was quickly identified as an influenza virus, named H1N1, related to ones that cause the seasonal flu. The illness spread rapidly, becoming a pandemic (global epidemic) that infected more than 600,000 people in 207 countries. The H1N1 virus was likely passed to humans after circulating among pigs for many years. In fact, scientists estimate that about three-quarters of new human diseases have originated in other animals.

The spread of a viral disease from a small, isolated human population can also lead to widespread epidemics. For instance, AIDS went unnamed and virtually unnoticed for decades before it began to spread around the world. In this case, technological and social factors—including affordable international travel, blood transfusions, sexual practices, and the abuse of intravenous drugs—allowed a previously rare disease in humans to become a global scourge. If we ever manage to control HIV and other emerging viruses, that success will likely develop out of our understanding of the structure and function of nucleic acids.

? **Why doesn't a flu shot one year give us immunity to flu in subsequent years?**

Influenza viruses evolve rapidly by frequent mutation; thus, the strains that infect us later will most likely be different from the ones to which we've been vaccinated.

10.20 The AIDS virus makes DNA on an RNA template

HIV, the virus that causes AIDS, is an RNA virus with some special properties. In outward appearance, HIV resembles the flu or mumps virus (**Figure 10.20A**). Its membranous envelope and glycoprotein spikes enable HIV to enter and leave a host cell much the way the mumps virus does (see Figure 10.18). Notice, however, that HIV contains two identical copies of its RNA instead of one. HIV also has a different mode of replication. It is a **retrovirus**, an RNA virus that reproduces by means of a DNA molecule. Retroviruses are so named because they reverse the usual DNA → RNA flow of genetic information. These viruses carry molecules of an enzyme called **reverse transcriptase**, which catalyzes reverse transcription: the synthesis of DNA on an RNA template.

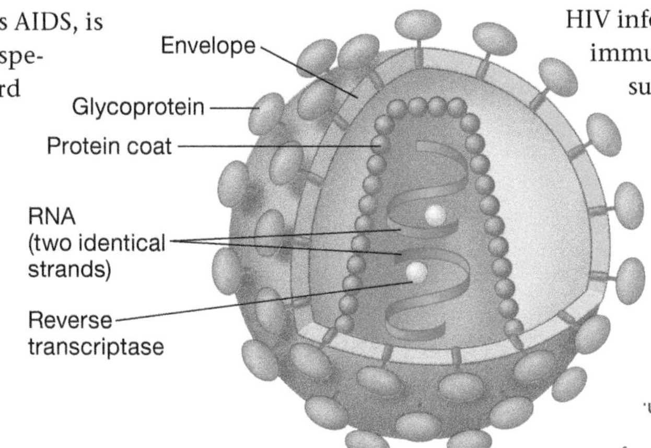

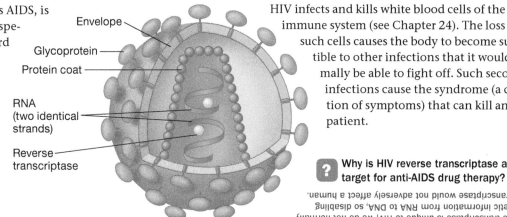

▲ **Figure 10.20A** A model of HIV structure

Figure 10.20B illustrates what happens after HIV RNA is uncoated in the cytoplasm of a host cell. ① Reverse transcriptase (●) uses the RNA as a template to make a DNA strand and then ② adds a second, complementary DNA strand. ③ The resulting double-stranded viral DNA enters the cell's nucleus and inserts itself into the chromosomal DNA. The host's RNA polymerase ④ transcribes the incorporated DNA into RNA, which can then be ⑤ translated into viral proteins. ⑥ New viruses assembled from these components leave the cell and can infect other cells.

HIV infects and kills white blood cells of the immune system (see Chapter 24). The loss of such cells causes the body to become susceptible to other infections that it would normally be able to fight off. Such secondary infections cause the syndrome (a collection of symptoms) that can kill an AIDS patient.

? **Why is HIV reverse transcriptase a good target for anti-AIDS drug therapy?**

■ Reverse transcriptase is unique to HIV; we do not normally copy genetic information from RNA to DNA, so disabling reverse transcriptase would not adversely affect a human.

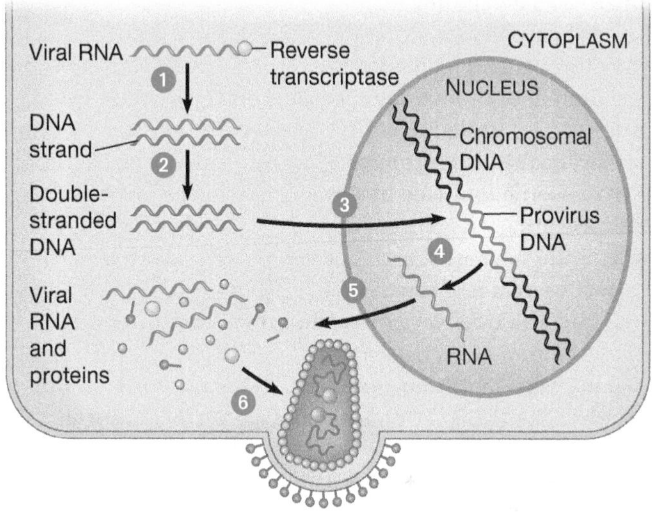

▲ **Figure 10.20B** The behavior of HIV nucleic acid in a host cell

10.21 Prions are infectious proteins

Prions are infectious proteins that cause a number of brain diseases in animals. While a virus uses DNA or RNA, a **prion** consists solely of a misfolded form of a normal brain protein (**Figure 10.21**). When the prion gets into a cell containing the normal form of the protein, the prion somehow converts normal protein molecules to misfolded versions. The misfolded proteins then clump together, disrupting brain functions.

Diseases caused by prions include scrapie in sheep; mad cow disease, which has plagued the European beef industry in recent years; and Creutzfeldt-Jakob disease in humans, which has caused the death of over 175 people in Great Britain. An early 1900s epidemic of kuru, another human disease caused by prions, in New Guinea, was halted after anthropologists identified the cause—ritualistic cannibalism of the brain—and convinced locals to stop that practice.

Prions act very slowly, with an incubation period of at least 10 years before symptoms develop. This can prevent the sources of infection from being identified until long after the first cases appear, allowing many more infections to occur. Additionally, prions are not destroyed in food by heating to normal cooking temperatures. To date, there is no known cure for prion diseases, and the only hope for developing effective treatments lies in understanding the process of infection.

▲ **Figure 10.21** A computer model of a prion

? **What makes prions different from all other known infectious agents?**

■ Prions are proteins and have no nucleic acid.

10.22 Bacteria can transfer DNA in three ways

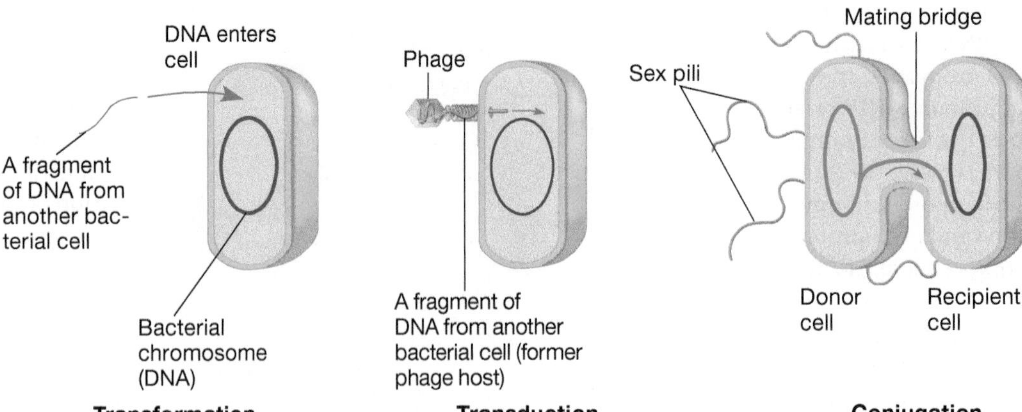

▲ **Figure 10.22A** Three ways that bacteria can transfer genes

By studying viral replication, researchers also learn about the mechanisms that regulate DNA replication and gene expression in living cells. Bacteria are equally valuable as microbial models in genetics research. As prokaryotic cells, bacteria allow researchers to investigate molecular genetics in the simplest living organisms.

Most of a bacterium's DNA is found in a single chromosome, a closed loop of DNA with associated proteins. In the diagrams here, we show the chromosome much smaller than it actually is relative to the cell. A bacterial chromosome is hundreds of times longer than its cell; it fits inside the cell because it is tightly folded.

Bacterial cells reproduce by replication of the bacterial chromosome followed by binary fission (see Module 8.2). Because binary fission is an asexual process involving only a single parent, the bacteria in a colony are genetically identical to the parental cell. But this does not mean that bacteria lack ways to produce new combinations of genes. In fact, in the bacterial world, there are three mechanisms by which genes can move from one cell to another: transformation, transduction, and conjugation (**Figure 10.22A**). The left side of the figure shows **transformation**, the uptake of foreign DNA from the surrounding environment. In Griffith's experiments (see Module 10.1), a harmless strain of bacteria took up pieces of DNA left over from the dead cells of a disease-causing strain. The DNA from the pathogenic bacteria carried a gene that made the cells resistant to an animal's defenses, and when the previously harmless bacteria acquired this gene and replaced its own with the pathogenic version, it caused pneumonia in infected animals.

Bacteriophages, the viruses that infect bacteria, provide the second means of bringing together genes of different bacteria (center of Figure 10.22A). The transfer of bacterial genes by a phage is called **transduction**. During a lytic infection, when new viruses are being assembled in an infected bacterial cell, a fragment of DNA belonging to the host cell may be mistakenly packaged within the phage's coat along with the phage's own DNA. When the phage infects a new bacterial cell, the DNA stowaway from the former host cell is injected into the new host.

In a third means of swapping genes, some bacteria cells can "mate" (right side of Figure 10.22A). This physical union of two bacterial cells—of the same or different species—and the DNA transfer between them is called **conjugation**. The donor cell has hollow appendages called sex pili, one of which is attached to the recipient cell in the figure. After attachment, the pilus retracts, pulling the two cells together, much like a grappling hook. The donor then transfers DNA (light blue in the figure) to the recipient. The donor cell replicates its DNA as it transfers it, so the cell doesn't end up lacking any genes. The DNA replication is a special type that allows one copy to peel off and transfer into the recipient cell.

Once new DNA gets into a bacterial cell, by whatever mechanism, part of it may then integrate into the recipient's chromosome. As **Figure 10.22B** indicates, integration occurs by crossing over between the donor and recipient DNA molecules, a process similar to crossing over between eukaryotic chromosomes (see Module 8.17). Here we see that two crossovers result in a piece of the donated DNA replacing part of the recipient cell's original DNA. The leftover pieces of DNA are broken down and degraded, leaving the recipient bacterium with a recombinant chromosome.

As we'll see in the next module, the transfer of genetic material between bacteria has important medical consequences.

? **The three modes of gene transfer between bacteria are __________, which is transfer via a virus; __________, which is the uptake of DNA from the surrounding environment; and __________, which is bacterial "mating."**

■ transduction ... transformation ... conjugation

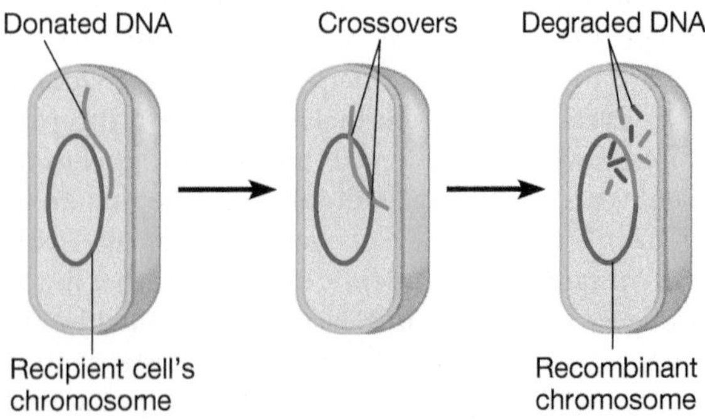

▲ **Figure 10.22B** The integration of donated DNA into the recipient cell's chromosome

10.23 Bacterial plasmids can serve as carriers for gene transfer

The ability of a donor *E. coli* cell to carry out conjugation is usually due to a specific piece of DNA called the **F factor** (F for *fertility*). The F factor carries about 25 genes for making sex pili and other requirements for conjugation; it also contains an origin of replication, where DNA replication starts.

Let's see how the F factor behaves during conjugation. (Figure 10.23A). First, the F factor (light blue) ① is integrated into the donor bacterium's chromosome. When this cell conjugates with a recipient cell, the donor chromosome ② starts replicating at the F factor's origin of replication, indicated in the figure by the blue dot on the DNA. The growing copy of the DNA peels off the chromosome and heads into the recipient cell. Thus, part of the F factor serves as the leading end of the transferred DNA, but right behind it are genes from the donor's original chromosome. The rest of the F factor stays in the donor cell. Once inside the recipient cell, the transferred donor genes can ③ recombine with the corresponding part of the recipient chromosome by crossing over. If crossing over occurs, the recipient cell may be genetically changed, but it usually remains a recipient because the two cells break apart before the rest of the F factor transfers.

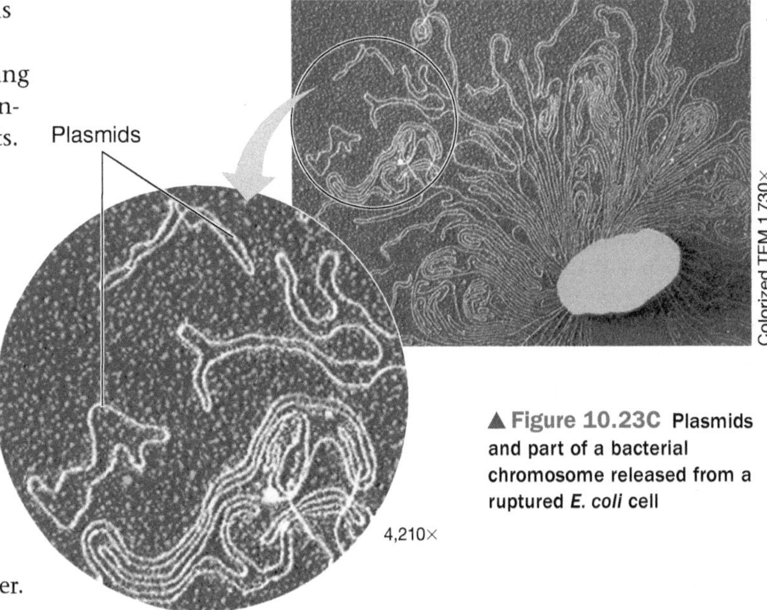

▲ **Figure 10.23C** **Plasmids and part of a bacterial chromosome released from a ruptured *E. coli* cell**

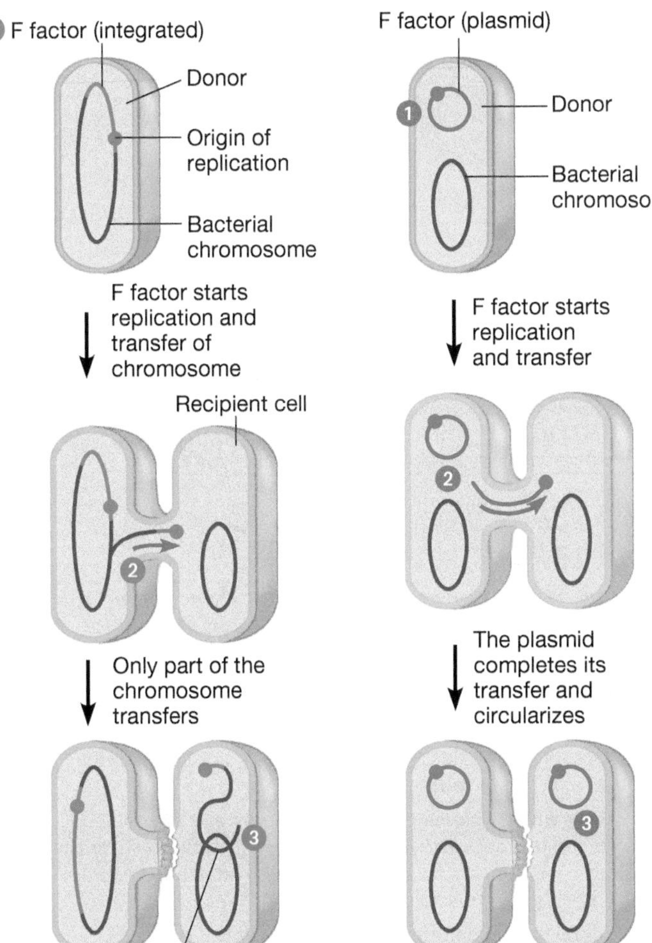

▲ **Figure 10.23A** **Transfer of chromosomal DNA by an integrated F factor**

▲ **Figure 10.23B** **Transfer of an F factor plasmid**

Alternatively, as Figure 10.23B shows, an F factor can exist as a ① **plasmid**, a small, circular DNA molecule separate from the bacterial chromosome. Every plasmid has an origin of replication, required for its replication within the cell. Some plasmids, including the F factor plasmid, can bring about conjugation and move to another cell. When the donor cell in Figure 10.23B mates with a recipient cell, ② the F factor replicates and at the same time transfers one whole copy of itself, in linear rather than circular form, to the recipient cell. The transferred plasmid ③ re-forms a circle in the recipient cell, and the cell becomes a donor.

E. coli and other bacteria have many different kinds of plasmids. You can see several from one cell in Figure 10.23C, along with part of the bacterial chromosome, which extends in loops from the ruptured cell. Some plasmids carry genes that can affect the survival of the cell. Plasmids of one class, called **R plasmids**, pose serious problems for human medicine. Transferable R plasmids carry genes for enzymes that destroy antibiotics, such as penicillin and tetracycline. Bacteria containing R plasmids are resistant (hence the designation R) to antibiotics that would otherwise kill them. The widespread use of antibiotics in medicine and agriculture has tended to kill off bacteria that lack R plasmids, whereas those with R plasmids have multiplied. As a result, an increasing number of bacteria that cause human diseases, such as food poisoning and gonorrhea, are becoming resistant to antibiotics (see Module 13.16).

We'll continue our study of molecular genetics and explore what is known about genes (see Chapter 11) and return to our discussion of plasmids (Chapter 12) in later chapters.

? **Plasmids are useful tools for genetic engineering. Can you guess why?**

■ Scientists can take advantage of the ability of plasmids to carry foreign genes, to replicate, and to be inherited by progeny cells.

CHAPTER 10 REVIEW

For practice quizzes, BioFlix animations, MP3 tutorials, video tutors, and more study tools designed for this textbook, go to MasteringBiology™

REVIEWING THE CONCEPTS

The Structure of the Genetic Material (10.1–10.3)

10.1 Experiments showed that DNA is the genetic material. By carefully choosing their model organism, Hershey and Chase were able to show that certain phages (bacterial viruses) reprogram host cells to produce more phages by injecting their DNA.

10.2 DNA and RNA are polymers of nucleotides.

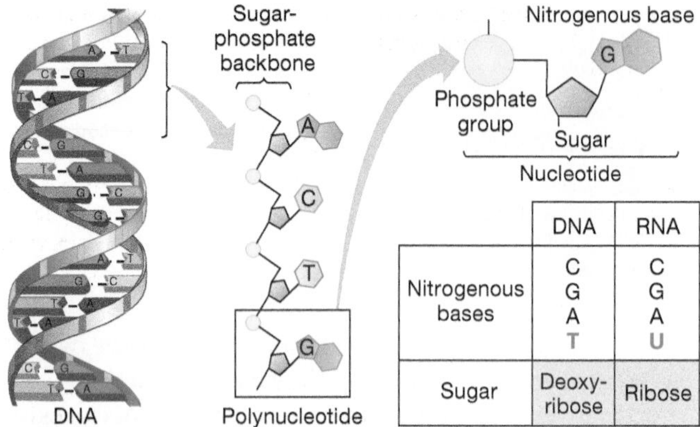

	DNA	RNA
Nitrogenous bases	C G A T	C G A U
Sugar	Deoxy-ribose	Ribose

10.3 DNA is a double-stranded helix. Watson and Crick worked out the three-dimensional structure of DNA: two polynucleotide strands wrapped around each other in a double helix. Hydrogen bonds between bases hold the strands together. Each base pairs with a complementary partner: A with T, G with C.

DNA Replication (10.4–10.5)

10.4 DNA replication depends on specific base pairing. DNA replication starts with the separation of DNA strands. The enzyme DNA polymerase then uses each strand as a template to assemble new nucleotides into a complementary strand.

10.5 DNA replication proceeds in two directions at many sites simultaneously. Using the enzyme DNA polymerase, the cell synthesizes one daughter strand as a continuous piece. The other strand is synthesized as a series of short pieces, which are then connected by the enzyme DNA ligase.

The Flow of Genetic Information from DNA to RNA to Protein (10.6–10.16)

10.6 Genes control phenotypic traits through the expression of proteins. The DNA of a gene—a linear sequence of many nucleotides—is transcribed into RNA, which is translated into a polypeptide.

10.7 Genetic information written in codons is translated into amino acid sequences. Codons are base triplets.

10.8 The genetic code dictates how codons are translated into amino acids. Nearly all organisms use an identical genetic code to convert the mRNA codons transcribed from a gene to the amino acid sequence of a polypeptide.

10.9 Transcription produces genetic messages in the form of RNA. In the nucleus, the DNA helix unzips, and RNA nucleotides line up and RNA polymerase joins them along one strand of the DNA, following the base-pairing rules.

10.10 Eukaryotic RNA is processed before leaving the nucleus as mRNA. Noncoding segments of RNA (introns) are spliced out, and a cap and tail are added to the ends of the mRNA.

10.11 Transfer RNA molecules serve as interpreters during translation. Translation takes place in the cytoplasm. A ribosome attaches to the mRNA and translates its message into a specific polypeptide, aided by transfer RNAs (tRNAs). Each tRNA is a folded molecule bearing a base triplet called an anticodon on one end and a specific amino acid attachment site at the other end.

10.12 Ribosomes build polypeptides. Made of rRNA and proteins, ribosomes have binding sites for tRNAs and mRNA.

10.13 An initiation codon marks the start of an mRNA message.

10.14 Elongation adds amino acids to the polypeptide chain until a stop codon terminates translation. As the mRNA moves one codon at a time relative to the ribosome, a tRNA with a complementary anticodon pairs with each codon, and its amino acid is added to the growing polypeptide chain.

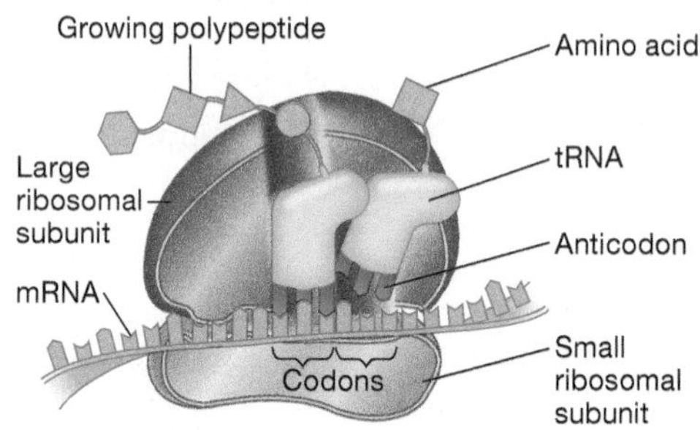

10.15 Review: The flow of genetic information in the cell is DNA → RNA → protein. The sequence of codons in DNA, via the sequence of codons in mRNA, spells out the primary structure of a polypeptide.

10.16 Mutations can affect genes. Mutations are changes in the genetic information of a cell or virus, caused by errors in DNA replication or recombination, or by mutagens. Substituting, inserting, or deleting nucleotides alters a gene, with varying effects.

The Genetics of Viruses and Bacteria (10.17–10.23)

10.17 Viral DNA may become part of the host chromosome. Viruses are infectious particles that contain genes packaged in protein. When phage DNA enters a lytic cycle inside a bacterium, it is replicated, transcribed, and translated; the new viral DNA and protein molecules then assemble into new phages, which burst from the host cell. In the lysogenic cycle, phage DNA inserts into the host chromosome and is passed on to generations of daughter cells. Later, it may initiate phage production.

10.18 Many viruses cause disease in animals and plants. Flu viruses and most plant viruses have RNA, rather than DNA, as their genetic material. Some animal viruses steal a bit of host cell membrane as a protective envelope.

10.19 Emerging viruses threaten human health.

10.20 The AIDS virus makes DNA on an RNA template. HIV is a retrovirus: Its enzyme, reverse transcriptase, uses its RNA genome as a template for making DNA, which then inserts into a host chromosome.

10.21 Prions are infectious proteins. Prions are infectious proteins that can cause brain diseases in animals.

10.22 Bacteria can transfer DNA in three ways. Bacteria can transfer genes from cell to cell by transformation, transduction, or conjugation.

10.23 Bacterial plasmids can serve as carriers for gene transfer. Plasmids are small, circular DNA molecules separate from the bacterial chromosome.

CONNECTING THE CONCEPTS

1. Check your understanding of the flow of genetic information through a cell by filling in the blanks.

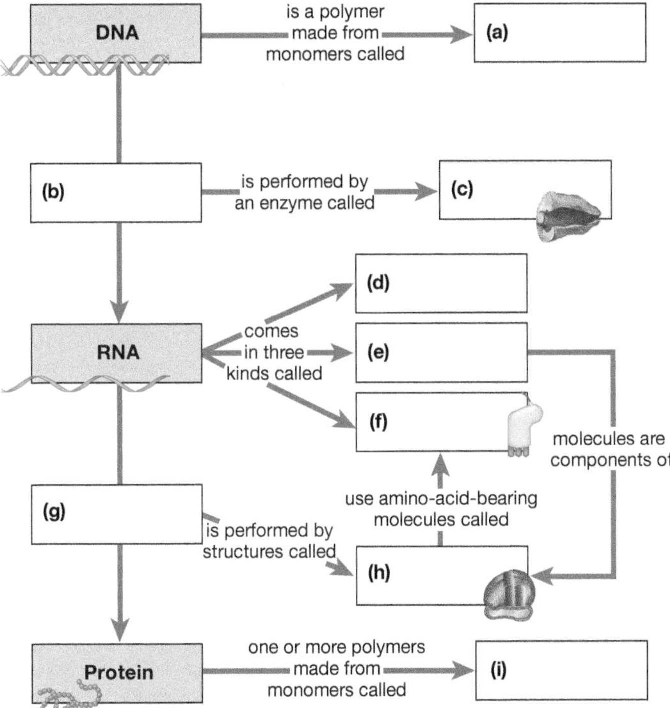

TESTING YOUR KNOWLEDGE

Level 1: Knowledge/Comprehension

2. Which of the following correctly ranks the structures in order of size, from largest to smallest?
   a. gene-chromosome-nucleotide-codon
   b. chromosome-gene-codon-nucleotide
   c. nucleotide-chromosome-gene-codon
   d. chromosome-nucleotide-gene-codon
3. Describe the process of DNA replication: the ingredients needed, the steps in the process, and the final product.
4. What is the name of the process that produces RNA from a DNA template? What is the name of the process that produces a polypeptide from an RNA template?

Level 2: Application/Analysis

5. Scientists have discovered how to put together a bacteriophage with the protein coat of phage T2 and the DNA of phage lambda. If this composite phage were allowed to infect a bacterium, the phages produced in the host cell would have ________. (*Explain your answer.*)
   a. the protein of T2 and the DNA of lambda
   b. the protein of lambda and the DNA of T2
   c. the protein and DNA of T2
   d. the protein and DNA of lambda
6. A geneticist found that a particular mutation had no effect on the polypeptide encoded by a gene. This mutation probably involved
   a. deletion of one nucleotide.
   b. alteration of the start codon.
   c. insertion of one nucleotide.
   d. substitution of one nucleotide.
7. Describe the process by which the information in a eukaryotic gene is transcribed and translated into a protein. Correctly use these words in your description: tRNA, amino acid, start codon, transcription, RNA splicing, exons, introns, mRNA, gene, codon, RNA polymerase, ribosome, translation, anticodon, peptide bond, stop codon.

Level 3: Synthesis/Evaluation

8. The nucleotide sequence of a DNA codon is GTA. A messenger RNA molecule with a complementary codon is transcribed from the DNA. In the process of protein synthesis, a transfer RNA pairs with the mRNA codon. What is the nucleotide sequence of the tRNA anticodon?
   a. CAT
   b. CUT
   c. GUA
   d. CAU
9. A cell containing a single chromosome is placed in a medium containing radioactive phosphate so that any new DNA strands formed by DNA replication will be radioactive. The cell replicates its DNA and divides. Then the daughter cells (still in the radioactive medium) replicate their DNA and divide, and a total of four cells are present. Sketch the DNA molecules in all four cells, showing a normal (nonradioactive) DNA strand as a solid line and a radioactive DNA strand as a dashed line.
10. The base sequence of the gene coding for a short polypeptide is CTACGCTAGGCGATTGACT. What would be the base sequence of the mRNA transcribed from this gene? Using the genetic code in Figure 10.8A, give the amino acid sequence of the polypeptide translated from this mRNA. (*Hint*: What is the start codon?)
11. Researchers working on the Human Genome Project have determined the nucleotide sequences of human genes and in many cases identified the proteins encoded by the genes. Knowledge of the nucleotide sequences of genes might be used to develop lifesaving medicines or treatments for genetic defects. In the United States, both government agencies and biotechnology companies have applied for patents on their discoveries of genes. In Britain, the courts have ruled that a naturally occurring gene cannot be patented. Do you think individuals and companies should be able to patent genes and gene products? Before answering, consider the following: What are the purposes of a patent? How might the discoverer of a gene benefit from a patent? How might the public benefit? What might be some positive and negative results of patenting genes?
12. SCIENTIFIC THINKING The success of an experiment often depends on choosing an appropriate organism to study. For example, Gregor Mendel was able to deduce the fundamental principles in genetics in part because of his choice of the pea plant. Reviewing module 10.1, how did Hershey and Chase take advantage of the unique structural properties of bacteriophage T2 to determine the genetic material?

Answers to all questions can be found in Appendix 4.

How Populations Evolve

CHAPTER 13

What does actor George Clooney have in common with George Washington, Ernest Hemingway, Christopher Columbus, and Mother Teresa? They all survived bouts with malaria, a disease caused by a microscopic parasite that is one of the worst killers in human history. In the 1960s, the World Health Organization (WHO) launched a campaign to eradicate malaria. Their strategy focused on killing the mosquitoes that carry the parasite from person to person. DDT, a widely used pesticide, was deployed in massive spraying operations. But in one location after another, early success was followed by rebounding mosquito populations in which resistance to DDT had evolved. Malaria continued to spread. Today, malaria causes more than a million deaths and 250 million cases of miserable illness each year.

How does evolution hinder attempts to eradicate disease?

Evolution has also hindered efforts to help malaria victims. At the same time that DDT was being celebrated as a miracle pesticide in the war against malaria, a drug called chloroquine was hailed as the miracle cure. But its effectiveness has diminished over time, as resistance to the drug has evolved in parasite populations. In some regions, chloroquine is powerless against the disease. The most effective antimalarial drug now is artemisinin, a compound extracted from a plant used in traditional Chinese medicine. But the effectiveness of this drug will eventually succumb to the power of evolution, too. Cases of malaria that don't respond to artemisinin have already appeared in Southeast Asia. The girl in the photo on the right is being tested to ensure that her treatment was effective.

An understanding of evolution informs all of biology, from exploring life's molecules to analyzing ecosystems. Applications of evolutionary biology are transforming fields as diverse as medicine, agriculture, and conservation biology. In this chapter, we begin our study of evolution with the enduring legacy of Charles Darwin's explanation for the unity and diversity of life. We also delve into the nitty-gritty of natural selection, the mechanism for evolution that Darwin proposed.

Darwin's Theory of Evolution

(13.1–13.7)

Darwin's theory of evolution explains the adaptations of organisms and the unity and diversity of life.

The Evolution of Populations

(13.8–13.11)

Genetic variation makes evolution possible within a population.

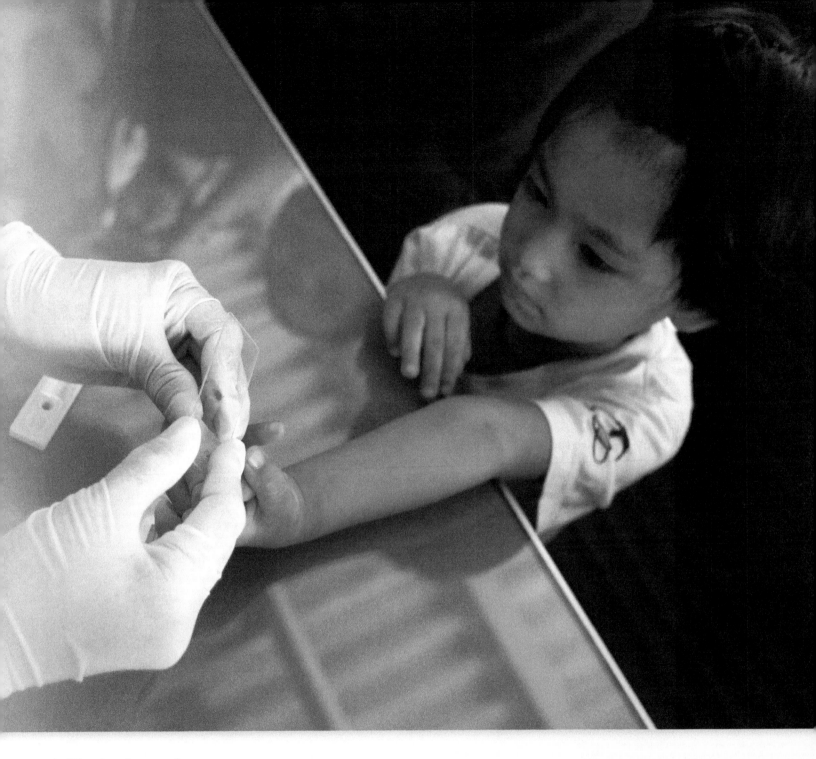

Mechanisms of Microevolution (13.12–13.18)

Natural selection, genetic drift, and gene flow can alter gene pools; natural selection leads to adaptive evolution.

Darwin's Theory of Evolution

13.1 A sea voyage helped Darwin frame his theory of evolution

If you have heard of the theory of evolution, you have probably heard of Charles Darwin. Although Darwin was born more than 200 years ago, his work had such an extraordinary impact that many biologists mark his birthday—February 12, the same as Abraham Lincoln's—with a celebration of his contributions to science. The publication of Darwin's best-known book, *On the Origin of Species by Means of Natural Selection*, commonly referred to as *The Origin of Species*, launched the era of evolutionary biology.

Darwin's Cultural and Scientific Context Darwin's early career gave no hint of his future fame. As a boy, he was fascinated with nature. When not reading books about nature, he was fishing, hunting, and collecting insects. His education was typical for a young man of his social class. Darwin's father, an eminent physician, could see no future for his son as a naturalist and sent him to medical school. But Darwin, finding medicine boring and surgery before the days of anesthesia horrifying, quit medical school. His father then enrolled him at Cambridge University with the intention that he should become a clergyman.

The cultural and scientific context of his time also instilled Darwin with a conventional view of Earth and its life. Most scientists accepted the views of the Greek philosopher Aristotle, who generally held that species are fixed, permanent forms that do not evolve. Judeo-Christian culture fortified this idea with a literal interpretation of the biblical book of Genesis, which tells the story of each form of life being individually created in its present-day form. In the 1600s, religious scholars used biblical accounts to estimate the age of Earth at 6,000 years. Thus, the idea that all living species came into being relatively recently and are unchanging in form dominated the intellectual climate of the Western world at the time.

Darwin's radical thinking stemmed from his postcollege life, when he returned to his childhood interests. At the age of 22, Darwin set sail on HMS *Beagle*, a survey ship preparing for a long expedition to chart poorly known stretches of the South American coast (Figure 13.1A).

Darwin's Sea Voyage During the five-year voyage of the *Beagle*, Darwin spent most of his time on shore collecting thousands of specimens of fossils and living plants and animals. He also kept detailed journals of his observations. For a naturalist (field biologist) from a small, temperate country, seeing the glorious diversity of unfamiliar life-forms on other continents was a revelation. He carefully noted the characteristics of plants and animals that made them well suited to such diverse environments as the jungles of Brazil, the grasslands of Argentina, the towering peaks of the Andes, and the desolate and frigid lands at the southern tip of South America.

Many of Darwin's observations indicated that geographic proximity is a better predictor of relationships among organism than similarity of environment. For example, the plants and animals living in temperate regions of South America more closely resembled species living in tropical regions of that continent than species living in temperate regions

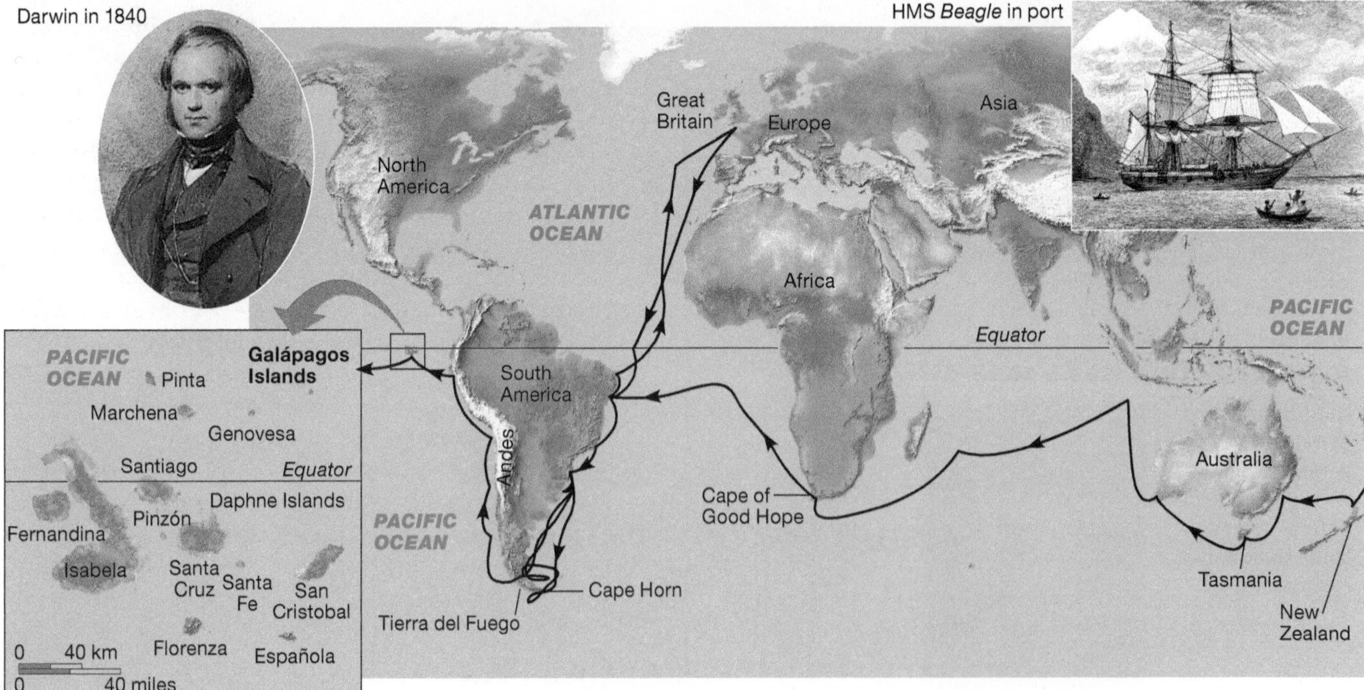

▲ Figure 13.1A The voyage of the *Beagle* (1831–1836), with insets showing a young Charles Darwin and the ship on which he sailed

of Europe. And the South American fossils Darwin found, though clearly species different from living ones, were distinctly South American in their resemblance to the contemporary plants and animals of that continent. For instance, he collected fossilized armor plates resembling those of living armadillo species. Paleontologists later reconstructed the creature to which the armor belonged—an extinct armadillo the size of a Volkswagen Beetle.

Darwin was particularly intrigued by the geographic distribution of organisms on the Galápagos Islands. The Galápagos are relatively young volcanic islands about 900 kilometers (540 miles) off the Pacific coast of South America. Most of the animals that inhabit these remote islands are found nowhere else in the world, but they resemble South American species. For example, Darwin noticed that Galápagos marine iguanas—with a flattened tail that aids in swimming—are similar to, but distinct from, land-dwelling iguanas on the islands and on the South American mainland (Figure 13.1B). Furthermore, each island had its own distinct variety of giant tortoise (Figure 13.1C), the strikingly unique inhabitant for which the islands were named (galápago means "tortoise" in Spanish).

▲ **Figure 13.1B** A marine iguana in the waters around the Galápagos Islands

▲ **Figure 13.1C** A giant tortoise, one of the unique inhabitants of the Galápagos Islands

While on his voyage, Darwin was strongly influenced by the newly published *Principles of Geology*, by Scottish geologist Charles Lyell. The book presented the case for an ancient Earth sculpted over millions of years by gradual geologic processes that continue today. Having witnessed an earthquake that raised part of the coastline of Chile almost a meter, Darwin realized that natural forces gradually changed Earth's surface and that these forces still operate. Thus, the fossils of marine snails that Darwin found high up in the Andes could have been lifted from sea level by natural mountain-building forces such as earthquakes.

By the time Darwin returned to Great Britain, he had begun to seriously doubt that Earth and all its living organisms had been specially created only a few thousand years earlier. As he reflected on his observations, analyzed his collections, and discussed his work with colleagues, he concluded that the evidence was better explained by the hypothesis that present-day species are the descendants of ancient ancestors that they still resemble in some ways. Over time, differences gradually accumulated by a process that Darwin called "descent with modification," his phrase for evolution. Darwin did not originate the concept of evolution—other scientists had explored the idea that organisms had changed over time. Unlike the others, however, Darwin also proposed a scientific mechanism for how life evolves. In the process he called **natural selection**, individuals with certain traits are more likely to survive and reproduce than are individuals who do not have those traits. He hypothesized that as the descendants of ancestral populations spread into various habitats over millions and millions of years, they accumulated diverse modifications, or **adaptations**, that fit them to specific ways of life in their environment.

Darwin's Writings By the early 1840s, Darwin had composed a long essay describing the major features of his theory of evolution by natural selection. Realizing that his ideas would cause an uproar, however, he delayed publication. Even as he procrastinated, Darwin continued to compile evidence in support of his hypothesis. In 1858, Alfred Russel Wallace, a British naturalist doing fieldwork in Indonesia, conceived a hypothesis almost identical to Darwin's. Faced with the possibility that Wallace's work would be published first, Darwin finally released his essay to the scientific community.

The following year, Darwin published *The Origin of Species*, a book that supported his hypothesis with immaculate logic and hundreds of pages of evidence drawn from observations and experiments in biology, geology, and paleontology. The hypothesis of evolution set forth in *The Origin of Species* also generated predictions that have been tested and verified by more than 150 years of research. Consequently, scientists regard Darwin's concept of evolution by means of natural selection as a **theory**—a widely accepted explanatory idea that is broader in scope than a hypothesis, generates new hypotheses, and is supported by a large body of evidence.

Next, we examine lines of evidence for Darwin's theory of **evolution**, the idea that living species are descendants of ancestral species that were different from present-day ones. We then return to the second main point Darwin made in *The Origin of Species*, that natural selection is the mechanism for evolutionary change. With our current understanding of how this mechanism works, we extend Darwin's definition of evolution to include "genetic changes in a population from generation to generation."

What was Darwin's phrase for evolution? What does it mean?

■ Descent with modification. An ancestral species could diversify into many descendant species by the accumulation of adaptations to various environments.

13.2 The study of fossils provides strong evidence for evolution

Fossils—imprints or remains of organisms that lived in the past—document differences between past and present organisms and the fact that many species have become extinct. The organic substances of a dead organism usually decay rapidly, but the hard parts of an animal that are rich in minerals, such as the bones and teeth of vertebrates and the shells of clams and snails, may remain as fossils. For example, the fossilized skull in Figure 13.2A is from one of our early relatives, *Homo erectus*, who lived some 1.5 million years ago in Africa.

Some fossils are not the actual remnants of organisms. The 375-million-year-old fossils shown in Figure 13.2B are casts of ammonites, shelled marine animals related to the present-day nautilus (see Figure 18.9E). Casts form when a dead organism captured in sediment decomposes and leaves an empty mold that is later filled by minerals dissolved in water. The minerals harden, making a replica of the organism. Fossils may also be imprints that remain after the organism decays. Footprints, burrows, and fossilized feces (known as coprolites) provide evidence of an ancient organism's behavior.

▲ Figure 13.2A Skull of *Homo erectus*

▲ Figure 13.2B Ammonite casts

In rare instances, an entire organism, including its soft parts, is encased in a medium that prevents bacteria and fungi from decomposing the body. Examples include insects trapped in amber (fossilized tree resin) and mammoths, bison, and even prehistoric humans frozen in ice or preserved in bogs.

Many fossils are found in fine-grained sedimentary rocks formed from the sand or mud that settles to the bottom of seas, lakes, swamps, and other aquatic habitats. New layers of sediment cover older ones and compress them into layers of rock called **strata** (singular, *stratum*). The fossils in a particular stratum provide a glimpse of some of the organisms that lived in the area at the time the layer formed. Because younger strata are on top of older ones, the relative ages of fossils can be determined by the layer in which they are found. Thus, the sequence in which fossils appear within layers of sedimentary rocks is a historical record of life on Earth.

Paleontologists (scientists who study fossils) sometimes gain access to very old fossils when erosion carves through upper (younger) strata, revealing deeper (older) strata that had been buried. Figure 13.2C shows strata of sedimentary rock at the Grand Canyon. The Colorado River has cut through more than 2,000 m (more than a mile) of rock, exposing sedimentary layers that can be read like huge pages from the book of life. Scan the canyon wall from rim to floor, and you look back through hundreds of millions of years. Each layer entombs fossils that represent some of the organisms from that period of Earth's history.

▲ Figure 13.2C Strata of sedimentary rock at the Grand Canyon

Of course, the **fossil record**—the chronicle of evolution over millions of years of geologic time engraved in the order in which fossils appear in rock strata—is incomplete. Many of Earth's organisms did not live in areas that favor fossilization. Many fossils that did form were in rocks later distorted or destroyed by geologic processes. Furthermore, not all fossils that have been preserved are accessible to paleontologists. Even with its limitations, however, the fossil record is remarkably detailed.

? **What types of animals do you think would be most represented in the fossil record? Explain your answer.**

■ Animals with hard parts, such as shells or bones that readily fossilize, and those that lived in areas where sedimentary rock may form

13.3 Fossils of transitional forms support Darwin's theory of evolution

SCIENTIFIC THINKING

In *The Origin of Species*, Darwin predicted the existence of fossils of transitional forms linking very different groups of organisms. For example, he hypothesized that whales evolved from land-dwelling mammals. If this hypothesis was correct, then fossils should show a series of changes in a lineage of mammals adapted to a fully aquatic habitat. Although Darwin lacked evidence with which to test this prediction, thousands of fossil discoveries have since shed light on the evolutionary origins of many groups of plants and animals, including the transition of fish to amphibian (see Module 19.4), the origin of birds from a lineage of dinosaurs (see Module 19.7), and the evolution of mammals from a reptilian ancestor. If Darwin were alive today, he would surely be delighted to know that evidence discovered over the past few decades has made the origin of whales from terrestrial mammals one of the best-documented evolutionary transitions to date.

Whales are cetaceans, a group that also includes dolphins and porpoises. They have forelimbs in the form of flippers but lack hind limbs. If cetaceans evolved from four-legged land animals, then transitional forms should have reduced hind limb and pelvic bones. Based on the few fossils available in the 1960s, paleontologists hypothesized the ancestors of whales were hoofed, wolflike carnivores.

Beginning in the late 1970s, an extraordinary series of transitional fossils unearthed in Pakistan and Egypt provided the evidence paleontologists needed to test the hypothesis. Figure 13.3 shows the progressive reduction in hind limb and pelvic bones in five of the fossil species. The 50-million-year-old *Pakicetus* ("whale of Pakistan") was a wolf-sized carnivore whose body shape and long limbs resembled those of land animals. However, other skeletal features, including distinctively cetacean middle ear structures, suggest adaptations to an aquatic environment. *Ambulocetus* ("walking whale"), roughly 48 million years old, was a perfect intermediate between modern whales and their land-dwelling ancestors: The joints of its forelimbs suggest mobility on land, while a powerful tail and large, paddle-like hind feet suggest the ability to swim. Adaptations for swimming are more apparent in the 46-million-year-old fossils of *Rodhocetus*, which had relatively short limbs and long-toed webbed feet. The fossil genus *Dorudon*, which lived between 40 and 35 million years ago, had completed the transition to aquatic life. The wrist and elbow joints of its paddle-like forelimbs could not have been used for walking. Its hind limbs were tiny, and as in modern whales, the remaining bit of its pelvis was not even connected to the vertebral column.

The new fossil discoveries were consistent with the earlier hypothesis, and paleontologists became more firmly convinced that whales did indeed arise from a wolflike carnivore. Meanwhile, molecular biologists were testing an alternative hypothesis using DNA analysis to infer relationships among living animals. They found a close relationship between whales and hippopotamuses, which are members of a group of mostly herbivorous, cloven-hoofed mammals that includes pigs, deer, and camels. Consequently, these researchers hypothesized that whales and hippos were both descendants of a cloven-hoofed ancestor. (A cloven hoof is a hoof split into two toes.)

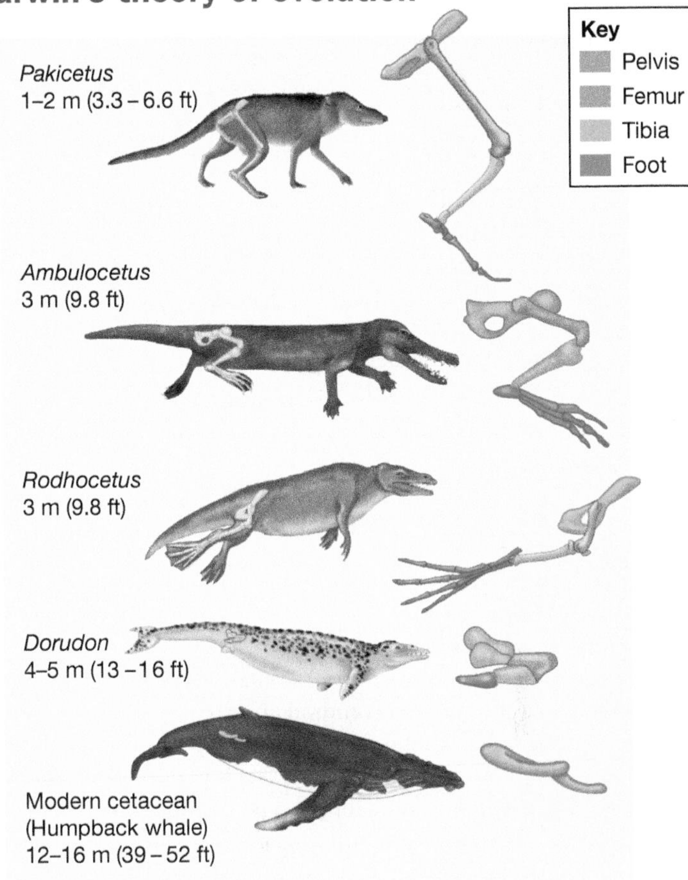

▲ **Figure 13.3** The transition to life in the sea; note positions of bones in animals (not drawn to scale)

TRY THIS List the animals shown, and describe how the structure of each animal's hind limbs reflects their function.

Paleontologists were taken aback by the contradictory results, but openness to new evidence is a hallmark of science. They turned their attention to seeking a fossil that would resolve the issue. Cloven-hoofed mammals have a unique ankle bone. If the ancestor of whales was a wolflike carnivore, then the shape of its ankle bone would be similar to most present-day mammals. Two fossils discovered in 2001 provided the answer. Both *Pakicetus* and *Rodhocetus* had the distinctive ankle bone of a cloven-hoofed mammal. Thus, as is often the case in science, scientists are becoming more certain about the evolutionary origin of whales as mounting evidence from different lines of inquiry converge.

? What anatomical feature did scientists predict in fossils of species transitional between terrestrial and aquatic mammals?

■ Reduced hind limb and pelvic bones

13.4 Homologies provide strong evidence for evolution

A second type of evidence for evolution comes from analyzing similarities among different organisms. Evolution is a process of descent with modification—characteristics present in an ancestral organism are altered over time by natural selection as its descendants face different environmental conditions. In other words, evolution is a remodeling process. As a result, related species can have characteristics that have an underlying similarity yet function differently. Similarity resulting from common ancestry is known as **homology**.

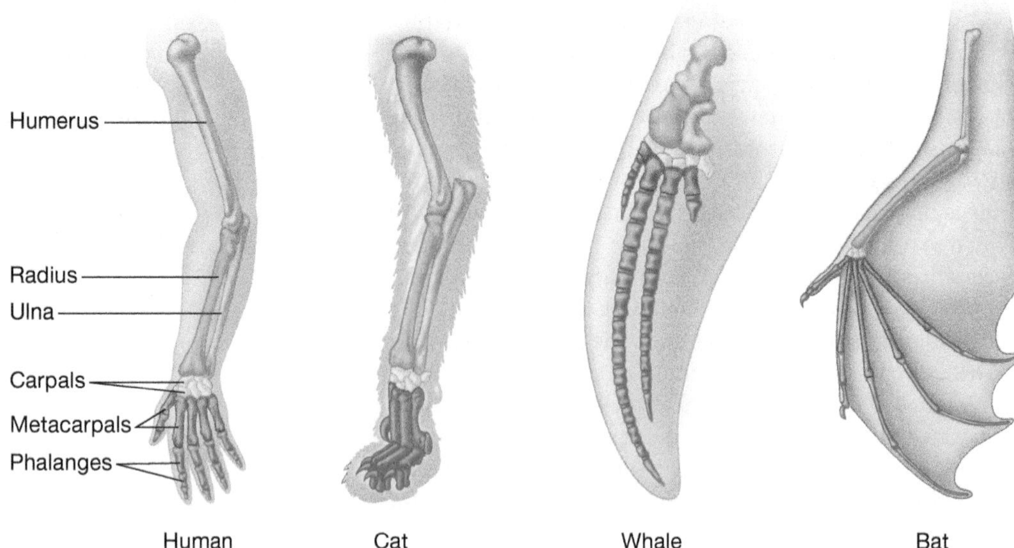

▲ Figure 13.4A Homologous structures: vertebrate forelimbs

Darwin cited the anatomical similarities among vertebrate forelimbs as evidence of common ancestry. As Figure 13.4A shows, the same skeletal elements make up the forelimbs of humans, cats, whales, and bats. The functions of these forelimbs differ. A whale's flipper does not do the same job as a bat's wing, so if these structures had been uniquely engineered, then we would expect that their basic designs would be very different. The logical explanation is that the arms, forelegs, flippers, and wings of these different mammals are variations on an anatomical structure of an ancestral organism that over millions of years has become adapted to different functions. Biologists call such anatomical similarities in different organisms **homologous structures**—features that often have different functions but are structurally similar because of common ancestry.

Because of advances in **molecular biology**, the study of the molecular basis of genes and gene expression, present-day scientists have a much deeper understanding of homologies than Darwin did. Just as your hereditary background is recorded in the DNA you inherit from your parents, the evolutionary history of each species is documented in the DNA inherited from its ancestral species. If two species have homologous genes with sequences that match closely, biologists conclude that these sequences must have been inherited from a relatively recent common ancestor. Conversely, the greater the number of sequence differences between species, the more distant is their last common ancestor. Molecular comparisons between diverse organisms have allowed biologists to develop hypotheses about the evolutionary divergence of major branches on the tree of life, as you learned in the previous module on the origin of whales.

Darwin's boldest hypothesis was that all life-forms are related. Molecular biology provides strong evidence for this claim: All forms of life use the same genetic language of DNA and RNA, and the genetic code—how RNA triplets are translated into amino acids—is essentially universal. Thus, it is likely that all species descended from common ancestors that used this code. Because of these homologies, bacteria engineered with human genes can produce human proteins such as insulin and human growth hormone (see Module 12.7). But molecular homologies go beyond a shared genetic code. For example, organisms as dissimilar as humans and bacteria share homologous genes inherited from a very distant common ancestor.

An understanding of homology can also explain observations that are otherwise puzzling. For example, comparing early stages of development in different animal species reveals similarities not visible in adult organisms. At some point in their development, all vertebrate embryos have a tail posterior to the anus, as well as structures called pharyngeal (throat) pouches. These pouches are homologous structures that ultimately develop to have very different functions, such as gills in fishes and parts of the ears and throat in humans. Note the pharyngeal pouches and tails of the bird embryo (left) and the human embryo (right) in Figure 13.4B.

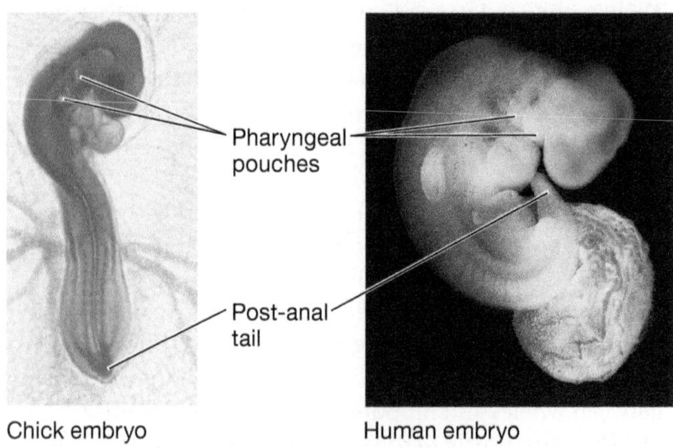

▲ Figure 13.4B Homologous structures in vertebrate embryos

Some of the most interesting homologies are "leftover" structures that are of marginal or perhaps no importance to the organism. These **vestigial structures** are remnants of features that served important functions in the organism's ancestors. For example, the small pelvis and hind-leg bones of ancient whales are vestiges (traces) of their walking ancestors. The eye remnants that are buried under scales in blind species of cave fishes—a vestige of their sighted ancestors—are another example.

Organisms may also retain genes that have lost their function, even though homologous genes in related species are fully functional. Researchers have identified many of these inactive "pseudogenes" in humans. One such gene encodes an enzyme known as GLO that is used in making vitamin C. Almost all mammals have a metabolic pathway to synthesize this essential vitamin from glucose. Although humans and other primates have functional genes for the first three steps in the pathway, the inactive GLO gene prevents vitamin C from being made—we must get sufficient amounts in our diet to maintain health.

Next we see how homologies help us trace evolutionary descent.

? What is homology? How does the concept of homology relate to molecular biology?

■ Homology is similarity in different species due to evolution from a common ancestor. Similarities in DNA sequences or proteins reflect the evolutionary relationship that is the basis of homology.

13.5 Homologies indicate patterns of descent that can be shown on an evolutionary tree

Darwin was the first to view the history of life as a tree, with multiple branchings from a common ancestral trunk to the descendant species at the tips of the twigs (see Figure 14.1). Biologists represent these patterns of descent with an **evolutionary tree**, although today they often turn the trees sideways.

Homologous structures, both anatomical and molecular, can be used to determine the branching sequence of such a tree. Some homologous characters, such as the genetic code, are shared by all species because they date to the deep ancestral past. In contrast, characters that evolved more recently are shared only within smaller groups of organisms. For example, all tetrapods (from the Greek *tetra*, four, and *pod*, foot) possess the same basic limb bone structure illustrated in Figure 13.4A, but their ancestors do not.

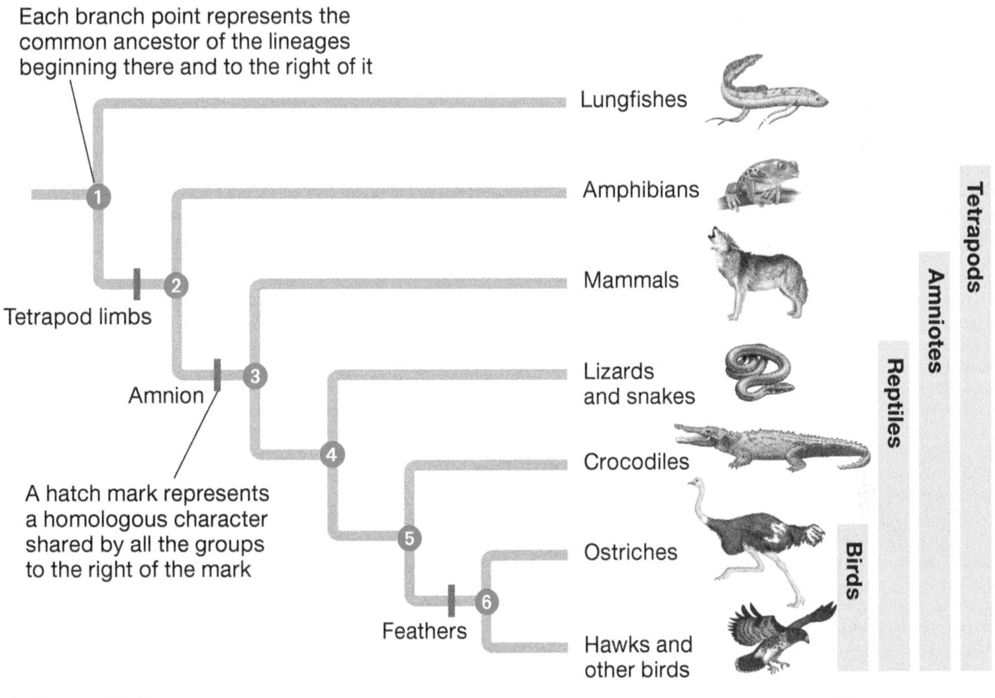

▲ **Figure 13.5** An evolutionary tree for tetrapods and their closest living relatives, the lungfishes

Figure 13.5 is an evolutionary tree of tetrapods (amphibians, mammals, and reptiles, including birds) and their closest living relatives, the lungfishes. In this diagram, each branch point represents the common ancestor of all species that descended from it. For example, lungfishes and all tetrapods descended from ancestor ①, whereas crocodiles and birds descended from ancestor ⑤. Three homologies are shown by the purple hatch marks on the tree—tetrapod limbs, the amnion (a protective embryonic membrane), and feathers. Tetrapod limbs were present in ancestor ② and hence are found in all of its descendants. The amnion was present only in ancestor ③ and thus is shared only by mammals and reptiles. Feathers were present only in ancestor ⑥ and hence are found only in birds.

Evolutionary trees are hypotheses reflecting our current understanding of patterns of evolutionary descent. Some trees, such as the one in Figure 13.5, are supported by a strong combination of fossil, anatomical, and molecular data. Others are more speculative because few data are available.

Now that you have learned about Darwin's view of evolution as descent with modification, let's examine the mechanism he proposed for how life evolves—natural selection.

? Refer to the evolutionary tree in Figure 13.5. Are crocodiles more closely related to lizards or birds?

■ Look for the most recent common ancestor of these groups. Crocodiles are more closely related to birds because they share a more recent common ancestor with birds (ancestor ⑤) than with lizards (ancestor ④).

13.6 Darwin proposed natural selection as the mechanism of evolution

Darwin's greatest contribution to biology was his explanation of *how* life evolves. Because he thought that species formed gradually over long periods of time, he knew that he would not be able to study the evolution of new species by direct observation. But he did have a way to gain insight into the process of incremental change—the practices used by plant and animal breeders.

All domesticated plants and animals are the products of selective breeding from wild ancestors. For example, the baseball-size tomatoes grown today are very different from their Peruvian ancestors, which were not much larger than blueberries, and dachshunds bear little resemblance to the wolves from which they were bred. Having conceived the notion that **artificial selection**—the selective breeding of domesticated plants and animals to promote the occurrence of desirable traits in the offspring—was the key to understanding evolutionary change, Darwin bred fancy pigeons (Figure 13.6) to gain firsthand experience. He also talked to farmers about livestock breeding. He learned that artificial selection has two essential components, variation and heritability.

Variation among individuals—for example, differences in coat type in a litter of puppies, size of corn ears, or milk production by the individual cows in a herd—allows the breeder to select the animals or plants with the most desirable combination of characters as breeding stock for the next generation. Heritability refers to the transmission of a trait from parent to offspring. Despite their lack of knowledge of the underlying genetics, breeders had long understood the importance of heritability in artificial selection.

Unlike most naturalists, who sought consistency of traits in order to classify organisms, Darwin was a careful observer of variations between individuals. He knew that individuals in natural populations have small but measurable differences. But what forces in nature played the role of the breeder by choosing which individuals became the breeding stock for the next generation?

Darwin found inspiration in an essay written by economist Thomas Malthus, who contended that much of human suffering—disease, famine, and war—was the consequence of human populations increasing faster than food supplies and other resources. Darwin applied Malthus's idea to populations of plants and animals. He deduced that the production of more individuals than the limited resources can support leads to a struggle for existence, with only some offspring surviving in each generation. Of the many eggs laid, young born, and seeds spread, only a tiny fraction complete development and leave offspring. The rest are eaten, starved, diseased, unmated, or unable to reproduce for other reasons. The essence of natural selection is this unequal reproduction. Individuals whose traits better enable them to obtain food or escape predators or tolerate physical conditions will survive and reproduce more successfully, passing these adaptive traits to their offspring (see Module 1.9).

Darwin reasoned that if artificial selection can bring about so much change in a relatively short period of time, then natural selection could modify species considerably over hundreds or thousands of generations. Over vast spans of time, many traits that adapt a population to its environment will accumulate. If the environment changes, however, or if individuals move to a new environment, natural selection will select for adaptations to these new conditions, sometimes producing changes that result in the origin of a completely new species in the process.

It is important to emphasize three key points about evolution by natural selection. First, although natural selection occurs through interactions between individual organisms and the environment, individuals do not evolve. Rather, it is the population—the group of organisms—that evolves over time as adaptive traits become more common in the group and other traits change or disappear.

Second, natural selection can amplify or diminish only heritable traits. Certainly, an organism may become modified through its own interactions with the environment during its lifetime, and those acquired characteristics may help the organism survive. But unless coded for in the genes of an organism's gametes, such acquired characteristics cannot be passed on to offspring. Thus, a championship female bodybuilder will not give birth to a muscle-bound baby.

Fantail

Frillback

Rock pigeon

Old Dutch Capuchine

Trumpeter

▲ **Figure 13.6** **Artificial selection: fancy pigeon varieties bred from the rock pigeon**

Third, evolution is not goal directed; it does not lead to perfectly adapted organisms. Whereas artificial selection is a deliberate attempt by humans to produce individuals with specific traits, natural selection is the result of environmental factors that vary from place to place and over time. A trait that is favorable in one situation may be useless—or even detrimental—in different circumstances. And as you will see, adaptations are often compromises. Now let's look at some examples of natural selection.

Compare artificial selection and natural selection.

In artificial selection, humans choose the desirable traits and breed only organisms with those traits. In natural selection, the environment does the choosing: Individuals with traits best suited to the environment survive and reproduce most successfully, passing those adaptive traits to offspring.

13.7 Scientists can observe natural selection in action

Look at any natural environment, and you will see the products of natural selection—adaptations that suit organisms to their environment. But can we see natural selection in action?

Indeed, biologists have documented evolutionary change in thousands of scientific studies. A classic example comes from work that Peter and Rosemary Grant and their students did with finches in the Galápagos Islands over more than 30 years (see Module 14.9). As part of their research, they measured changes in beak size in a population of a ground finch species. These birds eat mostly small seeds. In dry years, when all seeds are in short supply, birds must eat more large seeds. Birds with larger, stronger beaks have a feeding advantage and greater reproductive success, and the Grants measured an increase in the average beak depth for the population. During wet years, smaller beaks are more efficient for eating the now abundant small seeds, and the Grants found a decrease in average beak depth.

An unsettling example of natural selection in action is the evolution of pesticide resistance in hundreds of insect species. Pesticides control insects and prevent them from eating crops or transmitting diseases. Whenever a new type of pesticide is used to control pests, the story is similar (**Figure 13.7**): A relatively small amount of poison initially kills most of the insects, but subsequent applications are less and less effective. The few survivors of the first pesticide wave are individuals that are genetically resistant, carrying an allele (alternative form of a gene, colored red in the figure) that somehow enables them to survive the chemical attack. So the poison kills most members of the population, leaving the resistant survivors to reproduce and pass the alleles for pesticide resistance to their offspring. The proportion of pesticide-resistant individuals thus increases in each generation.

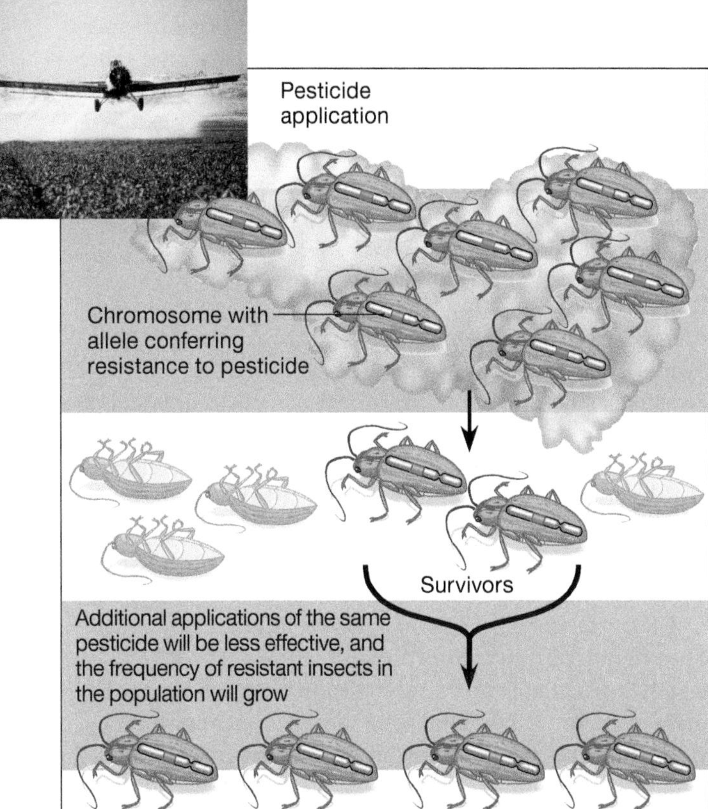

▲ **Figure 13.7** **Evolution of pesticide resistance in an insect population**

TRY THIS **Explain the failure of WHO's anti-malaria campaign by drawing a diagram similar to Figure 13.7.**

WHO's campaign against malaria described in the chapter introduction is a real-world example of the evolution of pesticide resistance. Some mosquitoes in the populations that were sprayed with DDT carried an allele that codes for an enzyme that detoxifies the pesticide. When the presence of DDT changed the environment, the individuals carrying that allele had an advantage. They survived to leave offspring, while nonresistant individuals did not. Thus, the process of natural selection defeated the efforts of WHO to control the spread of malaria by using DDT to kill mosquitoes.

These examples of evolutionary adaptation highlight two important points about natural selection. First, natural selection is more an editing process than a creative mechanism. A pesticide does not create new alleles that allow insects to survive. Rather, the presence of the pesticide leads to natural selection for insects in the population that already have those alleles. Second, natural selection is contingent on time and place: It favors those heritable traits in a varying population that fit the current, local environment. If the environment changes, different traits may be favored.

In the next few modules, we examine the genetic basis of evolution more closely.

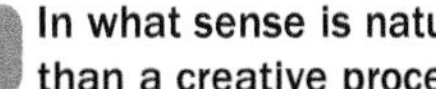

In what sense is natural selection more an editing process than a creative process?

Natural selection cannot create beneficial traits on demand but instead "edits" variation in a population by selecting for individuals with those traits that are best suited to the current environment.

The Evolution of Populations

13.8 Mutation and sexual reproduction produce the genetic variation that makes evolution possible

In *The Origin of Species*, Darwin provided evidence that life on Earth has evolved over time, and he proposed that natural selection, in favoring some heritable traits over others, was the primary mechanism for that change. But he could not explain the cause of variation among individuals, nor could he account for how those variations passed from parents to offspring.

Just a few years after the publication of *The Origin of Species*, Gregor Mendel wrote a groundbreaking paper on inheritance in pea plants (see Module 9.2). By breeding peas in his abbey garden, Mendel discovered the hereditary processes required for natural selection. Although the significance of Mendel's work was not recognized during his or Darwin's lifetime, its rediscovery in 1900 set the stage for understanding the genetic differences on which evolution is based.

Genetic Variation You have no trouble recognizing your friends in a crowd. The unique genome of each person is reflected in phenotypic variation, the expressed traits such as appearance that allow you to identify individuals. Indeed, individual variation occurs in all species, as illustrated by the garter snakes in Figure 13.8. All four of these snakes were captured in one Oregon field. In addition to obvious physical differences, such as the snakes' colors and patterns, most populations have a great deal of phenotypic variation that can be observed only at the molecular level, such as an enzyme that detoxifies DDT.

Of course, not all variation in a population is heritable. The phenotype results from a combination of the genotype, which is inherited, and many environmental influences. For instance, if you have dental work to straighten and whiten your teeth, you will not pass your environmentally produced smile to your offspring. Only the genetic component of variation is relevant to natural selection.

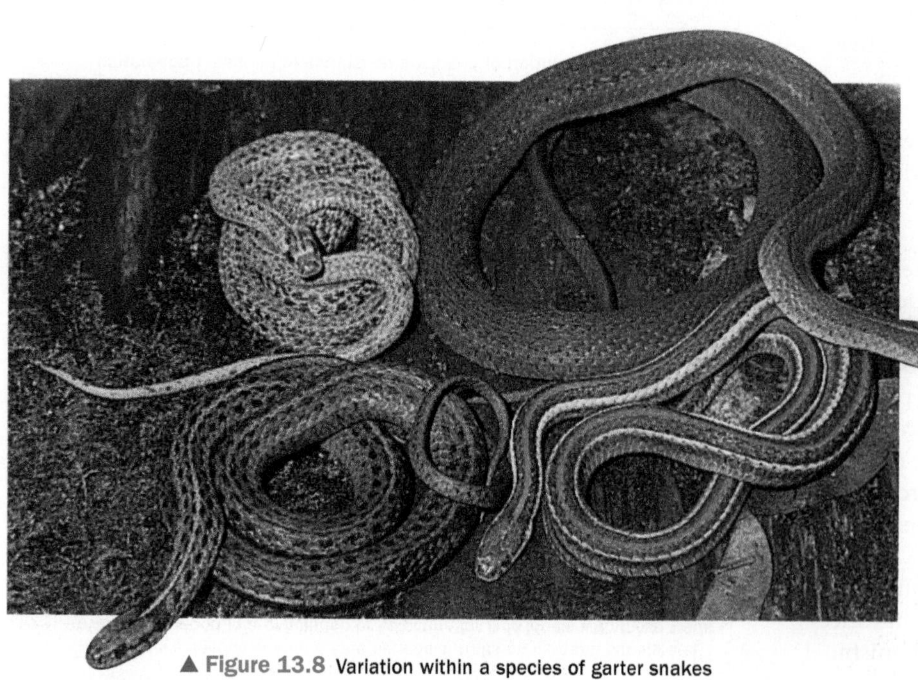

▲ Figure 13.8 Variation within a species of garter snakes

Many of the characters that vary in a population result from the combined effect of several genes. Polygenic inheritance produces characters that vary more or less continuously—in human height, for instance, from very short individuals to very tall ones (see Module 9.14). By contrast, other features, such as Mendel's purple and white pea flowers or human blood types, are determined by a single gene locus, with different alleles producing distinct phenotypes. But where do these alleles come from?

Mutation New alleles originate by **mutation**, a change in the genetic INFORMATION encoded in the nucleotide sequence of DNA. Thus, mutation is the ultimate source of the genetic variation that serves as raw material for evolution. In multicellular organisms, however, only mutations in cells that produce gametes can be passed to offspring and affect a population's genetic variability.

A change as small as a single nucleotide in a protein-coding gene can have a significant effect on phenotype, as in sickle-cell disease (see Module 9.13). An organism is a refined product of thousands of generations of past selection, and a random change in its DNA is not likely to improve its genome any more than randomly changing some letters on a page is likely to improve a story. In fact, mutation that affects a protein's function will probably be harmful. On rare occasions, however, a mutated allele may actually improve the adaptation of an individual to its environment and enhance its reproductive success. This kind of effect is more likely when the environment is changing in such a way that mutations that were once disadvantageous are favorable under the new conditions. For instance, mutations that endow houseflies with resistance to the pesticide DDT also reduce their growth rate. Before DDT was introduced, such mutations were a handicap to the flies that had them. But once DDT was part of the environment, the mutant alleles were advantageous, and natural selection increased their frequency in fly populations.

Chromosomal mutations that delete, disrupt, or rearrange many gene loci at once are almost certain to be harmful. But duplication of a gene or small pieces of DNA through errors in meiosis can provide an important source of genetic variation. If a repeated segment of DNA can persist over the generations, mutations may accumulate in the duplicate copies without affecting the function of the original gene, eventually leading to new genes with novel functions. This process may have played a major role in evolution.

For example, the remote ancestors of mammals carried a single gene for detecting odors that has since been duplicated repeatedly. As a result, mice have about 1,300 different olfactory receptor genes. It is likely that such dramatic increases helped early mammals by enabling them to distinguish among many different smells. And repeated duplications of genes that control development are linked to the origin of vertebrate animals from an invertebrate ancestor.

In prokaryotes, mutations can quickly generate genetic variation. Because bacteria multiply so rapidly, a beneficial mutation can increase in frequency in a matter of hours or days. And because bacteria are haploid, with a single allele for each gene, a new allele can have an effect immediately.

Mutation rates in animals and plants average about one in every 100,000 genes per generation. For these organisms, low mutation rates, long time spans between generations, and diploid genomes prevent most mutations from significantly affecting genetic variation from one generation to the next.

Sexual Reproduction In organisms that reproduce sexually, most of the genetic variation in a population results from the unique combination of alleles that each individual inherits. (Of course, the origin of those allele variations is past mutations.)

Fresh assortments of existing alleles arise every generation from three random components of sexual reproduction: crossing over, independent orientation of homologous chromosomes at metaphase I of meiosis, and random fertilization (see Modules 8.15 and 8.17). During meiosis, pairs of homologous chromosomes, one set inherited from each parent, trade some of their genes by crossing over. These homologous chromosomes separate into gametes independently of other chromosome pairs. Thus, gametes from any individual vary extensively in their genetic makeup. Finally, each zygote made by a mating pair has a unique assortment of alleles resulting from the random union of sperm and egg.

Now let's see why genetic variation is such an essential element of evolution.

? **What is the ultimate (original) source of genetic variation? What is the source of most genetic variation in a population that reproduces sexually?**

■ Mutation; unique combinations of alleles resulting from sexual reproduction

13.9 Evolution occurs within populations

A common misconception about evolution is that individual organisms evolve during their lifetimes. It is true that natural selection acts on individuals: Each individual's combination of traits affects its survival and reproductive success. But the evolutionary impact of natural selection is only apparent in the changes in a population of organisms over time.

A **population** is a group of individuals of the same species that live in the same area and can potentially interbreed. We can measure evolution as a change in the prevalence of certain heritable traits in a population over a span of generations. The increasing proportion of resistant insects in areas sprayed with pesticide is one example. Natural selection favored insects with alleles for pesticide resistance; these insects left more offspring than nonresistant individuals, changing the genetic makeup of the population.

Different populations of the same species may be geographically isolated from each other to such an extent that an exchange of genetic material never or only rarely occurs. Such isolation is common in populations confined to different lakes, as shown in Figure 13.9, or islands. For example, each population of Galápagos tortoises is restricted to its own island. Not all populations have such sharp boundaries. However, members of a population typically breed with one another and are therefore more closely related to each other than they are to members of a different population.

In studying evolution at the population level, biologists focus on the **gene pool**, which consists of all copies of every type of allele at every locus in all members of the population. For many loci, there are two or more alleles in the gene pool. For example, in a mosquito population, there may be two alleles relating to DDT breakdown, one that codes for an enzyme that breaks down DDT and one for a version of the enzyme that does not. In populations living in fields sprayed with DDT, the allele for the enzyme conferring resistance will increase in frequency and the other allele will decrease in frequency. When the relative frequencies of alleles in a population change like this over a number of generations, evolution is occurring on its smallest scale. Such a change in a gene pool is often called **microevolution**.

In the next module, we'll explore how to test whether evolution is occurring in a population.

? **Why can't an individual evolve?**

■ Evolution involves changes in the genetic makeup of a population over time. An individual's genetic makeup rarely changes during its lifetime.

▲ Figure 13.9 Lakes in Alaska containing isolated populations

13.10 The Hardy-Weinberg equation can test whether a population is evolving

To understand how microevolution works, let's first examine a simple population in which evolution is not occurring and thus the gene pool is not changing. Consider an imaginary population of iguanas with individuals that differ in foot webbing (**Figure 13.10A**). Let's assume that foot webbing is controlled by a single gene and that the allele for nonwebbed feet (*W*) is completely dominant to the allele for webbed feet (*w*). The term *dominant* (see Module 9.3) may seem to suggest that over many generations, the *W* allele will somehow come to "dominate," becoming more and more common at the expense of the recessive allele. In fact, this is not what happens. The shuffling of alleles that accompanies sexual reproduction does not alter the genetic makeup of the population. In other words, no matter how many times alleles are segregated into different gametes and united in different combinations by fertilization, the frequency of each allele in the gene pool will remain constant unless other factors are operating. This condition is known as the **Hardy-Weinberg equilibrium** named for the two scientists who derived it independently in 1908.

No webbing

Webbing

▲ **Figure 13.10A** Imaginary iguanas, with and without foot webbing

To test the Hardy-Weinberg equilibrium, let's look at two generations of our imaginary iguana population. **Figure 13.10B** shows the frequencies of alleles in the gene pool of the original population. We have a total of 500 animals; of these, 320 have the genotype *WW* (nonwebbed feet), 160 have the heterozygous genotype, *Ww* (also nonwebbed feet, because the nonwebbed allele *W* is dominant), and 20 have the genotype *ww* (webbed feet). The proportions or frequencies of the three genotypes are shown in the middle of Figure 13.10B: 0.64 for *WW* $\left(\frac{320}{500}\right)$, 0.32 for *Ww* $\left(\frac{160}{500}\right)$, and 0.04 for *ww* $\left(\frac{20}{500}\right)$.

From these genotype frequencies, we can calculate the frequency of each allele in the population. Because these are diploid organisms, this population of 500 has a total of 1,000 alleles for foot type. To determine the number of *W* alleles, we add the number in the *WW* iguanas, $2 \times 320 = 640$, to the number in the *Ww* iguanas, 160. The total number of *W* alleles is thus 800. The frequency of the *W* allele, which we will call p, is $\frac{800}{1,000}$, or 0.8. We can calculate the frequency of the *w* allele in a similar way; this frequency, called q, is 0.2.

The letters p and q are often used to represent allele frequencies. Notice that $p + q = 1$. The combined frequencies of all alleles for a gene in a population must equal 1. If there are only two alleles and you know the frequency of one allele, you can calculate the frequency of the other.

What happens when the iguanas of this parent population form gametes? At the end of meiosis, each gamete has one allele for foot type, either *W* or *w*. The frequencies of the two alleles in the gametes will be the same as their frequencies in the gene pool of the parental population, 0.8 for *W* and 0.2 for *w*.

Figure 13.10C shows a Punnett square that uses these gamete allele frequencies and the rule of multiplication (see Module 9.7) to calculate the frequencies of the three genotypes in the next generation. The probability of producing a *WW* individual (by combining two *W* alleles from the pool of gametes) is $p \times p = p^2$, or $0.8 \times 0.8 = 0.64$. Thus, the frequency of *WW* iguanas in the next generation would be 0.64. Likewise, the frequency of *ww* individuals would be $q^2 = 0.04$. For heterozygous individuals, *Ww*, the genotype can form in two ways, depending on whether the sperm or egg supplies the dominant allele. In other words, the frequency of *Ww* would be $2pq = 2 \times 0.8 \times 0.2 = 0.32$. Do these frequencies look familiar? Notice that the three genotypes have the same frequencies in the next generation as they did in the parent generation.

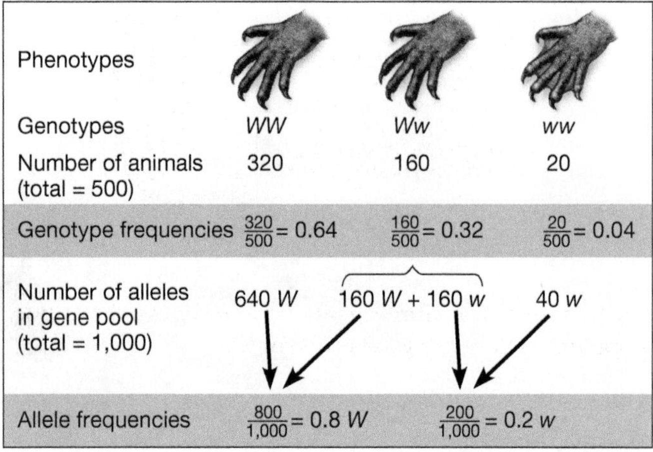

▲ **Figure 13.10B** Gene pool of the original population of imaginary iguanas

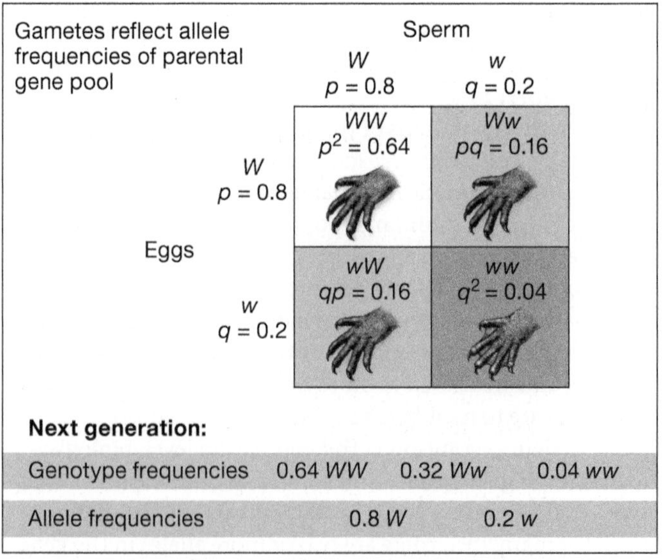

▲ **Figure 13.10C** Gene pool of the next generation of imaginary iguanas

Finally, what about the frequencies of the alleles in this new generation? Because the genotype frequencies are the same as in the parent population, the allele frequencies p and q are also the same. In fact, we could follow the frequencies of alleles and genotypes through many generations, and the results would continue to be the same. Thus, the gene pool of this population is in a state of equilibrium—Hardy-Weinberg equilibrium.

Now let's write a general formula for calculating the frequencies of genotypes in a population from the frequencies of alleles in the gene pool. In our imaginary iguana population, the frequency of the *W* allele (p) is 0.8, and the frequency of the *w* allele (q) is 0.2. Again note that $p + q = 1$. Also notice in Figures 13.10B and 13.10C that the frequencies of the three possible genotypes in the populations also add up to 1 (that is, $0.64 + 0.32 + 0.04 = 1$). We can represent these relationships symbolically with the Hardy-Weinberg equation:

$$p^2 + 2pq + q^2 = 1$$

p^2	$2pq$	q^2
Frequency of homozygous dominants	Frequency of heterozygotes	Frequency of homozygous recessives

If a population is in Hardy-Weinberg equilibrium, allele and genotype frequencies will remain constant generation after generation. Something other than the reshuffling processes of sexual reproduction is required to change allele frequencies in a population. One way to find out what factors *can* change a gene pool is to identify the conditions that must be met if genetic equilibrium is to be maintained.

For a population to be in Hardy-Weinberg equilibrium, it must satisfy five main conditions:

1. Very large population. The smaller the population, the more likely that allele frequencies will fluctuate by chance from one generation to the next.
2. No gene flow between populations. When individuals move into or out of populations, they add or remove alleles, altering the gene pool.
3. No mutations. By changing alleles or deleting or duplicating genes, mutations modify the gene pool.
4. Random mating. If individuals mate preferentially, such as with close relatives (inbreeding), random mixing of gametes does not occur, and genotype frequencies change.
5. No natural selection. The unequal survival and reproductive success of individuals (natural selection) can alter allele frequencies.

Because all five conditions are rarely met in real populations, allele and genotype frequencies often do change. The Hardy-Weinberg equation can be used to test whether evolution is occurring in a population. The equation also has medical applications, as we see next.

? Which is *least* likely to alter allele and genotype frequencies in a few generations of a large, sexually reproducing population: gene flow, mutation, or natural selection? Explain.

■ Mutation. Because mutations are rare, their effect on allele and genotype frequencies from one generation to the next is likely to be small.

13.11 The Hardy-Weinberg equation is useful in public health science

CONNECTION Public health scientists use the Hardy-Weinberg equation to estimate how many people carry alleles for certain inherited diseases. Consider the case of phenylketonuria (PKU), an inherited inability to break down the amino acid phenylalanine that results in brain damage if untreated. Newborns are routinely screened for PKU, which occurs in about one out of 10,000 babies born in the United States. The health problems associated with PKU can be prevented by strict adherence to a diet that limits the intake of phenylalanine. Packaged foods with ingredients such as aspartame, a common artificial sweetener that contains phenylalanine, must be labeled clearly (**Figure 13.11**).

PKU is due to a recessive allele, so the frequency of individuals born with PKU corresponds to the q^2 term in the Hardy-Weinberg equation. Given one PKU occurrence per 10,000 births, $q^2 = 0.0001$. Therefore, the frequency of the recessive allele for PKU in the population, q, equals the square root of 0.0001, or 0.01. And the frequency of the dominant allele, p, equals $1 - q$, or 0.99. The frequency of carriers, heterozygous people who do not have PKU but may pass the PKU allele on to offspring, is $2pq$, which equals $2 \times 0.99 \times 0.01$, or 0.0198. Thus, the equation tells us that about 2% (actually 1.98%) of the U.S. population are carriers of the PKU allele. Estimating the frequency of a harmful allele is part of any public health program dealing with genetic diseases.

INGREDIENTS: SORBITOL,
MAGNESIUM STEARATE,
ARTIFICIAL FLAVOR,
ASPARTAME† (SWEETENER),
ARTIFICIAL COLOR
(YELLOW 5 LAKE, BLUE 1
LAKE), ZINC GLUCONATE.
†PHENYLKETONURICS:
CONTAINS PHENYLALANINE
Diet
Soda

▲ **Figure 13.11** A warning to individuals with PKU

? Which term in the Hardy-Weinberg equation—p^2, $2pq$, or q^2—corresponds to the frequency of individuals who have no alleles for the disease PKU?

■ The frequency of individuals with no PKU alleles is p^2.

Mechanisms of Microevolution

13.12 Natural selection, genetic drift, and gene flow can cause microevolution

Deviations from the five conditions named in Module 13.10 for Hardy-Weinberg equilibrium can alter allele frequencies in a population (microevolution). Although new genes and new alleles originate by mutation, these random and rare events probably change allele frequencies little within a population of sexually reproducing organisms. Nonrandom mating can affect the frequencies of homozygous and heterozygous genotypes, but by itself usually does not affect allele frequencies. The three main causes of evolutionary change are natural selection, genetic drift, and gene flow.

Natural Selection The condition for Hardy-Weinberg equilibrium that there be no natural selection—that all individuals in a population be equal in ability to reproduce—is probably never met in nature. Populations consist of varied individuals, and some variants leave more offspring than others. In our imaginary iguana population, individuals with webbed feet (genotype *ww*) might survive better and produce more offspring because they are more efficient at swimming and catching food than individuals that lack webbed feet. Genetic equilibrium would be disturbed as the frequency of the *w* allele increased in the gene pool from one generation to the next.

Genetic Drift Flip a coin a thousand times, and a result of 700 heads and 300 tails would make you suspicious about that coin. But flip a coin 10 times, and an outcome of 7 heads and 3 tails would seem within reason. The smaller the sample, the more likely that chance alone will cause a deviation from an idealized result—in this case, an equal number of heads and tails. Let's apply that logic to a population's gene pool. The frequencies of alleles will be more stable from one generation to the next when a population is large. In a process called **genetic drift**, chance events can cause allele frequencies to fluctuate unpredictably from one generation to the next. The smaller the population, the more impact genetic drift is likely to have. In fact, an allele can be lost from a small population by such chance fluctuations. Two situations in which genetic drift can have a significant impact on a population are those that produce the bottleneck effect and the founder effect.

Catastrophes such as hurricanes, floods, or fires may kill large numbers of individuals, leaving a small surviving population that is unlikely to have the same genetic makeup as the original population. Such a drastic reduction in population size is called a **bottleneck effect**. Analogous to shaking just a few marbles through a bottleneck (Figure 13.12A), certain alleles (purple marbles) may be present at higher frequency in the surviving population than in the original population, others (green marbles) may be present at lower frequency, and some (orange marbles) may not be present at all. After a population is drastically reduced, genetic drift may continue for many generations until the population is again large enough for fluctuations due to chance to have less of an impact. Even if a population that has passed through a bottleneck ultimately recovers its size, it may have low levels of genetic variation—a legacy of the genetic drift that occurred when the population was small.

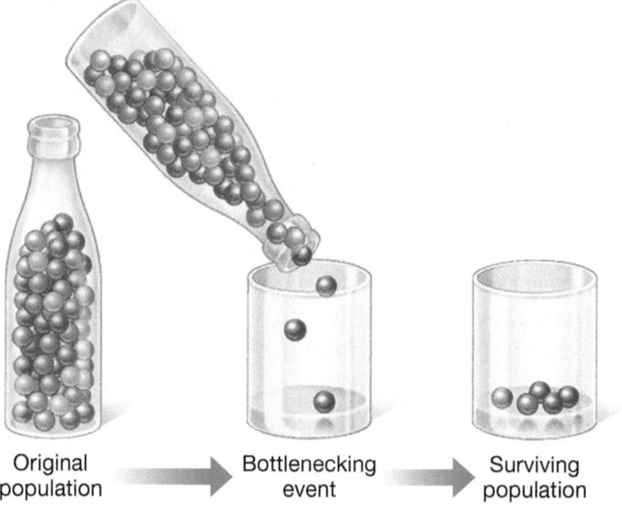

▲ **Figure 13.12A** The bottleneck effect

One reason it is important to understand the bottleneck effect is that human activities such as overhunting and habitat destruction may create severe bottlenecks for other species. Examples of species affected by bottlenecks include the endangered Florida panther, the African cheetah, and the greater prairie chicken (Figure 13.12B). Millions of these birds once lived on the prairies of Illinois. But as their habitat was converted to farmland and other uses during the 19th and 20th centuries, the number of greater prairie chickens plummeted. By 1993, only two Illinois populations remained, with a total of fewer than 50 birds. Less than 50% of the eggs of these birds hatched. Researchers compared the DNA of the 1993 population with DNA extracted from museum specimens dating back to the 1930s. They surveyed six gene loci and found that the modern birds had lost 30% of the alleles that were present in

▲ **Figure 13.12B** Greater prairie chicken (*Tympanuchus cupido*)

the museum specimens. Thus, genetic drift as a result of the bottleneck reduced the genetic variation of the population and may have increased the frequency of harmful alleles, leading to the low egg-hatching rate.

Genetic drift is also likely when a few individuals colonize an island or other new habitat, producing what is called the **founder effect**. The smaller the group, the less likely that the genetic makeup of the colonists will represent the gene pool of the larger population they left.

The founder effect explains the relatively high frequency of certain inherited disorders among some human populations established by small numbers of colonists. For example, in 1814, 15 people founded a colony on Tristan da Cunha, a group of small islands in the middle of the Atlantic Ocean. Apparently, one of the colonists carried a recessive allele for retinitis pigmentosa, a progressive form of blindness. Of the 240 descendants who still lived on the islands in the 1960s, four had retinitis pigmentosa, and at least nine others were known to be heterozygous carriers of the allele. The frequency of this allele is 10 times higher on Tristan da Cunha than in the British population from which the founders came.

Gene Flow Allele frequencies in a population can also change as a result of **gene flow**, by which a population may gain or lose alleles when fertile individuals move into or out of a population or when gametes (such as plant pollen) are transferred between populations. Gene flow tends to reduce differences between populations. For example, humans today move more freely about the world than in the past, and gene flow has become an important agent of microevolutionary change in previously isolated human populations.

Let's return to the Illinois greater prairie chickens and see how gene flow improved their fate. To counteract the lack of genetic diversity, researchers added a total of 271 birds from neighboring states to the Illinois populations. This strategy worked. New alleles entered the population, and the egg-hatching rate improved to more than 90%.

? **How might gene flow between populations living in different habitats actually interfere with each population's adaptation to its local environment?**

The introduction of alleles that may not be beneficial in a particular habitat prevents the population living there from becoming fully adapted to its local conditions.

13.13 Natural selection is the only mechanism that consistently leads to adaptive evolution

Genetic drift, gene flow, and even mutation can cause microevolution. But only by chance could these events result in improving a population's fit to its environment. In natural selection, on the other hand, only the events that produce genetic variation (mutation and sexual reproduction) are random. The process of natural selection, in which better-adapted individuals are more likely to survive and reproduce, is *not* random. Consequently, only natural selection consistently leads to adaptive evolution—evolution that results in a better fit between organisms and their environment.

The adaptations of organisms include many striking examples. Consider these examples of STRUCTURE AND FUNCTION that make the blue-footed booby suited to its home on the Galápagos Islands (Figure 13.13). The bird's body and bill are streamlined like a torpedo, minimizing friction as it dives from heights up to 24 m (more than 75 feet) into the shallow water below. To pull out of this high-speed dive once it hits the water, the booby uses its large tail as a brake. Its large, webbed feet make great flippers, propelling the bird through the water at high speeds—a huge advantage when hunting fish.

▲ **Figure 13.13** Blue-footed booby (*Sula nebouxii*)

Such adaptations are the result of natural selection. By consistently favoring some alleles over others, natural selection improves the match between organisms and their environment. However, the environment may change over time. As a result, what constitutes a "good match" between an organism and its environment is a moving target, making adaptive evolution a continuous, dynamic process.

Let's take a closer look at natural selection. The commonly used phrase "survival of the fittest" is misleading if we take it to mean direct competition between individuals. There are animal species in which individuals lock horns or otherwise do combat to determine mating privilege. But reproductive success is generally more subtle and passive. In a varied population of moths, certain individuals may produce more offspring than others because their wing colors hide them from predators better. Plants in a wildflower population may differ in reproductive success because the slight variations in color, shape, or fragrance of some flowers attract more pollinators. In a given environment, such traits can lead to greater **relative fitness**: the contribution an individual makes to the gene pool of the next generation *relative to* the contributions of other individuals. The fittest individuals in the context of evolution are those that produce the largest number of viable, fertile offspring and thus pass on the most genes to the next generation.

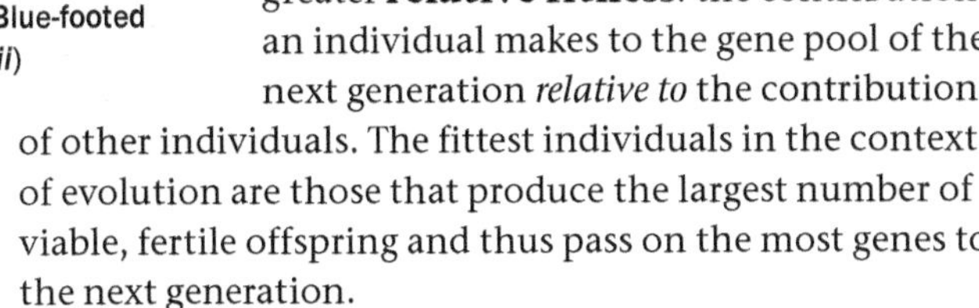

? **Explain how the phrase "survival of the fittest" differs from the biological definition of relative fitness.**

Survival alone does not guarantee reproductive success. An organism's relative fitness is determined by its number of fertile offspring and thus its relative contribution to the gene pool of the next generation.

VISUALIZING THE CONCEPT

13.14 Natural selection can alter variation in a population in three ways

Evolutionary fitness is related to genes, but it is an organism's phenotype—its physical traits, metabolism, and behavior—that is directly exposed to the environment. Depending on which phenotypes in a population are favored by natural selection, three general outcomes are possible. **Directional selection** shifts the overall makeup of the population by acting against individuals at one of the phenotypic extremes. **Stabilizing selection** favors intermediate phenotypes. **Disruptive selection** typically occurs when environmental conditions vary in a way that favors individuals at both ends of a phenotypic range over individuals with intermediate phenotypes. To visualize how each mode of selection affects the distribution of phenotypes, let's look at an imaginary mouse population that has a heritable variation in fur coloration. The graphs at the bottom of the page show an example of each mode of selection in a natural population.

Frequency of individuals

Distribution of phenotypes in original population

Phenotypes (fur color)

Adaptation to darker environment, such as a fire-blackened landscape

Adaptation to a patchy environment, such as light-colored soil with scattered dark rocks

Directional selection

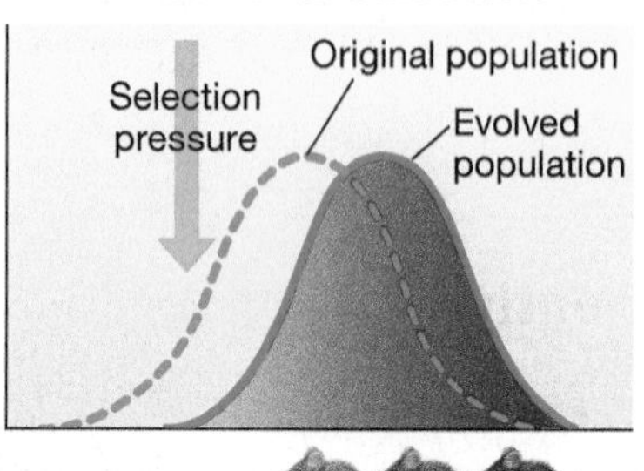

Common when a population's environment changes or when members of a population migrate to a different habitat

Stabilizing selection

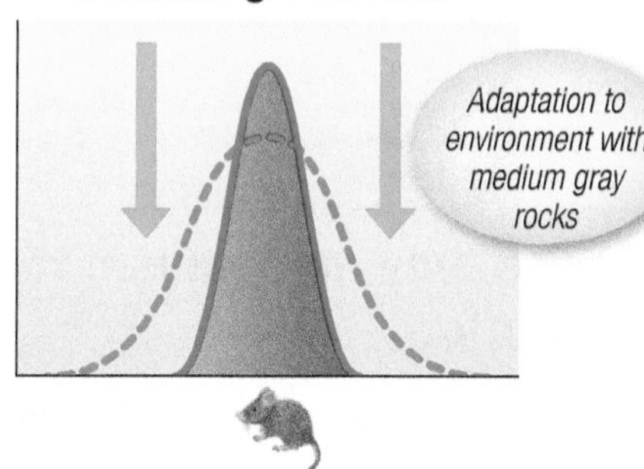

Adaptation to environment with medium gray rocks

Removes extreme phenotypes and maintains the status quo for a particular character

Disruptive selection

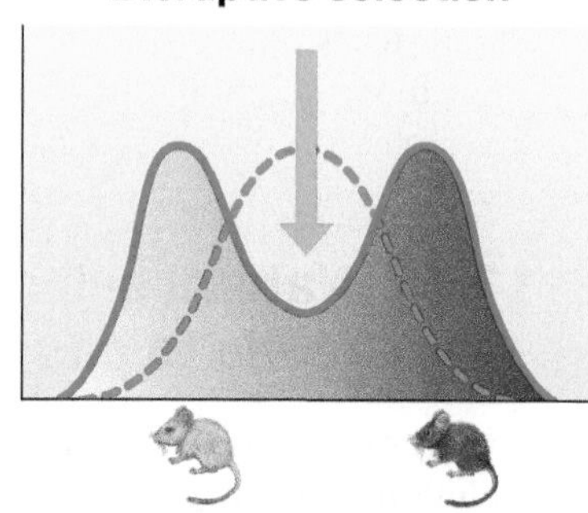

Favors extreme phenotypes, leading to two or more contrasting phenotypes in the same population

Cliff swallows

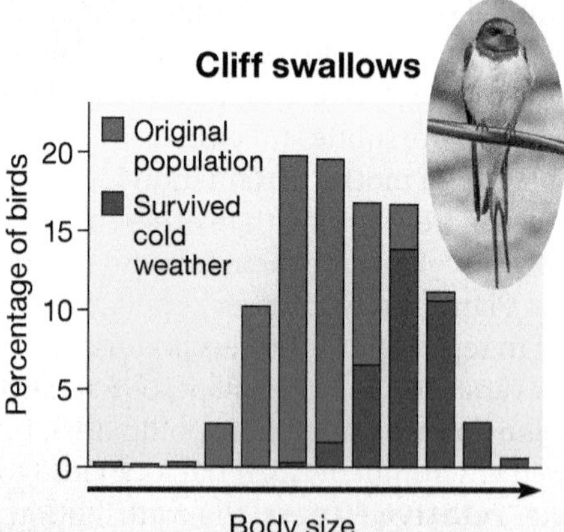

In a population of cliff swallows, birds with larger bodies survived an unusual period of cold weather.

Human birth weight

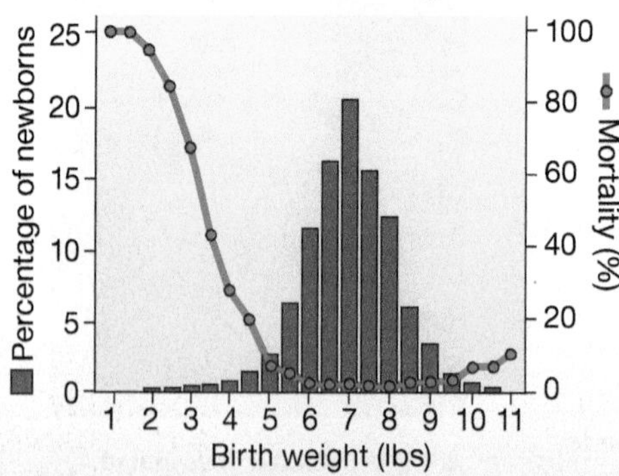

Birth weights of most human babies are in the range of 6 to 8 pounds. Babies who are either much smaller or much larger are less likely to survive.

African black-bellied finches

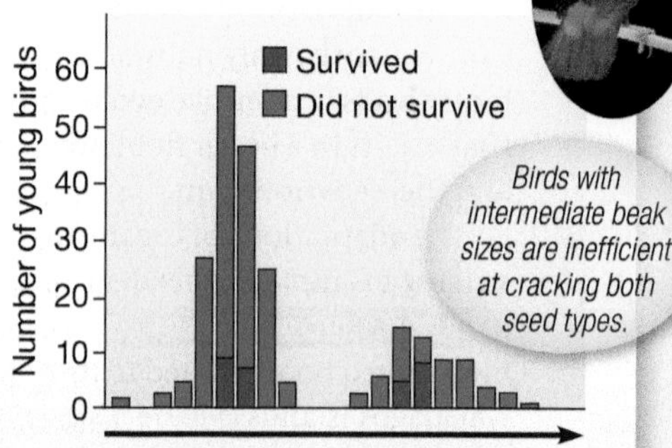

Birds with intermediate beak sizes are inefficient at cracking both seed types.

Young African black-bellied finches with small beaks, which feed mainly on soft seeds, and those with large beaks, which feed on mainly on hard seeds, are more likely to survive than those with medium-sized beaks.

? **What type of selection probably resulted in the color variations evident in the garter snakes in Figure 13.8?**

■ Disruptive selection

13.15 Sexual selection may lead to phenotypic differences between males and females

Darwin was the first to examine **sexual selection**, a form of natural selection in which individuals with certain traits are more likely than other individuals to obtain mates. The males and females of an animal species obviously have different reproductive organs. But they may also have secondary sexual characteristics, noticeable differences not directly associated with reproduction or survival. This distinction in appearance, called **sexual dimorphism**, is often manifested in a size difference, but it can also include forms of adornment, such as manes on lions or colorful plumage on birds (Figure 13.15A). Males are usually the showier sex, at least among vertebrates.

In some species, individuals compete directly with members of the same sex for mates (Figure 13.15B). This type of sexual selection is called intrasexual selection (within the same sex, most often the males). Contests may involve physical combat but are more often ritualized displays (see Module 35.19). Intrasexual selection is frequently found in species where the winning individual acquires a harem of mates.

In a more common type of sexual selection, called intersexual selection (between sexes) or mate choice, individuals of one sex (usually females) are choosy in selecting their mates. Males with the largest or most colorful adornments are often the most attractive to females. The extraordinary feathers of a peacock's tail are an example of this sort of "choose me" statement. What intrigued Darwin is that some of these mate-attracting features do not seem to be otherwise adaptive and may in fact pose some risks. For example, showy plumage may make male birds more visible to predators. But if such secondary sexual characteristics help a male gain a mate, then they will be reinforced over the generations for the most Darwinian of reasons—because they enhance reproductive success. Every time a female chooses a mate based on a certain appearance or behavior, she perpetuates the alleles that influenced her to make that choice and allows a male with that particular phenotype to perpetuate his alleles.

What is the advantage to females of being choosy? One hypothesis is that females prefer male traits that are correlated with "good genes." In several bird species, research has shown that traits preferred by females, such as bright beaks or long tails, are related to overall male health. The "good genes" hypothesis was also tested in gray tree frogs. Female frogs prefer to mate with males that give long mating calls (Figure 13.15C). Researchers collected eggs from wild gray tree frogs. Half of each female's eggs were fertilized with sperm from long-calling males, and the others with sperm from short-calling males. The offspring of long-calling male frogs grew bigger, grew faster, and survived better than their half-siblings fathered by short-calling males. The duration of a male's mating call was shown to be indicative of the male's overall genetic quality, supporting the hypothesis that female mate choice can be based on a trait that indicates whether the male has "good genes."

Next we return to the concept of directional selection, focusing on the evolution of drug resistance in microorganisms that cause disease.

▲ Figure 13.15A Extreme sexual dimorphism (peacock and peahen)

▲ Figure 13.15B A contest for access to mates between two male elks

▲ Figure 13.15C A male gray tree frog calling for mates

? Males with the most elaborate ornamentation may garner the most mates. How might choosing such a mate be advantageous to a female?

■ An elaborate display may signal good health and therefore good genes, which in turn could be passed along to the female's offspring.

13.16 The evolution of drug-resistant microorganisms is a serious public health concern

EVOLUTION CONNECTION

As you probably know, antibiotics are drugs that kill infectious microorganisms. Before antibiotics, people often died from bacterial diseases such as whooping cough, and a minor wound—a razor nick or a scratch from a rose thorn—could result in a fatal infection. A new era in human health followed the introduction of penicillin, the first widely used antibiotic, in the 1940s. Suddenly, many diseases that had often been fatal could easily be cured.

Medical experts now fear that the process of evolution could end the era of antibiotics. In the same way that pesticides select for resistant insects, antibiotics select for resistant bacteria. A gene that codes for an enzyme that breaks down an antibiotic or a mutation that alters the binding site of an antibiotic can make a bacterium and its offspring resistant to that antibiotic. Again we see both the random and nonrandom aspects of natural selection—the random genetic mutations in bacteria and the nonrandom selective effects as the environment favors the antibiotic-resistant phenotype. The same explanation applies to the evolution of chloroquine resistance in populations of the parasitic microbe that causes malaria, which you learned about in the chapter introduction. It's only a matter of time before the effectiveness of artemisinin is also lost to natural selection.

The rapid evolution of antibiotic resistance has been fueled by their widespread use—and misuse. Livestock producers add antibiotics to animal feed as a growth promoter and to prevent illness, practices that may select for bacteria resistant to standard antibiotics. Doctors may overprescribe antibiotics. Patients may stop taking the medication as soon as they feel better. This allows mutant bacteria that are killed more slowly by the drug to survive and multiply. Subsequent mutations in such bacteria may lead to full-blown antibiotic resistance.

A formidable "superbug" known as MRSA (methicillin-resistant *Staphylococcus aureus*) was the first sign that the power of antibiotics might be fading. *S. aureus* ("staph") is common in health-care facilities, where natural selection for antibiotic resistance is strong because of the extensive use of antibiotics. Staph outbreaks also occur in community settings such as athletic facilities, schools, and military barracks. Some staph infections cause relatively minor skin disorders, but when bacteria invade the bloodstream, staph infections can be fatal. Although deaths from invasive MRSA acquired at health-care facilities have declined recently as a result of preventative measures, MRSA remains a serious threat to public health.

Medical and pharmaceutical researchers are engaged in a race against the powerful force of evolution on many fronts. In 2013, the Centers for Disease Control (CDC) reported that drug-resistant microorganisms infect more than 2 million people and cause 23,000 deaths in the United States each year. The CDC identified 15 microorganisms that pose urgent or serious threats to public health. Some of the infections are associated with health-care facilities; others are passed on by contaminated food and water, sexual contact, or droplets exhaled from the respiratory tract of an infected person. Figure 13.16 shows the estimated percentage of infections by antibiotic-resistant strains for several diseases.

How does evolution hinder attempts to eradicate disease?

? **Explain why the following statement is incorrect: "Antibiotics have created resistant bacteria."**

The use of antibiotics did not cause bacteria to make new alleles. Rather, antibiotic use has increased the frequency of alleles for resistance that were already naturally present in bacterial populations.

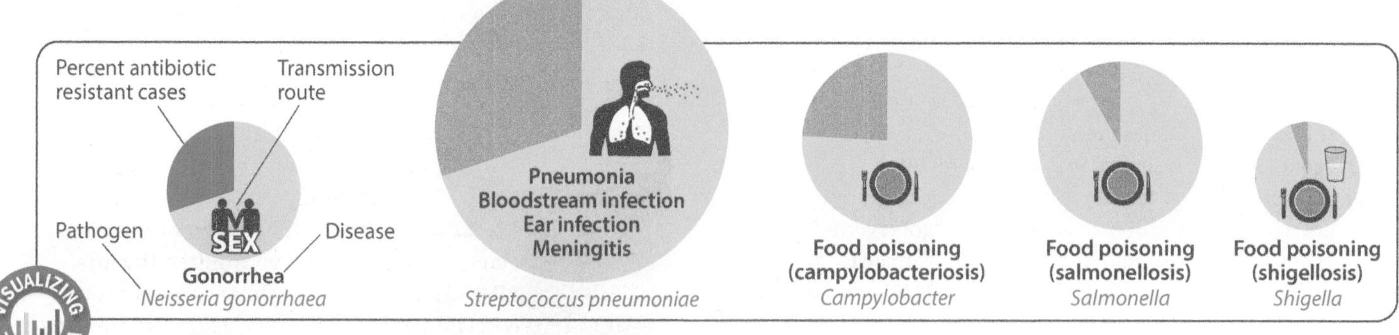

▲ **Figure 13.16 Urgent (red) and serious (orange) threats from antibiotic-resistant bacteria. Circle area represents the total numbers of infections; slices show the percent caused by antibiotic-resistant strains.**

Data from Centers for Disease Control and Prevention, cdc.gov.

13.17 Diploidy and balancing selection preserve genetic variation

As natural selection acts on variants within a population, the population becomes better suited for life in its environment. But what prevents natural selection from eliminating all variation as it selects against unfavorable genotypes? Why aren't less adaptive alleles eliminated as the "best" alleles are passed to the next generation? It turns out that the tendency for natural selection to reduce variation in a population is countered by mechanisms that maintain variation.

Most eukaryotes are diploid. Having two sets of chromosomes helps to prevent populations from becoming genetically uniform. As you know, natural selection acts on the phenotype, and recessive alleles only influence the phenotype of a homozygous recessive individual. In a heterozygote, a recessive allele is, in effect, protected from natural selection. The "hiding" of recessive alleles in heterozygotes can maintain a huge pool of alleles that may not be favored under present conditions but that could be advantageous if the environment changes.

In some cases, genetic variation is preserved rather than reduced by natural selection. **Balancing selection** occurs when natural selection maintains stable frequencies of two or more phenotypic forms in a population.

Heterozygote advantage is a type of balancing selection in which heterozygous individuals have greater reproductive success than either type of homozygote, with the result that two or more alleles for a gene are maintained in the population. An example of heterozygote advantage is the protection from malaria conferred by sickle-cell hemoglobin (see Module 9.13). The frequency of the sickle-cell allele is generally highest in areas where malaria is a major cause of death, such as West Africa (Figure 13.17). Heterozygotes are protected from the most severe effects of malaria. Individuals who are homozygous for the normal hemoglobin allele are selected against by malaria. Individuals homozygous for the sickle-cell allele are selected against by sickle-cell disease. Thus, sickle-cell hemoglobin is an evolutionary response to a fatal disease that first emerged in the environment of humans around 10,000 years ago. Notice that it is not an ideal solution—even heterozygotes may have health problems—but adaptations are often compromises.

Some of the genetic variation in a population probably has little or no impact on reproductive success. But even if only a fraction of the variation in a gene pool affects reproductive success, that is still an enormous resource of raw material for natural selection and the adaptive evolution it brings about.

? **Why would natural selection tend to reduce genetic variation more in populations of haploid organisms than in populations of diploid organisms?**

All alleles in a haploid organism are phenotypically expressed and are hence screened by natural selection.

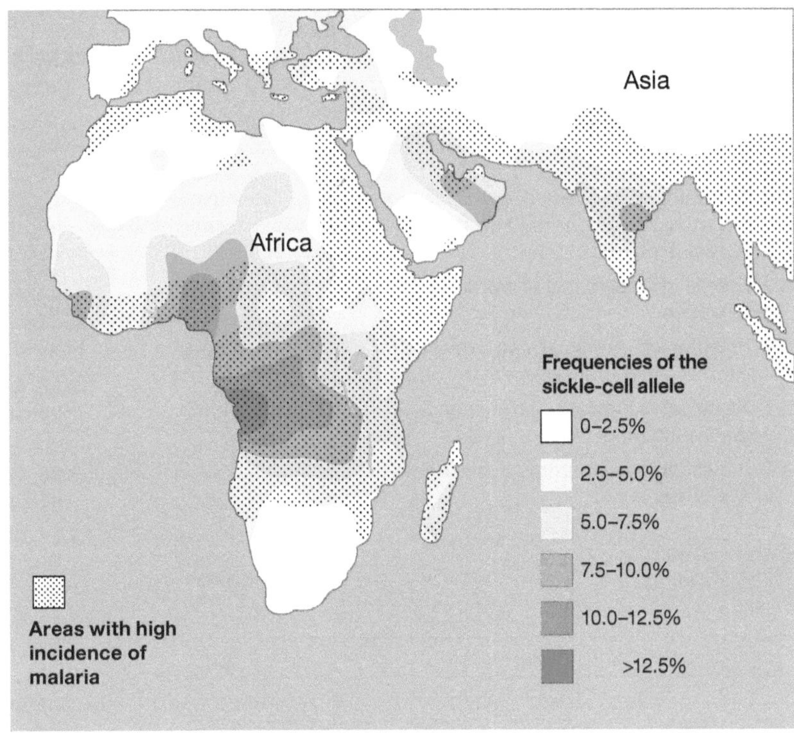

Adapted from A.C. Allison, Abnormal hemoglobins and erythrovute enzyme-deficiency traits, Genetic variation in human populations, G.A. Harrison, ed. Oxford, *Elsevier Science* (1961).

▲ **Figure 13.17** **Map of malaria and sickle-cell allele**

13.18 Natural selection cannot fashion perfect organisms

Though natural selection leads to adaptation, there are several reasons why nature abounds with organisms that seem to be less than ideally "engineered" for their lifestyles.

1. *Selection can act only on existing variations.* Natural selection favors only the fittest variants from the phenotypes that are available, which may not be the ideal traits. New, advantageous alleles do not arise on demand.
2. *Evolution is limited by historical constraints.* Each species has a legacy of descent with modification from ancestral forms. Evolution does not scrap ancestral anatomy and build each new complex structure from scratch. Rather, it co-opts existing structures and adapts them to new situations. Thus, as birds and bats evolved from four-legged ancestors, their existing forelimbs took on new functions for flight and each lineage was left with only two limbs for walking.
3. *Adaptations are often compromises.* Each organism must do many different things. A blue-footed booby uses its webbed feet to swim after prey in the ocean, but these same feet make for clumsy travel on land.
4. *Chance, natural selection, and the environment interact.* Chance events often affect the genetic makeup of populations. When a storm blows insects over an ocean to an island, the wind does not necessarily transport the individuals that are best suited to the new environment. In small populations, genetic drift can result in the loss of beneficial alleles. In addition, the environment may change unpredictably from year to year, again limiting the extent to which adaptive evolution results in a close match between organisms and the environment.

With all these constraints, we cannot expect evolution to craft perfect organisms. Natural selection operates on a "better than" basis. Evidence for evolution is seen in the imperfections of the organisms it produces as well as in adaptations.

? **Humans owe much of their physical versatility and athleticism to their flexible limbs and joints. But we are prone to sprains, torn ligaments, and dislocations. Why?**

Adaptations are compromises: Structural reinforcement has been compromised as agility was selected for.

CHAPTER

13 REVIEW

For practice quizzes, BioFlix animations, MP3 tutorials, video tutors, and more study tools designed for this textbook, go to MasteringBiology™

REVIEWING THE CONCEPTS

Darwin's Theory of Evolution 13.1–13.7

13.1 A sea voyage helped Darwin frame his theory of evolution. Darwin's theory differed greatly from the long-held notion of a young Earth inhabited by unchanging species. Darwin called his theory descent with modification, which explains that all of life is connected by common ancestry and that descendants have accumulated adaptations to changing environments over vast spans of time.

13.2 The study of fossils provides strong evidence for evolution. The fossil record reveals the historical sequence in which organisms have evolved.

13.3 Fossils of transitional forms support Darwin's theory of evolution.

13.4 Homologies provide strong evidence for evolution. Structural and molecular homologies reveal evolutionary relationships.

13.5 Homologies indicate patterns of descent that can be shown on an evolutionary tree.

13.6 Darwin proposed natural selection as the mechanism of evolution.

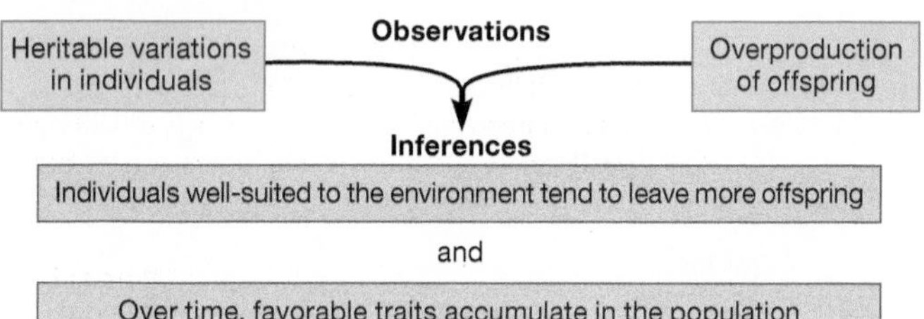

13.7 Scientists can observe natural selection in action.

The Evolution of Populations 13.8–13.11

13.8 Mutation and sexual reproduction produce the genetic variation that makes evolution possible.

13.9 Evolution occurs within populations. Microevolution is a change in the frequencies of alleles in a population's gene pool.

13.10 The Hardy-Weinberg equation can test whether a population is evolving. The Hardy-Weinberg equilibrium states that allele and genotype frequencies will remain constant if a population is large, mating is random, and there is no mutation, gene flow, or natural selection.

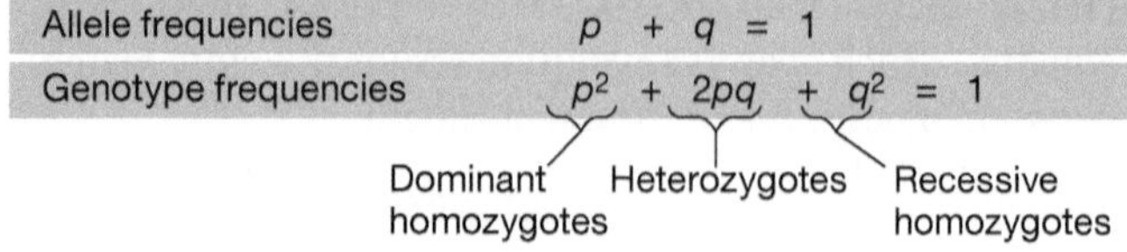

13.11 The Hardy-Weinberg equation is useful in public health science.

Mechanisms of Microevolution 13.12–13.18

13.12 Natural selection, genetic drift, and gene flow can cause microevolution. The bottleneck effect and founder effect lead to genetic drift.

13.13 Natural selection is the only mechanism that consistently leads to adaptive evolution. Relative fitness is the relative contribution an individual makes to the gene pool of the next generation. As a result of natural selection, favorable traits increase in a population.

13.14 Natural selection can alter variation in a population in three ways.

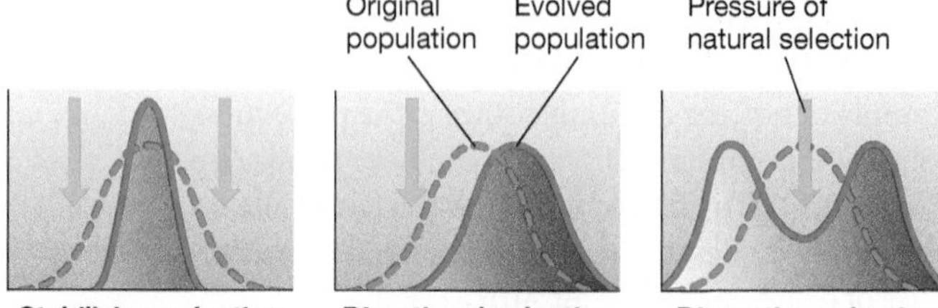

13.15 Sexual selection may lead to phenotypic differences between males and females. Secondary sex characteristics can give individuals an advantage in mating.

13.16 The evolution of drug-resistant microorganisms is a serious public health concern.

13.17 Diploidy and balancing selection preserve genetic variation. Diploidy preserves variation by "hiding" recessive alleles. Balancing selection may result from heterozygote advantage.

13.18 Natural selection cannot fashion perfect organisms. Natural selection can act only on available variation; anatomical structures result from modified ancestral forms; adaptations are often compromises; and chance, natural selection, and the environment interact.

CONNECTING THE CONCEPTS

1. Summarize the key points of Darwin's theory of descent with modification, including his proposed mechanism of evolution.
2. Complete this concept map describing potential causes of evolutionary change within populations.

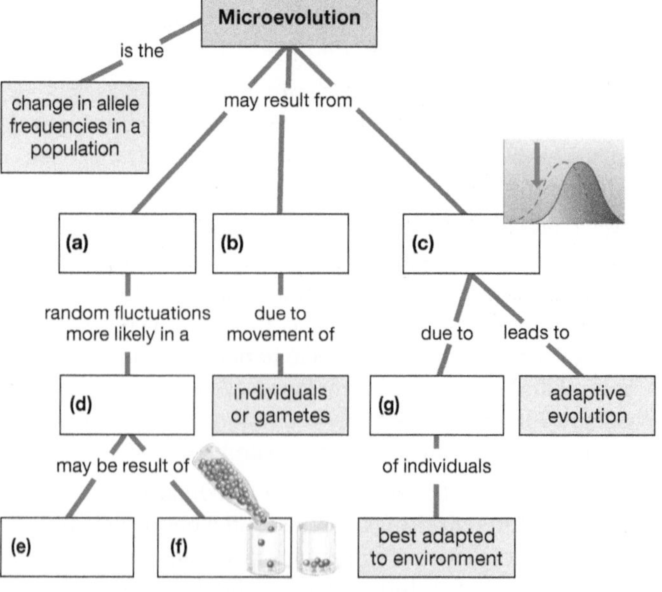

TESTING YOUR KNOWLEDGE

Level 1: Knowledge/Comprehension

3. Which of the following did *not* influence Darwin as he synthesized the theory of evolution by natural selection?
   a. examples of artificial selection that produce large and relatively rapid changes in domesticated species
   b. Lyell's *Principles of Geology*, on gradual geologic changes
   c. comparisons of fossils with living organisms
   d. Mendel's paper describing the laws of inheritance
4. Natural selection is sometimes described as "survival of the fittest." Which of the following best measures an organism's fitness?
   a. how many fertile offspring it produces
   b. how strong it is when pitted against others of its species
   c. its ability to withstand environmental extremes
   d. how much food it is able to make or obtain
5. In an area of erratic rainfall, a biologist found that grass plants with alleles for curled leaves reproduced better in dry years, and plants with alleles for flat leaves reproduced better in wet years. This situation would tend to ________. (*Explain your answer.*)
   a. cause genetic drift in the grass population.
   b. preserve genetic variation in the grass population.
   c. lead to stabilizing selection in the grass population.
   d. lead to uniformity in the grass population.
6. If an allele is recessive and lethal in homozygotes before they reproduce,
   a. the allele will be removed from the population by natural selection in approximately 1,000 years.
   b. the allele will likely remain in the population at a low frequency because it cannot be selected against in heterozygotes.
   c. the fitness of the homozygous recessive genotype is 0.
   d. both b and c are correct.
7. In a population with two alleles, B and b, the allele frequency of b is 0.4. B is dominant to b. What is the frequency of individuals with the dominant phenotype if the population is in Hardy-Weinberg equilibrium?
   a. 0.16
   b. 0.36
   c. 0.48
   d. 0.84
8. Within a few weeks of treatment with the drug 3TC, a patient's HIV population consists entirely of 3TC-resistant viruses. How can this result best be explained?
   a. HIV can change its surface proteins and resist vaccines.
   b. The patient must have become reinfected with a resistant virus.
   c. A few drug-resistant viruses were present at the start of treatment, and natural selection increased their frequency.
   d. HIV began making drug-resistant versions of its enzymes in response to the drug.

Level 2: Application/Analysis

9. In the late 1700s, machines that could blast through rock to build roads and railways were invented, exposing deep layers of rocks. How would you expect this development to aid the science of paleontology?
10. Write a paragraph briefly describing the kinds of scientific evidence for evolution.
11. In the early 1800s, French naturalist Jean Baptiste Lamarck suggested that the best explanation for the relationship of fossils to current organisms is that life evolves. He proposed that by using or not using its body parts, an individual may change its traits and then pass those changes on to its offspring. He suggested, for instance, that the ancestors of the giraffe had lengthened their necks by stretching higher and higher into the trees to reach leaves. Evaluate Lamarck's hypotheses from the perspective of present-day scientific knowledge.
12. Sickle-cell disease is caused by a recessive allele. Roughly one out of every 400 African Americans (0.25%) is afflicted with sickle-cell disease. Use the Hardy-Weinberg equation to calculate the percentage of African Americans who are carriers of the sickle-cell allele. (*Hint*: $q^2 = 0.0025$.)
13. It seems logical that natural selection would work toward genetic uniformity; the genotypes that are most fit produce the most offspring, increasing the frequency of adaptive alleles and eliminating less adaptive alleles. Yet there remains a great deal of genetic variation within populations. Describe factors that contribute to this variation.

Level 3: Synthesis/Evaluation

14. **SCIENTIFIC THINKING** Cetaceans are fully aquatic mammals that evolved from terrestrial ancestors. Gather information about the respiratory system of cetaceans and describe how it illustrates the statement made in Module 13.18 that "Evolution is limited by historical constraints."
15. A population of snails is preyed on by birds that break the snails open on rocks, eat the soft bodies, and leave the shells. The snails occur in both striped and unstriped forms. In one area, researchers counted both live snails and broken shells. Their data are summarized below:

	Striped	Unstriped	Total	Percent Striped
Living	264	296	560	47.1
Broken	486	377	863	56.3

   Which snail form seems better adapted to this environment? Why? Predict how the frequencies of striped and unstriped snails might change in the future.

16. Advocates of "scientific creationism" and "intelligent design" lobby school districts for such things as a ban on teaching evolution, equal time in science classes to teach alternative versions of the origin and history of life, or disclaimers in textbooks stating that evolution is "just a theory." They argue that it is only fair to let students evaluate both evolution and the idea that all species were created by God as the Bible relates or that, because organisms are so complex and well adapted, they must have been created by an intelligent designer. Do you think that alternative views of evolution should be taught in science courses? Why or why not?

Answers to all questions can be found in Appendix 4.

CHAPTER 14

The Origin of Species

Compared to many male birds that sport brilliant plumage—the shimmering eyes of the peacock's tail or the fire-engine red feathers of the cardinal, for example—the Vogelkop bowerbird (*Amblyornis inornata*) is a rather dull fellow. However, he does have a unique talent: He's a fabulous decorator. Bowerbirds, which are native to New Guinea and Australia, are named for the structure, called a bower, that the male weaves from twigs and grasses to attract females. The hut-style bower in the photo at the right built by a Vogelkop bowerbird, is about 2 meters (6.5 feet) wide and 1 meter high.

Can we observe speciation occurring?

After completing his elaborate construction project, the male bowerbird collects objects such as fruits, seeds, insect parts, rocks, flowers, and leaves and arranges them artfully by color and type. Individual males differ in their preferences for certain colors and arrangements of objects. Females tour the bowers of local males, inspecting each bower carefully while its owner courts her with a song and dance. A female may visit promising candidates multiple times before finally mating with one.

Not all Vogelkop bowerbirds construct displays like the one in the photo. The males of another population build a simpler structure consisting of sticks loosely woven around a central sapling. The objects ornamenting the display are all drab-colored. Researchers hypothesize that this divergence in display preferences has started the two populations on separate evolutionary paths that may eventually lead to two unique species of bowerbird.

In this chapter, we explore how natural selection and other processes may lead to speciation—the origin of new species. Speciation is responsible for the amazing diversity of life on Earth. We begin with the biological definition of a species and describe the mechanisms through which new species may evolve. We also explore some of the evidence for speciation and how scientists study this evolutionary process.

BIG IDEAS

Defining Species (14.1–14.3)

A species can be defined as a group of populations whose members can produce fertile offspring.

Mechanisms of Speciation (14.4–14.11)

Speciation can take place with or without geographic isolation, as long as reproductive barriers evolve that keep species separate.

Defining Species

14.1 The origin of species is the source of biological diversity

Darwin was eager to explore landforms newly emerged from the sea when he came to the Galápagos Islands. He noted that these volcanic islands, despite their geologic youth, were teeming with plants and animals found nowhere else in the world. He realized that these species, like the islands, were relatively new. He wrote in his diary: "Both in space and time, we seem to be brought somewhat near to that great fact—that mystery of mysteries—the first appearance of new beings on this Earth."

Even though Darwin titled his seminal work *On the Origin of Species by Means of Natural Selection*, most of his theory of evolution focused on the role of natural selection in the gradual adaptation of a population to its environment. We call this process microevolution—changes in the gene pool of a population from one generation to the next (see Module 13.9). But if microevolution were *all* that happened, then Earth would be inhabited only by a highly adapted version of the first form of life.

The "mystery of mysteries" that fascinated Darwin is **speciation**, the process by which one species splits into two or more species. He envisioned the history of life as a tree, with multiple branchings from a common trunk out to the tips of the youngest twigs (**Figure 14.1**).

Each time speciation occurs, the diversity of life increases. Over the course of 3.5 billion years, an ancestral species first gave rise to two or more different species, which then branched to new lineages, which branched again, until we arrive at the millions of species that live, or once lived, on Earth. This origin of species explains both the diversity and the unity of life. When one species splits into two, the new species share many characteristics because they are descended from a common ancestor.

? How does microevolution differ from speciation?

■ Microevolution involves evolutionary changes within a population; speciation occurs when a population changes enough that it diverges from its parent species and becomes a new species.

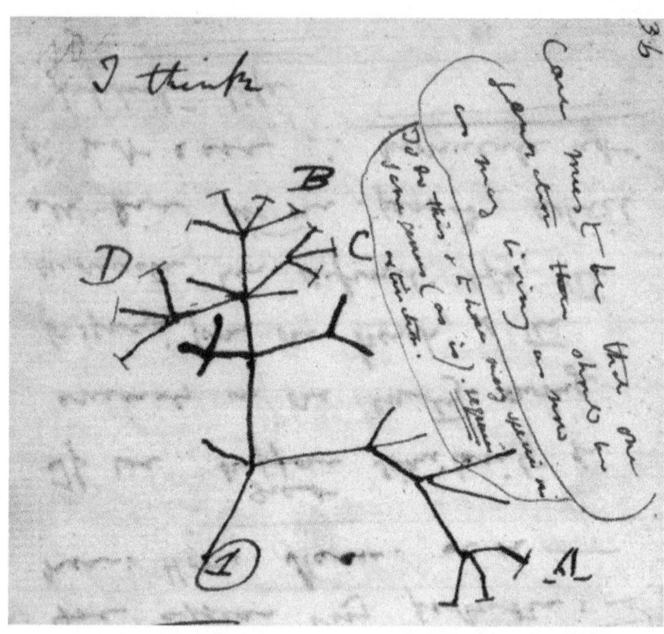

▲ **Figure 14.1** Sketch made by Darwin as he pondered the origin of species

14.2 There are several ways to define a species

The word *species* is from the Latin for "kind" or "appearance," and indeed, even young children learn to distinguish between kinds of plants and animals—between roses and dandelions or dogs and cats—from differences in their appearance. Although the basic idea of species as distinct life-forms seems intuitive, devising a more formal definition is not so easy.

In many cases, the differences between two species are obvious. In other cases, the differences between two species are not so plain to see. For example, the two birds in **Figure 14.2A** look much the same, but they are different species—the one on the left is an eastern meadowlark (*Sturnella magna*); the bird on the right is a western meadowlark (*Sturnella neglecta*). They are distinct species because their songs and other behaviors are different enough that each type of meadowlark breeds only with individuals of its own species.

▲ **Figure 14.2A** Similarity between two species: the eastern meadowlark (left) and western meadowlark (right)

How similar are members of the same species? Whereas the individuals of many species exhibit fairly limited variation in physical appearance, certain other species—our own, for example—seem extremely varied. Despite the physical diversity within our species (partly illustrated in **Figure 14.2B**, on the facing page) humans all belong to the same species, *Homo sapiens*.

▲ **Figure 14.2B** Diversity within one species

The Biological Species Concept How then do biologists define a species? The primary definition of species used in this book is called the **biological species concept**. It defines a **species** as a group of populations whose members have the potential to interbreed in nature and produce fertile offspring (offspring that themselves can reproduce). A businesswoman in Manhattan may be unlikely to meet a dairy farmer in Mongolia, but if the two should happen to meet and mate, they could have viable babies that develop into fertile adults. Thus, members of a biological species are united by being reproductively compatible, at least potentially. Conversely, it is reproductive incompatibility that keeps one species distinct from others. The existence of barriers that stop members of two species from producing viable, fertile offspring with each other is called **reproductive isolation**.

Identifying species solely on the basis of reproductive isolation can be more complex than it may seem. Many pairs of species are distinct and yet are capable of interbreeding. The offspring of pairs of clearly distinct species are called **hybrids**. An example is the grizzly bear (*Ursus arctos*) and the polar bear (*Ursus maritimus*), whose hybrid offspring have been called "grolar bears" (Figure 14.2C). The two species have been known to interbreed in zoos. With melting polar sea ice bringing the two species into contact more often in the wild, four grolar bears have been shot by hunters, and several other suspected hybrids have been sighted in recent years.

Grizzly bear

Polar bear

Hybrid "grolar" bear

▲ **Figure 14.2C** Hybridization between two species of bears

There are other instances in which applying the biological species concept is problematic. For example, there is no way to determine whether organisms that are now known only through fossils were once able to interbreed. Also, this criterion is useless for organisms such as prokaryotes that reproduce asexually. Because of such limitations, alternative species concepts are useful in certain situations.

Other Definitions of Species For most organisms—sexual, asexual, and fossils alike—classification is based mainly on physical traits such as shape, size, and other features of morphology (form). This **morphological species concept** has been used to identify most of the 1.8 million species that have been named to date. The advantages of this concept are that it can be applied to asexual organisms and fossils and does not require information on possible interbreeding. The disadvantage, however, is that this approach relies on subjective criteria, and researchers may disagree on which features distinguish a species.

Another species definition, the **ecological species concept**, identifies species in terms of their ecological niches, focusing on unique adaptations to particular roles in a biological community. For example, two species of fish may be similar in appearance but distinguishable based on what they eat or the depth of water in which they are usually found.

Finally, the **phylogenetic species concept** defines a species as the smallest group of individuals that share a common ancestor and thus form one branch on the tree of life. Biologists trace the phylogenetic history of such a species by comparing its characteristics, such as morphology, DNA sequences, or biochemical pathways, with those of other organisms. These sorts of analyses can distinguish groups that are generally similar yet different enough to be considered separate species. Of course, agreeing on the amount of difference required to establish separate species remains a challenge.

Each species definition is useful, depending on the situation and the questions being asked. The biological species concept, however, helps focus on how these discrete groups of organisms arise and are maintained by reproductive isolation. Because reproductive isolation is an essential factor in the evolution of many species, we look at it more closely next.

? **Which species concepts could you apply to both asexual and sexual species? Explain.**

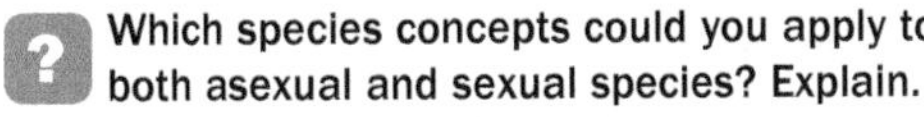

■ The morphological, ecological, and phylogenetic species
concepts could all be used because they do not rely on the
criterion of reproductive isolation.

VISUALIZING THE CONCEPT

14.3 Reproductive barriers keep species separate

Clearly, a fly will not mate with a frog or a fern. But what prevents species that are closely related from interbreeding? Reproductive isolation depends on one or more types of reproductive barriers—biological features of the organism that prevent individuals of different species from interbreeding successfully.

The various types of reproductive barriers that isolate the gene pools of species can be categorized as either prezygotic or postzygotic, depending on whether they function before or after zygotes (fertilized eggs) form. **Prezygotic barriers** prevent mating or fertilization between species. **Postzygotic barriers** operate after hybrid zygotes have formed.

PREZYGOTIC BARRIERS

Type of isolation

Habitat
Lack of opportunities to encounter each other

The garter snake *Thamnophis atratus* lives mainly in water.

The garter snake *Thamnophis sirtalis* lives on land.

Species are not necessarily separated by obvious physical barriers. These snakes occupy different habitats in the same area.

Temporal
Breeding at different times or seasons

The eastern spotted skunk (*Spilogale putorius*) breeds in late winter.

The western spotted skunk (*Spilogale gracilis*) breeds in the fall.

Temporal isolation also happens in plants that flower during different seasons or whose flowers open at different times during the day.

Behavioral
Failure to send or receive appropriate signals

The blue-footed booby (*Sula nebouxii*) performs an elaborate courtship dance.

The masked booby (*Sula dactylatra*) performs a different courtship ritual.

In another example, male fireflies signal to females of the same species by blinking their lights in the particular rhythm of their species. Females respond only to that rhythm.

Mechanical
Physical incompatibility of reproductive parts

Heliconia pogonantha is pollinated by hummingbirds with long, curved bills.

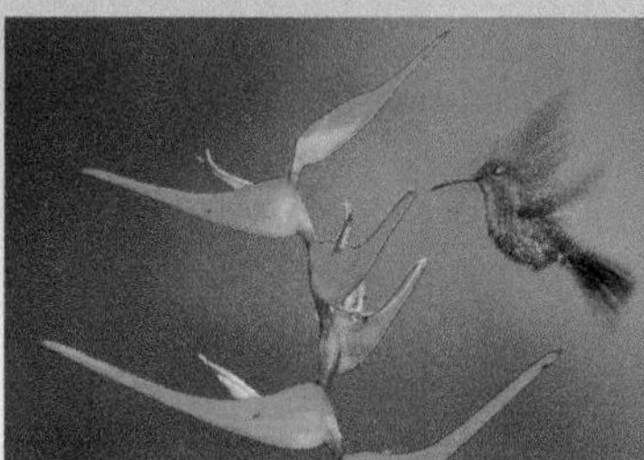

Heliconia latispatha is pollinated by hummingbirds with short, straight bills.

Pollinators pick up pollen from the male parts of one flower and transfer it to the female parts of another flower. Floral characteristics determine the best fit between pollinator and flower.

Purple sea urchin (*Strongylocentrotus purpuratus*)

Gametic
Molecular incompatibility of eggs and sperm or pollen and stigma

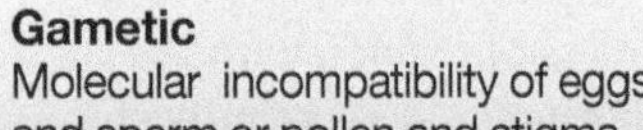

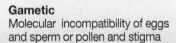

Red sea urchin (*Strongylocentrotus franciscanus*)

Sea urchins release their gametes into the water. Surface proteins prevent the gametes of different species from binding to each other.

POSTZYGOTIC BARRIERS

Reduced hybrid viability
Interaction of parental genes impairs the hybrid's development or survival.

Some species of salamander can hybridize, but their offspring do not develop fully or, like this one, are frail and will not survive long enough to reproduce.

Reduced hybrid fertility
Hybrids are vigorous but cannot produce viable offspring.

The hybrid offspring of a horse and a donkey is a mule, which is robust but sterile.

Hybrid breakdown
Hybrids are viable and fertile, but their offspring are feeble or sterile.

The rice hybrids on the left and right are fertile, but plants of the next generation (middle) are sterile.

If chromosomes of the parent species differ in number or structure, meiosis in hybrids may fail to produce normal gametes.

? **Two closely related fish live in the same lake, but one feeds along the shoreline and the other is a bottom feeder in deep water. This is an example of ________ isolation, which is a ________ reproductive barrier.**

habitat ... prezygotic

Mechanisms of Speciation

14.4 In allopatric speciation, geographic isolation leads to speciation

A key event in the origin of a new species is the interruption of gene flow between populations of the same species. In **allopatric speciation** (from the Greek *allos*, other, and *patra*, fatherland), a population is divided into geographically isolated subpopulations. With its gene pool isolated, a splinter population can follow its own evolutionary course. Changes in allele frequencies caused by natural selection, genetic drift, and mutation will not be diluted by alleles entering from other populations (gene flow). Populations separated by a geographic barrier are known as allopatric populations.

Several geologic processes can isolate populations. For example, a large lake may subside until there are several smaller lakes, isolating certain fish populations. A stream may change course and divide populations of animals that cannot cross it. Over time, a river flowing over rock may carve a deep canyon that separates the inhabitants on either side. On a larger scale, continents themselves can split and move apart. Allopatric speciation can also occur when individuals colonize a remote area and become geographically isolated from the parent population.

How large must a geographic barrier be to interrupt gene flow between allopatric populations? The answer depends on the ability of the organisms or their gametes to move. Birds, mountain lions, and coyotes can easily cross rivers and canyons. Nor do such barriers hinder the windblown pollen of trees and the seeds of many flowering plants. In contrast, small rodents may find a canyon or a wide river a formidable barrier. The Grand Canyon and Colorado River (Figure 14.4A) separate two species of antelope squirrels. Harris's antelope squirrel (*Ammospermophilus harrisii*) inhabits the south rim. Just a few kilometers away on the north rim, but separated by the deep and wide canyon, lives the closely related white-tailed antelope squirrel (*Ammospermophilus leucurus*).

Many studies provide evidence that speciation has occurred in allopatric populations. An interesting example is the 30 species of snapping shrimp in the genus *Alpheus* that live off the Isthmus of Panama, the land bridge that connects South and North America (Figure 14.4B). Snapping shrimp are named for their unique method of capturing prey—a snap of the shrimp's large, pistol-like claw fires a high-pressure shockwave that stuns the prey. Morphological and genetic data group these shrimp into 15 pairs of species, with the members of each pair being each other's closest relative. In each case, one member of the pair lives on the Atlantic side of the isthmus, while the other lives on the Pacific side, strongly suggesting that geographic separation of the ancestral species of these snapping shrimp led to allopatric speciation.

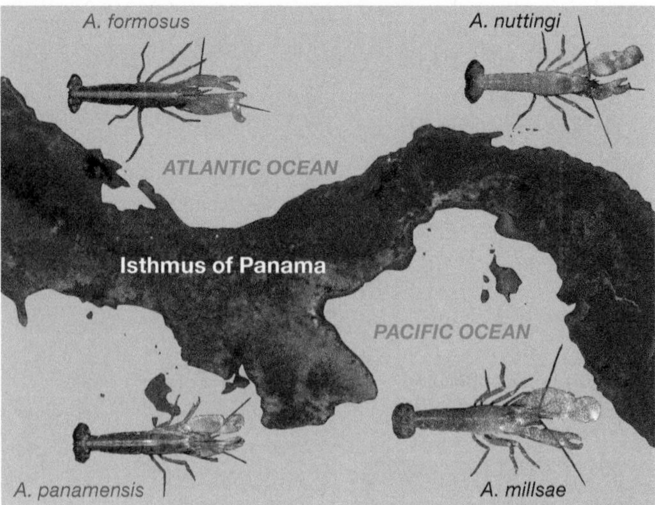

▲ Figure 14.4B Allopatric speciation in snapping shrimp: 2 of the 15 pairs of shrimp species that are separated by the Isthmus of Panama

? Geologic evidence indicates that the Isthmus of Panama gradually closed about 3 million years ago. Genetic analyses indicate that the various species of snapping shrimp originated from 9 to 3 million years ago, with the species pairs that live in deepest water diverging first. How would you interpret these data?

■ The deeper species would have been separated into two isolated populations first, which enabled them to diverge into new species first.

▲ Figure 14.4A Allopatric speciation of geographically isolated antelope squirrels

14.5 Reproductive barriers can evolve as populations diverge

Geographic isolation creates opportunities for speciation, but it does not necessarily lead to new species. Speciation occurs only when the gene pool undergoes changes that establish reproductive barriers such as those described in Module 14.3. What might cause such barriers to arise? The environment of an isolated population may include different food sources, different types of pollinators, and different predators. As a result of natural selection acting on preexisting variations—or as a result of genetic drift or mutation—a population's traits may change in ways that also establish reproductive barriers.

Researchers have successfully documented the evolution of reproductive isolation with laboratory experiments. While at Yale University, Diane Dodd tested the hypothesis that reproductive barriers can evolve as a by-product of changes in populations as they adapt to different environments. Dodd raised fruit flies on different food sources. Some populations were fed starch; others were fed maltose. After about 40 generations, populations raised on starch digested starch more efficiently, and those raised on maltose digested maltose more efficiently.

Dodd then combined flies from various populations in mating experiments. **Figure 14.5A** shows some of her results. When flies from "starch populations" were mixed with flies from "maltose populations," the flies mated more frequently with partners raised on the same food source (left grid), even when the partners came from different populations. In one of the control tests (right grid), flies taken from different populations adapted to starch were about as likely to mate with each other as with flies from their own populations. The mating preference shown in the experimental group is an example of a prezygotic barrier. The reproductive barrier was not absolute—some mating between maltose flies and starch flies did occur—but reproductive isolation was under way as these allopatric populations became adapted to different environments.

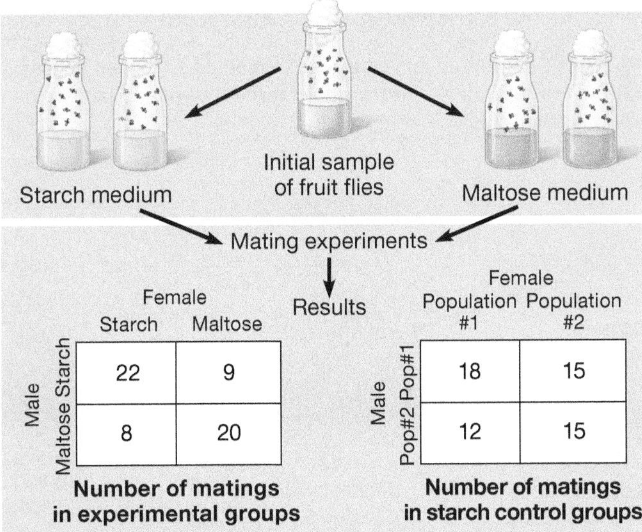

▲ **Figure 14.5A** **Evolution of reproductive barriers in laboratory populations of fruit flies adapted to different food sources**

TRY THIS In your own words, explain how the experiment was performed and interpret the results.

In plants, the preferences of pollinators may create reproductive barriers. Perhaps populations of an ancestral species became separated in environments that had either more hummingbirds than bees or vice versa. Flower color and shape would evolve through natural selection in ways that attracted the most common pollinator, and these changes would help separate the species should they later share the same region. For example, two closely related species of monkey flower are found in the same area of the Sierra Nevada, but they rarely interbreed. Bumblebees prefer the pink-flowered *Mimulus lewisii*, and hummingbirds prefer the red-flowered *Mimulus cardinalis*. Scientists experimentally exchanged the alleles for flower color between these two species. As a result, *M. lewisii* produced light orange flowers **(Figure 14.5B)** that received many more visits from hummingbirds than did the normal pink-flowered *M. lewisii*. *M. cardinalis* plants with the *M. lewisii* allele produced pinker flowers that received many more visits from bumblebees than the normal red-flowered plants. Thus, a change in flower color influenced pollinator preference, which normally provides a reproductive barrier between these two species.

Sometimes reproductive barriers can arise even when populations are not geographically separated, as we see next.

? Females of the Galápagos finch *Geospiza difficilis* respond to the songs of males from their island but ignore songs of males from other islands. How would you interpret these findings?

Behavioral barriers to reproduction have begun to develop in these allopatric (geographically separated) finch populations.

Pollinator choice in typical monkey flowers

Pollinator choice after color allele transfer

Typical *M. lewisii* (pink)

M. lewisii with red-color allele

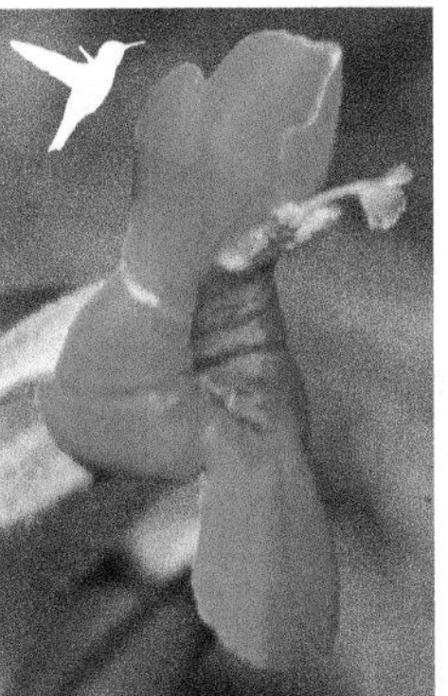

Typical *M. cardinalis* (red)

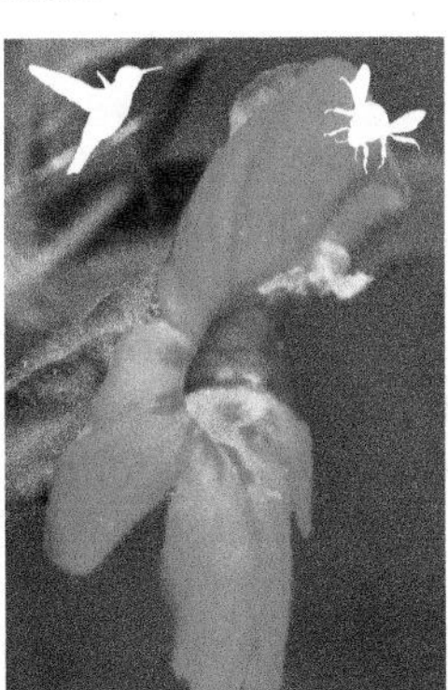

M. cardinalis with pink-color allele

▲ **Figure 14.5B** **Effect of changing color of monkey flowers on pollinator choice**

14.6 Sympatric speciation takes place without geographic isolation

In **sympatric speciation** (from the Greek *syn*, together, and *patra*, fatherland), a new species arises within the same geographic area as its parent species. Polyploidy, habitat differentiation, and sexual selection are factors that can reduce gene flow in sympatric populations.

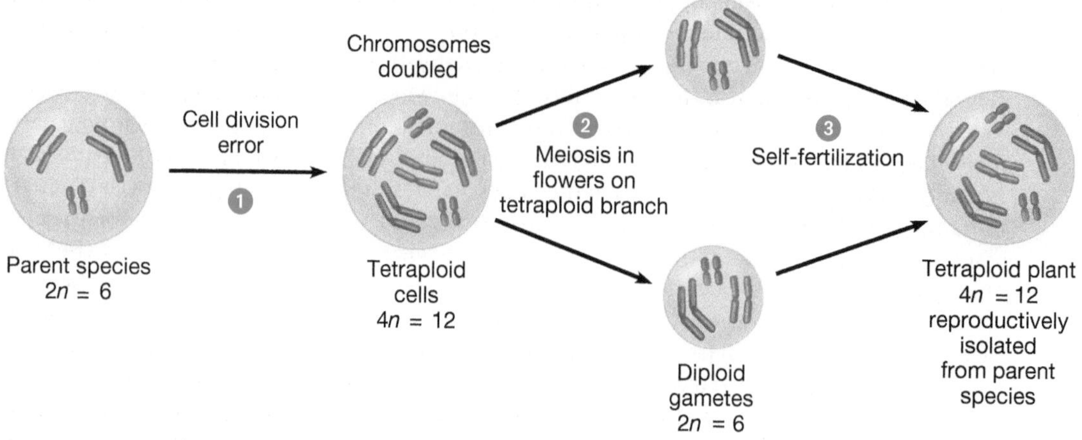

Parent species $2n = 6$
Cell division error ❶
Chromosomes doubled
Tetraploid cells $4n = 12$
❷ Meiosis in flowers on tetraploid branch
Diploid gametes $2n = 6$
❸ Self-fertilization
Tetraploid plant $4n = 12$ reproductively isolated from parent species

▲ **Figure 14.6A** Sympatric speciation by polyploidy within a single species

Many plant species have originated from sympatric speciation that occurs when accidents during cell division result in extra sets of chromosomes. New species formed in this way are **polyploid**, meaning that their cells have more than two complete sets of chromosomes. Figure 14.6A shows one way in which a tetraploid plant ($4n$, with four sets of chromosomes) can arise from a single diploid parent species. ❶ A failure of cell division after chromosome duplication could double a cell's chromosomes. ❷ If this $4n$ cell gives rise to a tetraploid branch, its flowers would produce diploid gametes. ❸ If self-fertilization occurs, as it commonly does in plants, the resulting tetraploid zygotes would develop into plants that can produce fertile tetraploid offspring by self-pollination or by mating with other tetraploids. However, the tetraploid plant cannot produce fertile offspring by mating with a parent plant. The fusion of a diploid ($2n$) gamete from the tetraploid plant and a haploid (n) gamete from the diploid parent would produce triploid ($3n$) offspring. Because odd numbers of chromosomes cannot form homologous pairs during meiosis, a triploid plant is sterile. Consequently, the tetraploid ($4n$) plant is reproductively isolated from its parent species and is a new species.

Most polyploid species, however, arise from hybridization of two different species. Figure 14.6B illustrates one way in which this can happen. ❶ Suppose the haploid gametes from two different species combine. The resulting hybrid has an odd number of chromosomes ($n = 5$), so it is sterile. ❷ However, the hybrid may reproduce asexually, as many plants can do. ❸ Subsequent errors in cell division may produce chromosome duplications that result in a diploid set of chromosomes ($2n = 10$). Now chromosomes *can* pair in meiosis, and haploid gametes will be produced; thus, a fertile polyploid species has formed. Again, this new species is reproductively isolated, this time from both parent species. Biologists have identified several plant species that originated through these mechanisms within the past 150 years—virtually instantaneously on an evolutionary time scale.

Does polyploid speciation occur in animals? It appears to happen occasionally. For example, the gray tree frog (see Figure 13.15C) is thought to have originated in this way. However, sympatric speciation in animals is more likely to happen through habitat differentiation or sexual selection than by polyploidy. Both habitat differentiation and sexual selection may have been involved in the origin of several hundred species of small fish called cichlids in Lake Victoria in East Africa. Adaptations for exploiting different food sources may have evolved in different subgroups of the original cichlid population. If those sources were in different habitats, mating between the populations would become rare, isolating their gene pools as each population becomes adapted to a different resource. As you will learn in the next module, speciation in these brightly colored fish may also have been driven by the type of sexual selection in which females choose mates based on coloration. Such mate choice can contribute to forming reproductive barriers that separate the gene pools of newly forming species. Of course, both habitat differentiation and sexual selection can also contribute to the formation of reproductive barriers between allopatric populations.

? **Revisit the reproductive barriers in Module 14.3, and choose the barrier that isolates a viable, fertile polyploid plant from its parental species.**

■ Reduced hybrid fertility

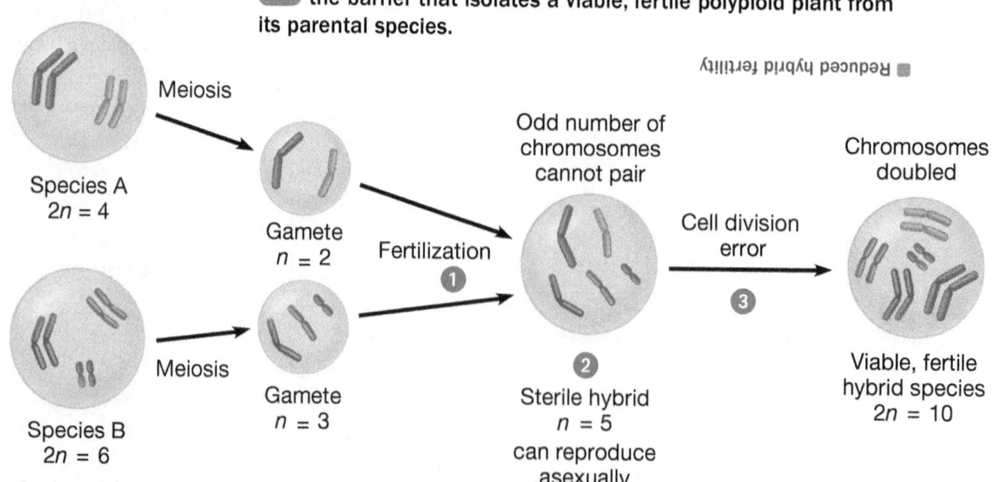

▲ **Figure 14.6B** Sympatric speciation producing a hybrid polyploid from two different species

TRY THIS Explain how a new species produced by the process shown in this figure differs from a new species produced by the process shown in Figure 14.6A.

14.7 Sexual selection can lead to speciation

SCIENTIFIC THINKING

In contrast to microevolutionary change, which may be apparent in a population within a few generations, the process of speciation is generally extremely slow. So you may be surprised to learn that we *can* see speciation occurring. Consider that life has been evolving over hundreds of millions of years and will continue to evolve. The species living today represent a snapshot, a brief instant in this vast span of time. The environment continues to change—sometimes rapidly due to human impact—and natural selection continues to act on affected populations. It is reasonable to assume that some of these populations are changing in ways that could eventually lead to speciation. Studying populations as they diverge gives biologists a window on the process of speciation. Researchers have documented at least two dozen cases in which populations are diverging as they exploit different food resources or breed in different habitats.

Can we observe speciation occurring?

The bowerbirds you read about in the chapter introduction provide an example of another means by which populations can diverge—sexual selection (see Module 13.15). Sexual selection is a form of natural selection in which individuals with certain traits are more likely to obtain mates. The authors of the bowerbird study hypothesized that the differences in male displays of the allopatric bowerbird populations resulted from changes in female preferences. Biologists have also identified several other animal populations that are diverging as a result of differences in how males attract females or how females choose mates. Because of its direct effect on reproductive success, sexual selection can interrupt gene flow within a population and may therefore be an important factor in sympatric speciation.

Biologists can also test hypotheses about the process of speciation by studying species that arose recently. Let's look at a series of investigations into the role of sexual selection in the diversification of cichlids in Lake Victoria (**Figure 14.7A**).

Cichlids are a family of fishes that live in tropical lakes and rivers. They come in all colors of the rainbow, making them favorites of the aquarium trade. Among evolutionary biologists, they are renowned for the spectacular speciations that stocked the large lakes of East Africa with more than a thousand species of cichlids in less than 100,000 years. In the largest of these lakes, Lake Victoria, roughly 500 species evolved in about 15,000 years. For comparison, there are approximately 525 species of fish in all the lakes and rivers of Europe combined. How can a single body of water host such diversity? The answer lies partly in the heterogeneity of the environment. Various species have adaptations that suit them to inhabit the lake's rocky shores, muddy bottom, or open water. Specialized feeding adaptations abound. For example, there are algae-scrapers, snail-crushers, leaf-biters, insect-eaters, and fish-hunters. The visual environment, including predominant wavelengths of light and water clarity, is also heterogeneous, a fact that is crucial to speciation via sexual selection.

▲ **Figure 14.7A** Map of East Africa showing Lake Victoria

In Lake Victoria, there are pairs of closely related cichlid species that differ only in color. Breeding males of *Pundamilia nyererei* have a bright red back and dorsal fin, while *Pundamilia pundamilia* males are metallic blue-gray (**Figure 14.7B**). Researchers hypothesized that sexual selection—divergent female preference for red or blue mates—led to reproductive isolation. Let's examine the evidence for this hypothesis.

Pundamilia nyererei

Pundamilia pundamilia

▲ **Figure 14.7B** Males of *Pundamilia nyererei* and *Pundamilia pundamilia*

Pundamilia females prefer brightly colored males. Mate-choice experiments performed in the laboratory showed that *P. nyererei* females prefer red males over blue males, and *P. pundamilia* females prefer blue males over red males. Furthermore, the vision of *P. nyererei* females is more sensitive to red light than blue light; *P. pundamilia* females are more sensitive to blue light. Researchers also demonstrated that this color sensitivity is heritable.

As mentioned above, the visual environment varies in Lake Victoria. As light travels through water, suspended particles selectively absorb and scatter the shorter (blue) wavelengths, so light becomes increasingly red with increasing depth. Thus, in deeper waters *P. nyererei* males are pleasingly apparent to females with red-sensitive vision but virtually invisible to *P. pundamilia* females. Accordingly, we would expect the two species to breed in different areas of the lake—and they do. When biologists sampled cichlid populations in Lake Victoria, they found that *P. nyererei* breeds in deep water, while *P. pundamilia* inhabits shallower habitats where the blue males shine brightly. As a consequence of their mating behavior, the two species encounter different environments that may result in further divergence.

In recent years, new environmental factors have had a dramatic impact on cichlids. Hybridization is rampant; a multitude of cichlid species have been genetically homogenized. You'll learn why in Module 14.10.

? **What lines of evidence support the conclusion that sexual selection led to reproductive isolation between *P. nyererei* and *P. pundamilia*?**

■ Mate-choice experiments performed in the laboratory; difference in color vision of females of the two species; difference in breeding location

14.8 Isolated islands are often showcases of speciation

Isolated island chains are often inhabited by unique collections of species. Islands that have physically diverse habitats and that are far enough apart to permit populations to evolve in isolation but close enough to allow occasional dispersals to occur are often the sites of multiple speciation events. The evolution of many diverse species from a common ancestor is known as **adaptive radiation**.

The Galápagos Archipelago, located about 900 km (560 miles) west of Ecuador, is one of the world's great showcases of adaptive radiation. Each island was born naked from underwater volcanoes from 5 million to 1 million years ago and was gradually covered by plants, animals, and microorganisms descended from strays that rode the ocean currents and winds from other islands and the South American mainland.

The Galápagos Islands today have numerous plants, snails, reptiles, and birds that are found nowhere else on Earth. For example, they are home to 14 species of closely related finches, which are often called Darwin's finches because Darwin collected them during his around-the-world voyage on the *Beagle* (see Module 13.1). These birds resemble each other in many ways, but they differ in their feeding habits and their beaks, which are specialized for what they eat—an example of the correlation between STRUCTURE AND FUNCTION. Their various foods include insects, large or small seeds, cactus fruits, and even eggs of other species. The woodpecker finch uses cactus spines or twigs as tools to pry insects from trees. The thin, probing bill of the warbler finch is well-suited for capturing small insects. Figure 14.8 shows some of these birds, with their distinctive beaks adapted for their specific diet.

Seed-eater (medium ground finch)

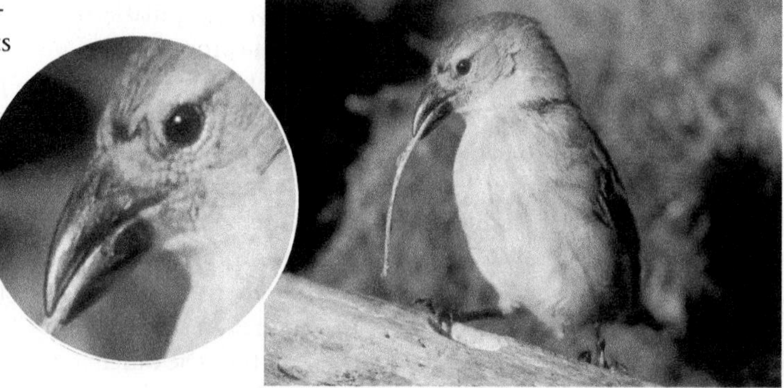

Tool-using insect-eater (woodpecker finch)

Insect-eater (warbler finch)

▲ Figure 14.8 Examples of differences in beak shape and size in Galápagos finches, each adapted for a specific diet

How might Darwin's finch species have evolved from a small population of ancestral birds that colonized one of the islands? Completely isolated on the island, the founder population may have changed significantly as natural selection favored different adaptations in the new environment, and eventually it became a new species. Later, a few individuals of this species may have migrated to a neighboring island, where, under different conditions, this new founder population was changed enough through natural selection to become another new species. Some of these birds may then have recolonized the first island and coexisted there with the original ancestral species if reproductive barriers kept the species distinct. Multiple colonizations and speciations on the many separate islands of the Galápagos probably followed.

Today, each of the Galápagos Islands has several species of finches, with as many as 10 on some islands. The effects of the adaptive radiation of Darwin's finches are evident not just in their many types of beaks but also in their different habitats—some live in trees and others spend most of their time on the ground. Reproductive isolation due to species-specific songs helps keep the species separate. However, occasional interbreeding happens when a male sings the song of a different species. For example, a cactus finch nestling whose father dies may learn a neighbor's song, even if the neighbor is not a cactus finch.

In the next module, we take a closer look at the evolution of Darwin's finches.

? Explain why isolated island chains provide opportunities for adaptive radiations.

The chance colonization of an island often presents a species with new resources and an absence of predators. Through natural selection acting on existing variation, the colonizing population becomes adapted to its new habitat and may evolve into a new species. Subsequent colonizations of nearby islands would provide additional opportunities for adaptation and genetic drift, which could lead to further speciations.

14.9 Long-term field studies document evolution in Darwin's finches

EVOLUTION CONNECTION As you learned in the previous module, the beaks of Darwin's finches are adapted to different food sources. How did such specialization evolve? Morphological, geographic, and genetic studies have provided a wealth of data on how and when new species emerged. In addition, remarkable field studies led by evolutionary ecologists Peter and Rosemary Grant documented the effect of natural selection on beak size in real time (see Module 13.7).

For 40 years, the Grants and their students have studied the finches on Daphne Major, an isolated island in the Galápagos (**Figure 14.9A**). The small size of the island, 100 acres, allowed the researchers to collect comprehensive data on its plant and animal inhabitants. They captured every medium ground finch (shown in Figure 14.8) and recorded the phenotypic variation in the population, including the depth, width, and length of each bird's beak. Additional studies established that these beak characters are highly heritable. Each bird was given a unique tag, allowing the scientists to observe the number of viable offspring it produced—its reproductive success.

▲ **Figure 14.9A** Peter and Rosemary Grant collecting data on medium ground finches on Daphne Major

With its rugged slopes and thin soils, Daphne is a challenging habitat for the plants that provide food for the medium ground finch. The climate alternates between two contrasting seasons. During the wet season, when almost all the rain falls, plants bloom and produce abundant seeds. Seeds are much less plentiful in the desert-like dry season. To measure this aspect of the finch's environment, the Grants and their students recorded data on availability of edible seeds. They also quantified seed toughness, using a formula that combines seed size and the amount of force required to crack it.

A few years after the Grants began their studies, the Galápagos were hit by a severe drought. In 1977, Daphne received a scant 24 mm (less than an inch) of rain. This dramatic environmental change was devastating to the finches, but it was a lucky break for the researchers. Because they had begun data collection before the drought, they were able to track the effect of natural selection on the finch populations. Seed production plummeted, resulting in a shortage of food to sustain the finches through the dry season (**Figure 14.9B**). After the finches exhausted the supply of small, soft seeds, the toughest seeds with thick, hard-to-crack coats became the only available food. Thus, birds with the ability to use this food resource were more likely to survive.

How did natural selection affect the population of medium ground finches on Daphne? Of the 1,200 adults present in June 1976, just 15% survived the drought. The birds did not breed that year, and almost all of the nestlings produced in the previous breeding season died. As the 1978 wet season began, rainfall returned to normal levels and the drought survivors resumed breeding. **Figure 14.9C** shows average beak depth, an indication of seed-crushing power, in the pre- and postdrought populations of medium ground finches. The proportion of birds with larger beaks in the population increased during this intense period of natural selection.

As the Grants continued their studies on Daphne, they observed additional droughts as well as other environmental changes that caused selection in the finch populations. Such periods of strong selection may be a key to explaining the rapid adaptive radiation of Darwin's finches.

By sequencing the genomes of Darwin's finches, scientists have begun to identify the genetic basis for the remarkable diversity of beaks. In 2015, for example, researchers discovered two variants of a gene, called *ALX1*, associated with beak formation. Birds with one of the *ALX1* variants had blunt, stout beaks capable of cracking open tough seeds. Birds possessing the other variant tended to have long, pointed beaks better suited to picking up small seeds from the ground. Although some species have only one *ALX1* variant and its associated beak type, medium ground finches have an intermediate beak shape and possess both *ALX1* variants. Researchers have also discovered that differences in the timing and location of gene expression during embryonic development contribute to beak diversity in Darwin's finches (see Module 15.11).

? **Why was it important for the researchers to establish that beak morphology is heritable?**

■ Natural selection can only modify heritable traits.

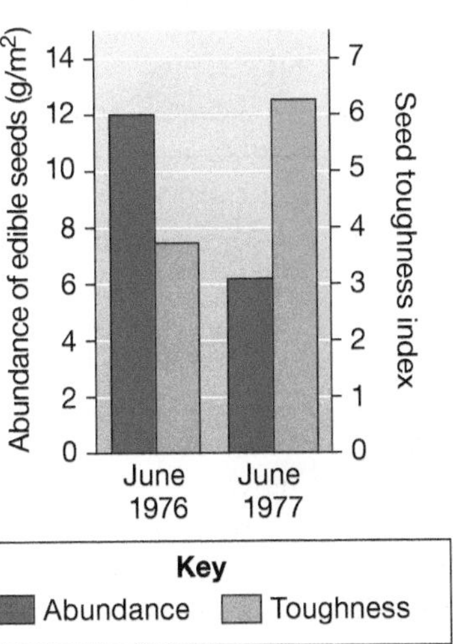

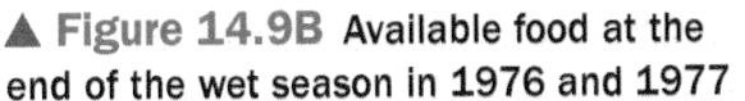

▲ **Figure 14.9B** Available food at the end of the wet season in 1976 and 1977

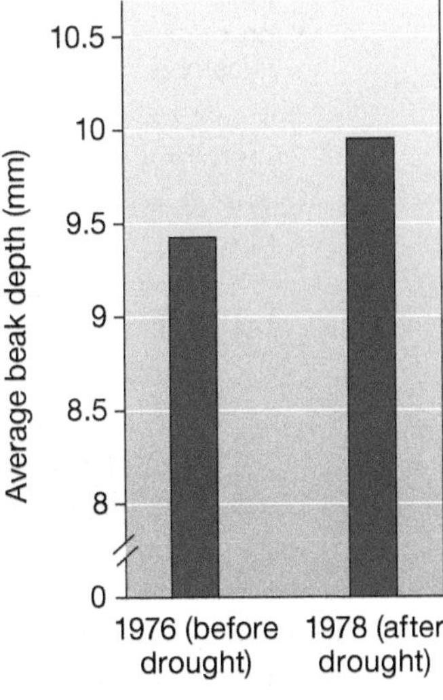

▲ **Figure 14.9C** Evidence of selection on beak depth by food source

Data from P. Boag and P. Grant, Intense selection in a population of Darwin's finches in the Galapagos, *Science 214:* 82–5 (1981); P. Grant and B. Grant, *Forty Years of Evolution: Darwin's Finches on Daphne Major Island*, 60–4. Princeton, Princeton University Press 2014.

14.10 Hybrid zones provide opportunities to study reproductive isolation

What happens when separated populations of closely related species come back into contact with one another? Will reproductive barriers be strong enough to keep the species separate? Or will the two species interbreed and become one? Biologists attempt to answer such questions by studying **hybrid zones**, regions in which members of different species meet and mate, producing at least some hybrid offspring.

Figure 14.10A illustrates the formation of a hybrid zone, starting with the ancestral species. ❶ Three populations are connected by gene flow. ❷ A barrier to gene flow separates one population. ❸ Over time, this population diverges from the other two. ❹ Later, gene flow is reestablished in the hybrid zone. Let's consider possible outcomes for this hybrid zone over time.

Three populations of a species
❶
❷
❸
Newly formed species
Hybrid zone
❹
Gene flow
Hybrid individual
Gene flow
Population
Barrier to gene flow

▲ Figure 14.10A Formation of a hybrid zone

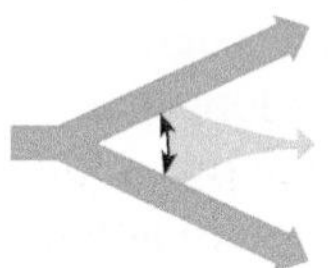

Reinforcement When hybrid offspring are less fit than members of both parent species, we might expect natural selection to strengthen, or reinforce, reproductive barriers, thus reducing the formation of unfit hybrids. And we would predict that barriers between species should be stronger where the species overlap (that is, where the species are sympatric).

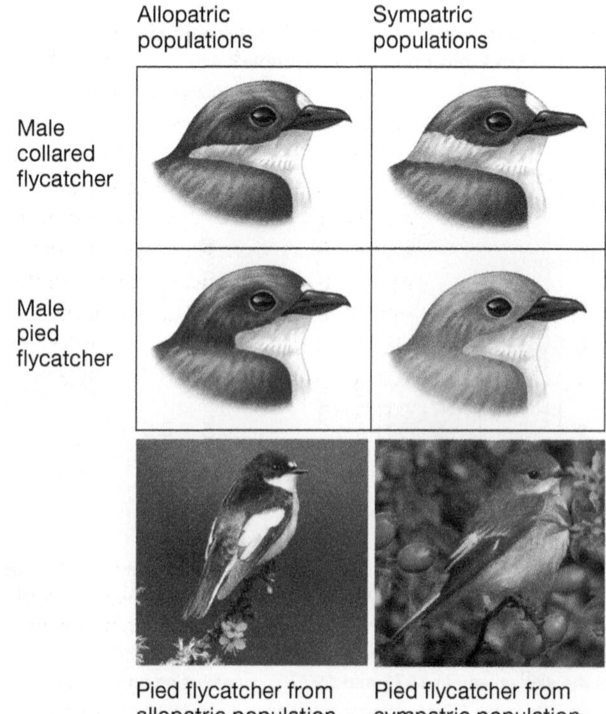

▲ Figure 14.10B Reinforcement of reproductive barriers

As an example, consider the closely related collared flycatcher and pied flycatcher illustrated in Figure 14.10B. When populations of these two species do not overlap (that is, when they are allopatric), males closely resemble each other, with similar black and white coloration (see left side of Figure 14.10B). However, when populations of the two species are sympatric, male collared flycatchers are still black but with enlarged patches of white, whereas male pied flycatchers are a dull brown (see right side of Figure 14.10B). The photographs at the bottom of the figure show two pied flycatchers, the one on the left from a population that has no overlap with collared flycatchers and the one on the right from a population in an area where both species coexist. When scientists performed mate choice experiments, they found that female flycatchers frequently made mistakes when presented with males from allopatric populations, which look similar. But females never selected mates from the other species when presented with males from sympatric populations, which look different. Thus, reproductive barriers are reinforced when populations of these two species overlap.

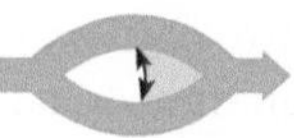

Fusion What happens when the reproductive barriers between species are weak and the species come into contact in a hybrid zone? So much gene flow may occur that the speciation process reverses, causing the two hybridizing species to fuse into one.

Such a situation has been occurring among the cichlid species in Lake Victoria that we discussed in Module 14.7. Since the 1980s, as many as 200 species of cichlids have disappeared from Lake Victoria. Some species were driven to extinction by an introduced predator, the Nile perch. But many species that are not prey for Nile perch are also disappearing. Pollution caused by development along the shores of Lake Victoria has turned the water murky. To understand how water clarity affects sexual selection in cichlids, think about how your eyes work in different lighting. It's easy to distinguish colors in bright light, but difficult in a dimly lit room. What happens when *P. nyererei* or *P. pundamilia* females can't tell red males from blue males? The behavioral barrier crumbles. Interbreeding is producing many viable hybrid offspring, and the once isolated gene pools of the parent species are combining—two species fusing into a single hybrid species (Figure 14.10C).

▲ Figure 14.10C Fusion: hybrid of *Pundamilia nyererei* and *Pundamilia pundamilia* from an area with turbid water

By mixing the unique alleles of separate species into a single gene pool, hybridization can increase a population's genetic variation, which in turn increases the phenotypic variation on which natural selection can act. Recently, pollution in Lake Victoria has been greatly reduced, and cichlid numbers—though not species diversity—have rebounded. If environmental conditions continue to improve, biologists may have an opportunity to study a new radiation of cichlid diversity.

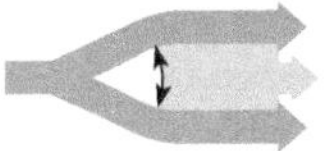

Stability One might predict that either reinforcement of reproductive barriers or fusion of gene pools into a single species would occur in a hybrid zone. However, many hybrid zones are fairly stable, and hybrids continue to be produced. Although these hybrids allow for some gene flow between populations, each species maintains its own integrity. The island inhabited by two finch species that occasionally interbreed (see Module 14.8) is an example of a stable hybrid zone.

? **Why might hybrid zones be called "natural laboratories" in which to study speciation?**

By studying the fate of hybrids over time, scientists can directly observe factors that cause (or fail to cause) reproductive isolation.

14.11 Speciation can occur rapidly or slowly

Biologists continue to make field observations and devise experiments to study evolution in progress. However, much of the evidence for evolution comes from fossils. What does the fossil record say about the process of speciation?

Many fossil species appear suddenly in a layer of rock and persist essentially unchanged through several layers (strata) until disappearing just as suddenly. Paleontologists coined the term **punctuated equilibria** to describe these long periods of little apparent morphological change (equilibria) interrupted (punctuated) by relatively brief periods of sudden change. Figure 14.11 (top) illustrates the evolution of two lineages of butterflies in a punctuated pattern. Notice that the butterfly species change little, if at all, once they appear.

Other fossil species appear to have diverged gradually over long periods of time. As shown in Figure 14.11 (bottom), differences gradually accumulate, and new species (represented by the two butterflies at the far right) evolve gradually from the ancestral population.

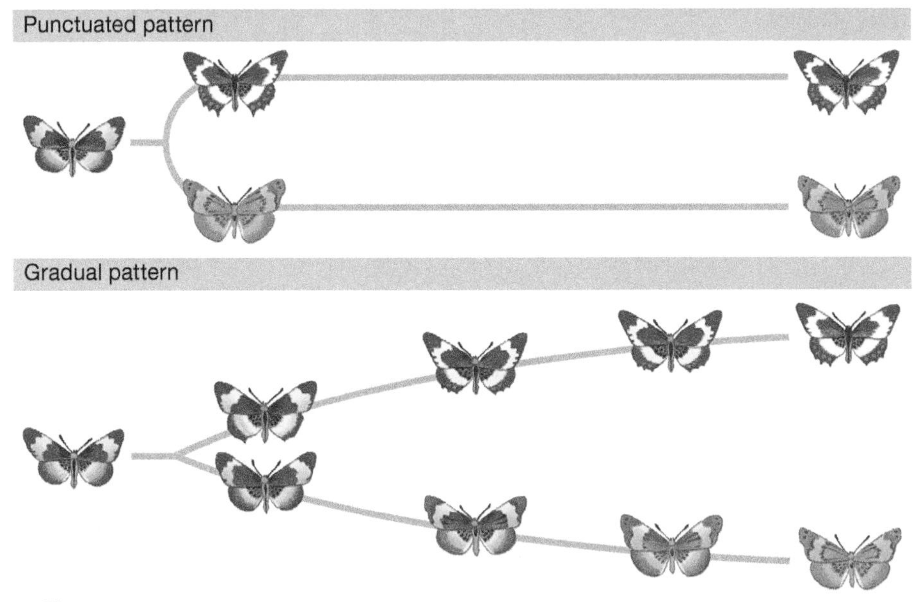

▲ **Figure 14.11** Two models for the tempo of speciation

Even when fossil evidence points to a punctuated pattern, species may not have originated as rapidly as it appears. Suppose that a species survived for 5 million years but that most of the changes in its features occurred during the first 50,000 years of its existence. Time periods this short often cannot be distinguished in fossil strata. And should a new species originate from a small, isolated population—as no doubt many species have—the chances of fossils being found are low.

What about the total length of time between speciation events—between when a new species forms and when its populations diverge enough to produce another new species? In a survey of 84 groups of plants and animals, this time ranged from 4,000 to 40 million years. Overall, the time between speciation events averaged 6.5 million years. Such long time frames tell us that it has taken vast spans of time for life on Earth to evolve.

As you've seen, speciation may begin with small differences. However, as speciation occurs again and again, these differences accumulate and may eventually lead to new groups that differ greatly from their ancestors, as in the origin of cetaceans from four-legged land animals (see Module 13.3), The cumulative effects of multiple speciations, as well as extinctions, have shaped the dramatic changes documented in the fossil record. (Such macroevolutionary changes are the subject of our next chapter.)

? **How does the punctuated equilibrium model account for the relative rarity of transitional fossils linking newer species to older ones?**

If speciation takes place in a relatively short time or in a small isolated population, the transition of one species to another may be difficult to find in the fossil record.

CHAPTER **14** REVIEW

For practice quizzes, BioFlix animations, MP3 tutorials, video tutors, and more study tools designed for this textbook, go to MasteringBiology™

REVIEWING THE CONCEPTS

Defining Species (14.1–14.3)

14.1 The origin of species is the source of biological diversity. Speciation, the process by which one species splits into two or more species, accounts for both the unity and diversity of life.

14.2 There are several ways to define a species. The biological species concept holds that a species is a group of populations whose members can interbreed and produce fertile offspring with each other but not with members of other species. This concept emphasizes reproductive isolation. Most organisms are classified based on observable traits—the morphological species concept.

14.3 Reproductive barriers keep species separate. Such barriers isolate a species' gene pool and prevent interbreeding.

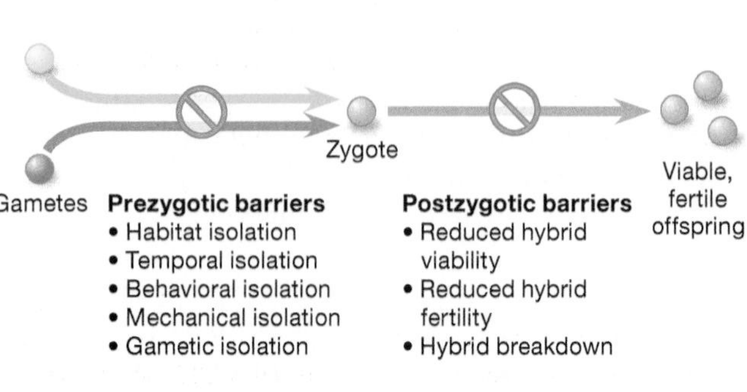

Mechanisms of Speciation (14.4–14.11)

14.4 In allopatric speciation, geographic isolation leads to speciation. Geographically separated from other populations, a small population may become genetically unique as its gene pool is changed by natural selection, mutation, or genetic drift.

14.5 Reproductive barriers can evolve as populations diverge. Researchers have documented the beginning of reproductive isolation in fruit fly populations adapting to different food sources and have identified a gene for flower color involved in the pollinator choice that helps separate monkey flower species.

14.6 Sympatric speciation takes place without geographic isolation. Many plant species have evolved by polyploidy, duplication of the chromosome number due to errors in cell division. Habitat differentiation and sexual selection, usually involving mate choice, can lead to sympatric (and allopatric) speciation.

14.7 Sexual selection can lead to speciation. Through the rapid diversification of cichlids, researchers have gained insight into speciation via sexual selection.

14.8 Isolated islands are often showcases of speciation. Repeated isolation, speciation, and recolonization events on isolated island chains have led to adaptive radiations of species, many of which are found nowhere else in the world.

14.9 Long-term field studies document evolution in Darwin's finches. Researchers studying finches on the island of Daphne Major have quantified the effect of natural selection on phenotypic variation in real time.

14.10 Hybrid zones provide opportunities to study reproductive isolation. Hybrid zones are regions in which populations of different species overlap and produce at least some hybrid offspring. Over time, reinforcement may strengthen barriers to reproduction, or fusion may reverse the speciation process as gene flow between species increases. In stable hybrid zones, a limited number of hybrid offspring continue to be produced.

14.11 Speciation can occur rapidly or slowly. Punctuated equilibrium describes an evolutionary pattern in which species change most as they arise from an ancestral species and then change relatively little for the rest of their existence. In other cases, species appear to have evolved more gradually. The time interval between speciation events varies from a few thousand years to tens of millions of years.

CONNECTING THE CONCEPTS

1. Name the two types of speciation represented by this diagram. For each type, describe how reproductive barriers may develop between the new species.

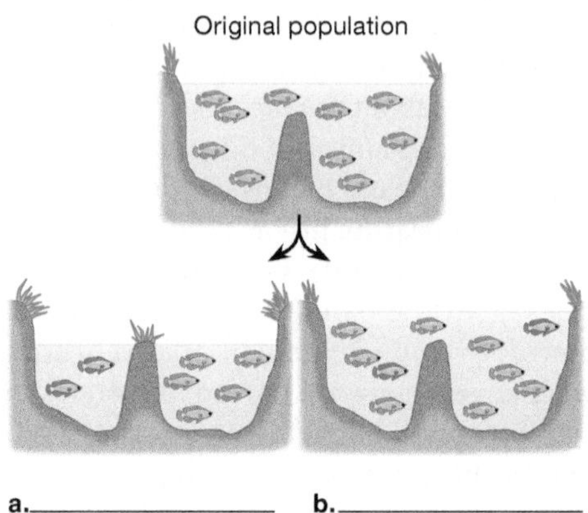

2. Fill in the blanks in the following concept map.

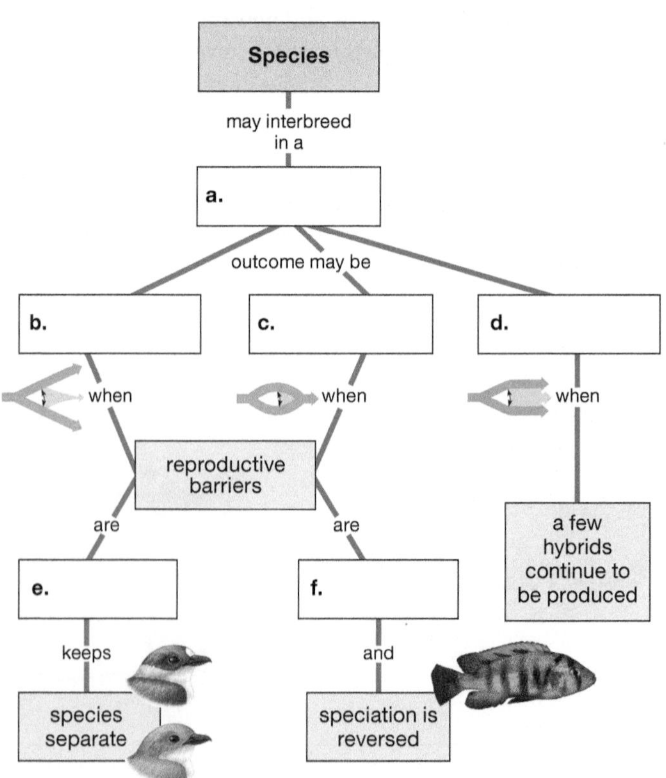

TESTING YOUR KNOWLEDGE

Level 1: Knowledge/Comprehension

3. Which concept of species would be most useful to a field biologist identifying new plant species in a tropical forest?
   a. biological
   b. ecological
   c. morphological
   d. phylogenetic
4. According to the biological species concept, species are defined by their
   a. particular roles in a biological community.
   b. ability to interbreed and produce viable, fertile offspring.
   c. reproductive isolation from nearby populations.
   d. common ancestry.
5. Bird guides once listed the myrtle warbler and Audubon's warbler as distinct species that lived side by side in parts of their ranges. However, recent books show them as eastern and western forms of a single species, the yellow-rumped warbler. Most likely, it has been found that these two kinds of warblers
   a. live in similar habitats and eat similar foods.
   b. interbreed often in nature, and the offspring are viable and fertile.
   c. are almost identical in appearance.
   d. have many genes in common.
6. Which of the following is an example of a postzygotic reproductive barrier?
   a. One *Ceanothus* shrub lives on acid soil, another on alkaline soil.
   b. Mallard and pintail ducks mate at different times of year.
   c. Two species of leopard frogs have different mating calls.
   d. Hybrid offspring of two species of jimsonweeds always die before reproducing.
7. Biologists have found more than 500 species of fruit flies on the various Hawaiian Islands, all apparently descended from a single ancestor species. This example illustrates
   a. polyploidy.
   b. temporal isolation.
   c. adaptive radiation.
   d. sympatric speciation.
8. A new plant species C, which formed from hybridization of species A ($2n = 16$) with species B ($2n = 12$), would probably produce gametes with a chromosome number of
   a. 12.
   b. 14.
   c. 16.
   d. 28.
9. A horse ($2n = 64$) and a donkey ($2n = 62$) can mate and produce a mule. How many chromosomes would there be in a mule's body cells?
   a. 31
   b. 62
   c. 63
   d. 126
10. What prevents horses and donkeys from hybridizing to form a new species?
    a. limited hybrid fertility
    b. limited hybrid viability
    c. hybrid breakdown
    d. gametic isolation
11. When hybrids produced in a hybrid zone can breed with each other and with both parent species, and they survive and reproduce as well as members of the parent species, one would predict that
    a. the hybrid zone would be stable.
    b. sympatric speciation would occur.
    c. reinforcement of reproductive barriers would keep the parent species separate.
    d. reproductive barriers would lessen and the two parent species would fuse.
12. Which of the following factors would *not* contribute to allopatric speciation?
    a. A population becomes geographically isolated from the parent population.
    b. The separated population is small, and genetic drift occurs.
    c. The isolated population is exposed to different selection pressures than the parent population.
    d. Gene flow between the two populations continues to occur.

Level 2: Application/Analysis

13. Explain how each of the following makes it difficult to clearly define a species: variation within a species, geographically isolated populations, asexual species, fossil organisms.
14. Explain why allopatric speciation would be less likely on an island close to a mainland than on a more isolated island.
15. What does the term *punctuated equilibria* describe?
16. Can factors that cause sympatric speciation also cause allopatric speciation? Explain.

Level 3: Synthesis/Evaluation

17. Cultivated American cotton plants have a total of 52 chromosomes ($2n = 52$). In each cell, there are 13 pairs of large chromosomes and 13 pairs of smaller chromosomes. Old World cotton plants have 26 chromosomes ($2n = 26$), all large. Wild American cotton plants have 26 chromosomes, all small. Propose a testable hypothesis to explain how cultivated American cotton probably originated.
18. **SCIENTIFIC THINKING** Explain how the murky waters of Lake Victoria may be contributing to the decline in cichlid species. How might these polluted waters affect the formation of new species?
19. The red wolf, *Canis rufus*, which was once widespread in the southeastern and south central United States, was declared extinct in the wild by 1980. Saved by a captive breeding program, the red wolf has been reintroduced in areas of eastern North Carolina. The current wild population is estimated to be about 100 individuals. It is presently being threatened with extinction due to hybridization with coyotes, *Canis latrans*, which have become more numerous in the area. Red wolves and coyotes differ in terms of morphology, DNA, and behavior, although these differences may disappear if interbreeding continues. Although the red wolf has been designated as an endangered species under the Endangered Species Act, some people think that its endangered status should be withdrawn and resources should not be spent to protect what is not a "pure" species. Do you agree? Why or why not?

Answers to all questions can be found in Appendix 4.

Tracing Evolutionary History

CHAPTER 15

The feathers and flight of birds are a marriage of structure and function. The skeleton, nervous system, internal organs, and especially feathers of birds, including those of the hoopoe on the right, are marvelously adapted for life on the wing. Clearly, feathers are essential to avian aeronautics. In a flight feather, separate filaments called barbs emerge from a central shaft that runs from base to tip. Each barb is linked to the next by tiny hooks that act like the teeth of a zipper. The result is a tightly connected sheet of barbs that is strong but flexible. In flight, the shapes and arrangements of various feathers produce lift, smooth airflow, and help with steering and balance. Layered like shingles over the bird's body, feathers also provide a waterproof, lightweight covering. How did such an intricate structure evolve? You'll learn the answer to this question later in this chapter, but here's a clue: Birds were not the first feathered animals on Earth—dinosaurs were.

How do brand-new structures arise by evolution?

The first feathered dinosaur to be discovered, a 130-million-year-old fossil found in northeastern China, was named *Sinosauropteryx* ("Chinese lizard-wing"). About the size of a turkey, it had short arms and ran on its hind legs, using its long tail for balance. Its unimpressive plumage consisted of a downy covering of hairlike feathers. Since the discovery of *Sinosauropteryx* in 1996, thousands of fossils of feathered dinosaurs have been found and classified into more than 30 different species. Although none was unequivocally capable of flying, many of these species had elaborate feathers that would be the envy of any modern bird.

The evolution of birds is an example of macroevolution, the major changes recorded in the history of life over vast tracts of time. In this chapter, we turn our attention to macroevolution, explore some of the mechanisms responsible for it, and consider how scientists organize the diversity of life according to evolutionary relationships. To approach these wide-ranging topics, we begin with the most basic of questions: How did life first arise on planet Earth?

BIG IDEAS

Early Earth and the Origin of Life (15.1–15.3)

Scientific experiments can test the four-stage hypothesis of how life originated on early Earth.

Major Events in the History of Life (15.4–15.6)

The fossil record and radiometric dating establish a geologic record of key events in life's history.

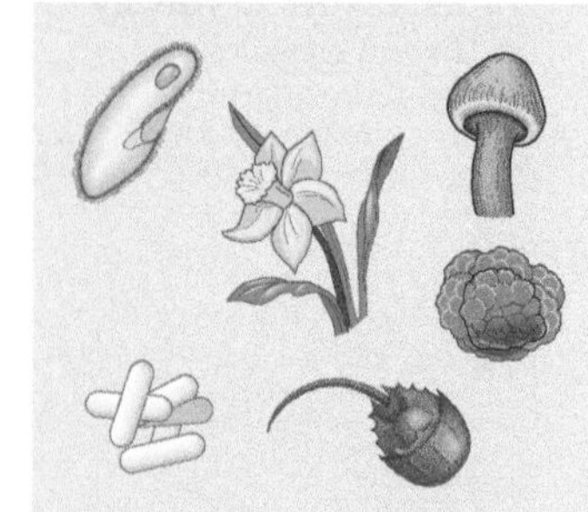

Mechanisms of Macroevolution (15.7–15.13)

Continental drift, mass extinctions, adaptive radiations, and changes in developmental genes have all contributed to macroevolution.

Phylogeny and the Tree of Life (15.14–15.19)

The evolutionary history of a species is reconstructed using fossils, homologies, and molecular systematics.

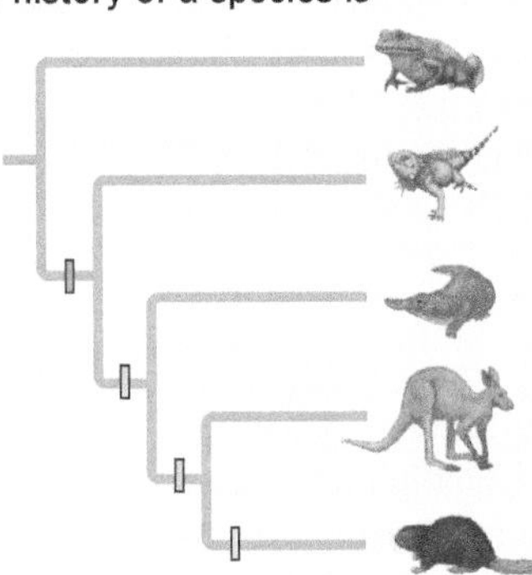

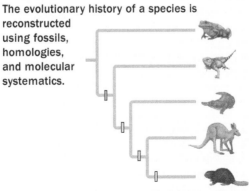

Early Earth and the Origin of Life

15.1 Conditions on early Earth made the origin of life possible

Earth is one of eight planets orbiting the sun, and the sun is one of billions of stars in the Milky Way. The Milky Way, in turn, is one of billions of galaxies in the universe. The star closest to our sun is 40 trillion kilometers away.

The universe has not always been so spread out. Physicists have evidence that before the universe existed in its present form, all matter was concentrated in one mass. The mass seems to have blown apart with a "big bang" sometime between 12 and 14 billion years ago and has been expanding ever since.

Scientific evidence indicates that Earth formed about 4.6 billion years ago from a vast swirling cloud of dust that surrounded the young sun. As gases, dust, and rocks collided and stuck together, larger bodies formed, and the gravity of the larger bodies in turn attracted more matter, eventually forming Earth and other planets.

Conditions on Early Earth Immense heat would have been generated by the impact of meteorites and compaction by gravity, and young planet Earth probably began as a molten mass. The mass then sorted into layers of varying densities, with the least dense material on the surface, solidifying into a thin crust.

As the bombardment of early Earth slowed about 4 billion years ago, conditions on the planet were extremely different from those of today. The first atmosphere was probably thick with water vapor, along with various compounds released by volcanic eruptions, including nitrogen and its oxides, carbon dioxide, methane, ammonia, hydrogen, and hydrogen sulfide. As Earth slowly cooled, the water vapor condensed into oceans. Not only was the atmosphere of young Earth very different from the atmosphere we know today, but lightning, volcanic activity, and ultraviolet radiation were much more intense.

When Did Life Begin? The earliest evidence of life on Earth comes from fossils that are about 3.5 billion years old. One of these fossils is pictured in the inset in Figure 15.1; the larger illustration is an artist's rendition of what Earth may have looked like at that time. Life is already present in this painting, as shown by the "stepping stones" that dominate the shoreline. These rocks, called **stromatolites**, were built up by ancient photosynthetic prokaryotes. As evident in the fossil stromatolite shown in the inset, the rocks are layered. The prokaryotes that built them bound thin films of sediment together, then migrated to the surface and started the next layer. Similar layered mats are still being formed today by photosynthetic prokaryotes in a few shallow, salty bays, such as Shark Bay, in western Australia.

Photosynthesis is not a simple process, so it is likely that significant time had elapsed before life as complex as the organisms that formed the ancient stromatolites had evolved. The evidence that these prokaryotes lived 3.5 billion years ago is strong support for the hypothesis that life in a simpler form arose much earlier, perhaps as early as 3.9 billion years ago.

How Did Life Arise? From the time of the ancient Greeks until well into the 1800s, it was commonly believed that nonliving matter could spontaneously generate living organisms. Many people believed, for instance, that flies came from rotting meat and fish from ocean mud. Experiments by the French scientist Louis Pasteur in 1862, however, confirmed that all life arises only by the reproduction of preexisting life.

Pasteur ended the argument over spontaneous generation of present-day organisms, but he did not address the question of how life arose in the first place. To attempt to answer that question, for which there is no fossil evidence available, scientists develop hypotheses and test their predictions.

Scientists hypothesize that chemical and physical processes on early Earth could have produced very simple cells through a sequence of four main stages:

1. The abiotic (nonliving) synthesis of small organic molecules, such as amino acids and nitrogenous bases
2. The joining of these small molecules into polymers, such as proteins and nucleic acids (see Module 3.3)
3. The packaging of these molecules into "protocells," droplets with membranes that maintained an internal chemistry different from that of their surroundings
4. The origin of self-replicating molecules that eventually made inheritance possible

In the next two modules, we examine some of the experimental evidence for each of these four stages.

? **Why do 3.5-billion-year-old stromatolites suggest that life originated *before* 3.5 billion years ago?**

■ If photosynthetic prokaryotes existed by 3.5 billion years ago, a simpler, nonphotosynthetic cell probably originated well before that time.

▲ Figure 15.1 A depiction of Earth about 3 billion years ago (inset: photo of a cross section of a fossilized stromatolite)

15.2 Experiments show that the abiotic synthesis of organic molecules is possible

SCIENTIFIC THINKING

Organic molecules are essential to the structures and functions of life, but Earth and its atmosphere are made up of inorganic molecules. How did the first organic molecules arise?

In the 1920s, Russian chemist A. I. Oparin and British scientist J. B. S. Haldane independently proposed that conditions on early Earth could have generated organic molecules. They reasoned that present-day conditions on Earth do not allow the spontaneous synthesis of organic compounds simply because the atmosphere is now rich in oxygen. As a strong oxidizing agent, O_2 tends to disrupt chemical bonds. However, before the early photosynthetic prokaryotes added O_2 to the air, Earth may have had a reducing (electron-adding) atmosphere. The energy for this abiotic synthesis of organic compounds could have come from lightning and intense UV radiation.

In 1953, Stanley Miller, then a graduate student in the laboratory of Nobel laureate Harold Urey, tested the Oparin-Haldane hypothesis. Miller devised the apparatus shown in **Figure 15.2**. A flask of warmed water represented the primeval sea. (1) The water was heated so that some vaporized and moved into a second, higher flask. (2) The "atmosphere" in this higher flask consisted of water vapor, hydrogen gas (H_2), methane (CH_4), and ammonia (NH_3)—the gases that scientists at the time thought prevailed in the ancient world. Electrodes discharged sparks into the flask to mimic lightning. (3) A condenser with circulating cold water cooled the atmosphere, raining water and any dissolved compounds back down into the miniature sea. (4) As material cycled through the apparatus, Miller periodically collected samples for chemical analysis.

Miller identified a variety of organic molecules that are common in organisms, including hydrocarbons (long chains of carbon and hydrogen) and some of the amino acids that make up proteins. His results—the first evidence that the molecules of life could have arisen spontaneously from inorganic precursors—attracted global attention. Many laboratories have since repeated Miller's classic experiment using various atmospheric mixtures and produced organic compounds.

Recent evidence indicates that the early atmosphere may not have been as strongly reducing as once assumed. However, results from experiments using such atmospheres have also produced organic molecules, corroborating Miller's results. And it is possible that small "pockets" of the early atmosphere—perhaps near volcanic openings—were reducing. In 2008, a former graduate student of Miller's discovered some samples from an experiment that Miller had designed to mimic volcanic conditions. Reanalyzing these samples using modern equipment, he identified additional organic compounds that had been synthesized. Indeed, 22 amino acids had been produced under Miller's simulated volcanic conditions, compared with the 11 produced with the atmosphere in his original 1953 experiment. (Miller had only found 5 amino acids using the analytical methods available to him at the time.)

Scientists continue to generate alternative hypotheses for the origin of organic molecules on Earth. Some researchers are exploring the hypothesis that life may have begun in submerged volcanoes or deep-sea hydrothermal vents, gaps in Earth's crust where hot water and minerals gush into deep oceans. These environments, among the most extreme environments in which life exists today, could have provided the initial chemical resources for life.

Another hypothesis proposes that meteorites were the source of Earth's first organic molecules. Fragments of a 4.5-billion-year-old meteorite that fell to Earth in Australia in 1969 contain more than 80 types of amino acids, some in large amounts. Recent studies have shown that this meteorite also contains other key organic molecules, including lipids, simple sugars, and nitrogenous bases such as uracil. Chemical analyses show that these organic compounds are not contaminants from Earth.

Research will continue on the possible origins of organic molecules on early Earth. We next turn our attention to the subsequent stages that scientists hypothesize gave rise to the earliest cells.

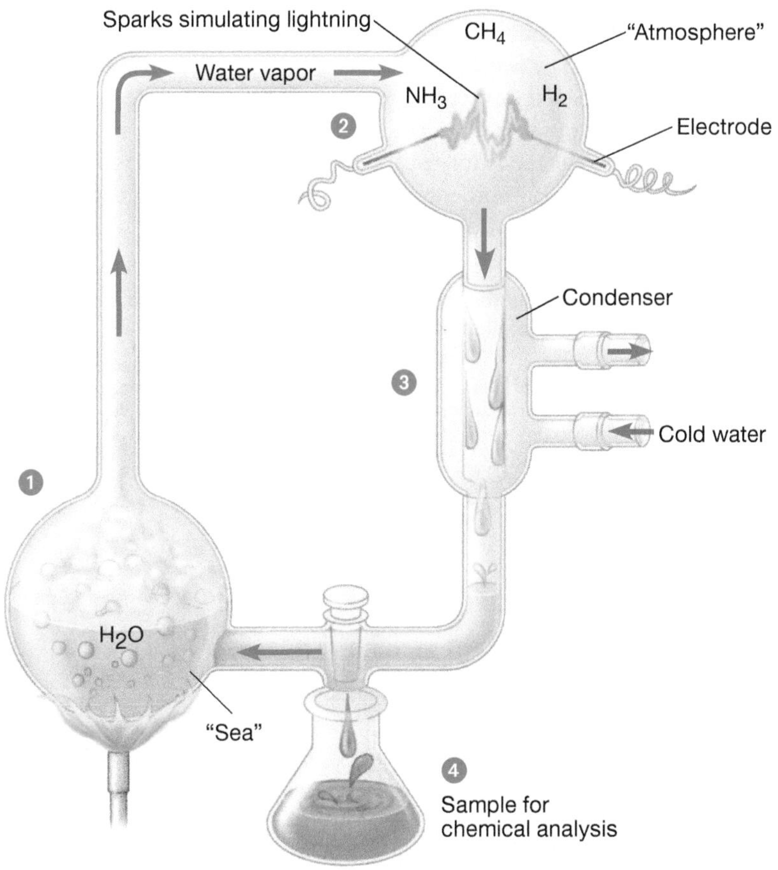

▲ **Figure 15.2** **Diagram showing the synthesis of organic compounds in Miller's 1953 experiment**

? What would a scientist change in Miller's apparatus to incorporate new evidence about Earth's early atmosphere?

■ The mixture of gases in the second flask (labeled 2 in Figure 15.2)

15.3 Stages in the origin of the first cells probably included the formation of polymers, protocells, and self-replicating RNA

The abiotic synthesis of small organic molecules would have been a first step in the origin of life. But what is the evidence that the next three stages—synthesis of polymers, formation of protocells, and self-replicating RNA—could have occurred on early Earth?

Abiotic Synthesis of Polymers In a cell, enzymes catalyze the joining of monomers to build polymers. But could this happen without enzymes? Scientists produced polymers in the laboratory by dripping dilute solutions of amino acids or RNA monomers onto hot sand, clay, or rock. The heat vaporizes the water and concentrates the monomers, some of which then spontaneously bond together in chains. A similar reaction might have happened on early Earth, when waves splashed organic monomers onto lava or hot rocks and then rinsed polypeptides and other polymers back into the sea.

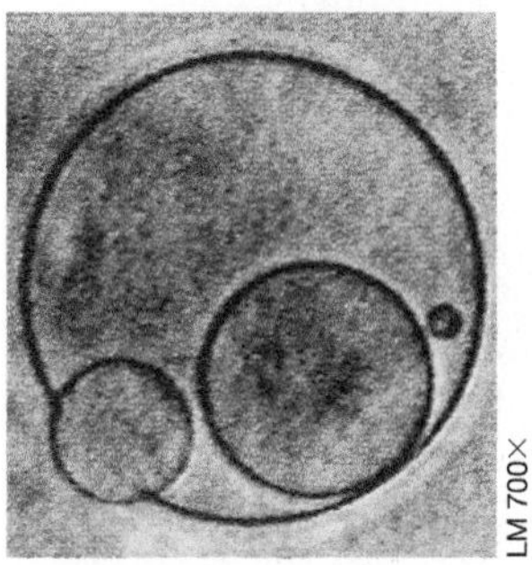

▲ **Figure 15.3A** Microscopic vesicle, with membranes made of lipids, "giving birth" to smaller vesicles

Formation of Protocells A key step in the origin of life would have been the isolation of a collection of organic molecules within a membrane-enclosed compartment. Laboratory experiments demonstrate that small membrane-enclosed sacs, or vesicles, form when lipids are mixed with water (see Module 5.2). When researchers add to the mixture a type of clay thought to have been common on early Earth, such vesicles form at a faster rate. Organic molecules become concentrated on the surface of this clay and thus more easily interact. As shown by the smaller droplets forming in Figure 15.3A, these abiotically created vesicles are able to grow and divide (reproduce). Researchers have shown that these vesicles can absorb clay particles to which RNA and other molecules are attached. In a similar fashion, protocells on early Earth may have been able to form, reproduce, and create and maintain an internal environment different from their surroundings.

Self-Replicating RNA Today's cells store their genetic information as DNA, transcribe the information into RNA, and then translate RNA messages into proteins. This DNA → RNA → protein assembly system is extremely intricate (as we saw in Chapter 10). Most likely, it emerged gradually through a series of refinements of much simpler processes.

What were the first genes like? One hypothesis is that they were short strands of self-replicating RNA. Laboratory experiments have shown that short RNA molecules can assemble spontaneously from nucleotide monomers. Furthermore, when RNA is added to a solution containing RNA monomers, new RNA molecules complementary to parts of the starting RNA sometimes assemble. We can imagine a scenario on early Earth like the one in Figure 15.3B: ❶ RNA monomers adhere to clay particles and become concentrated. ❷ Some monomers spontaneously join, which form the first small "genes." ❸ Then an RNA chain complementary to one of these genes assembles. If the new chain, in turn, serves as a template for another round of RNA assembly, a replica of the original gene results.

This replication process could have been aided by the RNA molecules themselves, acting as catalysts for their own replication. The discovery that some RNAs, which scientists call **ribozymes**, can carry out enzyme-like functions supports this hypothesis. Thus, the "chicken and egg" paradox of which came first, genes or enzymes, may be solved if the chicken and egg came together in the same RNA molecules. Scientists use the term "RNA world" for the hypothetical period in the evolution of life when RNA served as both rudimentary genes and catalytic molecules.

In 2013, researchers succeeded in constructing a protocell enclosing RNA that could self-replicate within the vesicle. On early Earth, once some protocells contained self-replicating RNA molecules, natural selection would have begun to shape their properties. Those that contained genetic information that helped them grow and reproduce more efficiently than others would have increased in number, passing their abilities on to subsequent generations. Mutations, errors in copying RNA "genes," would result in additional variation on which natural selection could work. At some point during millions of years of selection, DNA, a more stable molecule, replaced RNA as the repository of genetic information, and protocells passed a fuzzy border to become true cells. The stage was then set for the evolution of diverse life-forms.

? **Why would the formation of protocells represent a key step in the evolution of life?**

■ Segregating mixtures of molecules within compartments could concentrate organic molecules and facilitate chemical reactions. Natural selection could act on protocells once self-replicating "genes" evolved.

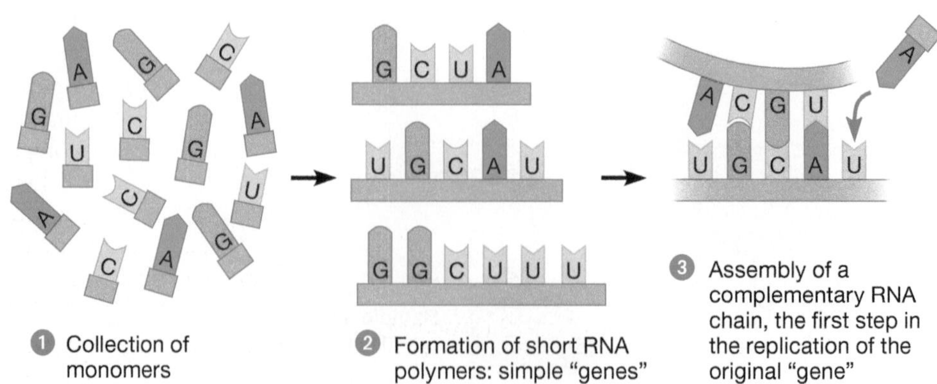

▲ **Figure 15.3B** A hypothesis for the origin of the first genes

Major Events in the History of Life

15.4 The origins of single-celled and multicellular organisms and the colonization of land were key events in life's history

We now begin our study of **macroevolution**, evolutionary change above the species level. Macroevolution encompasses the origin of a new group of organisms through a series of speciation events and the impact of mass extinctions on the diversity of life and its subsequent recovery. Figure 15.4 shows a timeline from the origin of Earth 4.6 billion years ago to the present. Earth's history can be divided into four eons of geologic time. The Hadean, Archaean, and Proterozoic eons together lasted about 4 billion years. The Phanerozoic eon includes the last half billion years.

Origin of Prokaryotes The earliest evidence of life comes from the fossil stromatolites described in Module 15.1. Prokaryotes (the gold band in Figure 15.4) were Earth's sole inhabitants from at least 3.5 billion years ago to about 2 billion years ago. Transformations of ENERGY AND MATTER by prokaryotes during this time had a lasting impact on the biosphere. As a result of prokaryotic photosynthesis, oxygen saturated the seas and began to appear in the atmosphere 2.7 billion years ago (the green band). By 2.2 billion years ago, atmospheric O_2 began to increase rapidly. Species of prokaryotes that were unable to live in this aerobic environment became extinct, but some species survived in anaerobic habitats. The evolution of cellular respiration, which uses O_2 in harvesting energy from organic molecules, allowed other prokaryotes to flourish.

Origin of Single-Celled Eukaryotes The oldest widely accepted fossils of eukaryotes are about 1.8 billion years old (the orange band). The more complex eukaryotic cell originated when small prokaryotic cells capable of aerobic respiration or photosynthesis took up life inside larger cells (Module 4.15). After the first eukaryotes appeared, a great range of unicellular forms evolved, giving rise to the diversity of single-celled eukaryotes that continue to flourish today.

Origin of Multicellular Eukaryotes Another wave of diversification followed: the origin of multicellular forms whose descendants include a variety of algae, plants, fungi, and animals. The oldest-known fossils of multicellular eukaryotes are of relatively small algae that lived 1.2 billion years ago (the light blue band).

Larger and more diverse multicellular organisms do not appear in the fossil record until about 600 million years ago. A great increase in the diversity of animal forms occurred 535–525 million years ago, during a span of time known as the Cambrian explosion (the bright blue band).

Colonization of Land There is fossil evidence that photosynthetic prokaryotes coated damp terrestrial surfaces well over a billion years ago. However, larger forms of life did not begin to colonize land until about 500 million years ago (the purple band).

Plants colonized land in the company of fungi. Even today, the roots of most plants are associated with fungi that aid in absorption of water and minerals; the fungi receive nutrients in return.

The most widespread and diverse land animals are arthropods (particularly insects and spiders) and tetrapods (vertebrates with four appendages). Tetrapods include humans, but we are late arrivals on the scene—the human lineage diverged from other primates around 6 to 7 million years ago, and our own species originated about 195,000 years ago. If the clock of Earth's history were rescaled to represent an hour, humans appeared less than 0.2 second ago! In the next two modules, we see how scientists have determined when these key episodes in Earth's history have occurred in geologic time.

? For how long did life on Earth consist solely of single-celled organisms?

More than 2 billion years: From the first fossils of prokaryotes (3.5 billion years old) until the oldest known fossils of multicellular eukaryotes (1.2 billion years old)

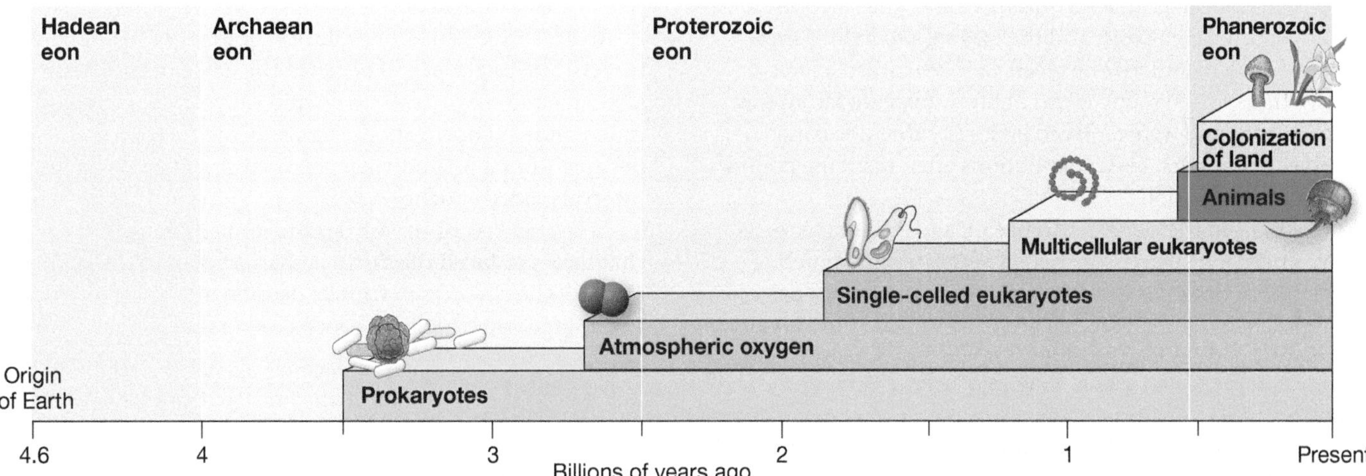

▲ Figure 15.4 Some key events in the history of life on Earth

15.5 The actual ages of rocks and fossils mark geologic time

Geologists use several techniques to determine the ages of rocks and the fossils they contain. The method most often used, called **radiometric dating**, is based on the decay of radioactive isotopes (unstable forms of an element; see Module 2.3). Fossils contain isotopes of elements that accumulated when the organisms were alive. For example, a living organism contains both the common isotope carbon-12 and the radioactive isotope carbon-14 in the same ratio as is present in the atmosphere. Once an organism dies, it stops accumulating carbon, and the stable carbon-12 in its tissues does not change. Its carbon-14, however, starts to decay to another element. The rate of decay is expressed as a half-life, the time required for 50% of the isotope in a sample to decay. Carbon-14 has a half-life of 5,730 years, so half the carbon-14 in a specimen decays in about 5,730 years, half the remaining carbon-14 decays in the next 5,730 years, and so on (Figure 15.5). Knowing both the half-life of a radioactive isotope and the ratio of radioactive to stable isotope in a fossil enables us to determine the age of the fossil.

Carbon-14 is useful for dating relatively young fossils—up to about 75,000 years old. Radioactive isotopes with longer half-lives are used to date older fossils.

There are indirect ways to estimate the age of much older fossils. For example, potassium-40, with a half-life of 1.3 billion years, can be used to date volcanic rocks hundreds of millions of years old. A fossil's age can be inferred from the ages of the rock layers above and below the stratum in which it is found.

By dating rocks and fossils, scientists have established a geologic record of Earth's history.

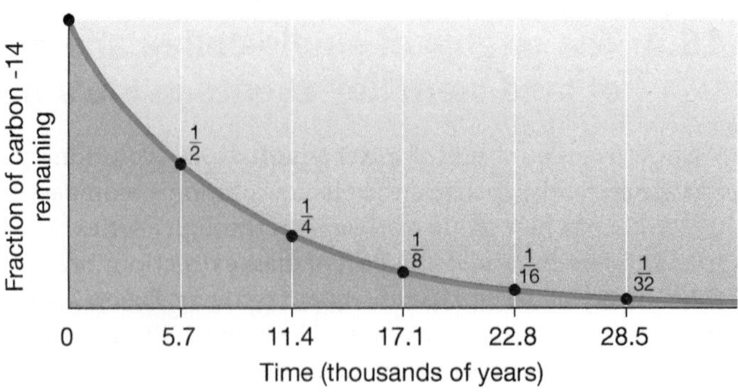

▲ **Figure 15.5** Radiometric dating using carbon-14

The fraction of carbon-14 remaining in a fossilized skull is found to be 1/64. Using Figure 15.5, what is the age of the fossil?

■ Approximately 34,230 thousand years old

15.6 The fossil record documents the history of life

The fossil record, the sequence in which fossils appear in rock strata, is an archive of evolutionary history (see Module 13.2). Based on this sequence and the ages of rocks and fossils, geologists have established a **geologic record**, as shown in Table 15.6, on the facing page. As you saw in Figure 15.4, Earth's history is divided into four eons, the Hadean, Archaean, Proterozoic, and Phanerozoic. The timeline in Table 15.6 shows the lengths and ages (in millions of years ago) of these eons. Note that the Phanerozoic eon, which is only the last 541 million years, is expanded in the table to show the key events in the evolution of multicellular eukaryotic life. This eon is divided into three eras: the Paleozoic, Mesozoic, and Cenozoic, and the eras are subdivided into periods. The boundaries between eras are marked by mass extinctions, when many forms of life disappeared from the fossil record and were replaced by species that diversified from the survivors. Lesser extinctions often mark the boundaries between periods.

Rocks from the Hadean, Archaean, and Proterozoic eons have undergone extensive change over time, and much of their fossil content is no longer visible. Nonetheless, paleontologists have pieced together ancient events in life's history. As mentioned earlier, the oldest-known fossils, dating from 3.5 billion years ago, are of prokaryotes; the oldest fossils of eukaryotic cells are from 1.8 billion years ago. Strata from the Ediacaran period (635–541 million years ago) bear diverse fossils of multicellular algae and soft-bodied animals.

Dating from about 541 million years ago, rocks of the Paleozoic ("ancient animal") era contain fossils of lineages that gave rise to present-day organisms, as well as many lineages that have become extinct. During the early Paleozoic, virtually all life was aquatic, but by about 400 million years ago, plants and animals were well established on land.

The Mesozoic ("middle animal") era is also known as the age of reptiles because of its abundance of reptilian fossils, including those of the dinosaurs. The Mesozoic era also saw the first mammals and flowering plants (angiosperms). By the end of the Mesozoic, dinosaurs had become extinct except for one lineage—the birds.

An explosive period of evolution of mammals, birds, insects, and angiosperms began at the dawn of the Cenozoic ("recent animal") era, about 66 million years ago. Because much more is known about the Cenozoic era than about earlier eras, our table subdivides the Cenozoic periods into finer intervals called epochs.

In the next section, we examine some of the processes that have produced the distinct changes seen in the geologic record. (The chapters in Unit IV describe the enormous diversity of life-forms that have evolved on Earth.)

What were the dominant animals during the Carboniferous period? When were gymnosperms the dominant plants? (*Hint*: Look at Table 15.6.)

■ Amphibians. Gymnosperms were dominant during the Triassic and Jurassic periods (252–145 million years ago).

TABLE 15.6 The Geologic Record

Relative Duration of Eons	Era	Period	Epoch	Age (millions of years ago)	Important Events in the History of Life
Phanerozoic	Cenozoic	Quaternary	Holocene	0.01	Historical time
			Pleistocene	2.6	Ice ages; origin of genus *Homo*
		Tertiary	Pliocene	5.3	Appearance of bipedal human ancestors
			Miocene	23	Continued radiation of mammals and angiosperms; earliest direct human ancestors
			Oligocene	34	Origins of many primate groups
			Eocene	56	Angiosperm dominance increases; continued radiation of most present-day mammalian orders
			Paleocene	66	Major radiation of mammals, birds, and pollinating insects
Proterozoic	Mesozoic	Cretaceous		145	Flowering plants (angiosperms) appear and diversify; many groups of organisms, including most dinosaurs, become extinct at end of period
		Jurassic		201	Gymnosperms continue as dominant plants; dinosaurs abundant and diverse
		Triassic		252	Cone-bearing plants (gymnosperms) dominate landscape; dinosaurs evolve and radiate; origin of mammals
	Paleozoic	Permian		299	Radiation of reptiles; origin of most present-day groups of insects; extinction of many marine and terrestrial organisms at end of period
		Carboniferous		359	Extensive forests of vascular plants form; first seed plants appear; origin of reptiles; amphibians dominant
		Devonian		419	Diversification of bony fishes; first tetrapods and insects appear
		Silurian		444	Diversification of early vascular plants
Archaean		Ordovician		485	Marine algae abundant; colonization of land by diverse fungi, plants, and animals
		Cambrian		541	Sudden increase in diversity of many animal phyla (Cambrian explosion)
		Ediacaran		635	Diverse algae and soft-bodied invertebrate animals appear
				1,800	Oldest fossils of eukaryotic cells appear
				2,500	
				2,700	Concentration of atmospheric oxygen begins to increase
Hadean				3,500	Oldest fossils of cells (prokaryotes) appear
				4,000	Oldest known rocks on Earth's surface
				Approx. 4,600	Origin of Earth

Mechanisms of Macroevolution

15.7 Continental drift has played a major role in macroevolution

The fossil record documents macroevolution, the major events in the history of life on Earth. In this section, we explore some of the factors that helped shape these evolutionary changes, such as plate tectonics, mass extinctions, and adaptive radiations.

Plate Tectonics If photographs of Earth were taken from space every 10,000 years and then spliced together, it would make a remarkable movie. The seemingly "rock solid" continents we live on move over time. Since the origin of multicellular eukaryotes roughly 1.5 billion years ago, there have been three occasions—1 billion, 600 million, and 250 million years ago—in which the landmasses of Earth came together to form a supercontinent, and later broke apart. Each time the landmasses split, they yielded a different configuration of continents. Geologists estimate that the continents will come together again and form a new supercontinent roughly 250 million years from now.

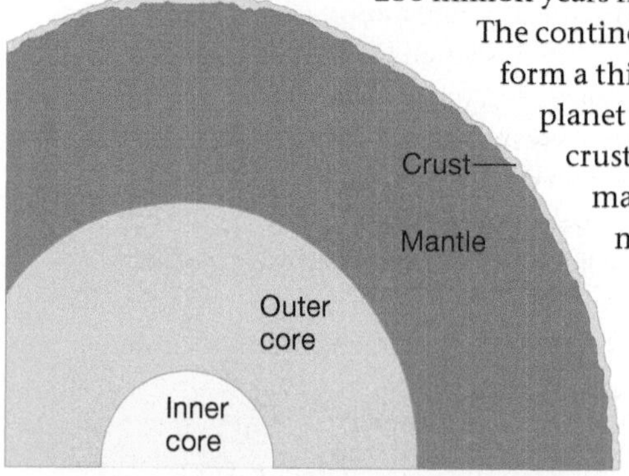

The continents and seafloors form a thin outer layer of planet Earth, called the crust, which covers a mass of hot, viscous material called the mantle. The outer core is liquid and the inner core is solid (Figure 15.7A). According to the theory of **plate tectonics**, Earth's crust is divided into giant, irregularly shaped plates (outlined in black in Figure 15.7B) that essentially float on the underlying mantle. In a process called continental drift, movements in the mantle cause the plates to move (black arrows in the figure). In some cases, the plates are moving away from each other. North America and Europe, for example, are drifting apart at a rate of about 2 cm per year. In other cases, two plates are sliding past each other, forming regions where earthquakes are common. In still other cases, two plates are colliding. Massive upheavals may occur, forming mountains along the plate boundaries. The red dots in Figure 15.7B indicate zones of violent geologic activity, most of which are associated with plate boundaries.

▲ Figure 15.7A Cross-sectional view of Earth (with the thickness of the crust exaggerated)

Consequences of Continental Drift Throughout Earth's history, continental drift has reshaped the physical features of the planet and altered the habitats in which organisms live. Figure 15.7C, on the facing page, shows continental movements that greatly influenced life during the Mesozoic and Cenozoic eras. (1) About 250 million years ago, near the end of the Paleozoic era, plate movements brought all the previously separated landmasses together into a supercontinent we call **Pangaea**, meaning "all land." When the landmasses fused, ocean basins became deeper, lowering the sea level and draining the shallow coastal seas. Then, as now, most marine species inhabited shallow waters, and much of that habitat was destroyed. The interior of the vast continent was cold and dry. Overall, the formation of Pangaea had a tremendous impact on the physical environment and climate. As the fossil record documents, biological diversity was reshaped. Many species were driven to extinction, and new opportunities arose for organisms that survived the crisis.

During the Mesozoic era, Pangaea started to break apart, causing a geographic isolation of colossal proportions. As the continents drifted apart, each became a separate evolutionary arena—a huge island on which organisms evolved in isolation from their previous neighbors. (2) At first, Pangaea split into northern and southern landmasses, which we call Laurasia and Gondwana, respectively. (3) By the end of the Mesozoic era, some 66 million years ago, the modern continents were beginning to take shape. Note that at that time Madagascar became isolated and India was still a large island. Then, around 45 million years ago, the India plate collided with the Eurasian plate, and the slow, steady buckling at the plate boundary formed the Himalayas, the tallest and youngest of Earth's mountain ranges. (4) The continents continue to drift today, and the Himalayas are still growing by about 1 cm per year.

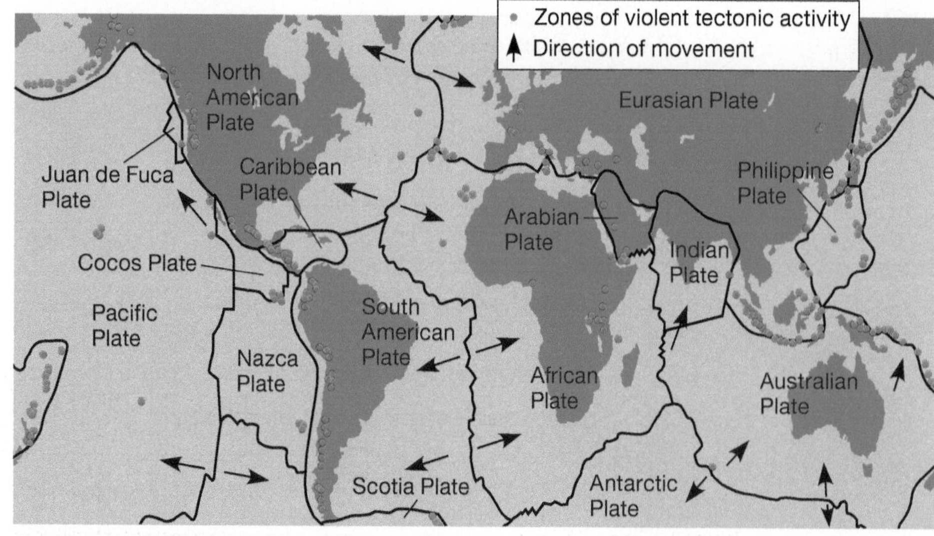

▲ Figure 15.7B Earth's tectonic plates

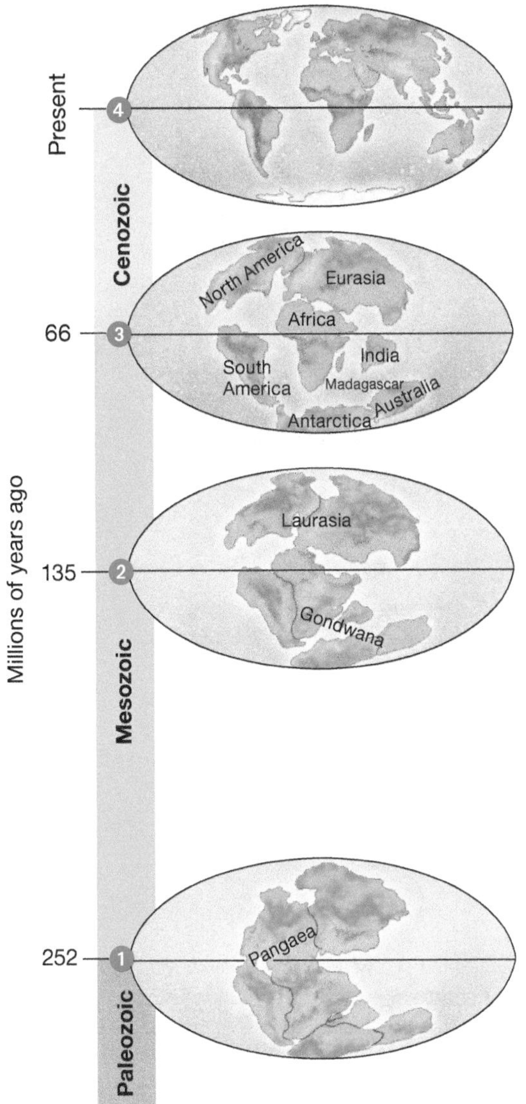

▲ **Figure 15.7C** Continental drift during the Phanerozoic eon

TRY THIS Use Table 15.6 to identify important events in the history of life that occurred while the continents occupied the positions shown at 1, 2, and 3.

The history of continental mergers and separations explains many patterns of **biogeography**, the study of the past and present distribution of organisms. For example, almost all the animals and plants that live on the island of Madagascar are unique—they diversified from ancestral populations after Madagascar was isolated from Africa and India. As in the Galápagos Islands, adaptive radiations occurred in many groups (see Module 14.8). The more than 50 species of lemurs that currently inhabit Madagascar, for instance, evolved from a common ancestor over the past 40 million years.

Continental drift solves the mystery of marsupials, mammals whose young complete their embryonic development in a pouch outside the mother's body, such as kangaroos, koalas, and wombats. Australia and its neighboring islands are home to more than 200 species of marsupials, most of which are found nowhere else in the world (**Figure 15.7D**).

What accounts for the predominance of marsupials in Australia, while the rest of the world is dominated by eutherian (placental) mammals whose young complete their development in the mother's uterus? Looking at a current map of the world, you might hypothesize that marsupials evolved only on this island continent. But marsupials are not unique to Australia. More than a hundred species live in Central and South America (**Figure 15.7E**); North America is home to only a few, including the Virginia opossum (**Figure 15.7F**). The distribution of marsupials only makes sense in the context of continental drift—marsupials must have originated when the continents were joined. Fossil evidence suggests that marsupials originated in what is now Asia and later dispersed to the tip of South America while it was still connected to Antarctica. They made their way to Australia before continental drift separated Antarctica from Australia, setting it "afloat" like a great raft of marsupials. The few early eutherians that lived there became extinct, while on other continents, most marsupials became extinct. Isolated on Australia, marsupials evolved and diversified, filling ecological roles analogous to those filled by eutherians on other continents.

Continental drift solves puzzles about the geographic distribution of extinct organisms as well as living ones. For example, paleontologists have discovered fossils of the same species of Permian freshwater reptiles in West Africa and Brazil, regions now separated by 3,000 km of ocean.

In the next module, we consider some of the perils associated with the movements of Earth's crustal plates.

? **If marsupials originated in Asia and reached Australia via South America, where else should paleontologists find fossil marsupials? (*Hint*: Look at Figure 15.7C.)**

■ Antarctica

▲ **Figure 15.7D** Greater bilby (*Macrotis lagotis*), an Australian marsupial

▲ **Figure 15.7E** Mexican mouse opossum (*Marmosa mexicana*)

▲ **Figure 15.7F** Virginia opossum female with young (*Didelphis virginiana*)

15.8 Plate tectonics may imperil human life

CONNECTION

Not only do moving crustal plates cause continents to collide, pile up, and build mountain ranges; they also produce volcanoes and earthquakes. The boundaries of plates are hot spots of such geologic activity. California's frequent earthquakes are a result of movement along the infamous San Andreas Fault, part of the border where the Pacific and North American plates grind together and gradually slide past each other in what geologists call a strike-slip fault (**Figure 15.8**). Two major earthquakes have occurred in the region in the past century: the San Francisco earthquake of 1906 and the 1989 Loma Prieta earthquake, also near San Francisco.

In such a strike-slip fault, the two plates do not slide smoothly past each other. They often stick in one spot until enough pressure builds along the fault that the landmasses suddenly jerk forward, releasing massive amounts of energy and causing the surrounding area to move or shake. A strike-slip fault running under Haiti is responsible for the devastating magnitude 7.0 earthquake of January 2010. In Haiti, the North American plate is moving west past the Caribbean plate (see Figure 15.7B). Undersea earthquakes can cause giant waves, such as the massive 2011 tsunami in Japan, a seismically active area where four tectonic plates meet.

A volcano is a rupture that allows hot, molten rock, ash, and gases to escape from beneath Earth's crust. Volcanoes are often found where tectonic plates are diverging or converging, as opposed to sliding past each other. Volcanoes can cause tremendous devastation, as when Mt. Vesuvius in southern Italy erupted in 79 AD, burying Pompeii in a layer of ash. But sometimes volcanoes imperil more than just local life, as we see in the next module.

▲ **Figure 15.8** **An aerial view of the San Andreas Fault, a boundary between two crustal plates, about 100 miles northwest of Los Angeles**

? **Volcanoes usually destroy life. How might undersea volcanoes create new opportunities for life?**

■ By creating new landmasses on which life can evolve, such as the Galápagos and Hawaiian Islands

15.9 Five mass extinctions have altered the course of evolution

Extinction is inevitable in a changing world. Indeed, the fossil record shows that the vast majority of species that have ever lived are now extinct. A species may become extinct because its habitat has been destroyed, because of unfavorable climatic changes, or because of changes in its biological community, such as the evolution of new predators or competitors. Extinctions occur all the time, but extinction rates have not been steady.

The fossil record chronicles five mass extinctions, occasions when global environmental changes were so rapid and disruptive that 50% or more of Earth's species were swept away in a relatively short amount of time. Of all the mass extinctions, the ones marking the ends of the Permian and Cretaceous periods have received the most attention.

The Permian Extinction The Permian extinction, which occurred about 252 million years ago and defines the boundary between the Paleozoic and Mesozoic eras, claimed about 96% of marine animal species and at least 70% of terrestrial life. This mass extinction occurred in less than 500,000 years, and possibly in just a few thousand years—an instant in the context of geologic time.

The Permian mass extinction occurred at a time of widespread volcanic eruptions in what is now Siberia. Besides spewing lava and sending ash and noxious gases into the atmosphere, the eruptions are thought to have produced enough carbon dioxide to warm the global climate by an estimated 6°C. Reduced temperature differences between the equator and the poles would have slowed the mixing of ocean water, leading to a widespread drop in oxygen concentration in the water. This oxygen deficit would have killed many marine organisms and promoted the growth of anaerobic bacteria that emit a poisonous by-product, hydrogen sulfide. As this gas bubbled out of the water, acid precipitation would have killed land plants and animals. Thus, a cascade of factors likely contributed to the Permian extinction.

The Cretaceous Extinction At the end of the Cretaceous period about 66 million years ago, the world again lost an enormous number of species—more than half of all marine species and many lineages of terrestrial plants and animals. At that point, dinosaurs had dominated the land and pterosaurs had ruled the air for some 150 million years. After the

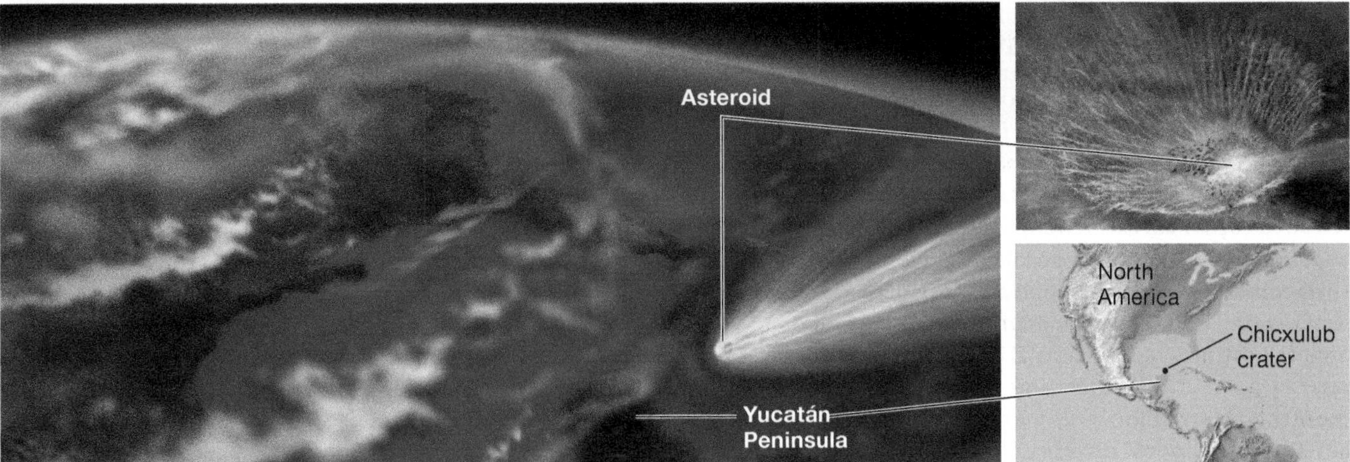

▲ **Figure 15.9** **The impact hypothesis for the Cretaceous mass extinction**

Cretaceous mass extinction, the pterosaurs and almost all the dinosaurs were gone, leaving behind only the descendants of one lineage, the birds.

One clue to a possible cause of the Cretaceous mass extinction is a thin layer of clay enriched in iridium that separates sediments from the Mesozoic and Cenozoic eras. Iridium is an element very rare on Earth but common in meteorites and other extraterrestrial objects that occasionally fall to Earth. The rocks of the Cretaceous boundary layer have many times more iridium than normal Earth levels. Most paleontologists conclude that the iridium layer is the result of fallout from a huge cloud of dust that billowed into the atmosphere when an asteroid or large comet hit Earth. The cloud would have blocked light and severely disturbed the global climate for months.

Is there evidence of such an asteroid? A large crater, the 65-million-year-old Chicxulub impact crater, has been found in the Caribbean Sea near the Yucatán Peninsula of Mexico (**Figure 15.9**). About 180 km wide (about 112 miles), the crater is the right size to have been caused by an object with a diameter of 10 km (about 6 miles). The horseshoe shape of the crater and the pattern of debris in sedimentary rocks indicate that an asteroid or comet struck at a low angle from the southeast. The artist's interpretation in Figure 15.9 represents the impact and its immediate effect—a cloud of hot vapor and debris that could have killed most of the plants and animals in North America within hours. The collision is estimated to have released more than a billion times the energy of the nuclear bombs dropped in Japan during World War II.

In March 2010, an international team of scientists reviewed two decades' worth of research on the Cretaceous extinction and endorsed the asteroid hypothesis as the triggering event. Nevertheless, research will continue on other contributing causes and the multiple and interrelated effects of this major ecological disaster.

A Sixth Mass Extinction? Currently, human activities are modifying the global environment to such an extent that many species are threatened with extinction (as we'll explore in Chapter 38). In the past 400 years, more than a thousand species are known to have become extinct. Scientists estimate that this rate is 100 to 1,000 times the normal rate seen in the fossil record.

Are we in the midst of a sixth mass extinction? In an extensive analysis published in 2011, researchers compared data from the fossil record of the "big five" mass extinctions with data from the modern era. They concluded that the current loss of biodiversity does not yet qualify as a mass extinction—but we are teetering on the brink of one. The loss of species that are now at critical risk of extinction would push our planet into a period of mass extinction. When the researchers included species that are endangered or threatened (lower categories of risk) in their calculations, the picture looks even bleaker. In contrast to the ancient mass extinctions, which unfolded over hundreds of thousands of years, a human-driven sixth mass extinction could be completed in just a few centuries.

Consequences of Mass Extinctions Whatever their causes, mass extinctions have profound effects. Loss of species can cause the collapse of an ecological community by disrupting the complex web of relationships that form its infrastructure. And once an evolutionary lineage disappears, it cannot reappear. The course of evolution is changed forever. Consider what would have happened if our early primate ancestors living 66 million years ago had died out in the Cretaceous mass extinction—or if a few large, predatory dinosaurs had *not* become extinct!

How long does it take for life to recover after a mass extinction? The fossil record shows that it typically takes 5–10 million years for the diversity of life to return to previous levels. In some cases, it has taken much longer: It took about 100 million years for the number of marine families to recover after the Permian mass extinction. But the fossil record also shows a creative side to the destruction. Mass extinctions can pave the way for adaptive radiations in which new groups rise to prominence, as we see next.

? **What groups of terrestrial organisms would have been affected by the Permian mass extinction? (*Hint*: Refer to Table 15.6.)**

■ Vascular plants, amphibians, insects, early reptiles

15.10 Adaptive radiations have increased the diversity of life

Adaptive radiations are periods of evolutionary change in which many new species evolve from a common ancestor, often following the colonization of new, unexploited areas (see Module 14.8). Adaptive radiations on a larger scale followed each mass extinction, when survivors became adapted to the many vacant ecological roles, or niches, in their communities. For example, fossil evidence indicates that mammals underwent a dramatic adaptive radiation after the extinction of terrestrial dinosaurs 66 million years ago (**Figure 15.10**). At that time, mammals had existed for more than 100 million years, but most were small creatures and there was limited diversity. Early mammals may have been eaten or outcompeted by the larger and more diverse dinosaurs. With the disappearance of the dinosaurs (except for the bird lineage), mammals expanded greatly in both diversity and size, filling the ecological roles once occupied by dinosaurs.

Adaptive radiations have also occurred following the appearance of evolutionary innovations that enabled a group of organisms to exploit an unused resource. The evolutionary history of land plants is one example (as you'll learn in Module 17.1). Major new adaptations also facilitated the colonization of land by insects and tetrapods (see Module 19.4). Organisms that originate in an adaptive radiation can themselves become a resource that spurs diversification in another group. For example, the proliferation of land plants stimulated a series of adaptive radiations in insects that pollinated or ate plants—helping to make insects the most diverse group of animals on Earth today.

Now that we've looked at geologic and environmental influences, let's take a look at the biological mechanisms of macroevolution.

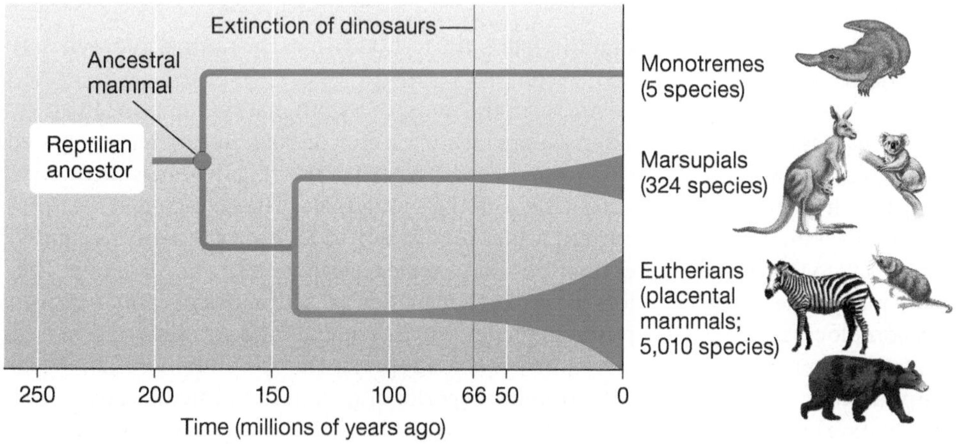

▲ **Figure 15.10** **Adaptive radiation of mammals (widening lines reflect increasing numbers of species)**

? Why did marsupial mammals undergo more diversification on the continent of Australia than elsewhere in the world (*Hint*: See Module 15.7).

Eutherians became extinct on Australia. Marsupials evolved and diversified, filling ecological roles that might otherwise have been filled by eutherians.

15.11 Genes that control development play a major role in evolution

The fossil record can tell us *what* the great events in the history of life have been and *when* they occurred. Continental drift, mass extinctions, and adaptive radiation provide the big picture of *how* those changes came about. But now we are increasingly able to understand the basic biological mechanisms that underlie the changes seen in the fossil record.

Scientists working at the interface of evolutionary biology and developmental biology—the research field abbreviated **"evo-devo"**—are studying how slight genetic changes can become magnified into major morphological differences between species. Genes that program development control the rate, timing, and spatial pattern of change in an organism's form as it develops from a zygote into an adult. A great many of these genes appear to have been conserved throughout evolutionary history: The same or very similar genes are involved in the development of form across multiple lineages.

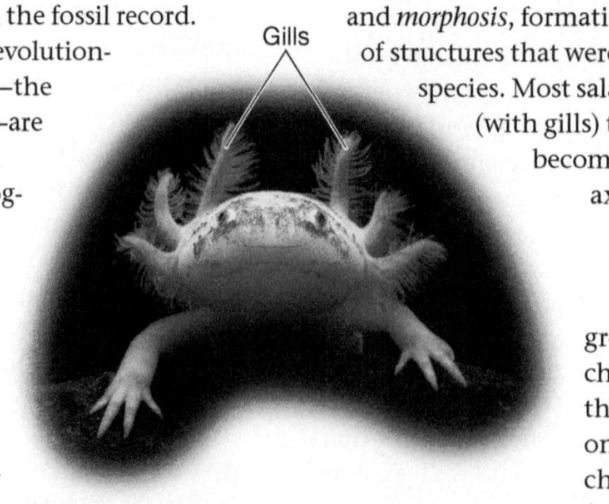

▲ **Figure 15.11A** **An axolotl, a paedomorphic salamander**

Changes in Rate and Timing Many striking evolutionary transformations are the result of a change in the rate or timing of developmental events. **Figure 15.11A** shows a photograph of an axolotl, a salamander that illustrates a phenomenon called **paedomorphosis** (from the Greek *paedos*, of a child, and *morphosis*, formation), the retention in the adult body of structures that were juvenile features in an ancestral species. Most salamander species have aquatic larvae (with gills) that undergo metamorphosis in becoming terrestrial adults (with lungs). The axolotl is a salamander that grows to a sexually mature adult while retaining gills and other larval features.

Slight changes in the relative growth of different body parts can change an adult form substantially. As the skulls and photo in **Figure 15.11B** on the next page show, humans and chimpanzees are much more alike as fetuses than they are as adults. As development proceeds, accelerated growth

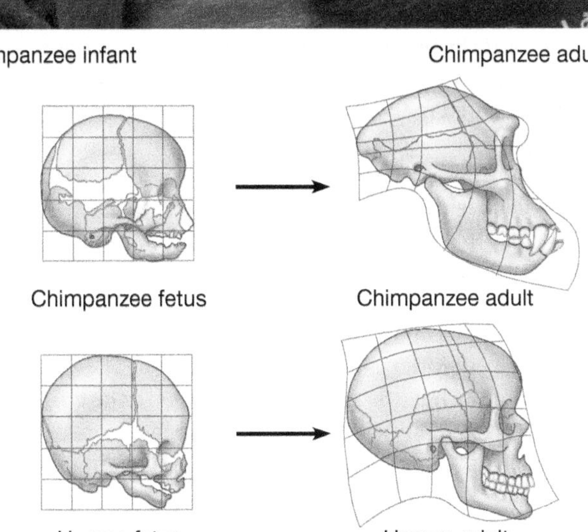

▲ **Figure 15.11B** **Chimpanzee and human skull shapes compared**

in the jaw produces the elongated skull, sloping forehead, and massive jaws of an adult chimpanzee. In the human lineage, genetic changes that slowed the growth of the jaw relative to other parts of the skull produced an adult whose head proportions still resembled that of a child (and that of a baby chimpanzee). Our large skull and complex brain are among our most distinctive features. Compared with the slow growth of a chimpanzee brain after birth, our brain continues to grow at the rapid rate of a fetal brain for the first year of life.

Changes in Spatial Pattern Homeotic genes, the master control genes, determine such basic features as where a pair of wings or legs will develop on a fruit fly (see Module 11.8). Changes in homeotic genes or in how or where such genes are expressed can have a profound impact on body form. Consider, for example, the evolution of snakes from a four-limbed lizard-like ancestor. Researchers have found that one pattern of expression of two homeotic genes in tetrapods results in the formation of forelimbs and of vertebrae with ribs, whereas a different pattern of expression of these two genes results in the development of vertebrae with ribs but no limbs, as in snakes (see Figure 30.3C).

New Genes and Changes in Genes New developmental genes that arose as a result of gene duplications may have facilitated the origin of new body forms. For example, a fruit fly (an invertebrate) has a single cluster of several homeotic genes that direct the development of major body parts. A mouse (a vertebrate) has four clusters of very similar genes that occur in the same linear order on chromosomes and direct the development of the same body regions as the fly genes (see Figure 27.14B). Two duplications of these gene clusters appear to have occurred in the evolution of vertebrates from invertebrate animals. Mutations in these duplicated genes may then have led to the origin of novel vertebrate characters, such as a backbone, jaws, and limbs.

Changes in Gene Regulation Researchers are finding that changes in the form of organisms often are caused by mutations that affect the regulation of developmental genes. As we just discussed, such a change in gene expression was shown to correlate with the lack of forelimbs in snakes.

Additional evidence for this type of change in gene regulation is seen in studies of the three-spined stickleback fish. In western Canada, these fish live in the ocean and also in lakes that formed when the coastline receded during the past 12,000 years. Ocean populations have bony plates that make up a kind of body armor and a set of pelvic spines that help deter predatory fish. The body armor and pelvic spines are reduced or absent in three-spined sticklebacks living in lakes that lack predatory fishes and that are also low in calcium. In the absence of predators, spineless sticklebacks may have a selective advantage because the limited calcium is needed for purposes other than constructing spines. Figure 15.11C shows specimens of an ocean and a lake stickleback, which have been stained to highlight their bony plates and spines.

Researchers have identified a key gene that influences the development of these spines. Was the reduction of spines in lake populations due to changes in the gene itself or to changes in where the gene is expressed? It turns out that the gene is identical in the two populations, and it is expressed in the mouth region and other tissues of embryos from both populations. Studies have shown, however, that while the gene is also expressed in the developing pelvic region of ocean sticklebacks, it is not turned on in the pelvic region in lake sticklebacks. This example shows how morphological change can be caused by altering the expression of a developmental gene in some parts of the body but not others.

? **Research shows that many differences in body form are caused by changes in gene regulation and not changes in the nucleotide sequence of the developmental gene itself. Why might this be the case?**

■ A change in sequence may affect a gene's function wherever that gene is expressed—with potentially harmful effects. Changes in the regulation of gene expression can be limited to specific areas in a developing embryo.

▲ **Figure 15.11C** **Stickleback fish from ocean (top) and lake (bottom), stained to show bony plates and spines. (Arrow indicates the absence of the pelvic spine in the lake fish.)**

15.12 Novel traits may arise in several ways

EVOLUTION CONNECTION

Let's see how the Darwinian theory of gradual change can account for the evolution of intricate structures such as eyes or of novel body structures such as wings (that is, new kinds of structures). Most complex structures have evolved in increments from simpler versions having the same basic function—a process of refinement.

Consider the amazing camera-like eyes of vertebrates and squids. Although these complex eyes evolved independently, the origin of both can be traced from a simple ancestral patch of photoreceptor cells through a series of incremental modifications that benefited their owners at each stage. Indeed, there appears to have been a single evolutionary origin of light-sensitive cells, and all animals with eyes—vertebrates and invertebrates alike—share the same master genes that regulate eye development.

Figure 15.12 illustrates the range of complexity in the structure of eyes among molluscs living today. Simple patches of pigmented cells enable limpets to distinguish light from dark, and they cling more tightly to their rock when a shadow falls on them—a behavioral adaptation that reduces the risk of being eaten. Other molluscs have eyecups that have no lenses or other means of focusing images but can indicate light direction. In those molluscs that do have complex eyes, the organs probably evolved in small steps of adaptation.

Although eyes have retained their basic function of vision throughout their evolutionary history, evolutionary novelty can also arise when structures that originally played one role gradually acquire a different one. Structures that evolve in one context but become co-opted for another function are called *exaptations*. However, exaptation does not mean that a structure evolves in anticipation of future use. Natural selection cannot predict the future; it can only improve an existing structure in the context of its current use. Novel features can arise gradually via a series of intermediate stages, each of which has some function in the organism's current situation.

The evolution of feathers is a good example of exaptation. Some paleontologists hypothesize that an entire lineage of dinosaurs—including the fearsome *Tyrannosaurus rex*—had feathers. But the feathers seen in these fossils could not have been used for flight, nor would their reptilian anatomy have been suited to flying. If feathers evolved before flight, what was their function? Their first utility may have been for insulation. It is possible that longer, winglike forelimbs and feathers, which increased the surface area of these forelimbs, were co-opted for flight after functioning in some other capacity, such as mating displays, thermoregulation, or camouflage (all functions that feathers still serve today). The first flights may have been only short glides to the ground or from branch to branch in tree-dwelling species. Once flight itself became an advantage, natural selection would have gradually remodeled feathers and wings to fit their additional function.

How do brand-new structures arise by evolution?

The flippers of penguins are another example of the modification of existing structures for different functions. Penguins cannot fly, but their modified wings are powerful oars that make them strong, fast underwater swimmers.

? **Explain why the concept of exaptation does not imply that a structure evolves in anticipation of some future environmental change.**

■ Although a structure is co-opted for new or additional functions in a new environment, the structure existed because it worked as an adaptation in the old environment.

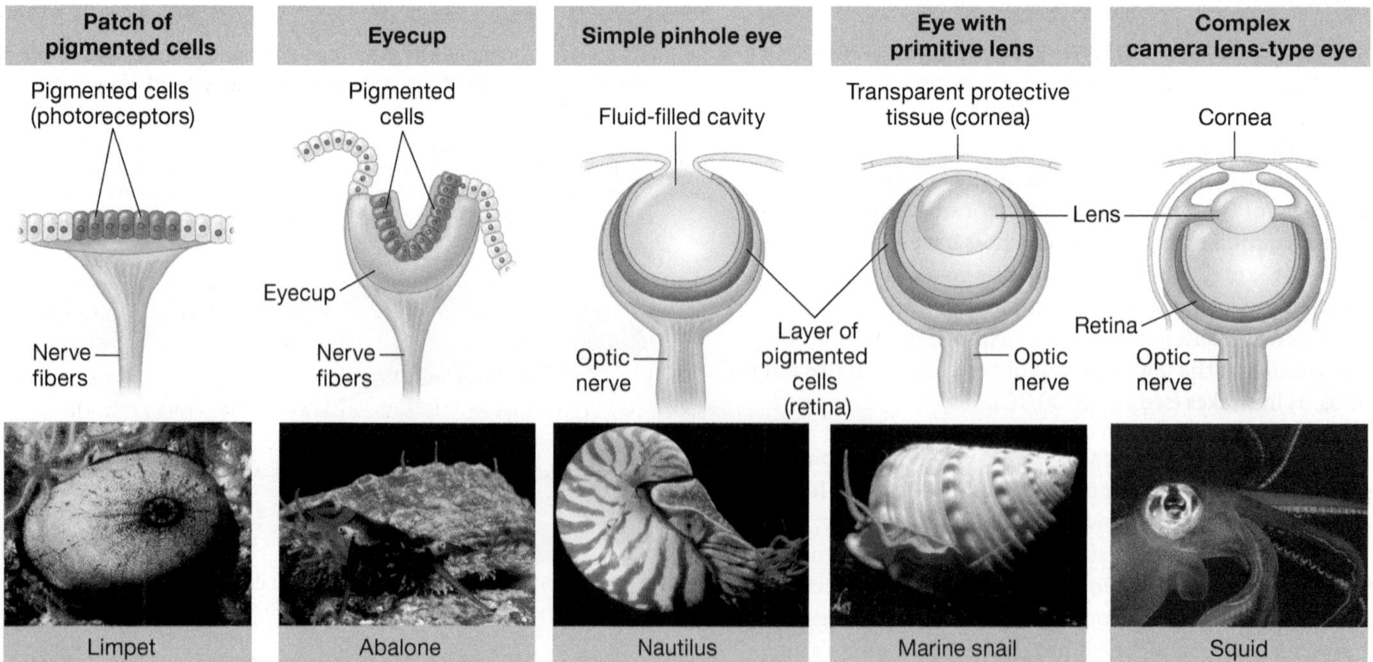

▲ **Figure 15.12** A range of eye complexity among molluscs

15.13 Evolutionary trends do not mean that evolution is goal directed

The fossil record seems to show trends in the evolution of many species, for example, toward larger or smaller body size. Let's look at apparent trends in the evolution of the modern horse (genus *Equus*), from an ancestor known as *Hyracotherium* that lived some 55 million years ago. *Hyracotherium*, which was about the size of a large dog, had four toes on its front feet and three toes on its hind feet. Its teeth were adapted to browsing on shrubs and trees. In contrast, the present-day horse has only one toe on each foot (the hoof) and teeth modified for grazing on grasses.

Did the horse lineage progress gradually toward larger size, reduced number of toes, and teeth adapted to grazing? **Figure 15.13** shows the fossil record of horses, with the vertical bars representing the period of time each group persisted in the record. If you follow the fossil species highlighted in yellow from the bottom to the top of Figure 15.13, it appears that modern horses evolved linearly from *Hyracotherium* to *Equus* through a series of intermediate forms. However, if we consider *all* fossil horses known today, this apparent trend vanishes. The genus *Equus* actually descended through a series of speciation episodes, not all of which led to large, one-toed grazers. The present-day horse is the only surviving twig of an evolutionary tree with many divergent branches.

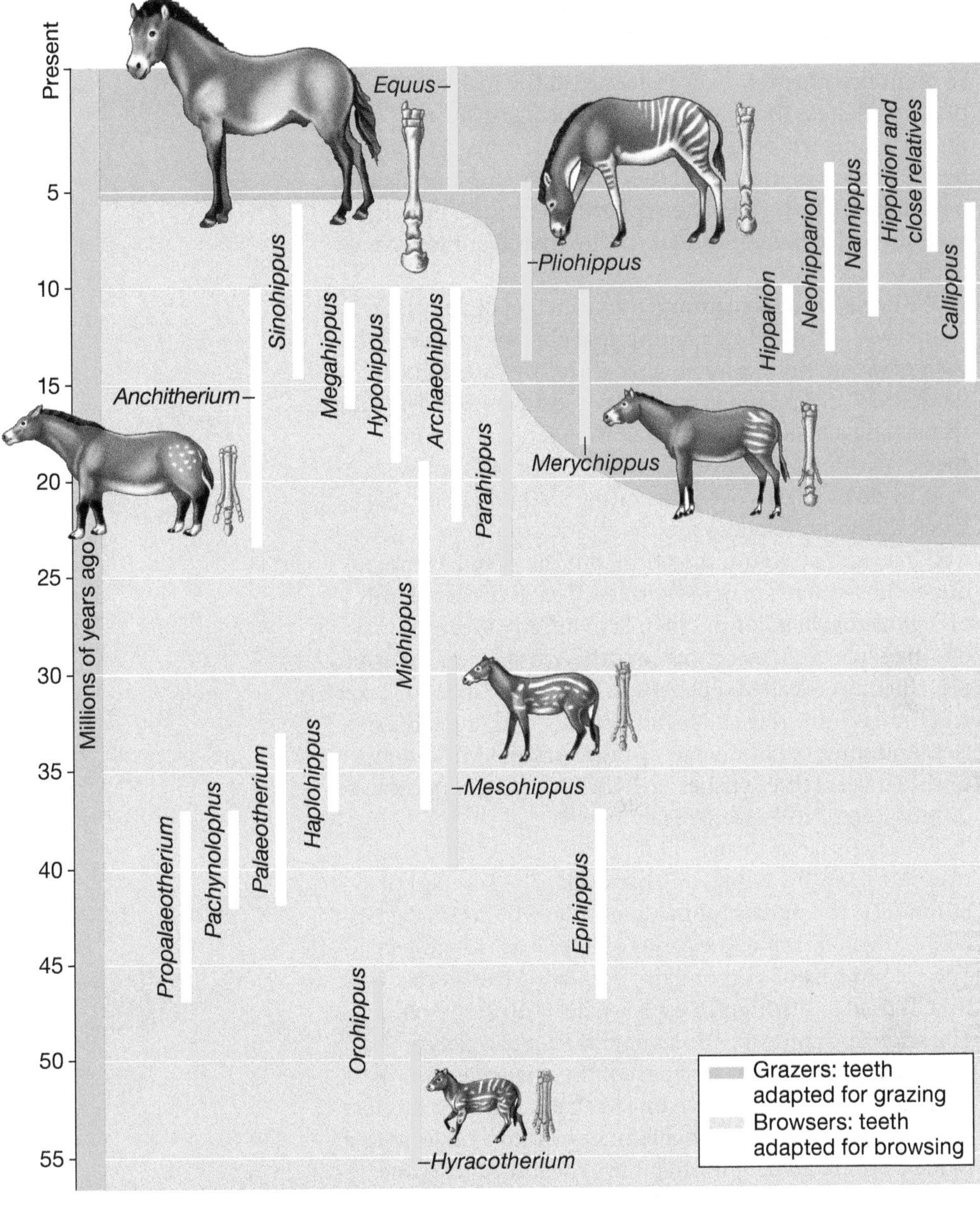

▲ **Figure 15.13** **The branched evolution of horses**

Branching evolution *can* lead to a real evolutionary trend, however. One model of long-term trends compares species with individuals: Speciation is their birth, extinction their death, and new species that diverge from them are their offspring. According to this model of species selection, unequal survival of species and unequal generation of new species play a role in macroevolution similar to the role of unequal reproduction in microevolution. In other words, the species that generate the greatest number of new species determine the direction of major evolutionary trends.

Evolutionary trends can also result directly from natural selection. For example, when horse ancestors invaded the grasslands that spread during the mid-Cenozoic, there was strong selection for grazers that could escape predators by running faster. This trend would not have occurred without open grasslands.

Whatever its cause, it is important to recognize that an evolutionary trend does not imply that evolution progresses toward a particular goal. Evolution is the result of interactions between organisms and the current environment. If conditions change, an apparent trend may cease or even reverse itself.

In the final section, we explore how biologists arrange life's astounding diversity into an evolutionary tree of life.

? A trend in the evolution of mammals was toward a larger brain size. Use the species selection model to explain how such a trend could occur.

■ Those species with larger brains persisted longer before extinction and gave rise to more "offspring" species than did species with smaller brains.

Phylogeny and the Tree of Life

15.14 Taxonomy names and classifies the diversity of life

So far in this chapter, we have looked at the major evolutionary changes that have occurred during the history of life on Earth and explored some of the mechanisms that underlie the process of macroevolution. Now we shift our focus to how biologists use the pattern of evolution to distinguish and categorize the millions of species that live, and have lived, on Earth.

We begin with **taxonomy**, the branch of biology concerned with identifying, naming, and classifying species. The basis of taxonomy is a system introduced by 18th-century naturalist Carolus Linneus, who devised a method of naming species and a hierarchical classification scheme that nests species within progressively broader groups of organisms.

Why do biologists need a scientific method for naming species? Common names such as squirrel and daisy may work well in everyday communication, but they can be ambiguous because there are many species of each of these kinds of organisms. In addition, people in different regions may use the same common name for different species. For example, the flowers called bluebells in Scotland, England, Texas, and the eastern United States are actually four unrelated species. And some common names are downright misleading. Consider these three "fishes": jellyfish (a cnidarian), crayfish (a crustacean), and silverfish (an insect).

In the Linnaean system, biologists assign each species a two-part scientific name, or **binomial**. The first part of a binomial is the **genus** (plural, *genera*) to which the species belongs. For example, the genus of large cats is *Panthera*. The second part of a binomial, often called the specific epithet, is used to distinguish each species within the genus. The scientific name for the leopard is *Panthera pardus*; the lion is *Panthera leo*. The first part of the scientific name is analogous to a person's surname in that it is shared by close relatives. The specific epithet is analogous to a person's first name—unrelated people often have the same first name. For example, "*pardus*," a Latin word meaning "leopard," is the second part of the binomial of diverse spotted species: The scientific name of the leopard toadfish is *Opsanus pardus* and *Maratus pardus* is a spider. Thus, both parts must be used together to name a species. Notice that the first letter of the genus name is capitalized and that the binomial is italicized. Once an organism's full scientific name has been used, biologists often use only the initial letter of the genus name, for example, *P. pardus*.

Linnaeus also introduced a system for grouping species into a hierarchy of increasingly inclusive categories. The first step of this classification is built into the binomial. For example, the genus *Panthera* includes three other species: the lion (*Panthera leo*), the tiger (*Panthera tigris*), and the jaguar (*Panthera onca*). Beyond the grouping of species within genera, the Linnaean system extends to progressively broader categories of classification. It places related genera in the same **family**, puts families into **orders**, orders into **classes**, classes into **phyla** (singular, *phylum*), phyla into **kingdoms**, and kingdoms into **domains**.

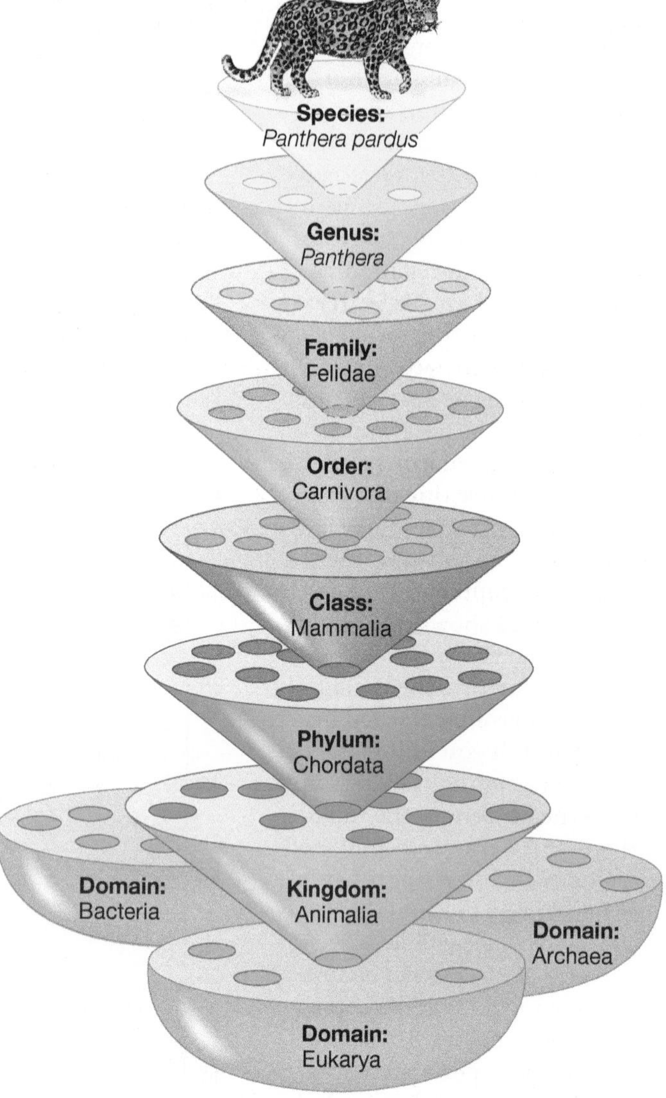

▲ **Figure 15.14 Hierarchical classification of the leopard**

Figure 15.14 uses the leopard (*Panthera pardus*) to illustrate this nested series of categories. *P. pardus* and the three other members of the genus *Panthera* are represented by small yellow circles in the figure. The genus *Panthera* is placed in the cat family, Felidae, along with other genera of cats, such as the genus *Lynx*, which includes the bobcat and the Canadian lynx. Family Felidae belongs to the order Carnivora, which also includes the family Canidae (for example, the wolf and coyote) and several other families. Order Carnivora is grouped with many other orders in the class Mammalia, the mammals. Class Mammalia is one of the classes belonging to the phylum Chordata in the kingdom Animalia, which is one of four kingdoms in the domain Eukarya (see Module 15.17). Each taxonomic unit at any level—family Felidae or class Mammalia, for instance—is called a **taxon** (plural, *taxa*).

Although it may satisfy our sense of order to know exactly where an organism fits in this hierarchical scheme, classifying species into higher (more inclusive) taxa is ultimately arbitrary. These broad groups are generally defined by morphological characters chosen by taxonomists rather than by quantitative measurements that could apply to the same taxon level across all lineages.

How much of the classification in Figure 15.14 do we share with the leopard?

■ We are classified the same from the domain to the class level: Both leopards and humans are mammals. We do not belong to the same order.

15.15 Phylogenies based on homologies reflect evolutionary history

Ever since Darwin, biologists have had a goal beyond simple organization: to have classification reflect evolutionary relationships. In other words, how an organism is named and classified should reflect its place within the evolutionary tree of life. The evolutionary history of a species or group of species is called **phylogeny** (from the Greek *phylon*, tribe, and *genesis*, origin). **Systematics**, which includes taxonomy, is a discipline of biology that focuses on classifying organisms and determining their evolutionary relationships.

Biologists traditionally use **phylogenetic trees** to depict hypotheses about the evolutionary history of species. These branching diagrams reflect the hierarchical classification of groups nested within more inclusive groups. Figure 15.15A illustrates the connection between classification and phylogeny by showing the classification of some of the taxa in the order Carnivora and the probable evolutionary relationships among these groups. Note that such a phylogenetic tree does not indicate when a particular species evolved but only the pattern of descent from the last common ancestors of the species shown.

To construct phylogenetic trees, systematists gather morphological and molecular data about the relevant organisms, including evidence from the fossil record. The important features are those that result from common ancestry, because only such features reflect evolutionary relationships. Recall that similarities attributable to shared ancestry are called homologies (see Module 13.4). An example of a morphological homology is the similarity in the forelimb bones of mammals due to their descent from a common ancestor with the same bone structure. In the same way, genes are homologous if they are descended from genes carried by a common ancestor.

Order	Family	Genus	Species
Carnivora	Felidae	*Panthera*	*Panthera pardus* (leopard)
	Mustelidae	*Mustela*	*Mustela frenata* (long-tailed weasel)
		Lutra	*Lutra lutra* (European otter)
	Canidae	*Canis*	*Canis latrans* (coyote)
			Canis lupus (wolf)

▲ Figure 15.15A Relating classification to phylogeny

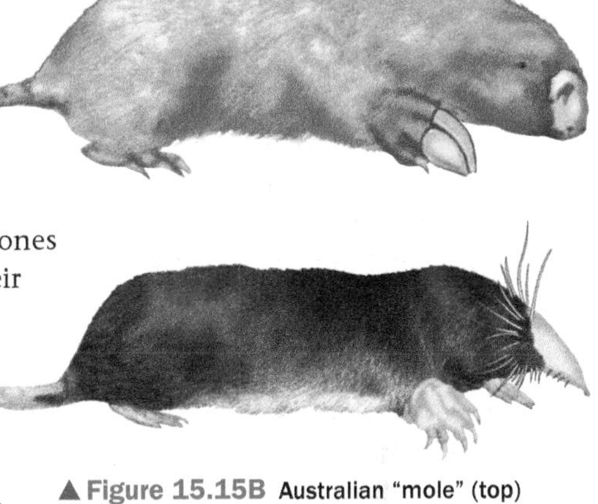

▲ Figure 15.15B Australian "mole" (top) and North American mole (bottom)

A potential source of confusion in constructing a phylogeny is similarity between organisms that is due to convergent evolution. **Convergent evolution** occurs when similar environments and natural selection produce similar adaptations in organisms from different evolutionary lineages. Similarity due to convergent evolution is called **analogy**. For example, the two mole-like animals shown in Figure 15.15B are very similar in external appearance. They both have enlarged front paws, small eyes, and a pad of protective thickened skin on the nose. Despite these similarities in STRUCTURE AND FUNCTION, the Australian "mole" (top) is a marsupial; the North American mole (bottom) is a eutherian. Genetic and fossil evidence indicates that the last common ancestor of these two animals lived 140 million years ago. And in fact, that ancestor and most of its descendants were not mole-like. Analogous traits evolved independently in these two mole lineages as they each became adapted to burrowing lifestyles.

In addition to molecular comparisons and fossil evidence, another clue to distinguishing homology from analogy is to consider the complexity of the structure being compared. For instance, the skulls of a human and a chimpanzee (see Figure 15.11B) consist of many bones fused together, and the composition of these skulls matches almost perfectly, bone for bone. It is highly improbable that such complex structures have separate origins. More likely, the genes involved in the development of both skulls were inherited from a common ancestor, and these complex structures are homologous.

? Human forearms and a bat's wings are ________. A bat's wings and a bee's wings are ________.

■ homologous ··· analogous

15.16 Shared characters are used to construct phylogenetic trees

In reconstructing a group's evolutionary history, biologists first sort homologous features, which reflect evolutionary relationship, from analogous features, which do not. They then infer phylogeny using these homologous characters.

Cladistics The most widely used method of constructing phylogenies is called cladistics. In **cladistics**, organisms are grouped by common ancestry. A **clade** (from the Greek *clados*, branch) consists of an ancestral species and all its evolutionary descendants—a distinct branch in the tree of life. Such an inclusive group of ancestor and descendants, be it a genus, family, or some broader taxon, is said to be **monophyletic** (meaning "single tribe"). Thus, identifying clades makes it possible to devise classification schemes that reflect the branching pattern of evolution.

Cladistics is based on the Darwinian concept of "descent with modification from a common ancestor"—species have some characters in common with their ancestors, but they also differ from them. Thus, systematists focus on two types of characters. A **shared ancestral character** is common to members of a particular clade, but originated in an ancestor that is not a member of the clade. For example, all mammals have backbones, but the presence of a backbone does not distinguish mammals from other vertebrates. The backbone predates the branching of the mammalian clade from other vertebrates. A **shared derived character** is common to members of a particular clade and is *not* found in its ancestors—it is an evolutionary novelty unique to that clade. Shared derived characters distinguish clades and thus mark branch points in the tree of life.

Inferring Phylogenies Using Shared Characters We'll use a simplified example to show how shared derived characters can be used to construct a phylogenetic tree. The table in Figure 15.16A compares five animals according to the presence (indicated by a 1) or absence (indicated by a 0) of a set of characters. Notice that the frog possesses none of these characters. The frog, representing amphibians, is an **outgroup**, a species from a lineage that is closely related to but not part of the group of species we are studying, the **ingroup** (the other four animals). In our example, the frog and the other four animals are all related in that they are tetrapods (vertebrates with four limbs). By comparing members of the ingroup with the outgroup and with each other, we can determine the clade in which each shared derived character first appeared in vertebrate evolution. That information is then used to infer evolutionary relationships.

Let's work through this example step by step. All four animals in the ingroup have an amnion, a membrane that encloses the embryo in a fluid-filled sac. The outgroup does not have this character. Now consider the next character—hair and mammary glands. This character is absent in the outgroup (frog) and in the iguana, but present in all other members of the ingroup (duck-billed platypus, kangaroo, and beaver). Hair and mammary glands are shared derived characters, evolutionary innovations unique to mammals.

The third character in the table is gestation, the carrying of developing offspring within the uterus of the female parent. Gestation is absent in the outgroup and in iguanas—frogs release their eggs into the water, and iguanas and most other reptiles lay eggs with a shell. Gestation is also absent in the duck-billed platypus, which also lays eggs with a shell. From this we might infer that the duck-billed platypus represents an early branch point in the mammalian clade. In fact, this hypothesis is strongly supported by structural,

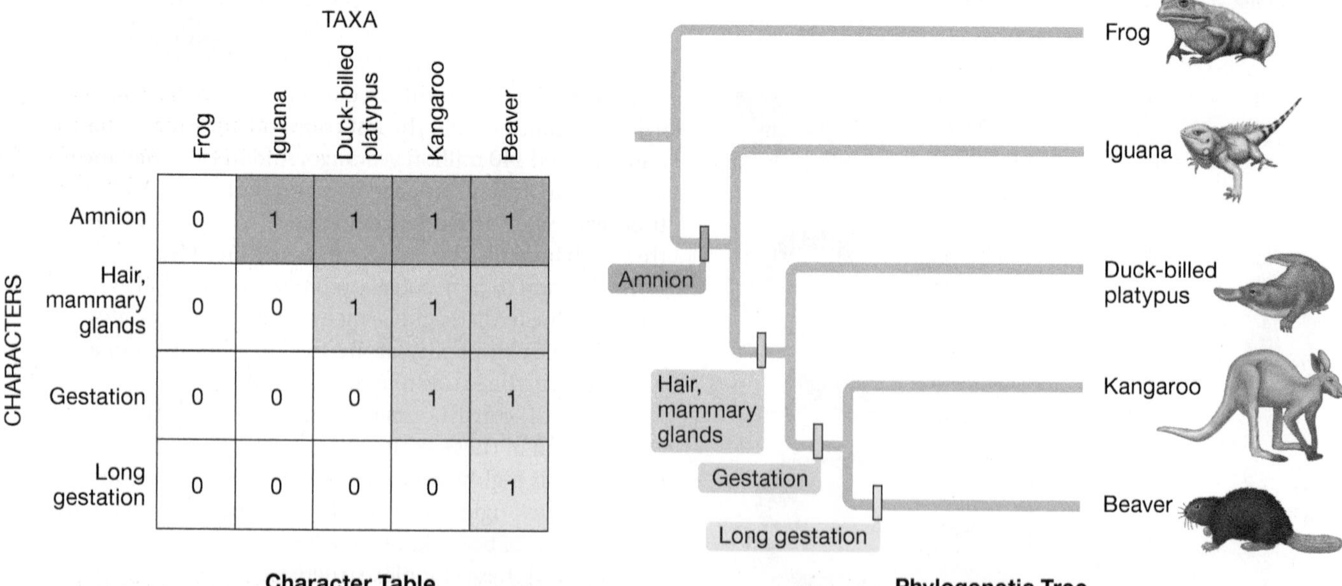

TAXA

CHARACTERS	Frog	Iguana	Duck-billed platypus	Kangaroo	Beaver
Amnion	0	1	1	1	1
Hair, mammary glands	0	0	1	1	1
Gestation	0	0	0	1	1
Long gestation	0	0	0	0	1

Character Table

Phylogenetic Tree

▲ **Figure 15.16A** Constructing a phylogenetic tree using cladistics

TRY THIS Label the outgroup and the ingroup. Circle the branch point that represents the most recent common ancestor of kangaroos and beavers, and name the derived character that defines this branch point.

fossil, and molecular evidence. The final character is long gestation, in which an offspring completes its embryonic development within the uterus. This is the case for a beaver, but a kangaroo has a very short gestation period and completes its embryonic development while nursing in its mother's pouch.

We can now translate the data in our table of characters into a phylogenetic tree. Such a tree is constructed from a series of two-way branch points (see Module 13.5). Each branch point represents the divergence of two groups from a common ancestor and the emergence of a lineage possessing a new set of derived characters. By tracing the distribution of shared derived characters, you can see how we inferred the sequence of branching and the evolutionary relationships of this group of animals.

Parsimony Useful in many areas of science, **parsimony** is the adoption of the simplest explanation for observed phenomena. Systematists use the principle of parsimony to construct phylogenetic trees that require the smallest number of evolutionary changes. For instance, parsimony leads to the hypothesis that a beaver is more closely related to a kangaroo than to a platypus, because in both the beaver and the kangaroo, embryos begin development within the female uterus. It is possible that gestation evolved twice, once in the kangaroo lineage and independently in the beaver lineage, but this explanation is more complicated and therefore less likely. Typical cladistic analyses involve much more complex data sets than the example in Figure 15.16A, often including comparisons of DNA sequences. Consequently, systematists use computer programs designed to construct parsimonious trees.

Phylogenetic Trees as Hypotheses Systematists use many kinds of evidence, including structural and developmental features, molecular data, and behavioral traits, to reconstruct evolutionary histories. However, even the best tree represents only the most likely hypothesis based on available evidence. As new data accumulate, hypotheses may be revised and new trees drawn.

An example of a redrawn tree is shown in Figure 15.16B. In traditional vertebrate taxonomy, crocodiles, snakes, lizards, and other reptiles were classified in the class Reptilia, while birds were placed in the separate class Aves. However, such a reptilian clade is not monophyletic—in other words, it does not include an ancestral species and all of its descendants, one group of which includes the birds. Many lines of evidence support the tree shown in Figure 15.16B, showing that birds belong to the clade of reptiles.

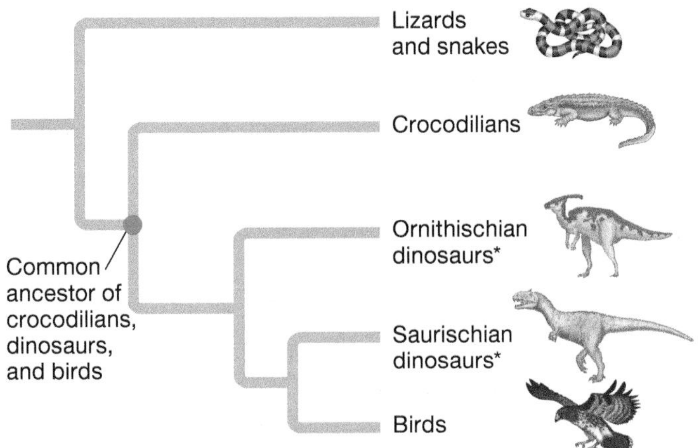

▲ **Figure 15.16B** A phylogenetic tree of reptiles (* indicates extinct lineages)

Thinking of phylogenetic trees as hypotheses allows us to use them to make and test predictions. For example, if our phylogeny is correct, then features shared by two groups of closely related organisms should be present in their common ancestor. Using this reasoning, consider the novel predictions that can be made about dinosaurs. As seen in the tree in Figure 15.16B, the closest *living* relatives of birds are crocodiles. Birds and crocodiles share numerous features: They have four-chambered hearts, they "sing" to defend territories and attract mates (although a crocodile "song" is more like a bellow), and they build nests. Both birds and crocodiles care for and warm their eggs by brooding. Birds brood by sitting on their eggs, whereas crocodiles cover their eggs with their neck. Reasoning that any feature shared by birds and crocodiles is likely to have been present in their common ancestor (denoted by the red circle in Figure 15.16B) and all of its descendants, biologists hypothesize that dinosaurs had four-chambered hearts, sang, built nests, and exhibited brooding.

Internal organs such as hearts rarely fossilize, and it is, of course, difficult to determine whether dinosaurs sang. However, fossilized dinosaur nests have been found. Figure 15.16C shows a fossil of an *Oviraptor* dinosaur thought to have died in a sandstorm while incubating or protecting its eggs. The hypothesis that dinosaurs built nests and exhibited brooding has been further supported by additional fossils that show other species of dinosaurs caring for their eggs.

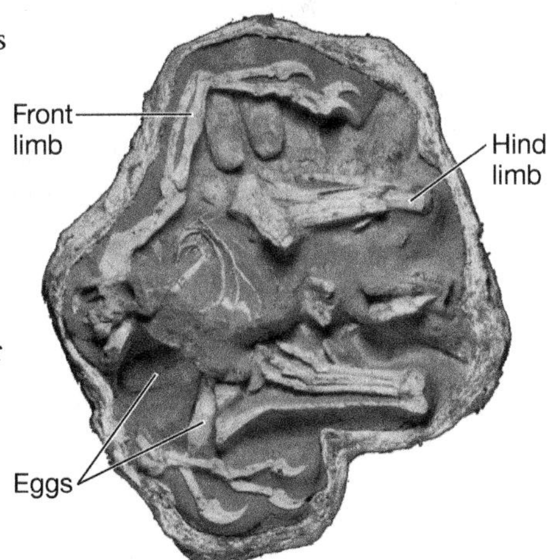

▲ **Figure 15.16C** Fossil remains of *Oviraptor* and eggs. The orientation of the bones, which surround the eggs, suggests that the dinosaur died while incubating or protecting its eggs.

The more we know about an organism and its relatives, the more accurately we can portray its phylogeny. In the next module, we consider how molecular biology is providing valuable data for tracing evolutionary history.

? To distinguish a particular clade of mammals within the larger clade that corresponds to class Mammalia, why is hair not a useful character?

■ Hair is a shared ancestral character common to all mammals and thus is not helpful in distinguishing different mammalian subgroups.

15.17 An organism's evolutionary history is documented in its genome

The more recently two species have branched from a common ancestor, the more similar their DNA sequences should be. The longer two species have been on separate evolutionary paths, the more their DNA is expected to have diverged.

Molecular Systematics A method called **molecular systematics**, which uses DNA or other molecules to infer relatedness, has fueled a boom in the study of phylogeny and clarified many evolutionary relationships. One early impact of molecular systematics was the addition of a new taxonomic category above the kingdom level, the domain. The previous classification system recognized five kingdoms, Monera (prokaryotes), Protista (a diverse kingdom consisting mostly of unicellular eukaryotes), Plantae, Fungi, and Animalia, By comparing the nucleotide sequences of ribosomal RNA (rRNA; see Module 10.12), researchers demonstrated that many prokaryotes once classified as bacteria are actually more closely related to eukaryotes. The **three-domain system** distinguishes two domains of prokaryotes, **Bacteria** and **Archaea**. The third domain, **Eukarya**, contains all of the eukaryotes, including kingdoms Fungi, Plantae, and Animalia, as well as the protists. (We'll take a closer look at the evolutionary relationships among these groups in Module 15.19.)

The observation that different genes evolve at different rates allows scientists to use molecular systematics for constructing phylogenetic trees that encompass both long and short periods of time. Because the DNA specifying ribosomal RNA (rRNA) changes relatively slowly, comparisons of DNA sequences in these genes are useful for investigating relationships between taxa that diverged hundreds of millions of years ago. Studies of the genes for rRNA have shown, for example, that fungi are more closely related to animals than to green plants—something that certainly could not have been deduced from morphological comparisons alone.

In contrast, the DNA in mitochondria (mtDNA) evolves relatively rapidly and can be used to investigate more recent evolutionary events. **Figure 15.17** presents a phylogenetic hypothesis for bears based on mtDNA analysis—with one exception, which is discussed below. Notice that the phylogenetic tree in Figure 15.17 includes a timeline, which is based on fossil evidence and molecular data that can estimate when many of these divergences occurred. (Most of the phylogenetic trees we have seen so far indicate only the relative order in which lineages diverged; they do not show the timing of those events.)

Mitochondria DNA has also been used to study human populations. For example, researchers have used mtDNA sequences to study the relationships between Native American groups. Their studies support earlier evidence that the Pima of Arizona, the Maya of Mexico, and the Yanomami of Venezuela are closely related, probably descending from the first wave of immigrants to cross the Bering Land Bridge from Asia to the Americas about 15,000 years ago.

Rapid advances in genomics (see Module 12.17) have vastly expanded the amount of data available to systematists and helped clarify many evolutionary relationships. For example, brown bears and polar bears are closely related and are even able to interbreed (see Figure 14.2C; grizzly bears are a subspecies of brown bear). Genetic evidence showed that polar bears and brown bears are separate species, but preliminary estimates of when the two species diverged ranged from 600,000 to 5 million years ago. In 2014, researchers published an analysis of the complete genomes of 89 individual bears. Using this extensive data set, they were able to show that the species diverged very recently, between 343,000 and 479,000 years ago, as shown in Figure 15.17.

Genome Evolution As new molecular technologies provide insight into how genomes evolved, some interesting

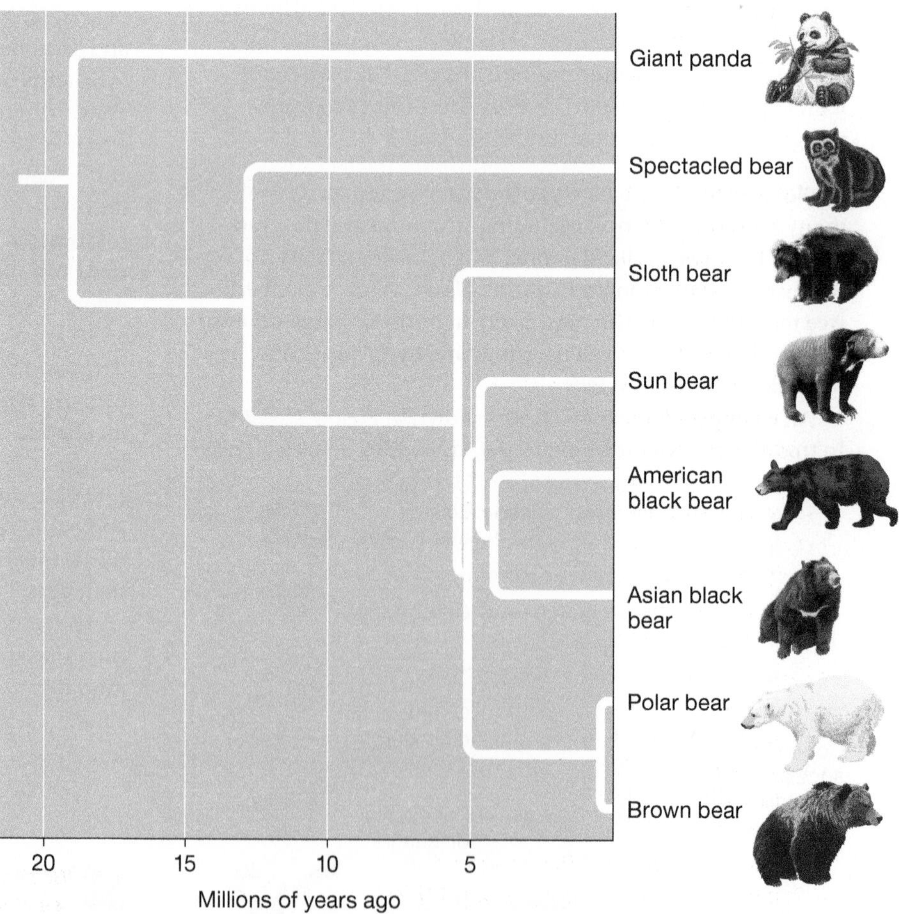

Data from J. Krause et al., Mitochondrial genomes reveal an explosive radiation of extinct and extant bears near the Miocene-Pliocene boundary, *BMC Evolutionary Biology* 8: 220–31 (2008).

▲ **Figure 15.17** **A phylogenetic tree of the bear family (Ursidae) based on mitochondrial DNA**

facts have emerged. As you may have heard, the genomes of humans and chimpanzees are strikingly similar. An even more remarkable fact is that homologous genes (similar genes that species share because of descent from a common ancestor) are widespread and can extend over huge evolutionary distances. Although the genes of humans and mice are certainly not identical, 99% of them are detectably homologous. And 50% of human genes are homologous with those of yeast. This remarkable commonality demonstrates that all living organisms share many biochemical and developmental pathways and provides overwhelming support for Darwin's theory of "descent with modification."

Gene duplication has played a particularly important role in evolution because it increases the number of genes in the genome, providing additional opportunities for further evolutionary changes (see Module 15.11). Molecular techniques now allow scientists to trace the evolutionary history of such duplications—in which lineage they occurred and how the multiple copies of genes have diverged from each other over time.

Another interesting fact evident from genome comparisons is that the number of genes has not increased at the same rate as the complexity of organisms. Humans have only about four times as many genes as yeasts. Yeasts are simple, single-celled eukaryotes; humans have a complex brain and a body that contains more than 200 different types of tissues. Evidence is emerging that many human genes are more versatile than those of yeast, but explaining the mechanisms of such versatility remains an exciting scientific challenge.

? **Why is the DNA that specifies rRNA useful for determining whether fungi are more closely related to plants or to animals?**

■ The DNA that specifies rRNA changes very slowly, which makes it useful for studying the relationships of organisms that diverged long ago.

15.18 Molecular clocks help track evolutionary time

The longer two groups have been separated, the greater the divergence of their genes. For example, sharks and tunas have been on separate evolutionary paths for more than 420 million years, whereas dolphins and bats diverged about 60 million years ago. Despite the obvious differences between dolphins and bats, their homologous genes are much more alike than are such genes in sharks and tuna. Indeed, molecular changes have kept better track of time than have changes in morphology. Biologists have found that some genes or other regions of genomes appear to accumulate changes at constant rates. Such observations form the basis for the concept of a **molecular clock**, a method that estimates the time required for a given amount of evolutionary change.

The molecular clock of a gene shown to have a reliable average rate of change can be calibrated in actual time by graphing the number of nucleotide differences against the dates of evolutionary branch points known from the fossil record. The graph line can then be used to estimate the dates of other evolutionary episodes not documented in the fossil record.

Molecular clocks have been used to date a wide variety of events. In one fascinating example published in 2011, researchers studied the divergence of human body lice (**Figure 15.18**) from head lice. Lice are tiny, blood-sucking insects that live in the fur of most mammal species. Early in human evolution, the loss of body hair restricted lice to the head—bare skin deprived the parasites of their refuge. When clothing offered a new habitat, populations diverged into two types, head lice and body lice, each with adaptations specific to its habitat. (Pubic lice have a different evolutionary history and are members of a different genus.) By comparing data from four different DNA sequences in head lice and body lice, the researchers estimated that people began to wear clothing between 83,000 and 170,000 years ago.

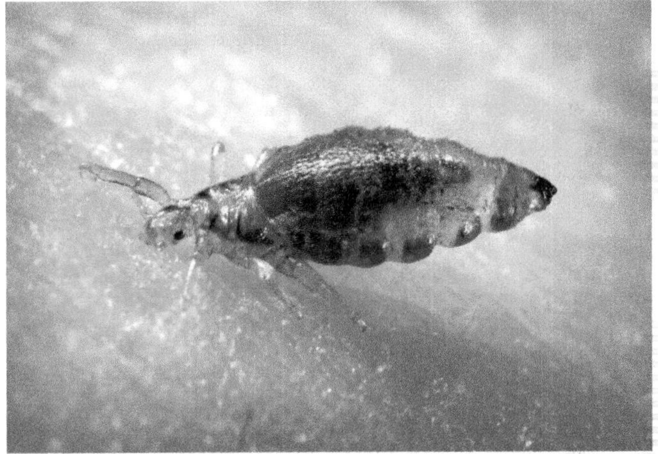

▲ **Figure 15.18** Human body louse (*Pediculus humanus humanus*)

Some biologists are skeptical about the accuracy of molecular clocks because the rate of molecular change may vary at different times, in different genes, and in different groups of organisms. In some cases, problems may be avoided by calibrating molecular clocks with many genes rather than just one or a few genes. One group of researchers used sequence data from 658 genes to construct a molecular clock that covered almost 600 million years of vertebrate evolution. Their estimates of divergence times agreed closely with fossil-based estimates. An abundant fossil record extends back only about 550 million years, and molecular clocks have been used to date evolutionary divergences that occurred a billion or more years ago. But the estimates assume that the clocks have been constant for all that time. Thus, such estimates are highly uncertain.

Evolutionary theory holds that all of life has a common ancestor. Molecular systematics is helping to link all living organisms into a comprehensive tree of life, as we see next.

? **What is a molecular clock? What assumption underlies the use of such a clock?**

■ A molecular clock estimates the actual time of evolutionary events based on the number of DNA changes. It is based on the assumption that some regions of genomes evolve at constant rates.

15.19 Constructing the tree of life is a work in progress

Phylogenetic trees are hypotheses about evolutionary history. Like all hypotheses, they are revised, or in some cases rejected, in accordance with new evidence. In recent years, the development of molecular techniques and new technologies for studying microorganisms have supplied an avalanche of new data, and cladistics has brought a new approach to tree construction.

As mentioned in Module 15.17, the three-domain system was a major revision to the tree of life. This classification system distinguishes two domains of prokaryotes, Bacteria and Archaea (**Figure 15.19A**). The third domain, Eukarya, contains all of the eukaryotes, including kingdoms Fungi, Plantae, and Animalia. The protists, indicated by purple labels in Figure 15.19A, are also placed in domain Eukarya. As you can see, protists are not monophyletic and thus cannot be considered a single kingdom. New data are accumulating so rapidly that questions of protist classification and phylogeny are far from settled (see Module 16.13).

Why are mitochondria and chloroplasts, the cellular organelles, found only in eukaryotes, shown as lineages in the domain Bacteria? The answer lies in the origin of eukaryotic cells from much smaller, simpler prokaryotes. **Figure 15.19B** is an evolutionary tree based largely on rRNA genes, which have evolved so slowly that homologies between distantly related organisms can still be detected. This tree shows that (1) the first major split in the history of life was the divergence of the bacteria from the other two domains, followed by the divergence of domains Archaea and Eukarya.

Comparisons of complete genomes from the three domains, however, show that, especially during the early history of life, there have been substantial interchanges of genes between organisms in the different domains. These took place through **horizontal gene transfer**, a process in which genes are transferred from one genome to another through mechanisms such as plasmid exchange and viral infection (see Modules 10.22 and 10.23) and even through the fusion of different organisms. Figure 15.19B shows two major episodes of horizontal gene transfer: (2) gene transfer between a mitochondrial ancestor and the ancestor of eukaryotes and (3) gene transfer between a chloroplast ancestor and the ancestor of green plants. Thus, mitochondria and chloroplasts in eukaryotic cells contain DNA from lineages in the domain Bacteria (see Module 4.15).

Based on molecular evidence, Figure 15.19B shows domain Eukarya originating from a prokaryotic lineage that diverged from the archaeal lineage some 2.8 billion years ago. However, some researchers have hypothesized that the eukaryotic ancestor was an archaean and therefore domains Archaea and Eukarya should be combined into a single domain. A controversial new group of archaea discovered in 2015 may lend support to this hypothesis. (In the next unit, we examine the enormous diversity of organisms that have populated Earth since life first arose more than 3.5 billion years ago.)

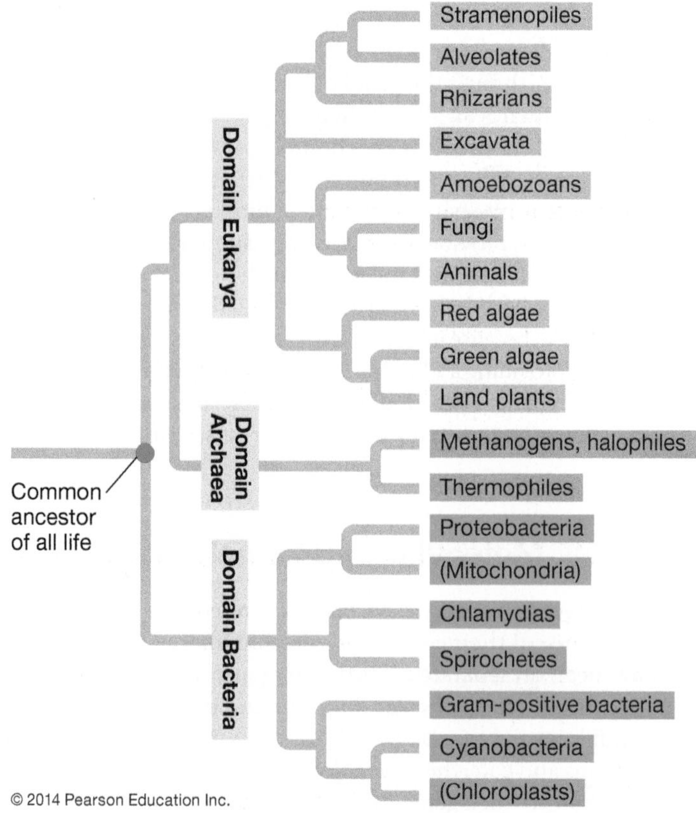

▲ **Figure 15.19A** The three domains of life (only some of the major branches in each domain are shown)

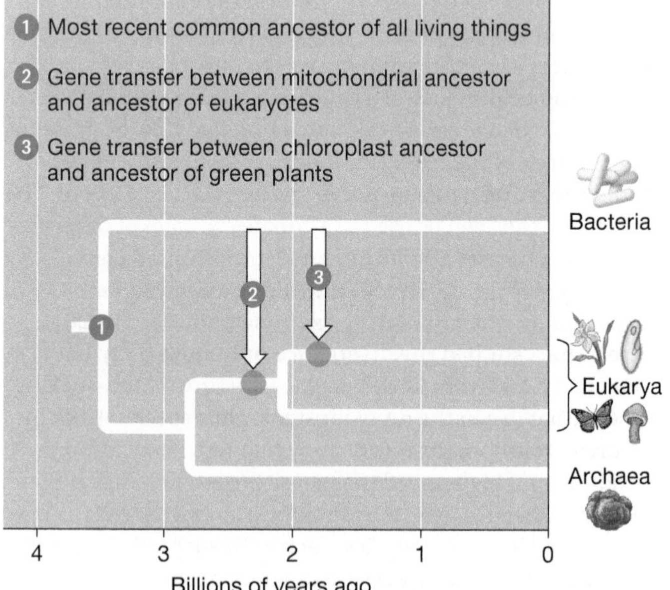

▲ **Figure 15.19B** Two major episodes of horizontal gene transfer in the history of life (dates are uncertain)

? **According to Figure 15.19A, which protists are most closely related to animals?**

■ Amoebas

CHAPTER **15 REVIEW**

For practice quizzes, BioFlix animations, MP3 tutorials, video tutors, and more study tools designed for this textbook, go to MasteringBiology™

REVIEWING THE CONCEPTS

Early Earth and the Origin of Life (15.1–15.3)

15.1 Conditions on early Earth made the origin of life possible. Earth formed some 4.6 billion years ago. Fossil stromatolites formed by prokaryotes date back 3.5 billion years.

15.2 Experiments show that the abiotic synthesis of organic molecules is possible.

15.3 Stages in the origin of the first cells probably included the formation of polymers, protocells, and self-replicating RNA. Natural selection could have acted on protocells that contained self-replicating molecules.

Major Events in the History of Life (15.4–15.6)

15.4 The origins of single-celled and multicellular organisms and the colonization of land were key events in life's history.

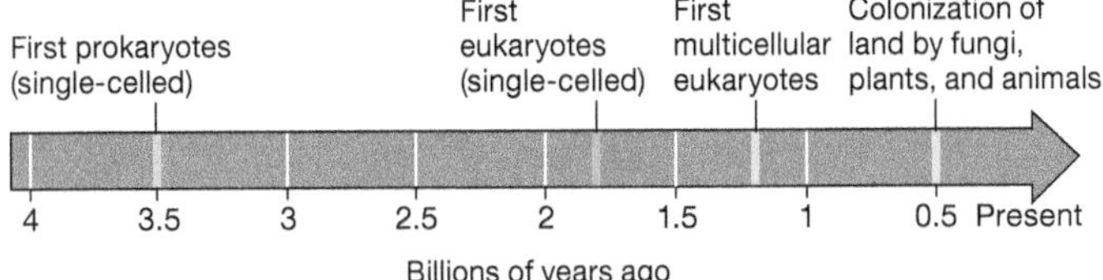

15.5 The actual ages of rocks and fossils mark geologic time. Radiometric dating can date rocks and fossils.

15.6 The fossil record documents the history of life. In the geologic record, eras and periods are separated by major transitions in life-forms, often caused by extinctions.

Mechanisms of Macroevolution (15.7–15.13)

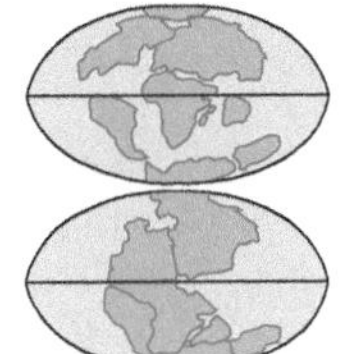

15.7 Continental drift has played a major role in macroevolution. The formation and split-up of Pangaea affected the distribution and diversification of organisms.

15.8 Plate tectonics may imperil human life. Volcanoes and earthquakes often occur at the boundaries of Earth's plates.

15.9 Five mass extinctions have altered the course of evolution. The Permian extinction is linked to the effects of extreme volcanic activity. The Cretaceous extinction, which included most dinosaurs, may have been caused by the impact of an asteroid.

15.10 Adaptive radiations have increased the diversity of life. The origin of many new species often follows mass extinctions, colonization of new habitats, and the evolution of new adaptations.

15.11 Genes that control development play a major role in evolution. "Evo-devo" combines evolutionary and developmental biology. New forms can evolve by changes in the number, sequences, or regulation of developmental genes.

15.12 Novel traits may arise in several ways. Complex structures may evolve in stages from simpler versions with the same basic function or from the gradual adaptation of existing structures to new functions.

15.13 Evolutionary trends do not mean that evolution is goal directed. An evolutionary trend may be a result of species selection or natural selection in changing environments.

Phylogeny and the Tree of Life (15.14–15.19)

15.14 Taxonomy names and classifies the diversity of life. Taxonomists assign each species a binomial—a genus and species name. Genera are grouped into progressively broader categories.

15.15 Phylogenies based on homologies reflect evolutionary history. A phylogenetic tree is a hypothesis of evolutionary relationships. Homologous structures and molecular sequences provide the evidence of common ancestry used to determine phylogeny.

15.16 Shared characters are used to construct phylogenetic trees. Cladistics uses shared derived characters to define clades. A parsimonious tree requires the fewest evolutionary changes.

15.17 An organism's evolutionary history is documented in its genome. Molecular systematics uses molecular comparisons to build phylogenetic trees. Homologous genes are found across distantly related species.

15.18 Molecular clocks help track evolutionary time. Regions of DNA that change at a constant rate can provide estimated dates of past events.

15.19 Constructing the tree of life is a work in progress. Life is currently classified in three domains: Bacteria, Archaea, and Eukarya. Multiple horizontal gene transfers occurred during the early history of life, including transfers that resulted in the origin of eukaryotic cells.

CONNECTING THE CONCEPTS

1. Using the figure below, describe the stages that may have led to the origin of life.

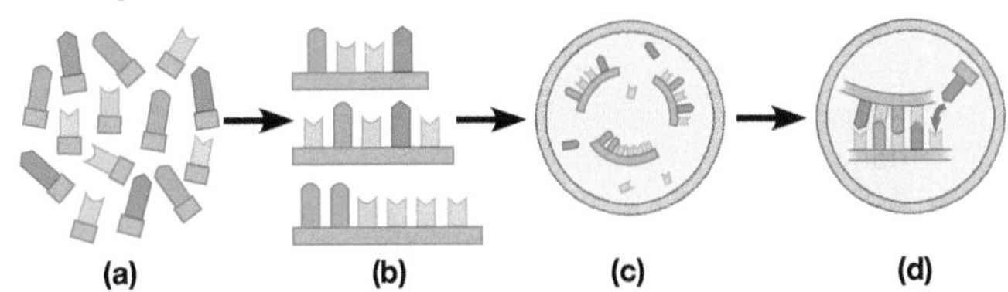

2. Fill in this concept map about systematics.

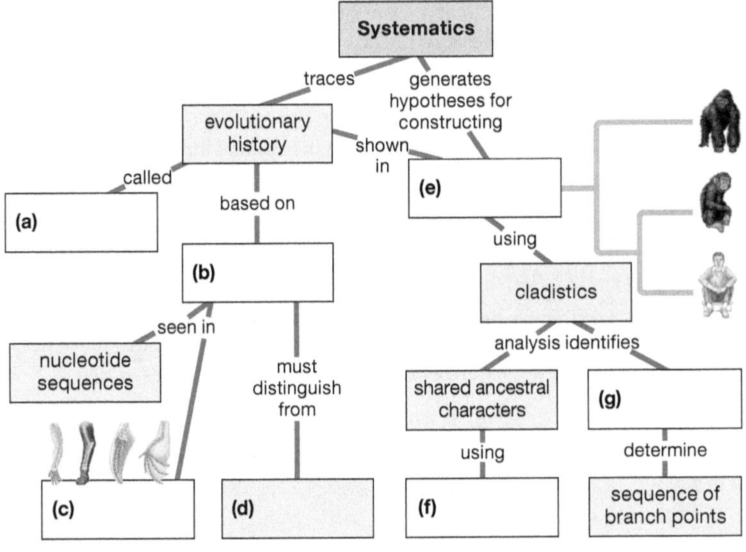

TESTING YOUR KNOWLEDGE

Level 1: Knowledge/Comprehension

3. You set your time machine for 3 billion years ago and push the start button. When the dust clears, you look out the window. Which of the following describes what you would probably see?
   a. a cloud of gas and dust in space
   b. green scum in the water
   c. land and water sterile and devoid of life
   d. an endless expanse of red-hot molten rock
4. Ancient photosynthetic prokaryotes were very important in the history of life because they
   a. produced the oxygen in the atmosphere.
   b. are the oldest-known archaea.
   c. were the first multicellular organisms.
   d. showed that life could evolve around deep-sea vents.
5. The animals and plants of India are very different from the species in nearby Southeast Asia. Why might this be true?
   a. India was once covered by oceans and Asia was not.
   b. India is in the process of separating from the rest of Asia.
   c. Life in India was wiped out by ancient volcanic eruptions.
   d. India was a separate continent until about 45 million years ago.
6. Adaptive radiations may be promoted by all of the following *except* one. Which one?
   a. mass extinctions that result in vacant ecological niches
   b. colonization of an isolated region with few competitors
   c. a gradual change in climate
   d. a novel adaptation
7. A swim bladder is a gas-filled sac that helps fish maintain buoyancy. Evidence indicates that early fish gulped air into primitive lungs, helping them survive in stagnant waters. The evolution of the swim bladder from lungs of an ancestral fish is an example of
   a. an evolutionary trend.
   b. paedomorphosis.
   c. the gradual refinement of a structure with the same function.
   d. exaptation.
8. If you were using cladistics to build a phylogenetic tree of cats, which would be the best choice for an outgroup?
   a. kangaroo
   b. leopard
   c. domestic cat
   d. iguana
9. Which of the following could provide the best data for determining the phylogeny of very closely related species?
   a. the fossil record
   b. their morphological differences and similarities
   c. a comparison of nucleotide sequences in homologous genes and mitochondrial DNA
   d. a comparison of their ribosomal DNA sequences
10. Major divisions in the geologic record are marked by
    a. radioactive dating.
    b. distinct changes in the types of fossilized life.
    c. regular time intervals measured in millions of years.
    d. the appearance, in order, of prokaryotes, eukaryotes, protists, animals, plants, and fungi.

Level 2: Application/Analysis

11. Distinguish between microevolution and macroevolution.
12. Which are more likely to be closely related: two species with similar appearance but divergent gene sequences or two species with different appearances but nearly identical genes? Explain.
13. How can the Darwinian concept of descent with modification explain the evolution of such complex structures as an eye?
14. Explain why changes in the regulation of developmental genes may have played such a large role in the evolution of new forms.
15. What types of molecular comparisons are used to determine the very early branching of the tree of life? Explain.

Level 3: Synthesis/Evaluation

16. Measurements indicate that a fossilized skull you unearthed has a carbon-14: carbon-12 ratio about 1/16th that of the skulls of present-day animals. What is the approximate age of the fossil? (The half-life of carbon-14 is 5,730 years.)
17. A paleontologist compares fossils from three dinosaurs and *Archaeopteryx*, the earliest-known bird. The following table shows the distribution of characters for each species, where 1 means that the character is present and 0 means it is not. The outgroup (not shown in the table) had none of the characters. Arrange these species on the phylogenetic tree below and indicate the derived character that defines each branch point.

Trait	*Velociraptor*	*Coelophysis*	*Archaeopteryx*	*Allosaurus*
Hollow bones	1	1	1	1
Three-fingered hand	1	0	1	1
Half-moon-shaped wrist bone	1	0	1	0
Reversed first toe	0	0	1	0

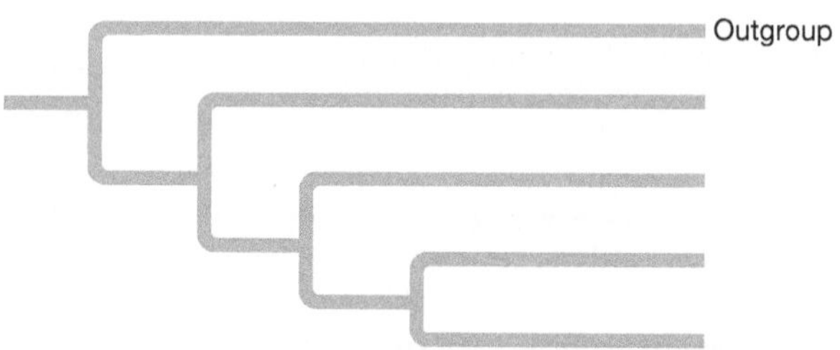

18. SCIENTIFIC THINKING When Stanley Miller's experiment was published in 1953, his results made global headlines. The general public thought Miller had answered the question of how life on Earth began by creating life in a test tube. However, scientists understood that Miller's experiment was neither a final answer nor a recipe for life. Rather, it was the first test of a long-standing hypothesis about the origin of life. Using the information in Module 15.2 (and additional research, if you wish) as an example, write an essay describing how the process of science progresses over time toward understanding how nature works. (You will find Module 1.7 helpful.)

Answers to all questions can be found in Appendix 4.

The Biosphere: *An Introduction to Earth's Diverse Environments*

CHAPTER 34

Why study ecology?

Did you ever think that a river could catch fire? In June 1969, fire broke out on the Cuyahoga River in Cleveland, Ohio. For a century, oil refineries, steel mills, rubber factories, and other industries in Cleveland and Akron, 40 miles upstream, had dumped wastes directly into the river, along with raw sewage from both cities. The stretch of river between the two cities was devoid of fish, and the most heavily polluted sections lacked any signs of life. Thick oil slicks clogged with trash and other debris were common sights. When the river caught fire, Clevelanders were not surprised—it had happened several times in the past. However, the notion of a flammable river captured the attention of the national media. Public outrage over the toxic conditions of the nation's waterways, along with growing awareness of widespread environmental abuse, spurred a flurry of legislation, including the creation of the Environmental Protection Agency.

Today, Cuyahoga Valley National Park (photo at right) surrounds a stretch of the river between Akron and Cleveland. Dozens of fish species thrive in it, and the park is home to abundant wildlife. Other parts of the river, however, are still polluted. Although the contamination is far from the noxious brew of earlier decades, it is unlikely that the river will ever be clean along its entire length. Wherever a river passes through populated areas, pollution is almost inevitable.

Environmental concerns are among the most pressing issues we face today. How can we manage Earth's resources in ways that meet the needs of people today without compromising the ability of future generations to meet theirs? Just as human health care requires learning about the structure and function of the body, preserving a healthy environment depends on understanding the structure and function of populations, communities, and ecosystems. In this unit, you will learn about the principles of ecology, beginning with an exploration of Earth's diverse environments.

BIG IDEAS

The Biosphere (34.1–34.5)

The distribution and abundance of life in the biosphere are influenced by living and nonliving components of the environment.

Aquatic Biomes (34.6–34.7)

The classification of aquatic biomes as marine or freshwater is determined by their salt concentration.

Terrestrial Biomes (34.8–34.18)

The distribution of terrestrial biomes is primarily determined by temperature and rainfall.

The Biosphere

34.1 Ecologists study how organisms interact with their environment at several levels

Ecology (from the Greek *oikos*, home) is the scientific study of the interactions between organisms and the environment. Ecologists describe the distribution and abundance of organisms—where they live and how many live there. Because the environment is complex, organisms can potentially be affected by many different variables. Ecologists group these variables into two major types, biotic factors and abiotic factors. **Biotic factors**, which include all of the organisms in the area, are the living component of the environment. **Abiotic factors** are the environment's nonliving component, the physical and chemical factors such as temperature, forms of energy available, water, and nutrients. An organism's **habitat**, the specific environment it lives in, includes the biotic and abiotic factors present in its surroundings.

As you might expect, field research is fundamental to ecology. But ecologists also test hypotheses using laboratory experiments, where conditions can be simplified and controlled. Some ecologists take a theoretical approach, devising mathematical and computer models that enable them to simulate large-scale experiments that are impossible to conduct in the field.

Ecologists study INTERACTIONS at several levels. Consider how researchers might investigate the ecology of an alpine meadow high in the Himalayan mountains. At the **organism** level, they may examine how one kind of organism meets the challenges and opportunities of its environment through its physiology or behavior. For example, an ecologist working at this level might study adaptations of the Himalayan blue poppy (*Meconopsis betonicifolia,* Figure 34.1A) to the freezing temperatures and short days of its abiotic environment.

Another level of study in ecology is the **population**, a group of individuals of the same species living in a particular geographic area. Blue poppies living in a particular Himalayan alpine meadow would constitute a population (Figure 34.1B). An ecologist studying blue poppies might investigate factors that affect the size of the population, such as the availability of chemical nutrients or seed dispersal.

A third level, the **community**, is an assemblage of all the populations of organisms living close enough together for potential interaction—all of the biotic factors in the environment. All the organisms in a particular alpine meadow would constitute a community (Figure 34.1C). An ecologist working at this level might focus on interspecies interactions, such as the effect of plant-eaters on poppies or the competition between poppies and other plants for soil nutrients.

The fourth level of ecological study, the **ecosystem**, includes both the biotic and abiotic components of the environment (Figure 34.1D). Some critical questions at the ecosystem level concern how chemicals cycle and how energy flows between organisms and their surroundings. For an alpine meadow, one ecosystem-level question would be, How rapidly does the decomposition of decaying plants release inorganic nutrients?

Some ecologists take a wider perspective by studying **landscapes**, which are arrays of ecosystems. Landscapes are usually visible from the air as distinctive patches. For example, Himalayan alpine meadows are part of a mountain landscape that also includes conifer and broadleaf forests. A landscape perspective emphasizes the absence of clearly defined ecosystem boundaries; energy, matter, and organisms may be exchanged by ecosystems within a landscape.

The **biosphere**, which extends from the atmosphere several kilometers above Earth to the depths of the oceans, is all of Earth that is inhabited by life. It is the home of us all, and as you will learn throughout this unit, our actions have consequences for the entire biosphere.

▲ Figure 34.1A An organism

▲ Figure 34.1B A population

▲ Figure 34.1C A community

▲ Figure 34.1D An ecosystem

List the biotic and abiotic factors shown in Figure 34.1D.

The biotic factors include the animals and plants (blue poppies and grass). Abiotic factors include the soil, temperature, and precipitation.

34.2 The science of ecology provides insight into environmental problems

SCIENTIFIC THINKING

The connections between human activities and environmental consequences are not always as visible as the pollution responsible for the Cuyahoga River fire. To understand how scientists identify less obvious environmental problems, let's take a look at another case that helped shape modern environmental policy.

In the 1950s, the prevailing view of the environment was that "Nature" was a force to be tamed and controlled for human purposes, in the same way that livestock had been domesticated. People were captivated by new technologies that promised an end to infectious disease and boundless increases in agricultural productivity. Chemical pesticides were an innovation that was enthusiastically embraced. The most widely used chemical was DDT, an insecticide that was employed against crop pests and disease-carrying insects such as mosquitoes (which transmit malaria), body lice (typhus), and fleas (plague). Despite its remarkable killing power against insects, DDT was considered harmless to vertebrates, including people (**Figure 34.2A**).

By the late 1950s, however, a heated debate was raging over the widespread use of chemical pesticides. Consumers raised questions about chemical residues in their food. Dairy farmers found their milk contaminated by aerial spraying on nearby crops. Fish and wildlife experts, along with private citizens, amassed dozens of reports of birds, fish, and other animals apparently poisoned by pesticides. In some of these instances, birds that had once been common simply disappeared from the area. Disturbingly, scientists found that small amounts of pesticides had accumulated in the fatty tissues of vertebrates thousands of miles from where pesticides were used. DDT was even detected in human milk.

Why study ecology?

Scientists also found that DDT remained in the soil or water long after application of the pesticide. For example, one study correlated bird deaths on a university campus with DDT sprayed in previous years to control disease-spreading beetles on elm trees. The paper suggested that the birds consumed a toxic dose of the poison when they ate earthworms that had fed on DDT-contaminated leaves decaying in the soil.

▲ **Figure 34.2A** Spraying DDT to control mosquitoes on Jones Beach, New York, in 1945

Other scientists reported similar correlations between the use of DDT and animals in aquatic ecosystems as well as in other terrestrial ecosystems. Birds of prey seemed to be especially vulnerable—populations of bald eagles, ospreys, peregrine falcons, and other predatory birds in Europe and North America had declined dramatically (**Figure 34.2B**). Studies suggested that pesticides, including DDT, caused the eggshells of these species to be abnormally thin and fragile.

▲ **Figure 34.2B** Peregrine falcon (*Falco peregrinus*)

Evaluating the degree of certainty in conclusions is an important part of science. Much of the initial evidence against DDT consisted of isolated observations and correlations, and thus was not conclusive. However, the accumulation of so many clues pointed to problems that merited thorough study.

Scientists often help people understand current issues by communicating with the general public. The publication of a book called *Silent Spring* in 1962 brought widespread attention to the pesticide issue. The author of *Silent Spring*, Rachel Carson (**Figure 34.2C**), used her talent for making scientific subjects come alive for readers to draw the public into the debate. Carson, a former marine biologist and writer with the U. S. Fish and Wildlife Service, compiled available evidence on the consequences of widespread pesticide use. Considering it reckless to mount aerial spraying campaigns, which broadcast massive amounts of toxic chemicals that persist in the environment for many years, Carson advocated a new approach to pest control that took the health of ecosystems into account. Awareness of the problems caused by pesticides developed into concern for a host of environmental issues and set the stage for the public outcry over the Cuyahoga River fire and similar manifestations of environmental abuses.

▲ **Figure 34.2C** Rachel Carson

The science of ecology can provide the understanding needed to resolve environmental problems. But these problems cannot be solved by ecologists alone, because they require making decisions based on values and ethics. Analyzing environmental issues and planning for better practices begin with an understanding of the basic concepts of ecology, so let's start to explore them now.

? **Why can't ecologists alone solve environmental problems?**

■ The science of ecology can inform the decision-making process, but solving environmental problems involves making ethical, economic, and political judgments that are outside the realm of science.

34.3 Physical and chemical factors influence life in the biosphere

You have learned that life thrives in a wide variety of habitats, from the mountaintops to the seafloor. To be successful, the organisms that live in each place must be adapted to the abiotic factors present in those environments.

Energy Sources Life depends on transformations of ENERGY AND MATTER. Thus, all organisms require a source of energy to live. Solar energy from sunlight, captured during the process of photosynthesis, powers most ecosystems. Lack of sunlight is seldom the most important factor limiting plant growth for terrestrial ecosystems, although shading by trees does create intense competition for light among plants growing on forest floors. In many aquatic environments, however, light is not uniformly available. Microorganisms and suspended particles, as well as the water itself, absorb light and prevent it from penetrating beyond certain depths. As a result, most photosynthesis occurs near the water's surface.

In dark environments such as caves or hydrothermal vents, bacteria that extract energy from inorganic chemicals power ecosystems. Sulfur bacteria perform this function in hydrothermal vent communities. Some of the animals there feed directly on the sulfur bacteria; others derive nutrition from bacteria living inside their bodies. For example, the red tips of the giant tube worms in Figure 34.3A are respiratory surfaces that acquire oxygen and sulfide from the water. Bacteria living in a specialized organ in the worm's body get energy from the sulfide—a lot of energy. These worms can grow to be over 2 m (6.5 feet) long.

▲ **Figure 34.3A** Giant tube worms

Temperature Temperature is an important abiotic factor because of its effect on metabolism (see Module 5.14). Few organisms can maintain a sufficiently active metabolism at temperatures close to 0°C, and temperatures above 45°C (113°F) destroy the enzymes of most organisms. However, extraordinary adaptations enable some species to live outside this temperature range. For example, archaeans living in hot springs have enzymes that function optimally at extremely high temperatures. Mammals and birds, such as the snowy owl in Figure 34.3B, can remain considerably warmer than their surroundings and can be active at a fairly wide range of temperatures. Amphibians and reptiles, which gain most of their warmth by absorbing heat from their surroundings, have a more limited distribution.

▼ **Figure 34.3B** A snowy owl

Water Water is essential to all life. Thus, for terrestrial organisms, dehydration is a major danger. Watertight coverings were key evolutionary adaptations enabling plants and vertebrates to be successful on land (see Modules 17.1 and 19.6). Aquatic organisms are surrounded by water; their problem is solute concentration. Freshwater organisms live in a hypotonic medium, while the environment of marine organisms is hypertonic. Animals maintain fluid balance by a variety of mechanisms (see Module 25.4).

Inorganic Nutrients The distribution and abundance of photosynthetic organisms, including plants, algae, and photosynthetic bacteria, depend on the availability of inorganic nutrients such as nitrogen and phosphorus. Plants obtain these from the soil. Soil structure, pH, and nutrient content often play major roles in determining the distribution of plants. In many aquatic ecosystems, low levels of nitrogen and phosphorus limit the growth of algae and photosynthetic bacteria.

Other Aquatic Factors Several abiotic factors are important in aquatic, but not terrestrial, ecosystems. While terrestrial organisms have a plentiful supply of oxygen from the air, aquatic organisms must depend on oxygen dissolved in water. Some species of fish—trout, for example—require high levels of dissolved oxygen. Cold, fast-moving water has a higher oxygen content than warm or stagnant water. Salinity, current, and tides may also play a role in aquatic ecosystems.

Other Terrestrial Factors On land, wind is often an important abiotic factor. Wind increases an organism's rate of water loss by evaporation. The resulting increase in evaporative cooling (see Module 25.2) can be advantageous on a hot summer day, but it can cause dangerous wind chill in the winter. In some ecosystems, fire occurs frequently enough that many plants have adapted to this disturbance.

Next we examine the interaction between one animal species and the abiotic and biotic factors of its environment.

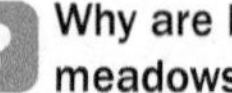

Why are birds and mammals found in Himalayan alpine meadows, but non-bird reptiles and amphibians are not?

■ As ectotherms (see Module 25.1), reptiles other than birds and amphibians do not have adaptations that enable them to withstand the cold temperatures of the alpine habitat.

34.4 Organisms are adapted to abiotic and biotic factors through natural selection

EVOLUTION CONNECTION

One of the fundamental goals of ecology is to explain the distribution of organisms. The presence of a species in a particular place has two possible explanations: The species may have evolved from ancestors living in that location, or it may have dispersed to that location and been able to survive once it arrived. The magnificent pronghorn "antelope" (*Antilocapra americana,* **Figure 34.4**) is the descendant of ancestors that roamed the open plains and shrub deserts of North America more than a million years ago. The animal is found nowhere else and is only distantly related to the many species of antelope in Africa. What selective factors in the abiotic and biotic environments of its ancestors produced the adaptations we see in the pronghorn that roams North America today?

The pronghorn's present-day habitat, like that of its ancestors, is arid, windswept, and subject to extreme temperature fluctuations both daily and seasonally. Individuals able to survive and reproduce under these conditions left offspring that carried their alleles forward into subsequent generations. Thus, we can infer that many of the adaptations that contribute to the success of present-day pronghorns must also have contributed to the success of their ancestors. For example, the pronghorn has a thick coat made of hollow hairs that trap air, insulating the animal in cold weather. If you drive through Wyoming or parts of Colorado in the winter, you will see herds of these animals foraging in the open when temperatures are well below 0°C. In hot weather, the pronghorn can raise patches of this stiff hair to release body heat.

▲ **Figure 34.4** A pronghorn (*Antilocapra americana*)

The biotic environment, which includes what the animal eats and any predators that threaten it, is also a factor in determining which members of a population survive and reproduce. The pronghorn's main foods are small broadleaf plants, grasses, and woody shrubs. Over time, characteristics that enabled the ancestors of the pronghorn to exploit these food sources more efficiently became established through natural selection. As a result, the teeth of a pronghorn are specialized for biting and chewing tough plant material. Like the stomach of a cow, the pronghorn's stomach contains cellulose-digesting bacteria. As the pronghorn eats plants, the bacteria digest the cellulose, and the animal obtains most of its nutrients from the bacteria.

While many factors in the pronghorn's environment have been fairly consistent throughout its evolutionary history, one aspect has changed significantly. Until around 12,000 years ago, one of the pronghorn's major predators was probably the American cheetah, a fleet-footed feline that bears some similarities to the more familiar African cheetah. The now-extinct American cheetah was one of many ferocious predators of Pleistocene North America, along with lions, jaguars, and saber-toothed cats with 7-inch canines. Ecologists hypothesize that the selection pressure of the cheetah's pursuit led to the pronghorn's blazing speed, which far exceeds that of its main present-day predator, the wolf. With a top speed of 97 km/hr (60 mph), the pronghorn is easily the fastest mammal on the continent, and an adult pronghorn can keep up a pace of 64 km/hr (40 mph) for at least 30 minutes. Unable to match the pronghorn's extravagant speed, wolves typically take adults that have been weakened by age or illness.

Like many large herbivores that live in open grasslands, the pronghorn also derives protection from living in herds. When one pronghorn starts to run, its white rump patch seems to alert other herd members to danger. Other adaptations that help the pronghorn foil predators include its tan and white coat, which provides camouflage, and its keen eyes, which can detect movement at great distances. Thus, the adaptations shaped by natural selection in the distant past still serve as protection from the predators of today's environment.

If the pronghorn's environment changed significantly, the adaptations that contribute to its current success might not be as advantageous. For example, if an increase in rainfall turned the open plains into woodlands, where predators would be more easily hidden by vegetation and could stalk their prey at close range, the pronghorn's adaptations for escaping predators might not be as effective. Thus, in adapting populations to local environmental conditions, natural selection may limit the distribution of organisms.

In the next module, we see how global climatic patterns determine temperature and precipitation, the major abiotic factors that influence the distribution of organisms. We examine the biotic components of the environment more closely in other chapters in this unit.

? **What is the role of the environment in adaptive evolution?**

■ The individuals whose phenotypes are best suited to the environment (including both abiotic and biotic factors) will pass their alleles to the next generation. But individuals with other phenotypes may not. For example, if the biotic environment includes wolves, a pronghorn that is not able to run at top speed for as long as the rest of the herd will probably not survive to reproduce.

34.5 Regional climate influences the distribution of terrestrial communities

When we ask what determines whether a particular organism or community of organisms lives in a certain area, the climate of the region—especially temperature and precipitation—is often a crucial part of the answer. Earth's global climate patterns are largely determined by the input of radiant energy from the sun and the planet's movement in space.

Figure 34.5A shows that because of its curvature, Earth receives an uneven distribution of solar energy. The sun's rays strike equatorial areas most directly (perpendicularly). Away from the equator, the rays strike Earth's surface at a slant. As a result, the same amount of solar energy is spread over a larger area. Thus, any particular area of land or ocean near the equator absorbs more heat than comparable areas in the more northern or southern latitudes.

The seasons of the year result from the permanent tilt of the planet on its axis as it orbits the sun. As Figure 34.5B shows, for instance, the Northern Hemisphere tilts toward the sun in June, resulting in the long days of summer in that hemisphere. But during this time, days are short in the Southern Hemisphere and it is winter there. Conversely, the Southern Hemisphere tilts toward the sun in December, causing summer there and winter in the Northern Hemisphere. The **tropics**, the region surrounding the equator between latitudes 23.5° north (the Tropic of Cancer) and 23.5° south (the Tropic of Capricorn), experience the greatest annual input and least seasonal variation in solar radiation. Distinct seasonal variation occurs in the **temperate zones**, the latitudes between the tropics and the Arctic Circle in the north and the Antarctic Circle in the south.

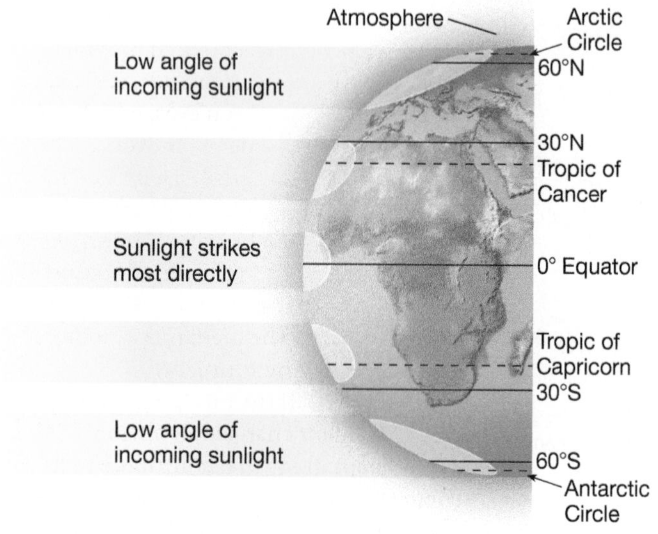

▲ Figure 34.5A How solar radiation varies with latitude

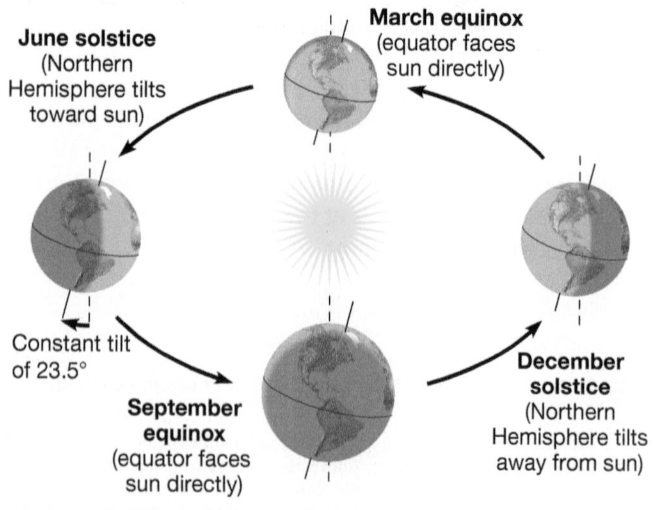

▲ Figure 34.5B How Earth's tilt causes the seasons

Figure 34.5C shows some of the effects of the intense solar radiation near the equator on global patterns of rainfall and winds. Arrows indicate air movements. High temperatures in the tropics evaporate water from Earth's surface and cause warm, moist air masses to rise and flow toward the poles. As the rising air cools, its ability to hold moisture diminishes. The water vapor condenses into clouds and rain falls. High temperatures throughout the year and ample rainfall largely explain why rain forests are concentrated near the equator.

After losing their moisture over equatorial zones, high-altitude air masses spread away in two opposing directions from the equator until they cool and descend again at latitudes of about 30° north and south. This descending dry air absorbs moisture from the land. Thus, many of the world's great deserts—the Sahara in North Africa and the Arabian on the Arabian Peninsula, for example—are centered at these latitudes. As the dry air descends, some of it spreads back toward the equator. This movement creates the cooling trade winds, which dominate the tropics. As the air moves back toward the equator, it warms and picks up moisture until it ascends again.

Notice in Figure 34.5C that some of the descending air heads into the latitudes above 30° north and south. At first these air masses pick up moisture, but they tend to drop it as they cool at higher latitudes. As a result, the north and south temperate zones, especially latitudes around 60°, tend to be relatively wet.

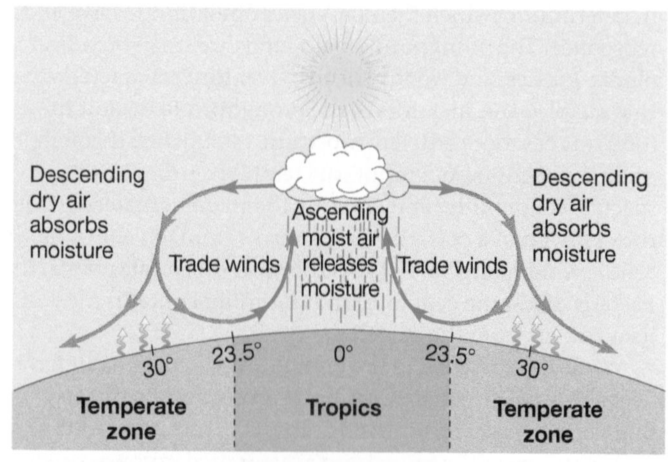

▲ Figure 34.5C How uneven heating causes rain and winds

Figure 34.5D shows the major global air movements, called the **prevailing winds**. Prevailing winds (pink arrows) result from the combined effects of the rising and falling of air masses (blue and brown arrows) and Earth's rotation (gray arrows). Because Earth is spherical, its surface moves faster at the equator, where its diameter is greatest, than at other latitudes. In the tropics, Earth's rapidly moving surface deflects vertically circulating air, making the trade winds blow from east to west. In temperate zones, the slower-moving surface produces the westerlies, winds that blow from west to east.

A combination of the prevailing winds, the planet's rotation, unequal heating of surface waters, and the locations and shapes of the continents creates **ocean currents**, river-like flow patterns at the oceans' surface (Figure 34.5E). Ocean currents have a profound effect on regional climates. For instance, the Gulf Stream circulates warm water northward from the Gulf of Mexico and makes the climate on the west coast of Great Britain warmer during winter than the coast of New England, which is actually farther south but is cooled by the Labrador Current flowing south from the coast of Greenland.

Landforms can also affect local climate. Air temperature declines by about 6°C with every 1,000-m increase in elevation, an effect you've probably experienced if you've ever hiked up a mountain. Figure 34.5F illustrates the effect of mountains on rainfall. This drawing represents major landforms across the state of California, but mountain ranges cause similar effects elsewhere. California is a temperate area in which the prevailing winds are westerlies. As moist air moves in off the Pacific Ocean and encounters the westernmost mountains (the Coast Range), it flows upward, cools at higher altitudes, and drops a large amount of water. The world's tallest trees, the coastal redwoods, thrive here. Farther inland, precipitation increases again as the air moves up and over higher mountains (the Sierra Nevada). Some of the world's deepest snowpacks occur here. On the eastern side of the Sierra, there is little precipitation, and the dry descending air also absorbs moisture. This effect, called a rain shadow, is responsible for the desert that covers much of central Nevada, for example, as well as other deserts located inland from coastal mountain ranges.

Climate and other abiotic factors of the environment control the global distribution of organisms. The influence of these abiotic factors results in **biomes**, major types of ecological associations that occupy broad geographic regions of land or water. Terrestrial biomes are determined primarily by temperature and precipitation—similar assemblages of plant and animal types are found in areas that have similar climates. Aquatic biomes are defined by different abiotic factors; the primary distinction is based on salinity. Marine biomes, which include oceans, intertidal zones, coral reefs, and estuaries, generally have salt concentrations around 3%, while freshwater biomes (lakes, streams and rivers, and wetlands) typically have a salt concentration of less than 1%. We describe several aquatic biomes in the next two modules.

? **What causes summer in the Northern Hemisphere?**

Because of the fixed angle of Earth's axis relative to the plane of its orbit around the sun, the Northern Hemisphere is tilted toward the sun during the portion of the annual orbit that corresponds to the summer months.

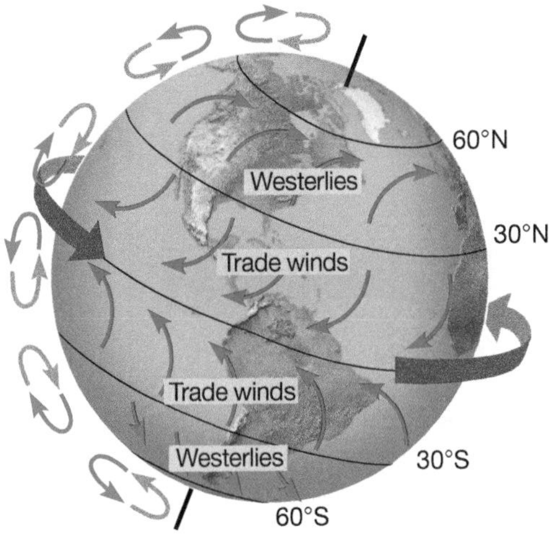

▲ Figure 34.5D Prevailing wind patterns

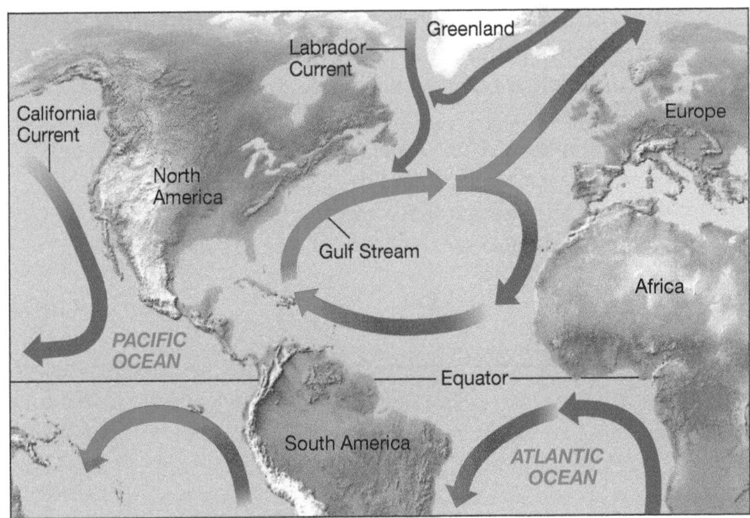

▲ Figure 34.5E Atlantic Ocean currents (red arrows indicate warming currents; blue arrows indicate cooling currents)

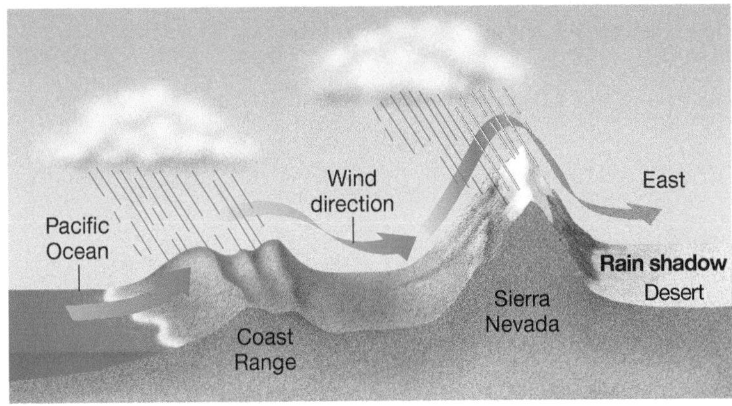

▲ Figure 34.5F How mountains affect precipitation (California)

Aquatic Biomes

34.6 Sunlight and substrate are key factors in the distribution of marine organisms

Gazing out over a vast ocean, you might think that it is the most uniform environment on Earth. But marine ecosystems can be as different as night and day. The deepest ocean, where hydrothermal vents are located, is perpetually dark. In contrast, the vivid coral reefs are utterly dependent on sunlight. Habitats near shore are different from those in mid-ocean, and the substrate, which varies with depth and distance from shore, hosts different communities from the open waters.

The **pelagic realm** of the oceans includes all open water, and the substrate—the seafloor—is known as the **benthic realm** (Figure 34.6A). The depth of light penetration, a maximum of 200 m (656 feet), marks the **photic zone**. In shallow areas such as the submerged parts of continents, called **continental shelves**, the photic zone includes both the pelagic and benthic realms. In these sunlit regions, photosynthesis by **phytoplankton** (microscopic algae and cyanobacteria) and multicellular algae provides energy and organic carbon for a diverse community of animals. Sponges, burrowing worms, clams, sea anemones, crabs, and echinoderms inhabit the benthic realm of the photic zone. **Zooplankton** (animals that drift in aquatic environments), fish, marine mammals, and many other types of animals are abundant in the pelagic photic zone.

Coral reefs, a visually spectacular and biologically diverse biome, are scattered around the globe in the photic zone of warm tropical waters above continental shelves, as shown in Figure 34.6B (also see the introduction to Chapter 2). A reef is built up slowly by successive generations of coral animals—a diverse group of cnidarians that secrete a hard external skeleton—and by multicellular algae encrusted with calcium carbonate. Unicellular algae live within the corals, providing the coral with food (see Module 18.6). Coral reefs support a huge variety of invertebrates and fishes.

▲ Figure 34.6B A coral reef with its immense variety of invertebrates and fishes

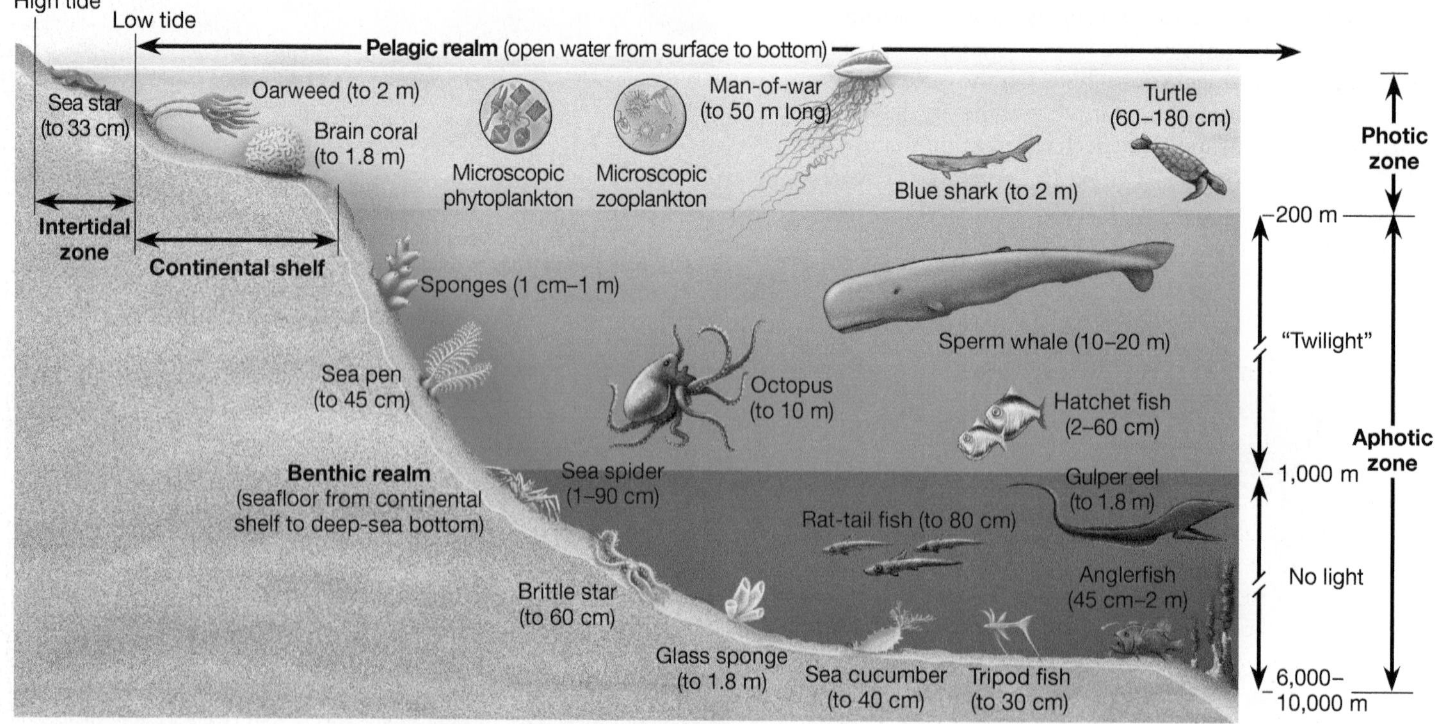

▲ Figure 34.6A Ocean life (zone depths and size of organisms not drawn to scale)

Below the photic zone of the ocean lies the **aphotic zone**. Although there is not enough light for photosynthesis between 200 and 1,000 m (0.6 mile), some light does reach these depths. This dimly lit world, sometimes called the twilight zone, is dominated by a fascinating variety of small fishes and crustaceans. Food sinking from the photic zone provides some sustenance for these animals. In addition, many of them migrate to the surface at night to feed. Some fishes in the twilight zone have enlarged eyes, enabling them to see in the very dim light, and luminescent organs that attract mates and prey.

Below 1,000 m, the ocean is completely and permanently dark. Adaptation to this environment has produced bizarre-looking creatures, such as the angler fish shown in Figure 34.6C. The scarcity of food probably explains the strangely outsized mouths of the angler and other fishes that inhabit this region of the ocean, a feature that allows them to grab any available prey, large or small. Inwardly angled teeth ensure that once caught, prey do not escape.

▲ **Figure 34.6C** An angler fish

The angler fish improves its chances of encountering prey by dangling a lure lit by bioluminescent bacteria. Most benthic organisms here are deposit feeders, animals that consume dead organic matter (detritus) on the substrate. Crustaceans, annelid worms, sea anemones, and echinoderms such as sea cucumbers, sea stars, and sea urchins are common. Because of the scarcity of food, however, the density of animals is low—except at hydrothermal vents, where chemoautotrophic bacteria support an abundance of life (see Module 34.3).

The marine environment also includes distinctive biomes where the ocean interfaces with land or with fresh water. In the **intertidal zone**, where the ocean meets land, the shore is pounded by waves during high tide and exposed to the sun and drying winds during low tide. The rocky intertidal zone is home to many sedentary organisms, such as algae, barnacles, and mussels, which attach to rocks and thus resist being washed away when the tide comes in. On sandy beaches, suspension-feeding worms, clams, and predatory crustaceans bury themselves in the ground.

Figure 34.6D shows an **estuary**, a biome that occurs where a freshwater stream or river merges with the ocean. The saltiness of estuaries ranges, across their length, from nearly that of fresh water to that of the ocean. With their waters enriched by nutrients from a river, estuaries are among the most productive biomes on Earth. Oysters, crabs, and many fishes live in estuaries or reproduce in them. Estuaries are also crucial nesting and feeding areas for waterfowl.

Wetlands constitute a biome that is transitional between an aquatic ecosystem—either marine or freshwater—and a terrestrial one. Covered with water either permanently or periodically, wetlands support the growth of aquatic plants (see Figure 34.7C). Mudflats and salt marshes are coastal wetlands that often border estuaries and experience tidal fluctuations.

For centuries, people viewed the ocean as a limitless resource, harvesting its bounty and using it as a dumping ground for wastes. The impact of these practices is now being felt in many ways, large and small. From worldwide declines in commercial fish species to dying coral reefs to beaches closed by pollution, danger signs abound. Because of their proximity to land, estuaries and wetlands are especially vulnerable. Many have been completely replaced by development on landfill. Other threats include nutrient pollution, contamination by pathogens or toxic chemicals, alteration of freshwater inflow, and introduction of nonnative species. Coral reefs have suffered from many of the same problems. In addition, overfishing has upset the species balance in some reef communities and greatly reduced diversity, and the widespread demise of reef-building corals in some regions has been attributed to climate change.

Freshwater biomes share many characteristics with marine biomes and experience some of the same threats. We introduce freshwater biomes in the next module.

? Oil from the 2010 Deepwater Horizon disaster in the Gulf of Mexico has polluted estuaries in Louisiana. Why does this pollution affect other animals in addition to those that live permanently in the estuaries?

Many species, including fishes and waterfowl, visit estuaries to feed or reproduce.

▲ **Figure 34.6D** An estuary in Georgia

34.7 Current, sunlight, and nutrients are important abiotic factors in freshwater biomes

Freshwater biomes cover less than 1% of Earth's surface and contain a mere 0.01% of its water. But they harbor a disproportionate share of biodiversity—an estimated 6% of all described species. Moreover, we depend on freshwater biomes for drinking water, crop irrigation, sanitation, and industry.

Freshwater biomes fall into two broad categories: standing water, which includes lakes and ponds, and flowing water, such as rivers and streams. Because these biomes are embedded in terrestrial landscapes, their characteristics are intimately connected with the soils and organisms of the ecosystems that surround them.

Lakes and Ponds In lakes and large ponds, as in the oceans, the communities of plants, algae, and animals are distributed according to the depth of the water and its distance from shore. Phytoplankton live in the photic zone, and rooted plants often inhabit shallow waters near shore (Figure 34.7A). If a lake or pond is deep enough or murky enough, it has an aphotic zone where light levels are too low to support photosynthesis. In the benthic realm, large populations of microorganisms decompose dead organisms that sink to the bottom. Respiration by microbes removes oxygen from water near the bottom, and in some lakes, benthic areas are unsuitable for any organisms except anaerobic microbes.

The mineral nutrients nitrogen and phosphorus typically determine the amount of phytoplankton growth in a lake or pond. Many lakes and ponds receive large inputs of nitrogen and phosphorus from sewage and runoff from fertilized lawns and farms. These nutrients may produce a heavy growth ("bloom") of algae, which reduces light penetration. When the algae die and decompose, a pond or lake can suffer severe oxygen depletion, killing fish that are adapted to high-oxygen conditions.

Rivers and Streams Rivers and streams generally support communities of organisms quite different from those of lakes and ponds. A river or a stream changes greatly between its source (perhaps a spring or snowmelt) and the point at which it empties into a lake or the ocean. Near the source, the water is usually clear, cold, and oxygen-rich, with a swift current that inhibits the growth of phytoplankton (Figure 34.7B). Most of the organisms found here are supported by the photosynthesis of algae attached to rocks or by organic material, such as leaves, carried into the stream from the surrounding land. The most abundant benthic animals are usually arthropods, such as small crustaceans and insect larvae, that have physical and behavioral adaptations that enable them to resist being swept away. Trout, which locate their insect prey mainly by sight in the clear water, are often the predominant fishes.

▲ **Figure 34.7B** A stream in the Great Smoky Mountains, Tennessee

Downstream, a river or stream generally widens and slows. The water is usually warmer, lower in oxygen, and may be murkier because of sediments and phytoplankton suspended in it. Worms and insects that burrow into mud are often abundant, as are waterfowl, frogs, and catfish and other fishes that find food more by scent and taste than by sight.

Wetlands Freshwater wetlands range from marshes, as shown in Figure 34.7C, to swamps and bogs. Like marine wetlands, freshwater wetlands are high in species diversity. They provide water storage areas that reduce flooding and improve water quality by filtering pollutants. Recognition of their ecological and economic value has led to government and private efforts to protect and restore wetlands.

? **Why does sewage cause algal blooms in lakes?**

■ The sewage adds nutrients, such as nitrates and phosphates, that stimulate growth of algae.

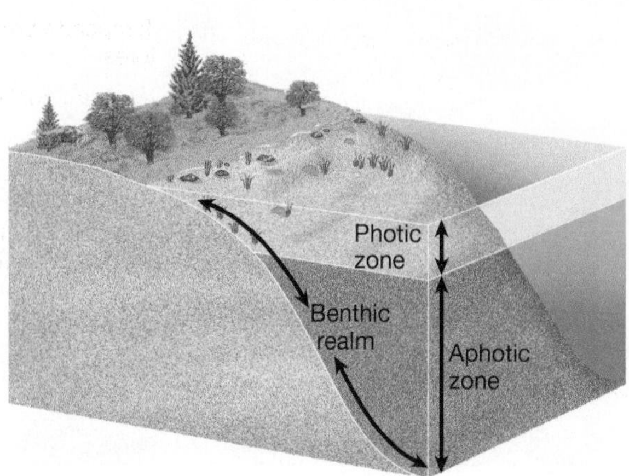

▲ **Figure 34.7A** Zones in a lake

▲ **Figure 34.7C** A marsh at Kent State University in Ohio

Terrestrial Biomes

34.8 Terrestrial biomes reflect regional variations in climate

Terrestrial ecosystems are grouped into nine major types of biomes, which are distinguished primarily by their predominant vegetation. By providing food, shelter, nesting sites, and much of the organic material for decomposers, plants build the foundation for the communities of animals, fungi, and microorganisms that are characteristic of each biome. The geographic distribution of plants, and thus of terrestrial biomes, largely depends on climate, with temperature and precipitation often the key factors determining the kind of biome that exists in a particular region.

Figure 34.8 shows the global distribution of the major terrestrial biomes. If the climate in two geographically separate areas is similar, the same type of biome may occur in both places; notice on the map that each kind of biome occurs on at least two continents. Each biome is characterized by a type of biological community, rather than an assemblage of particular species. For example, the species living in the deserts of the American Southwest and in the Sahara Desert of Africa are different, but all are adapted to desert conditions. Widely separated biomes may look alike because of convergent evolution, the appearance of similar traits in independently evolved species living in similar environments (see Module 15.15).

There is local variation within each biome that gives the vegetation a patchy, rather than uniform, appearance. For example, in northern coniferous forests, snowfall may break branches and small trees, causing openings where broadleaf trees such as aspen and birch can grow. Local disturbances such as storms and fires also create openings in many biomes.

The current global trend of rising temperatures is generating intense interest in the effect of climate change on vegetation patterns. Using powerful tools such as satellite imagery, scientists are documenting shifts in latitudes of biome borders, changes in snow and ice coverage, and changes in length of the growing season. At the same time, many natural biomes have been fragmented and altered by human activity. A high rate of biome alteration by humans is correlated with an unusually high rate of species loss throughout the globe (as we'll discuss in Module 38.2).

Now let's begin our survey of the major terrestrial biomes. To help you locate the biomes, an orientation map color-coded to Figure 34.8 is included with each module. Icons indicate a relative temperate range (in red) and average annual precipitation (in blue) for each biome. Icons also identify biomes in which fire plays a significant role.

? **As global temperatures continue to rise, which biome will most likely replace arctic tundra?**

Northern coniferous forest

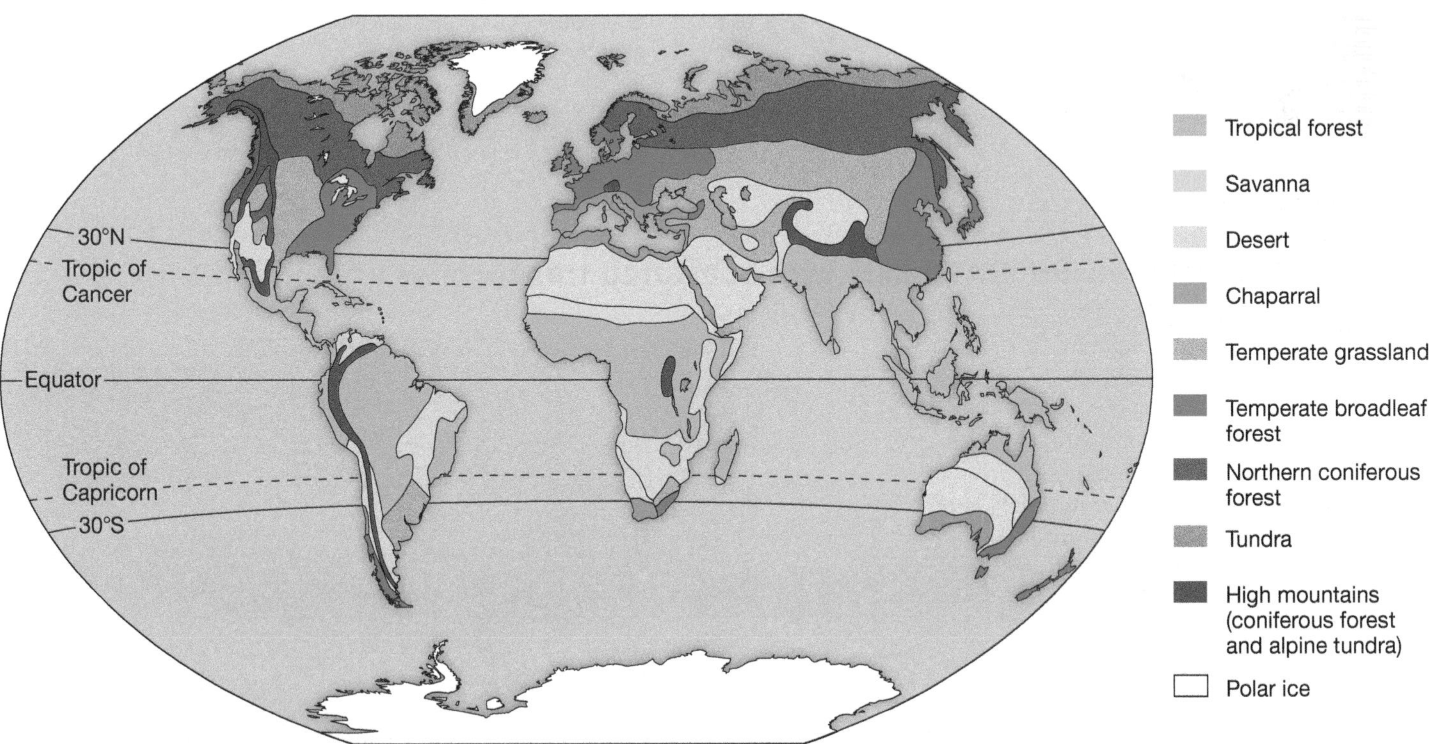

▲ **Figure 34.8** **Major terrestrial biomes**

TRY THIS **As you read Modules 34.9–34.17, construct a table showing the climate, characteristic plants and animals, and any special features of each biome.**

34.9 Tropical forests cluster near the equator

Tropical forests occur in equatorial areas where the temperature is warm and days are 11–12 hours long year-round. Rainfall in these areas is quite variable, and this variability, rather than temperature or day length, generally determines the vegetation that grows in a particular tropical forest. In areas where rainfall is scarce or there is a prolonged dry season, tropical dry forests predominate. The plants found there are a mixture of thorny shrubs and deciduous trees and succulents. Tropical rain forests are found in very humid equatorial areas where rainfall is abundant (200–400 cm, or 79–157 inches, per year).

Tropical rain forest, such as the lush area on the island of Borneo shown in Figure 34.9, is among the most complex of all biomes, harboring enormous numbers of different species. Up to 300 species of trees can be found in a single hectare (2.5 acres). The forest structure consists of distinct layers that provide many different habitats: emergent trees growing above a closed upper canopy, one or two layers of lower trees, a shrub understory, and a sparse ground layer of herbaceous plants. Because of the closed canopy, little sunlight reaches the forest floor. Many trees are covered by woody vines growing toward the light. Other plants, including bromeliads and orchids, gain access to sunlight by growing on the branches or trunks of tall trees. Many of the animals also dwell in trees, where food is abundant. Monkeys, birds, insects, snakes, bats, and frogs find food and shelter many meters above the ground.

The soils of tropical rain forests are typically poor. High temperatures and rainfall lead to rapid decomposition and release of nutrients. However, the nutrients are quickly taken up by the luxuriant vegetation or washed away by the frequent rains.

Human impact on the world's tropical rain forests is an ongoing source of great concern. It is a common practice to clear the forest for lumber, or simply to burn it, farm the land for a few years, and then abandon it. Mining has also devastated large tracts of rain forest. Once stripped, the tropical rain forest recovers very slowly because the soil is so nutrient-poor. (We will discuss the potential consequences of destroying tropical forests in Chapter 38, including the impact on world climate.)

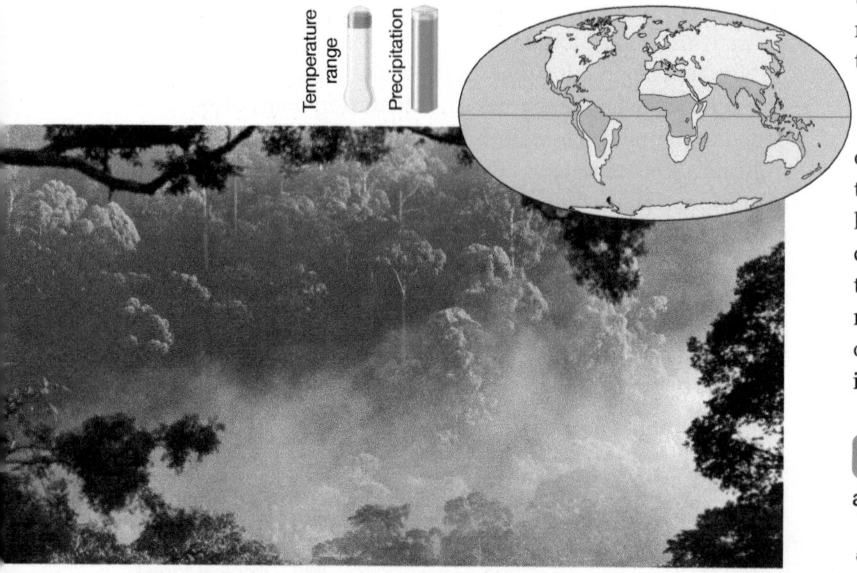

▲ Figure 34.9 Tropical rain forest

? Why are the soils in most tropical rain forests so poor in nutrients that they can only support farming for a few years after the forest is cleared?

Climate conditions favor rapid decomposition of organic litter in the soil and immediate uptake of the resulting nutrients by plants. Thus, most of the ecosystem's nutrients are tied up in the vegetation that is cleared away before farming rather than being stored in the soil.

34.10 Savannas are grasslands with scattered trees

▲ Figure 34.10 Savanna

Figure 34.10, a photograph taken in the Serengeti Plain in Tanzania, shows a typical **savanna**, a biome dominated by grasses and scattered trees. The temperature is warm year-round.

Rainfall averages 30–50 cm (about 12–20 inches) per year, almost all of it during a relatively brief rainy season. Poor soils and lack of moisture prevent the establishment of most trees. Grazing animals and frequent fires, caused by lightning or human activity, further limit invasion by trees. Grasses survive burning because the growing points of their shoots are below ground. Savanna plants have also been selected for their ability to survive prolonged periods of drought. Many trees and shrubs are deciduous, dropping their leaves during the dry season, an adaptation that helps conserve water.

Grasses and forbs (small broadleaf plants) grow rapidly during the rainy season, providing a good food source for many animal species. Large grazing mammals must migrate to greener pastures and scattered watering holes during seasonal drought. The dominant herbivores in savannas are actually insects, especially ants and termites. Also common are many burrowing animals, including mice, moles, gophers, snakes, ground squirrels, worms, and numerous arthropods.

Many of the world's large herbivores and their predators inhabit savannas. African savannas are home to giraffes, zebras, and many species of antelope, as well as to lions and cheetahs. Several species of kangaroo are the dominant mammalian herbivores of Australian savannas.

? **How do fires help to maintain savannas as grassland ecosystems?**

By repeatedly preventing the spread of trees and other woody plants; grasses survive because the growing points of their shoots are underground.

34.11 Deserts are defined by their dryness

Deserts are the driest of all terrestrial biomes, characterized by low and unpredictable rainfall (less than 30 cm—12 inches—per year). The large deserts in central Australia and northern Africa have average annual rainfalls of less than 2 cm, and in the Atacama Desert in Chile, the driest place on Earth, there is often no rain at all for decades at a time. But not all desert air is dry. Coastal sections of the Atacama and of the Namib Desert in Africa are often shrouded in fog, although the ground remains extremely dry.

As we discussed in Module 34.5, large tracts of desert occur in two regions of descending dry air centered around the 30° north and 30° south latitudes. At higher latitudes, large deserts may occur in the rain shadows of mountains (see Figure 34.5F); these encompass much of central Asia east of the Caucasus Mountains, and Washington and Oregon east of the Cascade Mountains. The Mojave Desert, shown in Figure 34.11, is in the rain shadow of the Sierra Nevada, along with much of the rest of Southern California and Nevada.

Some deserts, as represented by the temperature icon in Figure 34.11, are very hot, with daytime soil surface temperatures above 60°C (140°F) and large daily temperature fluctuations. Other deserts, such as those west of the Rocky Mountains, are relatively cold. Air temperatures in cold deserts may fall below −30°C (−22°F).

The cycles of growth and reproduction in the desert are keyed to rainfall. The driest deserts have no perennial vegetation at all, but less arid regions have scattered deep-rooted shrubs, often interspersed with water-storing succulents such as cacti. The leaves of some plants, including the Joshua tree shown in Figure 34.11, have a waxy coating that prevents water loss. Desert plants typically produce great numbers of seeds, which may remain dormant until a heavy rain triggers germination. After periods of rainfall, often in late winter, annual plants in deserts may display spectacular blooms.

Like desert plants, desert animals are adapted to drought and extreme temperatures. Many live in burrows and are active only at night, when temperatures drop, and most have special adaptations that conserve water. Seed-eaters such as ants, many birds, and rodents are common in deserts. Lizards, snakes, and hawks eat the seed-eaters.

The process of **desertification**, the conversion of semi-arid regions to desert, is a significant environmental problem. In northern Africa, for example, a burgeoning human population, overgrazing, and dryland farming are converting large areas of savanna to desert.

? **Why isn't "cold desert" an oxymoron?**

Because deserts are defined by low precipitation and dry soil, not by temperature

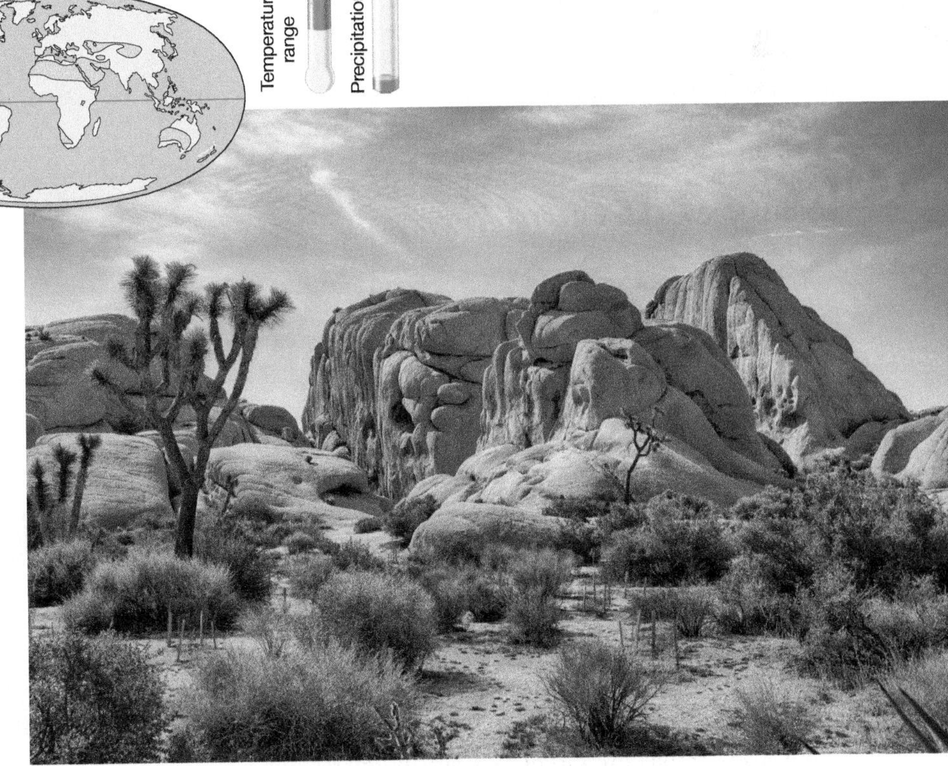

▲ **Figure 34.11** Desert

34.12 Spiny shrubs dominate the chaparral

Chaparral (a Spanish word meaning "place of evergreen scrub oaks") is characterized by dense, spiny shrubs with tough, evergreen leaves. The climate that supports chaparral vegetation results mainly from cool ocean currents circulating offshore, which produce mild, rainy winters and hot, dry summers. As a result, this biome is limited to small coastal areas, including California, where the photograph in Figure 34.12 was taken. In addition to the perennial shrubs that dominate chaparral, annual plants are also commonly seen, especially during the wet winter and spring months. Animals characteristic of the chaparral include browsers such as deer, fruit-eating birds, and seed-eating rodents, as well as lizards and snakes.

Chaparral vegetation is adapted to periodic fires, most often caused by lightning. Many plants contain flammable chemicals and burn fiercely, especially where dead brush has accumulated for some time. After a fire, shrubs use food reserves stored in the surviving roots to support rapid shoot regeneration. Some chaparral plant species produce seeds that will germinate only after exposure to a hot fire. The ashes of burned vegetation fertilize the soil with mineral nutrients, promoting regrowth of the plant community. Houses do not fare as well, and firestorms that race through the densely populated canyons of Southern California can be devastating.

? What is one way that homeowners in chaparral areas can protect their neighborhoods from fire?

They can keep the area clear of dead brush, which is highly flammable.

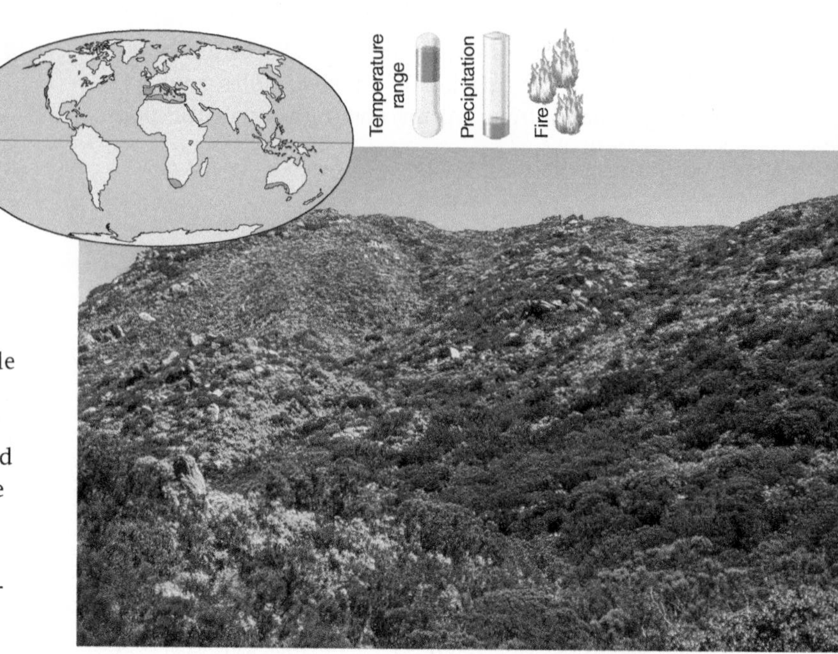

▲ **Figure 34.12** Chaparral

34.13 Temperate grasslands include the North American prairie

Temperate grasslands have some of the characteristics of tropical savannas, but they are mostly treeless, except along rivers or streams, and are found in regions with relatively cold winter temperatures. Annual precipitation averages 25–75 cm (about 10–30 inches) and periodic severe droughts occur, so conditions are too dry to support forest growth. Fires and grazing by large mammals also limit growth of woody plants but do not harm the belowground grass shoots.

Large grazing mammals, such as the bison and pronghorn of North America and the wild horses and sheep of the Asian steppes, are characteristic of grasslands. In the absence of trees, many birds nest on the ground, and some small mammals dig burrows to escape predators. Enriched by glacial deposits and mulch from decaying plant material, the soil of grasslands supports a great diversity of microorganisms and small animals, including annelids and arthropods.

The amount of annual precipitation influences the height of grassland vegetation. Shortgrass prairie is found in relatively dry regions; tallgrass prairie occurs in wetter areas. Figure 34.13 shows a mixed-grass prairie in Alberta, Canada. Little remains of North American prairies today. Most of the region is intensively farmed, and it is one of the most productive agricultural regions in the world.

? What factors prevent woody plants from growing in temperate grasslands?

Low rainfall, fires, and grazing by large mammals

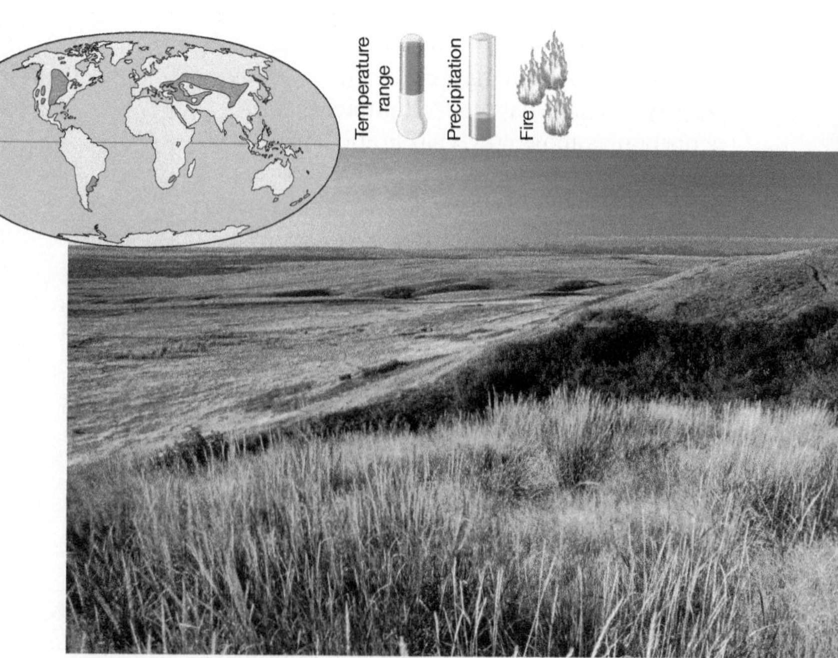

▲ **Figure 34.13** Temperate grassland

34.14 Broadleaf trees dominate temperate forests

Temperate broadleaf forests grow throughout midlatitude regions, where there is sufficient moisture to support the growth of large trees. In the Northern Hemisphere, deciduous trees (trees that drop their leaves seasonally) characterize temperate broadleaf forests. Some of the dominant trees are species of oak, hickory, birch, beech, and maple. The mix of tree species varies widely, depending on such factors as the climate at different latitudes, topography, and local soil conditions. Figure 34.14 features a photograph taken during the spectacular display of autumn color in West Virginia.

Temperatures in temperate broadleaf forests vary seasonally over a wide range, with hot summers and cold winters. Annual precipitation is relatively high at 75–150 cm (30–60 inches) and is usually evenly distributed throughout the year as either rain or snow. These forests typically have a growing season of five to six months and a distinct annual rhythm. Trees drop their leaves and become dormant in late autumn, preventing the loss of water from the tree at a time when frozen soil makes water less available. The trees produce new leaves in the spring.

The canopy of a temperate broadleaf forest is more open than that of a tropical rain forest, and the trees are not as tall or as diverse. However, the soils are richer in inorganic and organic nutrients. Rates of decomposition are lower in temperate forests than in the tropics, and a thick layer of leaf litter on forest floors conserves many of the biome's nutrients.

Numerous invertebrates live in the soil and leaf litter. Some vertebrates, such as mice, shrews, and ground squirrels, burrow for shelter and food, while others, including many species of birds, live in the trees. Predators include bobcats, foxes, black bears, and mountain lions.

▲ Figure 34.14 Temperate broadleaf forest

? How does the soil of a temperate broadleaf forest differ from that of a tropical rain forest?

■ The soil in temperate broadleaf forests is rich in inorganic and organic nutrients, while the soil in tropical rain forests is low in nutrients.

34.15 Coniferous forests are often dominated by a few species of trees

Cone-bearing evergreen trees, such as spruce, pine, fir, and hemlock, dominate **coniferous forests**. The northern coniferous forest, or **taiga**, is the largest terrestrial biome on Earth, stretching in a broad band across North America and Asia south of the Arctic Circle. Figure 34.15 shows taiga in Finland. Taiga is also found at cool, high elevations in more temperate latitudes, as in much of the mountainous region of western North America.

The taiga is characterized by long, cold winters and short, wet summers, which are sometimes warm. The soil is thin and acidic, and the slow decomposition of conifer needles makes few nutrients available for plant growth. Most of the precipitation is in the form of snow. The conical shape of many conifers prevents too much snow from accumulating on their branches and breaking them. Animals of the taiga include moose, elk, hares, bears, wolves, grouse, and migratory birds.

The **temperate rain forests** of coastal North America (from Alaska to Oregon) are also coniferous forests. Warm, moist air from the Pacific Ocean supports this unique biome, which, like most coniferous forests, is dominated by a few tree species, such as hemlock, Douglas fir, and redwood. These forests are heavily logged, and the old-growth stands of trees may soon disappear.

? How and why does the soil of the northern coniferous forests differ from that of a broadleaf forest?

■ The soil is thinner, nutrient-poor, and acidic because conifer needles decompose slowly in the low temperatures.

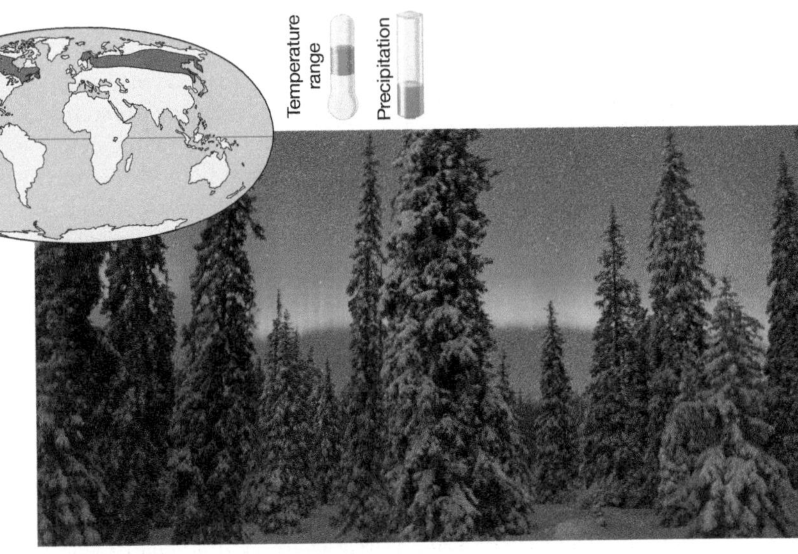

▲ Figure 34.15 Coniferous forest

34.16 Long, bitter-cold winters characterize the tundra

Tundra (from the Russian word for "marshy plain") covers expansive areas of the Arctic between the taiga and polar ice. Figure 34.16 shows the arctic tundra in the Brooks Range, Alaska, in the summer. The climate here is often extremely cold, with little light for much of the autumn and winter. The arctic tundra is characterized by **permafrost**, continuously frozen subsoil—only the upper part of the soil thaws in summer. The arctic tundra may receive as little precipitation as some deserts. But poor drainage, due to the permafrost, and slow evaporation keep the soil continually saturated.

Permafrost prevents the roots of plants from penetrating very far into the soil, which is one factor that explains the absence of trees. Extremely cold winter air temperatures and high winds also contribute to the exclusion of trees. Vegetation in the tundra includes dwarf shrubs, grasses and other herbaceous plants, mosses, and lichens. During the brief, warm summers, when there is nearly constant daylight, plants grow quickly and flower in a rapid burst.

High winds and cold temperatures create plant communities called alpine tundra on very high mountaintops at all latitudes, including the tropics (see Figure 34.8). Although these communities are similar to arctic tundra, there is no permafrost beneath alpine tundra.

Animals of the tundra withstand the cold by having good insulation that retains heat. Large herbivores include musk oxen and caribou. The principal smaller animals are rodents called lemmings and a few predators, such as the arctic fox and snowy owl. Many animals are migratory, using the tundra as a summer breeding ground. During the brief warm season, the marshy ground supports the aquatic larvae of insects, providing food for migratory waterfowl, and clouds of mosquitoes often fill the tundra air.

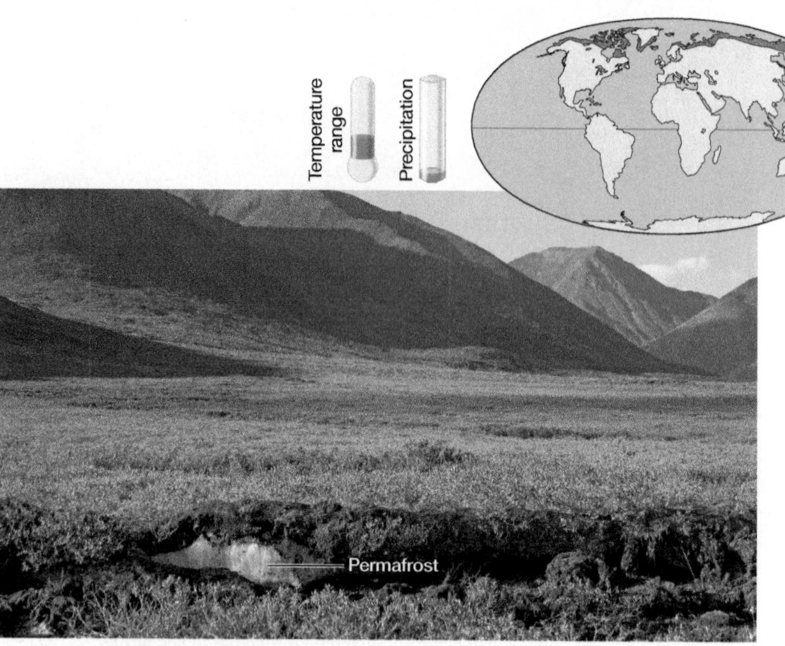

▲ Figure 34.16 Tundra

? What three abiotic factors account for the rarity of trees in arctic tundra?

Long, very cold winters (short growing season), high winds, and permafrost

34.17 Polar ice covers the land at high latitudes

In the Northern Hemisphere, **polar ice** covers land north of the tundra; much of the Arctic Ocean is continuously frozen as well. In the Southern Hemisphere, polar ice covers the continent of Antarctica (Figure 34.17), which is surrounded by a ring of sea ice, and numerous islands.

The temperature in these regions is extremely cold year-round, and precipitation is very low. Only a small portion of these landmasses is free of ice or snow, even during the summer. Nevertheless, lichens and small plants, such as mosses, manage to survive, and invertebrates such as nematodes, mites, and wingless insects called springtails inhabit the frigid soil.

The terrestrial polar biome is closely interconnected with the neighboring marine biome. Seals and marine birds, such as penguins, gulls, and skuas, feed in the ocean and visit the land or sea ice to rest and to breed. In the Northern Hemisphere, sea ice provides a feeding platform for polar bears (see Figure 38.5B).

? How does the vegetation found in polar ice regions compare with tundra vegetation?

Neither biome is hospitable to plants because of the cold temperatures. However, tundra supports the growth of small shrubs, while polar ice vegetation is limited to mosses and lichens.

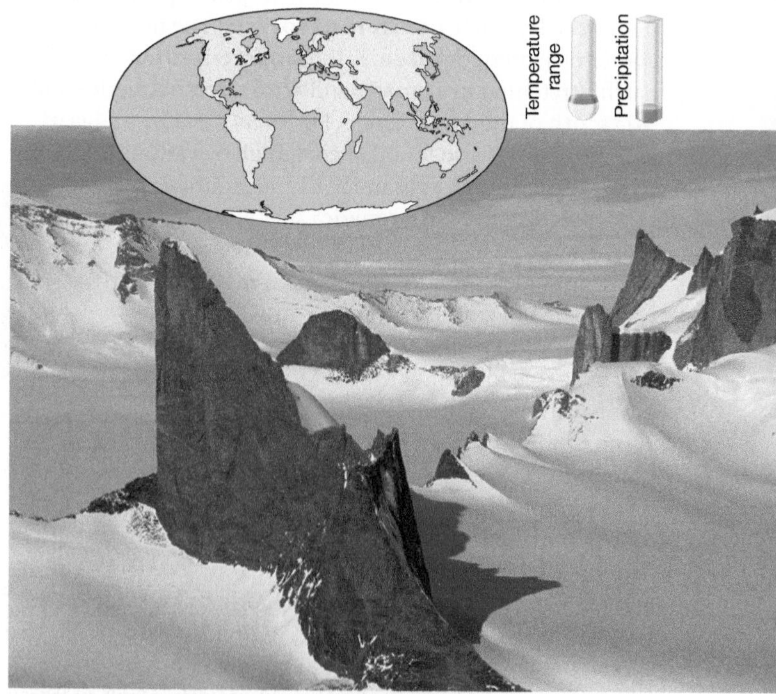

▲ Figure 34.17 Polar ice

VISUALIZING THE CONCEPT

34.18 The global water cycle connects aquatic and terrestrial biomes

Ecological subdivisions such as biomes are not self-contained units. Rather, all parts of the biosphere are linked by the global water cycle and by nutrient cycles (which you will learn about in Chapter 37). Consequently, events in one biome may reverberate throughout the biosphere. Recall from Module 34.5 that solar energy helps drive the movements of water and air in global patterns. In addition, precipitation and evaporation, as well as **transpiration** (evaporative water loss from plants; see Module 32.3), continuously move water between the land, oceans, and atmosphere.

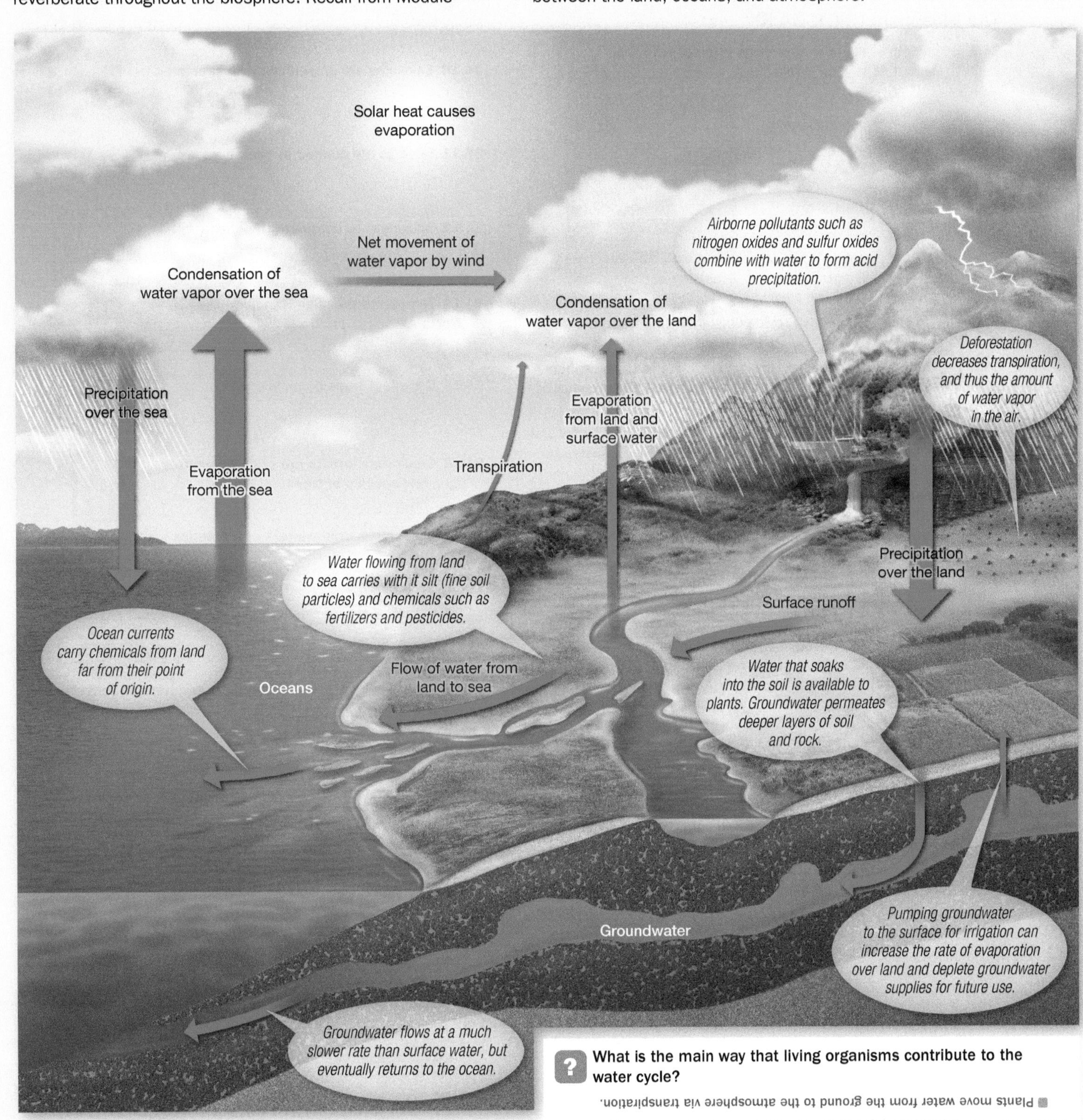

Solar heat causes evaporation
Net movement of water vapor by wind
Condensation of water vapor over the sea
Airborne pollutants such as nitrogen oxides and sulfur oxides combine with water to form acid precipitation.
Condensation of water vapor over the land
Deforestation decreases transpiration, and thus the amount of water vapor in the air.
Precipitation over the sea
Evaporation from land and surface water
Evaporation from the sea
Transpiration
Water flowing from land to sea carries with it silt (fine soil particles) and chemicals such as fertilizers and pesticides.
Precipitation over the land
Surface runoff
Ocean currents carry chemicals from land far from their point of origin.
Oceans
Flow of water from land to sea
Water that soaks into the soil is available to plants. Groundwater permeates deeper layers of soil and rock.
Groundwater
Pumping groundwater to the surface for irrigation can increase the rate of evaporation over land and deplete groundwater supplies for future use.
Groundwater flows at a much slower rate than surface water, but eventually returns to the ocean.

? What is the main way that living organisms contribute to the water cycle?

■ Plants move water from the ground to the atmosphere via transpiration.

TRY THIS Trace the path water molecules might follow as you explain how they move from the sea to the land and back to the sea.

CHAPTER

34 REVIEW

For practice quizzes, BioFlix animations, MP3 tutorials, video tutors, and more study tools designed for this textbook, go to MasteringBiology™

REVIEWING THE CONCEPTS

The Biosphere (34.1–34.5)

34.1 Ecologists study how organisms interact with their environment at several levels.

34.2 The science of ecology provides insight into environmental problems.

34.3 Physical and chemical factors influence life in the biosphere. Major factors include energy sources, temperature, the presence of water, and inorganic nutrients.

34.4 Organisms are adapted to abiotic and biotic factors by natural selection. The pronghorn's adaptations show the variety of factors that can affect an organism's fitness.

34.5 Regional climate influences the distribution of terrestrial communities. Most climatic variations are due to the uneven heating of Earth's surface as it orbits the sun, setting up patterns of precipitation and prevailing winds. Ocean currents influence coastal climate. Landforms such as mountains affect rainfall.

Aquatic Biomes (34.6–34.7)

34.6 Sunlight and substrate are key factors in the distribution of marine organisms. Marine biomes are found in both the pelagic and benthic realms, and the biomes are further distinguished by the availability of light. Coral reefs are found in warm, shallow waters above continental shelves. Other marine biomes are estuaries, wetlands, and the intertidal zone.

34.7 Current, sunlight, and nutrients are important abiotic factors in freshwater biomes. Standing water biomes (lakes and ponds) differ in structure from flowing water biomes (rivers and streams), and communities vary accordingly. Wetlands include marshes, swamps, and bogs.

Terrestrial Biomes (34.8–34.18)

34.8 Terrestrial biomes reflect regional variations in climate.

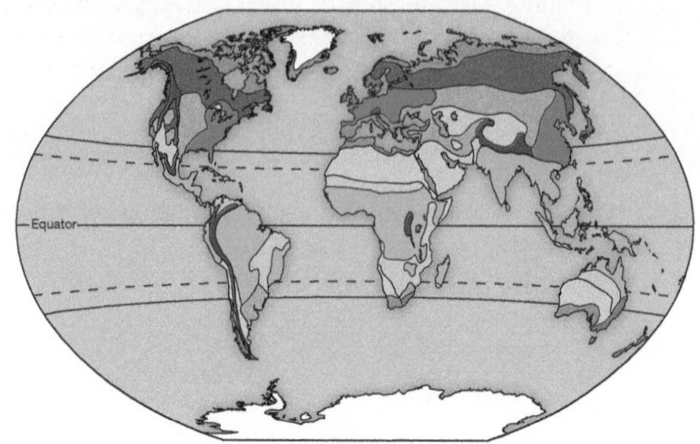

34.9 Tropical forests cluster near the equator.

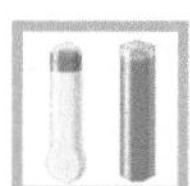

34.10 Savannas are grasslands with scattered trees.

34.11 Deserts are defined by their dryness.

34.12 Spiny shrubs dominate the chaparral.

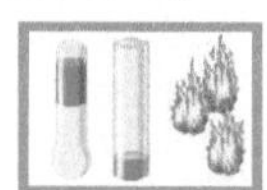

34.13 Temperate grasslands include the North American prairie.

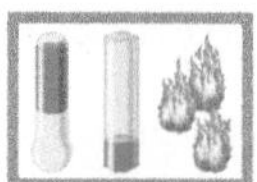

34.14 Broadleaf trees dominate temperate forests.

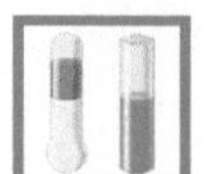

34.15 Coniferous forests are often dominated by a few species of trees.

34.16 Long, bitter-cold winters characterize the tundra.

34.17 Polar ice covers the land at high latitudes.

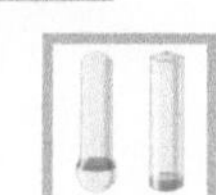

34.18 The global water cycle connects aquatic and terrestrial biomes.

CONNECTING THE CONCEPTS

1. You have seen that Earth's terrestrial biomes reflect regional variations in climate. But what determines these climatic variations? Interpret the following diagrams in reference to how each represents effects on global patterns of temperature, rainfall, and winds.
   a. Solar radiation and latitude:

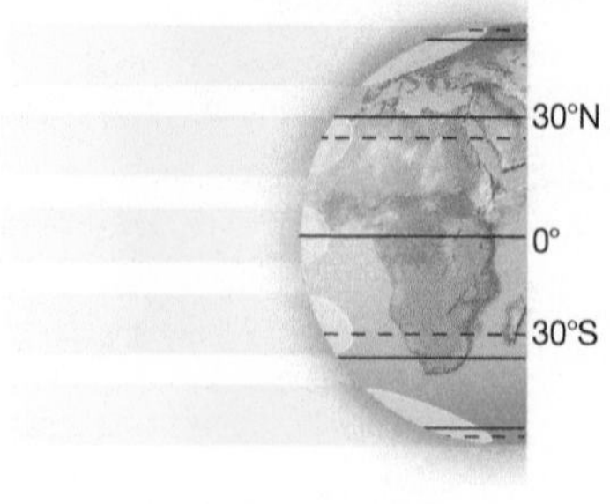

   b. Earth's orbit around the sun:

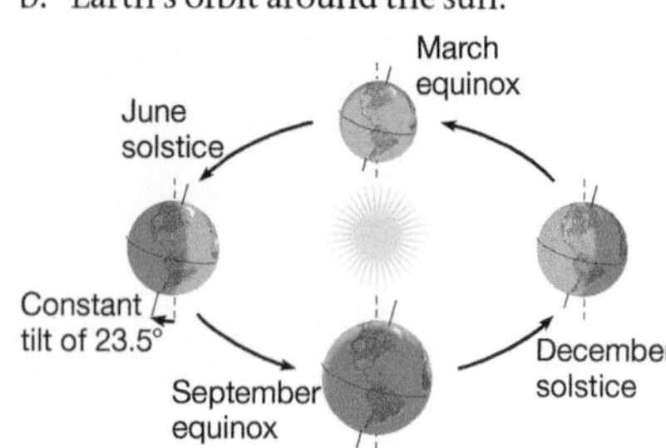

c. Global patterns of air circulation and rainfall:

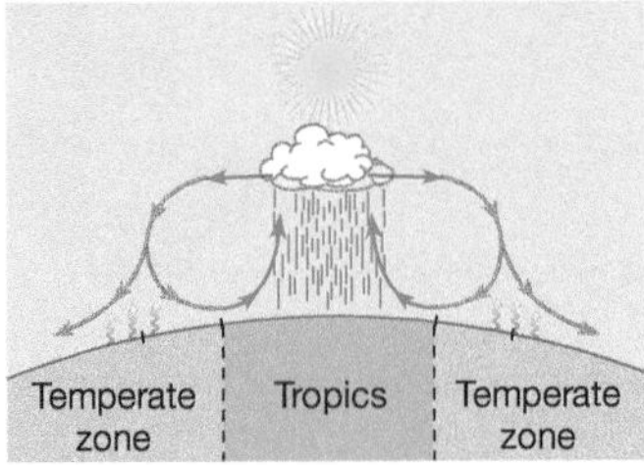

TESTING YOUR KNOWLEDGE

Level 1: Knowledge/Comprehension

Match each description on the left with the correct biome on the right.

2. The most complex and diverse biome	a. chaparral
3. Ground permanently frozen	b. savanna
4. Deciduous trees such as hickory and birch	c. taiga
5. Limited to small coastal areas	d. temperate broadleaf forest
6. Spruce, fir, pine, and hemlock trees	e. temperate grassland
7. Home of ants, antelopes, and lions	f. tropical rain forest
8. North American plains	g. arctic tundra

9. Changes in the seasons are caused by
   a. the tilt of Earth's axis toward or away from the sun.
   b. annual cycles of temperature and rainfall.
   c. variation in the distance between Earth and the sun.
   d. an annual cycle in the sun's energy output.
10. What makes the Gobi Desert of Asia a desert?
    a. The growing season there is very short.
    b. It is hot.
    c. Temperatures vary little from summer to winter.
    d. It is dry.
11. Which of the following sea creatures might be described as a pelagic animal of the aphotic zone?
    a. a coral reef fish
    b. an intertidal snail
    c. a deep-sea squid
    d. a harbor seal
12. Why do the tropics and the windward side of mountains receive more rainfall than areas around latitudes 30° north and south and the leeward side of mountains?
    a. Rising warm, moist air cools and drops its moisture as rain.
    b. Descending air condenses, creating clouds and rain.
    c. There is more solar radiation in the tropics and on the windward side of mountains.
    d. Earth's rotation creates seasonal differences in rainfall.
13. Phytoplankton are the major photosynthesizers in
    a. the benthic realm of the ocean.
    b. the ocean photic zone.
    c. the intertidal zone.
    d. the aphotic zone of a lake.
14. An ecologist monitoring the number of gorillas in a wildlife refuge over a five-year period is studying ecology at which level?
    a. organism
    b. population
    c. community
    d. ecosystem

Level 2: Application/Analysis

15. Tropical rain forests are the most diverse biomes. What factors contribute to this diversity?
16. What biome do you live in? Describe your climate and the factors that have produced that climate. What plants and animals are typical of this biome? If you live in an urban or agricultural area, how have human interventions changed the natural biome?
17. Use Figures 34.5C and 34.18 to predict how global warming (rapid increase in Earth's average temperature; see Module 7.14) might affect the water cycle.

Level 3: Synthesis/Evaluation

18. Aquatic biomes differ in levels of light, nutrients, oxygen, and water movement. These abiotic factors influence the productivity and diversity of freshwater ecosystems.
    a. Productivity, roughly defined as photosynthetic output, is high in estuaries, coral reefs, and shallow ponds. Describe the abiotic factors that contribute to high productivity in these ecosystems.
    b. How does extra input of nitrogen and phosphorus (for instance, by fertilizer runoff) affect the productivity of lakes and ponds? Is this nutrient input beneficial for the ecosystem? Explain.
19. In the climograph below, biomes are plotted by their range of annual mean temperature and annual mean precipitation. Identify the following biomes: arctic tundra, coniferous forest, desert, grassland, temperate forest, and tropical forest. Explain why there are areas in which biomes overlap on this graph.

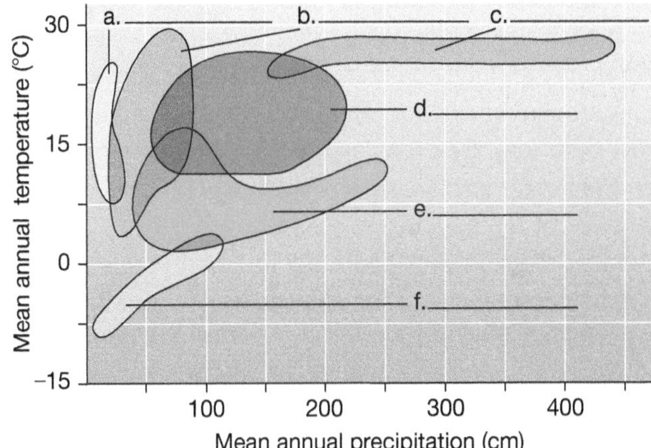

20. The North American pronghorn looks and acts like the antelopes of Africa. But the pronghorn is the only survivor of a family of mammals restricted to North America. Propose a hypothesis to explain how these widely separated animals came to be so much alike.
21. **SCIENTIFIC THINKING** In 1954, workers at Michigan State University began spraying the elm trees on campus annually with DDT to kill disease-carrying bark beetles. In the spring of 1955, large numbers of dead robins were found on the campus. Observers thought perhaps the robins died after eating earthworms contaminated by DDT the previous spring. Suggest how scientists could have investigated the scientific validity of this idea.

Answers to all questions can be found in Appendix 4.

CHAPTER 36

Population Ecology

Fish may not be the first animals that come to mind when you think about reproductive behavior, but a remarkable variety of mating systems and behaviors have evolved in various fish populations. Consider parental investment, the time and energy expended on offspring (see Module 35.15). For example, the males of some fish species build nests and guard their developing offspring from predators. The females of other species carry the embryos internally and give birth after they have hatched. These fish enhance their reproductive success by improving their offspring's chances of survival. Some fish don't provide any form of parental care. They invest in quantity, producing millions of eggs at a time. Most of the offspring will die, but the few that survive to maturity ensure the parents' reproductive success.

Has parental care evolved by natural selection?

There are also fish that hedge their bets by using more than one "strategy." For example, in a small Mediterranean species known as the peacock wrasse (photo at right), the largest males build seaweed nests, where they court and mate with females. After fertilizing a nestful of eggs, these males lose interest in mating, and instead guard the nest from predators. This may sound like a good deal for females, but it comes at a cost. The search for a nesting male takes time and energy and may be unsuccessful. The more abundant small males, which don't build nests, roam around looking for females. During the mating season, female wrasses typically lay eggs every other day. By choosing Mr. Right on some occasions, a female gains protection for some of her offspring; by choosing Mr. Right Now on other occasions, she ensures that she has at least a chance of reproductive success.

In this chapter, you'll learn about the structure and dynamics of populations and how traits such as parental care affect a population's growth rate and success in different types of habitats. As ecologists gain greater insight into natural populations, we become better equipped to assess the impact of human population growth and balance human needs with the conservation of biodiversity and resources.

Population Structure and Dynamics (36.1–36.8)

Population ecology is concerned with characteristics that describe populations, changes in population size, and factors that regulate populations over time.

The Human Population (36.9–36.11)

The principles of population ecology can be used to describe the growth of the human population and its limits.

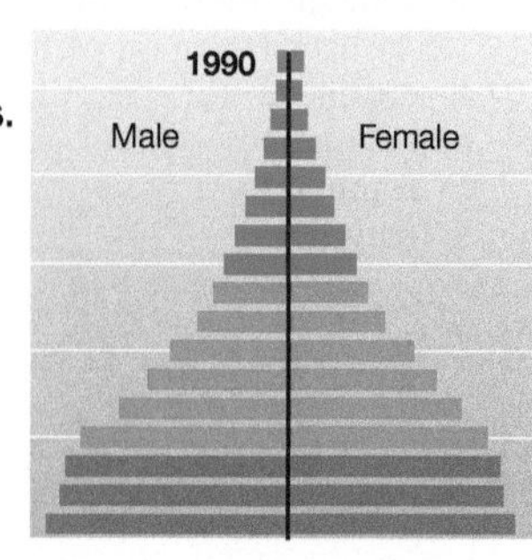

Population Structure and Dynamics

36.1 Population ecology is the study of how and why populations change

Ecologists usually define a **population** as a group of individuals of a single species that occupy the same general area. These individuals rely on the same resources, are influenced by the same environmental factors, and are likely to interact and breed with one another. For example, the red pandas living in central Nepal are a population. When a researcher chooses a population to study, he or she defines it by boundaries appropriate to the species being studied and to the purposes of the investigation.

Population ecology is concerned with changes in population size and the factors that regulate populations over time. A population ecologist might use statistics such as the number and distribution of individuals to describe a population. Population ecologists also examine population dynamics, the INTERACTIONS between biotic and abiotic factors that cause variation in population sizes. One important aspect of population dynamics—and a major topic for this chapter—is population growth. The red panda population of central Nepal increases through births and the immigration of red pandas from eastern and western Nepal. Deaths and the emigration of individuals away from central Nepal decrease the population. Population ecologists might investigate how various environmental factors, such as availability of food, hunting by humans, or forest fires affect the size, distribution, or dynamics of the population.

Population ecology plays a key role in applied research. Data from population ecology are used to manage wildlife populations, develop sustainable fisheries, and gain insight into controlling the spread of pests and pathogens. Conservationists use these concepts to help identify and save endangered species. Population ecology also includes the study of human population growth, one of the most critical environmental issues of our time.

? What is the relationship between a population and a species?

■ A population is a localized group of individuals of a single species.

36.2 Density and dispersion patterns are important population variables

Two important aspects of population structure are population density and dispersion pattern. **Population density** is the number of individuals of a species per unit area or volume—the number of oak trees per square kilometer (km^2) in a forest, for instance, or the number of earthworms per cubic meter (m^3) in forest soil. Because it is impractical or impossible to count all individuals in a population in most cases, ecologists use a variety of sampling techniques to estimate population densities. For example, they might base an estimate of the density of alligators in the Florida Everglades on a count of individuals in a few sample plots of 1 km^2 each. The larger the number and size of sample plots, the more accurate the estimates. In some cases, population densities are estimated not by counts of organisms but by indirect indicators, such as number of bird nests or rodent burrows.

Within a population's geographic range, local densities may vary greatly. The **dispersion pattern** of a population refers to the way individuals are spaced within their area. A **clumped dispersion pattern**, in which individuals are grouped in patches, is the most common in nature. Clumping often results from an unequal distribution of resources in the environment. For instance, plants or fungi may be clumped in areas where soil conditions and other factors favor germination and growth. Clumping of animals often results from uneven food distribution. For example, the sea stars shown in Figure 36.2A group together where food is abundant.

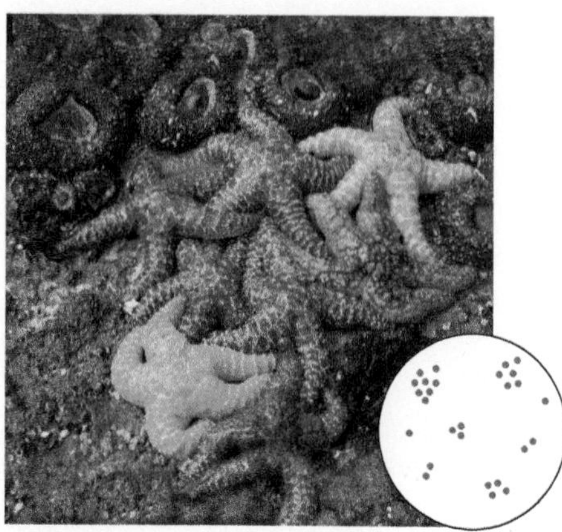

▲ Figure 36.2A Clumped dispersion of ochre sea stars at low tide

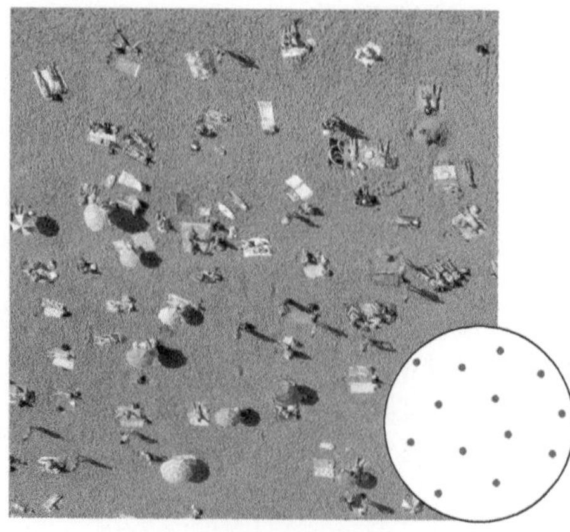

▲ Figure 36.2B Uniform dispersion of sunbathers on a beach

▲ Figure 36.2C Random dispersion of dandelions

Clumping may also reduce the risk of predation or be associated with social behavior.

A **uniform dispersion pattern** (an even one) often results from interactions between the individuals of a population. Some plants secrete chemicals, inhibiting the germination and growth of nearby plants that could compete for resources. Animals may exhibit uniform dispersion as a result of territorial behavior. Figure 36.2B (on the previous page) shows the uniform dispersion of sunbathers at a New York beach.

In a **random dispersion pattern**, individuals in a population are spaced in an unpredictable way, without a pattern. Plants, such as dandelions (Figure 36.2C), that grow from windblown seeds might be randomly dispersed. However, varying habitat conditions and social interactions make random dispersion rare.

Estimates of population density and dispersion patterns enable researchers to monitor changes in a population and to compare and contrast the growth and stability of populations in different areas. The next module describes another tool that ecologists use to study populations.

? **What dispersion pattern would you predict in a forest population of termites, which live in damp, rotting wood?**

■ Clumped (in fallen logs or dead trees).

36.3 Life tables track survivorship in populations

Life tables track survivorship, the chance of an individual in a given population surviving to various ages. Starting with a population of 100,000 people, Table 36.3 shows the number who are expected to be alive at the beginning of each age interval, based on U.S. death rates in 2011. For example, 94,281 out of every 100,000 people are expected to live to age 50. The chance of surviving from 50 to 60, shown in the last column of the table, is 0.941. The chance of surviving from age 80 to 90, however, is only 0.414. The life insurance industry uses life tables to estimate life expectancy. Population ecologists have adopted this technique and constructed life tables for various other species. By identifying the most vulnerable stages of an organism's life, life table data help conservationists develop effective measures for maintaining a viable population.

Life tables can be used to construct **survivorship curves**, which plot survivorship as the proportion of individuals from an initial population that are alive at each age (Figure 36.3). By using a percentage scale instead of actual ages on the *x* axis, we can compare species with widely varying life spans on the same graph. The curve for the human population shows that most people survive to the older age intervals, as we saw in the life table. Ecologists refer to the shape of this curve as Type I survivorship. Species that exhibit a Type I curve—humans and many other large mammals—usually produce few offspring but give them good care, increasing the likelihood that they will survive to maturity.

In contrast, a Type III curve indicates low survivorship for the very young, followed by a period when survivorship is high for those few individuals who live to a certain age. Species with this type of survivorship curve usually produce very large numbers of offspring but provide little or no care for them. Some fishes, for example, can produce millions of eggs at a time, but most offspring die as larvae from predation or other causes. Many invertebrates, such as clams, also have Type III survivorship curves.

A Type II curve is intermediate, with survivorship constant over the life span. That is, individuals are no more or less vulnerable at one stage of the life cycle than at another. This type of survivorship has been observed in some invertebrates, lizards, and rodents.

? **How does the chance of survival change with age in organisms with a Type III survivorship curve?**

■ The chance of survival is initially low but increases after an individual reaches a certain age.

TABLE 36.3 Life Table for the U.S. Population in 2011

Age Interval	Number Living at Start of Age Interval (*N*)	Number Dying During Interval (*D*)	Chance of Surviving Interval 1 − (*D*/*N*)
0–10	100,000	770	0.992
10–20	99,230	312	0.997
20–30	98,917	900	0.991
30–40	98,107	1,233	0.987
40–50	96,784	2,503	0.974
50–60	94,281	5,535	0.941
60–70	88,746	10,562	0.881
70–80	78,184	20,691	0.735
80–90	57,493	33,695	0.414
90+	23,798	23,798	0.000

Data from E. Arias, United States Life Tables, 2011, *National Vital Statistics Reports* 64: 11, September 22, 2015.

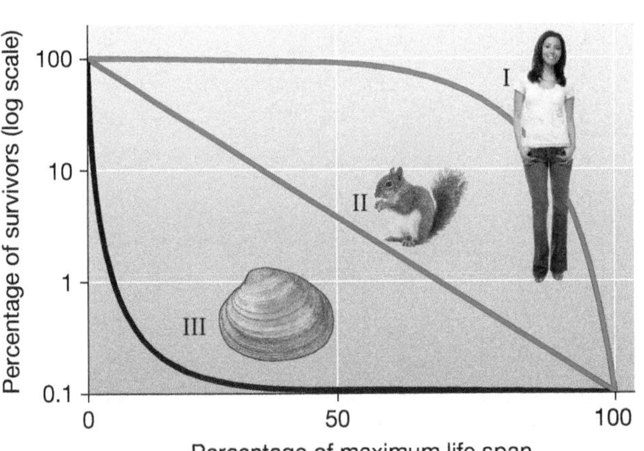

▲ Figure 36.3 Three types of survivorship curves

36.4 Idealized models predict patterns of population growth

Population size fluctuates as new individuals are born or immigrate into an area and others die or emigrate. Some populations—for example, trees in a mature forest—are relatively constant over time. Other populations change rapidly, even explosively. Consider a single bacterium that divides every 20 minutes. There would be two bacteria after 20 minutes, four after 40 minutes, eight after 60 minutes, and so on. In just 12 hours, the population would approach 70 billion cells. If reproduction continued at this rate for a day and a half—a mere 36 hours—there would be enough bacteria to form a layer a foot deep over Earth's entire surface. Using idealized models, population ecologists can predict how the size of a particular population will change over time under different conditions.

The Exponential Growth Model The rate of population increase under ideal conditions, called exponential growth, can be calculated using the simple equation $G = rN$. The G stands for the growth rate of the population (the number of new individuals added per time interval); N is the population size (the number of individuals in the population at a particular time); and r stands for the **per capita rate of increase** (the average contribution of each individual to population growth for the time interval; per capita means "per person").

How do we estimate the per capita rate of increase? Population growth reflects the number of births minus the number of deaths (the model assumes that immigration and emigration are equal). Suppose a population of rabbits has 100 individuals, and there are 50 births and 20 deaths in one month. The net increase is 30 rabbits. The per capita increase in the population, or r, is 30/100, or 0.3, for the month.

In a population growing in an ideal environment with unlimited space and resources, r is the maximum capacity of members of that population to reproduce. Thus, the value of r depends on the kind of organism. For example, rabbits have a higher r than elephants, and bacteria have a higher r than rabbits.

When a population is expanding without limits, r remains constant and the rate of population growth depends on the number of individuals already in the population (N). In Table 36.4A, a population begins with 20 rabbits. The growth rate (G) for this population, using $r = 0.3$, is shown in the right-hand column. Notice that the larger the population size, the more new individuals are added during each time interval.

Graphing these data, as shown in Figure 36.4A, produces a J-shaped curve, which is typical of exponential growth. The lower part of the J, where the slope of the line is almost flat, results from the relatively slow growth when N is small. As the population increases, the slope becomes steeper.

The **exponential growth model** gives an idealized picture of unlimited population growth. It includes no restriction on the abilities of the organisms to live, grow, and reproduce. Even elephants, the slowest breeders on the planet, would increase exponentially if enough resources were available. Although elephants typically produce only six young in a 100-year life span, Charles Darwin estimated that it would take only 750 years for a single pair to give rise to a population of 19 million. But any population—bacteria, rabbits, or elephants—will eventually be limited by the resources available.

TABLE 36.4A Exponential Growth of Rabbits, $r = 0.3$

Time (months)	N	$G = rN$
0	20	6
1	26	8
2	34	10
3	44	13
4	57	17
5	74	22
6	96	29
7	125	38
8	163	49
9	212	64
10	276	83
11	359	108
12	467	140

Limiting Factors and the Logistic Growth Model In nature, a population that is introduced to a new environment or is rebounding from a catastrophic decline in numbers may grow exponentially for a while. Eventually, however, one or more environmental factors will limit its growth rate as the population reaches its maximum sustainable size. Environmental factors that restrict population growth are called **limiting factors.**

You can see the effect of population-limiting factors in the graph in Figure 36.4B (see top of facing page), which illustrates the growth of a population of fur seals on St. Paul Island, off the coast of Alaska. (For simplicity, researchers counted only the mated bulls, each of which has a harem of females, as shown in the photograph.) Before 1925, the seal population on the island remained low because of uncontrolled

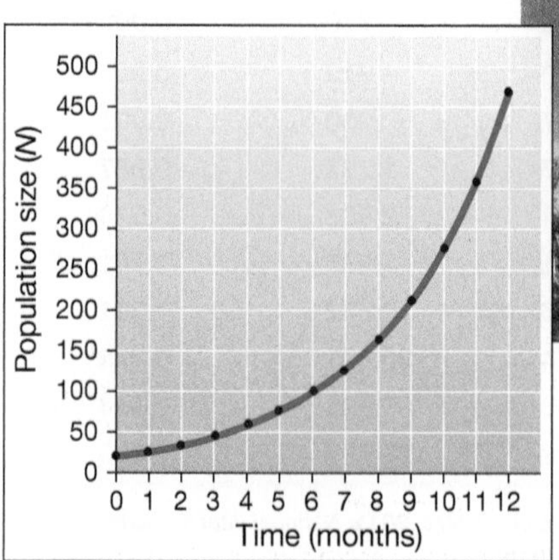

◀ **Figure 36.4A Exponential growth of rabbits**

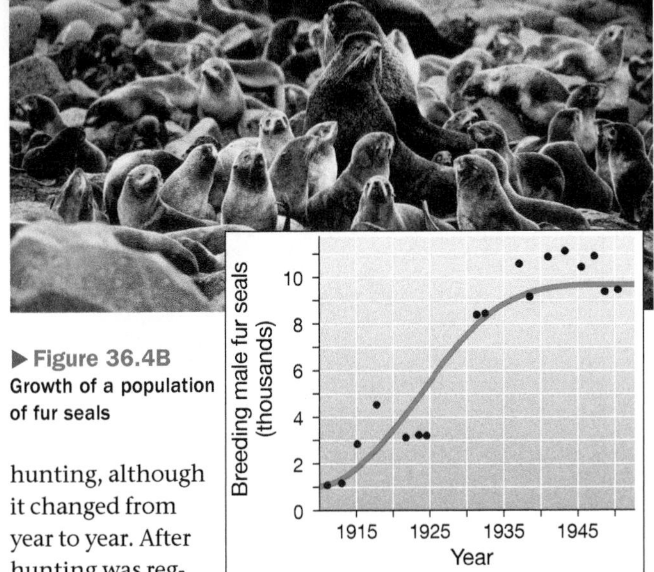

▶ **Figure 36.4B** **Growth of a population of fur seals**

Data from K. W. Kenyon et al., A population study of the Alaska fur-seal herd, *Federal Government Series: Special Scientific Report—Wildlife* 12 (1954).

hunting, although it changed from year to year. After hunting was regulated, the fur seal population increased rapidly until about 1935, when it began to level off and started fluctuating around a population size of about 10,000 bull seals. At this point, a number of limiting factors, including hunting and the amount of space suitable for breeding, restricted population growth.

The fur seal growth curve fits the **logistic growth model**, a description of idealized population growth that is slowed by limiting factors as the population size increases. Figure 36.4C compares the logistic growth model (red) with the exponential growth model (blue). As you can see, the logistic curve is J-shaped at first, but gradually levels off to resemble an S.

To model logistic growth, the formula for exponential growth, rN, is multiplied by an expression that describes the effect of limiting factors on an increasing population size:

$$G = rN\frac{(K - N)}{K}$$

This equation is actually simpler than it looks. The only symbol in the equation that is new to you is K, which stands for carrying capacity. **Carrying capacity** is the maximum population size that a particular environment can sustain ("carry"). For the fur seal population on St. Paul Island, for instance, K is about 10,000 mated males. The value of K varies, depending on the species and the resources available in the habitat. K might be considerably less than 10,000 for a fur seal population on a smaller island with fewer breeding sites. Even in one location, K is not a fixed number. Organisms interact with other organisms in their communities, including predators, parasites, and food sources, that may affect K. Changes in abiotic factors may also increase or decrease carrying capacity. In any case, the concept of carrying capacity expresses an essential fact of nature: Resources are finite.

The hypothetical example in Table 36.4B demonstrates how the expression $(K - N)/K$ in the logistic growth model produces the S-shaped curve. At the outset, N (the population size) is very small compared with K (the carrying capacity). Thus, $(K - N)/K$ nearly equals K/K, or 1, and population growth (G) is close to rN—that is, exponential growth. As the population increases and N gets closer to carrying capacity, $(K - N)/K$ becomes an increasingly smaller fraction. The growth rate slows as rN is multiplied by that fraction. At carrying capacity, the population is as large as it can theoretically get in its environment; at this point, $N = K$, and $(K - N)/K = 0$. The population growth rate (G) becomes zero.

What does the logistic growth model suggest to us about real populations in nature? The model predicts that a population's growth rate will be small when the population size is *either* small or large, and highest when the population is at an intermediate level relative to the carrying capacity. At a low population level, resources are abundant, and the population is able to grow nearly exponentially. At this point, however, the increase is small because N is small. In contrast, at a high population level, limiting factors strongly oppose the population's potential to increase. Reduced resources or increased predation, for example, may cause the birth rate to decrease, the death rate to increase, or both. Eventually, when the birth rate equals the death rate, the population stabilizes at the carrying capacity (K).

It is important to realize that the logistic growth model presents a mathematical ideal that is a useful starting point for studying population growth and for constructing more complex models. Like any good starting hypothesis, the logistic model has stimulated research, leading to a better understanding of the factors affecting population growth. We take a closer look at some of these factors next.

? **In logistic growth, at what population size—in terms of K—is the population increasing most rapidly? Explain why.**

■ When N is $\frac{1}{2}K$. At this population size, there are more reproducing individuals than at lower population sizes, and still lots of resources available for growth.

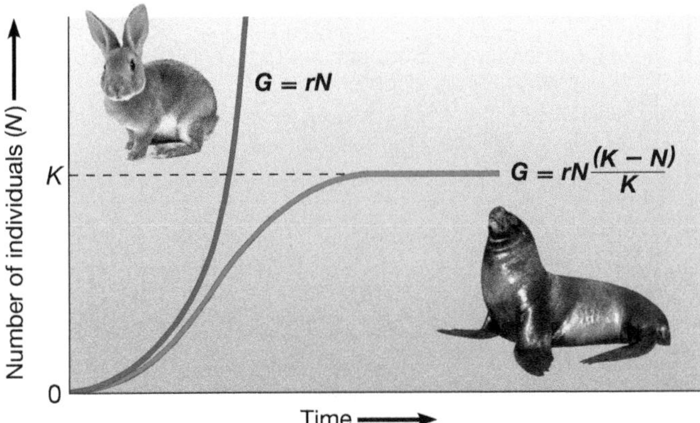

▲ **Figure 36.4C** **Logistic growth and exponential growth compared**

TABLE 36.4B Effect of K on Growth Rate as N Approaches K, where $K = 1{,}000$, $r = 0.1$

N	rN	$(K - N)/K$	$G = rN(K - N)/K$
10	1	0.99	0.99
100	10	0.9	9.00
400	40	0.6	24.00
500	50	0.5	25.00
600	60	0.4	24.00
700	70	0.3	21.00
950	95	0.05	4.75
1,000	100	0.00	0.00

36.5 Multiple factors may limit population growth

The logistic growth model predicts that population growth will slow and eventually stop as population density increases. That is, at higher population densities, the birth rate decreases, the death rate increases, or both. What are the possible causes of these density-dependent changes in birth and death rates?

Several **density-dependent factors**—limiting factors whose intensity is related to population density—appear to restrict growth in natural populations. The most obvious one is **intraspecific competition**—competition between individuals of the same species for limited resources. As a limited food supply is divided among more and more individuals, birth rates may decline because individuals have less energy available for reproduction. Density-dependent factors may also depress a population's growth by increasing the death rate. In a population of song sparrows, both factors reduced the number of offspring that survived and left the nest (Figure 36.5A). As the number of competitors for food increased, female song sparrows laid fewer eggs. Mortality of eggs and nestlings also increased with increasing population density.

The availability of space is a density-dependent factor for some populations. For instance, the number of nesting sites on rocky islands may limit the population size of seabirds such as gannets (see Figure 35.18A). Or, like a game of musical chairs, the number of safe hiding places may limit a prey population by exposing some individuals to a greater risk of predation. For example, young kelp perch hide from predators in "forests" of the large seaweed known as kelp (see Module 16.14). In the experiment shown in Figure 36.5B, the proportion of perch eaten by a predator increased with increasing perch density.

Intraspecific competition may limit plant population growth, too. Plants that grow close together may experience increased mortality as competition for resources increases. And those that survive will likely produce fewer flowers, fruits, and seeds than uncrowded individuals.

For some animal species, physiological factors may regulate population size. White-footed mice in a small field enclosure will multiply from a few to a colony of 30 to 40 individuals, but reproduction then declines until the population ceases to grow. This drop in reproduction occurs even when additional food and shelter are provided. High population densities in mice appear to induce a stress syndrome in which hormonal changes can delay sexual maturation, cause reproductive organs to shrink, and depress the immune system. In this case, high densities cause both a decrease in birth rate and an increase in death rate. Similar effects of crowding have been observed in wild populations of other rodents.

In many natural populations, abiotic factors such as weather may affect population size well before density-dependent factors become important. A population-limiting factor whose intensity is unrelated to population density is called a **density-independent factor**. If we look at the growth curve of such a population, we see something like exponential growth followed by a rapid decline, rather than a leveling off. Figure 36.5C shows this effect for a population of aphids, insects that feed on the sugary phloem sap of plants.

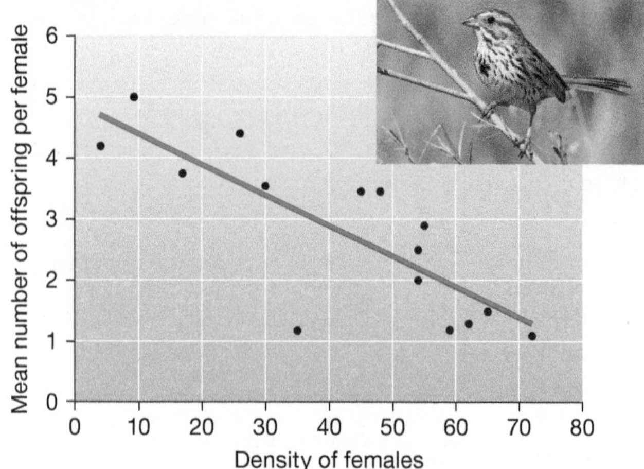

Data from P. Arcese et al., Stability, regulation, and the determination of abundance in an insular song sparrow population, *Ecology* 73: 805–82 (1992).

▲ **Figure 36.5A Declining reproductive success of song sparrows (*Melospiza melodia*, inset) with increasing population density**

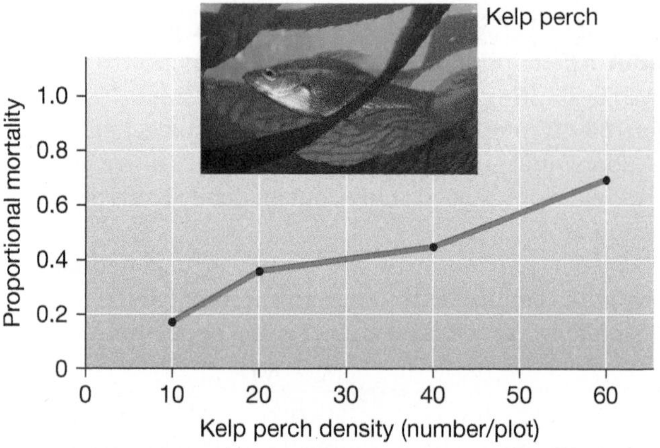

Data from T. W. Anderson, Predator responses, prey refuges, and density-dependent mortality of a marine fish, *Ecology* 82: 245–57 (2001).

▲ **Figure 36.5B Increasing mortality of kelp perch (*Brachyistius frenatus*, inset) with increasing density**

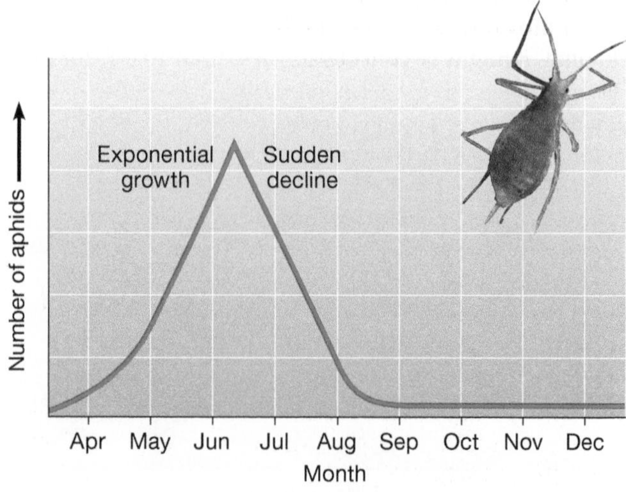

▲ **Figure 36.5C Weather change as a density-independent factor limiting aphid population growth**

These and many other insects undergo virtually exponential growth in the spring and then rapidly die off when the weather turns hot and dry in the summer. A few individuals may survive, and these may allow population growth to resume if favorable conditions return. In some populations of insects—many mosquitoes and grasshoppers, for instance—adults are killed by freezing temperatures, leaving only eggs, which initiate population growth the following year. In addition to seasonal changes in the weather, disturbances—such as fire, storms, and habitat disruption by human activity—can affect a population's size regardless of its density.

Over the long term, most populations are probably regulated by a mixture of factors. Some populations remain fairly stable in size and are presumably close to a carrying capacity that is determined by biotic factors such as competition or predation. Most populations for which we have long-term data, however, show fluctuations in numbers. Thus, the dynamics of many populations result from a complex interaction of both density-dependent factors and density-independent abiotic factors such as climate and disturbances. As you will see in the next module, ecologists must consider this complexity when they develop and test hypotheses.

? **List some of the factors that may reduce birth rate or increase death rate as population density increases.**

Limited food and nutrients, insufficient space, increase in disease and predation

36.6 Some populations have "boom-and-bust" cycles

SCIENTIFIC THINKING

Some populations of insects, birds, and mammals undergo dramatic fluctuations in density with remarkable regularity. "Booms" characterized by rapid exponential growth are followed by "busts," during which the population falls back to a minimal level. A striking example is illustrated in **Figure 36.6**, which shows estimated populations of the snowshoe hare and the lynx, based on the number of pelts sold by trappers in northern Canada to the Hudson Bay Company over a period of nearly 100 years. Both populations rise and fall at regular intervals of roughly 10 years, but not simultaneously. Changes in the lynx population lag behind changes in the hare population. The hare is the lynx's primary food source, so this pattern might be expected. For predators that depend heavily on a single species of prey, the availability of prey can have a strong influence on population size. Thus, the lynx population cycles probably result at least in part from the hare population cycles, and as the predator population declines, the prey population rebounds. But what causes the boom-and-bust cycles of snowshoe hares?

One hypothesis proposed that when hares are abundant, they overgraze their winter food supply, resulting in high mortality. This hypothesis was tested by providing extra food for experimental field populations of hares. Although the design of the experiment was simple, researchers had to collect data for more than 20 years to test the hypothesis. The cycles continued, leading to the conclusion that food supplies alone do not cause hare populations to cycle. However, other experiments indicate that factors such as the quality of available food may play a role.

Another hypothesis attributed hare population cycles to excessive predation. In addition to lynx, many other animals, including coyotes, foxes, and great-horned owls, prey on hares. Using radio collars to track individual hares, researchers determined that 95% of hares had been killed by predators. None had died of starvation. These results support the predation hypothesis. In a further experiment, researchers enclosed certain areas in electric fences to exclude predators. Compared with unfenced control areas, the survival rate of hares in the fenced areas was greater—the "bust" phase of the cycle was nearly eliminated. These results also support the predation hypothesis.

Now that we have looked at patterns of population growth, we turn our attention to the differences in reproductive patterns of populations and how they are shaped by natural selection.

? **Using the methods described above, propose an experiment to test the combined effect of food supply and predation on hare population cycles.**

Compare results for hares in fenced areas, hares in fenced areas that are given food supplements, hares in unfenced areas that are given food supplements, and hares in unfenced areas (control).

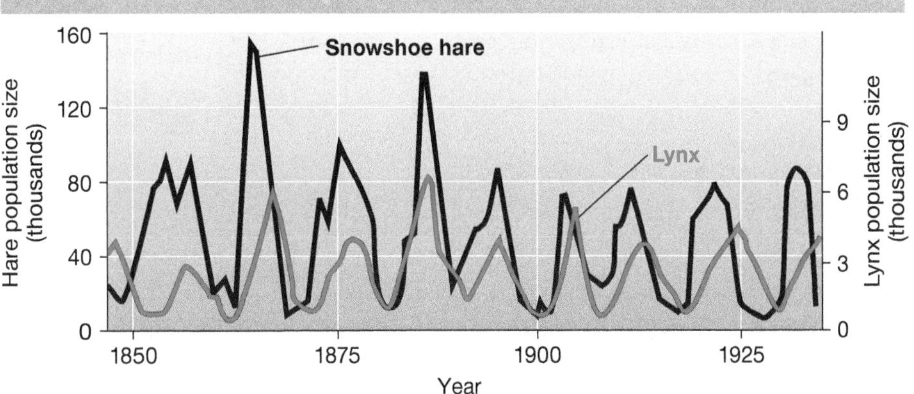

Data from C. Elton and M. Nicholson, The ten-year cycle in numbers of the lynx in Canada, *Journal of Animal Ecology* 11: 215-44 (1942).

▲ **Figure 36.6** **Population cycles of the snowshoe hare and the lynx**

36.7 Evolution shapes life histories

EVOLUTION CONNECTION

The traits that affect an organism's schedule of reproduction and death make up its **life history**. Some key life history traits are the age of first reproduction, the frequency of reproduction, the number of offspring, and the amount of parental care given. Natural selection cannot optimize all of these traits simultaneously because an organism has limited time, energy, and nutrients.

Has parental care evolved by natural selection?

For example, an organism that gives birth to a large number of offspring will not be able to provide a great deal of parental care. Consequently, the combination of life history traits in a population represents trade-offs that balance the demands of reproduction and survival. Because selective pressures vary, life histories are very diverse. Nevertheless, ecologists have observed some patterns that are useful for understanding how life history characteristics have been shaped by natural selection.

One life history pattern is typified by small-bodied, short-lived animals (for example, insects and small rodents) that develop and reach sexual maturity rapidly, have a large number of offspring, and offer little or no parental care. A similar pattern is seen in small, nonwoody plants such as dandelions that produce thousands of tiny seeds. Ecologists hypothesize that selection for this set of life history traits occurs in environments where resources are abundant, permitting exponential growth. It is sometimes called ***r*-selection** because *r* (the per capita rate of increase) is maximized. Most *r*-selected species have an advantage in habitats that experience unpredictable disturbances, such as fire, floods, hurricanes, drought, or cold weather, which create new opportunities by suddenly reducing a population to low levels. Human activity is a major cause of disturbance, producing road cuts, freshly cleared fields and woodlots, and poorly maintained lawns that are commonly colonized by *r*-selected plants and animals.

In contrast, large-bodied, long-lived animals (such as bears and elephants) develop slowly and produce few, but well-cared-for, offspring. Plants with comparable life history traits include coconut palms, which produce relatively few seeds that are well stocked with nutrient-rich material—the plant's version of parental care. Ecologists hypothesize that selection for this set of life history traits occurs in environments where the population size is near carrying capacity (*K*), so it is sometimes called ***K*-selection**. Population growth in these situations is limited by density-dependent factors. Because competition for resources is keen, *K*-selected organisms gain an advantage by allocating energy to their own survival and to the survival of their descendants. Thus, *K*-selected organisms are adapted to environments that typically have a stable climate and little opportunity for rapid population growth.

The concept of *r*- and *K*-selection has been criticized as an oversimplification, and most organisms fall somewhere between the extremes. However, this approach has stimulated a vigorous subfield of ecological research on the evolution of life histories.

A long-term project in Trinidad has provided direct evidence that life history traits can be shaped by natural selection. For years, researchers have been studying guppy populations living in small, relatively isolated pools. As shown in Figure 36.7, some guppy populations live in pools with predators called killifish, which eat mainly small,

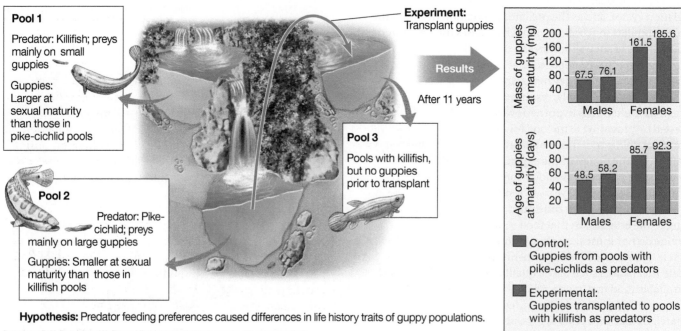

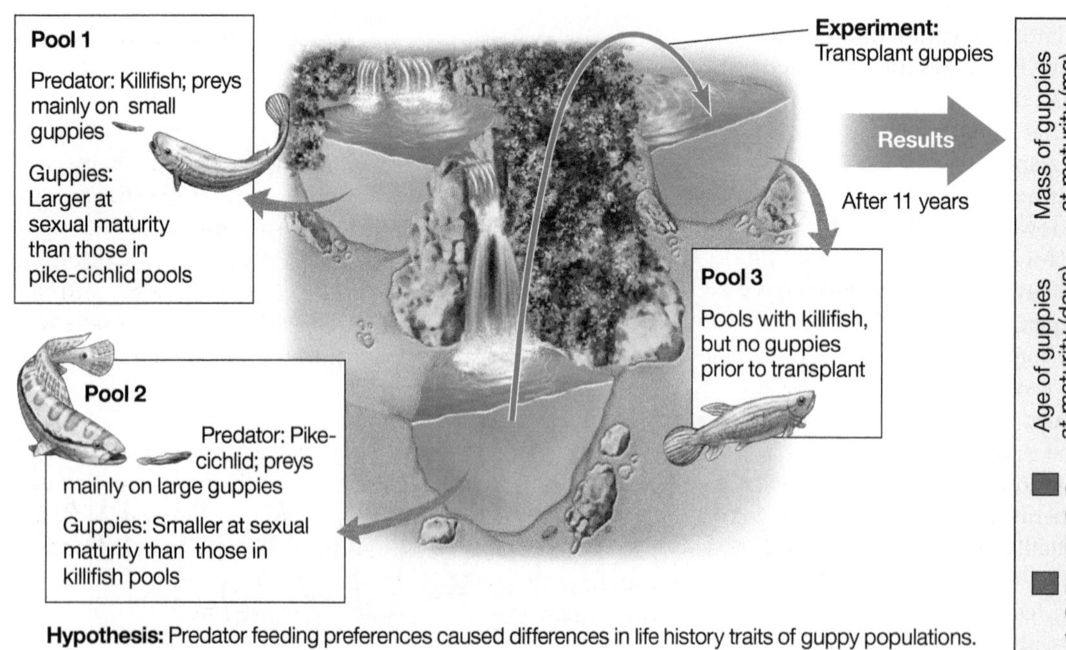

Data from D. N. Reznick and H. Bryga, Life-history evolution in guppies (*Poecilia reticulata*): 1. Phenotypic and genetic changes in an introduction experiment, *Evolution* 41: 1370–85 (1987).

▲ **Figure 36.7 The effect of predation on the life history traits of guppies**

TRY THIS Use the figure to explain how the hypothesis was tested.

immature guppies (Pool 1). Other guppy populations live where larger fish, called pike-cichlids, eat mostly mature, large-bodied guppies (Pool 2). Guppies in populations exposed to these pike-cichlids tend to be smaller, mature earlier, and produce more offspring at a time than those in areas with killifish. Thus, guppy populations differ in certain life history traits, depending on the kind of predator in their environment. For these differences to be the result of natural selection, the traits should be heritable. And indeed, guppies from both populations raised in the laboratory without predators retained their life history differences.

To test whether the feeding preferences of different predators caused these differences in life histories by natural selection, researchers introduced guppies from a pike-cichlid habitat into a guppy-free pool inhabited by killifish (Pool 3). The scientists tracked the weight and age at sexual maturity in the experimental guppy populations for 11 years, comparing these guppies with control guppies that remained in the pike-cichlid pools. The average weight and age at sexual maturity of the transplanted populations increased significantly as compared with the control populations. These studies demonstrate not only that life history traits are heritable and shaped by natural selection, but also that questions about evolution can be tested by field experiments.

As we have seen, population ecology involves theoretical model building as well as observations and experiments in the field. Next we look at how the principles of population ecology can be applied to conservation and management.

? **Refer to Module 36.3. Which type of survivorship curve would you expect to find in a population experiencing *r*-selection? *K*-selection?**

■ Type III for a population experiencing *r*-selection; Type I for *K*-selection

36.8 Principles of population ecology have practical applications

CONNECTION

Principles of population ecology can help guide us toward resource management goals, such as increasing populations we wish to harvest or save from extinction, or decreasing populations we consider pests. Wildlife managers, fishery biologists, and foresters implement **sustainable resource management**: practices that allow use of a natural resource without damaging it. In terms of population growth, this means maintaining a high population growth rate to replenish the resource. According to the logistic growth model, the fastest growth rate occurs when the population size is at roughly half the carrying capacity of the habitat. Theoretically, a resource manager should achieve the best results by harvesting the populations down to this level. However, the logistic model assumes that growth rate and carrying capacity are stable over time. Calculations based on these assumptions, which are not realistic for some populations, may lead to unsustainably high harvest levels that ultimately deplete the resource. Frequently, the amount of scientific information is insufficient to determine sustainable harvest levels. In addition, economic and political pressures often outweigh ecological concerns.

Fish, the only wild animals still hunted on a large scale, are particularly vulnerable to overharvesting. For example, in the northern Atlantic cod fishery, estimates of cod population sizes were too high. Fish were harvested at unsustainable levels, leading to the collapse of the fishery (Figure 36.8). Although commercial cod fishing was banned in 1992, cod populations have not recovered. Following the decline of many other fish and whale populations, resource managers are trying to minimize the risk of resource collapse by prohibiting harvest when population size reaches a pre-set minimum or establishing protected, harvest-free areas. For species that are in decline or facing extinction, resource managers try to provide additional habitat or improve the quality of existing habitat to raise the carrying capacity and thus increase population growth.

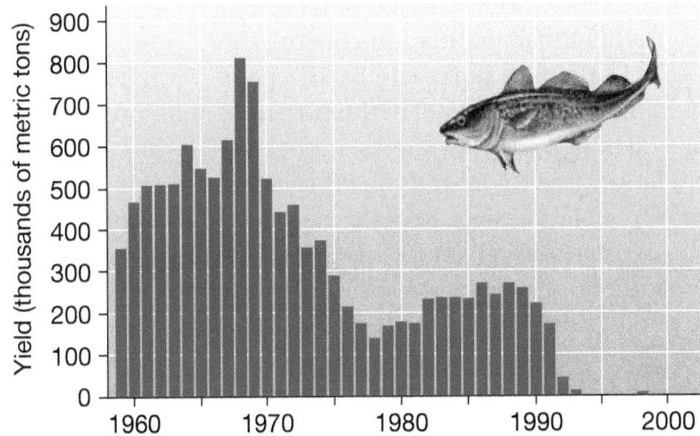

Data from Stock Assessment of Northern (2J3KL) Cod, *Science Advisory Report* 2011/041, Fisheries and Oceans Canada (2011).

▲ **Figure 36.8** **Collapse of northern cod fishery off Newfoundland**

Reducing the size of an undesired population may be a challenging task. Simply killing many individuals will not usually decrease the size of a pest population. Many insect and weed species have *r*-selected life history traits and adaptations that promote rapid population growth. Also, most pesticides kill both the pest and its natural predators. Because prey species often have a higher reproductive rate than predators, pest populations rapidly rebound before their predators can.

Integrated pest management (IPM) uses a combination of biological, chemical, and cultivation methods to control agricultural pests. IPM relies on knowledge of the population ecology of the pest and its associated predators and parasites, as well as crop growth dynamics.

As you've learned, there are many factors that influence a population's size. To effectively manage any population, we must identify those variables, account for the unpredictability of the environment, consider the organism's interactions with other species, and weigh the economic, political, and conservation issues. These same issues apply to the growth of the human population, which we explore next.

? **Explain why managers often try to maintain populations of fish and game species at about half their carrying capacity.**

■ To protect wildlife from overharvest yet maintain lower population levels so that growth rate is high and mortality from resource limitation is reduced

The Human Population

36.9 The human population continues to increase, but the growth rate is slowing

In the few seconds it takes you to read this sentence, 30 babies will be born somewhere in the world and 13 people will die. The statistics may have changed a bit since this book was printed, but births will still far outnumber deaths. An imbalance between births and deaths is the cause of population growth (or decline), and as the red curve in **Figure 36.9A** shows, the human population is expected to continue increasing for at least the next several decades. The blue bar graph in Figure 36.9A tells a different part of the story. The number of people added to the population each year has been declining since the 1980s. How do we explain these patterns of human population growth?

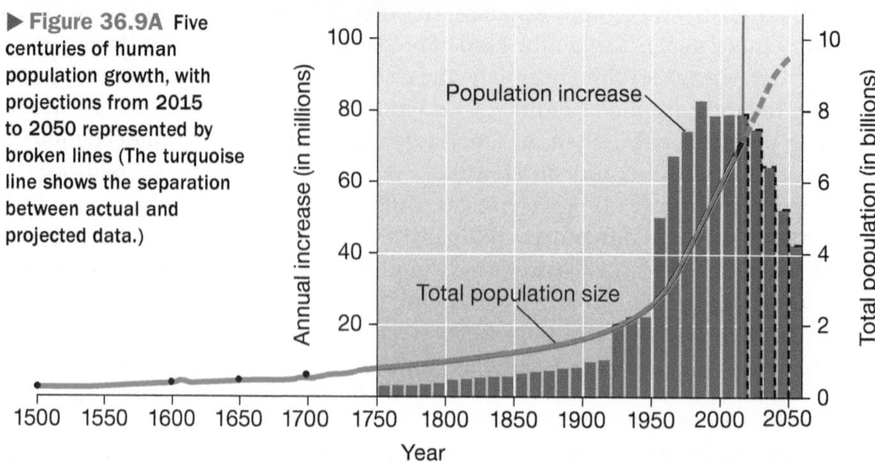

▶ **Figure 36.9A** Five centuries of human population growth, with projections from 2015 to 2050 represented by broken lines (The turquoise line shows the separation between actual and projected data.)

Adapted from The World at Six Billion, *United Nations Publications* (1999).

Let's begin with the rise in Earth's population from 480 million people in 1500 to the current population of more than 7.3 billion. In our simplest model (see Module 36.4), population growth depends on r (per capita rate of increase) and N (population size). Because the value of r was assumed to be constant in a given environment, the growth rate in the examples we used in Module 36.4 depended wholly on the population size. Throughout most of human history, the same was true of people. Although parents had many children, mortality was high, so r (birth rate - death rate) was only slightly higher than 0. As a result, population growth was very slow. (If we extended the x axis of Figure 36.9A back in time to year 1, when the population was roughly 300 million, the line would be almost flat for 1,500 years.) The 1 billion mark was not reached until the early 19th century.

As economic development in Europe and the United States led to advances in nutrition and sanitation and later, medical care, people took control of their population's rate of increase (r). At first, the death rate decreased, while the birth rate remained the same. The net rate of increase rose, and population growth began to pick up steam as the 20th century began. By mid-century, improvements in nutrition, sanitation, and health care had spread to the developing world, spurring growth at a breakneck pace as birth rates far outstripped death rates.

As the world population skyrocketed from 2 billion in 1927 to 3 billion just 33 years later, some scientists became alarmed. They feared that Earth's carrying capacity would be reached and that density-dependent factors (see Module 36.5) would maintain that population size through human suffering and death. But the overall growth rate peaked in 1962. In the more developed nations, advanced medical care continued to improve survivorship, but effective contraceptives held down the birth rate. As a result, the overall growth rate of the world's population began a downward trend.

Demographic Transition When the birth rate and death rate are equal, the population's rate of increase is zero. The world population is undergoing a change known as a **demographic transition**, a shift from birth rates and death rates that are high but roughly equal to birth and death rates that are low but roughly equal. **Figure 36.9B** shows the demographic transition of Mexico, which is projected to approach a zero net rate of increase, with low birth and death rates, in the next few decades. Notice that the death rate dropped sharply from 1925 to 1975 (the spike corresponds to the worldwide flu epidemic of 1918–1919), while the birth rate remained high until the 1960s. This is a typical pattern for demographic transitions.

Because economic development has occurred at different times in different regions, worldwide demographic transition is a mosaic of the changes occurring in different countries. The most developed nations have completed or are nearing completion of their demographic transitions. In these countries collectively, the rate of increase per 1,000 individuals was estimated at 0.8 in 2015 (**Table 36.9**, on the facing page). In the developing world, death rates have dropped, but high birth rates persist. As a result, these populations are growing

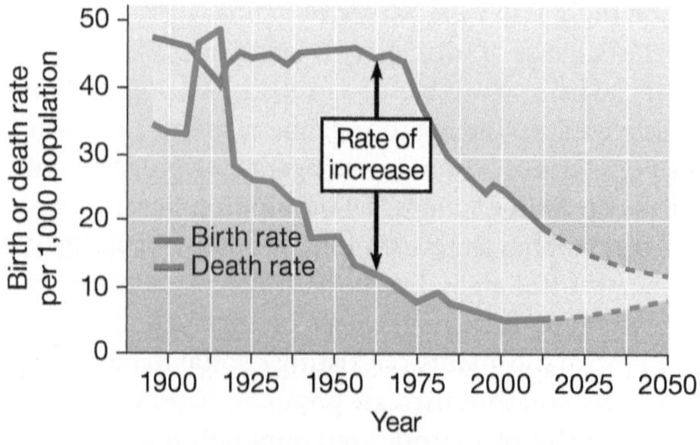

Adapted from Transitions in World Population, *Population Bulletin* 59: 1 (2004).

▲ **Figure 36.9B** Demographic transition in Mexico

TABLE 36.9 Population Changes in 2015 (Estimated)

Population	Birth Rate (per 1,000)	Death Rate (per 1,000)	Rate of Increase (per 1,000)
World	18.6	7.8	10.4
More developed nations	10.8	10.0	0.8
Less developed nations	20.2	7.4	12.8

Data from U.S. Census Bureau International Data Base.

rapidly. Of the roughly 79 million people added to the world in 2015, 74.5 million were in developing nations.

Reduced family size is the key to the demographic transition. As women's status and education increase, they delay reproduction and choose to have fewer children. This phenomenon has been observed in both developed and developing countries, wherever the lives of women have improved. Given access to affordable contraceptive methods, women generally practice birth control, and many countries now subsidize family planning services and have official population policies. In many other countries, however, issues of family planning remain socially and politically charged, with heated disagreement over how much support should be provided for family planning.

Age Structures A demographic tool called an age-structure diagram is helpful for predicting a population's future growth. The **age structure** of a population is the number of individuals in different age-groups. Figure 36.9C shows the age structure of Mexico's population in 1990 and 2015 and its projected age structure in 2040. In these diagrams, purple represents the portion of the population in their prereproductive years (0–14), pink indicates the part of the population in prime reproductive years (15–44), and blue is the proportion in postreproductive years (45 and older). Within each of these broader groups, each horizontal bar represents the population in a 5-year age-group. The area to the left of each vertical center line represents the number of males in each age-group; females are represented on the right side of the line.

An age structure with a broad base, such as Mexico's in 1990, reflects a population that has a high proportion of children and a high birth rate. The **fertility rate**—the average number of children produced by a woman over her lifetime—substantially exceeds the number of children needed to replace herself and her mate. As Figure 36.9B shows, the birth rate and the rate of increase have dropped 25 years later, but the population continues to be affected by its earlier expansion. This situation, which results from the increased proportion of women of childbearing age in the population, is known as **population momentum**. Girls 0–14 in the 1990 age structure (outlined in orange) are in their reproductive years in 2015, and girls who are 0–14 in 2015 (outlined in green) will carry the legacy of rapid growth forward to 2040. Putting the brakes on a rapidly expanding population is like stopping a freight train—the end result takes place long after the decision to do it was made. Even when the fertility rate is reduced to replacement level, the total population will continue to increase for several decades. The percentage of individuals under the age of 15 gives a rough idea of future growth. In the developing countries, 27.6% of the population is in this age-group. In contrast, 16.4% of the population of developed nations is under the age of 15. Population momentum also explains why the population size in Figure 36.9A continues to increase even though fewer people are added to the population each year. In the next module, we examine the age structure of the United States.

? During the demographic transition from high birth and death rates to low birth and death rates, countries usually undergo rapid population growth. Explain why.

■ The death rate declines before the birth rate declines, creating a period when births greatly outnumber deaths. This also sets up population momentum.

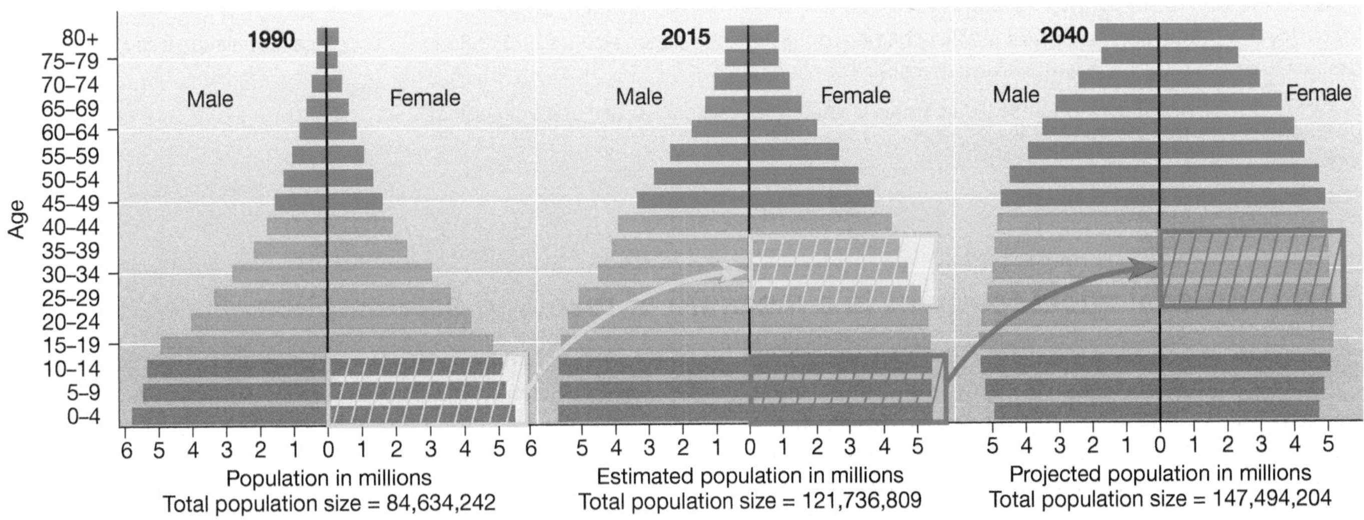

Adapted from International Data Base, U.S. Census Bureau (2015).

▲ **Figure 36.9C** Population momentum in Mexico

TRY THIS Use the orange and green boxes to follow an age-group through time.

36.10 Age structures reveal social and economic trends

CONNECTION Age-structure diagrams not only reveal a population's growth trends, but also indicate social conditions. For instance, an expanding population has an increasing need for schools, employment, and infrastructure. A large elderly population requires that extensive resources be allotted to health care. Let's look at trends in the age structure of the United States from 1990 to 2040 (**Figure 36.10**).

The large bulge in the 1990 age structure (tan screen) corresponds to the "baby boom" that lasted for about two decades after World War II ended in 1945. The large number of children swelled school enrollments, prompting construction of new schools and creating a demand for teachers. On the other hand, graduates who were born near the end of the boom faced stiff competition for jobs. Because they make up such a large segment of the population, boomers have had an enormous influence on social and economic trends. They also produced a "boomlet" of their own, seen in the 0–4 age-group in 1990 and the bump (green screen) in the 2015 age structure.

Where are the baby boomers now? The leading edge has reached retirement age, which will place pressure on programs such as Medicare and Social Security. In 2015, roughly 60% of the U.S. population was between 20 and 64, the ages most likely to be in the workforce, and 13.5% of the population was over 65. In 2040, these age-groups are projected to make up 55% and 22% of the population, respectively. In part, the increase in the elderly population is due to people living longer. The percentage of the population over 80, which was 2.8% in 1990, is projected to rise to 7.5%—more than 28.5 million people—in 2040.

? **Point out an example of population momentum in Figure 36.10.**

■ The 1981–1995 "boomlet" in the 2015 age structure is a consequence of rapid reproduction in 1946–1965, as girls born during the baby boom entered their reproductive years.

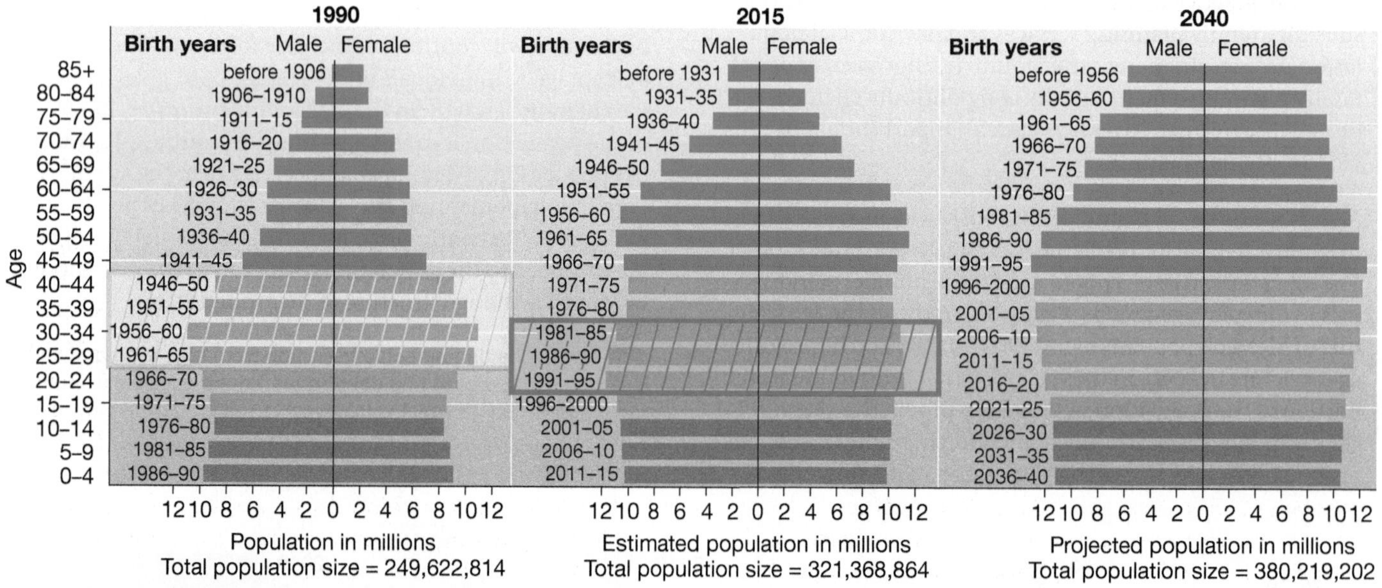

Data from International Data Base, U.S. Census Bureau website, (2015).

▲ **Figure 36.10 Age structures for the United States in 1990, 2015 (estimated), and 2040 (projected)**

TRY THIS **Locate your age-group in 2015.**

36.11 An ecological footprint is a measure of resource consumption

CONNECTION How large a population of humans can Earth hold? In Module 36.9, we saw that the world's population is growing rapidly, though at a slower rate than it did in the last century. The rate of increase, as well as population momentum, predicts that the populations of most developing nations will continue to increase for the foreseeable future. The U.S. Census Bureau projects a global population of 8 billion in 2025 and 9.7 billion by the mid-21st century. But these numbers are only part of the story. Trillions of bacteria can live in a petri dish if they have sufficient resources. Do we have sufficient resources to sustain 8 or 9 billion people? To accommodate all the people expected to live on our planet by 2025, the world will have to greatly increase food production. Already, agricultural lands are under pressure. Overgrazing by the world's growing herds of livestock is turning vast areas of grassland into desert. Water use, which increased sixfold from 1900 to 2000, continues to rise, causing rivers to run dry and levels of

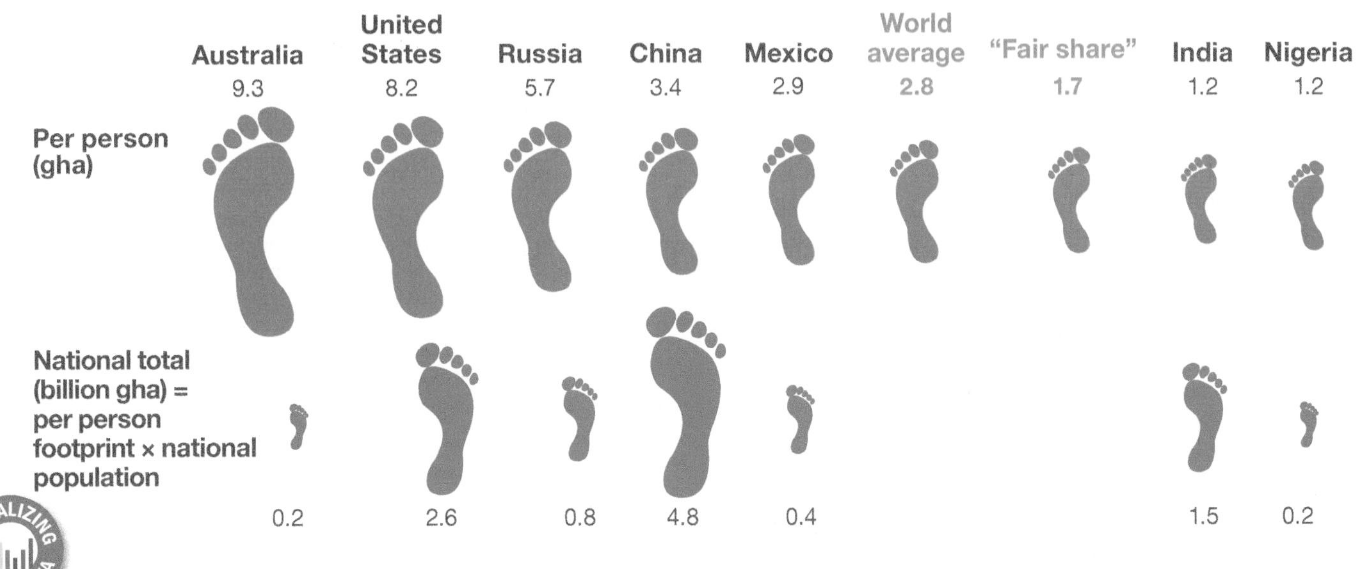

▲ **Figure 36.11** **Personal and national ecological footprints of several countries**

Data from Global Footprint Network © 2016 Global Footprint Network. National Footprint Accounts, 2016 Edition. www.footprintnetwork.org

groundwater to drop. The effects of climate change on precipitation patterns are likely to have a drastic impact on agriculture in some regions. And because so much open space will be needed to support the expanding human population, many other species, including some important to human survival, are expected to become extinct.

Applying the concept of an ecological footprint is one approach to understanding resource availability and usage. An **ecological footprint** is an estimate of the land and water area required to provide the resources an individual or a nation consumes—for example, food, fuel, and housing—and to absorb the waste it generates. Our carbon footprint, the emission of carbon dioxide and other greenhouse gases (see Module 7.14), is the largest component of humanity's ecological footprint. (You'll learn more about the carbon footprint in Module 38.4.)

Comparing our demand for resources with **biocapacity**, Earth's capacity to renew these resources, gives us a broad view of the sustainability of human activities. **Sustainability** is the goal of developing, managing, and conserving Earth's resources in ways that meet the needs of people today without compromising the ability of future generations to meet theirs. When used sustainably, resources such as crops, pastureland, forests, and fishing grounds will regenerate either naturally or with the assistance of technology.

Is humanity's current resource usage sustainable? When the total area of ecologically productive land on Earth is divided by the global population, we each have a share of about 1.7 global hectares (1 hectare, or ha, = 2.47 acres; a global hectare, or gha, is a hectare with world-average ability to produce resources and absorb wastes). According to the Global Footprint Network, in 2012 (the most recent year for which complete data are available), the average ecological footprint for the world's population was 2.8 global hectares (gha)—roughly 1.6 times the planet's biocapacity per person. To put it another way, Earth's total biocapacity for the year had been exhausted by August 22. By overshooting Earth's biocapacity, we are depleting our resources. The collapse of the northern cod fisheries (see Module 36.8) illustrates what happens when usage exceeds regenerative capacity.

The green footprints in Figure 36.11 compare the average ecological footprint per person for several countries with the "fair share" (1.7 gha) and world average (2.8 gha) footprints. As the giant footprints of the United States and Australia indicate, individuals in affluent nations consume a disproportionate amount of resources. Researchers estimate that providing everyone with the same standard of living as in the United States would require the resources of 4.8 planet Earths.

The impact of population size on sustainability is seen in the national total ecological footprints in Figure 36.11 (blue footprints), which is determined by multiplying each country's per-person footprint by its population. Earth's total biocapacity is estimated to be 12 billion gha. The United States alone uses more than 21% of that. China, with a massive population, uses nearly 40%, despite its modest per-person footprint. The ecological impact of India, too, is hugely amplified by its population size. In addition, India's population is growing rapidly. Thus, both overconsumption and overpopulation imperil the goal of sustainability.

? **What is your ecological footprint? Do a Web search to find a site that calculates personal resource consumption.**

CHAPTER

36 REVIEW

For practice quizzes, BioFlix animations, MP3 tutorials, video tutors, and more study tools designed for this textbook, go to MasteringBiology™

REVIEWING THE CONCEPTS

Population Structure and Dynamics (36.1–36.8)

36.1 Population ecology is the study of how and why populations change.

36.2 Density and dispersion patterns are important population variables. Population density is the number of individuals in a given area or volume. Environmental and social factors influence the spacing of individuals in various dispersion patterns: clumped (most common), uniform, or random.

36.3 Life tables track survivorship in populations. Life tables and survivorship curves predict an individual's statistical chance of dying or surviving during each interval in its life. The three types of survivorship curves reflect differences in species' reproduction and mortality.

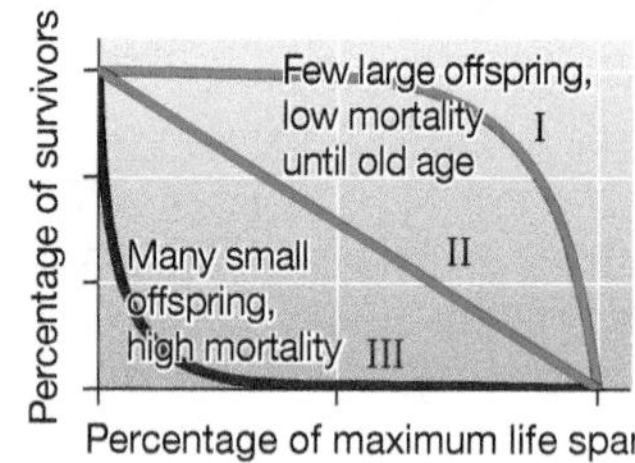

36.4 Idealized models predict patterns of population growth. Exponential growth is the accelerating increase that occurs when growth is unlimited. The equation $G = rN$ describes this J-shaped growth curve, where $G =$ the population growth rate, $r =$ an organism's inherent capacity to reproduce, and $N =$ the population size. Logistic growth is the model that represents the slowing of population growth as a result of limiting factors and the leveling off at carrying capacity, which is the number of individuals the environment can support. The equation $G = rN(K - N)/K$ describes a logistic growth curve, where $K =$ carrying capacity and the term $(K - N)/K$ accounts for the leveling off of the curve.

36.5 Multiple factors may limit population growth. As a population's density increases, factors such as limited food supply and increased disease or predation may increase the death rate, decrease the birth rate, or both. Abiotic, density-independent factors such as severe weather may limit many natural populations. Most populations are probably regulated by a mixture of factors, and fluctuations in numbers are common.

36.6 Some populations have "boom-and-bust" cycles. Researchers have tested hypotheses that explain the population cycles of the lynx and the snowshoe hare.

36.7 Evolution shapes life histories. Natural selection shapes a species' life history, the series of events from birth through reproduction to death. Populations with so-called *r*-selected life history traits produce many offspring and grow rapidly in unpredictable environments. Populations with *K*-selected traits raise few offspring and maintain relatively stable populations. Most species fall between these extremes.

36.8 Principles of population ecology have practical applications. For example, resource managers use population ecology to determine sustainable yields.

The Human Population (36.9–36.11)

36.9 The human population continues to increase, but the growth rate is slowing. The human population grew rapidly during the 20th century and currently stands at more than 7 billion. Demographic transition, the shift from high birth and death rates to low birth and death rates, has lowered the rate of growth in developed countries. In developing nations, death rates have dropped, but birth rates are still high. The age structure of a population—the proportion of individuals in different age-groups—affects its future growth. Population momentum is the continued growth that occurs despite reduction of the fertility rate to replacement level and is a result of girls in the 0–14 age-group of a previously expanding population reaching their childbearing years.

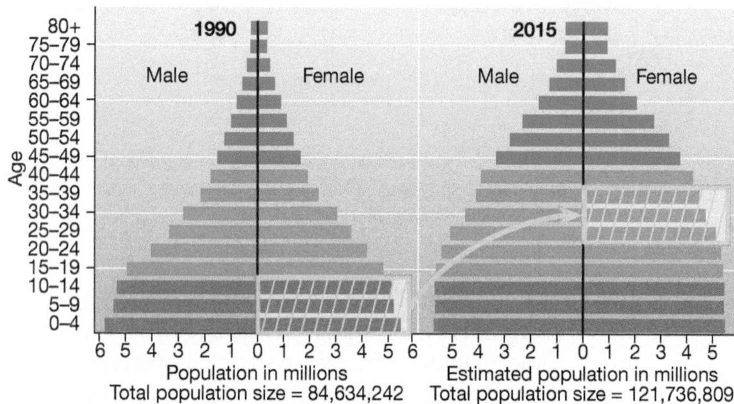

36.10 Age structures reveal social and economic trends.

36.11 An ecological footprint is a measure of resource consumption. An ecological footprint estimates the amount of land required by each person or country to produce all the resources it consumes and to absorb all its wastes. The global ecological footprint already exceeds a sustainable level. There is disparity between resource consumption in more developed and less developed nations.

CONNECTING THE CONCEPTS

1. Use this graph of the idealized exponential and logistic growth curves to complete the following.
   a. Label the axes and curves on the graph.
   b. Give the formula that describes the blue curve.
   c. What does the dotted line represent?
   d. For each curve, indicate and explain where population growth is the most rapid.
   e. Which of these curves best represents global human population growth?

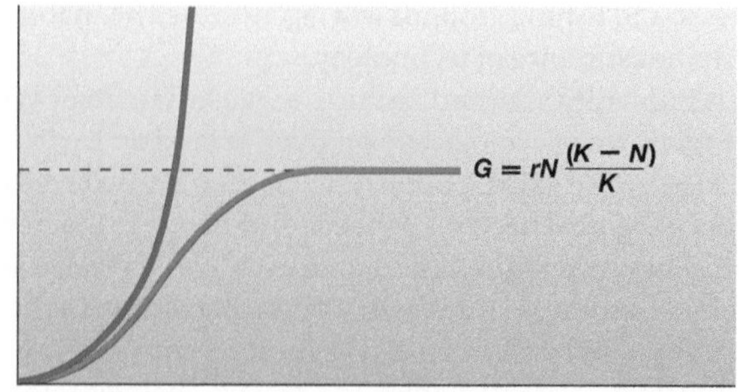

2. The graph below shows the demographic transition for a hypothetical country. Many developed countries that have achieved a stable population size have undergone a transition similar to this. Answer the following questions concerning this graph.
   a. What does the blue line represent? The red line?
   b. This diagram has been divided into four sections. Describe what is happening in each section.
   c. In which section(s) is the population size stable?
   d. In which section is the population growth rate the highest?

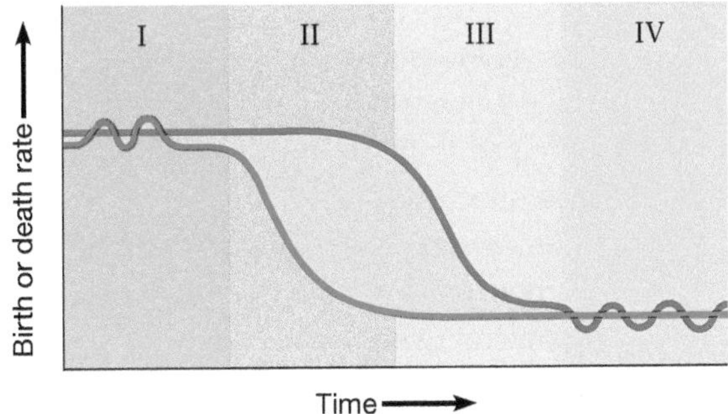

TESTING YOUR KNOWLEDGE

Level 1: Knowledge/Comprehension

3. After seeds have sprouted, gardeners often pull up some of the seedlings so that only a few grow to maturity. How does this practice help produce the best yield?
   a. by increasing K
   b. by decreasing r
   c. by reducing intraspecific competition
   d. by adding a density-independent factor to the environment
4. To figure out the human population density of your community, you would need to know the number of people living there and
   a. the land area in which they live.
   b. the birth rate of the population.
   c. the dispersion pattern of the population.
   d. the carrying capacity.
5. The term $(K - N)/K$
   a. is the carrying capacity for a population.
   b. is greatest when K is very large.
   c. is zero when population size equals carrying capacity.
   d. increases in value as N approaches K.
6. With regard to its rate of growth, a population that is growing logistically
   a. grows fastest when density is lowest.
   b. has a high intrinsic rate of increase.
   c. grows fastest at an intermediate population density.
   d. grows fastest as it approaches carrying capacity.
7. Which of the following represents a demographic transition?
   a. A population switches from exponential to logistic growth.
   b. A population reaches a fertility rate of zero.
   c. There are equal numbers of individuals in all age-groups.
   d. A population switches from high birth and death rates to low birth and death rates.
8. Skyrocketing growth of the human population appears to be mainly a result of
   a. a drop in death rate due to sanitation and health care.
   b. better nutrition boosting the birth rate.
   c. the concentration of humans in cities.
   d. social changes that make it desirable to have more children.
9. According to data on ecological footprints,
   a. the carrying capacity of the world is 10 billion.
   b. Earth's resources are sufficient to sustain future generations at current levels of consumption.
   c. the ecological footprint of the United States is more than twice the world average.
   d. nations with the largest ecological footprints have the fastest population growth rates.

Level 2: Application/Analysis

10. What are some factors that might have a density-dependent limiting effect on population growth?
11. What is survivorship? What does a survivorship curve show? Explain what the three survivorship curves tell us about humans, squirrels, and clams.
12. Describe the factors that might produce the following three types of dispersion patterns in populations.

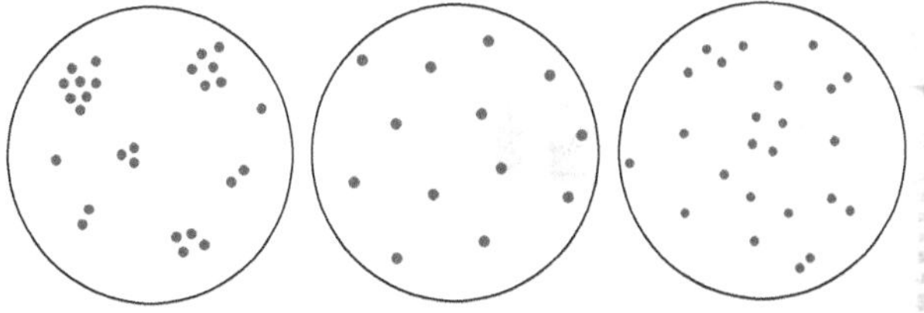

Level 3: Synthesis/Evaluation

13. The mountain gorilla, spotted owl, giant panda, snow leopard, and grizzly bear are all endangered by human encroachment on their environments. Another thing these animals have in common is their K-selected life history traits. Why might they be more easily endangered than animals with r-selected life history traits? What general type of survivorship curve would you expect these species to exhibit? Explain your answer.
14. **SCIENTIFIC THINKING** Another hypothesis for snowshoe hare population cycles proposes that they are caused by sunspot activity. According to this hypothesis, sunspot activity affects the chemicals present in the plants eaten by hares, which in turn affects the quality of the food. What testable predictions are generated by this hypothesis?
15. Many people regard the rapid population growth of developing countries as our most serious environmental problem. Others think that the growth of developed countries, though slower, is actually a greater threat to the environment. What kinds of environmental problems result from population growth in (a) developing countries and (b) developed countries? Which do you think is the greater threat? Why?

Answers to all questions can be found in Appendix 4.

Communities and Ecosystems

CHAPTER 37

Many drugs, including common medicines such as aspirin, are derived from plants. Morphine, a powerful pain reliever, for example, comes from opium poppies; a chemical found in certain *Ephedra* species relieves the symptoms of asthma; and a drug from foxglove is used to treat congestive heart failure. Many other plant substances have specific effects in the human body, as well. Caffeine, found in coffee berries, tea leaves, and kola nuts, is a stimulant; so is the nicotine in tobacco leaves. A plant called deadly nightshade (photo at right) provides several useful substances, including a mild sedative that is used to combat motion sickness and the drops used to dilate the pupils for an eye exam. Its ominous name is well-deserved, however—the leaves and berries contain deadly poisons that were used by ancient Romans to murder their enemies.

Why do plants make drugs?

We've listed only a fraction of the plants that are known to have medicinal properties. Researchers are eagerly testing newly discovered compounds that show pharmaceutical promise in treating cancer and infectious diseases such as malaria and HIV/AIDS, as pain relievers and sedatives, in promoting weight loss, and for many other uses. But why do plants make these substances? What is the adaptive value? The title of this chapter offers a clue: In a community, populations of many different species interact with each other, and some of these relationships are potentially harmful.

In this chapter, you'll examine the interactions among organisms and how those relationships determine the features of communities. On a larger scale, you'll explore the dynamics of ecosystems. And throughout the chapter, you'll learn how an understanding of these ecological relationships can help us manage Earth's resources wisely.

BIG IDEAS

Community Structure and Dynamics (37.1–37.13)

Community ecologists examine factors that influence the species composition of communities and factors that affect community stability.

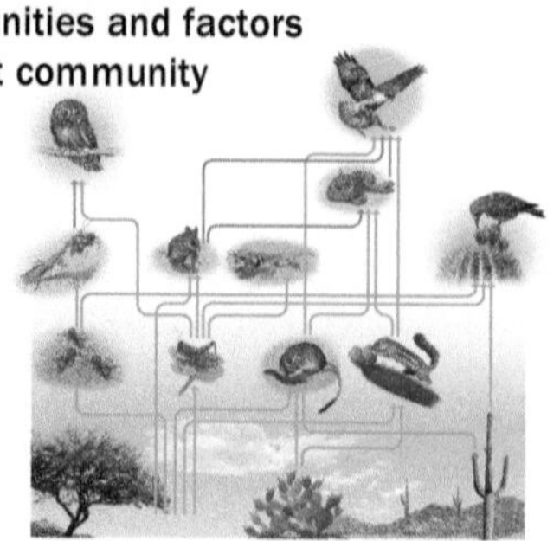

Ecosystem Structure and Dynamics (37.14–37.23)

Ecosystem ecology emphasizes energy flow and chemical cycling.

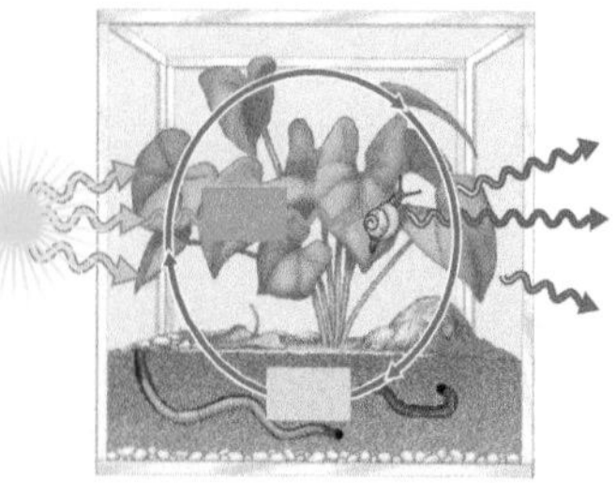

Community Structure and Dynamics

37.1 A community includes all the organisms inhabiting a particular area

In the hierarchy of life, a population is a group of interacting individuals of a particular species. The next step up is a biological **community**, an assemblage of all the populations of organisms living close enough together for potential interaction. Ecologists define the boundaries of the community according to the research questions they want to investigate. For example, one ecologist interested in wetland communities might study the shoreline plants and animals of a particular marsh, while another might investigate only the benthic (bottom-dwelling) microbes.

The structure of a community can be described by its species composition, including the number of species, their relative abundance, and their feeding relationships. Community ecologists focus on the INTERACTIONS among species. Some interactions occur between two species. For example, a community ecologist might investigate how alligator predation on sunfish affects the relative abundance of the two species in a marsh. Other interactions affect entire communities. For instance, a community ecologist might study how the presence of beavers affects the overall species composition of a pond community.

Community ecologists also investigate community dynamics, the variability or stability in the species composition of a community caused by biotic and abiotic factors. For example, a community ecologist might study changes in the species composition of a coastal wetlands community after a hurricane.

Community ecology is necessary for the conservation of endangered species and the management of wildlife, game, and fisheries. It is vital for controlling diseases, such as malaria, Zika, and Lyme disease, that are carried by animals. Community ecology also has applications in agriculture, where people attempt to control the species composition of communities they have established.

What is the relationship between a community and a population?

A community is a group of populations that interact with each other.

37.2 Interspecific interactions are fundamental to community structure

Members of communities engage in **interspecific interactions**—relationships with individuals of other species in the community—that greatly affect population structure and dynamics. In Table 37.2, interspecific interactions are classified according to the effect on the populations concerned, which may be helpful (+) or harmful (−). Other interactions, not discussed here, benefit one population without affecting the other population.

Members of a population may engage in intraspecific competition for limited resources such as food or space (see Module 36.5). **Interspecific competition** occurs when populations of two different species compete for the same limited resource. For example, desert plants compete for water, whereas plants in a tropical rain forest compete for light. Squirrels and black bears are among the animals that feed on acorns in a temperate broadleaf forest in autumn. When acorn production is low, the nut is a limited resource for which squirrels and bears compete. In general, the effect of interspecific competition is negative for both populations (−/−).

In **mutualism**, both populations benefit (+/+). Plants and mycorrhizae (see Module 17.12) and herbivores and the cellulose-digesting microbes that inhabit their digestive tracts (see Module 21.13) are examples of mutualism between symbiotic species—those that have a physically close association with each other. Mutualism can also occur between species that are not symbiotic. For example, flowers and their pollinators are mutualists (see Figure 17.10C).

There are three categories of interactions in which one species exploits another species (+/−). In **predation**, one species (the predator) kills and eats another species (the prey). **Herbivory** is consumption of plant parts or algae by an animal. Both plants and animals may be victimized by parasites (see Module 16.12) or pathogens (see Module 16.1). Thus, parasite-host and pathogen-host interactions are also +/−.

In the next several modules, you will learn more about these interspecific interactions and how they affect communities. You will also discover how interspecific interactions can act as powerful agents of natural selection.

TABLE 37.2 Interspecific Interactions

Interspecific Interaction	Effect on Species 1	Effect on Species 2	Example
Competition	−	−	Squirrels/black bears
Mutualism	+	+	Plants/mycorrhizae
Predation	+	−	Crocodiles/fish
Herbivory	+	−	Caterpillars/leaves
Parasites and pathogens	+	−	Heartworms/dogs; *Salmonella*/humans

? Populations of eastern bluebirds declined after the introduction of non-native house sparrows and European starlings. All three species nest in tree cavities. Suggest how an interspecific interaction could explain the bluebird's decline.

Based on the information given, interspecific competition for nest sites is a plausible explanation.

37.3 Competition may occur when a shared resource is limited

Each species in a community has an **ecological niche**, defined as the sum of its use of the biotic and abiotic resources in its environment. For example, the ecological niche of a small bird called the Virginia's warbler (Figure 37.3A) includes its nest sites and nest-building materials, the insects it eats, and climatic conditions such as the amount of precipitation and the temperature and humidity that enable it to survive. In other words, the ecological niche encompasses everything the Virginia's warbler needs for its existence.

▲ **Figure 37.3A** A Virginia's warbler (*Vermivora virginiae*)

−/−

Interspecific competition occurs when the niches of two populations overlap and both populations need a resource that is in short supply. Ecologists can study the effects of competition by removing all the members of one species from a study site. For example, in central Arizona, the niche of the orange-crowned warbler (Figure 37.3B) overlaps in some respects with the niche of the Virginia's warbler. When researchers removed either species, the remaining species was significantly more successful in raising their offspring. Thus, interspecific competition has a direct effect on reproductive fitness in these birds.

In general, competition lowers the carrying capacity (see Module 36.4) for competing populations because the resources used by one population are not available to the other population. In 1934, Russian ecologist G. F. Gause demonstrated the effects of interspecific competition using three closely related species of ciliates (see Module 16.14): *Paramecium caudatum*, *P. aurelia*, and *P. bursaria*. He first determined the carrying capacity for each species under laboratory conditions. Then he grew cultures of two species together. In a mixed culture of *P. caudatum* and *P. bursaria*, population sizes stabilized at lower numbers than each achieved in the absence of a competing species—competition lowered the carrying capacity of the environment. On the other hand, in a mixed culture of *P. caudatum* and *P. aurelia*, only *P. aurelia* survived. Gause concluded that the requirements of these two species were so similar that they could not coexist under those conditions; *P. aurelia* outcompeted *P. caudatum* for essential resources.

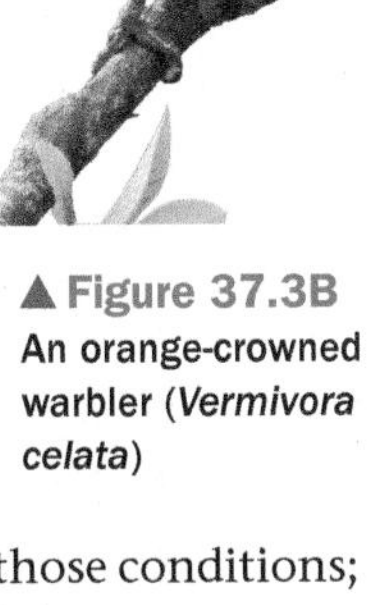

▲ **Figure 37.3B** An orange-crowned warbler (*Vermivora celata*)

? Which do you think has more severe effects, intraspecific competition or interspecific competition? Explain why.

■ Intraspecific competition is more severe because members of the same species have exactly the same niche. Thus, they compete for exactly the same resources.

37.4 Mutualism benefits both partners

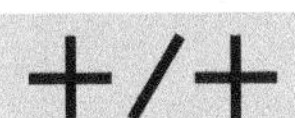

Reef-building corals and photosynthetic dinoflagellates (unicellular algae; see Module 16.14) provide a good example of how mutualists benefit from their relationship. Coral reefs are constructed by successive generations of colonial coral animals that secrete an external calcium carbonate ($CaCO_3$) skeleton. Deposition of the skeleton must outpace erosion and competition for space from fast-growing seaweeds. Corals could not build and sustain the massive reefs that provide the food, living space, and shelter to support the splendid diversity of the reef community without the millions of dinoflagellates that live in the cells of each coral polyp (Figure 37.4). The sugars that the dinoflagellates produce by photosynthesis provide at least half of the energy used by the coral animals. In return, the dinoflagellates gain a secure shelter that provides access to light. They also use the coral's waste products, including carbon dioxide (CO_2) and ammonia (NH_3), a valuable source of nitrogen for making proteins. Unicellular algae have similar mutually beneficial relationships with a wide variety of other marine invertebrates, including sponges, flatworms, and molluscs.

▲ **Figure 37.4** Coral polyps

? When corals are stressed by environmental conditions, they expel their dinoflagellates in a process called bleaching. How is widespread bleaching likely to affect coral reefs?

■ Without their dinoflagellate mutualists, corals do not have enough energy to maintain the reef structure. Bleached reefs will die.

37.5 Predation leads to diverse adaptations in prey species

EVOLUTION CONNECTION

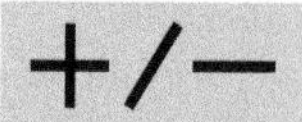

Predation benefits the predator but kills the prey. Because predation has such a negative impact on reproductive success in prey populations, numerous adaptations for predator avoidance have evolved in prey populations through natural selection.

Insect color patterns, including camouflage, provide protection against predators. Camouflage is also common in other animals (see Figure 1.5). As **Figure 37.5A** shows, the gray tree frog (*Hyla arenicolor*), an inhabitant of the southwestern United States, becomes almost invisible on a gray tree trunk.

Other protective devices include mechanical defenses, such as the sharp quills of a porcupine (see Figure 35.9) or the hard shells of clams and oysters. Chemical defenses are also widespread. Animals with effective chemical defenses usually have bright color patterns, often yellow, orange, or red in combination with black. Predators learn to associate these color patterns with undesirable consequences, such as noxious taste or a painful sting, and avoid potential prey with similar markings. The vivid orange and black pattern of monarch butterflies (**Figure 37.5B**) warns potential predators of a nasty taste. Monarchs acquire and store unpalatable chemicals during the larval stage, when the caterpillars feed on milkweed plants.

? **Explain why predation is a powerful factor in the adaptive evolution of prey species.**

■ The prey that avoid being eaten will most likely survive and reproduce, passing alleles for antipredator adaptations on to their offspring.

▲ **Figure 37.5A** Camouflage: a gray tree frog on bark

▲ **Figure 37.5B** Chemical defenses: the monarch butterfly

37.6 Herbivory leads to diverse adaptations in plants

EVOLUTION CONNECTION

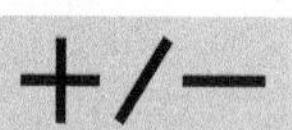

Although herbivory is not usually fatal, a plant whose body parts have been eaten by an animal must expend energy to replace the loss. Consequently, numerous defenses against herbivores have evolved in plants. Thorns and spines are obvious antiherbivore devices, as anyone who has plucked a rose from a thorny rosebush or brushed against a spiky cactus knows. The chemicals described in the chapter introduction—the substances that we use medicinally or for other purposes—are also adaptations that defend plants against herbivory.

Like the chemical defenses of animals, toxins in plants tend to be distasteful, and herbivores learn to avoid them. Among such chemical weapons are the poison strychnine, produced by a tropical vine called *Strychnos toxifera*; morphine, from the opium poppy; nicotine, produced by the tobacco plant; mescaline, from peyote cactus; and tannins, from a variety of plant species. A variety of sulfur compounds, including those that give brussels sprouts and cabbage their distinctive taste, are also toxic to herbivorous insects and mammals such as cattle. (The vegetables we eat are not toxic because the amount of chemicals in them has been reduced by crop breeders.) Some plants even produce chemicals that cause abnormal development in insects that eat them. Chemical companies have taken advantage of the poisonous properties of a certain species of chrysanthemum to produce a pesticide called pyrethrin. Nicotine is also used as an insecticide.

Why do plants make drugs?

Some herbivore-plant interactions illustrate the concept of **coevolution**, a series of reciprocal evolutionary adaptations in two species. Coevolution occurs when a change in one species acts as a new selective force on another species, and the resulting adaptations of the second species in turn affect the selection of individuals in the first species. **Figure 37.6** (top left of next page) illustrates an example of

▲ **Figure 37.6** **Coevolution: *Heliconius* and the passionflower vine (*Passiflora*)**

coevolution between an herbivorous insect (the caterpillar of the butterfly *Heliconius*, top) and a plant (the passionflower, *Passiflora*, a tropical vine).

Passiflora produces toxic chemicals that protect its leaves from most insects, but *Heliconius* caterpillars have digestive enzymes that break down the toxins. As a result, *Heliconius* gains access to a food source that few other insects can eat. These poison-resistant caterpillars seem to be a strong selective force for *Passiflora* plants, and defenses have evolved in some species. For instance, the leaves of some *Passiflora* species produce yellow spots that look like *Heliconius* eggs (Figure 37.6). Female butterflies avoid laying their eggs on leaves that already have eggs, presumably ensuring that only a few caterpillars will hatch and feed on any one leaf. Because the butterfly often mistakes the yellow spots for eggs, *Passiflora* species with these false eggs are less likely to be eaten.

? People find most bitter-tasting foods objectionable. In evolutionary terms, why do you suppose we have taste receptors for bitter-tasting chemicals?

■ Individuals having bitter taste receptors presumably survived better because they could identify potentially toxic food when they foraged.

37.7 Parasites and pathogens can affect community composition

+/−

A parasite lives on or in a host from which it obtains nourishment. Internal parasites include flukes and tapeworms (see Module 18.7) and a variety of nematodes (see Module 18.8) that live inside a host organism's body. External parasites include arthropods such as ticks, lice, mites, and mosquitoes, which attach to their victims temporarily to feed on blood or other body fluids. Plants are also attacked by parasites, including nematodes and aphids, tiny insects that tap into the phloem and suck plant sap (**Figure 37.7**). Pathogens are disease-causing bacteria, viruses, fungi, or protists that can be thought of as microscopic parasites. The potentially devastating effects of parasites and pathogens on cultivated plants, livestock, and humans are well known, but ecologists understand little about how these interactions affect natural communities. Non-native pathogens, whose impact is rapid and often dramatic, have provided some opportunities to study the effects of pathogens on communities. In one example, ecologists studied the consequences of an epidemic of chestnut blight that wiped out virtually all American chestnut trees during the first half of the 20th century; the disease is caused by a protist. Chestnuts were massive canopy trees that dominated many forest communities in North America. Their loss had a significant impact on species composition and community structure. Overall, the diversity of tree species increased as trees that had formerly competed with chestnuts, such as oaks and hickories, became more prominent. The dead chestnut trees furnished niches for other organisms, such as insects, cavity-nesting birds, and eventually decomposers. On the other hand, populations of organisms that depended heavily on living chestnut trees for their food and shelter declined.

◀ **Figure 37.7** **Aphids parasitizing a plant**

A fungus-like protist that causes a disease called sudden oak death is currently spreading on the West Coast. More than a million oaks have been lost so far, causing the decline of bird populations. Despite its name, sudden oak death affects many other species as well, including the majestic redwood and Douglas fir trees and flowering shrubs such as rhododendron and camellia. Because the epidemic is in its early stages, its full effect on forest communities will not be known for some time.

? Use your knowledge of interspecific interactions to explain why tree diversity increased after all the chestnuts died.

■ Chestnuts had many of the same niche characteristics as other trees, but apparently chestnuts were superior competitors. After they died, the remaining species may have had fewer niche similarities, or they may have been more equal as competitors, allowing more species to coexist.

37.8 Trophic structure is a key factor in community dynamics

Every community has a **trophic structure**, a pattern of feeding relationships consisting of several different levels. The sequence of food transfer up the trophic levels is known as a **food chain**. This transfer of food moves chemical nutrients and energy from organism to organism up through the trophic levels in a community.

Figure 37.8 compares a terrestrial food chain and an aquatic food chain. In this figure, the trophic levels are arranged vertically, and the names of the levels appear in colored boxes. The arrows connecting the organisms point from the food to the consumer, that is, in the direction of nutrient and energy transfer. Starting at the bottom, the trophic level that supports all others consists of autotrophs ("self-feeders"), which ecologists call **producers**. Photosynthetic producers use light energy to power the synthesis of organic compounds. Plants are the main producers on land. In water, the producers are mainly photosynthetic unicellular protists and cyanobacteria, collectively called phytoplankton. Multicellular algae and aquatic plants are also important producers in shallow waters. In a few communities, the producers are chemosynthetic prokaryotes. For example, in communities around hydrothermal vents, deep-sea sites near the adjoining edges of Earth's tectonic plates (see Module 15.7), the producers are bacteria that obtain energy by oxidizing hydrogen sulfide emitted from the vents.

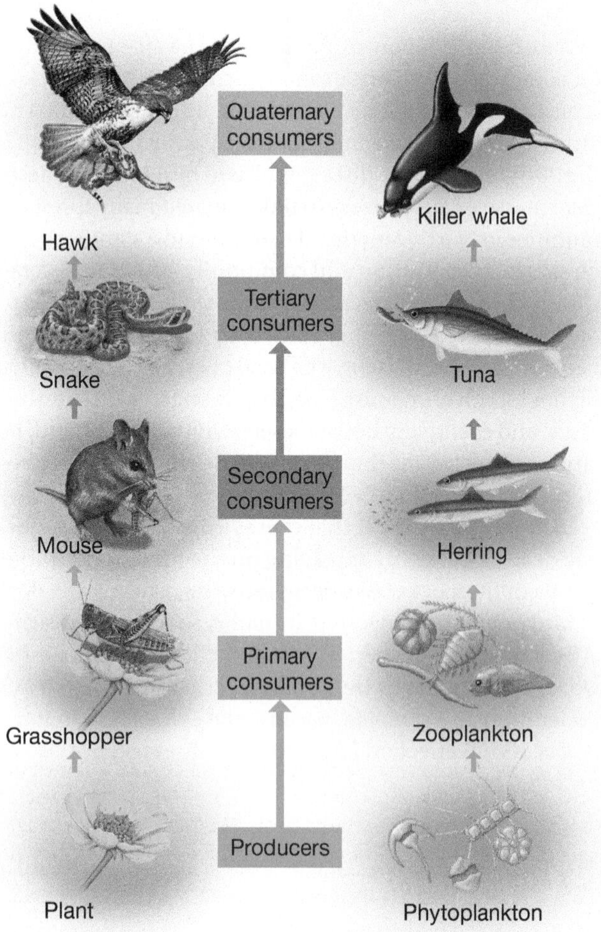

All organisms in trophic levels above the producers are heterotrophs ("other-feeders"), or consumers, and all consumers directly or indirectly depend on the output of producers. Herbivores, which eat plants, algae, or phytoplankton, are **primary consumers**. Primary consumers on land include grasshoppers and many other insects, snails, and certain vertebrates, such as grazing mammals and birds that eat seeds and fruits. In aquatic environments, primary consumers include a variety of zooplankton (mainly protists and microscopic animals such as small shrimps) that eat phytoplankton.

Above primary consumers, the trophic levels are made up of carnivores, including insectivores, which eat the consumers from the level below. On land, **secondary consumers** include many small mammals, such as the mouse shown here eating an herbivorous insect, and a great variety of birds, frogs, and spiders, as well as lions, wolves, and other large carnivores that eat grazers. In aquatic ecosystems, secondary consumers are mainly small fishes that eat zooplankton.

Higher trophic levels include **tertiary** (third-level) **consumers**, such as snakes that eat mice and other secondary consumers. Most ecosystems have secondary and tertiary consumers. As the figure indicates, some also have a higher level, **quaternary** (fourth-level) **consumers**, which eat tertiary consumers. These include hawks in terrestrial ecosystems and killer whales in the marine environment.

Not shown in Figure 37.8 is another trophic level—consumers that derive their energy from **detritus**, the dead material produced at all the trophic levels. Detritus includes animal wastes, plant litter, and the bodies of dead organisms. Different organisms consume detritus in different stages of decay. **Scavengers**, which are large animals such as crows and vultures, feast on carcasses left behind by predators or speeding cars. The diet of **detritivores** is made up primarily of decaying organic material. Examples of detritivores include earthworms and millipedes. **Decomposers**, mainly prokaryotes and fungi, secrete enzymes that digest molecules in organic material and convert them to inorganic forms. Enormous numbers of microscopic decomposers in the soil and in the mud at the bottom of lakes and oceans break down most of the community's organic materials to inorganic compounds that plants or phytoplankton can use. The breakdown of organic materials to inorganic ones is called **decomposition**. By breaking down detritus, decomposers link all trophic levels. Their role is essential for all communities and, indeed, for the continuation of life on Earth.

▲ Figure 37.8 Two food chains

? **I'm eating a cheese pizza. At which trophic level(s) am I feeding?**

■ Primary consumer (flour and tomato sauce) and secondary consumer (cheese, a product from cows, which are primary consumers)

VISUALIZING THE CONCEPT

37.9 Food chains interconnect, forming food webs

A more realistic view of the trophic structure of a community is a **food web**, a network of interconnecting food chains. In this Sonoran desert community, a consumer may eat more than one type of producer, and several species of primary consumers may feed on the same species of producer. Some consumers weave into the food web at more than one trophic level.

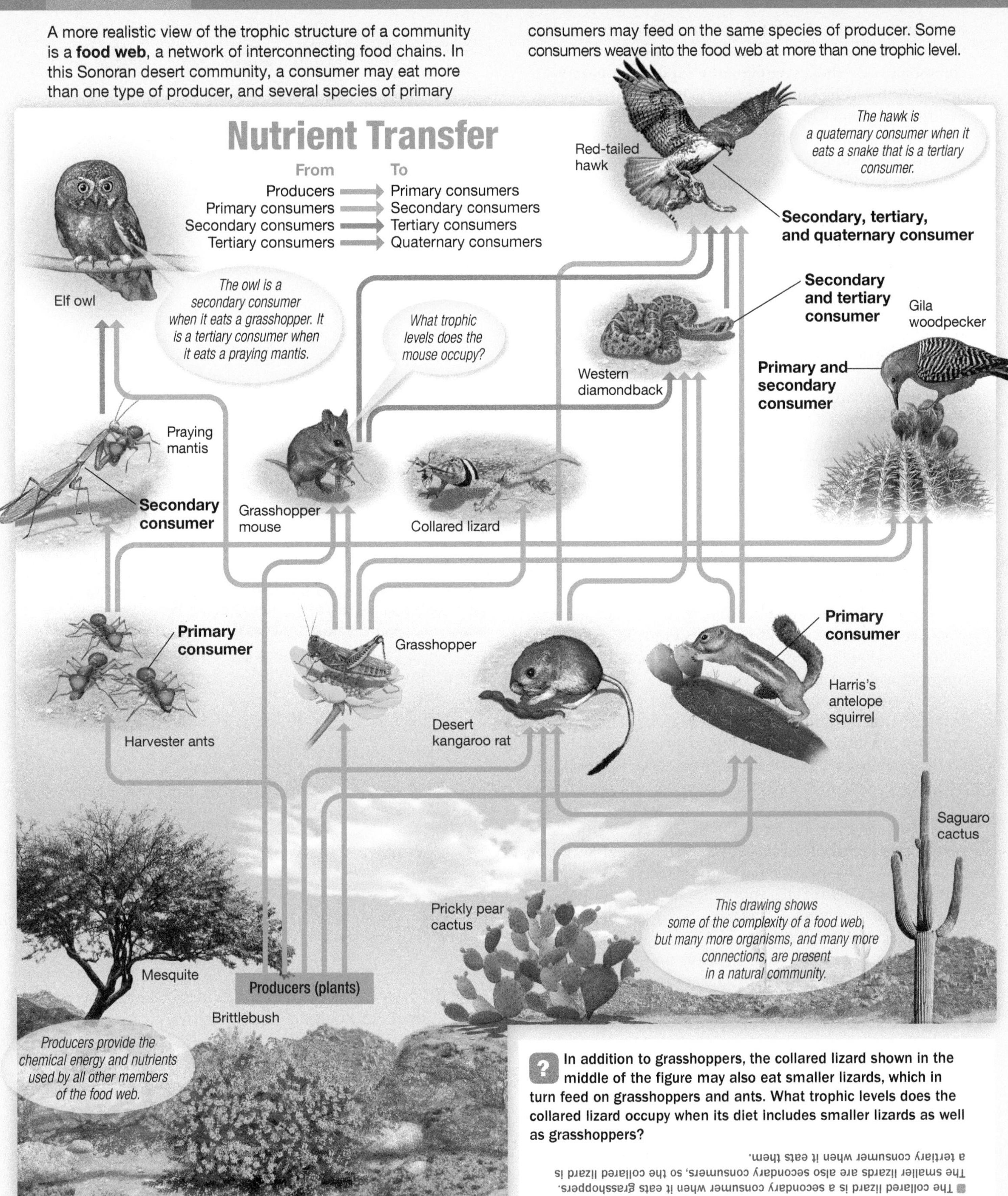

? **In addition to grasshoppers, the collared lizard shown in the middle of the figure may also eat smaller lizards, which in turn feed on grasshoppers and ants. What trophic levels does the collared lizard occupy when its diet includes smaller lizards as well as grasshoppers?**

■ The collared lizard is a secondary consumer when it eats grasshoppers. The smaller lizards are also secondary consumers, so the collared lizard is a tertiary consumer when it eats them.

37.10 Species diversity includes species richness and relative abundance

Now that we have looked at how populations in a community interact with each other, let's consider factors that affect the community as a whole. A community's **species diversity** is defined by two components: species richness, or the number of different species in a community, and relative abundance, the proportional representation of each species in a community. To understand why both components are important for describing species diversity, imagine walking through woodlot A on the path shown in Figure 37.10A. You would pass by four different species of trees, but most of the trees you encounter would be the same species. Now imagine walking on the path through woodlot B in Figure 37.10B. You would see the same four species of trees that you saw in woodlot A—the species richness of the two woodlots is the same. However, woodlot B would probably seem more diverse to you, because no single species predominates. As Table 37.10 shows, the relative abundance of one species in woodlot A is much higher than the relative abundances of the other three species. In woodlot B, all four species are equally abundant. As a result, species diversity is greater in woodlot B.

Plant species diversity in a community often has consequences for the species diversity of animals in the community. For example, suppose a species of caterpillar only eats the leaves of a tree that makes up just 5% of woodlot A. If the caterpillar is present at all, its population may be small and scattered. Birds that depend on those caterpillars to feed their young may be absent. But the caterpillars would easily be able to locate their food source in woodlot B, and their abundance would attract birds as well. By providing a broader range of habitats and food sources, a diverse tree community promotes animal diversity.

Species diversity also has consequences for pathogens. Most pathogens infect a limited range of host species or may even be restricted to a single host species. When many potential hosts are living close together, it is easy for a pathogen to spread from one to another. In woodlot A, for example, a pathogen that infects the most abundant tree would rapidly be transmitted through the entire forest. On the other hand, the more isolated trees in woodlot B are more likely to escape infection.

Low species diversity is characteristic of most modern agricultural ecosystems. For efficiency, crops and trees are often planted in monoculture—a single species grown over a wide area. Monocultures are especially vulnerable to attack by pathogens and herbivorous insects. Also, plants grown in monoculture have been bred for certain desirable characteristics, so their genetic variation is typically low, too. As a result, a pathogen can potentially devastate an entire field or more. Between 1845 and 1849, a pathogen wiped out a monoculture of genetically uniform potatoes throughout Ireland. A million people died of starvation, and well over a million more left the country.

To combat potential losses, many farmers and forest managers rely heavily on chemical methods of controlling pests. Modern crop scientists have bred varieties of plants that are genetically resistant to common pathogens, but these varieties can suddenly become vulnerable, too. In 1970, pathogen evolution led to an epidemic of a disease called corn leaf blight that resulted in a billion dollars of crop damage in the United States. Some researchers are now investigating the use of more diverse agricultural ecosystems—polyculture—as an alternative to monoculture.

▲ Figure 37.10A Species composition of woodlot A

▲ Figure 37.10B Species composition of woodlot B

TABLE 37.10 Relative Abundance of Tree Species in Woodlots A and B

Species	Relative Abundance in Woodlot A (%)	Relative Abundance in Woodlot B (%)
	80	25
	10	25
	5	25
	5	25

? **Which would you expect to have higher species diversity, a well-maintained lawn or one that is poorly maintained? Explain.**

A lawn that is poorly maintained would have higher species diversity. A well-maintained lawn should have low species diversity. While a lawn that is cared for may not be a perfect monoculture, any weeds that are present would have low relative abundance. The opposite is true if the lawn is not cared for.

37.11 Some species have a disproportionate impact on diversity

SCIENTIFIC THINKING What causes species diversity to vary among different communities? Ecologist Robert Paine hypothesized that the species diversity of a community is directly related to the ability of predators to prevent any one species from monopolizing local resources. Like many ecologists, Paine designed a field experiment to test his hypothesis. He chose a rocky intertidal community on the Pacific coast in Washington State as his study area (**Figure 37.11A**). In this rigorous environment, the rocks are pounded by waves during high tide and exposed to the sun and drying winds during low tide. Members of the community typically include algae, both herbivorous and carnivorous molluscs such as snails, suspension feeders such as sponges, sea anemones, barnacles, and mussels, and a predatory sea star known as *Pisaster*. Many of these organisms attach to the rocks to avoid being washed away; thus, space is an important but limited resource.

Paine manually removed *Pisaster* from certain areas of the intertidal zone and left comparable areas intact as controls. He then determined the species richness of these experimental and control areas over the next several years (**Figure 37.11B**). In the absence of *Pisaster*, species richness dropped from more than 15 species to fewer than 5. What accounted for the dramatic change? A mussel of the genus *Mytilus* proved to be a superior competitor for the available space, eliminating most other invertebrates and algae. In the control areas, *Mytilus*'s population growth was suppressed by *Pisaster*, a voracious predator on the mussel (**Figure 37.11C**). Thus, interspecific interactions can be an important factor in the species diversity of a community.

▲ **Figure 37.11A** A rocky intertidal zone on the Washington State coast

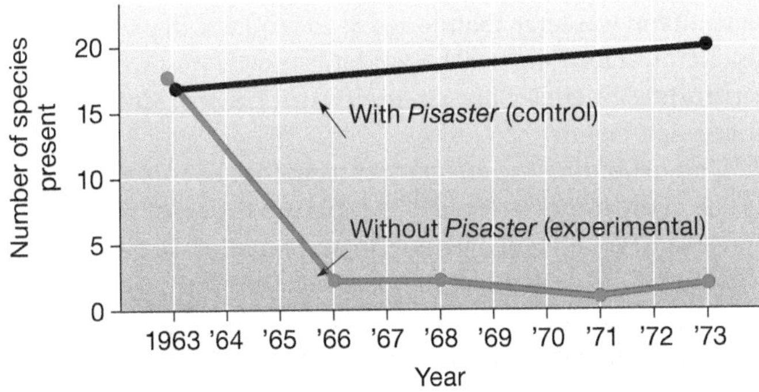

Data from R. T. Paine, Food web complexity and species diversity, *American Naturalist* 100: 65–75 (1966).

▲ **Figure 37.11B** Species richness in control areas and experimental areas after *Pisaster* removal

▲ **Figure 37.11C** A *Pisaster* sea star, a keystone species, eating a mussel

Paine's experiment and others like it gave rise to the concept of a keystone species. A **keystone species** is a species whose impact on its community is much larger than its abundance or total biological mass would indicate. The word "keystone" comes from the wedge-shaped stone at the top of an arch that locks the other pieces in place. If the keystone is removed, the arch collapses (**Figure 37.11D**). A keystone species occupies a niche that holds the rest of its community in place.

The keystone concept has practical application in efforts to restore or rehabilitate damaged ecosystems. One example focuses on the long-spined sea urchin, *Diadema antillarum*. Ecologists discovered that *Diadema* is a keystone species on Caribbean coral reefs when huge numbers of them were killed by a disease epidemic. Species diversity plummeted as the reefs were overgrown by fleshy seaweeds that had formerly been controlled by the herbivorous sea urchins. Recognition of *Diadema*'s key role in the community prompted conservationists to artificially replenish urchin populations to help restore damaged reefs.

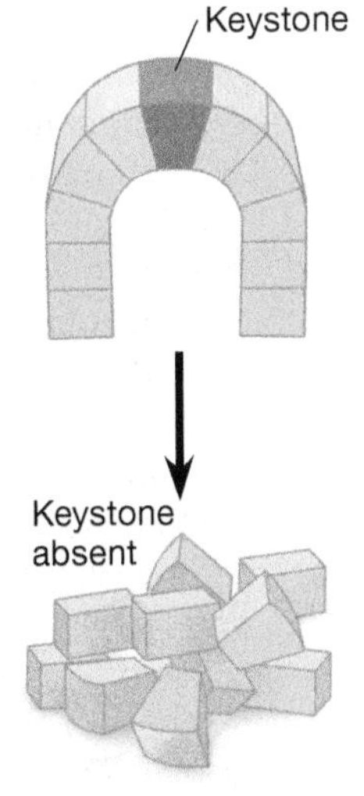

▲ **Figure 37.11D** Arch collapse with removal of keystone

? **Removing saguaro cacti from the Sonoran desert community (see Module 37.9) as part of a field study would have a drastic impact, and yet saguaro is not considered a keystone species. Why not?**

■ Saguaro is abundant and makes up a large part of the community, but its effect is not disproportionate to its mass or abundance. Keystone species have a large effect relative to their representation in the community just as a keystone is a small but vital piece of an arch.

37.12 Disturbance is a prominent feature of most communities

Early ecologists viewed biological communities as more or less stable in structure and species composition. But like many college campuses, where some construction or renovation project is always underway, many communities are frequently disrupted by sudden change. **Disturbances** are events such as storms, fires, floods, droughts, or human activities that change biological communities by removing organisms from it or altering the availability of resources. The types of disturbances and their frequency and severity vary from community to community.

Although we tend to think of disturbances in negative terms, small-scale disturbances often have positive effects. For example, new habitats are created when a large tree is uprooted in a windstorm. More light may reach the forest floor, giving small seedlings the opportunity to grow, or the hole left by the tree's roots may fill with water and be used as egg-laying sites by frogs, salamanders, and numerous insects. Communities change drastically following a severe disturbance that strips away vegetation and even soil. The disturbed area may be colonized by a variety of species, which are gradually replaced by a succession of other species, in a process called **ecological succession**.

When ecological succession begins in a virtually lifeless area with no soil, it is called **primary succession**. Examples of such areas are the rubble left by a retreating glacier or fresh volcanic lava flows (Figure 37.12A). Often the only life-forms initially present are autotrophic bacteria. Lichens and mosses, which grow from windblown spores, are commonly the first large photosynthesizers to colonize the area. Soil develops gradually as rocks break down and organic matter accumulates from the decomposed remains of the early colonizers. Lichens and mosses are gradually overgrown by larger plants that sprout from seeds blown in from nearby areas or carried in by animals. Eventually, the area is colonized by plants that become the community's prevalent form of vegetation. Primary succession can take hundreds or thousands of years.

Secondary succession occurs where a disturbance has cleared away an existing community but left the soil intact.

▲ **Figure 37.12A** Primary succession on a lava flow

▲ **Figure 37.12B** Secondary succession: Yellowstone National Park in November 1988, after a fire (top), and in July 1989

For example, secondary succession occurs as areas recover from fires or floods (Figure 37.12B). Some disturbances that lead to secondary succession are caused by human activities. Even before colonial times, people were clearing the forests of eastern North America for agriculture and settlements. Some of this land was later abandoned as the soil was depleted of its chemical nutrients or the residents moved west to new territories. Whenever human intervention stops, secondary succession begins.

Understanding the effects of disturbance in communities is especially important today; people are the most widespread and significant agents of disturbance (as we discuss in Chapter 38). Disturbances may also create opportunities for undesirable plants and animals that people transport to new habitats, which is the topic of the next module.

? **What is the main abiotic factor that distinguishes primary from secondary succession?**

■ Absence (primary) versus presence (secondary) of soil at the onset of succession

37.13 Invasive species can devastate communities

CONNECTION For as long as people have traveled from one region to another, they have carried organisms along, both intentionally and by accident. Many of these non-native species have established themselves firmly in their new locations. Furthermore, many have become **invasive species**, spreading far beyond the original point of introduction and causing environmental or economic damage by colonizing and dominating wherever they find a suitable habitat. In the United States alone, there are hundreds of invasive species, including plants, mammals, birds, fishes, arthropods, and molluscs. Worldwide, there are thousands more. Invasive species are a leading cause of local extinctions (a topic we'll return to in Module 38.1). The economic costs of invasive species are enormous—more than $100 billion a year in the United States. Regardless of where you live, an invasive plant or animal is probably nearby.

Community ecology offers some insights to explain why some non-native species become destructive pests, while others do not. Every population in a community is subject to harmful interspecific interactions, whether from competitors, predators, herbivores, or pathogens. Without biotic factors such as these to curb its growth, a population will continue to expand until limited by abiotic factors. The damage caused by an invasive species often results from interspecific interactions between it and native species. Let's look at three examples of invasive species in the United States.

Burmese pythons, one of the largest snake species on Earth—averaging 4.9 m (16 feet, the length of a minivan)—were brought from Asia to the United States by the pet trade. Accidently released in South Florida by damaging storms or deliberately set free by disenchanted owners, Burmese pythons found a hospitable habitat in the Florida Everglades, where they encountered few predators and abundant prey (Figure 37.13A). Since 2000, the enormous reptiles have established throughout the 600,000-acre Everglades National Park. Populations of native mammals, such as deer, marsh rabbits, and bobcats, which make up 75% of the python's diet, have declined steeply in the park over the same period.

Kudzu, a vine imported from Asia, is an example of an invasive plant (Figure 37.13B). Planted throughout the southern United States in the 1930s to control soil erosion, kudzu's remarkable growth rate—up to a foot a day—enabled it to become invasive. Kudzu spreads a blanket of vegetation over native ecosystems, starving plants of sunlight; animals that depend on those plants are deprived of food and shelter. An estimated 31,000 km^2 (roughly the area of Maryland) in southern states is now overrun with kudzu. Kudzu's range is limited by cold winters because its roots don't survive freezing. However, as climate change brings warmer winters, kudzu is advancing farther north.

▲ **Figure 37.13A** A Burmese python (*Python bivittatus*) captured in the Florida Everglades

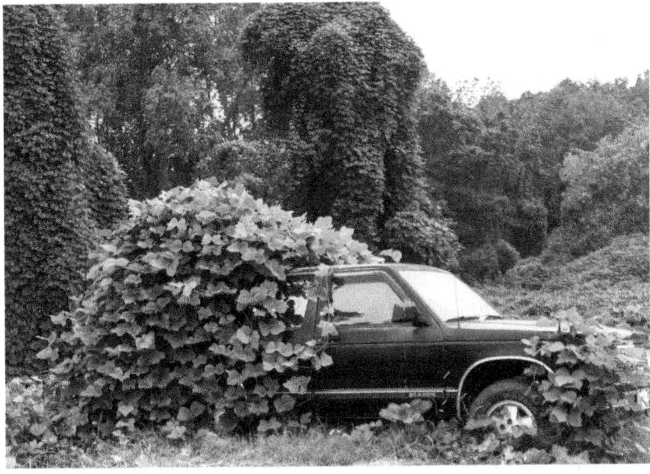

▲ **Figure 37.13B** Kudzu (*Pueraria lobata*), a fast-growing vine

Zebra mussels, fingernail-size molluscs native to western Asia, were first discovered in the Great Lakes in 1988, probably brought in the ballast water of oceangoing ships (Figure 37.13C). Their free-swimming larvae quickly dispersed the species to waterways beyond the Great Lakes region, and they are now widely distributed. The damage caused by these tiny molluscs results from their astronomically large populations. Adult zebra mussels attach themselves to any available object, forming thick layers that clog pipes and the water intakes of cities, power plants, and factories. Populations of native mussels have declined as a result of competition with zebra mussels for food and space. Zebra mussels also disrupt food webs by consuming vast quantities of phytoplankton, the producers in aquatic food webs. This depletes the food supply of zooplankton, which in turn affects higher-order consumers.

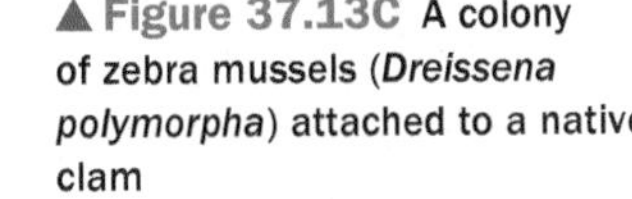

▲ **Figure 37.13C** A colony of zebra mussels (*Dreissena polymorpha*) attached to a native clam

In the next modules, we broaden our scope to look at ecosystems, the highest level of ecological complexity.

? What distinguishes invasive species from organisms that are introduced to non-native habitats but do not become invasive?

■ Invasive species spread far from where they have been introduced, and they cause environmental or economic damage.

Ecosystem Structure and Dynamics

37.14 Ecosystem ecology emphasizes energy flow and chemical cycling

An **ecosystem** consists of all the organisms in a community as well as the abiotic environment with which the organisms interact. Ecosystem ecologists are especially interested in **energy flow**, the passage of energy through the components of the ecosystem, and **chemical cycling**, the transfer of matter within the ecosystem. Thus, ecosystem ecology is a good example of the theme ENERGY AND MATTER.

The terrarium in Figure 37.14 represents a familiar type of ecosystem and illustrates the fundamentals of energy flow. Energy enters the terrarium in the form of sunlight (light energy arrow). Plants (producers) convert light energy to chemical energy (chemical energy arrow) through the process of photosynthesis. Animals (consumers) take in some of this chemical energy, which is stored in organic compounds, when they eat the plants.

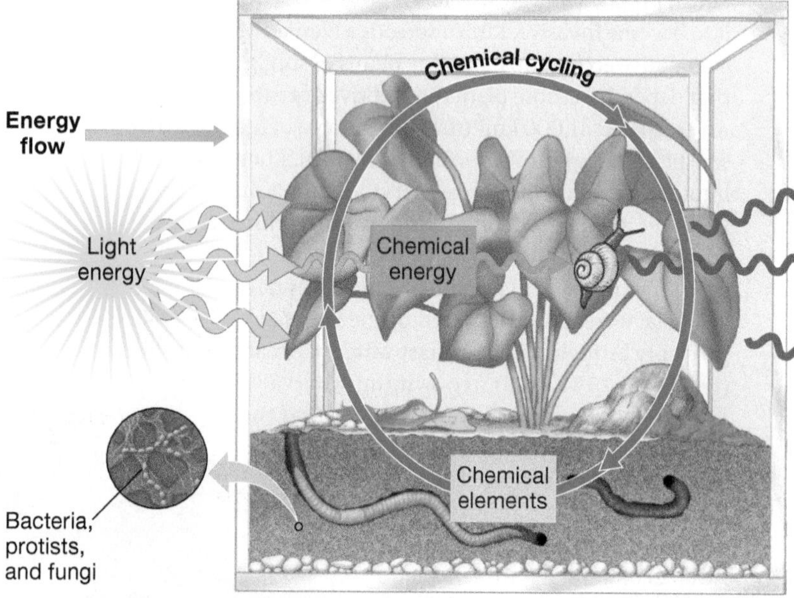

▲ **Figure 37.14** A terrarium ecosystem

TRY THIS In your own words, explain how energy flows through the terrarium. Explain how chemicals are cycled within the terrarium.

Decomposers, such as bacteria and fungi in the soil, obtain chemical energy when they decompose the dead remains of plants and animals. Every use of chemical energy by organisms involves a loss of some energy to the surroundings in the form of heat (heat arrow; see Module 5.10). Because so much of the energy captured by photosynthesis is lost as heat, the ecosystem would run out of energy if it were not powered by a continuous inflow of energy from the sun. A few ecosystems—for example, hydrothermal vents—are powered by chemical energy obtained from inorganic compounds.

In contrast to energy flow, chemical cycling (chemical cycling arrow) involves the transfer of matter *within* the ecosystem. While most ecosystems have a constant input of energy from sunlight, the supply of the chemical elements used to construct molecules is limited. Chemical elements such as carbon and nitrogen are cycled between the abiotic components of the ecosystem, including air, water, and soil, and the biotic component of the ecosystem (the community). Plants acquire these chemical elements in inorganic form from the air and soil and use them to build organic molecules. Animals, such as the snail in Figure 37.14, consume some of these organic molecules. When the plants and animals become detritus, decomposers return most of the elements to the soil and air in inorganic form. Some elements are also returned to the soil and air as the by-products of plant and animal metabolism.

In summary, both energy flow and chemical cycling involve the transfer of substances through the trophic levels of the ecosystem. However, energy flows through, and ultimately out of, ecosystems, whereas matter is recycled within ecosystems. We explore these fundamental ecosystem dynamics in the rest of the chapter.

? **How do chemical cycles in an ecosystem differ from food chains in a community?**

■ The components of food chains are solely biotic. In ecosystems, chemicals pass through one or more abiotic components as well as passing through the biotic components (food chain).

37.15 Primary production sets the energy budget for ecosystems

Each day, Earth receives about 10^{19} kcal of solar energy, the energy equivalent of 100 million atomic bombs. Most of this energy is absorbed, scattered, or reflected by the atmosphere or by Earth's surface. Of the visible light that reaches plants, algae, and cyanobacteria, only about 1% is used for **primary production**, the conversion of solar energy to chemical energy—as organic compounds—by photosynthesis. The total amount of primary production during a given time period is called **gross primary production**, expressed in units of energy or units of biomass (mass of vegetation). Earth's gross primary production is roughly 165 billion tons of organic material per year. Producers use some of this organic material to fuel their own cellular respiration. The remainder, or **net primary production**, is the amount of new organic material added to an ecosystem in a given period. Thus, net primary production represents the stored chemical energy available to consumers.

Different ecosystems vary considerably in their primary production as well as in their contribution to the total production of the biosphere. Figure 37.15 illustrates these differences

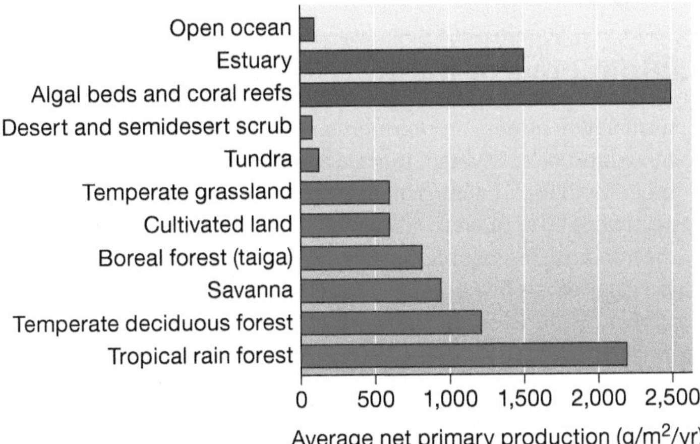

Data from R. H. Whittaker, *Communities and Ecosystems*, 2nd. ed. MacMillan, New York, 1975.

▲ **Figure 37.15** **Net primary production of various ecosystems**

by comparing the net primary production of several ecosystems. Tropical rain forests are among the most productive terrestrial ecosystems and contribute a large portion of the planet's total production. Coral reefs are also highly productive but their contribution to global production is small because they cover such a small area. Interestingly, although the open ocean has very low production, it contributes as much to Earth's total net primary production as terrestrial ecosystems do because it covers 65% of Earth's surface area.

? Deserts and semidesert scrub cover a similar surface area as tropical forests but contribute less than 1% of Earth's net primary production, while rain forests contribute 22%. Explain this difference.

■ The primary production of tropical rain forests is more than 20 times greater than that of desert and semidesert scrub ecosystems.

37.16 Energy supply limits the length of food chains

When organic material is transferred from one trophic level to the next (that is, when one organism consumes another), much of its stored energy is lost. Consider the transfer of organic matter from a producer to a primary consumer, such as the caterpillar shown in **Figure 37.16A**. The caterpillar might digest and absorb only about half the organic material it eats, passing the indigestible wastes as feces. Of the organic compounds it does absorb, the caterpillar typically uses two-thirds as fuel for cellular respiration. Only the chemical energy left over after respiration—15% of the organic material the caterpillar consumed—can be converted to caterpillar biomass. Thus, a secondary consumer that eats the caterpillar gets only 15% of the energy that was in the leaves the caterpillar ate.

Now let's apply the caterpillar example to ecosystems. **Figure 37.16B**, called an energy pyramid illustrates the cumulative loss of energy with each transfer in a food chain. Each tier of the pyramid represents the chemical energy present in all of the organisms at one trophic level of a food chain. The width of each tier indicates how much of the chemical energy of the tier below is actually incorporated into the biomass of that trophic level. Note that producers convert only about 1% of the energy in the sunlight available to them to primary production. In this idealized pyramid, 10% of the energy available at each trophic level becomes incorporated into the next higher level. Such efficiencies of energy transfer usually range from 5 to 20%. In other words, 80–95% of the energy at one trophic level never transfers to the next.

An important implication of this stepwise decline of energy in a trophic structure is that the amount of energy available to top-level consumers is small compared with that available to lower-level consumers. Only a tiny fraction of the energy stored by photosynthesis flows through a food chain all the way to a tertiary consumer. This explains why top-level consumers such as lions and hawks require so much geographic territory; it takes a lot of vegetation to support trophic levels so many steps removed from photosynthetic production. Energy pyramids help us understand why most food chains are limited to three to five levels; there is simply not enough energy at the very top of an ecological pyramid to support another trophic level.

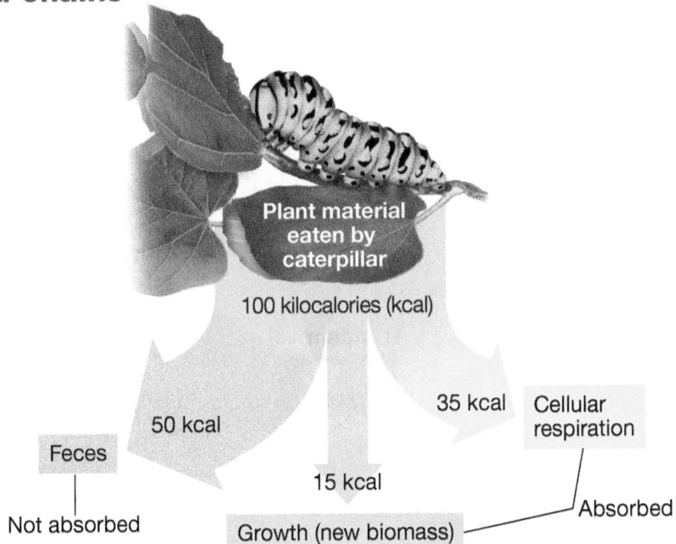

▲ **Figure 37.16A** **The fate of the energy in leaf biomass consumed by a caterpillar**

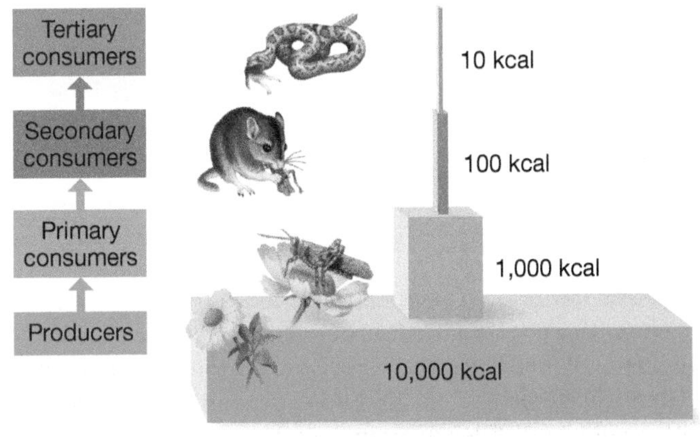

▲ **Figure 37.16B** **An idealized energy pyramid**

? Approximately what proportion of the energy produced by photosynthesis makes it to the snake in Figure 37.16B?

■ 1/1,000 of the 10,000 kcal produced by photosynthesis [(0.1 × 0.1 × 0.1) (10,000 kcal) = 10 kcal]

37.17 An energy pyramid explains the ecological cost of meat

CONNECTION The dynamics of energy flow apply to the human population as much as to other organisms. As omnivores, people eat both plant material and meat. When we eat grain or fruit, we are primary consumers; when we eat beef or other meat from herbivores, we are secondary consumers. When we eat fish like trout and salmon (which eat insects and other small animals), we are tertiary or quaternary consumers.

The energy pyramid on the left in Figure 37.17 indicates energy flow from producers to vegetarians (primary consumers). The energy in the producer trophic level comes from a corn crop. The pyramid on the right illustrates energy flow from the same corn crop, with people as secondary consumers, eating beef. These two pyramids are generalized models, based on the rough estimate that about 10% of the chemical energy available in a trophic level appears at the next higher trophic level. Thus, the pyramids indicate that the human population has about 10 times more energy available to it—10 times more people are supported—when people eat corn than when they process the same amount of corn through another trophic level and eat corn-fed beef.

Eating meat of any kind is both economically and environmentally expensive. Compared with growing plants for direct human consumption, producing meat usually requires that more land be cultivated, more water be used for irrigation, more fossil fuels be burned, and more chemical fertilizers and pesticides be applied to croplands used for growing grain. In many countries, people cannot afford to buy much meat and are vegetarians by necessity. Sometimes religion also plays a role in the decision. In India, for example, about 80% of the population practice Hinduism, a religion that discourages meat-eating. India's meat consumption was roughly 3.2 kg (7 pounds) per person annually in 2014. In Mexico, where many people are too poor to eat meat daily, per capita consumption in 2014 was 46.6 kg (103 pounds) per year. That is a large amount compared with India, but only about half the meat consumption of the United States, where the per capita rate was 90.1 kg (198 pounds) in 2014.

We turn next to the subject of chemical nutrients. Unlike energy, which is ultimately lost from an ecosystem, all chemical nutrients cycle within ecosystems.

? **Why does demand for meat also tend to drive up prices of grains such as wheat and rice, fruits, and vegetables?**

■ The potential supply of plants for direct consumption as food for humans is diminished by the use of agricultural land to grow feed for cattle, chickens, and other meat sources.

▶ **Figure 37.17** **Food energy available to people eating at different trophic levels**

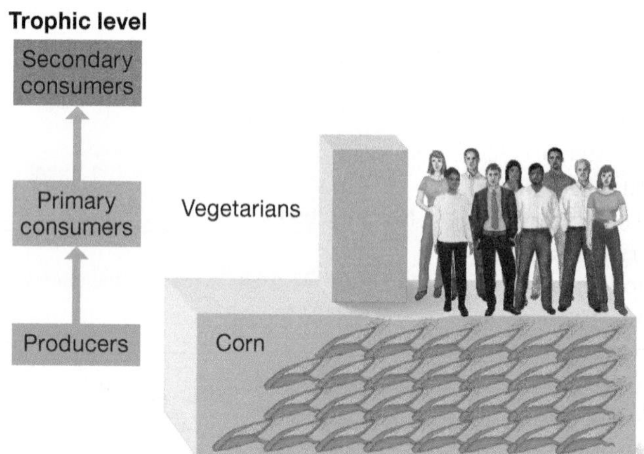

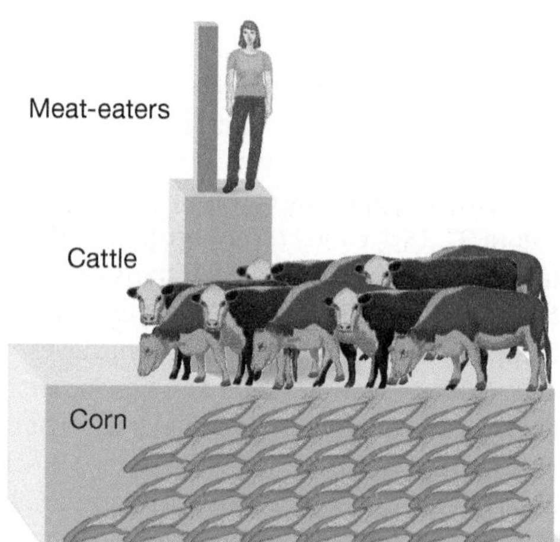

37.18 Chemicals are cycled between organic matter and abiotic reservoirs

The sun (or in some cases Earth's interior) supplies ecosystems with a continual influx of energy, but aside from an occasional meteorite, there are no extraterrestrial sources of chemical elements. Life, therefore, depends on the recycling of chemicals. While an organism is alive, much of its chemical stock changes continuously as it acquires nutrients and releases wastes. When the organism dies, decomposition returns the atoms that make up its complex molecules to the environment, thus replenishing the pool of inorganic nutrients that producers use to build new organic matter.

Because chemical cycles in an ecosystem include both biotic and abiotic (geologic and atmospheric) components, they are called **biogeochemical cycles**. Figure 37.18, at the top of the next page, is a general scheme for the cycling of a nutrient within an ecosystem. Note that the cycle has **abiotic reservoirs**, where chemicals accumulate or are stockpiled outside of living organisms. The atmosphere, for example, is an abiotic reservoir for carbon. Phosphorus, on the other hand, is available only from the soil. Both the atmosphere and soil are abiotic reservoirs for nitrogen.

Let's trace the general biogeochemical cycle in Figure 37.18. ❶ Producers incorporate chemicals from the abiotic reservoirs into organic compounds. ❷ Consumers feed on the producers, incorporating some of the chemicals into their

▶ **Figure 37.18**
A general model of the biogeochemical cycling of nutrients

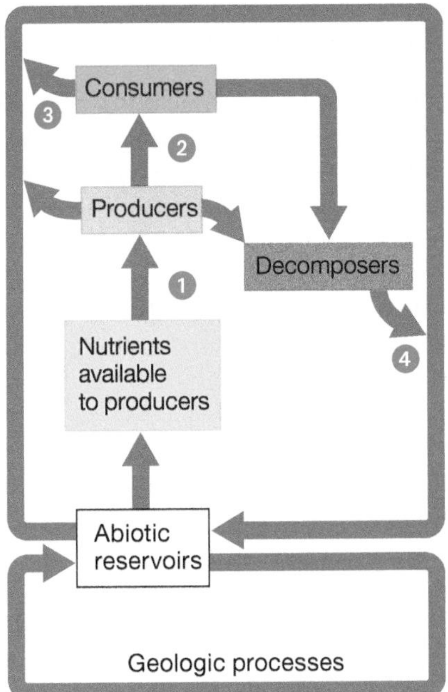

own bodies. ③ Both producers and consumers release some chemicals back to the environment in waste products (CO_2 and nitrogenous wastes of animals). ④ Decomposers play a central role by breaking down the complex organic molecules in detritus such as plant litter, animal wastes, and dead organisms. The products of this metabolism are inorganic compounds such as nitrates (NO_3^-), phosphates (PO_4^{3-}), and CO_2, which replenish the abiotic reservoirs. Geologic processes such as erosion and the weathering of rock also contribute to the abiotic reservoirs. Producers use the inorganic molecules from abiotic reservoirs as raw materials for synthesizing new organic molecules (carbohydrates and proteins, for example), and the cycle continues.

Biogeochemical cycles can be local or global. Soil is the main reservoir for nutrients in a local cycle, such as phosphorus. In contrast, for those chemicals that exist primarily in gaseous form—carbon and nitrogen are examples—the cycling is essentially global. For instance, some of the carbon a plant acquires from the air may have been released into the atmosphere by the respiration of an organism on another continent.

In the next three modules, we look at the cyclic movements of carbon, phosphorus, and nitrogen. As you study the cycles, look for the four basic steps we have cited, as well as the geologic processes that may move chemicals around and between ecosystems. In the diagrams, the main abiotic reservoirs are highlighted in white boxes.

? **Which boxes in Figure 37.18 represent biotic components of an ecosystem?**

■ Consumers, producers, and decomposers

37.19 The carbon cycle depends on photosynthesis and respiration

Carbon, the major ingredient of all organic molecules, has an atmospheric reservoir and cycles globally. Carbon also resides in plant and animal biomass, fossil fuels, soils, sedimentary rocks, and as dissolved carbon compounds in the oceans.

As shown in Figure 37.19, the reciprocal metabolic processes of photosynthesis and cellular respiration are mainly responsible for the cycling of carbon between the biotic and abiotic worlds. ① Photosynthesis removes CO_2 from the atmosphere and incorporates it into organic molecules, which are ② passed along the food chain by consumers. ③ Cellular respiration by producers and consumers returns CO_2 to the atmosphere. ④ Decomposers break down the carbon compounds in detritus; that carbon, too, is eventually released as CO_2.

On a global scale, the return of CO_2 to the atmosphere by cellular respiration closely balances its removal by photosynthesis. However, ⑤ the increased burning of wood and fossil fuels (coal and petroleum) is raising the level of CO_2 in the atmosphere. (As we will discuss in Module 38.4, this increase in CO_2 is leading to significant global warming.)

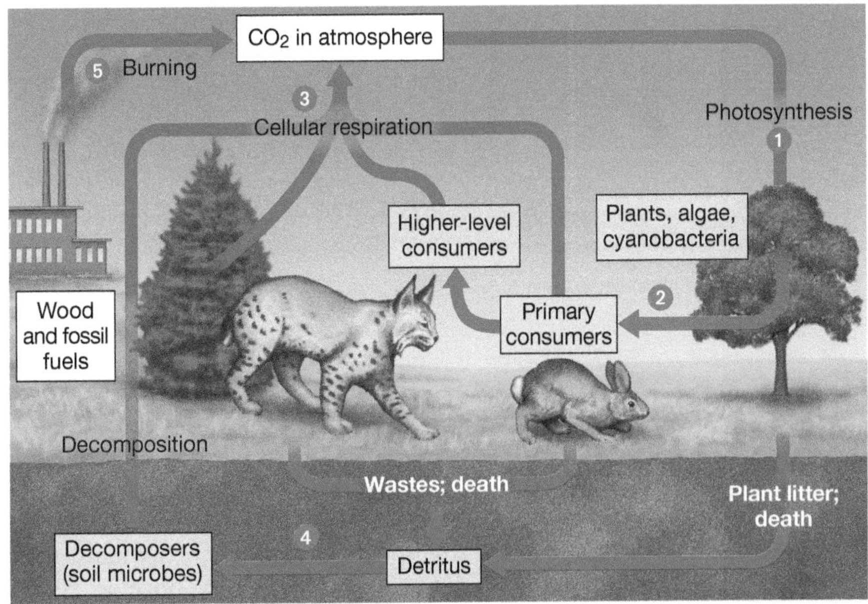

▲ **Figure 37.19** **The carbon cycle**

TRY THIS Identify all of the locations where carbon is stored; identify all of the sources that release carbon into the environment.

? **What would happen to the carbon cycle if all the decomposers suddenly "went on strike" and stopped working?**

■ Carbon would accumulate in organic material; the atmospheric reservoir of carbon would decline, and plants would eventually be starved for CO_2.

37.20 The phosphorus cycle depends on the weathering of rock

Organisms require phosphorus—usually in the form of the phosphate ion (PO_4^{3-})—as an ingredient of nucleic acids, phospholipids, and ATP, and (in vertebrates) as a mineral component of bones and teeth. In contrast to the carbon cycle and the other major biogeochemical cycles, the phosphorus cycle does not have an atmospheric component. Rocks are the only source of phosphorus for terrestrial ecosystems; in fact, rocks that have high phosphorus content are mined for agricultural fertilizer.

At the center of Figure 37.20, 1 the weathering (breakdown) of rock gradually adds inorganic phosphate (PO_4^{3-}) to the soil. 2 Plants assimilate the dissolved phosphate ions in the soil and build them into organic compounds. 3 Consumers obtain phosphorus in organic form by eating plants. 4 Phosphates are returned to the soil by the action of decomposers on animal waste and the remains of dead plants and animals. 5 Some phosphate drains from terrestrial ecosystems into the sea, where it may settle and eventually become part of new rocks. This phosphorus will not cycle back into living organisms until 6 geologic processes uplift the rocks and expose them to weathering, a process that takes millions of years.

Because phosphates are transferred from terrestrial to aquatic ecosystems more rapidly than they are replaced, the amount in terrestrial ecosystems gradually diminishes over time. Furthermore, much of the soluble phosphate released by weathering quickly binds to soil particles, rendering it inaccessible to plants. As a result, phosphate availability is often quite low and commonly a limiting factor. Mycorrhizal fungi (see Module 17.12) that facilitate phosphorus uptake are essential to many plants, especially those living in older, highly weathered soils. Soil erosion from land cleared for agriculture or development accelerates the loss of phosphates.

Farmers and gardeners often use crushed phosphate rock, bone meal (finely ground bones from slaughtered livestock), or guano, the droppings of seabirds and bats, to add phosphorus to the soil. Guano is mined from densely populated colonies or caves, where meters-deep deposits have accumulated. As you'll learn in Module 37.22, however, runoff of large amounts of phosphate fertilizer pollutes aquatic ecosystems.

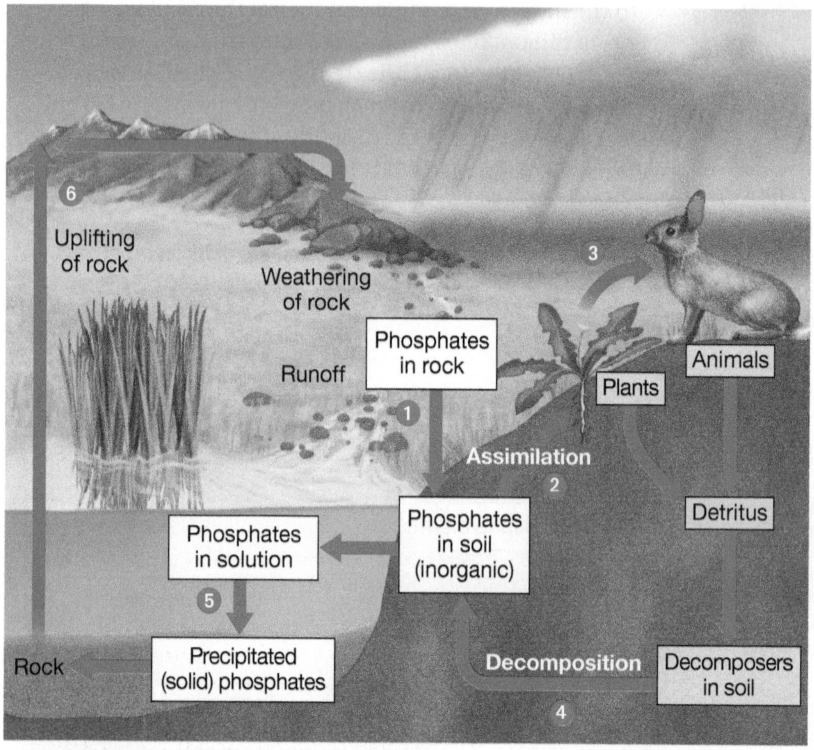

▲ Figure 37.20 The phosphorus cycle

? Over the short term, why does phosphorus cycling tend to be localized, whereas carbon and nitrogen cycle globally?

■ Because phosphorus is cycled almost entirely within the soil rather than transferred over long distances via the atmosphere

37.21 The nitrogen cycle depends on bacteria

As an ingredient of proteins and nucleic acids, nitrogen is essential to the structure and functioning of all organisms. In particular, it is a crucial and often limiting plant nutrient. Nitrogen has two abiotic reservoirs, the atmosphere and the soil. The atmospheric reservoir is huge; almost 80% of the atmosphere is nitrogen gas (N_2). However, plants cannot absorb nitrogen in the form of N_2. The process of **nitrogen fixation**, which is performed by some bacteria, converts N_2 to compounds of nitrogen that can be used by plants. Without these organisms, the natural reservoir of usable soil nitrogen would be extremely limited.

Figure 37.21, on the facing page, illustrates the actions of two types of nitrogen-fixing bacteria. Starting at the far right in the figure, 1 some bacteria live symbiotically in the roots of certain species of plants, supplying their hosts with a direct source of usable nitrogen. The largest group of plants with this mutualistic relationship is the legumes, a family that includes peanuts, soybeans, and alfalfa (see Module 32.14). A number of nonlegume plants that live in nitrogen-poor soils have a similar relationship with bacteria. 2 Free-living nitrogen-fixing bacteria in soil or water convert N_2 to ammonia (NH_3), which then picks up another H^+ to become ammonium (NH_4^+).

3 After nitrogen is "fixed," some of the NH_4^+ is taken up and used by plants. 4 Nitrifying bacteria in the soil also convert some of the NH_4^+ to nitrate (NO_3^-) which is more readily

▶ **Figure 37.21** The nitrogen cycle

TRY THIS The figure identifies five roles that bacteria play in the nitrogen cycle. Explain the effect of eliminating the bacteria that perform each of these roles.

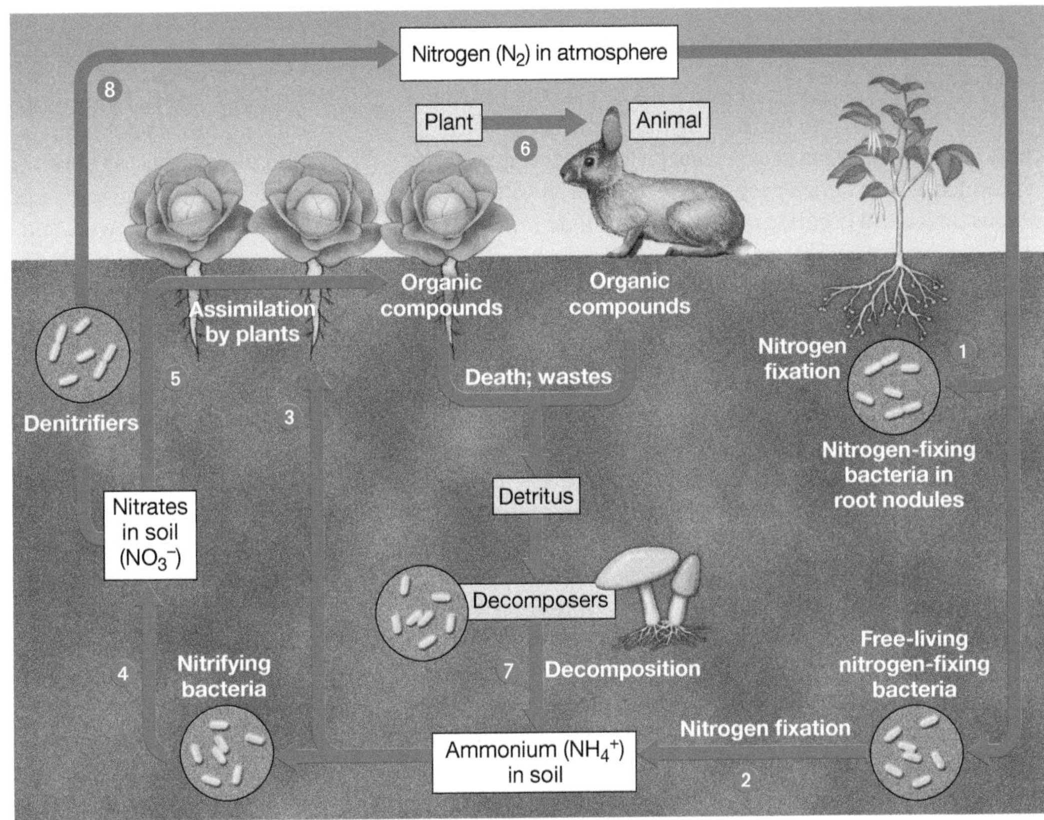

5 assimilated by plants. Plants use the nitrogen they assimilate to synthesize molecules such as amino acids, which are then incorporated into proteins.

6 When an herbivore (represented by the rabbit in Figure 37.21) eats a plant, it digests the proteins into amino acids, then uses the amino acids to build the proteins it needs. Higher-order consumers gain nitrogen from their prey. Nitrogen-containing waste products are formed during protein metabolism; consumers excrete some nitrogen as well as incorporate some into their body tissues (see Module 25.5). Mammals, such as the rabbit, excrete nitrogen as urea; industrially produced urea is widely used as an agricultural fertilizer.

Organisms that are not consumed eventually die and become detritus, which is decomposed by prokaryotes and fungi. 7 Decomposition releases NH_4^+ from organic compounds back into the soil, replenishing the soil reservoir of NH_4^+ and, with the help of nitrifying bacteria (step 4), NO_3^-. Under low-oxygen conditions, however, 8 soil bacteria known as denitrifiers strip the oxygen atoms from NO_3^-, releasing N_2 back into the atmosphere and depleting the soil reservoir of usable nitrogen.

Although not shown in the figure, some NH_4^+ and NO_3^- are made in the atmosphere by chemical reactions involving N_2 and ammonia gas (NH_3). These ions reach the soil in precipitation and dust, which are crucial sources of nitrogen for plants in some ecosystems.

Human activities are disrupting the nitrogen cycle by adding more nitrogen to the biosphere each year than that added by natural processes. Combustion of fossil fuels in motor vehicles and coal-fired power plants produces nitrogen oxides (NO and NO_2). Nitrogen oxides react with other gases in the lower atmosphere to increase the production of ozone (O_3). Unlike the ozone layer in the upper atmosphere, which protects Earth from harmful ultraviolet radiation, ground-level ozone is a health hazard. It irritates the respiratory system and can cause coughing and breathing difficulties. High ozone levels are especially dangerous for people with respiratory problems such as asthma. In many regions, ozone alerts are common during hot, dry summer weather. Nitrogen oxides also combine with water in the atmosphere to become nitric acid. The Clean Air Act Amendments of 1990 led to diminished acid precipitation from sulfur emissions, but environmental damage from nitric acid precipitation is causing new concern.

Modern agricultural practices are another major source of nitrogen. Animal wastes from intensive livestock production release ammonia into the atmosphere. Farmers use enormous amounts of nitrogen fertilizer to supplement natural nitrogen fixation by bacteria. Worldwide, the application of synthetic nitrogen fertilizer has increased 100-fold since the late 1950s. However, less than half the fertilizer is taken up by the crop plants. Some nitrogen escapes to the atmosphere, where it forms NO_2 or nitrous oxide (N_2O), an inert gas that lingers in the atmosphere and contributes to global warming (see Module 38.4). As you'll learn in the next module, nitrogen fertilizers also pollute aquatic systems.

? **What are the abiotic reservoirs of nitrogen? In what form does nitrogen occur in each reservoir?**

■ Atmosphere: N_2; soil: NH_4^+ and NO_3^-

37.22 A rapid inflow of nutrients degrades aquatic ecosystems

CONNECTION Low levels of nutrients, especially phosphorus and nitrogen, often limit the growth of algae and cyanobacteria—and thus primary production—in aquatic ecosystems. Standing-water ecosystems (lakes and ponds) gradually accumulate nutrients from the decomposition of organic matter and fresh influx from the land. As a result, primary production increases naturally over time in a process known as eutrophication. Human activities that add nutrients to aquatic ecosystems accelerate this process and also cause eutrophication in rivers, estuaries, coastal waters, and coral reefs.

You might think that an increase in primary production would be beneficial to a biological community. After all, Figure 37.15 shows that coral reefs and tropical rain forests, ecosystems renowned for spectacular species diversity, have the greatest net primary production. But rapid eutrophication actually lowers species diversity. In some ecosystems, cyanobacteria replace green algae as primary producers. These prokaryotes, which are often encased in a slimy coating, form extensive mats on the surface of the water that prevent light from penetrating the water (**Figure 37.22A**). Some species of cyanobacteria can fix nitrogen, which gives them an additional advantage when phosphate is the pollutant and nitrogen is scarce. Other ecosystems are overrun by blooms of unicellular diatoms, toxin-producing dinoflagellates (see Figure 16.14D), or multicellular algae. These heavy growths, or "blooms," of cyanobacteria or algae greatly reduce oxygen levels at night, when the photosynthesizers respire. As the cyanobacteria and algae die, microbes consume a great deal of oxygen as they decompose the extra biomass. Thus, rapid nutrient enrichment results in oxygen depletion of the water. Fishes that have a high oxygen requirement cannot survive in such an environment.

In many areas, phosphate pollution comes from agricultural fertilizers. Phosphates are also a common ingredient in pesticides. Other major sources of phosphates include outflow from sewage treatment facilities and runoff of animal waste from livestock feedlots (where hundreds of animals are penned together). Sewage treatment facilities may discharge large amounts of dissolved inorganic nitrogen compounds into rivers or streams when extreme conditions (such as unusually high rainfall) overwhelm their capacity. Agricultural sources of nitrogen include feedlots and the large amounts of inorganic nitrogen fertilizers that are routinely applied to crops, lawns, and golf courses. Plants take up some of the nitrogen compounds in fertilizer, and denitrifiers convert some to atmospheric N_2 or N_2O, but nitrate is not bound tightly by soil particles and is easily washed out of the soil by rain or irrigation. As a result, chemical fertilizers often exceed the soil's natural recycling capacity.

In an example of how far-reaching this problem can be, nitrogen runoff from midwestern farm fields has been linked to a "dead zone" observed each summer in the Gulf of Mexico. Vast algal blooms extend outward from the mouth of the Mississippi River where it deposits its nutrient-laden waters. As the algae die, decomposition of the huge quantities of biomass diminishes the supply of dissolved oxygen over an area that ranges from 13,000 to 22,000 km^2, or roughly 5,000 to 8,500 square miles (**Figure 37.22B**). Oxygen depletion disrupts benthic communities, displacing fishes and invertebrates that can move and killing organisms that are attached to the substrate. More than 400 recurring and permanent coastal dead zones totaling approximately 245,000 km^2 (about 95,000 square miles) have been documented in seas worldwide.

? **How would excessive addition of mineral nutrients to a lake eventually lead to the loss of many fish species?**

The nutrients initially cause population explosions of algae and cyanobacteria. Their respiration and that of the decomposers of all the detritus as the algae and cyanobacteria die consume most of the lake's oxygen, which the fish require.

▲ **Figure 37.22A** Growth of cyanobacteria in Lake Erie resulting from nutrient pollution

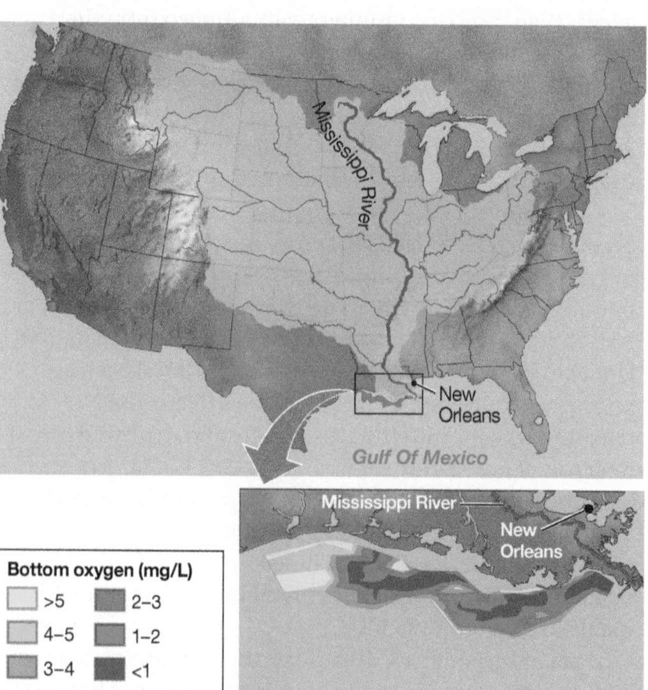

▲ **Figure 37.22B** Oxygen depletion in the Gulf of Mexico resulting from nutrient runoff, August 2015

37.23 Ecosystem services are essential to human well-being

CONNECTION Natural ecosystems provide direct benefits to people, for example, by supplying us with fresh water and food such as fish and shellfish (Figure 37.23A). Natural vegetation helps retain fertile soil and prevent landslides and mudslides. We also depend on healthy ecosystems to recycle nutrients, decompose wastes, and regulate climate and air quality. Wetlands buffer coastal populations against tidal waves and hurricanes, reduce the impact of flooding rivers, and filter pollutants.

Ecosystems that we create are also essential to our well-being. For example, agricultural ecosystems supply most of our food and fibers. Although we manage these ecosystems, they are modifications of natural ecosystems and make use of ecosystem services, such as control of agricultural pests by natural predators and pollination of crops. Soil fertility, the foundation for crop growth, depends on nutrient cycling, another ecosystem service. But agricultural methods introduced over the past several decades have pushed croplands beyond their natural capacity to produce food. Large inputs of chemical fertilizers are needed to supplement soil nutrients. Synthetic pesticides are used to control the population growth of crop-eating insects and pathogens that take advantage of vast monocultures of crop species. Herbicides are applied to kill weeds that would compete with crop plants for water and nutrients. In many areas, crops require additional water supplied by irrigation.

The growing demand of the human population for food, fibers, and water has largely been satisfied at the expense of other ecosystem services. The detrimental effects of nutrient runoff, discussed in the previous module, are affecting both freshwater and marine ecosystems as fertilizer use increases. Pesticides may kill beneficial organisms as well as pests, and as you learned previously, chemicals that persist in the environment can be carried far from their point of origin (see Modules 34.2, 34.18, and 35.16). Perhaps most worrisome is the deterioration of fertile soil. Clearing and cultivation expose land to wind and water that erode the rich topsoil.

Erosion and soil degradation are especially severe in grassland, savanna, and some forest ecosystems where low amounts of precipitation and high rates of evaporation result in low levels of soil moisture. In recent years, dust storms sweeping across overcultivated areas have removed millions of tons of topsoil from these stressed ecosystems. In China, for example, overgrazing and other poor agricultural practices are turning 2,330 km^2 of land—an area the size of Rhode Island—into desert each year, and generating massive dust storms that engulf cities (Figure 37.23B). Irrigation of arid land enables farmers to grow crops but leaves a salty residue that eventually prevents plant growth. In addition, population growth in these regions places increasing demands on the already scarce water supply.

The loss of ecosystem services is making some regions more vulnerable to the effects of climate change. Coastal wetlands are a critical line of defense against rising seas and the increasing intensity of hurricanes. As climate change brings more frequent episodes of torrential rains, inland wetlands provide essential flood protection for farms and cities downstream.

▲ Figure 37.23A Harvesting clams at low tide in a salt marsh near Charleston, South Carolina

They also store water in the soil and help recharge aquifers, ensuring the survival of biological communities—as well as crops—during periods of drought. However, half of the world's wetlands have been lost since 1900, destroyed by development, invasive species, nutrient pollution, drainage for agriculture, damming rivers, and siphoning off freshwater for burgeoning populations. In 2009 (the last year for which data are available), coastal wetlands were disappearing from the contiguous United States at a rate of 325 km^2 per year.

Ecosystem services are a key component of **sustainability**, the goal of developing, managing, and conserving Earth's resources in ways that meet the needs of people today without compromising the ability of future generations to meet theirs. Scientists are applying their knowledge of population, community, and ecosystem ecology to conserve natural ecosystems and even to repair some of the ecological damage that we have already done.

▲ Figure 37.23B A dust storm in Changling, China, caused by nearby degraded farmland.

? What ecosystem services are provided by wetlands?

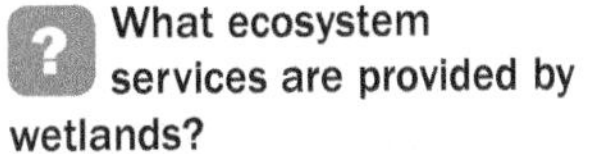

■ Wetlands protect coastal regions from damaging storms, provide fish and shellfish, filter pollutants, and reduce flooding.

CHAPTER

37 REVIEW

For practice quizzes, BioFlix animations, MP3 tutorials, video tutors, and more study tools designed for this textbook, go to MasteringBiology™

REVIEWING THE CONCEPTS

Community Structure and Dynamics (37.1–37.13)

37.1 A community includes all the organisms inhabiting a particular area. Community ecology is concerned with factors that influence the species composition of communities and with factors that affect community dynamics.

37.2 Interspecific interactions are fundamental to community structure. Interspecific interactions can be categorized according to their effect on the interacting populations.

37.3 Competition may occur when a shared resource is limited.

37.4 Mutualism benefits both partners.

37.5 Predation leads to diverse adaptations in prey species.

37.6 Herbivory leads to diverse adaptations in plants. Some herbivore-plant interactions illustrate coevolution or reciprocal evolutionary adaptations.

37.7 Parasites and pathogens can affect community composition.

37.8 Trophic structure is a key factor in community dynamics. Trophic structure can be represented by a food chain.

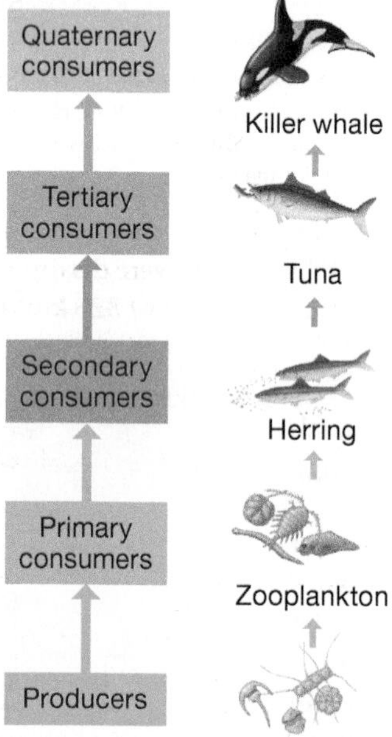

An aquatic food chain

37.9 Food chains interconnect, forming food webs.

37.10 Species diversity includes species richness and relative abundance. Thus, diversity takes into account both the number of species in a community and the proportion of the community that each species represents.

37.11 Some species have a disproportionate impact on diversity. Although a keystone species has low biomass or relative abundance, its removal from a community results in lower species diversity.

37.12 Disturbance is a prominent feature of most communities. Ecological succession is a transition in species composition of a community. Primary succession is the gradual colonization of barren rocks. Secondary succession occurs after a disturbance has destroyed a community but left the soil intact.

37.13 Invasive species can devastate communities. Organisms that have been introduced to non-native habitats by human actions and have established themselves at the expense of native communities are considered invasive.

Ecosystem Structure and Dynamics (37.14–37.23)

37.14 Ecosystem ecology emphasizes energy flow and chemical cycling. An ecosystem includes a community and the abiotic factors with which it interacts.

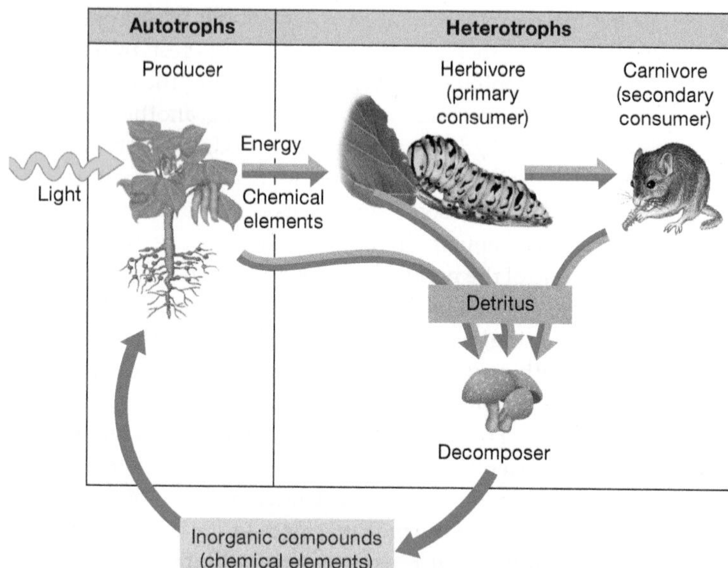

37.15 Primary production sets the energy budget for ecosystems.

37.16 Energy supply limits the length of food chains. An energy pyramid shows the flow of energy from producers to primary consumers and to higher trophic levels. Only about 10% of the energy stored at each trophic level is available to the next level.

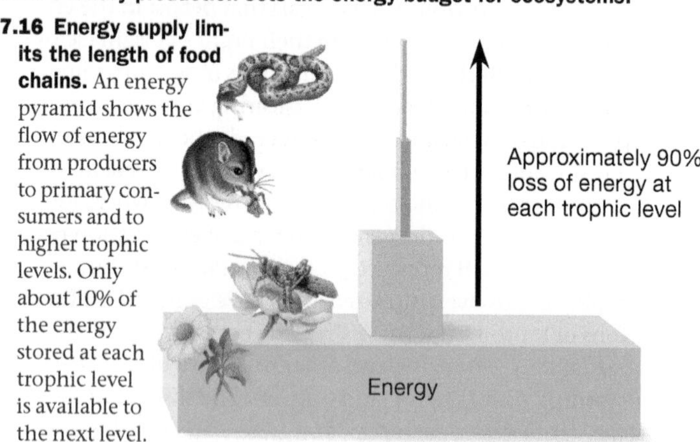

37.17 An energy pyramid explains the ecological cost of meat. A field of corn can support many more human vegetarians than meat-eaters.

37.18 Chemicals are cycled between organic matter and abiotic reservoirs.

37.19 The carbon cycle depends on photosynthesis and respiration.

37.20 The phosphorus cycle depends on the weathering of rock.

37.21 The nitrogen cycle depends on bacteria. Various bacteria in soil (and root nodules of some plants) convert gaseous N_2 to compounds that plants can use, such as ammonium (NH_4^+) and nitrate (NO_3^-).

37.22 A rapid inflow of nutrients degrades aquatic ecosystems. Nutrient input from fertilizer and other sources causes rapid eutrophication, resulting in decreased species diversity and oxygen depletion of lakes, rivers, and coastal waters.

37.23 Ecosystem services are essential to human well-being. We depend on services provided by natural ecosystems.

CONNECTING THE CONCEPTS

1. Fill in the blanks in the table below summarizing the interspecific interactions in a community.

Interspecific Interaction	Effect on Species 1	Effect on Species 2	Example
	+	−	
	−	−	
	+	−	
	+	−	
	+	+	

2. Fill in the blanks in the table below summarizing terrestrial nutrient cycles.

	Carbon	Phosphorus	Nitrogen
Main abiotic reservoir(s)			
Form in abiotic reservoir			
Form used by producers			
Human activities that alter cycle			
Effects of altering cycle			

TESTING YOUR KNOWLEDGE

Level 1: Knowledge/Comprehension

3. Which of the following groups is (are) absolutely essential to the functioning of an ecosystem?
   a. producers
   b. producers and herbivores
   c. producers, herbivores, and carnivores
   d. producers and decomposers
4. To ensure adequate nitrogen for a crop, a farmer would want to *decrease* ________ by soil bacteria.
   a. nitrification
   b. denitrification
   c. nitrogen fixation
   d. a and c
5. Which of the following organisms is mismatched with its trophic level?
   a. algae—producer
   b. phytoplankton—primary consumer
   c. carnivorous fish larvae—secondary consumer
   d. eagle—tertiary or quaternary consumer
6. Which of the following best illustrates ecological succession?
   a. A mouse eats seeds, and an owl eats the mouse.
   b. Decomposition in soil releases nitrogen that plants can use.
   c. Grasses grow in a deserted field, followed by shrubs and then trees.
   d. Imported pheasants increase in numbers, while local quail disappear.
7. The open ocean and tropical rain forests contribute the most to Earth's net primary production because
   a. both have high rates of net primary production.
   b. both cover huge surface areas of Earth.
   c. nutrients cycle fastest in these two ecosystems.
   d. the ocean covers a huge surface area and the tropical rain forest has a high rate of production.

Level 2: Application/Analysis

8. Explain how seed dispersal by animals is an example of mutualism in some cases.
9. What is rapid eutrophication? What steps might be taken to slow this process?
10. In Southeast Asia, there's an old saying: "There is only one tiger to a hill." In terms of energy flow in ecosystems, explain why big predatory animals such as tigers and sharks are relatively rare.
11. For which chemicals are biogeochemical cycles global? Explain.
12. What roles do bacteria play in the nitrogen cycle?

Level 3: Synthesis/Evaluation

13. SCIENTIFIC THINKING An ecologist studying plants in the desert performed the following experiment. She staked out two identical plots, which included a few sagebrush plants and numerous small, annual wildflowers. She found the same five wildflower species in roughly equal numbers on both plots. She then enclosed one of the plots with a fence to keep out kangaroo rats, the most common grain-eaters of the area. After two years, to her surprise, four of the wildflower species were no longer present in the fenced plot, but one species had increased dramatically. The control plot had not changed. Using the principles of ecology, propose a hypothesis to explain her results. What additional evidence would support your hypothesis?
14. In a classic study, John Teal measured energy flow in a salt marsh ecosystem. The table below shows some of his results.

Form of Energy	Kcal/m²/Year
Sunlight	600,000
Chemical energy in producers	6,585
Chemical energy in primary consumers	81

Data from J. M. Teal, Energy flow in the salt marsh ecosystem of Georgia, *Ecology* 43: 614–24 (1962).

   a. What percentage of the energy in sunlight was converted into chemical energy and incorporated into plant biomass? What term describes this new biomass?
   b. What percentage of the energy in plant biomass was incorporated into the bodies of the primary consumers? What became of the rest of the energy (see Figure 37.16A)?
   c. How much energy is available for secondary consumers? Based on the efficiency of energy transfer by primary consumers, estimate how much energy will be available to tertiary consumers.

Answers to all questions can be found in Appendix 4.

Conservation Biology

CHAPTER 38

Today, we face an environmental challenge that eclipses all others in scope: climate change caused by the unprecedented speed with which Earth's atmosphere is warming. The effects of climate change are already apparent in melting ice sheets, rising seas, and extreme weather, including record-shattering heat waves and precipitation. Biodiversity, the variety of living things, will be one casualty of the rapidly changing environment. You may know that climate change threatens polar bears and penguins, but thousands of other species are also imperiled, including the American pika *(Ochotona princeps*; photo at right). This diminutive relative of rabbits lives high up in the Rocky Mountains of the United States and Canada.

Can Earth's biodiversity be saved?

The pika's high body temperature is well suited to the chilly climate of its mountain habitat. On warm summer days, however, pikas must take refuge in crevices where pockets of cold air prevent fatal overheating. There is also a limit to the pika's tolerance of low temperatures. In winter, pikas depend on a blanket of snow to insulate their shelters and food stores from the cold. Climate change threatens pikas with sizzling summer temperatures and winters of diminishing snowfall. In 2010, the pika came within a whisker of being declared an endangered species. But after reviewing the research on pika populations, the U.S. Fish and Wildlife Service (the agency responsible for making the decision), found reason for optimism about the pika's future. In Module 38.11, you'll learn about a conservation project that offers hope for pikas and hundreds of other species in a changing world.

Climate change, which scientists worldwide agree is the result of human activities, is one of many impacts of our dominance over the environment that affect the nonhuman inhabitants of Earth. Biodiversity is rapidly diminishing despite conservation efforts. As you learn about the fight to save our biological heritage, you will see that conservation biology touches all levels of ecology, from a single pika to the ecosystem it calls home.

BIG IDEAS

The Loss of Biodiversity (38.1–38.6)

Biodiversity is declining rapidly worldwide as a result of human activities.

Conservation Biology and Restoration Ecology (38.7–38.13)

Biologists are applying their knowledge of ecology to slow the loss of biodiversity and help define a sustainable future for the planet.

The Loss of Biodiversity

38.1 Loss of biodiversity includes the loss of ecosystems, species, and genes

Why do we care about losing biodiversity? One reason is what Harvard biologist E. O. Wilson calls biophilia, our sense of connection to nature and to other forms of life. Another is that many people share a moral belief that other species have an inherent right to life. But our dependence on vital ecosystem services also gives us practical reasons for preserving biodiversity (see Module 37.23).

Biodiversity encompasses more than individual species—it includes ecosystem diversity, species diversity, and genetic diversity. Let's examine each level of diversity to see what we stand to lose if the decline is not stopped.

Ecosystem Diversity The world's natural ecosystems are rapidly disappearing. Nearly half of Earth's forests are gone, and thousands more square kilometers disappear every year. Grassland ecosystems in North America (see Figure 34.13), where millions of bison roamed as recently as the 19th century, have overwhelmingly been lost to agriculture and development.

The temperate coniferous forest of the Klamath-Siskiyou Wilderness (**Figure 38.1A**) is located in a region spanning parts of California and Oregon that is extraordinarily rich in ecosystem diversity. In addition to the distinctive chaparral ecosystem (see Figure 34.12), forests of sequoia, redwood, and Douglas fir, coastal dunes, salt marshes, and a wide variety of other ecosystems can be found in this rapidly vanishing treasure trove of biodiversity. Only about a quarter of the original area remains in its natural state.

Aquatic ecosystems are also threatened. For example, an estimated 20% of the world's coral reefs, ecosystems known for their species richness and productivity (see Figure 34.6B), have been destroyed by human activities, and 15% are in danger of collapse within the next two decades. The deteriorating state of freshwater ecosystems is particularly worrisome. Tens of thousands of species live in lakes and rivers, and these ecosystems supply food and water for many terrestrial species, as well—including us.

As natural ecosystems are lost, so are essential services. Water purification is one of the services provided free of charge by healthy ecosystems. As water moves slowly through forests, streams, and wetlands, pollutants and sediments are filtered out. Whether taken from surface waters such as lakes or subsurface sources (groundwater), the drinking water supplied by public water systems typically has passed through this natural filtration process. In some places, including New York City, no further filtration is required, although the water is chlorinated to kill microorganisms. As farm fields and housing developments replaced the naturally diverse ecosystems in New York City's watershed, however, the land's ability to purify water deteriorated. The additional pollution from agricultural runoff and sewage reduced water quality to the point where the city had to take action. Officials considered spending $8 billion to build a filtration plant, which would cost a further $1 million per day to operate. They decided to invest in lower-cost ecosystem services instead. Actions included more tightly restricting land use in the watershed, purchasing land to preserve natural ecosystems, and helping landowners better manage their land to protect the watershed. As a result of these measures, the quality of naturally filtered water supplied to New York City remains high.

Species Diversity When ecosystems are lost, populations of the species that make up their biological communities are also lost. A species may disappear from a local ecosystem but remain in others; for example, a population of American pika may be lost from one region of the Rocky Mountains while other populations survive elsewhere. Ecologists refer to the loss of a single population of a species as **extirpation**. Although extirpation and declining population sizes are strong signals that a species is in trouble, it may still be possible to save it. **Extinction** means that all populations of a species have disappeared, an irreversible situation.

How rapidly are species being lost? Because biologists are uncertain of the total number of species that exist, it is

▼ **Figure 38.1A** The Klamath-Siskiyou Wilderness, home to a wide variety of ecosystems

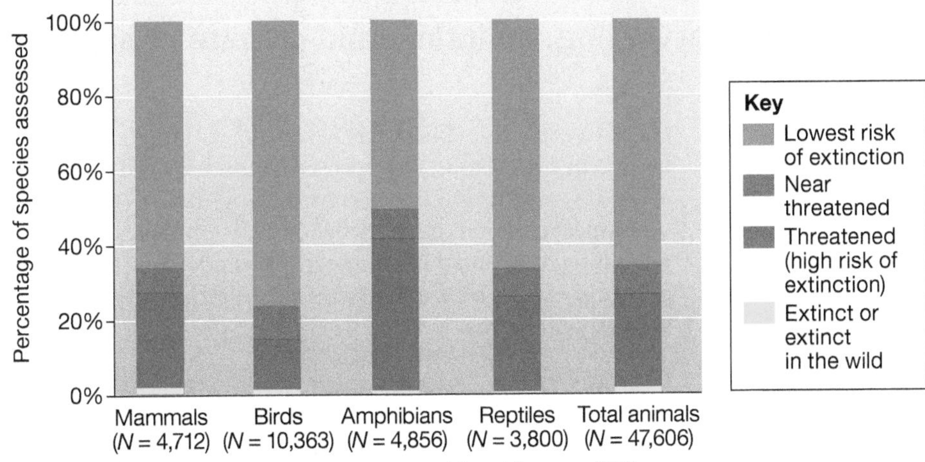

Data from International Union for Conservation of Nature and Natural Resources (2015).

▲ **Figure 38.1B Results of the 2015 IUCN assessment of species at risk for extinction (*N* = the number of species assessed)**

difficult to determine the actual rate of species loss. Some scientists estimate that current extinction rates are about 100 times greater than the natural rate of extinction. The International Union for Conservation of Nature (IUCN) is a global environmental network that keeps track of the status of species worldwide. **Figure 38.1B** shows the 2015 IUCN assessment of more than 47,000 species of animals plus those in four major groups. Notice the large proportions of amphibians that are considered threatened. Disease caused by chytrid fungi (see Module 17.14) is one reason for their decline. Amphibians are also vulnerable to climate change.

Because of the network of community interactions among populations of different species within an ecosystem, a good example of the INTERACTIONS that support life on Earth, the loss of one species can have a negative impact on the overall species richness of the ecosystem. Keystone species illustrate this effect (see Module 37.11). Other species modify their habitat in ways that encourage species diversity. In prairie ecosystems, for instance, plant and arthropod diversity is greatest near prairie dog burrows, where the soil has been altered by the animal's digging (**Figure 38.1C**). Abandoned burrows provide homes for cottontail rabbits, burrowing owls, and other animals. Thus, extirpation of prairie dogs results in lower species diversity in prairie communities.

In the United States, the Endangered Species Act protects species and the ecosystems on which they depend. Many other nations have also enacted laws to protect biodiversity, and an international agreement protects some 33,000 species of wild animals and plants from trade that would threaten their survival.

▼ **Figure 38.1C A group of young black-tailed prairie dogs (*Cynomys ludovicianus*) near their burrow**

Species loss also has practical consequences for human well-being. Many drugs have been developed from substances found in the natural world, including penicillin, aspirin, antimalarial agents, and anticancer drugs. Dozens more potentially useful chemicals from a variety of organisms are currently being investigated. For example, researchers are testing possible new antibiotics produced by microbial symbionts of marine sponges, painkillers extracted from a species of poison dart frog, and anti-HIV and anticancer drugs derived from compounds found in rain forest plants.

Genetic Diversity The genetic diversity within and between populations of a species is the raw material that makes microevolution and adaptation to the environment possible—a hedge against future environmental changes. If local populations disappear and the total number of individuals of a species declines, so, too, do the genetic resources for that species. Severe reduction in genetic variation threatens the survival of a species.

The enormous genetic diversity of all the organisms on Earth has great potential benefit for people, too. Breeding programs have narrowed the genetic diversity of crop plants to a handful of varieties, leaving them vulnerable to pathogens (see Module 17.11). For example, researchers are currently scrambling to stop the spread of a deadly new strain of wheat stem rust, a fungal pathogen that has devastated harvests in Africa and central Asia. Resistance genes found in the wild relatives of wheat (**Figure 38.1D**) may hold the key to the world's future food supply. Many research and biotechnology leaders are enthusiastic about the possibilities that "bioprospecting" for potentially useful genes in other organisms holds for the development of new medicines, industrial chemicals, and other products.

▲ **Figure 38.1D Einkorn wheat, a wild relative of modern cultivated varieties**

Now that you have some insight into the nature and value of biodiversity, let's examine in more detail the causes for its decline.

? **What are two reasons to be concerned about the impact of the biodiversity crisis on human welfare?**

■ The environmental degradation threatening other species may also harm us. We are dependent on biodiversity, both directly through the use of organisms and their products and indirectly through ecosystem services.

38.2 Habitat loss, invasive species, overharvesting, pollution, and climate change are major threats to biodiversity

CONNECTION The human population has grown exponentially over the past century. We have supported this growth by using increasingly effective technologies to capture or produce food, to extract resources from the environment, and to build cities. In industrialized countries, we consume far more resources than are required to meet our basic requirements for food and shelter (see Figure 36.11). Thus, it should not surprise you to learn that human activities are largely responsible for the current decline of biodiversity. In this section, we examine the major factors that threaten biodiversity.

Habitat Loss Human alteration of habitats poses the single greatest threat to biodiversity throughout the biosphere. Agriculture, urban development, forestry, mining, and environmental pollution have brought about massive destruction and fragmentation of habitats. Deforestation continues at a blistering pace in tropical and coniferous forests (**Figure 38.2A**).

▲ **Figure 38.2A** Clear-cut areas in Mount Baker-Snoqualmie National Forest, Washington

The amount of land surface altered by people is approaching 50%, and we use more than half of all accessible surface fresh water. The natural courses of most of the world's major rivers have been changed. Worldwide, tens of thousands of dams constructed for flood control, hydroelectric power, drinking water, and irrigation have damaged river and wetland ecosystems. Some of the most productive aquatic habitats in estuaries and intertidal wetlands have been overrun by commercial and residential development. The loss of marine habitat is severe, especially in coastal areas and coral reefs.

Invasive Species Ranking second behind habitat loss as a threat to biodiversity are invasive species, which disrupt communities by competing with, preying on, or parasitizing native species. The lack of interspecific interactions that keep the newcomer populations in check is often a key factor in a non-native species becoming invasive (see Module 37.13). Meanwhile, a newly arrived species is an unfamiliar biotic factor in the environment of native species. Natives are especially vulnerable when a new species poses an unprecedented threat. In the absence of an evolutionary history with predators, for example, animals may lack defense mechanisms or even a fundamental recognition of danger.

The Pacific island of Guam was home to 13 species of forest birds—but no native snakes—when brown tree snakes (**Figure 38.2B**) arrived as stowaways on a cargo plane. With no competitors, predators, or parasites to hinder them, the snakes proliferated rapidly on a diet of unwary birds. Six of the native species of birds were extirpated, although they survive on nearby islands. One species of bird that lived nowhere else but Guam is now extinct. As the populations of two other species of birds became perilously low, officials took the remaining individuals into protective custody; they now exist only in zoos. The brown tree snake also eliminated species of seabirds and lizards.

Overharvesting Another major threat to biodiversity is overexploitation of wildlife by harvesting at rates that exceed the ability of populations to rebound. Such overharvesting has threatened some rare trees that produce valuable wood, such as mahogany and rosewood. Animal species whose numbers have been drastically reduced by excessive commercial harvest, poaching, or sport hunting include tigers, whales, rhinoceroses, Galápagos tortoises, and numerous fishes. In parts of Africa, Asia, and South America, wild animals are heavily hunted for food, and the African term "bushmeat" is now used to refer generally to such meat. As once-impenetrable forests are opened to exploitation, the commercial bushmeat trade has become one of the greatest threats to primates, including gorillas, chimpanzees, and many species of monkeys, as well as other mammals and birds. No longer hunted only for local use, large quantities of bushmeat are sold at urban markets or exported worldwide, including to the United States.

Aquatic species are suffering overexploitation, too. Many edible marine fish and seafood species are in a precarious state (see Module 36.8). Worldwide, fishing fleets are working farther offshore and harvesting fish from greater depths to obtain hauls comparable with those of previous decades.

▲ **Figure 38.2B** A brown tree snake (*Boiga irregularis*)

Pollution Pollutants released by human activities can have local, regional, and global effects. Some pollutants, such as oil spills, contaminate a limited region (Figure 38.2C). The global water cycle, however, can transport pollutants—for instance, pesticides used on land—from terrestrial to aquatic ecosystems hundreds of miles away. Pollutants that are emitted into the atmosphere, such as nitrogen oxides from the burning of fossil fuels, may be carried aloft for many miles before falling to Earth in the form of acid precipitation.

Ozone depletion in the upper atmosphere is another example of the global impact of pollution. The **ozone layer** protects Earth from the harmful ultraviolet rays in sunlight. Beginning in the 1970s, scientists realized that the ozone layer was gradually thinning. The consequences of ozone depletion for life on Earth would be severe, increasing skin cancers and harming crops and natural communities, especially the phytoplankton that are responsible for much of Earth's primary production. International agreements to phase out the production of chemicals implicated in ozone destruction have been effective in slowing the rate of ozone depletion. Even so, complete ozone recovery is probably decades away.

In addition to being transported to areas far from where they originate, many toxins produced by industrial wastes or applied as pesticides become concentrated as they pass through the food chain. This concentration, or **biological magnification**, occurs because the biomass at any given trophic level is produced from a much larger toxin-containing biomass ingested from the level below (see Module 37.16). Thus, top-level consumers are usually the organisms most severely damaged by toxic compounds in the environment. In the Great Lakes food chain shown in Figure 38.2D, the concentration of industrial chemicals called PCBs increased at each successive trophic level. The PCB concentration measured in the eggs of herring gulls, top-level consumers, was almost 5,000 times higher than that measured in phytoplankton. Many other synthetic chemicals that cannot be degraded by microorganisms, including DDT and mercury, also become concentrated through biological magnification. Mercury, a by-product of plastic production and coal-fired power plants, enters the food chain after being converted to highly toxic methylmercury by benthic bacteria. Since people are top-level predators, too, eating fish from contaminated waters can be dangerous.

Recently, scientists have recognized a new type of pollutant in the oceans and the Great Lakes: plastic particles that are small enough to be eaten by zooplankton. Many body washes and facial cleansers include plastic "microbeads" to boost scrubbing power. Too small to be captured by wastewater treatment plants, these microparticles enter the watershed and eventually wash out to sea or collect in lakes. Larger particles called "nurdles," used in making plastic products, are also common aquatic pollutants. Nurdles may be broken down to microbead size in the ocean. Toxins such as PCBs and DDT adhere to these plastic spheres. Thus, toxins may be concentrated first on microparticles and concentrated again by biological magnification. A new federal law bans the use of microbeads in products after July 2017. However, microbeads are only part of the problem. In all, more than 8.8 million tons of plastic end up in the oceans every year.

▲ **Figure 38.2C** A brown pelican on the Louisiana coast suffering the effects of the 2010 British Petroleum oil rig explosion

Global Climate Change Changes in global climate that are occurring as a result of global warming are likely to become a leading cause of biodiversity loss. In the next four modules, you'll learn about some of the causes and consequences of climate change.

? **List four threats to biodiversity and give an example of each.**

■ Habitat loss—deforestation; invasive species—brown tree snake; overharvesting—bushmeat; pollution—biological magnification of PCBs, DDT, and mercury. (Other examples could be used.)

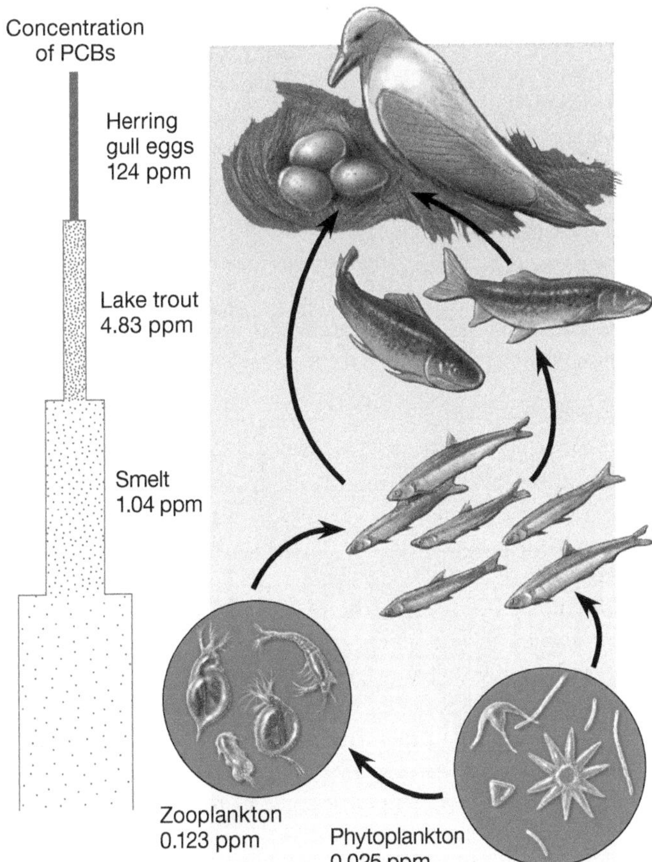

▲ **Figure 38.2D** Biological magnification of PCBs in a food web, measured in parts per million (ppm)

38.3 Rapid warming is changing the global climate

CONNECTION Rising concentrations of greenhouse gases in the atmosphere, such as carbon dioxide (CO_2), methane (CH_4), and nitrous oxide (N_2O), resulting from human activities, are changing global climate patterns (see Module 7.14). This was the overarching conclusion of the most recent assessment report released by the Intergovernmental Panel on Climate Change (IPCC) in 2014. Hundreds of scientists and policymakers from more than 100 countries participated in producing the report, which is based on data published in thousands of scientific papers.

The signature effect of increasing greenhouse gases is the rapid increase in the average global temperature, which has risen about 1°C (1.8°F) since 1900 at an accelerating pace (**Figure 38.3A**). But the temperature increases are not distributed evenly around the globe. The largest increases are in the northernmost regions of the Northern Hemisphere. In **Figure 38.3B** red and dark orange areas indicate the greatest temperature increases. In parts of Alaska and Canada, the average winter temperature has risen 3.4°C (more than 6°F) since 1961.

More than 90% of the heat trapped by greenhouse gases is being stored in the ocean. From 1995 to 2015, the heat content of the upper ocean increased by 1.3×10^{17} kcal per year, energy roughly equivalent to more than 5 million atomic bombs. Water expands as it warms, causing sea level to rise. Melting of the massive ice sheets of Greenland and Antarctica, as well as mountain glaciers, is also contributing to sea level rise. As this melting trend accelerates, rising sea levels will cause catastrophic flooding of coastal areas worldwide.

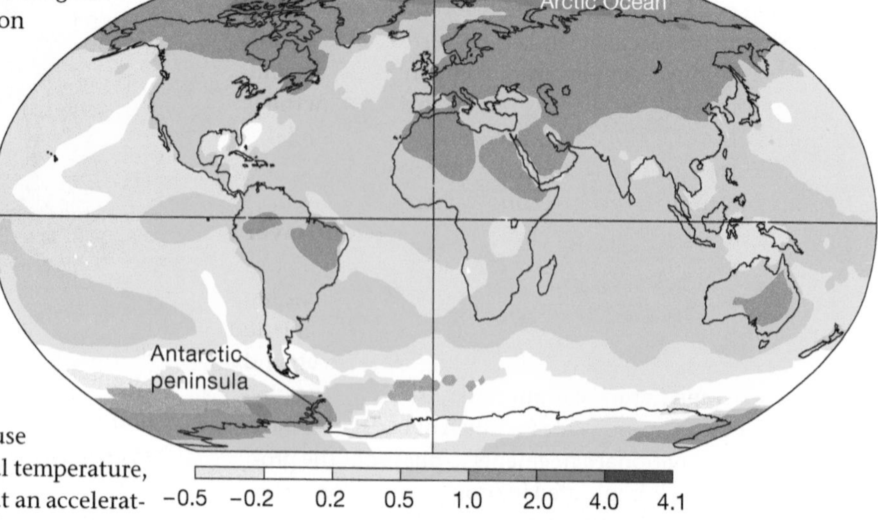

▲ **Figure 38.3B** Differences in average temperatures during 2005–2015 compared with long-term averages during 1951–1980 (in °C). (Gray areas lacked sufficient data to represent temperature differences.)

TRY THIS Identify the regions where the average temperature during 2005–2015 was 1°C or more above the long-term average.

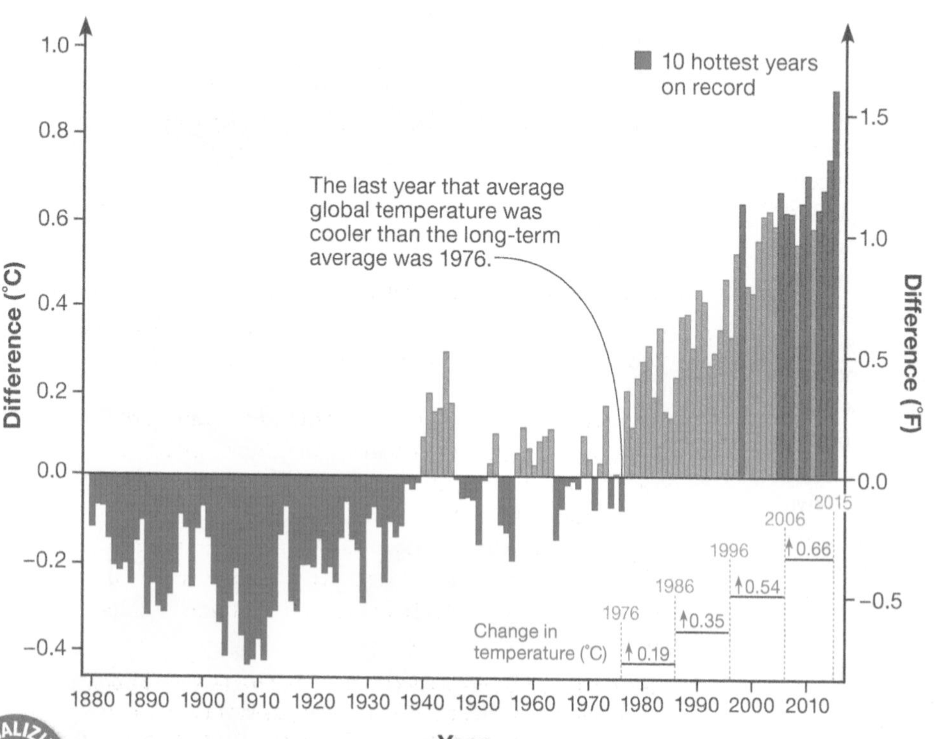

▲ **Figure 38.3A** Differences in average annual global temperatures compared with 20th-century average

Data from National Oceanic and Atmospheric Administration (2016).

The consequences of global warming include more extreme weather events. Precipitation patterns are changing, bringing longer and more intense drought to some areas. In other regions, a greater proportion of the total precipitation is falling in torrential downpours that cause flooding. Hurricane intensity is increasing, fueled by higher sea surface temperatures.

Seasonal changes are also occurring. Warm weather is beginning earlier each year. Cold days and nights and frosts have become less frequent; hot days and nights have become more frequent. Deadly heat waves are increasing in frequency and duration.

Many of these changes will have a profound impact on biodiversity, as we explore in Modules 38.5 and 38.6. In the next module, we examine the causes of rising greenhouse gas emissions.

? **From the map in Figure 38.3B, which biomes are likely to be most affected by global warming, and why?**

The high-latitude biomes of the Northern Hemisphere, tundra and taiga, and the polar ice biomes will be most affected. Those biomes are experiencing the greatest temperature increases. Also, the organisms that live there are adapted to cold weather and a short growing season, so their survival is on the line.

38.4 Human activities are responsible for rising concentrations of greenhouse gases

CONNECTION Without its blanket of natural greenhouse gases such as CO_2 and water vapor to trap heat, Earth would be too cold to support most life. However, increasing the insulation that the blanket provides is making the planet uncomfortably warm, and that increase is occurring rapidly. For 650,000 years, the atmospheric concentration of CO_2 did not exceed 300 parts per million (ppm); the preindustrial concentration was 280 ppm. The year 2016 began with CO_2 above 400 ppm. The levels of other heat-trapping gases, nitrous oxide (N_2O) and methane (CH_4), have increased dramatically, too (**Figure 38.4A**). CO_2 and N_2O are released when fossil fuels—oil, coal, and natural gas—are burned. N_2O is also released when nitrogen fertilizers are used in agriculture. Livestock and landfills are among the factors responsible for increases of atmospheric CH_4. The vast majority of scientists attribute rising concentrations of greenhouse gases—and thus, global warming—to human activities.

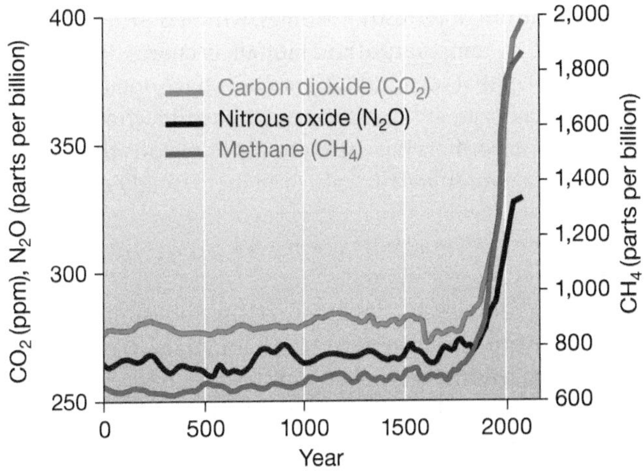

Data from Climate Change 2013: The physical science basis: Fifth assessment report of the International Panel on Climate Change, IPCC Secretariat and epa.gov/climatechange/indicators.

▲ **Figure 38.4A Atmospheric concentrations of CO_2, N_2O (*y* axis, left), and CH_4 (*y* axis, right), as of 2014**

Let's take a closer look at CO_2, the dominant greenhouse gas. The carbon cycle (see Module 37.19) illustrates the theme of **ENERGY AND MATTER** transformation. CO_2 is removed from the atmosphere by the process of photosynthesis and stored in organic molecules such as carbohydrates (**Figure 38.4B**; green arrows). Thus, all of the organic material in an ecosystem is a carbon reservoir. Purple arrows in Figure 38.4B represent carbon released in the form of CO_2. The carbon-containing molecules in living organisms may be used in the process of cellular respiration. Cellular respiration by microorganisms or fungi as they decompose nonliving organic material also releases CO_2. Overall, uptake of CO_2 by photosynthesis roughly equals the release of CO_2 by cellular respiration. In addition, CO_2 is exchanged between the atmosphere and the surface waters of the oceans.

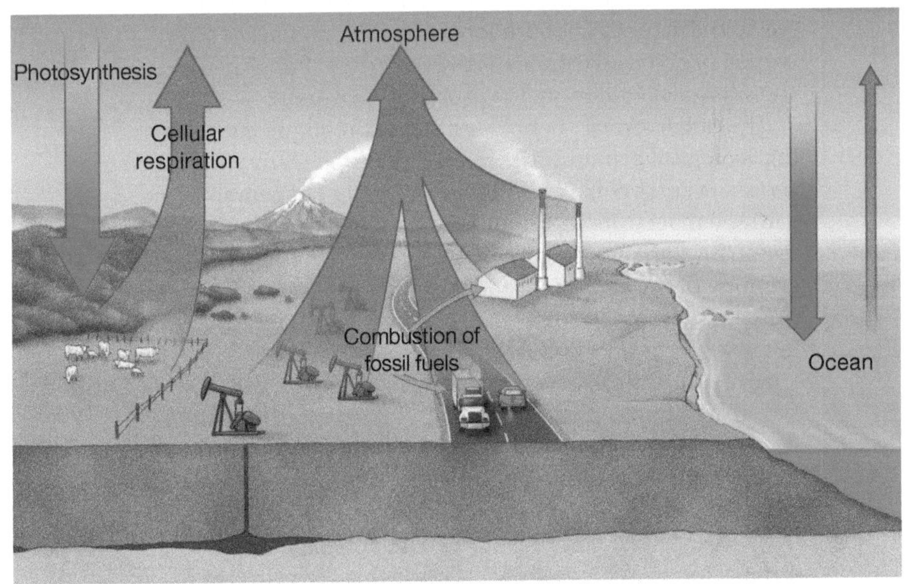

▲ **Figure 38.4B Carbon cycling (Arrow width indicates amount of carbon taken up or released.)**

TRY THIS **Label the diagram by writing the names of carbon-containing molecules (CO_2, organic molecules, carbonic acid) in the appropriate locations.**

Fossil fuels consist of dead organisms that lay buried under sediments for millions of years without being completely decomposed (see Module 17.4). The burning of fossil fuels and wood, which is also an organic material, can be thought of as a rapid form of decomposition. Whereas cellular respiration releases energy from organic molecules slowly and harnesses it to make ATP, combustion liberates the energy rapidly as heat and light. In both processes, the carbon atoms that make up the organic fuel are released in CO_2.

The CO_2 flooding into the atmosphere from combustion of fossil fuels may be absorbed by photosynthetic organisms and incorporated into biomass. But deforestation has significantly decreased the number of CO_2 molecules that can be accommodated by this pathway. CO_2 may also be absorbed into the ocean. For decades, the oceans have been absorbing considerably more CO_2 than they have released, and they will continue to do so, but the excess CO_2 is beginning to affect ocean chemistry. When CO_2 dissolves in water, it becomes carbonic acid. Recently, measurable decreases in ocean pH have raised concern among biologists. Organisms that construct shells or exoskeletons out of calcium carbonate ($CaCO_3$), including corals and many plankton, are most likely to be affected, as decreasing pH reduces the concentration of the carbonate ions (see Module 2.15).

Despite the attempts of many nations to curb carbon emissions (see Module 7.14), atmospheric CO_2 is increasing at an accelerating pace. At this rate, further climate change is inevitable.

? **Search for an online calculator that estimates your carbon footprint, the amount of greenhouse gases your activities are responsible for releasing every year (because CO_2 is the dominant greenhouse gas). What are the primary sources of the greenhouse gases you generate?**

■ Transportation and home energy use are the two major categories contributing to the footprint.

38.5 Climate change affects biomes, ecosystems, communities, and populations

The distribution of terrestrial biomes, which is primarily determined by temperature and rainfall, is changing as a consequence of global warming. Researchers have documented more than a dozen locations around the world where ranges of shrubs and conifers have stretched into regions that were once tundra. Prolonged droughts will increasingly extend the boundaries of deserts. Great expanses of the Amazonian tropical rain forest will gradually become savanna as increased temperatures dry out the soil.

The combined effects of climate change on components of forest ecosystems in western North America have spawned catastrophic wildfire seasons (**Figure 38.5A**). In these mountainous regions, spring snowmelt releases water into streams that sustain forest moisture levels over the summer dry season. With the earlier arrival of spring, snowmelt begins earlier and dwindles away before the dry season ends. As a result, the fire season has been getting longer since the 1980s. In addition, drought conditions have made trees more vulnerable to insect and pathogen attack; vast numbers of dead trees add fuel to the flames. Fires burn longer, and the number of acres burned has increased dramatically. As dry conditions persist and snowpacks diminish, the problem will worsen.

▲ **Figure 38.5A** A wildfire near San Andreas, California, in September 2015

The earlier arrival of warm weather in the spring is disturbing ecological communities in other ways. In many species, certain events are triggered by rising spring temperatures. Earlier temperature increases have hastened the breeding season for some animal species. Satellite images show earlier greening of the landscape, and flowering occurs sooner. For other species, day length is the cue that spring has arrived. Because global warming affects temperature but not day length, interactions between species may become out of sync. For example, plants may bloom before pollinators have emerged, or eggs may hatch before a dependable food source for the young is available. Because the magnitude of seasonal shifts increases from the tropics to the poles, migratory birds may also experience timing mismatches. For instance, birds arriving in the Arctic to breed may find that the period of peak food availability has already passed.

Warming oceans threaten tropical coral reef communities. When stressed by high temperatures, corals expel their symbiotic algae in a phenomenon called bleaching. Corals can recover if temperatures return to normal, but they cannot survive prolonged temperature increases. When corals die, the community is overrun by large algae, and species diversity plummets.

The distributions of populations and species are also shifting in response to climate change. Many species, including the pikas described in the chapter introduction, are adapted to the abiotic conditions in their environment. With rising temperatures, the ranges of many species have already shifted toward the poles or to higher elevations. For example, researchers in Europe and the United States have reported that the ranges of more than two dozen species of butterflies have moved north by as much as 150 miles. Shifts in the ranges of many bird species have also been reported; the Inuit peoples living north of the Arctic Circle have sighted birds such as robins in the region for the first time.

However, species that already live on mountaintops or in polar regions have nowhere to go. Researchers in Costa Rica have reported the disappearance of 20 species of frogs and toads as warmer Pacific Ocean temperatures reduce the dry-season mists in their mountain habitats. In the Arctic, polar bears (**Figure 38.5B**), which stalk their prey on ice and need to store up body fat for the warmer months, are showing signs of starvation as their hunting grounds melt away. Similarly, in the Antarctic, the disappearance of sea ice is blamed for recent decreases in populations of Emperor and Adélie penguins.

▲ **Figure 38.5B** A polar bear (*Ursus maritimus*) with her cubs on melting pack ice in Spitsbergen, Norway

Climate change has been a boon to some organisms, but so far the beneficiaries have been species that have a negative impact on humans. For example, in mountainous regions of Africa, Southeast Asia, and Central and South America, the ranges of mosquitoes that carry diseases such as malaria, yellow fever, and dengue are restricted to lower elevations by frost. With rising temperatures and fewer days of frost, these mosquitoes—and the diseases they carry—are appearing at higher elevations. In another example, longer summers in western North America have enabled bark beetles to complete their life cycle in one year instead of two, promoting beetle outbreaks that have destroyed millions of acres of conifers.

Undesirable plants such as poison ivy and kudzu have also benefited from rising temperatures (see the introduction to Chapter 7 and Module 37.13).

Environmental change has always been a part of life; in fact, it is a key ingredient of evolutionary change. In the next module, we consider the evidence of evolutionary adaptation to global warming.

? **How might timing mismatches caused by climate change affect an individual's reproductive fitness?**

■ Any factor that reduces the number of offspring an organism produces may affect fitness. Examples include flowers emerging too soon for pollinators and birds that arrive too late in the season to find food for offspring.

38.6 Climate change is an agent of natural selection

EVOLUTION CONNECTION

Climate change is already affecting habitats throughout the world. Why do some species appear to be adapting to these changes, while others, like the polar bear, are endangered by them?

In the previous module, we described several ways in which organisms have responded to climate change. For the most part, those examples can be attributed to **phenotypic plasticity**, the ability to change phenotype in response to local environmental conditions. Differences resulting from phenotypic plasticity are within the normal range of expression for an individual's genotype. Phenotypic plasticity allows organisms to cope with short-term environmental changes. On the other hand, phenotypic plasticity is itself a trait that has a genetic basis and can evolve. Researchers studying the effects of climate change on populations have detected microevolutionary changes in phenotypic plasticity.

▲ Figure 38.6A A great tit (*Parus major*)

A common bird in Europe, the great tit (Figure 38.6A) is the third link in a food chain that has been altered by climate change. As warm weather arrives earlier in the spring, tree leaves emerge earlier and caterpillars, which use the swelling buds and unfolding leaves as their food source, hatch sooner. The reproductive success of great tits depends on having an ample supply of these nutritious caterpillars to feed their offspring. Like many other birds, great tits have some phenotypic plasticity in the timing of their breeding, which helps them synchronize their reproduction with the availability of caterpillars. The range and degree of plasticity vary among great tits, and this variation has a genetic basis. Researchers have found evidence of directional selection (see Module 13.14) favoring individuals that have the greatest phenotypic plasticity and lay their eggs earlier, when the abundance of food gives their offspring a better chance of survival.

In another example, scientists studied reproduction in a population of red squirrels (Figure 38.6B) in the Yukon Territory of Canada, where spring temperatures have increased by approximately 2°C in the past three decades. These researchers also found earlier breeding times in the spring. Over a period of 10 years, the date on which female squirrels gave birth advanced by 18 days, a change of about 6 days per generation. Using statistical analysis, the scientists determined that phenotypic plasticity was responsible for most of the shift in breeding times. However, a small but significant portion of the change (roughly 15%) could be attributed to microevolution, directional selection for earlier breeding. The researchers hypothesize that red squirrels born earlier in the year are larger and more capable of gathering and storing food in the autumn and thus have a better chance of successful reproduction the following spring.

▲ Figure 38.6B A red squirrel (*Tamiasciurus hudsonicus*) eating the seeds from a spruce cone

From the scant evidence available at this time, it appears that some populations, especially those with high genetic variability and short life spans, may adapt quickly enough to avoid extinction. In addition to the studies on phenotypic plasticity in great tits and red squirrels, researchers have also documented microevolutionary changes in traits such as dispersal ability and timing of life cycle events in insect populations. However, evolutionary adaptation is unlikely to save species with long life spans and low reproductive rates, such as polar bears and penguins, that are experiencing rapid habitat loss. The rate of climate change is incredibly fast compared with major climate shifts in evolutionary history, and if it continues on its present course, thousands of species will likely become extinct.

? **How does a short generation time hasten the process of evolutionary adaptation?**

■ Each generation has the potential for "testing" new phenotypes in the environment. Shorter generation times result in more opportunities for testing new phenotypes, which in turn allows natural selection to proceed more rapidly.

Conservation Biology and Restoration Ecology

38.7 Protecting endangered populations is one goal of conservation biology

As we have seen in this unit, many of the environmental problems facing us today are consequences of human enterprises. But the science of ecology is not just useful for telling us how things have gone wrong. Ecological research is the foundation for finding solutions to these problems and for reversing the negative consequences of ecosystem alteration. Thus, we end the ecology unit with a section that highlights some of these applications of ecological research.

Conservation biology is a goal-oriented science that seeks to understand and counter the loss of biodiversity. Some conservation biologists focus on protecting populations of threatened species. This approach requires an understanding of the behavior and ecological niche of the target species, including its key habitat requirements and interactions with other members of its community. Threats posed by human activities are also assessed. With this knowledge, scientists can design a plan to expand or protect the resources needed. For example, the territory size required to support a tiger varies with the abundance of prey. Consequently, preserves set aside for Siberian tigers in Russia, where prey are scarce, must be 10 times as large as those provided for Bengal tigers in India.

The case of the black-footed ferret (Figure 38.7A) provides an example of the population approach to conservation. Little was known about this elusive nocturnal predator until the mid-20th century, and by then it was almost too late—population decline was already under way. Black-footed ferrets, one of three ferret species worldwide and the only one found in North America, feed almost exclusively on prairie dogs (see Figure 38.1C). Over the past century, prairie dogs have been extirpated from most of their former range by land-use changes and by poisoning or shooting. Epidemics of sylvatic plague, the animal version of bubonic plague, have devastated populations of black-footed ferrets as well as their prey. When an outbreak threatened to wipe out the last known population of black-footed ferrets, conservation biologists captured 18 remaining individuals and began breeding them in captivity to rebuild population numbers. Genetic variation, a prerequisite for adaptive evolutionary responses to environmental change, is a concern, given the bottleneck effect of near-extinction (see Module 13.12). Matings in the captive breeding facilities are carefully arranged to maintain as much genetic diversity as possible in the ferret populations.

In 1991, biologists began reintroducing captive-bred black-footed ferrets into the wild. Research carried out during these efforts has improved the success rate of reintroductions. For example, scientists found that the predatory behavior of ferrets has both innate and learned components, a discovery that led to more effective methods of preparing captive-bred animals to survive in the wild. Today, about 1,000 adult ferrets are living in the wild at sites scattered from Canada to Mexico. Despite the successes achieved thus far, however, the future of the black-footed ferret is far from secure. Biologists continue to monitor and manage the populations and their habitats.

▲ **Figure 38.7A** A black-footed ferret (*Mustela nigripes*)

Captive breeding programs are being used for numerous other species whose population numbers are perilously low. For example, efforts to save the whooping crane are under way (see Module 35.6). In Hawaii, biologists have planted thousands of greenhouse-grown silverswords (*Argyroxiphium sandwicense*; Figure 38.7B) on the cinder cone of the volcano Mauna Kea in hopes of reestablishing wild populations. Once so abundant that observers mistook their silvery color for snow on the distant peak, silverswords were grazed to near-extinction by goats and sheep that people had brought to the island.

▲ **Figure 38.7B** A Mauna Kea silversword (*Argyroxiphium sandwicense*)

By using a variety of methods, biologists have improved the conservation status of some endangered species, reintroduced many species to areas where they had been extirpated, and reversed declining population trends for others. However, we will not be able to save every threatened species. One way to select worthwhile targets is to identify and protect keystone species that may help preserve entire communities. And in many situations, conservation biologists must look beyond individual species to ecosystems.

? **What do you think is the first priority for conservation biologists when they select a site for ferret reintroduction?**

■ The presence of a sufficiently large population of prairie dogs

38.8 Sustaining ecosystems and landscapes is a conservation priority

One of the most harmful effects of habitat loss is population fragmentation, the splitting and consequent isolation of portions of populations. As you saw in Figure 38.2A, for example, logging carves once-continuous forest into a patchwork of disconnected fragments. For many species, fragmentation means the world instantly shrinks to a fraction of its former size. Populations are reduced, and so are resources such as food and shelter. To counteract the effects of fragmentation, conservation biology often aims to sustain the biodiversity of entire ecosystems and landscapes. Ecologically, a **landscape** is a regional assemblage of interacting ecosystems, such as a forest, adjacent fields, wetlands, streams, and streamside habitats. **Landscape ecology** is the application of ecological principles to the study of the structure and dynamics of a collection of ecosystems.

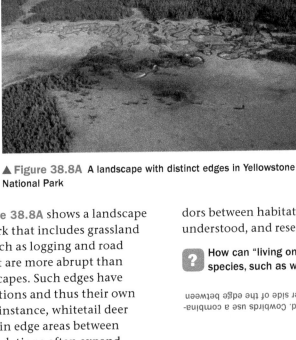

▲ **Figure 38.8A** A landscape with distinct edges in Yellowstone National Park

Edges, or boundaries between ecosystems, are prominent features of landscapes. The photograph in Figure 38.8A shows a landscape area in Yellowstone National Park that includes grassland and forest. Human activities, such as logging and road building, often create edges that are more abrupt than those delineating natural landscapes. Such edges have their own sets of physical conditions and thus their own communities of organisms. For instance, whitetail deer browse on woody shrubs found in edge areas between woods and fields, and their populations often expand when forests are logged or interrupted with housing developments.

Some organisms thrive in edges because they require resources from the two adjacent areas. In one example, populations of the brown-headed cowbird (Figure 38.8B), an edge-adapted species that lays its eggs in the nests of other birds, are currently expanding in many areas of North America. Cowbirds forage in open fields on insects disturbed by or attracted to cattle and other large herbivores. The cowbirds also need forests, where they can parasitize the nests of other birds. Declining populations of several songbird species are correlated with increasing cowbird parasitism and the loss of suitable nesting habitat.

▲ **Figure 38.8B** A male brown-headed cowbird (*Molothrus ater*)

Where habitats have been severely fragmented by human activities, a **movement corridor**, or wildlife corridor, a narrow strip or series of small clumps of high-quality habitat connecting otherwise isolated patches, can be a deciding factor in conserving biodiversity. In many areas, bridges or tunnels have reduced the number of animals killed as they try to cross highways (Figure 38.8C).

Corridors can also promote dispersal and reduce inbreeding in declining populations. Corridors are especially important to species that migrate between different habitats seasonally. In some European countries, amphibian tunnels have been constructed to help frogs, toads, and salamanders cross roads to access their breeding territories.

On the other hand, a corridor can be harmful—as, for example, in the spread of diseases, especially among small subpopulations in closely situated habitat patches. The effects of movement corridors between habitats in a landscape are not completely understood, and researchers continue to study them.

? How can "living on the edge" be a good thing for some species, such as whitetail deer and cowbirds?

■ Edges provide whitetail deer with a source of food. Cowbirds use a combination of resources from the two ecosystems on either side of the edge between field and forest.

▲ **Figure 38.8C** A wildlife bridge on the Flathead Indian Reservation in northwestern Montana

38.9 Establishing protected areas slows the loss of biodiversity

Conservation biologists are applying their understanding of population, community, ecosystem, and landscape dynamics in establishing parks, wilderness areas, and other legally protected nature reserves. Choosing locations for protection often focuses on biodiversity hot spots. A **biodiversity hot spot** is a relatively small area with numerous **endemic species**, those that are found nowhere else in the world, and a large number of endangered and threatened species (Figure 38.9A). The "hottest" of the terrestrial biodiversity hot spots total less than 1.5% of Earth's land but are home to a third of all species of plants and vertebrates. For example, all lemurs are endemic to Madagascar, which is home to more than 50 species. In fact, almost all of the mammals, reptiles, amphibians, and plants that inhabit Madagascar are endemic. There are also hot spots in aquatic ecosystems, such as certain river systems and coral reefs.

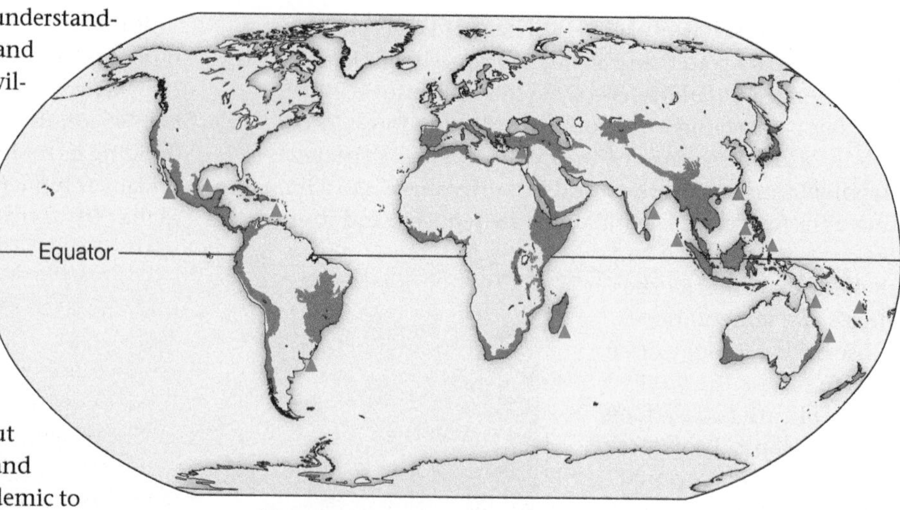

Adapted from Critical Ecosystem Partnership Fund, *Annual Report 2014*, Conservation International.

▲ **Figure 38.9A** Earth's terrestrial (purple) and marine (red) biodiversity hot spots

Because endemic species are limited to specific areas, they are highly sensitive to habitat degradation. Thus, biodiversity hot spots can also be hot spots of extinction. They rank high on the list of areas demanding strong global conservation efforts.

Concentrations of species provide an opportunity to protect many species in very limited areas. However, the "hot spot" designation tends to favor the most noticeable organisms, especially vertebrates and plants. Invertebrates and microorganisms are often overlooked. Furthermore, species endangerment is a truly global problem, and it is important that a focus on hot spots not detract from efforts to conserve habitats and species diversity in other areas.

Migratory species pose a special problem for conservationists. For example, monarch butterflies occupy much of the United States and Canada during the summer months, but migrate in the autumn to specific sites in Mexico and California, where they congregate in huge numbers. Overwintering populations are particularly susceptible to habitat disturbances because they are concentrated in small areas. Thus, habitat preservation must extend across all of the sites that monarchs inhabit in order to protect them. The situation is similar for many species of migratory songbirds, waterfowl, marine mammals, and sea turtles.

Sea turtles, such as the loggerhead turtle (Figure 38.9B), are threatened both in their ocean feeding grounds and on land. Loggerheads take about 20 years to reach sexual maturity, and great numbers of juveniles and adults are drowned at sea when caught in fishing nets. The adults mate at sea, and the females migrate to specific sites on sandy beaches to lay their eggs. Buried in shallow depressions, the eggs are susceptible to predators, especially raccoons. And many egg-laying sites have become housing developments and beachside resorts.

An ongoing international effort to conserve sea turtles focuses both on protecting egg-laying sites and minimizing the death rates of adults and juveniles at sea.

Currently, governments have set aside about 7% of the world's land in various forms of reserves. One major conservation question is whether it is better to create one large reserve or a group of smaller ones. Far-ranging animals with low-density populations—predators such as wolves and tigers—require extensive habitats. As conservation biologists learn more about the requirements for achieving minimum population sizes to sustain endangered species, it is becoming clear that most national parks and other reserves are far too small. Given political and economic realities, it is unlikely that many existing parks will be enlarged, and most new reserves will also be too small. In the next two modules, we look at two approaches to resolving this problem.

? **What is a biodiversity hot spot?**

■ A relatively small area with a disproportionate number of endangered and threatened species, many of which are endemic

▲ **Figure 38.9B** An adult loggerhead turtle (*Caretta caretta*) swimming off the coast of Belize

38.10 Zoned reserves are an attempt to reverse ecosystem disruption

Conservation of Earth's natural resources is not purely a scientific issue. The causes of declining biodiversity are rooted in complex social and economic issues, and the solutions must take these factors into account. Let's look at how the small Central American nation of Costa Rica is managing its biodiversity.

Despite its small size (about 51,000 km^2, the size of New Hampshire and Vermont combined), Costa Rica is a treasure trove of biodiversity. Its varied ecosystems, which extend over mountains and two coasts, are home to at least half a million species. As Figure 38.9A shows, the entire country is a biodiversity hot spot. Since the 1970s, the Costa Rican government and international agencies have worked together to preserve these unique assets. Approximately 25% of Costa Rica's territory is currently protected in some way (**Figure 38.10A**).

One type of protection is called a **zoned reserve**, an extensive region of land that includes one or more areas undisturbed by humans. The lands surrounding these areas continue to be used to support the human population, but they are protected from extensive alteration. As a result, they serve as a buffer zone, or shield, against further intrusion into the undisturbed areas. A primary goal of the zoned reserve approach is to develop a social and economic climate in the buffer zone that is compatible with the long-term viability of the protected area.

Costa Rica is making progress in managing its reserves so that the buffer zones provide a steady, lasting supply of forest products, water, and hydroelectric power and also support sustainable agriculture. An important goal is providing a stable economic base for people living there. Destructive practices that are not compatible with long-term ecosystem stability and from which there is often little local profit are gradually being discouraged. Such destructive practices include massive logging, large-scale single-crop agriculture, and extensive mining.

However, a recent analysis showed mixed results for Costa Rica's system of zoned reserves. The good news is that negligible deforestation has occurred within and just beyond protected parkland boundaries. However, some deforestation has taken place in the buffer zones, with plantations of cash crops such as banana and palm replacing the natural vegetation. Conservationists fear that continuing these practices will isolate protected areas, restricting gene flow and decreasing species and genetic diversity.

Costa Rica's commitment to conservation has resulted in a new source of income for the country—**ecotourism**, travel to natural areas for tourism and recreation (**Figure 38.10B**). People from all over the world come to experience Costa Rica's spectacular range of biodiversity, generating thousands of jobs and a significant chunk of the country's revenue. Worldwide, ecotourism has grown into a multibillion-dollar industry as tourists flock to the world's remaining natural areas. Whether ecotourism dollars ultimately help conserve Earth's biodiversity, however, remains to be seen.

? **Why is it important for zoned reserves to prevent large-scale alterations of habitat in the buffer zones? Why is it also important to support sustainable development for the people living there?**

■ Large-scale disruptions in buffer zones could impact the nearby undisturbed areas. Preservation is a realistic goal only if it is compatible with an acceptable standard of living for the local people.

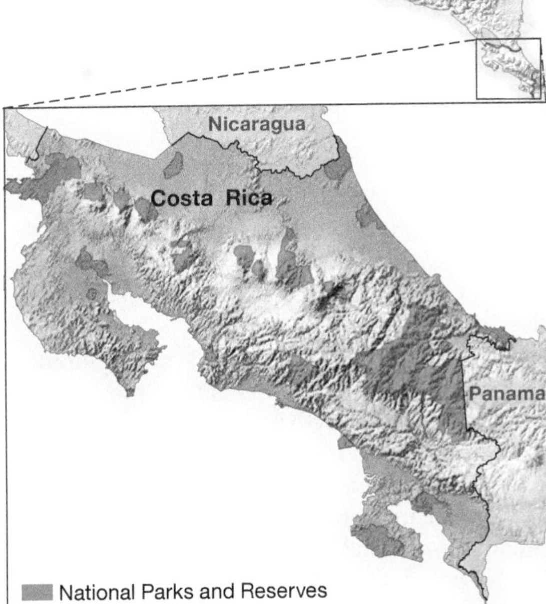

▲ **Figure 38.10A** Protected reserves in Costa Rica

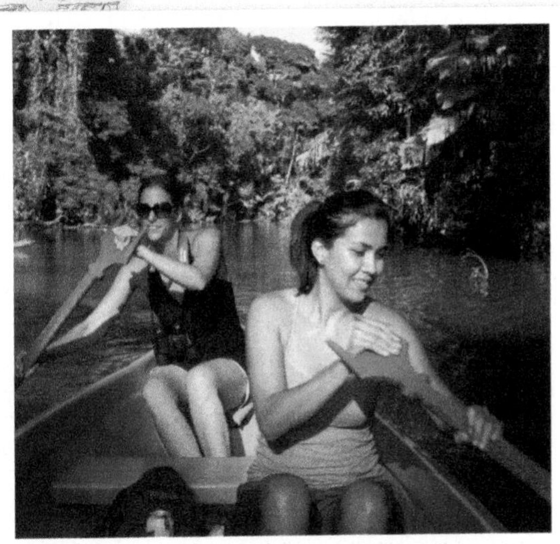

▲ **Figure 38.10B** Ecotourism: seeing the tropical rain forest by boat in Costa Rica's Tortuguero National Park

38.11 The Yellowstone to Yukon Conservation Initiative seeks to preserve biodiversity by connecting protected areas

SCIENTIFIC THINKING

In *The Once and Future King*, a fantasy novel about the childhood of King Arthur, the boy learns valuable lessons while magically inhabiting animal forms. As a bird flying high over the land and sea, he realizes that political boundaries exist only in human minds. The same lesson was emphatically driven home to biologists monitoring the travels of a gray wolf (Figure 38.11A) they called Pluie (French for "rain"). After capturing Pluie in western Canada in 1991, the scientists fitted her with a radio tracking collar and released her. They were stunned by what they learned. Over the next two years, the wolf roamed over an area of more than 100,000 km^2 (38,600 square miles). Heedless of the boundaries created by humans, she traveled from Alberta to British Columbia in Canada, then crossed into the United States and passed through Montana, Idaho, and Washington before returning to British Columbia—a loop of more than 900 miles—where she remained for a few weeks before heading south again. However, her ignorance of the line between protected reserves and legal hunting areas proved fatal. Pluie, her mate, and three cubs were shot while travelling outside the boundary of a national park.

▲ Figure 38.11A A gray wolf (*Canis lupus*)

Biologists who had studied Pluie realized that the wolf's life captured all the promise—and all the pitfalls—of efforts to protect her. She had thrived for nine years within the sporadic shelter of parks and other protected territory. But such lands were never big enough to hold her. Like others of her species (*Canis lupus*), Pluie needed more room. Reserves could shield animals briefly, the scientists realized, but true protection would have to include safe passages between reserves.

Can Earth's biodiversity be saved?

This research inspired the creation of the Yellowstone to Yukon Conservation Initiative (Y2Y), one of the world's most ambitious conservation biology efforts. The initiative aims to preserve the web of life that has long defined the Rocky Mountains of Canada and the northern United States. The area is dotted with famous parks, including Canada's Banff National Park and Yellowstone and Glacier National Parks in the United States. The idea is not to create one giant park, but rather to connect a string of more than 700 protected areas, including national, state, and provincial parks and national forests, with protected corridors where wildlife can travel safely.

Y2Y now stretches 3,200 km (roughly 2,000 miles) from Wyoming to the northern part of the Yukon Territory, encompassing temperate grasslands, coniferous forest, and alpine and arctic tundra (Figure 38.11B, on facing page). Its total area is 1.3 million km^2 (half a million square miles), roughly three times the size of California, but only about 10% of this land has protected status. Y2Y is also unique in its range of elevations. As mentioned in Module 38.5, some populations can respond to climate change by shifting their range to higher latitudes or higher altitudes. Y2Y can accommodate both types of movement. Studies show that populations of pikas (see chapter introduction) at low elevations are at greatest risk for extirpation; Y2Y offers upward mobility.

Conservationists must also seek ways that wildlife populations can coexist with industries such as logging, ranching, gas and oil exploration, and tourism that are important to the human population in the Y2Y region. For example, specially constructed road overpasses (see Figure 38.8C) used by wolves, elk, and grizzly bears are complemented by underground passages for animals such as black bears and cougars that prefer to travel under cover. In some areas, fences have been installed along railroad tracks to reduce the number of animals killed while scavenging spilled grains.

Many of the signature species that live in this vast region, such as grizzly bears, lynx, moose, and elk, don't confine themselves to human boundaries. But few have as great a range as the wolf. If Y2Y can provide safe passage for gray wolves, it will have also created secure zones for other animals in the Rockies.

Gray wolves once roamed all of North America. These carnivorous hunters live in packs that protect pups and search cooperatively for food. A pack may have a territory of about 130 km^2 or range much farther to find prey. The wolf's hunting prowess kept it the top predator of North American ecosystems as long as the human population was small. Things changed when large numbers of people migrated from Europe and pushed far into the continent.

Deeming wolves a dangerous predator and competitor that threatened people and livestock, settlers in the United States launched widespread campaigns to wipe out wolves. By the early 20th century, gray wolves were nearly extinct in the lower 48 states, with only a few hundred surviving in northern Minnesota. More managed to stay alive in the wilds of less populated western Canada and Alaska.

In Yellowstone National Park in Wyoming, wolves were extirpated by the mid-1920s. The decades that followed were marked by dramatic increases in the elk population.

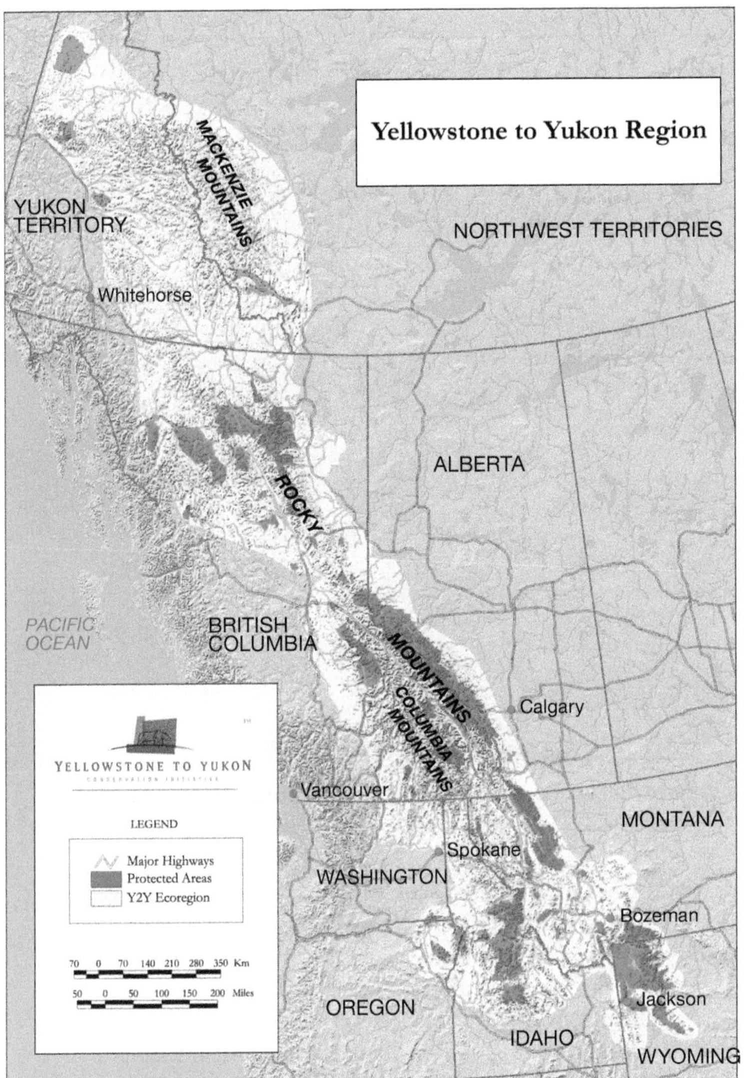

▲ **Figure 38.11B** A map showing the Yellowstone to Yukon Conservation Initiative region

In winter, elk descend from alpine meadows to the shelter of lower elevations, where they browse on the twigs and bark of young trees and shrubs (**Figure 38.11C**). Studies carried out over five decades showed the impact of the burgeoning elk herd on woody species such as aspen and willow. New shoots rarely grew taller than 80 cm (about 30 inches), the level at which elk browse, while the same species grown in elk-proof enclosures grew rapidly. Berry-producing shrubs were also heavily damaged by browsing. Over time, stream banks and nearby hillsides were stripped of plant cover, leading to soil erosion. To prevent further ecosystem deterioration, park managers took measures to reduce the elk herd. Large numbers of elk were captured and relocated; finally, park managers even resorted to killing them.

▲ **Figure 38.11C** Elk (*Cervus elaphus*) browsing

In 1991, the U.S. Fish and Wildlife Service launched a controversial campaign to bring wolves back to Yellowstone. After careful planning, about 30 wolves from Canada were released in the park in 1995 and 1996. The extirpation and later reintroduction of wolves into Yellowstone constituted a natural experiment, a type of observational experiment that takes advantage of treatments that were not intentionally created for a scientific experiment. This natural experiment provided an opportunity to compare community structure and dynamics with and without the gray wolf. In a report published in 2011, scientists summarized results from more than a dozen studies documenting the recovery of woody species such as aspen, cottonwood, and willow in some of the areas that had been overbrowsed. The largest elk herd decreased in size from pre-1995 highs of more than 15,000 to around 6,000 in 2005. But the presence of wolves has had further-reaching effects on species diversity in Yellowstone.

After the expanding elk herd decimated the willows, beavers, for which willows are a key resource, had all but disappeared from north Yellowstone. As predation by wolves reduced the elk population, willows and other vegetation once again flourished, and the beaver population recovered. Beaver dams created ponds and wetlands that attract waterfowl and support populations of amphibians, fish, and other animals. The resurgence of trees and shrubs in turn provided food and shelter for birds and small herbivores such as rodents and rabbits. Small herbivores also benefited from the wolf's impact on their main predator, coyotes. Within a few years of their reintroduction, wolves had reduced the population density of coyotes by 50%. That made more prey available for foxes, badgers, hawks, and owls. In addition, wolf kills provided a bonanza for scavengers, including ravens, magpies, eagles, black bears, and grizzly bears. The region was recovering its biodiversity.

In late 2013, 10 packs numbering approximately 95 gray wolves occupied the park. And true to their nature, Yellowstone's wolves haven't followed human-imposed borders; several packs have been found just outside the park. Meanwhile, the migrations of Canadian wolves, along with smaller release programs, have brought the animals back to Idaho and Montana. In 2011, federal officials removed gray wolves in those states from the endangered species list, making wolf hunting legal. When Yellowstone wolves cross the invisible park boundary they are fair game.

In addition to creating reserves to protect species and their habitats from human disruptions, conservation efforts also attempt to restore ecosystems degraded by human activities. We look at the field of restoration ecology next.

? **What hypothesis was tested by constructing elk-proof enclosures?**

■ Elk are responsible for the decline of woody plants such as aspen and willow.

38.12 The study of how to restore degraded habitats is a developing science

CONNECTION For centuries, humans have altered and degraded natural areas without considering the consequences. But as people have gradually come to realize the severity of some of the consequences of ecosystem alteration, they have sought ways to return degraded areas to their natural state. The expanding field of **restoration ecology** uses ecological principles to develop methods of achieving this goal.

One of the major strategies in restoration ecology is bioremediation, the use of living organisms to detoxify polluted ecosystems. For example, bacteria have been used to clean up oil spills and old mining sites. Bacteria are also employed to metabolize toxins in dump sites. Certain species of plants have successfully extracted potentially toxic metals such as zinc, nickel, and lead from contaminated soil. As the plants grow, they absorb large amounts of the toxins from the soil and store them in their bodies. The plants are then harvested and disposed of in hazardous waste landfills. Researchers are also investigating the use of trees and lichens to clean up soil polluted with uranium. In Japan, sunflowers are being planted in an attempt to decontaminate soil polluted by the nuclear disaster that followed the 2011 earthquake and tsunami (Figure 38.12A, at right).

▲ Figure 38.12A Sunflowers planted for bioremediation in Natori, Japan, after the 2011 tsunami

Some restoration projects have the broader goal of returning ecosystems to their natural state, which may involve replanting vegetation, fencing out non-native animals, or removing dams that restrict water flow. Hundreds of restoration projects are currently under way in the United States. One of the most ambitious endeavors is the Kissimmee River project in south central Florida.

▲ Figure 38.12B Restoring the natural water flow patterns of the Kissimmee River

The Kissimmee River was once a meandering shallow river that wound its way through central Florida from Lake Kissimmee southward into Lake Okeechobee (Figure 38.12B, inset). Periodic flooding of the river covered a wide floodplain during about half of the year, creating wetlands that provided critical habitat for vast numbers of birds, fishes, and invertebrates. As often happens, however, people saw the floodplain as wasted land that could be developed if the flooding were controlled. Between 1962 and 1971, the U.S. Army Corps of Engineers converted the 166-km wandering river into a straight canal 9 m deep, 100 m wide, and 90 km long. This project drained approximately 31,000 acres of wetlands, with significant negative impacts on fish and wetland bird populations. Spawning and foraging habitats for fishes were eliminated, and important sport fishes, such as largemouth bass, were replaced by nongame species more tolerant of the lower oxygen concentration in the deeper canal. The populations of waterfowl declined by 92%, and the number of bald eagle nesting territories decreased by 70%. Without the marshes to help filter and reduce agricultural runoff, phosphorus and other excess nutrients were transported through Lake Okeechobee into the Everglades ecosystem to the south.

As these negative ecological effects began to be recognized, public pressure to restore the river grew. In 1992, Congress authorized the

Kissimmee River Restoration Project, one of the largest landscape restoration projects and ecological experiments in the world. The plan involves removing water control structures such as dams, reservoirs, and channel modifications, and filling in about 35 km of the canal. Work began in 1999 and is slated to be completed in 2019. As shown in Figure 38.12B, the natural curves of the river are a pleasing contrast to the artificial linearity of the backfilled canal. Birds and other wildlife have returned in unexpected numbers to the 11,000 acres of wetlands that have been restored. The marshes are filled with native vegetation, and game fishes again swim in the river channels. However, drought conditions in recent years have threatened the southward flow of the Kissimmee River into Lake Okeechobee. The potential for water shortages in southern Florida has renewed attention to the urgent need to complete an even more ambitious project, the restoration of the Everglades.

? How will the Kissimmee River Restoration Project improve water quality in the Everglades ecosystem?

■ The wetlands filter agricultural runoff and prevent excess nutrients from entering the Everglades.

38.13 Sustainable development is an ultimate goal

The demand for the "provisioning" services of ecosystems, such as food, fibers, and water, is increasing as the world population grows and becomes more affluent. Although these demands are currently being met, they are satisfied at the expense of other critical ecosystem services, such as climate regulation and protection against natural disasters. Clearly, we have set ourselves and the rest of the biosphere on a precarious path into the future. How can we best manage Earth's resources to ensure that all generations inherit an adequate supply of natural and economic resources and a relatively stable environment?

Many nations, scientific societies, and private foundations have embraced the concept of **sustainable development**, development that meets the needs of people today without limiting the ability of future generations to meet their needs. The Ecological Society of America, the world's largest organization of ecologists, endorses a research agenda called the Sustainable Biosphere Initiative. The goal of this initiative is to acquire the basic ecological information necessary for the intelligent and responsible development, management, and conservation of Earth's resources. The research agenda includes devising ways to sustain the productivity of natural and artificial ecosystems and studying the relationship between biological diversity, climate change, and ecological processes.

Sustainable development doesn't only depend on continued research and application of ecological knowledge. It also requires us to connect the life sciences with the social sciences, economics, and humanities. Conservation and restoration of biodiversity is only one side of sustainable development; the other key facet is improving the human condition. Public education and the political commitment and cooperation of nations, especially the United States, are essential to the success of this endeavor.

The image of the red panda on this book's cover and in Figure 38.13 serves as a reminder of what we stand to lose if we fail to recognize and solve the ecological crises at hand. Red pandas are "living fossils," the only member of their family still in existence. Their habitat is increasingly fragmented as people claim ever more land for agriculture. Grazing cattle trample the bamboo that is the mainstay of the red panda's diet. When red pandas travel across cleared land to reach new feeding grounds, they are vulnerable to predators, including humans, who hunt them for their meat or fur or to use in medicines. In addition, captured red pandas are becoming popular pets in China and some other parts of Asia.

▲ Figure 38.13 Red panda (*Ailurus fulgens*)

Biology is the scientific expression of the human desire to know nature. We are most likely to save what we appreciate, and we are most likely to appreciate what we understand. By learning about the processes and diversity of life, we also become more aware of our dependence on healthy ecosystems. An awareness of our unique ability to alter the biosphere and jeopardize the existence of other species, as well as our own, may help us choose a path toward a sustainable future.

The risk of a world without adequate natural resources for all its people is not a vision of the distant future. It is a prospect for your children's lifetime, or perhaps even your own. But although the current state of the biosphere is grim, the situation is far from hopeless. Now is the time to aggressively pursue more knowledge about life and to work toward long-term sustainability.

Why is a concern for the well-being of future generations essential for progress toward sustainable development?

■ Sustainable development is a long-term goal—longer than a human lifetime. Preoccupation with the here and now is an obstacle to sustainable development because it discourages behavior that benefits future generations.

CHAPTER 38 REVIEW

For practice quizzes, BioFlix animations, MP3 tutorials, video tutors, and more study tools designed for this textbook, go to MasteringBiology™

REVIEWING THE CONCEPTS

The Loss of Biodiversity (38.1–38.6)

38.1 Loss of biodiversity includes the loss of ecosystems, species, and genes. Although valuable for its own sake, biodiversity also provides food, fibers, medicines, and ecosystem services.

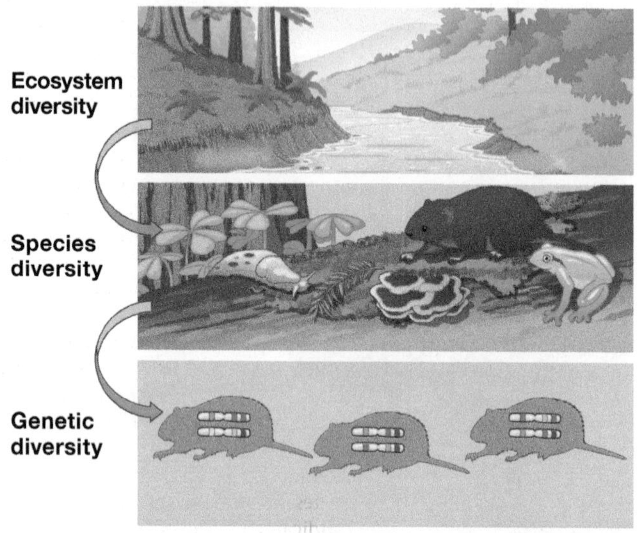

38.2 Habitat loss, invasive species, overharvesting, pollution, and climate change are major threats to biodiversity. Human alteration of habitats is the single greatest threat to biodiversity. Invasive species disrupt communities by competing with, preying on, or parasitizing native species. Harvesting at rates that exceed a population's ability to rebound is a threat to many species. Human activities produce diverse pollutants that may affect ecosystems far from their source. Biomagnification concentrates synthetic toxins that cannot be degraded by organisms.

38.3 Rapid warming is changing the global climate. Increased global temperature caused by rising concentrations of greenhouse gases is changing climate patterns, with grave consequences.

38.4 Human activities are responsible for rising concentrations of greenhouse gases. Much of the increase is the result of burning fossil fuels.

38.5 Climate change affects biomes, ecosystems, communities, and populations. Organisms that live at high latitudes and high elevations are experiencing the greatest impact.

38.6 Climate change is an agent of natural selection. Phenotypic plasticity has minimized the impact on some species, and several cases of microevolutionary change have been observed. However, the rapidity of the environmental changes makes it unlikely that evolutionary processes will save many species from extinction.

Conservation Biology and Restoration Ecology (38.7–38.13)

38.7 Protecting endangered populations is one goal of conservation biology. Conservation biology is a goal-driven science that seeks to understand and counter the rapid loss of biodiversity. Some conservation biologists direct their efforts at increasing populations that are endangered.

38.8 Sustaining ecosystems and landscapes is a conservation priority. Conservation efforts are increasingly aimed at sustaining ecosystems and landscapes. Edges between ecosystems have distinct sets of features and species. The increased frequency and abruptness of edges caused by human activities can accelerate species loss. Movement corridors connecting isolated habitats may be helpful to fragmented populations.

38.9 Establishing protected areas slows the loss of biodiversity. Biodiversity hot spots have high concentrations of endemic species.

38.10 Zoned reserves are an attempt to reverse ecosystem disruption. Zoned reserves are undisturbed wildlands surrounded by buffer zones of compatible economic development. Ecotourism has become an important source of revenue for conservation efforts.

38.11 The Yellowstone to Yukon Conservation Initiative seeks to preserve biodiversity by connecting protected areas. The success of this innovative international research and conservation effort hinged on the reintroduction of gray wolves.

38.12 The study of how to restore degraded habitats is a developing science. Restoration ecology uses ecological principles to return degraded areas to their natural state, a process that may include detoxifying polluted ecosystems, replanting native vegetation, and returning waterways to their natural course. Large-scale restoration projects attempt to restore damaged landscapes.

38.13 Sustainable development is an ultimate goal. Sustainable development depends on increasing and applying ecological knowledge as well as valuing our linkages to the biosphere.

CONNECTING THE CONCEPTS

1. Complete the following map, which organizes some of the key concepts of conservation biology.

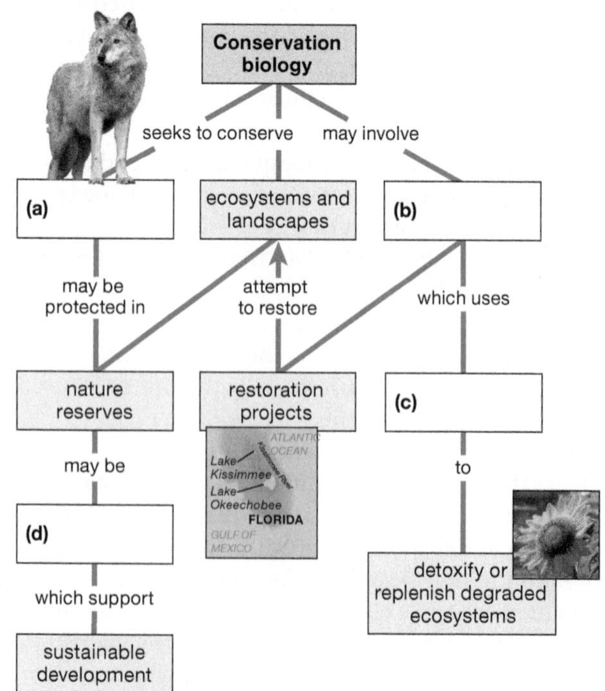

TESTING YOUR KNOWLEDGE

Level 1: Knowledge/Comprehension

2. Which of these statements best describes what conservation biologists mean by the "the rapid loss of biodiversity"?
   a. Introduced species, such as starlings and zebra mussels, have rapidly expanded their ranges.
   b. Harvests of marine fishes, such as cod and bluefin tuna, are declining.
   c. The current species extinction rate is as much as 100 times greater than at any time in the past 100,000 years.
   d. Many potential medicines are being lost as plant species become extinct.
3. Which of the following currently poses the single greatest threat to biodiversity?
   a. invasive species
   b. overhunting
   c. habitat loss
   d. pollution
4. Which of the following is characteristic of endemic species?
   a. They are often found in biodiversity hot spots.
   b. They are distributed widely in the biosphere.
   c. They require edges between ecosystems.
   d. They are often keystone species whose presence helps to structure a community.
5. Ospreys and other top predators are most severely affected by pesticides such as PCBs because they
   a. are especially sensitive to chemicals.
   b. have very long life spans.
   c. store the pesticides in their tissues.
   d. consume prey in which pesticides are concentrated.
6. Movement corridors are
   a. the routes taken by migratory animals.
   b. strips or clumps of habitat that connect isolated fragments of habitat.
   c. landscapes that include several different ecosystems.
   d. edges, or boundaries, between ecosystems.
7. With limited resources, conservation biologists need to prioritize their efforts. Of the following choices, which should receive the greatest attention for the goal of conserving biodiversity?
   a. a commercially important species
   b. all endangered vertebrate species
   c. a declining keystone species in a community
   d. all endangered species
8. Which of the following statements about protected areas is not correct?
   a. We now protect 25% of the land areas of the planet.
   b. National parks are only one type of protected area.
   c. Most reserves are smaller in size than the ranges of some of the species they are meant to protect.
   d. Management of protected areas must coordinate with the management of lands outside the protected zone.

Level 2: Application/Analysis

9. What are the three levels of biological diversity? Explain how human activities threaten each of these levels.
10. What are "greenhouse gases"? Why are they important to life on Earth?
11. What are the causes and possible consequences of climate change? Why is international cooperation necessary if we are to solve this problem?

Level 3: Synthesis/Evaluation

12. **SCIENTIFIC THINKING** The human-generated increase in greenhouse gases is a natural experiment (see Module 38.11) that provides many opportunities to study the effects of warming temperatures and climate change on populations, communities, and ecosystems. For example, snowshoe hares are adapted to the climate of their habitat in the taiga of the high mountains and northern regions of North America. One prominent adaptation is seasonal changes in fur color—a white winter coat that turns brown in the spring—that camouflage hares from a long list of predators, including lynx, bobcats, martens, weasels, foxes, owls, hawks, mountain lions, wolves, and coyotes. These color changes are triggered by day length. As increasing spring temperatures cause earlier snowmelt in the taiga, biologists have observed many white hares sitting on brown earth. Suggest how this natural experiment could be used to investigate the effects of climate change on populations and communities in the taiga ecosystem (assume historical data are available).
13. The price of energy does not reflect its real costs. What kinds of hidden environmental costs are not reflected in the price of fossil fuels? How are these costs paid, and by whom? Do you think these costs could or should be figured into the price of oil? How might that be done?
14. Research your country's per capita carbon emissions. Data can be found at a number of websites, including the World Bank (http://data.worldbank.org/indicator/EN.ATM.CO2E.PC) and the World Resources Institute (http://www.wri.org; http://carbonfootprintofnations.com/). Compare your carbon footprint with the average for your country. (See the question at the end of Module 38.4.) How can individuals reduce the greenhouse gas emissions for which they are directly responsible? Make a list of actions that you are willing to take to reduce your carbon footprint.
15. Until recently, response to environmental problems has been fragmented—an antipollution law here, incentives for recycling there. Meanwhile, the problems of the gap between rich and poor nations, diminishing resources, and pollution continue to grow. Now people and governments are starting to envision a sustainable society. The Worldwatch Institute, a respected environmental monitoring organization, estimates that we must reach sustainability by the year 2030 to avoid economic and environmental disaster. To get there, we must begin shaping a sustainable society during this decade. In what ways is our present system not sustainable? What might a sustainable society be like? Do you think a sustainable society is an achievable goal? Why or why not? What is the alternative? What might you do to work toward sustainability? What are the major roadblocks to achieving sustainability? How would your life be different in a sustainable society?

Answers to all questions can be found in Appendix 4.

APPENDIX 1

Metric Conversion Table

Measurement	Unit and Abbreviation	Metric Equivalent	Approximate Metric-to-English Conversion Factor	Approximate English-to-Metric Conversion Factor
Length	1 kilometer (km)	= 1,000 (10^3) meters	1 km = 0.6 mile	1 mile = 1.6 km
	1 meter (m)	= 100 (10^2) centimeters	1 m = 1.1 yards	1 yard = 0.9 m
		= 1,000 millimeters	1 m = 3.3 feet	1 foot = 0.3 m
			1 m = 39.4 inches	
	1 centimeter (cm)	= 0.01 (10^{-2}) meter	1 cm = 0.4 inch	1 foot = 30.5 cm
				1 inch = 2.5 cm
	1 millimeter (mm)	= 0.001 (10^{-3}) meter	1 mm = 0.04 inch	
	1 micrometer (μm)	= 10^{-6} meter (10^{-3} mm)		
	1 nanometer (nm)	= 10^{-9} meter (10^{-3} μm)		
	1 angstrom (Å)	= 10^{-10} meter (10^{-4} μm)		
Area	1 hectare (ha)	= 10,000 square meters	1 ha = 2.5 acres	1 acre = 0.4 ha
	1 square meter (m^2)	= 10,000 square centimeters	1 m^2 = 1.2 square yards	1 square yard = 0.8 m^2
			1 m^2 = 10.8 square feet	1 square foot = 0.09 m^2
	1 square centimeter (cm^2)	= 100 square millimeters	1 cm^2 = 0.16 square inch	1 square inch = 6.5 cm^2
Mass	1 metric ton (t)	= 1,000 kilograms	1 t = 1.1 tons	1 ton = 0.91 t
	1 kilogram (kg)	= 1,000 grams	1 kg = 2.2 pounds	1 pound = 0.45 kg
	1 gram (g)	= 1,000 milligrams	1 g = 0.04 ounce	1 ounce = 28.35 g
			1 g = 15.4 grains	
	1 milligram (mg)	= 10^{-3} gram	1 mg = 0.02 grain	
	1 microgram (μg)	= 10^{-6} gram		
Volume (Solids)	1 cubic meter (m^3)	= 1,000,000 cubic centimeters	1 m^3 = 1.3 cubic yards	1 cubic yard = 0.8 m^3
			1 m^3 = 35.3 cubic feet	1 cubic foot = 0.03 m^3
	1 cubic centimeter (cm^3 or cc)	= 10^{-6} cubic meter	1 cm^3 = 0.06 cubic inch	1 cubic inch = 16.4 cm^3
	1 cubic millimeter (mm^3)	= 10^{-9} cubic meter (10^{-3} cubic centimeter)		
Volume (Liquids and Gases)	1 kiloliter (kL or kl)	= 1,000 liters	1 kL = 264.2 gallons	
	1 liter (L or l)	= 1,000 milliliters	1 L = 0.26 gallon	1 gallon = 3.79 L
			1 L = 1.06 quarts	1 quart = 0.95 L
	1 milliliter (mL or ml)	= 10^{-3} liter	1 mL = 0.03 fluid ounce	1 quart = 946 mL
		= 1 cubic centimeter	1 mL = $^1/_4$ teaspoon	1 pint = 473 mL
			1 mL = 15–16 drops	1 fluid ounce = 29.6 mL
				1 teaspoon = 5 mL
	1 microliter (μL or μl)	= 10^{-6} liter (10^{-3} milliliter)		
Time	1 second (s)	= $^1/_{60}$ minute		
	1 millisecond (ms)	= 10^{-3} second		
Temperature	Degrees Celsius (°C)		°F = $^9/_5$ °C + 32	°C = $^5/_9$ (°F − 32)

APPENDIX 2

The Periodic Table

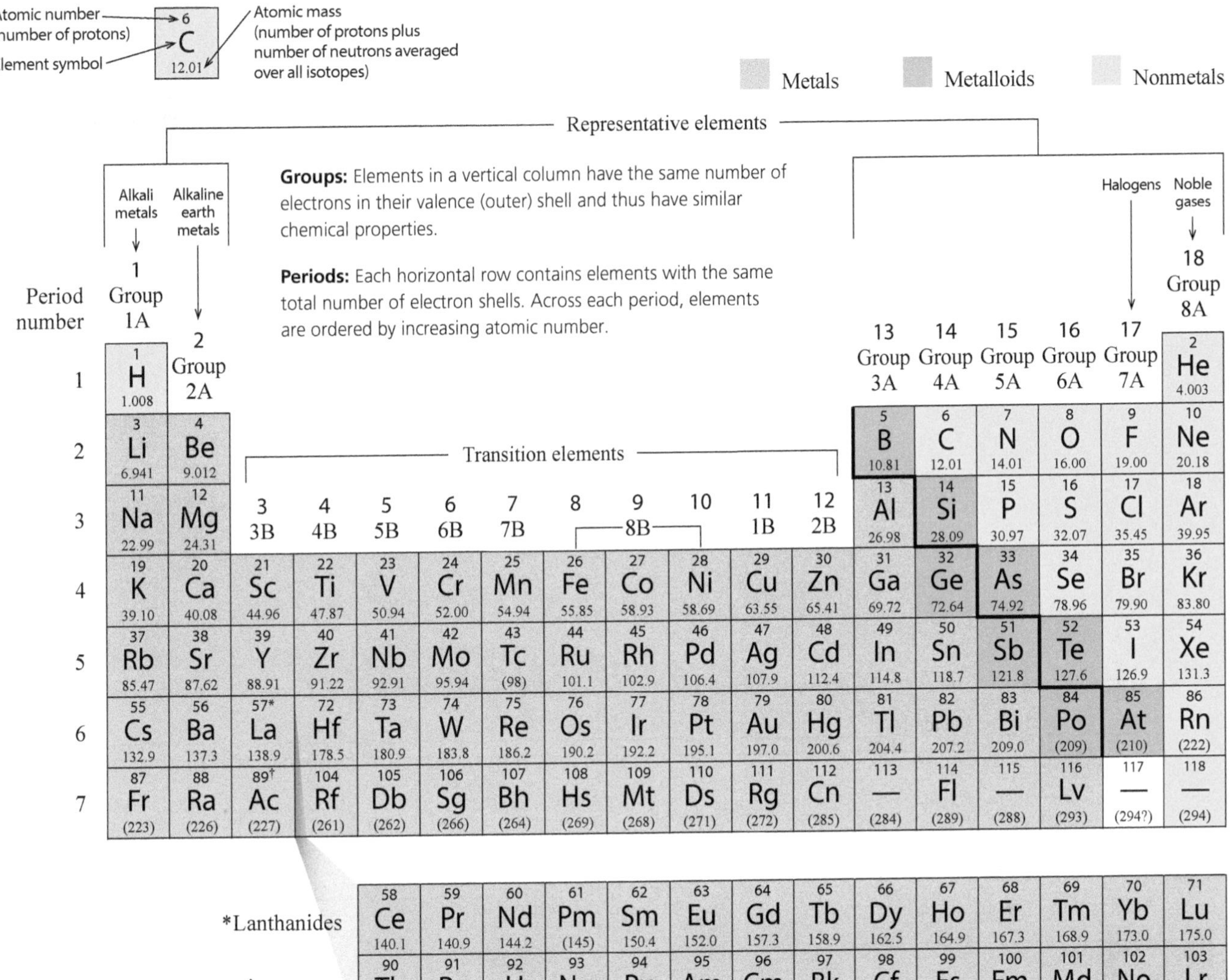

Name (Symbol)	Atomic Number	Name (Symbol)	Atomic Number	Name (Symbol)	Atomic Number	Name (Symbol)	Atomic Number	Name (Symbol)	Atomic Number
Actinium (Ac)	89	Copernicium (Cn)	112	Iodine (I)	53	Osmium (Os)	76	Silicon (Si)	14
Aluminum (Al)	13	Copper (Cu)	29	Iridium (Ir)	77	Oxygen (O)	8	Silver (Ag)	47
Americium (Am)	95	Curium (Cm)	96	Iron (Fe)	26	Palladium (Pd)	46	Sodium (Na)	11
Antimony (Sb)	51	Darmstadtium (Ds)	110	Krypton (Kr)	36	Phosphorus (P)	15	Strontium (Sr)	38
Argon (Ar)	18	Dubnium (Db)	105	Lanthanum (La)	57	Platinum (Pt)	78	Sulphur (S)	16
Arsenic (As)	33	Dysprosium (Dy)	66	Lawrencium (Lr)	103	Plutonium (Pu)	94	Tantalum (Ta)	73
Astatine (At)	85	Einsteinium (Es)	99	Lead (Pb)	82	Polonium (Po)	84	Technetium (Tc)	43
Barium (Ba)	56	Erbium (Er)	68	Lithium (Li)	3	Potassium (K)	19	Tellurium (Te)	52
Berkelium (Bk)	97	Europium (Eu)	63	Livermorium (Lv)	116	Praseodymium (Pr)	59	Terbium (Tb)	65
Beryllium (Be)	4	Fermium (Fm)	100	Lutetium (Lu)	71	Promethium (Pm)	61	Thallium (Tl)	81
Bismuth (Bi)	83	Flerovium (Fl)	114	Magnesium (Mg)	12	Protactinium (Pa)	91	Thorium (Th)	90
Bohrium (Bh)	107	Fluorine (F)	9	Manganese (Mn)	25	Radium (Ra)	88	Thulium (Tm)	69
Boron (B)	5	Francium (Fr)	87	Meitnerium (Mt)	109	Radon (Rn)	86	Tin (Sn)	50
Bromine (Br)	35	Gadolinium (Gd)	64	Mendelevium (Md)	101	Rhenium (Re)	75	Titanium (Ti)	22
Cadmium (Cd)	48	Gallium (Ga)	31	Mercury (Hg)	80	Rhodium (Rh)	45	Tungsten (W)	74
Calcium (Ca)	20	Germanium (Ge)	32	Molybdenum (Mo)	42	Roentgenium (Rg)	111	Uranium (U)	92
Californium (Cf)	98	Gold (Au)	79	Neodymium (Nd)	60	Rubidium (Rb)	37	Vanadium (V)	23
Carbon (C)	6	Hafnium (Hf)	72	Neon (Ne)	10	Ruthenium (Ru)	44	Xenon (Xe)	54
Cerium (Ce)	58	Hassium (Hs)	108	Neptunium (Np)	93	Rutherfordium (Rf)	104	Ytterbium (Yb)	70
Cesium (Cs)	55	Helium (He)	2	Nickel (Ni)	28	Samarium (Sm)	62	Yttrium (Y)	39
Chlorine (Cl)	17	Holmium (Ho)	67	Niobium (Nb)	41	Scandium (Sc)	21	Zinc (Zn)	30
Chromium (Cr)	24	Hydrogen (H)	1	Nitrogen (N)	7	Seaborgium (Sg)	106	Zirconium (Zr)	40
Cobalt (Co)	27	Indium (In)	49	Nobelium (No)	102	Selenium (Se)	34		

APPENDIX 3

The Amino Acids of Proteins

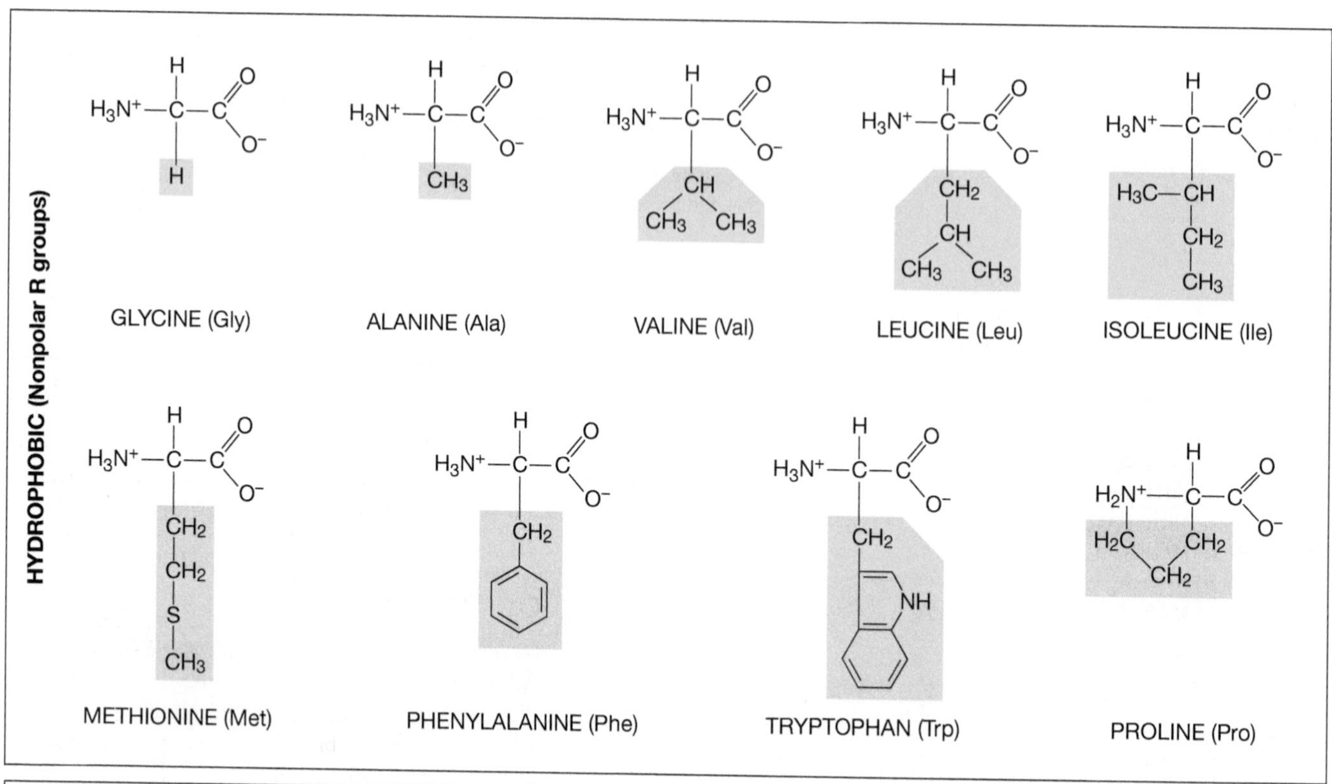

HYDROPHILIC (Polar or charged R groups)

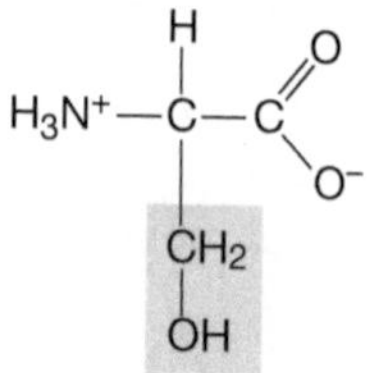

SERINE (Ser)
THREONINE (Thr) 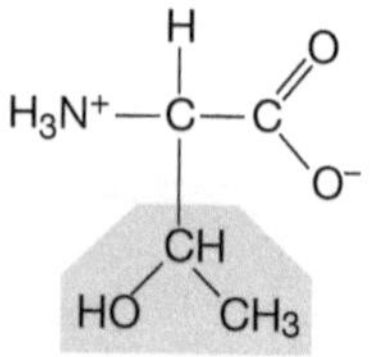
CYSTEINE (Cys) 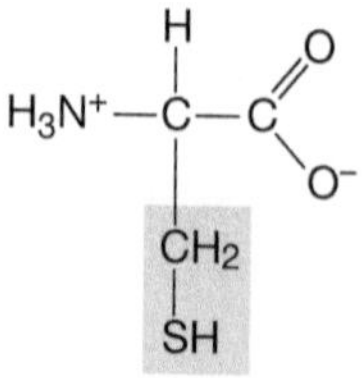
TYROSINE (Tyr) 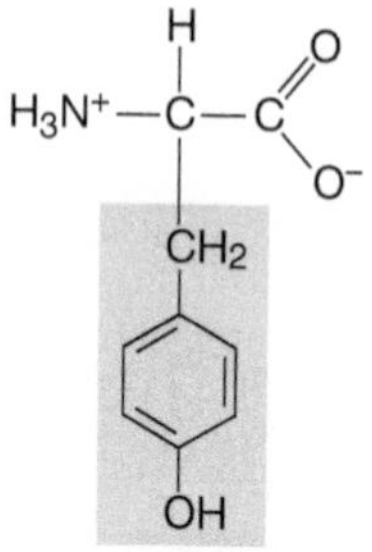
ASPARAGINE (Asn) 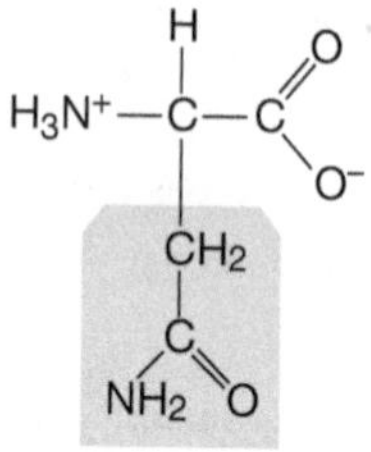
GLUTAMINE (Gln) 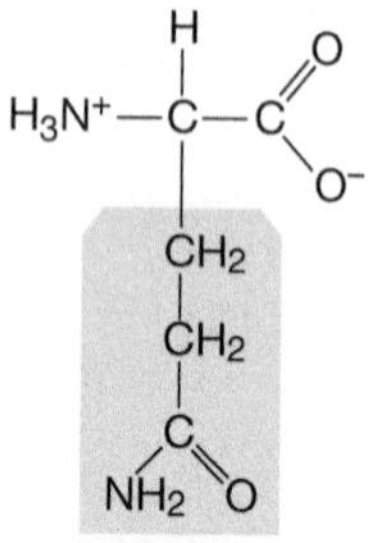

Acidic

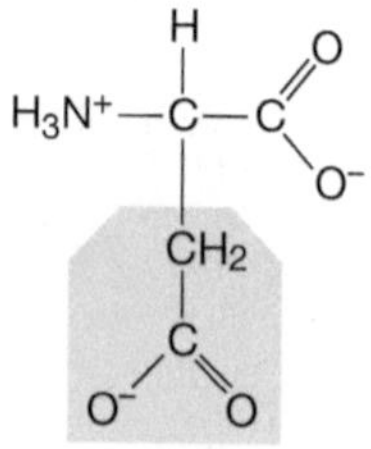

ASPARTIC ACID (Asp)
GLUTAMIC ACID (Glu) 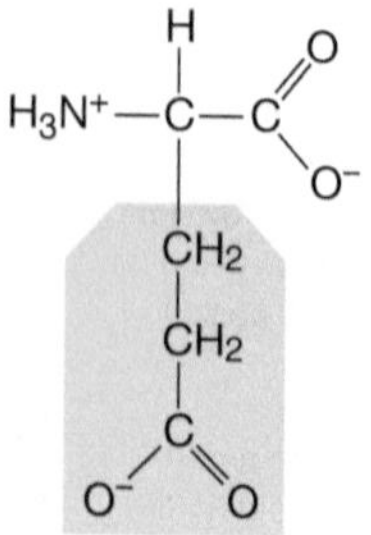

Basic

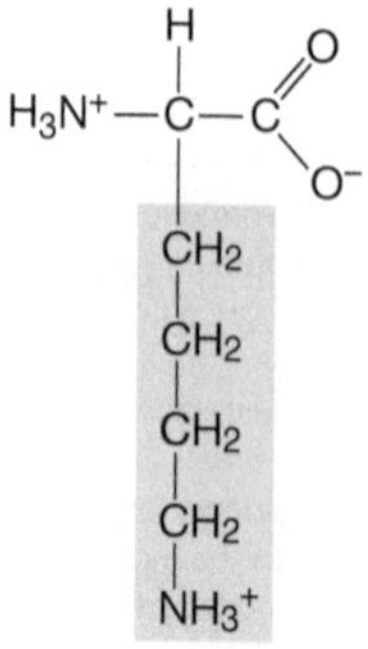

LYSINE (Lys)
ARGININE (Arg) 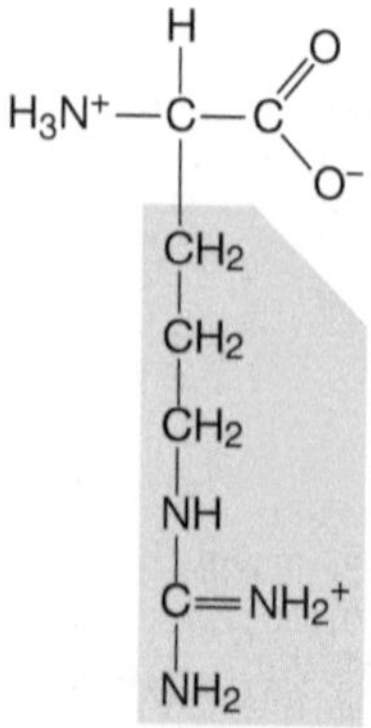
HISTIDINE (His)

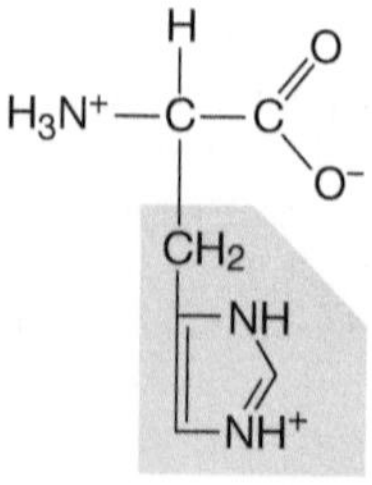

Chapter Review Answers

Chapter 1

1. a. life; b. evolution; c. natural selection; d. unity of life (or numerous kingdoms; 1.8 million species)
2. b 3. c 4. b 5. b 6. d 7. c 8. d (You may have been tempted to choose a, the population level. However, bacteria often have chemical communication or interactions with other bacteria. No bacteria, however, have organs.) 9. d
10. Both energy and matter are passed through an ecosystem from producers to consumers to decomposers. But energy enters most ecosystems as sunlight and leaves as heat. Chemicals are recycled from the soil or atmosphere through plants, consumers, and decomposers and returned to the air, soil, and water.
11. Darwin described how natural selection operates in populations whose individuals have varied traits that are inherited. When natural selection favors the reproductive success of certain individuals in a population more than others, the proportions of heritable variations change over the generations, and a population becomes better adapted to its environment. Should the environment change, however, natural selection may favor different traits.
12. In pursuit of answers to questions about nature, a scientist often uses a logical approach involving these key elements: observations about natural phenomena; questions derived from observations, reading scientific literature, and communicating with other scientists; hypotheses posed as tentative explanations of observations; logical predictions of the outcome of tests if the hypotheses are correct; actual tests of hypotheses; and analysis of results. Scientific research is not a rigid method because hypothesis generation and testing is often repetitive and nonlinear. Intuition, chance, and luck are also part of the scientific process.
13. Technology is the application of scientific knowledge. For example, the use of solar power to run a calculator or heat a home is an application of our knowledge, derived by the scientific process, of the nature of light as a type of energy and how light energy can be converted to other forms of energy. Another example is the use of genetic engineering to insert new genes into crop plants. Genetic engineering stems from decades of scientific research on the structure and function of DNA from many kinds of organisms.
14. The vertical scale of biology refers to the hierarchy of biological organization: from molecules to organelles, cells, tissues, organs, organ systems, organisms, populations, communities, ecosystems, and the biosphere. At each level, emergent properties arise from the interaction and organization of component parts. The horizontal scale of biology refers to the incredible diversity of life, past and present. Biologists seek to classify groups of organisms to reflect their evolutionary relationships.
15. Natural selection screens (edits) heritable variations by favoring the reproductive success of some individuals over others. It can only select from the variations that are present in the population; it does not create new genes or variations.
16. a. Hypothesis: Giving rewards to mice will improve their learning. Prediction: If mice are rewarded with food, they will learn to run a maze faster.
    b. The control group was the mice that were not rewarded. Without them, it would be impossible to know if the mice that were rewarded decreased their time running the maze only because of practice.
    c. Both groups of mice should not have run the maze before and should be about the same age. Both experiments should be run at the same time of day and under the same conditions.
    d. Yes, the results support the hypothesis because the data show that the rewarded mice began to run the maze faster by day 3 and improved their performance (ran faster than the control mice) each day thereafter.
17. The researcher needed to determine the percent of total attacks in each habitat that occurred on dark models. It may be that there were simply more predators in the inland habitat than in the beach habitat. The experiment needed proper data analysis.
18. If these cell division control genes are involved in producing the larger tomato, they may have similar effects if transferred to other fruits or vegetables. Cancer is a result of uncontrolled cell division. One could see if there are similarities between the tomato genes and any human genes that could be related to human development or disease. The control of cell division is a fundamental process in growth, repair, and asexual reproduction—all important topics in biology.
19. Virtually any news report or magazine contains stories that are about biology or at least have biological connections. How about biological connections in advertisements?

Chapter 2

1. a. protons; b. neutrons; c. electrons; d. different isotopes; e. covalent bonds; f. ionic bonds; g. polar covalent bonds; h. hydrogen bonding
2.

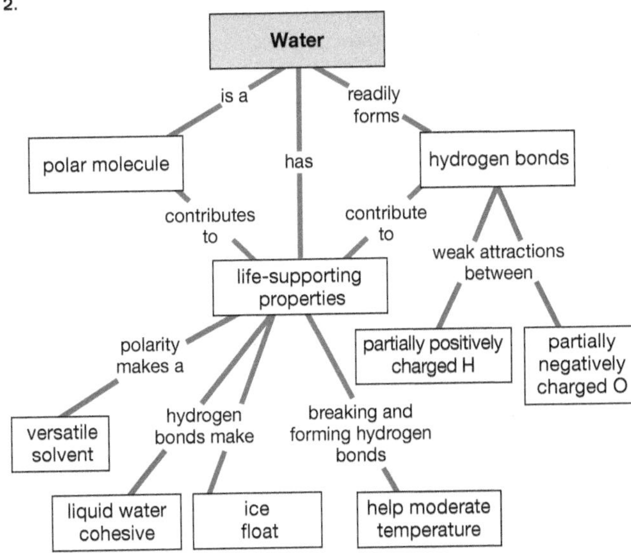

3. b 4. Each C has only 3 bonds instead of the 4 required to fill its valence shell. 5. b 6. d 7. c 8. b (Sulfur has 6 electrons in its valence shell. It reaches a full outer shell of 8 by sharing one pair of electrons with each of two hydrogen atoms. Each H then has a full valence shell of 2.)

9. Iodine (part of a thyroid hormone) and iron (part of hemoglobin in blood) are both trace elements, required in minute quantities. Calcium and phosphorus (components of bones and teeth) are needed by the body in much greater quantities.

10. The atoms of each element have a characteristic number of protons in their nuclei, which is referred to as the atomic number and is 6 for carbon. The mass number is an indication of the approximate mass of an atom and is equal to the number of protons and neutrons in the nucleus. Carbon-12 has 6 neutrons (and 6 protons, of course), so its mass number is 12. The valence usually equals the number of electrons needed to fill an atom's outer shell (the number of unpaired electrons). Carbon's valence or bonding capacity of 4 indicates that it will form 4 covalent bonds. Thus, an atom's valence is most related to its chemical behavior.

11. In nonpolar covalent bonds, electrons are equally shared between two atoms. Polar covalent bonds form when a more electronegative atom pulls the shared electrons closer to it, producing a partial negative charge associated with that portion of the molecule and a partial positive charge associated with the atom from which the electrons are pulled. In the formation of ions, an electron is completely pulled away from one atom and transferred to another, creating negatively and positively charged ions. These oppositely charged ions may be attracted to each other in an ionic bond.

12. Fluorine needs 1 electron for a full outer shell of 8, and if potassium loses 1 electron, its outer shell will have 8. Potassium will lose an electron (becoming a + ion), and fluorine will pick it up (becoming a – ion). The ions can form an ionic bond.

13. The elements in a row all have the same number of electron shells. In a column, all the elements have the same number of electrons in their outer shell. Elements in the same column should have similar chemical properties because they have the same valence or bonding capacity and thus would make the same number of covalent bonds. Or if they have only 1 or 2 electrons, or if they have 7 electrons in their outer shell, atoms of these elements would tend to lose or gain electrons, forming ions and participating in ionic bonds.

14. The O—H covalent bonds of water would nonpolar, and the special properties of water that relate to its polarity and ability to form hydrogen bonds would not exist.

15. The results indicate that both a lower pH and higher temperature negatively affected the growth of coral polyps and that the reduction in growth was much greater when both pH and temperature were varied at the same time. Because rising atmospheric levels of CO_2 are predicted to continue to acidify the oceans and raise ocean temperatures, it is beneficial to see how these two factors may interact.

16. When water is heated, much of the heat is absorbed in breaking hydrogen bonds before the water molecules increase their motion and the temperature increases. Conversely, when water is cooled, many hydrogen bonds are formed, which releases a significant amount of heat. This release of heat can provide some protection against freezing of the plants' leaves, thus protecting the cells from damage.

17. These extreme environments may be similar to those found on other planets. The fact that life may have evolved and continues to flourish in such extreme environments on Earth suggests that some form of life may have evolved on other planets. In addition to seeking evidence for the past or current presence of water on Mars or other planets, scientists now know to search in environments that previously would have been thought incapable of supporting life.

Chapter 3

1. a. glucose; b. energy storage; c. cellulose; d. fats; e. cell membrane component; f. steroids; g. amino group; h. carboxyl group; i. R group; j. enzyme; k. structural proteins; l. movement; m. membrane transport protein; n. defense; o. phosphate group; p. nitrogenous base; q. ribose or deoxyribose; r. DNA; s. code for proteins

2. d (The second kind of molecule is a polymer of the first.) 3. c 4. c 5. d 6. a 7. a 8. d 9. a

10. Circle NH_2, an amino group; COOH, a carboxyl group; and OH, a hydroxyl group on the R group. This is an amino acid, a monomer of proteins. The OH group makes it a polar amino acid.

11. Amino acids with hydrophobic R groups are most likely to be found clustered together in the interior of a protein, sheltered from the surrounding water.

12. This is a hydrolysis reaction, which consumes water. It is essentially the reverse of the diagram in Figure 3.5, except that fructose has a different shape than glucose.

13. The complementary base pairing of the two strands of DNA makes possible the precise copying of DNA every time a cell divides, ensuring that genetic information is faithfully transmitted. Complementary base pairing is involved in transferring information from DNA to RNA to specify the order of amino acids in a polypeptide. In some types of RNA, complementary base pairing enables RNA molecules to assume specific three-dimensional shapes that facilitate diverse functions.

14. Alpha helices and beta pleated sheets, the secondary structures of a polypeptide, are maintained by hydrogen bonds between oxygen and hydrogen atoms of the polypeptide backbone. The tertiary structure is formed by interactions among the R groups of constituent amino acids and stabilized by hydrogen bonds, ionic bonds, clustering of hydrophobic R groups, and covalent bonds between sulfur atoms of some amino acids.

15. Carbon forms four covalent bonds, either with other carbon atoms, producing chains or rings of various lengths and shapes, or with other atoms, such as characteristic chemical groups that confer specific properties on a molecule. This bonding capability is the basis for the incredible diversity of organic compounds. Organisms can link a small number of monomers into different arrangements to produce a huge variety of polymers.

16. The 20 amino acids that are found in proteins can be arranged in many different sequences into chains of many different lengths. The sequences of DNA nucleotides in the genes of a cell dictate the amino acid sequences of its polypeptide chains.

17. A developing chick is growing rapidly, increasing its number of cells. To build new cells it needs large stores of cell membrane components, including cholesterol and lipids, and amino acids for building its proteins. It also requires energy to fuel all this construction, and that is available in the form of fats, as fat molecules can be broken down to yield a lot of energy.

18. a. A: at about 37°C; B: at about 78°C
    b. A: from humans (human body temperature is about 37°C); B: from thermophilic bacteria
    c. Above 40°C, the human enzyme denatures and loses its shape and thus its function. The increased thermal energy disrupts the weak bonds that maintain secondary and tertiary structure in an enzyme.

19. These results indicate that replacing either saturated or trans fats in the diet with unsaturated fats reduces the risk of coronary heart disease. The benefit is greater (risk reduced the most) when trans fats are replaced, even though the quantity of energy in the diet replaced was only 2% rather than the 5% of saturated fats replaced.

Chapter 4

1. a. rough ER; b. nucleus; c. nucleolus; d. ribosomes; e. peroxisome; f. centrosome; g. cytoskeleton; h. mitochondrion; i. plasma membrane; j. lysosome; k. Golgi apparatus; l. smooth ER. For functions, see Table 4.22. A centrosome is a microtubule-organizing center.
2. c 3. b (Small cells have a greater ratio of surface area to volume.) 4. b 5. a
6. DNA as genetic material, ribosomes, plasma membrane, and cytosol
7. Cilia may propel a cell through its environment or sweep a fluid environment past the cell.
8. d 9. b 10. a 11. c
12. Different conditions and conflicting processes can occur simultaneously within separate, membrane-enclosed compartments. Also, there is increased area for membrane-attached enzymes that carry out metabolic processes.
13. Part true, part false. All animal *and* plant cells have mitochondria; plant cells do have chloroplasts, but animal cells do not. Both organelles process energy. A mitochondrion converts chemical energy (such as in sugar molecules) to another form of chemical energy (ATP). This process provides eukaryotic cells with ATP needed for cellular work. A chloroplast converts light energy to chemical energy (sugar molecules). These sugar molecules may then provide a plant cell's mitochondria with a source of energy. Or they may be stored in the plant body and passed to animals that eat plants or each other.
14. The plasma membrane is a phospholipid bilayer with the hydrophilic heads facing the aqueous environment on both sides and the hydrophobic fatty acid tails mingling in the center of the membrane. Proteins are embedded in and attached to this membrane. Microfilaments form a three-dimensional network just inside the plasma membrane. The extracellular matrix outside the membrane is composed largely of glycoproteins, which may be attached to membrane proteins called integrins. Integrins can transmit information from the ECM to microfilaments on the other side of the membrane.
15. Cell 1: $S = 1{,}256\,\mu m^2$; $V = 4{,}187\,\mu m^3$; $S/V = 0.3$. Cell 2: $S = 5{,}024\,\mu m^2$; $V = 33{,}493\,\mu m^3$; $S/V = 0.15$. The smaller cell has a larger surface area relative to volume, facilitating the uptake of sufficient nutrients and oxygen and the excretion of waste.
16. An mRNA molecule is transcribed from the gene for insulin and moves into the cytosol. There it joins with a ribosome that becomes attached to the outside of the rough ER (a bound ribosome). The ribosome produces a polypeptide that is threaded into the ER compartment. The polypeptide folds up and may be modified within the ER. It is then packaged into a transport vesicle. The vesicle joins with a Golgi sac, and the protein may be further modified during its journey through the Golgi apparatus. A transport vesicle pinches off from the "shipping" face of the Golgi and fuses with the plasma membrane, secreting insulin from the cell.
17. According to the endosymbiotic theory, an ancestral eukaryotic cell engulfed (ingested) an aerobic bacterium but did not digest its potential food item. The prokaryote took up residence within the cell, and its aerobic metabolism probably contributed ATP to the host cell. Over many generations of cells, the host and endosymbiont became mutually dependent and unable to exist on their own—they became a single organism. A similar process may have occurred when one of these mitochondria-containing cells ingested but did not digest a photosynthetic prokaryote.
18. Individuals with PCD have nonfunctional cilia and flagella because of a lack of dynein motor proteins. This defect would also mean that the cilia involved in left-right pattern formation in the embryo would not be able to set up the fluid flow that initiates the normal arrangement of organs.
19. As the chromosomes moved poleward, the microtubule segments on the chromosome side of the mark shortened, while those on pole side stayed the same length. Thus chromosome movement toward the poles of this dividing cell is correlated with the shortening (depolymerizing) of the microtubules at the end where the chromosome is attached. The experiment would have to be repeated on different types of cells from different organisms to determine whether the location where a spindle fiber depolymerizes is always the same. Indeed, other experiments have shown that in some cells, the microtubules depolymerize from the pole end of the spindle fibers.

Chapter 5

1. a. active transport; b. concentration gradient; c. small nonpolar molecules; d. facilitated diffusion; e. transport proteins
2. a. enzyme; b. active site of enzyme; c. substrate; d. substrate in active site; induced fit strains substrate bonds; e. substrate converted to products; f. product molecules released and enzyme ready to work again
3. b 4. d 5. c (Only active transport can move solute against a concentration gradient.) 6. a 7. b
8. The work of cells falls into three main categories: chemical, transport, and mechanical. ATP provides the energy for cellular work. During the hydrolysis of ATP, a phosphate group is often transferred to a substrate (chemical) or to a protein (transport and mechanical).
9. Energy is stored in the chemical bonds of a cell's organic molecules. The activation energy barrier prevents these molecules from spontaneously breaking down and releasing that energy. When a substrate fits into an enzyme's active site with an induced fit, its bonds may be strained and thus easier to break, amino acids or cofactors in the active site may facilitate or participate in the catalysis, or the active site may orient two substrates in such a way that expedites the conversion to products.
10. Energy is neither created nor destroyed but can be transferred and transformed. Plants transform the energy of sunlight into chemical energy stored in organic molecules. Almost all organisms rely on the products of photosynthesis for the source of their energy. In every energy transfer or transformation, disorder increases as some energy is lost to the random motion of thermal energy and released as heat.
11. Cell membranes are composed of diverse proteins suspended in a fluid phospholipid bilayer. The hydrophilic heads of the phospholipids face the aqueous environment on both sides of the membrane and the fatty acid tails cluster in the hydrophobic center of the membrane. The membrane forms a selectively permeable boundary between cells and their surroundings (or between organelles and the cytosol). The proteins perform many of the functions of membranes, such as enzyme action, transport, attachment, and signaling.
12. Inhibitors that are toxins or poisons irreversibly inhibit key cellular enzymes. Inhibitors that are designed as drugs are beneficial, such as when they interfere with the enzymes of bacterial or viral invaders or cancer cells. Cells use feedback inhibition of enzymes in metabolic pathways as important mechanisms that conserve resources.
13. Aquaporins are water transport channels that allow for very rapid diffusion of water through a cell membrane. It would be most important for your body to reabsorb water from the urine, thus preventing dehydration, after a run on a hot day.

14. The aquaporin RNA-injected oocytes had a high rate of water permeability. (Remember from Module 5.7 that they swelled and ruptured in 3 minutes.) Treatment with mercury chloride inhibited the aquaporins, and the water permeability of the oocytes was reduced. As expected, the higher the concentration of mercury, the greater the inhibition and reduction in water permeability.

When that inhibition was reversed by treatment with the chemical ME, the channels once again functioned and water permeability increased to almost the level of the uninhibited oocytes. The control oocytes were not injected with aquaporin RNA and thus did not have aquaporins. Thus, their water permeability should be very low and not affected by the mercury treatment. Indeed, their water permeability was much lower than any of the RNA-injected oocytes.

15. a. The more enzyme present, the faster the rate of reaction, because it is more likely that enzyme and substrate molecules will meet.

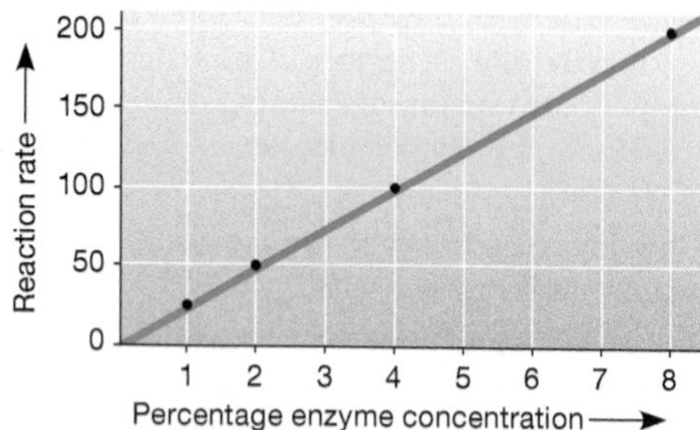

b. The more substrate present, the faster the reaction, for the same reason, but only up to a point. An enzyme molecule can work only so fast; once it is saturated (working at top speed), more substrate does not increase the rate.

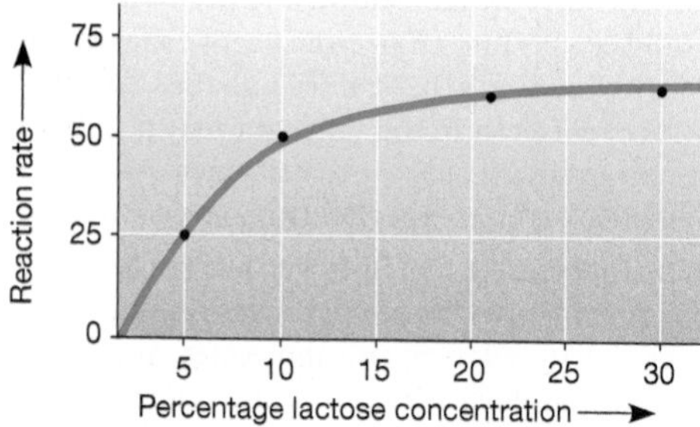

16. Some issues and questions to consider: Is improving crop yields of paramount importance in a world where many people can't get enough food? Does the fact that these compounds rapidly break down indicate that the risk to humans is low? How about the risks to people who work in agriculture or to other organisms, such as bees and other pollinating insects, birds, and small mammals? Might there be negative effects on ecosystems that are impossible to predict?

Chapter 6

1. a. glycolysis; b. pyruvate oxidation and citric acid cycle; c. oxidative phosphorylation; d. oxygen; e. electron transport chain; f. CO_2; g. H_2O

2. d 3. d 4. c. 5. b 6. a 7. c (NAD^+ and FAD, which are recycled by electron transport, are in limited supply in a cell.) 8. b (at the same time NADH is oxidized to NAD^+)

9. Glycolysis is considered the most ancient because it occurs in virtually all cells (including prokaryotic cells, which evolved before eukaryotic cells) and doesn't require oxygen or membrane-enclosed organelles.

10. In lactic acid fermentation (in muscle cells), pyruvate is reduced by NADH to form lactate, and NAD^+ is recycled. In alcohol fermentation, pyruvate is broken down to CO_2 and ethanol as NADH is oxidized to NAD^+. Both types of fermentation allow glycolysis to continue to produce 2 ATP per glucose by recycling NAD^+.

11. As carbohydrates are broken down in glycolysis and the oxidation of pyruvate, glycerol can be made from G3P and fatty acids can be made from acetyl CoA. Amino groups, containing N atoms, must be supplied to various intermediates of glycolysis and the citric acid cycle to produce amino acids.

12. 100 kcal per day is 700 kcal per week. According to Figure 6.4, walking 3 mph would require $\frac{700}{245}$ = about 2.8 hours; swimming, 1.7 hours; running, 0.7 hour.

13. NAD^+ and FAD are coenzymes that are not used up during the oxidation of glucose. NAD^+ and FAD are recycled when NADH and $FADH_2$ pass the electrons they are carrying to the electron transport chain. We need a small additional supply to replace those that are damaged.

14. As electrons from fuel molecules are passed from NADH or $FADH_2$ through the electron transport chain to oxygen, the energy released from some of these redox reactions is used to pump H^+ across the inner mitochondrial membrane into the intermembrane space. When hydrogen ions flow back through ATP synthase down their concentration gradient, they power the phosphorylation of ADP to ATP.

15. a. No, this shows the blue color getting more intense. The reaction decolorizes the blue dye.
b. No, this shows the dye being decolorized, but it also shows the three mixtures with different initial color intensities. The intensities should have started out the same, since all mixtures used the same concentration of dye.
c. Correct. The mixtures all start out the same, and then the ones with more malate (reactant) decolorize faster.

16. The presence of ATP synthase enzymes in prokaryotic plasma membranes and the inner membrane of mitochondria provides support for the theory of endosymbiosis—that mitochondria evolved from an engulfed prokaryote that used aerobic respiration (see Module 4.15).

17. The percentage of body fat is the independent variable and is plotted on the *x* axis. The activity of brown fat is the dependent variable, and it is plotted on the *y* axis. Your graph should show a negative correlation between body fat percentage and activity of brown fat (the data points are higher for lower body fat percentage and decrease as the body fat percentage increases). One hypothesis is that thin individuals have more active brown fat and thus burn more calories, which contributes to their thinness (lower percentage of body fat). A second hypothesis is that the higher percentage of body fat insulated the bodies of the more overweight subjects, thus their brown fat did not have to be as active to maintain their body temperatures when exposed to cold.

18. In a person treated with uncoupling agents like DNP, the proton gradient established during electron transport is no longer tied to ATP synthesis. As a result, oxidation of glucose during cellular respiration yields very little ATP, since ATP is normally produced as H^+ ions flow back through ATP synthase in the inner mitochondrial membrane. Without large amounts of ATP available, biosynthesis cannot take place and new organic molecules cannot be synthesized. Low ATP levels would signal the body to continue breaking down its own molecules and feeding them into the cellular respiration pathway, leading to excessive weight loss and severe overheating, sweating, and dehydration. One or a combination of these factors can cause death.

19. The mitochondria of brown fat cells have protein channels that make the inner mitochondrial membrane leaky to H^+ ions, producing the same effect that the drug DNP has on mitochondria. When these channels are activated, brown fat burns fuel without producing ATP. Drugs that could activate brown fat would help a patient burn more calories. Thus, excess calories from the diet would not be converted to fat, and fat stores of the body could be reduced. If these drugs somehow affected the mitochondria of all body cells, however, the results could be as disastrous as they were with DNP.

Chapter 7

1. a. light energy; b. light reactions; c. Calvin cycle; d. O_2 released; e. electron transport chain; f. NADPH; g. ATP; h. G3P (sugar)

2. c 3. b 4. a 5. c (NADPH and ATP from the light reactions are required by the Calvin cycle.) 6. d 7. b 8. c

9. 6 CO_2, 9 ATP, 6 NADPH

10. CO_2 and H_2O are the products of respiration; they are the reactants in photosynthesis. In respiration, glucose is oxidized to CO_2 as electrons are passed through an electron transfer chain from glucose to O_2, producing H_2O. In photosynthesis, H_2O is the source of electrons, which are energized by light, temporarily stored in NADPH, and used to reduce CO_2 to carbohydrate.

11. The light reactions require ADP and $NADP^+$, neither of which is recycled from ATP and NADPH when the Calvin cycle stops.

12. Plants can break down the sugar for energy in cellular respiration or use the sugar as a raw material for making other organic molecules, especially cellulose. Excess sugar is stored as starch.

13. Solar energy absorbed by pigment molecules drives low-energy electrons from water to NADPH. Light-driven electron flow also generates ATP by chemiosmosis. NADPH and ATP both store chemical energy, which is used in the Calvin cycle to reduce CO_2 to sugar.

14. Both organelles have electron transport chains that pump H^+ into a membrane-bound compartment, as well as ATP synthases. The higher H^+ concentration is found in the intermembrane space of the mitochondrion and in the thylakoid space of the chloroplast. a. electron transport chain; b. ATP synthase; c. thylakoid space; d. stroma; e. ATP.

15. In mitochondria: a. Electrons come from food molecules. b. Electrons have high potential energy in the bonds in organic molecules. c. Electrons are passed to oxygen, which picks up H^+ and forms water.

    In chloroplasts: a. Electrons come from splitting of water. b. Light energy excites the electrons to a higher energy level. c. Electrons flow from water to the reaction-center chlorophyll in photosystem II to the reaction-center chlorophyll in photosystem I to $NADP^+$, reducing it to NADPH.

    In both processes: d. Energy released by redox reactions in the electron transport chain is used to transport H^+ across a membrane. The flow of H^+ down its concentration gradient back through ATP synthase drives the phosphorylation of ADP to make ATP.

16. The hypothesis was that, because CO_2 is a raw material for photosynthesis, rising CO_2 levels would increase the growth and production of pollen by ragweed. Pollen production was positively correlated with CO_2 concentrations, and the results supported the hypothesis. Because rising CO_2 levels are associated with warmer temperatures, an experiment could also look at the effect of temperature on ragweed pollen production. One might also want to determine whether the growing season is getting longer, as this would expose hay fever sufferers to pollen for extended periods. It would also be interesting to measure whether ragweed pollen is more allergenic when grown in higher CO_2 levels, as poison ivy was shown to be. These types of experiments have been performed, and their results are as you would predict—the growing season for ragweed has gotten longer, and pollen that is more allergenic is produced in higher quantities under conditions of elevated CO_2.

17. Scientists will need to continue to research the causes and effects of global warming and climate change as well as the effectiveness of strategies to reduce emissions or otherwise mitigate climate change. Politicians will need to negotiate ways in which they can fulfill their pledges to reduce emissions and provide financial and other aid to less-developed countries, balancing shorter-term economic concerns with longer-term benefits. Citizens will need to consider their energy uses and the ways in which they can hold politicians and businesses accountable for the health of the planet.

Chapter 8

1.

	Mitosis	Meiosis
Number of chromosomal duplications	*1*	*1*
Number of cell divisions	*1*	*2*
Number of daughter cells produced	*2*	*4*
Number of chromosomes in the daughter cells	*Diploid (2n)*	*Haploid (n)*
How the chromosomes line up during metaphase	*Singly*	*In tetrads (metaphase I), then singly (metaphase II)*
Genetic relationship of the daughter cells to the parent cell	*Genetically identical*	*Genetically unique*
Functions performed in the human body	*Growth, development, and repair*	*Production of gametes*

2. b 3. c 4. b 5. b 6. b 7. a 8. b 9. d (A diploid cell would have an even number of chromosomes; the odd number suggests that meiosis I has been completed. Sister chromatids are together only in prophase and metaphase of meiosis II.) 10. c 11. d

12. Most of the cells are in interphase (a time of growth, DNA synthesis, metabolic activity), without recognizable compacted individual chromosomes. During prophase, chromosomes compact and thicken (e.g., the cell on the left edge, about halfway down) and the mitotic spindle forms. During metaphase, the chromosomes line up in the middle of the cell (e.g., the second cell from the top, near the top left corner). In anaphase, the chromosomes split into two groups (which you can see in two cells near the bottom right corner) as sister chromatids split. During telophase, the chromosomes reach opposite ends (e.g., at the very top, fifth cell from the right) as daughter nuclei form around the chromosomes and cytokinesis begins.

13. Mitosis without cytokinesis would result in a single cell with two nuclei. Multiple rounds of cell division like this could produce such a "megacell."

14. Various orientations of homologous chromosome pairs at metaphase I of meiosis lead to different combinations of chromosomes in gametes. Crossing over during prophase I results in an exchange of chromosome segments and new combinations of

genes. Random fertilization of eggs by sperm further increases possibilities for variation in offspring.

15. In culture, normal cells usually divide only when they are in contact with a surface but not touching other cells on all sides (the cells usually grow to form only a single layer). The density-dependent inhibition of cell division apparently results from local depletion of substances called growth factors. Growth factors are proteins secreted by certain cells that stimulate other cells to divide; they act via signal transduction pathways to signal the cell cycle control system of the affected cell to proceed past its checkpoints. The cell cycle control systems of cancer cells do not function properly. Cancer cells generally do not require externally supplied growth factors to complete the cell cycle, and they divide indefinitely (in contrast to normal mammalian cells, which stop dividing after 20 to 50 generations)—two reasons why cancer cells are relatively easy to grow in the lab. Furthermore, cancer cells can often grow without contacting a solid surface, making it possible to culture them in suspension in a liquid medium.

16. A ring of microfilaments pinches an animal cell in two, a process called cleavage. In a plant cell, membranous vesicles form a disk called the cell plate at the midline of the parent cell, cell plate membranes fuse with the plasma membrane, and a cell wall grows in the space, separating the daughter cells.

17. See Figure 8.18.

18.
   a. No. For this to happen, the chromosomes of the two gametes that fused would have to represent, together, a complete set of the donor's maternal chromosomes (the ones that originally came from the donor's mother) and a complete set of the donor's paternal chromosomes (from the donor's father). It is much more likely that the zygote would be missing one or more maternal chromosomes and would have an excess of paternal chromosomes, or vice versa.
   b. Correct. Consider what would have to happen to produce a zygote genetically identical to the gamete donor: The zygote would have to have a complete set of the donor's maternal chromosomes and a complete set of the donor's paternal chromosomes. The first gamete in this union could contain any mixture of maternal and paternal chromosomes, but once that first gamete was "chosen," the second one would have to have one particular combination of chromosomes—the combination that supplies whatever the first gamete did not supply. So, for example, if the first three chromosomes of the first gamete were maternal, maternal, and paternal, the first three of the second gamete would have to be paternal, paternal, and maternal. The chance that all 23 chromosome pairs would be complementary in this way is only one in 22^3 (that is, one in 8,388,608). Because of independent assortment, it is much more likely that the zygote would have an unpredictable combination of chromosomes from the donor's father and mother.
   c. No. First, the zygote could not be genetically identical to the gamete donor (*see answer b*). Second, the zygote could not be identical to either of the gamete donor's parents because the donor only has half the genetic material of each of his or her parents. For example, even if the zygote were formed by two gametes containing only paternal chromosomes, the combined set of chromosomes could not be identical to that of the donor's father because it would still be missing half of the father's chromosomes.
   d. No. *See answer c.*

19. Some possible hypotheses: The replication of the DNA of the bacterial chromosome takes less time than the replication of the DNA in a eukaryotic cell. The time required for a growing bacterium to roughly double its cytoplasm is much less than for a eukaryotic cell. Bacteria have a cell cycle control system much simpler than that of eukaryotes.

20. $1 \text{ cm}^3 = 1{,}000 \text{ mm}^3$, so $5{,}000 \text{ mm}^3$ of blood contains $5{,}000 \times 1{,}000 \times 5{,}000{,}000 = 25{,}000{,}000{,}000{,}000$, or 2.5×10^{13}, red blood cells. The number of cells replaced each day $= 2.5 \times 10^{13}/120 = 2.1 \times 10^{11}$ cells. There are $24 \times 60 \times 60 = 86{,}400$ seconds in a day. Therefore, the number of cells replaced each second $= 2.1 \times 10^{11}/86{,}400 =$ about 2×10^6, or 2 million. Thus, about 2 million cell divisions must occur each second to replace red blood cells that are lost.

21. Each chromosome is on its own in mitosis; chromosome replication and the separation of sister chromatids occur independently for each horse or donkey chromosome. Therefore, mitotic divisions, starting with the zygote, are not impaired. In meiosis, however, homologous chromosomes must pair in prophase I. This process of synapsis cannot occur properly because horse and donkey chromosomes do not match in number or content.

22. With three sets of chromosomes, there is no way for the sets to be separated equally to gametes during meiosis. Thus, taking cuttings from the plants and rooting them (a form of cloning) is the only way new plants can be grown. Sexual reproduction generates genetic diversity, whereas asexual reproduction does not. Genetic diversity would allow some plants to have a particular combination of genes that would allow them to resist a new pest. These genetic variants would not be possible in a population of plants that reproduces asexually.

23. Hypothetically, a study could be designed using a large group of women with a diagnosis of DCIS. The women could be divided into three groups. The first group receives lumpectomies. The second group receives mastectomy. The third group receives no treatment (and so serves as a control). The groups should be otherwise identical. The groups can then be monitored for outcomes (death, recurrence of the cancer, etc.) to compare which group fared better. However, such a study is clearly unethical. Instead, every patient must be given the best possible care for their particular cancer. This is why observational studies are more appropriate in this context.

Chapter 9

1. a. alleles; b. loci; c. homozygous; d. dominant; e. recessive; f. incomplete dominance

2. c 3. b 4. d (Neither parent is ruby-eyed, but some offspring are, so it is recessive. Different ratios among male and female offspring show that it is sex-linked.) 5. d

6. The trait of freckles is dominant, so Tim and Jan must both be heterozygous. There is a chance that they will produce a child with freckles and a chance that they will produce a child without freckles. The probability that the next two children will have freckles is $3/4 \times 3/4 = 9/16$.

7. As in problem 6, both Tim and Jan are heterozygous, and Mike is homozygous recessive. The probability of the next child having freckles is 3/4. The probability of the next child having a straight hairline is 1/4. The probability that the next child will have freckles and a straight hairline is $3/4 \times 1/4 = 3/16$.

8. The genotype of the black short-haired parent rabbit is *BBSS*. The genotype of the brown long-haired parent rabbit is *bbss*. The F_1 rabbits will all be black and short-haired, *BbSs*. The F_2 rabbits will be black short-haired, black long-haired, brown short-haired, and brown long-haired, in a proportion of 9:3:3:1.

9. If the genes are not linked, the proportions among the offspring will be 25% gray red, 25% gray purple, 25% black red, and 25% black purple. The actual percentages show that the genes are linked. The recombination frequency is 6%.

10. The recombination frequencies are black dumpy 36%, purple dumpy 41%, and black purple 6% (see problem 9). Because these recombination frequencies reflect distances between the genes, the sequence must be purple-black-dumpy (or dumpy-black-purple).

11. 1/4 will be boys suffering from hemophilia, and 1/4 will be female carriers. (The mother is a heterozygous carrier [X^HX^h], and the father is normal [X^HY].)

12. Genes on the single X chromosome in males are always expressed because there are no corresponding genes on the Y chromosome to mask them. A male needs only one recessive colorblindness allele (from his mother) to show the trait; a female must inherit the allele from both parents, which is less likely.

13. The parental gametes are *WS* and *ws*. Recombinant gametes are *Ws* and *wS*, produced by crossing over.

14. Height appears to be a quantitative trait resulting from polygenic inheritance, like human skin color. See Module 9.14.

15. For a woman to be colorblind, she must inherit X chromosomes bearing the colorblindness allele from both parents. Her father has only one X chromosome, which he passes on to all his daughters, so he must be colorblind. A male need only inherit the colorblindness allele from a carrier mother; both his parents are usually phenotypically normal.

16. Start out by breeding the cat to get a population to work with. If the curl allele is recessive, two curl cats can have only curl kittens. If the allele is dominant, curl cats can have "normal" kittens. If the curl allele is sex-linked, ratios will differ in male and female offspring of some crosses. If the curl allele is autosomal, the same ratios will be seen among males and females. Once you have established that the curl allele is dominant and autosomal, you can determine if a particular curl cat is true-breeding (homozygous) by doing a testcross with a normal cat. If the curl cat is homozygous, all offspring of the testcross will be curl; if heterozygous, half of the offspring will be curl and half normal.

17. If the genes are unlinked, you expect puppies in a 9:3:3:1 ratio: 90 black normal vision, 30 black blind, 30 chocolate normal, and 10 chocolate blind. If the genes are linked, you would expect a 3:1 ratio of black normal to chocolate blind, with a small number of black blind and chocolate normal recombinant offspring.

Chapter 10

1. a. nucleotides; b. transcription; c. RNA polymerase; d. mRNA; e. rRNA; f. tRNA; g. translation; h. ribosomes; i. amino acids

2. b

3. Ingredients: Original DNA, nucleotides, several enzymes and other proteins, including DNA polymerase and DNA ligase. Steps: Original DNA strands separate at a specific site (origin of replication), free nucleotides hydrogen-bond to each strand according to base-pairing rules, and DNA polymerase covalently bonds the nucleotides to form new strands. New nucleotides are added only to the 3' end of a growing strand. One new strand is made in one continuous piece; the other new strand is made in a series of short pieces that are then joined by DNA ligase. Product: Two identical DNA molecules, each with one old strand and one new strand.

4. transcription; translation

5. d (Only the phage DNA enters a host cell; lambda DNA determines both DNA and protein.)

6. d

7. A gene is the polynucleotide sequence with information for making one polypeptide. Each codon—a triplet of bases in DNA or RNA—codes for one amino acid. Transcription occurs when RNA polymerase produces RNA using one strand of DNA as a template. In prokaryotic cells, the RNA transcript may immediately serve as mRNA. In eukaryotic cells, the RNA is processed: A cap and tail are added, and RNA splicing removes introns and links exons together to form a continuous coding sequence. A ribosome is the site of translation, or polypeptide synthesis, and tRNA molecules serve as interpreters of the genetic code. Each folded tRNA molecule has an amino acid attached at one end and a three-base anticodon at the other end. Beginning at the start codon, mRNA is moved relative to the ribosome a codon at a time. A tRNA with a complementary anticodon pairs with each codon, adding its amino acid to the polypeptide chain. The amino acids are linked by peptide bonds. Translation stops at a stop codon, and the finished polypeptide is released. The polypeptide folds to form a functional protein, sometimes in combination with other polypeptides.

8. c

9.

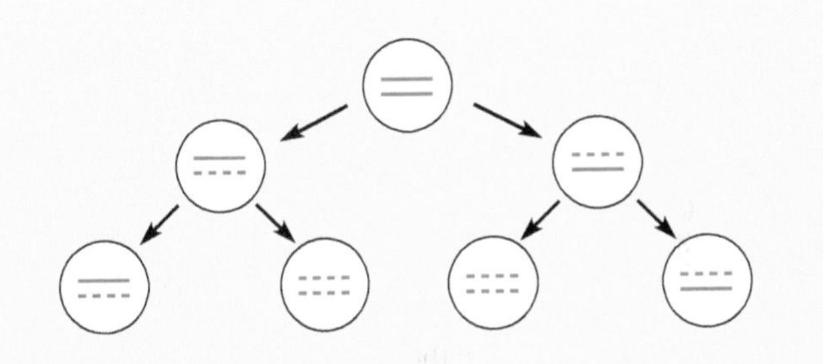

10. mRNA: GAUGCGAUCCGCUAACUGA; amino acids: Met-Arg-Ser-Ala-Asn

11. Some issues and questions to consider: Is it fair to issue a patent for a gene or gene product that occurs naturally in every human being? Or should a patent be issued only for something new that is invented rather than found? Suppose another scientist slightly modifies the gene or protein. How different does the gene or protein have to be to avoid patent infringement? Might patents encourage secrecy and interfere with the free flow of scientific information? What are the benefits to the holder of a patent? When research discoveries cannot be patented, what are the scientists' incentives for doing the research? What are the incentives for the institution or company that is providing financial support?

12. A bacteriophage is capable of easily infecting a host (bacterium) and therefore multiplying its genetic material. Most importantly, a bacteriophage has a very simple structure, allowing the outer structure (made entirely of protein) to be easily distinguished from the inner structure (made of DNA).

Chapter 11

1. a. proto-oncogene; b. repressor (or activator); c. cancer; d. operator; e. X inactivation; f. transcription factors; g. alternative RNA splicing

2. b 3. b 4. b 5. b (Different genes are active in different kinds of cells.) 6. c 7. Proto-oncogenes normally control cell division.

8. They will be black, because the DNA of the cell was obtained from a black mouse.

9. a. If the mutated repressor could still bind to the operator on the DNA, it would continuously repress the operon; enzymes

for lactose utilization would not be made, whether or not lactose was present.

b. The *lac* genes would continue to be transcribed and the enzymes made, whether or not lactose was present.

c. Same predicted result as for b.

d. RNA polymerase would not be able to transcribe the genes; no proteins would be made, whether or not lactose was present.

10. White, reflecting the genetic makeup of the nucleus donor

11. A mutation in a single gene can influence the actions of many other genes if the mutated gene is a control gene, such as a homeotic gene. A single control gene may encode a protein that affects (activates or represses) the expression of a number of other genes. In addition, some of the affected genes may themselves be control genes that in turn affect other batteries of genes. Cascades of gene expression are common in embryonic development.

12. The protein to which dioxin binds in the cell is probably a transcription factor that regulates multiple genes (see Module 11.3). If the binding of dioxin influences the activity of this transcription factor—either activating or inactivating it—dioxin could thereby affect multiple genes and thus have a variety of effects on the body. The differing effects in different animals might be explained by differing genetic details in the different species. It would be extremely difficult to demonstrate conclusively that dioxin exposure was the cause of illness in a particular individual, even if dioxin had been shown to be present in the person's tissues. However, if you had detailed information about how dioxin affects patterns of gene expression in humans and were able to show dioxin-specific abnormal patterns in the patient (perhaps using DNA microarrays; see Module 11.9), you might be able to establish a strong link between dioxin and the illness.

13. Wilmut was able to coordinate the cell cycle of the donor and host cells by depriving them of nutrients. When faced with starvation, both cells switched to the G_0 phase of the cell cycle. Wilmut could therefore be sure that, when placed in a growth medium with nutrients, the cell cycles within both the donor and host cell were synchronized. This allowed him to successfully clone a mammal from an adult cell for the first time.

Chapter 12

1. a. PCR; b. a restriction enzyme; c. gel electrophoresis; d. nucleic acid probe; e. cloning

2. d 3. b 4. b 5. c 6. c

7. Because it would be too expensive and time consuming to compare whole genomes. By choosing STR sites that vary considerably from person to person, investigators can get the necessary degree of specificity without sequencing the entire genome.

8. Medicine: Genes can be used to produce transgenic lab animals for AIDS research or for research related to human gene therapy. Proteins can be hormones, enzymes, blood-clotting factors, or the active ingredient of vaccines. Agriculture: Foreign genes can be inserted into plant cells or animal eggs to produce transgenic crop plants or farm animals. Animal growth hormones are examples of agriculturally useful proteins that can be made using recombinant DNA technology.

9. She could start with DNA isolated from liver cells (the entire genome) and carry out the procedure outlined in Module 12.1 to produce a collection of recombinant bacterial clones, each carrying a small piece of liver cell DNA. To find the clone with the desired gene, she could then make a probe of radioactive RNA with a nucleotide sequence complementary to part of the gene: GACCUGACUGU. This probe would bind to the gene, labeling it and identifying the clone that carries it. Alternatively, the biochemist could start with mRNA isolated from liver cells and use it as a template to make cDNA (using reverse transcriptase). Cloning this DNA rather than the entire genome would yield a smaller library of genes to be screened—only those active in liver cells. Furthermore, the genes would lack introns, making the desired gene easier to manipulate after isolation.

10. c (Bacteria lack the RNA-splicing machinery needed to delete eukaryotic introns.)

11. Isolate plasmids from a culture of *E. coli*. Cut the plasmids and the human DNA containing the HGH gene with the restriction enzyme to produce molecules with sticky ends. Join the plasmids and the fragments of human DNA with ligase. Allow *E. coli* to take up recombinant plasmids. Bacteria will then replicate plasmids and multiply, producing clones of bacterial cells. Identify a clone carrying and expressing the HGH gene using a nucleic acid probe. Grow large amounts of the bacteria, and extract and purify HGH from the culture.

12. Determining the nucleotide sequences is just the first step. Once researchers have written out the DNA "book," they will have to try to figure out what it means—what the nucleotide sequences code for and how they work.

13. Some issues and questions to consider: What are some of the unknowns in recombinant DNA experiments? Do we know enough to anticipate and deal with possible unforeseen and negative consequences? Do we want this kind of power over evolution? Who should make these decisions? If scientists doing the research were to make the decisions about guidelines, what factors might shape their judgment? What might shape the judgment of business executives in the decision-making process? Does the public have a right to a voice in the direction of scientific research? Does the public know enough about biology to get involved in this decision-making process? Who represents "the public," anyway?

14. Some issues and questions to consider: What kinds of impact will gene therapy have on the individuals who are treated? On society? Who will decide what patients and diseases will be treated? What costs will be involved, and who will pay them? How do we draw the line between treating disorders and "improving" the human species?

15. Some issues and questions to consider: Should genetic testing be mandatory or voluntary? Under what circumstances? Why might employers and insurance companies be interested in genetic data? Because genetic characteristics differ among ethnic groups and between the sexes, might such information be used to discriminate? Which of these questions do you think is most important? Which issues are likely to be the most serious in the future?

16. Gather two groups of volunteers. Have one group ingest a standard amount of GMO corn in their diet and the other group ingest a standard amount of traditional corn. Monitor the health of the individuals in both groups, looking for differences. In real life, such a study would be problematic because it is difficult to control and monitor what people eat, it would require many years to search for long-term health effects, and it may run afoul of ethics standards for human testing.

Chapter 13

1. According to Darwin's theory of descent with modification, all life has descended from a common ancestral form as a result of natural selection. Individuals in a population have hereditary variations. The overproduction of offspring in the face of limited resources leads to a struggle for existence. Individuals that are well suited to their environment tend to leave more offspring than other individuals, leading to the gradual accumulation of adaptations to the local environment in the population.

2. a. genetic drift; b. gene flow; c. natural selection; d. small population; e. founder effect; f. bottleneck effect; g. unequal reproductive success

3. d 4. a 5. b (Erratic rainfall and unequal reproductive success would ensure that a mixture of both forms remained in the population.) 6. d 7. d 8. c

9. Exposing deep rock strata made it easier to obtain older fossils.

10. Your paragraph should include such evidence as fossils and the fossil record, homologous structures, molecular homologies, artificial selection, and examples of natural selection.

11. Evidence strongly supports Lamarck's hypothesis that life evolves. However, our understanding of genetics refutes his hypothesis for the mechanism of evolution.

12. If $q^2 = 0.0025$, $q = 0.05$. Because $p + q = 1, p = 1 - q = 0.95$. The proportion of heterozygotes is $2pq = 2 \times 0.95 \times 0.05 = 0.095$. About 9.5% of African Americans are carriers.

13. Genetic variation is retained in a population by diploidy and balancing selection. Recessive alleles are hidden from selection when in the heterozygote; thus, less adaptive or even harmful alleles are maintained in the gene pool and are available should environmental conditions change. Heterozygote advantage tends to maintain alternate alleles in a population.

14. The terrestrial ancestors of cetaceans had lungs and breathed air. Evolution did not cause the invention of a new respiratory system for breathing underwater. Rather, the existing external structures were adapted. For example, the nostrils shifted position to the top of the head, where they form the blowhole, an opening to the trachea (windpipe), which leads to the lungs. The blowhole is closed while the cetacean is underwater. A cetacean must thrust its blowhole above the surface of the water periodically to obtain oxygen and expel carbon dioxide. Unlike other mammals, the cetacean respiratory system doesn't intersect with the digestive system, allowing the animal to take in food underwater.

15. The unstriped snails appear to be better adapted. Striped snails make up 47% of the living population but 56% of the broken shells. Assuming that all the broken shells result from the meals of birds, we would predict that bird predation would reduce the frequency of striped snails and the frequency of unstriped individuals would increase.

16. Some issues and questions to consider: Who should decide curriculum, scientific experts in a field or members of the community? Are these alternative versions scientific ideas? Who judges what is scientific? If it is fairer to consider alternatives, should the door be open to all alternatives? Are constitutional issues (separation of church and state) involved here? Can a teacher be compelled to teach an idea he or she disagrees with? Should a student be required to learn an idea he or she thinks is wrong?

Chapter 14

1. a. Allopatric speciation: Reproductive barriers may evolve between these two geographically separated populations as a by-product of the genetic changes associated with each population's adaptation to its own environment or as a result of genetic drift or mutation.
   b. Sympatric speciation: Some change, perhaps in resource use or female mate choice, may lead to a reproductive barrier that isolates the gene pools of these two populations, which are not separated geographically. Once the gene pools are separated, each species may go down its own evolutionary path. If speciation occurs by polyploidy—which is common in plants but unusual in animals—then the new species is instantly isolated from the parent species.

2. a. hybrid zone; b. reinforcement; c. fusion; d. stability; e. strengthened; f. weakened or eliminated

3. c 4. b 5. b 6. d 7. c 8. b 9. c 10. a 11. d 12. d

13. Different physical appearances may indicate that organisms belong in different species, but they may just be physical differences within a species. Isolated populations may or may not be able to interbreed; breeding experiments would need to be performed to determine this. Organisms that reproduce only asexually and fossil organisms do not have the potential to interbreed and produce fertile offspring; therefore, the biological species concept cannot apply to them.

14. There is more chance for gene flow between populations on a mainland and nearby island. This interbreeding would make it more difficult for reproductive isolation to develop and separate the two populations.

15. The term *punctuated equilibria* refers to a common pattern seen in the fossil record, in which most species diverge relatively quickly as they arise from an ancestral species and then remain fairly unchanged for the rest of their existence as a species.

16. Yes. Factors such as polyploidy, sexual selection, and habitat specialization can lead to reproductive barriers that would separate the gene pools of allopatric as well as sympatric populations.

17. A broad hypothesis would be that cultivated American cotton arose from a sequence of hybridization, mistakes in cell division, and self-fertilization. We can divide this broad statement into at least three hypotheses. *Hypothesis 1*: The first step in the origin of cultivated American cotton was hybridization between a wild American cotton plant (with 13 pairs of small chromosomes) and an Old World cotton plant (with 13 pairs of large chromosomes). If this hypothesis is correct, we would predict that the hybrid offspring would have had 13 small chromosomes and 13 large chromosomes. *Hypothesis 2*: The second step in the origin of cultivated American cotton was a failure of cell division in the hybrid offspring, such that all chromosomes were duplicated (now 26 small and 26 large). If this hypothesis is true, we would expect the resulting gametes to each have had 13 large chromosomes and 13 small chromosomes. *Hypothesis 3*: The third step in the origin of cultivated American cotton was self-fertilization of these gametes. If this hypothesis is true, we would expect the outcome of self-fertilization to be a hybrid plant with 52 chromosomes: 13 pairs of large ones and 13 pairs of small ones. Indeed, this is the genetic makeup of cultivated American cotton.

18. By decreasing the ability of females to distinguish males of their own species, the polluted turbid waters have increased the frequency of mating between members of species that had been reproductively isolated from one another. As the number of hybrid fish increase, the parent species' gene pools may fuse, resulting in a loss of the two separate parent species and the formation of a new hybrid species. Future speciation events in Lake Victoria cichlids are less likely to occur in turbid water because females are less able to base mate choice on male breeding color. Reducing the pollution in the lake may help reverse this trend.

19. Some issues and questions to consider: One could look at this question in two ways. If the biological species concept is followed strictly, one could argue that red wolves and coyotes are the same species, because they can interbreed. Because coyotes are not rare, this line of argument would suggest that red wolves should not be protected. On the other hand, because red wolves and coyotes differ in many ways, they can be viewed as distinct species by other species concepts. Protecting the remaining red wolves from hybridizing with coyotes can preserve their distinct

species status. The rationale behind protecting all endangered groups is the desire to preserve genetic diversity. Questions for society in general include the following: What is the value of any particular species and its genetically distinct subgroups? And how far are we willing to go to preserve a rare and distinct group of organisms? How should the costs of preserving genetic diversity compare with the costs of other public projects?

Chapter 15

1. a. Abiotic synthesis of important molecules from simpler chemicals in the atmosphere, with lightning or UV radiation as the energy source
   b. Polymerization of monomers, perhaps on hot rocks
   c. Enclosure within a lipid membrane, which maintained a distinct internal environment
   d. Beginnings of heredity as RNA molecules replicated themselves. Natural selection could have acted on protocells that enclosed self-replicating RNA.
2. a. phylogeny; b. homologies; c. morphology; d. analogies; e. phylogenetic tree; f. outgroup; g. shared derived characters
3. b 4. a 5. d 6. c 7. d 8. a 9. c 10. b
11. Microevolution is the change in the gene pool of a population from one generation to the next. Macroevolution involves the pattern of evolutionary changes over large time spans and includes the origin of new groups and evolutionary novelties as well as mass extinctions.
12. The latter are more likely to be closely related, because even small genetic changes can produce divergent physical appearances. But if genes have diverged greatly, it implies that lineages have been separate for some time, and the similar appearances may be analogous, not homologous.
13. Complex structures can evolve by the gradual refinement of earlier versions of those structures, all of which served a useful function in each ancestor.
14. Where and when key developmental genes are expressed in a developing embryo can greatly affect the final form and arrangement of body parts. The regulation of gene expression allows these genes to continue to be expressed in some areas, turned off in other areas, and/or expressed at different times during development.
15. The ribosomal RNA genes, which specify the RNA parts of ribosomes, have evolved so slowly that homologies between even distantly related organisms can still be detected. Analysis of other homologous genes is also used.
16. 22,920 years old, a result of four half-life reductions
17.

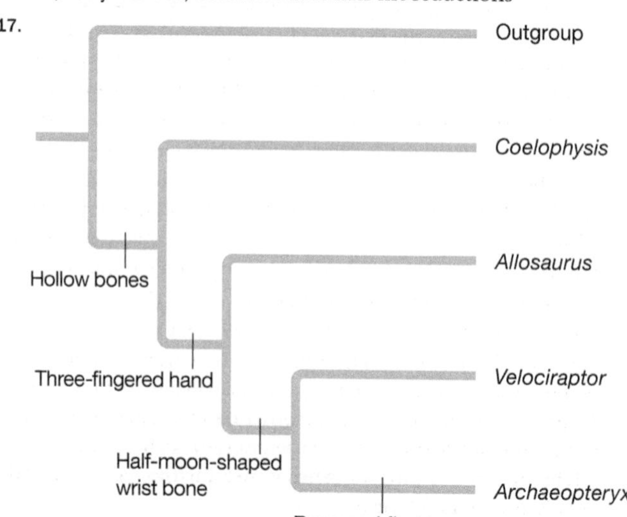

18. Your answer should include aspects of the process of science such as the following: how scientists develop hypotheses and test predictions; the importance of careful experimental design; generating and testing alternative hypotheses; using new technologies; and willingness to incorporate new evidence and revise hypotheses.

Chapter 16

1. Cell wall: maintains cell shape; provides physical protection; prevents cell from bursting in a hypotonic environment
   Capsule: enables cell to stick to substrate or to other individuals in a colony; shields pathogens from host's defensive cells
   Flagella: provide motility, enabling cell to respond to chemical or physical signals in the environment that lead to nutrients or other members of their species and away from toxic substances
   Fimbriae: allow cells to attach to surfaces, including host cells, or to each other
   Endospores: withstand harsh conditions
2. a. Archaeplastids; b. Charophytes; c. Unikonts; d. Fungi; e. Choanoflagellates; f. Animals
3. d (Algae are autotrophs; slime molds are heterotrophs.) 4. d 5. b 6. d 7. b
8. Rapid rate of reproduction enables prokaryotes to colonize favorable habitats quickly. Mutations during the rapid production of large numbers of cells results in a great deal of genetic variation, making it more likely that some individuals will survive—and be able to recolonize the habitat—if the environment changes again.
9. Multicellular organisms have a greater extent of cellular specialization and more interdependence of cells. New organisms are produced from a single cell, either an egg or an asexual spore.
10. *Chlamydomonas* is a eukaryotic cell, much more complex than a prokaryotic bacterium. It is autotrophic, whereas amoebas are heterotrophic. It is unicellular, unlike multicellular sea lettuce.
11. d
12. b. Antibiotics kill bacteria. If ulcers are caused by bacteria, then ulcers patients should be cured by antibiotics. (Assume that the researchers have chosen an antibiotic that is effective against the bacteria they hypothesize to be the cause of ulcers.) If the ulcers persist, then the bacteria did not cause the ulcers.
13. Dinoflagellates are autotrophs that provide most of the energy used by corals to sustain themselves and continue building reefs. Without this source of energy, corals will die and reefs will become barren of the communities that depend on coral reefs for food and shelter.
14. Use the links on the FDA's main page on dietary supplements to learn how dietary supplements are—and are not—regulated. While manufacturers must prove to the FDA that medicinal products are effective before they can be marketed, there is no such approval process for dietary supplements. The manufacturer is responsible for ensuring that the product is safe and that any claims made on the label are true. This web page also provides links to help you find information about specific supplements and to help you make informed decisions about supplement use. Once you are familiar with these resources, select a specific probiotic product to evaluate.
15. This is not a good idea; all life depends on prokaryotes, including bacteria. You could predict that eliminating all bacteria from an environment would result in a buildup of toxic wastes and dead organisms (both of which bacteria decompose), a shutdown of all chemical cycling, and the consequent death of all organisms.

16. Some issues and questions to consider: Could we determine beforehand whether the iron would really have the desired effect? How? Would the "fertilization" need to be repeated? Could it be a cure for the problem, or would it merely treat the symptoms? Might the iron treatment have side effects? What might they be?

Chapter 17

1. a. nonvascular plants (bryophytes); b. seedless vascular plants (lycophytes and monilophytes); c. gymnosperms; d. angiosperms; 1. apical meristems and embryos retained in the parent plant; 2. lignin-hardened vascular tissue; 3. seeds that protect and disperse embryos
2. a. This is a cloud of millions of pollen grains being released from a pollen cone of a pine tree. In pollen cones, haploid spores develop into haploid male gametophytes—the pollen grains. b. This is a cloud of haploid spores produced by a puffball fungus. Each spore may germinate to produce a haploid mycelium.
3. b 4. b (It is the only gametophyte among the possible answers.) 5. a 6. d 7. c 8. b 9. c
10. The alga is surrounded and supported by water, and it has no supporting tissues, vascular system, or special adaptations for obtaining or conserving water. Its whole body is photosynthetic, and its gametes and embryos are dispersed into the water. The seed plant has lignified vascular tissues that support it against gravity and carry food and water. The seed plant also has specialized organs that absorb water and minerals (roots), provide support (stems and roots), and photosynthesize (leaves and stems). It is covered by a waterproof cuticle and has stomata for gas exchange. Its sperm are carried by pollen grains, and embryos develop on the parent plant and are then protected and provided for by seeds.
11. Animals carry pollen from flower to flower and thus help fertilize the plants' eggs. They also disperse seeds by consuming fruit or carrying fruit that clings to their fur. In return, they get food (nectar, pollen, fruit).
12. Plants are autotrophs; they have chlorophyll and make their own food by photosynthesis. Fungi are heterotrophs that digest food externally and absorb nutrient molecules. There are also many structural differences; for example, the threadlike fungal mycelium is different from the plant body, and their cell walls are made of different substances. Plants evolved from green algae, which belong to the protist supergroup Archaeplastida; the ancestor of fungi was in the protist supergroup Unikonta. Molecular evidence indicates that fungi are more closely related to animals than to plants.
13. Fungi disperse their offspring as spores. Because the truffle's reproductive body is underground, its spores are not carried by wind like those of most other fungi. When a truffle is consumed by an animal, the spores pass through the animal's digestive tract and are later deposited at a distance from the parent fungus. The fleshy fruits of many angiosperms are dispersed by a similar mechanism.
14. Moss gametophytes, the dominant stage in the moss life cycle, are haploid plants. The diploid (sporophyte) generation is dominant in most other plants. Recessive mutations are not expressed in a diploid organism unless both homologous chromosomes carry the mutation. In haploid organisms, recessive mutations are apparent in the phenotype of the organism because haploid organisms have only one set of chromosomes. Some factors to consider in designing your experiment: What are the advantages and disadvantages of performing the experiment in the laboratory? In the field? What variables would be important to control? How many potted plants should you use? At what distances from the radiation source should you place them? What would serve as a control group for the experiment? What age of plants should you use?
15. Two possible hypotheses are (1) the lineage that led to present-day mosses diverged before plants and fungi established mycorrhizal relationships and (2) early mosses had mycorrhizae but lost them later in evolution.

Chapter 18

1. Sponges: sessile, saclike body with pores, suspension feeder; sponges
   Cnidarians: radial symmetry, gastrovascular cavity, cnidocytes, polyp or medusa body form; hydras, sea anemones, jellies, corals
   Flatworms: bilateral symmetry, gastrovascular cavity, no body cavity; free-living planarians, flukes, tapeworms
   Nematodes: body cavity, covered with cuticle, complete digestive tract, ubiquitous, free-living and parasitic; roundworms, heartworms, hookworms, trichinosis worms
   Molluscs: muscular foot, mantle, visceral mass, circulatory system, many with shells, radula in some; snails and slugs, bivalves, cephalopods (squids and octopuses)
   Annelids: segmented worms, closed circulatory system, many organs repeated in each segment; marine worms, tube-building worms, earthworms, leeches
   Arthropods: exoskeleton, jointed appendages, segmentation, open circulatory system; chelicerates (horseshoe crabs and arachnids), millipedes and centipedes, crustaceans (lobsters, crabs), insects
   Echinoderms: radial symmetry as adult, water vascular system with tube feet, endoskeleton, spiny skin; sea stars, sea urchins
   Chordates: (1) notochord, (2) dorsal, hollow nerve cord, (3) pharyngeal slits, (4) post-anal tail; lancelets, tunicates, hagfish, and all the vertebrates (lampreys, sharks, ray-finned fishes, lobe-fins, amphibians, reptiles (including birds)), mammals
2. a. Two tissue layers: cnidaria
   b. Protostomes: flatworms, molluscs, annelids, nematodes, arthropods
   c. Deuterostomes: echinoderms, chordates
3. c 4. d 5. a (The invertebrates include all animals except the vertebrates.) 6. c 7. c 8. i 9. f 10. b 11. c 12. a 13. d 14. h 15. e 16. g
17. The gastrovascular cavity of a flatworm is an incomplete digestive tract; the worm takes in food and expels waste through the same opening. An earthworm has a complete digestive tract; food travels one way, and different areas are specialized for different functions. The flatworm's body is solid and unsegmented. The earthworm has a fluid-filled body cavity, allowing its internal organs to grow and move independently of its outer body wall. Fluid in the body cavity cushions internal organs, acts as a skeleton, and aids circulation. Segmentation of the earthworm, including its body cavity, allows for greater flexibility and mobility.
18. Cnidarians and most adult echinoderms are radially symmetric, while most other animals, such as arthropods and chordates, are bilaterally symmetric. Most radially symmetric animals stay in one spot or float passively. Most bilateral animals are more active and move headfirst through their environment.
19. For example, the legs of a horseshoe crab are used for walking, while the antennae of a grasshopper have a sensory function. Some appendages on the abdomen of a lobster are used for swimming, while the scorpion catches prey with its pincers. (Note that the scorpion stinger and insect wings are not considered jointed appendages.)

20. Important characteristics include symmetry, the presence and type of body cavity, segmentation, type of digestive tract, type of skeleton, and appendages.

21.

When the lineages that became arthropods and velvet worms diverged from a common ancestor (indicated by arrow), they began with the same set of homeotic genes. The appendages on the body segments of velvet worms are identical, which is presumably the ancestral condition. If the arthropod body plan resulted from new genes that originated in the arthropod lineage, then velvet worms would lack those genes. Results showing that arthropods possess homeotic genes in addition to those found in velvet worms would support the hypothesis.

Chapter 19

1. a. Old World monkeys; b. gibbons; c. orangutans; d. gorillas; e. chimpanzees. All are anthropoids; gibbons, orangutans, gorillas, chimpanzees, and humans are apes.
2. a. vertebral column; b. jaws; c. lungs or lung derivatives; d. lobed fins; e. legs; f. amniotic egg; g. milk
3. c **4.** c **5.** b **6.** b **7.** b **8.** b **9.** a
10. Amphibians have four limbs adapted for locomotion on land, a skeletal structure that supports the body in a nonbuoyant medium, and lungs. However, most amphibians are tied to water because they obtain some of their oxygen through thin, moist skin and they require water for fertilization and development. Reptiles are completely adapted to life on land. They have amniotic eggs that contain food and water for the developing embryo and a shell to protect it from dehydration. Reptiles are covered by waterproof scales that enable them to resist dehydration (more efficient lungs eliminate the need for gas exchange through the skin).
11. Fossil evidence supports the evolution of birds from a small, bipedal, feathered dinosaur, which was probably endothermic. The last common ancestor that birds and mammals shared was the ancestral amniote. The four-chambered hearts of birds and mammals must have evolved independently.
12. In the phylogenetic tree of primates (Figure 19.10A), the last common ancestor of chimpanzees and humans lived more than 6 million years ago. The lineages that led to chimpanzees and humans have been evolving separately since that time.
13. Several primate characteristics make it easy for us to make and use tools: mobile digits, opposable fingers and thumb, and great sensitivity of touch. Primates also have forward-facing eyes, which enhances depth perception and eye-hand coordination, and a relatively large brain.
14. UV radiation is most intense in tropical regions and decreases farther north. Skin pigmentation is darkest in people indigenous to tropical regions and much lighter in northern latitudes. Scientists hypothesize that depigmentation was an adaptation to permit sufficient exposure to UV radiation, which catalyzes the production of vitamin D, a vitamin that permits the calcium absorption needed for both maternal and fetal bones. Dark pigmentation is hypothesized to protect against degradation of folate, a vitamin essential to normal embryonic development.
15. The paleontologists who discovered *Tiktaalik* hypothesized the existence of transitional forms between fishlike tetrapods such as *Panderichthys* and tetrapod-like fish such as *Acanthostega.* From the available evidence, they knew the time periods when fishlike tetrapods and tetrapod-like fish lived. From the rocks in which the fossils had been found, they knew the geographic region and the type of habitat these creatures occupied. With this knowledge, they predicted the type of rock formation where transitional fossils might be found.
16. Our intelligence and culture—accumulated and transmitted knowledge, beliefs, arts, and products—have enabled us to overcome our physical limitations and alter the environment to fit our needs and desires.
17. Most anthropologists think that humans and chimpanzees diverged from a common ancestor 6–7 million years ago. Primate fossils 4–8 million years old could help us understand how the human lineage first evolved.
18. The brain volume to body mass relationship of *H. floresiensis* is most similar to that of *Australopithecus afarensis*. If *H. floresiensis* were a dwarf form of *H. erectus*, we would expect the relationship to be roughly similar. This finding supports the hypothesis that the ancestor of *H. floresiensis* was an earlier hominin rather than *H. erectus*. (Keep in mind, however, that the available evidence is rather limited and includes only one skull.)

Chapter 20

1. a. epithelial tissue; b. connective tissue; c. smooth muscle tissue; d. connective tissue; e. epithelial tissue

   The structure of the specialized cells in each type of tissue fits their function. For example, columnar epithelial cells are specialized for absorption and secretion; the fibers and cells of the connective tissue provide support and connect the tissues. The hierarchy from cell to tissue to organ is evident in this diagram. The functional properties of a tissue or organ emerge from its structural organization and the coordination of its component parts. The many projections of the lining of the small intestine greatly increase the surface area for absorption of nutrients.
2. False. Each cell is bathed in interstitial fluid; blood remains inside the blood vessels.
3. d
4. a
5. Stratified squamous epithelium consists of many cell layers. The outer cells are flattened, filled with the protein keratin, and dead, providing a protective, waterproof covering for the body. Neurons are cells with long extensions that conduct signals to other cells, making multiple connections in the brain. Simple squamous epithelium is a single, thin layer of cells that allows for diffusion of gases across the lining of the lung. Bone cells are surrounded by a matrix that consists of fibers and mineral salts, forming a hard protective covering around the brain.
6. Extensive exchange surfaces are often located within the body. The surfaces of the intestine, urinary system, and lungs are highly folded and divided, increasing their surface area for exchange. These surfaces interface with many blood capillaries. Not all animals have such extensive exchange surfaces. Animals with small, simple bodies or thin, flat bodies have a greater surface-to-volume ratio, and their cells are closer to the surface, enabling direct exchange between cells and the outside environment.
7. c (Expelling salt opposes the increase in blood salt concentration, thereby maintaining a constant internal environment.)
8. The diaphragm is skeletal muscle, because you can control it voluntarily.
9. The words "perfectly designed" seem to imply that evolution is goal-oriented, but it is not. Structures are adapted from ancestral species and are not "perfect" forms. Take, for example, the laryngeal nerve in giraffes. Because the giraffe nerve is an adaptation

from an earlier fish ancestor, the nerve travels a length of 15 feet instead of taking a much more direct route of 1 foot.

10. Having some people use the cream and others not use it is an example of a controlled experiment, which is a necessary component of a well-designed study. However, since acne can clear up in certain individuals over time, possibly by face washing alone, it would be better to have each participant be their own control (one side of their face be the treated side and the other side be the control). Collecting data by asking participants to rate their own acne severity is biased, because in this case, participants will know if they are using the cream or not. Participants could be "blind" if all were given a cream to use, with only half of the participants receiving a cream with active medicine. Collecting data by counting pimples before, during, and after the study would be unbiased if done by a scientist who was also "blind" to which participants received which treatment. (When both participants and scientists are "blind," it is termed a double-blind study.)

11. Because the skin and blood vessels close to the skin's surface would be rapidly cooled by the ice, a likely hypothesis is that cold water will help cool you more quickly than simply waiting. Because the question considers the rate of cooling, we would need to test the hypothesis by measuring body temperature after a run over time (say every few minutes) and comparing the use of ice water to sitting and waiting

12. Maintaining a constant speed while driving over hilly terrain illustrates the concept of homeostasis. In this case, the set point is 55 miles per hour, and the driver uses different mechanisms to maintain this speed. When going downhill, gravity causes the car to speed up. The driver responds by pressing on the brakes, causing the car to slow down to 55 miles per hour. When going uphill, the car starts to slow down. Then the driver presses on the accelerator to increase the speed to 55 miles per hour. Similarly, homeostatic mechanisms maintain a steady state of blood sugar level, hormone levels, oxygen level, and much more in an animal's internal environment.

Chapter 21

1. a. oral cavity—ingests and chews food; b. salivary glands—produce saliva; c. liver—produces bile and processes nutrient-laden blood from intestines; d. gallbladder—stores bile; e. pancreas—produces digestive enzymes and bicarbonate; f. rectum—stores feces before elimination; g. pharynx—site of openings into esophagus and trachea; h. esophagus—transports bolus to stomach by peristalsis; i. stomach—stores food, mixes food with acid, begins digestion of proteins; j. small intestine—digestion and absorption; k. large intestine—absorbs water, compacts feces; l. anus—eliminates feces

2. a. fuel, chemical energy; b. raw materials, monomers; c. essential nutrients; d. overnutrition or obesity; e. vitamins and minerals; f. essential amino acids; g. malnutrition

3. d 4. b 5. a 6. b 7. d

8. You ingest the sandwich one bite at a time. In the oral cavity, chewing begins mechanical digestion, and salivary amylase action on starch begins chemical digestion. When you swallow, food passes through the pharynx and esophagus to the stomach. Mechanical and chemical digestion continues in the stomach, where HCl in gastric juice breaks apart food cells and pepsin begins protein digestion. In the small intestine, enzymes from the pancreas and intestinal wall break down starch, protein, and nucleic acids to monomers. Bile from the liver and gallbladder emulsifies fat droplets for attack by enzymes. Most nutrients are absorbed into the bloodstream through the villi of the small intestine. Fats travel through lymph vessels. In the large intestine, absorption of water is completed, and undigested material and intestinal bacteria are compacted into feces, which are eliminated through the anus.

9. a. 15% (The serving size is 2/3 cup, so a 1 cup serving has 10% × 3/2 = 15%.)
   b. Based on a 2,000-Calorie diet, this product supplies about 11.5% of daily Calories, and it supplies 10% of vitamin D and 20% of calcium. If all food consumed supplied a similar quantity, the daily requirement for vitamin D would be nearly met and the daily requirement of calcium would be met.
   c. The 1 g of saturated fat in this product represents 5% of the daily value. Thus, the daily value must be 20 g (1/0.05 = 20). This represents 180 Calories from saturated fat per day.

10. Our craving for fatty foods may have evolved from the feast-and-famine existence of our ancestors. Natural selection may have favored individuals who gorged on and stored high-energy molecules, as they were more likely to survive famines.

11. Sodas, chips, cookies, and candy provide many calories (high energy) but few vitamins, minerals, proteins, or other nutrients. Unprocessed, fresh foods such as fruits and vegetables are considered nutrient dense; they provide substantial amounts of vitamins, minerals, and other nutrients and relatively few calories.

12. Some issues and questions to consider: What are the roles of advertising, media, and government in providing nutritional information? How might the available information be improved? What types of scientific studies form the foundation of various nutritional claims?

13. Some issues and questions to consider: In wealthy countries, what are the factors that make it difficult for some people to get enough food? In your community, what types of help exist to feed hungry people? Think of two recent food crises in other countries and what caused them. Did other countries or international organizations provide aid? Which ones, and how did they help? Did that aid address the underlying causes of malnutrition and starvation in the stricken area or only provide temporary relief? How might that aid be changed to offer more permanent solutions to food shortages?

14. Freckles and red hair are correlated: When one occurs, the other also tends to occur. But these two traits have no causation: Freckles do not cause red hair, nor does red hair cause freckles. In terms of human nutrition studies, it can be difficult to correlate a particular dietary factor (the amount of fat, for example) with a particular health measure (high blood pressure, for example) because many other factors may be involved. It is thus hard to conduct strictly controlled human dietary studies.

Chapter 22

1. a. respiratory surface; b. circulatory system; c. lungs; d. hemoglobin; e. cellular respiration; f. negative pressure breathing; g. O_2

2. a. nasal cavity; b. pharynx; c. larynx; d. trachea; e. lung; f. bronchus; g. bronchiole; h. diaphragm

3. c 4. a 5. d 6. a 7. d 8. d 9. d

10. Advantages of breathing air: It has a higher concentration of O_2 than water and is easier to move over the respiratory surface. Disadvantage of breathing air: Living cells on the respiratory surface must remain moist, but breathing air dries out this surface.

11. Nasal cavity, pharynx, larynx, trachea, bronchus, bronchiole, alveolus, through wall of alveolus into blood vessel, blood plasma, into red blood cell, attaches to hemoglobin, carried by blood through heart, blood vessel in muscle, dropped off by hemoglobin, out of red blood cell, into blood plasma, through capillary wall, through interstitial fluid, and into muscle cell

12. Both these effects of carbon monoxide interfere with cellular respiration and the production of ATP. By binding more tightly to hemoglobin, CO would decrease the amount of O_2 picked up in the lungs and delivered to body cells. Without sufficient O_2 to act as the final electron acceptor, cellular respiration would slow. And by blocking electron flow in the electron transport chain, cellular respiration and ATP production would cease. Without ATP, cellular work stops and cells and organisms die.
13. Llama hemoglobin has a higher affinity for O_2 than does human hemoglobin. The dissociation curve shows that its hemoglobin becomes saturated with O_2 at the lower P_{O_2} of the high altitudes to which llamas are adapted. At that P_{O_2}, human hemoglobin is only 80% saturated.
14. The athlete's body would respond to training at high altitudes or sleeping in an artificial atmosphere with lower P_{O_2} by producing more red blood cells. Thus, the athlete's blood would carry more O_2, and this increase in aerobic capacity may improve endurance and performance.
15. Insects have a tracheal system for gas exchange. To provide O_2 to all the body cells in such a huge moth, the tracheal tubes would have to be wider (to provide enough ventilation across longer distances) and very extensive (to service large flight muscles and other tissues), thus presenting problems of water loss and increased weight. Both the tracheal system and the weight of the exoskeleton limit the size of insects.
16. The CDC website lists several conclusions along with links to references. You should find additional references, as well. Factors to consider include size and duration of studies, whether human studies are prospective or retrospective, what chemical compounds are inhaled during hookah smoking and whether they have carcinogenic or other harmful effects, and how passing through water affects hookah smoke. Also consider the smoking habits of the participants studied, for example, how frequently they smoked and the amount of tobacco used at each session.

Chapter 23

1. a. capillaries of head, chest, and arms; b. aorta; c. pulmonary artery; d. capillaries of left lung; e. pulmonary vein; f. left atrium; g. left ventricle; h. aorta; i. capillaries of abdominal region and legs; j. inferior vena cava; k. right ventricle; l. right atrium; m. pulmonary vein; n. capillaries of right lung; o. pulmonary artery; p. superior vena cava

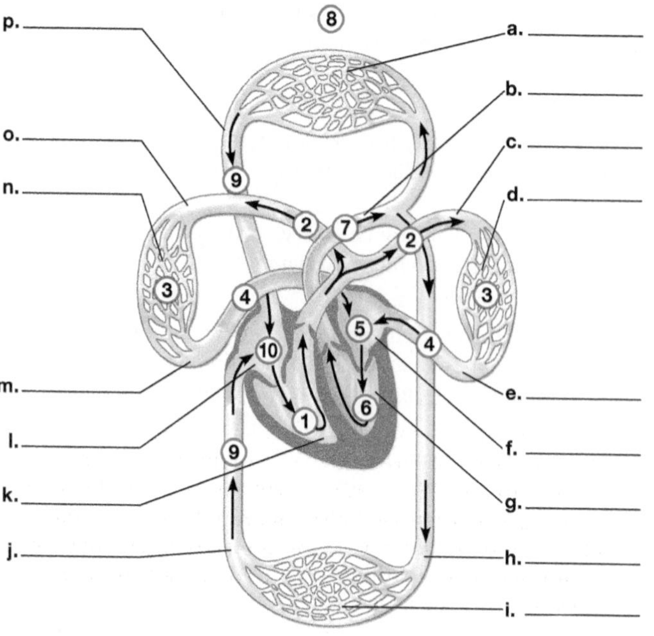

2. b 3. c (The second sound is the closing of the semilunar valves as the ventricles relax.) 4. b 5. b 6. a 7. d 8. b
9. Pulmonary vein, left atrium, left ventricle, aorta, artery, arteriole, body tissue capillary bed, venule, vein, vena cava, right atrium, right ventricle, pulmonary artery, capillary bed in lung, pulmonary vein
10. a
11. The clot would move from the leg vein to the inferior vena cava, to the right atrium, right ventricle, a pulmonary artery, an arteriole, and then to a capillary bed in a lung.
12. Capillaries are very numerous, producing a large surface area for exchange close to body cells. The capillary wall is only one epithelial cell thick. Pores in the wall allow fluid with small solutes to move out of the capillary.
13. a. Plasma (the straw-colored fluid) would contain water, inorganic salts (ions such as sodium, potassium, calcium, magnesium, chloride, and bicarbonate), plasma proteins such as fibrinogen and immunoglobulins (antibodies), and substances transported by blood, such as nutrients (for example, glucose, amino acids, vitamins), waste products of metabolism, respiratory gases (O_2 and CO_2), and hormones.
    b. The red portion would contain red blood cells (erythrocytes), white blood cells (basophils, eosinophils, neutrophils, lymphocytes, and monocytes), and platelets.
14. Oxygen content is reduced as oxygen-poor blood returning to the right ventricle from the systemic circuit mixes with oxygen-rich blood of the left ventricle.
15. Proteins are important solutes in blood, accounting for much of the osmotic pressure that counters the flow of fluid out of a capillary. If protein concentration is reduced, the inward pull of osmotic pressure will fail to balance the outward push of blood pressure, and more fluid will leave the capillary and accumulate in the tissues.
16. Points to consider in your essay may include the prevalence of heart disease; the personal and societal costs of heart disease (for example, costs of medical treatment; economic losses due to disability and death); research costs; who benefits from finding effective methods of prevention or treatment (for example, profit; common good); and the likelihood of producing valid scientific results.
17. With a three-chambered heart, there is some mixing of oxygen-rich blood returning from the lungs with oxygen-poor blood returning from the systemic circulation. Thus, the blood of a dinosaur might not have supplied enough O_2 to support the higher metabolism and strong cardiac muscle contractions needed to generate such a high systolic blood pressure. Also, with a single ventricle pumping simultaneously to both pulmonary and systemic circuits, the blood pumped to the lungs would be at such a high pressure that it would damage the lungs.

Chapter 24

1. a. innate immunity; b. adaptive immunity; c. B cells; d. helper T cells; e. cytotoxic T cells; f. antibodies; g. infected body cells
2. d 3. b 4. b 5. a
6. HIV is transmitted in semen, blood, or breast milk. The most effective way to avoid HIV transmission is to prevent contact with body fluids by practicing safe sex and avoiding intravenous drugs. AIDS is deadly because HIV infects helper T cells, crippling both the humoral and cell-mediated immune responses and leaving the body vulnerable to other infections.

7. Inflammation is triggered by tissue injury. Mast cells within injured tissue release histamine and other chemicals, which cause nearby blood vessels to dilate and become leakier. Blood plasma leaves vessels, and neutrophils are attracted to the site of injury. An increase in blood flow, fluid accumulation, and increased cell population cause redness, heat, and swelling. Inflammation disinfects and cleans the area and curtails the spread of infections from the injured area. Inflammation is considered part of the innate immune response because similar defenses are presented in response to any infection.
8. antigen presenting cells; infected body cells
9. d
10. c
11. Because flu viruses are constantly mutating, we need a flu vaccine every year to keep up with the evolution of flu viruses. Additionally, the immunity brought about by vaccination wanes over time (antibody levels decrease), so getting vaccinated every year provides the best protection.
12. The increase in pertussis cases in older children suggests that immunity declines with age. A solution would be to give children a booster shot, which is another dose of the vaccine. In fact, the number of cases is lower in 13-year-olds—the age most children receive the booster shot. Thus, one solution is to give the booster earlier than age 13.
13. One hypothesis is that your roommate's previous bee stings caused her to become sensitized to the allergens in bee venom. During sensitization, antibodies to allergens attach to receptor proteins on mast cells. In the sensitization stage, she would not have experienced allergy symptoms. When she was exposed to the bee venom again at a later time, the bee venom allergens bound to the mast cells, which triggered her allergic reaction.
14. Case 1: The new infection would cause a large number of people in the community to become ill because nobody would have natural immunity or have been vaccinated for the disease. Case 2: Nearly everyone in the community who comes in contact with the man would have an immediate adaptive response, due to previous vaccination. The disease would not take hold in the community—this is the concept of herd immunity.
15. Some issues and questions to consider: Possible directions include the idea that if the donor felt strongly about the process, then his or her wishes should be respected. The opposite direction would be that the next of kin should be able to approve or deny the procedure. Other considerations may be appropriate, including religious beliefs.
16. Some issues and questions to consider: How much do people in various nations stand to gain by the development of new drugs, in terms of both lives saved and profits made? How can oversight be used to ensure that drug companies are acting in the best interests of all their patients and not purely for profit? Can studies be modified so as to maximize the potential benefits to HIV-infected people while minimizing the risks to study participants? Or is such a trade-off impossible? Should studies on humans be banned altogether?

Chapter 25

1. a. thermoregulation; b. ectotherm; c. behavioral; d. water; e. solutes; f. filtration; g. reabsorption; h. secretion; i. excretion; j. ammonia; k. urea; l. uric acid; m. water; n. land
2. a. filtration: water, NaCl, other ions, urea, nutrients such as glucose and amino acids; b. reabsorption: water, nutrients such as glucose and amino acids, NaCl, other ions; c. secretion: some drugs and toxins, ions such as H^+; d. excretion: urine containing water, urea, and excess ions
3. b 4. a 5. d 6. c 7. b 8. c 9. c 10. b 11. d 12. b 13. a 14. b 15. c
16. In salt water, the fish loses water by osmosis. It drinks salt in water and disposes of salts through its gills. Its kidneys conserve water and excrete excess ions. In fresh water, the fish gains water by osmosis. Its kidneys excrete a lot of dilute urine. Its gills take up salt, and some ions are ingested with food.
17. Yes. Ectotherms that live in very stable environments, such as tropical seas or deep oceans, have stable body temperatures. Terrestrial ectotherms can maintain relatively stable temperatures by behavioral means.
18. A carnivore would produce more nitrogenous waste because it eats more protein and thus produces more breakdown products of protein digestion—nitrogenous wastes.
19. Diuretics increase the amount of water in urine output. An athlete who misuses a diuretic could rapidly lose weight without losing tissue mass. In some sports, such as wrestling, rapid weight loss just before a competition might allow an athlete to move to a lower weight class to potentially compete against someone of equal weight but with less muscle mass. Besides being unfair, the misuse of diuretics can lead to severe dehydration and even death.
20. You could take the reptile back to the laboratory and measure its body temperature under different ambient temperatures.
21. A scatter plot, as shown below, is ideal for graphing these data because both variables represent continuous numerical variables. The relationship between the two variables can be examined. (A bar chart, in which one of the variables represents different categories rather than continuous numerical values, would be less appropriate.) Although these data represent only a small sample, we see a trend that suggests penguins huddle for longer durations at colder temperatures compared to warmer temperatures.

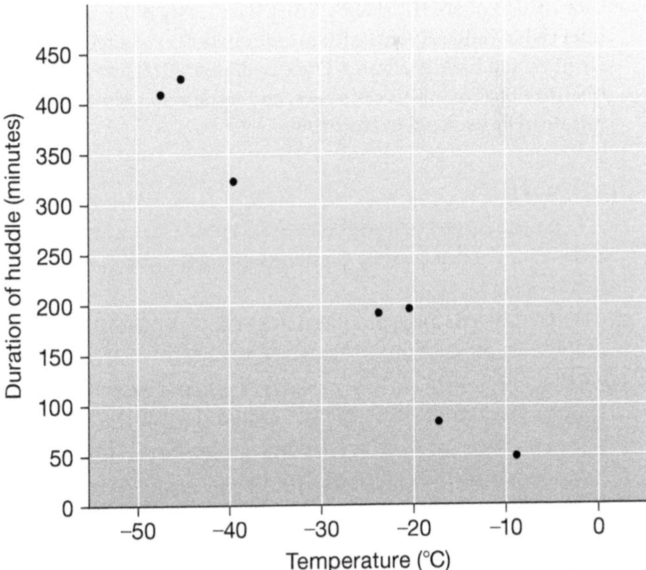

22. One hypothesis is that countercurrent heat exchange in dolphin flippers reduces the loss of heat from the body. Your experiment could measure the temperatures of blood at different locations in the circulatory system. You would expect the temperature of blood flowing back to the body from the flippers to be only slightly cooler than the blood flowing from the body to the flippers.

23. First consider the observation stated in the question: Birds and mammals at higher latitudes are larger. Next, gather other information relevant to the observation: (1) birds and mammals are endotherms; (2) animals living at higher latitudes would need to survive colder climates than those at lower latitudes; and (3) the ratio of surface area to volume is lower in a large animal compared with a small one. (For a review of the relationship between surface area to volume see Modules 4.2 and 20.13.) A possible hypothesis is that larger animals radiate less metabolic heat than smaller animals under the same cold conditions, making them more likely to survive and reproduce.

24. Some possible pros: A financial incentive might motivate more healthy donors to trade. More kidneys could become available, leading to less waiting time for recipients (saving more lives) and less financial burden on the health-care system compared to long-term dialysis. Some possible cons: A donor who is poor might put his or her own health at risk out of desperation. Donors and brokers would be motivated financially, and this could mean less healthy organs being traded (putting the recipients at risk). Crimes to obtain kidneys and coercion of donors could increase. Regulation to protect the donor and recipient would be complex.

25.

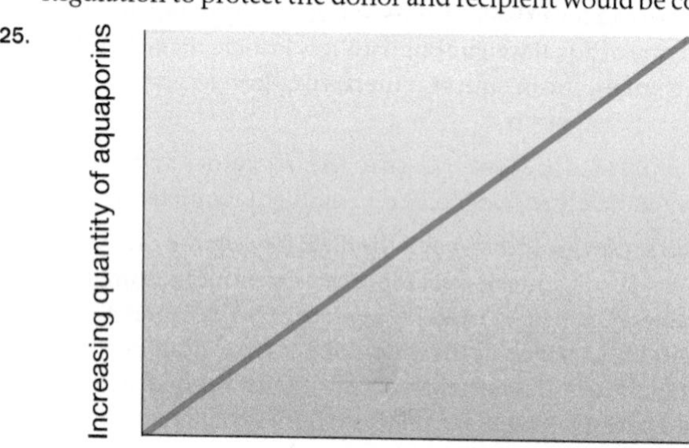

In times of dehydration, ADH levels rise and cause cells in the collecting ducts to reabsorb more water from the filtrate into the interstitial fluid of the tissues. Thus, with rising ADH, collecting duct cells would respond with more aquaporins at their surface. Urine would have less water. Once hydrated, ADH levels fall, the quantity of aquaporins decreases, and more water remains in the filtrate to be excreted in the urine.

Chapter 26

1. a. nervous system; b. hormones; c. receptors; d. inside target cells; e. endocrine glands; f. anterior pituitary gland; g. adrenal medulla

2. d (Thyroid hormone is produced by the thyroid; prolactin promotes milk production; androgens are produced by the testes.)

3. b (When thyroid hormone increases, it inhibits TRH and TSH, which reduces thyroid hormone secretion.)

4. The hypothalamus secretes releasing hormones and inhibiting hormones, which are carried by the blood to the anterior pituitary. In response to these signals from the hypothalamus, the anterior pituitary increases or decreases its secretion of a variety of hormones that directly affect body activities or influence other glands. Neurosecretory cells that extend from the hypothalamus into the posterior pituitary secrete hormones that are stored in the posterior pituitary until they are released into the blood.

5. Endocrine glands can be stimulated by a change in the level of certain ions and nutrients, direct stimulation by the nervous system, or hormones.

6. Both individuals have a rise in glucose blood level after glucose ingestion. The diabetic begins with a higher blood glucose concentration that peaks at approximately three times that of the normal individual about one hour after ingestion.

7. Yes. TSH stimulates the thyroid to grow and produce thyroid hormone. An enlarged thyroid, or goiter, is likely with excess TSH.

8. a and c. Glucagon and glucocorticoids both function to provide the body with cellular fuel. Glucagon breaks down glycogen stores in the liver, and glucocorticoids promote the synthesis of glucose from proteins and fats.

9. a. No. Blood sugar level drops too low. Diabetes would tend to make the blood sugar level too high after a meal.
   b. No. Insulin is working, as seen by the homeostatic blood sugar response to feeding.
   c. Correct. Exercise and fasting lower blood sugar, but without glucagon receptors, liver cells do not receive the glucagon signal to break glycogen down into glucose. The cells cannot mobilize any sugar reserves, and blood sugar level drops. Insulin (which lowers blood sugar) has no effect.
   d. No. If this were true, blood sugar level would increase too much after a meal.

10. Syngenta, the manufacturer of atrazine, has challenged the work. The U.S. Environmental Protection Agency (EPA) has reviewed studies, many conducted by Syngenta, and maintains that the chemical is safe. One summary: http://www.newsweek.com/does-epa-favor-industry-when-assessing-chemical-dangers-268168

Chapter 27

1. A. FSH; B. estrogen; C. LH; D. progesterone; P. menstruation; Q. growth of follicle; R. ovulation; S. development of corpus luteum

   If pregnancy occurs, the embryo produces human chorionic gonadotropin (hCG), which maintains the corpus luteum, keeping levels of estrogen and progesterone high.

2. e 3. g 4. d 5. h 6. f 7. a 8. b 9. c 10. c 11. c (The outer layer in a gastrula is the ectoderm; of the choices given, only the brain develops from ectoderm.) 12. a 13. c

14. The extraembryonic membranes provide a moist environment for the embryos of terrestrial vertebrates and enable the embryos to absorb food and oxygen and dispose of wastes. Such membranes are not needed when an embryo is surrounded by water, as are those of fishes and amphibians.

15. Both produce haploid gametes. Spermatogenesis produces four small sperm; oogenesis produces one large egg. In humans, the ovary contains all the primary oocytes at birth, while testes can keep making primary spermatocytes throughout life. Oogenesis is not complete until fertilization, but sperm mature without eggs.

16. The nerve cells may follow chemical trails to the muscle cells and identify and attach to them by means of specific surface proteins.

17. The researcher might find out whether chemicals from the notochord stimulate the nearby ectoderm to become the neural tube, a process called induction. Transplanted notochord tissue might cause ectoderm anywhere in the embryo to become neural tissue. Possible control experiment: Transplant non-notochord tissue under the ectoderm of the belly area.

18. Some issues and questions to consider: What characteristics might parents like to select for? If parents had the right to choose embryos based on these characteristics, what are some of the possible benefits? What are potential pitfalls? Could an imbalance of the population result?

19. You might be able to design an observational study, like the one used to test effectiveness of condoms (see Module 27.7). You could observe two at-risk populations, one who chose to use the vaccine, and one who didn't. Comparing rates of new infection among the two populations may provide insight into the effectiveness of the vaccine.

Chapter 28

1. a. sensory receptor; b. sensory neuron; c. synapse; d. spinal cord; e. interneuron; f. motor neuron; g. effector cells; h. CNS; i. PNS

2. negative

3. a. corpus callosum; b. amygdala ... limbic; c. cerebral cortex ... cerebrum; d. cerebellum; e. reticular ... hypothalamus

4. At the point where an action potential is triggered, Na^+ rushes into the neuron, depolarizing the membrane. Voltage-gated K^+ channels then open, and the membrane repolarizes. Meanwhile, Na^+ ions diffuse laterally and cause voltage-gated Na^+ channels to open in the adjacent part of the membrane, triggering another action potential. The moving wave of action potentials, each triggering the next, is a moving nerve signal. Behind the action potential, voltage-gated Na^+ channels are temporarily inactivated, so the action potential can only go forward. At a synapse, the transmitting cell releases a chemical neurotransmitter, which binds to receptors on the receiving cell and may trigger a nerve signal in the receiving cell.

5. b

6. b

7. a and c, because they would prevent action potentials from occurring; b could actually increase the generation of action potentials.

8. The controls are not given any drug, not even a placebo, so the placebo effect cannot be accounted for in the treatment group. In many SSRI studies, people believe the pill they receive helps them, even when it is only a placebo. Therefore, drugs must be compared against placebos and the drugs must be more effective than placebos. Additionally, placebos make the study double-blind—so that the patients don't know if they are receiving the treatment or not and so that the researchers are unaware of the assignments as well. Having patients evaluate their own mood allows too much variation among participants. Researchers could instead design surveys to help standardize the reporting (such as number of hours slept, mood on a quantitative scale, motivation, and so forth).

9. The results show the cumulative effect of all incoming signals on neuron D. Comparing experiments 1 and 2, we see that the more nerve signals D receives from C, the more it sends; C is excitatory. Because neuron A is not varied here, its action is unknown; it may be either excitatory or mildly inhibitory. Comparing experiments 2 and 3, we see that neuron B must release a strongly inhibitory neurotransmitter, because when B is transmitting, D stops.

10. Your answer should include a control and experimental group. Your experimental group would be individuals who became taxi drivers and continued successfully over the time period of the study. Your control group might have been a group of people who were not chosen to be taxi drivers. Thus, your two groups would differ in their knowledge of the city layout. To examine neuroplasticity, you might measure a change in gray matter. You might predict that only the successful taxi drivers who learned the city had a measurable increase in gray matter in regions of the brain involved in memory. In fact, a study in 2011 with London taxi drivers found these results.

Chapter 29

1. a. mechanoreceptors; b. chemoreceptors; c. light; d. electricity; e. magnetism; f. hair cells; g. photoreceptors

2. d 3. b 4. a 5. a

6. Louder sounds create pressure waves with greater amplitude, moving hair cells more and generating a greater frequency of action potentials. Different pitches affect different regions of the basilar membrane, stimulating different sensory neurons that transmit action potentials to different parts of the brain.

7. c (He could hear the tuning fork against his skull, so the cochlea, nerve, and brain are okay. Apparently, sounds are not being transmitted to the cochlea; therefore, the bones are the problem.)

8. The effect is called sensory adaptation. In this case, you become less sensitive to noise as the hair cells of the inner ear trigger fewer action potentials and the transmission of signals to the brain decreases.

9. **The dot disappears when the image gets close.** The blind spot, the part of the retina with no photoreceptor cells, is being identified by this vision challenge.

10.

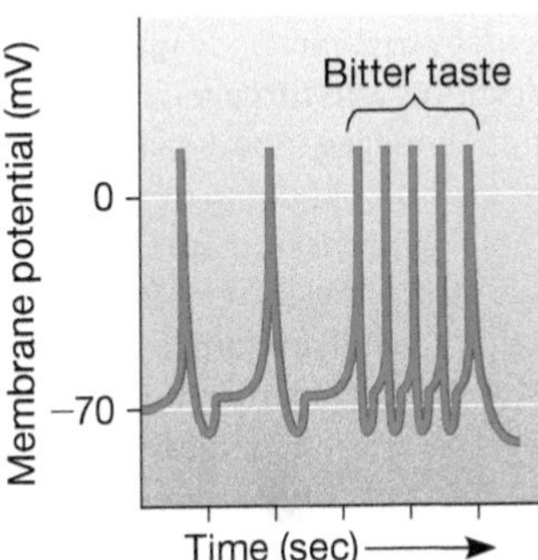

11. You could cover the eyes of some turtles but not others (covering the photoreceptor cells). If turtles with light-blocking masks don't make it to the ocean as frequently as unmasked turtles, they probably use moonlight to guide them. You could make observations on nights when there is no moon. If turtles are less likely to find the ocean on moonless nights, then moonlight likely guides them. You could also use artificial moonlight. If turtles move toward the light (and away from the water), this is evidence that turtles use moonlight in their orientation. (Indeed, many Florida beaches have "lights out" ordinances for beach-front residents during sea turtle nesting season to prevent disorientation of the hatchlings.)

12. Some issues and questions to consider: Assuming that the sound is loud enough to impair hearing, how long an exposure is necessary for this to occur? Does exposure have to occur all at once, or is damage cumulative? Who is responsible, concert promoters or listeners? Should there be regulations regarding sound exposure at concerts (as there are for job-related noise)? Are the young people who typically attend concerts sufficiently mature and aware to heed such warnings?

Chapter 30

1. a. skeleton; b. muscles; c. exoskeleton; d. sarcomeres; e. bone and cartilage

2. b 3. d 4. a (Water supports aquatic animals, reducing the effects of gravity.) 5. c 6. c 7. d 8. a 9. a (Each neuron controls a smaller number of muscle fibers.) 10. d

11. Advantages of an insect exoskeleton include strength, good protection for the body, flexibility at joints, and protection from water loss. The major disadvantage is that the exoskeleton must

be shed periodically as the insect grows, leaving the insect temporarily weak and vulnerable.

12. The bird's wings are airfoils, with convex upper surfaces and flat or concave lower surfaces. As the wings beat, air passing over them travels farther than air beneath. Air molecules above the wings are more spread out, lowering pressure. Higher pressure beneath the wings pushes them up.
13. Calcium is needed for healthy bone development. Calcium strengthens bones and makes them less susceptible to stress fractures.
14. Action potentials from the brain travel down the spinal cord and along a motor neuron to the muscle. The neuron releases a neurotransmitter, which triggers action potentials in a muscle fiber membrane. These action potentials initiate the release of calcium ions from the ER of the cell. Calcium enables myosin heads of the thick filaments to bind with the actin of the thin filaments. ATP provides energy for the movement of myosin heads, which causes the thick and thin filaments to slide along one another, shortening the muscle fiber. The shortening of muscle fibers pulls on bones, bending the arm. If more motor units are activated, the contraction is stronger.
15. The fundamental vertebrate body plan includes an axial skeleton (skull, backbone, and rib cage) and an appendicular skeleton (bones of the appendages). Species vary in the numbers of vertebrae and the numbers of different types of vertebrae they possess. For example, pythons have no cervical vertebrae. Almost all mammals have seven cervical vertebrae but may have different numbers of other types. For example, human coccygeal vertebrae are small and fused together, but cats and other animals with long tails have many coccygeal vertebrae. Limb bones have been modified into a variety of appendages, such as wings, fins, and limbs. Snakes have no appendages.
16. Chemical A would work better, because acetylcholine triggers contraction. Blocking it would prevent contraction. Chemical B would actually increase contraction, because Ca^{2+} allows contraction to occur.
17. Circular muscles in the earthworm body wall decrease the diameter of each segment, squeezing internal fluid and lengthening the segment. Longitudinal muscles shorten and thicken each segment. Different parts of the earthworm can lengthen while other parts shorten, producing a crawling motion. The whole roundworm body moves at once because of a lack of segmentation. The body can only shorten or bend, not lengthen, because of a lack of circular muscles. Roundworms simply thrash from side to side.
18. The binding of calcium ions causes the regulatory protein tropomyosin to move out of the way, enabling myosin heads to bind to actin. This results in muscle contraction. ATP causes the myosin heads of the thick filaments to detach from the thin filaments (Figure 30.9B, step 1). If there is no ATP present, the myosin heads remain attached to the thin filaments, and the muscle fiber remains fixed in position.
19. Some points to consider: (a) The study compared nonathletes with elite athletes, who are among the best in their field. Many people compete successfully without reaching this top rank. (b) The researchers studied athletes from sports that are either power events or endurance events. Some sports require a combination of characteristics. (c) The results did not provide a conclusive answer about the relationship between *ACTN3* genotype and endurance events. (d) Possession of a particular *ACTN3* genotype does not guarantee success in athletic endeavors. In addition to the fact that other genes are involved in physical prowess, athletic excellence requires appropriate training; psychological factors may also play a role.

Chapter 31

1. Here is one possible concept map:

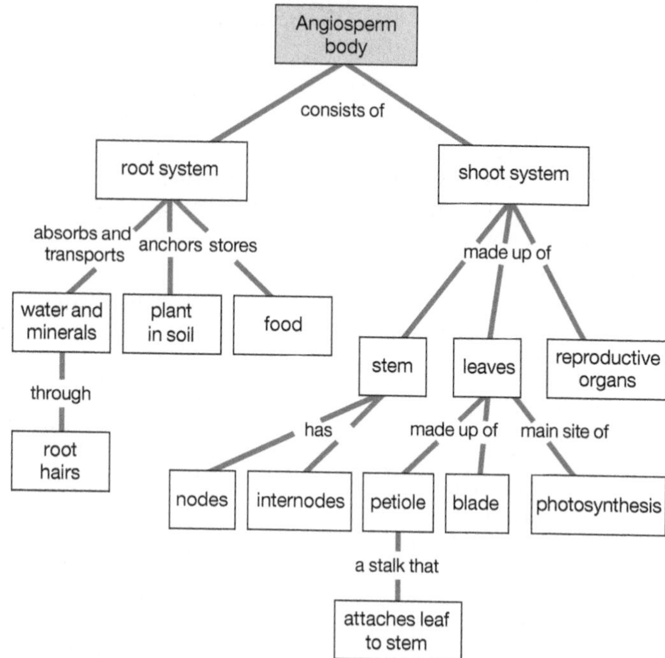

2. d 3. f 4. b 5. e 6. a 7. c 8. d
9. d, a, b, c
10. d
11. Pollen is deposited on the stigma of a carpel, and a pollen tube grows to the ovary at the base of the carpel. Sperm travel down the pollen tube and fertilize egg cells in ovules. The ovules grow into seeds, and the ovary grows into the flesh of the fruit. As the seeds mature, the fruit ripens and falls (or is picked).
12. Celery stalk—leaf stalk (petiole); peanut—seed (ovule); strawberry—fruit (ripened ovary); lettuce—leaf blades; beet—root
13. Fragmentation of bulbs and sprouting from roots are examples of asexual reproduction. Asexual reproduction is less wasteful and costly than sexual reproduction and less hazardous for young plants. The primary disadvantage of asexual reproduction is that it produces genetically identical offspring, decreasing genetic variability that can help a species survive times of environmental change.
14. Modern methods of plant breeding and propagation have increased crop yields but have decreased genetic variability, so plants have become more vulnerable to epidemics. Primitive varieties of crop plants could contribute to gene banks and be used for breeding new strains.
15. You may wish to discuss the benefits and drawbacks of the different lines of evidence, including archeological (remnants of plants left at ancient sites), anatomical (examination of the differences in plant anatomy between wild and domestic varieties), microscopic (examination of microscopic plant structures to reveal which varieties were used at an ancient site), and genetic (differences in DNA sequences derived from plant remains, corresponding to the accumulation of mutations during domestication).

Chapter 32

1. a. roots; b. xylem; c. sugar source; d. phloem; e. transpiration; f. sugar sink
2. d 3. d 4. d 5. b

6. If the plant starts to dry out, K^+ is pumped out of the guard cells. Water follows by osmosis, the guard cells become flaccid, and the stomata close. This prevents wilting, but it keeps leaves from taking in carbon dioxide, which is needed for photosynthesis.
7. The hypothesis is supported if transpiration varies with light intensity when humidity and temperature are about the same. These conditions are seen at two places in the table; at hours 11 and 12, recordings for temperature and humidity are about the same, but light intensity increased markedly from 11 to 12, as did the transpiration rate. The recordings made at hours 3 and 4 show the same effects. Also, the recordings made at hours 1 and 2 generally support the hypothesis. Here, both temperature and humidity decreased, so you might expect the transpiration rate to stay about the same or perhaps increase because the temperature decrease is small; however, transpiration rate dropped, as did light intensity.
8. Excessive amounts of fungicides could destroy mycorrhizae, symbiotic associations of fungi and plant root hairs. The fungal filaments provide lots of surface area for absorption of water and nutrients. Destroying the mycorrhizae could cause a water or nutrient deficiency in the plant.
9. An organic label indicates that the grower has been certified to be following standards meant to promote agricultural sustainability. The organic designation does not mean that the produce is more nutritious than conventionally grown produce.
10. Hypothesis: The hydrogen ions in acid precipitation displace positively charged nutrient ions from negatively charged clay particles. Test: In the laboratory, place equal amounts and types of soil in separate filters. The pore size of the filter must not allow any undissolved soil particles to pass through. Spray (to simulate rain) soil samples in the filters with solutions of different pH (for example, pH 4, 5, 6, 7, 8). Determine the concentration of nutrient ions in the solutions. (The only variable in the solutions should be the hydrogen ion concentration. Ideally, the solutions would contain no dissolved nutrient ions.) Collect fluid that drips through soil samples and filters. Determine the hydrogen ion concentration and the nutrient ion concentration in each sample of fluid. Prediction: If the hypothesis is correct, the fluid collected from the soil samples exposed to pH lower than that of acid rain (which is typically around pH 5.6) will contain the highest concentration of positively charged nutrient ions.
11. Some issues and questions to consider: How were the farmers assigned or sold "rights" to the water? How is the price established when a farmer buys or sells water rights? Is there enough water for everyone who "owns" it? What kinds of crops are these farmers growing? What will the water be used for in the city? Are there other users with no rights, such as wildlife? Is any effort being made to curb urban growth and conserve water? Should millions of people be living in what is essentially a desert? What are the reasons for farming desert land?
12. It is difficult to conduct properly controlled experiments on growing crops. To design a properly controlled experiment, only one variable (in this case, whether the crop is organic or not) should change between experimental groups. In the real world, this may be impossible to achieve, as soil conditions, weather, and other factors vary from location to location.

Chapter 33

1. a. auxin; b. gibberellin; c. auxin; d. cytokinin; e. auxin; f. ethylene; g. gibberellin; h. abscisic acid
2. b 3. b 4. a 5. d 6. b 7. d 8. f 9. e 10. d 11. a 12. b 13. g 14. c 15. c
16. Fruits produce ethylene gas, which triggers the ripening and aging of the fruit. Ventilation prevents a buildup of ethylene and delays its effects.
17. The terminal bud produces auxins, which counter the effects of cytokinins from the roots and inhibit the growth of axillary buds. If the terminal bud is removed, the cytokinins predominate, and lateral growth occurs at the axillary buds.
18. The red wavelengths in the room's lights quickly convert the phytochrome in the chrysanthemums to the P_{fr} form, which inhibits flowering in a long-night plant. The chrysanthemums will not flower unless the security guard can set up some far-red lights. Exposure to a burst of far-red light would convert the phytochrome to the P_r form, allowing flowering to occur.
19. The biologist could remove leaves at different stages of being eaten to see how long it takes for changes to occur in nearby leaves. The "hormone" could be captured in an agar block, as in the phototropism experiments in Module 33.1, and applied to an undamaged plant. Another experiment would be to block "hormone" movement out of a damaged leaf or into a nearby leaf.
20. Some issues and questions to consider: Is the chemical safe for human consumption? What are its effects on the environment? Could its production produce impurities or wastes that might be harmful? What kinds of tests need to be done to demonstrate its safety? How much does it cost to make and use? Are the benefits worth the costs and risks? Is it worth using an artificial chemical on food simply to improve its appearance?

    A scientist could seek answers by studying the stability of the chemical in a variety of laboratory simulations of natural conditions. The toxicity of the chemical, the materials used to produce it, and its breakdown products could be determined in laboratory tests.
21. Charles and Francis Darwin were the first to demonstrate that some signal moves through the plant and controls growth. Boysen-Jensen demonstrated that this signal must be a diffusible chemical. Went named auxin and demonstrated that a higher concentration of this chemical accumulated on the dark side of the shoot. You could make an argument that any one of these was the "discoverer" of auxin, depending on how you define the moment of discovery.

Chapter 34

1. a. The shape of Earth results in uneven heating, such that the tropics are warm and polar regions are cold.
   b. The seasonal differences of winter and summer in temperate and polar regions are produced as Earth tips toward or away from the sun during its orbit around the sun.
   c. Intense solar radiation in the tropics evaporates moisture; warm air rises, cools, and drops its moisture as rain; air circulates, cools, and drops around 30°N and S, warming as it descends and evaporating moisture from land, which creates arid regions in the temperate zones.
2. f 3. g 4. d 5. a 6. c 7. b 8. e 9. a 10. d 11. c 12. a 13. b 14. b
15. Tropical rain forests have a warm, moist climate, with favorable growing conditions year-round. The diverse plant growth provides various habitats for other organisms.
16. After identifying your biome by looking at the map in Figure 34.8, review Module 34.5 on climate and the module that describes your biome (Modules 34.9–34.17).
17. Warmer air causes more evaporation from the land and sea, and a warmer atmosphere holds more moisture. As a result, some areas would experience torrential rainstorms. In areas where rainfall is typically low, increased evaporation would lead to increasingly dry soils and drought.

18. a. All three areas have plenty of sunlight and nutrients.
    b. The addition of nitrogen or phosphorus "fertilizes" the algae living in ponds and lakes, leading to explosive population growth. (These nutrients are typically in short supply in aquatic ecosystems.) The effects are harmful to the ecosystem. Algae cover the surface, reducing light penetration. When the algae die, bacterial decomposition of the large amount of biomass can deplete the oxygen available in the pond or lake, which may adversely affect the animal community.
19. a. desert; b. grassland; c. tropical forest; d. temperate forest; e. coniferous forest; f. arctic tundra. The climograph is based on annual averages; areas of overlap have to do with seasonal variations in temperature and precipitation.
20. Through convergent evolution, these unrelated animals adapted in similar ways to similar environments—temperate grasslands and savanna.
21. The robin die-off appears to be correlated with the application of DDT, but this is weak evidence. Scientists would consider alternative explanations, for example, some kind of parasite or infectious disease; starvation due to a sudden lack of a critical food resource; or some other drastic change in the environment. To explore the correlation with DDT application, scientists would need to investigate factors such as the concentration of DDT present in earthworms, the number of earthworms typically consumed by robins, the concentrations of DDT in the tissues of living and dead robins, and the lethal dose of DDT for robins. Scientists would also determine whether the situation seen on the Michigan State campus, or circumstances similar to it, had been observed elsewhere. For example, they would try to find out whether robin mortality had been observed at other sites where DDT had been applied, as well as at locations where DDT had *not* been applied. They would also look for published evidence of the effects of DDT on other bird species or other wildlife.

Chapter 35

1. a. genetics; b. fixed action pattern (FAP); c. imprinting; d. spatial learning; e. associative learning; f. social learning
2. d 3. c 4. d 5. a
6. Main advantage: Flies do not live long. Innate behaviors can be performed the first time without learning, enabling flies to find food, mates, and so on without practice. Main disadvantage: Innate behaviors are rigid; flies cannot learn to adapt to specific situations.
7. In a stressful environment, for example, where predators are abundant, rats that behave cautiously are more likely to survive long enough to reproduce.
8. Courtship behaviors reduce aggression between potential mates and confirm their species, sex, and physical condition. Environmental changes such as rainfall, temperature, and day length probably lead frogs to start calling, so these would be the proximate causes. The ultimate cause relates to evolution. Fitness (reproductive success) is enhanced for frogs that engage in courtship behaviors.
9. a. Yes. The experimenter found that 5 m provided the most food for the least energy because the total flight height (number of drops × height per drop) was the lowest. Crows appear to be using an optimal foraging strategy.
    b. An experiment could measure the average drop height for juvenile and adult birds, or it could trace individual birds during a time span from juvenile to adult and see if their drop height changed.
10. One likely hypothesis is that the helper is closely related to one or both of the birds in the mated pair. Because closely related birds share relatively many genes, the helper bird is indirectly enhancing its own fitness by helping its relatives raise their young. (In other words, this behavior evolved by kin selection.) The easiest way to test the hypothesis would be to determine the relatedness of the birds by DNA analysis. If birds are closely related, their DNA should be more similar than those of more distantly related or unrelated birds.
11. Identical twins are genetically the same, so any differences between them are due to environment. Thus, the study of identical twins enables researchers to sort out the effects of "nature" and "nurture" on human behavior. The data suggest that many aspects of human behavior are inborn. Some people find these studies disturbing because they seem to leave less room for free will and self-improvement than we would like. Results of such studies may be carelessly cited in support of a particular social agenda.
12. Example of a hypothesis: The chimpanzee mating system is polygamous. To test this hypothesis, observe mating behavior in a chimpanzee group over an extended period of time (to obtain data from multiple hormonal cycles for each of the sexually mature females in the group). Record and compile data on behaviors such as how and when individuals solicit sexual intercourse; number of successful approaches made by individuals; number of rejected approaches made by individuals; stage of hormonal cycle at the time of each approach by a male (for females); which individuals mate with each other; and male attentiveness to or guarding of the female after mating. If one male or female mates with several members of the opposite sex, the evidence supports the hypothesis.

Chapter 36

1. a. The *x* axis is time; the *y* axis is the number of individuals (*N*). The blue curve represents exponential growth; red is logistic growth.
    b. $G = rN$
    c. The carrying capacity of the environment (*K*)
    d. In exponential growth, population growth continues to increase as the population size increases. In logistic growth, the population grows fastest when the population is about 1/2 the carrying capacity—when *N* is large enough so that rN produces a large increase, but the expression $(K - N)/K$ has not yet slowed growth as much as it will as *N* gets closer to *K*.
    e. Exponential growth curve, although the worldwide growth rate is slowing
2. a. The blue line is birth rate; the red line is death rate.
    b. I. Both birth and death rates are high. II. Birth rates remain high; death rates decrease, perhaps as a result of increased sanitation and health care. III. Birth rates decline, often coupled with increased opportunities for women and access to birth control; death rates are low. IV. Both birth and death rates are low.
    c. I and IV
    d. II, when death rate has fallen but birth rate remains high
3. c 4. a 5. c 6. c 7. d 8. a 9. c
10. Food and resource limitation, such as food or nesting sites; accumulation of toxic wastes; disease; increase in predation; stress responses, such as seen in some rodents
11. Survivorship is the fraction of individuals in a given age interval that survive to the next interval. It is a measure of the probability of surviving at any given age. A survivorship curve shows the fraction of individuals in a population surviving at each age interval during the life span. Clams produce large numbers of offspring, most of which die young, with a few living a full life span. Few humans die young; most live out a full life span and die of old age. Squirrels have approximately constant mortality and about an equal chance of surviving at all ages.

12. Clumped is the most common dispersion pattern, usually associated with unevenly distributed resources or social grouping. Uniform dispersion may be related to territories or inhibitory interactions between plants. A random dispersion is least common and may occur when no particular factor influences the distribution of organisms.
13. Populations with *K*-selected life history traits tend to live in fairly stable environments held near carrying capacity by density-dependent limiting factors. They reproduce later and have fewer offspring than species with *r*-selected traits. Their lower reproductive rate makes it hard for them to recover from human-caused disruption of their habitat. We would expect such species to have a Type I survivorship curve (see Figure 36.3).
14. Testable predictions include the following: If sunspot activity affects snowshoe hare population cycles, then the cycles should correlate with sunspot activity. Tests on food resources should reveal corresponding fluctuations in chemicals that affect its nutritional quality. Nutritional quality of hares' food should be shown to affect their reproductive output.
15. Some issues and questions to consider: How does population growth in developing countries relate to food supply, pollution, and the use of natural resources? How are these things affected by population growth in developed countries? Which of these factors are most critical to our survival? Are they affected more by the growth of developing or developed countries? What will happen as developing countries become more developed?

Chapter 37

1.

Interspecific Interaction	Effect on Species 1	Effect on Species 2	Example (many other answers possible)
Predation	+	–	Crocodile/fish
Competition	–	–	Squirrel/black bear
Herbivory	+	–	Caterpillar/leaves
Parasites and pathogens	+	–	Heartworms/dog; *Salmonella*/person
Mutualism	+	+	Plant/mycorrhizae

2.

	Carbon	Phosphorus	Nitrogen
Main abiotic reservoir(s)	Atmosphere	Rocks	Atmosphere, soil
Form in abiotic reservoir	Carbon dioxide (CO_2)	Phosphate in rock	N_2 in atmosphere; ammonium (NH_4^+) or nitrate (NO_3^-) in soil
Form used by producers	Carbon dioxide (CO_2)	Phosphate (PO_4^{3-})	NH_4^+ or NO_3^-
Human activities that alter cycle	Burning wood and fossil fuels	Agriculture (fertilizers, feedlots, pesticides, soil erosion)	Agriculture (fertilizers, feedlots); burning fossil fuels
Effects of altering cycle	Global climate change	Eutrophication of aquatic ecosystems; nutrient-depleted soils	Eutrophication of aquatic ecosystems; nutrient-depleted soils; global warming; depletion of ozone layer; acid precipitation

3. d 4. b 5. b 6. c 7. d
8. Plants benefit by having their seeds distributed away from the parent. Animals benefit when the seeds contain food, as in fleshy fruits.
9. Rapid eutrophication occurs when bodies of water receive nutrient pollution (for example, from agricultural runoff) that results in blooms of cyanobacteria and algae. Respiration from these organisms and their decomposers depletes oxygen levels, leading to fish kills. Reducing this type of pollution will require controlling the sources of excess inorganic nutrients, for example, runoff from feedlots and fertilizers.
10. These animals are secondary or tertiary consumers, at the top of the energy pyramid. Stepwise energy loss means not much energy is left for them; thus, they are rare and require large territories in which to hunt.
11. Chemicals with a gaseous form in the atmosphere, such as carbon and nitrogen, have a global biogeochemical cycle.
12. Nitrogen fixation of atmospheric N_2 into ammonium; decomposition of detritus into ammonium; nitrification of ammonium into nitrate; denitrification (by denitrifiers) of nitrates into N_2
13. Hypothesis: The kangaroo rat is a keystone species in the desert. (Apparently, herbivory by the rats kept the one plant from outcompeting the others; removing the rats reduced plant diversity.) Additional supporting evidence would include observations of the rats preferentially eating dominant plants and finding that the dominant plant recovers from damage from other herbivores faster.
14. a. 1.1% (6,585/600,000 × 100); net primary production
    b. 1.2% (81/6,585); cellular respiration and waste
    c. 81 kcal/m²/year; 1.0 kcal/m²/year (1.2% of 81 kcal/m²/year)

Chapter 38

1. a. species at risk of extinction; b. restoration ecology; c. bioremediation; d. zoned reserves
2. c 3. c 4. a 5. d 6. b 7. c 8. a
9. Genetic, species, and ecosystem diversity. As populations become smaller, genetic diversity is usually reduced. Genetic diversity is also threatened when local populations of a species are extirpated owing to habitat destruction or other assaults, or when entire species are lost. Many human activities have led to the extinction of species. The greatest threats include habitat loss, invasive species, and overharvesting. Species extinction or population extirpation may alter the structure of whole communities. Pollution and other widespread disruptions such as development and agriculture may lead to the loss of entire ecosystems.
10. Greenhouse gases in the atmosphere, including carbon dioxide, methane, and nitrous oxide, absorb infrared radiation and thus slow the escape of heat from Earth. This is called the greenhouse effect (see Module 7.13). Without greenhouse gases in the atmosphere, the temperature at the surface of Earth would be much colder and less hospitable for life.
11. Fossil fuel consumption, industry, and agriculture are increasing the quantity of greenhouse gases—such as CO_2, methane, and nitrous oxide—in the atmosphere. These gases are trapping more heat and raising atmospheric temperatures. Increases of 2–5°C are projected over the next century. Logging and the clearing of forests for farming contribute to global warming by reducing the uptake of CO_2 by plants (and adding CO_2 to the air when trees are burned). Global warming is having numerous effects already, including melting polar ice, permafrost, and glaciers, shifting patterns of precipitation, causing spring

temperatures to arrive earlier, and reducing the number of cold days and nights. In other words, global warming is causing climate change. Future consequences include rising sea levels and the extinction of many plants and animals. Climate change is an international problem because air and climate do not recognize international boundaries. Greenhouse gases are primarily produced by industrialized nations. Cooperation and commitment to reduce use of fossil fuels and to reduce deforestation will be necessary if the problem of climate change is to be solved.

12. Possible studies could include changes in the size or distribution of snowshoe hare populations, how changes in hare populations affect plant communities in the hares' habitat, how changes in hare populations affect predator populations, how changes in hare populations affect other prey populations, the effect on overall species diversity in taiga communities, and evolutionary changes in hare populations.
13. Some issues and questions to consider: How does the use of fossil fuels affect the environment? What about oil spills? Disruption of wildlife habitat for construction of oil fields and pipelines? Burning of fossil fuels that triggers climate change and flooding from global warming? Pollution of lakes and destruction of property by acid precipitation? Health effects of polluted air on humans? How are we paying for these "side effects" of fossil fuel use? In taxes? In health insurance premiums? Do we pay a nonfinancial price in terms of poorer health and quality of life? Could oil companies be required to pick up the tab for environmental effects of fossil fuel use? Could these costs be covered by an oil tax? How would this change the price of oil? How does a change in the price of oil change our pattern of energy use, our lifestyle, and our environment?
14. The per capita rankings of the United States and Canada are generally very high, along with other developed nations. Transportation and energy use are the major contributors to the carbon footprint. Any actions you can take to reduce these will help. For example, if you have a car, you can try to minimize the number of miles you drive by consolidating errands into fewer trips and using an alternative means of transportation (public transportation, walking, biking) whenever possible. To reduce energy consumption, be aware of the energy you use: Turn off lights, disconnect electronics that draw power when on standby, do laundry in cold water, for example. Websites such as http://www.nature.org/greenliving/carboncalculator/index.htm (The Nature Conservancy) and http://www.epa.gov/climatechange/ghgemissions/ind-calculator.html (U.S. Environmental Protection Agency) offer simple suggestions such as changing to energy-efficient lightbulbs. A Web search will turn up plenty of sites.
15. Some issues and questions to consider: How do population growth, resource consumption, pollution, and reduction in biodiversity relate to sustainability? How do poverty, economic growth and development, and political issues relate to sustainability? Why might developed and developing nations take different views of a sustainable society? What would life be like in a sustainable society? Have any steps toward sustainability been taken in your community? What are the obstacles to sustainability in your community? What steps have you taken toward a sustainable lifestyle? How old will you be in 2030? What do you think life will be like then?

Credits

Photo Credits

Cover Heather Angel /Natural Visions /Alamy Stock Photo

Detailed Table of Contents Reinhard Dirscherl/Alamy; Dougal Waters/Getty Images; SPL/Science Source; Peter B. Armstrong; StockLite/Shutterstock; ImageDJ/Jupiter Images; Ed Reschke/Getty Images; M. Lenke/Blickwinkel/AGE Fotostock; Biophoto Associates/Science Source; Ethan Bier; Hank Morgan/Science Source; Luis César Tejo/Shutterstock; ZUMA Press, Inc./Alamy; H Reinhard/Arco Images GmbH/Alamy; Jared Hobbs/SuperStock; Rick & Nora Bowers/Alamy; Eye of Science/Science Source; Bob Gibbons/Alamy; Danté Fenolio /Science Source; Jean-Philippe Varin /Science Source; Jeff Wheeler/MCT/Newscom; Jennette van Dyk/Getty Images; Corbis/AGE Fotostock; Science Source; Chris Bjornberg /Science Source; BERNARD CASTELEIN/Nature Picture Library; Belinda Images/SuperStock; Andaman/Shutterstock; Corey Ralston/Getty Images; Science Source; Manfred Kage/Science Source; N. F. Photography/Shutterstock; Nagel Photography/Shutterstock; Tim Hill/Alamy; Brian Capon; Fred Jensen; Don Fink/Shutterstock; Clive Bromhall/Getty Images; Simon Phillpotts/Alamy

Unit Openers **Unit I** Hero Images/Getty Images; **left** Doug Hodges; **right** Crista Shopis; **Unit II** SPL/Science Source; **left** Smantha Dube; **right** Jason Halal; **Unit III** ZUMA Press, Inc./Alamy Stock Photo; **left** Kevin Welzel; **right** Randy Olson; **Unit IV** Education Images/Getty Images; **left** Courtesy Traci McCollister and Dominik Mosur; **right** Courtesy Briana Pobiner; **Unit V** kali9/Getty Images; **left** Courtesy Corene Carpenter, Berkeley Dog & Cat Hospital; Berkeley, CA.; **right** Silvia Ramos; **Unit VI** Bill Hatcher/National Geographic/Getty Images; **left** Courtesy Francisca Coelho, New York Botanical Garden; **right** Brian Kemble; **Unit VII** Pete Mcbride/National Geographic/Getty Images; **left** Steven Veit; **right** Courtesy Jason Gorman, Finger Lakes Land Trust.

Chapter 1 **Chapter Opener** WILDLIFE GmbH/Alamy Stock Photo; **p. xxxviii left** asharkyu/Shutterstock; **p.xxxviii right** Sacha Vignieri; **p.xxxviii inset** Sacha Vignieri; **1.1.1** asharkyu/Shutterstock; **1.1.2** Werner Bollmann/AGE Fotostock; **1.1.3** WILDLIFE GmbH/Alamy; **1.1.4** ekawatchaow/Shutterstock; **1.1.4** Fabio Pupin/FLPA; **1.1.5** Vera Kutelvaserova/Fotolia; **1.1.6** kat334/Fotolia; **1.2 top to bottom** Meckes/Ottawa/Science Source; Dr. D. P. Wilson/Science Source; Florapix/Alamy; FLPA/Alamy; Doug Meek/Shutterstock; **1.3 left to right** Masa Ushioda/AGE Fotostock; seaphotoart/Fotolia; Alfredo Maiquez/Alamy Stock Photo; **1.5 left** Sacha Vignieri; Zoonar GmbH/Alamy Stock Photo; **1.5 right** Hopi Hoekstra, Harvard University; Shawn P. Carey; **1.6 center** leungchopan/Shutterstock; **1.6 top** Michel Loiselle/Zoonar GmbH/Alamy Stock Photo; **1.6 bottom** R Kaufung/AGE Fotostock; **1.9A top** StevenRussellSmithPhotos/Shutterstock; **1.9A left** zhaoyan/Shutterstock; **1.9A right** Volodymyr Goinyk/Shutterstock; **1.9C** Eric Isselée/Fotolia; **1.12A** Palto/Shutterstock; **1.12B** shahreen/Shutterstock; **1.12B inset** From "Functional anatomy of the red panda; forelimb", M. Antón et al, Journal Compilation, 6, Anatomical Society of Great Britain and Ireland, page 7; **1.13** Ron Erwin/AGE Fotostock; **1.14** gloriaclares/Fotolia; **p. 17** Ron Erwin/AGE Fotostock

Chapter 2 **Chapter Opener** Mark Conlin/Alamy; **2.1A left** Chip Clark/Fundamental Photographs; **2.1A Center** Pearson Education/Pearson Science; **2.1A right** Pearson Education; **2.2A** Alison Wright/Science Source; **2.2B** Robyn Mackenzie/Shutterstock; **2.2C** Anton Prado/Alamy; **2.4A** Will & Deni McIntyre/Science Source; **2.4B** Chester A. Mathis; **2.7B** Pearson Education/Pearson Science; **2.10** Herman Eisenbeiss/Science Source; **2.11** Radharc Images /Alamy; **2.12** Josef Friedhuber/Getty Images; **2.14 top** Ian 210/Fotolia; **2.14 center** VR Photos/Shutterstock; **2.14 bottom** Beth Van Trees/Shutterstock; **2.15B** Reinhard Dirscherl/Alamy

Chapter 3 **Chapter Opener** Jamie Gill/Getty Images; **3.2** george-sanker/Alamy; **3.4A** Douglas Waters/Getty Images; **3.7 left** Douglas Waters/Getty Images; **3.7 right** Biophoto Associates/Science Source; **3.7 center** Dr. Loyd M Beidler; **3.7 bottom** Biophoto Associates/Science Source; **3.8C top left** Stargazer/Shutterstock; **3.8C top right** Angel Simon/Shutterstock; **3.8C bottom left** Thomas M Perkins/Shutterstock; **3.8C bottom right** Alex Staroseltsev/Shutterstock; **3.9** panki/Shutterstock; **p. 46 center** Anetta/Shutterstock; **3.12C** Dieter Hopf/imageBROKER/AGE Fotostock; **3.16 left** Peter Horree/Alamy; **3.16 right** Ton Koene/Alamy

Chapter 4 **Chapter Opener** Jennifer C. Waters/Science Source; **p. 55 bottom right** Dr. Mary Osborn; **4.1A** Michael Abbey/Science Source; **4.1B** Andrew Syred/Science Source; **4.1C** Dr. Klaus Boller/Science Source; **4.1D** Spike Walker /Science Source; **4.3** Dr. Linda M. Stannard, University of Cape Town/Science Source; **4.5** David M. Phillips/Science Source; **4.6** Joseph F. Gennaro Jr./Science Source; **4.8A** Don Fawcett/Science Source; **4.9** Biophoto Associates/Science Source; **4.11A** Roland Birke/Getty Images; **4.11B** Biophoto Associates/Science Source; **4.13** Don Fawcett/Science Source; **4.16 left** Dr. Frank Solomon; **4.16 center** Mark Ladinsky; **4.16 right** Dr. Mary Osborn; **4.17** Albert Tousson; **4.18A** Omikron/Science Source; **4.18B** Meckes/Ottawa/Science Source; **4.18C** Bjorn Afzelius

Chapter 5 **Chapter Opener** B.L. de Groot; **5.2** Peter B. Armstrong; **5.16** Krista Kennell/Newscom

Chapter 6 **6.13C.1** StockLite/Shutterstock; **Chapter Opener** Stephen Marks/Getty Images; **p. 93 left** StockLite/Shutterstock; **p. 93 right** David & Micha Sheldon/AGE Fotostock; **6.2** UpperCut Images/Alamy; **6.12C right** Sean Lower/Marty Taylor; **6.2C left** Sean Lower/Marty Taylor; **6.14** Simon Smith/DK Images; **6.15** David & Micha Sheldon/AGE Fotostock

Chapter 7 **Chapter Opener** AGE Fotostock/Alamy; **p. 111 bottom** ImageDJ/Jupiter Images/Getty Images; **7.1A** ODM/Shutterstock; **7.1B** Mark Conlin/Alamy; **7.1C** Dr. Susan M. Barns; **7.2 top** Pearson Education; **7.2 center** Graham Kent/Pearson Education; **7.2 bottom** Dr. Jeremy Burgess/Science Source; **7.3** Martin Shields/Alamy; **7.6B** llaszlo/Shutterstock; **7.7A** Christine Case; **7.11 left** Dinodia/AGE Fotostock; **7.11 right** ImageDJ/Jupiter Images/Getty Images; **7.13A** Will Owens and William H. Schlesinger; **7.14B** Michael Boyny/LOOK Die Bildagentur der Fotografen GmbH/Alamy

Chapter 8 **Chapter Opener** Steve Gschmeissner/Science Source; **8.UN.1** Dr. Yorgos Nikas/Science Source; **p. 129 bottom right** Michelle Gilders/Alamy; **8.1A** Pick up from previous edition; add SPL/Science Source; **8.1B** Roger Steene/Image Quest Marine; **8.1C** Eric J. Simon; **8.1D** Zia Soleil/Getty Images; **8.1E** Dr. Yorgos Nikas/Science Source; **8.1F** Dr. Torsten Wittmann/Science Source; **8.2B** Lee D. Simon/Science Source; **8.3A** Dr. Andrew S. Bajer, University of Oregon; **8.3B** Biophoto Associates/Science Source; **8.5 p. 134 left** Conly L. Rieder, Ph.D.; **8.5 p. 134 center** Conly L. Rieder, Ph.D.; **8.5 p. 134 right** Conly L. Rieder, Ph.D.; **8.5 p. 135 left** Conly L. Rieder, Ph.D.; **8.5 p. 135 center** Conly L. Rieder, Ph.D.; **8.5 p. 135 right** Conly L. Rieder, Ph.D.; **8.6A** Don Fawcett/Science Source; **8.6B** Eldon Newcomb; **8.12A** Ron Chapple/Alamy; **8.13** Ed Reschke/Getty Images; **8.16A top** Jules Frazier/Getty Images, Inc.; **8.16A bottom** Roxana Gonzalez/Shutterstock; **8.16B** Mark Petronczki; **8.19 left** Hop Americain/Science Source; **8.19 right** CNRI/Science Source; **8.20A top** SPL/Science Source; **8.20A bottom** Lauren Shear/Science Source; **8.22** Michelle Gilders/Alamy; **p. 155** J.L. Carson/Photo Researchers, Inc./AGE Fotostock

Chapter 9 **Chapter Opener** Gordon Wiltsie/Getty Images; **p. 156 left** akg-images/Newscom; **p. 156 right** Jean Dickey; **9.1** Classic Image/Alamy Stock Photo; **9.2A** akg-images/Newscom; **9.5B1** Tracy Morgan/

Dorling Kindersley; **9.5B2** Tracy Morgan/Dorling Kindersley; **9.5B3** Eric Isselee/Shutterstock; **9.5B4** Victoria Rak/Shutterstock; **9.8 left** Photo Disc/Getty Images; **9.8 right** Photo Disc/Getty Images; **9.9A1** NinaMalyna/Fotolia.com; **9.9A2** Westend61/Getty Images; **9.9A3** Shell114/Shutterstock; **9.9A4** Milkos/Fotolia; **9.9C** Michael Ciesielski Photography; **9.10A** CNRI/Science Source; **9.10B** Monkey Business Images/Shutterstock; **9.10B inset** SPL /Science Source; **9.13A** Meckes/Ottawa/Science Source; **9.13B** Meckes/Ottawa/Science Source; **9.15A** Eric J. Simon; **9.15B** Jean Dickey; **9.18B** M. Lenke/AGE Fotostock; **9.20A** SPL/Science Source; **9.20B top left** People Images/Getty Images; **9.20B top right** Yuri Arcurs/Shutterstock; **9.20B bottom left** Anatoliy Samara/Shutterstock; **9.20B bottom right** Rubberball/Nicole Hill/Getty Images; **Table 9.20 top to bottom** fotosutra/Shutterstock; kosam/Shutterstock; anatchant/Fotolia; **9.21A left** Johner Images/AGE Fotostock; **9.21A right** blickwinkel/Kottmann/Alamy Stock Photo; **9.22** FPG/Getty; **9.23** PRISMA ARCHIVO/Alamy Stock Photo

Chapter 10 **10.CO** Public Health England Centre for Infections /Science Source; **10.1A** Biophoto Associates/Science Source; **10.3A** Library of Congress; **10.3A inset** Cold Spring Harbor Laboratory Archives; **10.3B** National Institute of Health; **10.6B** Kevin McCluskey, PhD; **10.8C** Yonhap Choi Byung-kil/AP Images; **10.12A** Joachim Frank; **p. 205 right** Hazel Appleton, Health Protection Agency Centre for Infections/Science Source; **10.19 clockwise from top left** Scott Camazine/Alamy Stock Photo; CDC/Dr. Terrence Tumpey; CDC/P.E. Rollin; National Institute of Allergy and Infectious Diseases (NIAID); CDC/Courtesy of Cynthia Goldsmith; Jacqueline Katz; Sherif R. Zaki; National Institute of Allergy and Infectious Diseases (NIAID); CDC/Cynthia Goldsmith; National Institute of Allergy and Infectious Diseases (NIAID); **10.23C** Huntington Potter

Chapter 11 **Chapter Opener** Handout/Getty Images; **p. 212 left** Martin Oeggerli/Science Source; **p. 212 right** Robyn Mackenzie/Shutterstock; **11.1A** Martin Oeggerli/Science Source; **11.2 left** Don. W. Fawcett/Science Source; **11.2 right** Biophoto Associates/Science Source; **11.2B** Eric Isselee/Shutterstock; **11.8A** F. Rudolf Turner; **11.9A** Ethan Bier; **11.9B** Alila Medical Media/Shutterstock; **11.12** Robyn Mackenzie/Shutterstock; **11.16A** Geo Martinez/Shutterstock

Chapter 12 **Chapter Opener** SunnyStock/Shutterstock; **p. 234 left** Pichi Chuang/Thomson Reuters; **p. 234 right** Hank Morgan/Science Source; **p. 235 left** F. Rudolf Turner/Repligen; **p. 235 right** Philippe Plailly & Atelier Daynes/Science Source; **12.1A** Pichi Chuang/Thomson Reuters; **12.1B top to bottom** Smileus/Dreamstime LLC; A.J. Sisco/UPI/Newscom; Dmitry Lobanov/Fotolia; CLIPAREA.com/Fotolia; **12.6A** Brad DeCecco Photography; **12.7A** Eli Lilly and Company; **12.7B** Hank Morgan/Science Source; **12.8A** Vladimir Nikitin/Shutterstock; **12.8B** Patti McConville/Alamy; **12.9 left** Borys Shevchuk/Fotolia; **12.9 center** Kirill Kurashov/Shutterstock; **12.9 right** Dionisvera/Shutterstock; **12.13** F. Rudolf Turner/Repligen; **p. 249** Steve Helber/AP Photo; **12.16** P. Morris/Garvan Institute of Medical Research; **12.20** Greg M. Herringer/Getty Images; **12.21** Philippe Plailly & Atelier Daynes/Look Sciences/Science Source

Chapter 13 **Chapter Opener** Sukree Sakplang/Reuters; **13.1A left** Archiv/Science Source; **13.1A right** National Maritime Museum Picture Library; **13.1B** Peter Scoones/Science Source; **13.1C** Stefan Huwiler/Corbis; **13.2A** Colin Keates/DK Images; **13.2B** Chip Clark/Courtesy of Smithsonian Institution; **13.2C** John Henshall/Alamy; **13.4B left** Dr. Keith Wheeler/Science Source; **13.4B right** TT Nyhetsbyra°n AB/Lennart Nilsson Photography; **13.6 center** Luis César Tejo/Shutterstock; **13.6 bottom right** Juniors Bildarchiv/Alamy; **13.6 bottom left** Kenneth W. Fink/Science Source; **13.6 top right** ZUMA Press, Inc./Alamy; **13.6 top left** Arco Images GmbH/Alamy; **13.7** Philip Wallick/Getty Images; **13.8** Edmund D. Brodie III; **13.9** Adam Jones/Getty Images; **13.11** Anne Dowie/Pearson Education; **13.12B** William Ervin/Science Source; **13.13** Steffen Foerster/Shutterstock; **13.14 left** Sergej Razvodovskij/Shutterstock; **13.14 right** Carlton Ward/Getty Images; **13.15A** Dave Blackey/Getty Images; **13.15B** George D. Lepp/Getty Images; **13.15C** Barry Mansell/Nature Picture Library

Chapter 14 **Chapter Opener** Barrie Britton/Nature Picture Library; **p. 280 left** Tier und Naturfotografie/SuperStock; **p. 280 right** Ole Seehausen; **14.1** Charles Darwin; **14.2A left** Malcom Schuyl/Alamy; **14.2A right** David Kjaer/Nature Picture Library; **14.2B left to right** XiXinXing/Shutterstock; Daxiao Productions/Shutterstock; Darren Baker/Fotolia.com; Radius Images/Getty Images; Zurijeta/Shutterstock; Masterfile Corporation; **14.2 top to bottom** CLFProductions/Shutterstock; janprchal/Shutterstock; Troy Maben/AP Images; **p. 284 1st column** Joe McDonald/Photoshot Holdings Ltd.; Joe Mcdonald/Getty Images; **p. 284 2nd column** USDA/APHIS Animal and Plant Health Inspection Service; Jared Hobbs/SuperStock; **p. 284 3rd column** J&C Sohns/AGE Fotostock; Tier und Naturfotografie/SuperStock; **p. 284 4th column** Phillippe Clement/Nature Picture Library; Oyvind Martinsen Wildlife Collection/Alamy Stock Photo; **p. 285 1st column** SERDAR/Alamy Stock Photo; WaterFrame/Alamy Stock Photo; **p. 285 2nd column** Chuck Brown/Science Source; FreeReinDesigns/fotolia; Kazutoshi Okuno; **14.4A** Corbis; **14.4A left** John Shaw/Photoshot; **14.4A right** Michael Fogden/Photoshot License Limited **14.4B** Arthur Anker/Florida Museum of Natural History; **14.5B** Douglas W. Schemske; **14.7B** Ole Seehausen; **14.8 top to bottom** imageBROKER/Alamy Stock Photo; Mary Plage/Getty Images; Ralph Lee Hopkins/National Geographic RF/Getty Images; **14.9A** Peter Grant; **14.10B left** Melvin Grey/Photoshot; **14.10B right** Juan Martin Simon; **14.10C** Ole Seehausen; **p. 294 bottom** Ole Seehausen

Chapter 15 **Chapter Opener** Paul Hobson/NaturePL; **p. 297 bottom** valon/Photoshot License/Alamy; **15.1 inset** Francois Gohier/Science Source; **15.1** Courtesy of Smithsonian Institution. Painting by P. Sawyer; **15.3A** Menger, Fred M.; **15.7D** Roland Seitre/Nature Picture Library; **15.7E** Phil Savoie/Nature Picture Library; **15.7F** Rick & Nora Bowers/Alamy Stock Photo; **15.8A** David Parker/Science Source; **15.11A** Avalon/Photoshot License/Alamy Stock Photo; **15.11B** Jean Kern; **15.11C** Dr. William A. Cresko; **15.12 left to right** Hal Beral/V & W/Image Quest Marine; Christophe Courteau/Biosphoto/Science Source; reinhard Diracherl/Alamy; Jim Greenfield/Image Quest Marine; James Watt/ImageQuestMarine; **15.16C** Image # 5789, American Museum of Natural History Library; **15.18** CDC/Frank Collins, Ph.D.

Chapter 16 **Chapter Opener** SPL/Science Source; **p. 322 left** SPL/Science Source; **p. 322 right** Steve Gschmeissner/Science Source; **16.1** SPL/Science Source; **16.2 left** Eye of Science/Science Source; **16.2A center** David McCarthy/SPL/Science Source; **16.2A right** Stem Jems/Science Source; **16.2B** ASM/Science Source; **16.2C** Rantala/Science Source; **16.2D** Meckes/Ottawa/Science Source; **16.3A** Huntington Potter; **16.3B** Scott Camazine/Science Source; **16.4 top left** Sinclair Stammers/Science Source; **16.4 top right** T. Stevens & P. McKinely/SPL/Science Source; **16.4 bottom left** Pasieka/SPL/Science Source; **16.4 bottom right** Dr. Gary Gaugler/Science Source; **16.5** Garry Palmateer; **16.6A** SPL/Science Source; **16.6B** SIPA USA/SIPA/Newscom; **16.7 left** Eye of Science/Science Source; **16.7 center** Eye of Science/Science Source; **16.7 right** Eric Isselée/Fotolia; **16.8A** A Jay Clark/Fotolia; **16.8B** Jim West /Alamy Stock Photo; **16.9A** National Library of Medicine; **16.9B** Meckes/Ottawa/Science Source; **16.9C** Susan M. Barns, Ph.D.; **16.9D** Moredun Animal Health/SPL/Science Source; **16.9E** Science Source; **16.10A** David M. Phillips/Science Source; **16.10B** Steve Lindridge/Alamy; **16.11 inset** Anders Wiklund/Reuters Limited; **16.11** James Cavallini/Science Source; **16.12A left** Carol Buchanan/AGE Fotostock; **16.12A center** Eye of Science/Science Source; **16.12A right** Wim Van Egmond/Science Source; **16.12B inset** Patrick Keeling; **16.12B** Eric V. Grave/Science Source; **16.13 top to bottom** Steve Gschmeissner/Science Source; Andrew Syred/Science Source; David Caron/Science Source; David M. Phillips/Science Source; Steve Gschmeissner/SPL/Science Source; Eye of Science/Science Source; Dr. George L. Barron; Alex Hyde/Nature Picture Library; Aaron J. Bell/Science Source; **16.14A** Steve Gschmeissner/Science Source; **16.14B** Georgie Holland/AGE Fotostock; **16.14C** Christine Smart; **16.14D** Miriam Godfrey/National Institute of Water and Atmospheric Research; **16.14E** Andrew Syred/Science Source; **16.14F inset** David Caron/Look Sciences/Science Source; **16.14F** Dee Breger/Photo Researchers; **16.14G** Steve Gschmeissner/SPL/Science Source; **16.15** Photoshot/Newscom; **16.16A** Meckes/Ottawa/Science Source; **16.16B** Eye of Science/Science Source; **16.17A** Biophoto Associates/Science Source; **16.17B inset** Ray Simons/Science Source; **16.17B** Dr. George L. Barron; **16.17C** Robert Kay; **16.18A**

Alex Hyde/Nature Picture Library; **16.18B left** Aaron J. Bell/Science Source; **16.18B right** Manfred Kage/SPL/Science Source; **16.18C** D. P. Wilson/Eric and David Hosking/Science Source; **16.19B** David J. Patterson; **p. 342 left** David M. Phillips/Science Source; **p. 342 right** Dr. Gary Gaugler/Science Source

Chapter 17 **Chapter Opener** Andrew Daymond/Alamy Stock Photo; **p. 345 bottom** Frank Young/Papilio/Getty Images; **17.1A** Bob Gibbons/Alamy; **17.1B** Dr. Linda E. Graham; **17.1D** Robert Marien/Corbis; **17.2B left** Matthijs Wetterauw/Alamy; **17.2B center** Dr. Jeremy Burgess/SPL/Science Source; **17.2B right** Hidden Forest; **17.2C left** Ed Reschke/Photolibrary, Inc.; **17.2C right** Colin Walton/Dorling Kindersley, Ltd.; **17.2D left to right** blickwinkel/Alamy; John Cancalosi/Getty Images; Bob Gibbons/Alamy; Pichugin Dmitry/Shutterstock; **17.2E left** Koos Van Der Lende/AGE Fotostock; **17.2E right** Nigel Cattlin/Alamy; **17.3.1** Sanamyan/Alamy; **17.3.2** Steffen Hauser/AGE Fotostock/SuperStock; **17.3.3** olesia/AGE Fotostock; **17.3.4** J Fieber/AGE Fotostock; **17.3.5** AGE Fotostock; **17.3.6** George Ostertag/AGE Fotostock; **17.4** Open University, Department of Earth Sciences; **17.5A left** Morales/AGE Fotostock; **17.5A bottom right** Trent Dietsche/Alamy; **17.5 top right** Brent Bergherm/AGE Fotostock; **17.6A** Jean Dickey; **17.7** Fortish/Shutterstock; **17.8A inset** Agita Leimane/Shutterstock; **17.8A** rakim/Shutterstock; **17.8B inset** Derek Hall/Dorling Kindersley, Ltd.; **17.8B** Scott Camazine/Science Source; **17.8C inset** Bryan Brunner; **17.8C** Cal Vornberg/AGE Fotostock; **17.9** Jethro Toe/Shutterstock; **17.10A** MShieldsPhotos/Alamy; **17.10B** Jean Dickey; **17.10C** D. Wilder/Wilder Nature Photography; **17.11A left** Bart Wursten; **17.11A right** SoFood/Superstock; **17.11B** NASA; **17.12A** Fred Rhoades; **17.12A inset** Dr. George L. Barron; **17.12B** BlueMoon Stock/Alamy; **17.14B** Gregory G. Dimijian/Science Source; **17.14D left** H Reinhard/AGE Fotostock; **17.14D right** Frank Young/Papilio/Getty Images; **17.14E top left** Phil Dotson/Science Source; **17.14E top right** Adrian Davies/Photoshot; **17.14E bottom** Inger Hogstrom/AGE Fotostock; **17.15** Emmanuel Lattes/Alamy; **17.16A** Filatov Alexey/Shutterstock; **17.16B** Christine Case; **17.16C** C Huetter/AGE Fotostock; **17.17A** NHPA/SuperStock; **17.17B** Eye of Science/Science Source; **17.17C** Jean Dickey; **17.19A** Long Photography, Inc.; **17.19B** Astrid/Hanns Frieder Michler//SPL/Science Source; **17.19C** Nigel Cattlin/Science Source; **p. 367 left** R.J. Erwin/Science Source; **p. 367 right** Adrian Davies/Photoshot

Chapter 18 **Chapter Opener** Jochen Tack/Alamy; **p. 368** Maximilian Weinzierl/Alamy; **18.1A** Gunter Ziesler/Getty Images; **18.2A left** South Australian Museum; **18.2A right** Regents of the University of California; **18.2B.1** John Sibbick/The Natural History Museum, London; **18.2B.2** Chip Clark; **18.5A left to right** James Watt/ImageQuestMarine; Andrew J. Martinez/Science Source; Paul Kay/Getty Images; **18.6A left** Jonathan Bird/Getty Images, Inc.; **18.6A top** SPL/Science Source; **18.6B** Reinhard Dirscherl /Getty Images; **18.7B** Meckes/Ottawa/Science Source; **18.8A** American Association for the Advancement of Science (AAAS); **18.8B** Gavin Parsons /Getty Images; **18.9C inset** Jez Tryner/Image Quest Marine; **18.9C** GK Hart/Vikki Hart/Getty Images, Inc.; **18.9D inset** Marevision/AGE Fotostock; **18.9D** Christophe Courteau/Nature Picture Library; **18.9E inset** Dante Fenolio/Science Source; **18.9E** blickwinkel/Alamy; **18.10A** A.N.T./Photoshot Holdings Ltd.; **18.10B left** SPL/Science Source; **18.10B right** Douglas P Wilson/AGE Fotostock; **18.10C left** Jurgen Freund/Nature Picture Library; **18.10C right** SPL/Science Source; **18.11B** Angelo Giampiccolo/Nature Picture Library; **18.11C left** EcoPrint/Shutterstock; **18.11C center** Scott Camazine/Alamy; **18.11C right** Meckes/Ottawa/Science Source; **18.11D** George Grall/Getty Images, Inc.; **18.11E** Mark Smith/Science Source; **18.11F inset** Colin Milkins/Getty Images, Inc.; **18.11F** Maximilian Weinzierl/Alamy; **18.12A.1** Hecker/Sauer/AGE Fotostock; **18.12A.2** W Holzenbecher/AGE Fotostock; **18.12A.3** M Woike/AGE Fotostock America Inc.; **18.12C left** Buddy Mays/Alamy; **18.12C center** Martin Shields/Alamy; **18.12C right** Matt Jeppson/Shutterstock; **18.12C center** Dante Fenolio/Science Source; **18.12E left** Alan Blank/Alamy; **18.12E right** Purestock/Getty Images, Inc.; **18.13B top left** Rod Williams/Nature Picture Library; **18.13B top right** Morley Read/Shutterstock; **18.13B bottom row** Stephen Paddock; **18.14B** Andrew J. Martinez/Science Source; **18.14C** Louise Murray/AGE Fotostock; **18.15A** Marevision/AGE Fotostock America Inc.; **18.15B** Jez Tryner/Image Quest Marine; **18.16A** Doug Perrine/Nature Picture Library; **18.16B** Linda Pitkin/220VISION/Nature Picture Library; **18.16C** S. Kuelcue/Shutterstock

Chapter 19 **Chapter Opener** Beawiharta/Thomson Reuters Pictures; **p. 392 left** Publiphoto/Photo Researchers, Inc.; **p. 392 right** David Tlipling/Nature Picture Library; **19.2A** Tom McHugh/Photo Researchers, Inc.; **19.2B inset** Marevision/AGE Fotostock America Inc.; **19.2B** Gary Meszaros/Science Source; **19.3B** George Grall/National Geographic Stock; **19.3C** Bernard Radvaner/AGE Fotostock; **19.3D** T. Leeson/Science Source; **19.3E.1** Andrey Nekrasov /Alamy; **19.3E.2** Marevision/AGE Fotostock; **19.3E.3** Jeff Rotman; **19.3F** Rudie Kuiter/OceanwideImages.com; **19.4B** Publiphoto/Science Source; **19.5A** Heinemann/Westend61 GmbH/Alamy; **19.5B** Dante Fenolio/Science Source; **19.5C** hotshotsworldwide/Fotolia; **19.5D** DE Photography/Fotolia; **19.5E** DP Wildlife Vertebrates/Alamy; **19.6A** Sylvain Cordier; **19.6C** Steven David Miller/Nature Picture Library; **19.7A** Huwiler Stefan/punchstock/Getty Images; **19.7B** Andy Rouse/Nature Picture Library; **19.8A** Jean-Philippe Varin/Science Source; **19.8B** Phillip Hayson; **19.8C** Mitch Reardon/Science Source; **19.9.1** E. H. Rao /Science Source; **19.9.2** Kevin Schafer/Alamy; **19.9.3** imageBROKER/Alamy; **19.9.4** Shutterstock; **19.9.5** Amazon-Images/Alamy; **19.9.6** Werner Bollmann/AGE Fotostock/SuperStock; **19.9.7** Steve Bloom/Alamy; **19.9.8** Arco Images GmbH/Alamy; **19.9.9** Anekoho/Shutterstock; **19.9.10** John Kelly/Getty Images, Inc.; **19.10B** David Tipling/Nature Picture Library; **19.12A left** Christian Musat/Fotolia; **19.12A right** Piotr Marcinski/Fotolia; **19.12B** SPL/Science Source; **19.14** avier Trueba/MSF/Science Source; **19.15** Achmad Ibrahim/AP Images; **19.16A** Sarah Leen/National Geographic Stock; **19.17A** SathyabhamaDasBiju, Used under a Creative Commons License. CC-BY-4.0; **19.17B** WaterFrame/Alamy Stock Photo; **19.17C** Hart JA, Detwiler KM, Gilbert CC, Burrell AS, Fuller JL, Emetshu M, et al. (212) Lesula A New Species of Cercopithecus Monkey Endemic to the Democratic Republic of Congo and Implications for Conservation of Congo's Central Basin. PLoS ONE 7(9) e44271. doi10.1371/journal.pone.0044271. © Hart et al. This is an open-access article distributed under the terms of the Creative Commons Attribution License, which permits unrestricted use, distribution, and reproduction in any medium, provided the original author and source are credited.

Chapter 20 **Chapter Opener** CSP_EcoPicture/AGE Fotostock; **20.2** Eric Isselee/Shutterstock; **20.4** Image Source/Getty Images; **20.5** Image Source/Getty Images; **20.5A** Nina Zanetti/Pearson Education; **20.5B** Ed Reschke/Getty Images, Inc.; **20.5C** Nina Zanetti/Pearson Education; **20.5D** Chuck Brown/Science Source; **20.5E** Nina Zanetti/Pearson Education; **20.5F** Gopal Murti/SPL/Science Source; **20.6** Paul Burns/Blend Images/Alamy; **20.6A** Nina Zanetti/Pearson Education; **20.6B** Ed Reschke/Getty Images, Inc; **20.6C** Ed Reschke/Getty Images, Inc; **20.9** Jeff Wheeler/MCT/Newscom; NA Paul Burns/Blend Images/Alamy; **20.10 p. 424 top** Douglas Pulsipher/Alamy; **20.10 p. 424 left center** Image Source/Corbis; **20.10 p. 424 top right** Rubberball/Getty Images; **20.10 p. 424 bottom left** Andy Crawford/DK Images; **20.10 p. 424 bottom right** Mixa/Alamy; **20.10 p. 425 top left** Laura Knox/DK Images; **20.10 p. 425 bottom left** Moodboard/Corbis; **20.10 p. 425 top right** Ryan McVay/Getty Images; **20.10 bottom right** Jeremy Woodhouse/Getty Images; **20.13B** SPL/Science Source; **20.14** Markus Varesvuo/Nature Picture Library; **p. 430 bottom** Nina Zanetti/Pearson Education

Chapter 21 **Chapter Opener** Alex Hubenov/Shutterstock; **p. 433 bottom** 6493829/Shutterstock; **21.1A** Mike Veitch/AlamyStockPhoto; **21.1B** Thomas Eisner; **21.1C** SPL/Science Source; **21.1D** Jennette van Dyk/Getty Images; **21.2A** 6493829/Shutterstock; **21.4** Geo Martinez/Shutterstock; **21.6C** Kletr/Shutterstock; **21.7** Science Photo Library/Alamy Stock Photo; **21.9** Meckes Ottawa/Science Source; **21.13** Kristin Piljay; **21.15A** atoss/Fotolia.com; **21.15 top** Corbis; **21.15 bottom** Debbie Hardin, Pearson Education; **21.15B** alexpro9500/Shutterstock; **21.16** Marlee/Shutterstock; **21.19B** The Jackson Laboratory; **21.21** Steve Allen/Brand X Pictures/Getty Images; **21.21.2** Maks Narodenko/Shutterstock; **p. 454 right** Geo Martinez/Shutterstock; **p. 455 left to right** Copyright © The Jackson Laboratory; atoss/Fotolia.com; Corbis

Chapter 22 Chapter Opener Tibanna79/Shutterstock; **p. 456 bottom left** F Rauschenbach/F1 ONLINE/SuperStock; **p. 456 bottom right** Douglas Pulsipher/Alamy; **22.1** Corbis/AGE Fotostock; **22.2D** Eric Isselée/Fotolia; **22.4A** Thomas Eisner; **22.4B** Valeriy Kirsanov/Fotolia; **22.4C** F Rauschenbach/F1 ONLINE/SuperStock; **22.5** University of Chicago Dept of Organismal Biology and Anatomy; **22.6** Douglas Pulsipher/Alamy; **p. 468 bottom** Douglas Pulsipher/Alamy

Chapter 23 Chapter Opener Hank Morgan/Science Source; **23.2A** GeorgePeters /E+ /Getty Images; **23.2B** Matt Antonino/Shutterstock; **23.2C** Eric Isselee/Shutterstock; **23.3** Hans Kim/Shutterstock; **23.5** Science Photo Library/Alamy Stock Photo; **23.6B left** Chuck Brown/Science Source; **23.6B right** Biophoto Associates/Science Source; **23.7B** Science Source; **23.11A** Meckes/Ottawa/Science Source; **23.13** Ingram Publishing/Photolibrary Royalty Free; **23.14B** The Gillette Co.

Chapter 24 Chapter Opener B BOISSONNET/BSIP/AGE Fotostock; **p. 489 bottom** SPL/Science Source; **24.4** Ryan McVay/Photodisc/Getty Images; **24.14A** Chris Bjornberg/Science Source; **24.17** Salisbury District Hospital/Science Source; **p. 505 center** David J. Green/Alamy Stock Photo

Chapter 25 Chapter Opener Fred Olivier/NaturePL; **p. 508 bottom** Mike Wilkes/Nature Picture Library; **25.1** Mike Wilkes/Nature Picture Library; **25.2** Leksele/Shutterstock; **25.5A** Andaman/Shutterstock; **25.5B left** GeorgePeters/Getty Images; **25.5B center** Eric Isselée/Fotolia; **25.5B right** Maksym Gorpenyuk/Shutterstock; **25.6A** Yuri Arcurs/Shutterstock; **p. 518 left column** Leksele/Shutterstock; Eric Isselée/Fotolia; Mike Wilkes/Nature Picture Library

Chapter 26 Chapter Opener Andrew McLachlan/All Canada Photos/SuperStock; **p. 521 bottom** Corey Ralston/Getty Images; **26.3A** Matteo photos/Shutterstock; **26.4** Laura Knox/DK Images; **26.5D** Mirrorpix/Splash News/Newscom; **26.6A** Eric Isselée/fotolia; **26.6A top** Eric Isselée/fotolia; **26.7C** National Geographic Creative/Alamy; **26.11** Corey Ralston/Getty Images; **p. 534 top** sianc/Shutterstock

Chapter 27 Chapter Opener Meckes/Ottawa/Science Source; **p. 536 bottom left** Courtesy John R. Finnerty; **p. 537 bottom** Ron Sutherland/Photo Researchers, Inc.; **27.1A** Biophoto Associates/Science Source; **27.1B** Allison J. Gong; **27.2A** Courtesy John R. Finnerty; **27.2B** Ken Preston-Mafham/PREMAPHOTOS/Nature Picture Library; **27.2C** Aneese/Shutterstock; **27.9A** David Phillips/Science Source; **27.10.1** Eric Isselée/fotolia; **27.10.2** Hintau Aliaksei/Shutterstock; **27.12B** Courtesy Dr. Thomas J. Poole, Upstate Medical University.; **27.12C** NHPA/Science Source; **27.13** David Barlow Photographer; **27.16A** TT Nyhetsbyra°n AB/Lennart Nilsson Photography; **27.16B** SPL/Science Source; **27.16C** TT Nyhetsbyra°n AB/Lennart Nilsson Photography; **27.16D** TT Nyhetsbyra°n AB/Lennart Nilsson Photography; **27.16E** SPL/Photo Researchers, Inc.

Chapter 28 Chapter Opener Tetra Images; **p. 566 bottom left** SPL/Science Source; **p. 566 bottom right** E.R. Lewis, Y.Y. Zeev, T.E. Everhart; University of California at Berkeley.; **28.1A left** corlaffra/Shutterstock; **28.1A right** Alice Day/Shutterstock; **28.2** SPL/Science Source; **28.7** E.R. Lewis, Y.Y. Zeev, T.E. Everhart; University of California at Berkeley.; **28.16B** Marcus E. Raichle, M.D.; **28.17A left** Science Source; **28.17A right** SPL/Science Source; **28.17B** Living Art Enterprises, LLC/Science Source; **28.21A** Jessica Wilson/Science Source; **28.21B** Amy Sancetta/ASSOCIATED PRESS

Chapter 29 Chapter Opener Brian J. Skerry/Getty Images; **p. 590 bottom** Jim Watt/Getty Images; **29.1A** Fuse/Getty Images; **29.3B** N. F. Photography/Shutterstock; **29.3D** Jim Watt/Perspectives/Getty Images; **29.4E** Keith Publicover/Shutterstock; **29.7A** Eric Grave /Science Source; **29.7B** MURGVI/Shutterstock; **29.9A** moodboard/Corbis; **29.9B** moodboard/Corbis; **29.9C** ARZTSAMUI/Shutterstock; **29.11** szefei/Shutterstock; **p. 603 bottom** Kelly Hogan

Chapter 30 Chapter Opener Christopher Futcher/Getty Images; **p. 606 bottom** Nagel Photography/Shutterstock; **30.1A** Danita Delimont/Alamy; **30.1B** Himagine/Getty Images; **30.1C** Dave Watts/NHPA/Science Source; **30.1D** Juniors Bildarchiv/AGE Fotostock; **30.1E** Nagel Photography/Shutterstock; **30.2A.1** Natural Visions/Alamy; **30.2A.2** Avalon/Photoshot License/Alamy; **30.2B** Tony Florio/Science Source; **30.2C** Carlos Villoch/Image Quest Marine; **30.2D.1** Jeff Rotman/The Image Bank/Getty Images; **30.2D.2** Kaj R. Svensson/SPL/Science Source; **30.2E** alle/Shutterstock; **30.5A.1** SPL/Science Source; **30.5A.2** P. Motta/SPL/Science Source; **30.8** Professor Clara Franzini-Armstrong/Pearson Education; **30.11** View Stock/Alamy; **p. 620** Allstar Picture Library/Alamy; **p. 621 left column** Himagine/Getty Images; NHPA/Science Source; Nagel Photography/Shutterstock; Stuart F. Westmorland/Danita Delimont /Alamy; **p. 621 right column** Nagel Photography/Shutterstock

Chapter 31 Chapter Opener sarawut/Getty Images; **p. 624** Don Mason/Corbis RF; **p. 625 bottom** Eric J. Simon; **31.1B.1** Cathleen A Clapper/Shutterstock; **31.1B.2** Nattika/Shutterstock; **31.1B.3** Vasilyev Alexandr/Shutterstock; **31.1B.4** zirconicusso/Shutterstock; **31.1B.5** panda3800/Shutterstock; **31.1B.6** Diana Mower/Shutterstock; **31.3** Adam Hart-Davis/Science Source; **31.4A** Eric J. Simon; **31.4B left** NHPA/NHPA; **31.4B top right** Donald Gregry Clever/Seelevel.com; **31.4B bottom right** FhF Greenmedia/AGE Fotostock America, Inc.; **31.4C** Scott Camazine/Science Source; **31.6B** Ed Reschke/Getty Images; **31.6C** Biophoto Associates/Science Source; **31.6D** Graham Kent/Pearson Education/Pearson Science; **31.6E** Scanning Electron Micrograph courtesy of the N.C Brown Center for Ultrastructure Studies, SUNY-ESF, Syracuse, NY.; **31.6F** Graham Kent/Pearson Education/Pearson Science; **31.7A** William Brooks/Alamy; **31.7C top** SeDmi/Shutterstock; **31.7C bottom** Ed Reschke/Getty Images; **31.7D** Ed Reschke/Getty Images; **31.8B** Don Mason/Corbis RF; **31.8C** Zack Frank/Shutterstock; **31.9A** Eric J. Simon; **31.12A** jopelka/Shutterstock; **31.12C top** Africa Studio/Shutterstock; **31.12C left center** Rolf Klebsattel/Shutterstock; **31.12C nuts** Elena Schweitzer/Shutterstock; **31.14A** Tim Hill/Alamy; **31.14B** Dennis Frates/Alamy; **31.15A** Alexandre Petzold/Science Source; **31.15B** Rosenfeld Images Ltd/Science Source; **31.16** David Welling/Nature Picture Library

Chapter 32 Chapter Opener mangostock/Shutterstock; **p. 646 bottom left** Brian Capon; **p. 647 bottom** USDA/ARS/Agricultural Research Service; **32.1B** Q-Images/Alamy; **32.2A** Brian Capon; **32.4.1** Brian Capon; **32.4.2** SPL/Science Source; **32.4 right** Jeremy Bur/Science Source; **32.5A** Professor Ray F. Evert; **32.5B** Lezh/E+/Getty Images; **32.6A** Henk Jacobs/Fotolia; **32.6B** TairA/Shutterstock; **32.8A** USDA/ARS/Agricultural Research Service; **32.8B** SPL/Science Source; **32.9A** USDA/ARS/Agricultural Research Service; **32.10A** U.S. Geological Survey, Denver; **32.10B** National Oceanic and Atmospheric Administration NOAA; **32.10C** Nagel Photography/Shutterstock; **32.12** Pallava Bagla/Corbis via Getty Images; **32.14B left** SPL/Science Source; **32.14B right** DR JEREMY BURGESS/Science Source; **32.15A** Stephen J. Krasemann/Science Source; **32.15B** Robert and Jean Pollock/Science Source; **32.15C** H. Reinhard/AGE Fotostock; **32.15D** Willi Rolfes/AGE Fotostock; **32.15E** James H. Robinson/Science Source

Chapter 33 Chapter Opener ton koene/Alamy; **p. 664 Bottom left** Ron and Patty Thomas Photography/Getty Images; **p. 684 Bottom right** Michael Evans; **33.1A** Martin Shields/Science Source; **33.3A** William M. Gray, Dept of Plant Biology, University of Minnesota.; **33.3C** SPL/Science Source; **33.4 left** Smit/Shutterstock; **33.4 right** Shotshop GmbH/Alamy; **33.5A** Courtesy of Alan Crozier, University of California; **33.5B** Kristin Piljay/Pearson Education/Pearson Science; **33.5C** Fred Jensen, UC Cooperative Extension; **33.6** Ron and Patty Thomas Photography/Getty Images; **33.7A** Kristin Piljay/Pearson Education/Pearson Science; **33.7B left** Ed Reschke/Getty Images; **33.7B right** Martin Ruegner/Getty Images; **33.8** Stockbyte/Getty Images; **p. 673 Center** Rudolf Madar/Shutterstock; **33.9A** Michael Evans; **33.9B** Ed Reschke/Getty Images; **33.10 left** Martin Shields/Science Source; **33.10 right** Martin Shields/Science Source; **33.13A** vainillaychile/Fotolia.com; **33.13B** Science Source; **33.13C** Courtesy Thomas Burr, School of Integrative Plant Science, Cornell University.

Chapter 34 Chapter Opener Paul L. Csizmadia/Spec3 Photography/Getty Images; **p. 682 Bottom left** WILDLIFE GmbH/Alamy; **p. 682 Bottom right** Don Fink/Shutterstock; **p. 683 Bottom right** Jorma Luhta/Nature Picture Library; **34.2A** Keystone-France/Getty Images; **34.2B** Arco Images GmbH/Alamy; **34.2C** Alfred Eisenstaedt/Time Life Pictures/

Getty Images; **34.3A** Ralph White/Getty Images; **34.3B** WILDLIFE GmbH/Alamy; **34.4** franzfoto.com/Alamy; **34.6B** Getty Images/Digital Vision; **34.6C** National Oceanography Centre/Image Quest Marine; **34.6D** James Randklev/Getty Images; **34.7B** Don Fink/Shutterstock; **34.7C** Jean Dickey; **34.9** Nick Garbutt/Nick Garbutt; **34.10** Eric Isselee/Shutterstock; **34.11** garytof/Fotolia.com; **34.12** Courtesy of Rick Halsey/California Chaparral Institute; **34.13** Mike Grandmaison/Getty Images; **34.14** Thomas R. Fletcher/Alamy; **34.15** Jorma Luhta/Nature Picture Library; **34.16** WILDLIFE GmbH/Alamy; **34.17** Gordon Wiltsie/National Geographic Stock; **p. 700 top** Getty Images/Digital Vision

Chapter 35 **Chapter Opener** Martin Harvey/Getty Images; **p. 702 Bottom left** Danita Delimont/Alamy; **p. 702 bottom right** John Cancalosi/Getty Images; **p. 703 bottom left** James Watt/Image Quest Marine; **p. 703 bottom right** Kitchin & Hurst/AGE Fotostock; **35.1** Tom McHugh/Science Source; **35.2B** Danita Delimont/Alamy; **35.3A** Wayne Lynch/AGE Fotostock; **35.5A** Thomas D. McAvoy/Getty Images; **35.5B** Terry Andrewartha/FLPA; **35.6A** Biological Resources Division, U.S. Geological Survey; **35.6B** Star Banner & Doug Engle/AP Photo; **35.7.1** Scott Camazine/Alamy; **35.7.2** Jeff Mondragon/Alamy; **35.7.3** Nick Upton/Nature Picture Library; **35.8A** Michael Nolan/AGE Fotostock; **35.8C** Juniors/Juniors; **35.9** John Cancalosi/Getty Images; **35.10** Richard Wrangham; **35.10 inset** Pal Teravagimov Photography/Getty Images; **35.11A** Clive Bromhall/Getty Images; **35.11B** Courtesy Dr. Bernd Heinrich; **35.12A** Jose B. Ruiz/Nature Picture Library; **35.13A** J. P. Varin/Jacana/Science Source; **35.14A** Steve Bloom Images/Alamy; **35.14B** Riverwalker/Fotolia; **35.14C** Carol Walker/Nature Picture Library; **35.15A** Kerstin Waurick/Getty Images; **35.15B** James Watt/Image Quest Marine; **35.16A** Barry Mansell/NaturePL; **35.16B** Jeff Mondragon/Alamy; **35.18A** JHVEPhoto/Shutterstock; **35.18B** Kitchin & Hurst/AGE Fotostock; **35.19** Rupert Barrington/Nature Picture Library; **35.20** Renne Lynn/Pearson Education/Pearson Science; **35.21A** Jennifer Jarvis, Dept of Biological Science, University of Capetown, South Africa; **35.21B** Shari L. Morris/AGE Fotostock; **35.22A** Michael Nichols/National Geographic Stock; **35.22B** Martin Harvey/Getty Images; **35.23A** DC5 WENN Photos/Newscom; **35.23B** Janet Mayer/Splash News/Newscom; **p. 724** Pal Teravagimov Photography/Getty Images

Chapter 36 **Chapter Opener** Jose B.Ruiz/NaturePL; **p. 726 bottom** Simon Phillpotts/Alamy; **36.2A** Matthew Banks/Alamy; **36.2B** Jon Ander Rabadan/Getty Images; **36.2C** mashe/Shutterstock; **36.3 left** Roger Phillips/DK Images; **36.3 Center** Jane Burton/DK Images; **36.3 right** Yuri Arcurs/Shutterstock; **36.4A** Simon Phillpotts/Alamy; **36.4B** bikeriderlondon/Shutterstock; **36.4C left** Joshua Lewis/Shutterstock; **36.4C right** WizData/Shutterstock; **36.5A** Rick & Nora Bowers/Alamy; **36.5B** National Geographic Creative/Alamy; **36.5C** Meul/ARCO/Nature Picture Library; **36.6** Alan Carey/Science Source

Chapter 37 **Chapter Opener** blickwinkel/Alamy; **37.3A** Doug Backlund; **37.3B** All Canada Photos/Alamy; **37.4** Jurgen Freund/Nature Picture Library; **37.5A** Kenneth M. Highfill /Science Source; **37.5B** Jean Dickey; **37.6 top** WILDLIFE GmbH/Alamy; **37.6 left** Geoffrey Peter Kidd/AGE Fotostock America Inc.; **37.6 right** Universal Images Group/Universal Images Group; **37.7** Joel Sartore/Getty Images; **37.9.11** Rolf Nussbaumer/Nature Picture Library; **37.9.14** aceshot1/shutterstock; **37.11A** Bernard Castelein/Nature Picture Library; **37.11C** Courtesy of Genevieve Anderson; **37.12A** Erich Schmidt/Getty Images; **37.12B** Bob Stevenson/NPS; **37.13A** Mike Rochford/USGS; **37.13B** U.S. Fish & Wildlife Service; **37.13C** Jean Dickey; **37.22A** Eric Albrecht/The Columbus Dispatch via AP; **37.23A** Jean Dickey; **37.23B** Fang Xinwu/Newscom

Chapter 38 **Chapter Opener** Arndt Sven-Erik/AGE Fotostock; **p. 784 Bottom left** Ingrid Visser/AGE Fotostock; **p. 784 bottom right** Rick & Nora Bowers/Alamy; **38.1A** Mike Dobel/Alamy; **38.1C** Jeff March/Alamy; **38.1D** James King-Holmes/Science Source; **38.2A** SuperStock; **38.2B** John Mitchell/Science Source; **38.2C** Charlie Riedel/AP Photo; **38.5A** Josh Edelson/AFP/Getty Images; **38.5B** Ingrid Visser/AGE Fotostock; **38.6A** William Osborn/Nature Picture Library; **38.6B** Paul McCormick/Getty Images; **38.7A** Rick & Nora Bowers/Alamy; **38.7B** DLILLC/Corbis RF; **38.8A** Yann Arthus-Bertrand/Corbis; **38.8B** CALVIN LARSEN/Science Source; **38.8C** AP Photo/The Missoulian, Kurt Wilson; **38.9B** Roger Kirkpatrick/Visual & Written/Image Quest Marine; **p. 776 left** Neo Edmund/Shutterstock; **38.10B** Chris Fredriksson/Alamy; **38.11A** Theo Allofs/Getty Images; **38.11C** Dancestrokes/Shutterstock; **38.12A** YOSHIKAZU TSUNO/Newscom; **38.12B** South Florida Water Management District; **38.13** Heather Angel/Natural Visions /Alamy Stock Photo

Illustration and Text Credits

Chapter 3 **3.14** Pearson Education

Chapter 8 **8.20B** Adapted from C. A. Huether et al., Maternal age specific risk rate estimates for Down syndrome among live births in whites and other races from Ohio and Metropolitan Atlanta, 1970–1989, Journal of Medical Genetics 35 482–90 (1998).

Chapter 10 **10.2B** Pearson Education

Chapter 11 **11.18** Data from American Cancer Society, Cancer Facts & ures. Atlanta, American Cancer Society, 215.

Chapter 16 **16.6A** Figure adapted from Microbiology An Introduction, 9th ed., by Gerard J. Tortora, Berdell R. Funke, and Christine L. Case. Copyright © 2007 by Pearson Education, Inc. Adapted and electronically reproduced by permission of Pearson Education, Inc., Upper Saddle River, New Jersey.

Chapter 22 **22.1** Figure adapted from Human Anatomy and Physiology, 4th ed., by Elaine N. Marieb. Copyright © 1998 by Pearson Education, Inc. Adapted and electronically reproduced by permission of Pearson Education, Inc., Upper Saddle River, New Jersey. **22.12** Figure adapted from Human Anatomy and Physiology, 4th ed., by Elaine N. Marieb. Copyright © 1998 by Pearson Education, Inc. Adapted and electronically reproduced by permission of Pearson Education, Inc., Upper Saddle River, New Jersey.

Chapter 27 **27.3A** Figure adapted from Human Anatomy and Physiology, 4th ed., by Elaine N. Marieb and Katja Hoehn. Copyright © 1998 by Pearson Education, Inc. Adapted and electronically reproduced by permission of Pearson Education, Inc., Upper Saddle River, New Jersey. **27.3C** Figure adapted from Human Anatomy and Physiology, 4th ed., by Elaine N. Marieb and Katja Hoehn. Copyright © 1998 by Pearson Education, Inc. Adapted and electronically reproduced by permission of Pearson Education, Inc., Upper Saddle River, New Jersey. **27.4B** Figure adapted from Human Anatomy and Physiology, 4th ed., by Elaine N. Marieb and Katja Hoehn. Copyright © 1998 by Pearson Education, Inc. Adapted and electronically reproduced by permission of Pearson Education, Inc., Upper Saddle River, New Jersey. **TABle 27.7** Table adapted from Microbiology An Introduction, 9th ed., by Gerard J. Tortora, Berdell R. Funke, and Christine L. Case. Copyright © 2007 by Pearson Education, Inc. Adapted and electronically reproduced by permission of Pearson Education, Inc., Upper Saddle River, New Jersey. **27.8** Original figure based loosely on this graphic from the United States Center for Disease Control http//www.cdc.gov/reproductivehealth/contraception/index.htm **27.12B** Pearson Education. **27.14B** Adapted from Campbell Biology, 10th ed., by Jane B. Reece et.al. Pearson Education, Inc. **27.17B** Figure adapted from Human Anatomy and Physiology, 4th ed., by Elaine N. Marieb and Katja Hoehn. Copyright © 1998 by Pearson Education, Inc. Adapted and electronically reproduced by permission of Pearson Education, Inc., Upper Saddle River, New Jersey.

Chapter 28 **28.9** Republished with permission of John Wiley & Sons, from Antidepressants Prevent Hierarchy Destabilization Induced by Lipopolysaccharide Administration in Mice A Neurobiological Approach to Depression, by Daniel W. H. Cohn, et al., from Annals of the New York Academy Of Sciences (July 212) 1262; Permission conveyed through Copyright Clearance Center, Inc.

Chapter 29 **29.5** Figure adapted from Human Anatomy and Physiology, 4th ed., by Elaine N. Marieb and Katja Hoehn. Copyright © 1998

by Pearson Education, Inc. Adapted and electronically reproduced by permission of Pearson Education, Inc., Upper Saddle River, New Jersey.

Chapter 29 **29.9A** Figure adapted from Human Anatomy and Physiology, 4th ed., by Elaine N. Marieb and Katja Hoehn. Copyright © 1998 by Pearson Education, Inc. Adapted and electronically reproduced by permission of Pearson Education, Inc., Upper Saddle River, New Jersey. **29.9B** Figure adapted from Human Anatomy and Physiology, 4th ed., by Elaine N. Marieb and Katja Hoehn. Copyright © 1998 by Pearson Education, Inc. Adapted and electronically reproduced by permission of Pearson Education, Inc., Upper Saddle River, New Jersey.

Chapter 30 **30.4** Figure adapted from Human Anatomy and Physiology, 4th ed., by Elaine N. Marieb. Copyright © 1998 by Pearson Education, Inc. Adapted and electronically reproduced by permission of Pearson Education, Inc., Upper Saddle River, New Jersey. **30.8** Figure adapted from Human Anatomy and Physiology, 4th ed., by Elaine N. Marieb. Copyright © 1998 by Pearson Education, Inc. Adapted and electronically reproduced by permission of Pearson Education, Inc., Upper Saddle River, New Jersey. **30.10A** Figure adapted from Human Anatomy and Physiology, 4th ed., by Elaine N. Marieb. Copyright © 1998 by Pearson Education, Inc. Adapted and electronically reproduced by permission of Pearson Education, Inc., Upper Saddle River, New Jersey. **TABle 30.12B** Data from N. Yang et al., ACTN3 genotype is associated with human elite athletic performance, American Journal of Human Genetics 73 627–31 (2003).

Chapter 31 **31.1B** "Multiple Birth" from "Seeking Agriculture's Ancient Roots" by Michael Balter from Science, June 2007, Volume 316(5833) by American Association for the Advancement of Science Reproduced with permission of AMERICAN ASSOCIATION FOR THE ADVANCEMENT OF SCIENCE in the format Educational/Instructional Program via Copyright Clearance Center.

Chapter 35 **35.12B** Data from Figure 8 in N. B. Davies, Prey selection and social behavior in wagtails (Aves Motacillidae), Journal of Animal Ecology 46 37–57 (1977).

Chapter 37 **37.9** Figure adapted from Ecology and Field Biology, 4th ed., by Robert L. Smith. Copyright © 1990 by Pearson Education, Inc. Adapted and electronically reproduced by permission of Pearson Education, Inc., Upper Saddle River, New Jersey.

Chapter 38 **38.3A** Data from National Oceanic and Atmospheric Administration (2016). **38.11B** "Yellowstone to Yukon Region" (map), from "Climate Change and the Yellowstone to Yukon Region." Copyright © 2012 by Yellowstone to Yukon Conservation Initiative. Reprinted with permission. www.y2y.net

Glossary

A

A site One of a ribosome's binding sites for tRNA during translation. The A site holds the tRNA that carries the next amino acid in the polypeptide chain. (A stands for aminoacyl tRNA.)

abiotic factor (ā´-bī-ot´-ik) A nonliving component of the environment, such as air, water, or temperature.

abiotic reservoir (ā´-bī-ot´-ik) The part of an ecosystem where a chemical, such as carbon or nitrogen, accumulates or is stockpiled outside of living organisms.

ABO blood groups Genetically determined classes of human blood that are based on the presence or absence of carbohydrates A and B on the surface of red blood cells. The ABO blood group phenotypes, also called blood types, are A, B, AB, and O.

abscisic acid (ABA) (ab-sis´-ik) A plant hormone that inhibits cell division, promotes dormancy, and interacts with gibberellins in regulating seed germination.

absorption The uptake of small nutrient molecules by an organism's body; the third main stage of food processing, following digestion.

acetyl CoA (a-sē´-til kō´-ā´) (acetyl coenzyme A) The entry compound for the citric acid cycle in cellular respiration; formed from a two-carbon fragment of pyruvate attached to a coenzyme.

acetylcholine (a-sē´-til-kō´-lēn) A neurotransmitter. Among other effects, it slows the heart rate and makes skeletal muscles contract.

acid A substance that increases the hydrogen ion (H^+) concentration in a solution.

acrosome (ak´-ruh-som) A membrane-enclosed sac at the tip of a sperm. The acrosome contains enzymes that help the sperm penetrate an egg.

actin A globular protein that links into chains, two of which twist helically around each other, forming microfilaments in muscle cells.

action potential A massive change in membrane voltage that transmits a nerve signal along an axon.

activation energy The amount of energy that reactants must absorb before a chemical reaction will start.

activator A protein that switches on a gene or group of genes.

active immunity Immunity conferred by recovering from an infectious disease or by receiving a vaccine.

active site The part of an enzyme where a substrate molecule attaches; typically, a pocket or groove on the enzyme's surface.

active transport The movement of a substance across a biological membrane against its concentration gradient, aided by specific transport proteins and requiring an input of energy (often as ATP)

adaptation An inherited character that enhances an organism's ability to survive and reproduce in a particular environment.

adaptive immunity A vertebrate-specific defense that is activated only after exposure to an antigen and is mediated by lymphocytes. It exhibits specificity, memory, and self-nonself recognition. Also called acquired immunity.

adaptive radiation Period of evolutionary change in which groups of organisms form many new species whose adaptations allow them to fill new or vacant ecological roles in their communities.

adenine (A) (ad´-uh-nēn) A double-ring nitrogenous base found in DNA and RNA.

adhesion The attraction between different kinds of molecules.

adipose tissue A type of connective tissue whose cells contain fat.

adrenal cortex (uh-drē´-nul) The outer portion of an adrenal gland, controlled by ACTH from the anterior pituitary; secretes hormones called glucocorticoids and mineralocorticoids.

adrenal gland (uh-drē´-nul) One of a pair of endocrine glands, located atop each kidney in mammals, composed of an outer cortex and a central medulla.

adrenal medulla (uh-drē´-nul muh-dul´-uh) The central portion of an adrenal gland, controlled by nerve signals; secretes the fight-or-flight hormones epinephrine and norepinephrine.

adrenocorticotropic hormone (ACTH) (uh-drē´-nō-cōr´-ti-kō-trop´-ik) A protein hormone secreted by the anterior pituitary that stimulates the adrenal cortex to secrete corticosteroids.

adult stem cell A cell present in adult tissues that generates replacements for nondividing differentiated cells. Adult stem cells are capable of differentiating into multiple cell types, but they are not as developmentally flexible as embryonic stem cells.

age structure The number of individuals in different age groups in a population.

agonistic behavior (a´-gō-nis´-tik) Confrontational behavior involving a contest waged by threats, displays, or actual combat that settles disputes over limited resources, such as food or mates.

AIDS (acquired immunodeficiency syndrome) The late stages of HIV infection, characterized by a reduced number of T cells and the appearance of characteristic opportunistic infections.

alcohol fermentation Glycolysis followed by the reduction of pyruvate to ethyl alcohol, regenerating NAD^+ and releasing carbon dioxide.

alga (al´-guh) (plural, **algae**) A protist that produces its food by photosynthesis.

alimentary canal (al´-uh-men´-tuh-rē) A complete digestive tract consisting of a tube running between a mouth and an anus.

allantois (al´-an-tō´-is) In animals, an extraembryonic membrane that develops from the yolk sac. The allantois helps dispose of the embryo's nitrogenous wastes and forms part of the umbilical cord in mammals.

allele (uh-lē´-ul) An alternative version of a gene.

allergen (al´-er-jen) An antigen that causes an allergy.

allergy A disorder of the immune system caused by an abnormally high sensitivity to an antigen. Symptoms are triggered by histamines released from mast cells.

allopatric speciation The formation of new species in populations that are geographically isolated from one another.

alternation of generations A life cycle in which there is both a multicellular diploid form, the sporophyte, and a multicellular haploid form, the gametophyte; a characteristic of plants and multicellular green algae.

alternative RNA splicing A type of regulation at the RNA-processing level in which multiple mRNA molecules are produced from the same primary transcript, depending on which RNA segments are treated as exons and which as introns.

altruism (al´-trū-iz-um) Behavior that reduces an individual's fitness while increasing the fitness of another individual in the population.

Alveolata (al-vē´-uh-let-uh) A clade of the SAR supergroup of protists that includes dinoflagellates, ciliates, and certain parasites.

alveolus (al-vē´-oh-lus) (plural, **alveoli**) One of the dead-end air sacs within the mammalian lung where gas exchange occurs.

Alzheimer's disease An age-related dementia (mental deterioration) characterized by confusion, memory loss, and other symptoms.

amino acid (uh-mēn´-ō) An organic molecule containing a carboxyl group and an amino group; serves as the monomer of proteins.

amino group (uh-mēn´-ō) A chemical group consisting of a nitrogen atom bonded to two hydrogen atoms.

ammonia NH_3; a small and very toxic nitrogenous waste produced by metabolism.

amniocentesis (am´-nē-ō-sen-tē´-sis) A technique for diagnosing genetic defects while a fetus is in the uterus. A sample of amniotic fluid, obtained by a needle inserted into the uterus, is analyzed for telltale chemicals and defective fetal cells.

amnion (am´-nē-on) In vertebrate animals, the extraembryonic membrane that encloses the fluid-filled amniotic sac containing the embryo.

amniote Member of a clade of tetrapods that have an amniotic egg containing specialized membranes that protect the embryo. Amniotes include mammals and birds and other reptiles.

amniotic egg (am´-nē-ot´-ik) A shelled egg in which an embryo develops within a fluid-filled amniotic sac and is nourished by yolk. Produced by reptiles (including birds) and egg-laying mammals, the amniotic egg enables them to complete their life cycles on dry land.

amoeba (uh-mē´-buh) A general term for a protist that moves and feeds by means of pseudopodia.

amoebocyte (uh-mē´-buh-sīt) An amoeba-like cell that moves by pseudopodia and is found in most animals; depending on the species, may digest and distribute food, dispose of wastes, form skeletal fibers, fight infections, and change into other cell types.

amoebozoan A member of a clade of protists in the supergroup Unikonta that includes amoebas and slime molds and is characterized by tube-shaped or lobe-shaped pseudopodia.

amphibian Member of a clade of tetrapods that includes frogs, toads, salamanders, and caecilians.

amygdala (uh-mig´-duh-la) An integrative center of the cerebrum; functionally, the part of the limbic system that is central in laying down emotional memories.

anabolic steroid (an´-uh-bol´-ik ster´-oyd) A synthetic variant of the male hormone testosterone that mimics some of its effects.

analogy The similarity between two species that is due to convergent evolution rather than to descent from a common ancestor with the same trait.

anaphase The fourth stage of mitosis, beginning when sister chromatids separate from each other and ending when a complete set of daughter chromosomes arrives at each of the two poles of the cell.

anatomy The study of the structures of an organism.

anchorage dependence The requirement that to divide, a cell must be attached to a solid surface.

androgen (an´-drō-jen) A steroid sex hormone secreted by the gonads that promotes the development and maintenance of the male reproductive system and male body features.

anemia (uh-nē´-me-ah) A condition in which an abnormally low amount of hemoglobin or a low number of red blood cells results in the body cells receiving too little oxygen.

angiosperm (an´-jē-ō-sperm) A flowering plant, which forms seeds inside a protective chamber called an ovary.

annelid (uh-nel´-id) A segmented worm. Annelids include earthworms, marine worms, and leeches.

annual A plant that completes its life cycle in a single year or growing season.

antagonistic hormones Two hormones that have opposite effects.

anterior Pertaining to the front, or head, of a bilaterally symmetric animal.

anterior pituitary (puh-tū´-uh-tār-ē) An endocrine gland, adjacent to the hypothalamus and the posterior pituitary, that synthesizes several hormones, including some that control the activity of other endocrine glands.

anther A sac located at the tip of a flower's stamen; contains male sporangia in which meiosis occurs to produce spores that form the male gametophytes, or pollen grains.

anthropoid (an´-thruh-poyd) A member of a primate group made up of the apes (gibbons, orangutans, gorillas, chimpanzees, bonobos, and humans) and monkeys.

antibody (an´-tih-bod´-ē) A protein dissolved in blood plasma that attaches to a specific kind of antigen and helps counter its effects; secreted by plasma cells.

anticodon (an´-tī-kō´-don) On a tRNA molecule, a specific sequence of three nucleotides that is complementary to a codon triplet on mRNA.

antidiuretic hormone (ADH) (an´-tē-dī´-yū-ret´-ik) A hormone made by the hypothalamus and secreted by the posterior pituitary that promotes water retention by the kidneys.

antigen (an´-tuh-jen) A foreign (nonself) molecule that elicits an adaptive immune response.

antigen receptor (an´-tuh-jen) The general term for a surface protein, located on B cells and T cells, that binds to antigens and initiates the adaptive immune response.

antigen-binding site (an´-tuh-jen) A region of the antigen receptor or antibody that binds the antigenic determinant on the antigen.

antigen-presenting cell (an´-tuh-jen) One of a family of white blood cells that ingests a foreign substance or a microbe and attaches antigenic portions of the ingested material to its own surface, thereby displaying the antigens to a helper T cell.

antihistamine (an´-tē-his´-tuh-mēn) A drug that interferes with the action of histamine, providing relief from an allergic reaction.

anus The opening through which undigested materials are expelled.

aorta (ā-or´-tuh) A large artery that conveys blood directly from the left ventricle of the heart to other arteries.

aphotic zone (ā-fō´-tik) The region of an aquatic ecosystem beneath the photic zone, where light does not penetrate enough for photosynthesis to take place.

apical dominance (ā´-pik-ul) In a plant, the hormonal inhibition of axillary buds by a terminal bud.

apical meristem (ā´-pik-ul mer´-uh-stem) A growth-producing region of cell division consisting of undifferentiated cells located at the tip of a plant root or in the terminal or axillary bud of a shoot.

apoptosis (ā-puh-tō´-sus) The timely and tidy suicide of cells; also called programmed cell death.

appendicular skeleton (ap´-en-dik´-yū-ler) Components of the skeletal system that support the fins of a fish or the arms and legs of a land vertebrate; in land vertebrates, the cartilage and bones of the shoulder girdle, pelvic girdle, forelimbs, and hind limbs. *See also* axial skeleton.

appendix (uh-pen´-dix) A small, finger-like extension of the vertebrate cecum; contains a mass of white blood cells that contribute to immunity.

aquaporin A transport protein in the plasma membrane of an animal, plant, or microorganism cell that facilitates the diffusion of water across the membrane (osmosis).

aqueous solution (ā´-kwē-us) A solution in which water is the solvent.

arachnid A member of a major arthropod group (chelicerates) that includes spiders, scorpions, ticks, and mites.

Archaea (ar´-kē-uh) One of two prokaryotic domains of life, the other being Bacteria.

Archaeplastida One of four monophyletic supergroups proposed in a current hypothesis of the evolutionary history of eukaryotes. The other four supergroups are SAR (Stramenopila, Alveolata, and Rhizaria), Excavata, and Unikonta.

arteriole (ar-ter´-ē-ōl) A vessel that conveys blood between an artery and a capillary bed.

artery A vessel that carries blood away from the heart to other parts of the body.

arthropod (ar´-thrō-pod) A member of the most diverse phylum in the animal kingdom. Arthropods include the horseshoe crab, arachnids (for example, spiders, ticks, scorpions, and mites), crustaceans (for example, crayfish, lobsters, crabs, and barnacles), millipedes, centipedes, and insects. Arthropods are characterized by a chitinous exoskeleton, molting, jointed appendages, and a body formed of distinct groups of segments.

artificial selection The selective breeding of domesticated plants and animals to promote the occurrence of desirable traits.

ascomycete (as´-kuh-mī´-sēt) Member of a group of fungi characterized by saclike structures called asci that produce spores in sexual reproduction.

asexual reproduction The creation of genetically identical offspring by a single parent, without the participation of sperm and egg.

assisted reproductive technology Procedure that involves surgically removing eggs from a woman's ovaries, fertilizing them, and then returning them to the woman's body. *See also in vitro* fertilization.

associative learning The ability to associate one environmental feature with another. In one type of associative learning, the animal learns to link a particular stimulus with a particular outcome. Trial-and-error learning is also a type of associative learning.

astigmatism (uh-stig´-muh-tizm) Blurred vision caused by a misshapen lens or cornea.

atherosclerosis (ath´-uh-rō´-skluh-rō´-sis) A cardiovascular disease in which fatty deposits called plaques develop on the inner walls of the arteries, narrowing their inner diameters.

atom The smallest unit of matter that retains the properties of an element.

atomic mass The total mass of an atom; also called atomic weight. Given as a whole number, the atomic mass approximately equals the mass number.

atomic number The number of protons in each atom of a particular element.

ATP Adenosine triphosphate, the main energy source for cells. ATP releases energy when its phosphate bonds are hydrolyzed.

ATP synthase A cluster of several membrane proteins that function in chemiosmosis with adjacent electron transport chains, using the energy of a hydrogen ion concentration gradient to make ATP.

atrium (ā´-trē-um) (plural, **atria**) A heart chamber that receives blood from the veins.

autoimmune disorder An immunological disorder in which the immune system attacks the body's own molecules.

autonomic nervous system (ot´-ō-nom´-ik) The component of the vertebrate peripheral nervous system that regulates the internal environment; made up of sympathetic and parasympathetic subdivisions. Most actions of the autonomic nervous system are involuntary.

autosome A chromosome not directly involved in determining the sex of an organism; in mammals, for example, any chromosome other than X or Y.

autotroph (ot´-ō-trōf) An organism that makes its own food (often by photosynthesis), thereby sustaining itself without eating other organisms or their molecules. Plants, algae, and numerous bacteria are autotrophs.

auxin (ok´-sin) A plant hormone (indoleacetic acid or a related compound) that promotes seedling elongation. Auxin performs multiple functions in the body of a plant, most of which promote growth.

AV (atrioventricular) node A region of specialized heart muscle tissue between the left and right atria where electrical impulses are delayed for about 0.1 second before spreading to both ventricles and causing them to contract.

axial skeleton (ak´-sē-ul) Components of the skeletal system that support the central trunk of the body: the skull, backbone, and rib cage in a vertebrate. *See also* appendicular skeleton.

axillary bud (ak´-sil-ār-ē) An embryonic shoot present in the angle formed by a leaf and stem.

axon (ak´-son) A neuron extension that conducts signals to another neuron or to an effector cell. A neuron has one long axon.

B

B cell A type of lymphocyte that completes its development in the bone marrow and is responsible for the humoral immune response.

bacillus (buh-sil´-us) (plural, **bacilli**) A rod-shaped prokaryotic cell.

Bacteria One of two prokaryotic domains of life, the other being Archaea.

bacteriophage (bak-tēr´-ē-ō-fāj) A virus that infects bacteria; also called a phage.

balancing selection Natural selection that maintains stable frequencies of two or more phenotypic forms in a population.

ball-and-socket joint A joint that allows rotation and movement in several planes. Examples in humans include the hip and shoulder joints.

bark All the tissues external to the vascular cambium in a plant that is growing in thickness. Bark is made up of secondary phloem, cork cambium, and cork.

Barr body A dense body formed from a deactivated X chromosome found in the nuclei of female mammalian cells.

basal metabolic rate (BMR) The number of kilocalories a resting animal requires to fuel its essential body processes for a given time.

basal nuclei (bā´-sul nū´-klē-ī) Clusters of neuron cell bodies located deep within the cerebrum that are important in motor coordination.

base A substance that decreases the hydrogen ion (H^+) concentration in a solution.

basidiomycete (buh-sid´-ē-ō-mī´-sēt) Member of a group of fungi characterized by club-shaped, spore-producing structures called basidia.

basilar membrane The floor of the middle canal of the inner ear.

behavior Individually, an action carried out by the muscles or glands under control of the nervous system in response to a stimulus; collectively, the sum of an animal's responses to external and internal cues.

behavioral ecology The study of behavior in an evolutionary context.

benign tumor An abnormal mass of cells that remains at its original site in the body.

benthic realm A seafloor or the bottom of a freshwater lake, pond, river, or stream.

biennial A plant that completes its life cycle in two years.

bilateral symmetry An arrangement of body parts such that an organism can be divided equally by a single cut passing longitudinally through it. A bilaterally symmetric organism has mirror-image right and left sides.

Bilateria Clade of animals exhibiting bilateral symmetry.

bile A mixture of substances that is produced by the liver and stored and concentrated in the gallbladder. Bile emulsifies fats and aids in their digestion.

binary fission A means of asexual reproduction in which a parent organism, often a single cell, divides into two genetically identical individuals of about equal size.

binomial The two-part format for naming a species, consisting of a genus and specific epithet; for example, *Homo sapiens*.

biocapacity Earth's capacity to provide and renew the land and water resources an individual or nation needs and to absorb the carbon emissions it generates, measured in global hectares (gha).

biodiversity The variety of living things; includes genetic diversity, species diversity, and ecosystem diversity.

biodiversity hot spot A small geographic area with an exceptional concentration of endangered and threatened species, especially endemic species (those found nowhere else).

biofilm A surface-coating colony of prokaryotes that engage in metabolic cooperation.

biogeochemical cycle Any of the various chemical circuits that involve both biotic and abiotic components of an ecosystem.

biogeography The study of the past and present distribution of organisms.

bioinformatics The use of computers, software, and mathematical models to process and integrate biological information from large sets of data.

biological clock An internal timekeeper that controls an organism's biological rhythms, marking time with or without environmental cues but often requiring signals from the environment to remain tuned to an appropriate period. *See also* circadian rhythm.

biological magnification The concentration of harmful chemicals that are retained in the living tissues of consumers in food chains.

biological species concept Definition of a species as a group of populations whose members have the potential to interbreed in nature and produce viable, fertile offspring but do not produce viable, fertile offspring with members of other such groups.

biology The scientific study of life.

biome (bī´-ōm) A major type of ecological association that occupies a broad geographic region of land or water and is characterized by organisms adapted to the particular environment.

bioremediation The use of living organisms to detoxify and restore polluted and degraded ecosystems.

biosphere The entire portion of Earth inhabited by life; the sum of all the planet's ecosystems.

biotechnology The manipulation of living organisms or their components to make useful products.

biotic factor (bī-o´-tik) A living component of the environment; an organism, or a factor pertaining to one or more organisms.

bipolar disorder Depressive mental illness characterized by extreme mood swings; also called manic-depressive disorder.

birds Members of a clade of reptiles that have feathers and adaptations for flight.

bivalve A member of a group of molluscs that includes clams, mussels, scallops, and oysters.

blastocyst (blas´-tō-sist) A mammalian embryo (equivalent to an amphibian blastula) made up of a hollow ball of cells that results from cleavage and that implants in the mother's endometrium.

blastula (blas´-tyū-luh) An embryonic stage that marks the end of cleavage during animal development; a hollow ball of cells in many species.
blood A type of connective tissue with a fluid matrix called plasma in which red blood cells, white blood cells, and platelets are suspended.
blood pressure The force that blood exerts against the walls of blood vessels.
body cavity A fluid-containing space between the digestive tract and the body wall.
body mass index (BMI) A ratio of weight to height.
bolus A lubricated ball of chewed food.
bone A type of connective tissue consisting of living cells held in a rigid matrix of collagen fibers embedded in calcium salts.
bottleneck effect Genetic drift resulting from a drastic reduction in population size. Typically, the surviving population is no longer genetically representative of the original population.
Bowman's capsule A cup-shaped swelling at the receiving end of a nephron in the vertebrate kidney; collects the filtrate from the blood.
brain The master control center of the nervous system, involved in regulating and controlling body activity and interpreting information from the senses transmitted through the nervous system.
brainstem A functional unit of the vertebrate brain, composed of the midbrain, the medulla oblongata, and the pons; serves mainly as a sensory filter, selecting which information reaches higher brain centers.
breathing Ventilation of the lungs through alternating inhalation and exhalation of air.
bronchiole (bron´-kē-ōl) A fine branch of the bronchi that transports air to alveoli.
bronchus (bron´-kus) (plural, **bronchi**) One of a pair of breathing tubes that branch from the trachea into the lungs.
brown alga One of a group of marine, multicellular, autotrophic protists belonging to the stramenopile clade of the SAR supergroup; the most common and largest type of seaweed. Brown algae include the kelps.
bryophyte (brī´-uh-fīt) A plant that lacks xylem and phloem; a seedless nonvascular plant. Bryophytes include mosses, liverworts, and hornworts.
buffer A chemical substance that minimizes changes in pH by accepting hydrogen ions from or donating hydrogen ions to solutions.
bulbourethral gland (bul´-bō-yū-rē´-thrul) One of a pair of glands near the base of the penis in the human male that secrete a clear alkaline mucus.
bulk feeder An animal that eats relatively large pieces of food.

C

C_3 plant A plant that uses the Calvin cycle for the initial steps that incorporate CO_2 into organic material, forming a three-carbon compound as the first stable intermediate.
C_4 plant A plant in which the Calvin cycle is preceded by reactions that incorporate CO_2 into a four-carbon compound, which then supplies CO_2 for the Calvin cycle.
Calvin cycle The second of two stages of photosynthesis; a cyclic series of chemical reactions that occur in the stroma of a chloroplast, using the carbon in CO_2 and the ATP and NADPH produced by the light reactions to make the energy-rich sugar molecule G3P.
CAM plant A plant that uses an adaptation for photosynthesis in arid conditions in which carbon dioxide entering open stomata during the night is converted to organic acids, which release CO_2 for the Calvin cycle during the day, when stomata are closed.
cancer A disease characterized by the presence of malignant tumors (rapidly growing and spreading masses of abnormal body cells) in the body.
capillary (kap´-il-er-ē) A microscopic blood vessel that conveys blood between an arteriole and a venule; enables the exchange of nutrients and dissolved gases between the blood and interstitial fluid.
capillary bed (kap´-il-er-ē) A network of capillaries in a tissue or organ.
capsid The protein shell that encloses a viral genome.
carbohydrate (kar´-bō-hī´-drāt) Member of the class of biological molecules consisting of single-monomer sugars (monosaccharides), two-monomer sugars (disaccharides), and polymers (polysaccharides).
carbon fixation The incorporation of carbon from atmospheric CO_2 into an organic compound. During photosynthesis in a C_3 plant, carbon is fixed into a three-carbon sugar as it enters the Calvin cycle. In C_4 and CAM plants, carbon is first fixed into a four-carbon sugar.
carbonyl group (kar´-buh-nēl´) A chemical group consisting of a carbon atom linked by a double bond to an oxygen atom.
carboxyl group (kar-bok´-sil) A chemical group consisting of a carbon atom double-bonded to an oxygen atom and also bonded to a hydroxyl group.
carcinogen (kar-sin´-uh-jin) A cancer-causing agent, either high-energy radiation (such as X-rays or UV light) or a chemical.
cardiac cycle (kar´-dē-ak) The alternating contractions and relaxations of the heart.
cardiac muscle (kar´-dē-ak) A type of striated muscle that forms the contractile wall of the heart.
cardiac output (kar´-dē-ak) The volume of blood pumped per minute by each ventricle of the heart.
cardiovascular disease (kar´-dē-ō-vas´-kyū-ler) Disorders of the heart and blood vessels.
cardiovascular system A closed circulatory system with a heart and a branching network of arteries, capillaries, and veins.
carnivore An animal that mainly eats other animals. *See also* herbivore; omnivore.
carpel (kar´-pul) The female part of a flower, consisting of a stalk with an ovary at the base and a stigma, which traps pollen, at the tip.
carrier An individual who is heterozygous for a recessively inherited disorder and who therefore does not show symptoms of that disorder but who may pass on the recessive allele to offspring.
carrying capacity In a population, the number of individuals that an environment can sustain.
cartilage (kar´-ti-lij) A flexible connective tissue consisting of living cells and collagenous fibers embedded in a rubbery matrix.
Casparian strip (kas-par´-ē-un) A waxy barrier in the walls of endodermal cells in a plant root that prevents water and ions from entering the xylem without crossing one or more cell membranes.
cataract A clouding of the eye's lens that results in less light reaching the retina; results in blurred images and faded colors.
cation exchange A process in which positively charged minerals are made available to a plant when hydrogen ions in the soil displace mineral ions from the clay particles.
cecum (sē´-kum) (plural, **ceca**) A blind outpocket at the beginning of the large intestine.
cell A basic unit of living matter separated from its environment by a plasma membrane; the fundamental structural unit of life.
cell body The part of a cell, such as a neuron, that houses the nucleus.
cell cycle An ordered sequence of events (including interphase and the mitotic phase) that extends from the time a eukaryotic cell is first formed from a dividing parent cell until its own division into two cells.
cell cycle control system A cyclically operating set of proteins that triggers and coordinates events in the eukaryotic cell cycle.
cell division The reproduction of a cell through duplication of the genome and division of the cytoplasm.
cell plate A double membrane across the midline of a dividing plant cell, between which the new cell wall forms during cytokinesis.
cell theory The theory that all living things are composed of cells and that all cells come from other cells.
cell wall A protective layer external to the plasma membrane in plant cells, bacteria, fungi, and some protists; protects the cell and helps maintain its shape.
cell-mediated immune response The branch of adaptive immunity that involves the activation of cytotoxic T cells, which defend against infected cells.
cellular metabolism (muh-tab´-uh-lizm) All the chemical activities of a cell.

cellular respiration The aerobic harvesting of energy from food molecules; the energy-releasing chemical breakdown of food molecules, such as glucose, and the storage of potential energy in a form that cells can use to perform work; involves glycolysis, pyruvate oxidation and the citric acid cycle, and oxidative phosphorylation (the electron transport chain and chemiosmosis).

cellular slime mold A type of protist that has unicellular amoeboid cells and aggregated reproductive bodies in its life cycle; a member of the amoebozoan clade.

cellulose (sel´-yū-lōs) A structural polysaccharide of plant cell walls composed of glucose monomers. Cellulose molecules are linked by hydrogen bonds into cable-like fibrils.

centipede A carnivorous terrestrial arthropod that has one pair of long legs for each of its numerous body segments, with the front pair modified as poison claws.

central nervous system (CNS) The integration and command center of the nervous system; the brain and, in vertebrates, the spinal cord.

central vacuole In a plant cell, a large membranous sac with diverse roles in growth and the storage of chemicals and wastes.

centralization The presence of a central nervous system (CNS) distinct from a peripheral nervous system.

centromere (sen´-trō-mēr) The region of a duplicated chromosome where two sister chromatids are joined (often appearing as a narrow "waist") and where spindle microtubules attach during mitosis and meiosis. The centromere divides at the onset of anaphase during mitosis and anaphase II during meiosis.

centrosome A structure found in animal cells from which microtubules originate and that is important during cell division. A centrosome has two centrioles.

cephalization (sef´-uh-luh-zā´-shun) An evolutionary trend toward concentration of the nervous system at the head end.

cephalopod A member of a group of molluscs that includes squids, cuttlefish, octopuses, and nautiluses.

cerebellum (sār´-ruh-bel´-um) Part of the vertebrate hindbrain; mainly a planning center that interacts closely with the cerebrum in coordinating body movement.

cerebral cortex (suh-rē´-brul kor´-teks) A folded sheet of gray matter forming the surface of the cerebrum. In humans, it contains integrating centers for higher brain functions such as reasoning, speech, language, and imagination.

cerebral hemisphere (suh-rē´-brul) The right or left half of the vertebrate cerebrum.

cerebrospinal fluid (suh-rē´-brō-spī´-nul) Blood-derived fluid that surrounds, nourishes, and cushions the brain and spinal cord.

cervix (ser´-viks) The neck of the uterus, which opens into the vagina.

chaparral (shap´-uh-ral´) A biome dominated by spiny evergreen shrubs adapted to periodic drought and fires; found where cold ocean currents circulate offshore, creating mild, rainy winters and long, hot, dry summers.

character A heritable feature that varies among individuals within a population, such as flower color in pea plants or eye color in humans.

chelicerate (kē-lih-suh´-rāte) A lineage of arthropods that includes horseshoe crabs, scorpions, ticks, and spiders.

chemical bond An attraction between two atoms resulting from a sharing of outer-shell electrons or the presence of opposite charges on the atoms. The bonded atoms gain complete outer electron shells.

chemical cycling The transfer of materials, such as carbon, within an ecosystem.

chemical energy Energy available in molecules for release in a chemical reaction; a form of potential energy.

chemical reaction The making and breaking of chemical bonds, leading to changes in the composition of matter.

chemiosmosis (kem´-ē-oz-mō´-sis) An energy-coupling mechanism that uses the energy of hydrogen ion (H^+) gradients across membranes to drive cellular work, such as the phosphorylation of ADP; powers most ATP synthesis in cells.

chemoautotroph An organism that obtains both energy and carbon from inorganic chemicals. A chemoautotroph makes its own organic compounds from CO_2 without using light energy.

chemoheterotroph An organism that obtains both energy and carbon from organic compounds.

chemoreceptor A sensory receptor that detects chemical changes within the body or a specific kind of molecule in the external environment.

chiasma (kī-az´-muh) (plural, **chiasmata**) The microscopically visible site where crossing over has occurred between chromatids of homologous chromosomes during prophase I of meiosis.

chitin (kī-tin) A structural polysaccharide found in many fungal cell walls and in the exoskeletons of arthropods.

chlamydia A member of a group of bacteria that live inside eukaryotic host cells; a common sexually transmitted disease caused by the bacterium *Chlamydia trachomatis*.

chlorophyll A green pigment located within the chloroplasts of plants and algae and in the membranes of certain prokaryotes. Chlorophyll *a* participates directly in the light reactions, which convert solar energy to chemical energy.

chloroplast (klō´-rō-plast) An organelle found in plants and algae that absorbs sunlight and uses it to drive the synthesis of organic compounds (sugars) from carbon dioxide and water.

choanocyte (kō-an´-uh-sīt) A flagellated feeding cell found in sponges. Also called a collar cell, it has a collar-like ring that traps food particles around the base of its flagellum.

cholesterol (kō-les´-tuh-rol) A steroid that is an important component of animal cell membranes and that acts as a precursor molecule for the synthesis of other steroids, such as hormones.

chondrichthyan (kon-drik´-thē-an) Cartilaginous fish; member of a clade of jawed vertebrates with skeletons made mostly of cartilage, such as sharks and rays.

chorion (kōr´-ē-on) In animals, the outermost extraembryonic membrane, which becomes the mammalian embryo's part of the placenta.

chorionic villus (kōr´-ē-on´-ik vil´-us) Outgrowth of the chorion, containing embryonic blood vessels. As part of the placenta, chorionic villi absorb nutrients and oxygen from, and pass wastes into, the mother's bloodstream.

chorionic villus sampling (CVS) A technique for diagnosing genetic defects while the fetus is in an early development stage within the uterus. A small sample of the fetal portion of the placenta is removed and analyzed.

chromatin (krō´-muh-tin) The complex of DNA and proteins that makes up eukaryotic chromosomes; often used to refer to the diffuse, very extended form taken by chromosomes when a cell is not dividing.

chromosome (krō´-muh-sōm) A gene-carrying structure found in the nucleus of a eukaryotic cell and most visible during mitosis and meiosis; also, the main gene-carrying structure of a prokaryotic cell. A chromosome consists of one very long DNA molecule and associated proteins.

chromosome theory of inheritance (krō´-muh-sōm) A basic principle in biology stating that genes are located on chromosomes and that the behavior of chromosomes during meiosis accounts for inheritance patterns.

chronic traumatic encephalopathy A dementia (mental deterioration) caused by brain trauma such as sports concussions and characterized by depression, memory loss, and other symptoms.

chyme (kīm) The mixture of partially digested food and digestive juices formed in the stomach.

chytrid (kī-trid) Member of a group of fungi that are mostly aquatic and have flagellated spores. They probably represent the most primitive fungal lineage.

ciliate (sil´-ē-it) A type of protist that moves and feeds by means of cilia. Ciliates belong to the alveolate clade of the SAR supergroup.

cilium (plural, **cilia**) A short cellular appendage specialized for locomotion or moving fluid past the cell, formed from a core of nine outer doublet microtubules and two single microtubules (the "9 + 2" arrangement) covered by the cell's plasma membrane.

circadian rhythm (ser-kā´-dē-un) In an organism, a biological cycle of about 24 hours that is controlled by a biological clock, usually under the influence of environmental cues; a pattern of activity that is repeated daily. *See also* biological clock.

circulatory system The organ system that transports materials such as nutrients, O_2, and hormones to body cells and transports CO_2 and other wastes from body cells.

citric acid cycle The chemical cycle that completes the metabolic breakdown of glucose molecules begun in glycolysis by oxidizing acetyl CoA (derived from pyruvate) to carbon dioxide. The cycle occurs in the matrix of mitochondria and supplies most of the NADH molecules that carry electrons to the electron transport chains. Together with pyruvate oxidation, the second major stage of cellular respiration.

clade A group of species that includes an ancestral species and all its descendants.

cladistics (kluh-dis´-tiks) An approach to systematics in which common descent is the primary criterion used to classify organisms by placing them into groups called clades.

class In Linnaean classification, the taxonomic category above order.

cleavage (klē´-vij) (1) Cytokinesis in animal cells and in some protists, characterized by pinching in of the plasma membrane. (2) In animal development, the first major phase of embryonic development, in which rapid cell divisions without cell growth transforms the animal zygote into a ball of cells.

cleavage furrow (klē´-vij) The first sign of cytokinesis during cell division in an animal cell; a shallow groove in the cell surface near the old metaphase plate.

climate change Increase in temperature and change in weather patterns all around the planet, due mostly to increasing atmospheric CO_2 levels from the burning of fossil fuels. The increase in temperature, called global warming, is a major aspect of global climate change.

clitoris An organ in the female that engorges with blood and becomes erect during sexual arousal.

clonal selection The process by which an antigen selectively binds to and activates only those lymphocytes bearing receptors specific for the antigen. The selected lymphocytes proliferate and differentiate into a clone of effector cells and a clone of memory cells specific for the stimulating antigen.

clone As a verb, to produce genetically identical copies of a cell, organism, or DNA molecule. As a noun, the collection of cells, organisms, or molecules resulting from cloning; colloquially, a single organism that is genetically identical to another because it arose from the cloning of a somatic cell.

closed circulatory system A circulatory system in which blood is confined to vessels and is kept separate from the interstitial fluid.

club fungus *See* basidiomycete.

clumped dispersion pattern A pattern in which the individuals of a population are aggregated in patches.

cnidarian (nī-dār´-ē-un) An animal characterized by cnidocytes, radial symmetry, a gastrovascular cavity, and a polyp and medusa body form. Cnidarians include the hydras, jellies, sea anemones, corals, and related animals.

cnidocyte (nī´-duh-sīt) A specialized cell for which the phylum Cnidaria is named; consists of a capsule containing a fine coiled thread, which, when discharged, functions in defense and prey capture.

coccus (kok´-us) (plural, **cocci**) A spherical prokaryotic cell.

cochlea (kok´-lē-uh) A coiled tube in the inner ear of birds and mammals that contains the hearing organ, the organ of Corti.

codominant Inheritance pattern in which a heterozygote expresses the distinct trait of both alleles.

codon (kō´-don) A three-nucleotide sequence in mRNA that specifies a particular amino acid or polypeptide termination signal; the basic unit of the genetic code.

coelom (sē´-lom) A body cavity completely lined with mesoderm.

coenzyme An organic molecule serving as a cofactor. Most vitamins function as coenzymes in important metabolic reactions.

coevolution Evolutionary change in which adaptations in one species act as a selective force on a second species, inducing adaptations that in turn act as a selective force on the first species; a series of reciprocal evolutionary adaptations in two interacting species.

cofactor A nonprotein molecule or ion that is required for the proper functioning of an enzyme. *See also* coenzyme.

cognition The process carried out by an animal's nervous system to perceive, store, integrate, and use information obtained by the animal's sensory receptors.

cohesion (kō-hē´-zhun) The sticking together of molecules of the same kind, often by hydrogen bonds.

collecting duct A tube in the vertebrate kidney that concentrates urine while conveying it to the renal pelvis.

collenchyma cell (kō-len´-kim-uh) In plants, a cell with a thick primary wall and no secondary wall, functioning mainly in supporting growing parts.

colon (kō´-lun) The largest section of the large intestine.

communication Animal behavior including transmission of, reception of, and response to signals.

community An assemblage of all the populations of organisms living close enough together for potential interactions.

companion cell In a plant, a cell connected to a sieve-tube element whose nucleus and ribosomes provide proteins for the sieve-tube element.

competitive inhibitor A substance that reduces the activity of an enzyme by entering the active site in place of the substrate. A competitive inhibitor's structure mimics that of the enzyme's substrate.

complement system A family of innate defensive blood proteins that cooperate with other components of the vertebrate defense system to protect against microbes; can enhance phagocytosis, cause the rupture of pathogens, and amplify the inflammatory response.

complementary DNA (cDNA) A DNA molecule made *in vitro* using mRNA as a template and the enzyme reverse transcriptase. A cDNA molecule therefore corresponds to a gene but lacks the introns present in the DNA of the genome.

complete digestive tract A digestive tube with two openings, a mouth and an anus.

complete dominance A type of inheritance in which the phenotypes of the heterozygote and dominant homozygote are indistinguishable.

complete metamorphosis (met´-uh-mōr´-fuh-sis) A type of development in certain insects in which development from larva to adult is achieved by multiple molts that are followed by a pupal stage. While encased in its pupa, the body rebuilds from clusters of embryonic cells that have been held in reserve. The adult emerges from the pupa.

compost Decomposing organic material that can be used to add nutrients to soil.

compound A substance containing two or more elements in a fixed ratio. For example, table salt (NaCl) consists of one atom of the element sodium (Na) for every atom of chlorine (Cl).

compound eye The photoreceptor in many invertebrates; made up of many tiny light detectors, each of which detects light from a tiny portion of the field of view.

concentration gradient A region along which the density of a chemical substance increases or decreases. Cells often maintain concentration gradients of ions across their membranes. When a concentration gradient exists, substances tend to move from where they are more concentrated to where they are less concentrated.

conception The fertilization of the egg by a sperm cell in humans.

condom A form of contraception; a sheath that fits over the penis to prevent the transfer of sperm to the vagina.

cone (1) In vertebrates, a photoreceptor cell in the retina stimulated by bright light and enabling color vision. (2) In conifers, a reproductive structure bearing pollen or ovules.

coniferous forest A biome characterized by conifers, cone-bearing evergreen trees.

conjugation The union (mating) of two bacterial cells or protist cells and the transfer of DNA between the two cells.

connective tissue Animal tissue that functions mainly to bind and support other tissues, having a sparse population of cells scattered through an extracellular matrix, which they produce. *See* adipose tissue; cartilage; bone; blood.

conservation biology A goal-oriented science that endeavors to understand and counter the loss of biodiversity.

continental shelf The submerged part of a continent.

contraception The deliberate prevention of pregnancy.

controlled experiment An experiment in which an experimental group is compared with a control group that varies only in the factor being tested.

convergent evolution The evolution of similar features in different evolutionary lineages, which can result from living in very similar environments.

cork The outermost protective layer of a plant's bark, produced by the cork cambium.

cork cambium (kam´-bē-um) Meristematic tissue that produces cork cells during secondary growth of a plant.

cornea (kor´-nē-uh) The transparent frontal portion of the sclera, which admits light into the vertebrate eye.

corpus callosum (kor´-pus kuh-lō´-sum) The thick band of nerve fibers that connect the right and left cerebral hemispheres in mammals, enabling the hemispheres to process information together.

corpus luteum (kor´-pus lū´-tē-um) A small body of endocrine tissue that develops from an ovarian follicle after ovulation and secretes progesterone and estrogen during pregnancy.

cortex In plants, the part of the ground tissue system that is between the vascular tissue and the dermal tissue in a root or eudicot stem.

corticosteroid A hormone synthesized and secreted by the adrenal cortex. The corticosteroids include the mineralocorticoids and glucocorticoids.

cotyledon (kot´-uh-lē´-don) The first leaf that appears on an embryo of a flowering plant; a seed leaf. Monocot embryos have one cotyledon; dicot embryos have two.

countercurrent exchange The transfer of a substance or heat between two fluids flowing in opposite directions.

countercurrent heat exchange A circulatory adaptation in which parallel blood vessels convey warm and cold blood in opposite directions, maximizing heat transfer to the cold blood.

covalent bond (ko-vā´-lent) A type of strong chemical bond in which two atoms share one or more pairs of valence electrons.

crop A pouch-like organ in a digestive tract where food is softened and may be stored temporarily.

cross A mating of two sexually reproducing individuals; often used to describe a genetics experiment involving a controlled mating (a "genetic cross").

crossing over The exchange of segments between chromatids of homologous chromosomes during synapsis in prophase I of meiosis; also, the exchange of segments between DNA molecules in prokaryotes.

crustacean A member of a major arthropod group that includes lobsters, crayfish, crabs, shrimps, and barnacles.

cuticle (kyū´-tuh-kul) (1) In animals, a tough, nonliving outer layer of the skin. (2) In plants, a waxy coating on the surface of stems and leaves that helps retain water.

cyanobacteria (sī-an´-ō-bak-tēr´-ē-uh) Photoautotrophic prokaryotes with plantlike, oxygen-generating photosynthesis.

cytokinesis (sī´-tō-kuh-nē´-sis) The division of the cytoplasm to form two separate daughter cells. Cytokinesis usually occurs in conjunction with telophase of mitosis. Mitosis and cytokinesis make up the mitotic (M) phase of the cell cycle.

cytokinin (sī´-tō-kī´-nin) One of a family of plant hormones that promotes cell division, retards aging in flowers and fruits, and may interact antagonistically with auxins in regulating plant growth and development.

cytoplasm (si´-tō-plaz´-um) The contents of a eukaryotic cell between the plasma membrane and the nucleus; consists of a semifluid medium and organelles; can also refer to the interior of a prokaryotic cell.

cytosine (C) (sī´-tuh-sin) A single-ring nitrogenous base found in DNA and RNA.

cytoskeleton A network of protein fibers in the cytoplasm of a eukaryotic cell; includes microfilaments, intermediate filaments, and microtubules.

cytosol (si´-tō-sol) The semifluid portion of the cytoplasm.

cytotoxic T cell (sī´-tō-tok´-sik) A type of lymphocyte that attacks body cells infected with pathogens.

D

data Recorded observations.

decomposer A prokaryote or fungus that secretes enzymes that digest molecules in organic material and convert them to inorganic forms.

decomposition The breakdown of organic materials into inorganic ones.

dehydration reaction (dē-hī-drā´-shun) A chemical reaction in which two molecules become covalently bonded to each other with the removal of a water molecule.

deletion The loss of one or more nucleotides from a gene by mutation; the loss of a fragment of a chromosome.

demographic transition A shift from zero population growth in which birth rates and death rates are high to zero population growth characterized by low birth and death rates.

denaturation (dē-nā´-chur-ā´-shun) A process in which a protein unravels, losing its specific structure and hence function; can be caused by changes in pH or salt concentration or by high temperature. Denaturation also refers to the separation of the two strands of the DNA double helix, caused by similar factors.

dendrite (den´-drīt) A neuron fiber that conveys signals from its tip inward, toward the rest of the neuron. A neuron typically has many short dendrites.

density-dependent factor A population-limiting factor whose intensity is linked to population density. For example, there may be a decline in birth rates or a rise in death rates in response to an increase in the number of individuals living in a designated area.

density-dependent inhibition The ceasing of cell division that occurs when cells touch one another.

density-independent factor A population-limiting factor whose intensity is unrelated to population density.

deoxyribonucleic acid (DNA) (dē-ok´-sē-rī´-bō-nū-klā´-ik) A double-stranded helical nucleic acid molecule consisting of nucleotide monomers with deoxyribose sugar and the nitrogenous bases adenine (A), cytosine (C), guanine (G), and thymine (T). Capable of replicating, DNA is an organism's genetic material. *See also* gene.

dependent variable A factor whose value is measured in an experiment to see whether it is influenced by changes in another factor (the independent variable).

dermal tissue system The outer protective covering of plants.

dermis A thick layer of skin under the epidermis that contains hair follicles, oil and sweat glands, muscles, nerves, and blood vessels.

desert A biome characterized by organisms adapted to sparse rainfall (less than 30 cm per year).

desertification The conversion of semi-arid regions to desert.

determinate growth Growth that ends after an organisms reaches a certain size, as in most animals. *See also* indeterminate growth.

detritivore (duh-trī´-tuh-vor) An organism that consumes decaying organic material.

detritus (duh-trī´-tus) Dead organic matter, including animal wastes, plant litter, and the bodies of dead organisms.

deuterostome (dū-ter´-ō-stōm) A mode of animal development in which the opening formed during gastrulation becomes the anus. Animals with the deuterostome pattern of development include the echinoderms and the chordates.

Deuterostomia A lineage of bilaterian animals, including the echinoderms and chordates, whose members all have a deuterostome pattern of development.

diabetes mellitus (dī´-uh-bē´-tis me-lī´-tis) A human hormonal disease in which body cells cannot absorb enough glucose from the blood and become energy starved; body fats and proteins are then consumed for their energy. Type 1 (insulin-dependent) diabetes results when the pancreas does not produce insulin; type 2 (non–insulin-dependent) diabetes results when body cells fail to respond to insulin.

dialysis (dī-al´-uh-sis) Separation and disposal of metabolic wastes from the blood by mechanical means; an artificial method of performing the functions of the kidneys that can be life sustaining in the event of kidney failure.

diaphragm (dī´-uh-fram) The sheet of muscle separating the chest cavity from the abdominal cavity in mammals. Its contraction expands the chest cavity, and its relaxation reduces it.

diastole (dȳ´-as´-tō-lē) The stage of the heart cycle in which the heart muscle is relaxed, allowing the chambers to fill with blood. *See also* systole.

diatom (dī´-uh-tom) A unicellular, autotrophic protist that belongs to the stramenopile clade of the SAR supergroup. Diatoms possess a unique glassy cell wall containing silica.

differentiation The specialization in the structure and function of cells that occurs during the development of an organism; results from selective activation and deactivation of the cells' genes.

diffusion The random movement of particles that results in the net movement of a substance down its concentration gradient from a region where it is more concentrated to a region where it is less concentrated.

digestion The mechanical and chemical breakdown of food into molecules small enough for the body to absorb; the second stage of food processing in animals.

dihybrid cross (dī´-hī´-brid) An experimental mating of individuals that are each heterozygous for both of two characters (or the self-pollination of a plant that is heterozygous for both characters).

dinoflagellate (dī´-nō-flaj´-uh-let) A member of a group of protists belonging to the alveolate clade of the SAR supergroup. Dinoflagellates are common components of marine and freshwater phytoplankton.

diploid In an organism that reproduces sexually, a cell containing two homologous sets of chromosomes, one set inherited from each parent; a 2*n* cell.

directional selection Natural selection in which individuals at one end of the phenotypic range survive and reproduce more successfully than do other individuals.

disaccharide (dī-sak´-uh-rīd) A sugar molecule consisting of two monosaccharides linked by a dehydration reaction.

dispersion pattern The manner in which individuals in a population are spaced within their area. Three types of dispersion patterns are clumped (individuals are aggregated in patches), uniform (individuals are evenly distributed), and random (unpredictable distribution).

disruptive selection Natural selection in which individuals on both extremes of a phenotypic range are favored over intermediate phenotypes.

distal tubule In the vertebrate kidney, the portion of a nephron after the loop of Henle that helps refine filtrate and empties it into a collecting duct.

disturbance In ecology, an event that changes a biological community by removing organisms from it or altering the availability of resources.

DNA *See* deoxyribonucleic acid (DNA).

DNA cloning The production of many identical copies of a specific segment of DNA.

DNA ligase (lī´-gās) An enzyme, essential for DNA replication, that catalyzes the covalent bonding of adjacent DNA polynucleotide strands. DNA ligase is used in genetic engineering to paste a specific piece of DNA containing a gene of interest into a bacterial plasmid or other vector.

DNA microarray A glass slide carrying thousands of different kinds of single-stranded DNA fragments arranged in an array (grid). A DNA microarray is used to detect and measure the expression of thousands of genes at one time. Tiny amounts of a large number of single-stranded DNA fragments representing different genes are fixed to the glass slide. These fragments, ideally representing all the genes of an organism, are tested for hybridization with various samples of cDNA molecules.

DNA polymerase (puh-lim´-er-ās) A large molecular complex that assembles DNA nucleotides into polynucleotides using a preexisting strand of DNA as a template.

DNA profiling A procedure that analyzes DNA samples to determine if they came from the same individual.

DNA technology Methods used to study and/or manipulate DNA, including recombinant DNA technology.

domain A taxonomic category above the kingdom level. The three domains of life are Archaea, Bacteria, and Eukarya.

dominance hierarchy The ranking of individuals within a group, based on social interactions and usually maintained by agonistic behavior.

dominant allele (uh-lē´-ul) The allele that determines the phenotype of a gene when the individual is heterozygous for that gene.

dorsal Pertaining to the back of a bilaterally symmetric animal.

dorsal, hollow nerve cord One of the four hallmarks of chordates, a tube that forms on the dorsal side of the body, above the notochord.

double circulation A circulatory system with separate pulmonary and systemic circuits, in which blood passes through the heart after completing each circuit; ensures vigorous blood flow to all organs.

double fertilization In flowering plants, the formation of both a zygote and a cell with a triploid nucleus, which develops into the endosperm.

double helix The form of native DNA, referring to its two adjacent polynucleotide strands interwound into a spiral shape.

Down syndrome *See* trisomy 21.

duodenum (dū-ō-dē´-num) The first portion of the vertebrate small intestine after the stomach, where chyme from the stomach mixes with bile and digestive enzymes.

duplication Repetition of part of a chromosome resulting from fusion with a fragment from a homologous chromosome; can result from an error in meiosis or from mutagenesis.

E

eardrum A sheet of connective tissue separating the outer ear from the middle ear that vibrates when stimulated by sound waves and passes the waves to the middle ear.

Ecdysozoa A lineage of bilaterian animals that includes the nematodes and arthropods.

echinoderm (uh-kī´-nō-derm) Member of a phylum of slow-moving or sessile marine animals characterized by a rough or spiny skin, a water vascular system, an endoskeleton, and radial symmetry in adults. Echinoderms include sea stars, sea urchins, and sand dollars.

ecological footprint An estimate of the amount of land and water area required to provide the resources an individual or nation consumes and to absorb the waste it generates, measured in global hectares (gha).

ecological niche (nich) The role of a species in its community; the sum total of a species' use of the biotic and abiotic resources of its environment.

ecological species concept A definition of species in terms of ecological niche, the sum of how members of the species interact with the nonliving and living parts of their environment.

ecological succession The process of biological community change resulting from disturbance; transition in the species composition of a biological community. *See also* primary succession; secondary succession.

ecology The scientific study of the interactions between organisms and the environment.

ecosystem (ē´-kō-sis-tem) All the organisms in a given area, along with the nonliving (abiotic) factors with which they interact; a biological community and its physical environment.

ecotourism Travel to natural areas for tourism and recreation.

ectoderm (ek´-tō-derm) The outer layer of three embryonic cell layers in a gastrula. The ectoderm forms the skin of the gastrula and gives rise to the epidermis and nervous system in the adult.

ectopic pregnancy (ek-top´-ik) The implantation and development of an embryo outside the uterus.

ectothermic (ek´-tō-therm-ik) Referring to organisms for which external sources provide most of the heat for temperature regulation.

effector cell (1) A muscle cell or gland cell that performs the body's response to stimuli, responding to signals from the brain or other processing center of the nervous system. (2) A lymphocyte that has undergone clonal selection and is capable of mediating an acquired immune response.

egg A female gamete.

ejaculation (ih-jak´-yū-lā´-shun) The expulsion of semen from the penis.

electromagnetic receptor A sensory receptor that detects energy of different wavelengths, such as electricity, magnetism, and light.

electromagnetic spectrum The entire spectrum of electromagnetic radiation ranging in wavelength from less than a nanometer to more than a kilometer.

electron A subatomic particle with a single negative electrical charge. One or more electrons move around the nucleus of an atom.

electron microscope (EM) A microscope that uses magnets to focus an electron beam through, or onto the surface of, a specimen. An electron microscope achieves a hundredfold greater resolution than a light microscope.

electron shell A level of electrons at a characteristic average distance from the nucleus of an atom.

electron transport chain A series of electron carrier molecules that shuttle electrons during a series of redox reactions that release energy used to make ATP; located in the inner membrane of mitochondria, the thylakoid membranes of chloroplasts, and the plasma membranes of prokaryotes.

electronegativity The attraction of a given atom for the electrons of a covalent bond.

element A substance that cannot be broken down to other substances by chemical means.

elimination The passing of undigested material out of the digestive compartment; the fourth and final stage of food processing in animals.

embryo (em´-brē-ō) A developing stage of a multicellular organism. In humans, the stage in development from the first division of the zygote until body structures begin to appear, about the 9th week of gestation.

embryo sac (em´-brē-ō) The female gametophyte contained in the ovule of a flowering plant.

embryonic stem cell (ES cell) Cell in the early animal embryo that differentiates during development to give rise to all the different kinds of specialized cells in the body.

embryophyte Another name for land plants, recognizing that land plants share the common derived trait of multicellular, dependent embryos.

emergent properties New properties that arise with each step upward in the hierarchy of life, owing to the arrangement and interactions of parts as complexity increases.

emerging virus A virus that has appeared suddenly or has recently come to the attention of medical scientists.

endemic species A species whose distribution is limited to a specific geographic area.

endergonic reaction (en´-der-gon´-ik) An energy-requiring chemical reaction, which yields products with more potential energy than the reactants.

endocrine disruptor A chemical, usually synthetic, that interferes with the endocrine system's normal functions.

endocrine gland (en´-dō-krin) A ductless gland that synthesizes hormone molecules and secretes them into the interstitial fluid, from which they diffuse into the bloodstream.

endocrine system (en´-dō-krin) The organ system consisting of ductless glands that secrete hormones and the molecular receptors on or in target cells that respond to the hormones. The endocrine system cooperates with the nervous system in regulating body functions and maintaining homeostasis.

endocytosis (en´-dō-sī-tō´-sis) Cellular uptake of molecules or particles via formation of new vesicles from the plasma membrane.

endoderm (en´-dō-derm) The innermost of three embryonic cell layers in a gastrula; gives rise to the innermost linings of the digestive tract and other hollow organs in the adult.

endodermis The innermost layer (a one-cell-thick cylinder) of the cortex of a plant root; forms a selective barrier determining which substances pass from the cortex into the vascular tissue.

endomembrane system A network of membranes inside and surrounding a eukaryotic cell, related either through direct physical contact or by the transfer of membranous vesicles.

endometrium (en´-dō-mē´-trē-um) The inner lining of the uterus in mammals, richly supplied with blood vessels that provide the maternal part of the placenta and nourish the developing embryo.

endoplasmic reticulum (ER) (reh-tik´-yuh-lum) An extensive membranous network in a eukaryotic cell, continuous with the outer nuclear membrane and composed of ribosome-studded (rough) and ribosome-free (smooth) regions. *See also* rough ER; smooth ER.

endoskeleton A hard skeleton located within the soft tissues of an animal; includes spicules of sponges, the hard plates of echinoderms, and the cartilage and bony skeletons of vertebrates.

endosperm In flowering plants, a nutrient-rich mass formed by the union of a sperm cell with two nuclei during double fertilization; provides nourishment to the developing embryo in the seed.

endospore A thick-coated, protective cell produced within a bacterial cell. The endospore becomes dormant and is able to survive harsh environmental conditions.

endosymbiont theory (en´-dō-sim´-bī-ont) The theory that mitochondria and chloroplasts originated as prokaryotic cells engulfed by an ancestral eukaryotic cell. The engulfed cell and its host cell then evolved into a single organism.

endothermic Referring to organisms that use heat generated by their own metabolism to maintain a warm, steady body temperature.

endotoxin A poisonous component of the outer membrane of gram-negative bacteria that is released only when the bacteria die.

energy The capacity to cause change, especially to perform work.

energy coupling In cellular metabolism, the use of energy released from an exergonic reaction to drive an endergonic reaction.

energy flow The passage of energy through the components of an ecosystem.

enhancer A eukaryotic DNA sequence that helps stimulate the transcription of a gene at some distance from it. An enhancer functions by means of a transcription factor called an activator, which binds to it and then to the rest of the transcription apparatus.

enteric division Part of the autonomic nervous system consisting of complex networks of neurons in the digestive tract, pancreas, and gallbladder.

entropy (en´-truh-pē) A measure of disorder, or randomness. *See also* second law of thermodynamics.

enzyme (en´-zīm) A macromolecule, usually a protein, that serves as a biological catalyst, changing the rate of a chemical reaction without being consumed by the reaction.

epidermis (ep´-uh-der´-mis) (1) In animals, one or more living layers of cells forming the protective covering, or outer skin. (2) In plants, the tissue system forming the protective outer covering of leaves, young stems, and young roots.

epididymis (ep´-uh-did´-uh-mus) A long coiled tube into which sperm pass from the testis and are stored until mature and ejaculated.

epigenetic inheritance The inheritance of traits transmitted by mechanisms not directly involving the nucleotide sequence of a genome, such as the chemical modification of histone proteins or DNA bases.

epiglottis A flap of elastic cartilage that protects the entrance to the trachea. Normally, the epiglottis is positioned to allow air to enter the trachea; it changes position when food is swallowed, allowing food to enter the esophagus and preventing food from entering the trachea.

epinephrine (ep´-uh-nef´-rin) A hormone (also called adrenaline) secreted by the adrenal medulla in response to stress from a physical threat that prepares body organs for action (fight or flight); also serves as a neurotransmitter.

epithelial tissue (ep´-uh-thē´-lē-ul) A sheet of tightly packed cells lining organs, body cavities, and external surfaces; also called epithelium.

epitope A small region on the surface of an antigen molecule to which an antigen receptor or antibody binds.

errantian A member of a major annelid lineage that includes mostly marine worms with an active lifestyle.

erythropoietin (EPO) (eh-rith´-rō-poy´-uh-tin) A hormone that stimulates the production of erythrocytes. It is secreted by the kidney when tissues of the body do not receive enough oxygen.

esophagus (eh-sof´-uh-gus) A muscular tube that conducts food by peristalsis, usually from the pharynx to the stomach.

essential amino acid An amino acid that an animal cannot synthesize itself and must obtain from food. Eight amino acids are essential for human adults, and a ninth is essential for human infants.

essential element In plants, a chemical element required for the plant to complete its life cycle (to grow from a seed and produce another generation of seeds).

essential fatty acid A fatty acid that an animal cannot synthesize itself and must obtain from food.

essential nutrient A substance that an organism must absorb in preassembled form because it cannot synthesize it from any other material. In humans, there are essential vitamins, minerals, amino acids, and fatty acids.

estrogen (es´-trō-jen) One of several chemically similar steroid hormones secreted by the gonads; maintains the female reproductive system and promotes the development of female body features.

estuary (es´-chū-ār-ē) A biome that occurs where a freshwater stream or river merges with the ocean.

ethylene A gas that functions as a hormone in plants, triggering aging responses such as fruit ripening and leaf drop.

eudicot (yū-dī´-kot) Member of a group that consists of the vast majority of flowering plants that have two embryonic seed leaves, or cotyledons.

Eukarya (yū-kar´-ē-uh) Domain of life that includes all eukaryotic organisms.

eukaryotic cell (yū-kar-ē-ot´-ik) A type of cell that has a membrane-enclosed nucleus and membrane-enclosed organelles. All organisms except bacteria and archaea are composed of eukaryotic cells.

Eumetazoa (yū-met-uh-zō´-uh) Clade of "true animals," the animals with true tissues (all animals except sponges).

Eustachian tube (yū-stā´-shun) An air passage between the middle ear and throat of vertebrates that equalizes air pressure on either side of the eardrum.

eutherian (yū-thēr´-ē-un) Placental mammal; mammal whose young complete their embryonic development within the uterus, joined to the mother by the placenta.

evaporative cooling The process in which the surface of an object becomes cooler during evaporation, a result of the molecules with the greatest energy changing from the liquid to the gaseous state.

evo-devo Evolutionary developmental biology; the field of biology that combines evolutionary biology with developmental biology.

evolution Descent with modification; the idea that living species are descendants of ancestral species that were different from present-day ones; also, the genetic changes in a population from generation to generation.

evolutionary tree A branching diagram that reflects a hypothesis about evolutionary relationships among groups of organisms.

Excavata One of four monophyletic supergroups proposed in a current hypothesis of the evolutionary history of eukaryotes. The other three supergroups are SAR (Stramenopila, Alveolata, and Rhizaria), Unikonta, and Archaeplastida.

excretion (ek-skrē´-shun) The disposal of nitrogen-containing metabolic wastes.

exergonic reaction (ek´-ser-gon´-ik) An energy-releasing chemical reaction in which the reactants contain more potential energy than the products.

exocytosis (ek´-sō-sī-tō´-sis) The movement of materials out of a cell by the fusion of vesicles with the plasma membrane.

exon The part of a gene that becomes part of the final messenger RNA and is therefore expressed.

exoskeleton A hard external skeleton that protects an animal and provides points of attachment for muscles.

exotoxin A poisonous protein secreted by certain bacteria.

experiment A scientific test. Often carried out under controlled conditions that involve manipulating one factor in a system in order to see the effects of changing that factor.

exponential growth model A mathematical description of idealized, unlimited population growth.

external fertilization The fusion of gametes that parents have discharged into the environment.

extinction The irrevocable loss of a species.

extirpation The loss of a single population of a species.

extracellular matrix (ECM) The meshwork surrounding animal cells; consists of glycoproteins and polysaccharides synthesized and secreted by cells.

extraembryonic membranes Four membranes (the yolk sac, amnion, chorion, and allantois) that form a life-support system for the developing embryo of a reptile, bird, or mammal.

extreme halophile A microorganism that lives in a highly saline environment, such as the Great Salt Lake or the Dead Sea.

extreme thermophile A microorganism that thrives in a hot environment (often 60–80°C).

eyecup The simplest type of photoreceptor, a cluster of photoreceptor cells shaded by a cuplike cluster of pigmented cells; detects light intensity and direction.

F

F factor A piece of DNA that can exist as a bacterial plasmid. The F factor carries genes for making sex pili and other structures needed for conjugation, as well as a site where DNA replication can start. F stands for fertility.

F_1 generation The offspring of two parental (P generation) individuals; F_1 stands for first filial.

F_2 generation The offspring of the F_1 generation; F_2 stands for second filial.

facilitated diffusion The passage of a substance through a specific transport protein across a biological membrane down its concentration gradient.

family In Linnaean classification, the taxonomic category above genus.

farsightedness An inability to focus on close objects; occurs when the eyeball is shorter than normal and the focal point of the lens is behind the retina; also called hyperopia.

fat A lipid composed of three fatty acids linked to one glycerol molecule; a triglyceride. Most fats function as energy-storage molecules.

feces The wastes of the digestive tract.

feedback inhibition A method of metabolic control in which a product of a metabolic pathway acts as an inhibitor of an enzyme within that pathway.

fertility rate In a human population, the average number of children produced by a woman over her lifetime.

fertilization The union of the nucleus of a sperm cell with the nucleus of an egg cell, producing a zygote.

fertilizer A compound given to plants to promote their growth.

fetus (fē´-tus) A developing human from the 9th week of gestation until birth. The fetus has all the major structures of an adult.

fiber (1) In animals, an elongate, supportive thread in the matrix of connective tissue; an extension of a neuron; a muscle cell. (2) In plants, a long, slender sclerenchyma cell that usually occurs in a bundle.

fibrin (fī´-brin) The activated form of the blood-clotting protein fibrinogen, which aggregates into threads that form the fabric of a blood clot.

fibrinogen (fī´-brin´-uh-jen) The plasma protein that is activated to form a clot when a blood vessel is injured.

fibrous connective tissue A dense tissue with large numbers of collagenous fibers organized into parallel bundles; the dominant tissue in tendons and ligaments.

filtrate Fluid extracted by the excretory system from the blood or body cavity. The excretory system produces urine from the filtrate after removing valuable solutes from it and concentrating it.

filtration In the vertebrate kidney, the extraction of water and small solutes, including metabolic wastes, from the blood by the nephrons.

fimbria (plural, **fimbriae**) One of the short, hairlike projections on some prokaryotic cells that help attach the cells to their substrate or to other cells.

first law of thermodynamics The principle of conservation of energy. Energy can be transferred and transformed, but it cannot be created or destroyed.

fixed action pattern (FAP) A genetically programmed, unchangeable behavioral sequence performed in response to a certain stimulus.

flagellum (fluh-jel´-um) (plural, **flagella**) A long cellular appendage specialized for locomotion. The flagella of prokaryotes and eukaryotes differ in both structure and function. Like cilia, eukaryotic flagella have a "9 + 2" arrangement of microtubules covered by the cell's plasma membrane.
flatworm A member of the phylum Platyhelminthes.
fluid feeder An animal that lives by sucking nutrient-rich fluids from another living organism.
fluid mosaic model The currently accepted model of cell membrane structure, depicting the membrane as a mosaic of protein molecules suspended in a fluid bilayer of phospholipid molecules.
fluke One of a group of parasitic flatworms.
follicle (fol´-uh-kul) A cluster of cells in the ovary that includes a developing egg and cells that surround, protect, and nourish it. Follicles secrete the hormone estrogen.
food chain A sequence of food transfers from producers through one to four levels of consumers in an ecosystem.
food web A network of interconnecting food chains.
foot In an invertebrate animal, a structure used for locomotion or attachment, such as the muscular organ extending from the ventral side of a mollusc.
foraging Behavior used in recognizing, searching for, capturing, and consuming food.
foraminiferan A protist that moves and feeds by means of threadlike pseudopodia and has porous shells composed of calcium carbonate. Forams belong to the Rhizaria clade of the SAR supergroup.
forebrain One of three ancestral and embryonic regions of the vertebrate brain; develops into the thalamus, hypothalamus, and cerebrum.
forensics The scientific analysis of evidence for crime scene and other legal proceedings. Also referred to as forensic science.
fossil A preserved remnant or impression of an organism.
fossil fuel An energy-containing deposit of organic material formed from the remains of ancient organisms.
fossil record The chronicle of evolution over millions of years of geologic time engraved in the order in which fossils appear in rock strata.
founder effect Genetic drift that occurs when a few individuals become isolated from a larger population and form a new population whose gene pool is not reflective of that of the original population.
fovea (fō´-vē-uh) An eye's center of focus and the place on the retina where photoreceptors are highly concentrated.
fragmentation A means of asexual reproduction whereby a single parent breaks into parts that regenerate into whole new individuals.
frameshift mutation A change in the genetic material that involves the insertion or deletion of one or more nucleotides in a gene, resulting in a change in the triplet grouping of nucleotides.
free-living flatworm A nonparasitic flatworm.
fruit A ripened, thickened ovary of a flower, which protects developing seeds and aids in their dispersal.
functional group A specific configuration of atoms commonly attached to the carbon skeletons of organic molecules and involved in chemical reactions.
Fungi (fun´-jī) The kingdom that contains the fungi.

G

gallbladder An organ that stores bile and releases it as needed into the small intestine.
gametangium (gam´-uh-tan´-jē-um) (plural, **gametangia**) A reproductive organ that houses and protects the gametes of a plant.
gamete (gam´-ēt) A sex cell; a haploid egg or sperm. The union of two gametes of opposite sex (fertilization) produces a zygote.
gametogenesis The creation of gametes within the gonads.
gametophyte (guh-mē´-tō-fīt) The multicellular haploid form in the life cycle of organisms undergoing alternation of generations; mitotically produces haploid gametes that unite and grow into the sporophyte generation.
ganglion (gang´-glē-un) (plural, **ganglia**) A cluster of neuron cell bodies in a peripheral nervous system.
gas exchange The exchange of O_2 and CO_2 between an organism and its environment.
gastric juice The collection of fluids (mucus, enzymes, and acid) secreted by the stomach.
gastrin A digestive hormone that stimulates the secretion of gastric juice.
gastropod A member of the largest group of molluscs, including snails and slugs.
gastrovascular cavity A central compartment with a single opening, the mouth; functions in both digestion and nutrient distribution and may also function in circulation, body support, waste disposal, and gas exchange.
gastrula (gas´-trū-luh) The embryonic stage resulting from gastrulation in animal development. Most animals have a gastrula made up of three layers of cells: ectoderm, endoderm, and mesoderm.
gastrulation (gas´-trū-lā´-shun) The second major phase of embryonic development, which transforms the blastula into a gastrula. Gastrulation adds more cells to the embryo and sorts the cells into distinct cell layers.
gel electrophoresis (jel´ ē-lek´-trō-fōr-ē´-sis) A technique for separating and purifying macromolecules, either DNA or proteins. A mixture of the macromolecules is placed on a gel between a positively charged electrode and a negatively charged one. Negative charges on the molecules are attracted to the positive electrode, and the molecules migrate toward that electrode. The molecules separate in the gel according to their rates of migration, which is mostly determined by their size: Smaller molecules generally move faster through the gel, while larger molecules generally move more slowly.
gene A discrete unit of hereditary information consisting of a specific nucleotide sequence in DNA (or RNA, in some viruses). Most of the genes of a eukaryote are located in its chromosomal DNA; a few are carried by the DNA of mitochondria and chloroplasts.
gene cloning The production of multiple copies of a gene.
gene expression The process whereby genetic information flows from genes to proteins; the flow of genetic information from the genotype to the phenotype.
gene flow The transfer of alleles from one population to another as a result of the movement of individuals or their gametes.
gene pool All copies of every type of allele at every locus in all members of the population.
gene regulation The turning on and off of genes within a cell in response to environmental stimuli or other factors (such as developmental stage).
gene therapy A treatment for a disease in which the patient's defective gene is supplemented or altered.
genetic code The set of rules that dictates the amino acid translations of each mRNA nucleotide triplet.
genetic drift A change in the gene pool of a population due to chance. Effects of genetic drift are most pronounced in small populations.
genetic engineering The direct manipulation of genes for practical purposes.
genetic map An ordered listing of the relative locations of genes along a chromosome.
genetically modified organism (GMO) An organism that has acquired one or more genes by artificial means. If the gene is from another species, the organism is also known as a transgenic organism.
genetics The scientific study of heredity. Modern genetics began with the work of Gregor Mendel in the 19th century.
genital herpes A sexually transmitted disease caused by the herpes simplex virus type 2.
genomics The study of complete sets of genes and their interactions.
genotype (jē´-nō-tīp) The genetic makeup of an organism.
genus (jē´-nus) (plural, **genera**) In classification, the taxonomic category above species; the first part of a species' binomial; for example, *Homo*.
geologic record A time scale established by geologists that divides Earth's history into four eons—Hadean, Archaean, Proterozoic, and Phanerozoic—and further subdivides it into eras, periods, and epochs.
germinate To start developing or growing.
gestation (jes-tā´-shun) Pregnancy; the state of carrying developing young within the female reproductive tract.

gibberellin (jib´-uh-rel´-in) One of a family of plant hormones that triggers the germination of seeds and interacts with auxins in regulating growth and fruit development.

gill An extension of the body surface of an aquatic animal, specialized for gas exchange and/or suspension feeding.

gizzard A pouch-like organ in a digestive tract where food is mechanically ground.

glaucoma An eye disease, most often caused by a buildup of fluid in the eye; leads to increased pressure in the eye; damage to the optic nerve from pressure may result in irreversible loss of vision.

glia A network of supporting cells that is essential for the structural integrity and for the normal functioning of the nervous system.

glomeromycete (glō´-mer-ō-mī´-sēt) Member of a group of fungi characterized by a distinct branching form of mycorrhizae (symbiotic relationships with plant roots) called arbuscules.

glomerulus (glō-mer´-ū-lus) (plural, **glomeruli**) In the vertebrate kidney, the part of a nephron consisting of the capillaries that are surrounded by Bowman's capsule; together, a glomerulus and Bowman's capsule produce the filtrate from the blood.

glucagon (glū´-kuh-gon) A peptide hormone, secreted by the pancreas, that raises the level of glucose in the blood. It is antagonistic with insulin.

glucocorticoid (glū´-kuh-kor´-tih-koyd) A corticosteroid hormone secreted by the adrenal cortex that increases the blood glucose level and helps maintain the body's response to stress from low blood sugar or decreased blood volume or blood pressure.

glucose A six-carbon monosaccharide that serves as a building block for many polysaccharides and whose oxidation in cellular respiration is a major source of ATP for cells.

glycogen (glī´-kō-jen) An extensively branched glucose storage polysaccharide found in liver and muscle cells; the animal equivalent of starch.

glycolysis (glī-kol´-uh-sis) A series of reactions that ultimately splits glucose into two molecules of pyruvate; the first stage of cellular respiration in all organisms; occurs in the cytosol.

glycoprotein (glī´-kō-prō´-tēn) A protein with one or more short chains of sugars attached to it.

goiter An enlargement of the thyroid gland resulting from a dietary iodine deficiency.

Golgi apparatus (gol´-jē) An organelle in eukaryotic cells consisting of stacks of membranous sacs that modify, store, and ship products of the endoplasmic reticulum.

gonad A sex organ in an animal that secretes sex hormones and produces gametes; an ovary or testis.

Gram stain Microbiological technique to identify the cell wall composition of bacteria. Results categorize bacteria as gram-positive or gram-negative.

gram-positive bacteria Diverse group of bacteria with a cell wall that is structurally less complex and contains more peptidoglycan than that of gram-negative bacteria. Gram-positive bacteria are usually less toxic than gram-negative bacteria.

granum (gran´-um) (plural, **grana**) A stack of membrane-bounded thylakoids in a chloroplast. Grana are the sites where light energy is trapped by chlorophyll and converted to chemical energy during the light reactions of photosynthesis.

gravitropism (grav´-uh-trō´-pizm) A plant's directional growth in response to gravity.

gray matter Regions within the central nervous system composed mainly of neuron cell bodies and dendrites.

green alga A member of a group of photosynthetic protists that includes chlorophytes and charophyceans, the closest living relatives of land plants. Green algae include unicellular, colonial, and multicellular species and belong to the supergroup Archaeplastida.

greenhouse effect The warming of Earth due to the atmospheric accumulation of CO_2 and certain other gases, which absorb infrared radiation and reradiate some of it back toward Earth.

gross primary production The total primary production of an ecosystem during a given time period.

ground tissue system A tissue of mostly parenchyma cells that makes up the bulk of a young plant and is continuous throughout its body. The ground tissue system fills the space between the epidermis and the vascular tissue system.

growth factor A protein secreted by certain body cells that stimulates other cells to divide.

growth hormone (GH) A protein hormone secreted by the anterior pituitary that promotes development and growth and stimulates metabolism.

guanine (G) (gwa´-nēn) A double-ring nitrogenous base found in DNA and RNA.

guard cell A specialized epidermal cell in plants that regulates the size of a stoma, allowing gas exchange between the surrounding air and the photosynthetic cells in the leaf.

gymnosperm (jim´-nō-sperm) A naked-seed plant. Its seed is said to be naked because it is not enclosed in an ovary.

H

habitat A place where an organism lives; the environment in which an organism lives.

habituation Learning not to respond to a repeated stimulus that conveys little or no information.

hair cell A type of mechanoreceptor that detects sound waves and other forms of movement in air or water.

haploid In the life cycle of an organism that reproduces sexually, a cell containing a single set of chromosomes; an *n* cell.

Hardy-Weinberg equilibrium The state of a population in which frequencies of alleles and genotypes in a population remain constant from generation to generation, provided that only Mendelian segregation and recombination of alleles are at work.

heart A muscular pump that propels a circulatory fluid (blood) through vessels to the body.

heart attack The damage or death of cardiac muscle cells and the resulting failure of the heart to deliver enough blood to the body.

heart rate The frequency of heart contraction, usually expressed in number of beats per minute.

heartwood In the center of trees, the darkened, older layers of secondary xylem made up of cells that no longer transport water and are clogged with resins. *See also* sapwood.

heat Thermal energy in transfer from one body of matter to another.

helper T cell A type of lymphocyte that, when activated, secretes stimulatory signals that promote the response of B cells (humoral response) and cytotoxic T cells (cell-mediated response) to antigens.

hemoglobin (hē´-mō-glō-bin) An iron-containing protein in red blood cells that reversibly binds O_2.

hepatic portal vein A blood vessel that conveys nutrient-laden blood from capillaries surrounding the intestine directly to the liver.

herbivore An animal that mainly eats plants or algae. *See also* carnivore; omnivore.

herbivory Consumption of plant parts or algae by an animal.

herd immunity The protection that most members of a community have against an outbreak of disease because a critical portion of the community is immunized.

heredity The transmission of traits (inherited features) from one generation to the next.

hermaphroditism (her-maf´-rō-dī-tizm) A condition in which an individual has both female and male gonads and functions as both a male and female in sexual reproduction by producing both sperm and eggs.

heterokaryotic stage (het´-er-ō-ker-ē-ot´-ik) A fungal life cycle stage that contains two genetically different haploid nuclei in the same cell.

heterotroph (het´-er-ō-trōf) An organism that obtains organic food molecules by eating other organisms or substances derived from them; a consumer or a decomposer in a food chain.

heterozygote advantage (het´-er-ō-zī´-gōt) Greater reproductive success of heterozygous individuals compared with homozygotes; tends to preserve variation in gene pools.

heterozygous (het´-er-ō-zī´-gus) Having two different alleles for a given gene.

high-density lipoprotein (HDL) A cholesterol-carrying particle in the blood, made up of thousands of cholesterol molecules and other lipids bound to a protein. HDL scavenges excess cholesterol.

hindbrain One of three ancestral and embryonic regions of the vertebrate brain; develops into the medulla oblongata, pons, and cerebellum.

hinge joint A joint that allows movement in only one plane. In humans, examples include the elbow and knee.

hippocampus (hip´-uh-kam´-pus) An integrative center of the cerebrum; functionally, plays a central role in the formation of memories and their recall.

histamine (his´-tuh-mēn) A chemical alarm signal released by mast cells that causes blood vessels to dilate and become more permeable in inflammatory and allergic responses.

histone (his´-tōn) A small protein molecule important in DNA packing in the eukaryotic chromosome. Eukaryotic chromatin consists of roughly equal parts of DNA and histone protein.

HIV (human immunodeficiency virus) The retrovirus that attacks the human immune system and causes AIDS.

homeobox (hō´-mē-ō-boks´) A 180-nucleotide sequence within a homeotic gene and some other developmental genes.

homeostasis (hō´-mē-ō-stā´-sis) The steady state of body functioning; a state of equilibrium characterized by a dynamic interplay between outside forces that tend to change an organism's internal environment and the internal control mechanisms that oppose such changes.

homeotic gene (hō´-mē-ot´-ik) A master control gene that determines the identity of a body structure of a developing organism, presumably by controlling the developmental fate of groups of cells.

hominin (hah´-mi-nin) Member of a species on the human branch of the evolutionary tree; a species more closely related to humans than to chimpanzees.

homologous chromosomes (hō-mol´-uh-gus) The two chromosomes that make up a matched pair in a diploid cell. Homologous chromosomes are of the same length, centromere position, and staining pattern and possess genes for the same characters at corresponding loci. One homologous chromosome is inherited from the organism's father, the other from the mother.

homologous structures (hō-mol´-uh-gus) Structures in different species that are similar because of common ancestry.

homology (hō-mol´-uh-jē) Similarity in characters resulting from a shared ancestry.

homozygous (hō´-mō-zī´-gus) Having two identical alleles for a given gene.

horizontal gene transfer The transfer of genes from one genome to another through mechanisms such as transposable elements, plasmid exchange, viral activity, and perhaps fusions of different organisms.

hormone (1) In animals, a regulatory chemical that travels in the blood from its production site, usually an endocrine gland, to other sites, where target cells respond to the regulatory signal. (2) In plants, a chemical that is produced in one part of the plant and travels to another part, where it acts on target cells to change their functioning.

human chorionic gonadotropin (hCG) (kōr´-ē-on´-ik gō-na´-dō-trō´-pin) A hormone secreted by the chorion that maintains the production of estrogen and progesterone by the corpus luteum of the ovary during the first few months of pregnancy; hCG secreted in the urine is the target of many home pregnancy tests.

Human Genome Project (HGP) An international collaborative effort to map and sequence the DNA of the entire human genome. The project was begun in 1990 and completed in 2004.

humoral immune response The branch of adaptive immunity that involves the activation of B cells and that leads to the production of antibodies, which defend against bacteria and viruses in body fluids.

humus (hyū´-mus) Decomposing organic material found in topsoil.

Huntington's disease A human genetic disease caused by a single dominant allele; characterized by uncontrollable body movements and degeneration of the nervous system; usually fatal 10 to 20 years after the onset of symptoms.

hybrid Offspring that results from the mating of individuals from two different species or from two true-breeding varieties of the same species; an offspring of two parents that differ in one or more inherited traits; an individual that is heterozygous for one or more pairs of genes.

hybrid zone A geographic region in which members of different species meet and mate, producing at least some hybrid offspring.

hydrocarbon An organic compound composed only of the elements carbon and hydrogen.

hydrogen bond A type of weak chemical bond formed when the slightly positive hydrogen atom of a polar covalent bond in one molecule is attracted to the slightly negative atom of a polar covalent bond in another molecule (or in another region of the same molecule).

hydrolysis (hī-drol´-uh-sis) A chemical reaction that breaks bonds between two molecules by the addition of water; process by which polymers are broken down and an essential part of digestion.

hydrophilic (hī´-drō-fil´-ik) "Water-loving"; pertaining to polar or charged molecules (or parts of molecules) that are soluble in water.

hydrophobic (hī´-drō-fō´-bik) "Water-fearing"; pertaining to nonpolar molecules (or parts of molecules) that do not dissolve in water.

hydrostatic skeleton A skeletal system composed of fluid held under pressure in a closed body compartment; the main skeleton of most cnidarians, flatworms, nematodes, and annelids.

hydroxyl group (hī-drok´-sil) A chemical group consisting of an oxygen atom bonded to a hydrogen atom.

hyperglycemia An abnormally high level of glucose in the blood that results when the pancreas does not secrete enough insulin or cells do not respond to insulin. Hyperglycemia is a characteristic of diabetes.

hypertension A disorder in which blood pressure remains abnormally high.

hypertonic Referring to a solution that, when surrounding a cell, will cause the cell to lose water.

hypha (hī´-fuh) (plural, **hyphae**) One of many filaments making up the body of a fungus.

hypoglycemia (hī´-pō-glī-sē´-mē-uh) An abnormally low level of glucose in the blood that results when the pancreas secretes too much insulin into the blood.

hypothalamus (hī-pō-thal´-uh-mus) The master control center of the endocrine system, located in the ventral portion of the vertebrate forebrain. The hypothalamus functions in maintaining homeostasis, especially in coordinating the endocrine and nervous systems; secretes hormones of the posterior pituitary and releasing hormones that regulate the anterior pituitary.

hypothesis (hī-poth´-uh-sis) (plural, **hypotheses**) A testable explanation for a set of observations based on the available data.

hypotonic Referring to a solution that, when surrounding a cell, will cause the cell to take up water.

I

immune system An animal body's system of defenses against agents that cause disease.

immunodeficiency disorder An immunological disorder in which the immune system lacks one or more components, making the body susceptible to infectious agents that would ordinarily not be pathogenic.

imperfect fungus A fungus with no known sexual stage.

impotence The inability to maintain an erection; also called erectile dysfunction.

imprinting Learning that is limited to a specific critical period in an animal's life and that is generally irreversible.

***in vitro* fertilization (IVF)** (vē´-tro) Uniting sperm and egg in a laboratory container, followed by the placement of a resulting early embryo in the mother's uterus.

inclusive fitness An individual's success at perpetuating its genes by producing its own offspring and by helping close relatives to produce offspring.

incomplete dominance A type of inheritance in which the phenotype of a heterozygote (*Aa*) is intermediate between the phenotypes of the two types of homozygotes (*AA* and *aa*).

incomplete metamorphosis (met´-uh-mōr´-fuh-sis) A type of development in certain insects in which development from larva to adult is achieved by multiple molts, but without forming a pupa.

independent variable A factor whose value is manipulated or changed during an experiment to reveal possible effects on another factor (the dependent variable).

indeterminate growth Growth that continues throughout life, as in most plants. *See also* determinate growth.
induced fit The change in shape of the active site of an enzyme, caused by entry of the substrate so that it binds the substrate snugly.
induction During embryonic development, the influence of one group of cells on an adjacent group of cells.
inferior vena cava A large vein that returns oxygen-poor blood to the heart from the lower, or posterior, part of the body. *See also* superior vena cava.
infertility The inability to conceive after one year of regular, unprotected intercourse.
inflammatory response An innate body defense in vertebrates caused by a release of histamine and other chemical alarm signals that trigger increased blood flow, a local increase in white blood cells, and fluid leakage from the blood. The resulting inflammatory response includes redness, heat, and swelling in the affected tissues.
ingestion The act of eating; the first stage of food processing in animals.
ingroup In a cladistic study of evolutionary relationships, the group of taxa whose evolutionary relationships are being determined. *See also* outgroup.
inhibiting hormone A kind of hormone released from the hypothalamus that prompts the anterior pituitary to stop secreting one or more hormones.
innate behavior Behavior that is under strong genetic control and is performed in virtually the same way by all members of a species.
innate immunity The kind of immunity that is present in an animal before exposure to pathogens and is effective from birth. Innate immune defenses include barriers, phagocytic cells, antimicrobial proteins, the inflammatory response, and natural killer cells.
inner ear One of three main regions of the vertebrate ear; includes the cochlea, organ of Corti, and semicircular canals.
insulin A protein hormone, secreted by the pancreas, that lowers the level of glucose in the blood. It is antagonistic with glucagon.
integration The analysis and interpretation of sensory signals within neural processing centers of the central nervous system.
integrin A transmembrane protein that interconnects the extracellular matrix and the cytoskeleton in animal cells.
interferon (in´-ter-fer´-on) An innate defensive protein produced by virus-infected vertebrate cells and capable of helping other cells resist viruses.
intermediate One of the compounds that form between the initial reactant and the final product in a metabolic pathway, such as between glucose and pyruvate in glycolysis.
intermediate filament An intermediate-sized protein fiber that is one of the three main kinds of fibers making up the cytoskeleton of eukaryotic cells. Intermediate filaments are ropelike, made of fibrous proteins.
internal fertilization Reproduction in which sperm are typically deposited in or near the female reproductive tract and fertilization occurs within the tract.
interneuron (in´-ter-nyūr´-on) A nerve cell, located entirely within the central nervous system, that integrates sensory signals and relays signals to other interneurons and to motor neurons.
internode The portion of a plant stem between two nodes.
interphase The period in the eukaryotic cell cycle when the cell is not actually dividing. Interphase constitutes the majority of the time spent in the cell cycle. *See also* mitotic phase (M phase).
interspecific competition Competition between individuals or populations of two or more species that require the same limited resource.
interspecific interactions Relationships between individuals of different species in a community.
interstitial fluid (in´-ter-stish´-ul) An aqueous solution that surrounds body cells and through which materials pass back and forth between the blood and the body tissues.
intertidal zone (in´-ter-tīd´-ul) A shallow zone where the waters of an estuary or ocean meet land.
intestine The region of a digestive tract located between the gizzard or stomach and the anus and where chemical digestion and nutrient absorption usually occur.
intraspecific competition Competition between members of a population for a limited resource.
intrauterine device (IUD) A T-shaped device that, when placed within the uterus, acts as a female contraception.
intron (in´-tron) An internal, noncoding region of a gene that does not become part of the final messenger RNA molecule and is therefore not expressed.
invasive species A non-native species that spreads beyond its original point of introduction and causes environmental or economic damage.
inversion A change in a chromosome resulting from reattachment of a chromosome fragment to the original chromosome, but in the reverse direction. Mutagens and errors during meiosis can cause inversions.
invertebrate An animal that lacks a backbone.
ion (ī-on) An atom or group of atoms that has gained or lost one or more electrons, thus acquiring an electrical charge.
ion channel A transmembrane pore that allows a specific ion to diffuse across the membrane down its electrochemical gradient.
ionic bond (ī-on´-ik) A chemical bond resulting from the attraction between oppositely charged ions.
iris The colored part of the vertebrate eye, formed by the anterior portion of the choroid.
isomers (ī´-sō-mers) Organic compounds with the same molecular formula but different structures and, therefore, different properties.
isotonic (ī-sō-ton´-ik) Referring to a solution that, when surrounding a cell, causes no net movement of water into or out of the cell.
isotope (ī´-sō-tōp) One of several atomic forms of an element, each with the same number of protons but a different number of neutrons.

K

karyotype (kār´-ē-ō-tīp) A display of micrographs of the metaphase chromosomes of a cell, arranged by size and centromere position. Karyotypes may be used to identify certain chromosomal abnormalities.
kelp Large, multicellular brown algae that form undersea "forests."
keystone species A species whose impact on the community is much larger than its biomass or abundance would indicate.
kilocalorie (kcal) A quantity of heat equal to 1,000 calories. Used to measure the energy content of food, it is usually called a "Calorie."
kin selection The natural selection that favors altruistic behavior by enhancing reproductive success of relatives.
kinesis (kuh-nē´-sis) (plural, **kineses**) Random movement in response to a stimulus.
kinetic energy (kuh-net´-ik) The energy associated with the motion of objects. Moving matter does work by imparting motion to other matter.
kingdom In classification, the broad taxonomic category above phylum.
***K*-selection** Selection for life history traits that produce relatively few offspring that have a good chance of survival; occurs when population size is near carrying capacity (*K*).

L

labia majora (lā´-bē-uh muh-jor´-uh) A pair of outer thickened folds of skin that protect the female genital region.
labia minora (lā´-bē-uh mi-nor´-uh) A pair of inner folds of skin, bordering and protecting the female genital region.
labor The series of events that expel an infant from the mother's uterus.
lactic acid fermentation Glycolysis followed by the reduction of pyruvate to lactate, regenerating NAD^+.
lancelet One of a group of small, bladelike, invertebrate chordates.
landscape Several different ecosystems linked by exchanges of energy, materials, and organisms.
landscape ecology The application of ecological principles to the study of the structure and dynamics of a collection of ecosystems; the scientific study of the biodiversity of interacting ecosystems.
large intestine The portion of the alimentary canal between the small intestine and the anus; functions mainly in water absorption and the formation of feces.

larva (lar´-vuh) (plural, **larvae**) A free-living, sexually immature form in some animal life cycles that may differ from the adult in morphology, nutrition, and habitat.

larynx (lār´-inks) The upper portion of the respiratory tract containing the vocal cords; also called the voice box.

lateral line system A row of sensory organs along each side of a fish's body that is sensitive to changes in water pressure. It enables a fish to detect minor vibrations in the water.

lateral meristem (mer´-eh-stem) Plant tissue made up of undifferentiated cells that enable roots and shoots of woody plants to thicken. The vascular cambium and cork cambium are lateral meristems.

lateralization Difference of functions in the cortex of the left and right cerebral hemispheres.

law of independent assortment A general rule of inheritance (originally formulated by Gregor Mendel) that when gametes form during meiosis, each pair of alleles for a particular character segregates independently of other pairs; also known as Mendel's second law of inheritance.

law of segregation A general rule in inheritance (originally formulated by Gregor Mendel) that individuals have two alleles for each gene and that when gametes form by meiosis, the two alleles separate, each resulting gamete ending up with only one allele of each gene; also known as Mendel's first law of inheritance.

leaf The main site of photosynthesis in a plant; typically consists of a flattened blade and a stalk (petiole) that joins the leaf to the stem.

learning Modification of behavior as a result of specific experiences.

lens The structure in an eye that focuses light rays onto the retina.

leukemia (lū-kē´-mē-ah) A type of cancer of the blood-forming tissues, characterized by an excessive production of white blood cells and an abnormally high number of them in the blood; cancer of the bone marrow cells that produce leukocytes.

lichen (lī´-ken) A close association between a fungus and an alga or between a fungus and a cyanobacterium, some of which are known to be beneficial to both partners.

life cycle The entire sequence of stages in the life of an organism, from the adults of one generation to the adults of the next.

life history The traits that affect an organism's schedule of reproduction and death, including age at first reproduction, frequency of reproduction, number of offspring, and amount of parental care.

life table A listing of survivals and deaths in a population in a particular time period and predictions of how long, on average, an individual of a given age will live.

ligament A type of fibrous connective tissue that joins bones together at movable joints.

light microscope (LM) An optical instrument with lenses that refract (bend) visible light to magnify images and project them into a viewer's eye or onto photographic film.

light reactions The first of two stages in photosynthesis; the steps in which solar energy is absorbed and converted to the chemical energy of ATP and NADPH, releasing oxygen in the process.

lignin A chemical that hardens the cell walls of plants.

limiting factor An environmental factor that restricts population growth.

linkage map An ordered listing of the relative locations of genes along a chromosome, as determined by recombination frequencies.

linked genes Genes located near each other on the same chromosome that tend to be inherited together.

lipid An organic compound consisting mainly of carbon and hydrogen atoms linked by nonpolar covalent bonds, making the compound mostly hydrophobic. Lipids include fats, phospholipids, and steroids and are insoluble in water.

liver The largest organ in the vertebrate body. The liver performs diverse functions, such as producing bile, preparing nitrogenous wastes for disposal, and detoxifying poisonous chemicals in the blood.

lobe-fin A bony fish with strong, muscular fins supported by bones.

locomotion Active movement from place to place.

locus (plural, **loci**) The particular site where a gene is found on a chromosome. Homologous chromosomes have corresponding gene loci.

logistic growth model A mathematical description of idealized population growth that is restricted by limiting factors.

long-day plant A plant that flowers in late spring or early summer, when day length is long. Long-day plants actually flower in response to short nights.

long-term memory The ability to hold, associate, and recall information over one's lifetime.

loop of Henle (hen´-lē) In the vertebrate kidney, the portion of a nephron that helps concentrate the filtrate while conveying it between a proximal tubule and a distal tubule.

loose connective tissue A tissue with a loose weave of fibers in a watery fluid; binds epithelia to underlying tissues and functions as packing material, holding organs in place.

Lophotrochozoa (lo-phah´-truh-kō-zō´-uh) A lineage of bilaterian animals that includes the flatworms, annelids, and molluscs.

low-density lipoprotein (LDL) A cholesterol-carrying particle in the blood, made up of thousands of cholesterol molecules and other lipids bound to a protein. An LDL particle transports cholesterol from the liver for incorporation into cell membranes.

lung An infolded respiratory surface of terrestrial vertebrates that connects to the atmosphere by narrow tubes.

lymph A colorless fluid, derived from interstitial fluid, that circulates in the lymphatic system.

lymph node An organ of the immune system located along a lymph vessel. Lymph nodes filter lymph and contain cells that attack viruses and bacteria.

lymphatic system (lim-fat´-ik) The vertebrate organ system through which lymph circulates; includes lymph vessels, lymph nodes, and the spleen. The lymphatic system helps remove toxins and pathogens from the blood and interstitial fluid and returns fluid and solutes from the interstitial fluid to the circulatory system.

lymphocyte (lim´-fuh-sīt) A type of white blood cell that is chiefly responsible for the adaptive immune response and is found mostly in the lymphatic system. *See also* B cell; T cell.

lysogenic cycle (lī´-sō-jen´-ik) A type of bacteriophage replication cycle in which the viral genome is incorporated into the bacterial host chromosome as a prophage. New phages are not produced, and the host cell is not killed or lysed unless the viral genome leaves the host chromosome.

lysosome (lī-sō-sōm) A digestive organelle in eukaryotic cells; contains hydrolytic enzymes that digest engulfed food or damaged organelles.

lytic cycle (lit´-ik) A type of viral replication cycle resulting in the release of new viruses by lysis (breaking open) of the host cell.

M

macroevolution Evolutionary change above the species level, encompassing the origin of a new group of organisms through a series of speciation events and the impact of mass extinctions on the diversity of life and its subsequent recovery.

macromolecule A giant molecule (a polysaccharide, protein, or nucleic acid) formed by the joining of smaller molecules, usually by a dehydration reaction.

macronutrient An essential element that an organism must obtain in relatively large amounts. *See also* micronutrient.

macrophage (mak´-rō-fāj) A large, amoeboid, phagocytic white blood cell that functions in innate immunity by destroying microbes and in adaptive immunity as an antigen-presenting cell.

major histocompatibility complex (MHC) molecule *See* self protein.

malignant tumor An abnormal tissue mass that can spread into neighboring tissue and to other parts of the body; a cancerous tumor.

malnutrition Health problems caused by a diet that contains insufficient calories or nutrients.

mammal Member of a clade of amniotes that possess mammary glands and hair.

mantle In a mollusc, the outgrowth of the body surface that drapes over the animal. The mantle produces the shell and forms the mantle cavity.

marsupial (mar-sū´-pē-ul) A pouched mammal, such as a kangaroo, opossum, or koala. Marsupials give birth to embryonic offspring that complete development while housed in a pouch and attached to nipples on the mother's abdomen.

mass number The sum of the number of protons and neutrons in an atom's nucleus.

mast cell A type of white blood cell residing in connective tissue that releases histamine during inflammatory responses and allergic reactions.

matter Anything that occupies space and has mass.

mechanoreceptor (mek´-uh-nō-ri-sep´-ter) A sensory receptor that detects changes in the environment associated with pressure, touch, stretch, motion, or sound.

medulla oblongata (meh-duh´-luh ob´-long-got´-uh) Part of the vertebrate hindbrain, continuous with the spinal cord; passes data between the spinal cord and forebrain and controls autonomic, homeostatic functions, including breathing, heart rate, swallowing, and digestion.

medusa (med-ū´-suh) (plural, **medusae**) One of two types of cnidarian body forms; an umbrella-like body form.

meiosis (mī-ō´-sis) In a sexually reproducing organism, the division of a single diploid nucleus into four haploid daughter nuclei. Meiosis and cytokinesis produce haploid gametes from diploid cells in the reproductive organs of the parents.

membrane potential The charge difference between a cell's cytoplasm and extracellular fluid due to the differential distribution of ions.

memory The ability to store and retrieve information. *See also* long-term memory; short-term memory.

memory cell A clone of long-lived lymphocytes formed during the primary adaptive immune response. Memory cells remain in the lymph nodes until activated by exposure to the same antigen that triggered their formation. When activated, a memory cell forms a large clone that mounts the secondary immune response.

menstrual cycle (men´-strū-ul) The hormonally synchronized cyclic buildup and breakdown of the endometrium of some primates, including humans.

menstruation (men´-strū-ā´-shun) Uterine bleeding resulting from shedding of the endometrium during a menstrual cycle.

meristem (mer´-eh-stem) Plant tissue consisting of undifferentiated cells that divide and generate new cells and tissues.

mesoderm (mez´-ō-derm) The middle layer of the three embryonic cell layers in a gastrula. The mesoderm gives rise to muscles, bones, the dermis of the skin, and most other organs in the adult.

mesophyll (mes´-ō-fil) Leaf cells specialized for photosynthesis; a leaf's ground tissue system.

messenger RNA (mRNA) The type of ribonucleic acid that encodes genetic information from DNA and conveys it to ribosomes, where the information is translated into amino acid sequences.

metabolic pathway A series of chemical reactions that either builds a complex molecule or breaks down a complex molecule into simpler compounds.

metabolic rate The total amount of energy an animal uses in a unit of time.

metabolism The totality of an organism's chemical reactions.

metagenomics The application of genomic and bioinformatics technologies to environmental samples; collection and sequencing of DNA from a group of species, usually an environmental sample of microorganisms, followed by computer analysis that assembles the DNA into genome sequences of the individual species within the sample.

metamorphosis (met´-uh-mōr´-fuh-sis) The transformation of a larva into an adult. *See also* complete metamorphosis; incomplete metamorphosis.

metaphase (met´-eh-fāz) The third stage of mitosis, during which all the cell's duplicated chromosomes are lined up at an imaginary plane equidistant between the poles of the mitotic spindle.

metastasis (muh-tas´-tuh-sis) The spread of cancer cells beyond their original site.

methanogen (meth-an´-ō-jen) An archaean that produces methane as a metabolic waste product.

methyl group A chemical group consisting of a carbon atom bonded to three hydrogen atoms.

microbiome The collection of genomes of individual microbial species present in a particular environment.

microbiota The community of microorganisms that live in and on the body of an animal.

microevolution A change in a population's gene pool over generations.

microfilament The thinnest of the three main kinds of protein fibers making up the cytoskeleton of a eukaryotic cell; a solid, helical rod composed of the globular protein actin.

micronutrient An essential element that an organism needs in very small amounts. *See also* macronutrient.

microRNA (miRNA) A small, single-stranded RNA molecule that associates with one or more proteins in a complex that can degrade or prevent translation of an mRNA with a complementary sequence.

microtubule The thickest of the three main kinds of fibers making up the cytoskeleton of a eukaryotic cell; a hollow tube made of globular proteins called tubulins; found in cilia and flagella.

microvillus (plural, **microvilli**) One of many microscopic projections on the epithelial cells in the lumen of the small intestine. Microvilli increase the surface area of the small intestine.

midbrain One of three ancestral and embryonic regions of the vertebrate brain; develops into sensory integrating and relay centers that send sensory information to the cerebrum.

middle ear One of three main regions of the vertebrate ear; a chamber containing three small bones (the hammer, anvil, and stirrup) that convey vibrations from the eardrum to the oval window.

migration The regular back-and-forth movement of animals between two geographic areas at particular times of the year.

millipede A terrestrial arthropod that has two pairs of short legs for each of its numerous body segments and that eats decaying plant matter.

mineral In nutrition, a simple inorganic nutrient that an organism requires in small amounts for proper body functioning.

mineralocorticoid (min´-er-uh-lō-kort´-uh-koyd) A corticosteroid hormone secreted by the adrenal cortex that helps maintain salt and water homeostasis and may increase blood pressure in response to stress from low blood sugar or decreased blood volume or blood pressure.

missense mutation A change in the nucleotide sequence of a gene that alters the amino acid sequence of the resulting polypeptide. In a missense mutation, a codon is changed from encoding one amino acid to encoding a different amino acid.

mitochondrial matrix (mī´-tō-kon´-drē-ul) The compartment of the mitochondrion enclosed by the inner membrane and containing enzymes and substrates for the citric acid cycle.

mitochondrion (mī´-tō-kon´-drē-on) (plural, **mitochondria**) An organelle in eukaryotic cells where cellular respiration occurs. Enclosed by two membranes, it is where most of the cell's ATP is made.

mitosis (mī´-tō-sis) The division of a single nucleus into two genetically identical nuclei. Mitosis and cytokinesis make up the mitotic (M) phase of the cell cycle.

mitotic phase (M phase) The part of the cell cycle when the nucleus divides (via mitosis), its chromosomes are distributed to the daughter nuclei, and the cytoplasm divides (via cytokinesis), producing two daughter cells.

mitotic spindle A football-shaped structure formed of microtubules and associated proteins that is involved in the movement of chromosomes during mitosis and meiosis.

mixotroph A protist that is capable of both autotrophy and heterotrophy.

mold A rapidly growing fungus that reproduces asexually by producing spores.

molecular biology The study of biological structures, functions, and heredity at the molecular level.

molecular clock A method for estimating the time required for a given amount of evolutionary change, based on the observation that some regions of genomes evolve at constant rates.

molecular systematics A scientific discipline that uses nucleic acids or other molecules in different species to infer evolutionary relationships.

molecule Two or more atoms held together by covalent bonds.

mollusc (mol´-lusk) A soft-bodied animal characterized by a muscular foot, mantle, mantle cavity, and visceral mass. Molluscs include gastropods (snails and slugs), bivalves (clams, oysters, and scallops), and cephalopods (squids and octopuses).

molting The process of shedding an old exoskeleton or cuticle and secreting a new, larger one.

monocot (mon´-ō-kot) A flowering plant whose embryos have a single seed leaf, or cotyledon.

monogamous Referring to a type of relationship in which a male and a female mate exclusively with each other, and both parents care for the offspring.

monohybrid cross An experimental mating of individuals that are heterozygous for the character being followed (or the self-pollination of a heterozygous plant).

monomer (mon´-uh-mer) The subunit that serves as a building block of a polymer.

monophyletic (mon´-ō-fī-let´-ik) Pertaining to a group of taxa that consists of a common ancestor and all its descendants, equivalent to a clade.

monosaccharide (mon´-ō-sak´-uh-rīd) The simplest carbohydrate; a simple sugar with a molecular formula that is generally some multiple of CH_2O. Monosaccharides are the monomers of disaccharides and polysaccharides.

monotreme (mon´-uh-trēm) An egg-laying mammal, such as the duck-billed platypus.

morning after pill (MAP) A birth control pill taken within three days of unprotected intercourse to prevent fertilization or implantation.

morphological species concept A definition of species in terms of measurable anatomical criteria.

motor neuron A nerve cell that conveys command signals from the central nervous system to effector cells, such as muscle cells or gland cells.

motor output The conduction of signals from a processing center in the central nervous system to effector cells.

motor protein A protein that interacts with the cytoskeleton and other cell components, producing movement of the whole cell or parts of the cell.

motor system The component of the vertebrate peripheral nervous system that carries signals to and from skeletal muscles, mainly in response to external stimuli. Most actions of the motor system are voluntary.

motor unit A motor neuron and all the muscle fibers it controls.

movement corridor A series of small clumps or a narrow strip of quality habitat (usable by organisms) that connects otherwise isolated patches of quality habitat.

muscle fiber Muscle cell.

muscle tissue Tissue consisting of long muscle cells that can contract, either on their own or when stimulated by nerve impulses; the most abundant tissue in a typical animal. *See* skeletal muscle; cardiac muscle; smooth muscle.

mutagen (myū´-tuh-jen) A chemical or physical agent that interacts with DNA and causes a mutation.

mutant The version of a character that occurs less frequently in nature than the wild-type.

mutation A change in the genetic information of a cell; the ultimate source of genetic diversity. A mutation also can occur in the DNA or RNA of a virus.

mutualism An interspecific relationship in which both partners benefit.

mycelium (mī-sē´-lē-um) (plural, **mycelia**) The densely branched network of hyphae in a fungus.

mycorrhiza (mī´-kō-rī´-zuh) (plural, **mycorrhizae**) A close association of plant roots and fungi that is beneficial to both partners.

myelin sheath (mī´-uh-lin) A series of cells, each wound around, and thus insulating, the axon of a nerve cell in vertebrates. *See also* node of Ranvier.

myofibril (mī´-ō-fī´-bril) A contractile strand in a muscle cell (fiber), made up of many sarcomeres. Longitudinal bundles of myofibrils make up a muscle fiber.

myosin A type of protein filament that interacts with actin filaments to cause cell contraction.

myriapod A member of an arthropod lineage that includes centipedes and millipedes.

N

NAD^+ Nicotinamide adenine dinucleotide; a coenzyme that can accept electrons during the redox reactions of cellular metabolism. It cycles between oxidized (NAD^+) and reduced (NADH) states.

$NADP^+$ Nicotinamide adenine dinucleotide phosphate, an electron acceptor that, as NADPH, temporarily stores energized electrons produced during the light reactions.

natural killer cell A cell type that provides an innate immune response by attacking cancer cells and infected body cells, especially those harboring viruses.

natural selection A process in which individuals with certain inherited traits are more likely to survive and reproduce than are individuals that do not have those traits.

nearsightedness An inability to focus on distant objects; occurs when the eyeball is longer than normal and the lens focuses distant objects in front of the retina; also called myopia.

negative feedback A form of regulation in which the accumulation of an end product of a process slows that process; in physiology, a primary mechanism of homeostasis, whereby a change in a variable triggers a response that counteracts the initial change.

negative pressure breathing A breathing system in which air is pulled into the lungs.

nematode (nem´-uh-tōd) A roundworm, characterized by a cylindrical, wormlike body form with a complete digestive tract and a tough cuticle that is molted to permit growth.

nephron The tubular excretory unit and associated blood vessels of the vertebrate kidney; extracts filtrate from the blood and refines it into urine. The nephron is the functional unit of the urinary system.

nerve A cable-like bundle of neurons tightly wrapped in connective tissue.

nerve net A weblike system of interconnected neurons, characteristic of radially symmetric animals such as a hydra.

nervous system The organ system that forms a communication and coordination network between all parts of an animal's body.

nervous tissue A type of tissue that senses stimuli and rapidly transmits information; made up of neurons and supportive cells called glia.

net primary production The gross primary production of an ecosystem minus the energy used by the producers for respiration; the stored chemical energy that is available to consumers in an ecosystem.

neural tube (nyūr´-ul) An embryonic cylinder that develops from the ectoderm after gastrulation and gives rise to the brain and spinal cord.

neuron (nyūr´-on) A nerve cell; the fundamental structural and functional unit of the nervous system, specialized for carrying signals from one location in the body to another.

neuronal plasticity The capacity of a nervous system to change with experience.

neurosecretory cell A nerve cell that synthesizes hormones and secretes them into the blood and also conducts nerve signals.

neurotransmitter A chemical messenger that carries information from a transmitting neuron to a receiving cell, either another neuron or an effector cell.

neutron A subatomic particle having no electrical charge, found in the nucleus of an atom.

neutrophil (nyū´-truh-fil) The most abundant type of white blood cell; functions in innate immunity as a type of phagocytic cell that tends to self-destruct as it destroys foreign invaders.

nitrogen fixation The conversion of atmospheric nitrogen (N_2) to nitrogen compounds (NH_4^+, NO_3^-) that plants can absorb and use.

node The point of attachment of a leaf on a stem.

node of Ranvier (ron´-vē-ā) An unmyelinated region on a myelinated axon of a nerve cell, where nerve signals are regenerated.

noncompetitive inhibitor A substance that reduces the activity of an enzyme without entering an active site. By binding elsewhere on the enzyme, a noncompetitive inhibitor changes the shape of the enzyme so that the active site no longer effectively catalyzes the conversion of substrate to product.

nondisjunction An accident of meiosis or mitosis in which a pair of homologous chromosomes or a pair of sister chromatids fail to separate at anaphase.

nonpolar covalent bond A type of covalent bond in which electrons are shared equally between two atoms of similar electronegativity.

nonself molecule A foreign antigen; a protein or other macromolecule that is not part of an organism's body. *See also* self protein.

nonsense mutation A change in the nucleotide sequence of a gene that converts an amino-acid-encoding codon to a stop codon. A nonsense mutation results in a shortened polypeptide.

norepinephrine (nor´-ep-uh-nef´-rin) A hormone (also called noradrenaline) secreted by the adrenal medulla in response to stress from physical threat that prepares body organs for action (fight or flight); also serves as a neurotransmitter.

notochord (nō´-tuh-kord) A flexible, cartilage-like, longitudinal rod located between the digestive tract and nerve cord in chordate animals; present only in embryos in many species.

nuclear envelope A double membrane that encloses the nucleus, perforated with pores that regulate traffic with the cytoplasm.

nuclear transplantation A technique in which the nucleus of one cell is placed into another cell that already has a nucleus or in which the nucleus has been previously destroyed.

nucleic acid A polymer consisting of many nucleotide monomers; serves as a blueprint for proteins and, through the actions of proteins, for all cellular structures and activities. The two types of nucleic acids are DNA and RNA.

nucleic acid hybridization The process of base pairing between a gene and a complementary sequence on another nucleic acid molecule.

nucleic acid probe (nū-klā´-ik) In DNA technology, a radioactively or fluorescently labeled single-stranded nucleic acid molecule used to find a specific gene or other nucleotide sequence within a mass of DNA. The probe hydrogen-bonds to the complementary sequence in the targeted DNA.

nucleoid (nū´-klē-oyd) A non–membrane-bounded region in a prokaryotic cell where the DNA is concentrated.

nucleolus (nū-klē´-ō-lus) A structure within the nucleus where ribosomal RNA is made and assembled with proteins imported from the cytoplasm to make ribosomal subunits.

nucleosome (nū´-klē-ō-sōm) The bead-like unit of DNA packing in a eukaryotic cell; consists of DNA wound twice around a protein core made up of eight histone molecules.

nucleotide (nū´-klē-ō-tīd) A building block of nucleic acids, consisting of a five-carbon sugar covalently bonded to a nitrogenous base and one or more phosphate groups.

nucleus (plural, **nuclei**) (1) An atom's central core, containing protons and neutrons. (2) The organelle of a eukaryotic cell that contains the genetic material in the form of chromosomes, made of chromatin.

O

obesity The excessive accumulation of fat in the body.

ocean acidification Process by which the pH of the ocean is lowered (made more acidic) when excess atmospheric CO_2 dissolves in seawater.

ocean current One of the river-like flow patterns in the oceans.

omnivore An animal that frequently eats animals as well as plants or algae. *See also* carnivore; herbivore.

oncogene (on´-kō-jēn) A cancer-causing gene; usually contributes to malignancy by abnormally enhancing the amount or activity of a growth factor made by the cell.

oogenesis (ō´-uh-jen´-uh-sis) The development of mature egg cells.

open circulatory system A circulatory system in which fluid is pumped through open-ended vessels and bathes the tissues and organs directly. In an animal with an open circulatory system, blood and interstitial fluid are the same.

operator In prokaryotic DNA, a sequence of nucleotides near the start of an operon to which an active repressor protein can attach. The binding of a repressor prevents RNA polymerase from attaching to the promoter and transcribing the genes of the operon. The operator sequence thereby acts as a "genetic switch" that can turn all the genes in an operon on or off as a single functional unit.

operculum (ō-per´-kyuh-lum) (plural, **opercula**) A protective flap on each side of a fish's head that covers a chamber housing the gills. Movement of the operculum increases the flow of oxygen-bearing water over the gills.

operon (op´-er-on) A unit of genetic regulation common in prokaryotes; a cluster of genes with related functions, along with the promoter and operator that control their transcription.

opportunistic infection An infection that can be controlled by a normally functioning immune system but that causes illness in a person with an immunodeficiency.

opposable thumb An arrangement of the fingers such that the thumb can touch the fingertips of all four fingers.

optimal foraging model The basis for analyzing behavior as a compromise between feeding costs and feeding benefits.

oral cavity The mouth of an animal.

oral contraceptive A chemical contraceptive that contains synthetic estrogen and/or progesterone (or a synthetic progesterone-like hormone called progestin) and prevents the release of eggs. Also called a birth control pill.

order In Linnaean classification, the taxonomic category above family.

organ A specialized structure composed of several different types of tissues that together perform specific functions.

organ of Corti (kor´-tē) The hearing organ in birds and mammals, located within the cochlea.

organ system A group of organs that work together in performing vital body functions.

organelle (ōr-guh-nel´) A membrane-enclosed structure with a specialized function within a cell.

organic compound A chemical compound containing the element carbon and usually the element hydrogen.

organic farming A set of agricultural principles that are intended to promote biological diversity and ecological sustainability. The use of the term *organic* on food labels is regulated by the U.S. Department of Agriculture.

organism An individual living thing, consisting of one or more cells.

osmoconformer (oz´-mō-con-form´-er) An organism whose body fluids have a solute concentration equal to that of its surroundings.

osmoregulation The homeostatic maintenance of solute concentrations and water balance by a cell or organism.

osmoregulator An organism whose body fluids have a solute concentration different from that of its environment and that must use energy in controlling water loss or gain. Examples include most land-dwelling and freshwater animals.

osmosis (oz-mō´-sis) The diffusion of free water across a selectively permeable membrane.

osteoporosis (os´-tē-ō-puh-rō´-sis) A skeletal disorder characterized by thinning, porous, and easily broken bones.

outer ear One of three main regions of the ear in reptiles (including birds) and mammals; made up of the auditory canal and, in many birds and mammals, the pinna.

outgroup In a cladistic study, a taxon or group of taxa known to have diverged before the lineage that contains the group of species being studied. *See also* ingroup.

ovarian cycle (ō-vār´-ē-un) Hormonally synchronized cyclic events in the mammalian ovary, culminating in ovulation.

ovary (1) In animals, the female gonad, which produces egg cells and reproductive hormones. (2) In flowering plants, the basal portion of a carpel in which the egg-containing ovules develop.

oviduct (ō´-vuh-dukt) The tube that conveys egg cells away from an ovary; also called a fallopian tube. In humans, the oviduct is the normal site of fertilization.

ovulation (ah´-vyū-lā´-shun) The release of an egg cell from an ovarian follicle.

ovule (ō-vyūl) seed plants, a structure that develops within the female cone (in gymnosperms) or ovary (in angiosperms) that contains the female gametophyte.

oxidation The loss of electrons from a substance involved in a redox reaction; always accompanies reduction.

oxidative phosphorylation (fos´-fōr-uh-lā´-shun) The production of ATP using energy derived from the redox reactions of an electron transport chain; the third major stage of cellular respiration.
ozone layer The layer of ozone (O_3) in the upper atmosphere that protects life on Earth from the harmful ultraviolet rays in sunlight.

P

P generation The parent individuals from which offspring are derived in studies of inheritance; P stands for parental.
P site One of a ribosome's binding sites for tRNA during translation. The P site holds the tRNA carrying the growing polypeptide chain. (P stands for peptidyl tRNA.)
paedomorphosis (pē´-duh-mōr´-fuh-sis) The retention in an adult of juvenile features of its evolutionary ancestors.
pain receptor A sensory receptor that detects pain.
paleoanthropology (pā´-lē-ō-an´-thruh-pol´-uh-jē) The study of human origins and evolution.
paleontologist (pa´-lē-on-tol´-uh-jist) A scientist who studies fossils.
pancreas (pan´-krē-us) A gland with dual functions: The digestive portion secretes digestive enzymes and an alkaline solution into the small intestine via a duct. The endocrine portion secretes the hormones insulin and glucagon into the blood.
pancrustacean A member of a large and diverse arthropod lineage that includes crustaceans and insects.
Pangaea (pan-jē´-uh) The supercontinent that formed near the end of the Paleozoic era, when plate movements brought all the landmasses of Earth together.
parasite Organism that derives its nutrition from a living host, which is harmed by the interaction.
parasympathetic division The component of the autonomic nervous system that generally promotes body activities that gain and conserve energy, such as digestion and reduced heart rate. *See also* sympathetic division.
parenchyma cell (puh-ren´-kim-uh) In plants, a relatively unspecialized cell with a thin primary wall and no secondary wall; functions in photosynthesis, food storage, and aerobic respiration.
Parkinson's disease A motor disorder caused by a progressive brain disease and characterized by difficulty in initiating movements, slowness of movement, and rigidity.
parsimony (par´-suh-mō´-nē) In scientific studies, the search for the least complex explanation for an observed phenomenon.
partial pressure The pressure exerted by a particular gas in a mixture of gases; a measure of the relative amount of a gas.
passive immunity Temporary immunity obtained by acquiring ready-made antibodies, as occurs in the transfer of maternal antibodies to a fetus or nursing infant. Passive immunity lasts only a few weeks or months.
passive transport The diffusion of a substance across a biological membrane, with no expenditure of energy.
pathogen An agent, such as a virus, bacteria, or fungus, that causes disease.
pedigree A family genetic tree representing the occurrence of heritable traits in parents and offspring across a number of generations. A pedigree can be used to determine genotypes of matings that have already occurred.
pelagic realm (puh-laj´-ik) The region of an ocean occupied by seawater.
penis The copulatory structure of male mammals.
peptide bond The covalent bond between two amino acid units in a polypeptide, formed by a dehydration reaction.
peptidoglycan (pep´-tid-ō-glī´-kan) A polymer of complex sugars cross-linked by short polypeptides; a material unique to bacterial cell walls.
per capita rate of increase The average contribution of each individual in a population to population growth for a time interval.
perennial (puh-ren´-ē-ul) A plant that lives for many years.
peripheral nervous system (PNS) The network of nerves and ganglia carrying signals into and out of the central nervous system.
peristalsis (per´-uh-stal´-sis) Rhythmic waves of contraction of smooth muscles. Peristalsis propels food through a digestive tract and also enables many animals, such as earthworms, to crawl.
permafrost Continuously frozen ground found in the arctic tundra.
peroxisome An organelle containing enzymes that transfer hydrogen atoms from various substrates to oxygen, producing and then degrading hydrogen peroxide.
petal A modified leaf of a flowering plant. Petals are often the colorful or fragrant parts of a flower that advertise it to pollinators.
pH scale A measure of the acidity of a solution, ranging in value from 0 (most acidic) to 14 (most basic). The letters pH stand for potential hydrogen and refer to the concentration of hydrogen ions (H^+).
phage (fāj) *See* bacteriophage.
phagocyte (fag´-ō-sīt´) A white blood cell (for example, a neutrophil or macrophage) that engulfs bacteria, foreign proteins, and the remains of dead body cells.
phagocytosis (fag´-ō-sī-tō´-sis) Cellular "eating"; a type of endocytosis in which a cell engulfs macromolecules, other cells, or particles into its cytoplasm.
pharyngeal slit (fā-rin´-jē-ul) A gill structure in the pharynx; found in chordate embryos and some adult chordates.
pharynx (fār´-inks) The organ in a digestive tract that receives food from the oral cavity; in terrestrial vertebrates, the region of the throat that is a common passageway for air and food.
phenotype (fē´-nō-tīp) The expressed traits of an organism.
phenotypic plasticity An individual's ability to change phenotype in response to local environmental conditions.
phloem (flō´-um) The portion of a plant's vascular tissue system that transports sugars and other organic nutrients from leaves or storage tissues to other parts of the plant.
phloem sap (flō´-um) The solution of sugars, other nutrients, and hormones conveyed throughout a plant via phloem tissue.
phosphate group (fos´-fāt) A chemical group consisting of a phosphorus atom bonded to four oxygen atoms.
phospholipid (fos´-fō-lip´-id) A lipid made up of glycerol joined to two fatty acids and a phosphate group, giving the molecule two nonpolar hydrophobic tails and a polar hydrophilic head. Phospholipids form bilayers that function as biological membranes.
phosphorylation (fos´-fōr-uh-lā´-shun) The transfer of a phosphate group, usually from ATP, to a molecule. Nearly all cellular work depends on ATP energizing other molecules by phosphorylation.
photic zone (fō´-tik) The region of an aquatic ecosystem into which light penetrates and where photosynthesis occurs.
photoautotroph An organism that obtains energy from sunlight and carbon from CO_2 using the process of photosynthesis.
photoheterotroph An organism that obtains energy from sunlight and carbon from organic sources.
photon (fō´-ton) A fixed quantity of light energy. The shorter the wavelength of light, the greater the energy of a photon.
photoperiod The relative lengths of day and night; an environmental stimulus that plants use to detect the time of year.
photophosphorylation (fō´-tō-fos´-fōr-uh-lā´-shun) The production of ATP by chemiosmosis during the light reactions of photosynthesis.
photopsin (fō-top´-sin) One of a family of visual pigments in the cones of the vertebrate eye that absorb bright, colored light.
photoreceptor A type of electromagnetic sensory receptor that detects light.
photorespiration In a plant cell, a metabolic pathway that consumes oxygen, releases CO_2, and decreases photosynthetic output. Photorespiration generally occurs on hot, dry days, when stomata close, O_2 accumulates in the leaf, and rubisco fixes O_2 rather than CO_2. Photorespiration produces no sugar molecules or ATP.
photosynthesis (fō´-tō-sin´-thuh-sis) The process by which plants, algae, and some protists and prokaryotes convert light energy to chemical energy that is stored in sugars made from carbon dioxide and water.
photosystem A light-capturing unit of a chloroplast's thylakoid membrane, consisting of a reaction-center complex surrounded by numerous light-harvesting complexes.
phototropism (fō´-tō-trō´-pizm) The growth of a plant organ toward light (positive phototropism) or away from light (negative phototropism).

phylogenetic species concept (fī´-lō-juh-net´-ik) A definition of species as the smallest group of individuals that shares a common ancestor, forming one branch on the tree of life.

phylogenetic tree (fī´-lō-juh-net´-ik) A branching diagram that represents a hypothesis about the evolutionary history of a group of organisms.

phylogeny (fī-loj´-uh-nē) The evolutionary history of a species or group of related species.

phylum (fi´-lum) (plural, **phyla**) In Linnaean classification, the taxonomic category above class.

physiology (fi´-zē-ol´-uh-ji) The study of the functions of an organism's structures.

phytochrome (fī´-tuh-krōm) A plant protein that has a light-absorbing component.

phytoplankton (fī´-tō-plank´-ton) Algae and photosynthetic bacteria that drift passively in aquatic environments.

pineal gland (pin´-ē-ul) An outgrowth of the vertebrate brain that secretes the hormone melatonin, which coordinates daily and seasonal body activities such as the sleep/wake circadian rhythm with environmental light conditions.

pistil Part of the reproductive organ of an angiosperm, a single carpel or a group of fused carpels.

pith Part of the ground tissue system of a dicot plant. Pith fills the center of a stem and may store food.

pituitary gland (puh-tū´-uh-tār-ē) An endocrine gland at the base of the hypothalamus; consists of a posterior lobe, which stores and releases two hormones produced by the hypothalamus, and an anterior lobe, which produces and secretes many hormones that regulate diverse body functions.

pivot joint A joint that allows precise rotations in multiple planes. An example in humans is the joint that rotates the forearm at the elbow.

placenta (pluh-sen´-tuh) In most mammals, the organ that provides nutrients and oxygen to the embryo and helps dispose of its metabolic wastes; formed of the embryo's chorion and the mother's endometrial blood vessels.

placental mammal (pluh-sen´-tul) Mammal whose young complete their embryonic development in the uterus, nourished via the mother's blood vessels in the placenta; also called a eutherian.

plasma The liquid matrix of the blood in which the blood cells are suspended.

plasma membrane The membrane at the boundary of every cell that acts as a selective barrier to the passage of ions and molecules into and out of the cell; consists of a phospholipid bilayer with embedded proteins.

plasmid A small ring of independently replicating DNA separate from the main chromosome(s). Plasmids are found in prokaryotes and yeasts.

plasmodesma (plaz´-mō-dez´-muh) (plural, **plasmodesmata**) An open channel in a plant cell wall that connects the cytoplasm of adjacent cells.

plasmodesmata An open channel in a plant cell wall that connects the cytoplasm of adjacent cells.

plasmodial slime mold (plaz-mō´-dē-ul) A type of protist that has amoeboid cells, flagellated cells, and an amoeboid plasmodial feeding stage in its life cycle; a member of the amoebozoan clade.

plasmodium (1) A single mass of cytoplasm containing many nuclei. (2) The amoeboid feeding stage in the life cycle of a plasmodial slime mold.

plate tectonics (tek-tän´-iks) The theory that the continents are part of great plates of Earth's crust that float on the hot, underlying portion of the mantle. Movements in the mantle cause the continents to move slowly over time.

platelet A pinched-off cytoplasmic fragment of a bone marrow cell. Platelets circulate in the blood and are important in blood clotting.

pleiotropy (plī´-uh-trō-pē) The control of more than one phenotypic character by a single gene.

polar covalent bond A covalent bond between atoms that differ in electronegativity. The shared electrons are pulled closer to the more electronegative atom, making it slightly negative and the other atom slightly positive.

polar ice A terrestrial biome that includes regions of extremely cold temperature and low precipitation located at high latitudes north of the arctic tundra and in Antarctica.

polar molecule A molecule containing polar covalent bonds and having an unequal distribution of charges in different regions of the molecule.

pollen grain The structure that will produce the sperm in seed plants; the male gametophyte.

pollination In seed plants, the delivery by wind or animals of pollen from the pollen-producing parts of a plant to a female cone (in gymnosperms) or the stigma of a carpel (in angiosperms).

polygamous Referring to a type of relationship in which an individual of one sex mates with more than one of the other sex.

polygenic inheritance (pol´-ē-jen´-ik) The additive effects of two or more gene loci on a single phenotypic character.

polymer (pol´-uh-mer) A large molecule consisting of many identical or similar monomers linked together by covalent bonds.

polymerase chain reaction (PCR) (puh-lim´-uh-rās) A technique used to obtain many copies of a DNA molecule or a specific part of a DNA molecule. In the procedure, the starting DNA is mixed with a heat-resistant DNA polymerase, DNA nucleotides, and a few other ingredients. Specific nucleotide primers flanking the region to be copied ensure that it, and no other regions of the DNA, is replicated during the PCR procedure.

polynucleotide (pol´-ē-nū´-klē-ō-tīd) A polymer made up of many nucleotide monomers covalently bonded together.

polyp (pol´-ip) One of two types of cnidarian body forms; a columnar, hydra-like body.

polypeptide A polymer (chain) of amino acids linked by peptide bonds.

polyploid An organism that has more than two complete sets of chromosomes as a result of an accident of cell division.

polysaccharide (pol´-ē-sak´-uh-rīd) A carbohydrate polymer of many monosaccharides (sugars) linked by dehydration reactions.

pons (pahnz) Part of the vertebrate hindbrain that functions with the medulla oblongata in passing data between the spinal cord and forebrain and in controlling autonomic, homeostatic functions.

population A group of individuals belonging to one species and living in the same geographic area.

population density The number of individuals of a species per unit area or volume.

population ecology The study of how members of a population interact with their environment, focusing on factors that influence population density and growth.

population momentum In a population in which $r = 0$, the continuation of population growth as girls in the prereproductive age group reach their reproductive years.

positive feedback A form of regulation in which the accumulation of an end product of a process speeds up that process; in physiology, a control mechanism in which a change in a variable triggers a response that reinforces or amplifies the change.

post-anal tail A tail posterior to the anus; found in chordate embryos and most adult chordates.

posterior Pertaining to the rear, or tail, of a bilaterally symmetric animal.

posterior pituitary (puh-tū´-uh-tār-ē) An extension of the hypothalamus composed of nervous tissue that secretes hormones made in the hypothalamus; a temporary storage site for hypothalamic hormones.

postzygotic barriers A reproductive barrier that prevents hybrid zygotes produce by two different species from developing into viable, fertile adults. Includes reduced hybrid viability, reduced hybrid fertility, and hybrid breakdown.

potential energy The energy that matter possesses because of its location or spatial arrangement. Water behind a dam possesses potential energy, and so do chemical bonds.

precapillary sphincters Rings of smooth muscle that regulate the flow of blood into capillary beds.

predation An interaction between species in which one species, the predator, kills and eats the other, the prey.

pressure flow mechanism The method by which phloem sap is transported through a plant from a sugar source, where sugars are produced, to a sugar sink, where sugars are used.

prevailing winds Major global air movements; winds that result from the combined effects of Earth's rotation and the rising and falling of air masses.

prezygotic barriers A reproductive barrier that impedes mating between species or hinders fertilization if mating between two species is attempted. Includes temporal, habitat, behavioral, mechanical, and gametic isolation.

primary consumer An herbivore; an organism that eats plants or other autotrophs.

primary growth Growth in the length of a plant root or shoot, produced by an apical meristem.

primary immune response The initial adaptive immune response to an antigen, which appears after a lag of about 10 days.

primary production The conversion of solar energy to chemical energy (in organic compounds) by photosynthesis.

primary structure The first level of protein structure; the specific sequence of amino acids making up a polypeptide chain.

primary succession A type of ecological succession in which a biological community arises in an area without soil. *See also* secondary succession.

primers Short, artificially created, single-stranded DNA molecules that bind to each end of a target sequence during a PCR procedure.

prion An infectious form of protein that may multiply by converting related proteins to more prions. Prions cause several related diseases in different animals, including scrapie in sheep and mad cow disease.

problem solving Applying past experiences to overcome obstacles in novel situations.

producer An organism that makes organic food molecules from CO_2, H_2O, and other inorganic raw materials: a plant, alga, or autotrophic prokaryote.

product An ending material in a chemical reaction.

progesterone (prō-jes´-tuh-rōn) A steroid hormone that contributes to the menstrual cycle and prepares the uterus for pregnancy.

prokaryotic cell (prō-kār´-ē-ot´-ik) A type of cell lacking a membrane-enclosed nucleus and other membrane-enclosed organelles; found only in the domains Bacteria and Archaea.

prolactin (PRL) (prō-lak´-tin) A protein hormone secreted by the anterior pituitary that stimulates human mammary glands to produce and release milk and produces other responses in different animals.

prometaphase The second stage of mitosis, during which the nuclear envelope fragments and the spindle microtubules attach to the kinetochores of the sister chromatids.

promiscuous Referring to a type of relationship in which mating occurs with no strong pair-bonds or lasting relationships.

promotor A specific nucleotide sequence in DNA located near the start of a gene that is the binding site for RNA polymerase and the place where transcription begins.

prophage (prō´-fāj) Phage DNA that has inserted by genetic recombination into the DNA of a bacterial chromosome.

prophase The first stage of mitosis, during which the chromatin condenses to form structures (sister chromatids) visible with a light microscope and the mitotic spindle begins to form, but the nucleus is still intact.

prostate gland (pros´-tāt) A gland in human males that secretes a thin fluid that nourishes the sperm.

protein A functional biological molecule consisting of one or more polypeptides folded into a specific three-dimensional structure.

proteobacteria A clade of gram-negative bacteria that encompasses enormous diversity, including all four modes of nutrition.

proteomics The study of whole sets of proteins and their interactions.

protist A member of a diverse collection of eukaryotes. Most protists are unicellular, but some are colonial or multicellular.

proton A subatomic particle with a single positive electrical charge, found in the nucleus of an atom.

proto-oncogene (prō´-tō-on´-kō-jēn) A normal gene that, through mutation, can be converted to a cancer-causing gene.

protostome A mode of animal development in which the opening formed during gastrulation becomes the mouth. Animals with the protostome pattern of development include the flatworms, molluscs, annelids, nematodes, and arthropods.

proximal tubule In the vertebrate kidney, the portion of a nephron immediately downstream from Bowman's capsule that conveys and helps refine filtrate.

proximate cause In animal behavior, a condition in an animal's internal or external environment that is the immediate reason or mechanism for a behavior.

proximate question In animal behavior, a question that concerns the immediate reason for a behavior.

pseudopodium (sū´-dō-pō´-dē-um) (plural, **pseudopodia**) A temporary extension of an amoeboid cell. Pseudopodia function in moving cells and engulfing food.

pulmonary artery A large blood vessel that conveys blood from the heart to a lung.

pulmonary circuit The branch of the circulatory system that supplies the lungs. *See also* systemic circuit.

pulmonary vein A blood vessel that conveys blood from a lung to the heart.

pulse The rhythmic stretching of the arteries caused by the pressure of blood during contraction of ventricles in systole.

punctuated equilibria In the fossil record, long periods in which a species undergoes little or no morphological change (equilibria), interrupted (punctuated) by relatively brief periods of sudden change.

Punnett square A diagram used in the study of inheritance to show the results of random fertilization.

pupil The opening in the iris that admits light into the interior of the vertebrate eye. Muscles in the iris regulate the pupil's size.

pyruvate oxidation The oxidation of pyruvate to acetyl CoA, with the release of CO_2 and production of NADH. Preparatory reaction to the citric acid cycle.

Q

quaternary consumer (kwot´-er-ner-ē) An animal that eats tertiary consumers.

quaternary structure The fourth level of protein structure; the shape resulting from the association of two or more polypeptide subunits.

R

R plasmid A bacterial plasmid that carries genes for enzymes that destroy particular antibiotics, thus making the bacterium resistant to the antibiotics.

radial symmetry An arrangement of the body parts of an organism like pieces of a pie around an imaginary central axis. Any slice passing longitudinally through a radially symmetric organism's central axis divides the organism into mirror-image halves.

radioactive isotope An isotope whose nucleus decays spontaneously, giving off particles and energy.

radiolarian A protist that moves and feeds by means of threadlike pseudopodia and has a mineralized support structure composed of silica. Radiolarians belong to the Rhizaria clade of the SAR supergroup.

radiometric dating A method for determining the absolute ages of fossils and rocks, based on the half-life of radioactive isotopes.

radula (rad´-yū-luh) A toothed, rasping organ used to scrape up or shred food; found in many molluscs.

random dispersion pattern A pattern in which the individuals of a population are spaced in an unpredictable way.

ray-finned fish Bony fish; member of a clade of jawed vertebrates having fins supported by thin, flexible skeletal rays.

reabsorption In the vertebrate kidney, the reclaiming of water and valuable solutes from the filtrate.

reactant A starting material in a chemical reaction.

receptor potential The electrical signal produced by sensory transduction.

receptor-mediated endocytosis (en´-dō-sī-tō´-sis) The movement of specific molecules into a cell by the infolding of vesicles containing proteins with receptor sites specific to the molecules being taken in.

recessive allele An allele that has no noticeable effect on the phenotype of a gene when the individual is heterozygous for that gene.

recombinant chromosome A chromosome created when crossing over combines DNA from two parents into a single chromosome.

recombinant DNA A DNA molecule that has been manipulated in the laboratory to carry nucleotide sequences derived from two sources, often different species.

recombination frequency With respect to two given genes, the number of recombinant progeny from a mating divided by the total number of progeny. Recombinant progeny carry combinations of alleles different from those in either of the parents as a result of crossing over during meiosis.

Recommended Dietary Allowance (RDA) A recommendation for daily nutrient intake established by a national scientific panel.

rectum The terminal portion of the large intestine where the feces are stored until they are eliminated.

red alga A member of a group of marine, mostly multicellular, autotrophic protists, which includes the reef-building coralline algae. Red algae belong to the supergroup Archaeplastida.

red blood cell A blood cell containing hemoglobin, which transports oxygen; also called an erythrocyte.

red bone marrow A specialized tissue that is found in the cavities at the ends of bones and that produces blood cells.

redox reaction Short for reduction-oxidation reaction; a chemical reaction in which electrons are lost from one substance (oxidation) and added to another (reduction).

reduction The gain of electrons by a substance involved in a redox reaction; always accompanies oxidation.

reflex An automatic reaction to a stimulus, mediated by the spinal cord or lower brain.

regeneration The regrowth of body parts from pieces of an organism.

regulatory gene A gene that codes for a protein, such as a repressor, that controls the transcription of another gene or group of genes.

relative fitness The contribution an individual makes to the gene pool of the next generation, relative to the contributions of other individuals in the population.

releasing hormone A kind of hormone secreted by the hypothalamus that promotes the release of hormones from the anterior pituitary.

renal cortex The outer portion of the vertebrate kidney, above the renal medulla.

renal medulla The inner portion of the vertebrate kidney, beneath the renal cortex.

repetitive DNA Nucleotide sequences that are present in many copies in the DNA of a genome. The repeated sequences may be long or short and may be located next to each other (tandomly) or dispersed in the DNA.

repressor A protein that blocks the transcription of a gene or operon.

reproduction The creation of new individuals from existing ones.

reproductive cloning Using a somatic cell from a multicellular organism to make one or more genetically identical individuals.

reproductive cycle A recurring sequence of events that produces eggs, makes them available for fertilization, and prepares the female body for pregnancy.

reproductive isolation The existence of biological factors (barriers) that impede members of two species from producing viable, fertile offspring.

reptile Member of the clade of amniotes that includes snakes, lizards, turtles, crocodilians, and birds, along with a number of extinct groups, such as dinosaurs.

resting potential The voltage across the plasma membrane of a resting neuron. The resting potential in a vertebrate neuron is typically around −70 millivolts, with the inside of the cell negatively charged relative to the outside.

restoration ecology The use of ecological principles to develop ways to return degraded ecosystems to conditions as similar as possible to their natural state.

restriction enzyme A bacterial enzyme that cuts up foreign DNA (at specific DNA sequences called restriction sites), thus protecting bacteria against intruding DNA from phages and other organisms. Restriction enzymes are used in DNA technology to cut DNA molecules in reproducible ways. The pieces of cut DNA are called restriction fragments.

restriction fragments Molecules of DNA produced from a longer DNA molecule cut up by a restriction enzyme. Restriction fragments are used in genome mapping and other applications.

restriction site A specific sequence on a DNA strand that is recognized as a "cut site" by a restriction enzyme.

retina (ret´-uh-nuh) The light-sensitive layer in an eye, made up of photoreceptor cells and sensory neurons.

retrovirus An RNA virus that reproduces by means of a DNA molecule. It reverse-transcribes its RNA into DNA, inserts the DNA into a cellular chromosome, and then transcribes more copies of the RNA from the viral DNA. HIV and a number of cancer-causing viruses are retroviruses.

reverse transcriptase (tran-skrip´-tās) An enzyme encoded and used by retroviruses that catalyzes the synthesis of DNA on an RNA template.

Rhizaria A clade of the SAR supergroup of protists that includes foraminiferans and radiolarians.

rhizome (rī´-zōm) A horizontal stem of a plant that grows below the ground.

rhodopsin (ro-dop´-sin) A visual pigment that is located in the rods of the vertebrate eye and that absorbs dim light.

ribonucleic acid (RNA) (rī-bō-nū-klā´-ik) A type of nucleic acid consisting of nucleotide monomers with a ribose sugar and the nitrogenous bases adenine (A), cytosine (C), guanine (G), and uracil (U); usually single-stranded; functions in protein synthesis, gene regulation, and as the genome of some viruses.

ribosomal RNA (rRNA) (rī´-buh-sōm´-ul) The type of ribonucleic acid that, together with proteins, makes up ribosomes; the most abundant type of RNA in most cells.

ribosome (rī´-buh-sōm) A cell structure consisting of RNA and protein organized into two subunits and functioning as the site of protein synthesis in the cytoplasm. In eukaryotic cells, the ribosomal subunits are constructed in the nucleolus.

ribozyme (rī´-bō-zīm) An RNA molecule that functions as an enzyme.

RNA interference (RNAi) A biotechnology technique used to silence the expression of specific genes. Synthetic RNA molecules with sequences that correspond to particular genes trigger the breakdown of the gene's mRNA.

RNA polymerase (puh-lim´-uh-rās) A large molecular complex that links together the growing chain of RNA nucleotides during transcription, using a DNA strand as a template.

RNA splicing The removal of introns and joining of exons in eukaryotic RNA, forming an mRNA molecule with a continuous coding sequence; occurs before mRNA leaves the nucleus.

rod A photoreceptor cell in the vertebrate retina enabling vision in dim light.

root A plant organ that provides an anchor and enables the plant to absorb water and minerals from the soil.

root cap A cone of cells at the tip of a plant root that protects the root's apical meristem.

root hair An outgrowth of an epidermal cell on a root, which increases the root's absorptive surface area.

root system All of a plant's roots, which anchor it in the soil, absorb and transport minerals and water, and store food.

rough endoplasmic reticulum (reh-tik´-yuh-lum) That portion of the endoplasmic reticulum with ribosomes attached that make membrane proteins and secretory proteins.

***r*-selection** Selection for life history traits that maximize reproductive success in environments where resources are abundant.

rule of addition A rule stating that the probability that an event can occur in two or more alternative ways is the sum of the separate probabilities of the different ways.

rule of multiplication A rule stating that the probability of a compound event is the product of the separate probabilities of the independent events.

ruminant (rū´-min-ent) An animal, such as a cow or sheep, with multiple stomach compartments housing microorganisms that can digest cellulose.

S

SA (sinoatrial) node (sȳ´-nō´-ā´-trē-ul) The pacemaker of the heart, located in the wall of the right atrium, that sets the rate and timing at which all cardiac muscle cells contract.

sac fungus *See* ascomycete.

salivary glands Glands associated with the oral cavity that secrete substances to lubricate food and begin the process of chemical digestion.
salt A compound resulting from the formation of an ionic bond.
sapwood Light-colored, water-conducting secondary xylem in a tree. *See also* heartwood.
SAR (Stramenopila, Alveolata, and Rhizaria) One of four monophyletic supergroups proposed in a current hypothesis of the evolutionary history of eukaryotes. The other three supergroups are Excavata, Unikonta, and Archaeplastida.
sarcomere (sar´-kō-mēr) The fundamental unit of muscle contraction, composed of thin filaments of actin and thick filaments of myosin; in electron micrographs, the region between two narrow, dark lines, called Z lines, in a myofibril.
saturated fatty acid A fatty acid in which all carbons in the hydrocarbon tail are connected by single bonds and the maximum number of hydrogen atoms are attached to the carbon skeleton. Saturated fats and fatty acids solidify at room temperature.
savanna A biome dominated by grasses and scattered trees and maintained by occasional fires and drought.
scanning electron microscope (SEM) A microscope that uses an electron beam to study the surface details of a cell or other specimens.
scavenger An animal that feeds on the carcasses of dead animals.
schizophrenia Severe mental disturbance characterized by psychotic episodes in which patients have a distorted perception of reality.
science An approach to understanding the natural world based on verifiable evidence.
sclereid (sklār´-ē-id) In plants, a very hard sclerenchyma cell found in nutshells and seed coats.
sclerenchyma cell (skluh-ren´-kē-muh) In plants, a supportive cell with rigid secondary walls hardened with lignin.
scrotum A pouch of skin outside the abdomen that houses a testis and functions in cooling sperm, keeping them viable.
search image A mental picture of a desired food item that enables an animal to find a particular kind of food efficiently.
second law of thermodynamics The principle stating that every energy conversion reduces the order of the universe, increasing its entropy. Ordered forms of energy are at least partly converted to heat.
secondary consumer An animal that eats herbivores (primary consumers).
secondary growth An increase in a plant's diameter, involving cell division in the vascular cambium and cork cambium.
secondary immune response The adaptive immune response elicited when an animal encounters the same antigen at some later time. The secondary immune response is more rapid, of greater magnitude, and of longer duration than the primary immune response.
secondary phloem (flō´-um) A type of phloem plant tissue produced by the vascular cambium during secondary growth.
secondary structure The second level of protein structure; the regular local patterns of coils or folds of a polypeptide chain.
secondary succession A type of ecological succession that occurs where a disturbance has destroyed an existing biological community but left the soil intact. *See also* primary succession.
secondary xylem (zī´-lum) A type of xylem plant tissue produced by the vascular cambium during secondary growth.
secretion (1) The discharge of molecules synthesized by a cell. (2) In the vertebrate kidney, the discharge of wastes from the blood into the filtrate from the nephron tubules.
sedentarian A member of a major annelid lineage that includes earthworms, leeches, and many tube-building marine worms.
seed A plant embryo packaged with a food supply within a protective covering.
seed coat A tough outer covering of a seed, formed from the tissue surrounding an ovule. The seed coat encloses and protects the embryo and its food supply.
seedless vascular plants The informal collective name for lycophytes (club mosses and their relatives) and monilophytes (ferns and their relatives).
segmentation Subdivision along the length of an animal body into a series of repeated parts called segments; allows for greater flexibility and mobility.
selective permeability A property of biological membranes that allows them to regulate the passage of substances across them.
self protein A protein on the surface of an antigen-presenting cell that can hold a foreign antigen and display it to T cells. Each individual has a unique set of self proteins that serve as molecular markers for the body. The technical name for self proteins is *major histocompatibility complex (MHC) proteins. See also* nonself molecule.
semen (sē´-mun) The sperm-containing fluid that is ejaculated by the male during orgasm.
semicircular canals Fluid-filled channels in the inner ear that detect changes in the head's rate of rotation or angular movement.
semiconservative model Type of DNA replication in which the replicated double helix consists of one old strand, derived from the old molecule, and one newly made strand.
seminal vesicle (sem´-uh-nul ves´-uh-kul) A gland in males that secretes a thick fluid that contains fructose, which provides most of the sperm's energy.
sensitive period A limited phase in an individual animal's development when learning of particular behaviors can take place.
sensory adaptation The tendency of sensory neurons to become less sensitive when they are stimulated repeatedly. For example, a prominent smell becomes unnoticeable over time.
sensory input The conduction of signals from sensory receptors to processing centers in the central nervous system.
sensory neuron A nerve cell that receives information from sensory receptors and conveys signals into the central nervous system.
sensory receptor A specialized cell or neuron that detects specific stimuli from an organism's external or internal environment and sends information to the central nervous system.
sensory transduction The conversion of a stimulus signal to an electrical signal by a sensory receptor.
sepal (sē´-pul) A modified leaf of a flowering plant. A circle of sepals encloses and protects the flower bud before it opens.
sessile An organism that is anchored to its substrate.
sex chromosome A chromosome that determines whether an individual is male or female.
sex-linked gene A gene located on a sex chromosome. In humans, the vast majority of sex-linked genes are located on the X chromosome.
sexual dimorphism (dī-mōr´-fizm) Marked differences between the secondary sex characteristics of males and females.
sexual reproduction The creation of genetically unique offspring by the fusion of two haploid sex cells (gametes), forming a diploid zygote.
sexual selection A form of natural selection in which individuals with certain inherited traits are more likely than other individuals to obtain mates.
sexually transmitted infection (STI) A pathogen spread by sexual contact. If symptoms are present, then the person is said to have sexually transmitted disease (STD).
shared ancestral character A character shared by members of a particular clade that originated in an ancestor that is not a member of that clade.
shared derived character An evolutionary novelty that is unique to a particular clade.
shoot system All of a plant's stems, leaves, and reproductive structures.
short tandem repeat (STR) A series of short DNA sequences that are repeated many times in a row in the genome.
short-day plant A plant that flowers in late summer, fall, or winter, when day length is short. Short-day plants actually flower in response to long nights.
short-term memory The ability to hold information, anticipations, or goals for a time and then release them if they become irrelevant.
sickle-cell disease A genetic condition caused by a mutation in the gene for hemoglobin. The mutation causes the protein to crystallize, which deforms red blood cells into a curved shape. Such blood cells produce a cascade of symptoms that can be life-threatening.
sieve plate An end wall in a sieve-tube element that facilitates the flow of phloem sap.
sieve-tube element A food-conducting cell in a plant; also called a sieve-tube member. Chains of sieve-tube elements make up phloem tissue.

signal In behavioral ecology, a stimulus transmitted by one animal to another animal.

signal transduction pathway In cell biology, a series of molecular changes that converts a signal on a target cell's surface to a specific response inside the cell.

silent mutation A mutation in a gene that changes a codon to one that codes for the same amino acid as the original codon. The amino acid sequence of the resulting polypeptide is thus unchanged.

single circulation A circulatory system with a single pump and circuit, in which blood passes from the sites of gas exchange to the rest of the body before returning to the heart.

single-lens eye The camera-like eye found in some jellies, polychaetes, spiders, many molluscs, and vertebrates.

sister chromatid (krō´-muh-tid) One of the two identical parts of a duplicated chromosome in a eukaryotic cell. Prior to mitosis, sister chromatids remain attached to each another at the centromere.

skeletal muscle A type of striated muscle attached to the skeleton; generally responsible for voluntary movements of the body.

small interfering RNA (siRNA) A small, single-stranded RNA molecule that associates with one or more proteins in a complex that can degrade or prevent translation of an mRNA with a complementary sequence.

small intestine The longest section of the alimentary canal. It is the principal site of the enzymatic hydrolysis of food macromolecules and the absorption of nutrients.

smooth endoplasmic reticulum (reh-tik´-yuh-lum) That portion of the endoplasmic reticulum that lacks ribosomes.

smooth muscle A type of muscle lacking striations; responsible for involuntary body activities.

social behavior Any kind of interaction between two or more animals, usually of the same species.

social learning Learning by observing the behavior of other individuals.

sociobiology The study of the evolutionary basis of social behavior.

sodium-potassium (Na^+-K^+) pump A membrane protein that transports sodium ions out of, and potassium ions into, a cell against their concentration gradients. The process is powered by ATP.

solute (sol´-yūt) A substance that is dissolved in a solution.

solution A liquid that is a homogeneous mixture of two or more substances.

solvent The dissolving agent of a solution. Water is the most versatile solvent known.

somatic cell (sō-mat´-ik) Any cell in a multicellular organism except a sperm or egg cell or a cell that develops into a sperm or egg.

spatial learning Modification of behavior based on experience of the spatial structure of the environment.

speciation The evolution of a new species.

species A group of populations whose members have the potential to interbreed and produce viable, fertile offspring. *See also* biological species concept.

species diversity The variety of species that make up a community. Species diversity includes both species richness (the total number of different species) and the relative abundance of the different species in the community.

sperm A male gamete.

spermatogenesis (sper-mat´-ō-jen´-uh-sis) The formation of sperm cells.

spermicide A sperm-killing chemical (cream, jelly, or foam) that works with a barrier device as a method of contraception.

sphincter (sfink´-ter) A ringlike band of muscle fibers that controls the size of an opening in the body, such as the passage between the esophagus and the stomach.

spinal cord A bundle of nervous tissue that runs lengthwise inside the spine in vertebrates and integrates simple responses to certain stimuli.

spirochete (spī´-ruh-kēt) A member of a group of helical bacteria that spiral through the environment by means of rotating, internal filaments.

sponge An aquatic animal characterized by a highly porous body.

sporangium (spuh-ranj´-ē-um´) (plural, **sporangia**) A structure in fungi and plants in which meiosis occurs and haploid spores develop.

spore (1) In plants and algae, a haploid cell that can develop into a multicellular individual without fusing with another cell. (2) In prokaryotes, protists, and fungi, any of a variety of thick-walled life cycle stages capable of surviving unfavorable environmental conditions.

sporophyte (spōr´-uh-fīt) The multicellular diploid form in the life cycle of organisms undergoing alternation of generations; results from a union of gametes and meiotically produces haploid spores that grow into the gametophyte generation.

stabilizing selection Natural selection that favors intermediate variants by acting against extreme phenotypes.

stamen (stā´-men) A pollen-producing male reproductive part of a flower, consisting an anther supported by a filament (stalk).

starch A storage polysaccharide in plants; a polymer of glucose.

start codon (kō´-don) On mRNA, the specific three-nucleotide sequence (AUG) to which an initiator tRNA molecule binds, starting translation of genetic information.

stem The part of a plant's shoot system that supports the leaves and reproductive structures.

stem cell An unspecialized cell that can divide to produce an identical daughter cell and a more specialized daughter cell, which undergoes differentiation.

steroid (ster´-oyd) A type of lipid whose carbon skeleton is in the form of four fused rings with various chemical groups attached. Examples are cholesterol, testosterone, and estrogen.

stigma (stig´-muh) (plural, **stigmata**) The sticky tip of a flower's carpel, which traps pollen grains.

stimulus (plural, **stimuli**) (1) In the context of a nervous system, any factor that causes a nerve signal to be generated. (2) In behavioral biology, an environmental cue that triggers a specific response.

stoma (stō´-muh) (plural, **stomata**) A microscopic pore surrounded by guard cells in the epidermis of a leaf. When stomata are open, CO_2 enters a leaf, and H_2O and O_2 exit. A plant conserves water when its stomata are closed.

stomach An organ in a digestive tract that stores food and performs preliminary steps of digestion.

stop codon In mRNA, one of three triplets (UAG, UAA, UGA) that signal gene translation to stop.

STR analysis Short tandem repeat analysis; a method of DNA profiling that compares the lengths of short tandem repeats (STRs) selected from specific sites within the genome.

Stramenopila A clade of the SAR supergroup of protists that includes diatoms, brown algae, and water molds.

stratum (plural, **strata**) Rock layer formed when a new layer of sediment covers an older one and compresses it.

stretch receptor A type of mechanoreceptor sensitive to changes in muscle length; detects the position of body parts.

stroke The death of nervous tissue in the brain, usually resulting from rupture or blockage of arteries in the head.

stroma (strō´-muh) The dense fluid within the chloroplast that surrounds the thylakoid membrane. Sugars are made in the stroma by the enzymes of the Calvin cycle.

stromatolite (strō-mat´-uh-līt) Layered rock that results from the activities of prokaryotes that bind thin films of sediment together.

substrate (1) A specific substance (reactant) on which an enzyme acts. Each enzyme recognizes only the specific substrate or substrates of the reaction it catalyzes. (2) A surface in or on which an organism lives.

substrate feeder An organism that lives in or on its food source, eating its way through the food.

substrate-level phosphorylation (fos´-fōr-uh-lā´-shun) The formation of ATP by an enzyme directly transferring a phosphate group to ADP from an organic molecule (for example, one of the intermediates in glycolysis or the citric acid cycle).

sugar sink A plant organ that is a net consumer or storer of sugar. Growing roots, shoot tips, stems, and fruits are sugar sinks supplied by phloem.

sugar source A plant organ in which sugar is being produced by either photosynthesis or the breakdown of starch. Mature leaves are the primary sugar sources of plants.

sugar-phosphate backbone In a polynucleotide (DNA or RNA strand), the alternating chain of sugar and phosphate to which nitrogenous bases are attached.

superior vena cava A large vein that returns oxygen-poor blood to the heart from the upper body and head. *See also* inferior vena cava.

surface tension A measure of how difficult it is to stretch or break the surface of a liquid. Water has a high surface tension because of the hydrogen bonding of surface molecules.

surfactant A substance secreted by alveoli that decreases surface tension in the fluid that coats the alveoli.

survivorship curve A plot of the number of members of a cohort that are still alive at each age; one way to represent age-specific mortality.

suspension feeder An organism that captures food particles from the surrounding medium.

sustainability The goal of developing, managing, and conserving Earth's resources in ways that meet the needs of people today without compromising the ability of future generations to meet theirs.

sustainable agriculture Farming methods that are environmentally safe and can be practiced in the same manner for many years without depleting soil, water, or genetic diversity.**sustainable development** Development that meets the needs of people today without limiting the ability of future generations to meet their needs.

sustainable resource management Management practices that allow use of a natural resource without damaging it.

swim bladder A gas-filled internal sac that helps bony fishes maintain buoyancy.

symbiosis (sim´-bē-ō-sis) A physically close association between organisms of two or more species.

sympathetic division A set of neurons in the autonomic nervous system that generally prepares the body for energy-consuming activities, such as fleeing or fighting. *See also* parasympathetic division.

sympatric speciation The formation of new species in populations that live in the same geographic area.

synapse (sin´-aps) A junction between two neurons, or between a neuron and an effector cell. Electrical or chemical signals are relayed from one cell to another at a synapse.

synaptic terminal (sin-ap´-tik) The tip of a transmitting neuron's axon, where signals are sent to another neuron or to an effector cell.

systematics A scientific discipline focused on classifying organisms and determining their evolutionary relationships.

systemic circuit The branch of the circulatory system that supplies oxygen-rich blood to, and carries oxygen-poor blood away from, organs and tissues in the body. *See also* pulmonary circuit.

systems biology An approach to studying biology that aims to model the dynamic behavior of whole biological systems based on a study of the interactions among the system's parts.

systole (sis´-tō-lē) The contraction stage of the heart cycle, when the heart chambers actively pump blood. *See also* diastole.

T

T cell A type of lymphocyte that matures in the thymus; T cells include both effector cells for the cell-mediated immune response and helper cells required for both the humoral and cell-mediated adaptive responses.

taiga (tī´-guh) The northern coniferous forest, characterized by long, snowy winters and short, wet summers, extending across North America and Eurasia to the southern border of the arctic tundra; also found just below alpine tundra on mountainsides in temperate zones.

tapeworm A parasitic flatworm characterized by the absence of a digestive tract.

target cell A cell that responds to a regulatory signal, such as a hormone.

taxis (tak´-sis) (plural, **taxes**) Automatic orientation toward or away from a stimulus.

taxon A named taxonomic unit at any given level of classification.

taxonomy The scientific discipline concerned with naming and classifying the diverse forms of life.

technology The application of scientific knowledge for a specific purpose, often involving industry or commerce but also including uses in basic research.

telophase The fifth and final stage of mitosis, during which daughter nuclei form at the two poles of a cell. Telophase usually occurs together with cytokinesis.

temperate broadleaf forest A biome located throughout midlatitude regions, where there is sufficient moisture to support the growth of large, broadleaf deciduous trees.

temperate grassland A biome dominated by grasses and other nonwoody plants and maintained by seasonal drought, occasional fires, and grazing by large mammals.

temperate rain forest Coniferous forests of coastal North America (from Alaska to Oregon) supported by warm, moist air from the Pacific Ocean.

temperate zones Latitudes between the tropics and the Arctic Circle in the north and the Antarctic Circle in the south; regions with milder climates than the tropics or polar regions.

temperature A measure in degrees of the average thermal energy of the atoms and molecules in a body of matter.

tendon Fibrous connective tissue connecting a muscle to a bone.

tendril A modified leaf used by some plants to climb around a fixed structure.

terminal bud Embryonic tissue at the tip of a shoot, made up of developing leaves and a compact series of nodes and internodes.

terminator A special sequence of nucleotides in DNA that marks the end of a gene. It signals RNA polymerase to release the newly made RNA molecule and then to depart from the gene.

territory An area that one or more individuals defend and from which other members of the same species are usually excluded.

tertiary consumer (ter´-shē-ār-ē) An animal that eats secondary consumers.

tertiary structure The third level of protein structure; the overall three-dimensional shape of a polypeptide due to interactions of the R groups of the amino acids making up the chain.

testcross The mating between an individual of unknown genotype for a particular character and an individual that is homozygous recessive for that same character. The testcross can be used to determine the unknown genotype (homozygous dominant versus heterozygous).

testicle A testis and scrotum together.

testis (plural, **testes**) The male gonad in an animal. The testis produces sperm and, in many species, reproductive hormones.

testosterone (tes-tos´-tuh-rōn) An androgen hormone that stimulates an embryo to develop into a male and promotes male body features.

tetrapod A vertebrate with two pairs of limbs. Tetrapods include mammals, amphibians, and birds and other reptiles.

thalamus (thal´-uh-mus) An integrating and relay center of the vertebrate forebrain; sorts and relays selected information to specific areas in the cerebral cortex.

theory A widely accepted explanatory idea that is broader in scope than a hypothesis, generates new hypotheses, and is supported by a large body of evidence.

therapeutic cloning The cloning of human cells by nuclear transplantation for therapeutic purposes, such as the generation of embryonic stem cells. *See also* nuclear transplantation; reproductive cloning.

thermal energy Kinetic energy due to the random motion of atoms and molecules; energy in its most random form.

thermodynamics The study of energy transformation that occurs in a collection of matter. *See also* first law of thermodynamics; second law of thermodynamics.

thermoreceptor A sensory receptor that detects heat or cold.

thermoregulation The homeostatic maintenance of an organism's internal body temperature within a range that allows cells to function efficiently.

thick filament The thicker of the two protein filaments in muscle fibers, consisting of parallel arrays of myosin molecules.

thigmotropism (thig´-mō-trō´-pizm) A plant's directional growth in response to touch.

thin filament The thinner of the two protein filaments in muscle fibers, consisting of two strands of actin and two strands of regulatory protein coiled around each other.

three-domain system A system of taxonomic classification based on three basic groups: Bacteria, Archaea, and Eukarya.

thylakoid (thī´-luh-koyd) A flattened membranous sac inside a chloroplast. Thylakoid membranes contain chlorophyll and the molecular complexes of the light reactions of photosynthesis. A stack of thylakoids is called a granum.
thymine (T) (thī´-min) A single-ring nitrogenous base found in DNA.
thyroid gland (thī´-royd) An endocrine gland located in the neck that secretes thyroid hormone.
thyroid hormone A combination of two different water-soluble hormones (T_3 and T_4) secreted by the thyroid gland that affects many functions of the body, including metabolic rate, heart rate, blood pressure, and tolerance to the cold.
thyroid-stimulating hormone (TSH) (thī´-royd) A protein hormone secreted by the anterior pituitary that stimulates the thyroid gland to secrete thyroid hormone.
tissue An integrated group of cells with a common function, structure, or both.
tonicity The ability of a solution surrounding a cell to cause that cell to gain or lose water.
topsoil The uppermost soil layer, consisting of a mixture of particles derived from rock, living organisms, and humus.
totipotent (tō-tuh-pōt-ent) Describing a cell that can give rise to all of the different types of cells within an organism.
trace element An element that is essential for life but required in extremely minute amounts.
trachea (trā´-kē-uh) (plural, **tracheae**) In the mammalian respiratory system, the windpipe; the portion of the respiratory tube that passes from the larynx to the two bronchi. In the tracheal system of insects, the largest tubes, which connect to external openings.
tracheal system A system of branched, air-filled tubes in insects that extends throughout the body and carries oxygen directly to cells.
tracheid (trā´-kē-id) A tapered, porous, water-conducting, and supportive cell in plants. Chains of tracheids or vessel elements make up the water-conducting, supportive tubes in xylem.
trait A variant of a character found within a population, such as purple or white flowers in pea plants.
trans fat An unsaturated fat linked to health risks that is formed artificially during hydrogenation of vegetable oils.
transcription The synthesis of RNA on a DNA template.
transcription factor In the eukaryotic cell, a protein that functions in initiating or regulating transcription. Transcription factors bind to DNA or to other proteins that bind to DNA.
transduction (1) The transfer of bacterial genes from one bacterial cell to another by a phage. (2) *See* sensory transduction. (3) *See* signal transduction pathway.
transfer RNA (tRNA) A type of ribonucleic acid that functions as an interpreter in translation. Each tRNA molecule has a specific anticodon, picks up a specific amino acid, and conveys the amino acid to the appropriate codon on mRNA.
transformation The incorporation of new genes into a cell from DNA that the cell takes up from the surrounding environment.
transgenic organism An organism that contains genes from another species.
translation The synthesis of a polypeptide using the genetic information encoded in an mRNA molecule. There is a change of "language" from nucleotides to amino acids.
translocation (1) During protein synthesis, the movement of a tRNA molecule carrying a growing polypeptide chain from the A site to the P site on a ribosome. (The mRNA travels with it.) (2) A change in a chromosome resulting from a chromosomal fragment attaching to a nonhomologous chromosome; can occur as a result of an error in meiosis or from mutagenesis.
transmission electron microscope (TEM) A microscope that uses an electron beam to study the internal structure of thinly sectioned specimens.
transpiration The evaporative loss of water from a plant.
transport vesicle A small membranous sac in a eukaryotic cell's cytoplasm carrying molecules produced by the cell. The vesicle buds from the endoplasmic reticulum or Golgi and eventually fuses with another organelle or the plasma membrane, releasing its contents.
TRH (TSH-releasing hormone) A peptide hormone that triggers the release of TSH (thyroid-stimulating hormone), which in turn stimulates the thyroid gland.
trial-and-error learning Type of associative learning in which an animal learns to associate one of its own behaviors with a positive or negative effect.
trimester In human pregnancy, one of three periods lasting about 3 months.
triplet code A set of three-nucleotide-long "words" that specify the amino acids for polypeptide chains. *See also* genetic code.
trisomy 21 A human genetic disorder resulting from the presence of an extra chromosome 21; characterized by heart and respiratory defects and varying degrees of mental retardation.
trophic structure The pattern of feeding relationships in a community.
tropical forest A terrestrial biome characterized by high levels of precipitation and warm temperatures year-round.
tropics Latitudes between 23.5° north and south; the region surrounding the equator.
tropism (trō´-pizm) A growth response that makes a plant grow toward or away from a stimulus.
true-breeding Referring to organisms for which sexual reproduction produces offspring with inherited traits identical to those of the parents. The organisms are homozygous for the characters under consideration.
tubal ligation A means of sterilization in which a segment of each of a woman's two oviducts is removed. The ends of the tubes are then tied closed to prevent eggs from reaching the uterus (commonly referred to as having the "tubes tied").
tuber An enlargement at the end of a rhizome in which food is stored.
tumor An abnormal mass of rapidly growing cells that forms within otherwise normal tissue.
tumor-suppressor gene A gene whose product inhibits cell division, thereby preventing uncontrolled cell growth. A mutation that deactivates a tumor-suppressor gene may lead to cancer.
tundra A biome at the northernmost limits of plant growth and at high altitudes, characterized by dwarf woody shrubs, grasses, mosses, and lichens.
tunicate One of a group of invertebrate chordates, also known as sea squirts.

U

ultimate cause In animal behavior, the evolutionary reason for a behavior.
ultimate question In animal behavior, a question that addresses the evolutionary basis for behavior.
ultrasound imaging A technique for examining a fetus in the uterus. High-frequency sound waves echoing off the fetus are used to produce an image of the fetus.
uniform dispersion pattern A pattern in which the individuals of a population are evenly distributed over an area.
Unikonta One of four monophyletic supergroups proposed in a current hypothesis of the evolutionary history of eukaryotes. The other three supergroups are SAR (Stramenopila, Alveolata, and Rhizaria), Excavata, and Archaeplastida.
unsaturated fatty acid A fatty acid that has one or more double bonds between carbons in the hydrocarbon tail and thus lacks the maximum number of hydrogen atoms. Unsaturated fats and fatty acids do not solidify at room temperature.
uracil (U) (yū´-ruh-sil) A single-ring nitrogenous base found in RNA.
urea (yū-rē´-ah) A soluble form of nitrogenous waste excreted by mammals and most adult amphibians.
ureter (yū´-reh-ter or yū-rē´-ter) A duct that conveys urine from the kidney to the urinary bladder.

urethra (yū-rē´-thruh) A duct that conveys urine from the urinary bladder to the outside. In the male, the urethra also conveys semen out of the body during ejaculation.
uric acid (yū´-rik) An insoluble precipitate of nitrogenous waste excreted by land snails, insects, birds, and some reptiles.
urinary bladder The pouch where urine is stored prior to elimination.
urine Concentrated filtrate produced by the kidneys and excreted by the bladder.
uterus (yū´-ter-us) In the reproductive system of a mammalian female, the organ where the development of young occurs; the womb.

V

vaccination (vak´-suh-nā´-shun) A procedure that presents the immune system with a harmless variant or derivative of a pathogen, thereby stimulating the adaptive immune system to mount a long-term defense against the pathogen.
vaccine (vak-sēn´) A harmless variant or derivative of a pathogen used to stimulate a host organism's immune system to mount a long-term adaptive response against the pathogen.
vacuole (vak´-ū-ōl) A membrane-enclosed sac that is part of the endomembrane system of a eukaryotic cell and has diverse functions in different kinds of cells.
vagina (vuh-jī´-nuh) Part of the female reproductive system between the uterus and the outside opening; the birth canal in mammals; also accommodates the male's penis and receives sperm during copulation.
vas deferens (vas def´-er-enz) (plural, **vasa deferentia**) Part of the male reproductive system that conveys sperm away from the testis; the sperm duct; in humans, the tube that conveys sperm between the epididymis and the common duct that leads to the urethra.
vascular bundle (vas´-kyū-ler) A strand of vascular tissues (both xylem and phloem) in a plant stem.
vascular cambium (vas´-kyū-ler kam´-bē-um) During secondary growth of a plant, the cylinder of meristematic cells, surrounding the xylem and pith, that produces secondary xylem and phloem.
vascular cylinder The central cylinder of vascular tissue in a plant root.
vascular plant A plant with xylem and phloem, including club mosses, ferns, gymnosperms, and angiosperms.
vascular tissue Plant tissue consisting of cells joined into tubes that transport water and nutrients throughout the plant body.
vascular tissue system A transport system formed by xylem and phloem throughout the plant. Xylem transports water and minerals, while phloem transports sugars and other organic nutrients.
vasectomy (vuh-sek´-tuh-mē) Surgical removal of a section of the two sperm ducts (vasa deferentia) to prevent sperm from reaching the urethra; a means of sterilization in males.
vector In molecular biology, a piece of DNA, usually a plasmid or a viral genome, that is used to move genes from one cell to another.
vein (1) In animals, a vessel that returns blood to the heart. (2) In plants, a vascular bundle in a leaf, composed of xylem and phloem.
ventilation The flow of air or water over a respiratory surface.
ventral Pertaining to the underside, or bottom, of a bilaterally symmetric animal.
ventricle (ven´-truh-kul) (1) A heart chamber that pumps blood out of the heart. (2) A space in the vertebrate brain filled with cerebrospinal fluid.
venule (ven´-yūl) A vessel that conveys blood between a capillary bed and a vein.
vertebra (ver´-tuh-bruh) (plural, **vertebrae**) One of a series of segmented skeletal units that enclose the nerve cord, making up the backbone of a vertebrate animal.
vertebral column Backbone, composed of a series of segmented units called vertebrae.
vertebrate (ver´-tuh-brāt) A chordate animal with a backbone, including hagfishes, lampreys, chondrichthyans, ray-finned fishes, lobe-finned fishes, amphibians, reptiles (including birds), and mammals.
vesicle (ves´-i-kul) A sac made of membrane in the cytoplasm of a eukaryotic cell.
vessel element A short, open-ended, water-conducting, and supportive cell in plants. Chains of vessel elements or tracheids make up the water-conducting, supportive tubes in xylem.
vestigial structure A feature of an organism that is a historical remnant of a structure that served a function in the organism's ancestors.
villus (vil´-us) (plural, **villi**) (1) A finger-like projection of the inner surface of the small intestine. (2) A finger-like projection of the chorion of the mammalian placenta. Large numbers of villi increase the surface areas of these organs.
virus A microscopic particle capable of infecting cells of living organisms and inserting its genetic material. Viruses are generally not considered to be alive because they do not display all of the characteristics associated with life.
visceral mass (vis´-uh-rul) One of the three main parts of a mollusc, containing most of the internal organs.
visual acuity The ability of the eyes to distinguish fine detail. Normal visual acuity in humans is usually reported as 20/20 vision.
vital capacity The maximum volume of air that a mammal can inhale and exhale with each breath.
vitamin An organic nutrient that an organism requires in small quantities. Many vitamins serve as coenzymes or parts of coenzymes.
vocal cord A band of elastic tissue in the larynx. Air rushing past the tensed vocal cords makes them vibrate, producing sounds.
voltage-gated ion channel A specialized ion channel that opens or closes in response to changes in membrane potential.
vulva The collective term for the external female genitalia.

W

water mold A fungus-like protist in the stramenopile clade of the SAR supergroup.
water vascular system In echinoderms, a radially arranged system of water-filled canals that branch into extensions called tube feet. The system provides movement and circulates water, facilitating gas exchange and waste disposal.
wavelength The distance between crests of adjacent waves, such as those of the electromagnetic spectrum.
wetland An ecosystem intermediate between an aquatic ecosystem and a terrestrial ecosystem, where soil is saturated with water permanently or periodically.
white blood cell A blood cell that functions in fighting infections; also called a leukocyte.
white matter Regions within the central nervous system composed mainly of axons with their whitish myelin sheaths.
whole-genome shotgun method A method for determining the DNA sequence of an entire genome. After a genome is cut into small fragments, each fragment is sequenced and then placed in the proper order.
wild-type The version of a character that most commonly occurs in nature.
wood Secondary xylem of a plant. *See also* heartwood; sapwood.
wood ray A column of parenchyma cells that radiates from the center of a log and transports water to its outer living tissues.

X

X chromosome inactivation In female mammals, the inactivation of one X chromosome in each somatic cell.
X-linked gene A gene located on the X chromosome. X-linked genes display unique patterns of inheritance because males only have one copy whereas females have two.
xylem (zī´-lum) The nonliving portion of a plant's vascular system that provides support and conveys xylem sap from the roots to the rest of the plant. Xylem is made up of vessel elements and/or tracheids, water-conducting cells. Primary xylem is derived from the procambium. Secondary xylem is derived from the vascular cambium in plants exhibiting secondary growth.

Y

yeast A single-celled fungus that inhabits liquid or moist habitats and reproduces asexually by simple cell division or by the pinching of small buds off a parent cell.

yellow bone marrow A tissue found within the central cavities of long bones, consisting mostly of stored fat.

yolk sac An extraembryonic membrane that develops from the endoderm. The yolk sac produces the embryo's first blood cells and germ cells and gives rise to the allantois.

Z

zoned reserve An extensive region of land that includes one or more areas that are undisturbed by humans. The undisturbed areas are surrounded by lands that have been altered by human activity.

zooplankton (zō´-ō-plank´-tun) Animals that drift in aquatic environments.

zygomycete (zī´-guh-mī-sēt) Member of a group of fungi characterized by a sturdy structure called a zygosporangium, in which meiosis produces haploid spores.

zygote (zī´-gōt) The diploid fertilized egg, which results from the union of a sperm cell nucleus and an egg cell nucleus.

Index

Page numbers with *f* indicate figure, *t* indicate table, and those in **bold** indicate page where listed as a key term.

C

D

F

G

H

I

J

K

L

M

N

O

P

S

U

V

W

X

Y

Z